2017 Valuation Handbook
U.S. Industry Cost of Capital

Market Results Through March 2017

Duff & Phelps

WILEY

Cover image: Duff & Phelps
Cover design: James Harrington

Copyright © 2017 by John Wiley & Sons, Inc. All rights reserved.
Published by John Wiley & Sons, Inc., Hoboken, New Jersey.
Published simultaneously in Canada.

No part of this publication may be reproduced, stored in a retrieval system, or transmitted in any form or by any means, electronic, mechanical, photocopying, recording, scanning, or otherwise, except as permitted under Section 107 or 108 of the 1976 United States Copyright Act, without either the prior written permission of the Publisher, or authorization through payment of the appropriate per-copy fee to the Copyright Clearance Center, Inc., 222 Rosewood Drive, Danvers, MA 01923, (978) 750-8400, fax (978) 646-8600, or on the Web at www.copyright.com. Requests to the Publisher for permission should be addressed to the Permissions Department, John Wiley & Sons, Inc., 111 River Street, Hoboken, NJ 07030, (201) 748-6011, fax (201) 748-6008, or online at http://www.wiley.com/go/permissions.

The foregoing does not preclude End-users from using the *2017 Valuation Handbook – U.S. Industry Cost of Capital* and data published therein in connection with their internal business operations.

Limit of Liability/Disclaimer of Warranty: While the publisher and author have used their best efforts in preparing this book, they make no representations or warranties with respect to the accuracy or completeness of the contents of this book and specifically disclaim any implied warranties of merchantability or fitness for a particular purpose. No warranty may be created or extended by sales representatives or written sales materials. The advice and strategies contained herein may not be suitable for your situation. You should consult with a professional where appropriate. Neither the publisher nor author shall be liable for any loss of profit or any other commercial damages, including but not limited to special, incidental, consequential, or other damages.

For general information on our other products and services or for technical support, please contact our Customer Care Department within the United States at (800) 762-2974, outside the United States at (317) 572-3993 or fax (317) 572-4002.

Wiley publishes in a variety of print and electronic formats and by print-on-demand. Some material included with standard print versions of this book may not be included in e-books or in print-on-demand. If this book refers to media such as a CD or DVD that is not included in the version you purchased, you may download this material at http://booksupport.wiley.com. For more information about Wiley products, visit www.wiley.com. For more information about Duff & Phelps valuation data resources published by John Wiley & Sons, please go to: www.wiley.com/go/ValuationHandbooks.

ISBN 978-1-119-36692-8 (Hardcover)
ISBN 978-1-119-36688-1 (ePDF)

Printed in the United States of America
10 9 8 7 6 5 4 3 2 1

About the Data

The information and data presented in the *2017 Valuation Handbook – U.S. Industry Cost of Capital* and its associated intra-year quarterly updates has been obtained with the greatest of care from sources believed to be reliable, but is not guaranteed to be complete, accurate or timely. Duff & Phelps, LLC (www.duffandphelps.com) and/or its data providers expressly disclaim any liability, including incidental or consequential damages, arising from the use of the *2017 Valuation Handbook – U.S. Industry Cost of Capital* and its associated intra-year quarterly updates or any errors or omissions that may be contained in the *2017 Valuation Handbook – U.S. Industry Cost of Capital* and its associated intra-year quarterly updates, or any other product (existing or to be developed) based upon the methodology and/or data published herein. One of the sources of raw data used to produce the derived data and information herein is Morningstar, Inc. Use of raw data from Morningstar to produce the derived data and information herein does not necessarily constitute agreement by Morningstar, Inc. of any investment philosophy or strategy presented in this publication.

About Duff & Phelps

Duff & Phelps is the premier global valuation and corporate finance advisor with expertise in complex valuation, disputes and investigations, M&A, real estate, restructuring, and compliance and regulatory consulting. The firm's more than 2,000 employees serve a diverse range of clients from offices around the world. For more information, visit www.duffandphelps.com.

M&A advisory, capital raising and secondary market advisory services in the United States are provided by Duff & Phelps Securities, LLC. Member FINRA/SIPC. Pagemill Partners is a Division of Duff & Phelps Securities, LLC. M&A advisory and capital raising services in Canada are provided by Duff & Phelps Securities Canada Ltd., a registered Exempt Market Dealer. M&A advisory and capital raising services in the United Kingdom and across Europe are provided by Duff & Phelps Securities Ltd. (DPSL), which is authorized and regulated by the Financial Conduct Authority. In Germany M&A advisory and capital raising services are also provided by Duff & Phelps GmbH, which is a Tied Agent of DPSL. Valuation Advisory Services in India are provided by Duff & Phelps India Private Limited under a category 1 merchant banker license issued by the Securities and Exchange Board of India.

Additional Resources

Duff & Phelps authors *five* books that focus on U.S. and international valuation theory, data, and risk premia (e.g., equity risk premia, risk-free rates, size premia, industry risk premia, betas, industry multiples and other statistics, etc.) for use in valuation models. The *Valuation Handbook – U.S. Industry Cost of Capital* (this book) is one of these five books.

Duff & Phelps produces *one* book that focuses on U.S. capital markets performance data (i.e., the history of returns of the capital markets in the U.S. from 1926 to the present). This resource, the *Stocks, Bonds, Bills, and Inflation® (SBBI®) Yearbook*, has been published for over 30 years.[i.1] The *SBBI Yearbook* does not provide extensive valuation data or methodology.[i.2]

The six books are:[i.3]

U.S. and International Valuation Theory and Data

- *Cost of Capital: Applications and Examples (5th edition)*
- *Valuation Handbook – U.S. Guide to Cost of Capital*
- *Valuation Handbook – U.S. Industry Cost of Capital*
- *Valuation Handbook – International Guide to Cost of Capital*
- *Valuation Handbook – International Industry Cost of Capital*

U.S. Capital Markets Performance Data

- *Stocks, Bonds, Bills, and Inflation (SBBI) Yearbook*

All six Duff & Phelps books are published by John Wiley & Sons (Hoboken, NJ). Each of the six books is summarized in the following sections.

To learn more about cost of capital issues, and to ensure that you are using the most recent Duff & Phelps Recommended ERP, visit www.duffandphelps.com/CostofCapital.

[i.1] "Stocks, Bonds, Bills, and Inflation" and "SBBI" are registered trademarks of Morningstar, Inc. All rights reserved. Used with permission.

[i.2] Morningstar previously published two "Ibbotson SBBI" yearbooks: (i) The *SBBI "Classic" Yearbook*, which is now produced by Duff & Phelps and published by John Wiley & Sons as the "SBBI Yearbook" starting in 2016 (the word "Classic" was dropped from the title), and (ii) the *SBBI "Valuation"* Yearbook, which was discontinued by Morningstar in 2013. The former *SBBI Valuation Yearbook* was replaced by the *Valuation Handbook – U.S. Guide to Cost of Capital* (this book), also produced by Duff & Phelps and published by John Wiley & Sons, starting in 2014.

[i.3] In 2014, 2015, and 2016 the four books comprising the Valuation Handbook series were named as follows: *Valuation Handbook – Guide to Cost of Capital*, *Valuation Handbook – Industry Cost of Capital*, *International Valuation Handbook – Guide to Cost of Capital*, and *International Valuation Handbook – Industry Cost of Capital*. Starting with the 2017 Valuation Handbook editions, the names of the four books were changed to: *Valuation Handbook – U.S. Guide to Cost of Capital*, *Valuation Handbook – U.S. Industry Cost of Capital*, *Valuation Handbook – International Guide to Cost of Capital*, and *Valuation Handbook – International Industry Cost of Capital*, respectively. For simplicity, in all 2017 books, intra-year updates, marketing materials, online tools, etc., the new names are used (even when referring to pre-2017 editions).

Cost of Capital: Applications and Examples 5th edition

The authoritative, comprehensive overview of valuation theory, best practices, and proper use of data. This book puts an emphasis on practical application.

To learn more about the latest theory and practice in cost of capital estimation, see *Cost of Capital: Applications and Examples* 5th edition, by Shannon P. Pratt and Roger J. Grabowski (John Wiley & Sons, Inc., 2014).

The *Cost of Capital: Applications and Examples* 5th edition is a one-stop shop for background and current thinking on the development and uses of rates of return on capital. This book contains expanded materials on estimating the basic building blocks of the cost of equity capital, the risk-free rate, and equity risk premium, plus in-depth discussion of the volatility created by the 2008 financial crisis, the subsequent recession and uncertain recovery, and how those events have fundamentally changed how we need to interpret the inputs to the models we use to develop these estimates.

The *Cost of Capital: Applications and Examples* 5th edition includes case studies providing comprehensive discussion of cost of capital estimates for valuing a business and damages calculations for small and medium-sized businesses, cross-referenced to the chapters covering the theory and data. This book puts an emphasis on practical application. To that end, this updated edition provides readers with exclusive access to a companion website filled with supplementary materials, allowing you to continue to learn in a hands-on fashion long after closing the book.

The *Cost of Capital: Applications and Examples* has been published since 1998, and is updated every three to four years. The 6th edition of this book is scheduled to be available in early 2018.

"Shannon Pratt and Roger Grabowski have produced a remarkably comprehensive review of the subject...it is a work that valuation practitioners, CFOs, and others will find an invaluable reference".

– **Professor Richard Brealey**, Emeritus Professor of Finance, London Business School (from the Foreword)

"Estimating the cost of capital is critical in determining the valuation of assets, in evaluating the capital structure of corporations, and in estimating the long-run expected return of investments. Shannon Pratt and Roger Grabowski have the most thorough text on the subject, not only providing various estimation methods, but also numerous ways to use the cost of capital".

– **Professor Roger G. Ibbotson**, Professor Emeritus of Finance at the Yale School of Management, Chairman and Chief Investment Officer of Zebra Capital LLC, and former Chairman and founder of Ibbotson Associates, now part of Morningstar, Inc.

Valuation Handbook – U.S. Guide to Cost of Capital

This annual book includes the U.S. cost of capital data inputs (equity risk premia, size premia, industry risk premia, risk premia over the risk-free rate, risk-free rates) that were previously published in the Morningstar/Ibbotson *Stocks, Bonds, Bills, and Inflation (SBBI) Valuation Yearbook* and the Duff & Phelps *Risk Premium Report*.

The *Valuation Handbook – U.S. Guide to Cost of Capital* can be used to develop cost of equity capital estimates (using both the build-up method and CAPM) for an individual business, business ownership interest, security, or intangible asset. This book includes many examples for using the data properly.

The *Valuation Handbook – U.S. Guide to Cost of Capital* has been published since 2014, and is updated annually with data through December 31 of the previous year (e.g., the *2014 Valuation Handbook – U.S. Guide to Cost of Capital* is "data through" December 31, 2013; the *2015 Valuation Handbook – U.S. Guide to Cost of Capital* is "data through" December 31, 2014, etc.). This book includes three optional intra-year quarterly updates (March, June, and September).

Valuation Handbook – U.S. Industry Cost of Capital (this book)

This annual book provides industry-level cost of capital estimates (cost of equity capital, cost of debt capital, and weighted average cost of capital, or WACC), plus detailed industry-level statistics for sales, market capitalization, capital structure, various levered and unlevered beta estimates (e.g., ordinary-least squares (OLS) beta, sum beta, peer group beta, downside beta, etc.), valuation (trading) multiples, financial and profitability ratios, equity returns, aggregate forward-looking earnings-per share (EPS) growth rates, and more. Over 300 critical industry-level data points are calculated for approximately 180 U.S. industries (depending on data availability). Industries are organized by standard industrial classification (SIC) code.

The *Valuation Handbook – U.S. Industry Cost of Capital* can be used to benchmark, augment, and support the analyst's own custom analysis of the industry in which a subject business, business ownership interest, security, or intangible asset resides.

The *Valuation Handbook – U.S. Industry Cost of Capital* has been published since 2014, and is updated annually with data through March 31 of the current year (e.g., the *2014 Valuation Handbook – U.S. Industry Cost of Capital* is "data through" March 31, 2014; the *2015 Valuation Handbook – U.S. Industry Cost of Capital* is "data through" March 31, 2015, etc.). This book includes three optional intra-year quarterly updates (June, September, and December).

Valuation Handbook – International Guide to Cost of Capital

This annual book provides country-level equity risk premia (ERPs), relative volatility (RV) factors, and country risk premia (CRPs).

This book can be used to estimate country-level cost of equity capital globally, for up to 188 countries, from the perspective of investors based in any one of up to 56 countries (depending on data availability).

The *Valuation Handbook – International Guide to Cost of Capital* has been published since 2014, and is updated annually with data through December of the previous year and March of the current year (e.g., the *2014 Valuation Handbook – International Guide to Cost of Capital* is "data through" December 31, 2013 and March 31, 2014; the *2015 Valuation Handbook – International Guide to Cost of Capital* is "data through" December 31, 2014 and March 31, 2015, etc.). This book includes one optional semi-annual update with data through June and September.

"Measuring the impact of country risk in determining the international cost of capital is one of the most vexing issues in finance. Any company doing international cost of capital estimation must, at minimum, consult the Valuation Handbook – International Guide to Cost of Capital".

– **Campbell R. Harvey,** Professor of International Business at the Fuqua School of Business, Duke University

Valuation Handbook – International Industry Cost of Capital

This annual book provides the same type of rigorous industry-level analysis published in the U.S.-centric *Valuation Handbook – U.S. Industry Cost of Capital*, on a global scale.

This book includes industry-level analyses for four global economic areas: (i) the "World", (ii) the European Union, (iii) the Eurozone, and (iv) the United Kingdom.[i.4] Industries in the book are identified by their Global Industry Classification Standard (GICS) code. Each of the four global economic area's industry analyses are presented in three currencies: (i) the euro (€ or EUR), (ii) the British pound (£ or GBP), and (iii) the U.S. dollar ($ or USD).

This annual book provides industry level cost of capital estimates (cost of equity capital, cost of debt capital, and weighted average cost of capital, or WACC), plus detailed industry-level statistics for sales, market capitalization, capital structure, various levered and unlevered beta estimates (e.g., ordinary-least squares (OLS) beta, sum beta, peer group beta, downside beta, etc.), valuation (trading) multiples, financial and profitability ratios, equity returns, aggregate forward-looking earnings-per share (EPS) growth rates, and more. Over 300 critical industry-level data points are calculated for each industry (depending on data availability). Industries are organized by global industry classification standard (GICS) code.

[i.4] In the *Valuation Handbook – International Industry Cost of Capital*, "World" companies are defined as companies that (i) are components of the MSCI ACWI IMI, and (ii) satisfy the rigorous screening requirements that are employed to define the company sets used therein.

The *Valuation Handbook – International Industry Cost of Capital* can be used to benchmark, augment, and support the analyst's own custom analysis of the industry in which a subject business, business ownership interest, security, or intangible asset resides.

The *Valuation Handbook – International Industry Cost of Capital* has been published since 2015, and is updated annually with data through March 31 of the current year (e.g., the *2015 Valuation Handbook – International Industry Cost of Capital* is "data through" March 31, 2015; the *2016 Valuation Handbook – International Industry Cost of Capital* is "data through" March 31, 2016, etc.). This book includes one optional semi-annual update with data through September.

Stocks, Bonds, Bills, and Inflation (SBBI) Yearbook

This annual book has been the definitive annual resource for historical U.S. capital markets performance data for over 30 years.

Starting with the 2016 edition, the *Stocks, Bonds, Bills, and Inflation (SBBI) Yearbook* is now produced by Duff & Phelps and published by John Wiley & Sons. The *SBBI Yearbook* was previously published by Morningstar, Inc. under the name "Ibbotson *Stocks, Bonds, Bills, and Inflation (SBBI) Classic Yearbook*".[i.5]

This book includes returns, index values, and statistical analyses of U.S. large company stocks, small company stocks, long-term corporate bonds, long-term government bonds, intermediate-term government bonds, U.S. Treasury bills, and inflation from January 1926 to present (monthly).

Anyone serious about investments or investing needs an appreciation of capital market history. Such an appreciation, which can be gained from this book, is equally valuable to the individual and institutional investor, practitioners and scholars in finance, economics, and business; portfolio strategists; and security analysts seeking to benchmark their own investment performance. The *SBBI Yearbook* is a thinking person's guide to using historical data to understand the financial markets and make decisions.

[i.5] The *SBBI Yearbook* was published by Morningstar, Inc. from 2007 through 2015, and by Ibbotson Associates in years prior to 2007.

Purchasing Information

U.S. and International Valuation Theory and Data

- *Cost of Capital: Applications and Examples (5th edition)*
- *Valuation Handbook – U.S. Guide to Cost of Capital*
- *Valuation Handbook – U.S. Industry Cost of Capital*
- *Valuation Handbook – International Guide to Cost of Capital*
- *Valuation Handbook – International Industry Cost of Capital*

To order additional copies of the *2017 Valuation Handbook – U.S. Industry Cost of Capital* (this book), or other Duff & Phelps valuation data resources published by John Wiley & Sons, please visit www.wiley.com/go/ValuationHandbooks, or call: U.S. (800) 762-2974
International (317) 572-3993 or fax (317) 572-4002.

U.S. Capital Markets Performance Data

- *Stocks, Bonds, Bills, and Inflation (SBBI) Yearbook*

To order copies of the *SBBI Yearbook*, please visit www.wiley.com/go/sbbiyearbook, or call: U.S. (800) 762-2974 International (317) 572-3993 or fax (317) 572-4002.

Table of Contents

Acknowledgements	**xiii**
Introduction	**1**
Who Should Use the *Valuation Handbook – U.S. Industry Cost of Capital*	1
Industry-Level Cost of Capital Estimates	2
Industry-Level Statistics, Capital Structure, Valuation Multiples, and Betas	2
Analysis of Capital Structure Including Off-Balance-Sheet Liabilities	3
New in the *2017 Valuation Handbook – U.S. Industry Cost of Capital*	3
Methodology	**5**
"Data Through" Date	5
County of Incorporation	5
Company Type	5
Industry Identification by SIC Code	5
Minimum Number of Companies Required	6
Data Sources	6
Company Screening Process	11
Medians and Industry Composites	16
"Latest" and "5-Year" Averages	18
Calculations of Industry Financial Statistics	**24**
Three Largest and Three Smallest Companies by Sales and Total Assets	24
Annualized Monthly Performance Statistics	24
Number of Companies in the Median, the Composites, and the High-Financial-Risk Category	25
Return Ratios	26
Liquidity Ratio	30
Profitability Ratio	31
Growth Rates	32
Beta Overview	33
Levered Betas	34
Adjusted Betas	37
Unlevered Betas	39
Equity Valuation Multiples	41
Enterprise Valuation (EV) Multiples	47
Fama-French (F-F) 5-Factor Model	53
Cost of Debt	56
Leverage Ratios	57
Cost of Equity Capital Estimates	61
CAPM	62
Cost of Equity Capital Estimates - Using the CRSP Deciles Size Study	64
CAPM + Size Premium	64
Build-up Method	66
Cost of Equity Capital Estimates - Using the Risk Premium Report Study	68
CAPM + Size Premium	69
Build-up 1 Method	71
Discounted Cash Flow (DCF) Models	74
1-Stage DCF	74
3-Stage DCF	75

Fama-French (F-F) 5-Factor Model	79
Weighted Average Cost of Capital (WACC)	81
WACC Calculations	84
Exhibit 11: Distribution of Company-level Average WACC by Industry	87
Exhibit 12: Average and Median of Average WACC by Industry for "Healthy" Companies and "High-Financial-Risk" Companies	88

Appendices

Appendix A
Relative Impact of Off-Balance-Sheet Debt-Equivalent Liabilities on the Capital Structure, as Measured by Total Capital

Appendix B
Leverage Ratios and Unlevered Betas Calculated Using (i) Book Debt, and (ii) Book Debt Plus Off-Balance-Sheet Debt

Appendix C
van Binsbergen-Graham-Yang Optimal Capital Structure Model

Appendix D
Definitions of Standard & Poor's *Compustat* Data Items Used in Calculations

Industry Data Exhibits

Division A: Agriculture, Forestry, and Fishing

Division B: Mining

Division C: Construction

Division D: Manufacturing

Division E: Transportation, Communications, Electric, Gas, and Sanitary Services

Division F: Wholesale Trade

Division G: Retail Trade

Division H: Finance, Insurance, and Real Estate

Division I: Services

Size Groupings: Large-, Mid-, Low-, and Micro-Capitalization Companies

Acknowledgements

Authors

Roger J. Grabowski, FASA
Managing Director, Duff & Phelps

James P. Harrington
Director, Duff & Phelps

Carla Nunes, CFA
Managing Director, Duff & Phelps

Thank you

The authors give special thanks to Senior Associate Kevin Madden and Analysts Aaron Russo and Andrew Vey of Duff & Phelps for their assistance in assembling the exhibits presented herein, analysis, editing, and quality control. We thank Executive Assistant Michelle Phillips for production assistance, and Director Kelly Hunter for securing data permissions.

Introduction

In 2014, Duff & Phelps introduced the *2014 Valuation Handbook – U.S. Industry Cost of Capital*. Now in its fourth year of printing, the *2017 Valuation Handbook – U.S. Industry Cost of Capital* (this book) provides the same type of rigorous industry-level analysis previously published in the green-cover Morningstar/Ibbotson *Cost of Capital Yearbook*.

The *2017 Valuation Handbook – U.S. Industry Cost of Capital* is published with data through March 31, 2017, and includes three intra-year Quarterly Updates (June, September, and December 2017).[2,3]

The *2017 Valuation Handbook – U.S. Industry Cost of Capital* provides cost of capital estimates (i.e., equity capital, debt capital, and WACC) for approximately 180 U.S. industries (identified by Standard Industrial Classification (SIC) code) and four size groupings (i.e., Large-, Mid-, Low-, and Micro-capitalization companies), plus a host of detailed statistics that can be used for benchmarking purposes. The *2017 Valuation Handbook – U.S. Industry Cost of Capital* contains data which the valuation analyst will find useful in benchmarking, augmenting, and supporting his or her own custom analysis of the industry in which a subject business, business ownership interest, security, or intangible asset resides.[4]

Who Should Use the *Valuation Handbook – U.S. Industry Cost of Capital*

In addition to the traditional professional valuation analyst, the *2017 Valuation Handbook – U.S. Industry Cost of Capital* is designed to serve the needs of:

- Corporate finance officers when pricing or evaluating proposed mergers and acquisitions (M&A), raising private or public equity, estimating property taxes, and/or dealing with stakeholder disputes.

- Corporate officers when evaluating investments for capital budgeting decisions.

- Investment bankers when pricing initial (or follow-on) public offerings, proposed M&A transactions, and private equity financing.

- Private equity investors when pricing or evaluating proposed M&A transactions, designing and awarding management equity-based compensation, or making capital budgeting decisions.

---

[2] Quarterly Updates are (i) optional, and (ii) are not sold separately.

[3] The 2014, 2015, and 2016 versions of the *Valuation Handbook – U.S. Industry Cost of Capital* were published with data through March 31, 2014, March 31, 2015, and March 31, 2016, respectively, and also included optional June, September, and December intra-year updates.

[4] Also published by John Wiley & Sons, the *2017 Valuation Handbook – U.S. Guide to Cost of Capital* (data through December 31, 2016) provides the key year-end data (risk-free rates, equity risk premia, size premia, industry risk premia) previously available in (i) the Morningstar/Ibbotson *SBBI Valuation Yearbook* and (ii) the Duff & Phelps *Risk Premium Report*. The *2017 Valuation Handbook – U.S. Guide to Cost of Capital* can be used to develop cost of equity capital estimates for an individual business, business ownership interest, security, or intangible asset. The *Valuation Handbook – U.S. Guide to Cost of Capital* has been published annually since 2014. This book includes three optional quarterly updates (March, June, and September).

- CPAs and valuators dealing with either valuations for financial and tax reporting purposes, or with dispute and bankruptcy valuations issues.

- Judges and attorneys dealing with valuation issues in M&A, shareholder and partner disputes, damage cases, solvency cases, bankruptcy reorganizations, property taxes, regulatory rate setting, transfer pricing, and financial reporting.

Industry-Level Cost of Capital Estimates

The *2017 Valuation Handbook – U.S. Industry Cost of Capital* provides eight (8) cost of equity capital estimates for each of the industries covered in the book:[5,6]

1) Capital Asset Pricing Model (CAPM)[7]

2) CAPM + Size Premium (using the CRSP Deciles Size Study)

3) Build-up + Industry Risk Premium (using the CRSP Deciles Size Study)

4) CAPM + Size Premium (using the Risk Premium Report Study)

5) Build-up + Risk Premium Over the Risk-free Rate (using Risk Premium Report Study)

6) 1-Stage Discounted Cash Flow (DCF) model

7) 3-Stage DCF model

8) Fama-French (F-F) 5-Factor Model

Cost of debt capital and weighted average cost of capital (WACC) are also presented for each industry.[8] WACC is calculated using the cost of equity capital estimated by *each* of the eight models, plus the cost of preferred capital input and the cost of debt capital input.

Industry-Level Statistics, Capital Structure, Valuation Multiples, and Betas

The *2017 Valuation Handbook – U.S. Industry Cost of Capital* also provides detailed statistics for sales, total assets, industry performance, capital structure, various levered and unlevered beta estimates (e.g., ordinary least squares (OLS) beta, sum beta, downside beta, etc.), valuation

---

[5] Depending on data availability; some industries may not include all estimates.
[6] In this list, the "CRSP Deciles Size Study" is the valuation data previously published on the "back page" of the Morningstar/Ibbotson *SBBI Valuation Yearbook*; the "Risk Premium Report Study" is the valuation data previously published in the Duff & Phelps *Risk Premium Report*. Both of these key valuation data sets are now published in the *2017 Valuation Handbook – U.S. Guide to Cost of Capital* (Wiley, 2017).
[7] This is CAPM calculated without any additional adjustments for "size", or other factors (i.e., the traditional "textbook" or "base" CAPM).
[8] Depending on data availability; some industries may not include all estimates.

(trading) multiples, financial and profitability ratios, equity returns, aggregate forward-looking earnings-per-share (EPS) growth rates, and more.

Analysis of Capital Structure Including Off-Balance-Sheet Liabilities

The *2017 Valuation Handbook – U.S. Industry Cost of Capital* provides statistics that enable the user to gauge the impact of "debt-like" off-balance-sheet items on the capital structure of the subject industry. These debt-equivalent liabilities (specifically, capitalized operating leases and unfunded pension obligations) are not only taken into account by credit rating agencies when assigning a debt rating for a company, but should likely be considered when ascertaining the true financial (and equity) risk of the subject company as well.

The capital structure (and unlevered betas) of each industry are calculated *with* and *without* these off-balance-sheet debt-equivalent items, so that the user can gauge how material these liabilities are for the subject industry (see Appendices A and B).

For a detailed discussion, see *Cost of Capital: Applications and Examples* 5th edition, by Shannon P. Pratt and Roger J. Grabowski, Chapter 20, "Other Components of a Business's Capital Structure".

New in the *2017 Valuation Handbook – U.S. Industry Cost of Capital*

The *Valuation Handbook – U.S. Industry Cost of Capital* is in its fourth year of publication with the release of the 2017 edition (this book). The inaugural 2014 edition was self-published by Duff & Phelps; starting with the 2015 edition, the *Valuation Handbook – U.S. Industry Cost of Capital* is published by John Wiley & Sons, marking a significant milestone in the evolution of the book.

Starting with the 2016 edition, we added a new Appendix C, the "van Binsbergen-Graham-Yang Optimal Capital Structure Model", based upon the work of Jules H. van Binsbergen, Associate Professor of Finance, The Wharton School, University of Pennsylvania, John R. Graham, Professor of Finance, Fuqua School of Business, Duke University, and Jie Yang, Senior Economist with the Board of Governors of the Federal Reserve System.[9] This new appendix provides estimates of (i) the optimal amount of debt that firms should use as a percentage of their total capital, and (ii) the incremental firm value potentially created by choosing an optimal capital structure (rather than using no debt at all).

In previous editions of the *Valuation Handbook – U.S. Industry Cost of Capital*, all beta estimates on each industry tearsheet were rounded to the nearest tenth (i.e., one decimal). Starting with the *2017 Valuation Handbook – U.S. Industry Cost of Capital* (this book), all beta estimates on each tearsheet are now rounded to the nearest hundredth (i.e., two decimals). At readers' request, this refinement was added to provide valuation practitioners with one more decimal of precision for this metric.

---

[9] In the *2014* and *2015 Valuation Handbook – U.S. Industry Cost of Capital*, Appendix C was "Definitions of Standard & Poor's Compustat Data Items Used in Calculations". Starting with the *2016 Valuation Handbook – U.S. Industry Cost of Capital*, "Definitions of Standard & Poor's Compustat Data Items Used in Calculations" has been moved to Appendix D.

In previous editions of the *Valuation Handbook – U.S. Industry Cost of Capital*, all SICs in Division H: Finance, Insurance, and Real Estate (major groups between SICs beginning with "60" and "67") included three equity valuation multiples (Price/Sales, Price/Earnings, and Market/Book) and two enterprise valuation multiples (EV/Sales and EV/EBITDA). Starting with the *2017 Valuation Handbook – U.S. Industry Cost of Capital* (this book), all SICs in Division H: Finance, Insurance, and Real Estate (Major groups between "60" and "67") now include four equity valuation multiples (Price/Sales, Price/Earnings, Price/Tangible Book, and Price/Earnings Before Taxes) and one enterprise valuation multiple (EV/EBITDA). This refinement is to provide more commonly used equity based metrics for valuation practitioners analyzing the financial services industry.

Methodology

"Data Through" Date

All cost of capital estimates and other statistics presented herein are calculated with the most recent monthly or fiscal year data through March 31, 2017.

County of Incorporation

All companies included in the analyses herein are incorporated in the U.S., in accordance with Standard & Poor's (S&P's) *Research Insight* database.

Company Type

All companies used in the analyses presented herein are publicly-held U.S. corporations.

Industry Identification by SIC Code

The *2017 Valuation Handbook – U.S. Industry Cost of Capital* is published with industries identified by Standard Industrial Classification (SIC) code.[10] The SIC is a system for classifying industries by 1-, 2-, 3-, and 4-digit codes (1-digit SIC codes are the broadest, *least* specific industry categories; 4-digit SIC codes are the narrowest, *most* specific industry categories).

The SIC codes can be grouped into progressively more specific industry levels: from division (1-digit SICs, the *least* specific (i.e., broadest) level), to major group (2-digit SICs), to industry group (3-digit SICs), and finally individual industry (4-digit SICs, the *most* specific (i.e., narrowest) level).

More specific (i.e., narrower) SICs "roll up" into less specific (i.e., broader) SICs. For example, in Exhibit 1, Division A: Agriculture, Forestry, and Fishing (i.e., those SICs beginning with "0") is a broader, less specific category than major group SIC 01 (Agricultural Production Crops), which in turn is less specific than industry group SIC 011 (Cash Grains). The most specific SIC shown in Exhibit 1 is the 4-digit SIC 0111 (Wheat), which represents the individual industry.

Only SIC descriptions listed on the United States Occupational Safety & Health Administration's (OSHA) website are presented here.

All industries that are "duplicative" are eliminated. For example, if SIC 131 and SIC 1311 were both comprised of the *same exact* companies, the broadest SIC (SIC 131) was kept, and the less broad SIC (SIC 1311) was discarded.

---

[10] All SIC naming conventions are from the U.S. Department of Labor Occupational Safety & Health Administration (OSHA) website. To learn more, visit https://www.osha.gov/.

Exhibit 1: Standard Industrial Classification Codes (SICs) Vary in Specificity

	SIC	SIC Description
Less Specific	0	Agriculture, Forestry, and Fishing
	01	Agricultural Production Crops
	011	Cash Grains
More Specific	0111	Wheat

Source: U.S. Department of Labor Occupational Safety & Health Administration (OSHA)

Minimum Number of Companies Required

An industry must have at least five (5) companies in order to be included in the analyses presented herein.

Data Sources

Company-level Data

The primary source of company-level data (income statement and balance sheet data, price data, shares outstanding, credit ratings, etc.) used in the calculation of the industry statistics presented herein is S&P's *Research Insight* database.[11]

Corporate Bond Yield and Credit Ratings

S&P is the source of U.S. corporate bond yield data (used as an input in the calculation of cost of debt). For companies that do not have an S&P credit rating, a long-term credit score from S&P Global Market Intelligence *Credit Analytics* is substituted. For companies without an S&P credit rating, *or* a credit score from S&P Global Market Intelligence *Credit Analytics*, an average credit rating for the most specific SIC code in which the company appears, and in which there are at least five companies with an S&P credit rating and credit score from S&P Global Market Intelligence *Credit Analytics*, is substituted. For example, if hypothetical Company ABC in SIC 3714 does not have a credit rating, the average credit rating for the other companies in SIC 3714 are used. If SIC 3714 does not have at least five other companies with credit ratings, then the calculation is performed using SIC 371 (up one level, and thus less specific), etc.

Beta Calculation Inputs

The market benchmark used in all beta calculations is the S&P 500 total return index. U.S. Treasury 30-day T-bill total returns are subtracted from the S&P 500 total return index returns, as well as

---

[11] Copyright © 1993–2017 Standard & Poor's, a Division of The McGraw-Hill Companies, Inc. All rights reserved.

from the individual company (or portfolio) total returns in order to arrive at the "excess" returns utilized in the regression analyses used to calculate betas. To calculate debt betas – used as an input in the calculation of "asset" (i.e., unlevered) betas – the Barclays U.S. Corporate total return indices were used.[12]

Fama-French (F-F) 5-Factor Model Inputs

To calculate cost of equity capital estimates using the Fama-French (F-F) 5-factor model, we used data available from Dr. Kenneth French.[13,14,15] The following monthly information was used:

- **SMB (small minus big) returns:** The difference between the monthly returns on diversified portfolios comprised of "small" company stocks and "big" (i.e., large) company stocks, as measured by market capitalization.

- **HML (high minus low) returns:** The difference between the monthly returns on diversified portfolios comprised of "value" company stocks (high book-to-market) and "growth" company stocks (low book-to-market).

- **RMW (robust minus weak) returns:** The difference between the monthly returns on diversified portfolios comprised of company stocks with "robust" profitability and "weak" profitability.

- **CMA (conservative minus aggressive) returns:** The difference between the monthly returns on diversified portfolios comprised of company stocks of low and high investment firms, which Fama and French define as "conservative" and "aggressive", respectively.

The expected SMB risk premium used in the F-F 5-factor model cost of equity capital estimates presented herein is calculated as the average annual return difference between diversified portfolios comprised of "small" company stocks and "big" (i.e., large) company stocks, as measured by market capitalization, over the period 1964–2016 (3.84%).[16]

---

[12] Bloomberg Barclays Indices © 2017. On August 24, 2016, Bloomberg L.P. announced today that it has completed its acquisition of Barclays Risk Analytics and Index Solutions Ltd. ("BRAIS") from Barclays PLC. To learn more, visit: https://www.bloomberg.com/company/announcements/bloomberg-acquisition-barclays-brais/.

[13] Source of Fama-French data: Dr. Kenneth French's website at: http://mba.tuck.dartmouth.edu/pages/faculty/ken.french/index.html. Professor French's website provides various "sorts" of the 5-factor model's factors: (i) "2x2" sorts, (ii) "2x2x2x2" sorts, and (iii) "2x3" sorts. In the analyses presented herein, the 2x3 sorts are used, as is suggested in "A Five-Factor Asset Pricing Model", *The Journal of Financial Economics* 116 (2015) 1–22, page 19: "*In the end, precedent, flexibility in accommodating more or fewer factors, and the fact that they perform as well as the 2x2 and 2x2x2x2 factors in our tests of asset pricing models lead us back to the factors from the 2x3 sorts*". The authors confirmed in correspondence with Professor French that the 2x3 factor sorts are indeed the indicated choice.

[14] Kenneth R. French is the co-author, together with Eugene Fama, of (i) the seminal paper introducing the 3-factor model: "The Cross-Section of Expected Stock Returns", *Journal of Finance*, 1992, and (ii) "A Five-Factor Asset Pricing Model", *The Journal of Financial Economics* 116 (2015): 1–22.

[15] The Fama-French 3-Factor Model used in the *2014 Valuation Handbook – U.S. Industry Cost of Capital* was replaced with the Fama-French 5-Factor Model starting with the *2015 Valuation Handbook – U.S. Industry Cost of Capital*.

[16] The Fama-French 3-Factor model utilizes data from July 1926–present. The Fama-French 5-Factor model utilizes data from July 1963–present.

The expected HML risk premium used in the F-F 5-factor model cost of equity capital estimates presented herein is calculated as the average annual return difference between diversified portfolios comprised of "value" company stocks (high book-to-market) and "growth" stocks portfolios (low book-to-market) over the period 1964–2016 (5.06%).

The expected RMW risk premium used in the F-F 5-factor model cost of equity capital estimates presented herein is calculated as the average annual return difference between diversified portfolios comprised of company stocks with "robust" profitability and "weak" profitability, over the period 1964–2016 (3.02%).

The expected CMA risk premium used in the F-F 5-factor model cost of equity capital estimates presented herein is calculated as the average annual return difference between diversified portfolios comprised of company stocks of low and high investment firms, which Fama and French define as "conservative" and "aggressive", respectively, over the period 1964–2016 (4.04%).

Growth Rates

Thomson Reuters *I/B/E/S* (Institutional Broker's Estimate System) *Consensus Estimates* database was the source used for analysts' estimates of future earnings growth. Most analysts define long-term growth as an estimated average rate of earnings growth for the next three to five years. The exact time frame will differ from broker to broker.[17] These growth rates are utilized in the 1-stage DCF model and in the first and second stages of the 3-stage DCF model. The *I/B/E/S* long-term growth rate estimates were retrieved from S&P's *Capital IQ* database.

The long-term growth rate (used as an input in the third stage of the 3-stage DCF model) is based upon average historical U.S. long-term real gross domestic product (GDP) adjusted for "dilution", plus the difference between the U.S. Treasury 20-year constant-maturity bond yield and the 20-year U.S. Treasury Inflation-Protected Securities (TIPS) (the so-called "breakeven inflation"). The sources used for this calculation are (i) the Bureau of Economic Analysis (BEA)[18], (ii) an estimate of dilution (due to a company's share issuances and repurchases, and to a larger degree by investors' dilution of current holdings to purchase shares in start-ups) is based on the work of Professor Bradford Cornell[19], and (iii) the Board of Governors of the Federal Reserve System's historical interest rate series (H.15).[20]

---

[17] As reported in S&P's *Capital IQ* database. Also, see "Methodology for Estimates – A Guide to Understanding Thomson Reuters Methodologies, Terms and Policies for I/B/E/S Estimates Databases", April 2014, by Thomson Reuters.

[18] The BEA is an agency of the U.S. Department of Commerce. Along with the U.S. Census Bureau, BEA is part of the Department's Economics and Statistics Administration. To learn more, visit: http://www.bea.gov/index.htm.

[19] Bradford Cornell, "Economic Growth and Equity Investing", *Financial Analysts Journal* 66, no. 1 (2010): pp. 54–64. To learn more, visit: http://www.hss.caltech.edu/~bcornell/.

[20] The H.15 release contains daily, weekly, monthly, and annual interest rates for selected U.S. Treasury and private money market and capital market instruments. To learn more, visit: http://www.federalreserve.gov/releases/h15/data.htm.

The expected long-term growth rate used as an input in the third stage of the 3-stage discounted cash flow model presented herein is calculated as of March 31, 2017 in the following fashion:

Long-term Growth Estimate = Long-term Real GDP (estimated) − Adjustment for Dilution + (U.S 20-year Government Bond Yield − U.S. 20-year TIPS yield)

3.24% = 3.22% − 2.00% + (2.76% − 0.74%) = 3.0% (rounded to the nearest 50 bps increment)

Company Tax Rates

Company tax rates (used as an input in the calculation of "asset" (i.e., unlevered) betas and the weighted average cost of capital (WACC)) were provided by John Graham, Professor of Finance, Fuqua School of Business, Duke University.[21] Professor Graham estimates firm-specific federal corporate income tax rates that account for the dynamics of the tax code and the probability that a firm will be taxable in a given year. His research has confirmed that tax rates calculated from financial statement data provide an accurate approximation to tax rates based on tax return data.[22]

Long-Term Risk-Free Rate and Long-Term Equity Risk Premium

There is no single universally accepted methodology for estimating the equity risk premium (ERP). A wide variety of premia are used in practice and recommended by academics and financial advisors. These differences are often due to differences in how ERP is estimated. The ERP is estimated relative to a risk-free rate. In estimating an ERP, valuation analysts should consider *not* simply using the long-term "historical" ERP. A likely better alternative is to examine approaches that are sensitive to the current economic conditions. Duff & Phelps employs a multi-step analysis to estimate the "conditional" ERP that takes into account a broad range of economic information and multiple ERP estimation methodologies to arrive at its recommendation, the steps of which are broadly outlined as follows:

- First, a reasonable *range* of normal or unconditional ERP is established.

- Second, based on current economic conditions, Duff & Phelps estimates *where* in the range the true ERP likely lies (e.g., top, bottom, or middle) by examining the current state of the economy (both by examining the level of stock prices indices as a forward indicator and examining economic forecasts), the implied volatility of the S&P 500 Index an indicator of perceived risk, corporate bond spreads, etc.

---

[21] Dr. Graham is the D. Richard Mead professor of finance at the Fuqua School of Business at Duke University. He has been co-editor of *The Journal of Finance*, associate editor of *The Journal of Finance*, *The Review of Financial Studies*, *Finance Research Letters*, and *Financial Management*, and has served on the board of directors of the American Finance Association, the Western Finance Association, and the Financial Management Association, three of the largest academic finance professional organizations. Graham is currently President-elect of the Financial Management Association and has been President of the Western Finance Association, is a Fellow of the Financial Management Association, and is a research associate of the National Bureau of Economic Research. Graham has published more than 50 articles and book chapters on corporate taxes, cost of capital, capital structure, financial reporting, and payout policy. His research has won numerous best paper awards. Since 1997 Graham has been the director of the Global Business Outlook (http://www.cfosurvey.org), a quarterly CFO survey that assesses the business climate and topical economic issues around the world.

[22] John R. Graham and Lilian Mills, "Using Tax Return Data to Simulate Corporate Marginal Tax Rates", *Journal of Accounting and Economics* 46 (2008): 366–380. (SSRN-id959245).

- Finally, other indicators are examined that may provide a more quantitative view of where we are within the range of reasonable long-term estimates for the U.S. ERP.[23]

In most circumstances we would prefer to use the "spot" yield on U. S. government bonds available in the market as a proxy for the U.S. risk-free rate. However, during times of flight to quality and/or high levels of central bank intervention, those lower observed yields imply a lower cost of capital (all other factors held the same) – just the opposite of what one would expect in times of relative economy-wide distress – so a "normalization" adjustment may be considered appropriate. By "normalization" we mean estimating a rate that more likely reflects the sustainable average return of long-term risk-free rates. *If spot yield-to-maturity were used at these times, without any other adjustments, one would arrive at an overall discount rate that is likely inappropriately low vis-à-vis the risks currently facing investors.*

After considering all of the evidence, the long-term risk-free rate (R_f) and long-term equity risk premium (ERP) used in all cost of capital calculations presented herein is the Duff & Phelps recommended ERP (5.5%) as of March 31, 2017, used in conjunction with a normalized risk-free rate (3.5%). This implies a "base" U.S. cost of equity capital of 9.0% (3.5% + 5.5%). To ensure that you are always using the most up-to-date recommendation, visit www.DuffandPhelps.com/CostofCapital and download the document "View Historical Equity Risk Premium Recommendations". The Duff & Phelps recommended ERP should be used with the risk-free rate that it was developed in relation to, per the schedule provided in "View Historical Equity Risk Premium Recommendations".

For a detailed discussion of the equity risk premium and risk-free rate, see the *2017 Valuation Handbook – U.S. Guide to Cost of Capital,* Chapter 3, "Basic Building Blocks of the Cost of Equity Capital – Risk-free Rate and Equity Risk Premium".

---

[23] These additional indicators may include a variation of Professor Aswath Damodaran's "implied ERP model", and/or a variation of the "default spread model" (and/or others). (i) In Damodaran's implied ERP model, a discount rate is first solved for that equates the current S&P 500 index level with estimates of cash distributions (dividends and stock buybacks) in future years, and then a risk-free rate is subtracted from the back-solved discount rate. Dr. Damodaran is Professor of Finance at the Stern School of Business at New York University. To learn more, visit http://pages.stern.nyu.edu/~adamodar/. (ii) The default spread model is based on the premise that the long-term average ERP (the unconditional ERP) is constant and deviations from that average over an economic cycle can be measured by reference to deviations from the long-term average of the default spread (e.g., Baa – Aaa). See Ravi Jagannathan and Zhenyu Wang, "The Conditional CAPM and the Cross-Section of Expected Returns", *The Journal of Finance* 51, no. 1 (March 1996): 3–53. See also Edwin J. Elton, and Martin J. Gruber, Deepak Agrawal, and Christopher Mann, "Is There a Risk Premium in Corporate Bonds?", Working Paper, http://citeseerx.ist.psu.edu/viewdoc/summary?doi=10.1.1.201.2928. See also, Michael Dobner and Joseph Lindsey, "The Default Spread Model: A Practical Method for Measuring Conditional Equity Risk Premium", *Business Valuation Review* 31–32, no. 4 (Fall 2013): pp. 171–178.

Size Premia and Risk Premia Over the Risk-free Rate

The source of the size premia and risk premia over the risk-free rate (used as inputs in the calculation of cost of equity capital estimates presented herein) is the *2017 Valuation Handbook – U.S. Guide to Cost of Capital*.[24] For a detailed discussion of the derivation of the size premia and risk premia over the risk-free rate used herein, see the *2017 Valuation Handbook – U.S. Guide to Cost of Capital*, Chapter 7, "The CRSP Deciles Size Premia Studies and the Risk Premium Report Studies – A Comparison".

Company Screening Process

The company screening process for the analyses presented herein mimics the screening process employed in the Risk Premium Report Study Exhibits that are published in the *2017 Valuation Handbook – U.S. Guide to Cost of Capital*. The result is a smaller set of "healthy" companies, but this is by design: the set of companies remaining after this screening process (i) are "seasoned" companies in that they have been traded for several years, (ii) have been selling at least a minimal quantity of product or services, and (iii) have been able to achieve a degree of positive cash flow from operations. "High-financial-risk" companies are identified and analyzed separately.

The results of the company screening process outlined in the following sections resulted in 1,986 companies in the main set of "healthy" companies, and 369 companies in the "high-financial-risk" set of companies.

Pre-screens

The company screening process begins with companies found in the predefined S&P's *Research Insight* database set that contains "publicly held U.S. corporations that trade common stock and wholly-owned subsidiaries that issue preferred stock or public debt".[25] In the next step, the following types of firms are excluded from the analysis:[26]

- American depositary receipts (ADRs)
- Non-operating holding companies
- Unseasoned companies
- High-financial-risk companies

---

[24] In the *2017 Valuation Handbook – U.S. Guide to Cost of Capital*, the data previously published in (i) the Morningstar/Ibbotson *SBBI Valuation Yearbook* and (ii) the Duff & Phelps *Risk Premium Report* have been renamed the "CRSP Deciles Size Study" and the "Risk Premium Report Study", respectively. Both of these key valuation data sets are now published in the *2017 Valuation Handbook – U.S. Guide to Cost of Capital*. The *Valuation Handbook – U.S. Guide to Cost of Capital* has been published annually since 2014.

[25] In S&P's *Research Insight* database terminology, this is the "$C" set.

[26] Financial service companies (companies in finance, insurance, or real estate; specifically, those companies in SIC code 6) are *excluded* in the Risk Premium Report Study screening process. Because companies in SIC code 6 are excluded from the calculation of Risk Premium Report Study size premia and risk premia, cost of equity capital and WACC calculations are *not* presented for those SICs that begin with 6 for the "Risk Premium Report "CAPM + Size Premia" or "Build-up 1" models.

Unseasoned Companies

The small-cap universe may consist of a disproportionate number of start-up companies and recent initial public offerings. These "unseasoned" companies may be inherently riskier than companies with a track record of viable performance. For this reason, the universe of companies is screened to exclude companies with any of the following characteristics:

- Companies lacking 5 years of publicly traded price history.

- Companies with sales below $1 million in any of the previous five fiscal years.

- Companies with a negative 5-year-average EBITDA (earnings before interest, taxes, depreciation and amortization) for the previous five fiscal years.[27]

- Companies not listed on one of the major US stock exchanges (NYSE, NYSE MKT, or NASDAQ).[28]

High-Financial-Risk Companies

After eliminating companies with the characteristics described above, the remaining companies are screened again to identify those considered to be in the "high-financial-risk" category. These companies have any of the following characteristics:

- Companies that are identified in S&P's *Research Insight* database as in bankruptcy or in liquidation.

- Companies with a negative "5-year average net income available to common equity" for the previous five years. Net income to common equity, as we have defined it in this book, is net income for the corporation minus dividends on preferred stock. While accounting rules define net income as after-tax earnings before payment of dividends (both on preferred and common equity capital), preferred capital is senior to common equity in the hierarchy of risk within the capital structure. Therefore, we subtract preferred dividends, the return on preferred equity, in arriving at the return on common equity and net income on common equity.

- Companies with negative book value of equity at any one of the company's previous five fiscal year-ends.

---

[27] Starting with the *2017 Valuation Handbook – U.S. Industry Cost of Capital* (this book), this screening step has been modified for companies in Division H: Finance, Insurance, and Real Estate (major groups between SICs beginning with "60" and "67"). For companies in SICs that begin with "60" (Depository Institutions), "61" (Non-depository Credit Institutions), and "62" (Security and Commodity Brokers, Dealers, Exchanges, and Services), a proxy for EBITDA is now calculated as follows: pre-tax income minus special items plus depreciation and amortization plus interest expense on long-term debt. For companies in SICs that begin with "63" (Insurance Carriers), "64" (Insurance Agents, Brokers, and Service), "65" (Real Estate), and "67" (Holding and other Investment Offices), a proxy for EBITDA is now calculated as follows: pre-tax income minus special items plus depreciation and amortization plus total interest expense. For more information, refer to Appendix D: Definitions of Standard & Poor's *Compustat* Data Items Used in Calculations.

[28] The "NYSE MKT" is the former American Stock Exchange, or AMEX.

- Companies with a negative "5-year-average operating income" (defined as net sales minus cost of goods sold; selling, general and administrative expenses; and depreciation) for the previous five years.[29]

- Companies with a debt-to-total capital ratio exceeding 80% (debt is measured in book value terms, and total capital is measured as book value of debt plus market value of equity) which fall in SICs in any of the following divisions.[30]

    - **Division A:** Agriculture, Forestry, and Fishing (Major groups between "01" and "09")
    - **Division B:** Mining (Major groups between "10" and "14")
    - **Division C:** Construction (Major groups between "15" and "17")
    - **Division D:** Manufacturing (Major groups between "20" and "39")
    - **Division E:** Transportation, Communications, Electric, Gas, and Sanitary Services (Major groups between "40" and "49")
    - **Division F:** Wholesale Trade (Major groups between "50" and "51")
    - **Division G:** Retail Trade (Major groups between "52" and "59")
    - **Division I:** Services (Major groups between "70" and "89")

- Companies that fall in SICs of the following division are screened in a slightly modified fashion:

    - **Division H:** Finance, Insurance, and Real Estate (Major groups between "60" and "67")

The same "80% debt-to-total-capital ratio" rule is applied to companies in SICs that begin with "62" (Security and Commodity Brokers, Dealers, Exchanges, and Services), "63" (Insurance Carriers), "64" (Insurance Agents, Brokers, and Service), and "67" (Holding and Other Investment Offices). Companies in these SICs, *and* with debt-to-total-capital ratios exceeding 80%, are identified and placed in the "high-financial-risk" category. Companies in SICs 62, 63, 64, and 67 tend to hold less debt than depository institutions, credit institutions, or real estate companies, and

---

[29] Starting with the 2017 Valuation Handbook – U.S. Industry Cost of Capital (this book), this screening step has been modified for companies in Division H: Finance, Insurance, and Real Estate (major groups between SICs starting with "60" and "67"). For companies in SICs that begin with "60" (Depository Institutions), "61" (Non-depository Credit Institutions), and "62" (Security and Commodity Brokers, Dealers, Exchanges, and Services), a proxy for operating income is now calculated as follows: pre-tax income minus special items plus interest expense on long-term debt. For companies in SICs that begin with "63" (Insurance Carriers), "64" (Insurance Agents, Brokers, and Service), "65" (Real Estate), and "67" (Holding and other Investment Offices), a proxy for operating income is now calculated as follows: pre-tax income minus special items plus total interest expense. For more information, refer to Appendix D: Definitions of Standard & Poor's *Compustat* Data Items Used in Calculations.

[30] Companies in Division J: Public Administration (Major groups between "91" and "99") are not included in the analysis presented herein.

therefore may be more similar to a non-financial company with respect to capital structure.

For companies in SICs that begin with "60" (Depository Institutions), "61" (Non-depository Credit Institutions), and "65" (Real Estate), a two-step process is applied:

In the first step, the threshold of debt-to-total-capital for being assigned to the "high-financial-risk" company set is increased from 80% to 95%. Given the nature of their business, companies in SICs 60, 61, and 65 tend to hold larger amounts of debt than (i) non-financial companies or (ii) companies in SICs 62, 63, 64, and 67.

In the second step, those companies that (i) were identified in the first step as having a debt-to-total-capital exceeding 95%, *and* (ii) which had been "bailed out" in the U.S. Treasury Department's Capital Purchase Program (CPP) during the 2008 Financial Crisis were identified.[31] These companies are *not* assigned to the "high-financial-risk" company set, but are returned to the main set of companies analyzed herein. This is done because it may not be unusual for companies that received these CPP funds to still have debt-to-total-capital ratios exceeding 95%, even though they may no longer be perceived to be in distress.

Identifying "Pure Play" Companies

The final step in the company screening process is identifying those companies that have at least 75% of their revenue derived from a single business segment (i.e., pure play companies). SIC codes are assigned by Standard & Poor's based on the activities of each segment as described in the company's 10-K and Annual Report.[32]

Companies that do *not* meet the 75% threshold (i.e., less than 75% of sales derived from a single SIC) are discarded from both the main "healthy" company set and the "high-financial-risk" set, and are *not* included in any further analysis. Companies that *do* meet the 75% threshold (i.e., greater than or equal to 75% of sales derived from a single SIC) are *included* in the analysis presented in this book. The 75% threshold is applied at the 4-, 3-, 2-, and 1-digit level, in turn, as we broaden the SIC level (i.e., we move from an individual industry into an industry group, major group, and division).

The "75% rule" ensures that *each* company in *each* level of industry analyzed in the *2017 Valuation Handbook – U.S. Industry Cost of Capital* is more or less a "pure play" participant in the industry being analyzed. Including "conglomerates" (i.e., companies that participate in many industry segments, with no clear industry segment dominating) would likely dilute the specificity of our analysis, which is designed to be (to the degree possible) a *targeted* industry analysis.

---

[31] The CPP was one of the various programs introduced within the broader Troubled Asset Recovery Program (TARP), which in turn was created in October 2008 to address the then ongoing financial crisis. The CPP program consisted primarily in U.S. government purchases of preferred stock in troubled banks. For more details on the various TARP programs, see the Congressional Research Service report entitled "Troubled Asset Relief Program (TARP): Implementation and Status", June 27, 2013. For a list of the financial institutions that used the CPP, visit CNN Money at http://money.cnn.com/news/specials/storysupplement/bankbailout/.

[32] Source: S&P's *Research Insight* database.

You may notice that companies may be included in *several* different (though related) industries, or you may also identify companies that are *not* included in an industry in which the company *does* participate. To demonstrate how this can occur, and to aid in understanding how the company sets are identified for each industry, consider the two hypothetical companies shown in Exhibit 2. Company 1 and Company 2 *both* derive 100% of their revenue from the same 4-digit SIC codes, but end up being included in the analysis for *different* sets of industries.

At the 4-digit SIC level, Company 1 will be included in the industry analysis for SIC 1382 (it derives 83% of its revenue from SIC 1382 and thus satisfies the 75% threshold). At the 3-digit SIC level, Company 1 will be included in the industry analysis for SIC 138 (again, it derives 83% of its revenue from SIC 138 and thus satisfies the 75% threshold). At the 2-digit SIC level, Company 1 derives 100% of its revenues from a single industry (SIC 13); at the 1-digit SIC level, Company 1 derives 100% of its revenues from a single industry (SIC 1), and will thus also be included in the industry analysis for both of those SIC levels.

The final result for Company 1 is summarized as follows: Company 1 will appear in the industry analysis for SICs 1382, 138, 13, and 1.

Exhibit 2: The "75% Rule" for Identifying "Pure Play" Companies in SICs

Company 1

SIC	SIC Description	Revenues
1311	Crude Petroleum and Natural Gas	$ 5
1321	Natural Gas Liquids	$ 12
1382	Oil and Gas Field Exploration Services	$ 83
	Total Revenues	$ 100

Company 2

SIC	SIC Description	Revenues
1311	Crude Petroleum and Natural Gas	$ 33
1321	Natural Gas Liquids	$ 33
1382	Oil and Gas Field Exploration Services	$ 34
	Total Revenues	$ 100

Look now to Company 2 in Exhibit 2. At the 4-digit level, Company 2 will *not* be included in the industry analysis for SICs 1311, 1321, or 1382 (the company does not derive at least 75% of its revenue from any one of these SICs, and thus does not satisfy the 75% threshold in any instance). Nor does Company 2 meet the 75% threshold at the 3-digit SIC level, and thus will not be included in the analysis for SICs 131, 132, or 138. However, at the 2-digit and 1-digit SIC level, Company 2 derives 100% of its revenue from SIC 13 and SIC 1, respectively, and thus will be included in the industry analysis for both SIC 13 and SIC 1.

The final result for Company 2 is summarized as follows: Company 2 will appear in the industry analysis for SICs 13 and 1 only.

Medians and Industry Composites

Statistics are presented in five ways for each industry: (i) the Median, (ii) the SIC Composite, (iii) the Large Composite, (iv) the Small Composite, and (v) High-Financial-Risk companies.[33] This is done in an effort to enrich the analysis by examining each industry's company set from different perspectives.

The Median, the SIC Composite, the Large Composite, and the Small Composite are calculated using the presumably "healthy" companies for each industry that (i) survived the company screening process, and (ii) were not placed in the high-financial-risk category.

The High-Financial-Risk statistics for each industry are calculated separately and reported on a separate line. The High-Financial-Risk statistics can be thought of as a "composite" of all *high-financial-risk* companies for each industry. For any given SIC, there must be at least five High-Financial-Risk companies in order for the SIC's High-Financial-Risk statistics to be calculated. In other words, even if the SIC itself has at least five companies in the main "Healthy" set of companies, if there are not at least 5 High-Financial-Risk companies, the High-Financial-Risk statistics will not be reported.

Median

A median is different than a simple average. A median's proximate definition is the *middle* value (i.e., the 50th percentile) of a set of values ranked from highest to lowest. As such, the median can be thought of as the "typical" observation. When compared to a simple average, the median can have the effect of dampening the effect of outliers (i.e., extreme values that are not "typical").

In this book, the median is calculated by first calculating the given statistic for each *individual* company in the industry's company set, and then identifying the median (i.e., middle value). For example, to calculate the median value of say, debt-to-equity for Industry ABC, the calculation of the debt-to-equity ratio for *each* of the individual companies in Industry ABC is first calculated, the results are ranked from highest to lowest, and then the middle value is identified.[34,35]

---

[33] Depending on data availability; some industries (or individual statistics within industries) may not have sufficient data available to calculate meaningful values.

[34] When the total number of observations is *odd*, the middle value is the single middle observation (there are an equal number of observations above and below this single observation). When the total number of observation is *even*, however, there is no single "middle" observation, and so the median is calculated as the average of the two middle observations.

[35] Medians in this book are all calculated in this fashion, with the exception of price to earnings (P/E), price to book (P/B), and price to sales (P/S), which are calculated by first calculating the *inverse* of each company's respective ratio, identifying the median, and then taking the inverse of this median result. See the Morningstar methodology paper entitled "Average Price Ratios" (August 31, 2005).

SIC Composite

The SIC Composite is calculated in order to give the analyst a sense of the characteristics of the industry *as a whole*. The SIC Composite includes all companies identified in the screening process as "healthy", and having at least 75% of their revenues derived from a single SIC code.

Large Composite

The Large Composite is calculated in order to give the analyst a sense of the characteristics of the *largest* companies in the specific industry. The Large Composite includes all companies identified in the screening process as "healthy", and having at least 75% of their revenues derived from a single SIC code.

Small Composite

The Small Composite is calculated in order to give the analyst a sense of the characteristics of the *smallest* companies in the specific industry. The Small Composite includes all companies identified in the screening process as "healthy", and having at least 75% of their revenues derived from a single SIC code.

Identification of the Companies that Comprise the Large and Small Composites

For industries that have fewer than 10 companies, the Large and Small Composites are not calculated due to the limited size of the sample. For industries that have 10 companies or more, the Large Composite and the Small Composite are identified as either (i) the largest three and the smallest three companies in terms of reported net sales amount (in U.S. dollars) for the most recent fiscal year, or (ii) the largest and smallest 10% (rounded down to the nearest integer), whichever is greater, as summarized in Exhibit 3.

Exhibit 3: Identification of Large and Small Composites

No. Companies	Large Composite	Small Composite
5–9 companies	Not Calculated	Not Calculated
10–39 companies	3 largest companies in terms of Sales	3 smallest companies in terms of Sales
40+ companies	Largest 10% of companies in terms of Sales (rounded *down* to nearest integer)	Smallest 10% of companies in terms of Sales (rounded *down* to nearest integer)

For example, if an industry is comprised of 64 companies, the Large Composite and Small Composite will each have 6 companies in them (10% of 64 companies is 6.4; this is then rounded down to the "nearest integer", which is 6).

Companies in the Large Composite and Small Composite are identified using the *most recent* fiscal year's sales data (in U.S. dollars); these companies are used in all calculations across all time periods, even if they are not necessarily the largest and smallest companies in prior periods (e.g., this could arise when computing 5-year averages).

Composites Are Aggregates

The main difference between the calculation of the median and "composite" values in the analysis presented herein is that the median calculation is performed at the *individual* company level, and the calculations done for the SIC Composite, Large Composite, Small Composite, or a composite of all high-financial-risk companies are performed on an *aggregate* basis.

"Aggregation" is employed to calculate the statistics for all composites to give the analyst a sense of the characteristics of all of the companies in the given composite (SIC Composite, Large Composite, Small Composite, or a composite of all high-financial-risk companies) if they were "rolled up" into a single entity. Alternatively, the analyst can look to the Median to get a sense of the "typical" company in the industry.

Aggregation is arguably a superior technique when discussing "industry" statistics to that of employing simple averages or some other non-aggregative technique. Aggregation also has the effect of *dampening* the effect of outliers (i.e., extreme values that are not "typical") on the analysis. Examples of how this aggregation technique is applied are provided in the following sections.

"Latest" and "5-Year" Averages

In most cases, the financial statistics presented herein are calculated over two different periods: (i) Latest and (ii) 5-Year Average. The "Latest" calculation is as of the "data through" date of this book (March 31, 2017), whereas the "5-Year Average" is the average statistic for the most recent 5-year period.[36] The Latest calculation can be thought of as a "snapshot" analysis of the industry's characteristics as of "now" (i.e., as of March 31, 2017), and the 5-Year Average calculation can be thought of as an "over time" analysis (i.e., over the last 5 years). Again, the Median calculation can be thought of as the "typical" observation in the sample.

The hypothetical data in Exhibit 4 will be used to demonstrate the aggregation methodology employed to calculate the Median, Latest, and 5-Year Average financial statistics presented herein. In all of these examples, calculation of a simple debt-to-equity ratio is performed for illustration purposes. In these examples, a generic "composite" is calculated, although these *same* steps are followed for the SIC Composite, the Large Composite, the Small Composite, or a composite of all high-financial-risk companies.

---

[36] Some data points used as inputs in the analyses presented herein are "annual" in nature, and some data points are "monthly" in nature. When "annual" in nature, the "Latest" statistics are calculated using the most recent fiscal year's data, while the "5-Year Average" statistics are calculated using the most recent five (or in some cases, six) years' fiscal data. When "monthly" in nature, the "Latest" statistics are calculated using the most recent month's data as of the "data through" date of this book (March 31, 2017), while the "5-Year Average" statistics are calculated using the most recent 60 months (or in some cases, 72 months).

Exhibit 4: Hypothetical Debt and Equity Data for Calculation Examples of Median, Latest, and 5-Year Average Debt-to-Equity Statistics

	A Year [-4] Total Debt	B Year [-3] Total Debt	C Year [-2] Total Debt	D Year [-1] Total Debt	E Year [0] Total Debt
Company 1	1	2	3	4	5
Company 2	6	7	8	9	10
Company 3	11	12	13	14	15

	F Year [-4] Total Equity	G Year [-3] Total Equity	H Year [-2] Total Equity	I Year [-1] Total Equity	J Year [0] Total Equity
Company 1	12	23	35	45	57
Company 2	9	21	32	44	54
Company 3	8	18	30	41	53

Calculating "Latest" Medians

To calculate the "Latest" Median debt-to-equity industry statistic, the debt-to-equity ratio of each *individual* company is first calculated as of the most recent (i.e., "Latest") period, and then the median is identified. The "Latest" total debt is in Column E of Exhibit 4 (i.e., "Year [0]" or the most recent fiscal year), and the "Latest" total equity is in Column J.

As shown in Exhibit 5, "Latest" debt-to-equity ratios for Company 1, Company 2, and Company 3 are 0.09, 0.19, and 0.28, respectively. The median (i.e., middle value) is 0.19.

Exhibit 5: Calculation Example of "Latest" Median Debt-to-Equity Statistic

	E Year [0] Total Debt		Debt-to-Equity (Latest)
Company 1	5	Company 1	5 ÷ 57 = 0.09
Company 2	10	Company 2	10 ÷ 54 = 0.19 ←
Company 3	15	Company 3	15 ÷ 53 = 0.28

	J Year [0] Total Equity
Company 1	57
Company 2	54
Company 3	53

Calculating "5-Year Average" Medians

To calculate the "5-Year Average" Median debt-to-equity statistic, the debt-to-equity ratio of each *individual* company is calculated by aggregating the most recent 5-years' debt, and dividing it by the aggregate of the most recent 5-years' equity, and then identifying the median.

Based on the procedure just described, the 5-Year Average debt-to-equity ratios for Company 1, Company 2, and Company 3 are 0.09, 0.25, and 0.43, respectively (see Exhibit 6). The median (i.e., middle value) is 0.25. Note that this differs from computing a straight 5-year arithmetic average of each company's debt-to-equity ratio over the last five years, and then taking a median. Such a calculation would have resulted in a median of 0.33 and would have given a greater weight to outlier observations.

Exhibit 6: Calculation Example of "5-Year Average" Median Debt-to-Equity Statistic

	A Year [-4] Total Debt	B Year [-3] Total Debt	C Year [-2] Total Debt	D Year [-1] Total Debt	E Year [0] Total Debt	5-Year Aggregate Debt
Company 1	1	2	3	4	5	1 + 2 + 3 + 4 + 5 = 15
Company 2	6	7	8	9	10	6 + 7 + 8 + 9 + 10 = 40
Company 3	11	12	13	14	15	11 + 12 + 13 + 14 + 15 = 65

	F Year [-4] Total Equity	G Year [-3] Total Equity	H Year [-2] Total Equity	I Year [-1] Total Equity	J Year [0] Total Equity	5-Year Aggregate Equity
Company 1	12	23	35	45	57	12 + 23 + 35 + 45 + 57 = 172
Company 2	9	21	32	44	54	9 + 21 + 32 + 44 + 54 = 160
Company 3	8	18	30	41	53	8 + 18 + 30 + 41 + 53 = 150

	5-Year Aggregate Debt		5-Year Average Debt-to-Equity
Company 1	15	Company 1	15 ÷ 172 = 0.09
Company 2	40	Company 2	40 ÷ 160 = 0.25
Company 3	65	Company 3	65 ÷ 150 = 0.43

	5-Year Aggregate Equity
Company 1	172
Company 2	160
Company 3	150

Calculating "Latest" Composites

To calculate the "Latest" SIC Composite, Large Composite, Small Composite, or a composite of all high-financial-risk Companies' debt-to-equity statistic, the most recent (i.e., "Latest") period's *aggregate* debt is divided by the most recent period's *aggregate* equity. The "Latest" total debt is in Column E of Exhibit 4 (i.e., "Year [0]" or the most recent fiscal year) and the "Latest" total equity is in Column J.

In Exhibit 7, the "Latest" aggregate total debt (for all companies in the industry) is 30, and the "Latest" aggregate total equity is 164. The "Latest" debt-to-equity ratio is therefore 0.18 (30 ÷ 164).

This *same* aggregation technique is used in the calculation of all "composite" statistics: the SIC Composite, the Large Composite, the Small Composite, and a composite of all high-financial-risk companies. The only item that will vary across these various composites is the number (and identity) of companies included in the set being aggregated.

Exhibit 7: Calculation Example of "Latest" Composite Debt-to-Equity Statistic

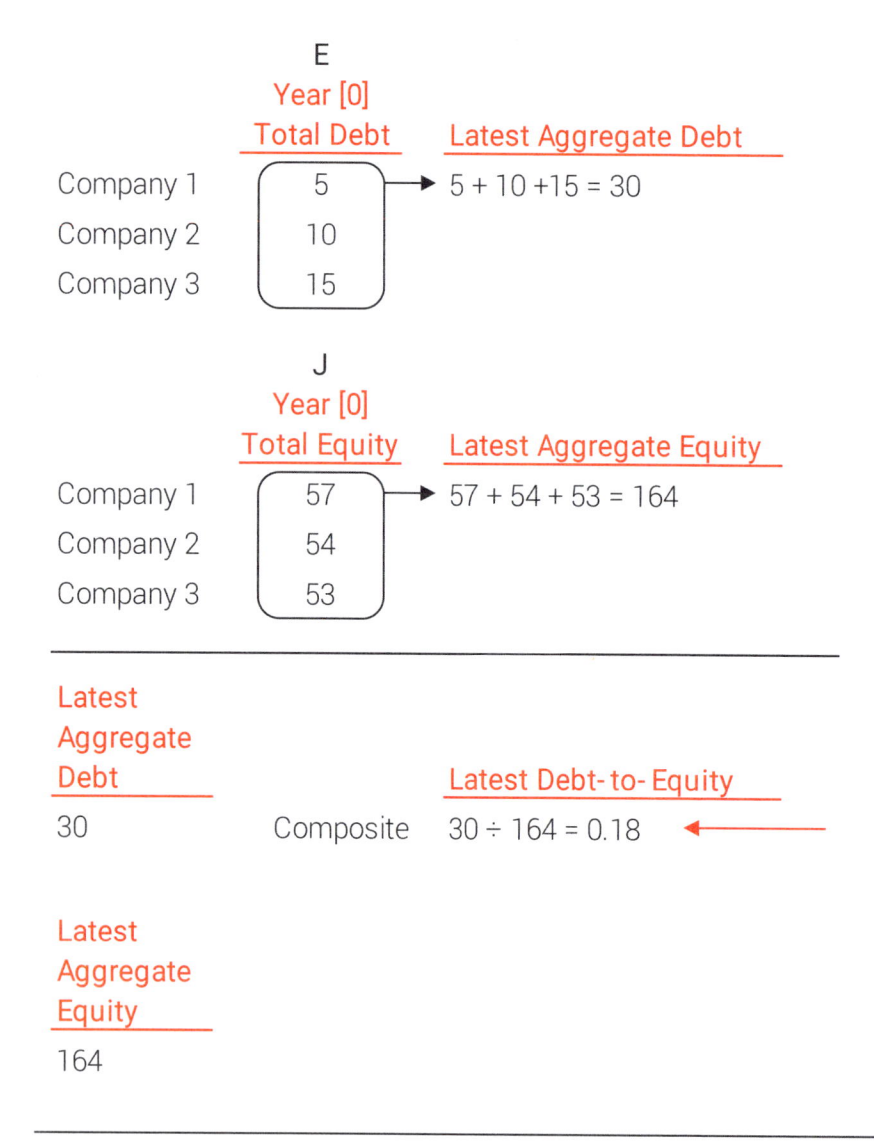

	E Year [0] Total Debt	Latest Aggregate Debt
Company 1	5	5 + 10 + 15 = 30
Company 2	10	
Company 3	15	

	J Year [0] Total Equity	Latest Aggregate Equity
Company 1	57	57 + 54 + 53 = 164
Company 2	54	
Company 3	53	

Latest Aggregate Debt		Latest Debt-to-Equity
30	Composite	30 ÷ 164 = 0.18

Latest Aggregate Equity
164

Calculating "5-Year Average" Composites

To calculate the "5-Year Average" Composite debt-to-equity statistic, the aggregate debt amount is first computed by summing the debt of all companies included in the Composite over the most recent 5 years. The same procedure is employed to arrive at an aggregate equity amount over the most recent 5 years. The "5-Year Average" Composite debt-to-equity statistic is then obtained by dividing the *aggregate* of the most recent 5-years' debt by the *aggregate* of the most recent 5 years' equity.

Based on the procedure just described, the 5-Year Average aggregate debt for Company 1, Company 2, and Company 3 is 120, while the 5-Year Average aggregate equity is 482. The "5-Year Average" Composite debt-to-equity is 0.25 (120 ÷ 482), as shown in Exhibit 8.

Exhibit 8: Calculation Example of "5-Year Average" Composite Debt-to-Equity Statistic

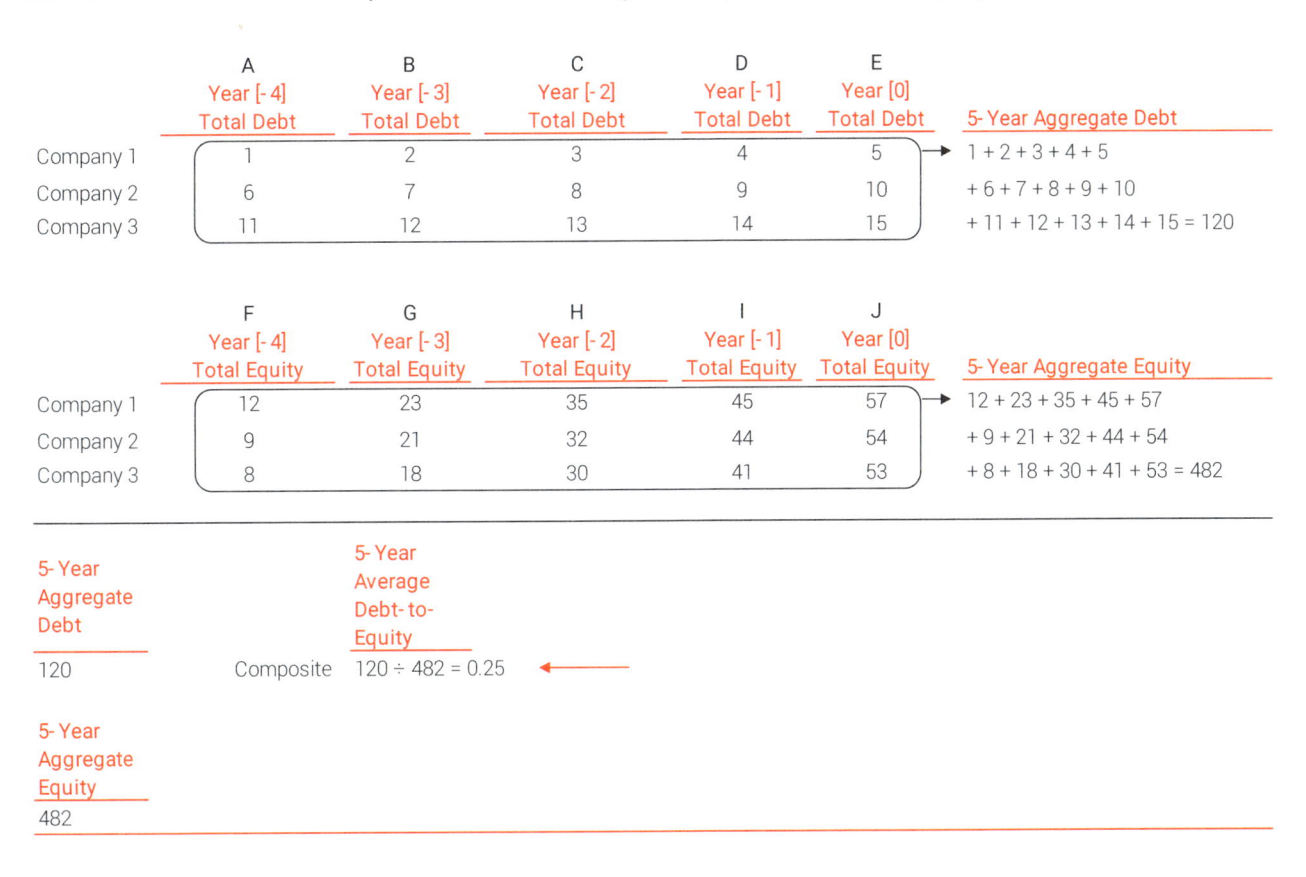

	A Year [-4] Total Debt	B Year [-3] Total Debt	C Year [-2] Total Debt	D Year [-1] Total Debt	E Year [0] Total Debt	5-Year Aggregate Debt
Company 1	1	2	3	4	5	1 + 2 + 3 + 4 + 5
Company 2	6	7	8	9	10	+ 6 + 7 + 8 + 9 + 10
Company 3	11	12	13	14	15	+ 11 + 12 + 13 + 14 + 15 = 120

	F Year [-4] Total Equity	G Year [-3] Total Equity	H Year [-2] Total Equity	I Year [-1] Total Equity	J Year [0] Total Equity	5-Year Aggregate Equity
Company 1	12	23	35	45	57	12 + 23 + 35 + 45 + 57
Company 2	9	21	32	44	54	+ 9 + 21 + 32 + 44 + 54
Company 3	8	18	30	41	53	+ 8 + 18 + 30 + 41 + 53 = 482

5-Year Aggregate Debt		5-Year Average Debt-to-Equity	
120	Composite	120 ÷ 482 = 0.25	
5-Year Aggregate Equity			
482			

Calculation of Industry Financial Statistics

Three Largest and Three Smallest Companies by Sales and Total Assets

The three largest and three smallest companies shown for each industry are determined and presented herein by (i) net sales (i.e., gross sales reduced by cash discounts, trade discounts, and returned sales and allowances for which credit is given to customers), and (ii) total assets (current assets *plus* net property, plant, and equipment *plus* other non-current assets) for the most recent fiscal year as of March 31, 2017.

Annualized Monthly Performance Statistics

Annualized monthly performance statistics (geometric return, arithmetic return, and standard deviation) are calculated using the total returns[37] of a portfolio comprised of all companies in each industry over the most recent five-year (60 months) period, the most recent three-year (36 months) period, and the most recent one-year (12 months) period as of the most recent month (in this book, the "most recent month" is March 31, 2017).

Portfolio formation

To compute the total returns for a portfolio comprised of each industry's company set, the portfolio returns are market-capitalization-weighted as follows: the end-of-month market capitalization in the *previous* month for *each* company in a specific industry (or composite) is used as the weight for *each* month in the period being examined (i.e., 60-, 36-, or 12-month periods).

Geometric returns

To calculate the annualized monthly geometric average (i.e., compound) return for an industry, the following formula is applied to the industry's monthly portfolio total returns over the given period:

$$R_g = \left[\prod_{m=1}^{n_m} (1+R_m) \right]^{\frac{1}{n_a}} - 1$$

where:

R_g	=	Annualized monthly geometric average return
R_m	=	Portfolio return in month m
n_m	=	Number of monthly periods (60, 36, or 12 months)
n_a	=	Number of annual periods (5, 3, or 1 year)

---

[37] "Total returns" assume dividend reinvestment.

Arithmetic returns

To calculate the annualized monthly arithmetic average return for an industry, the following formula is applied to the industry's monthly portfolio total returns over the given period (60, 36, or 12 months):

$$R_a = (1+Avg)^{12} - 1$$

where:
- R_a = Annualized monthly arithmetic average return
- Avg = Arithmetic average of monthly total return over the given period (60, 36, or 12 months)

Standard Deviation

To calculate the annualized monthly standard deviation for an industry, the following formula is applied to the industry's monthly portfolio total returns over the given period (60, 36, or 12 months):

$$SD_A = \sqrt{\left[SD_m^2 + (1+Avg)^2\right]^{12} - (1+Avg)^{24}}$$

where:
- SD_A = Annualized monthly standard deviation
- SD_m = Standard deviation of monthly total returns over the given period (60, 36, or 12 months)
- Avg = Arithmetic average of monthly total return over the given period (60, 36, or 12 months)

For performance benchmarking purposes, the same return statistics are also calculated and presented for the "market" (as represented by the S&P 500 total return index), over the same 60-, 36-, and 12-month periods.[38]

Number of Companies in the Median, the Composites, and the High-Financial-Risk Category

The number of companies in the Median, SIC Composite, Large Composite, Small Composite, and High-Financial-Risk category appears in the first occurrence of these designations (in the "Returns Ratios" section).

---

[38] Source of underlying returns for the S&P 500 total return index: Morningstar *Direct* database. All calculations by Duff & Phelps LLC.

The number of companies in the SIC Composite appears directly to the right of "SIC Composite", in parentheses (Example: "SIC Composite (114)"). This is the total number of companies (114) in the industry; this number will *match* the number that appears in the upper left of each Industry Data Exhibit (e.g., "Number of Companies: 114"). The number of companies in the "Large" and "Small" Composite are presented in the same fashion.

The SIC Composite number of companies is the number of "healthy" companies in the main company set for each industry; this number does *not* include the High-Financial-Risk set of companies. The High-Financial-Risk statistics are calculated *separately*. The number of companies in the High-Financial-Risk appears directly to the right of "High-Financial-Risk", in parentheses (Example: "High-Financial-Risk (10)").

Return Ratios

Return on Assets

Latest:

$$ROA_i = \frac{IBEI_i}{TA_i}$$

$$TA_i = \frac{BA + EA}{2}$$

5-Year Average:

$$ROA_{i,n} = \frac{\sum_{n=1}^{n} IBEI_{i,n}}{\sum_{n=1}^{n} TA_{i,n}}$$

where:

ROA_i	=	Return on total assets for company or portfolio *i*
$IBEI_i$	=	After-tax income before extraordinary items for company or portfolio *i*
TA_i	=	Total assets for company or portfolio *i*
BA	=	Beginning of year total assets
EA	=	End of year total assets
$ROA_{i,n}$	=	Return on total assets for company or portfolio *i* over *n* periods (in this case 5 years)
$IBEI_{i,n}$	=	After-tax income before extraordinary items for company or portfolio *i* over *n* periods
$TA_{i,n}$	=	Total assets for company or portfolio *i* over *n* periods

Latest

The "Latest" statistic is calculated as after-tax income before extraordinary items for the most recent fiscal year divided by average total assets for the most recent fiscal year. Average total assets for the most recent fiscal year is calculated as the average of the total assets as of the most recent fiscal year (FY[0]) and the total assets as of the second most recent fiscal year (FY[-1]).

5-Year Average

The "5-Year Average" statistic is calculated as the sum of after-tax income before extraordinary items for *each* of the previous five fiscal years divided by the sum of average total assets calculated for *each* of the previous five fiscal years. For example, average total assets for the most recent fiscal year is calculated as the average of the total assets as of the most recent fiscal year (FY[0]) and the total assets as of the second most recent fiscal year (FY[-1]). Average total assets for the second most recent fiscal year is calculated as the average of the total assets as of the second most recent fiscal year (FY[-1]) and total assets as of the third most recent fiscal year (FY[-2]), etc.

After-tax income *before* extraordinary (e.g., one-time) items is used in this calculation because after-tax income excluding extraordinary items is likely a better representation of an expected *sustainable* income stream.

Return on Equity

Latest:

$$ROE_i = \frac{IBEI_i - DVP_i}{BVE_i}$$

$$BVE_i = \frac{BBV + EBV}{2}$$

5-Year Average:

$$ROE_{i,n} = \frac{\sum_{n=1}^{n}(IBEI_{i,n} - DVP_{i,n})}{\sum_{n=1}^{n} BVE_{i,n}}$$

where:

ROE_i	=	Return on equity for company or portfolio i
$IBEI_i$	=	After-tax income before extraordinary items for company or portfolio i
DVP_i	=	Preferred dividends for company or portfolio i
BVE_i	=	Book value of equity for company or portfolio i
BBV	=	Beginning of year book value of equity
EBV	=	End of year book value of equity
$ROE_{i,n}$	=	Return on equity for company or portfolio i over n periods (in this case, 5 years)
$IBEI_{i,n}$	=	After-tax income before extraordinary items for company or portfolio i over n periods
$DVP_{i,n}$	=	Preferred dividends for company or portfolio i over n periods
$BVE_{i,n}$	=	Book value of equity for company or portfolio i over n periods

Latest

The "Latest" statistic is calculated as after-tax income before extraordinary items less preferred stock cash dividends in the most recent fiscal year divided by the average book value of equity for the most recent fiscal year. The average book value of equity for the most recent year is calculated as the average of the book value of equity as of the most recent fiscal year (FY[0]) and the book value of equity as of the second most recent fiscal year (FY[-1]).

5-Year Average

The "5-Year Average" statistic is calculated as the sum of after-tax income before extraordinary items less preferred stock cash dividends for *each* of the previous five fiscal years divided by the sum of average book value of equity calculated for *each* of the previous five fiscal years. For example, average book value of equity for the most recent fiscal year is calculated as the average of the book value of equity as of the most recent fiscal year (FY[0]) and the book value of equity as of the second most recent fiscal year (FY[-1]). Average book value of equity for the second most recent fiscal year is calculated as the average of the book value of equity as of the second most recent fiscal year (FY[-1]) and the book value of equity as of the third most recent fiscal year (FY[-2]), etc.

Again, after-tax income *before* extraordinary (e.g., one-time) items is also used in this calculation because income excluding extraordinary items is likely a better representation of an expected *sustainable* income stream.

Dividend Yield

$$DY_{A,i} = \frac{\sum_{m=1}^{n}(S_{i,m} \times D_{i,m})}{\sum_{m=1}^{n}(S_{i,m} \times P_{i,m})}$$

where:

$DY_{A,i}$ = Dividend yield for company or portfolio i

$S_{i,m}$ = Common shares outstanding for company or portfolio i in month m

$D_{i,m}$ = Dividends per share for company or portfolio i in month m

$P_{i,m}$ = Price per common share for company or portfolio i in month m

The "number of common shares outstanding" data point used is actually a quarterly data point, and so the number of common shares outstanding at the end of the *previous* quarter is assumed for the three months in the *subsequent* quarter. For example, the number of common shares outstanding as of the *end* of March 2012 was used as the number of common shares outstanding in April, May, and June of 2012; the number of common shares outstanding as of the *end* of June 2012 was used as the number of common shares outstanding in July, August, and September of 2012, etc.

Latest

The "Latest" statistic is calculated as the sum of common shares outstanding multiplied by dividends per common share for *each* of the 12 months ending March 31, 2017, which is then divided by the sum of common shares outstanding multiplied by price per common share for *each* of the 12 months ending March 31, 2017.

5-Year Average

The "5-Year Average" statistic is calculated as the sum of common shares outstanding multiplied by *dividends* per common share for *each* of the 60 months ending March 31, 2017, which is then divided by the sum of common shares outstanding multiplied by *price* per common share for *each* of the 60 months ending March 31, 2017.

Liquidity Ratio

Current Ratio

Latest:

$$CR_i = \frac{CA_i}{CL_i}$$

5-Year Average:

$$CR_{i,n} = \frac{\sum_{n=1}^{n} CA_{i,n}}{\sum_{n=1}^{n} CL_{i,n}}$$

where:

CR_i	=	Current ratio for company or portfolio i
CA_i	=	Current assets for company or portfolio i
CL_i	=	Current liabilities for company or portfolio i
$CR_{i,n}$	=	Current ratio for company or portfolio i over n periods (in this case, 5 years)
$CA_{i,n}$	=	Current assets for company or portfolio i over n periods
$CL_{i,n}$	=	Current liabilities for company or portfolio i over n periods

Latest

The "Latest" statistic is calculated as current assets in the most recent fiscal year divided by current liabilities in the most recent fiscal year.

5-Year Average

The "5-Year Average" statistic is calculated as the sum of current assets for *each* of the previous five fiscal years divided by the sum of current liabilities for *each* of the previous five fiscal years.

Profitability Ratio[39]

Operating Margin

Latest:

$$OM_i = \frac{OIAD_i}{NS_i}$$

5-Year Average:

$$OM_{A,i} = \frac{\sum_{n=1}^{n} OIAD_{i,n}}{\sum_{n=1}^{n} NS_{i,n}}$$

where:

OM_i	=	Operating margin for company or portfolio i
$OIAD_i$	=	Operating income after depreciation and amortization for company or portfolio i
NS_i	=	Net sales for company or portfolio i
$OM_{A,i}$	=	Operating margin for company i over n periods (in this case, 5 years)
$OIAD_{i,n}$	=	Operating income after depreciation and amortization for company or portfolio i over n periods
$NS_{i,n}$	=	Net sales for company or portfolio i over n periods

Latest

The "Latest" statistic is calculated as operating income after depreciation and amortization in the most recent fiscal year divided by net sales in the most recent fiscal year.

5-Year Average

The "5-Year Average" statistic is calculated as the sum of operating income after depreciation and amortization for *each* of the previous five fiscal years divided by the sum of net sales for *each* of the previous five fiscal years.

---

[39] The calculation of operating income shown here is used for all SICs (and companies), except for those SICs beginning in "6", or companies in SICs beginning with "6" (specifically, Division H: Finance, Insurance, and Real Estate; Major groups between SICs beginning with "60" and "67"). Starting with the *2017 Valuation Handbook – U.S. Industry Cost of Capital* (this book), for SICs that begin with (and companies that are in) "60" (Depository Institutions), "61" (Non-depository Credit Institutions), and "62" (Security and Commodity Brokers, Dealers, Exchanges, and Services), a proxy for operating income is now calculated as follows: pre-tax income minus special items plus interest expense on long-term debt. For SICs that begin with (and companies that are in) "63" (Insurance Carriers), "64" (Insurance Agents, Brokers, and Service), "65" (Real Estate), and "67" (Holding and other Investment Offices), a proxy for operating income is now calculated as follows: pre-tax income minus special items plus total interest expense. For more information, refer to Appendix D: Definitions of Standard & Poor's *Compustat* Data Items Used in Calculations.

Growth Rates

Long-Term Earnings Per Share (EPS)

Thomson Reuters *I/B/E/S Consensus Estimates* database is the source for analysts' estimates of future earnings growth. Growth rates for long-term earnings are calculated herein on a "Latest" basis only.

Latest

Growth rates for long-term earnings are calculated as the market-capitalization-weighted *I/B/E/S* long-term EPS growth rate. The market capitalization as of the end of the most recent month is used for the weighting (the "most recent month" in this book is March, 2017).

For companies that do *not* have an *I/B/E/S* long-term EPS growth rate, the market-capitalization-weighted growth rate for the most specific SIC code in which the company appears, *and* in which there are at least five companies with growth rates, is substituted. For example, if hypothetical Company ABC in SIC 3714 does not have a growth rate, the market-capitalization-weighted growth rate for the other companies in SIC 3714 are used. If SIC 3714 does not have at least five other companies with growth rates, then the calculation is performed using SIC 371 (up one level, and thus less specific), etc.

Beta Overview[40]

Beta is a measure of the systematic risk of a stock; the tendency of a stock's price to correlate with changes in the overall market. In all cases in the analyses presented herein:

"Excess" total returns of the company (or portfolio) and of the market benchmark are used in the regressions performed to calculate beta.

- A U.S. Treasury 30-day T-bill return is used to calculate monthly "excess" returns (i.e., total returns in excess of the risk-free rate). In other words, in every given month over the time period over which beta is being calculated, the corresponding U.S. 30-day T-bill return for that month is subtracted from the total returns of the company (or portfolio) and from the market benchmark total returns.

- The S&P 500 total return index is used as the "market" benchmark in the regressions performed to calculate beta.

- Beta is calculated over the 60-month period ending March, 2017.[41]

- Betas less than or equal to zero and betas greater than or equal to five are discarded and not included in any further calculations.

- All betas are presented in both "levered" and "unlevered" form:

Levered Betas: Published and calculated beta estimates for public stocks typically reflect the capital structure of each respective firm at market values. The historical beta estimates are typically made using realized returns for the subject business's stock and the stock market as a whole as measured by the market index (e.g., the S&P 500 total return index). These betas are sometimes referred to as "levered" betas, since these beta estimates reflect the actual leverage (i.e., debt) in the subject business's capital structure.

Unlevered Betas: Alternatively, "unlevered" betas (also called "asset" betas) have the effect of financial leverage (i.e., debt) removed, thereby reflecting only the effect of business risk. An unlevered beta is the beta that would be expected if a company were financed only with equity capital.

---

[40] In this book, beta calculations are summarized in equation form in order to document for the reader the methodologies employed; theory is not discussed in detail. To learn more, see the *2017 Valuation Handbook – U.S. Guide to Cost of Capital*, Chapter 5, "Basic Building Blocks of the Cost of Equity Capital – Betas and Industry Risk Premia". Also see *Cost of Capital: Applications and Examples* 5th edition, by Shannon P. Pratt and Roger J. Grabowski, Chapter 11, "Beta: Differing Definitions and Estimates", Appendix 11A, "Examples of Computing OLS Beta, Sum Beta, and Full-Information Beta Estimates", and Appendix 11B, "Estimating Beta: Interpreting Regression Statistics".

[41] Companies lacking 5 years (60 months) of publicly traded price history were discarded in the screening process used to identify the 1,986 "healthy" companies and the 369 "high-financial-risk" companies used in the analyses presented herein, and therefore all betas presented in this book have 60 months of return data. See the section entitled "Company Screening Process".

Levered Betas

Levered betas for companies and portfolios are calculated in the *2017 Valuation Handbook – U.S. Industry Cost of Capital* in three primary ways: (i) raw ordinary least squares (OLS) beta, (ii) sum beta, and (iii) downside beta.

Raw (OLS) Beta

$$(R_i - R_f) = \alpha + \beta_i \times (R_m - R_f) + \varepsilon$$

where:

R_i	=	Historical return on company or portfolio i
R_f	=	Expected return on a risk-free security
α	=	Regression constant
β_i	=	Beta coefficient of company or portfolio i
R_m	=	Historical return on market portfolio
ε	=	Regression error term

Raw (OLS) beta is calculated in this book as a linear regression with a company's (or portfolio's) excess monthly total returns (i.e., returns over the risk-free rate) acting as the dependent variable, and the excess monthly total returns of the market benchmark acting as the independent variable.

Sum Beta

$$(R_{i,n} - R_{f,n}) = \alpha + \beta_n \times (R_{m,n} - R_{f,n}) + \beta_{n-1} \times (R_{m,n-1} - R_{f,n-1}) + \varepsilon$$

$$\beta_{SumBeta} = \beta_n + \beta_{n-1}$$

where:

$(R_{i,n} - R_{f,n})$	=	Excess return on company or portfolio i in current month
α	=	Regression constant
β_n	=	Estimated market coefficient based on sensitivity to excess returns on market portfolio in current month
$(R_{m,n} - R_{f,n})$	=	Excess return on market portfolio in current month
β_{n-1}	=	Estimated market coefficient based on sensitivity to last month's excess returns on market portfolio
$(R_{m,n-1} - R_{f,n-1})$	=	Excess return on market portfolio last month
ε	=	Regression error term

For all but the largest companies, the prices of individual stocks tend to react (in part) to movements in the overall market with a lag. The smaller the company, generally the greater the lag in the price reaction. Sum beta is an attempt to capture more fully the lagged effect of co-movement in a company's returns with returns on the market.

Sum beta is calculated in this book as a multiple regression with a company's (or portfolio's) excess monthly total returns (i.e., returns over the risk-free rate) acting as the dependent variable, and the market's *current* month's excess returns and the market's *previous* month's (i.e., "lagged") excess returns acting as the independent variables, and then summing the resulting coefficients.

Downside Beta

$$\beta_{Downside} = \frac{\sum_{n=1}^{n}\{Min(R_i - B_i, 0) \times Min(R_m - B_m, 0)\}}{\sum_{n=1}^{n}\{Min(R_m - B_m, 0)\}^2}$$

where:

$\beta_{Downside}$ = Downside beta with respect to benchmark return
R_i = Historical return for company or portfolio *i*
B_i = Benchmark return for company or portfolio *i*
R_m = Historical return on market portfolio
B_m = Benchmark return for market portfolio

The "downside" beta attempts to isolate the *downside* potential of a security's returns relative to that of the market's returns. According to this measure, securities that magnify the market's upward swings are not necessarily risky; only those that magnify the market's downward swings are. The assumption made when using downside beta is that when assessing risk, investors are only interested in the relative downside potential with respect to any chosen benchmark.[42]

---

[42] As *paraphrased* from Javier Estrada, "Downside Risk in Practice", *Journal of Applied Corporate Finance* (Winter 2006): 117–125. The downside beta methodology employed in this book is based upon this same paper, as is the equation shown. Like all betas calculated and presented in the analyses herein, "excess" returns were used in the calculation of the downside betas as well.

Peer Group Beta

"Peer group" betas for composite portfolios are calculated based upon the sales-weighted "full-information" betas of the industries in which all companies in the SIC Composite, Large Composite, Small Composite, or composite of all high-financial-risk companies participate.[43] In Exhibit 9, an example of calculating a peer group beta is shown.

Exhibit 9: Calculation of Composite Peer Group Betas

2-digit SIC Code	2-digit SIC Description	Full Information Beta	Sales In Industry (in millions)	% of Sales in Industry	Sales-weighted Full-Information Beta Component
12	Coal Mining	0.90	$5	17%	(17% x 0.90) = 0.15
13	Oil and Gas Extraction	1.28	$7	23%	(23% x 1.28) = 0.29
14	Mining and Quarrying of Nonmetallic Minerals	1.40	$18	60%	(60% x 1.40) = 0.84
					Peer Group Beta
					0.15 + 0.29 + 0.84 = 1.29

At the composite-level (SIC Composite, Large Composite, Small Composite, or a composite of all high-financial-risk companies for each industry), this calculation is performed by *aggregation*. For the given set of companies in the composite, a unique list of all SICs (i.e., industries) from which any company in the set derives sales is first identified. The aggregate sales for each of these industries are then compiled, and, in conjunction with the corresponding full-information betas for the industries from which the company derives sales revenue, a sales-weighted peer group beta is calculated.

---

[43] The full-information betas calculated and used in the analyses presented in this book are based upon an article by Paul D. Kaplan and James D. Peterson, "Full-Information Industry Betas", *Financial Management*, Summer 1998, 85–93. The full-information beta methodology is based on the premise that a business can be thought of as a portfolio of assets. The full-information methodology is designed to capture the impact that the individual segments have upon the overall business beta. The full-information betas used in the calculations herein are calculated as of March 31, 2017 using groupings of companies at the 2-digit SIC level. There were a total of 55 2-digit SIC full-information betas calculated as of March 31, 2017.

Adjusted Betas

Cost of capital is inherently a forward-looking concept, and thus all of its inputs should also be forward-looking. Betas are generally calculated using historical data, and the betas calculated in this fashion may be "forward-looking" only to the degree that history repeats itself.

There are several "adjustment" techniques that can be used in an effort to make a historical beta more forward-looking. "Adjusted" betas for companies and portfolios are calculated in the *2017 Valuation Handbook – U.S. Industry Cost of Capital* using two commonly used techniques. The first of these (Blume)[44] adjusts to the market beta of 1.0; the second of these (Vasicek)[45] is used to adjust to the industry peer group beta, dependent on the statistical quality of the calculated raw (OLS) beta.

Blume-Adjusted Beta

This adjustment is sometimes referred to as the "Blume" adjustment, or the "one third/two thirds" adjustment. This technique has been popularized in Bloomberg terminals, even though many users may be unaware of what it really represents. The so-called "Bloomberg Adjusted Beta" is nothing more than the application of the "Blume" adjustment.

This is a mechanical "one size fits all" adjustment that has the net effect of adjusting historical betas toward the "market" beta of 1.0 (i.e., historical betas that are *less* than 1.0 are adjusted *upward*, and historical betas that are *greater* than 1.0 are adjusted *downward*). The adjustment is said to create a "forward" (or prospective) estimated beta because this adjustment is based on the assumption that betas tend to move toward the market's beta (1.0) over time. It does not indicate that any adjustment to the data used in calculating the historical beta estimate was made.

The formula used in this book to calculate "Blume" adjusted betas is:

$$\beta_{Blume} = 0.371 + 0.635(\beta_i)$$

where:
β_{Blume} = Blume-adjusted beta for company or portfolio i
β_i = Estimated beta based on historical data over the look-back period

---

[44] See M. E. Blume, "On the Assessment of Risk", *The Journal of Finance* 26 (1971): pp.1–10.
[45] See Oldrich A.Vasicek, "A Note on Using Cross-Sectional Information in Bayesian Estimation of Security Betas", *The Journal of Finance* 28, no. 5 (December 1973): 1233–1239.

Vasicek-Adjusted Beta

Another technique for adjusting historical beta estimates is sometimes referred to as Vasicek "shrinkage". The idea is that betas with *low* statistical quality (as measured by *high* standard error) are the least reliable estimates, and therefore should be adjusted toward the industry average (i.e., peer group beta) to a greater degree than betas with *high* statistical quality (as measured by *low* standard error).[46] Because high-beta stocks also tend to have the highest standard errors in their raw betas, they tend to be subject to the most significant adjustment toward their industry average.

The formula used in this book to calculate Vasicek-adjusted betas is:

$$\beta_{Vasicek\ Adj} = \frac{\sigma^2_{\beta_i}}{\sigma^2_{\beta_m} + \sigma^2_{\beta_i}} \beta_m + \frac{\sigma^2_{\beta_m}}{\sigma^2_{\beta_m} + \sigma^2_{\beta_i}} \beta_i$$

where:

$\beta_{Vasicek\ Adj}$ = Vasicek adjusted beta for company or portfolio i
β_i = Historical beta for company or portfolio i
β_m = Beta of the market industry or peer group
$\sigma^2_{\beta_m}$ = Variance of betas in the market industry or peer group
$\sigma^2_{\beta_i}$ = Square of the standard error of the historical beta for company or portfolio i

The Vasicek adjustment equation may look complex, but what it accomplishes is a straightforward "sliding scale" between the historical beta and the peer group beta, dependent on the statistical quality (as measured by standard error) of the historical beta.

The Vasicek adjustment can be re-written as follows:

Vasicek Adjusted Beta = [(1−weight) x peer group beta] + (weight x historical beta)

where:

$$weight = \frac{cross\ sectional\ standard\ error^2}{(cross\ sectional\ standard\ error)^2 + (raw\ beta\ standard\ error)^2}$$

The net result is that the *more* statistically significant the historical beta is (as measured by standard error), the *less* the adjustment toward the peer beta (i.e., "weight" will be closer to 1); the *less* statistically significant the historical beta is, the *greater* the adjustment toward the peer beta (i.e., "weight" will be closer to 0).

---

[46] The Vasicek shrinkage methodology is flexible in that it can be used to adjust a beta toward the industry, the market, or any other "target". In this book, the Vasicek shrinkage methodology is used to adjust *only* to the "industry" (i.e., the peer group beta). Whether betas tend to move toward market averages or industry averages over time is an issue open to debate, although it seems more intuitive that companies in say, the pharmaceuticals industry will become more like the average pharmaceutical company over time, rather than look more like the average company in *any* industry (i.e., the "market").

Unlevered Betas

"Unlevered" betas (also called "asset" betas) have the effect of financial leverage removed, thereby reflecting only the effect of business risk. An unlevered beta is the beta that would be expected if a company were financed only with equity capital (i.e., no debt).

The (levered) betas calculated in the industry analyses presented herein are as follows: (i) Raw (OLS) Beta, (ii) Blume-adjusted Raw (OLS) Beta, (iii) Peer Group Beta, (iv) Vasicek-adjusted Raw (OLS) Beta, (v) Sum Beta, and (vi) Downside Beta. *Each* of these levered betas is also presented in "unlevered" form.

There are several commonly used unlevering methodologies.[47] In the analyses presented in this book, the "Miles-Ezzell" formulas are used to unlever all beta estimates.[48] The Miles-Ezzell formula for unlevering beta is:

$$\beta_U = \frac{(M_e \times \beta_L) + M_d \times \beta_d \left(1 - \frac{t \times k_{d(pt)}}{1 + k_{d(pt)}}\right)}{M_e + M_d \left(1 - \frac{t \times k_{d(pt)}}{1 + k_{d(pt)}}\right)}$$

where:

β_U = Unlevered beta of equity capital for company or portfolio *i*
M_e = Market value of equity capital for company or portfolio *i*
β_L = Levered beta of equity capital for company or portfolio *i*
M_d = Market value of debt capital for company or portfolio *i*
β_d = Beta of debt capital for company or portfolio *i*
t = Tax rate for company or portfolio *i*
$k_{d(pt)}$ = Cost of debt (pre-tax) for company or portfolio *i*

---

[47] These include: (i) the Hamada formulas, (ii) the Miles-Ezzell formulas, (iii) the Harris-Pringle formulas, (iv) the Practitioners' method formulas, and (v) the Fernandez formulas. These alternative formulas tend to vary depending on the likelihood that tax deductions on interest will be realized. The Hamada formulas, for example, are likely the most commonly used, but are most applicable only in situations in which the absolute amount of debt is fixed, and there is no risk surrounding the ability to fully deduct interest expense for tax purposes. Alternatively, the Miles-Ezzell formulas assume that the market value of debt capital remains at a constant percentage of equity capital, which is equivalent to saying that debt *increases* in proportion to *increases* in the net cash flow of the firm (net cash flow to invested capital) in every period. The Miles-Ezzell formulas assume that the risk of realizing the interest tax deductions is greater than is assumed in the Hamada formulas. In this book, the Miles-Ezzell formulas are employed in all unlevering calculations. To learn more: see *Cost of Capital: Applications and Examples* 5th edition, by Shannon P. Pratt and Roger J. Grabowski, Chapter 12, "Unlevering and Levering Equity Betas".

[48] See James A. Miles and John R. Ezzell, "The Weighted Average Cost of Capital, Perfect Capital Markets and Project Life: A Clarification", *Journal of Financial and Quantitative Analysis* (1980): 719–730.

In the calculations in the main section of this book, debt is defined simply as the "book" value of interest-bearing debt (as a proxy for market value of debt). For example, "book" debt is the debt measure used as an input in the Miles-Ezzell formula to calculate the unlevered betas presented in the main Industry Data Exhibits. Appendices A and B, however, provide additional analysis in which an *alternative* definition of debt is used that includes "off-balance-sheet" debt (specifically, capitalized operating leases and unfunded pensions).

Appendix A focuses on the *impact* of these "debt-like" off-balance-sheet items on the capital structure of each of the 184 industries presented in this book, and also identifies which off-balance-sheet debt item is the main *driver* of the change in capital structure (capital operating leases *or* unfunded pension liabilities) for each industry. Appendix A is sorted by the "impact" of these debt-like off-balance-sheet items on the capital structure (from high to low).

Appendix B does not focus solely on "impact", but provides additional statistics (debt-to-equity, debt-to-total-capital, and unlevered betas) calculated using both (i) "book" debt and (ii) debt including off-balance-sheet items. Appendix B is sorted by SIC code.

Equity Valuation Multiples

Price to Sales

Latest:

$$PS_i = \frac{M_{e,i}}{NS_i}$$

5-Year Average:

$$PS_{Ai} = \frac{\sum_{n=1}^{n} M_{e,i,n}}{\sum_{n=1}^{n} NS_{i,n}}$$

$$M_{e,i,n} = \left(\sum_{m=1}^{p_n} M_{e,i,m,n}\right) \div p_n$$

where:

PS_i	=	Price-to-sales for company or portfolio i
$M_{e,i}$	=	Market value of equity capital for company or portfolio i
NS_i	=	Net sales for company or portfolio i
$PS_{A,i}$	=	Price-to-sales for company or portfolio i over n periods (in this case, 5 years)
$M_{e,i,n}$	=	Market value of equity capital for company or portfolio i over n periods
$NS_{i,n}$	=	Net sales for company or portfolio i over n periods
$M_{e,i,m,n}$	=	Market value of equity capital for company or portfolio i in month m over n periods
p_n	=	Number of months for which market value of equity capital data are available over n periods

Latest

The "Latest" statistic is calculated as total market capitalization of common equity at the end of the most recent month divided by net sales for the most recent fiscal year.

5-Year Average

The "5-Year Average" statistic is calculated as the sum of total market capitalization of common equity for *each* of the previous five fiscal years divided by the sum of net sales for *each* of the previous five fiscal years. For the 5-Year Average, total market capitalization of common equity is calculated as the sum of the monthly market capitalizations of common equity for each year divided by 12 for each of the most recent five fiscal years.

Price to Earnings

Latest:

$$PE_i = \frac{M_{e,i}}{IBEI_i - DVP_i}$$

5-Year Average:

$$PE_{A,i} = \frac{\sum_{n=1}^{n} M_{e,i,n}}{\sum_{n=1}^{n} (IBEI_{i,n} - DVP_{i,n})}$$

$$M_{e,i,n} = \left(\sum_{m=1}^{p_n} M_{e,i,m,n} \right) \div p_n$$

where:

PE_i	=	Price-earnings ratio for company or portfolio i
$M_{e,i}$	=	Market value of equity capital for company or portfolio i
$IBEI_i$	=	After-tax income before extraordinary items for company or portfolio i
DVP_i	=	Preferred dividends for company or portfolio i
$PE_{A,i}$	=	Price-earnings ratio for company or portfolio i over n periods (in this case, 5 years)
$M_{e,i,n}$	=	Market value of equity capital for company or portfolio i over n periods
$IBEI_{i,n}$	=	After-tax income before extraordinary items for company or portfolio i over n periods
$DVP_{i,n}$	=	Preferred dividends for company or portfolio i over n periods
$M_{e,i,m,n}$	=	Market value of equity capital for company or portfolio i in month m over n periods
p_n	=	Number of months for which market value of equity capital data are available over n periods

Latest

The "Latest" statistic is calculated as total market capitalization of common equity at the end of the most recent month divided by the after-tax income before extraordinary items less preferred dividends for the most recent fiscal year.

5-Year Average

The "5-Year Average" statistic is calculated as the sum of total market capitalization of common equity for *each* of the previous five fiscal years divided by the sum of after-tax income before extraordinary items less preferred dividends for *each* of the previous five fiscal years. For the 5-Year Average, total market capitalization of common equity is calculated as the sum of the monthly market capitalization of equity for *each* year divided by 12, for each of the most recent five fiscal years.

Market-to-Book

Latest:

$$MB_i = \frac{M_{e,i}}{BVE_i}$$

$$BVE_i = CE_i + DT_i + ITC_i$$

5-Year Average:

$$MB_{A,i} = \frac{\sum_{n=1}^{n} M_{e,i,n}}{\sum_{n=1}^{n} BVE_{i,n}}$$

$$M_{e,i,n} = \left(\sum_{m=1}^{p_n} M_{e,i,m,n}\right) \div p_n$$

where:

MB_i	=	Market-to-book ratio for company or portfolio *i*
$M_{e,i}$	=	Market value of equity capital for company or portfolio *i*
BVE_i	=	Book value of equity for company or portfolio *i*
CE_i	=	Common equity for company or portfolio *i*
DT_i	=	Deferred taxes (deferred tax assets minus deferred tax liabilities) for company or portfolio *i*
ITC_i	=	Investment tax credit for company or portfolio *i*
$MB_{A,i}$	=	Market-to-book ratio for company or portfolio *i* over *n* periods (in this case, 5 years)
$M_{e,i,n}$	=	Market value of equity capital for company or portfolio *i* over *n* periods
$BVE_{i,n}$	=	Book value of equity for company or portfolio *i* over *n* periods
$M_{e,i,m,n}$	=	Market value of equity capital for company or portfolio *i* in month *m* over *n* periods
p_n	=	Number of months for which market value of equity capital data are available over *n* periods

Latest

The "Latest" statistic is calculated as total market capitalization of common equity at the end of the most recent month divided by book value of common equity (plus net deferred taxes and investment tax credits) for the most recent fiscal year.

5-Year Average

The "5-Year Average" statistic is calculated as the sum of total market capitalization of common equity for *each* of the previous five fiscal years divided by the sum of book value of common equity (plus net deferred taxes and investment tax credits) for *each* of the previous five fiscal years. For the 5-Year Average, total market capitalization of common equity is calculated as the sum of the monthly market capitalizations of equity for each year divided by 12 for each of the most recent five fiscal years.

NOTE: In previous editions of the *Valuation Handbook – U.S. Industry Cost of Capital*, Market-to-Book was calculated for all SICs, including "Financial SICs" (i.e., Division H: Finance, Insurance, and Real Estate (Major groups between "60" and "67")). Starting with the *2017 Valuation Handbook – U.S. Industry Cost of Capital* (this book), Market-to-Book will continue to be calculated for non-Financial SICs (i.e., all SICs not included in Division H: Finance, Insurance, and Real Estate (Major groups between SICs beginning with "60" and "67")). Price to Tangible Book replaces Market-to-Book multiple for all Financial SICs.

Price to Tangible Book

Latest:

$$PTB_i = \frac{M_{e,i}}{TBVE_i}$$

$$TBVE_i = TCE_i + DT_i + ITC_i$$

5-Year Average:

$$PTB_{A,i} = \frac{\sum_{n=1}^{n} M_{e,i,n}}{\sum_{n=1}^{n} TBVE_{i,n}}$$

$$M_{e,i,n} = \left(\sum_{m=1}^{p_n} M_{e,i,m,n}\right) \div p_n$$

where:

PTB_i	=	Price to tangible book ratio for company or portfolio i
$M_{e,i}$	=	Market value of equity capital for company or portfolio i
$TBVE_i$	=	Tangible book value of equity for company or portfolio i
TCE_i	=	Tangible common equity for company or portfolio i
DT_i	=	Deferred taxes (deferred tax assets minus deferred tax liabilities) for company or portfolio i
ITC_i	=	Investment tax credit for company or portfolio i
$PTB_{A,i}$	=	Price to tangible book ratio for company or portfolio i over n periods (in this case, 5 years)
$M_{e,i,n}$	=	Market value of equity capital for company or portfolio i over n periods
$TBVE_{i,n}$	=	Tangible book value of equity for company or portfolio i over n periods
$M_{e,i,m,n}$	=	Market value of equity capital for company or portfolio i in month m over n periods
p_n	=	Number of months for which market value of equity capital data are available over n periods

Latest

The "Latest" statistic is calculated as total market capitalization of common equity at the end of the most recent month divided by tangible book value of common equity (plus net deferred taxes and investment tax credits) for the most recent fiscal year.

5-Year Average

The "5-Year Average" statistic is calculated as the sum of total market capitalization of common equity for *each* of the previous five fiscal years divided by the sum of tangible book value of common equity (plus net deferred taxes and investment tax credits) for *each* of the previous five fiscal years. For the 5-Year Average, total market capitalization of common equity is calculated as the sum of the monthly market capitalizations of equity for each year divided by 12 for each of the most recent five fiscal years.

NOTE: Starting with the *2017 Valuation Handbook – U.S. Industry Cost of Capital* (this book), Price to Earnings Before Taxes <u>replaces</u> the EV to Sales multiple for SICs beginning in "6", or companies in SICs beginning with "6" (specifically, Division H: Finance, Insurance, and Real Estate; Major groups between SICs beginning with "60" and "67"). EV to Sales will continue to be calculated for all non-financial SICs and non-financial companies.

Price to Earnings Before Taxes

Latest:

$$PEBT_i = \frac{M_{e,i}}{PI_i - SI_i}$$

5-Year Average:

$$PEBT_{A,i} = \frac{\sum_{n=1}^{n} M_{e,i,n}}{\sum_{n=1}^{n}(PI_{i,n} - SI_{i,n})}$$

$$M_{e,i,n} = \left(\sum_{m=1}^{p_n} M_{e,i,m,n}\right) \div p_n$$

where:

$PEBT_i$	=	Price to earnings before taxes ratio for company or portfolio *i*
$M_{e,i}$	=	Market value of equity capital for company or portfolio *i*
PI_i	=	Pre-tax income before extraordinary items for company or portfolio *i*
SI_i	=	Special (unusual or non-recurring) Items for company or portfolio *i*
$PEBT_{A,i}$	=	Price to earnings before taxes ratio for company or portfolio *i* over *n* periods (in this case, 5 years)
$M_{e,i,n}$	=	Market value of equity capital for company or portfolio *i* over *n* periods
$PI_{i,n}$	=	Pre-tax income before extraordinary items for company or portfolio *i* over *n* periods
$SI_{i,n}$	=	Special (unusual or non-recurring) Items for company or portfolio *i* over *n* periods
$M_{e,i,m,n}$	=	Market value of equity capital for company or portfolio *i* in month *m* over *n* periods
p_n	=	Number of months for which market value of equity capital data are available over *n* periods

Latest

The "Latest" statistic is calculated as total market capitalization of common equity at the end of the most recent month divided by the pre-tax income before extraordinary items less special items for the most recent fiscal year.

5-Year Average

The "5-Year Average" statistic is calculated as the sum of total market capitalization of common equity for *each* of the previous five fiscal years divided by the sum of pre-tax income before extraordinary items less special items for *each* of the previous five fiscal years. For the 5-Year Average, total market capitalization of common equity is calculated as the sum of the monthly market capitalization of equity for *each* year divided by 12, for each of the most recent five fiscal years.

Enterprise Valuation (EV) Multiples

"Enterprise value" is the firm's value to both equity and bond holders.

EV to Sales

Latest:

$$EVS_i = \frac{EV_i}{NS_i}$$

$$EV_i = \left(BD_i + M_{e,i} + MI_i - CCE_i\right)$$

$$BD_i = STD_i + LTD_i + NP_i + PSTK_i$$

5-Year Average:

$$EVS_{i,n} = \frac{\sum_{n=1}^{n} EV_{i,n}}{\sum_{t=1}^{n} NS_{i,n}}$$

$$EV_{i,n} = \left(BD_{i,n} + M_{e,i,n} + MI_{i,n} - CCE_{i,n}\right)$$

$$BD_{i,n} = STD_{i,n} + LTD_{i,n} + NP_{i,n} + PSTK_{i,n}$$

$$M_{e,i,n} = \left(\sum_{m=1}^{p_n} M_{e,i,m,n}\right) \div p_n$$

where:

EVS_i	=	Enterprise value to sales for company or portfolio i
EV_i	=	Enterprise value of company or portfolio i
NS_i	=	Net sales for company or portfolio i
BD_i	=	Book value of debt for company or portfolio i
$M_{e,i}$	=	Market value of equity capital for company or portfolio i
MI_i	=	Non-controlling interest (a.k.a. minority interest) for company or portfolio i
CCE_i	=	Cash and cash equivalents for company or portfolio i
STD_i	=	Book value of debt current portion for company or portfolio i
LTD_i	=	Book value of long-term debt for company or portfolio i
NP_i	=	Book value of notes payable for company or portfolio i
$PTSK_i$	=	Book value of preferred stock for company or portfolio i
$EVS_{i,n}$	=	Enterprise value to sales for company or portfolio i over n periods (in this case, 5 years)
$EV_{i,n}$	=	Enterprise value of company or portfolio i over n periods
$NS_{i,n}$	=	Net sales for company or portfolio i over n periods
$BD_{i,n}$	=	Book value of debt for company or portfolio i over n periods
$M_{e,i,n}$	=	Market value of equity capital for company or portfolio i over n periods
$MI_{i,n}$	=	Non-controlling interest (a.k.a. minority interest) for company or portfolio i over n periods
$CCE_{i,n}$	=	Cash and cash equivalents for company or portfolio i over n periods
$STD_{i,n}$	=	Book value of debt current portion for company or portfolio i over n periods
$LTD_{i,n}$	=	Book value of long-term debt for company or portfolio i over n periods
$NP_{i,n}$	=	Book value of notes payable for company or portfolio i over n periods
$PTSK_{i,n}$	=	Book value of preferred stock for company or portfolio i over n periods
$M_{e,i,m,n}$	=	Market value of equity capital for company or portfolio i in month m over n periods
p_n	=	Number of months for which market value of equity capital data are available over n periods

Latest

The "Latest" statistic is calculated as enterprise value in the most recent fiscal year divided by net sales in the most recent fiscal year.

Enterprise value is calculated as total debt, plus total market capitalization of common equity at the end of the most recent month, plus non-controlling interest (a.k.a. minority interest), minus cash and cash equivalents. With the exception of market capitalization of common equity, all other inputs are based on their book values as of the most recent fiscal year.

Total debt is calculated as the sum of long-term debt, the current portion of long-term debt, notes payable, and preferred stock.[49] Again, all of these inputs are based on their respective book values as of the most recent fiscal year.

5-Year Average

The "5-Year Average" statistic is calculated as the sum of enterprise value for *each* of the previous five fiscal years divided by the sum of net sales for *each* of the previous five fiscal years.

Enterprise value is calculated as total debt, plus total market capitalization of common equity, plus non-controlling interest (a.k.a. minority interest), minus cash and cash equivalents for *each* of the previous five fiscal years. For the 5-Year Average, total market capitalization of common equity is calculated as the sum of the monthly market capitalizations of equity for *each* year divided by 12 for each of the most recent five fiscal years.

Total debt is calculated as the sum of long-term debt, the current portion of long-term debt, notes payable, and preferred stock in each of the previous five fiscal years.

---

[49] Preferred stock is included in total debt calculations in the analyses presented herein because preferred stock has many of the same characteristics of debt: (i) companies generally have an obligation to pay dividends to preferred shareholders (similar to companies' obligation to pay coupon interest to debt holders), and (ii) preferred shareholders generally have *priority* of claims to assets relative to common shareholders in the event of liquidation. We acknowledge that this is a simplification, as certain types of preferred stock (e.g., convertible preferred) exhibit characteristics that are more similar to those of common stock.

EV to EBITDA[50]

Latest:

$$EVE_i = \frac{EV_i}{EBITDA_i}$$

$$EV_i = \left(BD_i + M_{e,i} + MI_i - CCE_i\right)$$

$$BD_i = STD_i + LTD_i + NP_i + PSTK_i$$

$$EBITDA_i = OIBD_i + NOPI_i$$

5-Year Average:

$$EVE_{A,i} = \frac{\sum_{n=1}^{n} EV_{i,n}}{\sum_{n=1}^{n} EBITDA_{i,n}}$$

$$EV_{i,n} = \left(BD_{i,n} + M_{e,i,n} + MI_{i,n} - CCE_{i,n}\right)$$

$$BD_{i,n} = STD_{i,n} + LTD_{i,n} + NP_{i,n} + PSTK_{i,n}$$

$$EBITDA_{i,n} = OIBD_{i,n} + NOPI_{i,n}$$

$$M_{e,i,n} = \left(\sum_{m=1}^{p_n} M_{e,i,m,n}\right) \div p_n$$

where:

EVE_i	=	Enterprise value to earnings before interest, tax, depreciation and amortization (EBITDA) for company or portfolio i
EV_i	=	Enterprise value of company or portfolio i
$EBITDA_i$	=	Earnings before interest expense, tax provisions, depreciation and amortization for company or portfolio i
BD_i	=	Book value of debt for company or portfolio i
$M_{e,i}$	=	Market value of equity capital for company or portfolio i
MI_i	=	Non-controlling interest (a.k.a. minority interest) for company or portfolio i

(continued on the next page)

---

[50] The calculation of EBITDA shown here is used for all SICs (and companies), <u>except</u> for those SICs beginning in "6", or companies in SICs beginning with "6" (specifically, Division H: Finance, Insurance, and Real Estate; Major groups between "60" and "67"). Starting with the *2017 Valuation Handbook – U.S. Industry Cost of Capital* (this book), for SICs that begin with (and companies that are in) "60" (Depository Institutions), "61" (Non-depository Credit Institutions), and "62" (Security and Commodity Brokers, Dealers, Exchanges, and Services), a proxy for EBITDA is now calculated as follows: pre-tax income minus special items plus depreciation and amortization plus interest expense on long-term debt. For SICs that begin with (and companies that are in) "63" (Insurance Carriers), "64" (Insurance Agents, Brokers, and Service), "65" (Real Estate), and "67" (Holding and other Investment Offices), a proxy for EBITDA is now calculated as follows: pre-tax income minus special items plus depreciation and amortization plus total interest expense. For more information, refer to Appendix D: Definitions of Standard & Poor's *Compustat* Data Items Used in Calculations.

CCE_i = Cash and cash equivalents for company or portfolio i

STD_i = Book value of debt current portion for company or portfolio i

LTD_i = Book value of long-term debt for company or portfolio i

NP_i = Book value of notes payable for company or portfolio i

$PTSK_i$ = Book value of preferred stock for company or portfolio i

$OIBD_i$ = Operating income before depreciation for company or portfolio i

$NOPI_i$ = Non-operating income (expense) for company or portfolio i

$EVE_{i,n}$ = Enterprise value to earnings before interest, tax, depreciation and amortization for company or portfolio i over n periods (in this case, 5 years)

$EV_{i,n}$ = Enterprise value of company or portfolio i over n periods

$EBITDA_{i,n}$ = Earnings before interest expense, tax provisions, depreciation and amortization for company or portfolio i over n periods

$BD_{i,n}$ = Book value of debt for company or portfolio i over n periods

$M_{e,i,n}$ = Market value of equity capital for company or portfolio i over n periods

$MI_{i,n}$ = Non-controlling interest (a.k.a. minority interest) for company or portfolio i over n periods

$CCE_{i,n}$ = Cash and cash equivalents for company or portfolio i over n periods

$STD_{i,n}$ = Book value of debt current portion for company or portfolio i over n periods

$LTD_{i,n}$ = Book value of long-term debt for company or portfolio i over n periods

$NP_{i,n}$ = Book value of notes payable for company or portfolio i over n periods

$PTSK_{i,n}$ = Book value of preferred stock for company or portfolio i over n periods

$OIBD_{i,n}$ = Operating income before depreciation for company or portfolio i over n periods

$NOPI_{i,n}$ = Non-operating income (expense) for company or portfolio i over n periods

$M_{e,i,m,n}$ = Market value of equity capital for company or portfolio i in month m over n periods

p_n = Number of months for which market value of equity capital data are available over n periods

Latest

The "Latest" statistic is calculated as enterprise value in the most recent fiscal year divided by EBITDA in the most recent fiscal year.

Enterprise value is calculated as total debt, plus total market capitalization of common equity capitalization at the end of the most recent month, plus non-controlling interest (a.k.a. minority interest), minus cash and cash equivalents. With the exception of market capitalization of common equity, all other inputs are based on their book values as of the most recent fiscal year.

Total debt is calculated as the sum of long-term debt, the current portion of long-term debt, notes payable, and preferred stock.[51] Again, all of these inputs are based on their respective book values as of the most recent fiscal year.

EBITDA is calculated as earnings before interest, taxes, depreciation and amortization plus non-operating income (as a proxy for an adjustment for non-recurring items) in the most recent fiscal year.

5-Year Average

The "5-Year Average" statistic is calculated as the sum of enterprise value for *each* of the previous five fiscal years divided by the sum of EBITDA for *each* of the previous five fiscal years.

Enterprise value is calculated as total debt, plus total market capitalization of common equity, plus non-controlling interest (a.k.a. minority interest), minus cash and cash equivalents for *each* of the previous five fiscal years. For the 5-Year Average, total market capitalization of common equity is calculated as the sum of the monthly market capitalization of equity for *each* year divided by 12 for each of the most recent five fiscal years.

Total debt is calculated as the sum of long-term debt, the current portion of long-term debt, notes payable, and preferred stock in *each* of the previous five fiscal years.

EBITDA is calculated as earnings before interest, taxes, depreciation and amortization plus non-operating income (as a proxy for an adjustment for non-recurring items) in *each* of the previous five fiscal years.

Graph – Enterprise Valuation Multiples

The "Enterprise Valuation" (EV) bar graph plots the "Latest" and "5-year Average" EV/Sales and EV/EBITDA multiples for the SIC Composite.

---

[51] Preferred stock is included in total debt calculations in the analyses presented herein because preferred stock has many of the same characteristics of debt. For example, (i) companies generally have an obligation to pay dividends to preferred shareholders (similar to companies' obligation to pay coupon interest to debt holders), and (ii) preferred shareholders generally have *priority* of claims to assets relative to common shareholders in the event of liquidation. We acknowledge that this is a simplification, as certain types of preferred stock (e.g., convertible preferred) exhibit characteristics that are more similar to those of common stock.

Fama-French (F-F) 5-Factor Model

In the inaugural *2014 Valuation Handbook – U.S. Industry Cost of Capital*, we presented cost of equity capital estimates and their underlying components using the Fama-French 3-Factor Model.[52,53]

The Fama-French 3-Factor Model is based on the seminal work of Professors Eugene Fama and Kenneth French, which focused on finding which risk factors could help explain realized equity returns. Their empirical study found that besides market betas, other risk factors such as size and "value" (captured through ratios such as earnings-to-price, debt-to-equity, and book-to-market, the latter being defined as book value of equity divided by market value of equity), could all help in explaining realized equity returns.

Starting with the *2015 Valuation Handbook – U.S. Industry Cost of Capital*, we present cost of equity capital estimates and its underlying components using the Fama-French 5-Factor Model.[54] The Fama-French 5-Factor Model includes the same three factors employed in the 3-Factor Model (market, SMB and HML; see below for definitions), plus two additional risk factors (RMW and CMA; see below for definitions).

The Fama-French 5-Factor Model is based on a multiple regression in which a company's (or portfolio's) excess monthly total returns (i.e., returns over the risk-free rate) are used as the *dependent* variable.

There are five *independent* variables (or risk factors):

Excess "market" returns: The excess monthly total returns of the market benchmark (in this book, the S&P 500 total return index is used as the market benchmark).[55]

SMB (small minus big) returns: The difference between the monthly returns on diversified portfolios comprised of "small" company stocks and "big" (i.e., large) company stocks, as measured by market capitalization.

HML (high minus low) returns: The difference between the monthly returns on diversified portfolios comprised of "value" company stocks (high book-to-market) and "growth" company stocks (low book-to-market).

---

[52] Eugene Fama and Kenneth French, "The Cross-Section of Expected Stock Returns", *The Journal of Finance* (June 1992): 427–486.
[53] Eugene Fama, the 2013 Nobel laureate in economic sciences, is the Robert R. McCormick Distinguished Service Professor of Finance and chairman of the Center for Research in Security Prices (CRSP) at the University of Chicago Booth School of Business. Ken French is the Roth Family Distinguished Professor of Finance at the Tuck School of Business at Dartmouth College. Fama and French are prolific researchers and authors who have contributed greatly to the field of modern finance. Fama and French's paper "The Cross-Section of Expected Stock Returns" was the winner of the 1992 Smith Breeden Prize for the best paper in *The Journal of Finance*.
[54] Eugene F. Fama and Kenneth R. French, "A five-factor asset pricing model", *The Journal of Financial Economics* 116 (2015): 1–22.
[55] "Excess" total returns are calculated herein by subtracting the monthly returns of a U.S. government 30-day T-bill from the equivalent monthly "market" total returns (the "market" is represented in the analyses herein by the S&P 500 total return index). Source of S&P 500 total returns: S&P. Source of 30-day T-bill returns: Morningstar *Direct* database.

RMW (robust minus weak) returns: The difference between the monthly returns on diversified portfolios comprised of company stocks with "robust" profitability and "weak" profitability.

CMA (conservative minus aggressive) returns: The difference between the monthly returns on diversified portfolios comprised of company stocks of low and high investment firms, which Fama and French define as "conservative" and "aggressive", respectively.

The multiple regression formula used in this book to calculate F-F 5-Factor model components is:

$$R_i - R_f = \alpha + \beta(R_m - R_f) + s_i(SMB) + h_i(HML) + r_i(RMW) + c_i(CMA) + \varepsilon$$

where:
- R_i = Return for company or portfolio i
- R_f = Rate of return on a risk-free security
- α = Regression constant
- β = Market risk coefficient (i.e., the Fama-French "beta")
- R_m = Historical average annual return on the "market" portfolio
- s_i = Small minus big (SMB) risk coefficient
- SMB = Historical average annual return on the small minus big (SMB) portfolio
- h_i = High minus low risk (HML) coefficient
- HML = Historical average annual return on the high minus low (HML) portfolio
- r_i = Robust minus weak (RMW) coefficient
- RMW = Historical average annual return on the robust minus weak (RMW) portfolio
- c_i = Conservative minus aggressive (CMA) coefficient
- CMA = Historical average annual return on the conservative minus aggressive (CMA) portfolio
- ε = Regression error term

The market coefficient (i.e., "F-F beta") is presented in this book. The F-F beta should not to be confused with the CAPM beta.

In the "Fama-French (F-F) Components" results, the actual SMB, HML, RMW, and CMA coefficients are *not* presented. Instead, each of these coefficients is multiplied, respectively, by the long-term average annual SMB return as measured over the 1964–2016 period (3.84%), the long-term average annual HML return as measured over the 1964–2016 period (5.06%), the long-term average annual RMW return as measured over the 1964–2016 period (3.02%), and the long-term average annual CMA return as measured over the 1964–2016 period (4.04%), which then form the "SMB Premium", "HML Premium", "RMW Premium", and "CMA Premium", respectively.[56]

The F-F 5-Factor cost of equity capital is estimated as follows:

$$k_e = R_f + (\beta_{F-F,i}) \times RP_m + SMB\ Premium + HML\ Premium + RMW\ Premium + CMA\ Premium + \varepsilon$$

where:

k_e	=	Return for company or portfolio i
R_f	=	Rate of return on a risk-free security
$\beta_{F-F,i}$	=	F-F beta of company or portfolio i
RP_m	=	Risk premium for the "market", (i.e., equity risk premium, or ERP)
SMB Premium	=	The Small Minus Big (SMB) coefficient multiplied by the long-term SMB return as measured over the 1964–2016 period (3.84%)
HML Premium	=	The High Minus Low (HML) coefficient multiplied by the long-term HML return as measured over the 1964–2016 period (5.06%)
RMW Premium	=	The Robust Minus Weak (RMW) coefficient multiplied by the long-term RMW return as measured over the 1964–2016 period (3.02%)
CMA Premium	=	The Conservative Minus Aggressive (CMA) coefficient multiplied by the long-term CMA return as measured over the 1964–2016 period (4.04%)
ε	=	Regression error term

---

[56] Source of Fama-French data: Dr. Kenneth French's website at: http://mba.tuck.dartmouth.edu/pages/faculty/ken.french/index.html. Professor French's website provides various "sorts" of the 5-Factor model's factors: (i) "2x2" sorts, (ii) "2x2x2x2" sorts, and (iii) "2x3" sorts. In the analyses presented herein, the 2x3 sorts are used, as is suggested in "A Five-Factor Asset Pricing Model", *The Journal of Financial Economics* 116 (2015): 1–22, page 19: *"In the end, precedent, flexibility in accommodating more or fewer factors, and the fact that they perform as well as the 2x2 and 2x2x2x2 factors in our tests of asset pricing models lead us back to the factors from the 2x3 sorts"*. The authors confirmed in correspondence with Professor French that the 2x3 factor sorts are indeed the preferred choice.

Cost of Debt

A cost of debt estimate is calculated for *each* company based upon (i) the S&P credit rating for the company, or (ii) for companies that do not have an S&P credit rating, a long-term credit score from S&P Global Market Intelligence *Credit Analytics* is substituted.[57,58] For companies without an S&P credit rating, *or* a credit score from S&P Global Market Intelligence *Credit Analytics*, an average credit rating for the most specific SIC code in which the company appears, and in which there are at least five companies with an S&P credit rating and credit score from S&P Global Market Intelligence *Credit Analytics*, is substituted. For example, if hypothetical Company ABC in SIC 3714 does not have a credit rating, the average credit rating for the other companies in SIC 3714 are used. If SIC 3714 does not have at least five other companies with credit ratings, then the calculation is performed using SIC 371 (up one level, and thus less specific), etc.

The credit rating for each is then mapped to 20-year corporate bond yields as of March 31, 2017 (AAA, AA, A, BBB).[59] For below-investment-grade ratings (BB, B, and CCC), composite non-investment-grade corporate bond credits spreads as of March 31, 2017 are added to the yield of a 20-year U.S. government bond as of March 31, 2017.[60]

Cost of debt is calculated herein on a "Latest" basis only. The median cost of debt is calculated as the middle value of all individual companies' cost of debt estimates. The cost of debt for the "SIC Composite", the "Large Composite", the "Small Composite", and a composite comprised of all companies in the "High-Financial-Risk" category is calculated as the debt-weighted average yield of all individual companies' cost of debt estimates.

---

[57] Source: S&P's *Capital IQ Credit Analytics*.
[58] In this analysis, all credit grade "notches" were removed (e.g., "AA-" was truncated to "AA", "B+" was truncated to "B", etc.).
[59] Source: S&P's *Global Fixed Income Research*, S&P's *RatingsDirect*® on the Global Credit Portal.
[60] Source of "composite non-investment-grade corporate credits spreads": S&P's Speculative-Grade Composite Credit Spreads By Rating Category, S&P's *RatingsDirect*® on the Global Credit Portal. Source of "20-year U.S. government bond" yield: Board of Governors of the Federal Reserve System historical interest rates (H.15) at
https://www.federalreserve.gov/datadownload/Choose.aspx?rel=H15.

Leverage Ratios

Debt-to-MV Equity

Latest:

$$DMVE_i = \frac{BD_i}{M_{e,i}}$$

$$BD_i = STD_i + LTD_i + NP_i + PSTK_i$$

$$M_{e,i} = P_i \times S_i$$

5-Year Average:

$$DMVE_{i,n} = \frac{\sum_{n=1}^{n} BD_{i,n}}{\sum_{n=1}^{n} M_{e,i,n}}$$

$$BD_{i,n} = STD_{i,n} + LTD_{i,n} + NP_{i,n} + PSTK_{i,n}$$

$$M_{e,i,n} = \left(\sum_{m=1}^{p_n} M_{e,i,m,n} \right) \div p_n$$

where:

$DMVE_i$	=	Debt-to-market value of equity capital for company or portfolio i
BD_i	=	Book value of debt for company or portfolio i
$M_{e,i}$	=	Market value of equity capital for company or portfolio i
STD_i	=	Book value of debt current portion for company or portfolio i
LTD_i	=	Book value of long-term debt for company or portfolio i
NP_i	=	Book value of notes payable for company or portfolio i
$PTSK_i$	=	Book value of preferred stock for company or portfolio i
P_i	=	Most recent month's price per share for company or portfolio i
S_i	=	Most recent common shares outstanding for company or portfolio i
$DMVE_{i,n}$	=	Debt-to-market value of equity capital for company or portfolio i over n periods (in this case, 5 years)
$BD_{i,n}$	=	Book value of debt for company or portfolio i over n periods
$M_{e,i,n}$	=	Market value of equity capital for company or portfolio i over n periods
$M_{e,i,m,n}$	=	Market value of equity capital for company or portfolio i in month m over n periods
p_n	=	Number of months for which market value of equity capital data are available over n periods

Latest

The "Latest" statistic is calculated as the most recent fiscal year total debt divided by total market capitalization of common equity at the end of the most recent month.

Total debt is calculated as the sum of long-term debt, the current portion of long-term debt, notes payable, and preferred stock.[61] Again, all of these inputs are based on their respective book values as of the most recent fiscal year.

5-Year Average

The "5-Year Average" statistic is calculated as the sum of total debt for *each* of the previous five fiscal years divided by the sum of total market capitalization of common equity for *each* of the previous five fiscal years.

Total debt is calculated as the sum of long-term debt, the current portion of long-term debt, notes payable, and preferred stock in *each* of the previous five fiscal years.

In the "5-Year Average" calculation, total market capitalization of common equity is calculated as the sum of the monthly market capitalizations of equity for *each* year divided by 12 for *each* of the most recent five fiscal years.

Debt-to-Total Capital

Latest:

$$DTC_i = \frac{BD_i}{TC_i}$$
$$BD_i = STD_i + LTD_i + NP_i + PSTK_i$$
$$TC_i = BD_i + M_{e,i}$$

---

[61] Preferred stock is included in total debt calculations in the analyses presented herein because preferred stock has many of the same characteristics of debt: (i) companies generally have an obligation to pay dividends to preferred shareholders (similar to companies' obligation to pay coupon interest to debt holders), and (ii) preferred shareholders generally have *priority* of claims to assets relative to common shareholders in the event of liquidation. We acknowledge that this is a simplification, as certain types of preferred stock (e.g., convertible preferred) exhibit characteristics that are more similar to those of common stock.

5-Year Average:

$$DTC_{A,i} = \frac{\sum_{n=1}^{n} BD_{i,n}}{\sum_{n=1}^{n} TC_{i,n}}$$

$$BD_{i,n} = STD_{i,n} + LTD_{i,n} + NP_{i,n} + PSTK_{i,n}$$

$$TC_{i,n} = BD_{i,n} + M_{e,i,n}$$

$$M_{e,i,n} = \left(\sum_{m=1}^{p_n} M_{e,i,m,n}\right) \div p_n$$

where:

DTC_i	=	Debt-to-total capital for company or portfolio i
BD_i	=	Book value of debt for company or portfolio i
TC_i	=	Total capital for company or portfolio i
STD_i	=	Book value of debt current portion for company or portfolio i
LTD_i	=	Book value of long-term debt for company or portfolio i
NP_i	=	Book value of notes payable for company or portfolio i
$PTSK_i$	=	Book value of preferred stock for company or portfolio i
$M_{e,i}$	=	Market value of equity capital for company or portfolio i
$DTC_{A,i}$	=	Debt-to-total capital for company or portfolio i over n periods (in this case, 5 years)
$BD_{i,n}$	=	Book value of debt for company or portfolio i over n periods
$STD_{i,n}$	=	Book value of debt current portion for company or portfolio i over n periods
$LTD_{i,n}$	=	Book value of long-term debt for company or portfolio i over n periods
$NP_{i,n}$	=	Book value of notes payable for company or portfolio i over n periods
$PTSK_{i,n}$	=	Book value of preferred stock for company or portfolio i over n periods
$M_{e,i,n}$	=	Market value of equity capital for company or portfolio i over n periods
$M_{e,i,m,n}$	=	Market value of equity capital for company or portfolio i in month m over n periods
p_n	=	Number of months for which market value of equity capital data are available over n periods

Latest

The "Latest" statistic is calculated as the most recent fiscal year total debt divided by total capital at the end of the most recent fiscal year.

Total debt is calculated as the sum of long-term debt, the current portion of long-term debt, notes payable, and preferred stock.[62] Again, all of these inputs are based on their respective book values as of the most recent fiscal year.

Total capital is measured as total debt plus total common equity capitalization at the end of the most recent month.

5-Year Average

The "5-Year Average" statistic is calculated as the sum of total debt for *each* of the previous five fiscal years divided by the sum of total capital for *each* of the previous five fiscal years.

Total debt is calculated as the sum of long-term debt, the current portion of long-term debt, notes payable, and preferred stock in *each* of the previous five fiscal years.

Total capital is calculated as total debt plus total market capitalization of common equity in *each* of the previous five fiscal years. In the "5-Year Average" calculation, total market capitalization of common equity is calculated as the sum of monthly market capitalizations of equity for *each* year divided by 12 for *each* of the most recent five fiscal years.

Graph – Latest Capital Structure

The "Latest Capital Structure (%)" pie chart plots the "Latest" debt-to-total-capital and equity-to-total-capital ratios for the SIC Composite. "Equity-to-total-capital" is calculated as (100% − "debt-to-total-capital").

---

[62] Preferred stock is included in total debt calculations in the analyses presented herein because preferred stock has many of the same characteristics of debt: (i) companies generally have an obligation to pay dividends to preferred shareholders (similar to companies' obligation to pay coupon interest to debt holders), and (ii) preferred shareholders generally have *priority* of claims to assets relative to common shareholders in the event of liquidation. We acknowledge that this is a simplification, as certain types of preferred stock (e.g., convertible preferred) exhibit characteristics that are more similar to those of common stock.

Cost of Equity Capital Estimates

The long-term equity risk premium (ERP) and long-term risk-free rate (R_f) used in all cost of capital calculations presented herein are the Duff & Phelps recommended ERP (5.5%) as of March 31, 2017, used in conjunction with a normalized risk-free rate (3.5%). This implies a "base" U.S. cost of equity capital of 9.0% (3.5% + 5.5%).[63]

The source of valuation data (ERPs, size premia, and risk premia over the risk-free rate) used to calculate the cost of capital estimates presented herein is the *2017 Valuation Handbook – U.S. Guide to Cost of Capital*. In the *2017 Valuation Handbook – U.S. Guide to Cost of Capital*, the size premia data previously published in the Morningstar/Ibbotson *SBBI Valuation Yearbook* is called the "CRSP Deciles Size Study", and the data previously published in the Duff & Phelps *Risk Premium Report* is called the "Risk Premium Report Study".

The cost of equity capital estimates using the CRSP Deciles Size Study, and the Risk Premium Report Study are each developed using two different estimation models in the analyses presented herein:

- **Capital Asset Pricing Model (CAPM):** The CAPM has evolved to become the preferred method to estimate the cost of equity capital in both classroom settings and by financial markets. The CAPM is now the most widely used method for estimating the cost of equity capital.

- **Build-up Method:** The build-up method is an additive model commonly used for calculating the required rate of return on equity capital. As the name implies, successive "building blocks" are summed, each representing the additional risk inherent to investing in alternative assets.[64]

Cost of capital estimates using the CRSP Deciles Size Study use "Vasicek-adjusted" OLS betas and OLS-beta-derived size premia (where applicable).

Cost of capital estimates using the Risk Premium Report Study use sum betas and sum-beta-derived size premia (where applicable).

All cost of capital estimates (and their inputs) are based on data from publicly-traded U.S. companies.

All cost of capital estimates are after corporate taxes, before personal taxes, and before any other company-specific adjustments (other than size) that the individual valuation analyst may deem necessary.

---

[63] To learn more about cost of capital issues, and to ensure that you are using the most recent Duff & Phelps Recommended ERP, visit www.duffandphelps.com/CostofCapital.

[64] The "build-up" model employed in the estimates using the CRSP Deciles Size Study exhibits is simply referred to here as "build-up"; the "build-up" model employed in the estimates using the Risk Premium Report Study is referred to here as "Build-up 1". "Build-up 1" is one of several build-up models that can be utilized when using the Risk Premium Report Study exhibits, and thus it is differentiated by putting the signifier "1" after its name.

CAPM

In the cost of equity capital calculations presented herein, an estimate is first calculated using the "base" CAPM, *without* any additional adjustments for "size" (or other risk factors). The formula used in this calculation is:

$$k_e = R_f + \beta_i \times (RP_m)$$

where:
- k_e = Cost of equity capital
- R_f = Rate of return on a risk-free security (a "normalized" 3.5% rate is used)
- β_i = Beta for company or portfolio *i*
- RP_m = Equity risk premium (a market risk premium of 5.5% is used)

Median

The median "base" CAPM cost of equity estimate is calculated differently from how the "base" CAPM cost of equity estimates for the composites (described in next section) are calculated. The median calculation is a multi-step process.

First, a 60-month raw (OLS) beta is calculated for *each* company in the industry, as described previously in the section "Raw (OLS) Beta".

Second, a "peer group" beta is calculated based upon the sales-weighted "full-information" betas of the industries in which all the companies included in the subject industry participate, as described previously in the section "Peer Betas".[65]

Third, the 60-month raw (OLS) beta for *each* company in the industry is then adjusted toward the peer group beta using the "Vasicek" adjustment, as described previously in the section "Vasicek-Adjusted Beta".

Fourth, the Vasicek-adjusted betas calculated in the previous step for each company is substituted into the CAPM equation to determine a base cost of equity capital estimate for *each* company in the industry.

Finally, the median (middle value) base cost of equity estimate is identified.

---

[65] "Peer" betas for composite portfolios are calculated based upon the sales-weighted 2-digit SIC "full-information" betas (calculated as of March 31, 2017) of the composite portfolio.

Composites

The composite-level "base" CAPM cost of equity estimate is calculated by *aggregation*. For illustration purposes, a generic "Composite" will be discussed here, although these *same* steps are followed for the SIC Composite, the Large Composite, the Small Composite, or a composite of all high-financial-risk companies. The composite-level calculation is also a multi-step process.

First, the market-cap-weighted total returns for a portfolio comprised of all of the companies in the Composite are calculated, as described previously in the section "Portfolio Formation".

Second, a 60-month raw (OLS) beta for the portfolio is calculated using the market-cap-weighted portfolio total returns calculated in the previous step.

Third, a "peer group" beta is calculated based upon the sales-weighted "full-information" betas of the industries in which all the companies included in the Composite participate, as described previously in the section "Peer Betas".

Fourth, the 60-month raw (OLS) beta for the Composite is adjusted toward the peer group beta using the "Vasicek" adjustment, as described previously in the section "Vasicek-Adjusted Beta".

Fifth, the Vasicek-adjusted Composite beta calculated in the previous step is substituted into the CAPM equation to determine a base cost of equity capital estimate for the Composite.

Using a Custom ERP and Risk-Free Rate

As previously discussed in the section "Risk-Free Rate and Equity Risk Premium", the long-term risk-free rate (R_f) and long-term equity risk premium (ERP) used in all cost of capital calculations presented herein are the Duff & Phelps recommended ERP (5.5%) as of March 31, 2017, used in conjunction with a normalized risk-free rate (3.5%).

If the valuation analyst would like to adjust the "base" CAPM cost of equity capital estimates to see what they would look like using a *custom* ERP and/or risk-free rate, this can be accomplished by substituting the custom ERP and risk-free rate values into the following equation:

Custom Estimate = (Custom Risk-free Rate) + (Custom ERP) x (Vasicek-Adjusted Beta)

As previously noted, the Vasicek-adjusted beta is used in the "base" CAPM estimated presented herein. A Vasicek-adjusted beta is calculated for each industry in four different ways: (i) Median, (ii) SIC Composite, (iii) Large Composite, and (iv) a composite comprised of the "high-financial-risk" companies in the industry. To calculate the custom *median* "base" CAPM cost of equity capital estimate, use the *median* Vasicek-adjusted beta; to calculate the custom *Large Composite* "base" CAPM cost of equity capital estimate, use the *Large Composite* Vasicek-adjusted beta; etc.

Cost of Equity Capital Estimates – Using the CRSP Deciles Size Study

Two cost of equity capital estimates are presented in the analyses herein using the CRSP Deciles Size Study: (i) CAPM plus a size premium (RP_s), and (ii) a "build-up" method that starts with the risk-free rate (R_f) and equity risk premium (ERP, or RP_m) and adds a size premium (RP_s) and an industry risk premium (RP_i).

All size premia used in the calculation of "CRSP Deciles Size Study – Cost of Equity Capital Estimates" are for CRSP standard market-cap-weighted NYSE/AMEX/NASDAQ Deciles 1–10 sourced from the *2017 Valuation Handbook – U.S. Guide to Cost of Capital,* Appendix 3, "CRSP Deciles Size Premia Study: Key Variables".[66]

All industry risk premia used in these calculations are sourced from the March 31, 2017 update to Appendix 3a, "Industry Risk Premia (RP_i)" from the *2017 Valuation Handbook – U.S. Guide to Cost of Capital).*[67]

CAPM + Size Premium

These cost of equity capital estimates are developed using the capital asset pricing model (CAPM), with an adjustment for "size". The formula used in this calculation is:

$$k_e = R_f + \beta_i \times (RP_m) + RP_s$$

where:

k_e	=	Cost of equity capital
R_f	=	Rate of return on a risk-free security (a "normalized" 3.5% rate is used)
β_i	=	Beta for company or portfolio *i*
RP_m	=	Equity risk premium (a market risk premium of 5.5% is used)
RP_s	=	Adjustment for size (i.e., "size premium")

---

[66] Appendix 3, "CRSP Deciles Size Premia Study: Key Variables" in the *2017 Valuation Handbook – U.S. Guide to Cost of Capital* is the equivalent of the (now-discontinued) Morningstar/Ibbotson *SBBI Valuation Handbook's* "back page", which was called "Key Variables in Estimating the Cost of Capital".

[67] Appendix 3a, "Industry Risk Premia (RP_i)", in the *2017 Valuation Handbook – U.S. Guide to Cost of Capital* is the equivalent of the (now-discontinued) Morningstar/Ibbotson *SBBI Valuation Handbook's* Table 3.5, which was called "Industry Risk Premia Estimates". Industry risk premia are "full-information" betas that have been adjusted so that they can be added as a simple "up or down" adjustment in the build-up method of estimating the cost of equity capital. [**Note:** In the previous 2014 and 2015 editions of the *Valuation Handbook – U.S. Guide to Cost of Capital*, industry risk premia were presented within Chapter 5 in Exhibit 5.7. The location of the industry risk premia in the book was changed in the *2016 Valuation Handbook – U.S. Guide to Cost of Capital*; industry risk premia are presented in Appendix 3a, "Industry Risk Premium (RP_i)", directly following Appendix 3, "CRSP Deciles Size Premia Study: Key Variables".] March, June, and September quarterly updates to Appendix 3a are available (Quarterly Updates are optional, and are not sold separately). For more information about Duff & Phelps valuation data resources published by John Wiley & Sons, please go to: www.wiley.com/go/ValuationHandbooks.

Median

For *each* company in the industry, the appropriate size premium is identified based on *each* company's market capitalization at the end of the most recent month (in this book, the "most recent month" is March, 2017), using the size premia as published in the *2017 Valuation Handbook – U.S. Guide to Cost of Capital*, Appendix 3, "CRSP Deciles Size Premia: Key Variables".

Then, the size premium for each company (as identified in the previous step) and the Vasicek-adjusted beta calculated for *each* company (as previously described in the previous section "CAPM, Median"), are substituted into the CAPM equation to determine a cost of equity capital estimate (adjusted for size) for each company in the industry.

Finally, the median (middle value) cost of equity capital estimate (adjusted for size) is identified.

Composites

The composite-level CAPM cost of equity estimate with an adjustment for size is calculated by *aggregation*. For example purposes, a generic Composite will be discussed here, although these *same* steps are followed for the SIC Composite, the Large Composite, the Small Composite, or a composite of all high-financial-risk companies. The composite-level calculation is also a multi-step process.

The first step in the Composite calculation is identical to the first step in the "Median" calculation: for each company in the industry, the appropriate size premium is identified based on each company's market capitalization at the end of the most recent month.

In the second step, a market-capitalization-weighted Composite size premium is calculated using the market capitalization of the individual companies as of the end of the most recent month.

The Vasicek-adjusted Composite beta (as previously described in the section entitled "CAPM, Composites") is also used as the beta in the calculation of the "CAPM + Size Premium" composites.

Finally, the market-capitalization-weighted Composite size premium and the Vasicek-adjusted Composite beta are substituted into the CAPM + Size Premium equation to determine a cost of equity capital estimate (adjusted for size) for the Composite.

Using a Custom ERP and Risk-Free Rate

As previously discussed in the section "Risk-Free Rate and Equity Risk Premium", the long-term risk-free rate (R_f) and long-term equity risk premium (ERP) used in all cost of capital calculations presented herein are the Duff & Phelps recommended ERP (5.5%) as of March 31, 2017, used in conjunction with a normalized risk-free rate (3.5%).

If the valuation analyst would like to adjust the "CAPM + Size Premium" cost of equity capital estimates to see what they would look like using a *custom* ERP and/or risk-free rate, this can be accomplished by substituting the custom ERP and risk-free rate values into the following equation:

Custom estimate =

(Custom Risk-free rate) + (Custom ERP) x ("Vasicek-Adjusted Beta")

+ ("Published CAPM + Size Premium cost of equity capital estimate") − ("Published 'Base' CAPM cost of equity capital estimate")

The Vasicek-adjusted beta is calculated for each industry in four different ways: (i) Median, (ii) SIC Composite, (iii) Large Composite, and (iv) a composite comprised of the high-financial-risk companies in the industry. To calculate the custom *median* "CAPM + Size Premium" cost of equity capital estimate, use the *median* Vasicek-adjusted beta; to calculate the custom *Large Composite* "CAPM + Size" cost of equity capital estimate, use the *Large Composite* Vasicek-adjusted beta; etc.

The term "*+ ('Published CAPM + Size Premium cost of equity capital estimate') − ('Published 'Base' CAPM cost of equity capital estimate')*" reverse engineers the size premium used in the published estimate. To reverse engineer the size premium used in the *median* cost of equity capital estimate, use the *median* "Published CAPM + Size Premium cost of equity capital estimate" and the *median* "Published "base" CAPM cost of equity capital estimate"; to reverse engineer the size premium used in the *Large Composite* cost of equity capital estimate, use the *Large Composite* "Published CAPM + Size Premium cost of equity capital estimate" and the *Large Composite* "Published "base" CAPM cost of equity capital estimate"; etc.

Build-up Method

The formula used to calculate a cost of equity estimate using the CRSP Deciles Size Study's "build-up" method is:

$$k_e = R_f + RP_m + RP_i + RP_s$$

where:

k_e = Cost of equity capital

R_f = Rate of return on a risk-free security (a "normalized" 3.5% rate is used)

RP_m = Equity risk premium (a market risk premium of 5.5% is used)

RP_i = Industry risk premium

RP_s = Adjustment for size (i.e., "size premium")

Median

The industry risk premium (RP_i) used here is the 2-digit SIC level industry risk premium for the given industry calculated as of the most recent month (in this book, "most recent month" is as of March 31, 2017).[68]

For each company in the industry, the appropriate size premium for each company in the industry is identified based on each company's market capitalization at the end of the most recent month, using the size premia published in Appendix 3 of the *2017 Valuation Handbook – U.S. Guide to Cost of Capital*.

Then, the size premium (RP_s) for each company (as identified in the previous step) and the industry risk premium (RP_i) are substituted into the build-up equation to determine a "build-up" cost of equity capital estimate for each company in the industry.

Finally, the median (middle value) build-up cost of equity capital estimate is identified.

Composites

The industry risk premium (RP_i) used here is the 2-digit SIC level industry risk premium for the given industry calculated as of the most recent month (in this book, "most recent month" is as of March 31, 2017).

The composite-level build-up cost of equity estimate is calculated by *aggregation*. For illustration purposes, a generic Composite will be discussed here, although these *same* steps are followed for the SIC Composite, the Large Composite, the Small Composite, or a composite of all high-financial-risk companies. The composite-level calculation is also a multi-step process.

The first step in the Composite calculation is identical to the first step in the "Median" calculation: for each company in the industry, the appropriate size premium is identified based on each company's market capitalization at the end of the most recent month.

In the second step, a market-capitalization-weighted Composite size premium is calculated using the market capitalization of the individual companies as of the end of the most recent month.

Finally, the market-capitalization-weighted Composite size premium and the industry risk premium (RP_i) are substituted into the build-up equation to determine a Composite build-up cost of equity capital estimate.

---

[68] Appendix 3a, "Industry Risk Premia (RP_i)", in the *2017 Valuation Handbook – U.S. Guide to Cost of Capital* is the equivalent of the (now-discontinued) Morningstar/Ibbotson *SBBI Valuation Handbook's* Table 3.5, which was called "Industry Risk Premia Estimates". Industry risk premia are "full-information" betas that have been adjusted so that they can be added as a simple "up or down" adjustment in the build-up method of estimating the cost of equity capital. [**Note:** In the previous 2014 and 2015 editions of the *Valuation Handbook – U.S. Guide to Cost of Capital*, industry risk premia were presented within Chapter 5 in Exhibit 5.7. The location of the industry risk premia in the book was changed in the *2017 Valuation Handbook – U.S. Guide to Cost of Capital*; industry risk premia are presented in Appendix 3a, "Industry Risk Premium (RP_i)", directly following Appendix 3, "CRSP Deciles Size Premia Study: Key Variables".] March, June, and September quarterly updates to Appendix 3a are available (Quarterly Updates are optional, and are not sold separately). For more information about Duff & Phelps valuation data resources published by John Wiley & Sons, please go to: www.wiley.com/go/ValuationHandbooks.

Using a Custom ERP and Risk-Free Rate

As previously discussed in the section "Risk-Free Rate and Equity Risk Premium", the long-term risk-free rate (R_f) and long-term equity risk premium (ERP) used in all cost of capital calculations presented herein are the Duff & Phelps recommended ERP (5.5%) as of March 31, 2017, used in conjunction with a normalized risk-free rate (3.5%).

If the valuation analyst would like to adjust the "Build-up" CAPM cost of equity capital estimates to see what they would look like using a *custom* ERP and/or risk-free rate, this can be accomplished by substituting the custom ERP and risk-free rate values into the following equation:

Custom estimate =

(Custom Risk-free rate) + (Custom ERP) + ("Published Build-up cost of equity capital" – 9.0%)

The third term, "*+ (Published Build-up cost of equity capital – 9.0%)*" reverse engineers the *sum* of (i) the size premium used and (ii) the industry risk premium used in the published estimate. To reverse engineer the sum of (i) the size premium used and (ii) the industry risk premium used in the *median* cost of equity capital estimate, use the *median* published "Build-up" cost of equity capital estimate"; to reverse engineer the sum of (i) the size premium used and (ii) the industry risk premium used in the *Large Composite* cost of equity capital estimate, use the *Large Composite* published "Build-up" cost of equity capital estimate"; etc.

Cost of Equity Capital Estimates – Using the Risk Premium Report Study

Unlike the CRSP Deciles Size Study, which measures size based solely on market capitalization, the Risk Premium Report Study measures size based on *eight* different measures, all of which have been shown to be good proxies for size as a predictor of returns: (i) market value of equity (i.e., market capitalization), (ii) book value of equity, (iii) 5-year average net income, (iv) market value of invested capital (MVIC), (v) total assets, (vi) 5-year average EBITDA, (vii) sales, and (viii) number of employees.

Two cost of equity capital estimates are presented in the analyses herein using the Risk Premium Report Study: (i) CAPM plus a size premium (RP_s), and (ii) a "build-up" method that starts with the risk-free rate (R_f) and adds a "risk premium over the risk-free rate" (RP_{m+s}).

All size premia (RP_s) used in the calculation of "Cost of Equity Capital Estimates – Using the Risk Premium Report Study" are for portfolios 1–25 as presented in the *2017 Valuation Handbook – U.S. Guide to Cost of Capital,* Appendix 4, "Risk Premia Report Study Exhibits", exhibits B-1 through B-8.

All "risk premium over the risk-free rate" (RP_{m+s}) used in the calculation of "Cost of Equity Capital Estimates – Using the Risk Premium Report Study" are for portfolios 1–25 of *2017 Valuation Handbook – U.S. Guide to Cost of Capital,* Appendix 4, "Risk Premia Report Study Exhibits", exhibits A-1 through A-8.

CAPM + Size Premium

These cost of equity capital estimates are developed using the capital asset pricing model (CAPM), with an adjustment for "size". The formula used in this calculation is:

$$k_e = R_f + \beta_i \times (RP_m) + RP_s$$

where:
- k_e = Cost of equity capital
- R_f = Rate of return on a risk-free security (a "normalized" 3.5% rate is used)
- β_i = Sum beta for company or portfolio i
- RP_m = Equity risk premium (a market risk premium of 5.5% is used)
- RP_s = Adjustment for size (i.e., "size premium")

Median

For *each* company in the industry, the appropriate size premium for *each* of the eight measures of size analyzed in the Risk Premium Report Study is identified using the Risk Premium Report's "Guideline Portfolio Method".[69] This identification is based upon the respective "size" of each company as measured by (i) market value of equity (i.e., market capitalization), (ii) book value of equity, (iii) 5-year average net income, (iv) market value of invested capital (MVIC), (v) total assets, (vi) 5-year average EBITDA, (vii) Sales, and (viii) number of employees.[70] The median of these size premia for *each* company is then identified.

Then, the (median) size premium for each company (as identified in the previous step) and the sum beta calculated for *each* company (as previously described in the section "Sum Beta"), are substituted into the CAPM equation to determine a cost of equity capital estimate (adjusted for size) for each company in the industry.

Finally, the median (middle value) cost of equity capital estimate (adjusted for size) is identified.

---

[69] The Risk Premium Report Study exhibits provide 25 size-ranked portfolios for each of the eight size measures (Portfolio 1 is comprised of the largest companies, Portfolio 25 is comprised of the smallest companies). With the "Guideline Portfolio Method", the portfolio (of the 25 portfolios) that has an average size that most closely matches the subject company's size (as measured by any one of the eight size measures) is identified, and the smoothed size premia associated with that portfolio is used in the CAPM calculation. A more sophisticated method of matching the subject company's size characteristics to the appropriate size premia, called the "Regression Equation Method", is provided by the Risk Premium Report Study. The Regression Equation Method allows for the interpolation of size premia "in-between" portfolios, and also for the interpolation of size premia for companies smaller than the average company in Portfolio 25 (Portfolio 25 is comprised of the smallest companies).

[70] All eight size measures are not always available for each company.

Composites

The composite-level CAPM cost of equity estimate with an adjustment for size is calculated by *aggregation*. For illustration purposes, a generic "Composite" will be discussed here, although these *same* steps are followed for the SIC Composite, the Large Composite, the Small Composite, or a composite of all high-financial-risk companies. The composite-level calculation is also a multi-step process.

The first step in the Composite calculation is identical to the first step in the Median calculation: for *each* company in the industry, the appropriate size premium for *each* of the eight measures of size analyzed in the Risk Premium Report Study is identified using the Risk Premium Report's "Guideline Portfolio Method". This identification is based upon the respective "size" of each company as measured by (i) market value of equity (i.e., market capitalization), (ii) book value of equity, (iii) 5-year average net income, (iv) market value of invested capital (MVIC), (v) total assets, (vi) 5-year average EBITDA, (vii) sales, and (viii) number of employees. The median of these size premia for *each* company is then identified.

In the second step, a market-capitalization-weighted Composite size premium is calculated using the individual (median) company size premia identified in the previous step and the market capitalization of the individual companies as of the end of the most recent month.

In the third step, market-capitalization-weighted portfolios are created for the Composite as described previously in the section "Portfolio Formation", and the total returns of these portfolios are used to calculate a sum beta for the portfolio, as described previously in the section "Sum Beta".

Finally, the market-capitalization-weighted Composite size premium and the Composite portfolio sum beta are substituted into the CAPM + Size Premium equation to determine a cost of equity capital estimate (adjusted for size) for the Composite.

Using a Custom ERP and Risk-Free Rate

As previously discussed in the section "Risk-Free Rate and Equity Risk Premium", the long-term risk-free rate (R_f) and long-term equity risk premium (ERP) used in all cost of capital calculations presented herein are the Duff & Phelps recommended ERP (5.5%) as of March 31, 2017, used in conjunction with a normalized risk-free rate (3.5%).

If the valuation analyst would like to adjust the "CAPM + Size Premium – Using the Risk Premium Report Study" cost of equity capital estimates to see what they would look like using a *custom* ERP and/or risk-free rate, this can be accomplished by substituting the custom ERP and risk-free rate values into the following equation:

Custom estimate =

(Custom Risk-free rate) + (Custom ERP) x ("Sum Beta")

+ ("CAPM + Size Premium – Using the Risk Premium Report Study") – (3.5% + "Sum beta" x 5.5%)

The "Sum" beta used here is calculated for each industry in four different ways: (i) Median, (ii) SIC Composite, (iii) Large Composite, and (iv) a composite comprised of the high-financial-risk companies in the industry. To calculate a custom *median* "CAPM + Size Premium " cost of equity capital estimate, use the *median* Sum beta; to calculate the custom *Large Composite* "CAPM + Size Premium" cost of equity capital estimate, use the *Large Composite* Sum beta; etc.

The third term, "+ ("CAPM + Size Premium – Using the Risk Premium Report Study") – (3.5% + "Sum beta" x 5.5%)" reverse engineers the size premium used in the published estimate. To reverse engineer the size premium used in the *median* cost of equity capital estimate, use the *median* "CAPM + Size Premium" and the *median* Sum beta; to reverse engineer the size premium used in the *Large Composite* cost of equity capital estimate, use the *Large Composite* "CAPM + Size Premium" and the *Large Composite* Sum beta, etc.

Build-up 1 Method

The build-up method is an additive model commonly used for calculating the required rate of return on equity capital. As the name implies, successive "building blocks" are summed, each representing the additional risk inherent to investing in alternative assets. The name Build-up "1" is used here merely to differentiate this particular build-up method from the other build-up methods available when using the Risk Premium Report Study.

The formula used to calculate a cost of equity estimate using the Risk Premium Report Study's "Build-up 1" method is:

$$k_e = R_f + RP_{m+s} + ERP\ Adjustment$$

where:
- k_e = Cost of equity capital
- R_f = Rate of return on a risk-free security (a "normalized" 3.5% rate is used)
- RP_{m+s} = Equity (market) risk premium plus size premium combined
- *ERP Adjustment* = Equity Risk Premium Adjustment (in the analyses herein the ERP Adjustment is 0.5%) [71,72]

---

[71] As calculated as the Duff & Phelps recommended ERP (5.5%) minus the historical average difference between the S&P 500 total return index and the income return on long-term (20-year) U.S. government bonds (5.0%) (rounded) as calculated over the period 1963–2016. Sources: (i) S&P and (ii) Morningstar *Direct* database, respectively.

[72] The ERP adjustment is needed to account for the difference between the forward-looking ERP as of the valuation date that the analyst has selected to use in his or her cost of equity capital calculations, and the historical (1963–present) ERP that was used as a convention in the calculations performed to create the Risk Premium Report exhibits. To learn more, see the *2017 Valuation Handbook – U.S. Guide to Cost of Capital*, Chapter 9, "Risk Premium Report Exhibits – General Information", in the section entitled "Proper Application of the Equity Risk Premium (ERP) Adjustment".

Median

For *each* company in the industry, the appropriate "risk premium over the risk-free rate" (RP_{m+s}) for *each* of the eight measures of size analyzed in the Risk Premium Report Study exhibits is identified using the Risk Premium Report's "Guideline Portfolio Method".[73] This identification is based upon the respective "size" of each company as measured by (i) market value of equity (i.e., market capitalization), (ii) book value of equity, (iii) 5-year average net income, (iv) market value of invested capital (MVIC), (v) total assets, (vi) 5-year average EBITDA, (vii) Sales, and (viii) number of employees.[74] The median of these "risk premia over the risk-free rate" (RP_{m+s}) for *each* company is then identified, and added to a normalized risk-free rate of 3.5%. This sum (median RP_{m+s} + 3.5%) is the cost of equity capital for each respective company.

Finally, the median (middle value) cost of equity capital estimate is identified.

Composites

The composite-level "Build-up 1" cost of equity estimate is calculated by *aggregation*. For illustration purposes, a generic "Composite" will be discussed here, although these *same* steps are followed for the SIC Composite, the Large Composite, the Small Composite, or a composite of all high-financial-risk companies. The composite-level calculation is also a multi-step process.

The first step in the Composite calculation is identical to the first step in the Median calculation: for *each* company in the industry, the appropriate "risk premium over the risk free rate" for *each* of the eight measures of size analyzed in the Risk Premium Report Study is identified using the Risk Premium Report's "Guideline Portfolio Method". This identification is based upon the respective "size" of each company as measured by (i) market value of equity (i.e., market capitalization), (ii) book value of equity, (iii) 5-year average net income, (iv) market value of invested capital (MVIC), (v) total assets, (vi) 5-year average EBITDA, (vii) sales, and (viii) number of employees. The median of these "risk premia over the risk-free rate" for *each* company is then identified.

In the second step, a market-capitalization-weighted Composite "risk premium over the risk-free rate" is calculated using the market capitalization of the individual companies as of the end of the most recent month.

Finally, the market-capitalization-weighted Composite "risk premium over the risk-free rate" (RP_{m+s}) is added to a normalized risk-free rate of 3.5%. This sum (market-capitalization-weighted RP_{m+s} + 3.5%) is the cost of equity capital estimate for the Composite.

---

[73] The Risk Premium Report Study exhibits provide 25 size-ranked portfolios for each of the eight size measures (Portfolio 1 is comprised of the largest companies, Portfolio 25 is comprised of the smallest companies). With the "Guideline Portfolio Method", the portfolio (of the 25 portfolios) that has an average size that most closely matches the subject company's size (as measured by any one of the eight size measures) is identified, and the smoothed size premia associated with that portfolio is used in the CAPM calculation. A more sophisticated method of matching the subject company's size characteristics to the appropriate size premia, called the "Regression Equation Method" is provided by the Risk Premium Report Study. The Regression Equation Method allows for the interpolation of size premia "in-between" portfolios, and also for the interpolation of size premia for companies smaller than the average company in Portfolio 25 (Portfolio 25 is comprised of the smallest companies).

[74] All eight size measures are not always available for each company.

Using a Custom ERP and Risk-Free Rate

As previously discussed in the section "Risk-Free Rate and Equity Risk Premium", the long-term risk-free rate (R_f) and long-term equity risk premium (ERP) used in all cost of capital calculations presented herein are the Duff & Phelps recommended ERP (5.5%) as of March 31, 2017, used in conjunction with a normalized risk-free rate (3.5%).

If the valuation analyst would like to adjust the "Build-up 1" cost of equity capital estimates to see what they would look like using a *custom* ERP and/or risk-free rate, this can be accomplished by substituting the custom ERP and risk-free rate values into the following equation:

Custom estimate =

(Custom Risk-free rate) + ("Published Build-up 1 cost of equity capital" – (0.5%))

+ (Custom ERP – 5.0%)

The term "+ (Published Build-up 1 cost of equity capital – (0.5%))" reverse engineers the cost of equity capital result published herein, less its embedded ERP Adjustment (0.5%). To reverse engineer the *median* cost of equity capital estimate less its embedded ERP Adjustment (0.5%), use the *median* "Published Build-up 1 cost of equity capital"; to reverse engineer the *Large Composite* cost of equity capital estimate less its embedded ERP Adjustment (0.5%), use the *Large Composite* "Published Build-up 1 cost of equity capital", etc.

The third term, "+ (Custom ERP – 5.0%)", adds back a new ERP Adjustment, based upon the custom ERP.

Discounted Cash Flow (DCF) Models[75]

1-Stage DCF

The 1-Stage DCF model presented in this book is essentially the constant growth model, commonly known as the Gordon Growth Model.[76] The constant growth model is a method of "capitalizing" cash flows. In capitalizing, the focus is on the cash flow of just a single period, as opposed to projecting the multiple expected cash flows from the subject investment over the life of the investment. The constant growth model can be written as:

$$P_i = \frac{D_i}{k_e - g_i}$$

where:

k_e	=	Cost of equity capital
D_i	=	Dividend per share for company or portfolio i at the end of year 1
g_i	=	Expected earnings growth rate for company or portfolio i
P_i	=	Most recent price per common share for company or portfolio i

Rewriting the constant growth model equation to solve for k_e yields:

$$k_e = \frac{D_i}{P_i} + g_i$$

In the 1-stage model presented in this book, dividends received at the end of year one are calculated as the sum of the dividends paid per share in the 12 months ending in the most recent month (D_0), increased by the expected growth rate (g_i):

$$k_e = \frac{D_0 \times (1 + g_i)}{P_i} + g_i$$

where:

D_0 = the sum of the dividends paid per share in the 12 months ending in the most recent month

---

[75] In this book, DCF calculations are summarized in equation form in order to document for the reader the methodologies employed; theory is not discussed in detail. To learn more, see *Cost of Capital: Applications and Examples* 5th edition, by Shannon P. Pratt and Roger J. Grabowski, Chapter 4, "Discounting versus Capitalizing".

[76] Named for Professor Myron Gordon. Myron J. Gordon and Eli Shapiro, "Capital Equipment Analysis: The Required Rate of Profit", *Management Science* 3 (October 1956): 102–110, reprinted in *Management of Corporate Capital* (Glencoe, IL: Free Press, 1959); Myron J. Gordon, *The Investment, Financing, and Valuation of the Corporation* (Homewood, IL: R.D. Irwin, 1962). This model is one of a general class of models referred to by some authors as the dividend discount model, indicating net cash flow to the investor.

The growth rates used are based on each company's expected growth rate from Thomson Reuters *I/B/E/S Consensus Estimates*.[77] If a company (or portfolio) paid no dividends in the 12 months ending in the most recent month, the cost of equity equals the growth rate.

Median

For *each* company in the industry, the cost of equity capital using the 1-Stage DCF model is first calculated. Then, the median (middle value) is identified.

Composites

The composite-level 1-Stage DCF cost of equity capital estimate is calculated by *aggregation*. For illustration purposes, a generic Composite will be discussed here, although these *same* steps are followed for the SIC Composite, the Large Composite, the Small Composite, or a composite of all high-financial-risk companies.

The aggregate growth rate is the market-capitalization-weighted growth rate of all companies in the Composite, based upon the market capitalization of *each* company as of the end of the *most recent month*. Aggregate dividends are the sum of all dividends for *each* company in the Composite in the 12 months ending in the most recent month. Price per share is the sum of the price per common share at the end of the most recent month for each company in the Composite.

3-Stage DCF

For most equity investments, it is probably not reasonable to expect a constant growth rate into perpetuity, as is assumed in the preceding 1-stage DCF model. This dilemma is typically dealt with by the use of "multi-stage" DCF models.

The 3-Stage DCF model presented in this book is defined as follows:

$$M_{e,i,l} = \sum_{n=1}^{5}\left[\frac{CF_{i,0} \times (1+g_{i,1})^n}{(1+k_e)^n}\right] + \sum_{n=6}^{10}\left[\frac{CF_{i,5} \times (1+g_2)^{n-5}}{(1+k_e)^n}\right] + \frac{\frac{IBEI_{i,10} \times (1+g_3)}{(k_e - g_3)}}{(1+k_e)^{10}}$$

$$CF_{i,0} = \frac{\sum_{n=1}^{n} CF_{i,n}}{\sum_{n=1}^{n} NS_{i,n}} \times NS_{i,l}$$

$$CF_{i,n} = IBEI_{i,n} + DEP_{i,n} + CE_{i,n} + DT_{i,n}$$

$$IBEI_{i,10} = \frac{\sum_{n=1}^{n} IBEI_{i,n}}{\sum_{n=1}^{n} NS_{i,n}} \times NS_{i,l}$$

---

[77] For companies that do not have an *I/B/E/S* growth rate, the growth rate is calculated as described previously in the section "Growth Rates; Long-Term Earnings Per Share (EPS)".

where:

$M_{e,i,l}$	=	Market value of equity capital for company or portfolio i in the most recent fiscal year
$CF_{i,0}$	=	Average cash flows for company or portfolio i
g_n	=	Expected earnings growth rate for company or portfolio i
k_e	=	Cost of equity capital
$CF_{i,n}$	=	Cash flow for company or portfolio i over n periods
$NS_{i,n}$	=	Net sales for company or portfolio i over n periods
$NS_{i,l}$	=	Net sales from company or portfolio i in the most recent fiscal year
$IBEI_{i,n}$	=	After-tax income before extraordinary items for company or portfolio i over n periods
$DEP_{i,n}$	=	Depreciation and amortization for company or portfolio i over n periods
$CE_{i,n}$	=	Capital expenditures for company or portfolio i over n periods
$DT_{i,n}$	=	Deferred taxes for company or portfolio i over n periods
$Cf_{i,5}$	=	Expected cash flow for company or portfolio i at the end of year 5
g_2	=	Expected growth rate for stage 2
$IBEI_{i,10}$	=	Expected income before extraordinary items for company or portfolio i at the end of year 10
g_3	=	Expected growth rate for stage 3

Solving for the cost of equity capital using the 3-stage DCF model presented herein is accomplished in all cases through an iterative process that equates the present value of all expected future cash flows for an individual company (or composite) to the market capitalization of the company (or composite) in the most recent month, dependent on the discount rate.

Median

For *each* company in the industry, the cost of equity capital using the 3-Stage DCF model is first calculated. Then, the median (middle value) cost of equity capital estimate is identified.

At the individual-company level, the growth rate used in Stage 1 is based on *each* company's expected growth rate from the Thomson Reuters *I/B/E/S Consensus Estimates* database.[78] The growth rate used in Stage 2 is the expected *industry* growth rate, measured as the market-capitalization-weighted growth rate of all companies in the industry as of the most recent month. The growth rate used in Stage 3 is the rounded expected growth rate of the *economy as a whole* (3.0%), the derivation of which was previously described in the section "Growth Rates". This is done based on the assumption that over time a company's growth rate will move toward its industry's growth rate, and ultimately will move toward the growth rate of the economy as a whole.

---

[78] For companies that do not have an *I/B/E/S* growth rate, the growth rate is calculated as described previously in the section "Growth Rates; Long-Term Earnings Per Share (EPS)".

Cash flows are used in Stage 1 (years 1–5) and Stage 2 (years 6–10) because many companies do not pay dividends. Cash flows for Stage 1 and Stage 2 are calculated in a multi-step process. First, cash flows for each company are calculated as after-tax income before extraordinary items, plus depreciation and amortization, plus deferred taxes, minus capital expenditures, for each of the most recent five fiscal years. This sum is then "normalized" by dividing by the sum of net sales for each company in each of most recent five fiscal years, and then multiplying this ratio by the net sales of each respective company in the most recent fiscal year.

Cash flows for Stage 3 (years 11+) are calculated differently. In Stage 3, after-tax income before extraordinary items alone is used in place of cash flows (as defined in Stages 1 and 2). This is done assuming that over long periods, capital expenditure and depreciation will be equal (i.e., net investment will be zero). This is consistent with a company ultimately reaching a "steady state" of operations and "[moving] toward the growth rate of the economy as a whole".[79]

Cash flows for Stage 3 are calculated in a multi-step process. First, the sum of income before extraordinary items for *each* company in *each* of the most recent five fiscal years is calculated. This sum is then "normalized" by dividing by the sum of net sales for *each* respective company in the most recent *five* fiscal years, and then multiplying this ratio by the net sales of *each* respective company in the most *recent* fiscal year.

Composites

The composite-level 3-Stage DCF cost of equity capital estimate is calculated by *aggregation*. For illustration purposes, a generic "Composite" will be discussed here, although these same steps are followed for the SIC Composite, the Large Composite, the Small Composite, or a composite of all high-financial-risk companies.

---

[79] We realize that in economies with positive inflation (i.e., inflation is generally greater than 0%), capital expenditures may exceed depreciation in the long-run for certain industries. In industries where long-term growth in capital expenditures is expected to be zero, then the assumption of depreciation equaling capital expenditures is reasonable. The long-term relationship between capital expenditures and depreciation has been subject to different opinions and various applications. For consistency between the (now discontinued) Morningstar/Ibbotson *Cost of Capital Yearbook*, which also employed this assumption, we have adopted the simplifying assumption in the analyses herein that capital expenditures and depreciation will be equal in the long-run. We do note that in Surface Transportation Board Ex Parte No. 664 (Sub-No. 1), *Use of a Multi-State Discounted Cash Flow Model in Determining the Railroad Industry's Cost of Capital*, Decided: January 23, 2009, the board noted the following: "We find reasonable the assumption regarding the terminal stage cash flows. In the terminal growth stage, the Morningstar/Ibbotson model sets capital expenditures equal to depreciation (i.e., net investment is assumed to be zero) because that assumption is consistent with an industry reaching a steady state of operations and growing at a rate equal to that of the overall economy. This assumption may run counter to the actual investment plans of the major railroads, but it does not bias the cost of equity upward. Rather, if we relaxed the assumption of zero net investment, we would also have to relax the assumption that the growth rate in the third stage is equal to the long-run growth rate of the overall economy. If the railroads were to continue making large capital expenditures in excess of depreciation during the third stage of the model, this stage of the model would have above normal growth prospects. Thus, lowering the cash flow would require a counterbalancing increase in growth rate. It would also require the Board to make a long-run forecast of the amount of capital investment in the railroad industry and the long-run growth rates. The difficulty of that endeavor probably explains why Morningstar/Ibbotson adopted the simplifying assumption of zero net investment for the terminal phase of the DCF model. We also find this simplifying assumption reasonable, as it permits a reasonable estimate of the cost of equity without a complex and detailed company-specific forecast of industry conditions 11 years into the future and beyond".

The net result of the aggregation process (i.e., a cost of equity is estimated for the group of companies – within an industry Composite – *as a whole* as opposed to estimating cost of equity for each company and then combining these estimates into a cost of equity for the group) is that when composites comprised of multiple companies are being calculated, the market-weighted average of the companies' expected growth rate is used for both Stage 1 and Stage 2. The growth rate used in Stage 3 is the rounded expected growth rate of the *economy as a whole* (3.0%), the derivation of which was previously described in the section "Growth Rates". This is done based on the assumption that over time a company's growth rate will move toward its industry's growth rate, and ultimately will move toward the growth rate of the economy as a whole.

Cash flows are used in Stage 1 (years 1–5) and Stage 2 (years 6–10) because many companies do not pay dividends. Cash flows for Stage 1 and Stage 2 are calculated in a multi-step process. First, the sum of income before extraordinary items, plus depreciation and amortization, plus deferred taxes, minus capital expenditures, for all companies in the Composite is calculated for *each* of the most recent five years. This sum is then "normalized" by dividing by the sum of net sales for all companies in the Composite in *each* of most recent *five* fiscal years, and then multiplying this ratio by the sum of net sales for all companies in the Composite in the most *recent* fiscal year.

Cash flows for Stage 3 (years 11+) are calculated differently. In Stage 3, after-tax income before extraordinary items alone is used in place of cash flows (as defined in Stages 1 and 2). Over long periods, it can be assumed that capital expenditure and depreciation will be equal (i.e., net investment will be zero). This is consistent with a company ultimately reaching a "steady state" of operations and "[moving] toward the growth rate of the economy as a whole" (see Footnote 74).

Cash flows for Stage 3 are calculated in a multi-step process. First, the sum of income before extraordinary items for all companies in the Composite in *each* of the most recent five fiscal years is calculated. This sum is then "normalized" by dividing by the sum of net sales for all companies in the Composite in the most recent five fiscal years, and then multiplying this ratio by the net sales of all companies in the Composite in the most *recent* fiscal year.

Fama-French (F-F) 5-Factor Model

In the inaugural *2014 Valuation Handbook – U.S. Industry Cost of Capital*, we presented cost of equity capital estimates using the Fama-French 3-Factor Model.[80]

Starting with the *2015 Valuation Handbook – U.S. Industry Cost of Capital*, we present cost of equity capital estimates using the Fama-French 5-Factor Model.[81]

The F-F 5-Factor Model cost of equity estimates for each industry are calculated using (i) a "normalized" long-term risk-free rate of 3.5%, (ii) a long-term equity risk premium of 5.5%, (iii) the F-F Beta calculated and presented in "Fama-French (F-F) Components",[82] (iv) the SMB Premium calculated and presented in "Fama-French (F-F) Components", (v) the HMB Premium calculated and presented in "Fama-French (F-F) Components", (vi) the RMW Premium calculated and presented in "Fama-French (F-F) Components", and (vii) the CMA Premium calculated and presented in "Fama-French (F-F) Components".

In the "Fama-French (F-F) Components" results, the actual SMB, HML, RMW, and CMA coefficients are *not* presented. Instead, each of these coefficients is multiplied, respectively, by the long-term average annual SMB return as measured over the 1964–2016 period (3.84%), the long-term average annual HML return as measured over the 1964–2016 period (5.06%), the long-term average annual RMW return as measured over the 1964–2016 period (3.02%), and the long-term average annual CMA return as measured over the 1964–2016 period (4.04%), which then form the "SMB Premium", "HML Premium", "RMW Premium", and "CMA Premium", respectively.[83]

---

[80] Eugene Fama and Kenneth French, "The Cross-Section of Expected Stock Returns", *Journal of Finance* (June 1992): 427–486.
[81] Eugene F. Fama and Kenneth R. French, "A five-factor asset pricing model", *The Journal of Financial Economics* 116 (2015): 1–22.
[82] The "F-F beta" should not to be confused with the CAPM beta.
[83] Source of Fama-French data: Dr. Kenneth French's website at: http://mba.tuck.dartmouth.edu/pages/faculty/ken.french/index.html.

The F-F 5-Factor cost of equity capital is estimated as follows:

$$k_e = R_f + (\beta_{F-F,i}) \times RP_m + SMB\ Premium + HML\ Premium + RMW\ Premium + CMA\ Premium + \varepsilon$$

where:

k_e	=	Return for company or portfolio i
R_f	=	Rate of return on a risk-free security
$\beta_{F-F,i}$	=	F-F beta of company or portfolio i
RP_m	=	Risk premium for the "market", (i.e., equity risk premium, or ERP)
SMB Premium	=	The Small Minus Big (SMB) coefficient multiplied by the long-term SMB return as measured over the 1964–2016 period (3.84%)
HML Premium	=	The High Minus Low (HML) coefficient multiplied by the long-term HML return as measured over the 1964–2016 period (5.06%)
RMW Premium	=	The Robust Minus Weak (RMW) coefficient multiplied by the long-term RMW return as measured over the 1964–2016 period (3.02%)
CMA Premium	=	The Conservative Minus Aggressive (CMA) coefficient multiplied by the long-term CMA return as measured over the 1964–2016 period (4.04%)
ε	=	Regression error term

Using a Custom ERP and Risk-Free Rate

As previously discussed in the section "Risk-Free Rate and Equity Risk Premium", the long-term risk-free rate (R_f) and long-term equity risk premium used in all cost of capital calculations presented in this book are the Duff & Phelps recommended ERP (5.5%) as of March 31, 2017, used in conjunction with a normalized risk-free rate (3.5%).

If the valuation analyst would like to adjust the "F-F" cost of equity capital estimates and use a *custom* ERP and/or risk-free rate instead, this can be accomplished by substituting the custom ERP and risk-free rate values into the following equation:

Custom estimate =

k_e = (Custom Risk-free rate) + ("F-F Beta" x Custom ERP) + SBM Premium + HML Premium + RMW Premium + CMA Premium

The "F-F Beta", "SMB Premium", "HML Premium", "RMW Premium", and "CMA Premium" used herein are calculated for each industry in four different ways: (i) Median, (ii) SIC Composite, (iii) Large Composite, and (iv) a composite comprised of the high-financial-risk companies in the industry. To calculate a custom *median* "F-F 5-Factor Model" cost of equity capital estimate, use the *median* "F-F Beta", "SMB Premium", "HML Premium", "RMW Premium", and "CMA Premium" calculated and presented in "Fama-French (F-F) Components"; likewise, to calculate a custom

Large Composite "F-F Model" cost of equity capital estimate, use the *Large Composite* "F-F Beta", "SMB Premium", "HML Premium", "RMW Premium", and "CMA Premium" calculated and presented in "Fama-French (F-F) Components"; etc.

Graph – Cost of Equity Capital

The "Cost of Equity Capital (%)" bar graph plots the SIC composite cost of equity estimates in five different ways: (i) the simple average of the CRSP Deciles Size Study "CAPM + Size Prem" and "Build-up" estimates, (ii) the simple average of the Risk Premium Report "CAPM + Size Prem" and "Build-up 1" estimates, (iii), the "Discounted Cash Flow" 1-stage estimate, (iv) the "Discounted Cash Flow" 3-stage estimate, and (v) the Fama-French 5-Factor Model estimate.

Weighted Average Cost of Capital (WACC)

All risks inherent in the assets of the business (i.e., overall business risk) are borne by the investors who provided *debt* and *equity* capital. The appropriate rate of return for overall business risk is not generally observable, and therefore must be imputed from the cost of capital for the debt capital and equity capital. This "blended" cost of capital is usually called the weighted average cost of capital, or WACC. The WACC represents the weighted cost for all of the company's invested capital (both equity and debt).

WACC can be applied in a single-year capitalization of net cash flows or multi-year discounted net cash flows valuation. It can also be used in valuing a control or minority interest position. The most obvious instance in which to use WACC is when the objective is to value the *overall* business enterprise.

WACC can be used in many valuation situations. It is especially appropriate for project selection in capital budgeting. The proportions of debt capital and equity capital that could be available to finance various projects might differ according to the project, and the cost of capital generally should be based on the debt capacity of the specific investment. The WACC can also be used to value highly leveraged companies, but *careful* adjustments need to be made, so that any financial distress risks are appropriately captured.

Alternatively, WACC can be used even when the objective is ultimately to value only the equity capital. This can be accomplished by valuing the *overall* business enterprise, and then subtracting the market value of the debt to estimate the value of the equity capital.[84]

---

[84] To learn more, see *Cost of Capital: Applications and Examples* 5th edition, by Shannon P. Pratt and Roger J. Grabowski, Chapter 21, "Weighted Average Cost of Capital".

WACC Formula

WACC is an after-tax concept (i.e., WACC is based on the cost of each capital structure component *net* of any corporate-level tax effect of that component). For example, in the United States interest expense on debt is a tax-deductible expense to a corporate taxpayer, and therefore the formula for computing the after-tax WACC for an entity with a three-tier capital structure (common equity, preferred equity, and debt) will make a tax-adjustment for the debt component.[85]

The WACC formula used in the calculations in this book is:

$$WACC = (k_e \times W_e) + (k_p \times W_p) + (k_{d(pt)}[1-t] \times W_d)$$

where:

WACC	=	Weighted average cost of capital (after-tax)
k_e	=	Cost of common equity capital
W_e	=	Weight of common equity capital in the capital structure
k_p	=	Cost of preferred equity capital
W_p	=	Weight of the preferred equity capital in the capital structure
$k_{d(pt)}$	=	Cost of debt (pre-tax)
t	=	Tax rate
W_d	=	Weight of debt capital in the capital structure

WACC Inputs

- **Cost of equity capital:** There are *eight* methods of cost of equity capital estimation presented in the analyses in this book. A WACC estimate is calculated using the cost of equity capital estimated by *each* of the eight models described previously (in each case), plus an estimate for the cost of preferred capital and the cost of debt capital inputs.[86]

  Note that for *each* company (or composite) a *single* cost of debt capital and a *single* cost of preferred capital estimate is calculated, unlike the cost of (common) equity capital which is computed using *eight* different methods. Therefore, the only item that varies across each company's (or composite's) WACC calculation is the cost of equity capital estimated using each of the eight respective cost of equity capital methods presented herein, as summarized in Exhibit 10.

---

[85] The company tax rates used herein are provided by John Graham. See footnote 21.
[86] Depending on data availability; some companies (or industries) may not include all estimates.

Exhibit 10: WACC is Calculated Using Up to *Eight* Cost of Equity Capital Estimation Methods, *One* Cost of Preferred Equity Capital Estimation Method, and *One* Cost of Debt Capital Estimation Method

WACC =

Cost of Equity Capital (up to 8 methods of estimation)

$(k_e \times W_e)$

Capital Asset Pricing Model (CAPM)	Build-up + Risk Premium Over the Risk-free Rate
CAPM + Size Premium (using the CRSP Deciles Size Study)	1-Stage Discounted Cash Flow (DCF) model
Build-up + Industry Risk Premium (using the CRSP Deciles Size Study)	3-Stage DCF model
CAPM + Size Premium (using the Risk Premium Report Study)	Fama-French (F-F) 5-Factor Model

+

Cost of Preferred Equity Capital (1 method of estimation)

$(k_p \times W_p)$

Cost of Preferred Equity Capital

+

Cost of Debt Capital (1 method of estimation)

$(k_{d(pt)} [1-t] \times W_d)$

Cost of Debt Capital

- **Cost of preferred equity capital:** Cost of preferred equity capital is calculated for each company used in the analysis in this book as preferred dividends in the most recent fiscal year, divided by the number of preferred shares at year-end multiplied by the par or stated value per share as presented in the company's balance sheet.[87] At the composite-level, this calculation is performed in an aggregative fashion. Cost of preferred equity is used in the calculation of the WACC estimates presented herein, but is not presented as a separate data point.

---

[87] Source: S&P's *Research Insight*.

- **Cost of debt capital:** Cost of debt capital is estimated for *each* company included in this book, the derivation of which was previously described in the section "Cost of Debt". Cost of debt is presented as a separate data point.

- **Weights:** The weight of each component in the WACC calculation is calculated as the percentage of total capital (common equity, preferred equity, and debt) it represents. See the section "Debt to Total Capital" for a detailed explanation of how total capital is calculated.[88]

- **Tax rate:** The company tax rates used herein are provided by Professor John Graham as explained under "Data Sources, Company Tax Rates".

WACC Calculations

Median

For *each* company in the industry, and for *each* of the eight methods of cost of equity capital estimation presented in this book, the WACC is first calculated. Then, for each, the median (middle value) WACC is identified.

Composites

Composite-level WACC estimates are calculated by using data points previously developed by *aggregation*.

For example, to calculate the *"Large Composite"* WACC estimate using the CRSP Deciles "CAPM + Size Premium" method, the (i) cost of common equity capital estimate calculated for the *"Large Composite"* using the CRSP Deciles "CAPM + Size Premium" method for the given industry is used, in conjunction with (ii) the cost of debt capital and (iii) the cost of preferred equity capital that were calculated for the *"Large Composite"* for the given industry.

The weights used in this example are the aggregate weights for (i) common equity capital, (ii) preferred equity capital, and (iii) debt capital for the *"Large Composite"* for the given industry in relation to aggregate total capital for the *"Large Composite"* for the given industry.

Alternatively, to calculate the *"Small Composite"* WACC estimate using the Risk Premium Report "Build-up" method, the (i) cost of common equity capital estimate calculated for the *"Small Composite"* using the Risk Premium Report "Build-up" method for the given industry is used, in conjunction with (ii) the cost of debt capital and (iii) the cost of preferred equity capital that were calculated for the *"Small Composite"* for the given industry.

---

[88] "Debt to Total Capital" is calculated and presented as a separate data point herein. The "Debt to Total Capital" data point *includes* preferred equity as part of "debt", because preferred stock has many of the same characteristics of debt: (i) companies generally have an obligation to pay dividends to preferred shareholders (similar to companies' obligation to pay coupon interest to debt holders), and (ii) preferred share holders generally have priority of claims to assets relative to common shareholders in the event of liquidation. We acknowledge that this is a simplification, as certain types of preferred stock (e.g., convertible preferred) exhibit characteristics that are more similar to those of common stock. For purposes of calculating WACC, however, *each* of the three capital components' "weight" (common equity, preferred equity, and debt) relative to total capital is developed *individually*.

The weights used in this example are the aggregate weights for (i) common equity capital, (ii) preferred equity capital, and (iii) debt capital for the *"Small Composite"* for the given industry in relation to aggregate total capital for the *"Small Composite"* for the given industry.

Graph – WACC

The "WACC (%)" horizontal line graph plots the *average* and *median* of the following seven estimates of WACC, at the SIC-Composite level: (i) CRSP Deciles Size Study "CAPM + Size Prem" estimate, (ii) the CRSP Deciles Size Study "Build-up" estimate, (iii) the Risk Premium Report "CAPM + Size Prem" estimate, (iv) the Risk Premium Report "Build-up" estimate, (v) the "Discounted Cash Flow" 1-stage estimate, (vi) the "Discounted Cash Flow" 3-stage estimate, and (vii) the Fama-French 5-Factor Model estimate. The "Low" and "High" of those seven estimates are also plotted.

Distribution of Company-level Average WACC by Industry

In this section the information portrayed in Exhibit 11 and Exhibit 12 are discussed. Exhibit 11 and Exhibit 12 are found on the pages following the discussion.

In Exhibit 11, a summary of the *distributions* of company-level average WACC estimates is shown for the 1,986 "healthy" companies (those not included in the high-financial-risk dataset) included in the analyses presented in this book.

The WACC for *each* company in *each* "division"-level industry (i.e., at the 1-digit SIC code level) was calculated as the company-level average WACC estimated using (i) the cost of debt estimate calculated for each company, (ii) the cost of preferred estimate calculated for each company, and (iii) *each* of the following seven cost of equity capital estimates (in turn) for each company:[89]

- CAPM + Size Premium using the CRSP Deciles Size Study

- Build-up + Industry Risk using the CRSP Deciles Size Study

- CAPM + Size Premium using the Risk Premium Report

- Build-up + Risk Premium Over the Risk-free Rate using the Risk Premium Report

- 1-Stage DCF Model

- 3-Stage DCF Model

- F-F 5-Factor Model

---

[89] The WACC estimate that utilizes the "base" CAPM cost of equity capital estimate as an input is *not* included in this average because "base" CAPM does *not* include an adjustment for size, whereas the seven other cost of equity estimates presented herein *do* include an adjustment for size.

Exhibit 11 illustrates the distribution of company-level average WACC calculated in this fashion at the 1-digit SIC level. The y-axis is the number of companies; the x-axis is the company-level average WACC.

The industries with the *highest* and *lowest* company-level average WACC were "SIC 1 – Mining & Construction" (12.3%) and "SIC 4 – Transportation, Communications, Electric, Gas, and Sanitary Services" (8.7%), respectively.

The industries with company-level average WACC distributions with the *highest* and *lowest* company-level standard deviation were "SIC 5 – Wholesale Trade & Retail Trade" (2.3%) and "SIC 7 – Services" (1.9%), respectively.[90]

Average and Median of Company-level Average WACC by Industry

In Exhibit 12, the *average* and *median* of the company-level average WACC estimates for the 1,986 "healthy" companies shown in Exhibit 11 are shown, as well as the *average* and *median* of the company-level average WACC estimates for the 369 high-financial-risk companies used in the analyses presented in this book. Company-level average WACCs for the high-financial-risk companies were calculated in exactly the same fashion as were the company-level average WACCs for the healthy companies.

The industry with the *largest* difference in company-level average WACC when "Healthy" and "High-Financial-Risk" companies are compared is "SIC 5 – Wholesale Trade & Retail Trade" (a difference of 8.4% to 9.3%, dependent on whether the "Average" or "Median" is being examined).

The industry with the *smallest* difference in company-level average WACC when "Healthy" and "High-Financial-Risk" companies are compared is "SIC 2 – Manufacturing" (a difference of 3.3% to 4.1%, dependent on whether the "Average" or "Median" is being examined).

In Exhibit 12, the "High-Financial-Risk" statistics for "SIC 6 – Finance, Insurance, And Real Estate" are not calculable because the Risk Premium Report Study (which provides risk premia for high-financial-risk companies in its Exhibits H-1 through H-3) also excludes financial service companies (those companies in finance, insurance, or real estate; i.e., in SIC codes that begin with "6").

---

[90] There are two occurrences (SIC 1 and SIC 5) of standard deviation of "2.3%" (rounded value) in Exhibit 11; the full-decimal values of these are 2.28% (SIC 1) and 2.34% (SIC 5). Thus, SIC 5 is the "highest".

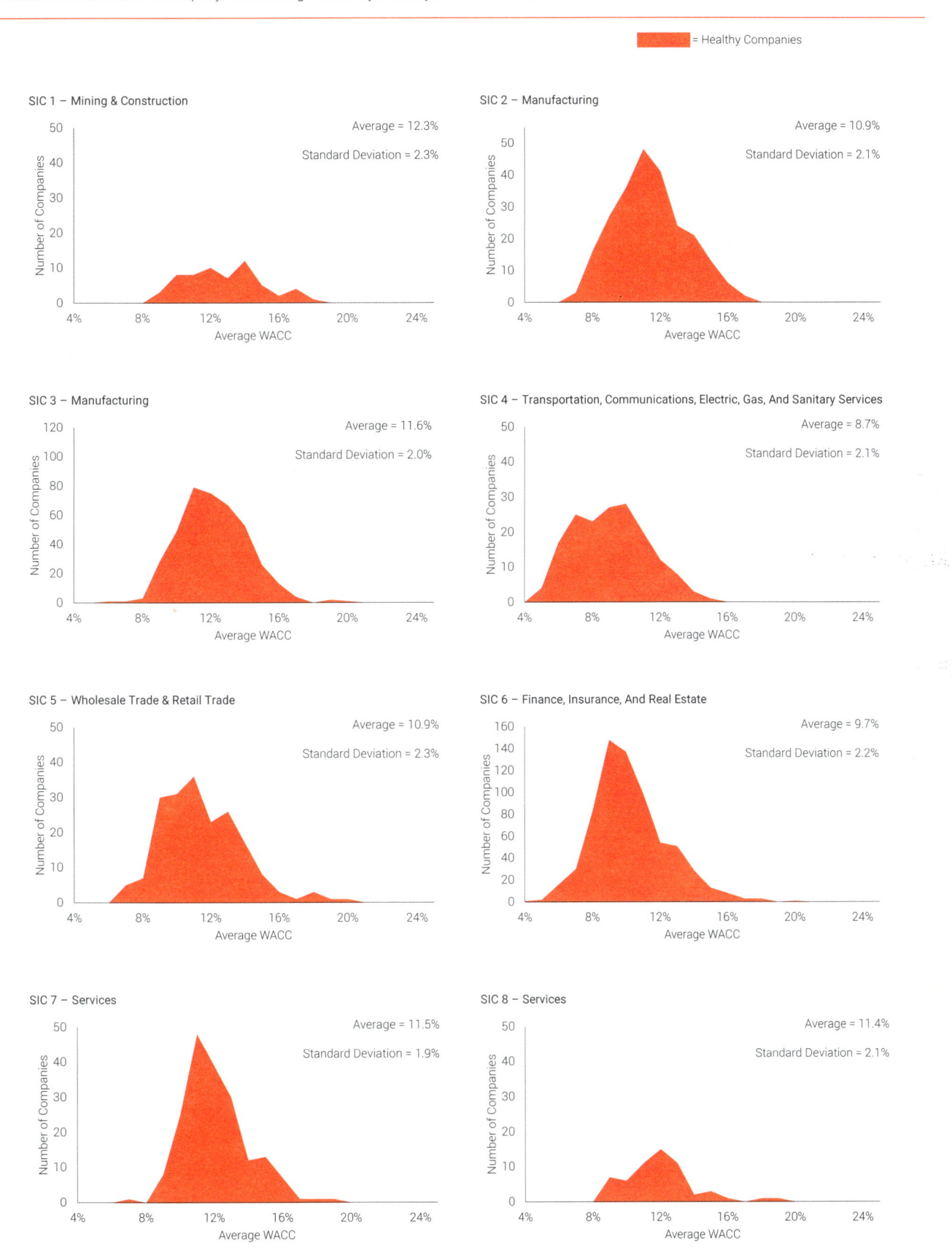

Exhibit 11: Distribution of Company-level Average WACC by Industry as of March 31, 2017

■ = Healthy Companies

SIC 1 – Mining & Construction
Average = 12.3%
Standard Deviation = 2.3%

SIC 2 – Manufacturing
Average = 10.9%
Standard Deviation = 2.1%

SIC 3 – Manufacturing
Average = 11.6%
Standard Deviation = 2.0%

SIC 4 – Transportation, Communications, Electric, Gas, And Sanitary Services
Average = 8.7%
Standard Deviation = 2.1%

SIC 5 – Wholesale Trade & Retail Trade
Average = 10.9%
Standard Deviation = 2.3%

SIC 6 – Finance, Insurance, And Real Estate
Average = 9.7%
Standard Deviation = 2.2%

SIC 7 – Services
Average = 11.5%
Standard Deviation = 1.9%

SIC 8 – Services
Average = 11.4%
Standard Deviation = 2.1%

2017 Valuation Handbook – U.S. Industry Cost of Capital (data through March 31, 2017)

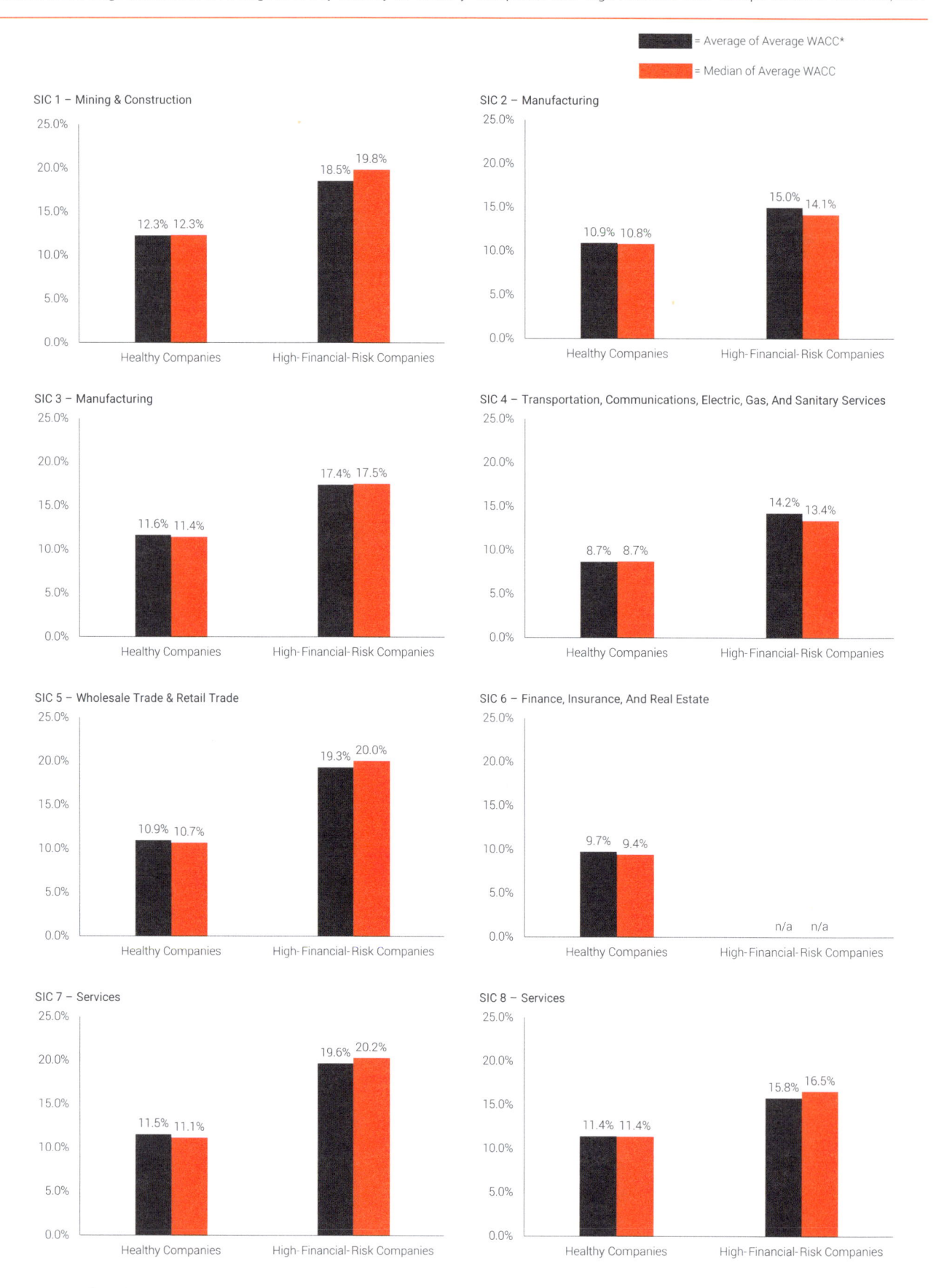

Exhibit 12: Average and Median of Average WACC by Industry for "Healthy" Companies and "High-Financial-Risk" Companies as of March 31, 2017

■ = Average of Average WACC*
■ = Median of Average WACC

SIC 1 – Mining & Construction
	Healthy Companies	High-Financial-Risk Companies
Average	12.3%	18.5%
Median	12.3%	19.8%

SIC 2 – Manufacturing
	Healthy Companies	High-Financial-Risk Companies
Average	10.9%	15.0%
Median	10.8%	14.1%

SIC 3 – Manufacturing
	Healthy Companies	High-Financial-Risk Companies
Average	11.6%	17.4%
Median	11.4%	17.5%

SIC 4 – Transportation, Communications, Electric, Gas, And Sanitary Services
	Healthy Companies	High-Financial-Risk Companies
Average	8.7%	14.2%
Median	8.7%	13.4%

SIC 5 – Wholesale Trade & Retail Trade
	Healthy Companies	High-Financial-Risk Companies
Average	10.9%	19.3%
Median	10.7%	20.0%

SIC 6 – Finance, Insurance, And Real Estate
	Healthy Companies	High-Financial-Risk Companies
Average	9.7%	n/a
Median	9.4%	n/a

SIC 7 – Services
	Healthy Companies	High-Financial-Risk Companies
Average	11.5%	19.6%
Median	11.1%	20.2%

SIC 8 – Services
	Healthy Companies	High-Financial-Risk Companies
Average	11.4%	15.8%
Median	11.4%	16.5%

* Average WACC for each company is based on an average of all of its respective WACCs, using the seven different cost of equity methods.

Appendices

Appendix A
Relative Impact of Off-Balance-Sheet Debt-Equivalent Liabilities on the Capital Structure, as Measured by Total Capital

Appendix A includes statistics that enable the user to gauge the impact of "debt-like" off-balance-sheet items on the capital structure (specifically, the impact on the debt-to-total-capital ratio) of the subject industry. These debt-equivalent liabilities (specifically, capitalized operating leases and unfunded pension liabilities) are not only taken into account by credit rating agencies when assigning a debt rating for a company, but should likely be considered as well when ascertaining the true financial (and equity) risk of the subject company.

Appendix A lists the "Latest" debt-to-total-capital ratios of all SICs analyzed herein (total 184) *before* and *after* adjusting for capitalized operating leases and unfunded liabilities, sorted by the *most* impacted (at the top of the table) to the *least* impacted (at the bottom of the table). "Impact" is measured as the absolute difference in the "Latest" debt-to-total-capital ratio for each SIC calculated using (i) book debt and (ii) book debt plus off-balance-sheet debt.

For example, when debt-to-total-capital is calculated using "Book Debt" (i.e., unadjusted debt), the "Latest" debt-to-total-capital ratio for "SIC 566 – Shoe Stores" is 1.5%, but when debt-to-total-capital is calculated using "Adjusted Debt" (i.e., including capitalized operating leases and unfunded pensions), the "Latest" debt-to-total-capital ratio for SIC 566 is 19.8%, a difference of 18.3% (19.8% – 1.5%).

Six of the ten SICs *most* impacted by the inclusion of off-balance-sheet debt were from Division G: Retail Trade (i.e., SIC codes beginning in "5"). The "Primary Driver" of the changes in debt-to-total-capital in these SICs is the operating leases that tend to be prevalent debt-like "off-balance-sheet" items reported by companies in the retail trade industry. For example, looking again to "SIC 566 – Shoe Stores", operating leases accounted for 99.4% of the 18.3% change in the "Latest" debt-to-total-capital ratio, while unfunded pension liabilities accounted for only 0.6% of the change.[A-1]

Alternatively, looking now to "SIC 372 – Aircraft and Parts", almost the exact opposite is true: operating leases accounted for only 0.9% of the change in "Latest" debt-to-total-capital ratio, while unfunded pension liabilities accounted for 99.1% of the change.[A-2]

[A-1] SIC 566 includes establishments primarily engaged in the retail sale of men's, women's, and children's footwear, including athletic footwear.

[A-2] SIC 372 includes establishments primarily engaged in manufacturing or assembling complete aircraft; aircraft engines and engine parts; aircraft parts and auxiliary equipment, not elsewhere classified.

2017 Valuation Handbook – U.S. Industry Cost of Capital (data through March 2017)

Appendix A: Relative Impact of Off-Balance-Sheet Debt-Equivalent Liabilities on the Capital Structure, as Measured by Total Capital (Latest)

		Calculated Using: Book Debt (Latest)	Calculated Using: Book Debt plus Off-Balance-Sheet Debt (Latest)	Relative Impact: Operating Leases versus Unfunded Pension Liabilities		
		Leverage Ratio (%)	Leverage Ratio (%)			
SIC Code	Industry Short Description	Debt-to-Total Capital Latest	Debt-to-Total Capital Latest	Primary Driver of Change	Operating Leases (%)	Unfunded Pension Liabilities (%)
562	Women's Clothing Stores	31.4	55.7	Operating Leases	100.0	0.0
566	Shoe Stores	1.5	19.8	Operating Leases	99.4	0.6
4512	Air Transportation, Scheduled	28.7	46.2	Operating Leases	69.0	31.0
451	Air Transportation, Scheduled, and Air Courier	28.7	46.1	Operating Leases	68.9	31.1
45	Transportation By Air	29.8	46.7	Operating Leases	69.6	30.4
57	Home Furniture, Furnishings, and Equipment Stores	12.1	28.3	Operating Leases	99.1	0.9
56	Apparel and Accessory Stores	7.3	22.9	Operating Leases	99.0	1.0
565	Family Clothing Stores	7.0	21.3	Operating Leases	98.8	1.2
314	Footwear, Except Rubber	10.6	24.7	Operating Leases	93.3	6.7
5411	Grocery Stores	28.9	42.3	Operating Leases	93.2	6.8
54	Food Stores	29.3	42.1	Operating Leases	93.7	6.3
541	Grocery Stores	27.8	40.4	Operating Leases	93.2	6.8
591	Drug Stores and Proprietary Stores	24.1	36.1	Operating Leases	99.6	0.4
31	Leather and Leather Products	8.6	20.2	Operating Leases	95.9	4.1
594	Miscellaneous Shopping Goods Stores	22.5	32.2	Operating Leases	92.6	7.4
0	Agriculture, Forestry, and Fishing	15.7	23.2	Operating Leases	99.2	0.8
372	Aircraft and Parts	14.2	21.6	Unfunded Pension Liabilities	0.9	99.1
23	Apparel and Other Finished Products Made From Fabrics and Similar Materials	11.3	18.7	Operating Leases	96.2	3.8
8742	Management Consulting Services	18.9	25.9	Operating Leases	100.0	0.0
55	Automotive Dealers and Gasoline Service Stations	36.5	43.3	Operating Leases	99.5	0.5
5812	Eating Places	15.2	22.0	Operating Leases	99.1	0.9
58	Eating and Drinking Places	15.2	22.0	Operating Leases	99.1	0.9
59	Miscellaneous Retail	13.3	19.9	Operating Leases	99.2	0.8
42	Motor Freight Transportation and Warehousing	13.1	19.6	Unfunded Pension Liabilities	15.4	84.6
5	Wholesale Trade & Retail Trade	16.9	23.3	Operating Leases	97.7	2.3
533	Variety Stores	19.7	26.1	Operating Leases	100.0	0.0
53	General Merchandise Stores	18.9	25.3	Operating Leases	98.0	2.0
348	Ordnance and Accessories, Except Vehicles and Guided Missiles	14.6	20.6	Unfunded Pension Liabilities	38.8	61.2
16	Heavy Construction Other Than Building Construction Contractors	17.2	23.0	Operating Leases	76.1	23.9
874	Management and Public Relations Services	16.5	22.2	Operating Leases	100.0	0.0
251	Household Furniture	22.1	27.7	Operating Leases	96.3	3.7
342	Cutlery, Handtools, and General Hardware	11.6	17.1	Unfunded Pension Liabilities	6.9	93.1
871	Engineering, Architectural, and Surveying	9.7	14.7	Operating Leases	100.0	0.0
738	Miscellaneous Business Services	25.7	30.4	Operating Leases	87.6	12.4
252	Office Furniture	11.0	15.7	Operating Leases	92.4	7.6
27	Printing, Publishing, and Allied Industries	17.8	22.4	Unfunded Pension Liabilities	30.2	69.8

Appendix A-2

Appendix A: Relative Impact of Off-Balance-Sheet Debt-Equivalent Liabilities on the Capital Structure, as Measured by Total Capital (Latest)

SIC Code	Industry Short Description	Calculated Using: Book Debt (Latest) Leverage Ratio (%) Debt-to-Total Capital Latest	Calculated Using: Book Debt plus Off-Balance-Sheet Debt (Latest) Leverage Ratio (%) Debt-to-Total Capital Latest	Relative Impact: Operating Leases versus Unfunded Pension Liabilities Primary Driver of Change	Operating Leases (%)	Unfunded Pension Liabilities (%)
344	Fabricated Structural Metal Products	15.0	19.3	Unfunded Pension Liabilities	21.2	78.8
7389	Business Services, Not Elsewhere Classified	26.7	30.9	Operating Leases	94.4	5.6
349	Miscellaneous Fabricated Metal Products	13.7	17.9	Unfunded Pension Liabilities	16.1	83.9
80	Health Services	32.4	36.5	Operating Leases	99.4	0.6
25	Furniture and Fixtures	18.2	22.3	Operating Leases	86.6	13.4
4813	Telephone Communications, Except Radiotelephone	47.1	51.1	Operating Leases	62.3	37.7
37	Transportation Equipment	40.4	44.4	Unfunded Pension Liabilities	10.5	89.5
506	Electrical Goods	31.2	35.2	Operating Leases	86.6	13.4
481	Telephone Communications	37.4	41.3	Operating Leases	75.1	24.9
64	Insurance Agents, Brokers, and Service	13.0	16.9	Operating Leases	75.3	24.7
8	Services	22.1	25.9	Operating Leases	97.0	3.0
34	Fabricated Metal Products, Except Machinery and Transportation Equipment	23.0	26.8	Unfunded Pension Liabilities	26.6	73.4
267	Converted Paper and Paperboard Products, Except	19.4	23.2	Unfunded Pension Liabilities	22.5	77.5
22	Textile Mill Products	19.2	22.9	Operating Leases	64.3	35.7
5045	Computers and Computer Peripheral Equipment and Software	22.6	26.3	Operating Leases	94.2	5.8
286	Industrial Organic Chemicals	22.0	25.6	Operating Leases	71.0	29.0
87	Engineering, Accounting, Research, Management, and Related Services	8.6	12.2	Operating Leases	98.2	1.8
26	Paper and Allied Products	24.4	27.9	Unfunded Pension Liabilities	32.7	67.3
30	Rubber and Miscellaneous Plastics Products	8.2	11.7	Operating Leases	79.1	20.9
3714	Motor Vehicle Parts and Accessories	19.5	23.0	Unfunded Pension Liabilities	29.5	70.5
353	Construction, Mining, and Materials Handling	19.8	23.3	Operating Leases	66.2	33.8
331	Steel Works, Blast Furnaces, and Rolling and Finishing Mills	24.2	27.6	Unfunded Pension Liabilities	13.5	86.5
281	Industrial Inorganic Chemicals	22.8	26.1	Unfunded Pension Liabilities	27.4	72.6
807	Medical and Dental Laboratories	23.9	27.2	Operating Leases	100.0	0.0
7363	Help Supply Services	8.2	11.5	Operating Leases	87.1	12.9
4	Transportation, Communications, Electric, Gas, and Sanitary Services	35.5	38.8	Operating Leases	60.3	39.7
806	Hospitals	40.2	43.5	Operating Leases	98.4	1.6
358	Refrigeration and Service Industry Machinery	9.4	12.6	Unfunded Pension Liabilities	38.0	62.0
48	Communications	33.7	37.0	Operating Leases	69.5	30.5
265	Paperboard Containers and Boxes	27.4	30.6	Operating Leases	50.6	49.4
508	Machinery, Equipment, and Supplies	20.7	23.9	Operating Leases	79.8	20.2
32	Stone, Clay, Glass, and Concrete Products	31.1	34.2	Unfunded Pension Liabilities	40.4	59.6
50	Wholesale Trade-durable Goods	18.9	22.0	Operating Leases	87.7	12.3
3672	Printed Circuit Boards	19.9	23.0	Operating Leases	90.5	9.5
82	Educational Services	5.2	8.2	Operating Leases	100.0	0.0
14	Mining and Quarrying Of Nonmetallic Minerals, Except Fuels	13.2	16.2	Operating Leases	72.2	27.8
736	Personnel Supply Services	9.0	12.0	Operating Leases	86.9	13.1

2017 Valuation Handbook – U.S. Industry Cost of Capital (data through March 2017)

Appendix A-3

2017 Valuation Handbook – U.S. Industry Cost of Capital (data through March 2017)

Appendix A-4

Appendix A: Relative Impact of Off-Balance-Sheet Debt-Equivalent Liabilities on the Capital Structure, as Measured by Total Capital (Latest)

		Calculated Using: Book Debt (Latest)	Calculated Using: Book Debt plus Off-Balance-Sheet Debt (Latest)	Relative Impact: Operating Leases versus Unfunded Pension Liabilities		
		Leverage Ratio (%)	Leverage Ratio (%)			
SIC Code	Industry Short Description	Debt-to-Total Capital Latest	Debt-to-Total Capital Latest	Primary Driver of Change	Operating Leases (%)	Unfunded Pension Liabilities (%)
33	Primary Metal Industries	23.3	26.3	Unfunded Pension Liabilities	25.0	75.0
65	Real Estate	35.1	38.1	Operating Leases	94.7	5.3
308	Miscellaneous Plastics Products	15.8	18.7	Unfunded Pension Liabilities	39.5	60.5
504	Professional and Commercial Equipment and Supplies	16.3	19.2	Operating Leases	94.4	5.6
162	Heavy Construction, Except Highway and Street	21.5	24.3	Operating Leases	100.0	0.0
3089	Plastics Products, Not Elsewhere Classified	17.7	20.5	Unfunded Pension Liabilities	44.5	55.5
6794	Patent Owners and Lessors	13.8	16.5	Operating Leases	100.0	0.0
394	Dolls, Toys, Games and Sporting and Athletic Goods	15.3	18.0	Operating Leases	76.9	23.1
514	Groceries and Related Products	21.6	24.2	Unfunded Pension Liabilities	46.2	53.8
3	Manufacturing	19.2	21.8	Unfunded Pension Liabilities	33.5	66.5
291	Petroleum Refining	15.6	18.2	Unfunded Pension Liabilities	40.8	59.2
29	Petroleum Refining and Related Industries	15.6	18.2	Unfunded Pension Liabilities	40.8	59.2
284	Soap, Detergents, and Cleaning Preparations; Perfumes, Cosmetics, and Other Toilet Preparations	8.5	11.1	Operating Leases	77.4	22.6
287	Agricultural Chemicals	32.2	34.7	Operating Leases	57.4	42.6
24	Lumber and Wood Products, Except Furniture	19.8	22.3	Operating Leases	84.2	15.8
39	Miscellaneous Manufacturing Industries	14.5	17.0	Operating Leases	77.0	23.0
356	General Industrial Machinery and Equipment	19.5	21.9	Unfunded Pension Liabilities	38.8	61.2
371	Motor Vehicles and Motor Vehicle Equipment	57.5	59.9	Unfunded Pension Liabilities	15.0	85.0
512	Drugs, Drug Proprietaries, and Druggists' Sundries	20.1	22.5	Operating Leases	81.8	18.2
4833	Television Broadcasting Stations	39.1	41.4	Operating Leases	68.1	31.9
47	Transportation Services	19.5	21.8	Operating Leases	96.3	3.7
52	Building Materials, Hardware, Garden Supply, and Mobile Home Dealers	12.8	15.1	Operating Leases	100.0	0.0
2	Manufacturing	16.3	18.5	Unfunded Pension Liabilities	41.9	58.1
28	Chemicals and Allied Products	15.9	18.0	Unfunded Pension Liabilities	37.6	62.4
289	Miscellaneous Chemical Products	15.7	17.7	Unfunded Pension Liabilities	41.0	59.0
3711	Motor Vehicles and Passenger Car Bodies	65.1	67.2	Unfunded Pension Liabilities	13.0	87.0
483	Radio and Television Broadcasting Stations	33.1	35.1	Operating Leases	72.0	28.0
51	Wholesale Trade-non-durable Goods	25.9	27.8	Operating Leases	75.2	24.8
633	Fire, Marine, and Casualty Insurance	16.1	17.9	Operating Leases	57.1	42.9
4924	Natural Gas Distribution	35.3	37.0	Unfunded Pension Liabilities	0.0	100.0
131	Crude Petroleum and Natural Gas	25.9	27.7	Operating Leases	77.2	22.8
6798	Real Estate Investment Trusts	37.4	39.1	Operating Leases	99.8	0.2
35	Industrial and Commercial Machinery and Computer Equipment	21.0	22.7	Unfunded Pension Liabilities	47.7	52.3
40	Railroad Transportation	19.2	20.9	Operating Leases	83.6	16.4
63	Insurance Carriers	21.5	23.2	Operating Leases	62.2	37.8
67	Holding and Other Investment Offices	37.0	38.7	Operating Leases	99.8	0.2
3621	Motors and Generators	25.6	27.2	Unfunded Pension Liabilities	40.1	59.9

Appendix A: Relative Impact of Off-Balance-Sheet Debt-Equivalent Liabilities on the Capital Structure, as Measured by Total Capital (Latest)

		Calculated Using: Book Debt (Latest)	Calculated Using: Book Debt plus Off-Balance-Sheet Debt (Latest)		Relative Impact: Operating Leases versus Unfunded Pension Liabilies		
		Leverage Ratio (%)	Leverage Ratio (%)				
SIC Code	Industry Short Description	Debt-to-Total Capital Latest	Debt-to-Total Capital Latest		Primary Driver of Change	Operating Leases (%)	Unfunded Pension Liabilities (%)
473	Arrangement Of Transportation Of Freight and Cargo	6.3	7.9		Operating Leases	100.0	0.0
596	Nonstore Retailers	5.9	7.6		Operating Leases	100.0	0.0
1	Mining & Construction	24.5	26.1		Operating Leases	77.8	22.2
13	Oil and Gas Extraction	25.2	26.9		Operating Leases	77.4	22.6
201	Meat Products	13.5	15.1		Operating Leases	50.0	50.0
262	Paper Mills	16.6	18.2		Operating Leases	59.1	40.9
7	Services	11.0	12.6		Operating Leases	82.3	17.7
73	Business Services	10.4	11.9		Operating Leases	80.3	19.7
357	Computer and Office Equipment	18.8	20.4		Operating Leases	53.4	46.6
20	Food and Kindred Products	19.2	20.7		Unfunded Pension Liabilities	43.6	56.4
7373	Computer Integrated Systems Design	7.9	9.4		Operating Leases	99.2	0.8
489	Communications Services, Not Elsewhere Classified	35.7	37.2		Operating Leases	96.7	3.3
737	Computer Programming, Data Processing, and Other Computer Related Services	9.5	10.9		Operating Leases	78.5	21.5
655	Land Subdividers and Developers	33.9	35.3		Operating Leases	95.7	4.3
362	Electrical Industrial Apparatus	22.2	23.6		Unfunded Pension Liabilities	39.7	60.3
3826	Laboratory Analytical Instruments	14.5	15.9		Operating Leases	66.9	33.1
494	Water Supply	30.0	31.3		Unfunded Pension Liabilities	2.5	97.5
38	Measuring, Analyzing, and Controlling Instruments; Photographic, Medical and Optical Goods; Watches and Clocks	14.3	15.5		Operating Leases	63.3	36.7
628	Services Allied With The Exchange Of Securities	19.2	20.4		Operating Leases	99.1	0.9
382	Laboratory Apparatus and Analytical, Optical, Measuring, and Controlling	13.3	14.5		Operating Leases	67.3	32.7
735	Miscellaneous Equipment Rental and Leasing	49.6	50.9		Operating Leases	100.0	0.0
2834	Pharmaceutical Preparations	12.4	13.6		Unfunded Pension Liabilities	36.6	63.4
7359	Equipment Rental and Leasing, Not Elsewhere Classified	56.4	57.6		Operating Leases	100.0	0.0
632	Accident and Health Insurance and Medical	20.3	21.5		Operating Leases	82.6	17.4
6324	Hospital and Medical Service Plans	19.4	20.6		Operating Leases	87.1	12.9
3841	Surgical and Medical Instruments and Apparatus	8.6	9.7		Operating Leases	66.2	33.8
493	Combination Electric and Gas, and Other Utility	39.2	40.3		Unfunded Pension Liabilities	0.0	100.0
206	Sugar and Confectionery Products	15.9	17.0		Operating Leases	70.8	29.2
495	Sanitary Services	26.7	27.8		Operating Leases	99.1	0.9
138	Oil and Gas Field Services	22.8	23.9		Operating Leases	78.4	21.6
36	Electronic and Other Electrical Equipment and Components, Except Computer Equipment	11.0	11.9		Operating Leases	77.1	22.9
49	Electric, Gas, and Sanitary Services	43.2	44.1		Unfunded Pension Liabilities	14.6	85.4
491	Electric Services	42.9	43.8		Unfunded Pension Liabilities	0.0	100.0
283	Drugs	15.1	16.0		Unfunded Pension Liabilities	44.8	55.2
7372	Prepackaged Software	8.4	9.3		Operating Leases	99.7	0.3

2017 Valuation Handbook – U.S. Industry Cost of Capital (data through March 2017)

Appendix A: Relative Impact of Off-Balance-Sheet Debt-Equivalent Liabilities on the Capital Structure, as Measured by Total Capital (Latest)

		Calculated Using: Book Debt (Latest)	Calculated Using: Book Debt plus Off-Balance-Sheet Debt (Latest)		Relative Impact: Operating Leases versus Unfunded Pension Liabilities	
SIC Code	Industry Short Description	Leverage Ratio (%) Debt-to-Total Capital Latest	Leverage Ratio (%) Debt-to-Total Capital Latest	Primary Driver of Change	Operating Leases (%)	Unfunded Pension Liabilities (%)
4213	Trucking, Except Local	8.1	9.0	Operating Leases	96.6	3.4
3679	Electronic Components, Not Elsewhere Classified	3.3	4.2	Unfunded Pension Liabilities	38.5	61.5
367	Electronic Components and Accessories	10.8	11.7	Operating Leases	65.3	34.7
7374	Computer Processing and Data Preparation and Processing Services	18.5	19.3	Operating Leases	95.7	4.3
384	Surgical, Medical, and Dental Instruments and Supplies	11.6	12.4	Operating Leases	59.9	40.1
366	Communications Equipment	10.7	11.4	Operating Leases	99.9	0.1
3663	Radio and Television Broadcasting and Communications Equipment	10.7	11.4	Operating Leases	100.0	0.0
3842	Orthopedic, Prosthetic, and Surgical Appliances and Supplies	20.6	21.4	Operating Leases	75.0	25.0
3674	Semiconductors and Related Devices	10.6	11.3	Operating Leases	66.1	33.9
208	Beverages	19.2	19.8	Unfunded Pension Liabilities	42.2	57.8
3823	Industrial Instruments for Measurement, Display, and Control of Process Variables; and Related Products	4.9	5.5	Operating Leases	86.7	13.3
6	Finance, Insurance, and Real Estate	47.5	48.1	Operating Leases	84.5	15.5
79	Amusement and Recreation Services	24.0	24.5	Operating Leases	96.5	3.5
799	Miscellaneous Amusement and Recreation	24.2	24.8	Operating Leases	96.4	3.6
2086	Bottled and Canned Soft Drinks and Carbonated Waters	18.1	18.6	Unfunded Pension Liabilities	45.0	55.0
46	Pipelines, Except Natural Gas	33.0	33.5	Operating Leases	91.7	8.3
3845	Electromedical and Electrotherapeutic Apparatus	6.5	7.0	Operating Leases	82.4	17.6
355	Special Industry Machinery, Except Metalworking	10.7	11.2	Unfunded Pension Liabilities	40.7	59.3
62	Security and Commodity Brokers, Dealers, Exchanges, and Services	59.8	60.3	Operating Leases	96.5	3.5
15	Building Construction General Contractors and Operative Builders	33.3	33.8	Operating Leases	95.4	4.6
492	Gas Production and Distribution	50.5	50.9	Operating Leases	52.1	47.9
3559	Special Industry Machinery, Not Elsewhere Classified	10.5	10.9	Unfunded Pension Liabilities	46.6	53.4
4922	Natural Gas Transmission	55.5	55.9	Operating Leases	85.8	14.2
2836	Biological Products, Except Diagnostic Substances	19.1	19.4	Operating Leases	98.8	1.2
517	Petroleum and Petroleum Products	40.0	40.3	Operating Leases	99.1	0.9
2835	In Vitro and In Vivo Diagnostic Substances	11.3	11.6	Operating Leases	100.0	0.0
61	Non-depository Credit Institutions	57.6	57.9	Operating Leases	91.2	8.8
609	Functions Related To Depository Banking	8.1	8.4	Operating Leases	98.3	1.7
615	Business Credit Institutions	76.4	76.6	Operating Leases	96.2	3.8
621	Security Brokers, Dealers, and Flotation	73.5	73.7	Operating Leases	96.1	3.9
616	Mortgage Bankers and Brokers	80.5	80.7	Operating Leases	100.0	0.0
651	Real Estate Operators (except Developers) and Lessors	59.8	59.9	Operating Leases	100.0	0.0
614	Personal Credit Institutions	62.1	62.2	Unfunded Pension Liabilities	49.9	50.1
6035	Savings Institutions, Federally Chartered	45.1	45.2	Unfunded Pension Liabilities	0.0	100.0
603	Savings Institutions	50.0	50.1	Unfunded Pension Liabilities	0.0	100.0
60	Depository Institutions	48.7	48.7	Unfunded Pension Liabilities	23.6	76.4
602	Commercial Banks	53.1	53.2	Unfunded Pension Liabilities	0.0	100.0
6036	Savings Institutions, Not Federally Chartered	55.5	55.5	Unfunded Pension Liabilities	0.0	100.0
6799	Investors, Not Elsewhere Classified	28.7	28.7	Operating Leases	100.0	0.0

Appendix B
Leverage Ratios and Unlevered Betas Calculated Using (i) Book Debt, and (ii) Book Debt Plus Off-Balance-Sheet Debt

Appendix B builds on the statistics provided in Appendix A for gauging the impact of "debt-like" off-balance-sheet items on the capital structure of the subject industry.[B-1] These debt-equivalent liabilities (specifically, capitalized operating leases and unfunded pension liabilities) are not only taken into account by credit rating agencies when assigning a debt rating for a company, but should likely be considered as well when ascertaining the true financial (and equity) risk of the subject company.

The "Latest" (i.e., using the "most recent" financial data) and "5-Year Average" capital structure (debt-to-equity, debt-to-total-capital) of each industry are calculated two ways in Appendix B: (i) *with*, and (ii) *without* capitalized operating leases and unfunded pension liabilities included.

The "unlevered" (i) Raw (OLS) betas, (ii) Blume-Adjusted betas, (iii) Peer Group betas, (iv) Vasicek-Adjusted betas, (v) Sum betas, and (vi) Downside betas of each industry are also calculated two ways: (i) *with*, and (ii) *without* capitalized operating leases and unfunded pension liabilities being considered in the unlevering formula (in the analyses presented in this book, the "Miles-Ezzell" formulas are used to unlever all beta estimates, as previously described in the section entitled "Unlevered Betas").

[B-1] While Appendix A focuses on the "impact" of "debt-like" off-balance-sheet items (specifically, capitalized operating leases and unfunded pension liabilities) on the capital structure (specifically, the debt-to-total-capital ratio) of the subject industry and is sorted by "impact", Appendix B provides additional statistics and does not focus solely on "impact", and is sorted by SIC code.

2017 Valuation Handbook – U.S. Industry Cost of Capital (data through March 2017)

Appendix B: Leverage Ratios and Unlevered Betas Calculated Using (i) Book Debt, and (ii) Book Debt Plus Off-Balance-Sheet Debt

Calculated Using Book Debt

SIC Code	Beta (Levered) Raw (OLS)	Blume Adjusted	Peer Group	Vasicek Adjusted	Sum	Downside	Leverage Ratio (%) Debt/MV Equity Latest	5-Yr Avg	Debt/Total Capital Latest	5-Yr Avg	Beta (Unlevered) (Using Latest Book Debt) Raw (OLS)	Blume Adjusted	Peer Group	Vasicek Adjusted	Sum	Downside
Division A: Agriculture, Forestry, and Fishing																
0	0.97	0.98	1.51	1.12	1.13	1.20	18.6	20.0	15.7	16.7	0.86	0.88	1.33	1.00	1.00	1.06
Division B: Mining																
1	1.07	1.05	1.24	1.09	1.35	1.10	32.5	30.4	24.5	23.3	0.85	0.83	0.97	0.86	1.05	0.87
13	1.10	1.07	1.27	1.13	1.56	1.16	33.8	29.0	25.2	22.5	0.85	0.83	0.98	0.87	1.19	0.90
131	1.09	1.07	1.27	1.12	1.53	1.15	35.0	30.8	25.9	23.5	0.83	0.81	0.97	0.85	1.16	0.87
138	1.14	1.09	1.28	1.18	1.64	1.30	29.5	23.4	22.8	19.0	0.91	0.88	1.02	0.94	1.30	1.03
14	1.24	1.16	1.37	1.25	0.84	1.36	15.2	21.3	13.2	17.6	1.09	1.02	1.21	1.10	0.75	1.20
Division C: Construction																
15	1.14	1.10	1.17	1.15	1.11	1.21	50.0	56.7	33.3	36.2	0.85	0.82	0.87	0.86	0.83	0.89
16	1.47	1.30	1.51	1.48	1.65	1.49	20.8	23.3	17.2	18.9	1.27	1.13	1.30	1.28	1.42	1.29
162	1.33	1.21	1.51	1.37	1.60	1.47	27.4	33.2	21.5	25.0	1.11	1.02	1.25	1.14	1.32	1.22
Division D: Manufacturing																
2	0.93	0.96	0.98	0.93	0.92	0.92	19.5	17.9	16.3	15.2	0.79	0.82	0.83	0.79	0.78	0.78
20	0.65	0.78	0.65	0.65	0.59	0.66	23.7	23.3	19.2	18.9	0.54	0.64	0.53	0.54	0.48	0.54
201	0.28	0.55	0.65	0.52	0.13	0.52	15.6	17.8	13.5	15.1	0.26	0.49	0.58	0.47	0.13	0.47
206	0.41	0.63	0.65	0.55	0.24	0.57	18.9	15.2	15.9	13.2	0.37	0.56	0.57	0.49	0.23	0.50
208	0.68	0.81	0.65	0.68	0.59	0.76	23.7	20.5	19.2	17.0	0.56	0.65	0.53	0.56	0.48	0.62
2086	0.66	0.79	0.65	0.65	0.61	0.76	22.1	20.7	18.1	17.2	0.54	0.64	0.53	0.54	0.50	0.62
22	1.22	1.15	1.06	1.21	1.38	1.57	23.8	22.8	19.2	18.6	1.04	0.98	0.91	1.03	1.17	1.33
23	0.61	0.76	0.61	0.61	0.84	0.77	12.7	11.4	11.3	10.2	0.56	0.69	0.57	0.56	0.77	0.71
24	1.63	1.41	1.66	1.64	1.52	1.62	24.6	24.7	19.8	19.8	1.38	1.20	1.40	1.38	1.29	1.37
25	1.18	1.12	1.14	1.17	1.48	1.22	22.3	22.5	18.2	18.4	1.01	0.96	0.97	1.00	1.25	1.04
251	1.15	1.13	1.15	1.17	2.14	1.46	26.4	23.6	22.1	19.1	1.00	0.98	0.96	0.98	1.73	1.21
252	1.28	1.18	1.17	1.20	1.13	1.35	12.4	14.0	11.0	12.3	1.16	1.08	1.07	1.09	1.03	1.23
26	1.14	1.09	1.00	1.13	1.22	1.15	32.2	34.0	24.4	25.4	0.89	0.85	0.79	0.88	0.95	0.90
262	0.76	0.86	1.00	0.84	0.54	0.83	19.9	20.8	16.6	17.2	0.65	0.73	0.85	0.71	0.46	0.71
265	1.56	1.36	1.00	1.45	1.87	1.69	37.8	44.2	27.4	30.7	1.13	0.99	0.77	1.09	1.40	1.27
267	1.04	1.03	1.00	1.01	1.12	1.08	24.0	26.8	19.4	21.2	0.86	0.85	0.83	0.84	0.92	0.89
27	1.15	1.10	1.44	1.20	0.95	1.05	21.7	28.5	17.8	22.2	1.00	0.96	1.24	1.05	0.83	0.92
28	1.09	1.06	1.11	1.09	1.12	1.09	18.9	17.6	15.9	14.9	0.93	0.91	0.94	0.93	0.96	0.93
281	1.12	1.08	1.11	1.12	1.17	1.13	29.5	26.6	22.8	21.0	0.89	0.86	0.88	0.89	0.93	0.90
283	1.06	1.04	1.11	1.06	1.08	1.09	17.7	15.1	15.1	13.1	0.90	0.89	0.95	0.91	0.93	0.93
2834	1.00	1.01	1.08	1.01	1.03	1.02	14.1	13.9	12.4	12.2	0.88	0.89	0.98	0.89	0.90	0.90
2835	0.60	0.75	1.11	0.84	0.58	0.88	12.7	12.0	11.3	10.7	0.57	0.71	1.03	0.78	0.55	0.82
2836	1.13	1.09	1.11	1.13	1.19	1.35	23.6	16.8	19.1	14.4	0.92	0.89	0.91	0.92	0.97	1.09
284	0.76	0.85	1.08	0.78	0.81	0.85	9.3	9.1	8.5	8.3	0.70	0.78	0.99	0.72	0.74	0.78
286	1.24	1.16	1.11	1.23	1.59	1.32	28.2	18.0	22.0	15.3	1.00	0.93	0.90	0.99	1.27	1.06
287	0.99	1.00	1.11	1.02	0.95	1.35	47.5	26.8	32.2	21.1	0.78	0.79	0.86	0.80	0.75	1.02
289	1.23	1.15	1.11	1.21	1.24	1.30	18.6	27.6	15.7	21.6	1.06	0.99	0.96	1.04	1.07	1.12
29	1.04	1.03	1.09	1.04	1.01	1.06	18.5	18.6	15.6	15.6	0.88	0.87	0.92	0.89	0.86	0.90
291	1.03	1.03	1.09	1.04	1.01	1.05	18.5	18.0	15.6	15.2	0.88	0.87	0.92	0.89	0.86	0.89
3	1.13	1.09	1.15	1.13	1.12	1.16	23.7	23.8	19.2	19.2	0.93	0.90	0.95	0.93	0.93	0.96
30	0.63	0.77	0.71	0.64	0.68	0.87	8.9	10.5	8.2	9.5	0.60	0.73	0.67	0.61	0.64	0.81
308	1.27	1.18	–	–	1.25	1.24	18.7	17.4	15.8	14.9	1.11	1.03	–	–	1.10	1.08
3089	1.26	1.17	–	–	1.28	1.23	21.6	19.7	17.7	16.4	1.08	1.01	–	–	1.10	1.05
31	0.40	0.62	0.66	0.54	0.44	0.77	9.4	8.0	8.6	7.4	0.38	0.59	0.62	0.51	0.42	0.72
314	0.42	0.64	–	–	0.60	1.11	11.9	15.6	10.6	13.5	0.41	0.60	–	–	0.56	1.03
32	1.29	1.19	1.35	1.32	1.21	1.44	45.2	49.6	31.1	33.2	0.96	0.90	1.00	0.98	0.91	1.07
33	1.64	1.41	1.99	1.68	1.56	1.57	30.4	37.0	23.3	27.0	1.32	1.15	1.59	1.35	1.26	1.27
331	1.68	1.44	2.03	1.74	1.63	1.63	31.9	42.4	24.2	29.8	1.34	1.15	1.60	1.38	1.30	1.30
34	1.06	1.04	0.95	1.05	1.16	1.08	29.8	30.1	23.0	23.1	0.87	0.86	0.79	0.87	0.95	0.89
342	1.31	1.20	1.04	1.23	0.99	1.36	13.2	12.9	11.6	11.4	1.20	1.10	0.96	1.13	0.92	1.24
344	0.86	0.92	0.91	0.87	1.11	1.00	17.6	14.1	15.0	12.3	0.76	0.81	0.81	0.77	0.98	0.88

Calculated Using Book plus Off-Balance-Sheet Debt

Leverage Ratio (%) Debt/MV Equity Latest	5-Yr Avg	Debt/Total Capital Latest	5-Yr Avg	Beta (Unlevered) (Using Latest Book plus Off-Balance-Sheet Debt) Raw (OLS)	Blume Adjusted	Peer Group	Vasicek Adjusted	Sum	Downside
30.3	35.8	23.2	26.4	0.82	0.83	1.24	0.94	0.94	0.99
35.4	33.5	26.1	25.1	0.83	0.82	0.95	0.84	1.03	0.85
36.7	32.0	26.9	24.2	0.84	0.81	0.96	0.86	1.17	0.88
38.3	34.0	27.7	25.4	0.82	0.80	0.95	0.83	1.13	0.85
31.4	25.5	23.9	20.3	0.90	0.87	1.01	0.93	1.28	1.02
19.3	26.4	16.2	20.9	1.06	0.99	1.17	1.07	0.73	1.17
51.0	57.9	33.8	36.7	0.85	0.82	0.86	0.85	0.83	0.89
29.9	34.6	23.0	25.7	1.20	1.08	1.23	1.21	1.34	1.22
32.1	38.0	24.3	27.6	1.08	1.00	1.22	1.11	1.29	1.19
22.7	21.4	18.5	17.6	0.77	0.80	0.81	0.77	0.76	0.76
26.2	25.8	20.7	20.5	0.53	0.63	0.53	0.53	0.48	0.53
17.8	20.2	15.1	16.8	0.26	0.48	0.57	0.46	0.13	0.46
20.4	16.4	17.0	14.1	0.37	0.55	0.56	0.48	0.23	0.50
24.7	21.7	19.8	17.8	0.55	0.65	0.52	0.55	0.47	0.62
22.9	21.8	18.6	17.9	0.53	0.64	0.53	0.53	0.50	0.62
29.7	27.8	22.9	21.8	1.01	0.95	0.88	1.00	1.13	1.28
23.0	20.6	18.7	17.1	0.53	0.65	0.53	0.53	0.72	0.66
28.7	28.9	22.3	22.4	1.35	1.17	1.37	1.35	1.26	1.34
28.7	29.7	22.3	22.9	0.97	0.92	0.94	0.96	1.20	1.00
38.3	32.4	27.7	24.5	0.95	0.90	0.91	0.93	1.63	1.14
18.7	22.4	15.7	18.3	1.11	1.03	1.02	1.06	0.96	1.18
38.7	42.0	27.9	29.6	0.85	0.82	0.76	0.85	0.91	0.86
22.2	23.7	18.2	19.2	0.64	0.71	0.84	0.70	0.45	0.69
44.1	53.6	30.6	34.9	1.13	0.99	0.74	1.05	1.35	1.22
30.2	34.1	23.2	25.4	0.82	0.81	0.79	0.80	0.88	0.85
28.8	39.2	22.4	28.2	0.96	0.92	1.19	1.01	0.80	0.89
21.9	20.7	18.0	17.2	0.91	0.89	0.92	0.91	0.93	0.91
35.4	31.7	26.1	24.1	0.86	0.83	0.85	0.86	0.89	0.86
19.0	16.4	16.0	14.1	0.89	0.88	0.94	0.90	0.92	0.92
15.7	15.6	13.6	13.5	0.87	0.87	0.97	0.88	0.89	0.89
13.1	12.8	11.6	11.3	0.57	0.71	1.02	0.78	0.55	0.82
24.1	17.4	19.4	14.8	0.92	0.89	0.90	0.91	0.96	1.09
12.4	12.4	11.1	11.1	0.68	0.76	0.96	0.70	0.72	0.76
34.4	22.6	25.6	18.5	0.96	0.90	0.86	0.95	1.22	1.02
53.2	30.6	34.7	23.4	0.76	0.77	0.84	0.78	0.73	1.00
21.5	31.5	17.7	23.9	1.03	0.97	0.94	1.02	1.04	1.09
22.2	16.0	18.2	13.8	0.85	0.85	0.90	0.86	0.84	0.87
22.2	16.0	18.2	13.8	0.85	0.85	0.90	0.86	0.83	0.87
27.8	28.8	21.8	22.3	0.90	0.87	0.92	0.90	0.90	0.93
13.2	16.0	11.7	13.8	0.59	0.71	0.66	0.59	0.63	0.79
23.0	21.9	18.7	18.0	1.08	1.00	–	–	1.07	1.05
25.9	24.2	20.5	19.5	1.05	0.98	–	–	1.07	1.02
25.4	18.1	20.2	15.3	0.36	0.54	0.56	0.47	0.39	0.66
32.9	34.3	24.7	25.5	0.39	0.55	–	–	0.52	0.91
52.0	58.8	34.2	37.0	0.93	0.87	0.97	0.95	0.88	1.03
35.6	42.1	26.3	29.6	1.28	1.11	1.54	1.31	1.22	1.23
38.1	48.5	27.6	32.6	1.29	1.11	1.54	1.33	1.25	1.25
36.6	38.4	26.8	27.7	0.84	0.83	0.77	0.84	0.92	0.86
20.6	23.4	17.1	19.0	1.15	1.06	0.92	1.08	0.88	1.18
23.9	21.8	19.3	17.9	0.74	0.78	0.78	0.74	0.94	0.84

Appendix B-2

	Calculated Using: Book Debt																Calculated Using: Book plus Off-Balance-Sheet Debt									
	Beta (Levered)						Leverage Ratio (%)				Beta (Unlevered) (Using Latest Book Debt)						Leverage Ratio (%)				Beta (Unlevered) (Using Latest Book plus Off-Balance-Sheet Debt)					
SIC Code	Raw (OLS)	Blume Adjusted	Peer Group	Vasicek Adjusted	Sum	Downside	Debt / MV Equity Latest	Debt / MV Equity 5-Yr Avg	Debt / Total Capital Latest	Debt / Total Capital 5-Yr Avg	Raw (OLS)	Blume Adjusted	Peer Group	Vasicek Adjusted	Sum	Downside	Debt / MV Equity Latest	Debt / MV Equity 5-Yr Avg	Debt / Total Capital Latest	Debt / Total Capital 5-Yr Avg	Raw (OLS)	Blume Adjusted	Peer Group	Vasicek Adjusted	Sum	Downside
348	0.53	0.71	0.92	0.86	0.57	0.87	17.0	22.7	14.6	18.5	0.50	0.65	0.83	0.77	0.53	0.79	25.9	35.3	20.6	26.1	0.48	0.62	0.79	0.74	0.51	0.75
349	1.28	1.18	1.00	1.18	1.42	1.40	15.9	17.0	13.7	14.5	1.12	1.03	0.87	1.03	1.24	1.22	21.9	23.7	17.9	19.1	1.07	0.99	0.84	0.98	1.18	1.16
35	1.33	1.22	1.36	1.34	1.31	1.57	26.5	28.7	21.0	22.3	1.08	0.98	1.10	1.08	1.05	1.26	29.3	32.7	22.7	24.6	1.05	0.96	1.07	1.06	1.03	1.24
353	1.22	1.15	1.36	1.26	1.85	1.45	24.7	20.8	19.8	17.2	1.02	0.96	1.13	1.05	1.53	1.20	30.3	26.2	23.3	20.8	0.99	0.93	1.09	1.01	1.47	1.16
355	1.61	1.40	1.35	1.58	1.56	1.77	12.0	13.8	10.7	12.1	1.45	1.26	1.22	1.42	1.40	1.59	12.6	14.9	11.2	13.0	1.44	1.25	1.21	1.41	1.39	1.58
3559	1.63	1.40	1.35	1.58	1.59	1.79	11.8	13.6	10.5	12.0	1.46	1.26	1.22	1.42	1.43	1.61	12.2	14.5	10.9	12.6	1.46	1.26	1.21	1.41	1.42	1.60
356	1.23	1.15	1.35	1.24	1.09	1.33	24.2	24.4	19.5	19.6	1.03	0.97	1.13	1.04	0.92	1.11	28.1	29.1	21.9	22.5	1.01	0.95	1.10	1.02	0.90	1.09
357	1.40	1.26	1.36	1.39	1.28	1.77	23.2	23.7	18.8	19.2	1.16	1.04	1.12	1.15	1.06	1.46	25.6	27.8	20.4	21.7	1.14	1.03	1.10	1.13	1.04	1.43
358	1.32	1.21	1.36	1.33	1.22	1.27	10.4	16.4	9.4	14.1	1.22	1.12	1.25	1.23	1.12	1.17	14.5	21.3	12.6	17.6	1.18	1.08	1.21	1.19	1.09	1.14
36	1.18	1.12	1.20	1.18	1.15	1.22	12.3	10.1	11.0	9.1	1.06	1.00	1.08	1.06	1.03	1.09	13.5	11.3	11.9	10.2	1.05	0.99	1.07	1.05	1.02	1.08
362	1.39	1.25	1.20	1.35	1.44	1.40	28.6	28.5	22.2	22.2	1.16	1.05	1.01	1.13	1.19	1.17	30.9	31.0	23.6	23.6	1.14	1.04	0.99	1.11	1.18	1.15
3621	1.45	1.29	1.19	1.39	1.46	1.43	34.4	31.6	25.6	24.0	1.16	1.05	0.97	1.12	1.17	1.15	37.4	34.6	27.2	25.7	1.14	1.03	0.96	1.10	1.15	1.13
366	1.18	1.12	1.20	1.18	1.09	1.34	11.9	7.5	10.7	7.0	1.06	1.00	1.07	1.06	0.98	1.20	12.9	8.3	11.4	7.7	1.05	0.99	1.07	1.05	0.97	1.19
3663	1.18	1.12	1.20	1.19	1.09	1.35	11.9	7.5	10.7	7.0	1.06	1.00	1.07	1.06	0.98	1.20	12.9	8.3	11.4	7.7	1.05	0.99	1.07	1.05	0.97	1.19
367	1.16	1.11	1.20	1.16	1.23	1.25	12.1	12.8	10.8	11.4	1.05	1.00	1.09	1.05	1.11	1.13	13.2	14.2	11.7	12.4	1.04	0.99	1.08	1.04	1.10	1.12
3672	0.92	0.96	1.20	1.07	0.80	1.53	24.8	31.1	19.9	23.7	0.77	0.80	1.00	0.89	0.68	1.26	29.8	36.8	23.0	26.9	0.75	0.78	0.96	0.87	0.66	1.22
3674	1.18	1.12	1.20	1.18	1.25	1.26	11.8	12.2	10.6	10.9	1.07	1.02	1.08	1.07	1.13	1.14	12.8	13.4	11.3	11.8	1.06	1.01	1.08	1.06	1.12	1.13
3679	1.03	1.03	1.20	1.07	0.71	1.18	3.4	4.9	3.3	4.7	1.01	1.00	1.17	1.04	0.70	1.15	4.4	6.6	4.2	6.2	1.00	0.99	1.16	1.04	0.69	1.14
37	1.12	1.08	1.09	1.11	1.15	1.19	67.9	62.9	40.4	38.6	0.70	0.68	0.69	0.70	0.72	0.75	79.8	77.1	44.4	43.5	0.66	0.64	0.65	0.66	0.68	0.71
371	1.24	1.16	1.09	1.23	1.33	1.40	135.4	110.8	57.5	52.6	0.58	0.55	0.52	0.57	0.62	0.65	149.3	127.4	59.9	56.0	0.55	0.52	0.49	0.55	0.59	0.61
3711	1.20	1.13	1.10	1.17	1.26	1.36	186.7	146.2	65.1	59.4	0.47	0.45	0.44	0.46	0.49	0.53	–	167.2	67.2	62.6	0.45	0.43	0.42	0.44	0.47	0.50
3714	1.34	1.22	1.05	1.31	1.47	1.52	24.3	24.8	19.5	19.9	1.12	1.03	0.89	1.10	1.23	1.27	29.9	30.9	23.0	23.6	1.09	1.00	0.86	1.06	1.18	1.22
372	1.11	1.08	1.10	1.11	1.15	1.36	16.5	17.9	14.2	15.2	0.98	0.95	0.96	0.98	1.01	1.19	27.6	30.2	21.6	23.2	0.91	0.88	0.89	0.91	0.94	1.10
38	0.97	0.99	0.92	0.97	1.10	1.03	16.6	15.3	14.3	13.2	0.85	0.86	0.80	0.85	0.96	0.90	18.4	17.4	15.5	14.8	0.84	0.85	0.79	0.84	0.94	0.89
382	1.12	1.08	0.93	1.11	1.37	1.35	15.3	16.1	13.3	13.9	0.99	0.96	0.82	0.97	1.20	1.19	17.0	18.0	14.5	15.3	0.98	0.94	0.81	0.96	1.19	1.17
3823	1.26	1.17	0.91	1.18	1.30	1.50	5.2	3.0	4.9	2.9	1.22	1.13	0.88	1.14	1.25	1.44	5.8	3.5	5.5	3.4	1.21	1.13	0.88	1.14	1.25	1.43
3826	1.01	1.01	0.93	0.96	1.41	1.34	17.0	18.2	14.5	15.4	0.88	0.88	0.82	0.84	1.22	1.16	18.9	20.4	15.9	16.9	0.87	0.87	0.80	0.83	1.21	1.14
384	0.83	0.90	0.91	0.84	0.85	0.84	13.1	12.0	11.6	10.7	0.74	0.81	0.82	0.75	0.77	0.76	14.2	13.5	12.4	11.9	0.74	0.80	0.81	0.75	0.76	0.75
3841	0.71	0.82	0.91	0.77	0.71	0.75	9.4	13.8	8.6	12.2	0.67	0.77	0.85	0.73	0.67	0.70	10.7	15.9	9.7	13.8	0.66	0.76	0.84	0.72	0.66	0.70
3842	0.96	0.98	0.91	0.95	0.98	0.99	26.0	20.1	20.6	16.7	0.79	0.80	0.74	0.78	0.80	0.81	27.2	21.5	21.4	17.7	0.78	0.80	0.74	0.77	0.80	0.80
3845	0.68	0.80	0.91	0.73	0.84	0.88	6.9	4.9	6.5	4.7	0.66	0.77	0.87	0.71	0.81	0.84	7.5	5.6	7.0	5.3	0.66	0.77	0.87	0.71	0.81	0.84
39	0.89	0.94	0.97	0.90	0.73	1.12	17.0	17.2	14.5	14.7	0.78	0.82	0.85	0.78	0.64	0.97	20.5	21.1	17.0	17.4	0.76	0.79	0.83	0.77	0.63	0.95
394	0.88	0.93	0.97	0.90	0.71	1.11	18.1	18.3	15.3	15.4	0.76	0.80	0.84	0.77	0.61	0.96	21.9	22.4	18.0	18.3	0.74	0.78	0.82	0.75	0.60	0.93
Division E: Transportation, Communications, Electric, Gas, and Sanitary Services																										
4	0.69	0.81	0.78	0.69	0.60	0.69	55.1	55.7	35.5	35.8	0.49	0.56	0.55	0.49	0.43	0.49	63.3	65.3	38.8	39.5	0.47	0.54	0.53	0.47	0.41	0.47
40	1.02	1.02	–	–	1.09	1.33	23.7	24.4	19.2	19.6	0.84	0.84	–	–	0.90	1.09	26.4	28.0	20.9	21.9	0.82	0.82	–	–	0.88	1.07
42	0.88	0.93	0.87	0.88	0.71	0.94	15.0	13.5	13.1	11.9	0.77	0.81	0.76	0.77	0.62	0.83	24.3	21.3	19.6	17.6	0.72	0.76	0.70	0.71	0.58	0.77
4213	0.85	0.91	0.87	0.85	0.73	0.94	8.8	9.4	8.1	8.6	0.80	0.86	0.82	0.81	0.69	0.88	9.9	10.8	9.0	9.7	0.80	0.85	0.81	0.80	0.69	0.88
45	0.98	0.99	1.32	1.01	0.50	1.06	42.4	52.3	29.8	34.3	0.77	0.78	1.01	0.80	0.44	0.83	87.7	114.9	46.7	53.5	0.66	0.66	0.84	0.67	0.40	0.70
451	0.94	0.97	1.32	0.98	0.42	1.09	40.3	51.0	28.7	33.8	0.75	0.77	1.02	0.78	0.38	0.86	85.6	115.0	46.1	53.5	0.64	0.65	0.84	0.66	0.35	0.72
4512	0.94	0.97	1.32	0.97	0.41	1.09	40.2	50.9	28.7	33.7	0.75	0.77	1.02	0.77	0.38	0.86	85.8	115.2	46.2	53.5	0.63	0.65	0.84	0.65	0.35	0.72
46	1.01	1.01	1.10	1.03	1.40	1.23	49.3	39.6	33.0	28.4	0.72	0.73	0.78	0.74	0.99	0.87	50.5	40.7	33.5	28.9	0.72	0.72	0.78	0.74	0.98	0.86
47	0.82	0.89	0.91	0.84	0.51	0.86	24.3	26.4	19.5	20.9	0.69	0.74	0.75	0.70	0.43	0.71	27.9	31.3	21.8	23.8	0.67	0.72	0.73	0.68	0.42	0.70
473	0.82	0.89	0.90	0.84	0.51	0.78	6.7	4.3	6.3	4.1	0.79	0.86	0.86	0.81	0.50	0.75	8.6	5.8	7.9	5.5	0.78	0.85	0.85	0.80	0.50	0.75
48	0.76	0.85	0.78	0.76	0.61	0.77	50.9	50.5	33.7	33.6	0.55	0.61	0.57	0.55	0.45	0.56	58.7	59.5	37.0	37.3	0.53	0.59	0.55	0.53	0.44	0.54
481	0.54	0.71	0.76	0.59	0.30	0.62	59.8	61.0	37.4	37.9	0.39	0.50	0.53	0.42	0.24	0.44	70.4	71.9	41.3	41.8	0.37	0.48	0.50	0.41	0.23	0.42
4813	0.90	0.94	0.76	0.86	0.47	1.01	88.9	95.2	47.1	48.8	0.62	0.64	0.54	0.60	0.39	0.67	104.5	111.3	51.1	52.7	0.59	0.61	0.52	0.57	0.38	0.64
483	1.27	1.18	0.85	1.25	1.27	1.18	49.5	42.4	33.1	29.8	0.91	0.85	0.63	0.90	0.92	0.85	54.1	46.6	35.1	31.8	0.89	0.83	0.62	0.88	0.90	0.83
4833	1.32	1.21	0.88	1.28	1.41	1.39	64.2	49.9	39.1	33.3	0.87	0.80	0.60	0.85	0.93	0.91	70.7	55.1	41.4	35.5	0.84	0.78	0.59	0.82	0.90	0.89
489	0.96	0.98	0.77	0.93	1.18	1.28	55.6	53.2	35.7	34.7	0.73	0.75	0.61	0.72	0.88	0.94	59.3	56.8	37.2	36.2	0.72	0.74	0.60	0.71	0.86	0.93
49	0.46	0.67	0.48	0.47	0.43	0.55	76.0	77.9	43.2	43.8	0.30	0.42	0.31	0.30	0.28	0.35	78.9	81.5	44.1	44.9	0.30	0.41	0.31	0.30	0.28	0.35
491	0.28	0.55	0.47	0.35	0.11	0.48	75.0	77.1	42.9	43.5	0.18	0.33	0.29	0.22	0.08	0.30	77.8	80.5	43.8	44.6	0.18	0.33	0.29	0.22	0.08	0.29
492	1.00	1.01	0.52	0.93	1.65	1.22	102.0	89.4	50.5	47.2	0.58	0.59	0.34	0.55	0.91	0.69	103.8	91.3	50.9	47.7	0.58	0.58	0.34	0.54	0.90	0.69
4922	1.27	1.18	0.54	1.12	2.28	1.55	124.9	96.1	55.5	49.0	0.68	0.64	0.35	0.61	1.13	0.81	126.9	98.4	55.9	49.6	0.68	0.63	0.35	0.61	1.12	0.80
4924	0.40	0.63	0.48	0.46	0.12	0.64	54.4	61.3	35.3	38.0	0.27	0.42	0.32	0.31	0.09	0.43	58.8	66.4	37.0	39.9	0.26	0.41	0.32	0.30	0.09	0.42

2017 Valuation Handbook – U.S. Industry Cost of Capital (data through March 2017)

Appendix B: Leverage Ratios and Unlevered Betas Calculated Using (i) Book Debt, and (ii) Book Debt Plus Off-Balance-Sheet Debt

Appendix B-4

Calculated Using: Book Debt

SIC Code	Beta (Levered) Raw (OLS)	Blume Adjusted	Peer Group	Vasicek Adjusted	Sum	Downside	Leverage Ratio (%) Debt/MV Equity Latest	5-Yr Avg	Debt/Total Capital Latest	5-Yr Avg	Beta (Unlevered) Raw (OLS)	Blume Adjusted	Peer Group	Vasicek Adjusted	Sum	Downside
Division F: Wholesale Trade																
493	0.25	0.53	0.47	0.37	-0.08	0.50	64.5	70.7	39.2	41.4	0.17	0.34	0.30	0.24	-0.04	0.32
494	0.35	0.59	0.47	0.40	-0.07	0.54	42.8	53.2	30.0	34.7	0.27	0.44	0.36	0.31	-0.02	0.40
495	0.58	0.74	0.52	0.58	0.48	0.65	36.5	44.2	26.7	30.7	0.45	0.57	0.41	0.45	0.37	0.50
5	0.87	0.92	0.87	0.87	0.83	0.85	20.3	19.0	16.9	16.0	0.74	0.79	0.74	0.74	0.71	0.72
50	1.02	1.02	1.07	1.02	0.94	1.05	23.2	20.6	18.9	17.1	0.87	0.87	0.91	0.87	0.81	0.90
504	1.07	1.05	1.07	1.07	0.76	1.09	19.5	16.5	16.3	14.2	0.93	0.92	0.94	0.94	0.67	0.95
5045	1.20	1.13	1.07	1.18	0.71	1.44	29.3	26.8	22.6	21.1	0.98	0.93	0.88	0.97	0.60	1.17
506	1.75	1.48	1.07	1.58	2.19	1.81	45.4	48.2	31.2	32.5	1.30	1.11	0.83	1.18	1.60	1.34
508	0.94	0.96	1.07	0.95	1.13	1.01	26.2	27.6	20.7	21.6	0.81	0.83	0.92	0.82	0.96	0.87
51	0.93	0.96	1.01	0.94	1.15	1.01	34.9	28.5	25.9	22.2	0.72	0.75	0.78	0.73	0.89	0.78
512	0.96	0.98	1.01	0.97	1.38	1.19	25.2	20.5	20.1	17.0	0.78	0.80	0.82	0.79	1.12	0.96
514	0.64	0.78	1.01	0.70	0.31	0.75	27.6	21.6	21.6	17.7	0.53	0.64	0.82	0.58	0.27	0.62
517	1.08	1.05	1.01	1.06	1.24	1.34	66.7	55.1	40.0	35.5	0.72	0.70	0.67	0.71	0.81	0.87
Division G: Retail Trade																
52	1.11	1.08	–	–	1.09	1.10	14.7	14.2	12.8	12.4	0.97	0.94	–	–	0.95	0.97
53	0.42	0.64	0.42	0.42	0.29	0.64	23.4	22.4	18.9	18.3	0.35	0.52	0.35	0.35	0.25	0.53
533	0.26	0.54	0.42	0.28	0.15	0.64	24.5	23.0	19.7	18.7	0.22	0.44	0.34	0.23	0.13	0.52
54	0.68	0.80	0.82	0.79	0.20	0.86	41.4	29.4	29.3	22.7	0.52	0.60	0.61	0.59	0.18	0.64
541	0.69	0.81	0.82	0.79	0.13	0.89	38.6	29.2	27.8	22.6	0.53	0.61	0.62	0.60	0.12	0.67
5411	0.70	0.82	0.82	0.81	0.09	0.94	40.7	29.7	28.9	22.9	0.53	0.61	0.61	0.60	0.09	0.70
55	1.03	1.03	0.91	1.01	0.90	1.21	57.5	51.8	36.5	34.1	0.75	0.75	0.67	0.74	0.67	0.87
56	0.83	0.90	0.76	0.82	0.52	0.78	7.8	6.2	7.3	5.8	0.78	0.85	0.72	0.77	0.50	0.74
562	1.09	1.06	0.73	0.97	1.38	1.21	45.7	8.1	31.4	7.5	0.84	0.82	0.59	0.79	0.39	0.93
565	0.83	0.90	0.76	0.81	0.43	1.21	7.5	6.8	7.0	6.4	0.78	0.84	0.72	0.77	0.48	0.73
566	0.67	0.79	0.78	0.70	0.51	0.77	1.5	1.5	1.5	1.5	0.66	0.79	0.77	0.70	0.70	0.79
57	1.01	1.01	1.30	1.12	0.71	0.80	13.8	8.5	12.1	7.8	0.90	0.91	1.16	1.00	0.92	1.10
58	0.65	0.79	0.66	0.65	1.03	1.23	18.0	13.9	15.2	12.2	0.58	0.69	0.58	0.58	0.46	0.63
5812	0.65	0.79	0.66	0.65	0.51	0.71	17.9	13.9	15.2	12.2	0.58	0.69	0.58	0.58	0.46	0.63
59	1.21	1.14	1.25	1.21	0.51	0.71	15.3	16.6	13.3	14.2	1.06	1.00	1.10	1.06	1.12	1.14
591	0.98	0.99	1.25	1.01	1.28	1.30	31.8	23.2	24.1	18.8	0.77	0.78	0.98	0.79	0.82	0.82
594	1.40	1.26	1.26	1.40	1.05	1.05	29.1	26.5	22.5	21.0	1.16	1.05	1.05	1.15	1.33	1.29
596	1.42	1.28	1.24	1.32	1.63	1.58	6.3	8.6	5.9	8.0	1.35	1.20	1.18	1.25	1.29	1.62
Division H: Finance, Insurance, and Real Estate																
6	1.08	1.06	1.11	1.09	1.37	1.72	90.4	116.3	47.5	53.8	0.60	0.59	0.62	0.60	0.69	0.65
60	1.13	1.09	1.14	1.13	1.43	1.30	94.8	126.1	48.7	55.8	0.60	0.58	0.61	0.60	0.76	0.69
602	1.16	1.11	1.14	1.16	1.56	1.38	113.4	153.1	53.1	60.5	0.57	0.54	0.56	0.57	0.75	0.67
603	0.63	0.77	1.14	0.70	0.68	0.79	100.1	122.1	50.0	55.0	0.35	0.43	0.62	0.39	0.38	0.44
6035	0.58	0.74	1.14	0.66	0.62	0.72	82.2	106.2	45.1	51.5	0.36	0.44	0.67	0.40	0.38	0.43
6036	0.67	0.80	1.14	0.78	0.73	0.89	124.5	141.2	55.5	58.5	0.35	0.40	0.56	0.39	0.37	0.44
609	1.06	1.04	1.14	1.09	0.98	1.16	8.8	4.2	8.1	4.0	0.98	0.96	1.05	1.01	0.90	1.06
61	1.22	1.15	1.61	1.27	1.50	1.43	135.9	134.1	57.6	57.3	0.61	0.58	0.78	0.63	0.73	0.70
614	1.25	1.16	1.69	1.31	1.36	1.38	163.7	174.0	62.1	63.5	0.53	0.50	0.70	0.56	0.57	0.58
615	1.51	1.33	1.66	1.55	1.23	1.70	–	184.8	76.4	64.9	0.58	0.54	0.61	0.59	0.51	0.62
616	1.27	1.18	1.70	1.49	0.89	1.67	–	–	80.5	78.7	0.48	0.46	0.57	0.52	0.41	0.56
62	1.52	1.34	1.55	1.52	1.84	1.66	148.9	–	59.8	67.1	0.66	0.58	0.67	0.66	0.79	0.71
621	1.56	1.36	1.53	1.55	1.96	1.76	–	–	73.5	79.4	0.47	0.42	0.47	0.47	0.58	0.53
628	1.60	1.39	1.56	1.60	1.89	1.68	23.7	27.2	19.2	21.4	1.30	1.13	1.27	1.30	1.54	1.37
63	1.00	1.00	0.98	1.00	1.00	1.06	27.4	32.1	21.5	24.3	0.80	0.80	0.79	0.80	0.80	0.85
632	0.71	0.82	0.99	0.78	0.55	0.83	25.5	27.0	20.3	21.3	0.58	0.67	0.81	0.64	0.45	0.68
6324	0.66	0.79	0.99	0.87	0.46	0.80	24.1	24.9	19.4	20.0	0.55	0.65	0.82	0.72	0.39	0.66
633	0.95	0.97	0.98	0.95	0.82	0.96	19.1	22.8	16.1	18.6	0.81	0.83	0.83	0.81	0.70	0.82
64	0.86	0.91	0.88	0.86	0.80	0.83	15.0	15.6	13.0	13.5	0.75	0.80	0.77	0.75	0.71	0.83
65	1.50	1.32	1.50	1.50	1.75	1.51	54.2	44.7	35.1	30.9	1.05	0.94	1.05	1.05	1.21	1.06
651	1.28	1.18	1.44	1.34	1.57	1.27	148.8	108.6	59.8	52.1	0.69	0.65	0.75	0.71	0.80	0.69

Calculated Using: Book plus Off-Balance-Sheet Debt

Leverage Ratio (%) Debt/MV Equity Latest	5-Yr Avg	Debt/Total Capital Latest	5-Yr Avg	Beta (Unlevered) (Using Latest Book plus Off-Balance-Sheet Debt) Raw (OLS)	Blume Adjusted	Peer Group	Vasicek Adjusted	Sum	Downside
67.5	74.3	40.3	42.6	0.17	0.33	0.30	0.24	-0.03	0.32
45.6	56.7	31.3	36.2	0.27	0.43	0.35	0.30	-0.02	0.40
38.5	46.8	27.8	31.9	0.45	0.56	0.40	0.44	0.37	0.50
30.4	30.1	23.3	23.1	0.70	0.74	0.69	0.70	0.67	0.68
28.1	25.8	22.0	20.5	0.84	0.84	0.88	0.84	0.78	0.87
23.8	21.6	19.2	17.7	0.91	0.90	0.91	0.91	0.66	0.93
35.6	34.9	26.3	25.9	0.94	0.89	0.85	0.93	0.59	1.12
54.3	57.5	35.2	36.5	1.24	1.07	0.80	1.13	1.53	1.28
31.4	32.8	23.9	24.7	0.79	0.81	0.90	0.80	0.94	0.85
38.5	32.1	27.8	24.3	0.71	0.73	0.77	0.71	0.87	0.76
29.0	23.6	22.5	19.1	0.76	0.78	0.80	0.77	1.09	0.94
32.0	26.0	24.2	20.7	0.52	0.62	0.80	0.56	0.26	0.60
67.6	57.5	40.3	36.5	0.71	0.70	0.67	0.70	0.81	0.87
17.8	19.1	15.1	16.0	0.95	0.92	–	–	0.93	0.94
33.8	30.8	25.3	23.6	0.32	0.49	0.32	0.32	0.23	0.49
35.3	31.2	26.1	23.8	0.20	0.41	0.32	0.21	0.12	0.48
72.6	54.2	42.1	35.1	0.44	0.52	0.53	0.51	0.17	0.55
67.9	54.5	40.4	35.3	0.45	0.53	0.53	0.51	0.12	0.57
73.3	56.8	42.3	36.2	0.45	0.51	0.51	0.51	0.09	0.59
76.3	71.3	43.3	41.6	0.70	0.70	0.63	0.69	0.62	0.80
29.6	26.2	22.9	20.7	0.68	0.73	0.62	0.67	0.44	0.64
125.6	43.4	55.7	30.3	0.65	0.64	0.49	0.62	0.36	0.70
27.0	25.2	21.3	20.1	0.68	0.73	0.62	0.67	0.42	0.63
24.8	27.6	19.8	21.6	0.59	0.69	0.68	0.62	0.63	0.70
39.4	32.1	28.3	24.3	0.76	0.76	0.97	0.84	0.78	0.92
28.2	24.6	22.0	19.7	0.55	0.65	0.55	0.55	0.44	0.59
28.2	24.6	22.0	19.7	0.55	0.65	0.55	0.55	0.44	0.59
24.9	30.4	19.9	23.3	0.99	0.93	1.02	0.99	1.05	1.06
56.5	48.7	36.1	32.7	0.67	0.68	0.84	0.69	0.71	0.71
47.5	49.8	32.2	33.2	1.05	0.95	0.95	1.05	1.20	1.17
8.2	11.3	7.6	10.1	1.32	1.19	1.16	1.22	1.27	1.59
92.5	118.9	48.1	54.3	0.60	0.58	0.61	0.60	0.68	0.64
95.0	126.5	48.7	55.8	0.60	0.58	0.61	0.60	0.75	0.69
113.6	153.5	53.2	60.5	0.57	0.54	0.56	0.57	0.75	0.67
100.4	122.6	50.1	55.1	0.35	0.43	0.61	0.39	0.38	0.44
82.5	106.8	45.2	51.6	0.36	0.44	0.67	0.40	0.38	0.43
124.7	141.6	55.5	58.6	0.35	0.40	0.56	0.39	0.37	0.44
9.1	4.4	8.4	4.2	0.97	0.96	1.05	1.00	0.90	1.06
137.4	136.1	57.9	57.6	0.61	0.58	0.78	0.63	0.73	0.70
164.7	175.0	62.2	63.6	0.53	0.50	0.70	0.56	0.57	0.58
–	187.6	76.6	65.2	0.58	0.53	0.61	0.59	0.51	0.62
–	–	80.7	78.9	0.48	0.46	0.56	0.52	0.41	0.56
151.7	–	60.3	67.5	0.65	0.58	0.66	0.65	0.78	0.71
–	–	73.7	79.5	0.47	0.42	0.46	0.47	0.57	0.52
25.7	29.5	20.4	22.8	1.28	1.11	1.25	1.28	1.51	1.35
30.2	35.8	23.2	26.3	0.78	0.79	0.77	0.78	0.78	0.83
27.3	29.8	21.5	23.0	0.58	0.66	0.80	0.63	0.45	0.67
25.9	27.6	20.6	21.6	0.54	0.65	0.81	0.71	0.38	0.65
21.8	26.2	17.9	20.7	0.79	0.81	0.82	0.79	0.69	0.81
20.3	22.3	16.9	18.2	0.72	0.77	0.74	0.72	0.68	0.80
61.4	51.9	38.1	34.2	1.01	0.91	1.01	1.01	1.17	1.02
149.6	109.6	59.9	52.3	0.69	0.65	0.75	0.71	0.80	0.68

Appendix B: Leverage Ratios and Unlevered Betas Calculated Using (i) Book Debt, and (ii) Book Debt Plus Off-Balance-Sheet Debt

Calculated Using: Book Debt

SIC Code	Beta (Levered) Raw (OLS)	Blume Adjusted	Peer Group	Vasicek Adjusted	Sum	Downside	Debt/MV Equity Latest	Leverage Ratio (%) 5-Yr Avg	Debt/Total Capital Latest	5-Yr Avg	Beta (Unlevered) Raw (OLS)	Blume Adjusted	Peer Group	Vasicek Adjusted	Sum	Downside
655	1.31	1.20	1.51	1.33	1.43	1.46	51.3	35.5	33.9	26.2	0.98	0.91	1.11	0.99	1.06	1.08
67	0.62	0.76	0.66	0.62	0.39	0.76	58.8	67.7	37.0	40.4	0.42	0.51	0.45	0.42	0.28	0.51
6794	0.74	0.84	0.66	0.73	0.55	0.89	16.0	19.2	13.8	16.1	0.68	0.77	0.61	0.67	0.52	0.81
6798	0.60	0.75	0.66	0.61	0.36	0.78	59.7	69.5	37.4	41.0	0.41	0.50	0.44	0.42	0.26	0.52
6799	1.14	1.10	0.66	1.03	1.46	1.33	40.2	42.0	28.7	29.6	0.84	0.81	0.49	0.76	1.07	0.97
7	1.10	1.07	1.08	1.10	1.00	1.06	12.4	12.0	11.0	10.7	0.99	0.96	0.98	0.99	0.90	0.95

Division I: Services

SIC Code	Raw (OLS)	Blume Adj	Peer Group	Vasicek Adj	Sum	Downside	Debt/MV Eq Latest	5-Yr Avg	Debt/TC Latest	5-Yr Avg	Raw (OLS)	Blume Adj	Peer Group	Vasicek Adj	Sum	Downside
73	1.09	1.06	1.06	1.09	1.00	1.04	11.6	11.0	10.4	9.9	0.98	0.96	0.96	0.98	0.90	0.94
735	1.82	1.53	1.06	1.76	2.05	2.05	98.6	111.2	49.6	52.7	1.02	0.87	0.63	0.99	1.13	1.13
7359	1.32	1.21	1.06	1.30	1.08	1.57	129.4	110.6	56.4	52.5	0.65	0.60	0.53	0.64	0.54	0.76
736	1.37	1.24	1.05	1.34	1.16	1.31	9.9	10.0	9.0	9.1	1.27	1.15	0.98	1.24	1.08	1.22
7363	1.43	1.28	1.05	1.40	1.16	1.38	13.0	9.1	8.2	8.4	1.33	1.19	0.98	1.30	1.08	1.28
737	1.07	1.05	1.06	1.07	0.97	1.02	12.2	9.7	9.5	8.8	0.98	0.96	0.97	0.98	0.88	0.93
7372	1.06	1.04	1.06	1.05	1.02	1.07	10.5	7.7	8.4	7.2	0.97	0.96	0.97	0.97	0.94	0.98
7373	1.05	1.04	1.06	1.05	1.07	1.24	8.5	6.8	7.9	6.4	0.99	0.97	0.99	0.99	1.00	1.16
7374	0.95	0.97	1.05	0.95	0.79	0.83	22.6	22.2	18.5	18.1	0.81	0.83	0.89	0.81	0.68	0.71
738	1.24	1.16	1.06	1.23	1.06	1.29	34.5	31.1	25.7	23.7	0.97	0.92	0.84	0.97	0.85	1.01
7389	1.21	1.14	1.06	1.20	1.02	1.29	36.4	31.2	26.7	23.8	0.95	0.90	0.84	0.94	0.81	1.01
79	1.60	1.39	1.55	1.59	1.17	1.51	31.5	30.9	24.0	23.6	1.27	1.10	1.23	1.26	0.94	1.20
799	1.63	1.40	1.55	1.61	1.19	1.54	31.9	31.0	24.2	23.7	1.28	1.11	1.22	1.27	0.95	1.22
8	0.94	0.97	0.92	0.94	0.96	1.01	28.3	25.9	22.1	20.6	0.79	0.81	0.77	0.79	0.80	0.84
80	0.86	0.92	0.92	0.87	1.03	1.11	47.8	45.4	32.4	31.2	0.67	0.71	0.72	0.68	0.79	0.84
806	1.09	1.06	0.92	0.98	1.33	1.39	67.3	59.5	40.2	37.3	0.78	0.76	0.68	0.71	0.93	0.96
807	0.74	0.84	0.92	0.75	0.85	1.02	31.3	40.6	23.9	28.9	0.59	0.67	0.73	0.61	0.68	0.81
82	1.02	1.02	0.83	0.99	0.78	1.19	5.4	6.8	5.2	6.4	0.99	0.98	0.80	0.95	0.76	1.14
87	0.95	0.98	0.94	0.96	0.92	0.97	9.4	8.2	8.6	7.6	0.91	0.92	0.89	0.90	0.86	0.91
871	1.02	1.02	0.94	0.99	0.89	1.08	10.7	10.5	9.7	9.5	0.95	0.95	0.88	0.93	0.84	1.01
874	1.07	1.05	0.94	1.06	1.01	1.16	19.7	13.8	16.5	12.1	0.94	0.92	0.83	0.92	0.88	1.01
8742	1.06	1.04	0.94	1.04	1.30	1.27	23.2	18.0	18.9	15.2	0.92	0.90	0.82	0.90	1.11	1.08

Calculated Using: Book plus Off-Balance-Sheet Debt

Leverage Ratio (%) Debt/MV Equity Latest	5-Yr Avg	Debt/Total Capital Latest	5-Yr Avg	Beta (Unlevered) (Using Latest Book plus Off-Balance-Sheet Debt) Raw (OLS)	Blume Adjusted	Peer Group	Vasicek Adjusted	Sum	Downside
54.6	39.1	35.3	28.1	0.97	0.90	1.10	0.98	1.04	1.06
63.1	71.7	38.7	41.8	0.41	0.50	0.44	0.42	0.27	0.50
19.8	24.5	16.5	19.7	0.67	0.75	0.60	0.66	0.51	0.80
64.2	73.7	39.1	42.4	0.40	0.49	0.43	0.41	0.25	0.51
40.3	42.1	28.7	29.6	0.84	0.81	0.49	0.76	1.07	0.97
14.4	14.3	12.6	12.5	0.98	0.95	0.95	0.98	0.89	0.93
13.5	13.2	11.9	11.7	0.97	0.95	0.95	0.97	0.89	0.93
103.6	118.0	50.9	54.1	1.00	0.85	0.62	0.97	1.11	1.11
135.8	117.8	57.6	54.1	0.64	0.59	0.52	0.63	0.53	0.74
13.6	15.2	12.0	13.2	1.23	1.12	0.95	1.21	1.05	1.18
13.0	14.0	11.5	12.3	1.29	1.15	0.95	1.26	1.05	1.24
12.2	11.6	10.9	10.4	0.96	0.94	0.96	0.96	0.87	0.92
10.2	8.9	9.3	8.2	0.96	0.95	0.96	0.96	0.93	0.97
10.3	8.8	9.4	8.1	0.97	0.96	0.98	0.97	0.99	1.15
23.9	23.9	19.3	19.3	0.80	0.82	0.88	0.80	0.67	0.71
43.6	41.9	30.4	29.5	0.93	0.87	0.80	0.92	0.81	0.96
44.7	40.5	30.9	28.8	0.91	0.86	0.80	0.90	0.78	0.96
32.5	31.9	24.5	24.2	1.26	1.10	1.22	1.25	0.93	1.19
32.9	32.1	24.8	24.3	1.28	1.11	1.21	1.26	0.96	1.21
35.0	32.8	25.9	24.7	0.76	0.78	0.75	0.76	0.78	0.81
57.5	54.8	36.5	35.4	0.65	0.68	0.69	0.65	0.76	0.81
76.9	67.2	43.5	40.2	0.75	0.74	0.66	0.69	0.89	0.92
37.4	48.6	27.2	32.7	0.57	0.65	0.71	0.58	0.65	0.78
8.9	13.7	8.2	12.0	0.97	0.96	0.79	0.93	0.74	1.12
13.9	13.0	12.2	11.5	0.88	0.90	0.86	0.88	0.84	0.88
17.2	18.3	14.7	15.4	0.91	0.92	0.85	0.90	0.81	0.97
28.6	22.9	22.2	18.7	0.89	0.88	0.79	0.88	0.84	0.96
35.0	30.9	25.9	23.6	0.86	0.85	0.77	0.85	1.04	1.02

Appendix C
van Binsbergen-Graham-Yang Optimal Capital Structure Model

From a corporate finance perspective, when an all-equity firm begins to use debt, this generally has the effect of reducing the firm's weighted average cost of capital (WACC), thereby increasing the value of the firm. This is only true, however, to the extent that the incremental benefit of using additional debt is not outweighed by the increased financial risk and associated costs borne by the firm (e.g., bankruptcy costs, agency costs, etc.). The optimal capital structure is achieved by finding the debt-to-total-capital ratio that minimizes the WACC for a given firm, and therefore maximizes the value of that firm.

Professors Jules van Binsbergen, John Graham and Jie Yang have conducted extensive research on the determination of a firm's optimal capital structure. Graham and Yang extended this research by developing an optimal capital structure model, which has been applied to actual firm-level data and whose results are displayed in this appendix (hereafter referred to as the "Optimal Capital Structure Model"). This model is also used to estimate the potential gain in firm value for firms that are presently using suboptimal amounts of debt in their capital structures. "Suboptimal" within the context of the model can mean either "too little debt" or "too much debt".[C-1, C-2]

While our description of the Optimal Capital Structure Model in the following sections includes conceptual discussions of both the "too little debt" and "too much debt" scenarios, when debating the capital structure of a firm it is not unusual for analysts to *start* with an "all equity" firm (i.e., a firm using 0% debt, a.k.a., a "no debt" firm, or a debt-free firm), and *then* ask the question, "What would happen if this firm used some debt financing"? Consistent with this approach, the data presented in Appendix C are applicable to the scenario where a firm starts at 0% debt financing and then increases the debt ratio to the estimated "optimal" level.

Appendix C provides estimates of (i) the optimal amount of debt that firms should use as a percentage of their total capital, and (ii) the incremental firm value potentially created by choosing an optimal capital structure (rather than using *no debt at all*).

[C-1] The estimates provided in Appendix C are based upon the work of Jules H. van Binsbergen, Associate Professor of Finance, The Wharton School, University of Pennsylvania; John R. Graham, Professor of Finance, Fuqua School of Business, Duke University; and Jie Yang, Assistant Professor of Finance at the McDonough School of Business at Georgetown University. See Jules H. van Binsbergen, John R. Graham, and Jie Yang, "The Cost of Debt", *The Journal of Finance* LXV, no. 6 (December 2010): pages 2089–2136. Also see Jules H. van Binsbergen, John R. Graham, and Jie Yang, "An Empirical Model of Optimal Capital Structure", *Journal of Applied Corporate Finance* 23 no. 4 (Fall 2011): pages 34–59. Calculations in Appendix C were performed by Professors Graham and Yang. The authors thank Kevin Madden of Duff & Phelps LLC for preparing materials for this appendix.

[C-2] In the *2014* and *2015 Valuation Handbook – U.S. Industry Cost of Capital*, Appendix C was "Definitions of Standard & Poor's *Compustat* Data Items Used in Calculations". Starting with the *2016 Valuation Handbook – U.S. Industry Cost of Capital,* "Definitions of Standard & Poor's *Compustat* Data Items Used in Calculations" has been moved to Appendix D.

In the following sections, we (i) briefly discuss the Optimal Capital Structure Model, (ii) provide a description of the data presented in Appendix C, and (iii) provide examples using the data presented in Appendix C.

Optimal Debt

In the context of the Optimal Capital Structure Model, the optimal amount of debt (D^*, which is expressed as ratio of debt over total capital) will maximize firm value, which is shown at the peak of the value function in Exhibit C-1.

Exhibit C-1: Firm Value as a Function of Debt

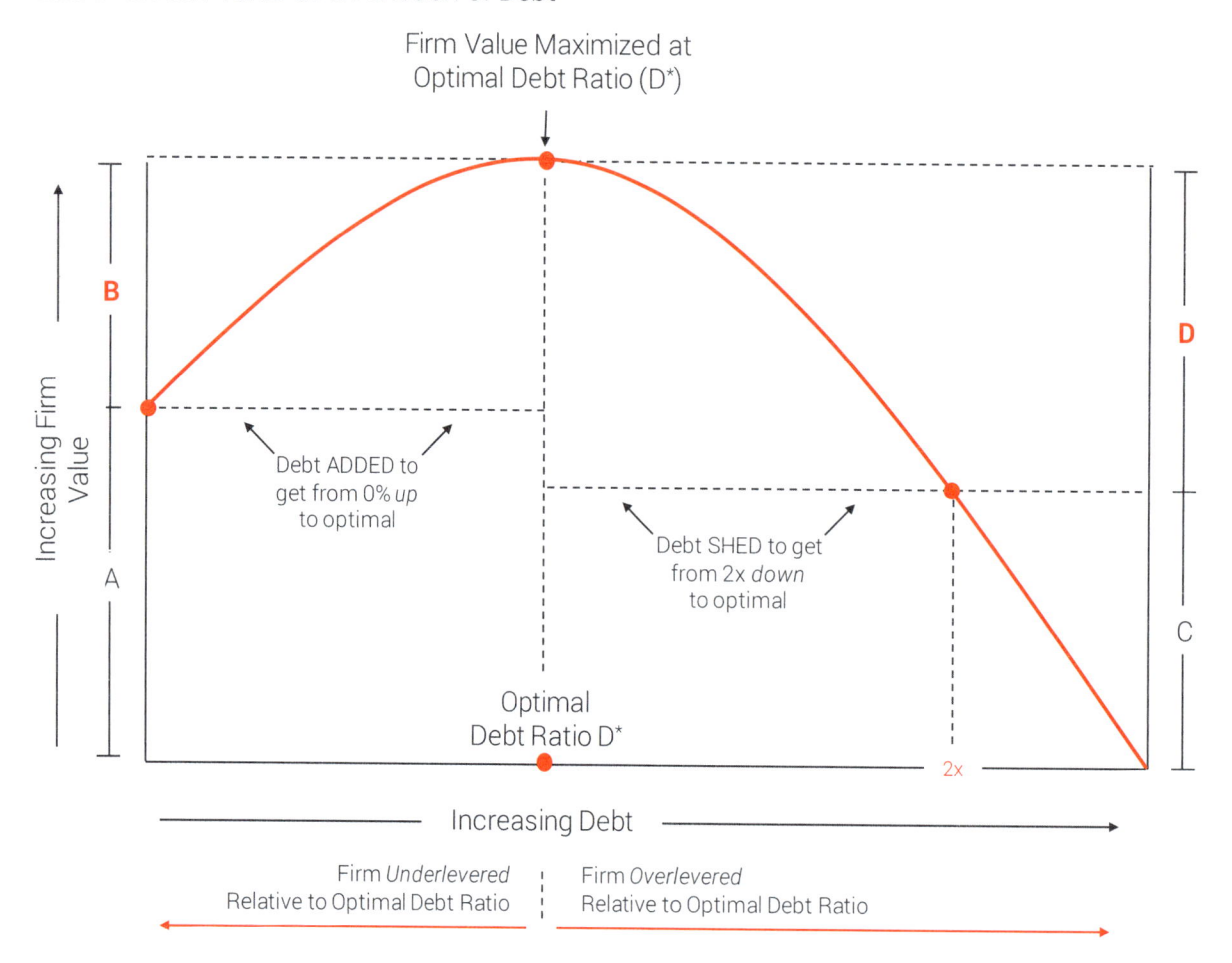

On the left-hand side of Exhibit C-1: The height of the range "A" represents a firm's value if the firm's debt percentage is equal to 0% (i.e., the firm's capital structure is 100% equity and 0% debt). Relative to the optimal debt ratio, this firm uses too little debt and so is *underlevered*.

2017 Valuation Handbook – U.S. Industry Cost of Capital (data through March 31, 2017)

The height of the range "B" represents the amount of firm value that could be created if a firm's debt percentage is *increased* from 0% debt *up* to the optimal debt ratio (D*). The amount of potential firm value created represented by the range "B" is the value reported in Appendix C shown in the columns entitled "Firm Value Created from Using Optimal Debt, Instead of 0% Debt, as a Percentage of Firm Value (%)".[C-3]

After the firm's debt percentage is *increased* from 0% debt up to the optimal debt ratio (D*), the firm's value is (A + B).

On the right-hand side of Exhibit C-1: The height of the range "C" represents a firm's value if the firm's debt percentage is equal to two times the optimal debt ratio (the point "2x" on the x-axis). Relative to the optimal debt ratio, this firm uses too much debt and so is *overlevered*. For example, if the optimal debt ratio is 20%, the 2x outcome would occur if the firm were to use 40% debt.

The height of the range "D" represents the amount of firm value that could be created if the firm's debt percentage is *decreased* from two times the optimal debt ratio *down* to the optimal debt ratio (D*).[C-4]

After the firm's debt percentage is *decreased* from twice the optimal debt down to the optimal debt ratio (D*), the firm's value is (C + D).

The following three observations about the relationships illustrated in Exhibit C-1 can be made:

- If a firm is using *less* debt than the optimal debt level, firm value can potentially be created by *increasing* the percentage of debt in the capital structure.

- If a firm is using *more* debt than the optimal debt level, firm value can potentially be created by *decreasing* the percentage of debt in the capital structure.

- The valuation penalty for being overlevered is greater than the penalty for being underlevered. This means that over-levered firms typically gain *more* firm value by reducing their debt levels down to the optimal level than under-levered firms gain from increasing their debt by a similar amount (e.g., D is bigger than B in Exhibit C-1).[C-5]

[C-3] "Firm value created from using optimal debt, instead of 0% debt, as a percentage of firm value" is presented in Appendix C for (i) the "Median" optimal debt ratio, and (ii) the "SIC Composite" optimal debt ratio.

[C-4] "Firm value created from using optimal debt, instead of a percentage of debt *greater* than the optimal debt ratio", is not presented in Appendix C.

[C-5] This relationship is not linear. The more a firm is overlevered, the greater the potential gain in firm value from reducing debt.

The Marginal Benefits versus the Marginal Costs of Debt in a Firm's Capital Structure

This optimal debt ratio D* is obtained by comparing the marginal benefit of using debt against the marginal cost of using debt. In Exhibit C-2, the value-maximizing amount of debt is identified as the debt ratio (D*) where the marginal *benefit* of using debt equals the marginal *cost* of that same level of debt. For example, if a firm were using a suboptimal amount of debt (e.g., too little debt), then the benefit would be *greater* than the cost of using additional debt, which means that firm value could be created by incurring more debt up to the point where the marginal benefit equals the marginal cost of debt (MB = MC).[C-6]

Exhibit C-2: "Value-Maximizing" Debt Is the Point at Which the Marginal Benefit Equals the Marginal Cost of Using the Optimal Amount of Debt (D*)

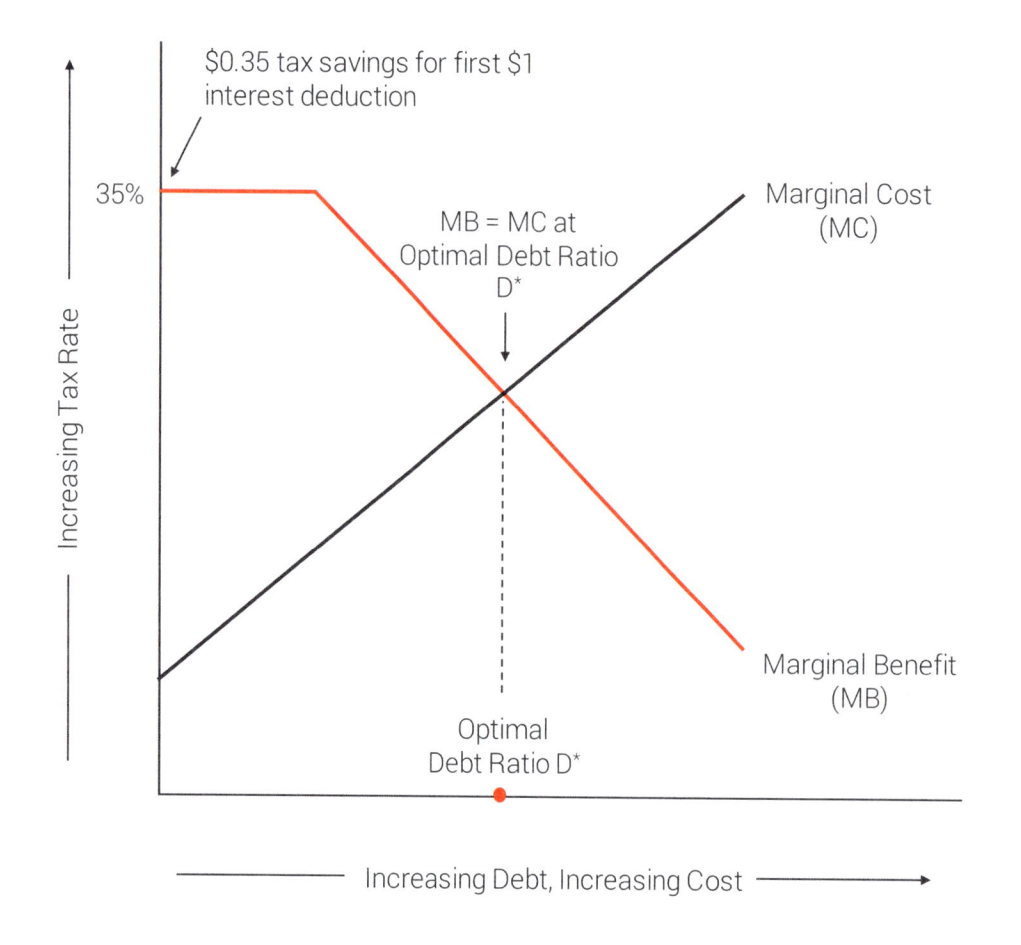

Recall that interest associated with servicing debt is tax deductible (at least in the United States and in several other countries). If a firm pays corporate income taxes at a rate of 35%, then $1 of interest deduction reduces the firm's tax payments by $0.35 (all other factors held the same). This

---

[C-6] It is important to be clear about what the Optimal Capital Structure Model's cost functions attempt to capture. The Optimal Capital Structure Model's cost functions attempt to capture *all* possible costs associated with using debt. The cost functions incorporate the summation of various possible costs of debt, including, for example, (i) expected bankruptcy costs, (ii) "debt overhang" effects that might discourage a company from investing in a profitable project because it currently has too much debt, or (iii) the implicit cost of management using too little debt perhaps due to managerial risk aversion, all of which are expected costs that are likely reflected in companies' actual capital structure choices.

$0.35 tax savings is shown as the left-most point on the marginal tax benefit function in Exhibit C-2. As a firm uses more debt, these incremental interest deductions would tend to become less valuable in some scenarios (i.e., the "marginal value" of an additional dollar of interest deductions *decreases*).

For example, if a hypothetical firm uses $1 million dollars in debt, it might accumulate enough interest expense so that there is a two-thirds chance that the firm will be fully taxable (at a 35% tax rate in the U.S.), and a one-third chance it will not be taxable at all (0% tax rate). In this case, the firm's *expected* tax rate is 23.3% (2/3 x 35% + 1/3 x 0%).

Alternatively, if our hypothetical firm were to use, say, $2 million dollars in debt, it might increase the chance of being non-taxable to one-half (50%), and its expected tax rate would decrease to 17.5% (1/2 x 35% + 1/2 x 0%). In this example, using more debt *reduces* the firm's expected tax rate, and at the same time *reduces* the expected marginal benefit of deducting another dollar of interest. This declining benefit of incremental debt is depicted in the declining marginal benefit (MB) function shown in Exhibit C-2.

Optimal Debt and the Cost of Capital

As long as debt policy does not affect the operating profits of the firm, the optimal debt ratio D^* is also where the cost of capital is *minimized* (as illustrated in Exhibit C-3). This is because if firm value equals the present value of future cash flows, *minimizing* the discount rate *maximizes* firm value.

Exhibit C-3: The Relationship Between Optimal Debt D^* and Cost of Capital

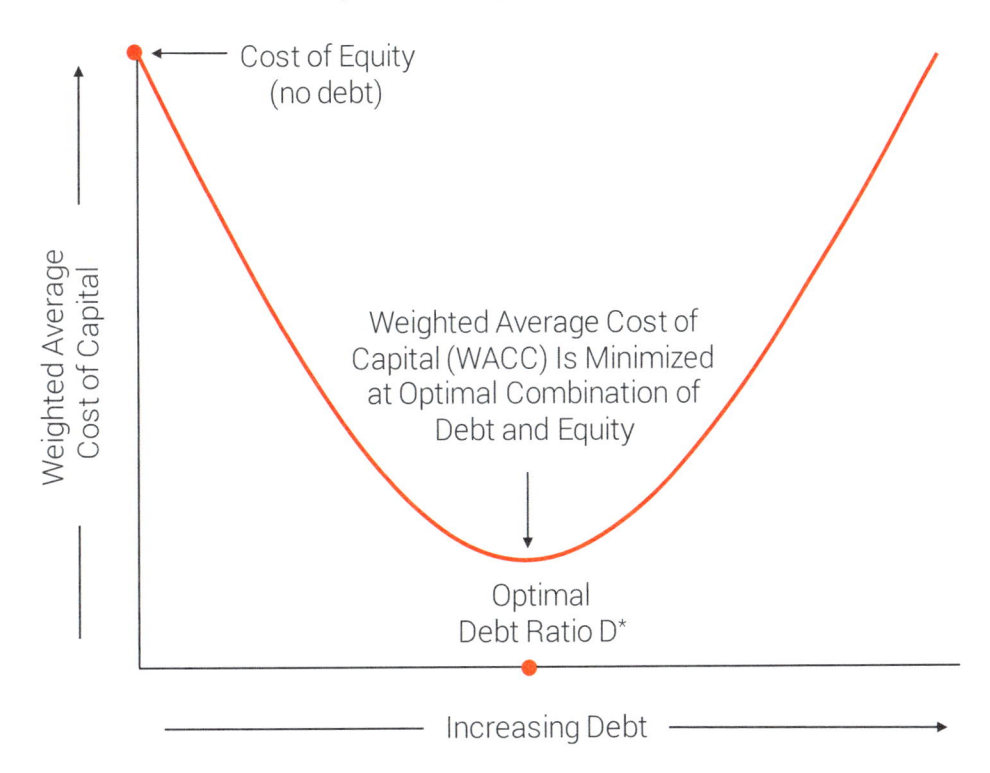

Identifying the Optimal Debt Ratio

The optimal debt ratio D^* is identified as follows:

Step 1: First, a marginal benefit of debt (MB) function is created for every firm. These "MB" functions capture the *decreasing* expected tax benefit from incurring additional debt (as described previously), and are modeled in a way that incorporates the loss carryback and carryforward tax code features that occur when a firm experiences a net operating loss (i.e. it ceases to be profitable). This entails forecasting future taxable income for every firm, so that the present value of taxes owed can be calculated and an estimated marginal tax rate can be derived. The marginal tax rate is then used to calculate the tax benefits of various amounts of debt for each firm.

Step 2: Given that in equilibrium the marginal benefit equals the marginal cost (MB = MC) for firms that optimally choose the D^* optimal debt ratio, statistical techniques are employed to identify the functional form (i.e., the shape of the curve) of each firm's MC function. For example, if a firm's MB function and D^* were to *shift* over time (perhaps because the corporate income tax rate changes), the authors can deduce the location of the MC function, as shown by the dashed line in Exhibit C-4.

Exhibit C-4: Identifying Marginal Cost of Debt (MC) Curves

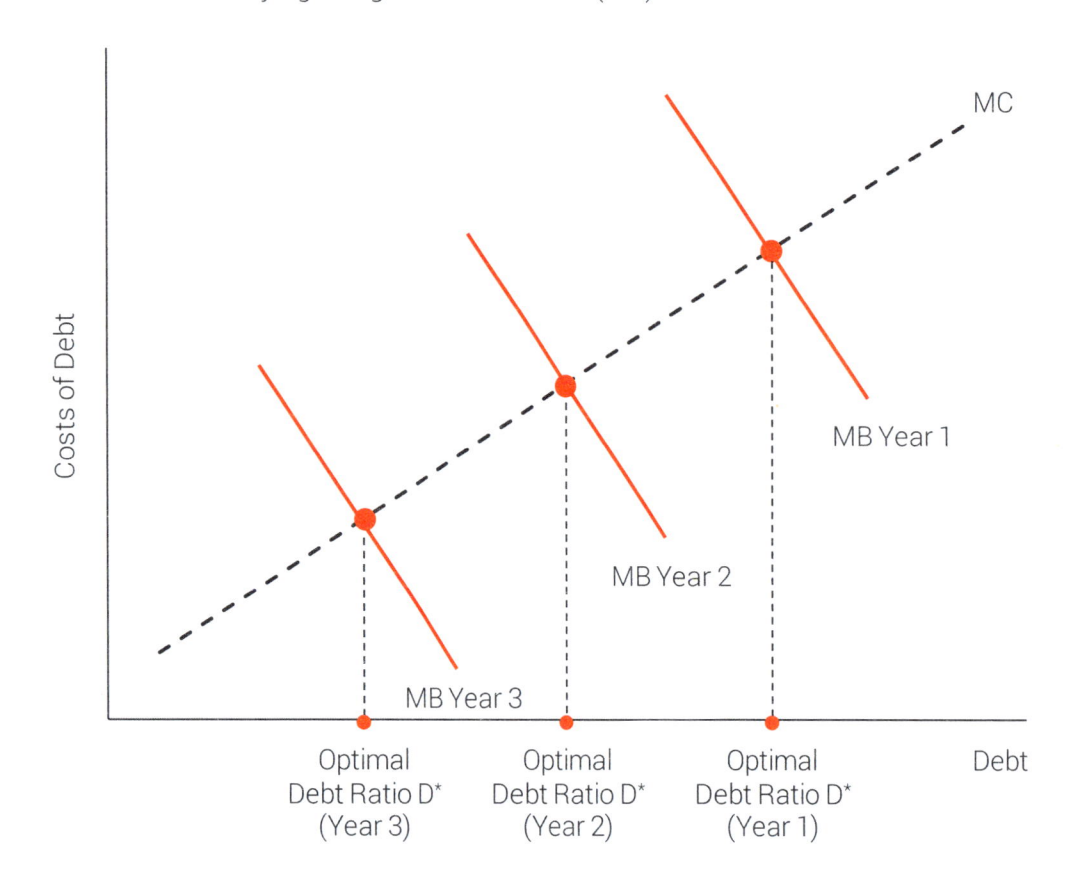

Knowing the functional form of both MB and MC for any given firm, one can deduce the optimal debt ratio D^* at the point where the marginal cost and the marginal benefit curves intersect (MB = MC) for any given firm. Once the MB and MC functions are known, the value function in Exhibit C-1 and WACC function in Exhibit C-3 can also be created.

Understanding the Appendix C Data Tables

All cost of capital estimates and other statistics presented in the *2017 Valuation Handbook – U.S. Industry Cost of Capital* (this book) are calculated with the most recent *monthly* or *fiscal* year data through March 31, 2017. The information in Appendix C is based upon the most recent *fiscal* year data for the companies used to calculate the statistics therein, and so can be best described as "data through" December 31, 2016.

In Appendix C, the Optimal Capital Structure Model is used to calculate (i) the Median optimal debt ratio (D^*) of companies in each industry (as identified by SIC code), and (ii) the SIC Composite optimal capital structure (i.e., the optimal capital structure for each industry, in *aggregate*).[C-7, C-8]

The "Median" is essentially the "middle" observation, and can be thought of as the "typical" observation in the industry. The "SIC Composite" is calculated in order to give the analyst a sense of the characteristics of the industry *as a whole*.

The columns to the table in Appendix C are defined as follows:

- **SIC:** The standard industrial code being analyzed.

- **SIC Description:** The short description of each SIC, as defined by the United States Occupational Safety & Health Administration (OSHA).[C-9]

- **No. of Co's:** The number of companies used in the calculations for each SIC.

- **Firm Value Created from Using Optimal Debt, Instead of 0% Debt, as a Percentage of Firm Value (%):** The value created by increasing debt *from* 0% debt *to* the optimal debt ratio. This is the value represented by the range "B" in Exhibit C-1.[C-10]

[C-7] The SICs presented in Appendix C are limited to the set of SICs that appear in the Industry Data Exhibits herein. In performing the analyses presented in Appendix C, Professors Graham and Yang started with the *same* company sets for each SIC as are used to calculate the information in the Industry Data Exhibits herein, but the number of companies was generally reduced in the analyses presented in Appendix C because of additional data requirements that are necessary to calculate the optimal capital structure for each individual company. All SICs that were reduced to fewer than 5 companies were eliminated from the analyses presented in Appendix C.

[C-8] The Optimal Capital Structure Model is not designed for financial firms, so SICs beginning with "6" (Finance, Insurance, and Real Estate) are *not* included in Appendix C.

[C-9] All SIC naming conventions are from the U.S. Department of Labor Occupational Safety & Health Administration (OSHA) website. To learn more, visit https://www.osha.gov/.

[C-10] "Firm value created" here is defined within the context of the Optimal Capital Structure Model as "gross" firm value created by a firm using the optimal debt ratio *minus* the all-in costs of debt associated with using the optimal debt ratio. "Gross" firm value created is defined here as the present value of tax savings that result from all current and future debt interest deductions, when the optimal amount of debt is used.

How an Analyst Can Use the Information in Appendix C

Analysts can use the information presented in Appendix C for various purposes.

First and foremost, this information can be used to select, or at least benchmark, the future "target" capital structure for a subject industry. When valuing a business or a controlling interest in a company, analysts will typically compute a WACC presuming that the capital structure of the Subject Company will migrate toward an optimal or a target level. The future "target" capital structure is typically selected based (in whole, or in part) on either the average or the median of the capital structures of other companies in the same industry in which the Subject Company operates. However, the average (or median) may not always be a good proxy for the optimal capital structure for any given industry.

The "optimal" debt ratios in Appendix C provide the analyst with an *additional* source of a "target" capital structure for use in these analyses. The optimal debt ratios in Appendix C can be used to (i) benchmark, and (ii) support the analyst's own capital structure selections.

A secondary use of the information in Appendix C is to gauge the benefits to a firm (expressed as a proportion of Firm Value) to be gained by using an optimal debt ratio, instead of financing the firm exclusively with equity (i.e., with 0% debt). Examples of this are provided in the following section.

Examples: Estimating the Firm Value Created From Using Optimal Debt

The analyst can use the information for each industry in Appendix C to calculate the estimated firm value created by using the optimal amount of debt in the capital structure relative to using 0% debt, as estimated by the Optimal Capital Structure Model.[C-11]

In the following two examples, the following assumptions are used:

- The Subject Company has a value of $100 million (and 0% debt)
- The Subject Company is in SIC 2 ("Manufacturing")

In each example, the information from Appendix C is used to calculate the "Median" and "SIC Composite" estimates of potential firm value created if the hypothetical Subject Company increases its debt ratio from 0% to the optimal debt ratio indicated for SIC 2.[C-12]

Example 1: Median Estimate of Potential Firm Value Created

- The Median "Optimal Debt Ratio" for SIC 2 ("Manufacturing") is 20.1%.
- The Median "Firm Value Created from Using Optimal Debt, Instead of 0% Debt, as a Percentage of Firm Value (%)" is 1.5%.

[C-11] Alternatively, this can be looked upon as the amount of firm value *lost* by using suboptimal amounts of debt in the capital structure.
[C-12] The "Median" estimate is essentially the "middle" observation, and can be thought of as the "typical" observation in the industry. The "SIC Composite" estimate can be thought of as the industry "as a whole".

In this example, the median estimate of firm value created if the hypothetical Subject Company *increases* its debt ratio from 0% to the median optimal debt ratio indicated for SIC 2 (20.1%) is $1.5 million ($100 million x 1.5%). The estimated value of the hypothetical Subject Company has increased to $101.5 million.

Example 2: SIC Composite Estimate of Potential Firm Value Created

- The SIC Composite "Optimal Debt Ratio" for SIC 2 ("Manufacturing") is 22.1%.

- The SIC Composite "Firm Value Created from Using Optimal Debt, Instead of 0% Debt, as a Percentage of Firm Value (%)" is 1.2%.

In this example, the SIC Composite estimate of firm value created if the hypothetical Subject Company *increases* its debt ratio from 0% to the SIC Composite optimal debt ratio indicated for SIC 1 (22.1%) is $1.2 million ($100 million x 1.2%). The estimated value of the hypothetical Subject Company has increased to $101.2 million.

The estimated increase in firm value in the previous two examples ranged from 1.2% (using the SIC Composite) to 1.5% (using the Median). These are useful benchmarks for gauging the value lost (as a proportion of "Firm Value) if a firm were to use 0% debt, versus using the optimal debt ratio. Of course, an individual firm may fare better (*more* firm value added) or fare worse (*less* firm value added) by using an optimal debt structure rather than no debt at all.

For example, when the expected increase in firm value for all 237 firms in SIC 2 ("Manufacturing") in Example 1 are ranked from largest to smallest, the median gain in firm value is 1.5%. The "median" is the 50th percentile. Alternatively, if we look at, say, the 25th percentile of expected increase in firm value for the 237 firms in SIC 2, the expected incremental benefit is only 0.8%. Alternatively, if we look at, say, the 75th percentile of expected increase in firm value for the 237 firms in SIC 2, the expected incremental benefit rises to 2.8%.

The 50th percentile (i.e., median) estimate of the amount of firm value created if a firm's debt percentage is *increased* from 0% debt *up* to the optimal debt ratio is already calculated and presented for each SIC in Appendix C. In Exhibit C-5 (see next page), we ranked the companies (by firm value created) for *each* of the SICs in Appendix C, and then calculated the 25th percentile and the 50th percentile estimate for each. An average of these results across all SICs presented in Appendix C is shown in Exhibit C-5.

Exhibit C-5: Average of the 25th, 50th (i.e., the median), and 75th Percentile Estimates of Firm Value Created If a Firm's Debt Percentage Is Increased from 0% Debt Up to the Optimal Debt Ratio, Across All SICs Presented in Appendix C

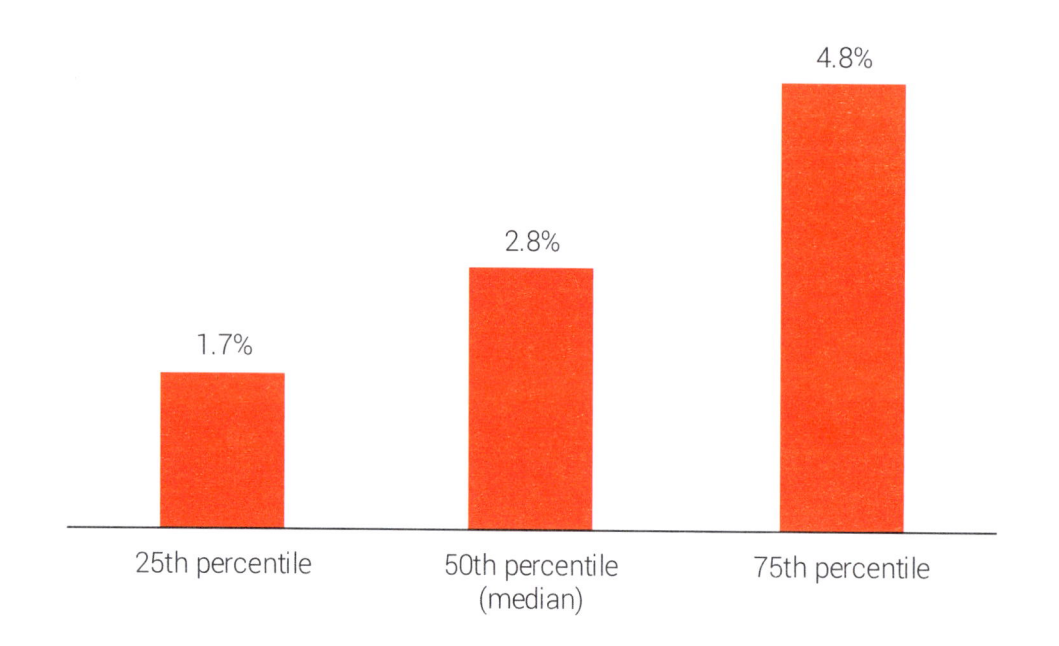

- 25th percentile: 1.7%
- 50th percentile (median): 2.8%
- 75th percentile: 4.8%

In Exhibit C-6 we performed the same analyses for all 1-digit-level SIC codes presented in Appendix C by calculating an average of the 25th, 50th (i.e., the median), and 75th percentile estimates of firm value created.[C-13]

[C-13] Each of the 98 SIC codes presented in Appendix C was trimmed to its first digit (e.g., SIC 1 remained "1", SIC 13 was trimmed to "1", SIC 208 was trimmed to "2", etc.), and then an average of all 25th, 50th, and 75th percentiles was calculated for all "1" SICs, "2" SICs, "3" SICs, etc.

Exhibit C-6: Average of the 25th, 50th (i.e., the median), and 75th Percentile Estimates of Firm Value Created If a Firm's Debt Percentage Is Increased from 0% Debt Up to the Optimal Debt Ratio, Across All 1-Digit-Level SICs Presented in Appendix C

		Firm Value Created from Using Optimal Debt, Instead of 0% Debt, as a Percentage of Firm Value (%)		
SIC	SIC Description	25th percentile	50th percentile	75th percentile
1	Mining & Construction	2.5	4.1	6.8
2	Manufacturing	1.1	1.7	2.6
3	Manufacturing	0.7	1.2	2.1
4	Transportation, Communications, Electric, Gas, and Sanitary Services	2.9	4.5	7.5
5	Wholesale Trade & Retail Trade	2.5	4.4	8.3
7	Services	2.0	3.1	5.3
8	Services	1.8	3.2	4.2

Appendix C: Firm Value Created from Using Optimal Debt, Instead of 0% Debt, as a Percentage of Firm Value (%) (as of December 31, 2016)*

van Binsbergen-Graham-Yang Optimal Capital Structure Model

			Optimal Debt Ratio (%)		Firm Value Created from Using Optimal Debt, Instead of 0% Debt, as a Percentage of Firm Value (%)	
SIC	SIC Description	No. of Co's	Median	SIC Composite	Median	SIC Composite
1	Mining & Construction	60	35.1	35.7	3.4	3.4
13	Oil and Gas Extraction	22	50.5	36.6	3.8	3.1
131	Crude Petroleum and Natural Gas	13	41.5	36.2	3.4	3.2
138	Oil and Gas Field Services	9	54.6	38.0	4.9	2.6
15	Building Construction General Contractors and Operative Builders	11	67.2	48.0	6.7	5.4
16	Heavy Construction Other Than Building Construction Contractors	10	34.3	29.2	3.3	4.9
162	Heavy Construction, Except Highway and Street	6	39.8	32.2	3.4	6.1
2	Manufacturing	237	20.1	22.1	1.5	1.2
20	Food and Kindred Products	47	24.2	22.8	1.6	0.9
206	Sugar and Confectionery Products	5	26.1	13.8	2.2	0.7
208	Beverages	12	16.2	18.2	1.6	0.2
23	Apparel and Other Finished Products Made From Fabrics and Similar Materials	14	7.4	10.4	2.0	1.6
24	Lumber and Wood Products, Except Furniture	7	20.1	17.6	1.5	1.5
25	Furniture and Fixtures	15	13.3	19.0	1.4	2.0
251	Household Furniture	8	12.0	11.4	1.9	1.6
252	Office Furniture	5	12.2	12.3	1.3	2.4
26	Paper and Allied Products	20	33.4	30.3	2.0	2.1
262	Paper Mills	7	33.7	31.0	1.9	1.8
265	Paperboard Containers and Boxes	5	27.5	31.8	2.3	2.4
27	Printing, Publishing, and Allied Industries	9	20.1	18.6	1.5	1.9
28	Chemicals and Allied Products	99	20.7	19.1	1.1	0.8
281	Industrial Inorganic Chemicals	11	34.6	25.9	1.5	0.7
283	Drugs	47	14.3	18.3	0.8	0.7
2834	Pharmaceutical Preparations	23	12.1	17.8	0.8	0.8
2836	Biological Products, Except Diagnostic Substances	11	17.6	15.5	0.5	0.4
284	Soap, Detergents, and Cleaning Preparations; Perfumes, Cosmetics, and Other Toilet Preparations	7	10.1	5.5	0.5	0.1
286	Industrial Organic Chemicals	7	17.8	7.7	0.7	0.4
287	Agricultural Chemicals	6	29.1	27.2	3.6	2.8
289	Miscellaneous Chemical Products	5	26.9	24.6	1.0	1.2
29	Petroleum Refining and Related Industries	13	35.9	35.6	3.4	2.7
291	Petroleum Refining	11	35.9	35.6	3.4	2.7
3	Manufacturing	402	18.8	21.7	1.2	1.0
30	Rubber and Miscellaneous Plastics Products	15	16.1	4.5	1.2	0.3
308	Miscellaneous Plastics Products	8	16.5	12.8	1.2	0.6
31	Leather and Leather Products	7	7.5	6.7	1.6	1.3
32	Stone, Clay, Glass, and Concrete Products	8	29.9	33.0	2.6	2.6
33	Primary Metal Industries	11	30.7	29.7	2.9	2.8

* All cost of capital estimates and other statistics presented in the 2017 Valuation Handbook – U.S. Industry Cost of Capital (this book) are calculated with the most recent monthly or fiscal year data through March 31, 2017. The information in Appendix C is based upon the most recent fiscal year data for the companies used to calculate the statistics therein, and so can be best described as "data through" December 31, 2016.

Appendix C: Firm Value Created from Using Optimal Debt, Instead of 0% Debt, as a Percentage of Firm Value (%) (as of December 31, 2016)*
van Binsbergen-Graham-Yang Optimal Capital Structure Model

SIC	SIC Description	No. of Co's	Optimal Debt Ratio (%) Median	Optimal Debt Ratio (%) SIC Composite	Firm Value Created from Using Optimal Debt, Instead of 0% Debt, as a Percentage of Firm Value (%) Median	Firm Value Created from Using Optimal Debt, Instead of 0% Debt, as a Percentage of Firm Value (%) SIC Composite
34	Fabricated Metal Products, Except Machinery and Transportation Equipment	29	22.7	28.2	1.7	1.6
344	Fabricated Structural Metal Products	5	18.0	18.7	1.5	1.6
349	Miscellaneous Fabricated Metal Products	7	24.0	18.3	0.9	0.5
35	Industrial and Commercial Machinery and Computer Equipment	70	21.9	30.2	1.4	1.0
353	Construction, Mining, and Materials Handling	11	30.1	30.7	2.9	2.6
355	Special Industry Machinery, Except Metalworking	12	17.7	16.3	1.3	0.3
3559	Special Industry Machinery, Not Elsewhere Classified	9	16.6	16.0	1.1	0.3
356	General Industrial Machinery and Equipment	12	22.4	19.5	0.7	1.0
357	Computer and Office Equipment	17	14.9	26.9	0.5	0.4
36	Electronic and Other Electrical Equipment and Components, Except Computer Equipment	90	22.6	14.8	1.3	0.7
362	Electrical Industrial Apparatus	6	26.6	26.0	1.5	1.5
366	Communications Equipment	11	3.3	1.1	0.5	0.4
367	Electronic Components and Accessories	54	25.9	14.9	1.3	0.7
3672	Printed Circuit Boards	7	28.4	27.5	2.2	2.1
3674	Semiconductors and Related Devices	34	20.3	15.6	0.8	0.6
37	Transportation Equipment	46	21.6	31.8	1.3	1.9
371	Motor Vehicles and Motor Vehicle Equipment	29	19.7	39.3	1.2	2.7
3714	Motor Vehicle Parts and Accessories	19	19.4	14.7	1.1	0.5
38	Measuring, Analyzing, and Controlling Instruments; Photographic, Medical and Optical Goods; Watches and Clocks	69	14.2	15.4	0.6	0.4
382	Laboratory Apparatus and Analytical, Optical, Measuring, and Controlling Instruments	24	6.0	10.6	0.6	0.4
3826	Laboratory Analytical Instruments	7	12.6	10.9	0.4	0.4
384	Surgical, Medical, and Dental Instruments and Supplies	32	17.2	14.9	0.6	0.4
3842	Orthopedic, Prosthetic, and Surgical Appliances and Supplies	6	21.1	24.2	0.6	0.6
3845	Electromedical and Electrotherapeutic Apparatus	13	15.2	13.5	0.2	0.3
39	Miscellaneous Manufacturing Industries	9	15.6	15.3	1.3	1.5
394	Dolls, Toys, Games and Sporting and Athletic Goods	5	12.3	15.3	1.0	1.5
4	Transportation, Communications, Electric, Gas, and Sanitary Services	168	31.8	32.7	4.5	4.0
40	Railroad Transportation	5	29.2	24.6	2.0	1.7
42	Motor Freight Transportation and Warehousing	14	29.1	21.5	1.5	1.1
4213	Trucking, Except Local	12	29.1	25.1	2.0	2.1
45	Transportation By Air	15	32.2	31.5	7.2	8.3
451	Air Transportation, Scheduled, and Air Courier	11	25.1	30.1	5.4	7.8
4512	Air Transportation, Scheduled	10	22.1	30.1	5.5	7.8
46	Pipelines, Except Natural Gas	6	30.6	31.0	0.4	0.5
47	Transportation Services	7	30.0	38.5	4.4	3.7
48	Communications	38	36.2	36.3	4.7	3.9
481	Telephone Communications	12	43.4	42.2	9.9	4.9

* All cost of capital estimates and other statistics presented in the *2017 Valuation Handbook – U.S. Industry Cost of Capital* (this book) are calculated with the most recent monthly or fiscal year data through March 31, 2017. The information in Appendix C is based upon the most recent fiscal year data for the companies used to calculate the statistics therein, and so can be best described as "data through" December 31, 2016.

Appendix C: Firm Value Created from Using Optimal Debt, Instead of 0% Debt, as a Percentage of Firm Value (%) (as of December 31, 2016)*

van Binsbergen-Graham-Yang Optimal Capital Structure Model

SIC	SIC Description	No. of Co's	Optimal Debt Ratio (%) Median	Optimal Debt Ratio (%) SIC Composite	Firm Value Created Median	Firm Value Created SIC Composite
4813	Telephone Communications, Except Radiotelephone	7	51.7	55.2	10.5	10.8
483	Radio and Television Broadcasting Stations	12	32.0	29.8	1.6	0.9
4833	Television Broadcasting Stations	8	32.0	33.4	1.5	1.0
489	Communications Services, Not Elsewhere Classified	7	61.4	57.3	6.2	10.2
5	Wholesale Trade & Retail Trade	192	20.8	18.8	3.5	2.3
50	Wholesale Trade-durable Goods	38	20.3	20.2	2.4	1.8
504	Professional and Commercial Equipment and Supplies	10	18.1	16.7	1.1	1.2
5045	Computers and Computer Peripheral Equipment and Software	7	18.1	18.1	1.1	1.4
506	Electrical Goods	5	31.2	35.2	5.3	4.5
508	Machinery, Equipment, and Supplies	8	31.1	24.5	3.0	2.2
51	Wholesale Trade-non-durable Goods	29	33.4	34.7	5.9	3.3
512	Drugs, Drug Proprietaries, and Druggists' Sundries	6	31.7	31.0	1.6	1.4
514	Groceries and Related Products	5	32.4	32.4	6.5	1.8
517	Petroleum and Petroleum Products	7	48.2	48.2	11.1	9.4
53	General Merchandise Stores	11	20.8	19.4	3.6	2.4
533	Variety Stores	7	12.4	20.0	3.1	2.5
54	Food Stores	8	24.1	24.4	5.6	3.5
55	Automotive Dealers and Gasoline Service Stations	13	62.8	39.1	4.4	2.7
56	Apparel and Accessory Stores	24	5.6	6.6	8.5	3.5
565	Family Clothing Stores	11	14.0	7.3	5.5	2.6
57	Home Furniture, Furnishings, and Equipment Stores	7	10.7	12.7	5.4	4.9
58	Eating and Drinking Places	26	15.7	14.6	3.2	1.6
5812	Eating Places	25	15.6	14.5	3.1	1.6
59	Miscellaneous Retail	27	18.7	15.3	4.0	1.9
591	Drug Stores and Proprietary Stores	5	19.0	20.2	1.7	2.1
594	Miscellaneous Shopping Goods Stores	6	15.2	15.6	9.5	8.2
596	Nonstore Retailers	7	15.4	9.1	2.5	0.9
7	Services	186	18.3	16.8	1.7	1.0
73	Business Services	155	16.4	15.7	1.4	0.9
735	Miscellaneous Equipment Rental and Leasing	6	69.4	57.7	10.2	9.2
736	Personnel Supply Services	13	18.2	17.8	2.3	2.7
7363	Help Supply Services	9	18.2	17.8	2.7	2.7
737	Computer Programming, Data Processing, and Other Computer Related Services	115	15.7	15.1	1.2	0.7
7372	Prepackaged Software	31	15.7	10.4	1.1	0.4
7373	Computer Integrated Systems Design	19	16.9	18.5	1.4	1.3
7374	Computer Processing and Data Preparation and Processing Services	17	27.1	24.6	2.2	1.3
738	Miscellaneous Business Services	14	25.3	23.6	3.1	2.2
7389	Business Services, Not Elsewhere Classified	12	25.3	23.6	2.0	2.1
79	Amusement and Recreation Services	16	39.5	39.0	3.5	2.4

* All cost of capital estimates and other statistics presented in the 2017 *Valuation Handbook – U.S. Industry Cost of Capital* (this book) are calculated with the most recent *monthly* or *fiscal* year data through March 31, 2017. The information in Appendix C is based upon the most recent *fiscal* year data for the companies used to calculate the statistics therein, and so can be best described as "data through" December 31, 2016.

Appendix C: Firm Value Created from Using Optimal Debt, Instead of 0% Debt, as a Percentage of Firm Value (%) (as of December 31, 2016)*
van Binsbergen-Graham-Yang Optimal Capital Structure Model

			Optimal Debt Ratio (%)		Firm Value Created from Using Optimal Debt, Instead of 0% Debt, as a Percentage of Firm Value (%)	
SIC	SIC Description	No. of Co's	Median	SIC Composite	Median	SIC Composite
799	Miscellaneous Amusement and Recreation	10	52.3	39.4	4.4	2.3
807	Medical and Dental Laboratories	5	15.3	26.0	3.3	2.3
82	Educational Services	11	11.1	11.1	3.3	2.8
87	Engineering, Accounting, Research, Management, and Related Services	22	17.3	15.4	2.1	1.8
874	Management and Public Relations Services	9	21.8	15.4	2.1	1.7
8742	Management Consulting Services	7	21.8	20.3	3.4	2.4
Large-Cap	Large-Cap Companies	329	20.6	22.1	1.0	1.5
Low-Cap	Low-Cap Companies	550	21.8	28.4	2.4	4.1
Micro-Cap	Micro-Cap Companies	580	26.2	32.1	3.7	7.5
Mid-Cap	Mid-Cap Companies	527	20.2	23.5	1.5	2.4

* All cost of capital estimates and other statistics presented in the 2017 Valuation Handbook – U.S. Industry Cost of Capital (this book) are calculated with the most recent monthly or fiscal year data through March 31, 2017. The information in Appendix C is based upon the most recent fiscal year data for the companies used to calculate the statistics therein, and so can be best described as "data through" December 31, 2016.

Appendix D
Definitions of Standard & Poor's *Compustat* Data Items Used in Calculations[D.1]

Cash and Equivalents: Data Item A1, Units: Millions of dollars

This item represents cash and all securities readily transferable to cash as listed in the Current Asset section.
This item includes, but is not limited to:
1. Cash in escrow (unless legally restricted, in which case it is included in *Current Assets - Other*)
2. Good faith and clearinghouse deposits for brokerage firms
3. Government and other marketable securities, including stocks and bonds, listed as short-term
4. Letters of credit
5. Margin deposits on commodity futures contracts
6. Time, demand, and certificates of deposit
7. The total of a bank's currency and coin, plus its reserves with the Federal Reserve Bank and balances with other banks

This item excludes
1. Money due from sale of debentures (included in *Receivables - Other Current*)
2. Commercial paper issued by unconsolidated subsidiaries to the parent company (included in *Receivables - Other Current*)
3. Bullion, bullion in transit, uranium in transit, etc. (included in *Inventories - Raw Materials*)

This item is not available for utilities.

Current Assets – Total: Data Item A4, Units: Millions of dollars

This item represents cash and other assets which, in the next 12 months, are expected to be realized in cash or used in the production of revenue. This item is the sum of:
1. Cash and Short-Term Investments
2. Current Assets – Other
3. Inventories – Total
4. Receivables – Total

Current Liabilities – Total: Data Item A5, Units: Millions of dollars

This item represents liabilities due within one year, including the current portion of long-term debt. This item is the sum of:
1. Accounts Payable
2. Current Liabilities – Other
3. Debt in Current Liabilities
4. Income Taxes

Assets – Total: Data Item A6, Units: Millions of dollars

This item represents current assets plus net property, plant, and equipment plus other non-current assets (including intangible assets, deferred items and investments and advances). Total liabilities and stockholders' equity represents current liabilities plus long-term debt plus other long-term liabilities plus stockholders' equity.
1. Accrued interest on long-term debt (included in *Liabilities – Other*)
2. Customers' deposits on bottles, kegs and cases (included in *Liabilities – Other*)
3. Deferred compensation

Long-term debt should be reported net of premium or discount. Standard & Poor's *Compustat* will collect the net figure.

[D.1] Source: S&P's *Research Insight Compustat* North America Data Guide

Long-Term Debt – Total: Data Item A9, Units: Millions of dollars

The item represents debt obligations due more than one year from the company's balance sheet date.
This item includes
1. Purchase obligations and payments to officers (when listed as long-term liabilities)
2. Notes payable, due within one year and to be refunded by long-term debt when carried as a non-current liability
3. Long-term lease obligations (capitalized lease obligations)
4. Industrial revenue bonds
5. Advances to finance construction
6. Loans on insurance policies
7. Indebtedness to affiliates
8. Bonds, mortgages, and similar debt
9. All obligations that require interest payments
10. Publishing companies' royalty contracts payable
11. Timber contracts for forestry and paper
12. Extractive industries' advances for exploration and development
13. Production payments and advances for exploration and development

This item excludes:
1. Subsidiary preferred stock (included in *Minority Interest*)
2. The current portion of long-term debt (included in *Current Liabilities*)
3. Accounts payable due after one year (included in *Liabilities – Other*)

Common Equity – Tangible: Data Item A11, Units: Millions of dollars

This item represents common stock plus the following items ...
1. Retained earnings
2. Capital surplus
3. Self-insurance reserves (when included in the Equity section)
4. Capital stock premium

Common equity deductions are ...
1. Treasury stock adjustments
2. Intangibles (except for property and casualty companies)
3. Accumulated unpaid preferred dividends
4. Excess of involuntary liquidating value of outstanding preferred stock over carrying value (not deducted on banks, utilities, or property and casualty companies)

Deferred Taxes and Investment Tax Credit are not included in this figure.
Negative equity figures are shown where applicable.

Sales (Net): Data Item A12, Units: Millions of dollars

This item represents gross sales (the amount of actual billings to customers for regular sales completed during the period) reduced by cash discounts, trade discounts, and returned sales and allowances for which credit is given to customers. This item is scaled in millions. For example the 1999 annual sales for GM is 173215.000 (or 173 billion, 215 million dollars).
This item includes:
1. Any revenue source that is expected to continue for the life of the company
2. Other operating revenue
3. Installment sales
4. Franchise sales (when corresponding expenses are available).

Special cases (by industry) include:
1. Royalty income when considered operating income (such as oil companies, extractive industries, publishing companies, etc.)
2. Retail companies' sales of leased departments when corresponding costs are available and included in expenses (if costs are not available, the net figure is included in *Non-operating Income [Expense]*)
3. Shipping companies' operating differential subsidies and income on reserve fund securities when shown separately
4. Airline companies, net mutual aid assistance and federal subsidies
5. Cigar, cigarette, oil, rubber, and liquor companies' net sales are after deducting excise taxes
6. Income derived from equipment rental is considered part of operating revenue
7. Utilities' net sales are total current operating revenue
8. Advertising companies' net sales are commissions earned, not gross billings
9. Franchise operations' franchise and license fees

10. Hospitals' sales net of provision for contractual allowances (will sometimes include doubtful accounts)

This item excludes:
1. Non-operating income
2. Interest income (included in *Non-operating Income ([Expense]*)
3. Equity in earnings of unconsolidated subsidiaries (included in *Non-operating Income [Expense]*)
4. Other income (included in *Non-operating Income [Expense]*)
5. Rental income (included in *Non-operating Income [Expense]*)
6. Gain on sale of securities or fixed assets (included in *Special Items*)
7. Discontinued operations (included in *Special Items*)
8. Excise taxes (excluded from sales and also deducted from *Cost of Goods Sold*)
9. Royalty income (included in *Non-operating Income [Expense]*)

Operating Income Before Depreciation: Data Item A13, Units: Millions of dollars

This item represents Net Sales less Cost of Goods Sold and Selling, General, and Administrative Expenses before deducting Depreciation, Depletion and Amortization. This item includes the effects of adjustments for Cost of Goods Sold and Selling, General, and Administrative Expenses. A partial listing of items which comprise Cost of Goods Sold and Selling, General, and Administrative Expenses is as follows:

This item includes:
1. Cost of Goods Sold
    - Rent and royalty expense
    - General taxes (other than income taxes)
    - Profit sharing contributions
    - Pension costs, including past service pension costs (except when written off in one year)
    - Motion picture and entertainment companies' amortization of film costs
2. Selling, General, and Administrative Expenses
    - Research and development expense
    - Strike expense
    - Bad debt expense (provisions for doubtful accounts)
    - Exploration expense
    - Parent company charges for administrative service

The following items, when separately listed, are treated as *Non-operating Income (Expense)* rather than as operating expenses:
1. Moving expenses
2. Recurring foreign exchange adjustments
3. Idle plant expenses
4. Profit on sales of properties (except for securities, etc.) for the companies in the oil, coal, airline, and other industries where these transactions are considered a normal part of doing business
5. Amortization of negative intangibles

The current year's results of discontinued operations are not considered operating expenses and are shown as an extraordinary item.

Interest Expense: Data Item A15, Units: Millions of dollars

This item represents the periodic expense to the company of securing short- and long-term debt. Where possible, this item is collected as a gross figure (for example, if interest expense is reported net by the company, interest income and/or interest capitalized will be added back to arrive at a gross figure).

This item includes:
1. Amortization of debt discount or premium
2. Amortization of deferred financing costs
3. Discount on the sale of receivables of a finance subsidiary
4. Dividends/interest expense on securities of Subsidiary Trusts
5. Expenses related to the issuance of debt (such as underwriting fees, brokerage costs, advertising costs, etc.)
6. Factoring charges (unless included in *Cost of Goods Sold* or *Selling, General, and Administrative Expenses*)
7. Financing charges
8. Interest expense net of income of unconsolidated finance subsidiaries for Retail companies
9. Interest expense on both short- and long-term debt
10. Interest expense on deferred compensation
11. Interest on tax settlements, when included with other interest expense
12. Non-debt interest expense, when it is not a *Special Item*
13. Underwriting fees

This item excludes:
1. Interest expense on deposits for Savings and Loan companies (include in *Cost of Goods Sold*)
2. Interest income
3. Interest on tax settlements, when reported as a separate line item (include in *Special Items*)

This item may be estimated if not reported.

Special Items: Data Item A17, Units: Millions of Dollars

This item represents unusual or non-recurring items presented above taxes by the company.

This item (when reported above taxes) includes
1. Adjustments applicable to prior years (except recurring prior year income tax adjustments)
2. After-tax adjustments to net income for the purchase portion of net income of partly pooled companies when the adjustment is carried over to retained earnings
3. Any significant non-recurring items
4. Current year's results of discontinued operations and operations to be discontinued
5. Flood, fire, and other natural disaster losses
6. Interest on tax settlements (when reported separately from other interest expense)
7. Inventory writedowns when reported separately or called "non-recurring"
8. Non-recurring profit or loss on the sale of assets, investments, securities, among others
9. Profit or loss on the repurchase of debentures
10. Purchased research and development
11. Relocation and moving expense
12. Reserve for litigation
13. Restructuring charges
14. Severance pay when reported separately on the Income Statement
15. Special allowances for facilities under construction
16. Transfers from reserves provided for in prior years
17. Write-down of assets
18. Write-downs or write-offs of receivables, intangibles, among others
19. Write-offs of capitalized computer software costs
20. Year 2000 expenses

This item excludes:
1. Any special item listed above as "include" that appears every year for the last three years, unless it has specifically been called Restructuring, Special, or Non-recurring. (Additionally, this does not apply to Year 2000 Expenses, Impairment of Goodwill, Extinguishment of Debt, Settlements, In Process R&D, or Purchased R&D.)
2. Foreign exchange (currency) adjustments (included in Non-operating Income [Expense])
3. Gain/Loss on Sale of Marketable Securities for companies that have adopted SFAS #115
4. Idle plant expense (included in Non-operating Income [Expense])
5. Interest on tax settlements, when included by the company with other interest expense (included in Interest Expense)
6. Milestone Payments or One-Time Contract Reimbursements for R&D companies
7. Nonrecurring items that are included in equity in earnings
8. Profit or loss on sale of properties (except for securities, etc.) for the companies in the oil, coal, transportation, and other industries where these transactions are considered a normal part of doing business (included in Non-operating Income [Expense])
9. Shipping firms' operating differential subsidies and estimated profit adjustments for preceding years. Prior years' operating differential subsidies are included in Non-operating Income (Expense). Current year operating differential subsidy is included in sales. Adjustments by shipping companies to estimated profits reported by this method are ignored

Income Before Extraordinary Items: Data Item A18, Units: Millions of dollars

This item represents the income of a company after all expenses, including special items, income taxes, and minority interest – but before provisions for common and/or preferred dividends. This item does not reflect discontinued operations (appearing below taxes) or extraordinary items.

This item includes (when reported below taxes):
1. Amortization of intangibles
2. Equity in earnings of unconsolidated subsidiaries
3. Gain or loss on the sale of securities when they are a regular part of a company's operations
4. Shipping companies' operating differential subsidies (current and prior years)

Cash Dividends – Preferred: Data Item A19, Units: Millions of dollars

This item represents the total amount of the preferred dividend requirement on cumulative preferred stock and dividends paid on non-cumulative preferred stock of the company during the year.
1. The amount of dividend requirements used by the company in calculating Available for Common
2. Preferred dividends of a merged company accounted for by the pooling of interest method are included for the year of the merger, unless the preferred stock was exchanged for common stock of the acquiring company (included in *Cash Dividends – Common*)

Utility companies' subsidiary preferred dividends are included.

This item excludes:
1. Preferred dividends deducted only for that portion of the year the stock was outstanding, if an entire issuance of convertible preferred stock is converted into common during the year
2. The dividends on the old preferred stock treated as common dividends, if common stock is issued by the company in exchange for preferred stock of another company
3. Subsidiary preferred dividends (included in *Minority Interest*)

Price – Calendar Year – Close: Data Item A24, Units: Dollars and cents

This item represents the absolute close transactions during the year for companies on national stock exchanges and bid prices for over-the-counter issues. Prices are reported on a calendar-year basis. Prices are adjusted for all stock splits and stock dividends that occurred in the fiscal year, except for 06-11 fiscal year companies which have declared stock splits and stock dividends between the end of their fiscal year and the end of the calendar year. In those instances, stated prices are not adjusted. When a 01-05 fiscal year company has a stock split or a stock dividend after the calendar year-end but before the fiscal year-end, prices will be adjusted. If a company suspends trading, the close price of the stock will be presented as of the last trading day.

Common Shares Outstanding – Company: Data Item A25, Units: Millions

This item represents the net number of all common shares outstanding at year-end, excluding treasury shares and scrip.
Common treasury shares carried on the asset side of the balance sheet are netted against the number of common shares issued.
Common shares paid in stock dividends are included when the ex-dividend date falls within the year and the payment date the next year.
Common shares will be excluded when a company nets shares held by a consolidated subsidiary against the capital account.

Employees: Data Item A29, Units: Thousands

This item represents the number of company workers as reported to shareholders. This is reported by some firms as an average number of employees and by some as the number of employees at year-end. No attempt has been made to differentiate between these bases of reporting. If both are given, the year-end figure is used.

This item, for banks always represents the number of year-end employees.

This item includes:
1. All part-time and seasonal employees
2. All employees of consolidated subsidiaries, both domestic and foreign

This item excludes:
1. Contract workers
2. Consultants
3. Employees of unconsolidated subsidiaries

Deferred Taxes and Investment Tax Credit: Data Item A35, Units: Millions of dollars

This item represents the accumulated tax deferrals due to timing differences between the reporting of revenues and expenses for financial statements and tax forms and investment tax credit. This item excludes deferred taxes reported as current liabilities (included in *Current Liabilities - Other*).

This item is not available for banks.

Debt Due in 1st Year: Data Item A44, Units: Millions of dollars

This item represents the current portion of long-term debt (included in *Current Liabilities*).

This item includes:
1. The installments on a loan
2. The sinking fund payments
3. The current portion of any item defined as long-term debt (for example, the current portion of a long-term lease obligation)

Minority Interest: Data Item A49, Units: Millions of dollars

This item represents the portion of the consolidated subsidiary income applicable to common stock not owned by the parent company. A negative number in this item increases *Net Income (Loss)* and a positive number decreases *Net Income (Loss)*.
This item includes subsidiary preferred dividends.
Participating departments are included for life insurance companies.
Subsidiary preferred dividends are excluded for utility companies (included in *Cash Dividends — Preferred*).
A Combined Figure data code (@CF) is entered in the income statement data item if minority interest appears on the Balance Sheet and an amount cannot be identified on the Income Statement.

Common Equity – Total: Data Item A60, Units: Millions of dollars

This item represents the common shareholders' interest in the company.
This item includes:
1. Common stock outstanding (including treasury stock adjustments)
2. Capital surplus
3. Retained earnings
4. Treasury stock adjustments for both common and non-redeemable preferred tock

This figure is not adjusted for excess liquidating value over carrying value of preferred stock or for intangibles.

Non-operating Income (Expense): Data Item A61, Units: Millions of dollars

This item represents any income or expense items resulting from secondary business-related activities, excluding those considered part of the normal operations of the business. Non-operating income and expense will be reported as a net figure with non-operating income treated as a positive number and non-operating expense treated as a negative number.
This item includes
1. Income
   - Discount on debt reacquired
   - Dividend income
   - Equity in earnings of a non-consolidated subsidiary
   - Franchise income when corresponding expenses are not included in the Income Statement
   - Interest charged to construction (interest capitalized)
   - Leased department income when corresponding expenses are not included in the Income Statement
   - Other income, Rental income, Royalty income, and Interest income
2. Expense
   - Amortization of deferred credit
   - Amortization of negative intangibles
   - Foreign exchange adjustments
   - Idle plant expense
   - Miscellaneous expense
   - Moving expense
   - Other expense

Rental Commitments – Min. (1st Year): Data Item A96, Units: Millions of dollars

This item represents the minimum rental expense due in the first, second, third, fourth, and fifth years from the Balance Sheet date under all existing non-cancelable leases. The figure is gross (before rental or sublease income is deducted) excluding capital leases. This is the amount payable in each of the years, not cumulative figures.
This item is not available for banks or utilities.

Interest Expense on Long-term Debt: Data Item A101, Units: Millions of dollars

This item represents the amount of interest expense specifically applicable to long-term debt.
This item includes
1. Amortization of debt discount or premium
2. Long-term debt issuance expense
3. Financing charges on long-term debt

    4. Interest expense on refinanced short-term debt
    5. Underwriting fees on long-term debt
This item excludes interest reported as being "principally" on long-term debt.

Depreciation and Amortization: Data Item A125, Units: Millions of dollars

This item represents non-cash charges for obsolescence and wear and tear on property, allocation of the current portion of capitalized expenditures, and depletion charges.
This item includes:
    1. Amortization of patents, trademarks, and other intangibles
    2. Amortization of deferred charges
    3. Amortization of tools and dies
This item excludes:
    1. Amortization of negative intangibles
    2. Amortization of liability intangibles
    3. Amortization of goodwill on unconsolidated subsidiaries
This item is not available for banks or utilities.

Capital Expenditures: Data Item A128, Units: Millions of dollars

This item represents cash outflow or the funds used for additions to the company's property, plant, and equipment.
This item includes:
    1. Expenditures for capital leases
    2. Increase in funds for construction
    3. Reclassification of inventory to property, plant and equipment
This item excludes:
    1. Capital expenditures of discontinued operations
    2. Changes in property, plant and equipment resulting from foreign currency fluctuations when listed separately
    3. Decrease in funds for construction presented as a use of funds
    4. Property, plant and equipment of acquired companies

Preferred Stock: Data Item A130, Units: Millions of dollars

This item represents the net number of preferred shares at year-end multiplied by the par or stated value per share as presented in the company's Balance Sheet.
This item includes:
    1. Preferred stock subscriptions
    2. Utilities subsidiary preferred stock
    3. Redeemable preferred stock
    4. Preference stock
    5. Receivables on preferred stock
This item excludes:
    1. Preferred stock sinking funds reported in *Current Liabilities*
    2. Secondary classes of common stock
    3. Subsidiary preferred stock
This item is reduced by the effects of:
    1. Par or carrying value of non-redeemable preferred treasury stock which was netted against this item prior to annual and quarterly fiscal periods of 1982 and 1986, 1st quarter, respectively
    2. Cost of redeemable preferred treasury stock which is netted against *Preferred Stock – Redeemable*
    3. Notes payable – banks, others
    4. Telephone companies' interim notes payable and advances from parent company
    5. Commercial paper
This item excludes:
    1. Current portion of long-term notes payable (included in *Debt Due in One Year*)
    2. Due to factor (included in *Current Liabilities – Other*) This item is not available for utilities.

Cash: Data Item A162, Units: Millions of dollars

This item represents any immediately negotiable medium of exchange. It includes money and any instruments normally accepted by banks for deposit and immediate credit to a customer's account.

This item includes:
1. Bank drafts
2. Cash
3. Checks (cashiers or certified)
4. Demand certificates of deposit
5. Demand deposits
6. Letters of credit
7. Money orders

This item excludes:
1. Commercial paper
2. Government securities
3. Legally restricted cash
4. Marketable securities
5. Short-term investments
6. Time deposits
7. Time certificates of deposit

This item is not available for utilities.

Rental Commitments – Min. (2nd Year): Data Item A164, Units: Millions of dollars

This item represents the minimum rental expense due in the first, second, third, fourth, and fifth years from the Balance Sheet date under all existing non-cancelable leases. The figure is gross (before rental or sublease income is deducted) excluding capital leases. This is the amount payable in each of the years, not cumulative figures.

This item is not available for banks or utilities.

Rental Commitments – Min. (3rd Year): Data Item A165, Units: Millions of dollars

This item represents the minimum rental expense due in the first, second, third, fourth, and fifth years from the Balance Sheet date under all existing non-cancelable leases. The figure is gross (before rental or sublease income is deducted) excluding capital leases. This is the amount payable in each of the years, not cumulative figures.

This item is not available for banks or utilities.

Rental Commitments – Min. (4th Year): Data Item A166, Units: Millions of dollars

This item represents the minimum rental expense due in the first, second, third, fourth, and fifth years from the Balance Sheet date under all existing non-cancelable leases. The figure is gross (before rental or sublease income is deducted) excluding capital leases. This is the amount payable in each of the years, not cumulative figures.

This item is not available for banks or utilities.

Rental Commitments – Min. (5th Year): Data Item A167, Units: Millions of dollars

This item represents the minimum rental expense due in the first, second, third, fourth, and fifth years from the Balance Sheet date under all existing non-cancelable leases. The figure is gross (before rental or sublease income is deducted) excluding capital leases. This is the amount payable in each of the years, not cumulative figures.

This item is not available for banks or utilities.

Pre-tax Income: Data Item A170, Units: Millions of dollars

This item represents operating and nonoperating income before provisions for income taxes and minority interest.

This item specifically excludes
1. Extraordinary items
2. Discontinued operations

Operating Income After Depreciation: Data Item A178, Units: Millions of dollars

This item represents the operating income of a company after deducting expenses for cost of goods sold, selling, general, and administrative expenses, and depreciation.

Liabilities – Total: Data Item A181, Units: Millions of dollars

This item represents the sum of:
1. Current Liabilities – Total
2. Deferred Taxes and Investment Tax Credit (Balance Sheet)
3. Liabilities – Other
4. Long-Term Debt – Total
5. Minority Interest (Balance Sheet)

Notes Payable: Data Item A206, Units: Millions of dollars

This item represents the total amount of short-term notes.
This item includes
1. Bank acceptances
2. Bank overdrafts
3. Loans payable to officers of the company
4. Loans payable to parents, and consolidated and unconsolidated subsidiaries
5. Loans payable to stockholders

Income Before Extraordinary Items - Available for Common: Data Item A237, Units: Millions of dollars

This item represents income before extraordinary items and discontinued operations less preferred dividend requirements, but before adding savings due to common stock equivalents. The preferred dividend requirements used in this calculation will normally be the same as the preferred dividends declared.
1. If more or less than one quarterly preferred dividend is declared in one quarter (where preferred dividends are normally declared quarterly), then either preferred dividend requirements or actual preferred dividends paid will be used, depending on the method used by the company in reporting.
2. If all convertible preferred stock is converted into common during the year, preferred dividends are deducted only for that portion of the year in which the stock was outstanding.
3. If the pooling of interest method was used to account for a merger, preferred dividends of the acquired company are included. If preferred stock was exchanged for common stock of the acquiring company, preferred dividends of the merger company are treated as common dividends. On a preliminary basis, this item may be obtained by subtracting the latest reported dividend requirements on preferred shares outstanding from net income.

Pension – Prepaid/Accrued Cost: Data Item A290, Units: Millions of dollars

Prior to January 1999, this item was called Pension – Prepaid/Accrued Cost (Overfunded). In February 1998, FASB issued a new statement that standardized employers' disclosures of pensions and other post-retirement benefits. Effective for companies whose fiscal years began after December 15, 1997, Statement of Financial Accounting Standards (SFAS) #132 permits companies to combine their disclosures regarding over- and underfunded accounts in particular circumstances. Previously, companies were required to report a breakout between over- and underfunded plans on the pension side. This breakout is no longer required under SFAS 132. Due to this accounting change, Standard & Poor's will no longer differentiate pension information between over- and underfunded, regardless of company presentation.

Prepaid pension cost represents cumulative employer contributions in excess of accrued net pension cost and is equal to the difference between plan assets and the projected benefit obligation. It is adjusted for unrecognized net gains and losses, unrecognized net assets, and obligations, among others. Prepaid pension cost is an asset on the Balance Sheet and appears as a positive number. Accrued pension cost represents cumulative net pension cost in excess of the employer's contributions and is equal to the excess of the projected benefit obligation over the plan assets. It is adjusted for unrecognized prior service cost, unrecognized net gains and losses, unrecognized net assets, and obligations, etc.

Accrued pension cost is a liability on the Balance Sheet and appears as a negative number.

Rental Commitments – Thereafter: Data Item A389, Units: Millions of dollars

This represents the cumulative total of all future rental commitments after year five. This item excludes Capitalized Lease Obligations (DCLO).

Stock Compensation Expense: Data Item A398, Units: Millions of dollars

This item represents compensation to employees/executives in the form of company stock.
This item includes:
1. Stock Bonus
2. Deferred Compensation
3. Amortization of Deferred Compensation
4. Non-cash compensation expense that is expensed in the current period

This item can also include options given to consultants in addition to other stock based compensation that a company voluntarily elects to expense.

Market Value: Data Item N/A, Units: Millions of dollars

Market Value is the Monthly Close Price multiplied by the Quarterly Common Shares Outstanding. The MKVAL concept provides company-level information based upon the monthly close price (PRCCM) for the company's primary trading issue and multiplies it by the company's shares outstanding. The common shares outstanding used in this calculation are those collected by Standard & Poor's from the company quarterly reports. (It is also important to notice that a 3-month reporting lag on shares outstanding has been built into this concept, whereas the shares used in the calculation are the ones for the fiscal quarter in effect 3-months prior to the monthly price used. If shares outstanding are not available for that quarter, the previous quarter figure will be used). This concept is accessed using a company-level key (Ex: IBM).

If Common Shares Outstanding for the current quarter is not available, the value for the previous quarter will be used. This calculation will search up to 2 prior quarters. If a company's CSHOQ is not available for any of these time periods, no market value will appear.

Industry Data Exhibits

To view the full list of companies in any of the Industry Data Exhibits (or Size Groupings), download the "March 2017 Industry Data Exhibit Company List Report" at www.DuffandPhelps.com/CostofCapital.

Division A:
Agriculture, Forestry, and Fishing

This division includes establishments primarily engaged in agricultural production, forestry, commercial fishing, hunting and trapping, and related services. Major groups between "01" and "09" are in this division.

Data Updated Through March 31, 2017

0

Number of Companies: 5
Agriculture, Forestry, and Fishing

Industry Description
This division includes establishments primarily engaged in agricultural production, forestry, commercial fishing, hunting and trapping, and related services.

Sales (in millions)

Three Largest Companies
VCA Inc.	$2,516.9
Cal-Maine Foods, Inc.	1,908.7
Alico Inc.	144.2

Three Smallest Companies
Alico Inc.	$144.2
Limoneira Company	111.8
First Financial Northwest, Inc.	44.4

Total Assets (in millions)

Three Largest Companies
VCA Inc.	$3,373.3
Cal-Maine Foods, Inc.	1,111.8
First Financial Northwest, Inc.	1,037.6

Three Smallest Companies
First Financial Northwest, Inc.	$1,037.6
Alico Inc.	458.7
Limoneira Company	305.4

Annualized Monthly Performance Statistics (%)

Industry	Geometric Mean	Arithmetic Mean	Standard Deviation	S&P 500 Index	Geometric Mean	Arithmetic Mean	Standard Deviation
1-year	27.9	31.0	31.3	1-year	17.2	17.4	7.2
3-year	28.0	30.3	24.9	3-year	10.4	10.9	11.5
5-year	25.5	27.6	23.4	5-year	13.3	13.9	11.5

Return Ratios (%)

	Return on Assets Latest	5-Yr Avg	Return on Equity Latest	5-Yr Avg	Dividend Yield Latest	5-Yr Avg	Current Ratio Latest	5-Yr Avg	Operating Margin Latest	5-Yr Avg	Long-term EPS Analyst Estimates
Median (5)	2.8	5.0	5.8	8.8	0.9	0.8	2.4	2.6	16.1	14.6	20.0
SIC Composite (5)	8.7	6.6	5.5	5.3	0.1	0.2	2.4	2.2	19.3	14.6	22.5
Large Composite (–)	–	–	–	–	–	–	–	–	–	–	–
Small Composite (–)	–	–	–	–	–	–	–	–	–	–	–
High-Financial Risk (–)	–	–	–	–	–	–	–	–	–	–	–

Betas (Levered)

	Raw (OLS)	Blume Adjusted	Peer Group	Vasicek Adjusted	Sum	Downside
Median	0.98	1.00	1.51	1.25	1.36	1.40
SIC Composite	0.97	0.98	1.51	1.12	1.13	1.20
Large Composite	–	–	–	–	–	–
Small Composite	–	–	–	–	–	–
High Financial Risk	–	–	–	–	–	–

Betas (Unlevered)

	Raw (OLS)	Blume Adjusted	Peer Group	Vasicek Adjusted	Sum	Downside
Median	0.81	0.83	1.21	1.06	0.87	1.24
SIC Composite	0.86	0.88	1.33	1.00	1.00	1.06
Large Composite	–	–	–	–	–	–
Small Composite	–	–	–	–	–	–
High Financial Risk	–	–	–	–	–	–

Equity Valuation Multiples

	Price/Sales Latest	5-Yr Avg	Price/Earnings Latest	5-Yr Avg	Market/Book Latest	5-Yr Avg
Median	2.7	2.3	31.4	20.4	1.8	2.2
SIC Composite	2.1	1.6	18.1	18.9	3.2	2.4
Large Composite	–	–	–	–	–	–
Small Composite	–	–	–	–	–	–
High Financial Risk	–	–	–	–	–	–

Enterprise Valuation (EV) Multiples

	EV/Sales Latest	5-Yr Avg	EV/EBITDA Latest	5-Yr Avg
Median	3.5	3.0	17.7	11.8
SIC Composite	2.4	1.9	10.3	9.8
Large Composite	–	–	–	–
Small Composite	–	–	–	–
High Financial Risk	–	–	–	–

Enterprise Valuation SIC Composite
- EV/Sales: Latest 2.4, 5-Yr Avg 1.9
- EV/EBITDA: Latest 10.3, 5-Yr Avg 9.8

Fama-French (F-F) 5-Factor Model

	F-F Beta	SMB Premium	HML Premium	RMW Premium	CMA Premium
Median	1.1	2.2	0.8	-5.8	3.5
SIC Composite	0.9	1.1	-0.7	-0.5	0.2
Large Composite	–	–	–	–	–
Small Composite	–	–	–	–	–
High Financial Risk	–	–	–	–	–

Leverage Ratios (%)

	Debt/MV Equity Latest	5-Yr Avg	Debt/Total Capital Latest	5-Yr Avg
Median	34.7	32.8	25.8	24.7
SIC Composite	18.6	20.0	15.7	16.7
Large Composite	–	–	–	–
Small Composite	–	–	–	–
High Financial Risk	–	–	–	–

Cost of Debt

	Cost of Debt (%) Latest
Median	7.1
SIC Composite	6.9
Large Composite	–
Small Composite	–
High Financial Risk	–

Capital Structure

SIC Composite (%) Latest
- D/TC: 15.7
- E/TC: 84.3

Cost of Equity Capital (%)

	CAPM	CRSP Deciles CAPM +Size Prem	Build-Up	Risk Premium Report CAPM +Size Prem	Build-Up	Discounted Cash Flow 1-Stage	3-Stage	Fama-French 5-Factor Model
Median	10.4	13.4	11.7	14.5	15.6	12.1	19.0	9.9
SIC Composite	9.7	10.9	10.3	13.4	13.3	22.6	16.9	8.8
Large Composite	–	–	–	–	–	–	–	–
Small Composite	–	–	–	–	–	–	–	–
High Financial Risk	–	–	–	–	–	–	–	–

Cost of Equity Capital (%) SIC Composite
- Avg CRSP: 10.6
- Avg RPR: 13.4
- 1-Stage: 22.6
- 3-Stage: 16.9
- 5-Factor Model: 8.8

Weighted Average Cost of Capital (WACC) (%)

	CAPM	CRSP Deciles CAPM +Size Prem	Build-Up	Risk Premium Report CAPM +Size Prem	Build-Up	Discounted Cash Flow 1-Stage	3-Stage	Fama-French 5-Factor Model
Median	9.7	11.3	10.2	10.9	12.1	11.3	11.9	7.7
SIC Composite	9.1	10.2	9.6	12.2	12.2	20.0	15.2	8.4
Large Composite	–	–	–	–	–	–	–	–
Small Composite	–	–	–	–	–	–	–	–
High Financial Risk	–	–	–	–	–	–	–	–

WACC (%) SIC Composite
- Low: 8.4
- High: 20.0
- Average: 12.6
- Median: 12.2

© 2017 Duff & Phelps. All Rights Reserved. Duff & Phelps has used the utmost care in compiling the data presented herein, but cannot guarantee the accuracy, completeness, or timeliness of the information.

Division B: Mining

This division includes all establishments primarily engaged in mining. The term "mining" is used in the broad sense to include the extraction of minerals occurring naturally: solids, such as coal and ores; liquids, such as crude petroleum; and gases such as natural gas. The term mining is also used in the broad sense to include quarrying, well operations, milling (e.g., crushing, screening, washing, flotation), and other preparation customarily done at the mine site, or as a part of mining activity. Major groups between "10" and "14" are in this division.

Data Updated Through March 31, 2017

1

Number of Companies: 60
Mining & Construction

Industry Description
Mining division includes all establishments primarily engaged in mining. The term mining is used in the broad sense to include the extraction of minerals occurring naturally: solids, such as coal and ores; liquids, such as crude petroleum; and gases such as natural gas. Construction division includes establishments primarily engaged in construction. The term construction includes new work, additions, alterations, reconstruction, installations, and repairs.

Sales (in millions)

Three Largest Companies
ConocoPhillips	$23,693.0
Enterprise Products Partners L.P.	23,022.3
Halliburton Co.	15,887.0

Three Smallest Companies
Enservco Corporation	$38.8
Evolution Petroleum Corp.	26.4
VOC Energy Trust	8.6

Annualized Monthly Performance Statistics (%)

Industry	Geometric Mean	Arithmetic Mean	Standard Deviation
1-year	28.4	29.8	20.3
3-year	-1.9	0.1	20.4
5-year	7.0	8.6	19.0

Total Assets (in millions)

Three Largest Companies
ConocoPhillips	$89,772.0
Enterprise Products Partners L.P.	52,194.0
EOG Resources, Inc.	29,459.4

Three Smallest Companies
VOC Energy Trust	$93.5
Goldfield Corp.	81.2
Enservco Corporation	47.2

S&P 500 Index	Geometric Mean	Arithmetic Mean	Standard Deviation
1-year	17.2	17.4	7.2
3-year	10.4	10.9	11.5
5-year	13.3	13.9	11.5

Return Ratios (%)

	Return on Assets Latest	5-Yr Avg	Return on Equity Latest	5-Yr Avg	Dividend Yield Latest	5-Yr Avg	Current Ratio Latest	5-Yr Avg	Operating Margin Latest	5-Yr Avg	Long-term EPS Analyst Estimates
Median (60)	3.9	5.1	7.4	10.1	0.6	0.8	1.7	1.7	5.8	9.2	15.9
SIC Composite (60)	-0.2	3.8	-0.2	3.8	2.1	2.5	1.6	1.6	4.7	9.9	37.4
Large Composite (6)	-2.4	3.4	-2.5	3.8	3.0	3.3	1.4	1.5	2.5	9.5	-3.4
Small Composite (6)	1.6	8.8	1.2	5.1	1.5	2.3	2.2	1.9	-6.8	22.9	52.1
High-Financial Risk (56)	-11.0	-3.9	-14.3	-5.5	0.7	0.8	1.7	1.4	—	-6.2	18.5

Liquidity Ratio — Profitability Ratio (%) — Growth Rates (%)

Betas (Levered)

	Raw (OLS)	Blume Adjusted	Peer Group	Vasicek Adjusted	Sum	Downside
Median	1.21	1.14	1.24	1.22	1.39	1.63
SIC Composite	1.07	1.05	1.24	1.09	1.35	1.10
Large Composite	1.05	1.04	1.28	1.12	1.44	1.07
Small Composite	0.53	0.71	1.28	0.92	0.45	1.02
High Financial Risk	1.25	1.17	1.26	1.25	1.71	1.26

Betas (Unlevered)

	Raw (OLS)	Blume Adjusted	Peer Group	Vasicek Adjusted	Sum	Downside
Median	0.88	0.85	0.97	0.90	1.04	1.21
SIC Composite	0.85	0.83	0.97	0.86	1.05	0.87
Large Composite	0.78	0.78	0.95	0.83	1.07	0.80
Small Composite	0.50	0.66	1.15	0.84	0.44	0.93
High Financial Risk	0.94	0.88	0.95	0.94	1.25	0.94

Equity Valuation Multiples

	Price/Sales Latest	5-Yr Avg	Price/Earnings Latest	5-Yr Avg	Market/Book Latest	5-Yr Avg
Median	1.1	1.2	25.8	21.5	1.7	1.7
SIC Composite	2.0	1.6	—	26.0	2.1	1.9
Large Composite	2.0	1.4	—	26.5	2.1	1.8
Small Composite	3.7	3.4	85.3	19.7	1.9	2.6
High Financial Risk	3.0	2.1	—	—	1.7	1.4

Enterprise Valuation (EV) Multiples

	EV/Sales Latest	5-Yr Avg	EV/EBITDA Latest	5-Yr Avg
Median	1.4	1.7	10.0	9.2
SIC Composite	2.5	1.9	14.8	9.0
Large Composite	2.6	1.8	17.6	8.6
Small Composite	4.1	3.7	16.2	8.9
High Financial Risk	4.0	2.8	—	11.6

Enterprise Valuation SIC Composite: Latest 14.8 / 5-Yr Avg 9.0; EV/Sales 2.5 / 1.9

Fama-French (F-F) 5-Factor Model

	F-F Beta	SMB Premium	HML Premium	RMW Premium	CMA Premium
Median	1.5	2.1	2.1	-2.7	0.9
SIC Composite	1.0	0.9	3.5	-1.2	0.8
Large Composite	1.0	0.1	3.2	-1.1	-1.5
Small Composite	0.4	2.6	4.1	0.4	-1.1
High Financial Risk	—	—	—	—	—

Leverage Ratios (%)

	Debt/MV Equity Latest	5-Yr Avg	Debt/Total Capital Latest	5-Yr Avg
Median	37.5	33.1	27.2	24.9
SIC Composite	32.5	30.4	24.5	23.3
Large Composite	37.8	33.1	27.4	24.9
Small Composite	15.8	12.8	13.6	11.4
High Financial Risk	46.1	41.3	31.6	29.2

Cost of Debt

	Cost of Debt (%) Latest
Median	6.1
SIC Composite	5.2
Large Composite	4.6
Small Composite	7.1
High Financial Risk	6.5

Capital Structure

SIC Composite (%) Latest: D/TC 75.5, E/TC 24.5

Cost of Equity Capital (%)

	CAPM	CRSP Deciles CAPM +Size Prem	Build-Up	Risk Premium Report CAPM +Size Prem	Build-Up	Discounted Cash Flow 1-Stage	3-Stage	Fama-French 5-Factor Model
Median	10.2	12.0	11.8	14.7	13.3	13.4	21.8	14.3
SIC Composite	9.5	9.9	10.8	13.1	11.2	40.1	20.6	13.1
Large Composite	9.7	9.8	10.6	13.1	10.3	—	4.1	9.8
Small Composite	8.6	12.5	14.1	11.8	16.4	—	31.2	11.9
High Financial Risk	—	—	—	27.0	26.4	—	—	—

Cost of Equity Capital (%) SIC Composite: Avg CRSP 10.4, Avg RPR 12.2, 1-Stage 40.1, 3-Stage 20.6, 5-Factor Model 13.1

Weighted Average Cost of Capital (WACC) (%)

	CAPM	CRSP Deciles CAPM +Size Prem	Build-Up	Risk Premium Report CAPM +Size Prem	Build-Up	Discounted Cash Flow 1-Stage	3-Stage	Fama-French 5-Factor Model
Median	8.8	9.9	9.7	12.0	10.8	10.6	18.2	12.1
SIC Composite	8.2	8.5	9.2	11.0	9.5	31.3	16.6	11.0
Large Composite	8.0	8.1	8.7	10.5	8.5	—	4.0	8.2
Small Composite	8.2	11.6	13.0	11.0	15.0	47.3	27.8	11.1
High Financial Risk	—	—	—	20.4	20.0	—	—	—

WACC (%) SIC Composite: Low 8.5, High 31.3, Average 13.9, Median 11.0

© 2017 Duff & Phelps. All Rights Reserved. Duff & Phelps has used the utmost care in compiling the data presented herein, but cannot guarantee the accuracy, completeness, or timeliness of the information.

Data Updated Through March 31, 2017

13
Number of Companies: 22
Oil and Gas Extraction

Industry Description
This major group includes establishments primarily engaged in: (1) producing crude petroleum and natural gas; (2) extracting oil from oil sands and oil shale; (3) producing natural gasoline and cycle condensate; and (4) producing gas and hydrocarbon liquids from coal at the mine site. Types of activities included are exploration, drilling, oil and gas well operation and maintenance, the operation of natural gasoline and cycle plants, and the gasification, liquefaction, and pyrolysis of coal at the mine site.

Sales (in millions)

Three Largest Companies
ConocoPhillips	$23,693.0
Enterprise Products Partners L.P.	23,022.3
Halliburton Co.	15,887.0

Three Smallest Companies
Enservco Corporation	$38.8
Evolution Petroleum Corp.	26.4
VOC Energy Trust	8.6

Annualized Monthly Performance Statistics (%)

Industry	Geometric Mean	Arithmetic Mean	Standard Deviation
1-year	29.5	31.9	27.5
3-year	-6.0	-3.0	24.9
5-year	4.6	6.9	22.8

Total Assets (in millions)

Three Largest Companies
ConocoPhillips	$89,772.0
Enterprise Products Partners L.P.	52,194.0
EOG Resources, Inc.	29,459.4

Three Smallest Companies
Evolution Petroleum Corp.	$97.5
VOC Energy Trust	93.5
Enservco Corporation	47.2

S&P 500 Index	Geometric Mean	Arithmetic Mean	Standard Deviation
1-year	17.2	17.4	7.2
3-year	10.4	10.9	11.5
5-year	13.3	13.9	11.5

Return Ratios (%)

	Return on Assets Latest	Return on Assets 5-Yr Avg	Return on Equity Latest	Return on Equity 5-Yr Avg	Dividend Yield Latest	Dividend Yield 5-Yr Avg
Median (22)	-2.6	3.7	-5.8	7.5	1.9	2.2
SIC Composite (22)	-3.2	2.8	-3.1	2.8	2.7	2.9
Large Composite (3)	-4.1	3.0	-4.2	3.3	3.4	3.7
Small Composite (3)	13.2	16.3	9.3	7.6	3.3	2.4
High-Financial Risk (45)	-12.7	-4.5	-15.9	-6.2	0.7	0.7

Liquidity Ratio

	Current Ratio Latest	Current Ratio 5-Yr Avg
	1.5	1.7
	1.4	1.5
	1.4	1.4
	3.9	3.1
	1.6	1.4

Profitability Ratio (%)

	Operating Margin Latest	Operating Margin 5-Yr Avg
	-1.3	13.3
	-2.5	10.0
	-1.1	9.8
	13.7	41.4
	–	-9.1

Growth Rates (%)

	Long-term EPS Analyst Estimates
	17.6
	48.3
	-5.7
	56.1
	20.2

Betas (Levered)

	Raw (OLS)	Blume Adjusted	Peer Group	Vasicek Adjusted	Sum	Downside
Median	1.15	1.10	1.27	1.19	1.72	1.71
SIC Composite	1.10	1.07	1.27	1.13	1.56	1.16
Large Composite	1.02	1.02	1.27	1.20	1.46	1.09
Small Composite	0.94	0.97	1.28	1.19	1.19	1.20
High Financial Risk	1.34	1.22	1.28	1.33	1.90	1.34

Betas (Unlevered)

	Raw (OLS)	Blume Adjusted	Peer Group	Vasicek Adjusted	Sum	Downside
Median	0.85	0.86	0.95	0.94	1.24	1.21
SIC Composite	0.85	0.83	0.98	0.87	1.19	0.90
Large Composite	0.75	0.75	0.93	0.88	1.07	0.80
Small Composite	0.91	0.93	1.22	1.14	1.14	1.15
High Financial Risk	1.00	0.92	0.95	0.99	1.38	1.00

Equity Valuation Multiples

	Price/Sales Latest	Price/Sales 5-Yr Avg	Price/Earnings Latest	Price/Earnings 5-Yr Avg	Market/Book Latest	Market/Book 5-Yr Avg
Median	2.8	2.1	–	30.6	1.5	2.1
SIC Composite	3.2	1.9	–	35.3	2.1	1.9
Large Composite	2.6	1.6	–	30.6	2.2	1.9
Small Composite	4.6	5.3	11.0	13.3	1.7	2.5
High Financial Risk	3.7	2.4	–	–	1.7	1.3

Enterprise Valuation (EV) Multiples

	EV/Sales Latest	EV/Sales 5-Yr Avg	EV/EBITDA Latest	EV/EBITDA 5-Yr Avg
Median	4.3	2.7	11.5	9.1
SIC Composite	4.2	2.3	18.4	8.6
Large Composite	3.5	2.0	20.6	8.5
Small Composite	4.4	5.3	13.0	10.7
High Financial Risk	5.1	3.2	–	11.8

Enterprise Valuation SIC Composite
- Latest: EV/Sales 4.2, EV/EBITDA 18.4
- 5-Yr Avg: EV/Sales 2.3, EV/EBITDA 8.6

Fama-French (F-F) 5-Factor Model

	F-F Beta	SMB Premium	HML Premium	RMW Premium	CMA Premium
Median	2.0	-0.9	6.4	-0.8	-2.8
SIC Composite	1.1	0.6	4.9	-1.4	1.1
Large Composite	1.0	-0.2	4.0	-1.2	-1.7
Small Composite	0.9	-0.8	10.7	-0.9	-4.6
High Financial Risk	–	–	–	–	–

Leverage Ratios (%)

	Debt/MV Equity Latest	Debt/MV Equity 5-Yr Avg	Debt/Total Capital Latest	Debt/Total Capital 5-Yr Avg
Median	39.6	33.1	28.4	24.9
SIC Composite	33.8	29.0	25.2	22.5
Large Composite	38.9	32.0	28.0	24.3
Small Composite	6.4	4.1	6.0	3.9
High Financial Risk	46.1	40.5	31.5	28.8

Cost of Debt

	Cost of Debt (%) Latest
Median	6.1
SIC Composite	4.9
Large Composite	4.5
Small Composite	7.1
High Financial Risk	6.4

Capital Structure
SIC Composite (%) Latest: D/TC 25.2, E/TC 74.8

Cost of Equity Capital (%)

	CRSP Deciles CAPM	CRSP Deciles CAPM +Size Prem	Build-Up	Risk Premium Report CAPM	Risk Premium Report CAPM +Size Prem	Build-Up	Discounted Cash Flow 1-Stage	Discounted Cash Flow 3-Stage	Fama-French 5-Factor Model
Median	10.1	11.8	11.8	16.2	12.7		17.7	18.1	16.5
SIC Composite	9.7	9.9	10.7	14.0	10.6		–	16.0	14.5
Large Composite	10.1	10.1	10.5	13.1	10.0		–	–	9.9
Small Composite	10.0	13.3	13.8	15.9	16.6		–	41.2	12.7
High Financial Risk	–	–	–	28.9	27.3		–	–	–

Cost of Equity Capital (%) SIC Composite: Avg CRSP 10.3, Avg RPR 12.3, 1-Stage n/a, 3-Stage 16.0, 5-Factor Model 14.5

Weighted Average Cost of Capital (WACC) (%)

	CRSP Deciles CAPM	CRSP Deciles CAPM +Size Prem	Build-Up	Risk Premium Report CAPM	Risk Premium Report CAPM +Size Prem	Build-Up	Discounted Cash Flow 1-Stage	Discounted Cash Flow 3-Stage	Fama-French 5-Factor Model
Median	8.7	10.0	9.6	13.6	10.0		13.4	14.2	13.0
SIC Composite	8.3	8.4	9.0	11.5	9.0		40.0	12.9	11.9
Large Composite	8.2	8.2	8.6	10.4	8.2		–	–	8.1
Small Composite	9.8	12.9	13.4	15.4	16.0		–	39.1	12.3
High Financial Risk	–	–	–	21.7	20.6		–	–	–

WACC (%) SIC Composite: Low 8.4, High 40.0, Average 14.7, Median 11.5

© 2017 Duff & Phelps. All Rights Reserved. Duff & Phelps has used the utmost care in compiling the data presented herein, but cannot guarantee the accuracy, completeness, or timeliness of the information.

Data Updated Through March 31, 2017

131

Number of Companies: 13
Crude Petroleum and Natural Gas

Industry Description
Establishments primarily engaged in operating oil and gas field properties.

Sales (in millions)

Three Largest Companies
ConocoPhillips	$23,693.0
Enterprise Products Partners L.P.	23,022.3
EOG Resources, Inc.	7,363.4

Three Smallest Companies
Panhandle Oil & Gas Inc.	$39.1
Evolution Petroleum Corp.	26.4
VOC Energy Trust	8.6

Total Assets (in millions)

Three Largest Companies
ConocoPhillips	$89,772.0
Enterprise Products Partners L.P.	52,194.0
EOG Resources, Inc.	29,459.4

Three Smallest Companies
Panhandle Oil & Gas Inc.	$198.1
Evolution Petroleum Corp.	97.5
VOC Energy Trust	93.5

Annualized Monthly Performance Statistics (%)

Industry	Geometric Mean	Arithmetic Mean	Standard Deviation
1-year	29.6	32.0	27.1
3-year	-4.9	-2.0	24.9
5-year	4.8	7.0	22.3

S&P 500 Index	Geometric Mean	Arithmetic Mean	Standard Deviation
1-year	17.2	17.4	7.2
3-year	10.4	10.9	11.5
5-year	13.3	13.9	11.5

Return Ratios (%)

	Return on Assets Latest	Return on Assets 5-Yr Avg	Return on Equity Latest	Return on Equity 5-Yr Avg	Dividend Yield Latest	Dividend Yield 5-Yr Avg
Median (13)	-2.8	4.1	-6.0	6.6	2.8	3.1
SIC Composite (13)	-1.1	2.8	-1.1	2.9	3.0	3.2
Large Composite (3)	-1.3	2.8	-1.2	3.0	3.0	3.4
Small Composite (3)	5.7	11.6	3.5	6.0	1.9	1.6
High-Financial Risk (35)	-12.4	-4.4	-15.1	-5.8	0.7	0.7

Liquidity Ratio

	Current Ratio Latest	Current Ratio 5-Yr Avg
Median (13)	1.0	1.2
SIC Composite (13)	1.1	1.1
Large Composite (3)	1.1	1.1
Small Composite (3)	3.4	3.1
High-Financial Risk (35)	1.6	1.3

Profitability Ratio (%)

	Operating Margin Latest	Operating Margin 5-Yr Avg
Median (13)	-18.4	12.9
SIC Composite (13)	-4.9	8.3
Large Composite (3)	-4.9	8.0
Small Composite (3)	-11.5	42.1
High-Financial Risk (35)	–	-11.3

Growth Rates (%)

	Long-term EPS Analyst Estimates
Median (13)	57.5
SIC Composite (13)	57.5
Large Composite (3)	66.3
Small Composite (3)	57.5
High-Financial Risk (35)	21.2

Betas (Levered)

	Raw (OLS)	Blume Adjusted	Peer Group	Vasicek Adjusted	Sum	Downside
Median	1.13	1.09	1.27	1.16	1.71	1.67
SIC Composite	1.09	1.07	1.27	1.12	1.53	1.15
Large Composite	0.99	1.00	1.27	1.18	1.41	1.02
Small Composite	0.85	0.91	1.28	1.27	1.11	1.17
High Financial Risk	1.29	1.19	1.28	1.29	1.79	1.28

Betas (Unlevered)

	Raw (OLS)	Blume Adjusted	Peer Group	Vasicek Adjusted	Sum	Downside
Median	0.85	0.85	0.94	0.91	1.31	1.24
SIC Composite	0.83	0.81	0.97	0.85	1.16	0.87
Large Composite	0.76	0.77	0.97	0.90	1.07	0.78
Small Composite	0.82	0.87	1.22	1.21	1.06	1.12
High Financial Risk	0.97	0.90	0.96	0.97	1.32	0.96

Equity Valuation Multiples

	Price/Sales Latest	Price/Sales 5-Yr Avg	Price/Earnings Latest	Price/Earnings 5-Yr Avg	Market/Book Latest	Market/Book 5-Yr Avg
Median	4.8	3.3	–	29.8	1.7	2.2
SIC Composite	3.5	2.0	–	34.2	2.1	1.8
Large Composite	3.3	1.9	–	33.6	2.1	1.8
Small Composite	8.7	6.7	29.7	16.9	2.0	2.3
High Financial Risk	4.1	2.6	–	–	1.7	1.4

Enterprise Valuation (EV) Multiples

	EV/Sales Latest	EV/Sales 5-Yr Avg	EV/EBITDA Latest	EV/EBITDA 5-Yr Avg
Median	6.3	4.8	13.9	9.7
SIC Composite	4.6	2.5	15.3	8.6
Large Composite	4.2	2.4	16.0	8.5
Small Composite	8.8	6.8	23.8	10.3
High Financial Risk	5.6	3.5	–	12.3

Enterprise Valuation SIC Composite
Latest: EV/Sales 4.6, EV/EBITDA 15.3
5-Yr Avg: EV/Sales 2.5, EV/EBITDA 8.6

Fama-French (F-F) 5-Factor Model

	F-F Beta	SMB Premium	HML Premium	RMW Premium	CMA Premium
Median	0.8	-0.9	12.7	-2.4	-2.3
SIC Composite	1.0	0.9	4.5	-1.3	1.0
Large Composite	1.0	0.5	4.0	-1.3	-1.7
Small Composite	0.8	0.7	10.8	-0.1	-1.3
High Financial Risk	–	–	–	–	–

Leverage Ratios (%)

	Debt/MV Equity Latest	Debt/MV Equity 5-Yr Avg	Debt/Total Capital Latest	Debt/Total Capital 5-Yr Avg
Median	40.5	33.3	28.8	25.0
SIC Composite	35.0	30.8	25.9	23.5
Large Composite	32.9	29.2	24.7	22.6
Small Composite	6.9	5.7	6.5	5.4
High Financial Risk	44.1	37.9	30.6	27.5

Cost of Debt

	Cost of Debt (%) Latest
Median	6.1
SIC Composite	4.8
Large Composite	4.4
Small Composite	7.1
High Financial Risk	6.4

Capital Structure

SIC Composite (%) Latest: D/TC 25.9, E/TC 74.1

Cost of Equity Capital (%)

	CAPM	CRSP Deciles CAPM +Size Prem	CRSP Deciles Build-Up	Risk Premium Report CAPM +Size Prem	Risk Premium Report Build-Up	Discounted Cash Flow 1-Stage	Discounted Cash Flow 3-Stage	Fama-French 5-Factor Model
Median	9.9	11.6	11.5	15.8	12.6	11.8	19.5	14.8
SIC Composite	9.6	9.8	10.7	13.7	10.4	–	18.9	14.3
Large Composite	10.0	10.0	10.5	12.8	10.1	–	24.1	10.2
Small Composite	10.5	13.4	13.5	15.4	16.4	–	32.1	18.1
High Financial Risk	–	–	–	28.4	27.4	–	–	–

Cost of Equity Capital (%) SIC Composite
Avg CRSP: 10.2, Avg RPR: 12.1, 1-Stage: n/a, 3-Stage: 18.9, 5-Factor Model: 14.3

Weighted Average Cost of Capital (WACC) (%)

	CAPM	CRSP Deciles CAPM +Size Prem	CRSP Deciles Build-Up	Risk Premium Report CAPM +Size Prem	Risk Premium Report Build-Up	Discounted Cash Flow 1-Stage	Discounted Cash Flow 3-Stage	Fama-French 5-Factor Model
Median	8.4	10.3	9.6	13.8	9.9	9.6	15.9	12.5
SIC Composite	8.1	8.3	8.9	11.1	8.7	46.8	15.0	11.6
Large Composite	8.4	8.4	8.8	10.5	8.4	–	19.0	8.5
Small Composite	10.2	12.9	13.0	14.7	15.7	–	30.4	17.3
High Financial Risk	–	–	–	21.5	20.8	–	–	–

WACC (%) SIC Composite
Low 8.3, High 46.8, Average 15.8, Median 11.1

© 2017 Duff & Phelps. All Rights Reserved. Duff & Phelps has used the utmost care in compiling the data presented herein, but cannot guarantee the accuracy, completeness, or timeliness of the information.

Data Updated Through March 31, 2017

138

Number of Companies: 9
Oil and Gas Field Services

Industry Description
Establishments primarily engaged in drilling oil and gas wells; oil and gas field exploration services; oil and gas field services not elsewhere classified.

Sales (in millions)

Three Largest Companies
Halliburton Co.	$15,887.0
Oceaneering International, Inc.	2,271.6
Helmerich & Payne, Inc.	1,624.2

Three Smallest Companies
RPC Inc.	$729.0
Archrock Partners, L.P.	562.4
Enservco Corporation	38.8

Total Assets (in millions)

Three Largest Companies
Halliburton Co.	$27,000.0
Helmerich & Payne, Inc.	6,832.0
Diamond Offshore Drilling Inc.	6,371.9

Three Smallest Companies
Archrock Partners, L.P.	$1,903.4
RPC Inc.	1,035.5
Enservco Corporation	47.2

Annualized Monthly Performance Statistics (%)

	Industry Geometric Mean	Arithmetic Mean	Standard Deviation		S&P 500 Index Geometric Mean	Arithmetic Mean	Standard Deviation
1-year	28.9	32.3	32.5	1-year	17.2	17.4	7.2
3-year	-9.0	-5.2	28.2	3-year	10.4	10.9	11.5
5-year	4.0	7.6	28.4	5-year	13.3	13.9	11.5

Return Ratios (%)

	Return on Assets Latest	5-Yr Avg	Return on Equity Latest	5-Yr Avg	Dividend Yield Latest	5-Yr Avg
Median (9)	-2.4	3.4	-5.5	8.3	0.9	1.8
SIC Composite (9)	-11.7	2.9	-9.9	2.5	1.7	2.0
Large Composite (–)	–	–	–	–	–	–
Small Composite (–)	–	–	–	–	–	–
High-Financial Risk (9)	-16.3	-5.5	–	-12.6	0.0	0.3

Liquidity Ratio

	Current Ratio Latest	5-Yr Avg
Median (9)	2.9	2.5
SIC Composite (9)	2.9	2.8
Large Composite	–	–
Small Composite	–	–
High-Financial Risk	2.0	2.0

Profitability Ratio (%)

	Operating Margin Latest	5-Yr Avg
Median (9)	3.5	13.8
SIC Composite (9)	3.4	14.5
Large Composite	–	–
Small Composite	–	–
High-Financial Risk	-18.6	4.2

Growth Rates (%)

	Long-term EPS Analyst Estimates
Median (9)	17.6
SIC Composite (9)	17.6
Large Composite	–
Small Composite	–
High-Financial Risk	3.6

Betas (Levered)

	Raw (OLS)	Blume Adjusted	Peer Group	Vasicek Adjusted	Sum	Downside
Median	1.21	1.14	1.28	1.24	1.75	1.75
SIC Composite	1.14	1.09	1.28	1.18	1.64	1.30
Large Composite	–	–	–	–	–	–
Small Composite	–	–	–	–	–	–
High Financial Risk	2.55	1.99	1.27	1.58	5.06	3.22

Betas (Unlevered)

	Raw (OLS)	Blume Adjusted	Peer Group	Vasicek Adjusted	Sum	Downside
Median	0.97	0.87	1.00	0.94	1.24	1.21
SIC Composite	0.91	0.88	1.02	0.94	1.30	1.03
Large Composite	–	–	–	–	–	–
Small Composite	–	–	–	–	–	–
High Financial Risk	1.56	1.25	0.85	1.02	2.97	1.94

Equity Valuation Multiples

	Price/Sales Latest	5-Yr Avg	Price/Earnings Latest	5-Yr Avg	Market/Book Latest	5-Yr Avg
Median	2.0	2.0	–	37.7	1.2	2.1
SIC Composite	2.6	1.7	–	39.4	2.2	2.0
Large Composite	–	–	–	–	–	–
Small Composite	–	–	–	–	–	–
High Financial Risk	1.4	0.8	–	–	1.7	0.9

Enterprise Valuation (EV) Multiples

	EV/Sales Latest	5-Yr Avg	EV/EBITDA Latest	5-Yr Avg
Median	3.2	2.1	6.4	9.0
SIC Composite	3.1	1.9	–	8.8
Large Composite	–	–	–	–
Small Composite	–	–	–	–
High Financial Risk	2.5	1.5	26.1	7.3

Enterprise Valuation SIC Composite
Latest: EV/Sales 3.1, EV/EBITDA 8.8
5-Yr Avg: EV/Sales 1.9, EV/EBITDA n/a

Fama-French (F-F) 5-Factor Model

	F-F Beta	SMB Premium	HML Premium	RMW Premium	CMA Premium
Median	1.1	-0.8	4.7	-1.4	5.8
SIC Composite	1.1	0.0	5.9	-1.5	1.2
Large Composite	–	–	–	–	–
Small Composite	–	–	–	–	–
High Financial Risk	–	–	–	–	–

Leverage Ratios (%)

	Debt/MV Equity Latest	5-Yr Avg	Debt/Total Capital Latest	5-Yr Avg
Median	29.9	24.5	23.0	19.7
SIC Composite	29.5	23.4	22.8	19.0
Large Composite	–	–	–	–
Small Composite	–	–	–	–
High Financial Risk	79.3	88.0	44.2	46.8

Cost of Debt

	Cost of Debt (%) Latest
Median	6.1
SIC Composite	5.3
Large Composite	–
Small Composite	–
High Financial Risk	6.6

Capital Structure

SIC Composite (%) Latest
D/TC: 22.8
E/TC: 77.2

Cost of Equity Capital (%)

	CRSP Deciles CAPM	CAPM +Size Prem	Build-Up	Risk Premium Report CAPM +Size Prem	Build-Up	Discounted Cash Flow 1-Stage	3-Stage	Fama-French 5-Factor Model
Median	10.3	11.8	12.0	16.3	12.9	17.9	7.6	18.0
SIC Composite	10.0	10.4	10.9	14.9	11.3	19.6	7.0	15.2
Large Composite	–	–	–	–	–	–	–	–
Small Composite	–	–	–	–	–	–	–	–
High Financial Risk	–	–	–	45.4	26.6	–	–	–

Cost of Equity Capital (%) SIC Composite
Avg CRSP: 10.6; Avg RPR: 13.1; 1-Stage: 19.6; 3-Stage: 7.0; 5-Factor Model: 15.2

Weighted Average Cost of Capital (WACC) (%)

	CRSP Deciles CAPM	CAPM +Size Prem	Build-Up	Risk Premium Report CAPM +Size Prem	Build-Up	Discounted Cash Flow 1-Stage	3-Stage	Fama-French 5-Factor Model
Median	8.9	9.8	10.0	12.8	10.2	17.0	6.8	14.4
SIC Composite	8.8	9.1	9.5	12.6	9.9	16.2	6.5	12.8
Large Composite	–	–	–	–	–	–	–	–
Small Composite	–	–	–	–	–	–	–	–
High Financial Risk	–	–	–	27.8	17.3	–	–	–

WACC (%) SIC Composite
Low 6.5, High 16.2; Average 10.9; Median 9.9

© 2017 Duff & Phelps. All Rights Reserved. Duff & Phelps has used the utmost care in compiling the data presented herein, but cannot guarantee the accuracy, completeness, or timeliness of the information.

Data Updated Through March 31, 2017

14

Number of Companies: 5
Mining and Quarrying Of Nonmetallic Minerals, Except Fuels

Industry Description
This major group includes establishments primarily engaged in mining or quarrying, developing mines, or exploring for nonmetallic minerals, except fuels. Also included are certain well and brine operations, and primary preparation plants, such as those engaged in crushing, grinding, washing, or other concentration.

Sales (in millions)

Three Largest Companies
Martin Marietta Materials	$3,818.7
Vulcan Materials Company	3,592.7
Compass Minerals Int'l Inc.	1,138.0

Three Smallest Companies
Compass Minerals Int'l Inc.	$1,138.0
U.S. Silica Holdings, Inc.	559.6
U.S. Lime & Minerals	139.3

Total Assets (in millions)

Three Largest Companies
Vulcan Materials Company	$8,471.5
Martin Marietta Materials	7,300.9
Compass Minerals Int'l Inc.	2,466.5

Three Smallest Companies
Compass Minerals Int'l Inc.	$2,466.5
U.S. Silica Holdings, Inc.	2,073.2
U.S. Lime & Minerals	210.2

Annualized Monthly Performance Statistics (%)

Industry	Geometric Mean	Arithmetic Mean	Standard Deviation
1-year	26.7	28.8	25.0
3-year	18.3	21.1	27.1
5-year	20.1	23.0	27.5

S&P 500 Index	Geometric Mean	Arithmetic Mean	Standard Deviation
1-year	17.2	17.4	7.2
3-year	10.4	10.9	11.5
5-year	13.3	13.9	11.5

Return Ratios (%)

	Return on Assets Latest	5-Yr Avg	Return on Equity Latest	5-Yr Avg	Dividend Yield Latest	5-Yr Avg
Median (5)	6.0	4.7	9.0	9.8	0.8	1.2
SIC Composite (5)	4.8	3.5	2.7	2.7	1.0	1.1
Large Composite (–)	–	–	–	–	–	–
Small Composite (–)	–	–	–	–	–	–
High-Financial Risk (–)	–	–	–	–	–	–

Liquidity Ratio / Profitability Ratio (%) / Growth Rates (%)

	Current Ratio Latest	5-Yr Avg	Operating Margin Latest	5-Yr Avg	Long-term EPS Analyst Estimates
Median (5)	3.1	2.9	16.9	13.7	21.7
SIC Composite (5)	2.8	2.9	16.4	13.4	21.8
Large Composite (–)	–	–	–	–	–
Small Composite (–)	–	–	–	–	–
High-Financial Risk (–)	–	–	–	–	–

Betas (Levered)

	Raw (OLS)	Blume Adjusted	Peer Group	Vasicek Adjusted	Sum	Downside
Median	1.20	1.13	1.37	1.22	0.76	1.44
SIC Composite	1.24	1.16	1.37	1.25	0.84	1.36
Large Composite	–	–	–	–	–	–
Small Composite	–	–	–	–	–	–
High Financial Risk	–	–	–	–	–	–

Betas (Unlevered)

	Raw (OLS)	Blume Adjusted	Peer Group	Vasicek Adjusted	Sum	Downside
Median	1.18	1.12	1.23	1.21	0.66	1.44
SIC Composite	1.09	1.02	1.21	1.10	0.75	1.20
Large Composite	–	–	–	–	–	–
Small Composite	–	–	–	–	–	–
High Financial Risk	–	–	–	–	–	–

Equity Valuation Multiples

	Price/Sales Latest	5-Yr Avg	Price/Earnings Latest	5-Yr Avg	Market/Book Latest	5-Yr Avg
Median	3.6	2.6	32.4	35.7	2.9	2.1
SIC Composite	3.9	2.9	36.8	37.6	2.9	2.3
Large Composite	–	–	–	–	–	–
Small Composite	–	–	–	–	–	–
High Financial Risk	–	–	–	–	–	–

Enterprise Valuation (EV) Multiples

	EV/Sales Latest	5-Yr Avg	EV/EBITDA Latest	5-Yr Avg
Median	4.0	3.1	15.9	14.5
SIC Composite	4.4	3.4	17.7	15.1
Large Composite	–	–	–	–
Small Composite	–	–	–	–
High Financial Risk	–	–	–	–

Enterprise Valuation SIC Composite
Latest: EV/Sales 4.4, EV/EBITDA 17.7
5-Yr Avg: EV/Sales 3.4, EV/EBITDA 15.1

Fama-French (F-F) 5-Factor Model

	F-F Beta	SMB Premium	HML Premium	RMW Premium	CMA Premium
Median	1.3	1.0	2.1	-2.2	-1.6
SIC Composite	1.2	1.3	1.0	-1.1	-0.4
Large Composite	–	–	–	–	–
Small Composite	–	–	–	–	–
High Financial Risk	–	–	–	–	–

Leverage Ratios (%)

	Debt/MV Equity Latest	5-Yr Avg	Debt/Total Capital Latest	5-Yr Avg
Median	12.4	22.2	11.1	18.2
SIC Composite	15.2	21.3	13.2	17.6
Large Composite	–	–	–	–
Small Composite	–	–	–	–
High Financial Risk	–	–	–	–

Cost of Debt

	Cost of Debt (%) Latest
Median	6.1
SIC Composite	5.3
Large Composite	–
Small Composite	–
High Financial Risk	–

Capital Structure

SIC Composite (%) Latest
D/TC: 13.2
E/TC: 86.8

Cost of Equity Capital (%)

	CAPM	CRSP Deciles CAPM +Size Prem	Build-Up	Risk Premium Report CAPM +Size Prem	Build-Up	Discounted Cash Flow 1-Stage	3-Stage	Fama-French 5-Factor Model
Median	10.2	11.7	12.2	11.4	13.4	21.1	11.0	9.7
SIC Composite	10.4	11.1	12.0	11.1	12.3	22.9	10.6	10.8
Large Composite	–	–	–	–	–	–	–	–
Small Composite	–	–	–	–	–	–	–	–
High Financial Risk	–	–	–	–	–	–	–	–

Cost of Equity Capital (%) SIC Composite
Avg CRSP: 11.5, Avg RPR: 11.7, 1-Stage: 22.9, 3-Stage: 10.6, 5-Factor Model: 10.8

Weighted Average Cost of Capital (WACC) (%)

	CAPM	CRSP Deciles CAPM +Size Prem	Build-Up	Risk Premium Report CAPM +Size Prem	Build-Up	Discounted Cash Flow 1-Stage	3-Stage	Fama-French 5-Factor Model
Median	10.1	10.9	11.0	9.7	11.3	19.2	10.3	9.1
SIC Composite	9.6	10.2	11.0	10.2	11.2	20.5	9.8	9.9
Large Composite	–	–	–	–	–	–	–	–
Small Composite	–	–	–	–	–	–	–	–
High Financial Risk	–	–	–	–	–	–	–	–

WACC (%) SIC Composite
Low 9.8 — High 20.5
▲ Average 11.8   ◆ Median 10.2

© 2017 Duff & Phelps. All Rights Reserved. Duff & Phelps has used the utmost care in compiling the data presented herein, but cannot guarantee the accuracy, completeness, or timeliness of the information.

Division C: Construction

This division includes establishments primarily engaged in construction. The term "construction" includes new work, additions, alterations, reconstruction, installations, and repairs. Construction activities are generally administered or managed from a relatively fixed place of business, but the actual construction work is performed at one or more different sites. Major groups between "15" and "17" are in this division.

Data Updated Through March 31, 2017

15

Number of Companies: 11
Building Construction General Contractors and Operative Builders

Industry Description
This major group includes general contractors and operative builders primarily engaged in the construction of residential, farm, industrial, commercial, or other buildings. General building contractors who combine a special trade with the contracting are included in this major group.

Sales (in millions)

Three Largest Companies
D R Horton Inc.	$12,170.9
Lennar Corp.	10,950.0
PulteGroup, Inc.	7,668.5

Three Smallest Companies
MDC Holdings Inc.	$2,326.8
Beazer Homes USA Inc.	1,822.1
M/I Homes, Inc.	1,691.3

Total Assets (in millions)

Three Largest Companies
Lennar Corp.	$15,361.8
D R Horton Inc.	11,558.9
PulteGroup, Inc.	10,178.2

Three Smallest Companies
MDC Holdings Inc.	$2,528.6
Beazer Homes USA Inc.	2,213.2
M/I Homes, Inc.	1,548.5

Annualized Monthly Performance Statistics (%)

Industry	Geometric Mean	Arithmetic Mean	Standard Deviation	S&P 500 Index	Geometric Mean	Arithmetic Mean	Standard Deviation
1-year	16.4	17.6	17.6	1-year	17.2	17.4	7.2
3-year	9.2	11.5	23.5	3-year	10.4	10.9	11.5
5-year	15.7	18.5	26.0	5-year	13.3	13.9	11.5

Return Ratios (%)

	Return on Assets Latest	5-Yr Avg	Return on Equity Latest	5-Yr Avg	Dividend Yield Latest	5-Yr Avg
Median (11)	5.4	5.7	11.2	15.3	0.4	0.2
SIC Composite (11)	5.7	6.5	7.4	9.0	0.7	0.6
Large Composite (3)	6.5	7.3	7.5	9.5	1.0	0.8
Small Composite (3)	2.6	4.0	6.4	9.7	2.2	2.1
High-Financial Risk (–)	–	–	–	–	–	–

Liquidity Ratio

	Current Ratio Latest	5-Yr Avg
Median (11)	–	–
SIC Composite (11)	–	–
Large Composite (3)	–	–
Small Composite (3)	–	–
High-Financial Risk	–	–

Profitability Ratio (%)

	Operating Margin Latest	5-Yr Avg
Median	10.1	9.7
SIC Composite	10.2	9.6
Large Composite	11.6	10.7
Small Composite	5.0	4.5
High-Financial Risk	–	–

Growth Rates (%)

	Long-term EPS Analyst Estimates
Median	10.8
SIC Composite	11.6
Large Composite	11.0
Small Composite	11.2
High-Financial Risk	–

Betas (Levered)

	Raw (OLS)	Blume Adjusted	Peer Group	Vasicek Adjusted	Sum	Downside
Median	1.23	1.15	1.17	1.22	1.23	1.48
SIC Composite	1.14	1.10	1.17	1.15	1.11	1.21
Large Composite	1.17	1.11	1.18	1.18	1.21	1.26
Small Composite	1.44	1.29	1.16	1.42	1.47	1.70
High Financial Risk	–	–	–	–	–	–

Betas (Unlevered)

	Raw (OLS)	Blume Adjusted	Peer Group	Vasicek Adjusted	Sum	Downside
Median	0.87	0.82	0.83	0.85	0.83	0.98
SIC Composite	0.85	0.82	0.87	0.86	0.83	0.89
Large Composite	0.90	0.86	0.90	0.90	0.93	0.97
Small Composite	0.84	0.77	0.71	0.83	0.85	0.96
High Financial Risk	–	–	–	–	–	–

Equity Valuation Multiples

	Price/Sales Latest	5-Yr Avg	Price/Earnings Latest	5-Yr Avg	Market/Book Latest	5-Yr Avg
Median	0.7	0.8	14.0	11.4	1.2	1.4
SIC Composite	0.9	1.0	13.5	11.2	1.6	1.6
Large Composite	1.0	1.1	13.3	10.5	1.7	1.7
Small Composite	0.4	0.5	16.0	10.5	1.0	1.2
High Financial Risk	–	–	–	–	–	–

Enterprise Valuation (EV) Multiples

	EV/Sales Latest	5-Yr Avg	EV/EBITDA Latest	5-Yr Avg
Median	1.2	1.2	9.8	10.6
SIC Composite	1.3	1.4	9.5	10.7
Large Composite	1.4	1.5	9.3	10.3
Small Composite	0.9	1.1	10.2	12.2
High Financial Risk	–	–	–	–

Enterprise Valuation SIC Composite
- Latest: EV/Sales 1.3, EV/EBITDA 9.5
- 5-Yr Avg: EV/Sales 1.4, EV/EBITDA 10.7

Fama-French (F-F) 5-Factor Model

	F-F Beta	SMB Premium	HML Premium	RMW Premium	CMA Premium
Median	1.1	4.3	-1.1	0.5	-3.7
SIC Composite	1.0	2.9	-3.9	-1.3	0.9
Large Composite	1.1	2.5	-4.9	-1.2	-1.5
Small Composite	1.2	6.1	-0.5	-0.2	0.1
High Financial Risk	–	–	–	–	–

Leverage Ratios (%)

	Debt/MV Equity Latest	5-Yr Avg	Debt/Total Capital Latest	5-Yr Avg
Median	64.3	67.1	39.2	40.2
SIC Composite	50.0	56.7	33.3	36.2
Large Composite	40.7	48.3	28.9	32.6
Small Composite	116.8	126.9	53.9	55.9
High Financial Risk	–	–	–	–

Cost of Debt

	Cost of Debt (%) Latest
Median	6.1
SIC Composite	6.1
Large Composite	5.8
Small Composite	6.8
High Financial Risk	–

Capital Structure

SIC Composite (%) Latest
- D/TC: 33.3
- E/TC: 66.7

Cost of Equity Capital (%)

	CRSP Deciles CAPM	CAPM +Size Prem	Build-Up	Risk Premium Report CAPM +Size Prem	Build-Up	Discounted Cash Flow 1-Stage	3-Stage	Fama-French 5-Factor Model
Median	10.2	11.3	10.8	13.2	12.5	11.6	18.4	9.6
SIC Composite	9.8	10.7	10.7	12.3	11.9	12.3	18.1	7.8
Large Composite	10.0	10.6	10.5	12.6	11.5	12.0	17.8	4.3
Small Composite	11.3	13.3	11.8	15.5	13.7	13.4	17.8	15.8
High Financial Risk	–	–	–	–	–	–	–	–

Cost of Equity Capital (%) SIC Composite
- Avg CRSP: 10.7
- Avg RPR: 12.1
- 1-Stage: 12.3
- 3-Stage: 18.1
- 5-Factor Model: 7.8

Weighted Average Cost of Capital (WACC) (%)

	CRSP Deciles CAPM	CAPM +Size Prem	Build-Up	Risk Premium Report CAPM +Size Prem	Build-Up	Discounted Cash Flow 1-Stage	3-Stage	Fama-French 5-Factor Model
Median	8.6	9.2	9.1	10.1	9.9	9.3	13.3	9.2
SIC Composite	8.4	9.0	9.0	10.1	9.8	10.0	13.9	7.0
Large Composite	8.7	9.2	9.1	10.6	9.8	10.2	14.3	4.7
Small Composite	8.8	9.8	9.1	10.8	10.0	9.8	11.8	10.9
High Financial Risk	–	–	–	–	–	–	–	–

WACC (%) SIC Composite
Low 7.0 — Average 9.8, Median 9.8 — High 13.9

© 2017 Duff & Phelps. All Rights Reserved. Duff & Phelps has used the utmost care in compiling the data presented herein, but cannot guarantee the accuracy, completeness, or timeliness of the information.

Data Updated Through March 31, 2017

16

Number of Companies: 10
Heavy Construction Other Than Building Construction Contractors

Industry Description
This major group includes general contractors primarily engaged in heavy construction other than building, such as highways and streets, bridges, sewers, railroads, irrigation projects, flood control projects and marine construction, and special trade contractors primarily engaged in activities of a type that are clearly specialized to such heavy construction and are not normally performed on buildings or building-related projects. Specialized activities that are covered here include grading for highways and airport runways; installation of highway signs; and asphalt and concrete construction of roads, highways, streets and public sidewalks.

Sales (in millions)

Three Largest Companies
Jacobs Engineering Group Inc.	$10,964.2
Mastec, Inc.	5,134.7
Dycom Industries Inc.	2,672.5

Three Smallest Companies
Great Lakes Dredge & Dock Co.	$767.6
Ameresco, Inc.	651.2
Goldfield Corp.	120.6

Annualized Monthly Performance Statistics (%)

Industry
	Geometric Mean	Arithmetic Mean	Standard Deviation
1-year	32.7	35.1	27.4
3-year	1.7	4.7	26.3
5-year	9.9	12.7	25.8

Total Assets (in millions)

Three Largest Companies
Jacobs Engineering Group Inc.	$7,360.0
Mastec, Inc.	3,183.1
Granite Construction Inc.	1,733.5

Three Smallest Companies
Ameresco, Inc.	$797.3
MYR Group Inc.	573.5
Goldfield Corp.	81.2

S&P 500 Index
	Geometric Mean	Arithmetic Mean	Standard Deviation
1-year	17.2	17.4	7.2
3-year	10.4	10.9	11.5
5-year	13.3	13.9	11.5

Return Ratios (%)

	Return on Assets Latest	5-Yr Avg	Return on Equity Latest	5-Yr Avg	Dividend Yield Latest	5-Yr Avg
Median (10)	3.1	3.7	6.0	7.7	0.0	0.0
SIC Composite (10)	3.3	3.5	3.4	4.4	0.3	0.3
Large Composite (3)	3.8	4.1	3.6	4.9	0.2	0.0
Small Composite (3)	0.5	1.1	1.3	2.3	0.0	0.5
High-Financial Risk (−)	−	−	−	−	−	−

Liquidity Ratio

	Current Ratio Latest	5-Yr Avg
	1.7	1.8
	1.8	1.8
	1.7	1.8
	1.5	1.7
	−	−

Profitability Ratio (%)

	Operating Margin Latest	5-Yr Avg
	4.7	5.1
	4.9	4.9
	5.6	5.4
	3.3	3.1
	−	−

Growth Rates (%)

	Long-term EPS Analyst Estimates
	12.6
	14.1
	16.2
	10.6
	−

Betas (Levered)

	Raw (OLS)	Blume Adjusted	Peer Group	Vasicek Adjusted	Sum	Downside
Median	1.38	1.25	1.51	1.45	1.46	1.81
SIC Composite	1.47	1.30	1.51	1.48	1.65	1.49
Large Composite	1.53	1.35	1.51	1.52	1.86	1.56
Small Composite	1.17	1.12	1.51	1.30	1.18	1.54
High Financial Risk	−	−	−	−	−	−

Betas (Unlevered)

	Raw (OLS)	Blume Adjusted	Peer Group	Vasicek Adjusted	Sum	Downside
Median	1.19	1.06	1.28	1.21	1.14	1.49
SIC Composite	1.27	1.13	1.30	1.28	1.42	1.29
Large Composite	1.36	1.20	1.34	1.35	1.64	1.38
Small Composite	0.75	0.72	0.91	0.81	0.75	0.93
High Financial Risk	−	−	−	−	−	−

Equity Valuation Multiples

	Price/Sales Latest	5-Yr Avg	Price/Earnings Latest	5-Yr Avg	Market/Book Latest	5-Yr Avg
Median	0.6	0.6	30.8	23.3	2.3	1.7
SIC Composite	0.7	0.6	29.7	23.0	2.0	1.6
Large Composite	0.7	0.5	27.5	20.4	2.0	1.6
Small Composite	0.4	0.5	78.5	43.0	1.0	1.2
High Financial Risk	−	−	−	−	−	−

Enterprise Valuation (EV) Multiples

	EV/Sales Latest	5-Yr Avg	EV/EBITDA Latest	5-Yr Avg
Median	0.8	0.7	9.7	8.1
SIC Composite	0.8	0.6	10.3	8.3
Large Composite	0.8	0.6	9.6	8.1
Small Composite	0.9	0.9	18.8	11.1
High Financial Risk	−	−	−	−

Enterprise Valuation SIC Composite

Latest: EV/Sales 0.8, EV/EBITDA 10.3
5-Yr Avg: EV/Sales 0.6, EV/EBITDA 8.3

Fama-French (F-F) 5-Factor Model

Fama-French (F-F) Components
	F-F Beta	SMB Premium	HML Premium	RMW Premium	CMA Premium
Median	1.1	4.2	8.8	-3.5	-1.3
SIC Composite	1.3	3.2	3.0	-2.4	-0.5
Large Composite	1.4	2.3	3.2	-3.2	-4.3
Small Composite	0.9	7.7	3.9	0.5	-3.2
High Financial Risk	−	−	−	−	−

Leverage Ratios (%)

	Debt/MV Equity Latest	5-Yr Avg	Debt/Total Capital Latest	5-Yr Avg
Median	23.2	33.5	18.8	25.1
SIC Composite	20.8	23.3	17.2	18.9
Large Composite	16.5	19.7	14.2	16.4
Small Composite	104.8	71.0	51.2	41.5
High Financial Risk	−	−	−	−

Cost of Debt

	Cost of Debt (%) Latest
Median	7.1
SIC Composite	6.7
Large Composite	6.3
Small Composite	7.1
High Financial Risk	−

Capital Structure

SIC Composite (%) Latest
D/TC: 17.2
E/TC: 82.8

Cost of Equity Capital (%)

	CRSP Deciles CAPM	CAPM +Size Prem	Build-Up	Risk Premium Report CAPM +Size Prem	Build-Up	Discounted Cash Flow 1-Stage	3-Stage	Fama-French 5-Factor Model
Median	11.5	13.6	13.7	15.8	14.3	10.3	10.7	17.6
SIC Composite	11.6	13.1	13.3	16.0	13.1	14.4	11.3	14.1
Large Composite	11.8	13.0	13.0	16.8	12.6	16.3	13.4	9.0
Small Composite	10.7	15.0	16.1	15.2	15.7	10.6	5.7	17.3
High Financial Risk	−	−	−	−	−	−	−	−

Cost of Equity Capital (%) SIC Composite
Avg CRSP 13.2, Avg RPR 14.6, 1-Stage 14.4, 3-Stage 11.3, 5-Factor Model 14.1

Weighted Average Cost of Capital (WACC) (%)

	CRSP Deciles CAPM	CAPM +Size Prem	Build-Up	Risk Premium Report CAPM +Size Prem	Build-Up	Discounted Cash Flow 1-Stage	3-Stage	Fama-French 5-Factor Model
Median	10.0	11.3	11.7	13.5	11.7	8.9	9.5	14.8
SIC Composite	10.6	11.8	11.9	14.2	11.8	12.9	10.3	12.6
Large Composite	11.0	12.0	11.9	15.2	11.6	14.8	12.3	8.5
Small Composite	8.5	10.6	11.2	10.7	11.0	8.5	6.1	11.8
High Financial Risk	−	−	−	−	−	−	−	−

WACC (%) SIC Composite
Low 10.3, High 14.2
Average 12.2, Median 11.9

© 2017 Duff & Phelps. All Rights Reserved. Duff & Phelps has used the utmost care in compiling the data presented herein, but cannot guarantee the accuracy, completeness, or timeliness of the information.

Data Updated Through March 31, 2017

162

Number of Companies: 6
Heavy Construction, Except Highway and Street

Industry Description
Contractors primarily engaged in bridge, tunnel, and elevated highway construction; water, sewer, pipeline, communication and power line construction; heavy construction not elsewhere classified.

Sales (in millions)

Three Largest Companies
Mastec, Inc.	$5,134.7
Dycom Industries Inc.	2,672.5
Primoris Services Corp.	1,969.4

Three Smallest Companies
Aegion Corporation	$1,221.9
MYR Group Inc.	1,142.5
Goldfield Corp.	120.6

Total Assets (in millions)

Three Largest Companies
Mastec, Inc.	$3,183.1
Dycom Industries Inc.	1,719.7
Aegion Corporation	1,193.6

Three Smallest Companies
Primoris Services Corp.	$1,170.8
MYR Group Inc.	573.5
Goldfield Corp.	81.2

Annualized Monthly Performance Statistics (%)

Industry	Geometric Mean	Arithmetic Mean	Standard Deviation		S&P 500 Index	Geometric Mean	Arithmetic Mean	Standard Deviation
1-year	47.3	49.1	25.1		1-year	17.2	17.4	7.2
3-year	7.7	11.8	32.1		3-year	10.4	10.9	11.5
5-year	18.1	21.6	29.7		5-year	13.3	13.9	11.5

Return Ratios (%)

	Return on Assets Latest	Return on Assets 5-Yr Avg	Return on Equity Latest	Return on Equity 5-Yr Avg	Dividend Yield Latest	Dividend Yield 5-Yr Avg
Median (6)	4.1	5.3	8.9	11.0	0.0	0.0
SIC Composite (6)	4.3	3.6	3.8	4.3	0.2	0.1
Large Composite (–)	–	–	–	–	–	–
Small Composite (–)	–	–	–	–	–	–
High-Financial Risk (–)	–	–	–	–	–	–

Liquidity Ratio

	Current Ratio Latest	Current Ratio 5-Yr Avg
Median (6)	2.0	1.9
SIC Composite (6)	1.9	1.8
Large Composite (–)	–	–
Small Composite (–)	–	–
High-Financial Risk (–)	–	–

Profitability Ratio (%)

	Operating Margin Latest	Operating Margin 5-Yr Avg
Median (6)	5.3	5.7
SIC Composite (6)	5.5	5.5
Large Composite (–)	–	–
Small Composite (–)	–	–
High-Financial Risk (–)	–	–

Growth Rates (%)

	Long-term EPS Analyst Estimates
Median (6)	14.0
SIC Composite (6)	20.5
Large Composite (–)	–
Small Composite (–)	–
High-Financial Risk (–)	–

Betas (Levered)

	Raw (OLS)	Blume Adjusted	Peer Group	Vasicek Adjusted	Sum	Downside
Median	1.52	1.33	1.51	1.50	1.49	1.81
SIC Composite	1.33	1.21	1.51	1.37	1.60	1.47
Large Composite	–	–	–	–	–	–
Small Composite	–	–	–	–	–	–
High Financial Risk	–	–	–	–	–	–

Betas (Unlevered)

	Raw (OLS)	Blume Adjusted	Peer Group	Vasicek Adjusted	Sum	Downside
Median	1.19	1.06	1.29	1.21	1.20	1.49
SIC Composite	1.11	1.02	1.25	1.14	1.32	1.22
Large Composite	–	–	–	–	–	–
Small Composite	–	–	–	–	–	–
High Financial Risk	–	–	–	–	–	–

Equity Valuation Multiples

	Price/Sales Latest	Price/Sales 5-Yr Avg	Price/Earnings Latest	Price/Earnings 5-Yr Avg	Market/Book Latest	Market/Book 5-Yr Avg
Median	0.6	0.6	28.2	22.3	2.5	1.8
SIC Composite	0.7	0.6	26.3	23.4	2.7	1.9
Large Composite	–	–	–	–	–	–
Small Composite	–	–	–	–	–	–
High Financial Risk	–	–	–	–	–	–

Enterprise Valuation (EV) Multiples

	EV/Sales Latest	EV/Sales 5-Yr Avg	EV/EBITDA Latest	EV/EBITDA 5-Yr Avg
Median	0.8	0.7	9.5	8.0
SIC Composite	0.9	0.7	9.8	7.8
Large Composite	–	–	–	–
Small Composite	–	–	–	–
High Financial Risk	–	–	–	–

Enterprise Valuation SIC Composite
- Latest: EV/Sales 0.9, EV/EBITDA 9.8
- 5-Yr Avg: EV/Sales 0.7, EV/EBITDA 7.8

Fama-French (F-F) 5-Factor Model

	F-F Beta	SMB Premium	HML Premium	RMW Premium	CMA Premium
Median	1.1	4.2	8.8	-3.5	-1.3
SIC Composite	1.2	2.8	4.2	-3.2	-2.0
Large Composite	–	–	–	–	–
Small Composite	–	–	–	–	–
High Financial Risk	–	–	–	–	–

Leverage Ratios (%)

	Debt/MV Equity Latest	Debt/MV Equity 5-Yr Avg	Debt/Total Capital Latest	Debt/Total Capital 5-Yr Avg
Median	23.2	33.5	18.8	25.1
SIC Composite	27.4	33.2	21.5	25.0
Large Composite	–	–	–	–
Small Composite	–	–	–	–
High Financial Risk	–	–	–	–

Cost of Debt

	Cost of Debt (%) Latest
Median	7.1
SIC Composite	6.4
Large Composite	–
Small Composite	–
High Financial Risk	–

Capital Structure

SIC Composite (%) Latest
- D/TC: 21.5
- E/TC: 78.5

Cost of Equity Capital (%)

	CAPM	CRSP Deciles CAPM +Size Prem	CRSP Deciles Build-Up	Risk Premium Report CAPM +Size Prem	Risk Premium Report Build-Up	Discounted Cash Flow 1-Stage	Discounted Cash Flow 3-Stage	Fama-French 5-Factor Model
Median	11.7	13.5	13.7	15.8	14.3	13.2	13.0	17.6
SIC Composite	11.0	12.7	13.5	16.1	13.7	20.6	14.7	11.7
Large Composite	–	–	–	–	–	–	–	–
Small Composite	–	–	–	–	–	–	–	–
High Financial Risk	–	–	–	–	–	–	–	–

Cost of Equity Capital (%) SIC Composite
- Avg CRSP: 13.1
- Avg RPR: 14.9
- 1-Stage: 20.6
- 3-Stage: 14.7
- 5-Factor Model: 11.7

Weighted Average Cost of Capital (WACC) (%)

	CAPM	CRSP Deciles CAPM +Size Prem	CRSP Deciles Build-Up	Risk Premium Report CAPM +Size Prem	Risk Premium Report Build-Up	Discounted Cash Flow 1-Stage	Discounted Cash Flow 3-Stage	Fama-French 5-Factor Model
Median	10.0	11.3	11.7	13.5	12.1	11.5	11.6	14.8
SIC Composite	9.7	11.0	11.6	13.7	11.7	17.2	12.5	10.2
Large Composite	–	–	–	–	–	–	–	–
Small Composite	–	–	–	–	–	–	–	–
High Financial Risk	–	–	–	–	–	–	–	–

WACC (%) SIC Composite
- Low: 10.2
- High: 17.2
- Average: 12.6
- Median: 11.7

© 2017 Duff & Phelps. All Rights Reserved. Duff & Phelps has used the utmost care in compiling the data presented herein, but cannot guarantee the accuracy, completeness, or timeliness of the information.

Division D: Manufacturing

The manufacturing division includes establishments engaged in the mechanical or chemical transformation of materials or substances into new products. Major groups between "20" and "39" are in this division.

Data Updated Through March 31, 2017

2

Number of Companies: 237
Manufacturing

Industry Description

The manufacturing division includes establishments engaged in the mechanical or chemical transformation of materials or substances into new products. These establishments are usually described as plants, factories, or mills and characteristically use power driven machines and materials handling equipment. Establishments engaged in assembling component parts of manufactured products are also considered manufacturing if the new product is neither a structure nor other fixed improvement. Also included is the blending of materials, such as lubricating oils, plastics resins, or liquors.

Sales (in millions)

Three Largest Companies
Exxon Mobil Corp.	$197,518.0
Chevron Corp.	103,310.0
Phillips 66	70,898.0

Three Smallest Companies
Flexible Solutions International Inc.	$15.9
United-Guardian Inc.	14.0
ImmuCell Corp.	10.2

Annualized Monthly Performance Statistics (%)

Industry
	Geometric Mean	Arithmetic Mean	Standard Deviation
1-year	9.1	9.3	7.1
3-year	7.2	7.7	10.8
5-year	12.1	12.6	11.4

Total Assets (in millions)

Three Largest Companies
Exxon Mobil Corp.	$330,314.0
Chevron Corp.	260,078.0
Pfizer Inc.	171,615.0

Three Smallest Companies
United-Guardian Inc.	$15.7
ImmuCell Corp.	14.6
Flexible Solutions International Inc.	14.1

S&P 500 Index
	Geometric Mean	Arithmetic Mean	Standard Deviation
1-year	17.2	17.4	7.2
3-year	10.4	10.9	11.5
5-year	13.3	13.9	11.5

Return Ratios (%)

	Return on Assets Latest	Return on Assets 5-Yr Avg	Return on Equity Latest	Return on Equity 5-Yr Avg	Dividend Yield Latest	Dividend Yield 5-Yr Avg	Current Ratio Latest	Current Ratio 5-Yr Avg	Operating Margin Latest	Operating Margin 5-Yr Avg	Long-term EPS Analyst Estimates
Median (237)	7.3	7.2	13.5	13.3	1.6	1.6	2.1	2.3	12.2	11.0	9.2
SIC Composite (237)	6.1	7.4	4.2	5.3	2.7	2.6	1.5	1.5	13.3	12.9	13.5
Large Composite (23)	5.6	7.3	4.2	5.7	3.1	3.0	1.4	1.4	12.2	12.4	14.8
Small Composite (23)	4.2	9.1	1.7	4.3	0.0	0.0	2.2	2.8	14.6	14.4	23.2
High-Financial Risk (30)	-4.9	-2.1	-10.6	-4.2	1.1	2.7	1.4	1.7	4.9	5.7	11.1

Betas (Levered)

	Raw (OLS)	Blume Adjusted	Peer Group	Vasicek Adjusted	Sum	Downside
Median	1.07	1.05	0.98	1.03	1.10	1.41
SIC Composite	0.93	0.96	0.98	0.93	0.92	0.92
Large Composite	0.92	0.96	1.00	0.92	0.91	0.91
Small Composite	1.18	1.12	0.95	1.16	1.43	1.45
High Financial Risk	1.17	1.12	0.94	1.17	1.27	1.25

Betas (Unlevered)

	Raw (OLS)	Blume Adjusted	Peer Group	Vasicek Adjusted	Sum	Downside
Median	0.90	0.88	0.86	0.86	0.94	1.15
SIC Composite	0.79	0.82	0.83	0.79	0.78	0.78
Large Composite	0.78	0.80	0.84	0.78	0.76	0.76
Small Composite	1.12	1.06	0.90	1.09	1.34	1.36
High Financial Risk	0.72	0.69	0.61	0.72	0.76	0.75

Equity Valuation Multiples

	Price/Sales Latest	Price/Sales 5-Yr Avg	Price/Earnings Latest	Price/Earnings 5-Yr Avg	Market/Book Latest	Market/Book 5-Yr Avg
Median	1.5	1.4	22.6	21.3	3.0	2.6
SIC Composite	2.3	1.7	24.1	19.0	3.1	2.9
Large Composite	2.3	1.6	24.1	17.6	2.8	2.5
Small Composite	4.1	3.0	57.9	23.4	3.6	3.0
High Financial Risk	0.5	0.6	–	–	2.3	2.0

Enterprise Valuation (EV) Multiples

	EV/Sales Latest	EV/Sales 5-Yr Avg	EV/EBITDA Latest	EV/EBITDA 5-Yr Avg
Median	1.8	1.5	10.5	9.8
SIC Composite	2.5	1.9	12.2	9.7
Large Composite	2.5	1.8	11.8	9.0
Small Composite	4.0	2.8	20.1	14.8
High Financial Risk	1.1	1.0	10.5	9.2

Enterprise Valuation SIC Composite
Latest: EV/Sales 2.5, EV/EBITDA 12.2
5-Yr Avg: EV/Sales 1.9, EV/EBITDA 9.7

Fama-French (F-F) 5-Factor Model

Fama-French (F-F) Components
	F-F Beta	SMB Premium	HML Premium	RMW Premium	CMA Premium
Median	0.1	4.9	-0.2	6.2	-2.1
SIC Composite	0.9	-0.4	-1.5	-0.3	2.3
Large Composite	1.0	-0.8	-1.3	-0.4	-0.5
Small Composite	1.1	4.8	-5.0	0.3	2.3
High Financial Risk	–	–	–	–	–

Leverage Ratios (%)

	Debt/MV Equity Latest	Debt/MV Equity 5-Yr Avg	Debt/Total Capital Latest	Debt/Total Capital 5-Yr Avg
Median	17.6	16.0	15.0	13.8
SIC Composite	19.5	17.9	16.3	15.2
Large Composite	19.3	17.4	16.2	14.8
Small Composite	8.0	7.0	7.4	6.5
High Financial Risk	118.0	93.8	54.1	48.4

Cost of Debt

	Cost of Debt (%) Latest
Median	6.1
SIC Composite	4.5
Large Composite	4.1
Small Composite	6.7
High Financial Risk	7.1

Capital Structure

SIC Composite (%) Latest
D/TC: 16.3
E/TC: 83.7

Cost of Equity Capital (%)

	CAPM	CRSP Deciles CAPM +Size Prem	CRSP Deciles Build-Up	Risk Premium Report CAPM +Size Prem	Risk Premium Report Build-Up	Discounted Cash Flow 1-Stage	Discounted Cash Flow 3-Stage	Fama-French 5-Factor Model
Median	9.1	11.0	10.7	13.4	13.8	11.1	9.4	12.8
SIC Composite	8.6	8.8	9.1	10.1	10.2	16.4	9.8	8.9
Large Composite	8.6	8.6	9.1	9.5	9.4	18.4	9.5	5.9
Small Composite	9.9	12.4	12.0	16.3	15.4	23.2	14.3	11.8
High Financial Risk	–	–	–	22.0	23.7	–	–	–

Cost of Equity Capital (%) SIC Composite
Avg CRSP: 9.0, Avg RPR: 10.1, 1-Stage: 16.4, 3-Stage: 9.8, 5-Factor Model: 8.9

Weighted Average Cost of Capital (WACC) (%)

	CAPM	CRSP Deciles CAPM +Size Prem	CRSP Deciles Build-Up	Risk Premium Report CAPM +Size Prem	Risk Premium Report Build-Up	Discounted Cash Flow 1-Stage	Discounted Cash Flow 3-Stage	Fama-French 5-Factor Model
Median	8.3	9.7	9.5	11.8	11.9	10.3	8.5	11.2
SIC Composite	7.8	8.0	8.3	9.1	9.1	14.3	8.8	8.0
Large Composite	7.7	7.8	8.1	8.5	8.4	15.9	8.5	5.5
Small Composite	9.6	11.9	11.6	15.5	14.7	21.9	13.7	11.4
High Financial Risk	–	–	–	13.6	14.3	–	–	–

WACC (%) SIC Composite
Low 8.0, High 14.3, Average 9.4, Median 8.8

© 2017 Duff & Phelps. All Rights Reserved. Duff & Phelps has used the utmost care in compiling the data presented herein, but cannot guarantee the accuracy, completeness, or timeliness of the information.

Data Updated Through March 31, 2017

20

Number of Companies: 47
Food and Kindred Products

Industry Description
This major group includes establishments manufacturing or processing foods and beverages for human consumption, and certain related products, such as manufactured ice, chewing gum, vegetable and animal fats and oils, and prepared feeds for animals and fowls.

Sales (in millions)

Three Largest Companies
Pepsico, Inc.	$62,799.0
Archer-Daniels-Midland Co.	62,346.0
Coca-Cola Co.	41,863.0

Three Smallest Companies
Lifeway Foods Inc.	$118.6
SkyPeople Fruit Juice, Inc.	86.4
Willamette Valley Vineyards	17.9

Annualized Monthly Performance Statistics (%)

Industry	Geometric Mean	Arithmetic Mean	Standard Deviation
1-year	3.8	4.3	10.0
3-year	10.2	10.8	11.9
5-year	12.1	12.7	11.9

Total Assets (in millions)

Three Largest Companies
Coca-Cola Co.	$87,270.0
Pepsico, Inc.	74,129.0
Mondelez International Inc.	61,538.0

Three Smallest Companies
Bridgford Foods Corp.	$87.3
Lifeway Foods Inc.	64.9
Willamette Valley Vineyards	38.7

S&P 500 Index	Geometric Mean	Arithmetic Mean	Standard Deviation
1-year	17.2	17.4	7.2
3-year	10.4	10.9	11.5
5-year	13.3	13.9	11.5

Return Ratios (%)

	Return on Assets Latest	Return on Assets 5-Yr Avg	Return on Equity Latest	Return on Equity 5-Yr Avg	Dividend Yield Latest	Dividend Yield 5-Yr Avg
Median (47)	7.4	6.3	16.1	11.6	1.8	1.8
SIC Composite (47)	6.6	6.8	4.0	4.5	2.5	2.5
Large Composite (4)	7.1	7.4	4.1	4.7	3.0	2.8
Small Composite (4)	3.2	5.4	4.3	5.7	0.0	0.1
High-Financial Risk (5)	1.0	0.0	1.3	0.1	0.0	0.0

Liquidity Ratio / Profitability Ratio (%) / Growth Rates (%)

	Current Ratio Latest	Current Ratio 5-Yr Avg	Operating Margin Latest	Operating Margin 5-Yr Avg	Long-term EPS Analyst Estimates
Median (47)	2.0	2.0	13.2	10.8	6.9
SIC Composite (47)	1.2	1.3	13.0	11.9	6.9
Large Composite (4)	1.4	1.3	12.3	11.0	5.1
Small Composite (4)	2.1	2.7	8.6	9.4	8.3
High-Financial Risk (5)	2.6	2.5	10.5	9.6	8.7

Betas (Levered)

	Raw (OLS)	Blume Adjusted	Peer Group	Vasicek Adjusted	Sum	Downside
Median	0.60	0.75	0.65	0.62	0.68	0.97
SIC Composite	0.65	0.78	0.65	0.65	0.59	0.66
Large Composite	0.63	0.77	0.65	0.63	0.56	0.64
Small Composite	0.61	0.76	0.65	0.61	1.22	0.94
High Financial Risk	0.59	0.74	0.68	0.62	0.74	0.96

Betas (Unlevered)

	Raw (OLS)	Blume Adjusted	Peer Group	Vasicek Adjusted	Sum	Downside
Median	0.55	0.66	0.55	0.56	0.54	0.84
SIC Composite	0.54	0.64	0.53	0.54	0.48	0.54
Large Composite	0.50	0.62	0.52	0.51	0.45	0.51
Small Composite	0.53	0.65	0.56	0.53	1.04	0.80
High Financial Risk	0.48	0.58	0.54	0.50	0.58	0.72

Equity Valuation Multiples

	Price/Sales Latest	Price/Sales 5-Yr Avg	Price/Earnings Latest	Price/Earnings 5-Yr Avg	Market/Book Latest	Market/Book 5-Yr Avg
Median	1.9	1.3	24.7	23.2	3.3	2.8
SIC Composite	2.0	1.7	24.9	22.0	4.4	3.6
Large Composite	1.9	1.6	24.5	21.3	5.3	4.1
Small Composite	0.9	1.1	23.5	17.6	1.2	1.4
High Financial Risk	1.2	1.4	95.4	–	1.7	1.7

Enterprise Valuation (EV) Multiples

	EV/Sales Latest	EV/Sales 5-Yr Avg	EV/EBITDA Latest	EV/EBITDA 5-Yr Avg
Median	1.9	1.6	12.6	11.8
SIC Composite	2.4	1.9	13.9	12.5
Large Composite	2.2	1.8	13.5	12.3
Small Composite	0.9	1.0	7.3	7.8
High Financial Risk	1.8	2.1	13.6	16.0

Enterprise Valuation SIC Composite
- Latest: EV/Sales 2.4, EV/EBITDA 13.9
- 5-Yr Avg: EV/Sales 1.9, EV/EBITDA 12.5

Fama-French (F-F) 5-Factor Model

	F-F Beta	SMB Premium	HML Premium	RMW Premium	CMA Premium
Median	0.9	0.1	1.5	-3.0	1.8
SIC Composite	0.7	-1.3	-2.6	0.7	3.0
Large Composite	0.8	-1.8	-2.4	1.2	1.7
Small Composite	0.6	3.7	-2.1	1.9	2.0
High Financial Risk	–	–	–	–	–

Leverage Ratios (%)

	Debt/MV Equity Latest	Debt/MV Equity 5-Yr Avg	Debt/Total Capital Latest	Debt/Total Capital 5-Yr Avg
Median	22.4	21.3	18.3	17.6
SIC Composite	23.7	23.3	19.2	18.9
Large Composite	24.6	23.8	19.7	19.2
Small Composite	20.0	13.4	16.7	11.8
High Financial Risk	58.3	52.5	36.8	34.4

Cost of Debt

	Cost of Debt (%) Latest
Median	4.8
SIC Composite	4.4
Large Composite	4.0
Small Composite	5.1
High Financial Risk	6.9

Capital Structure

SIC Composite (%) Latest
- D/TC: 19.2
- E/TC: 80.8

Cost of Equity Capital (%)

	CRSP Deciles CAPM	CRSP Deciles CAPM +Size Prem	CRSP Deciles Build-Up	Risk Premium Report CAPM +Size Prem	Risk Premium Report Build-Up	Discounted Cash Flow 1-Stage	Discounted Cash Flow 3-Stage	Fama-French 5-Factor Model
Median	6.9	8.3	8.0	10.4	13.0	10.2	8.1	8.8
SIC Composite	7.1	7.3	7.3	8.6	10.6	9.3	8.2	7.2
Large Composite	7.0	7.0	7.1	7.9	9.8	8.1	7.7	6.5
Small Composite	6.9	12.5	12.7	16.1	16.7	8.3	10.7	12.1
High Financial Risk	–	–	–	19.0	23.4	–	–	–

Cost of Equity Capital (%) SIC Composite
- Avg CRSP: 7.3
- Avg RPR: 9.6
- 1-Stage: 9.3
- 3-Stage: 8.2
- 5-Factor Model: 7.2

Weighted Average Cost of Capital (WACC) (%)

	CRSP Deciles CAPM	CRSP Deciles CAPM +Size Prem	CRSP Deciles Build-Up	Risk Premium Report CAPM +Size Prem	Risk Premium Report Build-Up	Discounted Cash Flow 1-Stage	Discounted Cash Flow 3-Stage	Fama-French 5-Factor Model
Median	6.6	7.5	7.3	9.1	11.0	9.5	7.6	8.7
SIC Composite	6.5	6.7	6.7	7.7	9.4	8.3	7.5	6.6
Large Composite	6.4	6.4	6.5	7.1	8.7	7.3	7.0	6.0
Small Composite	6.4	11.0	11.2	14.1	14.5	7.6	9.5	10.7
High Financial Risk	–	–	–	14.4	17.3	–	–	–

WACC (%) SIC Composite
- Low: 6.6
- High: 9.4
- Average: 7.6
- Median: 7.5

© 2017 Duff & Phelps. All Rights Reserved. Duff & Phelps has used the utmost care in compiling the data presented herein, but cannot guarantee the accuracy, completeness, or timeliness of the information.

Data Updated Through March 31, 2017

201

Number of Companies: 5
Meat Products

Industry Description
Establishments primarily engaged in processing or manufacturing meat products including meat packing plants; sausages and other prepared meat products; poultry slaughtering and processing.

Sales (in millions)

Three Largest Companies
Tyson Foods, Inc.	$36,881.0
Hormel Foods Corp.	9,523.2
Pilgrim's Pride Corp.	7,931.1

Three Smallest Companies
Pilgrim's Pride Corp.	$7,931.1
Sanderson Farms Inc.	2,816.1
Bridgford Foods Corp.	140.1

Total Assets (in millions)

Three Largest Companies
Tyson Foods, Inc.	$22,373.0
Hormel Foods Corp.	6,370.1
Pilgrim's Pride Corp.	3,008.2

Three Smallest Companies
Pilgrim's Pride Corp.	$3,008.2
Sanderson Farms Inc.	1,422.7
Bridgford Foods Corp.	87.3

Annualized Monthly Performance Statistics (%)

Industry	Geometric Mean	Arithmetic Mean	Standard Deviation	S&P 500 Index	Geometric Mean	Arithmetic Mean	Standard Deviation
1-year	-9.8	-7.9	19.3	1-year	17.2	17.4	7.2
3-year	13.9	15.8	21.3	3-year	10.4	10.9	11.5
5-year	25.0	27.4	24.6	5-year	13.3	13.9	11.5

Return Ratios (%)

	Return on Assets Latest	5-Yr Avg	Return on Equity Latest	5-Yr Avg	Dividend Yield Latest	5-Yr Avg
Median (5)	13.9	12.1	20.8	18.4	1.7	1.6
SIC Composite (5)	9.9	8.3	6.8	6.6	2.6	2.4
Large Composite (–)	–	–	–	–	–	–
Small Composite (–)	–	–	–	–	–	–
High-Financial Risk (–)	–	–	–	–	–	–

Liquidity Ratio

	Current Ratio Latest	5-Yr Avg
	1.9	2.2
	1.8	1.9
	–	–
	–	–
	–	–

Profitability Ratio (%)

	Operating Margin Latest	5-Yr Avg
	9.0	9.4
	9.0	6.8
	–	–
	–	–
	–	–

Growth Rates (%)

	Long-term EPS Analyst Estimates
	6.9
	6.0
	–
	–
	–

Betas (Levered)

	Raw (OLS)	Blume Adjusted	Peer Group	Vasicek Adjusted	Sum	Downside
Median	0.42	0.64	0.65	0.58	0.10	0.89
SIC Composite	0.28	0.55	0.65	0.52	0.13	0.52
Large Composite	–	–	–	–	–	–
Small Composite	–	–	–	–	–	–
High Financial Risk	–	–	–	–	–	–

Betas (Unlevered)

	Raw (OLS)	Blume Adjusted	Peer Group	Vasicek Adjusted	Sum	Downside
Median	0.41	0.63	0.64	0.58	0.13	0.84
SIC Composite	0.26	0.49	0.58	0.47	0.13	0.47
Large Composite	–	–	–	–	–	–
Small Composite	–	–	–	–	–	–
High Financial Risk	–	–	–	–	–	–

Equity Valuation Multiples

	Price/Sales Latest	5-Yr Avg	Price/Earnings Latest	5-Yr Avg	Market/Book Latest	5-Yr Avg
Median	0.7	0.6	12.7	14.1	2.7	2.8
SIC Composite	0.8	0.6	14.7	15.0	2.6	2.3
Large Composite	–	–	–	–	–	–
Small Composite	–	–	–	–	–	–
High Financial Risk	–	–	–	–	–	–

Enterprise Valuation (EV) Multiples

	EV/Sales Latest	5-Yr Avg	EV/EBITDA Latest	5-Yr Avg
Median	0.8	0.6	7.2	7.8
SIC Composite	1.0	0.7	8.7	8.3
Large Composite	–	–	–	–
Small Composite	–	–	–	–
High Financial Risk	–	–	–	–

Enterprise Valuation SIC Composite
- EV/Sales: Latest 1.0, 5-Yr Avg 0.7
- EV/EBITDA: Latest 8.7, 5-Yr Avg 8.3

Fama-French (F-F) 5-Factor Model

	F-F Beta	SMB Premium	HML Premium	RMW Premium	CMA Premium
Median	0.5	-0.1	-4.8	-0.9	4.7
SIC Composite	–	–	–	–	–
Large Composite	–	–	–	–	–
Small Composite	–	–	–	–	–
High Financial Risk	–	–	–	–	–

Leverage Ratios (%)

	Debt/MV Equity Latest	5-Yr Avg	Debt/Total Capital Latest	5-Yr Avg
Median	1.4	2.7	1.3	2.6
SIC Composite	15.6	17.8	13.5	15.1

Cost of Debt

	Cost of Debt (%) Latest
Median	6.1
SIC Composite	4.9

Capital Structure

SIC Composite (%) Latest
- D/TC: 13.5
- E/TC: 86.5

Cost of Equity Capital (%)

	CRSP Deciles CAPM	CAPM +Size Prem	Build-Up	Risk Premium Report CAPM +Size Prem	Build-Up	Discounted Cash Flow 1-Stage	3-Stage	Fama-French 5-Factor Model
Median	6.7	7.8	8.0	6.9	12.2	11.4	8.9	5.3
SIC Composite	6.4	7.1	7.8	6.6	11.4	9.0	9.3	–
Large Composite	–	–	–	–	–	–	–	–
Small Composite	–	–	–	–	–	–	–	–
High Financial Risk	–	–	–	–	–	–	–	–

Cost of Equity Capital (%) SIC Composite
- Avg CRSP: 7.4
- Avg RPR: 9.0
- 1-Stage: 9.0
- 3-Stage: 9.3
- 5-Factor Model: n/a

Weighted Average Cost of Capital (WACC) (%)

	CRSP Deciles CAPM	CAPM +Size Prem	Build-Up	Risk Premium Report CAPM +Size Prem	Build-Up	Discounted Cash Flow 1-Stage	3-Stage	Fama-French 5-Factor Model
Median	6.7	7.8	7.7	6.8	11.5	11.3	8.9	5.3
SIC Composite	6.1	6.7	7.3	6.3	10.4	8.3	8.6	–
Large Composite	–	–	–	–	–	–	–	–
Small Composite	–	–	–	–	–	–	–	–
High Financial Risk	–	–	–	–	–	–	–	–

WACC (%) SIC Composite
- Low: 6.3, High: 10.4
- Average 7.9, Median 7.8

© 2017 Duff & Phelps. All Rights Reserved. Duff & Phelps has used the utmost care in compiling the data presented herein, but cannot guarantee the accuracy, completeness, or timeliness of the information.

Data Updated Through March 31, 2017

206

Number of Companies: 5
Sugar and Confectionery Products

Industry Description
Establishments primarily engaged in cane sugar; cane sugar refining; beet sugar; candy and other confectionery products; chocolate and cocoa products; chewing gum; salted and roasted nuts and seeds.

Sales (in millions)

Three Largest Companies
Hershey Co.	$7,440.2
Treehouse Foods, Inc.	6,185.0
John B Sanfilippo & Son	952.1

Three Smallest Companies
John B Sanfilippo & Son	$952.1
Tootsie Roll Industries Inc.	521.1
American Lorain Corp.	215.3

Total Assets (in millions)

Three Largest Companies
Treehouse Foods, Inc.	$6,545.8
Hershey Co.	5,524.3
Tootsie Roll Industries Inc.	920.1

Three Smallest Companies
Tootsie Roll Industries Inc.	$920.1
John B Sanfilippo & Son	391.4
American Lorain Corp.	309.5

Annualized Monthly Performance Statistics (%)

Industry	Geometric Mean	Arithmetic Mean	Standard Deviation
1-year	16.0	18.9	28.0
3-year	4.9	6.3	18.2
5-year	14.1	15.5	18.2

S&P 500 Index	Geometric Mean	Arithmetic Mean	Standard Deviation
1-year	17.2	17.4	7.2
3-year	10.4	10.9	11.5
5-year	13.3	13.9	11.5

Return Ratios (%)

	Return on Assets Latest	5-Yr Avg	Return on Equity Latest	5-Yr Avg	Dividend Yield Latest	5-Yr Avg
Median (5)	7.4	6.4	9.0	8.5	1.7	1.8
SIC Composite (5)	4.3	7.8	1.9	3.3	2.0	1.9
Large Composite (−)	−	−	−	−	−	−
Small Composite (−)	−	−	−	−	−	−
High-Financial Risk (−)	−	−	−	−	−	−

Liquidity Ratio

	Current Ratio Latest	5-Yr Avg
Median (5)	2.3	2.7
SIC Composite (5)	1.4	1.6
Large Composite (−)	−	−
Small Composite (−)	−	−
High-Financial Risk (−)	−	−

Profitability Ratio (%)

	Operating Margin Latest	5-Yr Avg
Median (5)	6.5	10.4
SIC Composite (5)	12.0	14.5
Large Composite (−)	−	−
Small Composite (−)	−	−
High-Financial Risk (−)	−	−

Growth Rates (%)

	Long-term EPS Analyst Estimates
Median (5)	6.9
SIC Composite (5)	8.9
Large Composite (−)	−
Small Composite (−)	−
High-Financial Risk (−)	−

Betas (Levered)

	Raw (OLS)	Blume Adjusted	Peer Group	Vasicek Adjusted	Sum	Downside
Median	0.57	0.74	0.65	0.64	0.57	0.94
SIC Composite	0.41	0.63	0.65	0.55	0.24	0.57
Large Composite	−	−	−	−	−	−
Small Composite	−	−	−	−	−	−
High Financial Risk	−	−	−	−	−	−

Betas (Unlevered)

	Raw (OLS)	Blume Adjusted	Peer Group	Vasicek Adjusted	Sum	Downside
Median	0.47	0.57	0.58	0.50	0.38	0.57
SIC Composite	0.37	0.56	0.57	0.49	0.23	0.50
Large Composite	−	−	−	−	−	−
Small Composite	−	−	−	−	−	−
High Financial Risk	−	−	−	−	−	−

Equity Valuation Multiples

	Price/Sales Latest	5-Yr Avg	Price/Earnings Latest	5-Yr Avg	Market/Book Latest	5-Yr Avg
Median	0.9	1.0	32.2	28.4	3.1	1.8
SIC Composite	2.0	2.1	52.6	30.7	6.3	5.9
Large Composite	−	−	−	−	−	−
Small Composite	−	−	−	−	−	−
High Financial Risk	−	−	−	−	−	−

Enterprise Valuation (EV) Multiples

	EV/Sales Latest	5-Yr Avg	EV/EBITDA Latest	5-Yr Avg
Median	1.2	1.4	13.0	11.9
SIC Composite	2.4	2.4	14.9	13.4
Large Composite	−	−	−	−
Small Composite	−	−	−	−
High Financial Risk	−	−	−	−

Enterprise Valuation SIC Composite
- EV/Sales: Latest 2.4, 5-Yr Avg 2.4
- EV/EBITDA: Latest 14.9, 5-Yr Avg 13.4

Fama-French (F-F) 5-Factor Model

	F-F Beta	SMB Premium	HML Premium	RMW Premium	CMA Premium
Median	0.6	1.1	−2.8	2.8	−0.3
SIC Composite	0.4	−0.1	−4.8	−0.3	5.6
Large Composite	−	−	−	−	−
Small Composite	−	−	−	−	−
High Financial Risk	−	−	−	−	−

Leverage Ratios (%)

	Debt/MV Equity Latest	5-Yr Avg	Debt/Total Capital Latest	5-Yr Avg
Median	12.9	18.8	11.4	15.8
SIC Composite	18.9	15.2	15.9	13.2
Large Composite	−	−	−	−
Small Composite	−	−	−	−
High Financial Risk	−	−	−	−

Cost of Debt

	Cost of Debt (%) Latest
Median	6.1
SIC Composite	5.1
Large Composite	−
Small Composite	−
High Financial Risk	−

Capital Structure

SIC Composite (%) Latest
- D/TC: 15.9
- E/TC: 84.1

Cost of Equity Capital (%)

	CRSP Deciles CAPM	CAPM +Size Prem	Build-Up	Risk Premium Report CAPM +Size Prem	Build-Up	Discounted Cash Flow 1-Stage	3-Stage	Fama-French 5-Factor Model
Median	7.0	8.9	8.7	10.1	13.9	11.3	7.5	7.7
SIC Composite	6.5	7.3	7.9	7.6	12.0	11.0	7.7	6.3
Large Composite	−	−	−	−	−	−	−	−
Small Composite	−	−	−	−	−	−	−	−
High Financial Risk	−	−	−	−	−	−	−	−

Cost of Equity Capital (%) SIC Composite
- Avg CRSP: 7.6
- Avg RPR: 9.8
- 1-Stage: 11.0
- 3-Stage: 7.7
- 5-Factor Model: 6.3

Weighted Average Cost of Capital (WACC) (%)

	CRSP Deciles CAPM	CAPM +Size Prem	Build-Up	Risk Premium Report CAPM +Size Prem	Build-Up	Discounted Cash Flow 1-Stage	3-Stage	Fama-French 5-Factor Model
Median	6.6	7.2	7.3	7.1	10.5	9.8	7.2	10.1
SIC Composite	6.1	6.7	7.2	7.0	10.7	9.8	7.0	5.9
Large Composite	−	−	−	−	−	−	−	−
Small Composite	−	−	−	−	−	−	−	−
High Financial Risk	−	−	−	−	−	−	−	−

WACC (%) SIC Composite
- Low: 5.9
- High: 10.7
- Average 7.8
- Median 7.0

© 2017 Duff & Phelps. All Rights Reserved. Duff & Phelps has used the utmost care in compiling the data presented herein, but cannot guarantee the accuracy, completeness, or timeliness of the information.

Data Updated Through March 31, 2017

208

Number of Companies: 12
Beverages

Industry Description
Establishments primarily engaged in manufacturing malt beverages; malt; wines, brandy, and brandy spirits; distilled and blended liquors; bottled and canned soft drinks and carbonated waters; flavoring extracts and flavoring syrups.

Sales (in millions)

Three Largest Companies
Coca-Cola Co.	$41,863.0
Dr Pepper Snapple Group, Inc.	6,440.0
Molson Coors Brewing Co.	4,885.0

Three Smallest Companies
Craft Brew Alliance, Inc.	$204.2
SkyPeople Fruit Juice, Inc.	86.4
Willamette Valley Vineyards	17.9

Total Assets (in millions)

Three Largest Companies
Coca-Cola Co.	$87,270.0
Molson Coors Brewing Co.	29,341.5
Dr Pepper Snapple Group, Inc.	9,791.0

Three Smallest Companies
MGP Ingredients Inc.	$194.3
Craft Brew Alliance, Inc.	190.3
Willamette Valley Vineyards	38.7

Annualized Monthly Performance Statistics (%)

Industry	Geometric Mean	Arithmetic Mean	Standard Deviation	S&P 500 Index	Geometric Mean	Arithmetic Mean	Standard Deviation
1-year	-2.0	-1.7	7.4	1-year	17.2	17.4	7.2
3-year	9.2	10.1	14.2	3-year	10.4	10.9	11.5
5-year	8.9	9.8	14.1	5-year	13.3	13.9	11.5

Return Ratios (%)

	Return on Assets Latest	Return on Assets 5-Yr Avg	Return on Equity Latest	Return on Equity 5-Yr Avg	Dividend Yield Latest	Dividend Yield 5-Yr Avg
Median (12)	9.3	7.0	18.2	16.1	1.1	1.5
SIC Composite (12)	8.2	8.5	4.2	4.3	2.7	2.7
Large Composite (3)	7.4	8.0	4.2	4.5	3.1	2.9
Small Composite (3)	1.4	3.8	2.2	5.8	–	–
High-Financial Risk (–)	–	–	–	–	–	–

Liquidity Ratio / Profitability Ratio (%) / Growth Rates (%)

	Current Ratio Latest	Current Ratio 5-Yr Avg	Operating Margin Latest	Operating Margin 5-Yr Avg	Long-term EPS Analyst Estimates
Median (12)	2.2	2.1	14.9	16.1	6.0
SIC Composite (12)	1.3	1.2	22.7	22.1	5.8
Large Composite (3)	1.3	1.1	22.7	22.2	3.7
Small Composite (3)	1.6	2.1	6.5	9.0	21.2
High-Financial Risk	–	–	–	–	–

Betas (Levered)

	Raw (OLS)	Blume Adjusted	Peer Group	Vasicek Adjusted	Sum	Downside
Median	0.66	0.79	0.65	0.65	0.63	1.21
SIC Composite	0.68	0.81	0.65	0.68	0.59	0.76
Large Composite	0.66	0.79	0.65	0.66	0.55	0.75
Small Composite	0.61	0.76	0.65	0.61	1.65	1.32
High Financial Risk	–	–	–	–	–	–

Betas (Unlevered)

	Raw (OLS)	Blume Adjusted	Peer Group	Vasicek Adjusted	Sum	Downside
Median	0.59	0.68	0.57	0.55	0.55	0.99
SIC Composite	0.56	0.65	0.53	0.56	0.48	0.62
Large Composite	0.52	0.62	0.51	0.52	0.43	0.59
Small Composite	0.51	0.63	0.55	0.52	1.35	1.08
High Financial Risk	–	–	–	–	–	–

Equity Valuation Multiples

	Price/Sales Latest	Price/Sales 5-Yr Avg	Price/Earnings Latest	Price/Earnings 5-Yr Avg	Market/Book Latest	Market/Book 5-Yr Avg
Median	2.8	2.1	24.4	25.4	5.0	3.4
SIC Composite	4.2	3.8	24.0	23.3	5.5	4.7
Large Composite	4.1	3.7	23.6	22.4	5.1	4.4
Small Composite	1.0	1.0	45.8	17.4	0.9	0.9
High Financial Risk	–	–	–	–	–	–

Enterprise Valuation (EV) Multiples

	EV/Sales Latest	EV/Sales 5-Yr Avg	EV/EBITDA Latest	EV/EBITDA 5-Yr Avg
Median	3.0	2.3	16.2	14.2
SIC Composite	4.8	4.2	16.3	14.5
Large Composite	4.9	4.2	15.7	14.0
Small Composite	1.1	1.0	8.7	6.6
High Financial Risk	–	–	–	–

Enterprise Valuation SIC Composite
Latest: EV/Sales 4.8, EV/EBITDA 16.3
5-Yr Avg: EV/Sales 4.2, EV/EBITDA 14.5

Fama-French (F-F) 5-Factor Model

	F-F Beta	SMB Premium	HML Premium	RMW Premium	CMA Premium
Median	0.9	-0.5	-3.2	0.3	2.5
SIC Composite	0.8	-1.4	-2.8	1.2	2.2
Large Composite	0.8	-1.8	-2.4	1.3	1.8
Small Composite	0.4	4.8	2.4	2.4	-5.2
High Financial Risk	–	–	–	–	–

Leverage Ratios (%)

	Debt/MV Equity Latest	Debt/MV Equity 5-Yr Avg	Debt/Total Capital Latest	Debt/Total Capital 5-Yr Avg
Median	16.0	13.9	13.4	12.0
SIC Composite	23.7	20.5	19.2	17.0
Large Composite	28.2	23.7	22.0	19.2
Small Composite	24.6	19.4	19.8	16.3
High Financial Risk	–	–	–	–

Cost of Debt / Capital Structure

	Cost of Debt (%) Latest	SIC Composite (%) Latest
Median	4.8	
SIC Composite	4.1	D/TC 19.2, E/TC 80.8
Large Composite	4.1	
Small Composite	5.1	
High Financial Risk	–	

Cost of Equity Capital (%)

	CRSP Deciles CAPM	CRSP Deciles CAPM +Size Prem	CRSP Deciles Build-Up	Risk Premium Report CAPM +Size Prem	Risk Premium Report Build-Up	Discounted Cash Flow 1-Stage	Discounted Cash Flow 3-Stage	Fama-French 5-Factor Model
Median	7.1	8.5	8.4	11.1	13.9	7.0	7.5	7.7
SIC Composite	7.3	7.4	7.2	8.3	10.4	8.5	7.8	6.8
Large Composite	7.1	7.2	7.2	7.7	9.9	6.9	7.3	6.8
Small Composite	6.9	12.5	12.7	18.4	16.6	21.2	15.6	10.3
High Financial Risk	–	–	–	–	–	–	–	–

Cost of Equity Capital (%) SIC Composite
Avg CRSP 7.3, Avg RPR 9.3, 1-Stage 8.5, 3-Stage 7.8, 5-Factor Model 6.8

Weighted Average Cost of Capital (WACC) (%)

	CRSP Deciles CAPM	CRSP Deciles CAPM +Size Prem	CRSP Deciles Build-Up	Risk Premium Report CAPM +Size Prem	Risk Premium Report Build-Up	Discounted Cash Flow 1-Stage	Discounted Cash Flow 3-Stage	Fama-French 5-Factor Model
Median	6.5	7.8	7.3	9.8	11.6	6.1	7.3	7.2
SIC Composite	6.6	6.8	6.6	7.5	9.2	7.6	7.1	6.3
Large Composite	6.4	6.5	6.5	6.9	8.6	6.3	6.6	6.2
Small Composite	6.4	10.9	11.0	15.7	14.2	17.9	13.4	9.2
High Financial Risk	–	–	–	–	–	–	–	–

WACC (%) SIC Composite: Low 6.3, High 9.2, Average 7.3, Median 7.1

© 2017 Duff & Phelps. All Rights Reserved. Duff & Phelps has used the utmost care in compiling the data presented herein, but cannot guarantee the accuracy, completeness, or timeliness of the information.

Data Updated Through March 31, 2017

2086

Number of Companies: 5
Bottled and Canned Soft Drinks and Carbonated Waters

Industry Description
Establishments primarily engaged in manufacturing soft drinks and carbonated waters.

Sales (in millions)

Three Largest Companies
Coca-Cola Co.	$41,863.0
Dr Pepper Snapple Group, Inc.	6,440.0
Coca-Cola Bottling Co.	3,156.4

Three Smallest Companies
Coca-Cola Bottling Co.	$3,156.4
Monster Beverage Corp.	3,043.7
National Beverage Corp.	704.8

Annualized Monthly Performance Statistics (%)

Industry	Geometric Mean	Arithmetic Mean	Standard Deviation
1-year	-2.1	-1.7	8.5
3-year	9.4	10.4	14.8
5-year	8.0	9.0	14.5

Total Assets (in millions)

Three Largest Companies
Coca-Cola Co.	$87,270.0
Dr Pepper Snapple Group, Inc.	9,791.0
Monster Beverage Corp.	4,153.5

Three Smallest Companies
Monster Beverage Corp.	$4,153.5
Coca-Cola Bottling Co.	2,449.5
National Beverage Corp.	305.5

S&P 500 Index	Geometric Mean	Arithmetic Mean	Standard Deviation
1-year	17.2	17.4	7.2
3-year	10.4	10.9	11.5
5-year	13.3	13.9	11.5

Return Ratios (%)

	Return on Assets Latest	5-Yr Avg	Return on Equity Latest	5-Yr Avg	Dividend Yield Latest	5-Yr Avg
Median (5)	9.1	8.7	22.9	23.9	1.5	1.8
SIC Composite (5)	7.9	8.8	3.5	4.2	2.8	2.7
Large Composite (−)	−	−	−	−	−	−
Small Composite (−)	−	−	−	−	−	−
High-Financial Risk (−)	−	−	−	−	−	−

Liquidity Ratio

	Current Ratio Latest	5-Yr Avg
Median (5)	2.6	1.4
SIC Composite (5)	1.4	1.2
Large Composite (−)	−	−
Small Composite (−)	−	−
High-Financial Risk (−)	−	−

Profitability Ratio (%)

	Operating Margin Latest	5-Yr Avg
Median (5)	22.4	20.0
SIC Composite (5)	23.6	22.7
Large Composite (−)	−	−
Small Composite (−)	−	−
High-Financial Risk (−)	−	−

Growth Rates (%)

	Long-term EPS Analyst Estimates
Median (5)	8.7
SIC Composite (5)	5.9
Large Composite (−)	−
Small Composite (−)	−
High-Financial Risk (−)	−

Betas (Levered)

	Raw (OLS)	Blume Adjusted	Peer Group	Vasicek Adjusted	Sum	Downside
Median	0.63	0.77	0.65	0.64	0.61	1.08
SIC Composite	0.66	0.79	0.65	0.65	0.61	0.76
Large Composite	−	−	−	−	−	−
Small Composite	−	−	−	−	−	−
High Financial Risk	−	−	−	−	−	−

Betas (Unlevered)

	Raw (OLS)	Blume Adjusted	Peer Group	Vasicek Adjusted	Sum	Downside
Median	0.52	0.63	0.54	0.52	0.55	0.75
SIC Composite	0.54	0.65	0.53	0.54	0.50	0.62
Large Composite	−	−	−	−	−	−
Small Composite	−	−	−	−	−	−
High Financial Risk	−	−	−	−	−	−

Equity Valuation Multiples

	Price/Sales Latest	5-Yr Avg	Price/Earnings Latest	5-Yr Avg	Market/Book Latest	5-Yr Avg
Median	4.3	2.1	36.7	25.8	6.8	5.3
SIC Composite	4.2	3.7	28.3	23.6	6.9	5.3
Large Composite	−	−	−	−	−	−
Small Composite	−	−	−	−	−	−
High Financial Risk	−	−	−	−	−	−

Enterprise Valuation (EV) Multiples

	EV/Sales Latest	5-Yr Avg	EV/EBITDA Latest	5-Yr Avg
Median	4.9	2.5	15.3	14.3
SIC Composite	4.7	4.1	15.8	14.3
Large Composite	−	−	−	−
Small Composite	−	−	−	−
High Financial Risk	−	−	−	−

Enterprise Valuation SIC Composite

Latest: EV/Sales 4.7, EV/EBITDA 15.8
5-Yr Avg: EV/Sales 4.1, EV/EBITDA 14.3

Fama-French (F-F) 5-Factor Model

	Fama-French (F-F) Components				
	F-F Beta	SMB Premium	HML Premium	RMW Premium	CMA Premium
Median	0.5	4.2	-4.4	1.9	-1.1
SIC Composite	0.7	-1.6	-2.9	1.4	2.4
Large Composite	−	−	−	−	−
Small Composite	−	−	−	−	−
High Financial Risk	−	−	−	−	−

Leverage Ratios (%)

	Debt/MV Equity Latest	5-Yr Avg	Debt/Total Capital Latest	5-Yr Avg
Median	25.0	22.5	20.0	18.4
SIC Composite	22.1	20.7	18.1	17.2
Large Composite	−	−	−	−
Small Composite	−	−	−	−
High Financial Risk	−	−	−	−

Cost of Debt

	Cost of Debt (%) Latest
Median	4.8
SIC Composite	4.0
Large Composite	−
Small Composite	−
High Financial Risk	−

Capital Structure

SIC Composite (%) Latest
D/TC: 18.1
E/TC: 81.9

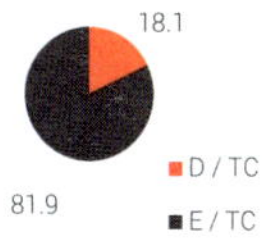

Cost of Equity Capital (%)

	CRSP Deciles			Risk Premium Report		Discounted Cash Flow		Fama-French
	CAPM	CAPM +Size Prem	Build-Up	CAPM +Size Prem	Build-Up	1-Stage	3-Stage	5-Factor Model
Median	7.0	7.4	7.7	9.2	12.0	8.8	7.6	7.0
SIC Composite	7.1	7.2	7.1	8.2	10.2	8.9	7.7	6.8
Large Composite	−	−	−	−	−	−	−	−
Small Composite	−	−	−	−	−	−	−	−
High Financial Risk	−	−	−	−	−	−	−	−

Cost of Equity Capital (%) SIC Composite

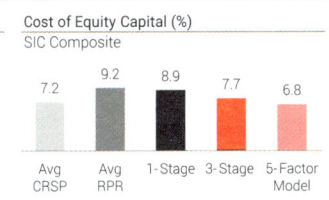

Avg CRSP: 7.2; Avg RPR: 9.2; 1-Stage: 8.9; 3-Stage: 7.7; 5-Factor Model: 6.8

Weighted Average Cost of Capital (WACC) (%)

	CRSP Deciles			Risk Premium Report		Discounted Cash Flow		Fama-French
	CAPM	CAPM +Size Prem	Build-Up	CAPM +Size Prem	Build-Up	1-Stage	3-Stage	5-Factor Model
Median	6.4	6.8	7.1	8.7	10.5	7.8	7.6	7.0
SIC Composite	6.5	6.6	6.5	7.4	9.0	8.0	7.0	6.3
Large Composite	−	−	−	−	−	−	−	−
Small Composite	−	−	−	−	−	−	−	−
High Financial Risk	−	−	−	−	−	−	−	−

WACC (%) SIC Composite
Low 6.3 — High 9.0
▲ Average 7.3   ◆ Median 7.0

© 2017 Duff & Phelps. All Rights Reserved. Duff & Phelps has used the utmost care in compiling the data presented herein, but cannot guarantee the accuracy, completeness, or timeliness of the information.

Data Updated Through March 31, 2017

22
Number of Companies: 5
Textile Mill Products

Industry Description
This major group includes establishments engaged in performing any of the following operations: (1) preparation of fiber and subsequent manufacturing of yarn, thread, braids, twine, and cordage; (2) manufacturing broad woven fabrics, narrow woven fabrics, knit fabrics, and carpets and rugs from yarn; (3) dyeing and finishing fiber, yarn, fabrics, and knit apparel; (4) coating, waterproofing, or otherwise treating fabrics; (5) the integrated manufacture of knit apparel and other finished articles from yarn; and (6) the manufacture of felt goods, lace goods, non-woven fabrics, and miscellaneous textiles.

Sales (in millions)

Three Largest Companies
Interface Inc.	$958.6
Albany Int'l Corp.	779.8
Unifi Inc.	643.6

Three Smallest Companies
Unifi Inc.	$643.6
Culp Inc.	312.9
Crown Crafts Inc.	84.3

Annualized Monthly Performance Statistics (%)

Industry	Geometric Mean	Arithmetic Mean	Standard Deviation
1-year	15.6	16.9	18.8
3-year	6.1	8.1	21.3
5-year	14.7	16.8	23.0

Total Assets (in millions)

Three Largest Companies
Albany Int'l Corp.	$1,263.4
Interface Inc.	839.6
Unifi Inc.	526.9

Three Smallest Companies
Unifi Inc.	$526.9
Culp Inc.	175.1
Crown Crafts Inc.	52.4

S&P 500 Index	Geometric Mean	Arithmetic Mean	Standard Deviation
1-year	17.2	17.4	7.2
3-year	10.4	10.9	11.5
5-year	13.3	13.9	11.5

Return Ratios (%)

	Return on Assets Latest	5-Yr Avg	Return on Equity Latest	5-Yr Avg	Dividend Yield Latest	5-Yr Avg
Median (5)	6.9	5.6	13.5	13.5	1.3	0.9
SIC Composite (5)	5.8	4.6	4.5	3.8	1.2	1.1
Large Composite (–)	–	–	–	–	–	–
Small Composite (–)	–	–	–	–	–	–
High-Financial Risk (–)	–	–	–	–	–	–

Liquidity Ratio

	Current Ratio Latest	5-Yr Avg
	3.0	2.8
	2.8	2.8
	–	–
	–	–
	–	–

Profitability Ratio (%)

	Operating Margin Latest	5-Yr Avg
	10.9	9.8
	10.6	8.9
	–	–
	–	–
	–	–

Growth Rates (%)

	Long-term EPS Analyst Estimates
	13.6
	13.6
	–
	–
	–

Betas (Levered)

	Raw (OLS)	Blume Adjusted	Peer Group	Vasicek Adjusted	Sum	Downside
Median	0.70	0.81	1.06	0.79	1.24	1.33
SIC Composite	1.22	1.15	1.06	1.21	1.38	1.57
Large Composite	–	–	–	–	–	–
Small Composite	–	–	–	–	–	–
High Financial Risk	–	–	–	–	–	–

Betas (Unlevered)

	Raw (OLS)	Blume Adjusted	Peer Group	Vasicek Adjusted	Sum	Downside
Median	0.63	0.72	0.92	0.70	1.06	1.14
SIC Composite	1.04	0.98	0.91	1.03	1.17	1.33
Large Composite	–	–	–	–	–	–
Small Composite	–	–	–	–	–	–
High Financial Risk	–	–	–	–	–	–

Equity Valuation Multiples

	Price/Sales Latest	5-Yr Avg	Price/Earnings Latest	5-Yr Avg	Market/Book Latest	5-Yr Avg
Median	1.2	0.9	22.6	16.9	2.9	2.1
SIC Composite	1.3	1.1	22.3	26.0	2.7	2.3
Large Composite	–	–	–	–	–	–
Small Composite	–	–	–	–	–	–
High Financial Risk	–	–	–	–	–	–

Enterprise Valuation (EV) Multiples

	EV/Sales Latest	5-Yr Avg	EV/EBITDA Latest	5-Yr Avg
Median	1.1	0.9	9.8	8.1
SIC Composite	1.5	1.2	9.6	9.1
Large Composite	–	–	–	–
Small Composite	–	–	–	–
High Financial Risk	–	–	–	–

Enterprise Valuation SIC Composite
- Latest: EV/Sales 1.5, EV/EBITDA 9.6
- 5-Yr Avg: EV/Sales 1.2, EV/EBITDA 9.1

Fama-French (F-F) 5-Factor Model

	F-F Beta	SMB Premium	HML Premium	RMW Premium	CMA Premium
Median	0.2	4.9	7.3	0.2	-3.3
SIC Composite	1.1	4.6	2.5	-0.1	-2.5
Large Composite	–	–	–	–	–
Small Composite	–	–	–	–	–
High Financial Risk	–	–	–	–	–

Leverage Ratios (%)

	Debt/MV Equity Latest	5-Yr Avg	Debt/Total Capital Latest	5-Yr Avg
Median	22.1	22.0	18.1	18.1
SIC Composite	23.8	22.8	19.2	18.6
Large Composite	–	–	–	–
Small Composite	–	–	–	–
High Financial Risk	–	–	–	–

Cost of Debt

	Cost of Debt (%) Latest
Median	7.1
SIC Composite	6.3
Large Composite	–
Small Composite	–
High Financial Risk	–

Capital Structure

SIC Composite (%) Latest
- D/TC: 19.2
- E/TC: 80.8

Cost of Equity Capital (%)

	CRSP Deciles CAPM	CAPM +Size Prem	Build-Up	Risk Premium Report CAPM +Size Prem	Build-Up	Discounted Cash Flow 1-Stage	3-Stage	Fama-French 5-Factor Model
Median	7.8	11.8	11.7	14.7	15.1	15.0	12.7	14.0
SIC Composite	10.1	12.2	11.0	15.6	14.6	14.7	10.0	13.8
Large Composite	–	–	–	–	–	–	–	–
Small Composite	–	–	–	–	–	–	–	–
High Financial Risk	–	–	–	–	–	–	–	–

Cost of Equity Capital (%) SIC Composite
- Avg CRSP: 11.6
- Avg RPR: 15.1
- 1-Stage: 14.7
- 3-Stage: 10.0
- 5-Factor Model: 13.8

Weighted Average Cost of Capital (WACC) (%)

	CRSP Deciles CAPM	CAPM +Size Prem	Build-Up	Risk Premium Report CAPM +Size Prem	Build-Up	Discounted Cash Flow 1-Stage	3-Stage	Fama-French 5-Factor Model
Median	7.7	10.7	10.8	13.1	13.5	13.0	12.2	13.5
SIC Composite	9.3	11.0	10.1	13.8	13.0	13.1	9.2	12.3
Large Composite	–	–	–	–	–	–	–	–
Small Composite	–	–	–	–	–	–	–	–
High Financial Risk	–	–	–	–	–	–	–	–

WACC (%) SIC Composite
- Low: 9.2
- High: 13.8
- Average: 11.8
- Median: 12.3

© 2017 Duff & Phelps. All Rights Reserved. Duff & Phelps has used the utmost care in compiling the data presented herein, but cannot guarantee the accuracy, completeness, or timeliness of the information.

Data Updated Through March 31, 2017

23

Number of Companies: 14
Apparel and Other Finished Products Made From Fabrics and Similar Materials

Industry Description
This major group, known as the cutting-up and needle trades, includes establishments producing clothing and fabricating products by cutting and sewing purchased woven or knit textile fabrics and related materials, such as leather, rubberized fabrics, plastics, and furs. Also included are establishments that manufacture clothing by cutting and joining (for example, by adhesives) materials such as paper and non-woven textiles. Included in the apparel industries are three types of establishments: (1) the regular or inside factories; (2) contract factories; and (3) apparel jobbers.

Sales (in millions)

Three Largest Companies
V.F. Corp.	$12,019.0
PVH Corp.	8,203.1
Cintas Corporation	4,905.5

Three Smallest Companies
Delta Apparel Inc.	$425.2
Ever-Glory Int'l Group Inc.	421.4
Superior Uniform Group Inc.	252.6

Annualized Monthly Performance Statistics (%)

Industry	Geometric Mean	Arithmetic Mean	Standard Deviation
1-year	-13.6	-12.9	12.0
3-year	-0.2	0.8	14.4
5-year	11.6	12.7	15.5

Total Assets (in millions)

Three Largest Companies
PVH Corp.	$11,067.9
V.F. Corp.	9,739.3
Cintas Corporation	4,104.4

Three Smallest Companies
Delta Apparel Inc.	$344.7
Ever-Glory Int'l Group Inc.	228.7
Superior Uniform Group Inc.	196.8

S&P 500 Index	Geometric Mean	Arithmetic Mean	Standard Deviation
1-year	17.2	17.4	7.2
3-year	10.4	10.9	11.5
5-year	13.3	13.9	11.5

Return Ratios (%)

	Return on Assets Latest	Return on Assets 5-Yr Avg	Return on Equity Latest	Return on Equity 5-Yr Avg	Dividend Yield Latest	Dividend Yield 5-Yr Avg
Median (14)	8.5	8.1	14.1	15.1	0.7	0.5
SIC Composite (14)	8.6	8.0	4.8	4.1	1.4	1.1
Large Composite (3)	8.7	7.9	4.9	4.7	2.1	1.6
Small Composite (3)	4.8	4.0	8.4	7.9	1.2	1.4
High-Financial Risk (−)	−	−	−	−	−	−

Liquidity Ratio / Profitability Ratio (%) / Growth Rates (%)

	Current Ratio Latest	Current Ratio 5-Yr Avg	Operating Margin Latest	Operating Margin 5-Yr Avg	Long-term EPS Analyst Estimates
Median (14)	2.9	3.0	9.5	9.3	11.5
SIC Composite (14)	2.5	2.5	11.3	11.3	11.1
Large Composite (3)	2.1	2.2	13.1	13.1	9.0
Small Composite (3)	2.1	2.2	5.1	4.3	13.4
High-Financial Risk	−	−	−	−	−

Betas (Levered)

	Raw (OLS)	Blume Adjusted	Peer Group	Vasicek Adjusted	Sum	Downside
Median	0.59	0.75	0.61	0.60	0.70	1.14
SIC Composite	0.61	0.76	0.61	0.61	0.84	0.77
Large Composite	0.73	0.84	0.62	0.67	1.17	1.03
Small Composite	0.34	0.59	0.59	0.35	0.48	0.75
High Financial Risk	−	−	−	−	−	−

Betas (Unlevered)

	Raw (OLS)	Blume Adjusted	Peer Group	Vasicek Adjusted	Sum	Downside
Median	0.58	0.74	0.58	0.59	0.67	1.00
SIC Composite	0.56	0.69	0.57	0.56	0.77	0.71
Large Composite	0.65	0.74	0.56	0.60	1.04	0.92
Small Composite	0.34	0.51	0.51	0.34	0.43	0.62
High Financial Risk	−	−	−	−	−	−

Equity Valuation Multiples

	Price/Sales Latest	Price/Sales 5-Yr Avg	Price/Earnings Latest	Price/Earnings 5-Yr Avg	Market/Book Latest	Market/Book 5-Yr Avg
Median	1.2	1.3	18.9	21.2	2.5	2.4
SIC Composite	1.6	1.7	20.8	24.2	3.2	3.5
Large Composite	1.8	1.7	20.3	21.2	3.4	3.1
Small Composite	0.4	0.3	11.9	12.7	1.3	1.2
High Financial Risk	−	−	−	−	−	−

Enterprise Valuation (EV) Multiples

	EV/Sales Latest	EV/Sales 5-Yr Avg	EV/EBITDA Latest	EV/EBITDA 5-Yr Avg
Median	1.4	1.3	9.3	10.5
SIC Composite	1.7	1.8	11.5	12.7
Large Composite	1.9	1.9	12.0	11.9
Small Composite	0.6	0.5	7.3	7.8
High Financial Risk	−	−	−	−

Enterprise Valuation SIC Composite
- EV/Sales: Latest 1.7, 5-Yr Avg 1.8
- EV/EBITDA: Latest 11.5, 5-Yr Avg 12.7

Fama-French (F-F) 5-Factor Model

	F-F Beta	SMB Premium	HML Premium	RMW Premium	CMA Premium
Median	0.6	1.5	0.3	1.6	1.6
SIC Composite	0.6	0.4	-1.6	0.6	1.8
Large Composite	0.8	0.1	-0.8	1.5	2.0
Small Composite	0.3	4.0	-1.7	1.3	4.9
High Financial Risk	−	−	−	−	−

Leverage Ratios (%)

	Debt/MV Equity Latest	Debt/MV Equity 5-Yr Avg	Debt/Total Capital Latest	Debt/Total Capital 5-Yr Avg
Median	10.0	10.7	9.1	9.6
SIC Composite	12.7	11.4	11.3	10.2
Large Composite	15.5	15.4	13.4	13.3
Small Composite	45.7	53.6	31.3	34.9
High Financial Risk	−	−	−	−

Cost of Debt / Capital Structure

	Cost of Debt (%) Latest	SIC Composite (%) Latest
Median	6.1	
SIC Composite	5.4	D/TC 11.3, E/TC 88.7
Large Composite	5.2	
Small Composite	6.9	

Cost of Equity Capital (%)

	CRSP Deciles CAPM	CRSP Deciles CAPM +Size Prem	Build-Up	Risk Premium Report CAPM	Risk Premium Report CAPM +Size Prem Build-Up	Discounted Cash Flow 1-Stage	Discounted Cash Flow 3-Stage	Fama-French 5-Factor Model
Median	6.8	8.4	8.3	11.8	13.5	12.1	11.0	11.5
SIC Composite	6.9	7.7	7.6	11.0	12.2	12.5	10.9	8.0
Large Composite	7.2	7.9	7.4	12.5	11.6	10.7	10.3	10.7
Small Composite	5.4	9.3	10.6	11.8	16.4	14.7	16.1	13.7
High Financial Risk	−	−	−	−	−	−	−	−

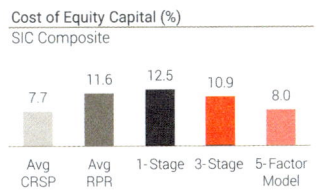

Cost of Equity Capital (%) SIC Composite
- Avg CRSP: 7.7
- Avg RPR: 11.6
- 1-Stage: 12.5
- 3-Stage: 10.9
- 5-Factor Model: 8.0

Weighted Average Cost of Capital (WACC) (%)

	CRSP Deciles CAPM	CRSP Deciles CAPM +Size Prem	Build-Up	Risk Premium Report CAPM	Risk Premium Report CAPM +Size Prem Build-Up	Discounted Cash Flow 1-Stage	Discounted Cash Flow 3-Stage	Fama-French 5-Factor Model
Median	6.8	8.3	7.9	11.0	12.5	11.2	10.3	10.7
SIC Composite	6.6	7.4	7.3	10.3	11.3	11.6	10.2	7.6
Large Composite	6.8	7.4	7.1	11.4	10.6	9.8	9.5	9.9
Small Composite	5.3	8.0	8.9	9.7	12.9	11.7	12.7	11.0
High Financial Risk	−	−	−	−	−	−	−	−

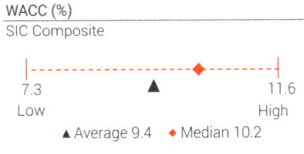

WACC (%) SIC Composite
- Low: 7.3
- High: 11.6
- Average: 9.4
- Median: 10.2

© 2017 Duff & Phelps. All Rights Reserved. Duff & Phelps has used the utmost care in compiling the data presented herein, but cannot guarantee the accuracy, completeness, or timeliness of the information.

Data Updated Through March 31, 2017

24

Number of Companies: 7
Lumber and Wood Products, Except Furniture

Industry Description
This major group includes establishments engaged in cutting timber and pulpwood; merchant sawmills, lath mills, shingle mills, cooperage stock mills, planning mills, and plywood mills and veneer mills engaged in producing lumber and wood basic materials; and establishments engaged in manufacturing finished articles made entirely or mainly of wood or related materials.

Sales (in millions)

Three Largest Companies
Builders FirstSource, Inc.	$6,367.3
Universal Forest Products Inc.	3,240.5
Patrick Industries Inc.	1,221.9

Three Smallest Companies
Cavco Industries Inc.	$712.4
Trex Co. Inc.	479.6
Deltic Timber Corp.	219.4

Annualized Monthly Performance Statistics (%)

Industry
	Geometric Mean	Arithmetic Mean	Standard Deviation
1-year	30.7	34.7	35.0
3-year	21.8	26.2	34.7
5-year	26.3	30.1	32.2

Total Assets (in millions)

Three Largest Companies
Builders FirstSource, Inc.	$2,909.9
Universal Forest Products Inc.	1,292.1
Deltic Timber Corp.	554.7

Three Smallest Companies
Patrick Industries Inc.	$535.0
American Woodmark Corp.	466.7
Trex Co. Inc.	221.4

S&P 500 Index
	Geometric Mean	Arithmetic Mean	Standard Deviation
1-year	17.2	17.4	7.2
3-year	10.4	10.9	11.5
5-year	13.3	13.9	11.5

Return Ratios (%)

	Return on Assets Latest	Return on Assets 5-Yr Avg	Return on Equity Latest	Return on Equity 5-Yr Avg	Dividend Yield Latest	Dividend Yield 5-Yr Avg	Current Ratio Latest	Current Ratio 5-Yr Avg	Operating Margin Latest	Operating Margin 5-Yr Avg	Long-term EPS Analyst Estimates
Median (7)	8.4	6.2	23.0	8.8	0.0	0.0	2.1	2.3	7.4	5.7	13.6
SIC Composite (7)	7.1	4.5	4.5	3.3	0.3	0.4	2.1	2.3	6.0	4.9	14.3
Large Composite (–)	–	–	–	–	–	–	–	–	–	–	–
Small Composite (–)	–	–	–	–	–	–	–	–	–	–	–
High-Financial Risk (–)	–	–	–	–	–	–	–	–	–	–	–

Betas (Levered)

	Raw (OLS)	Blume Adjusted	Peer Group	Vasicek Adjusted	Sum	Downside
Median	1.66	1.42	1.66	1.66	1.47	1.57
SIC Composite	1.63	1.41	1.66	1.64	1.52	1.62
Large Composite	–	–	–	–	–	–
Small Composite	–	–	–	–	–	–
High Financial Risk	–	–	–	–	–	–

Betas (Unlevered)

	Raw (OLS)	Blume Adjusted	Peer Group	Vasicek Adjusted	Sum	Downside
Median	1.35	1.22	1.58	1.46	1.24	1.50
SIC Composite	1.38	1.20	1.40	1.38	1.29	1.37
Large Composite	–	–	–	–	–	–
Small Composite	–	–	–	–	–	–
High Financial Risk	–	–	–	–	–	–

Equity Valuation Multiples

	Price/Sales Latest	Price/Sales 5-Yr Avg	Price/Earnings Latest	Price/Earnings 5-Yr Avg	Market/Book Latest	Market/Book 5-Yr Avg
Median	1.5	1.1	25.4	35.0	5.3	3.9
SIC Composite	0.8	0.7	22.1	30.3	4.3	3.3
Large Composite	–	–	–	–	–	–
Small Composite	–	–	–	–	–	–
High Financial Risk	–	–	–	–	–	–

Enterprise Valuation (EV) Multiples

	EV/Sales Latest	EV/Sales 5-Yr Avg	EV/EBITDA Latest	EV/EBITDA 5-Yr Avg
Median	1.4	0.9	12.0	13.5
SIC Composite	0.9	0.9	12.1	13.0
Large Composite	–	–	–	–
Small Composite	–	–	–	–
High Financial Risk	–	–	–	–

Enterprise Valuation SIC Composite
Latest: EV/Sales 0.9, EV/EBITDA 12.1
5-Yr Avg: EV/Sales 0.9, EV/EBITDA 13.0

Fama-French (F-F) 5-Factor Model

Fama-French (F-F) Components
	F-F Beta	SMB Premium	HML Premium	RMW Premium	CMA Premium
Median	1.6	3.0	0.5	0.7	-3.4
SIC Composite	1.5	5.5	1.1	1.7	-2.6
Large Composite	–	–	–	–	–
Small Composite	–	–	–	–	–
High Financial Risk	–	–	–	–	–

Leverage Ratios (%)

	Debt/MV Equity Latest	Debt/MV Equity 5-Yr Avg	Debt/Total Capital Latest	Debt/Total Capital 5-Yr Avg
Median	6.6	12.2	6.2	10.9
SIC Composite	24.6	24.7	19.8	19.8
Large Composite	–	–	–	–
Small Composite	–	–	–	–
High Financial Risk	–	–	–	–

Cost of Debt

	Cost of Debt (%) Latest
Median	6.1
SIC Composite	7.0
Large Composite	–
Small Composite	–
High Financial Risk	–

Capital Structure

SIC Composite (%) Latest: D/TC 19.8, E/TC 80.2

Cost of Equity Capital (%)

	CAPM	CRSP Deciles CAPM +Size Prem	CRSP Deciles Build-Up	Risk Premium Report CAPM +Size Prem	Risk Premium Report Build-Up	Discounted Cash Flow 1-Stage	Discounted Cash Flow 3-Stage	Fama-French 5-Factor Model
Median	12.6	14.3	14.3	16.3	14.7	13.6	8.6	13.0
SIC Composite	12.5	14.2	14.3	16.2	14.4	14.6	8.8	17.3
Large Composite	–	–	–	–	–	–	–	–
Small Composite	–	–	–	–	–	–	–	–
High Financial Risk	–	–	–	–	–	–	–	–

Cost of Equity Capital (%) SIC Composite: Avg CRSP 14.3, Avg RPR 15.3, 1-Stage 14.6, 3-Stage 8.8, 5-Factor Model 17.3

Weighted Average Cost of Capital (WACC) (%)

	CAPM	CRSP Deciles CAPM +Size Prem	CRSP Deciles Build-Up	Risk Premium Report CAPM +Size Prem	Risk Premium Report Build-Up	Discounted Cash Flow 1-Stage	Discounted Cash Flow 3-Stage	Fama-French 5-Factor Model
Median	11.5	13.2	13.7	13.0	13.2	12.5	8.6	13.7
SIC Composite	11.1	12.5	12.6	14.1	12.6	12.8	8.2	14.9
Large Composite	–	–	–	–	–	–	–	–
Small Composite	–	–	–	–	–	–	–	–
High Financial Risk	–	–	–	–	–	–	–	–

WACC (%) SIC Composite: Low 8.2, High 14.9, Average 12.5, Median 12.6

© 2017 Duff & Phelps. All Rights Reserved. Duff & Phelps has used the utmost care in compiling the data presented herein, but cannot guarantee the accuracy, completeness, or timeliness of the information.

Data Updated Through March 31, 2017

25

Number of Companies: 15
Furniture and Fixtures

Industry Description
This major group includes establishments engaged in manufacturing household, office, public building, and restaurant furniture, and office and store fixtures.

Sales (in millions)

Three Largest Companies
Lear Corp.	$18,557.6
Tempur Sealy Int'l Inc.	3,127.3
Steelcase Inc.	3,032.4

Three Smallest Companies
Bassett Furniture Industries, Inc.	$432.0
Hooker Furniture Corp.	247.0
Nova Lifestyle, Inc.	108.8

Total Assets (in millions)

Three Largest Companies
Lear Corp.	$9,900.6
B/E Aerospace Inc.	3,370.1
Tempur Sealy Int'l Inc.	2,702.6

Three Smallest Companies
Flexsteel Industries Inc.	$246.9
Hooker Furniture Corp.	181.7
Nova Lifestyle, Inc.	89.7

Annualized Monthly Performance Statistics (%)

Industry	Geometric Mean	Arithmetic Mean	Standard Deviation	S&P 500 Index	Geometric Mean	Arithmetic Mean	Standard Deviation
1-year	17.3	19.9	26.4	1-year	17.2	17.4	7.2
3-year	7.5	9.3	20.7	3-year	10.4	10.9	11.5
5-year	11.3	13.5	22.6	5-year	13.3	13.9	11.5

Return Ratios (%) | Liquidity Ratio | Profitability Ratio (%) | Growth Rates (%)

	Return on Assets Latest	5-Yr Avg	Return on Equity Latest	5-Yr Avg	Dividend Yield Latest	5-Yr Avg	Current Ratio Latest	5-Yr Avg	Operating Margin Latest	5-Yr Avg	Long-term EPS Analyst Estimates
Median (15)	9.6	6.9	14.8	14.5	1.7	2.0	1.6	1.9	8.2	6.9	11.7
SIC Composite (15)	9.1	7.4	7.1	6.3	1.4	1.1	1.5	1.6	9.2	7.9	11.7
Large Composite (3)	9.0	7.9	9.1	8.6	1.1	1.0	1.4	1.4	8.6	6.9	12.5
Small Composite (3)	6.2	6.5	5.0	6.2	2.6	3.6	3.0	3.1	7.1	6.0	11.7
High-Financial Risk (–)	–	–	–	–	–	–	–	–	–	–	–

Betas (Levered) | Betas (Unlevered)

	Raw (OLS)	Blume Adjusted	Peer Group	Vasicek Adjusted	Sum	Downside	Raw (OLS)	Blume Adjusted	Peer Group	Vasicek Adjusted	Sum	Downside
Median	1.15	1.10	1.14	1.14	1.28	1.53	1.04	0.98	1.06	1.00	1.19	1.41
SIC Composite	1.18	1.12	1.14	1.17	1.48	1.22	1.01	0.96	0.97	1.00	1.25	1.04
Large Composite	1.32	1.21	1.13	1.22	1.65	1.42	1.06	0.98	0.92	0.99	1.32	1.14
Small Composite	1.00	1.00	1.14	1.07	0.13	1.27	0.98	0.99	1.12	1.05	0.14	1.25
High Financial Risk	–	–	–	–	–	–	–	–	–	–	–	–

Equity Valuation Multiples | Enterprise Valuation (EV) Multiples

	Price/Sales Latest	5-Yr Avg	Price/Earnings Latest	5-Yr Avg	Market/Book Latest	5-Yr Avg	EV/Sales Latest	5-Yr Avg	EV/EBITDA Latest	5-Yr Avg
Median	0.8	0.8	16.6	18.2	3.0	2.4	0.9	0.8	8.3	8.8
SIC Composite	0.8	0.8	14.1	15.8	4.0	3.2	0.9	0.9	7.9	8.4
Large Composite	0.6	0.5	11.0	11.7	3.6	2.9	0.7	0.6	6.3	6.8
Small Composite	0.9	0.7	20.2	16.2	1.7	1.4	0.8	0.6	8.3	8.0
High Financial Risk	–	–	–	–	–	–	–	–	–	–

Enterprise Valuation SIC Composite
EV/Sales: Latest 0.9, 5-Yr Avg 0.9
EV/EBITDA: Latest 7.9, 5-Yr Avg 8.4

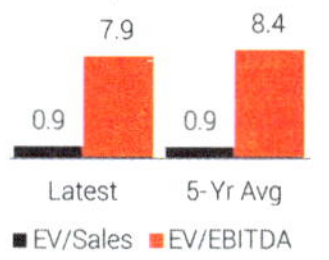

Fama-French (F-F) 5-Factor Model | Leverage Ratios (%) | Cost of Debt | Capital Structure

	F-F Beta	SMB Premium	HML Premium	RMW Premium	CMA Premium	Debt/MV Equity Latest	5-Yr Avg	Debt/Total Capital Latest	5-Yr Avg	Cost of Debt (%) Latest	SIC Composite (%) Latest
Median	0.9	6.3	8.6	3.9	-7.9	10.5	10.5	9.5	9.5	6.1	
SIC Composite	1.1	3.5	5.3	2.8	-4.7	22.3	22.5	18.2	18.4	5.7	D/TC 18.2
Large Composite	1.2	2.9	6.2	2.4	3.2	28.8	27.4	22.4	21.5	5.4	E/TC 81.8
Small Composite	0.9	2.1	3.0	0.1	-2.5	2.5	2.4	2.5	2.4	7.1	
High Financial Risk	–	–	–	–	–	–	–	–	–	–	

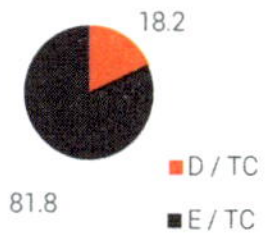

Cost of Equity Capital (%)

	CRSP Deciles CAPM	CAPM +Size Prem	Build-Up	Risk Premium Report CAPM +Size Prem	Build-Up	Discounted Cash Flow 1-Stage	3-Stage	Fama-French 5-Factor Model
Median	9.8	11.7	11.6	14.9	14.4	13.3	12.2	19.2
SIC Composite	9.9	11.2	11.2	15.0	13.0	13.0	12.8	16.3
Large Composite	10.2	11.3	11.0	15.3	12.1	13.7	15.3	24.7
Small Composite	9.4	12.2	12.7	9.7	16.1	12.9	11.7	11.1
High Financial Risk	–	–	–	–	–	–	–	–

Cost of Equity Capital (%) SIC Composite
Avg CRSP 11.2, Avg RPR 14.0, 1-Stage 13.0, 3-Stage 12.8, 5-Factor Model 16.3

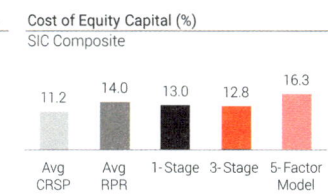

Weighted Average Cost of Capital (WACC) (%)

	CRSP Deciles CAPM	CAPM +Size Prem	Build-Up	Risk Premium Report CAPM +Size Prem	Build-Up	Discounted Cash Flow 1-Stage	3-Stage	Fama-French 5-Factor Model
Median	9.0	11.4	11.6	13.8	14.2	13.2	11.1	18.6
SIC Composite	9.1	10.2	10.1	13.3	11.6	11.6	11.4	14.3
Large Composite	9.1	10.0	9.7	13.1	10.6	11.8	13.1	20.3
Small Composite	9.3	12.1	12.5	9.6	15.8	12.7	11.5	11.0
High Financial Risk	–	–	–	–	–	–	–	–

WACC (%) SIC Composite
Low 10.1, High 14.3
Average 11.8, Median 11.6

© 2017 Duff & Phelps. All Rights Reserved. Duff & Phelps has used the utmost care in compiling the data presented herein, but cannot guarantee the accuracy, completeness, or timeliness of the information.

Data Updated Through March 31, 2017

251

Number of Companies: 8
Household Furniture

Industry Description
Establishments primarily engaged in manufacturing both upholstered and unupholstered wood household furniture; metal household furniture; mattresses, foundations, and convertible beds; wood television, radio, phonograph, and sewing machine cabinets; household furniture, not elsewhere classified.

Sales (in millions)

Three Largest Companies
Tempur Sealy Int'l Inc.	$3,127.3
La-Z-Boy Inc.	1,525.4
Select Comfort Corp.	1,311.3

Three Smallest Companies
Bassett Furniture Industries, Inc.	$432.0
Hooker Furniture Corp.	247.0
Nova Lifestyle, Inc.	108.8

Total Assets (in millions)

Three Largest Companies
Tempur Sealy Int'l Inc.	$2,702.6
La-Z-Boy Inc.	800.0
Ethan Allen Interiors Inc.	577.4

Three Smallest Companies
Flexsteel Industries Inc.	$246.9
Hooker Furniture Corp.	181.7
Nova Lifestyle, Inc.	89.7

Annualized Monthly Performance Statistics (%)

	Industry			S&P 500 Index		
	Geometric Mean	Arithmetic Mean	Standard Deviation	Geometric Mean	Arithmetic Mean	Standard Deviation
1-year	-7.1	1.5	45.7	17.2	17.4	7.2
3-year	3.0	7.3	31.1	10.4	10.9	11.5
5-year	-2.9	2.9	35.1	13.3	13.9	11.5

Return Ratios (%)

	Return on Assets		Return on Equity		Dividend Yield		Current Ratio		Operating Margin		Long-term EPS
	Latest	5-Yr Avg	Latest	5-Yr Avg	Latest	5-Yr Avg	Latest	5-Yr Avg	Latest	5-Yr Avg	Analyst Estimates
Median (8)	9.4	7.7	13.4	13.3	1.6	2.0	2.5	2.5	7.6	7.2	11.7
SIC Composite (8)	8.4	6.8	6.5	4.7	0.5	0.5	1.7	2.0	9.5	8.9	14.8
Large Composite (−)	−	−	−	−	−	−	−	−	−	−	−
Small Composite (−)	−	−	−	−	−	−	−	−	−	−	−
High-Financial Risk (−)	−	−	−	−	−	−	−	−	−	−	−

Liquidity Ratio Profitability Ratio (%) Growth Rates (%)

Betas (Levered)

	Raw (OLS)	Blume Adjusted	Peer Group	Vasicek Adjusted	Sum	Downside
Median	1.11	1.08	1.15	1.13	1.46	1.69
SIC Composite	1.19	1.13	1.15	1.17	2.14	1.46
Large Composite	−	−	−	−	−	−
Small Composite	−	−	−	−	−	−
High Financial Risk	−	−	−	−	−	−

Betas (Unlevered)

	Raw (OLS)	Blume Adjusted	Peer Group	Vasicek Adjusted	Sum	Downside
Median	1.04	0.97	1.14	0.99	1.46	1.54
SIC Composite	1.00	0.95	0.96	0.98	1.73	1.21
Large Composite	−	−	−	−	−	−
Small Composite	−	−	−	−	−	−
High Financial Risk	−	−	−	−	−	−

Equity Valuation Multiples

	Price/Sales		Price/Earnings		Market/Book	
	Latest	5-Yr Avg	Latest	5-Yr Avg	Latest	5-Yr Avg
Median	0.8	0.9	17.4	17.8	2.2	1.8
SIC Composite	0.9	1.0	15.3	21.3	3.7	3.8
Large Composite	−	−	−	−	−	−
Small Composite	−	−	−	−	−	−
High Financial Risk	−	−	−	−	−	−

Enterprise Valuation (EV) Multiples

	EV/Sales		EV/EBITDA	
	Latest	5-Yr Avg	Latest	5-Yr Avg
Median	0.8	0.8	8.1	8.9
SIC Composite	1.0	1.2	8.7	10.3
Large Composite	−	−	−	−
Small Composite	−	−	−	−
High Financial Risk	−	−	−	−

Enterprise Valuation SIC Composite
EV/Sales Latest 1.0, 5-Yr Avg 1.2
EV/EBITDA Latest 8.7, 5-Yr Avg 10.3

Fama-French (F-F) 5-Factor Model

	F-F Beta	SMB Premium	HML Premium	RMW Premium	CMA Premium
Median	1.1	4.1	-0.2	2.2	3.0
SIC Composite	1.1	5.2	5.3	4.8	-8.0
Large Composite	−	−	−	−	−
Small Composite	−	−	−	−	−
High Financial Risk	−	−	−	−	−

Leverage Ratios (%)

	Debt/MV Equity		Debt/Total Capital	
	Latest	5-Yr Avg	Latest	5-Yr Avg
Median	1.3	1.8	1.2	1.8
SIC Composite	28.4	23.6	22.1	19.1

Cost of Debt

	Cost of Debt (%) Latest
Median	7.1
SIC Composite	6.2

Capital Structure
SIC Composite (%) Latest
D / TC 22.1
E / TC 77.9

Cost of Equity Capital (%)

	CRSP Deciles			Risk Premium Report		Discounted Cash Flow		Fama-French
	CAPM	CAPM +Size Prem	Build-Up	CAPM +Size Prem	Build-Up	1-Stage	3-Stage	5-Factor Model
Median	9.7	11.9	12.2	16.7	15.2	14.6	13.4	18.7
SIC Composite	10.0	11.8	11.7	19.5	14.3	15.3	14.1	16.7
Large Composite	−	−	−	−	−	−	−	−
Small Composite	−	−	−	−	−	−	−	−
High Financial Risk	−	−	−	−	−	−	−	−

Cost of Equity Capital (%) SIC Composite
Avg CRSP 11.8, Avg RPR 16.9, 1-Stage 15.3, 3-Stage 14.1, 5-Factor Model 16.7

Weighted Average Cost of Capital (WACC) (%)

	CRSP Deciles			Risk Premium Report		Discounted Cash Flow		Fama-French
	CAPM	CAPM +Size Prem	Build-Up	CAPM +Size Prem	Build-Up	1-Stage	3-Stage	5-Factor Model
Median	8.9	11.4	12.1	15.4	14.5	13.7	13.1	18.4
SIC Composite	8.9	10.3	10.2	16.3	12.2	13.1	12.1	14.1
Large Composite	−	−	−	−	−	−	−	−
Small Composite	−	−	−	−	−	−	−	−
High Financial Risk	−	−	−	−	−	−	−	−

WACC (%) SIC Composite
Low 10.2, High 16.3, Average 12.6, Median 12.2

© 2017 Duff & Phelps. All Rights Reserved. Duff & Phelps has used the utmost care in compiling the data presented herein, but cannot guarantee the accuracy, completeness, or timeliness of the information.

Data Updated Through March 31, 2017

252

Number of Companies: 5
Office Furniture

Industry Description
Establishments primarily engaged in manufacturing office furniture.

Sales (in millions)

Three Largest Companies
Steelcase Inc.	$3,032.4
Herman Miller Inc.	2,264.9
HNI Corp.	2,203.5

Three Smallest Companies
HNI Corp.	$2,203.5
Knoll, Inc.	1,164.3
Kimball International, Inc.	635.1

Total Assets (in millions)

Three Largest Companies
Steelcase Inc.	$1,792.0
HNI Corp.	1,330.2
Herman Miller Inc.	1,235.2

Three Smallest Companies
Herman Miller Inc.	$1,235.2
Knoll, Inc.	858.6
Kimball International, Inc.	273.6

Annualized Monthly Performance Statistics (%)

Industry
	Geometric Mean	Arithmetic Mean	Standard Deviation
1-year	15.3	21.9	43.6
3-year	6.0	10.3	32.0
5-year	13.1	17.0	31.0

S&P 500 Index
	Geometric Mean	Arithmetic Mean	Standard Deviation
1-year	17.2	17.4	7.2
3-year	10.4	10.9	11.5
5-year	13.3	13.9	11.5

Return Ratios (%)

	Return on Assets Latest	5-Yr Avg	Return on Equity Latest	5-Yr Avg	Dividend Yield Latest	5-Yr Avg
Median (5)	7.8	6.2	16.6	14.5	2.4	2.6
SIC Composite (5)	8.2	6.0	5.9	4.8	2.6	2.6
Large Composite (−)	−	−	−	−	−	−
Small Composite (−)	−	−	−	−	−	−
High-Financial Risk (−)	−	−	−	−	−	−

Liquidity Ratio

	Current Ratio Latest	5-Yr Avg
	1.2	1.4
	1.3	1.4
	−	−
	−	−
	−	−

Profitability Ratio (%)

	Operating Margin Latest	5-Yr Avg
	8.4	6.6
	8.4	6.8
	−	−
	−	−
	−	−

Growth Rates (%)

	Long-term EPS Analyst Estimates
	11.7
	10.4
	−
	−
	−

Betas (Levered)

	Raw (OLS)	Blume Adjusted	Peer Group	Vasicek Adjusted	Sum	Downside
Median	1.40	1.26	1.17	1.21	1.19	1.49
SIC Composite	1.28	1.18	1.17	1.20	1.13	1.35
Large Composite	−	−	−	−	−	−
Small Composite	−	−	−	−	−	−
High Financial Risk	−	−	−	−	−	−

Betas (Unlevered)

	Raw (OLS)	Blume Adjusted	Peer Group	Vasicek Adjusted	Sum	Downside
Median	1.28	1.16	1.08	1.12	1.05	1.30
SIC Composite	1.16	1.08	1.07	1.09	1.03	1.23
Large Composite	−	−	−	−	−	−
Small Composite	−	−	−	−	−	−
High Financial Risk	−	−	−	−	−	−

Equity Valuation Multiples

	Price/Sales Latest	5-Yr Avg	Price/Earnings Latest	5-Yr Avg	Market/Book Latest	5-Yr Avg
Median	0.9	0.8	15.8	23.3	3.3	3.1
SIC Composite	0.8	0.7	17.0	21.0	3.1	3.0
Large Composite	−	−	−	−	−	−
Small Composite	−	−	−	−	−	−
High Financial Risk	−	−	−	−	−	−

Enterprise Valuation (EV) Multiples

	EV/Sales Latest	5-Yr Avg	EV/EBITDA Latest	5-Yr Avg
Median	0.9	0.9	8.8	8.6
SIC Composite	0.9	0.8	8.2	8.5
Large Composite	−	−	−	−
Small Composite	−	−	−	−
High Financial Risk	−	−	−	−

Enterprise Valuation SIC Composite
- EV/Sales: Latest 0.9, 5-Yr Avg 0.8
- EV/EBITDA: Latest 8.2, 5-Yr Avg 8.5

Fama-French (F-F) 5-Factor Model

Fama-French (F-F) Components
	F-F Beta	SMB Premium	HML Premium	RMW Premium	CMA Premium
Median	1.3	4.2	7.7	4.3	-6.1
SIC Composite	1.1	6.7	7.3	3.9	-4.7
Large Composite	−	−	−	−	−
Small Composite	−	−	−	−	−
High Financial Risk	−	−	−	−	−

Leverage Ratios (%)

	Debt/MV Equity Latest	5-Yr Avg	Debt/Total Capital Latest	5-Yr Avg
Median	11.7	15.2	10.5	13.2
SIC Composite	12.4	14.0	11.0	12.3
Large Composite	−	−	−	−
Small Composite	−	−	−	−
High Financial Risk	−	−	−	−

Cost of Debt

	Cost of Debt (%) Latest
Median	6.1
SIC Composite	5.7
Large Composite	−
Small Composite	−
High Financial Risk	−

Capital Structure

SIC Composite (%) Latest
- D/TC: 11.0
- E/TC: 89.0

Cost of Equity Capital (%)

	CRSP Deciles CAPM	CAPM +Size Prem	Build-Up	Risk Premium Report CAPM +Size Prem	Build-Up	Discounted Cash Flow 1-Stage	3-Stage	Fama-French 5-Factor Model
Median	10.1	11.8	11.5	14.4	13.8	13.0	10.0	20.6
SIC Composite	10.1	11.8	11.6	13.8	14.0	12.5	10.1	22.5
Large Composite	−	−	−	−	−	−	−	−
Small Composite	−	−	−	−	−	−	−	−
High Financial Risk	−	−	−	−	−	−	−	−

Cost of Equity Capital (%) SIC Composite
- Avg CRSP: 11.7
- Avg RPR: 13.9
- 1-Stage: 12.5
- 3-Stage: 10.1
- 5-Factor Model: 22.5

Weighted Average Cost of Capital (WACC) (%)

	CRSP Deciles CAPM	CAPM +Size Prem	Build-Up	Risk Premium Report CAPM +Size Prem	Build-Up	Discounted Cash Flow 1-Stage	3-Stage	Fama-French 5-Factor Model
Median	9.8	11.3	10.9	13.1	13.0	12.4	9.6	19.7
SIC Composite	9.6	11.1	10.9	12.8	13.1	11.7	9.5	20.6
Large Composite	−	−	−	−	−	−	−	−
Small Composite	−	−	−	−	−	−	−	−
High Financial Risk	−	−	−	−	−	−	−	−

WACC (%) SIC Composite
- Low: 9.5
- High: 20.6
- Average: 12.8
- Median: 11.7

© 2017 Duff & Phelps. All Rights Reserved. Duff & Phelps has used the utmost care in compiling the data presented herein, but cannot guarantee the accuracy, completeness, or timeliness of the information.

Data Updated Through March 31, 2017

26

Number of Companies: 20
Paper and Allied Products

Industry Description
This major group includes establishments primarily engaged in the manufacture of pulps from wood and other cellulose fibers, and from rags; the manufacture of paper and paperboard; and the manufacture of paper and paperboard into converted products, such as paper coated off the paper machine, paper bags, paper boxes, and envelopes. Also included are establishments primarily engaged in manufacturing bags of plastics film and sheet.

Sales (in millions)

Three Largest Companies
Int'l Paper Co.	$21,079.0
Kimberly-Clark Corp.	18,202.0
WestRock Company	14,171.8

Three Smallest Companies
CSS Industries Inc.	$317.0
Orchids Paper Products	168.4
Orient Paper, Inc.	135.3

Annualized Monthly Performance Statistics (%)

Industry
	Geometric Mean	Arithmetic Mean	Standard Deviation
1-year	15.7	16.4	13.2
3-year	8.7	9.9	16.7
5-year	14.7	15.8	16.0

Total Assets (in millions)

Three Largest Companies
Int'l Paper Co.	$33,345.0
WestRock Company	23,038.2
Kimberly-Clark Corp.	14,602.0

Three Smallest Companies
CSS Industries Inc.	$309.9
Orchids Paper Products	251.4
Orient Paper, Inc.	238.6

S&P 500 Index
	Geometric Mean	Arithmetic Mean	Standard Deviation
1-year	17.2	17.4	7.2
3-year	10.4	10.9	11.5
5-year	13.3	13.9	11.5

Return Ratios (%)

	Return on Assets Latest	5-Yr Avg	Return on Equity Latest	5-Yr Avg	Dividend Yield Latest	5-Yr Avg
Median (20)	5.0	5.1	9.4	9.9	2.9	2.5
SIC Composite (20)	4.7	4.8	4.3	4.9	3.0	2.9
Large Composite (3)	4.5	4.7	4.0	4.5	3.2	3.1
Small Composite (3)	5.3	6.4	8.4	8.2	4.6	4.5
High-Financial Risk (–)	–	–	–	–	–	–

Liquidity Ratio

	Current Ratio Latest	5-Yr Avg
Median (20)	1.8	1.9
SIC Composite (20)	1.4	1.5
Large Composite (3)	1.3	1.4
Small Composite (3)	3.0	3.6
High-Financial Risk (–)	–	–

Profitability Ratio (%)

	Operating Margin Latest	5-Yr Avg
Median (20)	9.9	9.1
SIC Composite (20)	11.1	10.5
Large Composite (3)	12.4	11.7
Small Composite (3)	10.5	10.8
High-Financial Risk (–)	–	–

Growth Rates (%)

	Long-term EPS Analyst Estimates
Median (20)	8.5
SIC Composite (20)	8.5
Large Composite (3)	8.1
Small Composite (3)	8.5
High-Financial Risk (–)	–

Betas (Levered)

	Raw (OLS)	Blume Adjusted	Peer Group	Vasicek Adjusted	Sum	Downside
Median	1.21	1.14	1.00	1.14	1.31	1.49
SIC Composite	1.14	1.09	1.00	1.13	1.22	1.15
Large Composite	1.03	1.03	1.01	1.03	1.09	1.08
Small Composite	1.09	1.06	1.00	1.02	1.00	1.12
High Financial Risk	–	–	–	–	–	–

Betas (Unlevered)

	Raw (OLS)	Blume Adjusted	Peer Group	Vasicek Adjusted	Sum	Downside
Median	0.95	0.89	0.79	0.90	0.97	1.09
SIC Composite	0.89	0.85	0.79	0.88	0.95	0.90
Large Composite	0.81	0.80	0.79	0.81	0.85	0.84
Small Composite	0.92	0.90	0.86	0.87	0.85	0.95
High Financial Risk	–	–	–	–	–	–

Equity Valuation Multiples

	Price/Sales Latest	5-Yr Avg	Price/Earnings Latest	5-Yr Avg	Market/Book Latest	5-Yr Avg
Median	0.9	0.8	19.2	18.4	2.1	1.9
SIC Composite	1.3	1.0	23.2	20.5	3.3	2.8
Large Composite	1.5	1.2	25.0	22.4	3.8	3.4
Small Composite	0.8	0.8	11.9	12.1	0.8	1.0
High Financial Risk	–	–	–	–	–	–

Enterprise Valuation (EV) Multiples

	EV/Sales Latest	5-Yr Avg	EV/EBITDA Latest	5-Yr Avg
Median	1.3	1.1	8.9	7.6
SIC Composite	1.6	1.4	9.6	8.5
Large Composite	1.9	1.6	10.1	9.0
Small Composite	0.9	0.8	5.4	5.2
High Financial Risk	–	–	–	–

Enterprise Valuation SIC Composite
Latest: EV/Sales 1.6, EV/EBITDA 9.6
5-Yr Avg: EV/Sales 1.4, EV/EBITDA 8.5

Fama-French (F-F) 5-Factor Model

Fama-French (F-F) Components
	F-F Beta	SMB Premium	HML Premium	RMW Premium	CMA Premium
Median	1.2	3.2	0.8	-0.9	-0.3
SIC Composite	1.1	0.5	-2.9	-0.9	3.8
Large Composite	–	–	–	–	–
Small Composite	1.0	2.9	-2.0	-1.9	3.8
High Financial Risk	–	–	–	–	–

Leverage Ratios (%)

	Debt/MV Equity Latest	5-Yr Avg	Debt/Total Capital Latest	5-Yr Avg
Median	36.9	37.1	26.9	27.0
SIC Composite	32.2	34.0	24.4	25.4
Large Composite	30.5	30.8	23.4	23.5
Small Composite	26.3	13.7	20.8	12.0
High Financial Risk	–	–	–	–

Cost of Debt

	Cost of Debt (%) Latest
Median	6.1
SIC Composite	5.0
Large Composite	4.6
Small Composite	6.1
High Financial Risk	–

Capital Structure

SIC Composite (%) Latest
D/TC: 24.4
E/TC: 75.6

Cost of Equity Capital (%)

	CAPM	CRSP Deciles CAPM +Size Prem	Build-Up	Risk Premium Report CAPM +Size Prem	Build-Up	Discounted Cash Flow 1-Stage	3-Stage	Fama-French 5-Factor Model
Median	9.8	12.1	10.7	14.4	13.2	11.8	10.6	12.8
SIC Composite	9.7	10.3	9.6	12.6	11.3	11.6	9.6	10.2
Large Composite	9.2	9.4	9.3	11.4	10.5	11.4	8.7	–
Small Composite	9.1	14.7	14.6	14.4	16.0	11.6	11.0	11.7
High Financial Risk	–	–	–	–	–	–	–	–

Cost of Equity Capital (%) SIC Composite
Avg CRSP: 10.0, Avg RPR: 12.0, 1-Stage: 11.6, 3-Stage: 9.6, 5-Factor Model: 10.2

Weighted Average Cost of Capital (WACC) (%)

	CAPM	CRSP Deciles CAPM +Size Prem	Build-Up	Risk Premium Report CAPM +Size Prem	Build-Up	Discounted Cash Flow 1-Stage	3-Stage	Fama-French 5-Factor Model
Median	8.7	9.7	8.7	11.9	10.7	9.8	8.7	10.6
SIC Composite	8.3	8.8	8.2	10.5	9.5	9.8	8.2	8.7
Large Composite	7.8	8.0	7.9	9.5	8.8	9.5	7.4	–
Small Composite	8.1	12.5	12.4	12.3	13.5	10.0	9.5	10.1
High Financial Risk	–	–	–	–	–	–	–	–

WACC (%) SIC Composite
Low 8.2 — High 10.5
Average 9.1, Median 8.8

© 2017 Duff & Phelps. All Rights Reserved. Duff & Phelps has used the utmost care in compiling the data presented herein, but cannot guarantee the accuracy, completeness, or timeliness of the information.

Data Updated Through March 31, 2017

262

Number of Companies: 7
Paper Mills

Industry Description
Establishments primarily engaged in manufacturing paper from wood pulp and other fiber pulp, and which may also manufacture converted paper products.

Sales (in millions)

Three Largest Companies
Kimberly-Clark Corp.	$18,202.0
Domtar Corp.	5,098.0
Clearwater Paper Corp.	1,734.8

Three Smallest Companies
Neenah Paper, Inc.	$941.5
Schweitzer-Mauduit Int'l Inc.	839.9
Orient Paper, Inc.	135.3

Total Assets (in millions)

Three Largest Companies
Kimberly-Clark Corp.	$14,602.0
Domtar Corp.	5,680.0
Clearwater Paper Corp.	1,684.3

Three Smallest Companies
Schweitzer-Mauduit Int'l Inc.	$1,173.7
Neenah Paper, Inc.	765.6
Orient Paper, Inc.	238.6

Annualized Monthly Performance Statistics (%)

Industry	Geometric Mean	Arithmetic Mean	Standard Deviation	S&P 500 Index	Geometric Mean	Arithmetic Mean	Standard Deviation
1-year	1.8	3.1	17.5	1-year	17.2	17.4	7.2
3-year	8.7	9.9	17.0	3-year	10.4	10.9	11.5
5-year	14.9	16.1	17.0	5-year	13.3	13.9	11.5

Return Ratios (%)

	Return on Assets Latest	5-Yr Avg	Return on Equity Latest	5-Yr Avg	Dividend Yield Latest	5-Yr Avg
Median (7)	4.8	7.6	8.2	9.7	2.3	2.1
SIC Composite (7)	9.9	7.8	4.7	4.6	3.0	3.0
Large Composite (–)	–	–	–	–	–	–
Small Composite (–)	–	–	–	–	–	–
High-Financial Risk (–)	–	–	–	–	–	–

Liquidity Ratio

	Current Ratio Latest	5-Yr Avg
Median (7)	1.5	2.0
SIC Composite (7)	1.1	1.2
Large Composite (–)	–	–
Small Composite (–)	–	–
High-Financial Risk (–)	–	–

Profitability Ratio (%)

	Operating Margin Latest	5-Yr Avg
Median (7)	13.0	11.2
SIC Composite (7)	14.4	13.4
Large Composite (–)	–	–
Small Composite (–)	–	–
High-Financial Risk (–)	–	–

Growth Rates (%)

	Long-term EPS Analyst Estimates
Median (7)	7.4
SIC Composite (7)	7.3
Large Composite (–)	–
Small Composite (–)	–
High-Financial Risk (–)	–

Betas (Levered)

	Raw (OLS)	Blume Adjusted	Peer Group	Vasicek Adjusted	Sum	Downside
Median	1.20	1.14	1.00	1.04	1.09	1.43
SIC Composite	0.76	0.86	1.00	0.84	0.54	0.83
Large Composite	–	–	–	–	–	–
Small Composite	–	–	–	–	–	–
High Financial Risk	–	–	–	–	–	–

Betas (Unlevered)

	Raw (OLS)	Blume Adjusted	Peer Group	Vasicek Adjusted	Sum	Downside
Median	0.90	0.86	0.80	0.78	0.69	0.94
SIC Composite	0.65	0.73	0.85	0.71	0.46	0.71
Large Composite	–	–	–	–	–	–
Small Composite	–	–	–	–	–	–
High Financial Risk	–	–	–	–	–	–

Equity Valuation Multiples

	Price/Sales Latest	5-Yr Avg	Price/Earnings Latest	5-Yr Avg	Market/Book Latest	5-Yr Avg
Median	0.6	0.6	17.9	15.0	1.5	1.7
SIC Composite	1.9	1.6	21.2	21.8	8.7	5.6
Large Composite	–	–	–	–	–	–
Small Composite	–	–	–	–	–	–
High Financial Risk	–	–	–	–	–	–

Enterprise Valuation (EV) Multiples

	EV/Sales Latest	5-Yr Avg	EV/EBITDA Latest	5-Yr Avg
Median	0.9	0.9	8.7	7.5
SIC Composite	2.2	1.8	11.4	9.8
Large Composite	–	–	–	–
Small Composite	–	–	–	–
High Financial Risk	–	–	–	–

Enterprise Valuation SIC Composite

Latest: EV/Sales 2.2, EV/EBITDA 11.4
5-Yr Avg: EV/Sales 1.8, EV/EBITDA 9.8

Fama-French (F-F) 5-Factor Model

	F-F Beta	SMB Premium	HML Premium	RMW Premium	CMA Premium
Median	1.3	6.3	-1.6	0.6	-0.7
SIC Composite	0.8	-0.7	-5.3	-0.3	6.3
Large Composite	–	–	–	–	–
Small Composite	–	–	–	–	–
High Financial Risk	–	–	–	–	–

Leverage Ratios (%)

	Debt/MV Equity Latest	5-Yr Avg	Debt/Total Capital Latest	5-Yr Avg
Median	39.4	38.2	28.2	27.7
SIC Composite	19.9	20.8	16.6	17.2
Large Composite	–	–	–	–
Small Composite	–	–	–	–
High Financial Risk	–	–	–	–

Cost of Debt

	Cost of Debt (%) Latest
Median	6.1
SIC Composite	4.5
Large Composite	–
Small Composite	–
High Financial Risk	–

Capital Structure

SIC Composite (%) Latest: D/TC 16.6, E/TC 83.4

Cost of Equity Capital (%)

	CRSP Deciles CAPM	CAPM +Size Prem	Build-Up	Risk Premium Report CAPM +Size Prem	Build-Up	Discounted Cash Flow 1-Stage	3-Stage	Fama-French 5-Factor Model
Median	9.2	11.6	10.7	13.6	14.1	10.4	11.8	15.1
SIC Composite	8.1	8.3	9.3	8.6	10.9	10.4	8.3	7.9
Large Composite	–	–	–	–	–	–	–	–
Small Composite	–	–	–	–	–	–	–	–
High Financial Risk	–	–	–	–	–	–	–	–

Cost of Equity Capital (%) SIC Composite
Avg CRSP 8.8, Avg RPR 9.7, 1-Stage 10.4, 3-Stage 8.3, 5-Factor Model 7.9

Weighted Average Cost of Capital (WACC) (%)

	CRSP Deciles CAPM	CAPM +Size Prem	Build-Up	Risk Premium Report CAPM +Size Prem	Build-Up	Discounted Cash Flow 1-Stage	3-Stage	Fama-French 5-Factor Model
Median	8.0	9.1	8.5	11.1	9.9	9.3	9.4	10.8
SIC Composite	7.3	7.5	8.2	7.7	9.6	9.2	7.5	7.1
Large Composite	–	–	–	–	–	–	–	–
Small Composite	–	–	–	–	–	–	–	–
High Financial Risk	–	–	–	–	–	–	–	–

WACC (%) SIC Composite
Low 7.1, High 9.6, Average 8.1, Median 7.7

© 2017 Duff & Phelps. All Rights Reserved. Duff & Phelps has used the utmost care in compiling the data presented herein, but cannot guarantee the accuracy, completeness, or timeliness of the information.

Data Updated Through March 31, 2017

265

Number of Companies: 5
Paperboard Containers and Boxes

Industry Description
Establishments primarily engaged in manufacturing paperboard products; paperboard containers and boxes; corrugated and solid fiber boxes; fiber cans, tubes, drums, and similar products; sanitary food containers; folding paperboard boxes, including sanitary.

Sales (in millions)

Three Largest Companies
WestRock Company	$14,171.8
Packaging Corp. Of America	5,779.0
Sonoco Products Co.	4,782.9

Three Smallest Companies
Sonoco Products Co.	$4,782.9
Graphic Packaging Holding Co.	4,298.1
Greif, Inc.	3,323.6

Total Assets (in millions)

Three Largest Companies
WestRock Company	$23,038.2
Packaging Corp. Of America	5,777.0
Graphic Packaging Holding Co.	4,603.4

Three Smallest Companies
Graphic Packaging Holding Co.	$4,603.4
Sonoco Products Co.	3,923.2
Greif, Inc.	3,153.0

Annualized Monthly Performance Statistics (%)

	Industry Geometric Mean	Arithmetic Mean	Standard Deviation		S&P 500 Index Geometric Mean	Arithmetic Mean	Standard Deviation
1-year	38.6	39.9	19.6	1-year	17.2	17.4	7.2
3-year	8.4	11.1	24.6	3-year	10.4	10.9	11.5
5-year	16.0	18.4	24.2	5-year	13.3	13.9	11.5

Return Ratios (%)

	Return on Assets Latest	5-Yr Avg	Return on Equity Latest	5-Yr Avg	Dividend Yield Latest	5-Yr Avg	Current Ratio Latest	5-Yr Avg	Operating Margin Latest	5-Yr Avg	Long-term EPS Analyst Estimates
Median (5)	5.1	3.6	16.1	12.5	3.0	2.9	1.7	1.6	9.3	8.7	8.7
SIC Composite (5)	2.9	3.9	3.6	5.4	3.0	2.5	1.8	1.7	9.8	9.4	9.5
Large Composite (–)	–	–	–	–	–	–	–	–	–	–	–
Small Composite (–)	–	–	–	–	–	–	–	–	–	–	–
High-Financial Risk (–)	–	–	–	–	–	–	–	–	–	–	–

Betas (Levered)

	Raw (OLS)	Blume Adjusted	Peer Group	Vasicek Adjusted	Sum	Downside
Median	1.45	1.29	1.00	1.23	2.01	1.88
SIC Composite	1.56	1.36	1.00	1.45	1.87	1.69
Large Composite	–	–	–	–	–	–
Small Composite	–	–	–	–	–	–
High Financial Risk	–	–	–	–	–	–

Betas (Unlevered)

	Raw (OLS)	Blume Adjusted	Peer Group	Vasicek Adjusted	Sum	Downside
Median	1.13	1.01	0.79	0.97	1.53	1.45
SIC Composite	1.17	1.03	0.77	1.09	1.40	1.27
Large Composite	–	–	–	–	–	–
Small Composite	–	–	–	–	–	–
High Financial Risk	–	–	–	–	–	–

Equity Valuation Multiples

	Price/Sales Latest	5-Yr Avg	Price/Earnings Latest	5-Yr Avg	Market/Book Latest	5-Yr Avg
Median	0.9	0.8	19.2	19.8	2.8	2.6
SIC Composite	1.0	0.8	28.2	18.7	1.8	1.7
Large Composite	–	–	–	–	–	–
Small Composite	–	–	–	–	–	–
High Financial Risk	–	–	–	–	–	–

Enterprise Valuation (EV) Multiples

	EV/Sales Latest	5-Yr Avg	EV/EBITDA Latest	5-Yr Avg
Median	1.3	1.1	9.2	8.2
SIC Composite	1.4	1.2	8.5	7.9
Large Composite	–	–	–	–
Small Composite	–	–	–	–
High Financial Risk	–	–	–	–

Enterprise Valuation SIC Composite
- EV/Sales: Latest 1.4, 5-Yr Avg 1.2
- EV/EBITDA: Latest 8.5, 5-Yr Avg 7.9

Fama-French (F-F) 5-Factor Model

	F-F Beta	SMB Premium	HML Premium	RMW Premium	CMA Premium
Median	1.7	1.3	-1.7	-2.2	-0.4
SIC Composite	1.5	1.2	-0.2	-2.1	0.1
Large Composite	–	–	–	–	–
Small Composite	–	–	–	–	–
High Financial Risk	–	–	–	–	–

Leverage Ratios (%)

	Debt/MV Equity Latest	5-Yr Avg	Debt/Total Capital Latest	5-Yr Avg
Median	39.0	49.3	28.0	33.0
SIC Composite	37.8	44.2	27.4	30.7
Large Composite	–	–	–	–
Small Composite	–	–	–	–
High Financial Risk	–	–	–	–

Cost of Debt

	Cost of Debt (%) Latest
Median	4.8
SIC Composite	5.3
Large Composite	–
Small Composite	–
High Financial Risk	–

Capital Structure

SIC Composite (%) Latest
- D/TC: 27.4
- E/TC: 72.6

Cost of Equity Capital (%)

	CAPM	CRSP Deciles CAPM +Size Prem	Build-Up	Risk Premium Report CAPM +Size Prem	Build-Up	Discounted Cash Flow 1-Stage	3-Stage	Fama-French 5-Factor Model
Median	10.3	11.8	10.0	18.1	12.6	12.0	11.5	10.0
SIC Composite	11.5	12.3	9.9	16.5	11.9	12.5	11.3	10.7
Large Composite	–	–	–	–	–	–	–	–
Small Composite	–	–	–	–	–	–	–	–
High Financial Risk	–	–	–	–	–	–	–	–

Cost of Equity Capital (%) SIC Composite
- Avg CRSP: 11.1
- Avg RPR: 14.2
- 1-Stage: 12.5
- 3-Stage: 11.3
- 5-Factor Model: 10.7

Weighted Average Cost of Capital (WACC) (%)

	CAPM	CRSP Deciles CAPM +Size Prem	Build-Up	Risk Premium Report CAPM +Size Prem	Build-Up	Discounted Cash Flow 1-Stage	3-Stage	Fama-French 5-Factor Model
Median	8.6	9.4	8.7	14.1	10.4	9.7	8.9	8.7
SIC Composite	9.5	10.1	8.3	13.2	9.8	10.2	9.3	8.9
Large Composite	–	–	–	–	–	–	–	–
Small Composite	–	–	–	–	–	–	–	–
High Financial Risk	–	–	–	–	–	–	–	–

WACC (%) SIC Composite
- Low: 8.3
- High: 13.2
- Average: 10.0
- Median: 9.8

© 2017 Duff & Phelps. All Rights Reserved. Duff & Phelps has used the utmost care in compiling the data presented herein, but cannot guarantee the accuracy, completeness, or timeliness of the information.

Data Updated Through March 31, 2017

267

Number of Companies: 5
Converted Paper and Paperboard Products, Except

Industry Description
Establishments primarily engaged in manufacturing packaging paper and plastics film; coated and laminated paper; plastics, foil, and coated paper bags; uncrated paper and multiwall bags; die-cut paper and paperboard and cardboard; sanitary paper products; envelopes; stationery, tablets, and related products; converted paper and paperboard products, not elsewhere classified.

Sales (in millions)

Three Largest Companies
Avery Dennison Corp.	$6,086.5
Bemis Co. Inc.	4,004.4
ZAGG Inc.	401.9

Three Smallest Companies
ZAGG Inc.	$401.9
CSS Industries Inc.	317.0
Orchids Paper Products	168.4

Annualized Monthly Performance Statistics (%)

Industry	Geometric Mean	Arithmetic Mean	Standard Deviation
1-year	5.5	6.3	13.3
3-year	14.7	16.2	19.3
5-year	17.4	18.7	17.8

Total Assets (in millions)

Three Largest Companies
Avery Dennison Corp.	$4,396.4
Bemis Co. Inc.	3,715.7
ZAGG Inc.	310.7

Three Smallest Companies
ZAGG Inc.	$310.7
CSS Industries Inc.	309.9
Orchids Paper Products	251.4

S&P 500 Index	Geometric Mean	Arithmetic Mean	Standard Deviation
1-year	17.2	17.4	7.2
3-year	10.4	10.9	11.5
5-year	13.3	13.9	11.5

Return Ratios (%)

	Return on Assets Latest	5-Yr Avg	Return on Equity Latest	5-Yr Avg	Dividend Yield Latest	5-Yr Avg
Median (5)	6.4	5.7	9.9	9.7	2.3	2.6
SIC Composite (5)	6.4	5.6	4.6	5.2	2.3	2.6
Large Composite (–)	–	–	–	–	–	–
Small Composite (–)	–	–	–	–	–	–
High-Financial Risk (–)	–	–	–	–	–	–

Liquidity Ratio

	Current Ratio Latest	5-Yr Avg
Median (5)	2.0	2.3
SIC Composite (5)	1.2	1.5
Large Composite	–	–
Small Composite	–	–
High-Financial Risk	–	–

Profitability Ratio (%)

	Operating Margin Latest	5-Yr Avg
Median	9.9	8.5
SIC Composite	9.9	8.6
Large Composite	–	–
Small Composite	–	–
High-Financial Risk	–	–

Growth Rates (%)

	Long-term EPS Analyst Estimates
Median	8.5
SIC Composite	9.4
Large Composite	–
Small Composite	–
High-Financial Risk	–

Betas (Levered)

	Raw (OLS)	Blume Adjusted	Peer Group	Vasicek Adjusted	Sum	Downside
Median	1.02	1.02	1.00	1.00	0.95	1.24
SIC Composite	1.04	1.03	1.00	1.01	1.12	1.08
Large Composite	–	–	–	–	–	–
Small Composite	–	–	–	–	–	–
High Financial Risk	–	–	–	–	–	–

Betas (Unlevered)

	Raw (OLS)	Blume Adjusted	Peer Group	Vasicek Adjusted	Sum	Downside
Median	0.89	0.89	0.86	0.87	0.95	1.09
SIC Composite	0.86	0.85	0.83	0.84	0.92	0.89
Large Composite	–	–	–	–	–	–
Small Composite	–	–	–	–	–	–
High Financial Risk	–	–	–	–	–	–

Equity Valuation Multiples

	Price/Sales Latest	5-Yr Avg	Price/Earnings Latest	5-Yr Avg	Market/Book Latest	5-Yr Avg
Median	1.1	0.8	19.2	19.8	1.7	2.1
SIC Composite	1.1	0.9	21.6	19.4	4.2	2.9
Large Composite	–	–	–	–	–	–
Small Composite	–	–	–	–	–	–
High Financial Risk	–	–	–	–	–	–

Enterprise Valuation (EV) Multiples

	EV/Sales Latest	5-Yr Avg	EV/EBITDA Latest	5-Yr Avg
Median	1.3	1.0	10.0	8.4
SIC Composite	1.4	1.1	10.1	8.6
Large Composite	–	–	–	–
Small Composite	–	–	–	–
High Financial Risk	–	–	–	–

Enterprise Valuation SIC Composite
- EV/Sales: Latest 1.4, 5-Yr Avg 1.1
- EV/EBITDA: Latest 10.1, 5-Yr Avg 8.6

Fama-French (F-F) 5-Factor Model

	F-F Beta	SMB Premium	HML Premium	RMW Premium	CMA Premium
Median	1.0	0.0	-2.2	-0.9	6.3
SIC Composite	1.0	1.0	-2.5	-0.4	4.4
Large Composite	–	–	–	–	–
Small Composite	–	–	–	–	–
High Financial Risk	–	–	–	–	–

Leverage Ratios (%)

	Debt/MV Equity Latest	5-Yr Avg	Debt/Total Capital Latest	5-Yr Avg
Median	25.5	13.8	20.3	12.2
SIC Composite	24.0	26.8	19.4	21.2
Large Composite	–	–	–	–
Small Composite	–	–	–	–
High Financial Risk	–	–	–	–

Cost of Debt

	Cost of Debt (%) Latest
Median	6.1
SIC Composite	4.9
Large Composite	–
Small Composite	–
High Financial Risk	–

Capital Structure

SIC Composite (%) Latest
- D/TC: 19.4
- E/TC: 80.6

Cost of Equity Capital (%)

	CRSP Deciles CAPM	CAPM +Size Prem	Build-Up	Risk Premium Report CAPM +Size Prem	Build-Up	Discounted Cash Flow 1-Stage	3-Stage	Fama-French 5-Factor Model
Median	9.0	14.6	14.6	14.2	15.5	11.7	10.0	12.1
SIC Composite	9.1	10.3	10.2	13.0	12.8	11.8	9.9	11.5
Large Composite	–	–	–	–	–	–	–	–
Small Composite	–	–	–	–	–	–	–	–
High Financial Risk	–	–	–	–	–	–	–	–

Cost of Equity Capital (%) SIC Composite
- Avg CRSP: 10.2
- Avg RPR: 12.9
- Build-Up: 11.8
- 1-Stage: 9.9
- 3-Stage: 11.5
- 5-Factor Model: (11.5)

Weighted Average Cost of Capital (WACC) (%)

	CRSP Deciles CAPM	CAPM +Size Prem	Build-Up	Risk Premium Report CAPM +Size Prem	Build-Up	Discounted Cash Flow 1-Stage	3-Stage	Fama-French 5-Factor Model
Median	8.1	12.2	12.2	12.9	13.5	10.3	9.0	10.3
SIC Composite	8.2	9.2	9.1	11.4	11.2	10.4	8.9	10.2
Large Composite	–	–	–	–	–	–	–	–
Small Composite	–	–	–	–	–	–	–	–
High Financial Risk	–	–	–	–	–	–	–	–

WACC (%) SIC Composite
Low 8.9 — High 11.4
▲ Average 10.1 ♦ Median 10.2

© 2017 Duff & Phelps. All Rights Reserved. Duff & Phelps has used the utmost care in compiling the data presented herein, but cannot guarantee the accuracy, completeness, or timeliness of the information.

Data Updated Through March 31, 2017

27

Number of Companies: 9
Printing, Publishing, and Allied Industries

Industry Description
This major group includes establishments engaged in printing by one or more common processes, such as letterpress; lithography (including offset), gravure, or screen; and those establishments which perform services for the printing trade, such as bookbinding and platemaking. This major group also includes establishments engaged in publishing newspapers, books, and periodicals, regardless of whether or not they do their own printing.

Sales (in millions)

Three Largest Companies
Deluxe Corp.	$1,849.1
John Wiley & Sons	1,727.0
Scholastic Corp.	1,672.8

Three Smallest Companies
Multi-Color Corp.	$870.8
A. H. Belo Corp.	272.1
Value Line, Inc.	34.5

Annualized Monthly Performance Statistics (%)

Industry
	Geometric Mean	Arithmetic Mean	Standard Deviation
1-year	18.0	19.2	17.8
3-year	6.8	8.0	16.4
5-year	12.3	13.7	18.3

Total Assets (in millions)

Three Largest Companies
John Wiley & Sons	$2,921.1
New York Times Co.	2,185.4
Deluxe Corp.	2,184.3

Three Smallest Companies
Multi-Color Corp.	$1,078.1
A. H. Belo Corp.	221.5
Value Line, Inc.	86.5

S&P 500 Index
	Geometric Mean	Arithmetic Mean	Standard Deviation
1-year	17.2	17.4	7.2
3-year	10.4	10.9	11.5
5-year	13.3	13.9	11.5

Return Ratios (%)

	Return on Assets Latest	Return on Assets 5-Yr Avg	Return on Equity Latest	Return on Equity 5-Yr Avg	Dividend Yield Latest	Dividend Yield 5-Yr Avg
Median (9)	4.8	4.3	11.8	10.6	1.2	0.9
SIC Composite (9)	4.4	4.8	4.0	5.3	1.1	1.4
Large Composite (–)	–	–	–	–	–	–
Small Composite (–)	–	–	–	–	–	–
High-Financial Risk (–)	–	–	–	–	–	–

Liquidity Ratio

Current Ratio Latest	5-Yr Avg
1.8	1.9
1.5	1.5
–	–
–	–
–	–

Profitability Ratio (%)

Operating Margin Latest	5-Yr Avg
9.3	9.7
11.0	11.1
–	–
–	–
–	–

Growth Rates (%)

Long-term EPS Analyst Estimates
14.4
14.4
–
–
–

Betas (Levered)

	Raw (OLS)	Blume Adjusted	Peer Group	Vasicek Adjusted	Sum	Downside
Median	1.02	1.02	1.44	1.28	0.94	1.32
SIC Composite	1.15	1.10	1.44	1.20	0.95	1.05
Large Composite	–	–	–	–	–	–
Small Composite	–	–	–	–	–	–
High Financial Risk	–	–	–	–	–	–

Betas (Unlevered)

	Raw (OLS)	Blume Adjusted	Peer Group	Vasicek Adjusted	Sum	Downside
Median	0.90	0.91	1.26	1.14	0.78	1.24
SIC Composite	1.00	0.96	1.24	1.05	0.83	0.92
Large Composite	–	–	–	–	–	–
Small Composite	–	–	–	–	–	–
High Financial Risk	–	–	–	–	–	–

Equity Valuation Multiples

	Price/Sales Latest	Price/Sales 5-Yr Avg	Price/Earnings Latest	Price/Earnings 5-Yr Avg	Market/Book Latest	Market/Book 5-Yr Avg
Median	1.4	1.1	25.2	19.4	2.7	2.3
SIC Composite	1.4	1.2	24.9	19.0	2.4	2.1
Large Composite	–	–	–	–	–	–
Small Composite	–	–	–	–	–	–
High Financial Risk	–	–	–	–	–	–

Enterprise Valuation (EV) Multiples

	EV/Sales Latest	EV/Sales 5-Yr Avg	EV/EBITDA Latest	EV/EBITDA 5-Yr Avg
Median	1.5	1.7	9.9	7.5
SIC Composite	1.5	1.3	9.6	8.0
Large Composite	–	–	–	–
Small Composite	–	–	–	–
High Financial Risk	–	–	–	–

Enterprise Valuation SIC Composite

Latest: EV/Sales 1.5, EV/EBITDA 9.6
5-Yr Avg: EV/Sales 1.3, EV/EBITDA 8.0

Fama-French (F-F) 5-Factor Model

Fama-French (F-F) Components

	F-F Beta	SMB Premium	HML Premium	RMW Premium	CMA Premium
Median	0.7	3.0	4.9	-0.8	-4.9
SIC Composite	1.1	2.9	1.2	0.6	-0.7
Large Composite	–	–	–	–	–
Small Composite	–	–	–	–	–
High Financial Risk	–	–	–	–	–

Leverage Ratios (%)

	Debt/MV Equity Latest	5-Yr Avg	Debt/Total Capital Latest	5-Yr Avg
Median	19.6	21.3	16.4	17.6
SIC Composite	21.7	28.5	17.8	22.2
Large Composite	–	–	–	–
Small Composite	–	–	–	–
High Financial Risk	–	–	–	–

Cost of Debt

Cost of Debt (%) Latest
6.1
6.5
–
–
–

Capital Structure

SIC Composite (%) Latest
D/TC: 17.8
E/TC: 82.2

Cost of Equity Capital (%)

	CAPM	CRSP Deciles CAPM +Size Prem	Build-Up	Risk Premium Report CAPM +Size Prem	Build-Up	Discounted Cash Flow 1-Stage	3-Stage	Fama-French 5-Factor Model
Median	10.6	12.4	13.1	13.0	14.0	10.0	13.7	9.7
SIC Composite	10.1	11.8	13.1	12.5	13.6	15.1	13.6	13.3
Large Composite	–	–	–	–	–	–	–	–
Small Composite	–	–	–	–	–	–	–	–
High Financial Risk	–	–	–	–	–	–	–	–

Cost of Equity Capital (%) SIC Composite

Avg CRSP 12.5, Avg RPR 13.1, 1-Stage 15.1, 3-Stage 13.6, 5-Factor Model 13.3

Weighted Average Cost of Capital (WACC) (%)

	CAPM	CRSP Deciles CAPM +Size Prem	Build-Up	Risk Premium Report CAPM +Size Prem	Build-Up	Discounted Cash Flow 1-Stage	3-Stage	Fama-French 5-Factor Model
Median	9.8	11.3	11.8	12.3	12.7	8.7	12.1	9.7
SIC Composite	9.4	10.8	11.8	11.3	12.2	13.4	12.2	12.0
Large Composite	–	–	–	–	–	–	–	–
Small Composite	–	–	–	–	–	–	–	–
High Financial Risk	–	–	–	–	–	–	–	–

WACC (%) SIC Composite
Low 10.8, High 13.4, Average 12.0, Median 12.0

© 2017 Duff & Phelps. All Rights Reserved. Duff & Phelps has used the utmost care in compiling the data presented herein, but cannot guarantee the accuracy, completeness, or timeliness of the information.

Data Updated Through March 31, 2017

28

Number of Companies: 99
Chemicals and Allied Products

Industry Description
This major group includes establishments producing basic chemicals, and establishments manufacturing products by predominantly chemical processes. Establishments classified in this major group manufacture three general classes of products: (1) basic chemicals, such as acids, alkalies, salts, and organic chemicals; (2) chemical products to be used in further manufacture, such as synthetic fibers, plastics materials, dry colors, and pigments; and (3) finished chemical products to be used for ultimate consumption, such as drugs, cosmetics, and soaps; or to be used as materials or supplies in other industries, such as paints.

Sales (in millions)

Three Largest Companies
Pfizer Inc.	$52,824.0
Dow Chemical	48,158.0
Merck & Co.	39,807.0

Three Smallest Companies
Flexible Solutions International Inc.	$15.9
United-Guardian Inc.	14.0
ImmuCell Corp.	10.2

Total Assets (in millions)

Three Largest Companies
Pfizer Inc.	$171,615.0
Merck & Co.	95,377.0
Dow Chemical	79,511.0

Three Smallest Companies
United-Guardian Inc.	$15.7
ImmuCell Corp.	14.6
Flexible Solutions International Inc.	14.1

Annualized Monthly Performance Statistics (%)

Industry	Geometric Mean	Arithmetic Mean	Standard Deviation
1-year	11.4	12.1	13.6
3-year	7.3	8.3	15.0
5-year	14.8	15.8	15.1

S&P 500 Index	Geometric Mean	Arithmetic Mean	Standard Deviation
1-year	17.2	17.4	7.2
3-year	10.4	10.9	11.5
5-year	13.3	13.9	11.5

Return Ratios (%)

	Return on Assets Latest	5-Yr Avg	Return on Equity Latest	5-Yr Avg	Dividend Yield Latest	5-Yr Avg
Median (99)	7.3	8.0	13.3	16.1	1.2	1.1
SIC Composite (99)	7.5	7.9	4.4	4.8	2.2	2.1
Large Composite (9)	7.3	7.5	4.8	5.2	2.8	2.8
Small Composite (9)	3.2	8.4	1.3	3.8	0.0	0.1
High-Financial Risk (14)	-6.7	-1.6	-11.9	-2.4	0.3	0.3

Liquidity Ratio

	Current Ratio Latest	5-Yr Avg
	2.5	2.7
	2.0	2.0
	2.0	2.0
	–	–
	1.9	2.1

Profitability Ratio (%)

	Operating Margin Latest	5-Yr Avg
	16.5	16.4
	24.0	21.7
	26.7	23.7
	9.8	13.8
	5.1	6.5

Growth Rates (%)

	Long-term EPS Analyst Estimates
	8.9
	9.1
	7.1
	10.6
	13.9

Betas (Levered)

	Raw (OLS)	Blume Adjusted	Peer Group	Vasicek Adjusted	Sum	Downside
Median	1.15	1.10	1.11	1.14	1.21	1.60
SIC Composite	1.09	1.06	1.11	1.09	1.12	1.09
Large Composite	1.04	1.03	1.10	1.04	1.08	1.03
Small Composite	1.09	1.06	1.11	1.09	1.04	1.39
High Financial Risk	1.20	1.14	1.11	1.20	1.35	1.54

Betas (Unlevered)

	Raw (OLS)	Blume Adjusted	Peer Group	Vasicek Adjusted	Sum	Downside
Median	0.99	0.95	0.99	0.96	1.03	1.32
SIC Composite	0.93	0.91	0.94	0.93	0.96	0.93
Large Composite	0.87	0.86	0.92	0.87	0.91	0.87
Small Composite	1.06	1.04	1.09	1.07	1.02	1.36
High Financial Risk	0.77	0.73	0.72	0.76	0.84	0.93

Equity Valuation Multiples

	Price/Sales Latest	5-Yr Avg	Price/Earnings Latest	5-Yr Avg	Market/Book Latest	5-Yr Avg
Median	2.4	2.2	26.0	23.2	3.4	3.1
SIC Composite	3.3	3.0	23.0	21.1	4.1	3.8
Large Composite	3.5	3.1	20.9	19.4	3.6	3.2
Small Composite	3.4	3.0	76.0	26.2	3.0	2.7
High Financial Risk	0.9	1.0	–	–	2.8	2.6

Enterprise Valuation (EV) Multiples

	EV/Sales Latest	5-Yr Avg	EV/EBITDA Latest	5-Yr Avg
Median	2.5	2.2	11.5	10.3
SIC Composite	3.6	3.2	11.4	10.9
Large Composite	3.8	3.3	10.4	10.0
Small Composite	3.0	2.5	20.5	13.4
High Financial Risk	1.6	1.6	13.1	11.9

Enterprise Valuation SIC Composite
- EV/Sales: Latest 3.6, 5-Yr Avg 3.2
- EV/EBITDA: Latest 11.4, 5-Yr Avg 10.9

Fama-French (F-F) 5-Factor Model

	F-F Beta	SMB Premium	HML Premium	RMW Premium	CMA Premium
Median	1.2	1.4	-0.2	0.0	1.4
SIC Composite	1.1	0.3	-2.8	-1.0	2.0
Large Composite	–	–	–	–	–
Small Composite	1.0	0.8	-0.9	-0.9	-2.2
High Financial Risk	–	–	–	–	–

Leverage Ratios (%)

	Debt/MV Equity Latest	5-Yr Avg	Debt/Total Capital Latest	5-Yr Avg
Median	13.9	12.4	12.2	11.0
SIC Composite	18.9	17.6	15.9	14.9
Large Composite	20.0	19.0	16.7	16.0
Small Composite	3.2	2.6	3.1	2.6
High Financial Risk	105.1	77.9	51.2	43.8

Cost of Debt

	Cost of Debt (%) Latest
Median	6.1
SIC Composite	4.5
Large Composite	4.1
Small Composite	6.4
High Financial Risk	7.3

Capital Structure

SIC Composite (%) Latest
- D/TC: 15.9
- E/TC: 84.1

Cost of Equity Capital (%)

	CRSP Deciles CAPM	CAPM +Size Prem	Build-Up	Risk Premium Report CAPM +Size Prem	Build-Up	Discounted Cash Flow 1-Stage	3-Stage	Fama-French 5-Factor Model
Median	9.8	11.6	11.3	14.0	14.1	10.8	9.2	12.9
SIC Composite	9.5	9.7	9.8	11.4	10.3	11.4	10.5	7.9
Large Composite	9.2	9.2	9.6	10.6	9.6	10.1	10.5	–
Small Composite	9.5	13.6	13.7	15.1	16.5	10.6	9.4	5.9
High Financial Risk	–	–	–	22.0	23.4	–	–	–

Cost of Equity Capital (%) SIC Composite
- Avg CRSP: 9.7
- Avg RPR: 10.9
- 1-Stage: 11.4
- 3-Stage: 10.5
- 5-Factor Model: 7.9

Weighted Average Cost of Capital (WACC) (%)

	CRSP Deciles CAPM	CAPM +Size Prem	Build-Up	Risk Premium Report CAPM +Size Prem	Build-Up	Discounted Cash Flow 1-Stage	3-Stage	Fama-French 5-Factor Model
Median	8.9	10.4	10.3	12.3	12.6	10.0	8.5	11.6
SIC Composite	8.6	8.7	8.8	10.1	9.3	10.2	9.4	7.2
Large Composite	8.2	8.2	8.5	9.4	8.5	8.9	9.3	–
Small Composite	9.4	13.3	13.4	14.7	16.2	10.4	9.3	5.9
High Financial Risk	–	–	–	13.9	14.5	–	–	–

WACC (%) SIC Composite
- Low: 7.2
- High: 10.2
- Average: 9.1
- Median: 9.3

© 2017 Duff & Phelps. All Rights Reserved. Duff & Phelps has used the utmost care in compiling the data presented herein, but cannot guarantee the accuracy, completeness, or timeliness of the information.

Data Updated Through March 31, 2017

281

Number of Companies: 11
Industrial Inorganic Chemicals

Industry Description
This group includes establishments primarily engaged in manufacturing basic industrial inorganic chemicals.

Sales (in millions)

Three Largest Companies
Praxair Inc.	$10,534.0
Air Products & Chemicals Inc.	9,524.4
Olin Corp.	5,550.6

Three Smallest Companies
Calgon Carbon Corp.	$514.2
Gulf Resources, Inc.	149.7
Flexible Solutions International Inc.	15.9

Total Assets (in millions)

Three Largest Companies
Praxair Inc.	$19,332.0
Air Products & Chemicals Inc.	18,055.3
Olin Corp.	8,762.6

Three Smallest Companies
Innophos Holdings Inc.	$643.0
Gulf Resources, Inc.	365.7
Flexible Solutions International Inc.	14.1

Annualized Monthly Performance Statistics (%)

Industry	Geometric Mean	Arithmetic Mean	Standard Deviation	S&P 500 Index	Geometric Mean	Arithmetic Mean	Standard Deviation
1-year	12.5	13.1	13.0	1-year	17.2	17.4	7.2
3-year	2.8	3.9	15.1	3-year	10.4	10.9	11.5
5-year	5.6	6.6	14.8	5-year	13.3	13.9	11.5

Return Ratios (%)

	Return on Assets Latest	5-Yr Avg	Return on Equity Latest	5-Yr Avg	Dividend Yield Latest	5-Yr Avg
Median (11)	7.3	5.6	12.2	10.9	2.5	2.1
SIC Composite (11)	5.8	6.2	4.0	4.4	2.5	2.2
Large Composite (3)	6.5	6.8	4.4	4.6	2.6	2.4
Small Composite (3)	4.5	6.1	6.1	6.3	1.2	0.5
High-Financial Risk (–)	–	–	–	–	–	–

Liquidity Ratio

	Current Ratio Latest	5-Yr Avg
Median	2.9	2.9
SIC Composite	1.5	1.5
Large Composite	1.3	1.2
Small Composite	4.5	4.5
High Financial Risk	–	–

Profitability Ratio (%)

	Operating Margin Latest	5-Yr Avg
Median	11.6	11.2
SIC Composite	16.6	16.6
Large Composite	18.6	18.4
Small Composite	13.5	13.8
High Financial Risk	–	–

Growth Rates (%)

	Long-term EPS Analyst Estimates
Median	8.9
SIC Composite	8.3
Large Composite	9.4
Small Composite	8.9
High Financial Risk	–

Betas (Levered)

	Raw (OLS)	Blume Adjusted	Peer Group	Vasicek Adjusted	Sum	Downside
Median	1.14	1.10	1.11	1.14	1.63	1.65
SIC Composite	1.12	1.08	1.11	1.12	1.17	1.13
Large Composite	1.07	1.05	1.11	1.08	1.03	1.04
Small Composite	1.09	1.06	1.11	1.10	1.25	1.29
High Financial Risk	–	–	–	–	–	–

Betas (Unlevered)

	Raw (OLS)	Blume Adjusted	Peer Group	Vasicek Adjusted	Sum	Downside
Median	0.93	0.89	0.93	0.93	1.31	1.24
SIC Composite	0.89	0.86	0.88	0.89	0.93	0.90
Large Composite	0.85	0.84	0.88	0.86	0.82	0.82
Small Composite	0.93	0.91	0.95	0.94	1.06	1.09
High Financial Risk	–	–	–	–	–	–

Equity Valuation Multiples

	Price/Sales Latest	5-Yr Avg	Price/Earnings Latest	5-Yr Avg	Market/Book Latest	5-Yr Avg
Median	1.4	1.3	22.5	24.8	3.0	2.1
SIC Composite	2.5	2.3	24.9	22.9	4.0	3.8
Large Composite	2.7	2.6	22.8	21.7	4.0	3.8
Small Composite	1.2	1.4	16.3	15.8	1.1	1.3
High Financial Risk	–	–	–	–	–	–

Enterprise Valuation (EV) Multiples

	EV/Sales Latest	5-Yr Avg	EV/EBITDA Latest	5-Yr Avg
Median	1.6	1.4	12.0	10.4
SIC Composite	3.1	2.8	11.7	11.0
Large Composite	3.4	3.2	11.2	11.0
Small Composite	1.3	1.3	10.7	6.5
High Financial Risk	–	–	–	–

Enterprise Valuation SIC Composite

	Latest	5-Yr Avg
EV/Sales	3.1	2.8
EV/EBITDA	11.7	11.0

Fama-French (F-F) 5-Factor Model

Fama-French (F-F) Components

	F-F Beta	SMB Premium	HML Premium	RMW Premium	CMA Premium
Median	1.1	3.8	3.3	-2.5	-0.3
SIC Composite	1.1	1.2	0.9	-0.1	0.9
Large Composite	1.1	1.0	0.6	0.1	0.1
Small Composite	0.9	2.1	3.1	-3.0	1.1
High Financial Risk	–	–	–	–	–

Leverage Ratios (%)

	Debt/MV Equity Latest	5-Yr Avg	Debt/Total Capital Latest	5-Yr Avg
Median	21.1	20.0	17.5	16.7
SIC Composite	29.5	26.6	22.8	21.0
Large Composite	28.2	26.8	22.0	21.1
Small Composite	27.2	11.1	21.4	10.0
High Financial Risk	–	–	–	–

Cost of Debt

	Cost of Debt (%) Latest
Median	6.1
SIC Composite	4.7
Large Composite	4.4
Small Composite	7.1
High Financial Risk	–

Capital Structure

SIC Composite (%) Latest
- D/TC: 22.8
- E/TC: 77.2

Cost of Equity Capital (%)

	CAPM	CRSP Deciles CAPM +Size Prem	Build-Up	Risk Premium Report CAPM +Size Prem	Build-Up	Discounted Cash Flow 1-Stage	3-Stage	Fama-French 5-Factor Model
Median	9.8	11.9	11.3	15.9	14.1	10.9	8.6	13.7
SIC Composite	9.7	9.9	9.9	12.3	11.2	10.9	8.5	12.3
Large Composite	9.4	9.5	9.7	11.2	10.8	12.2	9.0	11.1
Small Composite	9.6	12.1	12.1	15.1	14.9	10.1	13.4	12.1
High Financial Risk	–	–	–	–	–	–	–	–

Cost of Equity Capital (%) SIC Composite
- Avg CRSP: 9.9
- Avg RPR: 11.7
- 1-Stage: 10.9
- 3-Stage: 8.5
- 5-Factor Model: 12.3

Weighted Average Cost of Capital (WACC) (%)

	CAPM	CRSP Deciles CAPM +Size Prem	Build-Up	Risk Premium Report CAPM +Size Prem	Build-Up	Discounted Cash Flow 1-Stage	3-Stage	Fama-French 5-Factor Model
Median	8.8	9.5	10.2	13.4	12.6	9.3	8.0	12.0
SIC Composite	8.5	8.7	8.7	10.5	9.7	9.5	7.6	10.5
Large Composite	8.3	8.4	8.5	9.7	9.4	10.5	8.0	9.6
Small Composite	9.0	10.9	11.0	13.3	13.2	9.4	12.0	10.9
High Financial Risk	–	–	–	–	–	–	–	–

WACC (%) SIC Composite
Low 7.6 — High 10.5
▲ Average 9.3 ♦ Median 9.5

© 2017 Duff & Phelps. All Rights Reserved. Duff & Phelps has used the utmost care in compiling the data presented herein, but cannot guarantee the accuracy, completeness, or timeliness of the information.

Data Updated Through March 31, 2017

283

Number of Companies: 47
Drugs

Industry Description
Establishments primarily engaged in medicinal chemicals and botanical products; pharmaceutical preparations; in vitro and in vivo diagnostic substances; biological products, except diagnostic substances.

Sales (in millions)

Three Largest Companies
Pfizer Inc.	$52,824.0
Merck & Co.	39,807.0
Gilead Sciences Inc.	30,390.0

Three Smallest Companies
Biospecifics Technologies Co.	$22.8
United-Guardian Inc.	14.0
ImmuCell Corp.	10.2

Annualized Monthly Performance Statistics (%)

Industry	Geometric Mean	Arithmetic Mean	Standard Deviation
1-year	9.0	10.1	16.5
3-year	7.1	8.3	16.5
5-year	16.2	17.4	16.9

Total Assets (in millions)

Three Largest Companies
Pfizer Inc.	$171,615.0
Merck & Co.	95,377.0
Amgen Inc.	77,626.0

Three Smallest Companies
Reliv International Inc.	$24.3
United-Guardian Inc.	15.7
ImmuCell Corp.	14.6

S&P 500 Index	Geometric Mean	Arithmetic Mean	Standard Deviation
1-year	17.2	17.4	7.2
3-year	10.4	10.9	11.5
5-year	13.3	13.9	11.5

Return Ratios (%)

	Return on Assets Latest	5-Yr Avg	Return on Equity Latest	5-Yr Avg	Dividend Yield Latest	5-Yr Avg
Median (47)	8.7	9.1	11.3	16.8	0.0	0.0
SIC Composite (47)	8.1	8.3	4.5	4.6	2.2	2.1
Large Composite (4)	8.1	8.1	5.5	5.5	3.1	2.7
Small Composite (4)	10.3	14.0	2.2	3.1	0.0	0.0
High-Financial Risk (9)	-7.8	-2.2	-13.2	-3.2	0.0	0.0

Liquidity Ratio

	Current Ratio Latest	5-Yr Avg
	3.4	3.5
	2.1	2.1
	2.0	2.2
	–	–
	1.9	2.4

Profitability Ratio (%)

	Operating Margin Latest	5-Yr Avg
	24.4	20.7
	32.1	29.7
	36.1	33.5
	28.0	24.1
	3.4	6.7

Growth Rates (%)

	Long-term EPS Analyst Estimates
	10.9
	9.2
	4.8
	10.9
	14.2

Betas (Levered)

	Raw (OLS)	Blume Adjusted	Peer Group	Vasicek Adjusted	Sum	Downside
Median	1.13	1.09	1.11	1.12	1.14	1.71
SIC Composite	1.06	1.04	1.11	1.06	1.08	1.09
Large Composite	1.03	1.02	1.11	1.05	1.07	1.08
Small Composite	1.18	1.12	1.11	1.15	0.97	1.55
High Financial Risk	1.00	1.01	1.11	1.01	1.14	1.53

Betas (Unlevered)

	Raw (OLS)	Blume Adjusted	Peer Group	Vasicek Adjusted	Sum	Downside
Median	1.01	0.96	1.03	0.98	1.08	1.52
SIC Composite	0.90	0.89	0.95	0.91	0.93	0.93
Large Composite	0.85	0.84	0.92	0.87	0.88	0.89
Small Composite	1.16	1.10	1.10	1.13	0.96	1.52
High Financial Risk	0.68	0.68	0.74	0.69	0.75	0.95

Equity Valuation Multiples

	Price/Sales Latest	5-Yr Avg	Price/Earnings Latest	5-Yr Avg	Market/Book Latest	5-Yr Avg
Median	3.4	3.4	28.8	24.6	3.4	3.9
SIC Composite	4.4	4.3	22.3	21.9	3.9	3.6
Large Composite	4.1	4.1	18.3	18.2	3.2	2.9
Small Composite	6.4	5.6	45.7	31.8	5.7	5.3
High Financial Risk	1.4	1.7	–	–	2.1	2.0

Enterprise Valuation (EV) Multiples

	EV/Sales Latest	5-Yr Avg	EV/EBITDA Latest	5-Yr Avg
Median	3.3	3.6	10.5	11.0
SIC Composite	4.6	4.5	11.1	11.3
Large Composite	4.4	4.3	9.1	9.3
Small Composite	5.9	5.1	18.6	18.5
High Financial Risk	2.5	2.6	14.3	13.1

Enterprise Valuation SIC Composite
Latest: EV/Sales 4.6, EV/EBITDA 11.1
5-Yr Avg: EV/Sales 4.5, EV/EBITDA 11.3

Fama-French (F-F) 5-Factor Model

	F-F Beta	SMB Premium	HML Premium	RMW Premium	CMA Premium
Median	0.6	3.1	-1.1	0.0	2.1
SIC Composite	1.0	0.3	-4.0	-1.6	2.6
Large Composite	–	–	–	–	–
Small Composite	1.1	0.2	-2.2	-1.1	-0.8
High Financial Risk	–	–	–	–	–

Leverage Ratios (%)

	Debt/MV Equity Latest	5-Yr Avg	Debt/Total Capital Latest	5-Yr Avg
Median	10.7	6.6	9.7	6.2
SIC Composite	17.7	15.1	15.1	13.1
Large Composite	21.6	19.4	17.8	16.3
Small Composite	2.2	1.8	2.1	1.8
High Financial Risk	95.1	73.7	48.7	42.4

Cost of Debt

	Cost of Debt (%) Latest
Median	6.1
SIC Composite	4.3
Large Composite	4.0
Small Composite	6.4
High Financial Risk	7.2

Capital Structure

SIC Composite (%) Latest
D/TC: 15.1
E/TC: 84.9

Cost of Equity Capital (%)

	CRSP Deciles CAPM	CAPM +Size Prem	Build-Up	Risk Premium Report CAPM +Size Prem	Build-Up	Discounted Cash Flow 1-Stage	3-Stage	Fama-French 5-Factor Model
Median	9.7	11.5	11.3	14.0	14.4	11.7	10.0	11.2
SIC Composite	9.3	9.4	9.7	10.9	10.0	11.5	11.3	6.6
Large Composite	9.3	9.3	9.6	10.3	9.3	8.0	10.9	–
Small Composite	9.8	13.2	13.0	14.6	16.5	10.9	8.2	5.8
High Financial Risk	–	–	–	20.0	22.6	–	–	–

Cost of Equity Capital (%) SIC Composite
Avg CRSP: 9.5, Avg RPR: 10.4, 1-Stage: 11.5, 3-Stage: 11.3, 5-Factor Model: 6.6

Weighted Average Cost of Capital (WACC) (%)

	CRSP Deciles CAPM	CAPM +Size Prem	Build-Up	Risk Premium Report CAPM +Size Prem	Build-Up	Discounted Cash Flow 1-Stage	3-Stage	Fama-French 5-Factor Model
Median	9.0	10.6	10.8	12.3	13.6	11.1	9.5	10.5
SIC Composite	8.4	8.5	8.7	9.8	9.0	10.3	10.1	6.1
Large Composite	8.2	8.2	8.5	9.0	8.2	7.1	9.5	–
Small Composite	9.7	13.0	12.8	14.4	16.2	10.8	8.1	5.8
High Financial Risk	–	–	–	13.0	14.3	–	–	–

WACC (%) SIC Composite
Low: 6.1, High: 10.3
Average 8.9, Median 9.0

© 2017 Duff & Phelps. All Rights Reserved. Duff & Phelps has used the utmost care in compiling the data presented herein, but cannot guarantee the accuracy, completeness, or timeliness of the information.

Data Updated Through March 31, 2017

2834

Number of Companies: 23
Pharmaceutical Preparations

Industry Description
Establishments primarily engaged in manufacturing, fabricating, or processing drugs in pharmaceutical preparations for human or veterinary use.

Sales (in millions)

Three Largest Companies
Pfizer Inc.	$52,824.0
Merck & Co.	39,807.0
Eli Lilly & Co.	21,222.1

Three Smallest Companies
Cumberland Pharmaceuticals, Inc.	$33.0
Biospecifics Technologies Co.	22.8
United-Guardian Inc.	14.0

Total Assets (in millions)

Three Largest Companies
Pfizer Inc.	$171,615.0
Merck & Co.	95,377.0
Eli Lilly & Co.	38,805.9

Three Smallest Companies
Biospecifics Technologies Co.	$45.7
Reliv International Inc.	24.3
United-Guardian Inc.	15.7

Annualized Monthly Performance Statistics (%)

Industry	Geometric Mean	Arithmetic Mean	Standard Deviation	S&P 500 Index	Geometric Mean	Arithmetic Mean	Standard Deviation
1-year	14.9	16.3	18.4	1-year	17.2	17.4	7.2
3-year	8.6	9.7	16.1	3-year	10.4	10.9	11.5
5-year	15.7	16.8	16.2	5-year	13.3	13.9	11.5

Return Ratios (%)

	Return on Assets Latest	5-Yr Avg	Return on Equity Latest	5-Yr Avg	Dividend Yield Latest	5-Yr Avg
Median (23)	7.4	9.6	19.0	20.3	0.0	0.0
SIC Composite (23)	5.8	6.4	3.1	3.8	2.4	2.7
Large Composite (3)	4.5	5.9	2.9	4.4	3.2	3.4
Small Composite (3)	8.6	8.7	2.3	2.9	0.0	0.0
High-Financial Risk (–)	–	–	–	–	–	–

Liquidity Ratio

	Current Ratio Latest	5-Yr Avg
Median (23)	2.1	3.1
SIC Composite (23)	1.6	1.8
Large Composite (3)	1.4	1.8
Small Composite (3)	–	–
High-Financial Risk (–)	–	–

Profitability Ratio (%)

	Operating Margin Latest	5-Yr Avg
Median (23)	24.4	20.7
SIC Composite (23)	26.1	25.4
Large Composite (3)	24.8	25.5
Small Composite (3)	27.7	24.4
High-Financial Risk (–)	–	–

Growth Rates (%)

	Long-term EPS Analyst Estimates
Median (23)	10.9
SIC Composite (23)	10.9
Large Composite (3)	7.6
Small Composite (3)	10.9
High-Financial Risk (–)	–

Betas (Levered)

	Raw (OLS)	Blume Adjusted	Peer Group	Vasicek Adjusted	Sum	Downside
Median	1.13	1.09	1.11	1.12	1.21	1.84
SIC Composite	1.00	1.01	1.11	1.01	1.03	1.02
Large Composite	0.80	0.88	1.11	0.84	0.91	0.87
Small Composite	1.25	1.16	1.11	1.16	1.10	1.48
High Financial Risk	–	–	–	–	–	–

Betas (Unlevered)

	Raw (OLS)	Blume Adjusted	Peer Group	Vasicek Adjusted	Sum	Downside
Median	1.02	1.02	1.04	1.01	1.16	1.65
SIC Composite	0.88	0.89	0.98	0.89	0.90	0.90
Large Composite	0.69	0.76	0.96	0.72	0.78	0.74
Small Composite	1.24	1.16	1.11	1.16	1.09	1.47
High Financial Risk	–	–	–	–	–	–

Equity Valuation Multiples

	Price/Sales Latest	5-Yr Avg	Price/Earnings Latest	5-Yr Avg	Market/Book Latest	5-Yr Avg
Median	3.4	3.4	28.8	22.3	3.9	4.2
SIC Composite	4.6	4.1	32.0	26.1	3.9	3.2
Large Composite	4.1	3.6	34.0	23.0	3.1	2.5
Small Composite	8.2	6.2	43.0	34.5	4.3	3.4
High Financial Risk	–	–	–	–	–	–

Enterprise Valuation (EV) Multiples

	EV/Sales Latest	5-Yr Avg	EV/EBITDA Latest	5-Yr Avg
Median	3.0	3.5	10.5	10.0
SIC Composite	4.9	4.3	13.0	11.6
Large Composite	4.5	3.8	11.7	9.7
Small Composite	6.9	5.0	21.3	17.4
High Financial Risk	–	–	–	–

Enterprise Valuation SIC Composite
- Latest: EV/Sales 4.9, EV/EBITDA 13.0
- 5-Yr Avg: EV/Sales 4.3, EV/EBITDA 11.6

Fama-French (F-F) 5-Factor Model

	Fama-French (F-F) Components				
	F-F Beta	SMB Premium	HML Premium	RMW Premium	CMA Premium
Median	1.0	7.7	-8.9	-1.3	4.8
SIC Composite	1.0	0.0	-3.9	-1.7	3.6
Large Composite	–	–	–	–	–
Small Composite	1.2	0.9	-1.5	-0.7	0.2
High Financial Risk	–	–	–	–	–

Leverage Ratios (%)

	Debt/MV Equity Latest	5-Yr Avg	Debt/Total Capital Latest	5-Yr Avg
Median	10.7	7.8	9.7	7.3
SIC Composite	14.1	13.9	12.4	12.2
Large Composite	16.4	16.6	14.1	14.2
Small Composite	0.7	0.5	0.7	0.5
High Financial Risk	–	–	–	–

Cost of Debt

	Cost of Debt (%) Latest
Median	6.1
SIC Composite	4.1
Large Composite	3.9
Small Composite	7.1
High Financial Risk	–

Capital Structure

SIC Composite (%) Latest
- D/TC: 12.4
- E/TC: 87.6

Cost of Equity Capital (%)

	CRSP Deciles CAPM	CAPM +Size Prem	Build-Up	Risk Premium Report CAPM +Size Prem	Build-Up	Discounted Cash Flow 1-Stage	3-Stage	Fama-French 5-Factor Model
Median	9.7	12.1	11.3	14.6	14.4	10.9	11.7	11.6
SIC Composite	9.0	9.1	9.7	10.5	9.8	13.5	10.3	6.9
Large Composite	8.1	8.1	9.6	9.4	9.3	11.0	9.7	–
Small Composite	9.9	13.5	13.2	15.3	16.5	10.9	8.1	8.9
High Financial Risk	–	–	–	–	–	–	–	–

Cost of Equity Capital (%) SIC Composite
- Avg CRSP: 9.4
- Avg RPR: 10.1
- 1-Stage: 13.5
- 3-Stage: 10.3
- 5-Factor Model: 6.9

Weighted Average Cost of Capital (WACC) (%)

	CRSP Deciles CAPM	CAPM +Size Prem	Build-Up	Risk Premium Report CAPM +Size Prem	Build-Up	Discounted Cash Flow 1-Stage	3-Stage	Fama-French 5-Factor Model
Median	9.1	11.1	10.5	12.3	13.2	10.9	10.0	11.4
SIC Composite	8.3	8.3	8.8	9.5	9.0	12.2	9.4	6.4
Large Composite	7.3	7.3	8.6	8.5	8.3	9.8	8.6	–
Small Composite	9.9	13.4	13.2	15.3	16.4	10.9	8.1	8.9
High Financial Risk	–	–	–	–	–	–	–	–

WACC (%) SIC Composite
- Low: 6.4
- High: 12.2
- Average 9.1
- Median 9.0

© 2017 Duff & Phelps. All Rights Reserved. Duff & Phelps has used the utmost care in compiling the data presented herein, but cannot guarantee the accuracy, completeness, or timeliness of the information.

Data Updated Through March 31, 2017

2835

Number of Companies: 6
In Vitro and In Vivo Diagnostic Substances

Industry Description
Establishments primarily engaged in manufacturing in vitro and in vivo diagnostic substances whether or not packaged for retail sale.

Sales (in millions)

Three Largest Companies
IDEXX Labs. Inc.	$1,775.4
Myriad Genetics Inc.	753.8
AMAG Pharmaceuticals, Inc.	532.1

Three Smallest Companies
Luminex Corporation	$270.6
Heska Corp.	104.6
ImmuCell Corp.	10.2

Total Assets (in millions)

Three Largest Companies
AMAG Pharmaceuticals, Inc.	$2,478.4
IDEXX Labs. Inc.	1,530.7
Myriad Genetics Inc.	880.5

Three Smallest Companies
Luminex Corporation	$450.7
Heska Corp.	109.7
ImmuCell Corp.	14.6

Annualized Monthly Performance Statistics (%)

Industry	Geometric Mean	Arithmetic Mean	Standard Deviation
1-year	52.3	54.4	26.7
3-year	21.9	24.3	25.1
5-year	18.9	21.2	23.9

S&P 500 Index	Geometric Mean	Arithmetic Mean	Standard Deviation
1-year	17.2	17.4	7.2
3-year	10.4	10.9	11.5
5-year	13.3	13.9	11.5

Return Ratios (%)

	Return on Assets Latest	5-Yr Avg	Return on Equity Latest	5-Yr Avg	Dividend Yield Latest	5-Yr Avg
Median (6)	7.3	4.4	6.3	6.2	0.0	0.0
SIC Composite (6)	6.7	9.4	2.1	3.5	0.0	0.0
Large Composite (–)	–	–	–	–	–	–
Small Composite (–)	–	–	–	–	–	–
High-Financial Risk (–)	–	–	–	–	–	–

Liquidity Ratio

	Current Ratio Latest	5-Yr Avg
Median (6)	3.3	4.0
SIC Composite (6)	1.5	1.8
Large Composite	–	–
Small Composite	–	–
High-Financial Risk	–	–

Profitability Ratio (%)

	Operating Margin Latest	5-Yr Avg
Median	20.3	15.9
SIC Composite	20.0	21.4
Large Composite	–	–
Small Composite	–	–
High-Financial Risk	–	–

Growth Rates (%)

	Long-term EPS Analyst Estimates
Median	12.7
SIC Composite	12.5
Large Composite	–
Small Composite	–
High-Financial Risk	–

Betas (Levered)

	Raw (OLS)	Blume Adjusted	Peer Group	Vasicek Adjusted	Sum	Downside
Median	0.64	0.78	1.11	1.01	0.88	1.47
SIC Composite	0.60	0.75	1.11	0.84	0.58	0.88
Large Composite	–	–	–	–	–	–
Small Composite	–	–	–	–	–	–
High Financial Risk	–	–	–	–	–	–

Betas (Unlevered)

	Raw (OLS)	Blume Adjusted	Peer Group	Vasicek Adjusted	Sum	Downside
Median	0.61	0.68	1.08	0.91	0.85	1.15
SIC Composite	0.57	0.71	1.03	0.78	0.55	0.82
Large Composite	–	–	–	–	–	–
Small Composite	–	–	–	–	–	–
High Financial Risk	–	–	–	–	–	–

Equity Valuation Multiples

	Price/Sales Latest	5-Yr Avg	Price/Earnings Latest	5-Yr Avg	Market/Book Latest	5-Yr Avg
Median	2.5	3.2	59.0	35.7	2.1	2.7
SIC Composite	5.0	3.9	47.2	28.9	7.5	5.5
Large Composite	–	–	–	–	–	–
Small Composite	–	–	–	–	–	–
High Financial Risk	–	–	–	–	–	–

Enterprise Valuation (EV) Multiples

	EV/Sales Latest	5-Yr Avg	EV/EBITDA Latest	5-Yr Avg
Median	2.4	3.0	11.1	15.3
SIC Composite	5.3	4.0	19.8	15.3
Large Composite	–	–	–	–
Small Composite	–	–	–	–
High Financial Risk	–	–	–	–

Enterprise Valuation SIC Composite
- Latest: EV/Sales 5.3, EV/EBITDA 19.8
- 5-Yr Avg: EV/Sales 4.0, EV/EBITDA 15.3

Fama-French (F-F) 5-Factor Model

	F-F Beta	SMB Premium	HML Premium	RMW Premium	CMA Premium
Median	0.4	3.2	-4.0	-1.3	1.0
SIC Composite	0.5	3.0	-3.2	-1.0	0.9
Large Composite	–	–	–	–	–
Small Composite	–	–	–	–	–
High Financial Risk	–	–	–	–	–

Leverage Ratios (%)

	Debt/MV Equity Latest	5-Yr Avg	Debt/Total Capital Latest	5-Yr Avg
Median	4.5	5.1	4.1	4.7
SIC Composite	12.7	12.0	11.3	10.7
Large Composite	–	–	–	–
Small Composite	–	–	–	–
High Financial Risk	–	–	–	–

Cost of Debt

	Cost of Debt (%) Latest
Median	7.1
SIC Composite	7.1
Large Composite	–
Small Composite	–
High Financial Risk	–

Capital Structure

SIC Composite (%) Latest:
- D/TC: 11.3
- E/TC: 88.7

Cost of Equity Capital (%)

	CRSP Deciles CAPM	CAPM +Size Prem	Build-Up	Risk Premium Report CAPM +Size Prem	Build-Up	Discounted Cash Flow 1-Stage	3-Stage	Fama-French 5-Factor Model
Median	9.0	10.9	11.7	13.8	14.9	14.9	8.4	4.8
SIC Composite	8.1	9.0	10.5	10.4	13.4	12.5	8.7	5.9
Large Composite	–	–	–	–	–	–	–	–
Small Composite	–	–	–	–	–	–	–	–
High Financial Risk	–	–	–	–	–	–	–	–

Cost of Equity Capital (%) SIC Composite
- Avg CRSP: 9.8
- Avg RPR: 11.9
- 1-Stage: 12.5
- 3-Stage: 8.7
- 5-Factor Model: 5.9

Weighted Average Cost of Capital (WACC) (%)

	CRSP Deciles CAPM	CAPM +Size Prem	Build-Up	Risk Premium Report CAPM +Size Prem	Build-Up	Discounted Cash Flow 1-Stage	3-Stage	Fama-French 5-Factor Model
Median	8.6	10.5	11.5	12.1	14.7	14.3	7.9	8.1
SIC Composite	8.0	8.8	10.1	10.0	12.7	11.9	8.5	6.0
Large Composite	–	–	–	–	–	–	–	–
Small Composite	–	–	–	–	–	–	–	–
High Financial Risk	–	–	–	–	–	–	–	–

WACC (%) SIC Composite
- Low: 6.0
- High: 12.7
- Average: 9.7
- Median: 10.0

© 2017 Duff & Phelps. All Rights Reserved. Duff & Phelps has used the utmost care in compiling the data presented herein, but cannot guarantee the accuracy, completeness, or timeliness of the information.

Data Updated Through March 31, 2017

2836

Number of Companies: 11
Biological Products, Except Diagnostic Substances

Industry Description
Establishments primarily engaged in the production of bacterial and virus vaccines, toxoids, and analogous products, serums, plasmas, and other blood derivatives for human or veterinary use, other than in vitro or in vivo diagnostic substances.

Sales (in millions)

Three Largest Companies
Gilead Sciences Inc.	$30,390.0
Amgen Inc.	22,991.0
Biogen Inc.	11,448.8

Three Smallest Companies
MiMedx Group, Inc.	$245.0
Repligen Corp.	104.5
Anika Therapeutics Inc.	103.4

Total Assets (in millions)

Three Largest Companies
Amgen Inc.	$77,626.0
Gilead Sciences Inc.	56,977.0
Biogen Inc.	22,876.8

Three Smallest Companies
Repligen Corp.	$288.9
Anika Therapeutics Inc.	240.2
MiMedx Group, Inc.	193.3

Annualized Monthly Performance Statistics (%)

Industry	Geometric Mean	Arithmetic Mean	Standard Deviation
1-year	-4.0	-2.5	17.9
3-year	3.4	5.4	20.8
5-year	19.9	22.2	24.0

S&P 500 Index	Geometric Mean	Arithmetic Mean	Standard Deviation
1-year	17.2	17.4	7.2
3-year	10.4	10.9	11.5
5-year	13.3	13.9	11.5

Return Ratios (%)

	Return on Assets Latest	Return on Assets 5-Yr Avg	Return on Equity Latest	Return on Equity 5-Yr Avg	Dividend Yield Latest	Dividend Yield 5-Yr Avg
Median (11)	10.4	9.0	14.6	16.1	0.0	0.0
SIC Composite (11)	14.7	14.6	8.5	6.3	1.8	1.0
Large Composite (3)	15.8	15.2	9.3	6.8	2.0	1.1
Small Composite (3)	7.8	9.9	2.0	2.4	0.0	0.0
High-Financial Risk (–)	–	–	–	–	–	–

Liquidity Ratio

	Current Ratio Latest	Current Ratio 5-Yr Avg
	4.1	3.7
	3.2	3.1
	3.2	3.1
	–	–

Profitability Ratio (%)

	Operating Margin Latest	Operating Margin 5-Yr Avg
	42.5	37.5
	50.9	47.2
	52.6	48.2
	20.6	23.9
	–	–

Growth Rates (%)

	Long-term EPS Analyst Estimates
	6.4
	4.4
	2.7
	14.2
	–

Betas (Levered)

	Raw (OLS)	Blume Adjusted	Peer Group	Vasicek Adjusted	Sum	Downside
Median	1.26	1.17	1.11	1.20	1.14	1.77
SIC Composite	1.13	1.09	1.11	1.13	1.19	1.35
Large Composite	1.10	1.07	1.11	1.11	1.21	1.32
Small Composite	1.40	1.26	1.11	1.23	1.92	1.93
High Financial Risk	–	–	–	–	–	–

Betas (Unlevered)

	Raw (OLS)	Blume Adjusted	Peer Group	Vasicek Adjusted	Sum	Downside
Median	1.01	1.01	1.00	1.09	1.09	1.52
SIC Composite	0.92	0.89	0.91	0.92	0.97	1.09
Large Composite	0.88	0.86	0.89	0.89	0.97	1.06
Small Composite	1.36	1.23	1.09	1.20	1.87	1.88
High Financial Risk	–	–	–	–	–	–

Equity Valuation Multiples

	Price/Sales Latest	Price/Sales 5-Yr Avg	Price/Earnings Latest	Price/Earnings 5-Yr Avg	Market/Book Latest	Market/Book 5-Yr Avg
Median	5.2	5.5	19.5	23.2	3.7	5.5
SIC Composite	4.3	5.6	11.8	16.0	4.0	5.2
Large Composite	4.2	5.3	10.8	14.7	4.2	5.2
Small Composite	6.3	6.5	51.1	41.3	5.4	5.0
High Financial Risk	–	–	–	–	–	–

Enterprise Valuation (EV) Multiples

	EV/Sales Latest	EV/Sales 5-Yr Avg	EV/EBITDA Latest	EV/EBITDA 5-Yr Avg
Median	4.9	5.4	9.5	12.4
SIC Composite	4.5	5.8	7.8	10.8
Large Composite	4.3	5.5	7.2	10.1
Small Composite	5.9	5.8	24.8	21.0
High Financial Risk	–	–	–	–

Enterprise Valuation SIC Composite
- EV/Sales: Latest 4.5, 5-Yr Avg 7.8
- EV/EBITDA: Latest 5.8, 5-Yr Avg 10.8

Fama-French (F-F) 5-Factor Model

	F-F Beta	SMB Premium	HML Premium	RMW Premium	CMA Premium
Median	1.8	0.1	-12.4	-4.7	10.6
SIC Composite	1.1	0.6	-4.4	-1.9	1.2
Large Composite	–	–	–	–	–
Small Composite	1.3	4.9	-6.1	0.3	5.4
High Financial Risk	–	–	–	–	–

Leverage Ratios (%)

	Debt/MV Equity Latest	Debt/MV Equity 5-Yr Avg	Debt/Total Capital Latest	Debt/Total Capital 5-Yr Avg
Median	12.1	5.1	10.8	4.9
SIC Composite	23.6	16.8	19.1	14.4
Large Composite	25.1	18.2	20.0	15.4
Small Composite	3.3	1.2	3.2	1.1
High Financial Risk	–	–	–	–

Cost of Debt

	Cost of Debt (%) Latest
Median	7.1
SIC Composite	4.2
Large Composite	4.1
Small Composite	7.1
High Financial Risk	–

Capital Structure

SIC Composite (%) Latest
- D/TC: 19.1
- E/TC: 80.9

Cost of Equity Capital (%)

	CRSP Deciles CAPM	CRSP Deciles CAPM +Size Prem	CRSP Deciles Build-Up	Risk Premium Report CAPM +Size Prem	Risk Premium Report Build-Up	Discounted Cash Flow 1-Stage	Discounted Cash Flow 3-Stage	Fama-French 5-Factor Model
Median	10.1	11.2	11.3	13.6	14.1	10.0	9.2	6.9
SIC Composite	9.7	9.8	9.7	11.5	10.1	6.3	12.5	5.0
Large Composite	9.6	9.6	9.6	11.5	9.9	4.8	12.2	–
Small Composite	10.3	12.1	11.4	19.2	15.7	14.2	8.1	15.2
High Financial Risk	–	–	–	–	–	–	–	–

Cost of Equity Capital (%) SIC Composite
- Avg CRSP: 9.7
- Avg RPR: 10.8
- 1-Stage: 6.3
- 3-Stage: 12.5
- 5-Factor Model: 5.0

Weighted Average Cost of Capital (WACC) (%)

	CRSP Deciles CAPM	CRSP Deciles CAPM +Size Prem	CRSP Deciles Build-Up	Risk Premium Report CAPM +Size Prem	Risk Premium Report Build-Up	Discounted Cash Flow 1-Stage	Discounted Cash Flow 3-Stage	Fama-French 5-Factor Model
Median	9.5	10.6	10.5	13.6	12.7	10.0	8.8	6.9
SIC Composite	8.7	8.7	8.6	10.1	9.0	5.9	10.9	4.9
Large Composite	8.5	8.5	8.5	10.0	8.7	4.7	10.5	–
Small Composite	10.2	11.9	11.3	18.8	15.4	14.0	8.0	15.0
High Financial Risk	–	–	–	–	–	–	–	–

WACC (%) SIC Composite
Low 4.9 — High 10.9 — Average 8.3 — Median 8.7

© 2017 Duff & Phelps. All Rights Reserved. Duff & Phelps has used the utmost care in compiling the data presented herein, but cannot guarantee the accuracy, completeness, or timeliness of the information.

Data Updated Through March 31, 2017

284

Number of Companies: 7
Soap, Detergents, and Cleaning Preparations; Perfumes, Cosmetics, and Other Toilet Preparations

Industry Description
This industry group includes establishments primarily engaged in manufacturing soap and other detergents and in producing glycerin from vegetables and animal fats and oils; specialty cleaning, polishing, and sanitation preparations; surface active preparations; perfumes, cosmetics, and other toilet preparations.

Sales (in millions)

Three Largest Companies
Colgate-Palmolive Co.	$15,195.0
Estee Lauder Cos. Inc.	11,263.7
Church & Dwight Inc.	3,493.1

Three Smallest Companies
Inter Parfums Inc.	$521.1
Ocean Bio-Chem Inc.	34.0
Ikonics Corp.	17.6

Annualized Monthly Performance Statistics (%)

Industry
	Geometric Mean	Arithmetic Mean	Standard Deviation
1-year	2.3	3.2	14.5
3-year	8.1	9.0	13.7
5-year	10.7	11.5	13.5

Total Assets (in millions)

Three Largest Companies
Colgate-Palmolive Co.	$12,123.0
Estee Lauder Cos. Inc.	9,223.3
Church & Dwight Inc.	4,354.1

Three Smallest Companies
Inter Parfums Inc.	$682.4
Ocean Bio-Chem Inc.	24.0
Ikonics Corp.	18.3

S&P 500 Index
	Geometric Mean	Arithmetic Mean	Standard Deviation
1-year	17.2	17.4	7.2
3-year	10.4	10.9	11.5
5-year	13.3	13.9	11.5

Return Ratios (%)

	Return on Assets Latest	Return on Assets 5-Yr Avg	Return on Equity Latest	Return on Equity 5-Yr Avg	Dividend Yield Latest	Dividend Yield 5-Yr Avg
Median (7)	6.6	7.9	9.0	14.1	1.5	1.5
SIC Composite (7)	14.9	13.9	3.7	3.8	1.9	1.9
Large Composite (–)	–	–	–	–	–	–
Small Composite (–)	–	–	–	–	–	–
High-Financial Risk (–)	–	–	–	–	–	–

Liquidity Ratio

	Current Ratio Latest	Current Ratio 5-Yr Avg
Median (7)	2.3	2.3
SIC Composite (7)	1.4	1.5
Large Composite	–	–
Small Composite	–	–
High Financial Risk	–	–

Profitability Ratio (%)

	Operating Margin Latest	Operating Margin 5-Yr Avg
Median (7)	13.0	12.7
SIC Composite (7)	20.6	19.9
Large Composite	–	–
Small Composite	–	–
High Financial Risk	–	–

Growth Rates (%)

	Long-term EPS Analyst Estimates
Median (7)	7.8
SIC Composite (7)	8.7
Large Composite	–
Small Composite	–
High Financial Risk	–

Betas (Levered)

	Raw (OLS)	Blume Adjusted	Peer Group	Vasicek Adjusted	Sum	Downside
Median	0.75	0.85	1.08	0.90	0.76	1.23
SIC Composite	0.76	0.85	1.08	0.78	0.81	0.85
Large Composite	–	–	–	–	–	–
Small Composite	–	–	–	–	–	–
High Financial Risk	–	–	–	–	–	–

Betas (Unlevered)

	Raw (OLS)	Blume Adjusted	Peer Group	Vasicek Adjusted	Sum	Downside
Median	0.71	0.82	0.99	0.84	0.69	1.09
SIC Composite	0.70	0.78	0.99	0.72	0.74	0.78
Large Composite	–	–	–	–	–	–
Small Composite	–	–	–	–	–	–
High Financial Risk	–	–	–	–	–	–

Equity Valuation Multiples

	Price/Sales Latest	Price/Sales 5-Yr Avg	Price/Earnings Latest	Price/Earnings 5-Yr Avg	Market/Book Latest	Market/Book 5-Yr Avg
Median	2.2	1.6	27.9	24.7	3.0	2.3
SIC Composite	3.4	3.0	26.9	26.5	–	–
Large Composite	–	–	–	–	–	–
Small Composite	–	–	–	–	–	–
High Financial Risk	–	–	–	–	–	–

Enterprise Valuation (EV) Multiples

	EV/Sales Latest	EV/Sales 5-Yr Avg	EV/EBITDA Latest	EV/EBITDA 5-Yr Avg
Median	1.9	1.4	15.6	13.8
SIC Composite	3.7	3.2	15.2	13.7
Large Composite	–	–	–	–
Small Composite	–	–	–	–
High Financial Risk	–	–	–	–

Enterprise Valuation SIC Composite
- EV/Sales: Latest 3.7, 5-Yr Avg 3.2
- EV/EBITDA: Latest 15.2, 5-Yr Avg 13.7

Fama-French (F-F) 5-Factor Model

	F-F Beta	SMB Premium	HML Premium	RMW Premium	CMA Premium
Median	0.7	-1.0	3.0	-4.2	3.7
SIC Composite	0.8	-1.2	-2.7	0.5	1.6
Large Composite	–	–	–	–	–
Small Composite	–	–	–	–	–
High Financial Risk	–	–	–	–	–

Leverage Ratios (%)

	Debt/MV Equity Latest	Debt/MV Equity 5-Yr Avg	Debt/Total Capital Latest	Debt/Total Capital 5-Yr Avg
Median	9.6	6.6	8.8	6.2
SIC Composite	9.3	9.1	8.5	8.3
Large Composite	–	–	–	–
Small Composite	–	–	–	–
High Financial Risk	–	–	–	–

Cost of Debt

	Cost of Debt (%) Latest
Median	4.8
SIC Composite	4.1
Large Composite	–
Small Composite	–
High Financial Risk	–

Capital Structure

SIC Composite (%) Latest
- D/TC: 8.5
- E/TC: 91.5

Cost of Equity Capital (%)

	CRSP Deciles CAPM	CRSP Deciles CAPM +Size Prem	CRSP Deciles Build-Up	Risk Premium Report CAPM +Size Prem	Risk Premium Report Build-Up	Discounted Cash Flow 1-Stage	Discounted Cash Flow 3-Stage	Fama-French 5-Factor Model
Median	8.4	11.4	11.3	11.5	13.9	9.5	8.5	8.7
SIC Composite	7.8	7.9	9.7	10.1	10.9	10.7	8.1	6.1
Large Composite	–	–	–	–	–	–	–	–
Small Composite	–	–	–	–	–	–	–	–
High Financial Risk	–	–	–	–	–	–	–	–

Cost of Equity Capital (%) SIC Composite
- Avg CRSP: 8.8
- Avg RPR: 10.5
- 1-Stage: 10.7
- 3-Stage: 8.1
- 5-Factor Model: 6.1

Weighted Average Cost of Capital (WACC) (%)

	CRSP Deciles CAPM	CRSP Deciles CAPM +Size Prem	CRSP Deciles Build-Up	Risk Premium Report CAPM +Size Prem	Risk Premium Report Build-Up	Discounted Cash Flow 1-Stage	Discounted Cash Flow 3-Stage	Fama-French 5-Factor Model
Median	8.1	10.6	10.5	10.9	12.7	9.1	8.2	8.8
SIC Composite	7.4	7.5	9.1	9.5	10.2	10.0	7.7	5.8
Large Composite	–	–	–	–	–	–	–	–
Small Composite	–	–	–	–	–	–	–	–
High Financial Risk	–	–	–	–	–	–	–	–

WACC (%) SIC Composite
- Low: 5.8
- High: 10.2
- Average: 8.6
- Median: 9.1

© 2017 Duff & Phelps. All Rights Reserved. Duff & Phelps has used the utmost care in compiling the data presented herein, but cannot guarantee the accuracy, completeness, or timeliness of the information.

Data Updated Through March 31, 2017

286

Number of Companies: 7
Industrial Organic Chemicals

Industry Description
Establishments primarily engaged in manufacturing industrial organic chemicals.

Sales (in millions)

Three Largest Companies
Westlake Chemical Corp.	$5,075.5
NewMarket Corp.	2,049.5
Koppers Holdings Inc.	1,416.2

Three Smallest Companies
REX American Resources Corp.	$453.8
KMG Chemicals Inc.	298.0
FutureFuel Corp.	253.2

Total Assets (in millions)

Three Largest Companies
Westlake Chemical Corp.	$10,890.3
Sensient Technologies Corp.	1,667.9
NewMarket Corp.	1,416.4

Three Smallest Companies
FutureFuel Corp.	$529.0
REX American Resources Corp.	454.0
KMG Chemicals Inc.	237.0

Annualized Monthly Performance Statistics (%)

Industry	Geometric Mean	Arithmetic Mean	Standard Deviation	S&P 500 Index	Geometric Mean	Arithmetic Mean	Standard Deviation
1-year	35.2	36.5	19.6	1-year	17.2	17.4	7.2
3-year	5.3	7.6	22.8	3-year	10.4	10.9	11.5
5-year	18.4	20.6	23.3	5-year	13.3	13.9	11.5

Return Ratios (%)

	Return on Assets Latest	5-Yr Avg	Return on Equity Latest	5-Yr Avg	Dividend Yield Latest	5-Yr Avg
Median (7)	7.4	8.4	14.3	11.2	1.4	1.7
SIC Composite (7)	5.5	9.1	4.5	6.1	1.9	2.2
Large Composite (–)	–	–	–	–	–	–
Small Composite (–)	–	–	–	–	–	–
High-Financial Risk (–)	–	–	–	–	–	–

Liquidity Ratio

	Current Ratio Latest	5-Yr Avg
Median (7)	2.8	3.3
SIC Composite (7)	2.3	3.2
Large Composite	–	–
Small Composite	–	–
High-Financial Risk	–	–

Profitability Ratio (%)

	Operating Margin Latest	5-Yr Avg
Median (7)	14.4	14.5
SIC Composite (7)	15.2	16.1
Large Composite	–	–
Small Composite	–	–
High-Financial Risk	–	–

Growth Rates (%)

	Long-term EPS Analyst Estimates
Median (7)	8.4
SIC Composite (7)	8.3
Large Composite	–
Small Composite	–
High-Financial Risk	–

Betas (Levered)

	Raw (OLS)	Blume Adjusted	Peer Group	Vasicek Adjusted	Sum	Downside
Median	1.00	1.00	1.11	1.04	1.15	1.57
SIC Composite	1.24	1.16	1.11	1.23	1.59	1.32
Large Composite	–	–	–	–	–	–
Small Composite	–	–	–	–	–	–
High Financial Risk	–	–	–	–	–	–

Betas (Unlevered)

	Raw (OLS)	Blume Adjusted	Peer Group	Vasicek Adjusted	Sum	Downside
Median	0.89	0.90	1.02	0.90	1.06	1.20
SIC Composite	1.00	0.93	0.90	0.99	1.27	1.06
Large Composite	–	–	–	–	–	–
Small Composite	–	–	–	–	–	–
High Financial Risk	–	–	–	–	–	–

Equity Valuation Multiples

	Price/Sales Latest	5-Yr Avg	Price/Earnings Latest	5-Yr Avg	Market/Book Latest	5-Yr Avg
Median	1.8	1.7	22.1	18.8	3.6	2.1
SIC Composite	1.8	1.5	22.2	16.4	2.7	2.8
Large Composite	–	–	–	–	–	–
Small Composite	–	–	–	–	–	–
High Financial Risk	–	–	–	–	–	–

Enterprise Valuation (EV) Multiples

	EV/Sales Latest	5-Yr Avg	EV/EBITDA Latest	5-Yr Avg
Median	1.9	1.0	10.0	7.9
SIC Composite	2.2	1.7	11.1	8.5
Large Composite	–	–	–	–
Small Composite	–	–	–	–
High Financial Risk	–	–	–	–

Enterprise Valuation SIC Composite
Latest: EV/Sales 2.2, EV/EBITDA 11.1
5-Yr Avg: EV/Sales 1.7, EV/EBITDA 8.5

Fama-French (F-F) 5-Factor Model

	F-F Beta	SMB Premium	HML Premium	RMW Premium	CMA Premium
Median	0.5	5.5	0.1	1.7	3.6
SIC Composite	1.2	1.7	3.4	-0.7	-1.0
Large Composite	–	–	–	–	–
Small Composite	–	–	–	–	–
High Financial Risk	–	–	–	–	–

Leverage Ratios (%)

	Debt/MV Equity Latest	5-Yr Avg	Debt/Total Capital Latest	5-Yr Avg
Median	9.5	18.2	8.6	15.4
SIC Composite	28.2	18.0	22.0	15.3
Large Composite	–	–	–	–
Small Composite	–	–	–	–
High Financial Risk	–	–	–	–

Cost of Debt

	Cost of Debt (%) Latest
Median	6.1
SIC Composite	5.2
Large Composite	–
Small Composite	–
High Financial Risk	–

Capital Structure

SIC Composite (%) Latest: D/TC 22.0, E/TC 78.0

Cost of Equity Capital (%)

	CRSP Deciles CAPM	CAPM +Size Prem	Build-Up	Risk Premium Report CAPM +Size Prem	Build-Up	Discounted Cash Flow 1-Stage	3-Stage	Fama-French 5-Factor Model
Median	9.2	11.3	11.7	13.2	14.3	8.9	10.3	17.2
SIC Composite	10.2	11.4	10.8	15.6	12.8	10.1	9.8	13.3
Large Composite	–	–	–	–	–	–	–	–
Small Composite	–	–	–	–	–	–	–	–
High Financial Risk	–	–	–	–	–	–	–	–

Cost of Equity Capital (%) SIC Composite
Avg CRSP 11.1, Avg RPR 14.2, 1-Stage 10.1, 3-Stage 9.8, 5-Factor Model 13.3

Weighted Average Cost of Capital (WACC) (%)

	CRSP Deciles CAPM	CAPM +Size Prem	Build-Up	Risk Premium Report CAPM +Size Prem	Build-Up	Discounted Cash Flow 1-Stage	3-Stage	Fama-French 5-Factor Model
Median	8.6	10.2	10.4	12.8	12.4	8.4	8.9	16.5
SIC Composite	9.0	9.9	9.5	13.2	11.0	8.9	8.7	11.4
Large Composite	–	–	–	–	–	–	–	–
Small Composite	–	–	–	–	–	–	–	–
High Financial Risk	–	–	–	–	–	–	–	–

WACC (%) SIC Composite
Low 8.7, High 13.2, Average 10.4, Median 9.9

© 2017 Duff & Phelps. All Rights Reserved. Duff & Phelps has used the utmost care in compiling the data presented herein, but cannot guarantee the accuracy, completeness, or timeliness of the information.

Data Updated Through March 31, 2017

287
Number of Companies: 6
Agricultural Chemicals

Industry Description
This group includes establishments primarily engaged in manufacturing nitrogenous and phosphatic basic fertilizers, pesticides, and other agricultural chemicals.

Sales (in millions)

Three Largest Companies
CF Industries Holdings Inc.	$3,685.0
Scotts Miracle-Gro Co.	2,836.1
Terra Nitrogen Co. LP	418.3

Three Smallest Companies
American Vanguard Corp.	$312.1
CVR Partners, LP	289.2
China Green Agriculture, Inc.	268.8

Total Assets (in millions)

Three Largest Companies
CF Industries Holdings Inc.	$15,131.0
Scotts Miracle-Gro Co.	2,808.8
CVR Partners, LP	536.5

Three Smallest Companies
American Vanguard Corp.	$430.0
China Green Agriculture, Inc.	418.8
Terra Nitrogen Co. LP	373.3

Annualized Monthly Performance Statistics (%)

Industry	Geometric Mean	Arithmetic Mean	Standard Deviation
1-year	5.0	7.7	25.6
3-year	-6.8	-4.1	23.5
5-year	-0.6	2.0	23.6

S&P 500 Index	Geometric Mean	Arithmetic Mean	Standard Deviation
1-year	17.2	17.4	7.2
3-year	10.4	10.9	11.5
5-year	13.3	13.9	11.5

Return Ratios (%)

	Return on Assets Latest	5-Yr Avg	Return on Equity Latest	5-Yr Avg	Dividend Yield Latest	5-Yr Avg
Median (6)	7.7	9.2	11.1	20.6	3.3	2.7
SIC Composite (6)	1.5	10.8	1.9	8.8	3.8	3.4
Large Composite (−)	−	−	−	−	−	−
Small Composite (−)	−	−	−	−	−	−
High-Financial Risk (−)	−	−	−	−	−	−

Liquidity Ratio

Current Ratio	Latest	5-Yr Avg
	3.1	3.1
	2.9	2.4
	−	−
	−	−
	−	−

Profitability Ratio (%)

Operating Margin	Latest	5-Yr Avg
	13.6	26.8
	15.6	28.6
	−	−
	−	−
	−	−

Growth Rates (%)

Long-term EPS	Analyst Estimates
	9.9
	35.8
	−
	−
	−

Betas (Levered)

	Raw (OLS)	Blume Adjusted	Peer Group	Vasicek Adjusted	Sum	Downside
Median	0.91	0.95	1.11	1.01	0.98	1.54
SIC Composite	0.99	1.00	1.11	1.02	0.95	1.35
Large Composite	−	−	−	−	−	−
Small Composite	−	−	−	−	−	−
High Financial Risk	−	−	−	−	−	−

Betas (Unlevered)

	Raw (OLS)	Blume Adjusted	Peer Group	Vasicek Adjusted	Sum	Downside
Median	0.75	0.76	0.96	0.80	0.76	1.25
SIC Composite	0.78	0.79	0.86	0.80	0.75	1.02
Large Composite	−	−	−	−	−	−
Small Composite	−	−	−	−	−	−
High Financial Risk	−	−	−	−	−	−

Equity Valuation Multiples

	Price/Sales Latest	5-Yr Avg	Price/Earnings Latest	5-Yr Avg	Market/Book Latest	5-Yr Avg
Median	1.8	2.0	12.5	11.3	1.5	2.3
SIC Composite	2.0	2.1	54.0	11.3	2.1	2.6
Large Composite	−	−	−	−	−	−
Small Composite	−	−	−	−	−	−
High Financial Risk	−	−	−	−	−	−

Enterprise Valuation (EV) Multiples

	EV/Sales Latest	5-Yr Avg	EV/EBITDA Latest	5-Yr Avg
Median	2.2	2.4	8.3	7.7
SIC Composite	2.7	2.5	9.8	6.8
Large Composite	−	−	−	−
Small Composite	−	−	−	−
High Financial Risk	−	−	−	−

Enterprise Valuation SIC Composite
Latest: EV/Sales 2.7, EV/EBITDA 9.8
5-Yr Avg: EV/Sales 2.5, EV/EBITDA 6.8

Fama-French (F-F) 5-Factor Model

	F-F Beta	SMB Premium	HML Premium	RMW Premium	CMA Premium
Median	1.6	0.2	1.7	-0.2	-0.4
SIC Composite	0.9	1.9	1.9	0.1	0.0
Large Composite	−	−	−	−	−
Small Composite	−	−	−	−	−
High Financial Risk	−	−	−	−	−

Leverage Ratios (%)

	Debt/MV Equity Latest	5-Yr Avg	Debt/Total Capital Latest	5-Yr Avg
Median	23.6	17.9	19.1	14.9
SIC Composite	47.5	26.8	32.2	21.1
Large Composite	−	−	−	−
Small Composite	−	−	−	−
High Financial Risk	−	−	−	−

Cost of Debt

Cost of Debt (%)	Latest
Median	6.6
SIC Composite	6.9
Large Composite	−
Small Composite	−
High Financial Risk	−

Capital Structure

SIC Composite (%) Latest
D/TC: 32.2
E/TC: 67.8

Cost of Equity Capital (%)

	CRSP Deciles CAPM	CAPM +Size Prem	Build-Up	Risk Premium Report CAPM +Size Prem	Build-Up	Discounted Cash Flow 1-Stage	3-Stage	Fama-French 5-Factor Model
Median	9.1	11.5	11.8	11.9	14.6	15.3	29.3	13.4
SIC Composite	9.1	10.3	10.8	11.9	12.6	40.9	30.2	12.5
Large Composite	−	−	−	−	−	−	−	−
Small Composite	−	−	−	−	−	−	−	−
High Financial Risk	−	−	−	−	−	−	−	−

Cost of Equity Capital (%) SIC Composite
Avg CRSP: 10.5, Avg RPR: 12.2, 1-Stage: 40.9, 3-Stage: 30.2, 5-Factor Model: 12.5

Weighted Average Cost of Capital (WACC) (%)

	CRSP Deciles CAPM	CAPM +Size Prem	Build-Up	Risk Premium Report CAPM +Size Prem	Build-Up	Discounted Cash Flow 1-Stage	3-Stage	Fama-French 5-Factor Model
Median	8.1	10.3	11.1	10.2	12.9	14.5	21.9	12.1
SIC Composite	8.2	9.0	9.4	10.1	10.6	29.8	22.5	10.5
Large Composite	−	−	−	−	−	−	−	−
Small Composite	−	−	−	−	−	−	−	−
High Financial Risk	−	−	−	−	−	−	−	−

WACC (%) SIC Composite
Low: 9.0, High: 29.8
Average 14.6, Median 10.5

© 2017 Duff & Phelps. All Rights Reserved. Duff & Phelps has used the utmost care in compiling the data presented herein, but cannot guarantee the accuracy, completeness, or timeliness of the information.

Data Updated Through March 31, 2017

289

Number of Companies: 5
Miscellaneous Chemical Products

Industry Description
Establishments primarily engaged in the production of adhesives and sealants, explosives, printing ink, carbon black, and chemicals and chemical preparations not elsewhere classified.

Sales (in millions)

Three Largest Companies
Cabot Corp.	$2,411.0
HB Fuller Co.	2,094.6
Cabot Microelectronics Corp.	430.4

Three Smallest Companies
Cabot Microelectronics Corp.	$430.4
WD-40 Co.	380.7
Chase Corp.	238.1

Total Assets (in millions)

Three Largest Companies
Cabot Corp.	$3,044.0
HB Fuller Co.	2,058.3
Cabot Microelectronics Corp.	727.9

Three Smallest Companies
Cabot Microelectronics Corp.	$727.9
WD-40 Co.	339.7
Chase Corp.	262.8

Annualized Monthly Performance Statistics (%)

Industry	Geometric Mean	Arithmetic Mean	Standard Deviation	S&P 500 Index	Geometric Mean	Arithmetic Mean	Standard Deviation
1-year	32.3	32.8	11.3	1-year	17.2	17.4	7.2
3-year	9.0	10.4	18.2	3-year	10.4	10.9	11.5
5-year	13.6	15.4	20.4	5-year	13.3	13.9	11.5

Return Ratios (%)

	Return on Assets Latest	5-Yr Avg	Return on Equity Latest	5-Yr Avg	Dividend Yield Latest	5-Yr Avg
Median (5)	8.6	8.6	13.3	13.3	1.3	1.4
SIC Composite (5)	6.5	3.9	3.9	3.6	1.7	1.5
Large Composite (–)	–	–	–	–	–	–
Small Composite (–)	–	–	–	–	–	–
High-Financial Risk (–)	–	–	–	–	–	–

Liquidity Ratio

	Current Ratio Latest	5-Yr Avg
	2.7	2.2
	2.7	2.3

Profitability Ratio (%)

	Operating Margin Latest	5-Yr Avg
	18.1	16.3
	12.7	11.1

Growth Rates (%)

	Long-term EPS Analyst Estimates
	8.9
	9.5

Betas (Levered)

	Raw (OLS)	Blume Adjusted	Peer Group	Vasicek Adjusted	Sum	Downside
Median	1.29	1.19	1.11	1.20	1.43	1.59
SIC Composite	1.23	1.15	1.11	1.21	1.24	1.30
Large Composite	–	–	–	–	–	–
Small Composite	–	–	–	–	–	–
High Financial Risk	–	–	–	–	–	–

Betas (Unlevered)

	Raw (OLS)	Blume Adjusted	Peer Group	Vasicek Adjusted	Sum	Downside
Median	1.25	1.11	1.05	1.16	1.19	1.36
SIC Composite	1.06	0.99	0.96	1.04	1.07	1.12
Large Composite	–	–	–	–	–	–
Small Composite	–	–	–	–	–	–
High Financial Risk	–	–	–	–	–	–

Equity Valuation Multiples

	Price/Sales Latest	5-Yr Avg	Price/Earnings Latest	5-Yr Avg	Market/Book Latest	5-Yr Avg
Median	3.7	1.7	27.2	24.6	3.8	2.5
SIC Composite	1.9	1.2	25.5	27.7	3.4	2.3
Large Composite	–	–	–	–	–	–
Small Composite	–	–	–	–	–	–
High Financial Risk	–	–	–	–	–	–

Enterprise Valuation (EV) Multiples

	EV/Sales Latest	5-Yr Avg	EV/EBITDA Latest	5-Yr Avg
Median	3.6	1.8	13.5	9.6
SIC Composite	2.1	1.4	11.7	9.0
Large Composite	–	–	–	–
Small Composite	–	–	–	–
High Financial Risk	–	–	–	–

Enterprise Valuation SIC Composite
- EV/Sales: Latest 2.1, 5-Yr Avg 1.4
- EV/EBITDA: Latest 11.7, 5-Yr Avg 9.0

Fama-French (F-F) 5-Factor Model

	F-F Beta	SMB Premium	HML Premium	RMW Premium	CMA Premium
Median	1.3	5.3	0.3	3.8	-4.8
SIC Composite	1.1	3.2	0.8	1.4	-0.3
Large Composite	–	–	–	–	–
Small Composite	–	–	–	–	–
High Financial Risk	–	–	–	–	–

Leverage Ratios (%)

	Debt/MV Equity Latest	5-Yr Avg	Debt/Total Capital Latest	5-Yr Avg
Median	8.1	16.0	7.5	13.8
SIC Composite	18.6	27.6	15.7	21.6

Cost of Debt

	Cost of Debt (%) Latest
Median	6.1
SIC Composite	5.1

Capital Structure

SIC Composite (%) Latest
- D/TC: 15.7
- E/TC: 84.3

Cost of Equity Capital (%)

	CAPM	CRSP Deciles CAPM +Size Prem	Build-Up	Risk Premium Report CAPM +Size Prem	Build-Up	Discounted Cash Flow 1-Stage	3-Stage	Fama-French 5-Factor Model
Median	10.1	12.2	11.3	15.2	14.2	10.2	7.9	15.3
SIC Composite	10.2	11.6	11.0	14.2	13.8	11.0	7.1	14.8
Large Composite	–	–	–	–	–	–	–	–
Small Composite	–	–	–	–	–	–	–	–
High Financial Risk	–	–	–	–	–	–	–	–

Cost of Equity Capital (%) SIC Composite
- Avg CRSP: 11.3
- Avg RPR: 14.0
- 1-Stage: 11.0
- 3-Stage: 7.1
- 5-Factor Model: 14.8

Weighted Average Cost of Capital (WACC) (%)

	CAPM	CRSP Deciles CAPM +Size Prem	Build-Up	Risk Premium Report CAPM +Size Prem	Build-Up	Discounted Cash Flow 1-Stage	3-Stage	Fama-French 5-Factor Model
Median	9.8	11.3	10.9	12.9	13.7	10.0	7.7	14.6
SIC Composite	9.3	10.5	10.1	12.8	12.4	10.0	6.8	13.2
Large Composite	–	–	–	–	–	–	–	–
Small Composite	–	–	–	–	–	–	–	–
High Financial Risk	–	–	–	–	–	–	–	–

WACC (%) SIC Composite
- Low: 6.8
- High: 13.2
- Average: 10.8
- Median: 10.5

© 2017 Duff & Phelps. All Rights Reserved. Duff & Phelps has used the utmost care in compiling the data presented herein, but cannot guarantee the accuracy, completeness, or timeliness of the information.

Data Updated Through March 31, 2017

29

Number of Companies: 13
Petroleum Refining and Related Industries

Industry Description
This major group includes establishments primarily engaged in petroleum refining, manufacturing paving and roofing materials, and compounding lubricating oils and greases from purchased materials.

Sales (in millions)

Three Largest Companies
Exxon Mobil Corp.	$197,518.0
Chevron Corp.	103,310.0
Phillips 66	70,898.0

Three Smallest Companies
NuStar Energy L.P.	$1,756.7
Quaker Chemical Corp.	746.7
Trecora Resources	212.4

Total Assets (in millions)

Three Largest Companies
Exxon Mobil Corp.	$330,314.0
Chevron Corp.	260,078.0
Phillips 66	51,653.0

Three Smallest Companies
Renewable Energy Group, Inc.	$1,136.6
Quaker Chemical Corp.	692.0
Trecora Resources	292.1

Annualized Monthly Performance Statistics (%)

Industry	Geometric Mean	Arithmetic Mean	Standard Deviation
1-year	6.2	7.0	13.6
3-year	-0.5	0.5	15.0
5-year	4.4	5.6	15.8

S&P 500 Index	Geometric Mean	Arithmetic Mean	Standard Deviation
1-year	17.2	17.4	7.2
3-year	10.4	10.9	11.5
5-year	13.3	13.9	11.5

Return Ratios (%)

	Return on Assets Latest	Return on Assets 5-Yr Avg	Return on Equity Latest	Return on Equity 5-Yr Avg	Dividend Yield Latest	Dividend Yield 5-Yr Avg
Median (13)	2.4	6.5	5.3	11.5	4.0	3.0
SIC Composite (13)	1.5	6.8	1.7	7.2	3.7	3.3
Large Composite (3)	1.4	6.9	1.5	7.1	3.6	3.2
Small Composite (3)	3.8	2.3	3.8	2.6	6.4	6.7
High-Financial Risk (–)	–	–	–	–	–	–

Liquidity Ratio

	Current Ratio Latest	Current Ratio 5-Yr Avg
	1.7	1.7
	1.1	1.2
	0.9	1.1
	1.8	1.6
	–	–

Profitability Ratio (%)

	Operating Margin Latest	Operating Margin 5-Yr Avg
	2.4	7.0
	0.2	6.9
	-1.1	7.3
	17.0	9.9
	–	–

Growth Rates (%)

	Long-term EPS Analyst Estimates
	32.8
	38.4
	40.0
	-0.1
	–

Betas (Levered)

	Raw (OLS)	Blume Adjusted	Peer Group	Vasicek Adjusted	Sum	Downside
Median	1.26	1.17	1.09	1.18	1.50	1.63
SIC Composite	1.04	1.03	1.09	1.04	1.01	1.06
Large Composite	1.02	1.02	1.09	1.03	0.97	1.05
Small Composite	1.29	1.19	–	–	1.56	1.40
High Financial Risk	–	–	–	–	–	–

Betas (Unlevered)

	Raw (OLS)	Blume Adjusted	Peer Group	Vasicek Adjusted	Sum	Downside
Median	1.00	0.94	0.84	0.90	1.12	1.28
SIC Composite	0.88	0.87	0.92	0.89	0.86	0.90
Large Composite	0.87	0.87	0.93	0.89	0.83	0.90
Small Composite	0.95	0.88	–	–	1.13	1.02
High Financial Risk	–	–	–	–	–	–

Equity Valuation Multiples

	Price/Sales Latest	Price/Sales 5-Yr Avg	Price/Earnings Latest	Price/Earnings 5-Yr Avg	Market/Book Latest	Market/Book 5-Yr Avg
Median	0.5	0.4	30.5	14.4	1.4	1.4
SIC Composite	1.3	0.9	57.5	13.9	1.5	1.5
Large Composite	1.6	1.0	65.7	14.2	1.5	1.6
Small Composite	2.2	1.2	26.6	39.3	9.7	2.5
High Financial Risk	–	–	–	–	–	–

Enterprise Valuation (EV) Multiples

	EV/Sales Latest	EV/Sales 5-Yr Avg	EV/EBITDA Latest	EV/EBITDA 5-Yr Avg
Median	0.7	0.4	12.1	5.5
SIC Composite	1.5	0.9	11.9	6.1
Large Composite	1.8	1.1	12.6	6.2
Small Composite	3.4	1.9	12.9	12.5
High Financial Risk	–	–	–	–

Enterprise Valuation SIC Composite
- Latest: EV/Sales 1.5, EV/EBITDA 11.9
- 5-Yr Avg: EV/Sales 0.9, EV/EBITDA 6.1

Fama-French (F-F) 5-Factor Model

	F-F Beta	SMB Premium	HML Premium	RMW Premium	CMA Premium
Median	1.4	-0.2	-0.5	0.9	5.2
SIC Composite	1.0	0.0	2.8	-0.2	2.4
Large Composite	1.0	-0.1	2.5	-0.3	-0.4
Small Composite	1.3	1.1	0.5	0.7	3.9
High Financial Risk	–	–	–	–	–

Leverage Ratios (%)

	Debt/MV Equity Latest	Debt/MV Equity 5-Yr Avg	Debt/Total Capital Latest	Debt/Total Capital 5-Yr Avg
Median	44.5	25.4	30.8	20.3
SIC Composite	18.5	12.0	15.6	10.7
Large Composite	16.9	10.5	14.5	9.5
Small Composite	52.8	55.5	34.5	35.7
High Financial Risk	–	–	–	–

Cost of Debt

	Cost of Debt (%) Latest
Median	6.1
SIC Composite	4.2
Large Composite	4.0
Small Composite	6.2
High Financial Risk	–

Capital Structure

SIC Composite (%) Latest
- D/TC: 15.6
- E/TC: 84.4

Cost of Equity Capital (%)

	CRSP Deciles CAPM	CRSP Deciles CAPM +Size Prem	CRSP Deciles Build-Up	Risk Premium Report CAPM +Size Prem	Risk Premium Report Build-Up	Discounted Cash Flow 1-Stage	Discounted Cash Flow 3-Stage	Fama-French 5-Factor Model
Median	10.0	11.3	10.4	15.0	12.8	18.8	28.5	16.7
SIC Composite	9.2	9.3	9.4	9.8	8.9	43.7	25.1	14.1
Large Composite	9.2	9.2	9.4	9.4	8.7	45.2	25.5	11.1
Small Composite	–	–	10.6	15.8	13.4	5.8	4.2	16.9
High Financial Risk	–	–	–	–	–	–	–	–

Cost of Equity Capital (%) SIC Composite
- Avg CRSP: 9.4
- Avg RPR: 9.4
- 1-Stage: 43.7
- 3-Stage: 25.1
- 5-Factor Model: 14.1

Weighted Average Cost of Capital (WACC) (%)

	CRSP Deciles CAPM	CRSP Deciles CAPM +Size Prem	CRSP Deciles Build-Up	Risk Premium Report CAPM +Size Prem	Risk Premium Report Build-Up	Discounted Cash Flow 1-Stage	Discounted Cash Flow 3-Stage	Fama-French 5-Factor Model
Median	8.5	9.1	8.5	12.7	9.5	16.5	22.2	13.0
SIC Composite	8.3	8.3	8.4	8.8	8.0	37.4	21.7	12.4
Large Composite	8.3	8.3	8.4	8.5	7.9	39.1	22.2	9.9
Small Composite	–	–	8.5	11.9	10.4	5.4	4.3	12.7
High Financial Risk	–	–	–	–	–	–	–	–

WACC (%) SIC Composite
- Low: 8.0
- High: 37.4
- Average 15.0 ◆ Median 8.8

© 2017 Duff & Phelps. All Rights Reserved. Duff & Phelps has used the utmost care in compiling the data presented herein, but cannot guarantee the accuracy, completeness, or timeliness of the information.

Data Updated Through March 31, 2017

291

Number of Companies: 11
Petroleum Refining

Industry Description
Establishments primarily engaged in producing gasoline, kerosene, distillate fuel oils, residual fuel oils, and lubricants, through fractionation or straight distillation of crude oil, redistillation of unfinished petroleum derivatives, cracking or other process.

Sales (in millions)

Three Largest Companies
Exxon Mobil Corp.	$197,518.0
Chevron Corp.	103,310.0
Phillips 66	70,898.0

Three Smallest Companies
Alon USA Energy, Inc.	$3,831.8
NuStar Energy L.P.	1,756.7
Trecora Resources	212.4

Annualized Monthly Performance Statistics (%)

Industry
	Geometric Mean	Arithmetic Mean	Standard Deviation
1-year	6.1	6.9	13.6
3-year	-0.6	0.5	15.0
5-year	4.4	5.5	15.8

Total Assets (in millions)

Three Largest Companies
Exxon Mobil Corp.	$330,314.0
Chevron Corp.	260,078.0
Phillips 66	51,653.0

Three Smallest Companies
Delek US Holdings, Inc.	$2,985.1
Alon USA Energy, Inc.	2,110.2
Trecora Resources	292.1

S&P 500 Index
	Geometric Mean	Arithmetic Mean	Standard Deviation
1-year	17.2	17.4	7.2
3-year	10.4	10.9	11.5
5-year	13.3	13.9	11.5

Return Ratios (%)

	Return on Assets Latest	5-Yr Avg	Return on Equity Latest	5-Yr Avg	Dividend Yield Latest	5-Yr Avg
Median (11)	2.2	6.5	3.8	11.5	4.2	3.5
SIC Composite (11)	1.5	6.8	1.7	7.2	3.7	3.3
Large Composite (3)	1.4	6.9	1.5	7.1	3.6	3.2
Small Composite (3)	1.2	1.4	1.7	2.0	7.9	7.2
High-Financial Risk (−)	−	−	−	−	−	−

Liquidity Ratio

	Current Ratio Latest	5-Yr Avg
	1.5	1.5
	1.1	1.2
	0.9	1.1
	1.2	1.2
	−	−

Profitability Ratio (%)

	Operating Margin Latest	5-Yr Avg
	2.0	7.0
	0.1	6.9
	-1.1	7.3
	5.6	5.4
	−	−

Growth Rates (%)

	Long-term EPS Analyst Estimates
	32.8
	38.5
	40.0
	2.4
	−

Betas (Levered)

	Raw (OLS)	Blume Adjusted	Peer Group	Vasicek Adjusted	Sum	Downside
Median	1.26	1.17	1.09	1.17	1.50	1.55
SIC Composite	1.03	1.03	1.09	1.04	1.01	1.05
Large Composite	1.02	1.02	1.09	1.03	0.97	1.05
Small Composite	1.23	1.15	−	−	1.79	1.40
High Financial Risk	−	−	−	−	−	−

Betas (Unlevered)

	Raw (OLS)	Blume Adjusted	Peer Group	Vasicek Adjusted	Sum	Downside
Median	0.97	0.91	0.84	0.87	1.08	1.17
SIC Composite	0.88	0.87	0.92	0.89	0.86	0.89
Large Composite	0.87	0.87	0.93	0.89	0.83	0.90
Small Composite	0.85	0.80	−	−	1.18	0.95
High Financial Risk	−	−	−	−	−	−

Equity Valuation Multiples

	Price/Sales Latest	5-Yr Avg	Price/Earnings Latest	5-Yr Avg	Market/Book Latest	5-Yr Avg
Median	0.5	0.4	43.4	14.4	1.4	1.4
SIC Composite	1.3	0.9	57.8	13.8	1.5	1.5
Large Composite	1.6	1.0	65.7	14.2	1.5	1.6
Small Composite	0.9	0.5	61.7	51.2	4.7	1.9
High Financial Risk	−	−	−	−	−	−

Enterprise Valuation (EV) Multiples

	EV/Sales Latest	5-Yr Avg	EV/EBITDA Latest	5-Yr Avg
Median	0.7	0.4	12.1	5.5
SIC Composite	1.5	0.9	11.9	6.1
Large Composite	1.8	1.1	12.6	6.2
Small Composite	1.5	0.9	12.3	9.9
High Financial Risk	−	−	−	−

Enterprise Valuation SIC Composite
- EV/Sales: Latest 1.5, 5-Yr Avg 0.9
- EV/EBITDA: Latest 11.9, 5-Yr Avg 6.1

Fama-French (F-F) 5-Factor Model

Fama-French (F-F) Components
	F-F Beta	SMB Premium	HML Premium	RMW Premium	CMA Premium
Median	1.4	-0.2	-0.5	0.9	5.2
SIC Composite	1.0	0.0	2.8	-0.2	2.4
Large Composite	1.0	-0.1	2.5	-0.3	-0.4
Small Composite	1.3	0.6	2.2	0.8	1.9
High Financial Risk	−	−	−	−	−

Leverage Ratios (%)

	Debt/MV Equity Latest	5-Yr Avg	Debt/Total Capital Latest	5-Yr Avg
Median	44.5	25.4	30.8	20.3
SIC Composite	18.5	12.0	15.6	10.7
Large Composite	16.9	10.5	14.5	9.5
Small Composite	70.4	67.1	41.3	40.2
High Financial Risk	−	−	−	−

Cost of Debt

	Cost of Debt (%) Latest
Median	6.1
SIC Composite	4.2
Large Composite	4.0
Small Composite	6.3
High Financial Risk	−

Capital Structure

SIC Composite (%) Latest
- D/TC: 15.6
- E/TC: 84.4

Cost of Equity Capital (%)

	CRSP Deciles CAPM	CAPM +Size Prem	Build-Up	Risk Premium Report CAPM +Size Prem	Build-Up	Discounted Cash Flow 1-Stage	3-Stage	Fama-French 5-Factor Model
Median	9.9	10.9	10.4	15.0	12.4	24.9	28.7	16.7
SIC Composite	9.2	9.3	9.4	9.8	8.9	43.8	25.1	14.1
Large Composite	9.2	9.2	9.4	9.4	8.7	45.2	25.5	11.1
Small Composite	−	−	10.6	16.9	13.2	10.0	4.1	15.9
High Financial Risk	−	−	−	−	−	−	−	−

Cost of Equity Capital (%) SIC Composite
- Avg CRSP: 9.3
- Avg RPR: 9.3
- 1-Stage: 43.8
- 3-Stage: 25.1
- 5-Factor Model: 14.1

Weighted Average Cost of Capital (WACC) (%)

	CRSP Deciles CAPM	CAPM +Size Prem	Build-Up	Risk Premium Report CAPM +Size Prem	Build-Up	Discounted Cash Flow 1-Stage	3-Stage	Fama-French 5-Factor Model
Median	8.2	8.9	8.4	11.6	9.2	20.7	22.4	13.0
SIC Composite	8.3	8.3	8.4	8.7	8.0	37.4	21.7	12.4
Large Composite	8.3	8.3	8.4	8.5	7.9	39.1	22.2	9.9
Small Composite	−	−	8.1	11.7	9.6	7.7	4.2	11.2
High Financial Risk	−	−	−	−	−	−	−	−

WACC (%) SIC Composite
- Low: 8.0
- High: 37.4
- Average: 15.0
- Median: 8.7

© 2017 Duff & Phelps. All Rights Reserved. Duff & Phelps has used the utmost care in compiling the data presented herein, but cannot guarantee the accuracy, completeness, or timeliness of the information.

Data Updated Through March 31, 2017

3

Number of Companies: 402
Manufacturing

Industry Description
The manufacturing division includes establishments engaged in the mechanical or chemical transformation of materials or substances into new products. These establishments are usually described as plants, factories, or mills and characteristically use power driven machines and materials handling equipment. Establishments engaged in assembling component parts of manufactured products are also considered manufacturing if the new product is neither a structure nor other fixed improvement. Also included is the blending of materials, such as lubricating oils, plastics resins, or liquors.

Sales (in millions)

Three Largest Companies
Apple Inc.	$215,091.0
General Motors Co.	166,380.0
Ford Motor Co.	151,800.0

Three Smallest Companies
Interlink Electronics, Inc.	$10.5
Electro-Sensors Inc.	7.6
NF Energy Saving Corp.	6.7

Annualized Monthly Performance Statistics (%)

Industry	Geometric Mean	Arithmetic Mean	Standard Deviation
1-year	27.2	27.7	12.7
3-year	13.8	14.8	15.5
5-year	13.7	14.6	14.7

Total Assets (in millions)

Three Largest Companies
Apple Inc.	$321,686.0
Ford Motor Co.	237,951.0
General Motors Co.	221,690.0

Three Smallest Companies
Electromed, Inc.	$20.6
Electro-Sensors Inc.	13.4
Interlink Electronics, Inc.	7.6

S&P 500 Index	Geometric Mean	Arithmetic Mean	Standard Deviation
1-year	17.2	17.4	7.2
3-year	10.4	10.9	11.5
5-year	13.3	13.9	11.5

Return Ratios (%)

	Return on Assets Latest	5-Yr Avg	Return on Equity Latest	5-Yr Avg	Dividend Yield Latest	5-Yr Avg	Current Ratio Latest	5-Yr Avg	Operating Margin Latest	5-Yr Avg	Long-term EPS Analyst Estimates
Median (402)	5.4	6.0	10.2	11.1	0.9	1.0	2.7	2.7	10.2	10.3	10.6
SIC Composite (402)	6.4	6.9	4.7	5.9	2.0	2.0	1.6	1.7	13.8	13.4	10.6
Large Composite (40)	6.8	7.2	5.5	6.7	2.4	2.3	1.4	1.5	14.1	13.7	9.9
Small Composite (40)	0.4	5.4	0.3	4.1	0.8	1.2	5.0	4.7	4.2	9.6	14.2
High-Financial Risk (80)	-2.9	-3.5	-3.9	-6.5	0.3	0.5	1.6	1.8	4.8	3.7	18.0

Betas (Levered)

	Raw (OLS)	Blume Adjusted	Peer Group	Vasicek Adjusted	Sum	Downside
Median	1.16	1.11	1.15	1.16	1.19	1.45
SIC Composite	1.13	1.09	1.15	1.13	1.12	1.16
Large Composite	1.12	1.08	1.14	1.13	1.11	1.16
Small Composite	0.93	0.96	1.16	0.96	0.92	1.02
High Financial Risk	1.63	1.40	1.24	1.61	1.65	1.72

Betas (Unlevered)

	Raw (OLS)	Blume Adjusted	Peer Group	Vasicek Adjusted	Sum	Downside
Median	1.00	0.96	1.04	1.00	1.04	1.27
SIC Composite	0.93	0.90	0.95	0.93	0.93	0.96
Large Composite	0.90	0.87	0.91	0.90	0.89	0.93
Small Composite	0.90	0.93	1.12	0.93	0.90	0.99
High Financial Risk	1.20	1.05	0.94	1.19	1.22	1.26

Equity Valuation Multiples

	Price/Sales Latest	5-Yr Avg	Price/Earnings Latest	5-Yr Avg	Market/Book Latest	5-Yr Avg
Median	1.6	1.4	27.5	22.0	2.7	2.3
SIC Composite	1.9	1.5	21.3	17.0	3.7	3.0
Large Composite	1.8	1.4	18.2	15.1	3.8	3.1
Small Composite	1.8	1.7	—	24.5	1.6	1.6
High Financial Risk	1.1	0.7	—	—	4.8	2.6

Enterprise Valuation (EV) Multiples

	EV/Sales Latest	5-Yr Avg	EV/EBITDA Latest	5-Yr Avg
Median	1.7	1.5	12.2	10.2
SIC Composite	2.2	1.6	11.2	8.9
Large Composite	2.1	1.6	10.3	8.3
Small Composite	1.6	1.4	16.2	10.1
High Financial Risk	1.5	1.1	14.2	11.9

Enterprise Valuation SIC Composite: Latest EV/Sales 2.2, EV/EBITDA 11.2; 5-Yr Avg EV/Sales 1.6, EV/EBITDA 8.9

Fama-French (F-F) 5-Factor Model

	Fama-French (F-F) Components				
	F-F Beta	SMB Premium	HML Premium	RMW Premium	CMA Premium
Median	1.2	1.7	3.9	-0.1	-2.1
SIC Composite	1.1	1.4	0.4	1.5	-2.6
Large Composite	1.1	0.7	0.4	2.2	3.0
Small Composite	0.8	3.7	0.0	-0.3	3.0
High Financial Risk	—	—	—	—	—

Leverage Ratios (%)

	Debt/MV Equity Latest	5-Yr Avg	Debt/Total Capital Latest	5-Yr Avg
Median	13.8	12.4	12.1	11.0
SIC Composite	23.7	23.8	19.2	19.2
Large Composite	27.2	26.6	21.4	21.0
Small Composite	4.7	4.6	4.5	4.4
High Financial Risk	48.3	63.9	32.6	39.0

Cost of Debt

	Cost of Debt (%) Latest
Median	6.1
SIC Composite	4.8
Large Composite	4.5
Small Composite	6.6
High Financial Risk	6.7

Capital Structure

SIC Composite (%) Latest: D/TC 19.2, E/TC 80.8

Cost of Equity Capital (%)

	CRSP Deciles			Risk Premium Report		Discounted Cash Flow		Fama-French
	CAPM	CAPM +Size Prem	Build-Up	CAPM +Size Prem	Build-Up	1-Stage	3-Stage	5-Factor Model
Median	9.9	11.8	11.6	14.0	14.0	11.8	9.9	13.7
SIC Composite	9.7	10.0	10.1	11.5	10.6	12.5	11.1	10.2
Large Composite	9.7	9.7	9.9	10.8	9.6	12.1	11.6	15.9
Small Composite	8.8	13.7	14.7	14.4	16.5	14.8	11.3	14.5
High Financial Risk	—	—	—	22.5	21.9	—	—	—

Cost of Equity Capital (%) SIC Composite: Avg CRSP 10.1, Avg RPR 11.1, Build-Up 12.5, 1-Stage 11.1, 3-Stage / 5-Factor Model 10.2

Weighted Average Cost of Capital (WACC) (%)

	CRSP Deciles			Risk Premium Report		Discounted Cash Flow		Fama-French
	CAPM	CAPM +Size Prem	Build-Up	CAPM +Size Prem	Build-Up	1-Stage	3-Stage	5-Factor Model
Median	9.0	10.7	10.6	12.6	12.5	10.8	9.2	12.3
SIC Composite	8.6	8.9	8.9	10.1	9.3	10.8	9.7	9.0
Large Composite	8.4	8.4	8.5	9.2	8.3	10.3	9.9	13.3
Small Composite	8.6	13.3	14.2	14.0	16.0	14.4	11.0	14.1
High Financial Risk	—	—	—	17.0	16.6	—	—	—

WACC (%) SIC Composite: Low 8.9, High 10.8, Average 9.5, Median 9.3

© 2017 Duff & Phelps. All Rights Reserved. Duff & Phelps has used the utmost care in compiling the data presented herein, but cannot guarantee the accuracy, completeness, or timeliness of the information.

Data Updated Through March 31, 2017

30

Number of Companies: 15
Rubber and Miscellaneous Plastics Products

Industry Description
This major group includes establishments manufacturing products, not elsewhere classified, from plastics resins and from natural, synthetic, or reclaimed rubber, gutta percha, balata, or gutta siak.

Sales (in millions)

Three Largest Companies
Nike, Inc.	$32,376.0
Goodyear Tire & Rubber Co.	15,158.0
Cooper Tire & Rubber Co.	2,924.9

Three Smallest Companies
CTI Industries Corp.	$59.4
Alpha Pro Tech, Ltd.	46.2
Female Health Co.	22.1

Total Assets (in millions)

Three Largest Companies
Nike, Inc.	$21,396.0
Goodyear Tire & Rubber Co.	16,511.0
Cooper Tire & Rubber Co.	2,619.4

Three Smallest Companies
CTI Industries Corp.	$41.8
Female Health Co.	38.6
Alpha Pro Tech, Ltd.	35.9

Annualized Monthly Performance Statistics (%)

Industry	Geometric Mean	Arithmetic Mean	Standard Deviation
1-year	-3.7	-2.8	14.0
3-year	14.1	15.2	16.3
5-year	16.6	18.1	18.9

S&P 500 Index	Geometric Mean	Arithmetic Mean	Standard Deviation
1-year	17.2	17.4	7.2
3-year	10.4	10.9	11.5
5-year	13.3	13.9	11.5

Return Ratios (%)

	Return on Assets Latest	5-Yr Avg	Return on Equity Latest	5-Yr Avg	Dividend Yield Latest	5-Yr Avg
Median (15)	6.7	7.7	8.2	12.0	1.1	1.1
SIC Composite (15)	11.8	9.8	4.8	4.8	1.6	1.6
Large Composite (3)	13.0	10.5	5.1	4.9	1.1	0.9
Small Composite (3)	3.9	8.8	4.8	5.3	0.0	1.8
High-Financial Risk (–)	–	–	–	–	–	–

Liquidity Ratio

	Current Ratio Latest	5-Yr Avg
Median (15)	2.7	2.4
SIC Composite (15)	2.1	2.1
Large Composite (3)	2.1	2.2
Small Composite (3)	3.1	3.2
High-Financial Risk (–)	–	–

Profitability Ratio (%)

	Operating Margin Latest	5-Yr Avg
Median (15)	10.3	10.2
SIC Composite (15)	12.9	11.3
Large Composite (3)	13.3	11.3
Small Composite (3)	8.6	8.8
High-Financial Risk (–)	–	–

Growth Rates (%)

	Long-term EPS Analyst Estimates
Median (15)	12.7
SIC Composite (15)	12.7
Large Composite (3)	12.6
Small Composite (3)	12.7
High-Financial Risk (–)	–

Betas (Levered)

	Raw (OLS)	Blume Adjusted	Peer Group	Vasicek Adjusted	Sum	Downside
Median	1.07	1.05	0.71	0.96	1.00	1.38
SIC Composite	0.63	0.77	0.71	0.64	0.68	0.87
Large Composite	0.54	0.71	0.71	0.55	0.61	0.86
Small Composite	1.03	1.03	0.71	0.95	-0.01	1.57
High Financial Risk	–	–	–	–	–	–

Betas (Unlevered)

	Raw (OLS)	Blume Adjusted	Peer Group	Vasicek Adjusted	Sum	Downside
Median	1.06	0.96	0.66	0.90	0.94	1.20
SIC Composite	0.60	0.73	0.67	0.61	0.64	0.81
Large Composite	0.52	0.68	0.68	0.53	0.58	0.81
Small Composite	0.91	0.90	0.64	0.84	0.05	1.35
High Financial Risk	–	–	–	–	–	–

Equity Valuation Multiples

	Price/Sales Latest	5-Yr Avg	Price/Earnings Latest	5-Yr Avg	Market/Book Latest	5-Yr Avg
Median	1.3	1.0	23.4	22.3	2.2	2.4
SIC Composite	2.0	1.7	20.7	21.1	5.6	5.1
Large Composite	2.1	1.7	19.7	20.6	5.8	5.5
Small Composite	0.7	1.5	20.6	18.9	1.2	2.4
High Financial Risk	–	–	–	–	–	–

Enterprise Valuation (EV) Multiples

	EV/Sales Latest	5-Yr Avg	EV/EBITDA Latest	5-Yr Avg
Median	1.2	1.0	9.6	9.3
SIC Composite	2.1	1.7	12.5	11.6
Large Composite	2.1	1.7	12.4	11.8
Small Composite	0.8	1.5	7.3	12.9
High Financial Risk	–	–	–	–

Enterprise Valuation SIC Composite
- EV/Sales Latest: 2.1; 5-Yr Avg: 1.7
- EV/EBITDA Latest: 12.5; 5-Yr Avg: 11.6

Fama-French (F-F) 5-Factor Model

	F-F Beta	SMB Premium	HML Premium	RMW Premium	CMA Premium
Median	0.9	4.3	0.7	-1.1	3.3
SIC Composite	0.6	0.9	-0.8	2.4	-2.3
Large Composite	0.6	0.5	-0.8	2.6	3.5
Small Composite	1.0	2.8	0.4	2.7	1.2
High Financial Risk	–	–	–	–	–

Leverage Ratios (%)

	Debt/MV Equity Latest	5-Yr Avg	Debt/Total Capital Latest	5-Yr Avg
Median	13.9	17.0	12.2	14.6
SIC Composite	8.9	10.5	8.2	9.5
Large Composite	7.6	9.2	7.1	8.4
Small Composite	22.6	9.9	18.4	9.0
High Financial Risk	–	–	–	–

Cost of Debt

	Cost of Debt (%) Latest
Median	6.1
SIC Composite	5.7
Large Composite	5.5
Small Composite	7.1
High Financial Risk	–

Capital Structure

SIC Composite (%) Latest
- D/TC: 8.2
- E/TC: 91.8

Cost of Equity Capital (%)

	CRSP Deciles CAPM	CAPM +Size Prem	Build-Up	Risk Premium Report CAPM +Size Prem	Build-Up	Discounted Cash Flow 1-Stage	3-Stage	Fama-French 5-Factor Model
Median	8.8	11.4	9.1	13.7	14.9	13.3	10.9	15.7
SIC Composite	7.0	7.3	7.7	9.2	10.8	13.1	10.6	7.1
Large Composite	6.5	6.7	7.5	8.5	10.4	12.8	10.7	12.4
Small Composite	8.7	14.3	13.0	9.4	16.7	12.7	19.0	16.3
High Financial Risk	–	–	–	–	–	–	–	–

Cost of Equity Capital (%) SIC Composite
- Avg CRSP: 7.5
- Avg RPR: 10.0
- 1-Stage: 13.1
- 3-Stage: 10.6
- 5-Factor Model: 7.1

Weighted Average Cost of Capital (WACC) (%)

	CRSP Deciles CAPM	CAPM +Size Prem	Build-Up	Risk Premium Report CAPM +Size Prem	Build-Up	Discounted Cash Flow 1-Stage	3-Stage	Fama-French 5-Factor Model
Median	8.4	10.5	8.9	12.6	12.9	12.7	9.9	12.6
SIC Composite	6.9	7.2	7.5	8.9	10.4	12.5	10.1	7.0
Large Composite	6.5	6.6	7.4	8.3	10.0	12.2	10.3	11.9
Small Composite	8.1	12.7	11.6	8.7	14.6	11.4	16.5	14.3
High Financial Risk	–	–	–	–	–	–	–	–

WACC (%) SIC Composite
Low 7.0 — High 12.5
▲ Average 9.1 ◆ Median 8.9

© 2017 Duff & Phelps. All Rights Reserved. Duff & Phelps has used the utmost care in compiling the data presented herein, but cannot guarantee the accuracy, completeness, or timeliness of the information.

Data Updated Through March 31, 2017

308

Number of Companies: 8
Miscellaneous Plastics Products

Industry Description
Establishments primarily engaged in unsupported plastics film and sheet; unsupported plastics profile shapes; laminated plastics plate, sheet, and profile shapes; plastic bottles; plastics foam products; custom compounding of purchased plastics resins, plastics plumbing fixtures; plastic products, not elsewhere classified.

Sales (in millions)

Three Largest Companies
AptarGroup Inc.	$2,330.9
Tupperware Brands Corp.	2,213.1
Tredegar Corp.	828.3

Three Smallest Companies
Core Molding Technologies	$174.9
UFP Technologies, Inc.	146.1
Alpha Pro Tech, Ltd.	46.2

Annualized Monthly Performance Statistics (%)

Industry
	Geometric Mean	Arithmetic Mean	Standard Deviation
1-year	11.8	12.4	11.6
3-year	0.4	1.6	16.1
5-year	5.6	7.0	17.6

Total Assets (in millions)

Three Largest Companies
AptarGroup Inc.	$2,606.8
Tupperware Brands Corp.	1,587.8
Tredegar Corp.	651.2

Three Smallest Companies
Core Molding Technologies	$134.8
UFP Technologies, Inc.	127.9
Alpha Pro Tech, Ltd.	35.9

S&P 500 Index
	Geometric Mean	Arithmetic Mean	Standard Deviation
1-year	17.2	17.4	7.2
3-year	10.4	10.9	11.5
5-year	13.3	13.9	11.5

Return Ratios (%)

	Return on Assets Latest	Return on Assets 5-Yr Avg	Return on Equity Latest	Return on Equity 5-Yr Avg	Dividend Yield Latest	Dividend Yield 5-Yr Avg	Current Ratio Latest	Current Ratio 5-Yr Avg	Operating Margin Latest	Operating Margin 5-Yr Avg	Long-term EPS Analyst Estimates
Median (8)	6.6	7.8	7.8	10.9	1.9	1.8	2.7	2.2	7.6	9.1	12.7
SIC Composite (8)	8.5	8.3	4.7	4.9	2.7	2.5	1.8	1.8	11.8	11.9	10.3
Large Composite (–)	–	–	–	–	–	–	–	–	–	–	–
Small Composite (–)	–	–	–	–	–	–	–	–	–	–	–
High-Financial Risk (–)	–	–	–	–	–	–	–	–	–	–	–

(Liquidity Ratio / Profitability Ratio (%) / Growth Rates (%))

Betas (Levered)

	Raw (OLS)	Blume Adjusted	Peer Group	Vasicek Adjusted	Sum	Downside
Median	1.13	1.09	–	–	1.07	1.58
SIC Composite	1.27	1.18	–	–	1.26	1.24
Large Composite	–	–	–	–	–	–
Small Composite	–	–	–	–	–	–
High Financial Risk	–	–	–	–	–	–

Betas (Unlevered)

	Raw (OLS)	Blume Adjusted	Peer Group	Vasicek Adjusted	Sum	Downside
Median	1.11	1.05	–	–	1.04	1.47
SIC Composite	1.11	1.03	–	–	1.10	1.08
Large Composite	–	–	–	–	–	–
Small Composite	–	–	–	–	–	–
High Financial Risk	–	–	–	–	–	–

Equity Valuation Multiples

	Price/Sales Latest	Price/Sales 5-Yr Avg	Price/Earnings Latest	Price/Earnings 5-Yr Avg	Market/Book Latest	Market/Book 5-Yr Avg
Median	1.1	1.0	23.3	20.9	2.4	2.1
SIC Composite	1.6	1.4	21.1	20.4	4.4	3.8
Large Composite	–	–	–	–	–	–
Small Composite	–	–	–	–	–	–
High Financial Risk	–	–	–	–	–	–

Enterprise Valuation (EV) Multiples

	EV/Sales Latest	EV/Sales 5-Yr Avg	EV/EBITDA Latest	EV/EBITDA 5-Yr Avg
Median	1.1	0.9	10.0	8.8
SIC Composite	1.8	1.6	10.8	9.6
Large Composite	–	–	–	–
Small Composite	–	–	–	–
High Financial Risk	–	–	–	–

Enterprise Valuation SIC Composite: EV/Sales Latest 1.8, 5-Yr Avg 1.6; EV/EBITDA Latest 10.8, 5-Yr Avg 9.6

Fama-French (F-F) 5-Factor Model

	F-F Beta	SMB Premium	HML Premium	RMW Premium	CMA Premium
Median	1.7	1.6	-3.3	2.4	3.2
SIC Composite	1.2	2.1	-1.6	1.2	2.8
Large Composite	–	–	–	–	–
Small Composite	–	–	–	–	–
High Financial Risk	–	–	–	–	–

Leverage Ratios (%)

	Debt/MV Equity Latest	Debt/MV Equity 5-Yr Avg	Debt/Total Capital Latest	Debt/Total Capital 5-Yr Avg
Median	11.8	13.0	10.4	11.4
SIC Composite	18.7	17.4	15.8	14.9

Cost of Debt

	Cost of Debt (%) Latest
Median	7.1
SIC Composite	6.3

Capital Structure

SIC Composite (%) Latest: D/TC 15.8, E/TC 84.2

Cost of Equity Capital (%)

	CRSP Deciles CAPM	CRSP Deciles CAPM +Size Prem	CRSP Deciles Build-Up	Risk Premium Report CAPM +Size Prem	Risk Premium Report Build-Up	Discounted Cash Flow 1-Stage	Discounted Cash Flow 3-Stage	Fama-French 5-Factor Model
Median	–	–	9.8	15.3	15.2	12.7	9.8	16.8
SIC Composite	–	–	8.9	14.2	13.5	13.1	10.2	14.6
Large Composite	–	–	–	–	–	–	–	–
Small Composite	–	–	–	–	–	–	–	–
High Financial Risk	–	–	–	–	–	–	–	–

Cost of Equity Capital (%) SIC Composite: Avg CRSP 8.9, Avg RPR 13.8, 1-Stage 13.1, 3-Stage 10.2, 5-Factor Model 14.6

Weighted Average Cost of Capital (WACC) (%)

	CRSP Deciles CAPM	CRSP Deciles CAPM +Size Prem	CRSP Deciles Build-Up	Risk Premium Report CAPM +Size Prem	Risk Premium Report Build-Up	Discounted Cash Flow 1-Stage	Discounted Cash Flow 3-Stage	Fama-French 5-Factor Model
Median	–	–	9.1	14.0	14.2	12.7	9.6	14.6
SIC Composite	–	–	8.4	12.9	12.3	12.0	9.5	13.3
Large Composite	–	–	–	–	–	–	–	–
Small Composite	–	–	–	–	–	–	–	–
High Financial Risk	–	–	–	–	–	–	–	–

WACC (%) SIC Composite: Low 8.4, High 13.3, Average 11.4, Median 12.1

© 2017 Duff & Phelps. All Rights Reserved. Duff & Phelps has used the utmost care in compiling the data presented herein, but cannot guarantee the accuracy, completeness, or timeliness of the information.

Data Updated Through March 31, 2017

3089

Number of Companies: 5
Plastics Products, Not Elsewhere Classified

Industry Description
Establishments primarily engaged in manufacturing plastics products, not elsewhere classified.

Sales (in millions)

Three Largest Companies
AptarGroup Inc.	$2,330.9
Tupperware Brands Corp.	2,213.1
Myers Industries, Inc.	558.1

Three Smallest Companies
Myers Industries, Inc.	$558.1
Core Molding Technologies	174.9
Alpha Pro Tech, Ltd.	46.2

Total Assets (in millions)

Three Largest Companies
AptarGroup Inc.	$2,606.8
Tupperware Brands Corp.	1,587.8
Myers Industries, Inc.	381.7

Three Smallest Companies
Myers Industries, Inc.	$381.7
Core Molding Technologies	134.8
Alpha Pro Tech, Ltd.	35.9

Annualized Monthly Performance Statistics (%)

Industry	Geometric Mean	Arithmetic Mean	Standard Deviation	S&P 500 Index	Geometric Mean	Arithmetic Mean	Standard Deviation
1-year	6.5	7.1	12.3	1-year	17.2	17.4	7.2
3-year	1.1	2.4	16.7	3-year	10.4	10.9	11.5
5-year	6.6	8.0	18.0	5-year	13.3	13.9	11.5

Return Ratios (%)

	Return on Assets Latest	5-Yr Avg	Return on Equity Latest	5-Yr Avg	Dividend Yield Latest	5-Yr Avg	Current Ratio Latest	5-Yr Avg	Operating Margin Latest	5-Yr Avg	Long-term EPS Analyst Estimates
Median (5)	8.1	7.7	9.0	12.0	1.6	1.7	2.3	2.1	8.0	7.9	12.0
SIC Composite (5)	9.3	9.0	5.1	5.2	2.8	2.6	1.7	1.6	13.1	12.8	9.8
Large Composite (–)	–	–	–	–	–	–	–	–	–	–	–
Small Composite (–)	–	–	–	–	–	–	–	–	–	–	–
High-Financial Risk (–)	–	–	–	–	–	–	–	–	–	–	–

Betas (Levered)

	Raw (OLS)	Blume Adjusted	Peer Group	Vasicek Adjusted	Sum	Downside
Median	1.15	1.10	–	–	1.13	1.59
SIC Composite	1.26	1.17	–	–	1.28	1.23
Large Composite	–	–	–	–	–	–
Small Composite	–	–	–	–	–	–
High Financial Risk	–	–	–	–	–	–

Betas (Unlevered)

	Raw (OLS)	Blume Adjusted	Peer Group	Vasicek Adjusted	Sum	Downside
Median	1.15	1.05	–	–	1.07	1.56
SIC Composite	1.08	1.01	–	–	1.10	1.05
Large Composite	–	–	–	–	–	–
Small Composite	–	–	–	–	–	–
High Financial Risk	–	–	–	–	–	–

Equity Valuation Multiples

	Price/Sales Latest	5-Yr Avg	Price/Earnings Latest	5-Yr Avg	Market/Book Latest	5-Yr Avg
Median	0.9	0.9	18.4	19.7	4.0	2.9
SIC Composite	1.6	1.4	19.5	19.2	5.2	4.5
Large Composite	–	–	–	–	–	–
Small Composite	–	–	–	–	–	–
High Financial Risk	–	–	–	–	–	–

Enterprise Valuation (EV) Multiples

	EV/Sales Latest	5-Yr Avg	EV/EBITDA Latest	5-Yr Avg
Median	1.2	1.0	9.5	8.8
SIC Composite	1.9	1.6	10.2	9.5
Large Composite	–	–	–	–
Small Composite	–	–	–	–
High Financial Risk	–	–	–	–

Enterprise Valuation SIC Composite

Latest: EV/Sales 1.9, EV/EBITDA 10.2
5-Yr Avg: EV/Sales 1.6, EV/EBITDA 9.5

Fama-French (F-F) 5-Factor Model

	F-F Beta	SMB Premium	HML Premium	RMW Premium	CMA Premium
Median	1.1	2.6	-1.1	4.1	-2.0
SIC Composite	1.2	1.2	-2.2	1.0	2.9
Large Composite	–	–	–	–	–
Small Composite	–	–	–	–	–
High Financial Risk	–	–	–	–	–

Leverage Ratios (%)

	Debt/MV Equity Latest	5-Yr Avg	Debt/Total Capital Latest	5-Yr Avg
Median	19.8	17.0	16.5	14.6
SIC Composite	21.6	19.7	17.7	16.4
Large Composite	–	–	–	–
Small Composite	–	–	–	–
High Financial Risk	–	–	–	–

Cost of Debt

	Cost of Debt (%) Latest
Median	7.1
SIC Composite	6.2
Large Composite	–
Small Composite	–
High Financial Risk	–

Capital Structure

SIC Composite (%) Latest: D/TC 82.3, E/TC 17.7

Cost of Equity Capital (%)

	CAPM	CRSP Deciles CAPM +Size Prem	Build-Up	Risk Premium Report CAPM +Size Prem	Build-Up	Discounted Cash Flow 1-Stage	3-Stage	Fama-French 5-Factor Model
Median	–	–	10.1	15.7	15.5	12.7	12.4	13.2
SIC Composite	–	–	8.8	14.1	13.1	12.8	10.5	13.2
Large Composite	–	–	–	–	–	–	–	–
Small Composite	–	–	–	–	–	–	–	–
High Financial Risk	–	–	–	–	–	–	–	–

Cost of Equity Capital (%) SIC Composite
Avg CRSP: 8.8, Avg RPR: 13.6, 1-Stage: 12.8, 3-Stage: 10.5, 5-Factor Model: 13.2

Weighted Average Cost of Capital (WACC) (%)

	CAPM	CRSP Deciles CAPM +Size Prem	Build-Up	Risk Premium Report CAPM +Size Prem	Build-Up	Discounted Cash Flow 1-Stage	3-Stage	Fama-French 5-Factor Model
Median	–	–	9.1	14.2	12.9	12.2	11.4	13.6
SIC Composite	–	–	8.3	12.7	11.9	11.6	9.7	11.9
Large Composite	–	–	–	–	–	–	–	–
Small Composite	–	–	–	–	–	–	–	–
High Financial Risk	–	–	–	–	–	–	–	–

WACC (%) SIC Composite
Low 8.3, High 12.7
▲ Average 11.0, ◆ Median 11.7

© 2017 Duff & Phelps. All Rights Reserved. Duff & Phelps has used the utmost care in compiling the data presented herein, but cannot guarantee the accuracy, completeness, or timeliness of the information.

Data Updated Through March 31, 2017

31

Number of Companies: 7
Leather and Leather Products

Industry Description

This major group includes establishments engaged in tanning, currying, and finishing hides and skins, leather converters, and establishments manufacturing finished leather and artificial leather products and some similar products made of other materials.

Sales (in millions)

Three Largest Companies
Coach, Inc.	$4,491.8
Skechers U.S.A., Inc.	3,563.3
Caleres, Inc.	2,579.4

Three Smallest Companies
Steven Madden, LTD	$1,411.4
Vera Bradley, Inc.	485.9
Rocky Brands Inc.	260.3

Annualized Monthly Performance Statistics (%)

Industry
	Geometric Mean	Arithmetic Mean	Standard Deviation
1-year	2.6	3.5	14.1
3-year	0.6	2.2	18.3
5-year	-2.5	-0.4	20.7

Total Assets (in millions)

Three Largest Companies
Coach, Inc.	$4,892.7
Wolverine World Wide	2,431.7
Skechers U.S.A., Inc.	2,393.7

Three Smallest Companies
Steven Madden, LTD	$973.0
Vera Bradley, Inc.	373.5
Rocky Brands Inc.	180.6

S&P 500 Index
	Geometric Mean	Arithmetic Mean	Standard Deviation
1-year	17.2	17.4	7.2
3-year	10.4	10.9	11.5
5-year	13.3	13.9	11.5

Return Ratios (%)

	Return on Assets Latest	Return on Assets 5-Yr Avg	Return on Equity Latest	Return on Equity 5-Yr Avg	Dividend Yield Latest	Dividend Yield 5-Yr Avg
Median (7)	5.2	8.2	10.1	12.5	1.0	1.0
SIC Composite (7)	7.8	11.1	4.5	5.5	2.0	1.9
Large Composite (–)	–	–	–	–	–	–
Small Composite (–)	–	–	–	–	–	–
High-Financial Risk (–)	–	–	–	–	–	–

Liquidity Ratio

	Current Ratio Latest	Current Ratio 5-Yr Avg
Median (7)	3.0	2.9
SIC Composite (7)	2.6	2.7
Large Composite (–)	–	–
Small Composite (–)	–	–
High-Financial Risk (–)	–	–

Profitability Ratio (%)

	Operating Margin Latest	Operating Margin 5-Yr Avg
Median (7)	8.4	9.1
SIC Composite (7)	11.0	13.9
Large Composite (–)	–	–
Small Composite (–)	–	–
High-Financial Risk (–)	–	–

Growth Rates (%)

	Long-term EPS Analyst Estimates
Median (7)	10.6
SIC Composite (7)	10.0
Large Composite (–)	–
Small Composite (–)	–
High-Financial Risk (–)	–

Betas (Levered)

	Raw (OLS)	Blume Adjusted	Peer Group	Vasicek Adjusted	Sum	Downside
Median	0.56	0.73	0.66	0.63	0.58	1.35
SIC Composite	0.40	0.62	0.66	0.54	0.44	0.77
Large Composite	–	–	–	–	–	–
Small Composite	–	–	–	–	–	–
High Financial Risk	–	–	–	–	–	–

Betas (Unlevered)

	Raw (OLS)	Blume Adjusted	Peer Group	Vasicek Adjusted	Sum	Downside
Median	0.53	0.66	0.61	0.58	0.57	1.12
SIC Composite	0.38	0.59	0.62	0.51	0.42	0.72
Large Composite	–	–	–	–	–	–
Small Composite	–	–	–	–	–	–
High Financial Risk	–	–	–	–	–	–

Equity Valuation Multiples

	Price/Sales Latest	Price/Sales 5-Yr Avg	Price/Earnings Latest	Price/Earnings 5-Yr Avg	Market/Book Latest	Market/Book 5-Yr Avg
Median	1.0	1.2	19.3	17.8	2.2	2.5
SIC Composite	1.4	1.5	22.3	18.1	3.0	3.5
Large Composite	–	–	–	–	–	–
Small Composite	–	–	–	–	–	–
High Financial Risk	–	–	–	–	–	–

Enterprise Valuation (EV) Multiples

	EV/Sales Latest	EV/Sales 5-Yr Avg	EV/EBITDA Latest	EV/EBITDA 5-Yr Avg
Median	1.0	1.3	11.2	8.5
SIC Composite	1.4	1.5	10.2	9.1
Large Composite	–	–	–	–
Small Composite	–	–	–	–
High Financial Risk	–	–	–	–

Enterprise Valuation SIC Composite

EV/Sales: Latest 1.4, 5-Yr Avg 1.5
EV/EBITDA: Latest 10.2, 5-Yr Avg 9.1

Fama-French (F-F) 5-Factor Model

Fama-French (F-F) Components
	F-F Beta	SMB Premium	HML Premium	RMW Premium	CMA Premium
Median	0.5	2.7	-0.4	5.1	-0.9
SIC Composite	0.4	1.6	-1.9	2.8	1.4
Large Composite	–	–	–	–	–
Small Composite	–	–	–	–	–
High Financial Risk	–	–	–	–	–

Leverage Ratios (%)

	Debt/MV Equity Latest	Debt/MV Equity 5-Yr Avg	Debt/Total Capital Latest	Debt/Total Capital 5-Yr Avg
Median	7.6	3.7	7.0	3.6
SIC Composite	9.4	8.0	8.6	7.4
Large Composite	–	–	–	–
Small Composite	–	–	–	–
High Financial Risk	–	–	–	–

Cost of Debt

	Cost of Debt (%) Latest
Median	6.1
SIC Composite	5.6
Large Composite	–
Small Composite	–
High Financial Risk	–

Capital Structure

SIC Composite (%) Latest
- D / TC: 8.6
- E / TC: 91.4

Cost of Equity Capital (%)

	CRSP Deciles CAPM	CRSP Deciles CAPM +Size Prem	CRSP Deciles Build-Up	Risk Premium Report CAPM +Size Prem	Risk Premium Report Build-Up	Discounted Cash Flow 1-Stage	Discounted Cash Flow 3-Stage	Fama-French 5-Factor Model
Median	7.0	8.7	10.7	11.4	13.8	11.8	12.2	12.6
SIC Composite	6.5	7.5	10.0	9.0	12.5	12.1	12.0	9.4
Large Composite	–	–	–	–	–	–	–	–
Small Composite	–	–	–	–	–	–	–	–
High Financial Risk	–	–	–	–	–	–	–	–

Cost of Equity Capital (%) SIC Composite
- Avg CRSP: 8.7
- Avg RPR: 10.7
- 1-Stage: 12.1
- 3-Stage: 12.0
- 5-Factor Model: 9.4

Weighted Average Cost of Capital (WACC) (%)

	CRSP Deciles CAPM	CRSP Deciles CAPM +Size Prem	CRSP Deciles Build-Up	Risk Premium Report CAPM +Size Prem	Risk Premium Report Build-Up	Discounted Cash Flow 1-Stage	Discounted Cash Flow 3-Stage	Fama-French 5-Factor Model
Median	6.8	8.2	9.9	10.9	12.9	10.5	11.5	14.0
SIC Composite	6.4	7.3	9.6	8.7	11.8	11.5	11.4	9.1
Large Composite	–	–	–	–	–	–	–	–
Small Composite	–	–	–	–	–	–	–	–
High Financial Risk	–	–	–	–	–	–	–	–

WACC (%) SIC Composite
Low 7.3 — High 11.8
Average 9.9 ♦ Median 9.6

© 2017 Duff & Phelps. All Rights Reserved. Duff & Phelps has used the utmost care in compiling the data presented herein, but cannot guarantee the accuracy, completeness, or timeliness of the information.

Data Updated Through March 31, 2017

314

Number of Companies: 5
Footwear, Except Rubber

Industry Description
Establishments primarily engaged in house slippers; men's footwear, except athletic; women's footwear, except athletic.

Sales (in millions)

Three Largest Companies
Skechers U.S.A., Inc.	$3,563.3
Caleres, Inc.	2,579.4
Wolverine World Wide	2,494.6

Three Smallest Companies
Wolverine World Wide	$2,494.6
Steven Madden, LTD	1,411.4
Rocky Brands Inc.	260.3

Total Assets (in millions)

Three Largest Companies
Wolverine World Wide	$2,431.7
Skechers U.S.A., Inc.	2,393.7
Caleres, Inc.	1,475.3

Three Smallest Companies
Caleres, Inc.	$1,475.3
Steven Madden, LTD	973.0
Rocky Brands Inc.	180.6

Annualized Monthly Performance Statistics (%)

	Industry				S&P 500 Index		
	Geometric Mean	Arithmetic Mean	Standard Deviation		Geometric Mean	Arithmetic Mean	Standard Deviation
1-year	2.3	3.4	16.1	1-year	17.2	17.4	7.2
3-year	8.0	11.1	27.2	3-year	10.4	10.9	11.5
5-year	16.7	19.9	28.3	5-year	13.3	13.9	11.5

Return Ratios (%)

	Return on Assets		Return on Equity		Dividend Yield		Current Ratio		Operating Margin		Long-term EPS
	Latest	5-Yr Avg	Latest	5-Yr Avg	Latest	5-Yr Avg	Latest	5-Yr Avg	Latest	5-Yr Avg	Analyst Estimates
Median (5)	4.7	5.0	10.1	11.7	1.0	1.0	3.0	2.9	8.4	8.0	10.6
SIC Composite (5)	6.9	6.4	5.0	4.9	0.4	0.4	2.6	2.7	8.5	8.0	10.1
Large Composite (–)	–	–	–	–	–	–	–	–	–	–	–
Small Composite (–)	–	–	–	–	–	–	–	–	–	–	–
High-Financial Risk (–)	–	–	–	–	–	–	–	–	–	–	–

Liquidity Ratio · Profitability Ratio (%) · Growth Rates (%)

Betas (Levered)

	Raw (OLS)	Blume Adjusted	Peer Group	Vasicek Adjusted	Sum	Downside
Median	0.56	0.73	–	–	0.72	1.35
SIC Composite	0.42	0.64	–	–	0.60	1.11
Large Composite	–	–	–	–	–	–
Small Composite	–	–	–	–	–	–
High Financial Risk	–	–	–	–	–	–

Betas (Unlevered)

	Raw (OLS)	Blume Adjusted	Peer Group	Vasicek Adjusted	Sum	Downside
Median	0.53	0.66	–	–	0.72	1.12
SIC Composite	0.41	0.60	–	–	0.56	1.03
Large Composite	–	–	–	–	–	–
Small Composite	–	–	–	–	–	–
High Financial Risk	–	–	–	–	–	–

Equity Valuation Multiples

	Price/Sales		Price/Earnings		Market/Book	
	Latest	5-Yr Avg	Latest	5-Yr Avg	Latest	5-Yr Avg
Median	1.0	1.0	19.3	18.4	2.2	2.3
SIC Composite	1.0	1.0	19.8	20.5	2.4	2.4
Large Composite	–	–	–	–	–	–
Small Composite	–	–	–	–	–	–
High Financial Risk	–	–	–	–	–	–

Enterprise Valuation (EV) Multiples

	EV/Sales		EV/EBITDA		Enterprise Valuation SIC Composite
	Latest	5-Yr Avg	Latest	5-Yr Avg	
Median	1.0	1.0	11.2	10.1	Latest 9.5 / 5-Yr Avg 10.1
SIC Composite	1.0	1.0	9.5	10.1	EV/Sales 1.0 / EV/EBITDA 1.0
Large Composite	–	–	–	–	
Small Composite	–	–	–	–	
High Financial Risk	–	–	–	–	

Fama-French (F-F) 5-Factor Model

	F-F Beta	SMB Premium	HML Premium	RMW Premium	CMA Premium
Median	0.5	2.7	-0.4	5.1	-0.9
SIC Composite	0.4	2.1	-1.8	2.9	0.3
Large Composite	–	–	–	–	–
Small Composite	–	–	–	–	–
High Financial Risk	–	–	–	–	–

Leverage Ratios (%)

	Debt/MV Equity		Debt/Total Capital	
	Latest	5-Yr Avg	Latest	5-Yr Avg
Median	17.0	22.4	14.5	18.3
SIC Composite	11.9	15.6	10.6	13.5
Large Composite	–	–	–	–
Small Composite	–	–	–	–
High Financial Risk	–	–	–	–

Cost of Debt

	Cost of Debt (%) Latest
Median	6.1
SIC Composite	6.2
Large Composite	–
Small Composite	–
High Financial Risk	–

Capital Structure

SIC Composite (%) Latest
D/TC 10.6
E/TC 89.4

Cost of Equity Capital (%)

	CRSP Deciles			Risk Premium Report		Discounted Cash Flow		Fama-French 5-Factor Model
	CAPM	CAPM +Size Prem	Build-Up	CAPM +Size Prem	Build-Up	1-Stage	3-Stage	
Median	–	–	10.7	11.5	13.8	11.8	11.8	12.6
SIC Composite	–	–	10.4	10.5	13.4	10.5	11.0	9.1
Large Composite	–	–	–	–	–	–	–	–
Small Composite	–	–	–	–	–	–	–	–
High Financial Risk	–	–	–	–	–	–	–	–

Cost of Equity Capital (%) SIC Composite: Avg CRSP 10.4, Avg RPR 11.9, 1-Stage 10.5, 3-Stage 11.0, 5-Factor Model 9.1

Weighted Average Cost of Capital (WACC) (%)

	CRSP Deciles			Risk Premium Report		Discounted Cash Flow		Fama-French 5-Factor Model
	CAPM	CAPM +Size Prem	Build-Up	CAPM +Size Prem	Build-Up	1-Stage	3-Stage	
Median	–	–	9.9	11.3	12.9	10.5	11.2	14.2
SIC Composite	–	–	9.9	9.9	12.6	10.0	10.4	8.8
Large Composite	–	–	–	–	–	–	–	–
Small Composite	–	–	–	–	–	–	–	–
High Financial Risk	–	–	–	–	–	–	–	–

WACC (%) SIC Composite: Low 8.8, High 12.6, Average 10.3, Median 10.0

© 2017 Duff & Phelps. All Rights Reserved. Duff & Phelps has used the utmost care in compiling the data presented herein, but cannot guarantee the accuracy, completeness, or timeliness of the information.

Data Updated Through March 31, 2017

32

Number of Companies: 8
Stone, Clay, Glass, and Concrete Products

Industry Description
This major group includes establishments engaged in manufacturing flat glass and other glass products, cement, structural clay products, pottery, concrete and gypsum products, cut stone, abrasive and asbestos products, and other products from materials taken principally from the earth in the form of stone, clay, and sand.

Sales (in millions)

Three Largest Companies
Owens-Illinois Inc.	$6,702.0
Owens Corning	5,677.0
USG Corporation	3,017.0

Three Smallest Companies
Libbey Inc.	$796.2
Oil-Dri Corp. America	262.3
CARBO Ceramics Inc.	103.1

Annualized Monthly Performance Statistics (%)

Industry
	Geometric Mean	Arithmetic Mean	Standard Deviation
1-year	26.9	28.1	18.8
3-year	-3.1	-1.2	20.0
5-year	6.1	8.4	22.8

Total Assets (in millions)

Three Largest Companies
Owens-Illinois Inc.	$9,135.0
Owens Corning	7,741.0
USG Corporation	3,869.0

Three Smallest Companies
Libbey Inc.	$818.2
CARBO Ceramics Inc.	723.5
Oil-Dri Corp. America	204.9

S&P 500 Index
	Geometric Mean	Arithmetic Mean	Standard Deviation
1-year	17.2	17.4	7.2
3-year	10.4	10.9	11.5
5-year	13.3	13.9	11.5

Return Ratios (%)

	Return on Assets Latest	5-Yr Avg	Return on Equity Latest	5-Yr Avg	Dividend Yield Latest	5-Yr Avg	Current Ratio Latest	5-Yr Avg	Operating Margin Latest	5-Yr Avg	Long-term EPS Analyst Estimates
Median (8)	4.6	3.3	12.4	12.0	0.0	0.9	2.2	2.1	11.2	8.9	10.4
SIC Composite (8)	3.9	3.3	4.4	4.2	0.6	0.5	1.5	1.6	11.6	9.6	10.5
Large Composite (−)	−	−	−	−	−	−	−	−	−	−	−
Small Composite (−)	−	−	−	−	−	−	−	−	−	−	−
High-Financial Risk (−)	−	−	−	−	−	−	−	−	−	−	−

Betas (Levered)

	Raw (OLS)	Blume Adjusted	Peer Group	Vasicek Adjusted	Sum	Downside
Median	1.30	1.20	1.35	1.34	1.22	1.54
SIC Composite	1.29	1.19	1.35	1.32	1.21	1.44
Large Composite	−	−	−	−	−	−
Small Composite	−	−	−	−	−	−
High Financial Risk	−	−	−	−	−	−

Betas (Unlevered)

	Raw (OLS)	Blume Adjusted	Peer Group	Vasicek Adjusted	Sum	Downside
Median	1.12	1.03	1.11	1.12	0.88	1.25
SIC Composite	0.96	0.90	1.00	0.98	0.91	1.07
Large Composite	−	−	−	−	−	−
Small Composite	−	−	−	−	−	−
High Financial Risk	−	−	−	−	−	−

Equity Valuation Multiples

	Price/Sales Latest	5-Yr Avg	Price/Earnings Latest	5-Yr Avg	Market/Book Latest	5-Yr Avg
Median	1.4	1.0	24.1	22.3	2.4	3.7
SIC Composite	1.2	1.0	22.8	24.0	2.7	2.5
Large Composite	−	−	−	−	−	−
Small Composite	−	−	−	−	−	−
High Financial Risk	−	−	−	−	−	−

Enterprise Valuation (EV) Multiples

	EV/Sales Latest	5-Yr Avg	EV/EBITDA Latest	5-Yr Avg
Median	1.7	1.4	8.5	9.5
SIC Composite	1.7	1.5	8.9	9.1
Large Composite	−	−	−	−
Small Composite	−	−	−	−
High Financial Risk	−	−	−	−

Enterprise Valuation SIC Composite
Latest: EV/Sales 1.7, EV/EBITDA 8.9
5-Yr Avg: EV/Sales 1.5, EV/EBITDA 9.1

Fama-French (F-F) 5-Factor Model

Fama-French (F-F) Components
	F-F Beta	SMB Premium	HML Premium	RMW Premium	CMA Premium
Median	1.5	0.9	0.6	-1.8	1.6
SIC Composite	1.2	2.5	1.7	-1.7	-1.4
Large Composite	−	−	−	−	−
Small Composite	−	−	−	−	−
High Financial Risk	−	−	−	−	−

Leverage Ratios (%)

	Debt/MV Equity Latest	5-Yr Avg	Debt/Total Capital Latest	5-Yr Avg
Median	26.9	38.9	21.1	28.0
SIC Composite	45.2	49.6	31.1	33.2
Large Composite	−	−	−	−
Small Composite	−	−	−	−
High Financial Risk	−	−	−	−

Cost of Debt

	Cost of Debt (%) Latest
Median	6.1
SIC Composite	5.8
Large Composite	−
Small Composite	−
High Financial Risk	−

Capital Structure

SIC Composite (%) Latest
D/TC: 31.1
E/TC: 68.9

Cost of Equity Capital (%)

	CRSP Deciles CAPM	CAPM +Size Prem	Build-Up	Risk Premium Report CAPM +Size Prem	Build-Up	Discounted Cash Flow 1-Stage	3-Stage	Fama-French 5-Factor Model
Median	10.9	12.7	12.4	13.8	13.5	12.7	9.4	12.8
SIC Composite	10.7	11.9	12.1	13.5	12.8	11.0	9.2	11.2
Large Composite	−	−	−	−	−	−	−	−
Small Composite	−	−	−	−	−	−	−	−
High Financial Risk	−	−	−	−	−	−	−	−

Cost of Equity Capital (%) SIC Composite
Avg CRSP: 12.0; Avg RPR: 13.1; 1-Stage: 11.0; 3-Stage: 9.2; 5-Factor Model: 11.2

Weighted Average Cost of Capital (WACC) (%)

	CRSP Deciles CAPM	CAPM +Size Prem	Build-Up	Risk Premium Report CAPM +Size Prem	Build-Up	Discounted Cash Flow 1-Stage	3-Stage	Fama-French 5-Factor Model
Median	9.8	10.8	10.8	11.5	11.5	9.5	8.0	11.8
SIC Composite	8.9	9.7	9.9	10.8	10.3	9.1	7.8	9.3
Large Composite	−	−	−	−	−	−	−	−
Small Composite	−	−	−	−	−	−	−	−
High Financial Risk	−	−	−	−	−	−	−	−

WACC (%) SIC Composite
Low: 7.8; High: 10.8; Average: 9.6; Median: 9.7

© 2017 Duff & Phelps. All Rights Reserved. Duff & Phelps has used the utmost care in compiling the data presented herein, but cannot guarantee the accuracy, completeness, or timeliness of the information.

Data Updated Through March 31, 2017

33

Number of Companies: 11
Primary Metal Industries

Industry Description
This major group includes establishments engaged in smelting and refining ferrous and nonferrous metals from ore, pig, or scrap; in rolling, drawing, and alloying metals; in manufacturing castings and other basic metal products; and in manufacturing nails, spikes, and insulated wire and cable. This major group includes the production of coke.

Sales (in millions)

Three Largest Companies
Steel Dynamics Inc.	$7,777.1
Belden Inc.	2,351.1
Mueller Industries	2,055.6

Three Smallest Companies
Insteel Industries Inc.	$418.5
Haynes International Inc.	406.4
Friedman Industries, Inc.	81.6

Annualized Monthly Performance Statistics (%)

Industry	Geometric Mean	Arithmetic Mean	Standard Deviation
1-year	31.9	36.0	37.4
3-year	6.1	9.4	28.5
5-year	10.9	13.8	26.5

Total Assets (in millions)

Three Largest Companies
Steel Dynamics Inc.	$6,423.7
Belden Inc.	3,806.8
Carpenter Technology Corp.	2,794.3

Three Smallest Companies
Haynes International Inc.	$649.6
Insteel Industries Inc.	292.9
Friedman Industries, Inc.	66.9

S&P 500 Index	Geometric Mean	Arithmetic Mean	Standard Deviation
1-year	17.2	17.4	7.2
3-year	10.4	10.9	11.5
5-year	13.3	13.9	11.5

Return Ratios (%)

	Return on Assets		Return on Equity		Dividend Yield		Current Ratio		Operating Margin		Long-term EPS
	Latest	5-Yr Avg	Latest	5-Yr Avg	Latest	5-Yr Avg	Latest	5-Yr Avg	Latest	5-Yr Avg	Analyst Estimates
Median (11)	3.6	3.6	5.8	6.8	2.0	1.8	4.0	3.3	7.8	6.7	19.0
SIC Composite (11)	4.1	3.0	4.2	3.7	2.5	1.7	3.6	3.2	9.5	7.5	13.6
Large Composite (3)	5.2	3.2	4.6	3.8	2.8	1.9	3.5	3.2	10.7	7.3	12.7
Small Composite (3)	4.2	4.6	3.5	4.3	3.4	2.4	–	–	7.0	6.5	19.0
High-Financial Risk (8)	-6.3	-5.4	-11.7	-14.9	0.8	1.6	2.0	1.9	1.2	1.9	12.7

Betas (Levered)

	Raw (OLS)	Blume Adjusted	Peer Group	Vasicek Adjusted	Sum	Downside
Median	1.48	1.31	1.99	1.63	1.45	1.80
SIC Composite	1.64	1.41	1.99	1.68	1.56	1.57
Large Composite	1.66	1.43	1.90	1.71	1.43	1.61
Small Composite	1.78	1.50	2.05	1.82	1.90	1.82
High Financial Risk	2.59	2.01	2.05	2.47	2.57	2.69

Betas (Unlevered)

	Raw (OLS)	Blume Adjusted	Peer Group	Vasicek Adjusted	Sum	Downside
Median	1.24	1.16	1.81	1.47	1.15	1.57
SIC Composite	1.32	1.15	1.59	1.35	1.26	1.27
Large Composite	1.33	1.15	1.52	1.37	1.16	1.29
Small Composite	1.77	1.50	2.05	1.81	1.89	1.81
High Financial Risk	1.68	1.34	1.36	1.61	1.67	1.74

Equity Valuation Multiples

	Price/Sales		Price/Earnings		Market/Book	
	Latest	5-Yr Avg	Latest	5-Yr Avg	Latest	5-Yr Avg
Median	1.0	0.8	26.0	24.9	1.6	1.6
SIC Composite	1.0	0.8	24.5	27.4	2.0	1.7
Large Composite	1.1	0.7	22.5	26.5	2.3	1.8
Small Composite	1.3	1.0	28.4	23.2	2.0	1.7
High Financial Risk	0.5	0.3	–	–	2.7	1.4

Enterprise Valuation (EV) Multiples

	EV/Sales		EV/EBITDA	
	Latest	5-Yr Avg	Latest	5-Yr Avg
Median	1.1	0.9	8.9	8.9
SIC Composite	1.2	1.0	8.6	8.7
Large Composite	1.3	1.0	8.7	9.1
Small Composite	1.2	0.9	11.1	9.8
High Financial Risk	0.7	0.5	11.8	9.0

Enterprise Valuation SIC Composite
- Latest: EV/Sales 1.2, EV/EBITDA 8.6
- 5-Yr Avg: EV/Sales 1.0, EV/EBITDA 8.7

Fama-French (F-F) 5-Factor Model

	Fama-French (F-F) Components				
	F-F Beta	SMB Premium	HML Premium	RMW Premium	CMA Premium
Median	2.0	6.5	-0.7	0.9	4.5
SIC Composite	1.5	4.4	3.5	1.7	2.6
Large Composite	1.6	4.0	4.2	2.5	3.4
Small Composite	1.6	8.9	3.0	3.7	6.1
High Financial Risk	–	–	–	–	–

Leverage Ratios (%)

	Debt/MV Equity		Debt/Total Capital	
	Latest	5-Yr Avg	Latest	5-Yr Avg
Median	11.6	13.3	10.4	11.7
SIC Composite	30.4	37.0	23.3	27.0
Large Composite	31.5	46.6	23.9	31.8
Small Composite	0.4	0.4	0.4	0.4
High Financial Risk	67.5	87.4	40.3	46.6

Cost of Debt

	Cost of Debt (%) Latest
Median	6.1
SIC Composite	6.0
Large Composite	6.1
Small Composite	7.1
High Financial Risk	7.1

Capital Structure
SIC Composite (%) Latest
- D/TC: 23.3
- E/TC: 76.7

Cost of Equity Capital (%)

	CRSP Deciles			Risk Premium Report		Discounted Cash Flow		Fama-French
	CAPM	CAPM +Size Prem	Build-Up	CAPM +Size Prem	Build-Up	1-Stage	3-Stage	5-Factor Model
Median	12.5	14.6	16.9	15.4	14.4	19.7	10.7	25.4
SIC Composite	12.7	14.1	16.2	15.6	13.2	16.2	9.5	24.0
Large Composite	12.9	14.0	15.9	14.6	12.6	15.6	9.2	26.4
Small Composite	13.5	15.9	17.2	18.9	15.4	22.6	12.5	34.3
High Financial Risk	–	–	–	30.1	24.4	–	–	–

Cost of Equity Capital (%) SIC Composite
- Avg CRSP: 15.2
- Avg RPR: 14.4
- 1-Stage: 16.2
- 3-Stage: 9.5
- 5-Factor Model: 24.0

Weighted Average Cost of Capital (WACC) (%)

	CRSP Deciles			Risk Premium Report		Discounted Cash Flow		Fama-French
	CAPM	CAPM +Size Prem	Build-Up	CAPM +Size Prem	Build-Up	1-Stage	3-Stage	5-Factor Model
Median	11.6	13.5	15.3	13.9	12.9	15.6	9.1	20.0
SIC Composite	11.1	12.1	13.7	13.3	11.4	13.8	8.6	19.7
Large Composite	11.2	12.1	13.5	12.5	11.0	13.3	8.4	21.5
Small Composite	13.5	15.9	17.2	18.9	15.3	22.6	12.5	34.2
High Financial Risk	–	–	–	20.7	17.3	–	–	–

WACC (%) SIC Composite
- Low: 8.6
- High: 19.7
- ▲ Average 13.2
- ◆ Median 13.3

© 2017 Duff & Phelps. All Rights Reserved. Duff & Phelps has used the utmost care in compiling the data presented herein, but cannot guarantee the accuracy, completeness, or timeliness of the information.

Data Updated Through March 31, 2017

331

Number of Companies: 6
Steel Works, Blast Furnaces, and Rolling and Finishing Mills

Industry Description
Establishments primarily engaged in steel works, blast furnaces and rolling mills; electrometallurigcal products, except steel; steel wiredrawing and steel nails and spikes; cold-rolled steel sheet, strip and bars; steel pipe and tubes.

Sales (in millions)

Three Largest Companies
Steel Dynamics Inc.	$7,777.1
Carpenter Technology Corp.	1,813.4
SunCoke Energy Inc.	1,223.3

Three Smallest Companies
Insteel Industries Inc.	$418.5
Haynes International Inc.	406.4
Friedman Industries, Inc.	81.6

Total Assets (in millions)

Three Largest Companies
Steel Dynamics Inc.	$6,423.7
Carpenter Technology Corp.	2,794.3
SunCoke Energy Inc.	2,120.9

Three Smallest Companies
Haynes International Inc.	$649.6
Insteel Industries Inc.	292.9
Friedman Industries, Inc.	66.9

Annualized Monthly Performance Statistics (%)

Industry	Geometric Mean	Arithmetic Mean	Standard Deviation	S&P 500 Index	Geometric Mean	Arithmetic Mean	Standard Deviation
1-year	42.7	49.3	49.5	1-year	17.2	17.4	7.2
3-year	7.8	12.5	34.5	3-year	10.4	10.9	11.5
5-year	10.1	14.1	31.0	5-year	13.3	13.9	11.5

Return Ratios (%)

	Return on Assets Latest	5-Yr Avg	Return on Equity Latest	5-Yr Avg	Dividend Yield Latest	5-Yr Avg	Current Ratio Latest	5-Yr Avg	Operating Margin Latest	5-Yr Avg	Long-term EPS Analyst Estimates
Median (6)	0.7	3.5	1.9	6.0	2.0	1.9	3.7	3.3	7.3	6.8	19.0
SIC Composite (6)	3.6	2.5	3.8	3.4	2.0	2.0	3.7	3.3	9.7	7.2	15.9
Large Composite (–)	–	–	–	–	–	–	–	–	–	–	–
Small Composite (–)	–	–	–	–	–	–	–	–	–	–	–
High-Financial Risk (–)	–	–	–	–	–	–	–	–	–	–	–

Betas (Levered)

	Raw (OLS)	Blume Adjusted	Peer Group	Vasicek Adjusted	Sum	Downside
Median	1.55	1.35	2.03	1.68	1.55	2.00
SIC Composite	1.68	1.44	2.03	1.74	1.63	1.63
Large Composite	–	–	–	–	–	–
Small Composite	–	–	–	–	–	–
High Financial Risk	–	–	–	–	–	–

Betas (Unlevered)

	Raw (OLS)	Blume Adjusted	Peer Group	Vasicek Adjusted	Sum	Downside
Median	1.40	1.19	1.83	1.45	1.40	1.66
SIC Composite	1.34	1.15	1.60	1.38	1.30	1.30
Large Composite	–	–	–	–	–	–
Small Composite	–	–	–	–	–	–
High Financial Risk	–	–	–	–	–	–

Equity Valuation Multiples

	Price/Sales Latest	5-Yr Avg	Price/Earnings Latest	5-Yr Avg	Market/Book Latest	5-Yr Avg
Median	1.0	0.8	56.3	25.1	1.5	1.6
SIC Composite	1.0	0.7	26.6	29.1	2.1	1.5
Large Composite	–	–	–	–	–	–
Small Composite	–	–	–	–	–	–
High Financial Risk	–	–	–	–	–	–

Enterprise Valuation (EV) Multiples

	EV/Sales Latest	5-Yr Avg	EV/EBITDA Latest	5-Yr Avg
Median	1.2	1.0	9.3	8.7
SIC Composite	1.3	1.0	8.6	8.4
Large Composite	–	–	–	–
Small Composite	–	–	–	–
High Financial Risk	–	–	–	–

Enterprise Valuation SIC Composite
- EV/Sales: Latest 1.3, 5-Yr Avg 1.0
- EV/EBITDA: Latest 8.6, 5-Yr Avg 8.4

Fama-French (F-F) 5-Factor Model

Fama-French (F-F) Components

	F-F Beta	SMB Premium	HML Premium	RMW Premium	CMA Premium
Median	2.0	6.5	-0.7	0.9	4.5
SIC Composite	1.6	2.9	4.8	1.3	2.8
Large Composite	–	–	–	–	–
Small Composite	–	–	–	–	–
High Financial Risk	–	–	–	–	–

Leverage Ratios (%)

	Debt/MV Equity Latest	5-Yr Avg	Debt/Total Capital Latest	5-Yr Avg
Median	14.4	12.4	11.3	10.0
SIC Composite	31.9	42.4	24.2	29.8
Large Composite	–	–	–	–
Small Composite	–	–	–	–
High Financial Risk	–	–	–	–

Cost of Debt

	Cost of Debt (%) Latest
Median	6.1
SIC Composite	5.9
Large Composite	–
Small Composite	–
High Financial Risk	–

Capital Structure
SIC Composite (%) Latest: D/TC 24.2, E/TC 75.8

Cost of Equity Capital (%)

	CRSP Deciles CAPM	CAPM +Size Prem	Build-Up	Risk Premium Report CAPM +Size Prem	Build-Up	Discounted Cash Flow 1-Stage	3-Stage	Fama-French 5-Factor Model
Median	12.8	15.1	16.9	16.2	14.8	21.3	11.5	25.4
SIC Composite	13.0	14.3	16.0	15.7	12.8	17.9	9.6	24.1
Large Composite	–	–	–	–	–	–	–	–
Small Composite	–	–	–	–	–	–	–	–
High Financial Risk	–	–	–	–	–	–	–	–

Cost of Equity Capital (%) SIC Composite
- Avg CRSP: 15.1
- Avg RPR: 14.3
- 1-Stage: 17.9
- 3-Stage: 9.6
- 5-Factor Model: 24.1

Weighted Average Cost of Capital (WACC) (%)

	CRSP Deciles CAPM	CAPM +Size Prem	Build-Up	Risk Premium Report CAPM +Size Prem	Build-Up	Discounted Cash Flow 1-Stage	3-Stage	Fama-French 5-Factor Model
Median	11.6	13.5	15.2	14.9	13.2	17.0	10.4	19.1
SIC Composite	11.2	12.2	13.5	13.3	11.1	14.9	8.6	19.6
Large Composite	–	–	–	–	–	–	–	–
Small Composite	–	–	–	–	–	–	–	–
High Financial Risk	–	–	–	–	–	–	–	–

WACC (%) SIC Composite
Low 8.6, High 19.6
▲ Average 13.3 ◆ Median 13.3

© 2017 Duff & Phelps. All Rights Reserved. Duff & Phelps has used the utmost care in compiling the data presented herein, but cannot guarantee the accuracy, completeness, or timeliness of the information.

Data Updated Through March 31, 2017

34

Number of Companies: 29
Fabricated Metal Products, Except Machinery and Transportation Equipment

Industry Description
This major group includes establishments engaged in fabricating ferrous and nonferrous metal products, such as metal cans, tinware, handtools, cutlery, general hardware, nonelectric heating apparatus, fabricated structural metal products, metal forgings, metal stampings, ordnance (except vehicles and guided missiles), and a variety of metal and wire products, not elsewhere classified.

Sales (in millions)

Three Largest Companies
Parker-Hannifin Corp.	$11,360.8
Ball Corp.	9,061.0
Crown Holdings Inc.	8,284.0

Three Smallest Companies
Graham Corp.	$90.0
Chicago Rivet & Machine Co.	36.2
NF Energy Saving Corp.	6.7

Annualized Monthly Performance Statistics (%)

Industry	Geometric Mean	Arithmetic Mean	Standard Deviation
1-year	22.1	22.6	10.8
3-year	7.9	8.9	15.3
5-year	12.5	13.5	15.0

Total Assets (in millions)

Three Largest Companies
Ball Corp.	$16,173.0
Parker-Hannifin Corp.	12,056.7
Crown Holdings Inc.	9,599.0

Three Smallest Companies
OmegaFlex, Inc.	$66.3
NF Energy Saving Corp.	44.4
Chicago Rivet & Machine Co.	30.1

S&P 500 Index	Geometric Mean	Arithmetic Mean	Standard Deviation
1-year	17.2	17.4	7.2
3-year	10.4	10.9	11.5
5-year	13.3	13.9	11.5

Return Ratios (%)

	Return on Assets Latest	5-Yr Avg	Return on Equity Latest	5-Yr Avg	Dividend Yield Latest	5-Yr Avg	Current Ratio Latest	5-Yr Avg	Operating Margin Latest	5-Yr Avg	Long-term EPS Analyst Estimates
Median (29)	5.1	6.0	10.4	13.6	1.1	1.0	2.5	2.5	10.1	10.5	10.5
SIC Composite (29)	4.5	5.6	3.7	5.2	1.2	1.3	1.8	1.8	11.2	11.1	10.4
Large Composite (3)	4.1	5.8	3.7	5.7	1.2	1.2	1.4	1.4	11.4	11.2	9.8
Small Composite (3)	3.1	6.0	2.5	4.5	–	–	3.2	3.1	6.4	12.1	10.5
High-Financial Risk (5)	-1.2	-0.9	-2.5	-1.6	0.4	2.4	1.8	1.9	3.7	2.3	21.6

Betas (Levered)

	Raw (OLS)	Blume Adjusted	Peer Group	Vasicek Adjusted	Sum	Downside
Median	0.98	0.99	0.95	0.97	1.05	1.45
SIC Composite	1.06	1.04	0.95	1.05	1.16	1.08
Large Composite	1.20	1.13	0.96	1.14	1.35	1.28
Small Composite	1.00	1.00	0.92	0.97	1.12	1.31
High Financial Risk	1.22	1.15	0.97	1.17	1.55	1.57

Betas (Unlevered)

	Raw (OLS)	Blume Adjusted	Peer Group	Vasicek Adjusted	Sum	Downside
Median	0.87	0.84	0.83	0.82	0.88	1.37
SIC Composite	0.87	0.86	0.79	0.87	0.95	0.89
Large Composite	0.94	0.89	0.77	0.90	1.05	1.00
Small Composite	0.98	0.98	0.91	0.95	1.10	1.28
High Financial Risk	0.92	0.87	0.75	0.88	1.13	1.15

Equity Valuation Multiples

	Price/Sales Latest	5-Yr Avg	Price/Earnings Latest	5-Yr Avg	Market/Book Latest	5-Yr Avg
Median	1.5	1.2	25.8	18.4	2.6	2.2
SIC Composite	1.5	1.1	27.0	19.1	3.9	3.3
Large Composite	1.5	1.0	26.7	17.4	4.6	4.2
Small Composite	2.0	1.8	39.4	22.3	1.6	1.7
High Financial Risk	0.5	0.6	–	–	2.5	2.2

Enterprise Valuation (EV) Multiples

	EV/Sales Latest	5-Yr Avg	EV/EBITDA Latest	5-Yr Avg
Median	1.6	1.3	10.3	9.1
SIC Composite	1.8	1.3	12.1	9.4
Large Composite	1.9	1.3	12.4	9.6
Small Composite	1.5	1.5	14.8	9.7
High Financial Risk	0.7	0.7	10.6	12.2

Enterprise Valuation SIC Composite

	Latest	5-Yr Avg
EV/Sales	1.8	1.3
EV/EBITDA	12.1	9.4

Fama-French (F-F) 5-Factor Model

	F-F Beta	SMB Premium	HML Premium	RMW Premium	CMA Premium
Median	1.0	0.9	0.6	-1.7	5.6
SIC Composite	1.0	2.0	0.3	0.2	1.2
Large Composite	1.2	1.4	0.4	0.5	0.6
Small Composite	0.7	6.6	3.0	-0.7	-0.7
High Financial Risk	–	–	–	–	–

Leverage Ratios (%)

	Debt/MV Equity Latest	5-Yr Avg	Debt/Total Capital Latest	5-Yr Avg
Median	21.6	16.3	17.8	14.0
SIC Composite	29.8	30.1	23.0	23.1
Large Composite	37.1	37.7	27.0	27.4
Small Composite	3.1	3.4	3.0	3.3
High Financial Risk	50.6	44.5	33.6	30.8

Cost of Debt

	Cost of Debt (%) Latest
Median	6.1
SIC Composite	5.8
Large Composite	5.7
Small Composite	6.1
High Financial Risk	6.6

Capital Structure

SIC Composite (%) Latest: D/TC 23.0, E/TC 77.0

Cost of Equity Capital (%)

	CRSP Deciles CAPM	CAPM +Size Prem	Build-Up	Risk Premium Report CAPM +Size Prem	Build-Up	Discounted Cash Flow 1-Stage	3-Stage	Fama-French 5-Factor Model
Median	8.8	11.5	10.6	14.0	14.8	11.4	10.6	14.2
SIC Composite	9.3	10.4	9.6	13.0	12.5	11.5	9.8	12.6
Large Composite	9.8	10.4	9.2	13.5	11.6	10.9	9.5	12.8
Small Composite	8.8	14.4	14.1	15.4	16.6	10.5	9.6	15.6
High Financial Risk	–	–	–	20.0	19.9	–	–	–

Cost of Equity Capital (%) SIC Composite

Avg CRSP 10.0, Avg RPR 12.8, 1-Stage 11.5, 3-Stage 9.8, 5-Factor Model 12.6

Weighted Average Cost of Capital (WACC) (%)

	CRSP Deciles CAPM	CAPM +Size Prem	Build-Up	Risk Premium Report CAPM +Size Prem	Build-Up	Discounted Cash Flow 1-Stage	3-Stage	Fama-French 5-Factor Model
Median	8.1	9.9	9.8	12.3	12.8	9.9	10.0	13.1
SIC Composite	8.2	9.0	8.4	11.1	10.7	9.9	8.6	10.8
Large Composite	8.3	8.8	7.9	11.0	9.6	9.1	8.1	10.5
Small Composite	8.7	14.1	13.8	15.1	16.2	10.3	9.5	15.3
High Financial Risk	–	–	–	15.1	15.1	–	–	–

WACC (%) SIC Composite: Low 8.4, High 11.1, Average 9.8, Median 9.9

© 2017 Duff & Phelps. All Rights Reserved. Duff & Phelps has used the utmost care in compiling the data presented herein, but cannot guarantee the accuracy, completeness, or timeliness of the information.

Data Updated Through March 31, 2017

342

Number of Companies: 6
Cutlery, Handtools, and General Hardware

Industry Description
Establishments primarily engaged in manufacturing cutlery; hand and edge tools, except machine tools and handsaws; saw blades and handsaws; hardware not else classified.

Sales (in millions)

Three Largest Companies
Simpson Manufacturing Inc.	$860.7
Handy & Harman LTD	828.3
Lifetime Brands, Inc.	592.6

Three Smallest Companies
Eastern Co.	$144.6
Acme United Corp.	124.6
CompX International Inc.	109.0

Annualized Monthly Performance Statistics (%)

Industry	Geometric Mean	Arithmetic Mean	Standard Deviation
1-year	18.3	19.2	16.1
3-year	9.6	12.1	24.9
5-year	8.8	11.4	24.2

Total Assets (in millions)

Three Largest Companies
Simpson Manufacturing Inc.	$980.0
Handy & Harman LTD	836.5
Lifetime Brands, Inc.	399.9

Three Smallest Companies
CompX International Inc.	$134.8
Eastern Co.	121.7
Acme United Corp.	92.1

S&P 500 Index	Geometric Mean	Arithmetic Mean	Standard Deviation
1-year	17.2	17.4	7.2
3-year	10.4	10.9	11.5
5-year	13.3	13.9	11.5

Return Ratios (%)

	Return on Assets Latest	5-Yr Avg	Return on Equity Latest	5-Yr Avg	Dividend Yield Latest	5-Yr Avg
Median (6)	5.7	5.5	7.6	8.4	1.6	1.7
SIC Composite (6)	4.5	4.8	3.7	4.4	1.5	1.5
Large Composite (–)	–	–	–	–	–	–
Small Composite (–)	–	–	–	–	–	–
High-Financial Risk (–)	–	–	–	–	–	–

Liquidity Ratio

	Current Ratio Latest	5-Yr Avg
Median (6)	–	4.7
SIC Composite (6)	3.6	4.0
Large Composite	–	–
Small Composite	–	–
High-Financial Risk	–	–

Profitability Ratio (%)

	Operating Margin Latest	5-Yr Avg
Median (6)	6.9	7.6
SIC Composite (6)	9.8	9.0
Large Composite	–	–
Small Composite	–	–
High-Financial Risk	–	–

Growth Rates (%)

	Long-term EPS Analyst Estimates
Median (6)	10.5
SIC Composite (6)	14.1
Large Composite	–
Small Composite	–
High-Financial Risk	–

Betas (Levered)

	Raw (OLS)	Blume Adjusted	Peer Group	Vasicek Adjusted	Sum	Downside
Median	0.97	0.99	1.04	1.01	1.11	1.41
SIC Composite	1.31	1.20	1.04	1.23	0.99	1.36
Large Composite	–	–	–	–	–	–
Small Composite	–	–	–	–	–	–
High Financial Risk	–	–	–	–	–	–

Betas (Unlevered)

	Raw (OLS)	Blume Adjusted	Peer Group	Vasicek Adjusted	Sum	Downside
Median	0.86	0.83	0.94	0.84	1.02	1.37
SIC Composite	1.20	1.10	0.96	1.13	0.92	1.24
Large Composite	–	–	–	–	–	–
Small Composite	–	–	–	–	–	–
High Financial Risk	–	–	–	–	–	–

Equity Valuation Multiples

	Price/Sales Latest	5-Yr Avg	Price/Earnings Latest	5-Yr Avg	Market/Book Latest	5-Yr Avg
Median	0.8	0.6	21.8	17.9	1.8	1.4
SIC Composite	1.2	1.1	26.8	23.0	2.1	1.8
Large Composite	–	–	–	–	–	–
Small Composite	–	–	–	–	–	–
High Financial Risk	–	–	–	–	–	–

Enterprise Valuation (EV) Multiples

	EV/Sales Latest	5-Yr Avg	EV/EBITDA Latest	5-Yr Avg
Median	0.9	0.7	8.0	7.6
SIC Composite	1.2	1.1	9.3	9.0
Large Composite	–	–	–	–
Small Composite	–	–	–	–
High Financial Risk	–	–	–	–

Enterprise Valuation
SIC Composite
EV/Sales: Latest 1.2, 5-Yr Avg 1.1
EV/EBITDA: Latest 9.3, 5-Yr Avg 9.0

Fama-French (F-F) 5-Factor Model

	Fama-French (F-F) Components				
	F-F Beta	SMB Premium	HML Premium	RMW Premium	CMA Premium
Median	0.9	1.4	3.2	-0.1	0.5
SIC Composite	1.1	5.6	0.1	1.8	1.3
Large Composite	–	–	–	–	–
Small Composite	–	–	–	–	–
High Financial Risk	–	–	–	–	–

Leverage Ratios (%)

	Debt/MV Equity Latest	5-Yr Avg	Debt/Total Capital Latest	5-Yr Avg
Median	17.5	27.1	13.5	19.0
SIC Composite	13.2	12.9	11.6	11.4
Large Composite	–	–	–	–
Small Composite	–	–	–	–
High Financial Risk	–	–	–	–

Cost of Debt

	Cost of Debt (%) Latest
Median	6.1
SIC Composite	7.0
Large Composite	–
Small Composite	–
High Financial Risk	–

Capital Structure

SIC Composite (%) Latest
D/TC: 11.6
E/TC: 88.4

Cost of Equity Capital (%)

	CRSP Deciles			Risk Premium Report		Discounted Cash Flow		Fama-French
	CAPM	CAPM +Size Prem	Build-Up	CAPM +Size Prem	Build-Up	1-Stage	3-Stage	5-Factor Model
Median	9.1	13.0	12.6	15.5	16.1	11.6	13.5	13.5
SIC Composite	10.3	12.7	10.9	13.4	14.6	15.6	12.6	18.6
Large Composite	–	–	–	–	–	–	–	–
Small Composite	–	–	–	–	–	–	–	–
High Financial Risk	–	–	–	–	–	–	–	–

Cost of Equity Capital (%) SIC Composite
Avg CRSP: 11.8, Avg RPR: 14.0, 1-Stage: 15.6, 3-Stage: 12.6, 5-Factor Model: 18.6

Weighted Average Cost of Capital (WACC) (%)

	CRSP Deciles			Risk Premium Report		Discounted Cash Flow		Fama-French
	CAPM	CAPM +Size Prem	Build-Up	CAPM +Size Prem	Build-Up	1-Stage	3-Stage	5-Factor Model
Median	8.3	11.7	10.8	12.4	13.7	10.3	11.8	15.4
SIC Composite	9.8	11.9	10.4	12.6	13.6	14.5	11.9	17.2
Large Composite	–	–	–	–	–	–	–	–
Small Composite	–	–	–	–	–	–	–	–
High Financial Risk	–	–	–	–	–	–	–	–

WACC (%) SIC Composite
Low 10.4, High 17.2
Average 13.2, Median 12.6

© 2017 Duff & Phelps. All Rights Reserved. Duff & Phelps has used the utmost care in compiling the data presented herein, but cannot guarantee the accuracy, completeness, or timeliness of the information.

Data Updated Through March 31, 2017

344

Number of Companies: 5
Fabricated Structural Metal Products

Industry Description
Establishments primarily engaged in fabricated structural metal; metal doors, sash, frames, molding, and trim manufacturing; fabricated plate work; sheet metal work; architectural and ornamental metal work; prefabricated metal buildings and components; miscellaneous structural metal work.

Sales (in millions)

Three Largest Companies
Valmont Industries Inc.	$2,521.7
BWX Technologies, Inc.	1,550.6
Chart Industries Inc.	859.2

Three Smallest Companies
Chart Industries Inc.	$859.2
PGT, Inc.	458.5
Graham Corp.	90.0

Total Assets (in millions)

Three Largest Companies
Valmont Industries Inc.	$2,391.7
BWX Technologies, Inc.	1,579.8
Chart Industries Inc.	1,233.1

Three Smallest Companies
Chart Industries Inc.	$1,233.1
PGT, Inc.	436.6
Graham Corp.	143.1

Annualized Monthly Performance Statistics (%)

Industry	Geometric Mean	Arithmetic Mean	Standard Deviation
1-year	35.9	36.8	17.1
3-year	6.5	8.0	18.8
5-year	9.4	10.8	17.6

S&P 500 Index	Geometric Mean	Arithmetic Mean	Standard Deviation
1-year	17.2	17.4	7.2
3-year	10.4	10.9	11.5
5-year	13.3	13.9	11.5

Return Ratios (%)

	Return on Assets Latest	5-Yr Avg	Return on Equity Latest	5-Yr Avg	Dividend Yield Latest	5-Yr Avg
Median (5)	6.1	7.8	16.0	14.3	0.5	0.5
SIC Composite (5)	7.2	6.2	4.1	4.5	0.8	0.7
Large Composite (–)	–	–	–	–	–	–
Small Composite (–)	–	–	–	–	–	–
High-Financial Risk (–)	–	–	–	–	–	–

Liquidity Ratio / Profitability Ratio (%) / Growth Rates (%)

	Current Ratio Latest	5-Yr Avg	Operating Margin Latest	5-Yr Avg	Long-term EPS Analyst Estimates
Median (5)	3.6	3.5	10.0	11.7	10.5
SIC Composite (5)	2.6	2.3	11.7	10.8	11.8
Large Composite	–	–	–	–	–
Small Composite	–	–	–	–	–
High-Financial Risk	–	–	–	–	–

Betas (Levered)

	Raw (OLS)	Blume Adjusted	Peer Group	Vasicek Adjusted	Sum	Downside
Median	0.99	1.00	0.91	0.97	1.21	1.42
SIC Composite	0.86	0.92	0.91	0.87	1.11	1.00
Large Composite	–	–	–	–	–	–
Small Composite	–	–	–	–	–	–
High Financial Risk	–	–	–	–	–	–

Betas (Unlevered)

	Raw (OLS)	Blume Adjusted	Peer Group	Vasicek Adjusted	Sum	Downside
Median	0.83	0.84	0.80	0.81	1.12	1.30
SIC Composite	0.76	0.81	0.81	0.77	0.98	0.88
Large Composite	–	–	–	–	–	–
Small Composite	–	–	–	–	–	–
High Financial Risk	–	–	–	–	–	–

Equity Valuation Multiples

	Price/Sales Latest	5-Yr Avg	Price/Earnings Latest	5-Yr Avg	Market/Book Latest	5-Yr Avg
Median	1.4	1.4	25.8	22.6	3.2	2.7
SIC Composite	1.8	1.3	24.3	22.3	4.8	3.1
Large Composite	–	–	–	–	–	–
Small Composite	–	–	–	–	–	–
High Financial Risk	–	–	–	–	–	–

Enterprise Valuation (EV) Multiples

	EV/Sales Latest	5-Yr Avg	EV/EBITDA Latest	5-Yr Avg
Median	1.6	1.7	11.4	10.6
SIC Composite	2.0	1.4	12.7	9.4
Large Composite	–	–	–	–
Small Composite	–	–	–	–
High Financial Risk	–	–	–	–

Enterprise Valuation SIC Composite
- EV/Sales: Latest 2.0, 5-Yr Avg 1.4
- EV/EBITDA: Latest 12.7, 5-Yr Avg 9.4

Fama-French (F-F) 5-Factor Model

	F-F Beta	SMB Premium	HML Premium	RMW Premium	CMA Premium
Median	1.0	0.9	0.6	-1.7	5.6
SIC Composite	0.8	2.0	1.4	-1.5	0.2
Large Composite	–	–	–	–	–
Small Composite	–	–	–	–	–
High Financial Risk	–	–	–	–	–

Leverage Ratios (%)

	Debt/MV Equity Latest	5-Yr Avg	Debt/Total Capital Latest	5-Yr Avg
Median	21.6	14.8	17.8	12.9
SIC Composite	17.6	14.1	15.0	12.3
Large Composite	–	–	–	–
Small Composite	–	–	–	–
High Financial Risk	–	–	–	–

Cost of Debt

	Cost of Debt (%) Latest
Median	6.1
SIC Composite	5.7
Large Composite	–
Small Composite	–
High Financial Risk	–

Capital Structure

SIC Composite (%) Latest
- D/TC: 15.0
- E/TC: 85.0

Cost of Equity Capital (%)

	CAPM	CRSP Deciles CAPM +Size Prem	Build-Up	Risk Premium Report CAPM +Size Prem	Build-Up	Discounted Cash Flow 1-Stage	3-Stage	Fama-French 5-Factor Model
Median	8.8	10.3	10.2	14.3	14.4	11.4	10.2	14.2
SIC Composite	8.3	9.7	9.9	13.3	13.4	12.6	9.4	9.8
Large Composite	–	–	–	–	–	–	–	–
Small Composite	–	–	–	–	–	–	–	–
High Financial Risk	–	–	–	–	–	–	–	–

Cost of Equity Capital (%) SIC Composite
- Avg CRSP: 9.8
- Avg RPR: 13.4
- 1-Stage: 12.6
- 3-Stage: 9.4
- 5-Factor Model: 9.8

Weighted Average Cost of Capital (WACC) (%)

	CAPM	CRSP Deciles CAPM +Size Prem	Build-Up	Risk Premium Report CAPM +Size Prem	Build-Up	Discounted Cash Flow 1-Stage	3-Stage	Fama-French 5-Factor Model
Median	7.8	9.3	9.5	12.3	12.7	9.9	9.9	12.3
SIC Composite	7.8	9.0	9.2	12.1	12.1	11.5	8.7	9.1
Large Composite	–	–	–	–	–	–	–	–
Small Composite	–	–	–	–	–	–	–	–
High Financial Risk	–	–	–	–	–	–	–	–

WACC (%) SIC Composite
- Low: 8.7
- High: 12.1
- Average: 10.2
- Median: 9.2

© 2017 Duff & Phelps. All Rights Reserved. Duff & Phelps has used the utmost care in compiling the data presented herein, but cannot guarantee the accuracy, completeness, or timeliness of the information.

Data Updated Through March 31, 2017

348

Number of Companies: 5
Ordnance and Accessories, Except Vehicles and Guided Missiles

Industry Description
Establishments primarily engaged in manufacturing ammunition; small arms; ordnance and accessories.

Sales (in millions)

Three Largest Companies
Orbital ATK, Inc.	$3,399.1
American Outdoor Brands Corporati	722.9
Sturm, Ruger & Co. Inc.	665.5

Three Smallest Companies
Sturm, Ruger & Co. Inc.	$665.5
National Presto Inds Inc.	341.9
TASER International Inc.	268.2

Total Assets (in millions)

Three Largest Companies
Orbital ATK, Inc.	$5,353.6
American Outdoor Brands Corpora	619.5
National Presto Inds Inc.	417.6

Three Smallest Companies
National Presto Inds Inc.	$417.6
Sturm, Ruger & Co. Inc.	355.4
TASER International Inc.	278.2

Annualized Monthly Performance Statistics (%)

Industry	Geometric Mean	Arithmetic Mean	Standard Deviation	S&P 500 Index	Geometric Mean	Arithmetic Mean	Standard Deviation
1-year	4.6	5.9	17.2	1-year	17.2	17.4	7.2
3-year	11.6	13.3	20.1	3-year	10.4	10.9	11.5
5-year	25.9	28.1	24.3	5-year	13.3	13.9	11.5

Return Ratios (%)

	Return on Assets Latest	5-Yr Avg	Return on Equity Latest	5-Yr Avg	Dividend Yield Latest	5-Yr Avg
Median (5)	10.4	10.3	12.1	15.1	3.1	4.6
SIC Composite (5)	6.0	6.7	4.3	5.9	2.4	3.3
Large Composite (−)	−	−	−	−	−	−
Small Composite (−)	−	−	−	−	−	−
High-Financial Risk (−)	−	−	−	−	−	−

Liquidity Ratio

	Current Ratio Latest	5-Yr Avg
Median (5)	2.7	2.6
SIC Composite (5)	2.5	2.4
Large Composite	−	−
Small Composite	−	−
High-Financial Risk	−	−

Profitability Ratio (%)

	Operating Margin Latest	5-Yr Avg
Median	18.4	17.1
SIC Composite	12.7	13.2
Large Composite	−	−
Small Composite	−	−
High-Financial Risk	−	−

Growth Rates (%)

	Long-term EPS Analyst Estimates
Median	10.5
SIC Composite	12.5
Large Composite	−
Small Composite	−
High-Financial Risk	−

Betas (Levered)

	Raw (OLS)	Blume Adjusted	Peer Group	Vasicek Adjusted	Sum	Downside
Median	0.43	0.65	0.92	0.90	0.25	1.54
SIC Composite	0.53	0.71	0.92	0.86	0.57	0.87
Large Composite	−	−	−	−	−	−
Small Composite	−	−	−	−	−	−
High Financial Risk	−	−	−	−	−	−

Betas (Unlevered)

	Raw (OLS)	Blume Adjusted	Peer Group	Vasicek Adjusted	Sum	Downside
Median	0.43	0.65	0.92	0.86	0.25	1.54
SIC Composite	0.50	0.65	0.83	0.77	0.53	0.79
Large Composite	−	−	−	−	−	−
Small Composite	−	−	−	−	−	−
High Financial Risk	−	−	−	−	−	−

Equity Valuation Multiples

	Price/Sales Latest	5-Yr Avg	Price/Earnings Latest	5-Yr Avg	Market/Book Latest	5-Yr Avg
Median	1.7	1.5	16.9	14.3	3.5	4.2
SIC Composite	1.8	1.2	23.1	16.8	3.2	2.8
Large Composite	−	−	−	−	−	−
Small Composite	−	−	−	−	−	−
High Financial Risk	−	−	−	−	−	−

Enterprise Valuation (EV) Multiples

	EV/Sales Latest	5-Yr Avg	EV/EBITDA Latest	5-Yr Avg
Median	1.8	1.5	7.6	6.6
SIC Composite	2.0	1.4	12.0	8.6
Large Composite	−	−	−	−
Small Composite	−	−	−	−
High Financial Risk	−	−	−	−

Enterprise Valuation SIC Composite
- EV/Sales: Latest 2.0, 5-Yr Avg 1.4
- EV/EBITDA: Latest 12.0, 5-Yr Avg 8.6

Fama-French (F-F) 5-Factor Model

	F-F Beta	SMB Premium	HML Premium	RMW Premium	CMA Premium
Median	0.6	1.2	-6.3	4.6	3.8
SIC Composite	0.5	1.9	-2.2	0.6	2.2
Large Composite	−	−	−	−	−
Small Composite	−	−	−	−	−
High Financial Risk	−	−	−	−	−

Leverage Ratios (%)

	Debt/MV Equity Latest	5-Yr Avg	Debt/Total Capital Latest	5-Yr Avg
Median	0.0	0.0	0.0	0.0
SIC Composite	17.0	22.7	14.6	18.5
Large Composite	−	−	−	−
Small Composite	−	−	−	−
High Financial Risk	−	−	−	−

Cost of Debt

	Cost of Debt (%) Latest
Median	6.1
SIC Composite	6.2
Large Composite	−
Small Composite	−
High Financial Risk	−

Capital Structure

SIC Composite (%) Latest
- D/TC: 14.6
- E/TC: 85.4

Cost of Equity Capital (%)

	CRSP Deciles CAPM	CAPM +Size Prem	Build-Up	Risk Premium Report CAPM +Size Prem	Build-Up	Discounted Cash Flow 1-Stage	3-Stage	Fama-French 5-Factor Model
Median	8.4	10.2	10.2	9.7	14.7	15.4	11.3	9.9
SIC Composite	8.2	9.5	9.8	10.4	13.6	13.3	11.5	8.6
Large Composite	−	−	−	−	−	−	−	−
Small Composite	−	−	−	−	−	−	−	−
High Financial Risk	−	−	−	−	−	−	−	−

Cost of Equity Capital (%) SIC Composite
- Avg CRSP: 9.7
- Avg RPR: 12.0
- 1-Stage: 13.3
- 3-Stage: 11.5
- 5-Factor Model: 8.6

Weighted Average Cost of Capital (WACC) (%)

	CRSP Deciles CAPM	CAPM +Size Prem	Build-Up	Risk Premium Report CAPM +Size Prem	Build-Up	Discounted Cash Flow 1-Stage	3-Stage	Fama-French 5-Factor Model
Median	8.2	10.2	10.2	9.7	14.7	15.4	11.3	10.2
SIC Composite	7.7	8.8	9.0	9.5	12.3	12.0	10.4	8.0
Large Composite	−	−	−	−	−	−	−	−
Small Composite	−	−	−	−	−	−	−	−
High Financial Risk	−	−	−	−	−	−	−	−

WACC (%) SIC Composite
- Low: 8.0
- High: 12.3
- Average: 10.0
- Median: 9.5

© 2017 Duff & Phelps. All Rights Reserved. Duff & Phelps has used the utmost care in compiling the data presented herein, but cannot guarantee the accuracy, completeness, or timeliness of the information.

Data Updated Through March 31, 2017

349

Number of Companies: 7
Miscellaneous Fabricated Metal Products

Industry Description
Establishments primarily engaged in industrial valves; fluid power valves and hose fittings; steel springs except wire; valves and pipe fittings, not elsewhere classified; wire springs; miscellaneous fabricated wire products; metal foil and leaf; fabricated pipe and pipe fittings; fabricated metal products, not elsewhere classified.

Sales (in millions)

Three Largest Companies
Parker-Hannifin Corp.	$11,360.8
Crane Co.	2,748.0
Watts Water Technologies Inc.	1,398.4

Three Smallest Companies
Sun Hydraulics Corp.	$196.9
OmegaFlex, Inc.	93.3
NF Energy Saving Corp.	6.7

Total Assets (in millions)

Three Largest Companies
Parker-Hannifin Corp.	$12,056.7
Crane Co.	3,428.0
Watts Water Technologies Inc.	1,800.3

Three Smallest Companies
Sun Hydraulics Corp.	$444.8
OmegaFlex, Inc.	66.3
NF Energy Saving Corp.	44.4

Annualized Monthly Performance Statistics (%)

Industry	Geometric Mean	Arithmetic Mean	Standard Deviation	S&P 500 Index	Geometric Mean	Arithmetic Mean	Standard Deviation
1-year	41.2	42.7	21.9	1-year	17.2	17.4	7.2
3-year	9.2	10.9	20.2	3-year	10.4	10.9	11.5
5-year	14.5	16.5	21.6	5-year	13.3	13.9	11.5

Return Ratios (%)

	Return on Assets Latest	5-Yr Avg	Return on Equity Latest	5-Yr Avg	Dividend Yield Latest	5-Yr Avg
Median (7)	4.8	5.9	10.4	17.3	1.6	2.0
SIC Composite (7)	5.7	7.0	3.5	5.6	1.8	1.9
Large Composite (−)	−	−	−	−	−	−
Small Composite (−)	−	−	−	−	−	−
High-Financial Risk (−)	−	−	−	−	−	−

Liquidity Ratio

	Current Ratio Latest	5-Yr Avg
Median (7)	2.4	2.4
SIC Composite (7)	2.3	2.0
Large Composite (−)	−	−
Small Composite (−)	−	−
High-Financial Risk (−)	−	−

Profitability Ratio (%)

	Operating Margin Latest	5-Yr Avg
Median (7)	11.4	11.6
SIC Composite (7)	11.7	11.9
Large Composite (−)	−	−
Small Composite (−)	−	−
High-Financial Risk (−)	−	−

Growth Rates (%)

	Long-term EPS Analyst Estimates
Median (7)	10.6
SIC Composite (7)	10.4
Large Composite (−)	−
Small Composite (−)	−
High-Financial Risk (−)	−

Betas (Levered)

	Raw (OLS)	Blume Adjusted	Peer Group	Vasicek Adjusted	Sum	Downside
Median	1.32	1.21	1.00	1.12	1.21	1.81
SIC Composite	1.28	1.18	1.00	1.18	1.42	1.40
Large Composite	−	−	−	−	−	−
Small Composite	−	−	−	−	−	−
High Financial Risk	−	−	−	−	−	−

Betas (Unlevered)

	Raw (OLS)	Blume Adjusted	Peer Group	Vasicek Adjusted	Sum	Downside
Median	1.19	1.08	0.87	0.99	1.05	1.50
SIC Composite	1.12	1.03	0.87	1.03	1.24	1.22
Large Composite	−	−	−	−	−	−
Small Composite	−	−	−	−	−	−
High Financial Risk	−	−	−	−	−	−

Equity Valuation Multiples

	Price/Sales Latest	5-Yr Avg	Price/Earnings Latest	5-Yr Avg	Market/Book Latest	5-Yr Avg
Median	1.7	1.2	35.9	26.0	3.8	2.9
SIC Composite	1.9	1.3	28.6	18.0	4.1	2.8
Large Composite	−	−	−	−	−	−
Small Composite	−	−	−	−	−	−
High Financial Risk	−	−	−	−	−	−

Enterprise Valuation (EV) Multiples

	EV/Sales Latest	5-Yr Avg	EV/EBITDA Latest	5-Yr Avg
Median	2.0	1.4	18.8	10.5
SIC Composite	2.0	1.4	13.1	9.3
Large Composite	−	−	−	−
Small Composite	−	−	−	−
High Financial Risk	−	−	−	−

Enterprise Valuation
SIC Composite
- EV/Sales: Latest 2.0, 5-Yr Avg 1.4
- EV/EBITDA: Latest 13.1, 5-Yr Avg 9.3

Fama-French (F-F) 5-Factor Model

	F-F Beta	SMB Premium	HML Premium	RMW Premium	CMA Premium
Median	1.2	2.8	2.1	1.9	0.5
SIC Composite	1.2	3.0	2.3	1.5	0.7
Large Composite	−	−	−	−	−
Small Composite	−	−	−	−	−
High Financial Risk	−	−	−	−	−

Leverage Ratios (%)

	Debt/MV Equity Latest	5-Yr Avg	Debt/Total Capital Latest	5-Yr Avg
Median	16.9	16.3	14.5	14.0
SIC Composite	15.9	17.0	13.7	14.5
Large Composite	−	−	−	−
Small Composite	−	−	−	−
High Financial Risk	−	−	−	−

Cost of Debt

	Cost of Debt (%) Latest
Median	6.1
SIC Composite	4.6
Large Composite	−
Small Composite	−
High Financial Risk	−

Capital Structure

SIC Composite (%) Latest
- D/TC: 13.7
- E/TC: 86.3

Cost of Equity Capital (%)

	CRSP Deciles CAPM	CAPM +Size Prem	Build-Up	Risk Premium Report CAPM +Size Prem	Build-Up	Discounted Cash Flow 1-Stage	3-Stage	Fama-French 5-Factor Model
Median	9.7	11.5	10.6	13.6	14.8	12.2	8.5	17.7
SIC Composite	10.0	10.8	9.4	14.2	12.1	12.1	10.2	17.6
Large Composite	−	−	−	−	−	−	−	−
Small Composite	−	−	−	−	−	−	−	−
High Financial Risk	−	−	−	−	−	−	−	−

Cost of Equity Capital (%) SIC Composite
- Avg CRSP: 10.1
- Avg RPR: 13.1
- 1-Stage: 12.1
- 3-Stage: 10.2
- 5-Factor Model: 17.6

Weighted Average Cost of Capital (WACC) (%)

	CRSP Deciles CAPM	CAPM +Size Prem	Build-Up	Risk Premium Report CAPM +Size Prem	Build-Up	Discounted Cash Flow 1-Stage	3-Stage	Fama-French 5-Factor Model
Median	9.0	10.2	9.6	12.6	11.7	10.8	8.2	19.2
SIC Composite	9.1	9.8	8.5	12.7	10.9	10.9	9.3	15.7
Large Composite	−	−	−	−	−	−	−	−
Small Composite	−	−	−	−	−	−	−	−
High Financial Risk	−	−	−	−	−	−	−	−

WACC (%) SIC Composite: Low 8.5, High 15.7, Average 11.1, Median 10.9

© 2017 Duff & Phelps. All Rights Reserved. Duff & Phelps has used the utmost care in compiling the data presented herein, but cannot guarantee the accuracy, completeness, or timeliness of the information.

Data Updated Through March 31, 2017

35

Number of Companies: 70
Industrial and Commercial Machinery and Computer Equipment

Industry Description
This major group includes establishments engaged in manufacturing industrial and commercial machinery and equipment and computers.

Sales (in millions)

Three Largest Companies
Cisco Systems, Inc.	$49,247.0
HP Inc.	48,238.0
Deere & Co.	26,006.0

Three Smallest Companies
WSI Industries Inc.	$35.2
Innovative Solutions and Support, Inc.	28.0
Art's Way Mfg. Co. Inc.	21.6

Total Assets (in millions)

Three Largest Companies
Cisco Systems, Inc.	$121,652.0
Deere & Co.	57,981.4
Western Digital Corp.	32,862.0

Three Smallest Companies
TransAct Technologies Inc.	$32.0
Art's Way Mfg. Co. Inc.	27.2
WSI Industries Inc.	26.0

Annualized Monthly Performance Statistics (%)

Industry	Geometric Mean	Arithmetic Mean	Standard Deviation
1-year	36.1	36.8	14.6
3-year	10.1	11.6	18.1
5-year	11.4	13.0	18.8

S&P 500 Index	Geometric Mean	Arithmetic Mean	Standard Deviation
1-year	17.2	17.4	7.2
3-year	10.4	10.9	11.5
5-year	13.3	13.9	11.5

Return Ratios (%)

	Return on Assets Latest	Return on Assets 5-Yr Avg	Return on Equity Latest	Return on Equity 5-Yr Avg	Dividend Yield Latest	Dividend Yield 5-Yr Avg
Median (70)	4.1	5.2	7.2	10.1	0.8	1.1
SIC Composite (70)	4.7	4.9	3.9	5.2	2.3	2.1
Large Composite (7)	5.1	4.9	4.6	5.9	2.9	2.6
Small Composite (7)	0.0	3.2	0.0	3.3	1.8	4.3
High-Financial Risk (16)	-3.9	-2.9	-6.6	-5.0	0.9	0.9

Liquidity Ratio

	Current Ratio Latest	Current Ratio 5-Yr Avg
Median (70)	2.7	2.6
SIC Composite (70)	2.2	2.0
Large Composite (7)	2.2	1.9
Small Composite (7)	3.6	3.5
High-Financial Risk (16)	1.6	1.9

Profitability Ratio (%)

	Operating Margin Latest	Operating Margin 5-Yr Avg
Median (70)	9.0	10.1
SIC Composite (70)	12.5	12.4
Large Composite (7)	13.6	12.9
Small Composite (7)	7.1	8.0
High-Financial Risk (16)	4.6	5.1

Growth Rates (%)

	Long-term EPS Analyst Estimates
Median (70)	12.8
SIC Composite (70)	13.1
Large Composite (7)	13.1
Small Composite (7)	12.3
High-Financial Risk (16)	21.0

Betas (Levered)

	Raw (OLS)	Blume Adjusted	Peer Group	Vasicek Adjusted	Sum	Downside
Median	1.22	1.15	1.36	1.27	1.27	1.58
SIC Composite	1.33	1.22	1.36	1.34	1.31	1.57
Large Composite	1.35	1.23	1.36	1.35	1.37	1.66
Small Composite	1.00	1.00	1.36	1.04	1.24	1.19
High Financial Risk	1.82	1.53	1.36	1.78	1.96	2.00

Betas (Unlevered)

	Raw (OLS)	Blume Adjusted	Peer Group	Vasicek Adjusted	Sum	Downside
Median	1.07	1.02	1.23	1.11	1.13	1.37
SIC Composite	1.08	0.98	1.10	1.08	1.05	1.26
Large Composite	1.05	0.96	1.06	1.05	1.06	1.29
Small Composite	0.94	0.95	1.28	0.98	1.16	1.12
High Financial Risk	1.04	0.90	0.82	1.02	1.11	1.13

Equity Valuation Multiples

	Price/Sales Latest	Price/Sales 5-Yr Avg	Price/Earnings Latest	Price/Earnings 5-Yr Avg	Market/Book Latest	Market/Book 5-Yr Avg
Median	1.7	1.4	34.2	25.2	2.4	2.0
SIC Composite	2.0	1.3	26.0	19.2	3.2	2.2
Large Composite	2.0	1.2	21.9	17.0	3.1	2.1
Small Composite	0.9	1.1	–	30.3	1.1	1.2
High Financial Risk	0.9	0.9	–	–	6.2	2.8

Enterprise Valuation (EV) Multiples

	EV/Sales Latest	EV/Sales 5-Yr Avg	EV/EBITDA Latest	EV/EBITDA 5-Yr Avg
Median	1.9	1.4	13.4	10.3
SIC Composite	2.0	1.3	11.9	7.8
Large Composite	2.0	1.2	10.9	6.9
Small Composite	0.8	1.0	7.9	8.3
High Financial Risk	1.8	1.5	12.4	11.6

Enterprise Valuation SIC Composite

Latest: EV/Sales 2.0, EV/EBITDA 11.9
5-Yr Avg: EV/Sales 1.3, EV/EBITDA 7.8

Fama-French (F-F) 5-Factor Model

Fama-French (F-F) Components

	F-F Beta	SMB Premium	HML Premium	RMW Premium	CMA Premium
Median	0.8	3.8	0.9	2.6	0.1
SIC Composite	1.3	0.6	1.8	-0.4	-2.2
Large Composite	1.3	-0.5	1.8	-0.6	-0.8
Small Composite	1.0	-0.5	-1.1	-1.6	1.4
High Financial Risk	–	–	–	–	–

Leverage Ratios (%)

	Debt/MV Equity Latest	Debt/MV Equity 5-Yr Avg	Debt/Total Capital Latest	Debt/Total Capital 5-Yr Avg
Median	14.1	14.0	12.3	12.3
SIC Composite	26.5	28.7	21.0	22.3
Large Composite	30.1	33.0	23.2	24.8
Small Composite	8.9	9.1	8.2	8.3
High Financial Risk	109.5	95.6	52.3	48.9

Cost of Debt

	Cost of Debt (%) Latest
Median	6.1
SIC Composite	4.7
Large Composite	4.5
Small Composite	6.6
High Financial Risk	6.8

Capital Structure

SIC Composite (%) Latest
D/TC: 21.0
E/TC: 79.0

Cost of Equity Capital (%)

	CRSP Deciles CAPM	CRSP Deciles CAPM +Size Prem	Build-Up	Risk Premium Report CAPM +Size Prem	Risk Premium Report Build-Up	Discounted Cash Flow 1-Stage	Discounted Cash Flow 3-Stage	Fama-French 5-Factor Model
Median	10.5	12.5	12.6	14.9	14.1	13.5	10.6	15.4
SIC Composite	10.8	11.3	11.4	12.7	10.8	15.2	11.7	10.4
Large Composite	10.9	11.0	11.1	12.2	9.6	15.9	12.6	10.6
Small Composite	9.2	14.8	16.6	16.2	16.7	13.3	9.6	7.2
High Financial Risk	–	–	–	25.9	23.7	–	–	–

Cost of Equity Capital (%) SIC Composite

Avg CRSP: 11.4, Avg RPR: 11.7, 1-Stage: 15.2, 3-Stage: 11.7, 5-Factor Model: 10.4

Weighted Average Cost of Capital (WACC) (%)

	CRSP Deciles CAPM	CRSP Deciles CAPM +Size Prem	Build-Up	Risk Premium Report CAPM +Size Prem	Risk Premium Report Build-Up	Discounted Cash Flow 1-Stage	Discounted Cash Flow 3-Stage	Fama-French 5-Factor Model
Median	9.7	11.2	11.5	13.4	12.5	12.1	9.8	13.5
SIC Composite	9.5	9.9	10.0	11.0	9.5	12.9	10.2	9.2
Large Composite	9.4	9.5	9.5	10.4	8.4	13.2	10.7	9.1
Small Composite	8.9	14.0	15.7	15.4	15.8	12.7	9.3	7.0
High Financial Risk	–	–	–	15.5	14.5	–	–	–

WACC (%) SIC Composite
Low: 9.2, Average: 10.4, Median: 10.0, High: 12.9

© 2017 Duff & Phelps. All Rights Reserved. Duff & Phelps has used the utmost care in compiling the data presented herein, but cannot guarantee the accuracy, completeness, or timeliness of the information.

Data Updated Through March 31, 2017

353

Number of Companies: 11
Construction, Mining, and Materials Handling

Industry Description

Establishments primarily engaged in construction machinery and equipment; mining machinery and equipment; oil and gas field machinery and equipment; elevators and moving stairways; conveyors and conveying equipment; overhead traveling cranes, hoists, and monorail systems; and industrial trucks, tractors, trailers and stackers.

Sales (in millions)

Three Largest Companies
National Oilwell Varco, Inc.	$7,251.0
Terex Corp.	4,443.1
Joy Global, Inc.	2,371.4

Three Smallest Companies
Douglas Dynamics, Inc.	$416.3
Manitex International Inc.	289.0
Natural Gas Services Group	71.7

Annualized Monthly Performance Statistics (%)

Industry	Geometric Mean	Arithmetic Mean	Standard Deviation
1-year	30.7	34.7	35.1
3-year	-13.2	-10.0	25.3
5-year	-5.9	-3.1	24.1

Total Assets (in millions)

Three Largest Companies
National Oilwell Varco, Inc.	$21,140.0
Terex Corp.	5,006.8
Joy Global, Inc.	3,426.4

Three Smallest Companies
Douglas Dynamics, Inc.	$671.9
Manitex International Inc.	318.0
Natural Gas Services Group	293.5

S&P 500 Index	Geometric Mean	Arithmetic Mean	Standard Deviation
1-year	17.2	17.4	7.2
3-year	10.4	10.9	11.5
5-year	13.3	13.9	11.5

Return Ratios (%)

	Return on Assets Latest	5-Yr Avg	Return on Equity Latest	5-Yr Avg	Dividend Yield Latest	5-Yr Avg	Current Ratio Latest	5-Yr Avg	Operating Margin Latest	5-Yr Avg	Long-term EPS Analyst Estimates
Median (11)	-1.8	2.7	-4.5	4.6	0.1	0.5	2.6	2.9	3.0	9.1	19.2
SIC Composite (11)	-7.9	2.7	-10.0	3.2	0.5	1.4	2.6	2.4	-0.1	11.7	28.0
Large Composite (3)	-9.0	2.5	-12.5	3.1	0.6	1.6	2.4	2.4	-1.4	12.2	40.7
Small Composite (3)	1.9	3.9	2.1	4.6	1.9	2.3	2.8	2.8	10.6	13.4	15.9
High-Financial Risk (−)	−	−	−	−	−	−	−	−	−	−	−

Betas (Levered)

	Raw (OLS)	Blume Adjusted	Peer Group	Vasicek Adjusted	Sum	Downside
Median	1.46	1.30	1.36	1.42	1.80	1.90
SIC Composite	1.22	1.15	1.36	1.26	1.85	1.45
Large Composite	1.21	1.14	1.36	1.24	1.87	1.45
Small Composite	1.25	1.17	−	−	1.54	1.34
High Financial Risk	−	−	−	−	−	−

Betas (Unlevered)

	Raw (OLS)	Blume Adjusted	Peer Group	Vasicek Adjusted	Sum	Downside
Median	1.13	1.05	1.09	1.16	1.38	1.44
SIC Composite	1.02	0.96	1.13	1.05	1.53	1.20
Large Composite	0.99	0.93	1.10	1.01	1.50	1.18
Small Composite	0.99	0.92	−	−	1.19	1.04
High Financial Risk	−	−	−	−	−	−

Equity Valuation Multiples

	Price/Sales Latest	5-Yr Avg	Price/Earnings Latest	5-Yr Avg	Market/Book Latest	5-Yr Avg
Median	1.2	1.1	−	29.5	1.6	1.6
SIC Composite	1.5	1.2	−	30.8	1.3	1.4
Large Composite	1.5	1.1	−	31.8	1.2	1.3
Small Composite	1.5	1.3	46.6	21.8	1.8	1.5
High Financial Risk	−	−	−	−	−	−

Enterprise Valuation (EV) Multiples

	EV/Sales Latest	5-Yr Avg	EV/EBITDA Latest	5-Yr Avg
Median	1.5	1.3	11.9	8.9
SIC Composite	1.7	1.3	29.1	8.4
Large Composite	1.8	1.2	35.6	7.9
Small Composite	1.9	1.7	11.6	8.7
High Financial Risk	−	−	−	−

Enterprise Valuation SIC Composite
- Latest: EV/Sales 1.7, EV/EBITDA 29.1
- 5-Yr Avg: EV/Sales 1.3, EV/EBITDA 8.4

Fama-French (F-F) 5-Factor Model

	Fama-French (F-F) Components				
	F-F Beta	SMB Premium	HML Premium	RMW Premium	CMA Premium
Median	1.4	5.8	3.3	-9.0	9.4
SIC Composite	1.1	3.2	5.6	-1.0	0.1
Large Composite	1.1	2.6	5.6	-0.9	-1.2
Small Composite	1.2	3.7	2.6	1.5	2.1
High Financial Risk	−	−	−	−	−

Leverage Ratios (%)

	Debt/MV Equity Latest	5-Yr Avg	Debt/Total Capital Latest	5-Yr Avg
Median	35.3	27.8	26.1	21.7
SIC Composite	24.7	20.8	19.8	17.2
Large Composite	27.2	20.1	21.4	16.7
Small Composite	40.2	33.7	28.7	25.2
High Financial Risk	−	−	−	−

Cost of Debt

	Cost of Debt (%) Latest
Median	7.1
SIC Composite	5.7
Large Composite	5.4
Small Composite	6.4
High Financial Risk	−

Capital Structure

SIC Composite (%) Latest: D/TC 19.8, E/TC 80.2

Cost of Equity Capital (%)

	CRSP Deciles CAPM	CAPM +Size Prem	Build-Up	Risk Premium Report CAPM +Size Prem	Build-Up	Discounted Cash Flow 1-Stage	3-Stage	Fama-French 5-Factor Model
Median	11.3	13.4	12.7	17.0	14.0	16.9	14.0	20.9
SIC Composite	10.4	11.6	12.1	16.6	12.2	28.6	15.8	17.3
Large Composite	10.3	11.2	11.8	16.2	11.5	41.4	21.8	15.7
Small Composite	−	−	13.6	17.2	15.6	18.1	15.1	20.0
High Financial Risk	−	−	−	−	−	−	−	−

Cost of Equity Capital (%) SIC Composite
- Avg CRSP: 11.8
- Avg RPR: 14.4
- 1-Stage: 28.6
- 3-Stage: 15.8
- 5-Factor Model: 17.3

Weighted Average Cost of Capital (WACC) (%)

	CRSP Deciles CAPM	CAPM +Size Prem	Build-Up	Risk Premium Report CAPM +Size Prem	Build-Up	Discounted Cash Flow 1-Stage	3-Stage	Fama-French 5-Factor Model
Median	9.8	11.5	10.7	13.6	11.7	13.2	12.0	17.4
SIC Composite	9.4	10.3	10.8	14.4	10.8	24.0	13.7	14.9
Large Composite	9.2	9.9	10.4	13.9	10.1	33.7	18.3	13.4
Small Composite	−	−	10.9	13.5	12.4	14.1	12.0	15.5
High Financial Risk	−	−	−	−	−	−	−	−

WACC (%) SIC Composite
Low 10.3 — High 24.0 — Average 14.1 — Median 13.7

© 2017 Duff & Phelps. All Rights Reserved. Duff & Phelps has used the utmost care in compiling the data presented herein, but cannot guarantee the accuracy, completeness, or timeliness of the information.

Data Updated Through March 31, 2017

355

Number of Companies: 12
Special Industry Machinery, Except Metalworking

Industry Description
Establishment primarily engaged in special industry machinery including textile, woodworking, paper industries, printing trades, food products and special industry machinery not elsewhere classified.

Sales (in millions)

Three Largest Companies
Applied Materials, Inc.	$10,825.0
Lam Research Corp.	5,885.9
John Bean Technologies	1,350.5

Three Smallest Companies
PDF Solutions Inc.	$107.5
Cleantech Solutions Int'l Inc.	49.6
CVD Equipment Corp.	39.0

Total Assets (in millions)

Three Largest Companies
Applied Materials, Inc.	$14,588.0
Lam Research Corp.	12,271.5
Entegris, Inc.	1,699.5

Three Smallest Companies
PDF Solutions Inc.	$222.3
Cleantech Solutions Int'l Inc.	94.6
CVD Equipment Corp.	41.1

Annualized Monthly Performance Statistics (%)

	Industry				S&P 500 Index		
	Geometric Mean	Arithmetic Mean	Standard Deviation		Geometric Mean	Arithmetic Mean	Standard Deviation
1-year	69.8	73.0	34.9	1-year	17.2	17.4	7.2
3-year	26.1	29.5	30.8	3-year	10.4	10.9	11.5
5-year	25.2	28.3	28.7	5-year	13.3	13.9	11.5

Return Ratios (%)

	Return on Assets		Return on Equity		Dividend Yield		Current Ratio		Operating Margin		Long-term EPS
	Latest	5-Yr Avg	Latest	5-Yr Avg	Latest	5-Yr Avg	Latest	5-Yr Avg	Latest	5-Yr Avg	Analyst Estimates
Median (12)	6.2	6.0	10.8	10.3	0.3	0.5	3.8	3.6	11.8	13.6	17.3
SIC Composite (12)	8.7	6.1	3.8	4.1	1.2	1.5	3.0	2.8	17.7	14.7	18.8
Large Composite (3)	9.6	6.2	4.1	4.1	1.4	1.7	2.8	2.5	18.9	15.3	19.4
Small Composite (3)	-0.1	7.2	-0.1	3.9	0.0	0.0	–	–	10.3	17.9	18.4
High-Financial Risk (–)	–	–	–	–	–	–	–	–	–	–	–

Betas (Levered)

	Raw (OLS)	Blume Adjusted	Peer Group	Vasicek Adjusted	Sum	Downside
Median	1.37	1.24	1.35	1.37	1.33	1.72
SIC Composite	1.61	1.40	1.35	1.58	1.56	1.77
Large Composite	1.73	1.47	1.36	1.57	1.64	1.86
Small Composite	1.41	1.27	1.36	1.40	1.36	1.64
High Financial Risk	–	–	–	–	–	–

Betas (Unlevered)

	Raw (OLS)	Blume Adjusted	Peer Group	Vasicek Adjusted	Sum	Downside
Median	1.24	1.12	1.28	1.24	1.20	1.61
SIC Composite	1.45	1.26	1.22	1.42	1.40	1.59
Large Composite	1.55	1.31	1.21	1.40	1.47	1.66
Small Composite	1.40	1.26	1.35	1.39	1.35	1.63
High Financial Risk	–	–	–	–	–	–

Equity Valuation Multiples

	Price/Sales		Price/Earnings		Market/Book	
	Latest	5-Yr Avg	Latest	5-Yr Avg	Latest	5-Yr Avg
Median	2.8	2.1	32.8	25.6	3.1	2.1
SIC Composite	3.5	2.4	26.3	24.6	4.4	2.6
Large Composite	3.6	2.4	24.2	24.2	4.9	2.8
Small Composite	4.0	3.1	–	25.9	2.5	2.2
High Financial Risk	–	–	–	–	–	–

Enterprise Valuation (EV) Multiples

	EV/Sales		EV/EBITDA		Enterprise Valuation SIC Composite
	Latest	5-Yr Avg	Latest	5-Yr Avg	
Median	2.7	2.0	14.0	11.9	Latest: 15.2 / 3.3
SIC Composite	3.3	2.2	15.2	11.2	5-Yr Avg: 11.2 / 2.2
Large Composite	3.5	2.3	15.2	11.3	■ EV/Sales ■ EV/EBITDA
Small Composite	3.3	2.5	24.0	11.4	
High Financial Risk	–	–	–	–	

Fama-French (F-F) 5-Factor Model

	Fama-French (F-F) Components				
	F-F Beta	SMB Premium	HML Premium	RMW Premium	CMA Premium
Median	1.7	3.3	1.2	-1.0	-2.8
SIC Composite	1.5	2.5	1.3	-0.2	-2.7
Large Composite	1.6	2.0	1.3	-0.7	-0.9
Small Composite	1.3	5.8	1.1	1.8	0.8
High Financial Risk	–	–	–	–	–

Leverage Ratios (%)

	Debt/MV Equity		Debt/Total Capital	
	Latest	5-Yr Avg	Latest	5-Yr Avg
Median	6.9	7.6	6.5	7.1
SIC Composite	12.0	13.8	10.7	12.1
Large Composite	12.8	15.1	11.4	13.1
Small Composite	1.0	1.5	1.0	1.4
High Financial Risk	–	–	–	–

Cost of Debt

	Cost of Debt (%)
	Latest
Median	6.1
SIC Composite	4.7
Large Composite	4.6
Small Composite	6.6
High Financial Risk	–

Capital Structure

SIC Composite (%)
Latest: D/TC 10.7, E/TC 89.3

Cost of Equity Capital (%)

	CRSP Deciles		Risk Premium Report		Discounted Cash Flow		Fama-French
	CAPM	CAPM +Size Prem	Build-Up	CAPM +Size Prem	Build-Up	1-Stage	3-Stage	5-Factor Model
Median	11.0	12.8	12.7	15.0	14.6	16.8	12.2	13.4
SIC Composite	12.2	12.6	11.4	14.8	11.9	19.9	12.0	12.7
Large Composite	12.1	12.4	11.2	15.0	11.5	20.7	12.4	14.1
Small Composite	11.2	13.6	13.4	16.3	15.8	18.4	11.3	20.0
High Financial Risk	–	–	–	–	–	–	–	–

Cost of Equity Capital (%) SIC Composite:
Avg CRSP 12.0, Avg RPR 13.3, 1-Stage 19.9, 3-Stage 12.0, 5-Factor Model 12.7

Weighted Average Cost of Capital (WACC) (%)

	CRSP Deciles		Risk Premium Report		Discounted Cash Flow		Fama-French
	CAPM	CAPM +Size Prem	Build-Up	CAPM +Size Prem	Build-Up	1-Stage	3-Stage	5-Factor Model
Median	10.3	12.1	12.5	14.2	14.4	14.8	11.6	13.5
SIC Composite	11.3	11.7	10.7	13.7	11.1	18.2	11.2	11.8
Large Composite	11.2	11.5	10.4	13.8	10.7	18.8	11.5	13.0
Small Composite	11.1	13.5	13.3	16.2	15.7	18.3	11.2	19.8
High Financial Risk	–	–	–	–	–	–	–	–

WACC (%) SIC Composite:
Low 10.7, High 18.2, Average 12.6, Median 11.7

© 2017 Duff & Phelps. All Rights Reserved. Duff & Phelps has used the utmost care in compiling the data presented herein, but cannot guarantee the accuracy, completeness, or timeliness of the information.

Data Updated Through March 31, 2017

3559

Number of Companies: 9
Special Industry Machinery, Not Elsewhere Classified

Industry Description
Establishments primarily engaged in manufacturing special industry machinery, not elsewhere classified, such as smelting and refining equipment, cement making, clayworking, cotton ginning, glass making, hat making, incandescent lamp making, leather working, paint making, rubber working, cigar and cigarette making, tobacco working, shoe making, and stone working machinery, and industrial sewing machines, and automotive maintenance machinery and equipment.

Sales (in millions)

Three Largest Companies
Applied Materials, Inc.	$10,825.0
Lam Research Corp.	5,885.9
Entegris, Inc.	1,175.3

Three Smallest Companies
Ultratech, Inc.	$194.1
PDF Solutions Inc.	107.5
CVD Equipment Corp.	39.0

Annualized Monthly Performance Statistics (%)

Industry	Geometric Mean	Arithmetic Mean	Standard Deviation
1-year	70.8	74.1	35.7
3-year	25.8	29.3	31.2
5-year	24.9	28.1	29.1

Total Assets (in millions)

Three Largest Companies
Applied Materials, Inc.	$14,588.0
Lam Research Corp.	12,271.5
Entegris, Inc.	1,699.5

Three Smallest Companies
Proto Labs, Inc.	$414.2
PDF Solutions Inc.	222.3
CVD Equipment Corp.	41.1

S&P 500 Index	Geometric Mean	Arithmetic Mean	Standard Deviation
1-year	17.2	17.4	7.2
3-year	10.4	10.9	11.5
5-year	13.3	13.9	11.5

Return Ratios (%)

	Return on Assets Latest	5-Yr Avg	Return on Equity Latest	5-Yr Avg	Dividend Yield Latest	5-Yr Avg
Median (9)	5.8	6.1	10.3	10.2	0.0	0.0
SIC Composite (9)	8.9	6.2	3.9	4.0	1.3	1.5
Large Composite (–)	–	–	–	–	–	–
Small Composite (–)	–	–	–	–	–	–
High-Financial Risk (–)	–	–	–	–	–	–

Liquidity Ratio

	Current Ratio Latest	5-Yr Avg
Median (9)	–	4.2
SIC Composite (9)	3.0	2.9
Large Composite	–	–
Small Composite	–	–
High-Financial Risk	–	–

Profitability Ratio (%)

	Operating Margin Latest	5-Yr Avg
Median	13.9	14.0
SIC Composite	18.4	15.3
Large Composite	–	–
Small Composite	–	–
High-Financial Risk	–	–

Growth Rates (%)

	Long-term EPS Analyst Estimates
Median	18.3
SIC Composite	18.9
Large Composite	–
Small Composite	–
High-Financial Risk	–

Betas (Levered)

	Raw (OLS)	Blume Adjusted	Peer Group	Vasicek Adjusted	Sum	Downside
Median	1.26	1.17	1.35	1.30	1.29	1.67
SIC Composite	1.63	1.40	1.35	1.58	1.59	1.79
Large Composite	–	–	–	–	–	–
Small Composite	–	–	–	–	–	–
High Financial Risk	–	–	–	–	–	–

Betas (Unlevered)

	Raw (OLS)	Blume Adjusted	Peer Group	Vasicek Adjusted	Sum	Downside
Median	1.21	1.13	1.35	1.26	1.14	1.64
SIC Composite	1.46	1.26	1.22	1.42	1.43	1.61
Large Composite	–	–	–	–	–	–
Small Composite	–	–	–	–	–	–
High Financial Risk	–	–	–	–	–	–

Equity Valuation Multiples

	Price/Sales Latest	5-Yr Avg	Price/Earnings Latest	5-Yr Avg	Market/Book Latest	5-Yr Avg
Median	3.5	2.5	31.7	26.7	3.5	2.2
SIC Composite	3.7	2.5	26.0	24.8	4.4	2.6
Large Composite	–	–	–	–	–	–
Small Composite	–	–	–	–	–	–
High Financial Risk	–	–	–	–	–	–

Enterprise Valuation (EV) Multiples

	EV/Sales Latest	5-Yr Avg	EV/EBITDA Latest	5-Yr Avg
Median	3.0	2.1	14.9	14.2
SIC Composite	3.5	2.3	15.1	11.2
Large Composite	–	–	–	–
Small Composite	–	–	–	–
High Financial Risk	–	–	–	–

Enterprise Valuation SIC Composite
- EV/Sales: Latest 3.5, 5-Yr Avg 2.3
- EV/EBITDA: Latest 15.1, 5-Yr Avg 11.2

Fama-French (F-F) 5-Factor Model

	F-F Beta	SMB Premium	HML Premium	RMW Premium	CMA Premium
Median	1.7	3.3	1.2	-1.0	-2.8
SIC Composite	1.5	2.4	1.2	-0.2	-2.7
Large Composite	–	–	–	–	–
Small Composite	–	–	–	–	–
High Financial Risk	–	–	–	–	–

Leverage Ratios (%)

	Debt/MV Equity Latest	5-Yr Avg	Debt/Total Capital Latest	5-Yr Avg
Median	0.3	0.6	0.3	0.6
SIC Composite	11.8	13.6	10.5	12.0
Large Composite	–	–	–	–
Small Composite	–	–	–	–
High Financial Risk	–	–	–	–

Cost of Debt

	Cost of Debt (%) Latest
Median	7.1
SIC Composite	4.6
Large Composite	–
Small Composite	–
High Financial Risk	–

Capital Structure

SIC Composite (%) Latest
- D/TC: 10.5
- E/TC: 89.5

Cost of Equity Capital (%)

	CRSP Deciles CAPM	CAPM +Size Prem	Build-Up	Risk Premium Report CAPM +Size Prem	Build-Up	Discounted Cash Flow 1-Stage	3-Stage	Fama-French 5-Factor Model
Median	10.6	12.4	12.7	14.4	14.5	17.5	12.0	13.4
SIC Composite	12.2	12.6	11.4	14.9	11.8	20.1	12.1	12.7
Large Composite	–	–	–	–	–	–	–	–
Small Composite	–	–	–	–	–	–	–	–
High Financial Risk	–	–	–	–	–	–	–	–

Cost of Equity Capital (%) SIC Composite
- Avg CRSP: 12.0
- Avg RPR: 13.3
- 1-Stage: 20.1
- 3-Stage: 12.1
- 5-Factor Model: 12.7

Weighted Average Cost of Capital (WACC) (%)

	CRSP Deciles CAPM	CAPM +Size Prem	Build-Up	Risk Premium Report CAPM +Size Prem	Build-Up	Discounted Cash Flow 1-Stage	3-Stage	Fama-French 5-Factor Model
Median	10.4	12.1	12.7	13.5	14.5	16.4	11.3	12.7
SIC Composite	11.3	11.7	10.6	13.8	11.0	18.4	11.3	11.8
Large Composite	–	–	–	–	–	–	–	–
Small Composite	–	–	–	–	–	–	–	–
High Financial Risk	–	–	–	–	–	–	–	–

WACC (%) SIC Composite
- Low: 10.6, High: 18.4
- Average 12.7, Median 11.7

© 2017 Duff & Phelps. All Rights Reserved. Duff & Phelps has used the utmost care in compiling the data presented herein, but cannot guarantee the accuracy, completeness, or timeliness of the information.

Data Updated Through March 31, 2017

356

Number of Companies: 12
General Industrial Machinery and Equipment

Industry Description
Establishments primarily engaged in pumps and pumping equipment; ball and roller bearings; air and gas compressors; industrial and commercial fans and blowers and air purification equipment; packaging machinery; speed changers, industrial high speed drive and gears; industrial process furnaces and ovens; mechanical power transmission equipment not elsewhere classified; general industrial equipment not elsewhere classified.

Sales (in millions)

Three Largest Companies
Xylem Inc.	$3,771.0
Timken Co.	2,669.8
Rexnord Corporation	1,923.8

Three Smallest Companies
Gencor Industries Inc.	$70.0
Taylor Devices Inc.	35.7
WSI Industries Inc.	35.2

Annualized Monthly Performance Statistics (%)

Industry
	Geometric Mean	Arithmetic Mean	Standard Deviation
1-year	32.0	33.0	17.0
3-year	10.9	12.7	20.6
5-year	13.1	14.8	20.2

Total Assets (in millions)

Three Largest Companies
Xylem Inc.	$6,474.0
Rexnord Corporation	3,354.8
Timken Co.	2,758.3

Three Smallest Companies
Gencor Industries Inc.	$128.7
Taylor Devices Inc.	37.5
WSI Industries Inc.	26.0

S&P 500 Index
	Geometric Mean	Arithmetic Mean	Standard Deviation
1-year	17.2	17.4	7.2
3-year	10.4	10.9	11.5
5-year	13.3	13.9	11.5

Return Ratios (%)

	Return on Assets Latest	5-Yr Avg	Return on Equity Latest	5-Yr Avg	Dividend Yield Latest	5-Yr Avg
Median (12)	5.1	5.7	8.8	10.8	1.5	1.5
SIC Composite (12)	4.5	6.2	2.8	4.5	1.5	1.5
Large Composite (3)	3.8	4.6	3.2	4.3	1.7	1.8
Small Composite (3)	5.9	4.2	4.2	4.6	0.0	0.3
High-Financial Risk (−)	−	−	−	−	−	−

Liquidity Ratio

	Current Ratio Latest	5-Yr Avg
Median (12)	2.8	2.5
SIC Composite (12)	2.2	2.5
Large Composite (3)	2.0	2.3
Small Composite (3)	−	−
High-Financial Risk (−)	−	−

Profitability Ratio (%)

	Operating Margin Latest	5-Yr Avg
Median (12)	11.1	11.8
SIC Composite (12)	14.0	14.3
Large Composite (3)	11.6	12.3
Small Composite (3)	9.6	5.8
High-Financial Risk (−)	−	−

Growth Rates (%)

	Long-term EPS Analyst Estimates
Median (12)	10.2
SIC Composite (12)	11.3
Large Composite (3)	10.0
Small Composite (3)	10.2
High-Financial Risk (−)	−

Betas (Levered)

	Raw (OLS)	Blume Adjusted	Peer Group	Vasicek Adjusted	Sum	Downside
Median	1.18	1.12	1.35	1.23	1.26	1.40
SIC Composite	1.23	1.15	1.35	1.24	1.09	1.33
Large Composite	1.24	1.16	1.35	1.30	1.10	1.36
Small Composite	0.68	0.80	1.36	0.83	0.42	0.79
High Financial Risk	−	−	−	−	−	−

Betas (Unlevered)

	Raw (OLS)	Blume Adjusted	Peer Group	Vasicek Adjusted	Sum	Downside
Median	1.03	0.98	1.18	1.10	1.09	1.22
SIC Composite	1.03	0.97	1.13	1.04	0.92	1.11
Large Composite	0.98	0.91	1.05	1.02	0.87	1.06
Small Composite	0.67	0.79	1.33	0.81	0.42	0.78
High Financial Risk	−	−	−	−	−	−

Equity Valuation Multiples

	Price/Sales Latest	5-Yr Avg	Price/Earnings Latest	5-Yr Avg	Market/Book Latest	5-Yr Avg
Median	1.8	1.5	34.6	22.2	2.9	2.5
SIC Composite	2.3	1.7	35.5	22.4	4.1	3.2
Large Composite	1.8	1.4	30.9	23.3	3.2	2.6
Small Composite	1.9	1.4	23.8	21.9	1.6	1.1
High Financial Risk	−	−	−	−	−	−

Enterprise Valuation (EV) Multiples

	EV/Sales Latest	5-Yr Avg	EV/EBITDA Latest	5-Yr Avg
Median	2.0	1.6	14.4	10.6
SIC Composite	2.8	2.0	14.9	10.9
Large Composite	2.3	1.7	13.2	9.7
Small Composite	1.2	0.6	8.6	5.2
High Financial Risk	−	−	−	−

Enterprise Valuation SIC Composite

Latest: EV/Sales 2.8, EV/EBITDA 14.9
5-Yr Avg: EV/Sales 2.0, EV/EBITDA 10.9

Fama-French (F-F) 5-Factor Model

	F-F Beta	SMB Premium	HML Premium	RMW Premium	CMA Premium
Median	0.6	4.2	-1.9	3.8	1.9
SIC Composite	1.1	3.3	0.8	1.0	-0.3
Large Composite	1.1	3.7	-0.4	0.4	0.6
Small Composite	0.6	2.9	-0.8	2.0	-0.4
High Financial Risk	−	−	−	−	−

Leverage Ratios (%)

	Debt/MV Equity Latest	5-Yr Avg	Debt/Total Capital Latest	5-Yr Avg
Median	17.2	16.2	14.7	13.9
SIC Composite	24.2	24.4	19.5	19.6
Large Composite	33.2	32.4	24.9	24.5
Small Composite	3.1	5.9	3.0	5.6
High Financial Risk	−	−	−	−

Cost of Debt

	Cost of Debt (%) Latest
Median	6.1
SIC Composite	5.7
Large Composite	5.3
Small Composite	6.1
High Financial Risk	−

Capital Structure

SIC Composite (%) Latest
D/TC: 19.5
E/TC: 80.5

Cost of Equity Capital (%)

	CRSP Deciles CAPM	CAPM +Size Prem	Build-Up	Risk Premium Report CAPM +Size Prem	Build-Up	Discounted Cash Flow 1-Stage	3-Stage	Fama-French 5-Factor Model
Median	10.3	12.4	12.7	15.4	14.4	11.8	9.2	14.6
SIC Composite	10.3	11.5	12.2	13.0	13.1	12.6	9.7	14.5
Large Composite	10.6	11.8	12.1	12.7	12.6	11.4	8.8	14.1
Small Composite	8.0	13.6	16.6	11.7	16.7	10.2	9.3	10.6
High Financial Risk	−	−	−	−	−	−	−	−

Cost of Equity Capital (%) SIC Composite
Avg CRSP: 11.9, Avg RPR: 13.0, 1-Stage: 12.6, 3-Stage: 9.7, 5-Factor Model: 14.5

Weighted Average Cost of Capital (WACC) (%)

	CRSP Deciles CAPM	CAPM +Size Prem	Build-Up	Risk Premium Report CAPM +Size Prem	Build-Up	Discounted Cash Flow 1-Stage	3-Stage	Fama-French 5-Factor Model
Median	9.6	10.9	11.1	12.1	12.2	10.3	8.7	13.5
SIC Composite	9.3	10.3	10.8	11.4	11.5	11.1	8.8	12.6
Large Composite	9.2	10.1	10.3	10.8	10.7	9.8	7.8	11.8
Small Composite	7.9	13.4	16.2	11.5	16.3	10.0	9.1	10.4
High Financial Risk	−	−	−	−	−	−	−	−

WACC (%) SIC Composite
Low 8.8, Average 10.9, Median 11.1, High 12.6

© 2017 Duff & Phelps. All Rights Reserved. Duff & Phelps has used the utmost care in compiling the data presented herein, but cannot guarantee the accuracy, completeness, or timeliness of the information.

Data Updated Through March 31, 2017

357

Number of Companies: 17
Computer and Office Equipment

Industry Description
Establishments primarily engaged in electronic computers; computer storage devices; computer terminals; computer peripheral equipment, not elsewhere classified; calculating and accounting machines, except electronic computers; office machines, not elsewhere classified.

Sales (in millions)

Three Largest Companies
Cisco Systems, Inc.	$49,247.0
HP Inc.	48,238.0
Western Digital Corp.	12,994.0

Three Smallest Companies
Digi International Inc.	$203.0
TransAct Technologies Inc.	57.2
Innovative Solutions and Support, Inc.	28.0

Total Assets (in millions)

Three Largest Companies
Cisco Systems, Inc.	$121,652.0
Western Digital Corp.	32,862.0
HP Inc.	29,010.0

Three Smallest Companies
PAR Technology Corporation	$125.1
Innovative Solutions and Support, Inc	36.5
TransAct Technologies Inc.	32.0

Annualized Monthly Performance Statistics (%)

Industry	Geometric Mean	Arithmetic Mean	Standard Deviation	S&P 500 Index	Geometric Mean	Arithmetic Mean	Standard Deviation
1-year	29.6	30.7	18.0	1-year	17.2	17.4	7.2
3-year	12.1	14.0	21.5	3-year	10.4	10.9	11.5
5-year	11.9	14.2	23.5	5-year	13.3	13.9	11.5

Return Ratios (%)

	Return on Assets Latest	5-Yr Avg	Return on Equity Latest	5-Yr Avg	Dividend Yield Latest	5-Yr Avg
Median (17)	3.9	5.1	7.3	8.1	0.0	0.0
SIC Composite (17)	6.8	5.0	5.6	5.5	3.0	2.5
Large Composite (3)	7.4	5.2	6.1	5.9	3.4	2.8
Small Composite (3)	4.7	2.6	4.5	2.5	0.6	1.8
High-Financial Risk (8)	-4.7	-4.8	-9.3	-9.6	1.0	1.3

Liquidity Ratio

	Current Ratio Latest	5-Yr Avg
Median (17)	2.6	2.6
SIC Composite (17)	2.1	1.9
Large Composite (3)	2.2	1.9
Small Composite (3)	–	–
High-Financial Risk (8)	1.6	1.8

Profitability Ratio (%)

	Operating Margin Latest	5-Yr Avg
Median (17)	7.6	7.3
SIC Composite (17)	14.7	12.6
Large Composite (3)	15.9	12.9
Small Composite (3)	8.5	5.0
High-Financial Risk (8)	2.8	2.6

Growth Rates (%)

	Long-term EPS Analyst Estimates
Median (17)	9.0
SIC Composite (17)	9.0
Large Composite (3)	8.1
Small Composite (3)	9.0
High-Financial Risk (8)	28.9

Betas (Levered)

	Raw (OLS)	Blume Adjusted	Peer Group	Vasicek Adjusted	Sum	Downside
Median	1.39	1.25	1.36	1.37	1.01	1.80
SIC Composite	1.40	1.26	1.36	1.39	1.28	1.77
Large Composite	1.42	1.27	1.36	1.38	1.37	1.83
Small Composite	1.27	1.18	1.36	1.31	0.86	1.64
High Financial Risk	1.72	1.47	1.36	1.67	1.61	1.89

Betas (Unlevered)

	Raw (OLS)	Blume Adjusted	Peer Group	Vasicek Adjusted	Sum	Downside
Median	1.22	1.09	1.28	1.20	0.96	1.55
SIC Composite	1.16	1.04	1.12	1.15	1.06	1.46
Large Composite	1.17	1.05	1.12	1.14	1.12	1.50
Small Composite	–	–	–	–	–	–
High Financial Risk	0.92	0.81	0.76	0.89	0.87	0.99

Equity Valuation Multiples

	Price/Sales Latest	5-Yr Avg	Price/Earnings Latest	5-Yr Avg	Market/Book Latest	5-Yr Avg
Median	1.8	1.7	24.3	27.7	2.1	2.0
SIC Composite	2.0	1.2	17.9	18.1	3.1	2.2
Large Composite	2.0	1.2	16.4	16.8	3.1	2.1
Small Composite	1.5	1.4	22.2	40.8	1.2	1.2
High Financial Risk	0.9	0.8	–	–	–	4.9

Enterprise Valuation (EV) Multiples

	EV/Sales Latest	5-Yr Avg	EV/EBITDA Latest	5-Yr Avg
Median	1.4	1.2	9.9	9.8
SIC Composite	1.8	1.1	9.4	6.2
Large Composite	1.8	1.0	9.0	5.8
Small Composite	0.9	0.9	8.7	11.6
High Financial Risk	1.9	1.7	13.0	13.4

Enterprise Valuation SIC Composite

Latest: EV/Sales 1.8, EV/EBITDA 9.4
5-Yr Avg: EV/Sales 1.1, EV/EBITDA 6.2

Fama-French (F-F) 5-Factor Model

	F-F Beta	SMB Premium	HML Premium	RMW Premium	CMA Premium
Median	1.6	3.6	5.3	1.4	-8.0
SIC Composite	1.4	-0.8	1.3	-0.7	-3.5
Large Composite	1.4	-1.3	1.2	-0.5	-0.7
Small Composite	1.1	4.2	5.8	-1.5	-2.2
High Financial Risk	–	–	–	–	–

Leverage Ratios (%)

	Debt/MV Equity Latest	5-Yr Avg	Debt/Total Capital Latest	5-Yr Avg
Median	7.7	8.1	7.2	7.5
SIC Composite	23.2	23.7	18.8	19.2
Large Composite	23.5	24.9	19.0	19.9
Small Composite	0.0	0.0	0.0	0.0
High Financial Risk	140.8	127.6	58.5	56.1

Cost of Debt

	Cost of Debt (%) Latest
Median	6.1
SIC Composite	4.9
Large Composite	4.7
Small Composite	–
High Financial Risk	7.0

Capital Structure

SIC Composite (%) Latest
D/TC: 18.8
E/TC: 81.2

Cost of Equity Capital (%)

	CRSP Deciles CAPM	CAPM +Size Prem	Build-Up	Risk Premium Report CAPM +Size Prem	Build-Up	Discounted Cash Flow 1-Stage	3-Stage	Fama-French 5-Factor Model
Median	11.0	12.3	12.5	13.6	13.7	9.0	9.8	14.7
SIC Composite	11.1	11.4	11.2	11.8	9.8	11.7	10.6	7.6
Large Composite	11.1	11.2	11.0	11.8	9.2	11.3	10.6	10.0
Small Composite	10.7	14.2	14.4	14.1	16.5	9.6	7.2	15.5
High Financial Risk	–	–	–	21.9	21.6	–	–	–

Cost of Equity Capital (%) SIC Composite
Avg CRSP 11.3, Avg RPR 10.8, 1-Stage 11.7, 3-Stage 10.6, 5-Factor Model 7.6

Weighted Average Cost of Capital (WACC) (%)

	CRSP Deciles CAPM	CAPM +Size Prem	Build-Up	Risk Premium Report CAPM +Size Prem	Build-Up	Discounted Cash Flow 1-Stage	3-Stage	Fama-French 5-Factor Model
Median	10.2	11.1	11.9	12.6	13.2	9.0	8.8	12.1
SIC Composite	9.9	10.1	10.0	10.5	8.8	10.4	9.5	7.0
Large Composite	9.9	9.9	9.8	10.5	8.3	10.0	9.5	9.0
Small Composite	10.7	14.2	14.4	14.1	16.5	9.6	7.2	15.5
High Financial Risk	–	–	–	12.4	12.3	–	–	–

WACC (%) SIC Composite
Low 7.0, High 10.5, Average 9.5, Median 10.0

© 2017 Duff & Phelps. All Rights Reserved. Duff & Phelps has used the utmost care in compiling the data presented herein, but cannot guarantee the accuracy, completeness, or timeliness of the information.

Data Updated Through March 31, 2017

358

Number of Companies: 5
Refrigeration and Service Industry Machinery

Industry Description
Establishments primarily engaged in automatic vending machines; commercial laundry, dry-cleaning and pressing machines; air conditioning and warm air heating equipment and commercial industrial refrigeration equipment; measuring and dispensing pumps; service industry machinery, not elsewhere classified.

Sales (in millions)

Three Largest Companies
Lennox International Inc.	$3,641.6
Middleby Corp.	2,267.9
SPX Corp.	1,472.3

Three Smallest Companies
SPX Corp.	$1,472.3
Tennant Co.	808.6
AAON Inc.	384.0

Annualized Monthly Performance Statistics (%)

Industry	Geometric Mean	Arithmetic Mean	Standard Deviation
1-year	29.0	30.9	23.8
3-year	13.1	15.2	22.6
5-year	22.1	24.1	22.9

S&P 500 Index	Geometric Mean	Arithmetic Mean	Standard Deviation
1-year	17.2	17.4	7.2
3-year	10.4	10.9	11.5
5-year	13.3	13.9	11.5

Total Assets (in millions)

Three Largest Companies
Middleby Corp.	$2,917.1
SPX Corp.	1,912.5
Lennox International Inc.	1,760.3

Three Smallest Companies
Lennox International Inc.	$1,760.3
Tennant Co.	470.0
AAON Inc.	256.5

Return Ratios (%)

	Return on Assets Latest	Return on Assets 5-Yr Avg	Return on Equity Latest	Return on Equity 5-Yr Avg	Dividend Yield Latest	Dividend Yield 5-Yr Avg
Median (5)	10.3	9.5	21.7	19.2	0.8	1.2
SIC Composite (5)	9.2	5.8	3.5	3.8	0.6	0.8
Large Composite (–)	–	–	–	–	–	–
Small Composite (–)	–	–	–	–	–	–
High-Financial Risk (–)	–	–	–	–	–	–

Liquidity Ratio / Profitability Ratio (%) / Growth Rates (%)

	Current Ratio Latest	Current Ratio 5-Yr Avg	Operating Margin Latest	Operating Margin 5-Yr Avg	Long-term EPS Analyst Estimates
Median (5)	1.7	1.7	12.5	10.0	14.8
SIC Composite (5)	1.4	1.5	13.2	10.1	14.5
Large Composite (–)	–	–	–	–	–
Small Composite (–)	–	–	–	–	–
High-Financial Risk (–)	–	–	–	–	–

Betas (Levered)

	Raw (OLS)	Blume Adjusted	Peer Group	Vasicek Adjusted	Sum	Downside
Median	1.09	1.06	1.36	1.19	1.20	1.52
SIC Composite	1.32	1.21	1.36	1.33	1.22	1.27
Large Composite	–	–	–	–	–	–
Small Composite	–	–	–	–	–	–
High Financial Risk	–	–	–	–	–	–

Betas (Unlevered)

	Raw (OLS)	Blume Adjusted	Peer Group	Vasicek Adjusted	Sum	Downside
Median	1.00	1.01	1.27	1.17	1.12	1.26
SIC Composite	1.22	1.12	1.25	1.23	1.12	1.17
Large Composite	–	–	–	–	–	–
Small Composite	–	–	–	–	–	–
High Financial Risk	–	–	–	–	–	–

Equity Valuation Multiples

	Price/Sales Latest	Price/Sales 5-Yr Avg	Price/Earnings Latest	Price/Earnings 5-Yr Avg	Market/Book Latest	Market/Book 5-Yr Avg
Median	2.0	1.4	27.6	26.1	5.8	4.7
SIC Composite	2.2	1.5	28.4	26.6	9.3	4.7
Large Composite	–	–	–	–	–	–
Small Composite	–	–	–	–	–	–
High Financial Risk	–	–	–	–	–	–

Enterprise Valuation (EV) Multiples

	EV/Sales Latest	EV/Sales 5-Yr Avg	EV/EBITDA Latest	EV/EBITDA 5-Yr Avg
Median	2.2	1.6	15.3	12.9
SIC Composite	2.4	1.7	15.9	13.4
Large Composite	–	–	–	–
Small Composite	–	–	–	–
High Financial Risk	–	–	–	–

Enterprise Valuation SIC Composite: EV/Sales Latest 2.4, 5-Yr Avg 1.7; EV/EBITDA Latest 15.9, 5-Yr Avg 13.4

Fama-French (F-F) 5-Factor Model

	F-F Beta	SMB Premium	HML Premium	RMW Premium	CMA Premium
Median	0.8	5.9	-0.5	1.5	-1.0
SIC Composite	1.2	3.7	-0.9	-0.3	-0.6
Large Composite	–	–	–	–	–
Small Composite	–	–	–	–	–
High Financial Risk	–	–	–	–	–

Leverage Ratios (%)

	Debt/MV Equity Latest	Debt/MV Equity 5-Yr Avg	Debt/Total Capital Latest	Debt/Total Capital 5-Yr Avg
Median	9.3	11.8	8.5	10.5
SIC Composite	10.4	16.4	9.4	14.1
Large Composite	–	–	–	–
Small Composite	–	–	–	–
High Financial Risk	–	–	–	–

Cost of Debt

	Cost of Debt (%) Latest
Median	6.1
SIC Composite	5.5
Large Composite	–
Small Composite	–
High Financial Risk	–

Capital Structure

SIC Composite (%) Latest: D/TC 9.4, E/TC 90.6

Cost of Equity Capital (%)

	CRSP Deciles CAPM	CRSP Deciles CAPM +Size Prem	CRSP Deciles Build-Up	Risk Premium Report CAPM +Size Prem	Risk Premium Report Build-Up	Discounted Cash Flow 1-Stage	Discounted Cash Flow 3-Stage	Fama-French 5-Factor Model
Median	10.1	11.8	12.6	14.3	14.1	15.4	11.1	14.0
SIC Composite	10.8	11.9	12.0	13.8	13.3	15.1	10.6	11.9
Large Composite	–	–	–	–	–	–	–	–
Small Composite	–	–	–	–	–	–	–	–
High Financial Risk	–	–	–	–	–	–	–	–

Cost of Equity Capital (%) SIC Composite: Avg CRSP 12.0, Avg RPR 13.6, 1-Stage 15.1, 3-Stage 10.6, 5-Factor Model 11.9

Weighted Average Cost of Capital (WACC) (%)

	CRSP Deciles CAPM	CRSP Deciles CAPM +Size Prem	CRSP Deciles Build-Up	Risk Premium Report CAPM +Size Prem	Risk Premium Report Build-Up	Discounted Cash Flow 1-Stage	Discounted Cash Flow 3-Stage	Fama-French 5-Factor Model
Median	9.9	11.6	11.4	12.9	12.4	14.1	10.2	14.0
SIC Composite	10.3	11.3	11.4	13.0	12.6	14.2	10.1	11.3
Large Composite	–	–	–	–	–	–	–	–
Small Composite	–	–	–	–	–	–	–	–
High Financial Risk	–	–	–	–	–	–	–	–

WACC (%) SIC Composite: Low 10.1, High 14.2, Average 12.0, Median 11.4

© 2017 Duff & Phelps. All Rights Reserved. Duff & Phelps has used the utmost care in compiling the data presented herein, but cannot guarantee the accuracy, completeness, or timeliness of the information.

Data Updated Through March 31, 2017

36

Number of Companies: 90
Electronic and Other Electrical Equipment and Components, Except Computer Equipment

Industry Description
This major group includes establishments engaged in manufacturing machinery, apparatus, and supplies for the generation, storage, transmission, transformation, and utilization of electrical energy. Included are the manufacturing of electricity distribution equipment; electrical industrial apparatus; household appliances; electrical lighting and wiring equipment; radio and television receiving equipment; communications equipment; electronic components and accessories; and other electrical equipment and supplies.

Sales (in millions)

Three Largest Companies
Apple Inc.	$215,091.0
Intel Corp.	59,387.0
Whirlpool Corp.	20,718.0

Three Smallest Companies
Espey Mfg. & Electronics Corp.	$27.5
LRAD Corp.	16.4
Interlink Electronics, Inc.	10.5

Annualized Monthly Performance Statistics (%)

Industry	Geometric Mean	Arithmetic Mean	Standard Deviation
1-year	35.0	36.9	23.3
3-year	21.7	23.7	22.8
5-year	14.1	15.9	20.7

Total Assets (in millions)

Three Largest Companies
Apple Inc.	$321,686.0
Intel Corp.	113,327.0
Micron Technology Inc.	27,540.0

Three Smallest Companies
Servotronics Inc.	$34.4
RF Industries, LTD	25.8
Interlink Electronics, Inc.	7.6

S&P 500 Index	Geometric Mean	Arithmetic Mean	Standard Deviation
1-year	17.2	17.4	7.2
3-year	10.4	10.9	11.5
5-year	13.3	13.9	11.5

Return Ratios (%)

	Return on Assets Latest	5-Yr Avg	Return on Equity Latest	5-Yr Avg	Dividend Yield Latest	5-Yr Avg
Median (90)	5.1	5.9	9.7	9.6	0.2	0.3
SIC Composite (90)	10.6	12.6	5.1	6.7	2.0	2.0
Large Composite (9)	11.9	14.2	5.5	7.3	2.1	2.1
Small Composite (9)	4.4	8.3	2.4	5.3	2.2	2.5
High-Financial Risk (20)	-3.2	-2.5	-5.7	-7.2	0.6	0.6

Liquidity Ratio

	Current Ratio Latest	5-Yr Avg
	3.9	3.7
	1.8	1.8
	1.5	1.5
	–	–
	1.8	1.9

Profitability Ratio (%)

	Operating Margin Latest	5-Yr Avg
	9.6	10.0
	21.7	22.6
	23.5	24.6
	9.8	12.6
	2.8	2.8

Growth Rates (%)

	Long-term EPS Analyst Estimates
	10.7
	10.0
	9.3
	17.4
	30.8

Betas (Levered)

	Raw (OLS)	Blume Adjusted	Peer Group	Vasicek Adjusted	Sum	Downside
Median	1.16	1.11	1.20	1.17	1.14	1.46
SIC Composite	1.18	1.12	1.20	1.18	1.15	1.22
Large Composite	1.17	1.11	1.20	1.18	1.14	1.27
Small Composite	0.80	0.88	1.19	0.89	0.92	0.80
High Financial Risk	1.98	1.63	1.19	1.93	2.04	2.13

Betas (Unlevered)

	Raw (OLS)	Blume Adjusted	Peer Group	Vasicek Adjusted	Sum	Downside
Median	1.06	1.00	1.10	1.06	1.04	1.34
SIC Composite	1.06	1.00	1.08	1.06	1.03	1.09
Large Composite	1.05	1.00	1.07	1.05	1.02	1.14
Small Composite	0.80	0.87	1.18	0.88	0.92	0.79
High Financial Risk	1.48	1.24	0.93	1.45	1.52	1.59

Equity Valuation Multiples

	Price/Sales Latest	5-Yr Avg	Price/Earnings Latest	5-Yr Avg	Market/Book Latest	5-Yr Avg
Median	2.1	1.7	29.3	23.3	2.6	2.3
SIC Composite	3.1	2.5	19.8	14.9	4.1	3.3
Large Composite	3.1	2.5	18.0	13.6	4.3	3.5
Small Composite	2.9	2.1	42.2	18.8	2.1	1.8
High Financial Risk	1.3	0.8	–	–	4.0	2.4

Enterprise Valuation (EV) Multiples

	EV/Sales Latest	5-Yr Avg	EV/EBITDA Latest	5-Yr Avg
Median	1.9	1.7	12.1	10.8
SIC Composite	3.2	2.5	10.9	8.4
Large Composite	3.2	2.5	10.4	8.0
Small Composite	2.4	1.6	18.7	10.4
High Financial Risk	1.7	1.1	20.7	14.1

Enterprise Valuation SIC Composite
EV/Sales: 3.2 (Latest), 2.5 (5-Yr Avg)
EV/EBITDA: 10.9 (Latest), 8.4 (5-Yr Avg)

Fama-French (F-F) 5-Factor Model

	F-F Beta	SMB Premium	HML Premium	RMW Premium	CMA Premium
Median	0.9	2.5	0.6	-0.4	0.0
SIC Composite	1.2	1.4	1.0	4.7	-6.8
Large Composite	1.2	1.1	1.1	5.7	7.6
Small Composite	0.7	3.2	-0.6	1.2	0.9
High Financial Risk	–	–	–	–	–

Leverage Ratios (%)

	Debt/MV Equity Latest	5-Yr Avg	Debt/Total Capital Latest	5-Yr Avg
Median	12.5	8.8	11.2	8.1
SIC Composite	12.3	10.1	11.0	9.1
Large Composite	12.2	9.5	10.9	8.7
Small Composite	0.9	1.0	0.9	1.0
High Financial Risk	43.0	70.3	30.1	41.3

Cost of Debt

	Cost of Debt (%) Latest
	6.1
	4.5
	4.2
	7.1
	6.9

Capital Structure
SIC Composite (%) Latest
D/TC: 11.0
E/TC: 89.0

Cost of Equity Capital (%)

	CRSP Deciles CAPM	CAPM +Size Prem	Build-Up	Risk Premium Report CAPM +Size Prem	Build-Up	Discounted Cash Flow 1-Stage	3-Stage	Fama-French 5-Factor Model
Median	10.0	12.0	11.8	14.3	14.2	12.0	9.6	11.0
SIC Composite	10.0	10.2	10.3	11.1	9.8	11.7	11.9	10.3
Large Composite	10.0	10.0	10.1	10.6	9.1	11.2	12.3	25.5
Small Composite	8.4	12.5	14.2	14.3	16.4	18.1	14.0	12.2
High Financial Risk	–	–	–	28.2	25.5	–	–	–

Cost of Equity Capital (%) SIC Composite
Avg CRSP: 10.2; Avg RPR: 10.4; 1-Stage: 11.7; 3-Stage: 11.9; 5-Factor Model: 10.3

Weighted Average Cost of Capital (WACC) (%)

	CRSP Deciles CAPM	CAPM +Size Prem	Build-Up	Risk Premium Report CAPM +Size Prem	Build-Up	Discounted Cash Flow 1-Stage	3-Stage	Fama-French 5-Factor Model
Median	9.3	11.1	11.1	13.2	13.0	11.0	9.1	10.6
SIC Composite	9.3	9.4	9.5	10.2	9.1	10.8	11.0	9.6
Large Composite	9.2	9.2	9.3	9.7	8.4	10.3	11.3	23.0
Small Composite	8.3	12.4	14.1	14.2	16.3	18.0	13.9	12.1
High Financial Risk	–	–	–	21.7	19.9	–	–	–

WACC (%) SIC Composite
Low: 9.1; High: 11.0; Average: 9.9; Median: 9.6

© 2017 Duff & Phelps. All Rights Reserved. Duff & Phelps has used the utmost care in compiling the data presented herein, but cannot guarantee the accuracy, completeness, or timeliness of the information.

Data Updated Through March 31, 2017

362

Number of Companies: 6
Electrical Industrial Apparatus

Industry Description
Establishments primarily engaged in motors and generators; carbon and graphite products; relays and industrial controls; electrical industrial apparatus, not elsewhere classified.

Sales (in millions)

Three Largest Companies
Regal Beloit Corporation	$3,224.5
Woodward, Inc.	2,023.1
Generac Holdings Inc.	1,444.5

Three Smallest Companies
Franklin Electric Co. Inc.	$949.9
Allied Motion Technologies	232.4
Servotronics Inc.	36.7

Total Assets (in millions)

Three Largest Companies
Regal Beloit Corporation	$4,358.5
Woodward, Inc.	2,642.4
Generac Holdings Inc.	1,861.7

Three Smallest Companies
Franklin Electric Co. Inc.	$1,039.9
Allied Motion Technologies	166.1
Servotronics Inc.	34.4

Annualized Monthly Performance Statistics (%)

Industry	Geometric Mean	Arithmetic Mean	Standard Deviation
1-year	21.5	23.0	20.1
3-year	2.1	4.6	23.6
5-year	10.4	12.5	22.3

S&P 500 Index	Geometric Mean	Arithmetic Mean	Standard Deviation
1-year	17.2	17.4	7.2
3-year	10.4	10.9	11.5
5-year	13.3	13.9	11.5

Return Ratios (%)

	Return on Assets Latest	5-Yr Avg	Return on Equity Latest	5-Yr Avg	Dividend Yield Latest	5-Yr Avg
Median (6)	6.8	7.2	16.2	13.3	0.9	1.1
SIC Composite (6)	5.7	5.6	4.8	4.8	0.8	2.2
Large Composite (–)	–	–	–	–	–	–
Small Composite (–)	–	–	–	–	–	–
High-Financial Risk (–)	–	–	–	–	–	–

Liquidity Ratio

	Current Ratio Latest	5-Yr Avg
	2.2	2.6
	2.2	2.6

Profitability Ratio (%)

	Operating Margin Latest	5-Yr Avg
	10.7	11.0
	11.6	12.4

Growth Rates (%)

	Long-term EPS Analyst Estimates
	8.1
	9.3

Betas (Levered)

	Raw (OLS)	Blume Adjusted	Peer Group	Vasicek Adjusted	Sum	Downside
Median	1.49	1.32	1.20	1.38	1.34	1.46
SIC Composite	1.39	1.25	1.20	1.35	1.44	1.40
Large Composite	–	–	–	–	–	–
Small Composite	–	–	–	–	–	–
High Financial Risk	–	–	–	–	–	–

Betas (Unlevered)

	Raw (OLS)	Blume Adjusted	Peer Group	Vasicek Adjusted	Sum	Downside
Median	1.16	1.04	1.02	1.09	1.21	1.26
SIC Composite	1.16	1.05	1.01	1.13	1.19	1.17
Large Composite	–	–	–	–	–	–
Small Composite	–	–	–	–	–	–
High Financial Risk	–	–	–	–	–	–

Equity Valuation Multiples

	Price/Sales Latest	5-Yr Avg	Price/Earnings Latest	5-Yr Avg	Market/Book Latest	5-Yr Avg
Median	1.3	1.2	19.6	20.0	2.9	2.6
SIC Composite	1.5	1.4	20.9	20.7	2.7	2.4
Large Composite	–	–	–	–	–	–
Small Composite	–	–	–	–	–	–
High Financial Risk	–	–	–	–	–	–

Enterprise Valuation (EV) Multiples

	EV/Sales Latest	5-Yr Avg	EV/EBITDA Latest	5-Yr Avg
Median	1.8	1.5	10.9	10.3
SIC Composite	1.9	1.7	11.8	10.2
Large Composite	–	–	–	–
Small Composite	–	–	–	–
High Financial Risk	–	–	–	–

Enterprise Valuation SIC Composite
- EV/EBITDA: Latest 11.8, 5-Yr Avg 10.2
- EV/Sales: Latest 1.9, 5-Yr Avg 1.7

Fama-French (F-F) 5-Factor Model

	Fama-French (F-F) Components
	F-F Beta	SMB Premium	HML Premium	RMW Premium	CMA Premium
Median	1.4	4.4	-0.4	1.9	3.9
SIC Composite	1.2	4.8	0.0	1.1	3.8
Large Composite	–	–	–	–	–
Small Composite	–	–	–	–	–
High Financial Risk	–	–	–	–	–

Leverage Ratios (%)

	Debt/MV Equity Latest	5-Yr Avg	Debt/Total Capital Latest	5-Yr Avg
Median	26.9	26.5	20.8	20.8
SIC Composite	28.6	28.5	22.2	22.2
Large Composite	–	–	–	–
Small Composite	–	–	–	–
High Financial Risk	–	–	–	–

Cost of Debt

	Cost of Debt (%) Latest
Median	7.1
SIC Composite	6.9

Capital Structure

SIC Composite (%) Latest
- D/TC: 22.2
- E/TC: 77.8

Cost of Equity Capital (%)

	CRSP Deciles			Risk Premium Report		Discounted Cash Flow		Fama-French
	CAPM	CAPM +Size Prem	Build-Up	CAPM +Size Prem	Build-Up	1-Stage	3-Stage	5-Factor Model
Median	11.1	12.7	11.8	14.8	13.7	8.6	9.9	21.3
SIC Composite	10.9	12.4	11.6	15.0	13.3	10.1	10.0	20.0
Large Composite	–	–	–	–	–	–	–	–
Small Composite	–	–	–	–	–	–	–	–
High Financial Risk	–	–	–	–	–	–	–	–

Cost of Equity Capital (%) SIC Composite
- Avg CRSP: 12.0
- Avg RPR: 14.2
- 1-Stage: 10.1
- 3-Stage: 10.0
- 5-Factor Model: 20.0

Weighted Average Cost of Capital (WACC) (%)

	CRSP Deciles			Risk Premium Report		Discounted Cash Flow		Fama-French
	CAPM	CAPM +Size Prem	Build-Up	CAPM +Size Prem	Build-Up	1-Stage	3-Stage	5-Factor Model
Median	10.0	11.1	10.8	13.6	12.6	8.1	9.3	17.1
SIC Composite	9.9	11.1	10.4	13.1	11.8	9.3	9.2	17.0
Large Composite	–	–	–	–	–	–	–	–
Small Composite	–	–	–	–	–	–	–	–
High Financial Risk	–	–	–	–	–	–	–	–

WACC (%) SIC Composite
- Low: 9.2
- High: 17.0
- Average: 11.7
- Median: 11.1

© 2017 Duff & Phelps. All Rights Reserved. Duff & Phelps has used the utmost care in compiling the data presented herein, but cannot guarantee the accuracy, completeness, or timeliness of the information.

Data Updated Through March 31, 2017

3621

Number of Companies: 5
Motors and Generators

Industry Description
Establishments primarily engaged in manufacturing electric motors (except engine starting motors) and power generators; motor generator sets; railway motors and control equipment; and motors, generators, and control equipment for gasoline, electric, and oil-electric buses and trucks.

Sales (in millions)

Three Largest Companies
Regal Beloit Corporation	$3,224.5
Generac Holdings Inc.	1,444.5
Franklin Electric Co. Inc.	949.9

Three Smallest Companies
Franklin Electric Co. Inc.	$949.9
Allied Motion Technologies	232.4
Servotronics Inc.	36.7

Annualized Monthly Performance Statistics (%)

Industry	Geometric Mean	Arithmetic Mean	Standard Deviation
1-year	17.0	18.8	22.1
3-year	-3.8	-1.1	24.1
5-year	10.4	13.0	24.8

S&P 500 Index	Geometric Mean	Arithmetic Mean	Standard Deviation
1-year	17.2	17.4	7.2
3-year	10.4	10.9	11.5
5-year	13.3	13.9	11.5

Total Assets (in millions)

Three Largest Companies
Regal Beloit Corporation	$4,358.5
Generac Holdings Inc.	1,861.7
Franklin Electric Co. Inc.	1,039.9

Three Smallest Companies
Franklin Electric Co. Inc.	$1,039.9
Allied Motion Technologies	166.1
Servotronics Inc.	34.4

Return Ratios (%)

	Return on Assets Latest	5-Yr Avg	Return on Equity Latest	5-Yr Avg	Dividend Yield Latest	5-Yr Avg
Median (5)	6.7	7.0	17.7	12.9	1.1	1.3
SIC Composite (5)	5.3	5.1	5.0	4.7	0.9	2.8
Large Composite (–)	–	–	–	–	–	–
Small Composite (–)	–	–	–	–	–	–
High-Financial Risk (–)	–	–	–	–	–	–

Liquidity Ratio

	Current Ratio Latest	5-Yr Avg
Median (5)	2.2	2.6
SIC Composite (5)	2.3	2.6
Large Composite	–	–
Small Composite	–	–
High-Financial Risk	–	–

Profitability Ratio (%)

	Operating Margin Latest	5-Yr Avg
Median	9.8	10.1
SIC Composite	11.3	12.4
Large Composite	–	–
Small Composite	–	–
High-Financial Risk	–	–

Growth Rates (%)

	Long-term EPS Analyst Estimates
Median	8.1
SIC Composite	7.6
Large Composite	–
Small Composite	–
High-Financial Risk	–

Betas (Levered)

	Raw (OLS)	Blume Adjusted	Peer Group	Vasicek Adjusted	Sum	Downside
Median	1.50	1.32	1.19	1.40	1.31	1.43
SIC Composite	1.45	1.29	1.19	1.39	1.46	1.43
Large Composite	–	–	–	–	–	–
Small Composite	–	–	–	–	–	–
High Financial Risk	–	–	–	–	–	–

Betas (Unlevered)

	Raw (OLS)	Blume Adjusted	Peer Group	Vasicek Adjusted	Sum	Downside
Median	1.27	1.13	0.96	1.12	1.23	1.25
SIC Composite	1.16	1.05	0.97	1.12	1.17	1.15
Large Composite	–	–	–	–	–	–
Small Composite	–	–	–	–	–	–
High Financial Risk	–	–	–	–	–	–

Equity Valuation Multiples

	Price/Sales Latest	5-Yr Avg	Price/Earnings Latest	5-Yr Avg	Market/Book Latest	5-Yr Avg
Median	1.1	0.9	17.1	21.2	2.8	2.7
SIC Composite	1.3	1.3	20.0	21.5	2.4	2.3
Large Composite	–	–	–	–	–	–
Small Composite	–	–	–	–	–	–
High Financial Risk	–	–	–	–	–	–

Enterprise Valuation (EV) Multiples

	EV/Sales Latest	5-Yr Avg	EV/EBITDA Latest	5-Yr Avg
Median	1.4	1.2	9.5	9.5
SIC Composite	1.7	1.6	11.0	9.8
Large Composite	–	–	–	–
Small Composite	–	–	–	–
High Financial Risk	–	–	–	–

Enterprise Valuation SIC Composite
- EV/Sales: Latest 1.7, 5-Yr Avg 1.6
- EV/EBITDA: Latest 11.0, 5-Yr Avg 9.8

Fama-French (F-F) 5-Factor Model

	F-F Beta	SMB Premium	HML Premium	RMW Premium	CMA Premium
Median	1.4	4.4	-0.4	1.9	3.9
SIC Composite	1.3	4.4	-0.5	1.6	5.7
Large Composite	–	–	–	–	–
Small Composite	–	–	–	–	–
High Financial Risk	–	–	–	–	–

Leverage Ratios (%)

	Debt/MV Equity Latest	5-Yr Avg	Debt/Total Capital Latest	5-Yr Avg
Median	36.4	32.0	26.7	24.2
SIC Composite	34.4	31.6	25.6	24.0
Large Composite	–	–	–	–
Small Composite	–	–	–	–
High Financial Risk	–	–	–	–

Cost of Debt

	Cost of Debt (%) Latest
Median	7.1
SIC Composite	7.1
Large Composite	–
Small Composite	–
High Financial Risk	–

Capital Structure

SIC Composite (%) Latest
- D/TC: 25.6
- E/TC: 74.4

Cost of Equity Capital (%)

	CRSP Deciles CAPM	CAPM +Size Prem	Build-Up	Risk Premium Report CAPM +Size Prem	Build-Up	Discounted Cash Flow 1-Stage	3-Stage	Fama-French 5-Factor Model
Median	11.2	12.8	11.8	14.9	13.9	8.0	11.0	21.3
SIC Composite	11.1	12.8	11.8	15.2	13.4	8.5	10.3	21.9
Large Composite	–	–	–	–	–	–	–	–
Small Composite	–	–	–	–	–	–	–	–
High Financial Risk	–	–	–	–	–	–	–	–

Cost of Equity Capital (%) SIC Composite
- Avg CRSP: 12.3
- Avg RPR: 14.3
- 1-Stage: 8.5
- 3-Stage: 10.3
- 5-Factor Model: 21.9

Weighted Average Cost of Capital (WACC) (%)

	CRSP Deciles CAPM	CAPM +Size Prem	Build-Up	Risk Premium Report CAPM +Size Prem	Build-Up	Discounted Cash Flow 1-Stage	3-Stage	Fama-French 5-Factor Model
Median	10.1	11.6	11.3	13.9	13.2	7.4	9.6	18.0
SIC Composite	9.9	11.2	10.4	13.0	11.6	8.0	9.3	18.0
Large Composite	–	–	–	–	–	–	–	–
Small Composite	–	–	–	–	–	–	–	–
High Financial Risk	–	–	–	–	–	–	–	–

WACC (%) SIC Composite
- Low: 8.0
- High: 18.0
- Average: 11.6
- Median: 11.2

© 2017 Duff & Phelps. All Rights Reserved. Duff & Phelps has used the utmost care in compiling the data presented herein, but cannot guarantee the accuracy, completeness, or timeliness of the information.

Data Updated Through March 31, 2017

366

Number of Companies: 11
Communications Equipment

Industry Description
Establishments primarily engaged in manufacturing wire telephone and telegraph equipment; radio and television broadcasting and communications equipment; communications and related equipment, not elsewhere classified.

Sales (in millions)

Three Largest Companies
Apple Inc.	$215,091.0
EchoStar Corporation	3,056.7
Plantronics, Inc.	856.9

Three Smallest Companies
Napco Security Technologies, Inc.	$82.5
ClearOne Inc.	48.6
RELM Wireless Corp.	29.7

Annualized Monthly Performance Statistics (%)

Industry	Geometric Mean	Arithmetic Mean	Standard Deviation
1-year	34.4	38.0	32.9
3-year	25.1	28.3	29.2
5-year	12.9	16.1	27.8

Total Assets (in millions)

Three Largest Companies
Apple Inc.	$321,686.0
EchoStar Corporation	9,008.9
Plantronics, Inc.	933.4

Three Smallest Companies
ClearOne Inc.	$88.1
Napco Security Technologies, Inc.	64.8
RELM Wireless Corp.	39.4

S&P 500 Index	Geometric Mean	Arithmetic Mean	Standard Deviation
1-year	17.2	17.4	7.2
3-year	10.4	10.9	11.5
5-year	13.3	13.9	11.5

Return Ratios (%)

	Return on Assets Latest	5-Yr Avg	Return on Equity Latest	5-Yr Avg	Dividend Yield Latest	5-Yr Avg
Median (11)	5.4	9.3	7.3	11.4	0.9	0.6
SIC Composite (11)	13.8	17.2	6.0	7.6	2.0	1.9
Large Composite (3)	13.9	17.2	6.0	7.6	2.0	1.9
Small Composite (3)	4.8	7.6	2.7	5.8	0.7	0.5
High-Financial Risk (5)	-0.7	-2.8	-0.7	-2.7	0.0	0.0

Liquidity Ratio

	Current Ratio Latest	5-Yr Avg
Median (11)	–	4.2
SIC Composite (11)	1.4	1.4
Large Composite (3)	1.4	1.3
Small Composite (3)	–	5.0
High-Financial Risk (5)	2.1	2.2

Profitability Ratio (%)

	Operating Margin Latest	5-Yr Avg
Median (11)	8.3	10.3
SIC Composite (11)	27.3	29.4
Large Composite (3)	27.4	29.6
Small Composite (3)	7.3	8.4
High-Financial Risk (5)	2.7	0.2

Growth Rates (%)

	Long-term EPS Analyst Estimates
Median (11)	9.2
SIC Composite (11)	9.2
Large Composite (3)	9.2
Small Composite (3)	9.2
High-Financial Risk (5)	19.6

Betas (Levered)

	Raw (OLS)	Blume Adjusted	Peer Group	Vasicek Adjusted	Sum	Downside
Median	1.18	1.12	1.20	1.19	1.09	1.44
SIC Composite	1.18	1.12	1.20	1.18	1.09	1.34
Large Composite	1.18	1.12	1.20	1.19	1.09	1.34
Small Composite	0.75	0.85	1.20	0.87	0.53	0.80
High Financial Risk	1.44	1.28	1.17	1.37	0.65	1.88

Betas (Unlevered)

	Raw (OLS)	Blume Adjusted	Peer Group	Vasicek Adjusted	Sum	Downside
Median	1.06	1.01	1.16	1.06	0.98	1.34
SIC Composite	1.06	1.00	1.07	1.06	0.98	1.20
Large Composite	1.06	1.00	1.07	1.06	0.97	1.20
Small Composite	0.75	0.84	1.19	0.86	0.52	0.79
High Financial Risk	1.17	1.05	0.97	1.12	0.57	1.50

Equity Valuation Multiples

	Price/Sales Latest	5-Yr Avg	Price/Earnings Latest	5-Yr Avg	Market/Book Latest	5-Yr Avg
Median	2.1	1.9	33.2	25.0	2.1	2.4
SIC Composite	3.5	2.9	16.6	13.2	4.8	4.0
Large Composite	3.5	2.9	16.6	13.2	4.8	4.0
Small Composite	2.2	1.6	37.6	17.2	2.1	1.6
High Financial Risk	1.2	1.1	–	–	3.2	3.4

Enterprise Valuation (EV) Multiples

	EV/Sales Latest	5-Yr Avg	EV/EBITDA Latest	5-Yr Avg
Median	2.1	1.7	13.3	12.9
SIC Composite	3.6	2.9	10.7	8.5
Large Composite	3.6	2.9	10.7	8.5
Small Composite	2.0	1.4	20.1	12.3
High Financial Risk	1.2	1.2	16.2	21.1

Enterprise Valuation SIC Composite
EV/Sales: 3.6 Latest, 2.9 5-Yr Avg
EV/EBITDA: 10.7 Latest, 8.5 5-Yr Avg

Fama-French (F-F) 5-Factor Model

	F-F Beta	SMB Premium	HML Premium	RMW Premium	CMA Premium
Median	1.2	1.3	0.9	7.6	-10.1
SIC Composite	1.2	1.4	0.9	7.5	-10.0
Large Composite	1.2	1.3	0.9	7.6	10.1
Small Composite	0.7	2.1	-0.9	-1.0	2.3
High Financial Risk	–	–	–	–	–

Leverage Ratios (%)

	Debt/MV Equity Latest	5-Yr Avg	Debt/Total Capital Latest	5-Yr Avg
Median	4.9	5.2	4.7	5.0
SIC Composite	11.9	7.5	10.7	7.0
Large Composite	12.0	7.5	10.7	7.0
Small Composite	1.4	5.2	1.4	5.0
High Financial Risk	30.8	38.1	23.5	27.6

Cost of Debt

	Cost of Debt (%) Latest
Median	7.1
SIC Composite	4.0
Large Composite	4.0
Small Composite	7.1
High Financial Risk	6.2

Capital Structure

SIC Composite (%) Latest
D/TC: 10.7
E/TC: 89.3

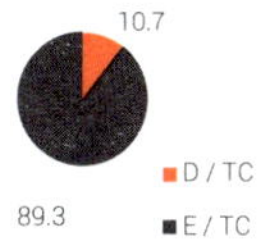

Cost of Equity Capital (%)

	CRSP Deciles CAPM	CAPM +Size Prem	Build-Up	Risk Premium Report CAPM +Size Prem	Build-Up	Discounted Cash Flow 1-Stage	3-Stage	Fama-French 5-Factor Model
Median	10.0	13.2	12.2	14.6	15.4	9.2	10.2	9.8
SIC Composite	10.0	10.0	10.1	10.1	8.8	11.0	13.1	9.9
Large Composite	10.0	10.0	10.1	10.0	8.7	11.0	13.1	30.0
Small Composite	8.3	13.9	15.7	12.3	16.7	9.8	10.3	9.8
High Financial Risk	–	–	–	21.6	27.1	–	–	–

Cost of Equity Capital (%) SIC Composite
Avg CRSP: 10.1, Avg RPR: 9.4, 1-Stage: 11.0, 3-Stage: 13.1, 5-Factor Model: 9.9

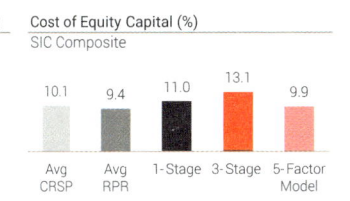

Weighted Average Cost of Capital (WACC) (%)

	CRSP Deciles CAPM	CAPM +Size Prem	Build-Up	Risk Premium Report CAPM +Size Prem	Build-Up	Discounted Cash Flow 1-Stage	3-Stage	Fama-French 5-Factor Model
Median	9.3	11.2	11.2	13.2	13.9	9.2	10.0	9.9
SIC Composite	9.2	9.3	9.3	9.3	8.1	10.1	12.0	9.1
Large Composite	9.2	9.2	9.3	9.3	8.1	10.1	12.0	27.1
Small Composite	8.2	13.8	15.6	12.2	16.5	9.7	10.3	9.7
High Financial Risk	–	–	–	18.0	22.1	–	–	–

WACC (%) SIC Composite
Low 8.1, High 12.0, Average 9.6, Median 9.3

© 2017 Duff & Phelps. All Rights Reserved. Duff & Phelps has used the utmost care in compiling the data presented herein, but cannot guarantee the accuracy, completeness, or timeliness of the information.

Data Updated Through March 31, 2017

3663

Number of Companies: 7
Radio and Television Broadcasting and Communications Equipment

Industry Description
Establishments primarily engaged in manufacturing radio and television broadcasting and communications equipment.

Sales (in millions)

Three Largest Companies
Apple Inc.	$215,091.0
EchoStar Corporation	3,056.7
Ubiquiti Networks, Inc.	666.4

Three Smallest Companies
Calamp Corp.	$280.7
ClearOne Inc.	48.6
RELM Wireless Corp.	29.7

Total Assets (in millions)

Three Largest Companies
Apple Inc.	$321,686.0
EchoStar Corporation	9,008.9
Comtech Telecommunications Co	921.2

Three Smallest Companies
Calamp Corp.	$384.4
ClearOne Inc.	88.1
RELM Wireless Corp.	39.4

Annualized Monthly Performance Statistics (%)

	Industry Geometric Mean	Arithmetic Mean	Standard Deviation		S&P 500 Index Geometric Mean	Arithmetic Mean	Standard Deviation
1-year	34.4	38.1	33.1	1-year	17.2	17.4	7.2
3-year	25.2	28.4	29.3	3-year	10.4	10.9	11.5
5-year	13.0	16.2	28.0	5-year	13.3	13.9	11.5

Return Ratios (%)

	Return on Assets Latest	5-Yr Avg	Return on Equity Latest	5-Yr Avg	Dividend Yield Latest	5-Yr Avg
Median (7)	2.7	11.0	4.0	13.2	1.8	1.1
SIC Composite (7)	13.8	17.2	6.0	7.6	2.0	1.9
Large Composite (–)	–	–	–	–	–	–
Small Composite (–)	–	–	–	–	–	–
High-Financial Risk (–)	–	–	–	–	–	–

Liquidity Ratio

	Current Ratio Latest	5-Yr Avg
Median (7)	–	4.2
SIC Composite (7)	1.4	1.3
Large Composite	–	–
Small Composite	–	–
High-Financial Risk	–	–

Profitability Ratio (%)

	Operating Margin Latest	5-Yr Avg
Median (7)	11.7	10.3
SIC Composite (7)	27.4	29.6
Large Composite	–	–
Small Composite	–	–
High-Financial Risk	–	–

Growth Rates (%)

	Long-term EPS Analyst Estimates
Median (7)	9.2
SIC Composite (7)	9.2
Large Composite	–
Small Composite	–
High-Financial Risk	–

Betas (Levered)

	Raw (OLS)	Blume Adjusted	Peer Group	Vasicek Adjusted	Sum	Downside
Median	1.18	1.12	1.20	1.19	1.09	1.44
SIC Composite	1.18	1.12	1.20	1.19	1.09	1.35
Large Composite	–	–	–	–	–	–
Small Composite	–	–	–	–	–	–
High Financial Risk	–	–	–	–	–	–

Betas (Unlevered)

	Raw (OLS)	Blume Adjusted	Peer Group	Vasicek Adjusted	Sum	Downside
Median	1.06	1.01	1.08	1.07	0.98	1.34
SIC Composite	1.06	1.00	1.07	1.06	0.98	1.20
Large Composite	–	–	–	–	–	–
Small Composite	–	–	–	–	–	–
High Financial Risk	–	–	–	–	–	–

Equity Valuation Multiples

	Price/Sales Latest	5-Yr Avg	Price/Earnings Latest	5-Yr Avg	Market/Book Latest	5-Yr Avg
Median	2.1	1.9	35.2	24.0	2.0	1.7
SIC Composite	3.5	2.9	16.6	13.2	4.8	4.0
Large Composite	–	–	–	–	–	–
Small Composite	–	–	–	–	–	–
High Financial Risk	–	–	–	–	–	–

Enterprise Valuation (EV) Multiples

	EV/Sales Latest	5-Yr Avg	EV/EBITDA Latest	5-Yr Avg
Median	1.9	1.7	11.5	8.6
SIC Composite	3.6	3.0	10.7	8.5
Large Composite	–	–	–	–
Small Composite	–	–	–	–
High Financial Risk	–	–	–	–

Enterprise Valuation SIC Composite
Latest: EV/Sales 3.6, EV/EBITDA 10.7
5-Yr Avg: EV/Sales 3.0, EV/EBITDA 8.5

Fama-French (F-F) 5-Factor Model

Fama-French (F-F) Components

	F-F Beta	SMB Premium	HML Premium	RMW Premium	CMA Premium
Median	1.2	1.3	0.9	7.6	-10.1
SIC Composite	1.2	1.4	0.9	7.5	-10.1
Large Composite	–	–	–	–	–
Small Composite	–	–	–	–	–
High Financial Risk	–	–	–	–	–

Leverage Ratios (%)

	Debt/MV Equity Latest	5-Yr Avg	Debt/Total Capital Latest	5-Yr Avg
Median	11.5	5.2	10.3	5.0
SIC Composite	11.9	7.5	10.7	7.0
Large Composite	–	–	–	–
Small Composite	–	–	–	–
High Financial Risk	–	–	–	–

Cost of Debt

	Cost of Debt (%) Latest
Median	7.1
SIC Composite	4.0
Large Composite	–
Small Composite	–
High Financial Risk	–

Capital Structure

SIC Composite (%) Latest
D/TC: 10.7
E/TC: 89.3

Cost of Equity Capital (%)

	CRSP Deciles CAPM	CAPM +Size Prem	Build-Up	Risk Premium Report CAPM +Size Prem	Build-Up	Discounted Cash Flow 1-Stage	3-Stage	Fama-French 5-Factor Model
Median	10.0	12.7	12.2	14.6	15.4	11.0	10.2	9.8
SIC Composite	10.0	10.0	10.1	10.1	8.7	11.0	13.1	9.9
Large Composite	–	–	–	–	–	–	–	–
Small Composite	–	–	–	–	–	–	–	–
High Financial Risk	–	–	–	–	–	–	–	–

Cost of Equity Capital (%) SIC Composite
Avg CRSP 10.1 | Avg RPR 9.4 | 1-Stage 11.0 | 3-Stage 13.1 | 5-Factor Model 9.9

Weighted Average Cost of Capital (WACC) (%)

	CRSP Deciles CAPM	CAPM +Size Prem	Build-Up	Risk Premium Report CAPM +Size Prem	Build-Up	Discounted Cash Flow 1-Stage	3-Stage	Fama-French 5-Factor Model
Median	9.3	10.3	10.8	13.2	13.2	10.2	9.9	9.9
SIC Composite	9.2	9.2	9.3	9.3	8.1	10.1	12.0	9.2
Large Composite	–	–	–	–	–	–	–	–
Small Composite	–	–	–	–	–	–	–	–
High Financial Risk	–	–	–	–	–	–	–	–

WACC (%) SIC Composite
Low 8.1 — High 12.0
▲ Average 9.6 ♦ Median 9.3

© 2017 Duff & Phelps. All Rights Reserved. Duff & Phelps has used the utmost care in compiling the data presented herein, but cannot guarantee the accuracy, completeness, or timeliness of the information.

Data Updated Through March 31, 2017

367

Number of Companies: 54
Electronic Components and Accessories

Industry Description
Establishments primarily engaged in electron tubes, printed circuit boards, semiconductors and related devices; electronic capacitors; electronic resistors; electronic coils, transformers and other inductors; electronic connectors; electronic components, not elsewhere classified.

Sales (in millions)

Three Largest Companies
Intel Corp.	$59,387.0
Jabil Circuit Inc.	18,353.1
Texas Instruments Inc.	13,370.0

Three Smallest Companies
NVE Corp.	$27.7
Espey Mfg. & Electronics Corp.	27.5
Interlink Electronics, Inc.	10.5

Annualized Monthly Performance Statistics (%)

Industry	Geometric Mean	Arithmetic Mean	Standard Deviation
1-year	39.5	40.7	18.9
3-year	18.7	20.4	20.9
5-year	16.0	17.5	18.9

Total Assets (in millions)

Three Largest Companies
Intel Corp.	$113,327.0
Micron Technology Inc.	27,540.0
Texas Instruments Inc.	16,431.0

Three Smallest Companies
Espey Mfg. & Electronics Corp.	$34.5
RF Industries, LTD	25.8
Interlink Electronics, Inc.	7.6

S&P 500 Index	Geometric Mean	Arithmetic Mean	Standard Deviation
1-year	17.2	17.4	7.2
3-year	10.4	10.9	11.5
5-year	13.3	13.9	11.5

Return Ratios (%)

	Return on Assets Latest	Return on Assets 5-Yr Avg	Return on Equity Latest	Return on Equity 5-Yr Avg	Dividend Yield Latest	Dividend Yield 5-Yr Avg
Median (54)	5.2	5.1	9.7	9.0	0.0	0.0
SIC Composite (54)	7.7	9.0	3.8	5.7	2.0	2.2
Large Composite (5)	8.8	10.2	4.4	6.7	2.3	2.6
Small Composite (5)	8.8	10.6	2.8	3.9	0.9	1.8
High-Financial Risk (11)	-10.7	-7.2	-7.9	-9.6	0.9	0.9

Liquidity Ratio / Profitability Ratio (%) / Growth Rates (%)

	Current Ratio Latest	Current Ratio 5-Yr Avg	Operating Margin Latest	Operating Margin 5-Yr Avg	Long-term EPS Analyst Estimates
Median (54)	4.2	4.2	11.6	10.3	10.8
SIC Composite (54)	2.4	2.6	18.2	18.0	10.6
Large Composite (5)	1.9	2.1	20.6	20.2	9.5
Small Composite (5)	–	–	18.4	20.4	18.1
High-Financial Risk (11)	1.7	1.8	-1.0	0.5	33.1

Betas (Levered)

	Raw (OLS)	Blume Adjusted	Peer Group	Vasicek Adjusted	Sum	Downside
Median	1.13	1.09	1.20	1.15	1.15	1.43
SIC Composite	1.16	1.11	1.20	1.16	1.23	1.25
Large Composite	1.14	1.09	1.20	1.15	1.24	1.34
Small Composite	0.95	0.98	1.20	1.00	1.28	1.03
High Financial Risk	2.25	1.80	1.20	2.14	2.49	2.40

Betas (Unlevered)

	Raw (OLS)	Blume Adjusted	Peer Group	Vasicek Adjusted	Sum	Downside
Median	1.03	0.99	1.10	1.05	1.04	1.31
SIC Composite	1.05	1.00	1.09	1.05	1.11	1.13
Large Composite	1.02	0.98	1.07	1.03	1.11	1.20
Small Composite	–	–	–	–	–	–
High Financial Risk	1.81	1.47	1.00	1.73	2.00	1.93

Equity Valuation Multiples

	Price/Sales Latest	Price/Sales 5-Yr Avg	Price/Earnings Latest	Price/Earnings 5-Yr Avg	Market/Book Latest	Market/Book 5-Yr Avg
Median	2.7	2.4	31.6	24.3	2.8	2.3
SIC Composite	3.2	2.3	26.2	17.7	3.5	2.6
Large Composite	3.2	2.3	22.6	14.9	3.6	2.6
Small Composite	4.5	3.9	36.2	25.7	3.4	2.9
High Financial Risk	1.6	0.8	–	–	4.7	2.6

Enterprise Valuation (EV) Multiples

	EV/Sales Latest	EV/Sales 5-Yr Avg	EV/EBITDA Latest	EV/EBITDA 5-Yr Avg
Median	2.6	1.9	12.6	10.8
SIC Composite	3.2	2.3	11.2	7.9
Large Composite	3.3	2.3	10.0	6.9
Small Composite	4.0	3.5	18.1	14.5
High Financial Risk	1.9	1.1	34.7	18.9

Enterprise Valuation — SIC Composite
Latest: EV/Sales 3.2, EV/EBITDA 11.2
5-Yr Avg: EV/Sales 2.3, EV/EBITDA 7.9

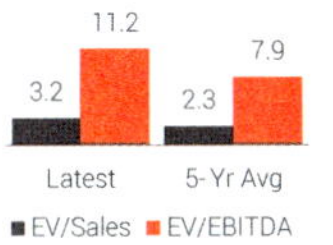

Fama-French (F-F) 5-Factor Model

	F-F Beta	SMB Premium	HML Premium	RMW Premium	CMA Premium
Median	0.8	4.4	-3.3	-2.1	3.8
SIC Composite	1.1	0.9	1.5	0.5	-2.7
Large Composite	1.1	-0.1	1.7	0.7	0.9
Small Composite	0.8	5.0	-2.0	0.2	1.8
High Financial Risk	–	–	–	–	–

Leverage Ratios (%)

	Debt/MV Equity Latest	Debt/MV Equity 5-Yr Avg	Debt/Total Capital Latest	Debt/Total Capital 5-Yr Avg
Median	12.4	8.5	11.0	7.9
SIC Composite	12.1	12.8	10.8	11.4
Large Composite	12.7	14.0	11.2	12.3
Small Composite	0.0	0.0	0.0	0.0
High Financial Risk	29.1	50.2	22.6	33.4

Cost of Debt / Capital Structure

	Cost of Debt (%) Latest	SIC Composite (%) Latest
Median	6.1	
SIC Composite	5.0	D/TC 10.8
Large Composite	4.6	E/TC 89.2
Small Composite	–	
High Financial Risk	6.9	

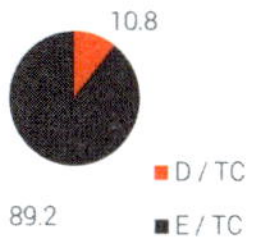

Cost of Equity Capital (%)

	CRSP Deciles CAPM	CRSP Deciles CAPM +Size Prem	CRSP Deciles Build-Up	Risk Premium Report CAPM +Size Prem	Risk Premium Report Build-Up	Discounted Cash Flow 1-Stage	Discounted Cash Flow 3-Stage	Fama-French 5-Factor Model
Median	9.8	11.4	11.6	13.6	13.9	12.3	9.1	10.9
SIC Composite	9.9	10.2	10.4	12.3	10.8	12.3	10.2	9.9
Large Composite	9.8	9.8	10.1	11.6	9.7	11.7	10.5	12.9
Small Composite	9.0	13.0	14.2	16.2	16.4	18.6	12.9	13.0
High Financial Risk	–	–	–	30.0	24.7	–	–	–

Cost of Equity Capital (%) — SIC Composite
Avg CRSP 10.3, Avg RPR 11.5, 1-Stage 12.3, 3-Stage 10.2, 5-Factor Model 9.9

Weighted Average Cost of Capital (WACC) (%)

	CRSP Deciles CAPM	CRSP Deciles CAPM +Size Prem	CRSP Deciles Build-Up	Risk Premium Report CAPM +Size Prem	Risk Premium Report Build-Up	Discounted Cash Flow 1-Stage	Discounted Cash Flow 3-Stage	Fama-French 5-Factor Model
Median	9.3	10.6	11.0	12.5	12.9	11.7	8.8	10.6
SIC Composite	9.3	9.6	9.7	11.4	10.1	11.4	9.5	9.3
Large Composite	9.1	9.1	9.4	10.7	9.1	10.8	9.7	11.9
Small Composite	9.0	13.0	14.2	16.2	16.4	18.6	12.9	13.0
High Financial Risk	–	–	–	24.8	20.6	–	–	–

WACC (%) — SIC Composite
Low 9.3, High 11.4, Average 10.2, Median 9.7

© 2017 Duff & Phelps. All Rights Reserved. Duff & Phelps has used the utmost care in compiling the data presented herein, but cannot guarantee the accuracy, completeness, or timeliness of the information.

Data Updated Through March 31, 2017

3672

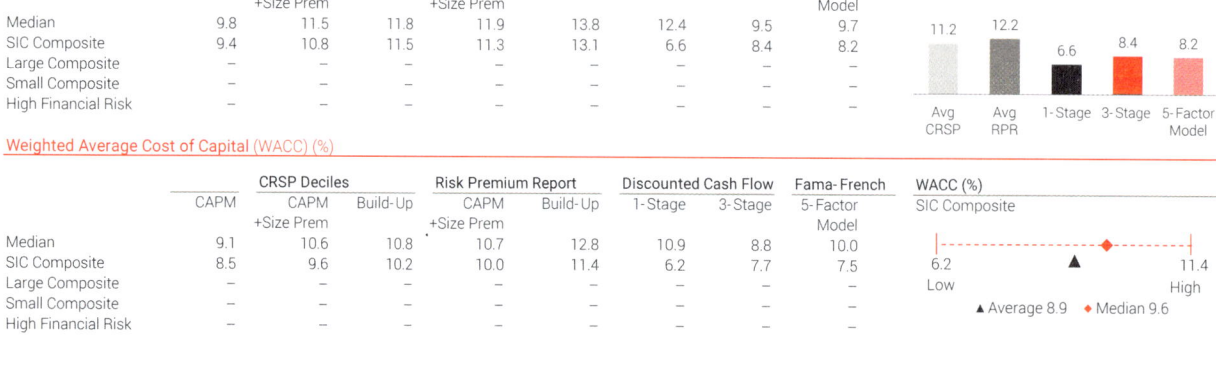

Number of Companies: 7
Printed Circuit Boards

Industry Description
Establishments primarily engaged in manufacturing printed circuit boards.

Sales (in millions)

Three Largest Companies
Jabil Circuit Inc.	$18,353.1
Sanmina Corp.	6,481.2
Plexus Corp.	2,556.0

Three Smallest Companies
Rogers Corp.	$656.3
Sigmatron International Inc.	253.9
Park Electrochemical Corp.	145.9

Annualized Monthly Performance Statistics (%)

Industry
	Geometric Mean	Arithmetic Mean	Standard Deviation
1-year	51.0	53.2	27.7
3-year	16.9	19.7	26.4
5-year	10.4	13.1	24.9

Total Assets (in millions)

Three Largest Companies
Jabil Circuit Inc.	$10,322.7
Sanmina Corp.	3,625.2
Benchmark Electronics Inc.	1,998.7

Three Smallest Companies
Rogers Corp.	$1,056.5
Park Electrochemical Corp.	314.8
Sigmatron International Inc.	136.9

S&P 500 Index
	Geometric Mean	Arithmetic Mean	Standard Deviation
1-year	17.2	17.4	7.2
3-year	10.4	10.9	11.5
5-year	13.3	13.9	11.5

Return Ratios (%)

	Return on Assets Latest	5-Yr Avg	Return on Equity Latest	5-Yr Avg	Dividend Yield Latest	5-Yr Avg
Median (7)	4.4	4.8	7.8	9.4	0.0	0.0
SIC Composite (7)	3.4	4.0	4.7	7.1	0.6	0.7
Large Composite (–)	–	–	–	–	–	–
Small Composite (–)	–	–	–	–	–	–
High-Financial Risk (–)	–	–	–	–	–	–

Liquidity Ratio

	Current Ratio Latest	5-Yr Avg
	2.2	2.3
	1.5	1.6

Profitability Ratio (%)

	Operating Margin Latest	5-Yr Avg
	3.8	3.8
	3.5	3.5

Growth Rates (%)

	Long-term EPS Analyst Estimates
	10.5
	6.1

Betas (Levered)

	Raw (OLS)	Blume Adjusted	Peer Group	Vasicek Adjusted	Sum	Downside
Median	0.95	0.98	1.20	1.14	0.91	1.43
SIC Composite	0.92	0.96	1.20	1.07	0.80	1.53
Large Composite	–	–	–	–	–	–
Small Composite	–	–	–	–	–	–
High Financial Risk	–	–	–	–	–	–

Betas (Unlevered)

	Raw (OLS)	Blume Adjusted	Peer Group	Vasicek Adjusted	Sum	Downside
Median	0.87	0.89	1.08	1.01	0.70	1.21
SIC Composite	0.77	0.80	1.00	0.89	0.68	1.26
Large Composite	–	–	–	–	–	–
Small Composite	–	–	–	–	–	–
High Financial Risk	–	–	–	–	–	–

Equity Valuation Multiples

	Price/Sales Latest	5-Yr Avg	Price/Earnings Latest	5-Yr Avg	Market/Book Latest	5-Yr Avg
Median	0.7	0.5	20.8	16.1	1.9	1.7
SIC Composite	0.4	0.3	21.1	14.0	1.9	1.5
Large Composite	–	–	–	–	–	–
Small Composite	–	–	–	–	–	–
High Financial Risk	–	–	–	–	–	–

Enterprise Valuation (EV) Multiples

	EV/Sales Latest	5-Yr Avg	EV/EBITDA Latest	5-Yr Avg
Median	0.5	0.3	7.7	5.9
SIC Composite	0.5	0.3	7.0	5.6
Large Composite	–	–	–	–
Small Composite	–	–	–	–
High Financial Risk	–	–	–	–

Enterprise Valuation SIC Composite
- EV/Sales: Latest 0.5, 5-Yr Avg 0.3
- EV/EBITDA: Latest 7.0, 5-Yr Avg 5.6

Fama-French (F-F) 5-Factor Model

Fama-French (F-F) Components

	F-F Beta	SMB Premium	HML Premium	RMW Premium	CMA Premium
Median	0.5	4.0	2.9	1.6	-5.2
SIC Composite	0.8	4.6	3.0	0.4	-7.5
Large Composite	–	–	–	–	–
Small Composite	–	–	–	–	–
High Financial Risk	–	–	–	–	–

Leverage Ratios (%)

	Debt/MV Equity Latest	5-Yr Avg	Debt/Total Capital Latest	5-Yr Avg
Median	15.8	20.4	13.7	17.0
SIC Composite	24.8	31.1	19.9	23.7

Cost of Debt

	Cost of Debt (%) Latest
Median	7.1
SIC Composite	5.5

Capital Structure

SIC Composite (%) Latest
- D/TC: 19.9
- E/TC: 80.1

Cost of Equity Capital (%)

	CAPM	CRSP Deciles CAPM +Size Prem	Build-Up	Risk Premium Report CAPM +Size Prem	Build-Up	Discounted Cash Flow 1-Stage	3-Stage	Fama-French 5-Factor Model
Median	9.8	11.5	11.8	11.9	13.8	12.4	9.5	9.7
SIC Composite	9.4	10.8	11.5	11.3	13.1	6.6	8.4	8.2
Large Composite	–	–	–	–	–	–	–	–
Small Composite	–	–	–	–	–	–	–	–
High Financial Risk	–	–	–	–	–	–	–	–

Cost of Equity Capital (%) SIC Composite
- Avg CRSP: 11.2
- Avg RPR: 12.2
- 1-Stage: 6.6
- 3-Stage: 8.4
- 5-Factor Model: 8.2

Weighted Average Cost of Capital (WACC) (%)

	CAPM	CRSP Deciles CAPM +Size Prem	Build-Up	Risk Premium Report CAPM +Size Prem	Build-Up	Discounted Cash Flow 1-Stage	3-Stage	Fama-French 5-Factor Model
Median	9.1	10.6	10.8	10.7	12.8	10.9	8.8	10.0
SIC Composite	8.5	9.6	10.2	10.0	11.4	6.2	7.7	7.5
Large Composite	–	–	–	–	–	–	–	–
Small Composite	–	–	–	–	–	–	–	–
High Financial Risk	–	–	–	–	–	–	–	–

WACC (%) SIC Composite
- Low: 6.2
- High: 11.4
- Average 8.9
- Median 9.6

© 2017 Duff & Phelps. All Rights Reserved. Duff & Phelps has used the utmost care in compiling the data presented herein, but cannot guarantee the accuracy, completeness, or timeliness of the information.

Data Updated Through March 31, 2017

3674

Number of Companies: 34
Semiconductors and Related Devices

Industry Description
Establishments primarily engaged in manufacturing semiconductors and related solid-state devices.

Sales (in millions)

Three Largest Companies
Intel Corp.	$59,387.0
Texas Instruments Inc.	13,370.0
Micron Technology Inc.	12,399.0

Three Smallest Companies
Vishay Precision Group, Inc.	$224.9
Universal Display Corp.	198.9
NVE Corp.	27.7

Total Assets (in millions)

Three Largest Companies
Intel Corp.	$113,327.0
Micron Technology Inc.	27,540.0
Texas Instruments Inc.	16,431.0

Three Smallest Companies
Ultra Clean Holdings Inc.	$380.7
Vishay Precision Group, Inc.	270.5
NVE Corp.	100.9

Annualized Monthly Performance Statistics (%)

Industry	Geometric Mean	Arithmetic Mean	Standard Deviation
1-year	39.8	41.0	19.6
3-year	18.9	20.8	21.8
5-year	16.1	17.7	19.6

S&P 500 Index	Geometric Mean	Arithmetic Mean	Standard Deviation
1-year	17.2	17.4	7.2
3-year	10.4	10.9	11.5
5-year	13.3	13.9	11.5

Return Ratios (%)

	Return on Assets Latest	5-Yr Avg	Return on Equity Latest	5-Yr Avg	Dividend Yield Latest	5-Yr Avg
Median (34)	5.6	6.4	9.9	9.4	0.0	0.0
SIC Composite (34)	8.1	9.6	3.8	5.7	2.1	2.3
Large Composite (3)	8.7	10.7	4.8	6.9	2.6	2.8
Small Composite (3)	6.7	6.0	1.4	2.2	0.0	0.0
High-Financial Risk (–)	–	–	–	–	–	–

Liquidity Ratio

	Current Ratio Latest	5-Yr Avg
Median (34)	4.4	4.4
SIC Composite (34)	2.6	2.7
Large Composite (3)	1.9	2.2
Small Composite (3)	–	–
High-Financial Risk (–)	–	–

Profitability Ratio (%)

	Operating Margin Latest	5-Yr Avg
Median (34)	11.6	11.3
SIC Composite (34)	21.9	21.9
Large Composite (3)	23.8	24.0
Small Composite (3)	22.1	17.0
High-Financial Risk (–)	–	–

Growth Rates (%)

	Long-term EPS Analyst Estimates
Median (34)	11.8
SIC Composite (34)	10.7
Large Composite (3)	9.0
Small Composite (3)	11.9
High-Financial Risk (–)	–

Betas (Levered)

	Raw (OLS)	Blume Adjusted	Peer Group	Vasicek Adjusted	Sum	Downside
Median	1.24	1.16	1.20	1.23	1.19	1.48
SIC Composite	1.18	1.12	1.20	1.18	1.25	1.26
Large Composite	1.13	1.09	1.20	1.14	1.29	1.33
Small Composite	1.46	1.30	1.20	1.27	3.08	2.51
High Financial Risk	–	–	–	–	–	–

Betas (Unlevered)

	Raw (OLS)	Blume Adjusted	Peer Group	Vasicek Adjusted	Sum	Downside
Median	1.13	1.08	1.10	1.13	1.08	1.36
SIC Composite	1.07	1.02	1.08	1.07	1.13	1.14
Large Composite	1.00	0.97	1.06	1.01	1.14	1.18
Small Composite	1.45	1.29	1.19	1.26	3.06	2.50
High Financial Risk	–	–	–	–	–	–

Equity Valuation Multiples

	Price/Sales Latest	5-Yr Avg	Price/Earnings Latest	5-Yr Avg	Market/Book Latest	5-Yr Avg
Median	4.5	3.3	36.9	28.3	3.4	3.0
SIC Composite	3.9	2.8	26.2	17.6	3.6	2.7
Large Composite	3.3	2.6	20.7	14.6	3.1	2.6
Small Composite	10.3	5.7	69.8	46.0	5.8	3.3
High Financial Risk	–	–	–	–	–	–

Enterprise Valuation (EV) Multiples

	EV/Sales Latest	5-Yr Avg	EV/EBITDA Latest	5-Yr Avg
Median	4.4	3.1	15.7	12.3
SIC Composite	3.9	2.8	11.3	7.9
Large Composite	3.5	2.7	9.0	6.8
Small Composite	9.5	4.8	31.7	20.5
High Financial Risk	–	–	–	–

Enterprise Valuation SIC Composite

Latest: EV/Sales 3.9, EV/EBITDA 11.3
5-Yr Avg: EV/Sales 2.8, EV/EBITDA 7.9

Fama-French (F-F) 5-Factor Model

	F-F Beta	SMB Premium	HML Premium	RMW Premium	CMA Premium
Median	0.8	3.1	0.1	-2.0	2.1
SIC Composite	1.2	0.8	1.5	0.5	-2.6
Large Composite	1.1	-0.5	1.0	0.4	0.6
Small Composite	–	–	–	–	–
High Financial Risk	–	–	–	–	–

Leverage Ratios (%)

	Debt/MV Equity Latest	5-Yr Avg	Debt/Total Capital Latest	5-Yr Avg
Median	10.4	7.8	9.4	7.3
SIC Composite	11.8	12.2	10.6	10.9
Large Composite	14.0	13.9	12.3	12.2
Small Composite	0.8	1.1	0.8	1.1
High Financial Risk	–	–	–	–

Cost of Debt

	Cost of Debt (%) Latest
Median	6.1
SIC Composite	5.0
Large Composite	4.6
Small Composite	7.1
High Financial Risk	–

Capital Structure

SIC Composite (%) Latest
D/TC: 10.6
E/TC: 89.4

Cost of Equity Capital (%)

	CRSP Deciles CAPM	CAPM +Size Prem	Build-Up	Risk Premium Report CAPM +Size Prem	Build-Up	Discounted Cash Flow 1-Stage	3-Stage	Fama-French 5-Factor Model
Median	10.2	11.5	11.3	13.5	13.5	12.3	8.6	11.2
SIC Composite	10.0	10.3	10.4	12.3	10.6	12.5	10.3	10.0
Large Composite	9.8	9.8	10.1	11.6	9.3	11.5	11.1	11.2
Small Composite	10.5	11.8	11.4	24.9	14.6	11.9	6.0	–
High Financial Risk	–	–	–	–	–	–	–	–

Cost of Equity Capital (%) SIC Composite

Avg CRSP: 10.3, Avg RPR: 11.5, 1-Stage: 12.5, 3-Stage: 10.3, 5-Factor Model: 10.0

Weighted Average Cost of Capital (WACC) (%)

	CRSP Deciles CAPM	CAPM +Size Prem	Build-Up	Risk Premium Report CAPM +Size Prem	Build-Up	Discounted Cash Flow 1-Stage	3-Stage	Fama-French 5-Factor Model
Median	9.8	10.9	10.8	12.9	12.6	11.9	8.1	11.1
SIC Composite	9.4	9.6	9.7	11.4	10.0	11.6	9.6	9.4
Large Composite	9.0	9.0	9.3	10.6	8.6	10.5	10.2	10.2
Small Composite	10.4	11.8	11.4	24.8	14.6	11.9	6.0	–
High Financial Risk	–	–	–	–	–	–	–	–

WACC (%) SIC Composite

Low 9.4 — High 11.6
Average 10.2, Median 9.7

© 2017 Duff & Phelps. All Rights Reserved. Duff & Phelps has used the utmost care in compiling the data presented herein, but cannot guarantee the accuracy, completeness, or timeliness of the information.

Data Updated Through March 31, 2017

3679

Number of Companies: 6
Electronic Components, Not Elsewhere Classified

Industry Description
Establishments primarily engaged in manufacturing electronic components, not elsewhere classified, such as receiving antennas, switches, and waveguides.

Sales (in millions)

Three Largest Companies
Advanced Energy Inds Inc.	$483.7
Sparton Corp.	419.4
Nortech Systems Inc.	115.2

Three Smallest Companies
Clearfield, Inc.	$75.3
Espey Mfg. & Electronics Corp.	27.5
Interlink Electronics, Inc.	10.5

Total Assets (in millions)

Three Largest Companies
Advanced Energy Inds Inc.	$571.5
Sparton Corp.	246.0
Clearfield, Inc.	70.6

Three Smallest Companies
Nortech Systems Inc.	$56.6
Espey Mfg. & Electronics Corp.	34.5
Interlink Electronics, Inc.	7.6

Annualized Monthly Performance Statistics (%)

Industry	Geometric Mean	Arithmetic Mean	Standard Deviation
1-year	72.9	74.8	27.4
3-year	25.6	29.0	30.6
5-year	34.1	38.0	33.6

S&P 500 Index	Geometric Mean	Arithmetic Mean	Standard Deviation
1-year	17.2	17.4	7.2
3-year	10.4	10.9	11.5
5-year	13.3	13.9	11.5

Return Ratios (%)

	Return on Assets Latest	5-Yr Avg	Return on Equity Latest	5-Yr Avg	Dividend Yield Latest	5-Yr Avg
Median (6)	10.9	8.6	11.9	9.8	0.0	0.0
SIC Composite (6)	9.2	7.7	2.8	4.6	0.1	0.2
Large Composite (–)	–	–	–	–	–	–
Small Composite (–)	–	–	–	–	–	–
High-Financial Risk (–)	–	–	–	–	–	–

Liquidity Ratio

	Current Ratio Latest	5-Yr Avg
Median (6)	–	–
SIC Composite (6)	3.7	3.3
Large Composite	–	–
Small Composite	–	–
High-Financial Risk	–	–

Profitability Ratio (%)

	Operating Margin Latest	5-Yr Avg
Median (6)	15.0	9.5
SIC Composite (6)	14.1	10.7
Large Composite	–	–
Small Composite	–	–
High-Financial Risk	–	–

Growth Rates (%)

	Long-term EPS Analyst Estimates
Median (6)	10.5
SIC Composite (6)	41.2
Large Composite	–
Small Composite	–
High-Financial Risk	–

Betas (Levered)

	Raw (OLS)	Blume Adjusted	Peer Group	Vasicek Adjusted	Sum	Downside
Median	1.00	1.00	1.20	1.07	0.89	1.39
SIC Composite	1.03	1.03	1.20	1.07	0.71	1.18
Large Composite	–	–	–	–	–	–
Small Composite	–	–	–	–	–	–
High Financial Risk	–	–	–	–	–	–

Betas (Unlevered)

	Raw (OLS)	Blume Adjusted	Peer Group	Vasicek Adjusted	Sum	Downside
Median	1.00	0.97	1.20	1.01	0.56	1.35
SIC Composite	1.01	1.00	1.17	1.04	0.70	1.15
Large Composite	–	–	–	–	–	–
Small Composite	–	–	–	–	–	–
High Financial Risk	–	–	–	–	–	–

Equity Valuation Multiples

	Price/Sales Latest	5-Yr Avg	Price/Earnings Latest	5-Yr Avg	Market/Book Latest	5-Yr Avg
Median	2.4	2.1	33.2	24.0	3.1	2.4
SIC Composite	2.9	1.5	36.2	21.7	5.5	2.6
Large Composite	–	–	–	–	–	–
Small Composite	–	–	–	–	–	–
High Financial Risk	–	–	–	–	–	–

Enterprise Valuation (EV) Multiples

	EV/Sales Latest	5-Yr Avg	EV/EBITDA Latest	5-Yr Avg
Median	2.0	1.7	14.8	9.6
SIC Composite	2.7	1.4	16.2	10.3
Large Composite	–	–	–	–
Small Composite	–	–	–	–
High Financial Risk	–	–	–	–

Enterprise Valuation SIC Composite
Latest: EV/Sales 2.7, EV/EBITDA 16.2
5-Yr Avg: EV/Sales 1.4, EV/EBITDA 10.3

Fama-French (F-F) 5-Factor Model

	F-F Beta	SMB Premium	HML Premium	RMW Premium	CMA Premium
Median	0.6	1.0	-0.4	2.7	-0.7
SIC Composite	0.8	4.3	-2.6	-2.8	3.1
Large Composite	–	–	–	–	–
Small Composite	–	–	–	–	–
High Financial Risk	–	–	–	–	–

Leverage Ratios (%)

	Debt/MV Equity Latest	5-Yr Avg	Debt/Total Capital Latest	5-Yr Avg
Median	0.0	0.1	0.0	0.1
SIC Composite	3.4	4.9	3.3	4.7
Large Composite	–	–	–	–
Small Composite	–	–	–	–
High Financial Risk	–	–	–	–

Cost of Debt

	Cost of Debt (%) Latest
Median	6.1
SIC Composite	6.3
Large Composite	–
Small Composite	–
High Financial Risk	–

Capital Structure

SIC Composite (%)
Latest
D/TC: 3.3
E/TC: 96.7

Cost of Equity Capital (%)

	CRSP Deciles CAPM	CAPM +Size Prem	Build-Up	Risk Premium Report CAPM +Size Prem	Build-Up	Discounted Cash Flow 1-Stage	3-Stage	Fama-French 5-Factor Model
Median	9.4	13.1	15.7	14.3	16.7	13.5	23.7	9.3
SIC Composite	9.4	11.6	12.3	11.9	14.6	41.3	23.1	10.1
Large Composite	–	–	–	–	–	–	–	–
Small Composite	–	–	–	–	–	–	–	–
High Financial Risk	–	–	–	–	–	–	–	–

Cost of Equity Capital (%) SIC Composite
Avg CRSP: 12.0; Avg RPR: 13.2; 1-Stage: 41.3; 3-Stage: 23.1; 5-Factor Model: 10.1

Weighted Average Cost of Capital (WACC) (%)

	CRSP Deciles CAPM	CAPM +Size Prem	Build-Up	Risk Premium Report CAPM +Size Prem	Build-Up	Discounted Cash Flow 1-Stage	3-Stage	Fama-French 5-Factor Model
Median	8.7	11.3	13.8	11.3	15.4	10.5	19.3	7.8
SIC Composite	9.3	11.4	12.1	11.7	14.3	40.1	22.5	10.0
Large Composite	–	–	–	–	–	–	–	–
Small Composite	–	–	–	–	–	–	–	–
High Financial Risk	–	–	–	–	–	–	–	–

WACC (%) SIC Composite
Low: 10.0; High: 40.1; Average 17.4; Median 12.1

© 2017 Duff & Phelps. All Rights Reserved. Duff & Phelps has used the utmost care in compiling the data presented herein, but cannot guarantee the accuracy, completeness, or timeliness of the information.

Data Updated Through March 31, 2017

37

Number of Companies: 46
Transportation Equipment

Industry Description
This major group includes establishments engaged in manufacturing equipment for transportation of passengers and cargo by land, air, and water. Important products produced by establishments classified in this major group include motor vehicles, aircraft, guided missiles and space vehicles, ships, boats, railroad equipment, and miscellaneous transportation equipment, such as motorcycles, bicycles, and snowmobiles.

Sales (in millions)

Three Largest Companies
General Motors Co.	$166,380.0
Ford Motor Co.	151,800.0
Boeing Co.	94,571.0

Three Smallest Companies
SORL Auto Parts Inc.	$218.7
Kandi Technologies Group, Inc.	201.1
SIFCO Industries	119.1

Total Assets (in millions)

Three Largest Companies
Ford Motor Co.	$237,951.0
General Motors Co.	221,690.0
Boeing Co.	89,997.0

Three Smallest Companies
SIFCO Industries	$130.5
Supreme Industries Inc.	121.7
Marine Products Corp.	88.5

Annualized Monthly Performance Statistics (%)

Industry
	Geometric Mean	Arithmetic Mean	Standard Deviation
1-year	21.3	22.0	13.1
3-year	8.2	9.3	16.0
5-year	15.1	16.3	16.7

S&P 500 Index
	Geometric Mean	Arithmetic Mean	Standard Deviation
1-year	17.2	17.4	7.2
3-year	10.4	10.9	11.5
5-year	13.3	13.9	11.5

Return Ratios (%)

	Return on Assets Latest	5-Yr Avg	Return on Equity Latest	5-Yr Avg	Dividend Yield Latest	5-Yr Avg
Median (46)	6.1	6.5	15.8	17.7	1.7	1.2
SIC Composite (46)	4.2	4.4	7.0	7.6	3.2	2.8
Large Composite (4)	3.8	3.9	7.9	8.6	3.7	3.1
Small Composite (4)	3.7	4.1	4.7	3.7	2.2	2.9
High-Financial Risk (6)	-4.6	-4.8	-12.1	-12.5	0.0	0.0

Liquidity Ratio

	Current Ratio Latest	5-Yr Avg
	1.9	2.0
	1.2	1.3
	1.1	1.2
	1.9	2.2
	1.3	1.4

Profitability Ratio (%)

	Operating Margin Latest	5-Yr Avg
	8.4	7.5
	8.0	7.3
	7.0	6.3
	3.3	6.1
	5.7	3.2

Growth Rates (%)

	Long-term EPS Analyst Estimates
	8.3
	7.8
	7.5
	8.6
	4.0

Betas (Levered)

	Raw (OLS)	Blume Adjusted	Peer Group	Vasicek Adjusted	Sum	Downside
Median	1.31	1.21	1.09	1.22	1.39	1.60
SIC Composite	1.12	1.08	1.09	1.11	1.15	1.19
Large Composite	1.05	1.04	1.10	1.06	1.06	1.14
Small Composite	1.67	1.43	1.06	1.57	1.68	1.53
High Financial Risk	1.92	1.59	1.07	1.82	2.31	2.33

Betas (Unlevered)

	Raw (OLS)	Blume Adjusted	Peer Group	Vasicek Adjusted	Sum	Downside
Median	1.08	1.03	0.94	1.01	1.15	1.36
SIC Composite	0.70	0.68	0.69	0.70	0.72	0.75
Large Composite	0.60	0.59	0.62	0.60	0.60	0.64
Small Composite	1.50	1.29	0.96	1.41	1.50	1.37
High Financial Risk	0.98	0.85	0.63	0.94	1.14	1.15

Equity Valuation Multiples

	Price/Sales Latest	5-Yr Avg	Price/Earnings Latest	5-Yr Avg	Market/Book Latest	5-Yr Avg
Median	0.9	0.7	18.9	16.2	2.9	2.7
SIC Composite	0.7	0.7	14.3	13.5	3.6	3.3
Large Composite	0.6	0.6	12.6	12.1	3.7	3.3
Small Composite	0.9	1.3	21.5	26.8	1.3	1.7
High Financial Risk	0.3	0.3	—	—	—	—

Enterprise Valuation (EV) Multiples

	EV/Sales Latest	5-Yr Avg	EV/EBITDA Latest	5-Yr Avg
Median	1.0	0.9	9.3	8.5
SIC Composite	1.1	0.9	8.0	7.6
Large Composite	1.0	0.8	7.5	7.1
Small Composite	0.9	1.3	11.2	12.3
High Financial Risk	0.7	0.7	8.4	11.2

Enterprise Valuation SIC Composite
Latest: 1.1 / 8.0 5-Yr Avg: 0.9 / 7.6
■ EV/Sales ■ EV/EBITDA

Fama-French (F-F) 5-Factor Model

	F-F Beta	SMB Premium	HML Premium	RMW Premium	CMA Premium
Median	0.9	5.4	0.2	2.8	-2.1
SIC Composite	1.1	1.4	1.4	0.6	-1.2
Large Composite	1.0	0.4	1.3	0.6	0.8
Small Composite	1.5	3.9	0.3	-2.2	2.7
High Financial Risk	—	—	—	—	—

Leverage Ratios (%)

	Debt/MV Equity Latest	5-Yr Avg	Debt/Total Capital Latest	5-Yr Avg
Median	20.9	17.9	17.3	15.2
SIC Composite	67.9	62.9	40.4	38.6
Large Composite	88.1	80.6	46.8	44.6
Small Composite	14.8	12.8	12.9	11.3
High Financial Risk	146.2	126.8	59.4	55.9

Cost of Debt

	Cost of Debt (%) Latest
Median	6.1
SIC Composite	4.9
Large Composite	4.8
Small Composite	6.1
High Financial Risk	6.9

Capital Structure

SIC Composite (%) Latest
D/TC: 40.4
E/TC: 59.6

Cost of Equity Capital (%)

	CRSP Deciles CAPM	CAPM +Size Prem	Build-Up	Risk Premium Report CAPM +Size Prem	Build-Up	Discounted Cash Flow 1-Stage	3-Stage	Fama-French 5-Factor Model
Median	10.2	12.0	10.9	14.9	13.6	10.5	10.4	14.8
SIC Composite	9.6	10.0	9.7	11.5	10.5	11.0	10.1	11.6
Large Composite	9.3	9.3	9.3	10.3	9.5	11.2	10.1	12.2
Small Composite	12.1	16.0	13.2	18.4	16.4	10.1	9.6	16.6
High Financial Risk	—	—	—	27.3	23.4	—	—	—

Cost of Equity Capital (%) SIC Composite
Avg CRSP: 9.8 Avg RPR: 11.0 1-Stage: 11.0 3-Stage: 10.1 5-Factor Model: 11.6

Weighted Average Cost of Capital (WACC) (%)

	CRSP Deciles CAPM	CAPM +Size Prem	Build-Up	Risk Premium Report CAPM +Size Prem	Build-Up	Discounted Cash Flow 1-Stage	3-Stage	Fama-French 5-Factor Model
Median	9.2	10.8	10.0	13.0	11.7	9.1	8.9	12.9
SIC Composite	7.3	7.5	7.3	8.4	7.8	8.1	7.6	8.5
Large Composite	6.5	6.5	6.5	7.0	6.6	7.5	6.9	8.1
Small Composite	11.1	14.5	12.0	16.6	14.8	9.3	8.8	15.0
High Financial Risk	—	—	—	14.5	12.9	—	—	—

WACC (%) SIC Composite
Low: 7.3 High: 8.5
▲ Average 7.9 ◆ Median 7.8

© 2017 Duff & Phelps. All Rights Reserved. Duff & Phelps has used the utmost care in compiling the data presented herein, but cannot guarantee the accuracy, completeness, or timeliness of the information.

Data Updated Through March 31, 2017

371

Number of Companies: 29
Motor Vehicles and Motor Vehicle Equipment

Industry Description
Establishments primarily motor vehicles and passenger car bodies; truck and bus bodies; motor vehicle parts and accessories; truck trailers; motor homes.

Sales (in millions)

Three Largest Companies
General Motors Co.	$166,380.0
Ford Motor Co.	151,800.0
PACCAR Inc.	17,033.3

Three Smallest Companies
Supreme Industries Inc.	$278.4
SORL Auto Parts Inc.	218.7
Kandi Technologies Group, Inc.	201.1

Total Assets (in millions)

Three Largest Companies
Ford Motor Co.	$237,951.0
General Motors Co.	221,690.0
PACCAR Inc.	20,638.9

Three Smallest Companies
Miller Industries Inc.	$270.9
STRATTEC Security Corp.	242.2
Supreme Industries Inc.	121.7

Annualized Monthly Performance Statistics (%)

Industry	Geometric Mean	Arithmetic Mean	Standard Deviation
1-year	10.4	11.6	17.1
3-year	1.6	3.3	19.6
5-year	8.3	10.2	20.6

S&P 500 Index	Geometric Mean	Arithmetic Mean	Standard Deviation
1-year	17.2	17.4	7.2
3-year	10.4	10.9	11.5
5-year	13.3	13.9	11.5

Return Ratios (%)

	Return on Assets Latest	5-Yr Avg	Return on Equity Latest	5-Yr Avg	Dividend Yield Latest	5-Yr Avg
Median (29)	6.0	6.6	15.6	17.9	1.6	1.2
SIC Composite (29)	3.4	3.7	9.9	9.7	3.5	2.9
Large Composite (3)	3.0	3.3	11.8	11.1	4.5	3.4
Small Composite (3)	5.0	4.2	6.8	4.8	2.5	2.2
High-Financial Risk (–)	–	–	–	–	–	–

Liquidity Ratio / Profitability Ratio (%) / Growth Rates (%)

	Current Ratio Latest	5-Yr Avg	Operating Margin Latest	5-Yr Avg	Long-term EPS Analyst Estimates
Median (29)	2.1	2.1	7.5	7.0	9.3
SIC Composite (29)	1.1	1.3	6.9	6.0	3.0
Large Composite (3)	1.1	1.2	6.3	5.4	0.0
Small Composite (3)	2.1	2.2	4.3	5.2	5.8
High-Financial Risk (–)	–	–	–	–	–

Betas (Levered)

	Raw (OLS)	Blume Adjusted	Peer Group	Vasicek Adjusted	Sum	Downside
Median	1.40	1.26	1.09	1.24	1.38	1.90
SIC Composite	1.24	1.16	1.09	1.23	1.33	1.40
Large Composite	1.20	1.13	1.10	1.13	1.26	1.36
Small Composite	2.13	1.72	1.06	1.82	2.40	2.36
High Financial Risk	–	–	–	–	–	–

Betas (Unlevered)

	Raw (OLS)	Blume Adjusted	Peer Group	Vasicek Adjusted	Sum	Downside
Median	1.02	1.01	0.94	1.00	1.14	1.36
SIC Composite	0.58	0.55	0.52	0.57	0.62	0.65
Large Composite	0.46	0.44	0.43	0.44	0.48	0.52
Small Composite	1.92	1.56	0.97	1.65	2.17	2.13
High Financial Risk	–	–	–	–	–	–

Equity Valuation Multiples

	Price/Sales Latest	5-Yr Avg	Price/Earnings Latest	5-Yr Avg	Market/Book Latest	5-Yr Avg
Median	0.9	0.5	17.7	15.2	2.6	2.5
SIC Composite	0.5	0.5	10.1	10.8	1.8	2.0
Large Composite	0.4	0.4	8.4	9.5	1.5	1.8
Small Composite	0.9	0.9	14.7	20.8	1.1	1.4
High Financial Risk	–	–	–	–	–	–

Enterprise Valuation (EV) Multiples

	EV/Sales Latest	5-Yr Avg	EV/EBITDA Latest	5-Yr Avg
Median	0.9	0.6	7.3	6.8
SIC Composite	0.9	0.8	6.5	6.6
Large Composite	0.9	0.8	6.1	6.4
Small Composite	0.8	0.9	6.6	9.3
High Financial Risk	–	–	–	–

Enterprise Valuation SIC Composite
- EV/Sales: Latest 0.9, 5-Yr Avg 0.8
- EV/EBITDA: Latest 6.5, 5-Yr Avg 6.6

Fama-French (F-F) 5-Factor Model

	F-F Beta	SMB Premium	HML Premium	RMW Premium	CMA Premium
Median	0.5	5.8	-1.2	3.5	-0.1
SIC Composite	1.2	2.0	3.1	0.0	-1.9
Large Composite	1.1	1.2	3.3	-0.5	-0.6
Small Composite	1.9	4.6	-6.2	-4.1	3.0
High Financial Risk	–	–	–	–	–

Leverage Ratios (%)

	Debt/MV Equity Latest	5-Yr Avg	Debt/Total Capital Latest	5-Yr Avg
Median	22.3	17.7	18.3	15.0
SIC Composite	135.4	110.8	57.5	52.6
Large Composite	192.1	148.8	65.8	59.8
Small Composite	12.6	16.3	11.2	14.0
High Financial Risk	–	–	–	–

Cost of Debt

	Cost of Debt (%) Latest
Median	6.1
SIC Composite	4.8
Large Composite	4.8
Small Composite	6.2
High Financial Risk	–

Capital Structure
SIC Composite (%) Latest
- D/TC: 42.5
- E/TC: 57.5

Cost of Equity Capital (%)

	CRSP Deciles CAPM	CAPM +Size Prem	Build-Up	Risk Premium Report CAPM +Size Prem	Build-Up	Discounted Cash Flow 1-Stage	3-Stage	Fama-French 5-Factor Model
Median	10.3	12.3	11.0	15.2	13.9	9.5	9.5	14.3
SIC Composite	10.3	10.8	9.8	12.5	10.5	6.4	8.6	13.1
Large Composite	9.7	9.8	9.4	11.3	9.4	4.5	7.7	13.1
Small Composite	13.5	17.4	13.2	22.3	16.3	7.0	7.8	11.2
High Financial Risk	–	–	–	–	–	–	–	–

Cost of Equity Capital (%) SIC Composite
- Avg CRSP: 10.3
- Avg RPR: 11.5
- 1-Stage: 6.4
- 3-Stage: 8.6
- 5-Factor Model: 13.1

Weighted Average Cost of Capital (WACC) (%)

	CRSP Deciles CAPM	CAPM +Size Prem	Build-Up	Risk Premium Report CAPM +Size Prem	Build-Up	Discounted Cash Flow 1-Stage	3-Stage	Fama-French 5-Factor Model
Median	9.1	11.0	10.3	13.3	12.3	9.3	8.4	12.9
SIC Composite	6.6	6.8	6.4	7.6	6.7	5.0	5.9	7.8
Large Composite	5.7	5.8	5.6	6.3	5.6	–	5.0	6.9
Small Composite	12.6	16.0	12.3	20.4	15.0	6.8	7.5	10.5
High Financial Risk	–	–	–	–	–	–	–	–

WACC (%) SIC Composite: Low 5.0 — High 7.8; Average 6.6, Median 6.7

© 2017 Duff & Phelps. All Rights Reserved. Duff & Phelps has used the utmost care in compiling the data presented herein, but cannot guarantee the accuracy, completeness, or timeliness of the information.

Data Updated Through March 31, 2017

3711

Number of Companies: 6
Motor Vehicles and Passenger Car Bodies

Industry Description
Establishments primarily engaged in manufacturing or assembling complete passenger automobiles, trucks, commercial cars and buses, and special purpose motor vehicles which are for highway use.

Sales (in millions)

Three Largest Companies
General Motors Co.	$166,380.0
Ford Motor Co.	151,800.0
PACCAR Inc.	17,033.3

Three Smallest Companies
Tower International, Inc.	$1,913.6
LCI Industries	1,678.9
Federal Signal Corp.	707.9

Total Assets (in millions)

Three Largest Companies
Ford Motor Co.	$237,951.0
General Motors Co.	221,690.0
PACCAR Inc.	20,638.9

Three Smallest Companies
Tower International, Inc.	$1,162.5
LCI Industries	786.9
Federal Signal Corp.	643.2

Annualized Monthly Performance Statistics (%)

	Industry			S&P 500 Index		
	Geometric Mean	Arithmetic Mean	Standard Deviation	Geometric Mean	Arithmetic Mean	Standard Deviation
1-year	7.9	9.0	16.5	17.2	17.4	7.2
3-year	1.1	2.8	19.2	10.4	10.9	11.5
5-year	7.2	9.2	21.3	13.3	13.9	11.5

Return Ratios (%)

	Return on Assets		Return on Equity		Dividend Yield	
	Latest	5-Yr Avg	Latest	5-Yr Avg	Latest	5-Yr Avg
Median (6)	4.6	4.9	19.1	20.4	2.3	2.8
SIC Composite (6)	3.1	3.3	11.7	11.0	4.4	3.4
Large Composite (–)	–	–	–	–	–	–
Small Composite (–)	–	–	–	–	–	–
High-Financial Risk (–)	–	–	–	–	–	–

Liquidity Ratio

	Current Ratio	
	Latest	5-Yr Avg
Median (6)	1.2	1.2
SIC Composite (6)	1.1	1.2
Large Composite	–	–
Small Composite	–	–
High-Financial Risk	–	–

Profitability Ratio (%)

	Operating Margin	
	Latest	5-Yr Avg
Median	8.2	7.3
SIC Composite	6.3	5.4
Large Composite	–	–
Small Composite	–	–
High-Financial Risk	–	–

Growth Rates (%)

	Long-term EPS
	Analyst Estimates
Median	3.9
SIC Composite	0.1
Large Composite	–
Small Composite	–
High-Financial Risk	–

Betas (Levered)

	Raw (OLS)	Blume Adjusted	Peer Group	Vasicek Adjusted	Sum	Downside
Median	1.28	1.18	1.10	1.21	1.42	1.53
SIC Composite	1.20	1.13	1.10	1.17	1.26	1.36
Large Composite	–	–	–	–	–	–
Small Composite	–	–	–	–	–	–
High Financial Risk	–	–	–	–	–	–

Betas (Unlevered)

	Raw (OLS)	Blume Adjusted	Peer Group	Vasicek Adjusted	Sum	Downside
Median	1.07	0.96	0.79	0.90	1.06	1.25
SIC Composite	0.47	0.45	0.44	0.46	0.49	0.53
Large Composite	–	–	–	–	–	–
Small Composite	–	–	–	–	–	–
High Financial Risk	–	–	–	–	–	–

Equity Valuation Multiples

	Price/Sales		Price/Earnings		Market/Book	
	Latest	5-Yr Avg	Latest	5-Yr Avg	Latest	5-Yr Avg
Median	0.5	0.5	13.2	10.4	2.3	2.4
SIC Composite	0.4	0.4	8.6	9.6	1.5	1.8
Large Composite	–	–	–	–	–	–
Small Composite	–	–	–	–	–	–
High Financial Risk	–	–	–	–	–	–

Enterprise Valuation (EV) Multiples

	EV/Sales		EV/EBITDA	
	Latest	5-Yr Avg	Latest	5-Yr Avg
Median	1.1	1.0	8.8	8.4
SIC Composite	0.9	0.8	6.2	6.4
Large Composite	–	–	–	–
Small Composite	–	–	–	–
High Financial Risk	–	–	–	–

Enterprise Valuation SIC Composite
- EV/Sales: Latest 0.9, 5-Yr Avg 0.8
- EV/EBITDA: Latest 6.2, 5-Yr Avg 6.4

Fama-French (F-F) 5-Factor Model

	F-F Beta	SMB Premium	HML Premium	RMW Premium	CMA Premium
Median	1.1	4.9	1.3	0.4	-0.2
SIC Composite	1.1	1.3	3.4	-0.4	-1.1
Large Composite	–	–	–	–	–
Small Composite	–	–	–	–	–
High Financial Risk	–	–	–	–	–

Leverage Ratios (%)

	Debt/MV Equity		Debt/Total Capital	
	Latest	5-Yr Avg	Latest	5-Yr Avg
Median	53.4	72.4	33.9	40.1
SIC Composite	186.7	146.2	65.1	59.4

Cost of Debt

	Cost of Debt (%)
	Latest
Median	5.5
SIC Composite	4.8

Capital Structure

SIC Composite (%) Latest
- D/TC: 34.9
- E/TC: 65.1

Cost of Equity Capital (%)

	CRSP Deciles			Risk Premium Report		Discounted Cash Flow		Fama-French
	CAPM	CAPM +Size Prem	Build-Up	CAPM +Size Prem	Build-Up	1-Stage	3-Stage	5-Factor Model
Median	10.1	11.1	10.4	13.6	12.4	10.2	7.6	15.8
SIC Composite	9.9	10.1	9.5	11.5	9.5	4.5	7.7	12.9
Large Composite	–	–	–	–	–	–	–	–
Small Composite	–	–	–	–	–	–	–	–
High Financial Risk	–	–	–	–	–	–	–	–

Cost of Equity Capital (%) SIC Composite
- Avg CRSP: 9.8
- Avg RPR: 10.5
- 1-Stage: 4.5
- 3-Stage: 7.7
- 5-Factor Model: 12.9

Weighted Average Cost of Capital (WACC) (%)

	CRSP Deciles			Risk Premium Report		Discounted Cash Flow		Fama-French
	CAPM	CAPM +Size Prem	Build-Up	CAPM +Size Prem	Build-Up	1-Stage	3-Stage	5-Factor Model
Median	8.7	9.7	9.0	12.1	10.0	7.9	6.5	14.2
SIC Composite	5.9	5.9	5.7	6.4	5.7	–	5.1	6.9
Large Composite	–	–	–	–	–	–	–	–
Small Composite	–	–	–	–	–	–	–	–
High Financial Risk	–	–	–	–	–	–	–	–

WACC (%) SIC Composite
- Low: 5.1
- High: 6.9
- Average: 6.0
- Median: 5.8

© 2017 Duff & Phelps. All Rights Reserved. Duff & Phelps has used the utmost care in compiling the data presented herein, but cannot guarantee the accuracy, completeness, or timeliness of the information.

Data Updated Through March 31, 2017

3714

Number of Companies: 19
Motor Vehicle Parts and Accessories

Industry Description
Establishments primarily engaged in manufacturing motor vehicle parts and accessories, but not engaged in manufacturing complete motor vehicles or passenger car bodies.

Sales (in millions)

Three Largest Companies
Autoliv, Inc.	$10,073.6
BorgWarner Inc.	9,071.0
Tenneco Inc.	8,599.0

Three Smallest Companies
STRATTEC Security Corp.	$401.4
SORL Auto Parts Inc.	218.7
Kandi Technologies Group, Inc.	201.1

Total Assets (in millions)

Three Largest Companies
BorgWarner Inc.	$8,834.7
Autoliv, Inc.	8,234.4
Dana Incorporated	4,860.0

Three Smallest Companies
Kandi Technologies Group, Inc.	$371.5
SORL Auto Parts Inc.	320.6
STRATTEC Security Corp.	242.2

Annualized Monthly Performance Statistics (%)

Industry	Geometric Mean	Arithmetic Mean	Standard Deviation
1-year	15.3	17.0	20.5
3-year	2.4	4.7	22.6
5-year	10.6	12.8	21.9

S&P 500 Index	Geometric Mean	Arithmetic Mean	Standard Deviation
1-year	17.2	17.4	7.2
3-year	10.4	10.9	11.5
5-year	13.3	13.9	11.5

Return Ratios (%)

	Return on Assets Latest	5-Yr Avg	Return on Equity Latest	5-Yr Avg	Dividend Yield Latest	5-Yr Avg
Median (19)	5.8	6.6	15.4	14.7	0.9	0.9
SIC Composite (19)	6.6	6.9	5.9	6.5	1.2	1.8
Large Composite (3)	4.9	6.6	4.9	5.7	1.6	1.3
Small Composite (3)	4.0	4.3	10.4	5.3	1.4	1.0
High-Financial Risk (–)	–	–	–	–	–	–

Liquidity Ratio

	Current Ratio Latest	5-Yr Avg
Median (19)	1.9	1.8
SIC Composite (19)	1.8	1.8
Large Composite (3)	1.4	1.5
Small Composite (3)	2.0	2.1
High-Financial Risk (–)	–	–

Profitability Ratio (%)

	Operating Margin Latest	5-Yr Avg
Median (19)	7.7	7.1
SIC Composite (19)	10.2	9.4
Large Composite (3)	9.2	9.4
Small Composite (3)	3.9	6.2
High-Financial Risk (–)	–	–

Growth Rates (%)

	Long-term EPS Analyst Estimates
Median (19)	9.3
SIC Composite (19)	9.1
Large Composite (3)	8.1
Small Composite (3)	9.3
High-Financial Risk (–)	–

Betas (Levered)

	Raw (OLS)	Blume Adjusted	Peer Group	Vasicek Adjusted	Sum	Downside
Median	1.41	1.26	1.05	1.23	1.40	1.91
SIC Composite	1.34	1.22	1.05	1.31	1.47	1.52
Large Composite	1.42	1.27	1.06	1.32	1.53	1.60
Small Composite	2.05	1.67	1.06	1.68	2.05	2.22
High Financial Risk	–	–	–	–	–	–

Betas (Unlevered)

	Raw (OLS)	Blume Adjusted	Peer Group	Vasicek Adjusted	Sum	Downside
Median	1.02	1.01	0.90	0.99	1.10	1.36
SIC Composite	1.12	1.03	0.89	1.10	1.23	1.27
Large Composite	1.17	1.05	0.88	1.09	1.25	1.31
Small Composite	1.71	1.41	0.91	1.41	1.71	1.85
High Financial Risk	–	–	–	–	–	–

Equity Valuation Multiples

	Price/Sales Latest	5-Yr Avg	Price/Earnings Latest	5-Yr Avg	Market/Book Latest	5-Yr Avg
Median	0.9	0.6	15.9	15.8	2.7	2.7
SIC Composite	1.0	0.9	17.0	15.7	3.1	2.9
Large Composite	0.8	0.9	20.3	17.5	2.8	2.9
Small Composite	0.4	0.8	9.6	18.8	0.6	1.3
High Financial Risk	–	–	–	–	–	–

Enterprise Valuation (EV) Multiples

	EV/Sales Latest	5-Yr Avg	EV/EBITDA Latest	5-Yr Avg
Median	0.8	0.6	6.5	6.1
SIC Composite	1.1	1.0	8.4	7.5
Large Composite	0.9	0.9	8.4	7.6
Small Composite	0.4	0.8	3.5	7.7
High Financial Risk	–	–	–	–

Enterprise Valuation SIC Composite: EV/Sales Latest 1.1, 5-Yr Avg 1.0; EV/EBITDA Latest 8.4, 5-Yr Avg 7.5

Fama-French (F-F) 5-Factor Model

	F-F Beta	SMB Premium	HML Premium	RMW Premium	CMA Premium
Median	1.4	4.6	2.3	3.3	-7.5
SIC Composite	1.2	3.8	2.4	1.2	-3.9
Large Composite	1.3	3.7	2.7	1.8	2.4
Small Composite	1.9	2.2	-2.6	-3.8	1.0
High Financial Risk	–	–	–	–	–

Leverage Ratios (%)

	Debt/MV Equity Latest	5-Yr Avg	Debt/Total Capital Latest	5-Yr Avg
Median	25.0	17.7	20.0	15.0
SIC Composite	24.3	24.8	19.5	19.9
Large Composite	24.2	18.6	19.5	15.7
Small Composite	24.6	14.5	19.7	12.6
High Financial Risk	–	–	–	–

Cost of Debt

	Cost of Debt (%) Latest
Median	6.1
SIC Composite	5.9
Large Composite	4.9
Small Composite	6.4
High Financial Risk	–

Capital Structure

SIC Composite (%) Latest: D/TC 19.5, E/TC 80.5

Cost of Equity Capital (%)

	CRSP Deciles CAPM	CAPM +Size Prem	Build-Up	Risk Premium Report CAPM +Size Prem	Build-Up	Discounted Cash Flow 1-Stage	3-Stage	Fama-French 5-Factor Model
Median	10.3	12.4	11.0	15.2	13.6	11.4	11.6	14.0
SIC Composite	10.7	11.9	10.5	14.8	12.6	10.3	11.3	13.6
Large Composite	10.8	11.8	10.3	14.7	12.0	9.8	11.0	21.1
Small Composite	12.7	18.3	14.9	20.4	16.4	9.9	12.6	10.7
High Financial Risk	–	–	–	–	–	–	–	–

Cost of Equity Capital (%) SIC Composite: Avg CRSP 11.2, Avg RPR 13.7, 1-Stage 10.3, 3-Stage 11.3, 5-Factor Model 13.6

Weighted Average Cost of Capital (WACC) (%)

	CRSP Deciles CAPM	CAPM +Size Prem	Build-Up	Risk Premium Report CAPM +Size Prem	Build-Up	Discounted Cash Flow 1-Stage	3-Stage	Fama-French 5-Factor Model
Median	9.0	10.4	10.3	12.6	11.7	10.3	9.7	12.3
SIC Composite	9.6	10.6	9.5	12.9	11.2	9.3	10.1	12.0
Large Composite	9.6	10.4	9.2	12.7	10.5	8.8	9.8	17.9
Small Composite	11.0	15.5	12.8	17.2	14.0	8.8	11.0	9.4
High Financial Risk	–	–	–	–	–	–	–	–

WACC (%) SIC Composite: Low 9.3, High 12.9, Average 10.8, Median 10.6

© 2017 Duff & Phelps. All Rights Reserved. Duff & Phelps has used the utmost care in compiling the data presented herein, but cannot guarantee the accuracy, completeness, or timeliness of the information.

Data Updated Through March 31, 2017

372

Number of Companies: 5
Aircraft and Parts

Industry Description
Establishments primarily engaged in manufacturing or assembling complete aircraft; aircraft engines and engine parts; aircraft parts and auxiliary equipment, not elsewhere classified.

Sales (in millions)

Three Largest Companies
Boeing Co.	$94,571.0
Spirit AeroSystems Holdings	6,792.9
TransDigm Group Inc.	3,171.4

Three Smallest Companies
TransDigm Group Inc.	$3,171.4
AeroVironment, Inc.	264.1
SIFCO Industries	119.1

Total Assets (in millions)

Three Largest Companies
Boeing Co.	$89,997.0
TransDigm Group Inc.	10,726.3
Spirit AeroSystems Holdings	5,405.2

Three Smallest Companies
Spirit AeroSystems Holdings	$5,405.2
AeroVironment, Inc.	410.4
SIFCO Industries	130.5

Annualized Monthly Performance Statistics (%)

Industry	Geometric Mean	Arithmetic Mean	Standard Deviation
1-year	38.6	39.9	20.0
3-year	15.4	17.4	22.3
5-year	21.9	23.9	22.8

S&P 500 Index	Geometric Mean	Arithmetic Mean	Standard Deviation
1-year	17.2	17.4	7.2
3-year	10.4	10.9	11.5
5-year	13.3	13.9	11.5

Return Ratios (%)

	Return on Assets Latest	5-Yr Avg	Return on Equity Latest	5-Yr Avg	Dividend Yield Latest	5-Yr Avg
Median (5)	5.3	3.9	2.5	11.1	1.8	1.6
SIC Composite (5)	5.6	5.1	4.6	5.4	3.8	3.0
Large Composite (−)	−	−	−	−	−	−
Small Composite (−)	−	−	−	−	−	−
High-Financial Risk (−)	−	−	−	−	−	−

Liquidity Ratio / Profitability Ratio (%) / Growth Rates (%)

	Current Ratio Latest	5-Yr Avg	Operating Margin Latest	5-Yr Avg	Long-term EPS Analyst Estimates
Median (5)	1.9	2.3	8.6	6.6	10.6
SIC Composite (5)	1.3	1.3	9.7	8.8	13.9
Large Composite	−	−	−	−	−
Small Composite	−	−	−	−	−
High-Financial Risk	−	−	−	−	−

Betas (Levered)

	Raw (OLS)	Blume Adjusted	Peer Group	Vasicek Adjusted	Sum	Downside
Median	1.16	1.11	1.10	1.14	1.40	1.48
SIC Composite	1.11	1.08	1.10	1.11	1.15	1.36
Large Composite	−	−	−	−	−	−
Small Composite	−	−	−	−	−	−
High Financial Risk	−	−	−	−	−	−

Betas (Unlevered)

	Raw (OLS)	Blume Adjusted	Peer Group	Vasicek Adjusted	Sum	Downside
Median	1.07	1.02	0.99	1.05	1.07	1.32
SIC Composite	0.98	0.95	0.96	0.98	1.01	1.19
Large Composite	−	−	−	−	−	−
Small Composite	−	−	−	−	−	−
High Financial Risk	−	−	−	−	−	−

Equity Valuation Multiples

	Price/Sales Latest	5-Yr Avg	Price/Earnings Latest	5-Yr Avg	Market/Book Latest	5-Yr Avg
Median	1.2	0.9	22.3	25.8	3.7	2.8
SIC Composite	1.2	1.0	21.6	18.6	−	9.8
Large Composite	−	−	−	−	−	−
Small Composite	−	−	−	−	−	−
High Financial Risk	−	−	−	−	−	−

Enterprise Valuation (EV) Multiples

	EV/Sales Latest	5-Yr Avg	EV/EBITDA Latest	5-Yr Avg
Median	1.2	1.0	14.1	9.6
SIC Composite	1.3	1.1	10.9	9.5
Large Composite	−	−	−	−
Small Composite	−	−	−	−
High Financial Risk	−	−	−	−

Enterprise Valuation SIC Composite
- Latest: EV/Sales 1.3, EV/EBITDA 10.9
- 5-Yr Avg: EV/Sales 1.1, EV/EBITDA 9.5

Fama-French (F-F) 5-Factor Model

	F-F Beta	SMB Premium	HML Premium	RMW Premium	CMA Premium
Median	1.2	3.0	3.1	3.7	-6.8
SIC Composite	1.1	0.3	0.1	2.2	-2.2
Large Composite	−	−	−	−	−
Small Composite	−	−	−	−	−
High Financial Risk	−	−	−	−	−

Leverage Ratios (%)

	Debt/MV Equity Latest	5-Yr Avg	Debt/Total Capital Latest	5-Yr Avg
Median	15.4	22.1	13.4	18.1
SIC Composite	16.5	17.9	14.2	15.2

Cost of Debt

	Cost of Debt (%) Latest
Median	6.1
SIC Composite	5.2

Capital Structure

SIC Composite (%) Latest: D/TC 14.2, E/TC 85.8

Cost of Equity Capital (%)

	CRSP Deciles CAPM	CAPM +Size Prem	Build-Up	Risk Premium Report CAPM +Size Prem	Build-Up	Discounted Cash Flow 1-Stage	3-Stage	Fama-French 5-Factor Model
Median	9.8	11.1	10.2	14.8	12.4	16.1	11.7	13.3
SIC Composite	9.6	9.7	9.4	11.2	10.0	17.7	12.7	10.2
Large Composite	−	−	−	−	−	−	−	−
Small Composite	−	−	−	−	−	−	−	−
High Financial Risk	−	−	−	−	−	−	−	−

Cost of Equity Capital (%) SIC Composite: Avg CRSP 9.6, Avg RPR 10.6, 1-Stage 17.7, 3-Stage 12.7, 5-Factor Model 10.2

Weighted Average Cost of Capital (WACC) (%)

	CRSP Deciles CAPM	CAPM +Size Prem	Build-Up	Risk Premium Report CAPM +Size Prem	Build-Up	Discounted Cash Flow 1-Stage	3-Stage	Fama-French 5-Factor Model
Median	9.2	10.4	9.6	11.9	11.6	13.1	9.1	12.6
SIC Composite	8.8	8.9	8.6	10.2	9.2	15.7	11.5	9.3
Large Composite	−	−	−	−	−	−	−	−
Small Composite	−	−	−	−	−	−	−	−
High Financial Risk	−	−	−	−	−	−	−	−

WACC (%) SIC Composite: Low 8.6, High 15.7, Average 10.5, Median 9.3

© 2017 Duff & Phelps. All Rights Reserved. Duff & Phelps has used the utmost care in compiling the data presented herein, but cannot guarantee the accuracy, completeness, or timeliness of the information.

Data Updated Through March 31, 2017

38

Number of Companies: 69
Measuring, Analyzing, and Controlling Instruments; Photographic, Medical and Optical Goods; Watches and Clocks

Industry Description
This major group includes establishments engaged in manufacturing instruments (including professional and scientific) for measuring, testing, analyzing, and controlling, and their associated sensors and accessories; optical instruments and lenses; surveying and drafting instruments; hydrological, hydrographic, meteorological, and geophysical equipment; search, detection, navigation, and guidance systems and equipment; surgical, medical, and dental instruments, equipment, and supplies; ophthalmic goods; photographic equipment and supplies; and watches and clocks.

Sales (in millions)

Three Largest Companies
Thermo Fisher Scientific Inc.	$18,274.1
Danaher Corp.	16,882.4
Becton Dickinson & Co.	12,483.0

Three Smallest Companies
Utah Medical Products Inc.	$39.3
Electromed, Inc.	23.0
Electro-Sensors Inc.	7.6

Annualized Monthly Performance Statistics (%)

Industry	Geometric Mean	Arithmetic Mean	Standard Deviation
1-year	21.4	22.2	14.2
3-year	14.7	15.6	15.1
5-year	16.4	17.3	14.4

Total Assets (in millions)

Three Largest Companies
Thermo Fisher Scientific Inc.	$45,907.5
Danaher Corp.	45,295.3
Zimmer Biomet Holdings, Inc.	26,684.4

Three Smallest Companies
InTEST Corp.	$42.8
Electromed, Inc.	20.6
Electro-Sensors Inc.	13.4

S&P 500 Index	Geometric Mean	Arithmetic Mean	Standard Deviation
1-year	17.2	17.4	7.2
3-year	10.4	10.9	11.5
5-year	13.3	13.9	11.5

Return Ratios (%)

	Return on Assets Latest	5-Yr Avg	Return on Equity Latest	5-Yr Avg	Dividend Yield Latest	5-Yr Avg	Current Ratio Latest	5-Yr Avg	Operating Margin Latest	5-Yr Avg	Long-term EPS Analyst Estimates
Median (69)	6.0	6.2	10.0	8.6	0.0	0.1	3.2	3.3	15.2	12.4	11.1
SIC Composite (69)	5.5	6.4	2.9	3.8	0.6	0.8	2.1	2.4	18.3	17.9	11.3
Large Composite (6)	4.4	5.4	3.1	4.0	0.9	0.9	1.5	2.0	18.9	18.6	10.4
Small Composite (6)	2.3	6.3	1.3	4.3	0.8	1.1	–	–	10.7	12.0	11.5
High-Financial Risk (17)	1.5	-3.2	0.9	-3.4	0.0	0.0	1.3	1.6	12.9	8.6	12.5

Betas (Levered)

	Raw (OLS)	Blume Adjusted	Peer Group	Vasicek Adjusted	Sum	Downside
Median	0.88	0.93	0.92	0.90	1.10	1.24
SIC Composite	0.97	0.99	0.92	0.97	1.10	1.03
Large Composite	1.01	1.01	0.92	0.98	1.15	1.03
Small Composite	0.73	0.83	0.93	0.76	0.57	0.81
High Financial Risk	1.22	1.14	0.95	1.17	1.02	1.35

Betas (Unlevered)

	Raw (OLS)	Blume Adjusted	Peer Group	Vasicek Adjusted	Sum	Downside
Median	0.83	0.85	0.86	0.82	0.97	1.11
SIC Composite	0.85	0.86	0.80	0.85	0.96	0.90
Large Composite	0.82	0.82	0.75	0.79	0.93	0.83
Small Composite	0.72	0.83	0.92	0.75	0.56	0.81
High Financial Risk	1.04	0.98	0.83	1.00	0.88	1.15

Equity Valuation Multiples

	Price/Sales Latest	5-Yr Avg	Price/Earnings Latest	5-Yr Avg	Market/Book Latest	5-Yr Avg
Median	3.1	2.3	35.2	28.5	3.1	2.4
SIC Composite	3.9	3.1	34.5	26.4	3.7	3.0
Large Composite	3.6	3.0	32.6	25.1	3.0	2.5
Small Composite	2.6	2.1	75.8	23.4	2.1	1.8
High Financial Risk	2.9	1.8	–	–	4.2	2.5

Enterprise Valuation (EV) Multiples

	EV/Sales Latest	5-Yr Avg	EV/EBITDA Latest	5-Yr Avg
Median	3.1	2.4	15.9	13.4
SIC Composite	4.3	3.3	17.2	13.9
Large Composite	4.4	3.4	16.0	13.4
Small Composite	2.2	1.7	15.7	10.9
High Financial Risk	3.3	2.2	15.5	12.9

Enterprise Valuation SIC Composite: EV/Sales: Latest 4.3, 5-Yr Avg 3.3; EV/EBITDA: Latest 17.2, 5-Yr Avg 13.9

Fama-French (F-F) 5-Factor Model

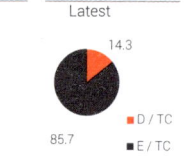

	F-F Beta	SMB Premium	HML Premium	RMW Premium	CMA Premium
Median	0.9	2.8	2.8	0.3	-4.5
SIC Composite	0.9	1.4	-3.1	-1.2	0.7
Large Composite	–	–	–	–	–
Small Composite	0.7	3.9	-1.1	1.0	3.8
High Financial Risk	–	–	–	–	–

Leverage Ratios (%)

	Debt/MV Equity Latest	5-Yr Avg	Debt/Total Capital Latest	5-Yr Avg
Median	9.1	8.0	8.3	7.4
SIC Composite	16.6	15.3	14.3	13.2
Large Composite	25.6	21.2	20.4	17.5
Small Composite	1.3	3.2	1.3	3.1
High Financial Risk	20.3	33.7	16.9	25.2

Cost of Debt

	Cost of Debt (%) Latest
Median	6.1
SIC Composite	4.9
Large Composite	4.6
Small Composite	7.1
High Financial Risk	5.5

Capital Structure

SIC Composite (%) Latest: D/TC 14.3, E/TC 85.7

Cost of Equity Capital (%)

	CAPM	CRSP Deciles CAPM +Size Prem	Build-Up	Risk Premium Report CAPM +Size Prem	Build-Up	Discounted Cash Flow 1-Stage	3-Stage	Fama-French 5-Factor Model
Median	8.5	10.1	10.0	12.8	13.9	11.5	8.9	9.9
SIC Composite	8.8	9.3	8.9	12.1	11.7	12.0	9.0	6.3
Large Composite	8.9	8.9	8.6	11.7	10.5	11.3	9.2	–
Small Composite	7.7	13.3	14.1	12.5	16.7	12.2	9.1	14.7
High Financial Risk	–	–	–	15.1	18.0	–	–	–

Cost of Equity Capital (%) SIC Composite: Avg CRSP 9.1, Avg RPR 11.9, 1-Stage 12.0, 3-Stage 9.0, 5-Factor Model 6.3

Weighted Average Cost of Capital (WACC) (%)

	CAPM	CRSP Deciles CAPM +Size Prem	Build-Up	Risk Premium Report CAPM +Size Prem	Build-Up	Discounted Cash Flow 1-Stage	3-Stage	Fama-French 5-Factor Model
Median	8.1	9.5	9.5	11.7	12.9	11.2	8.6	9.4
SIC Composite	8.2	8.5	8.2	11.0	10.6	10.8	8.3	6.0
Large Composite	7.8	7.9	7.6	10.1	9.1	9.8	8.1	–
Small Composite	7.6	13.2	14.0	12.4	16.5	12.2	9.1	14.6
High Financial Risk	–	–	–	13.3	15.6	–	–	–

WACC (%) SIC Composite: Low 6.0, High 11.0; Average 9.1, Median 8.5

© 2017 Duff & Phelps. All Rights Reserved. Duff & Phelps has used the utmost care in compiling the data presented herein, but cannot guarantee the accuracy, completeness, or timeliness of the information.

Data Updated Through March 31, 2017

382

Number of Companies: 24
Laboratory Apparatus and Analytical, Optical, Measuring, and Controlling Instruments

Industry Description
Establishments primarily engaged in laboratory apparatus and furniture; automatic controls for regulating residential and commercial environments and appliances; industrial instruments for measurement, display, and control of process variables; and related products; totalizing fluid meters and counting devices; instruments for measuring and testing of electricity and electrical signals; laboratory analytical instruments; optical instruments and lenses; measuring and controlling devices, not elsewhere classified.

Sales (in millions)

Three Largest Companies
Thermo Fisher Scientific Inc.	$18,274.1
KLA-Tencor Corp.	2,984.5
Mettler-Toledo Int'l Inc.	2,508.3

Three Smallest Companies
Frequency Electronics Inc.	$60.4
InTEST Corp.	40.2
Electro-Sensors Inc.	7.6

Annualized Monthly Performance Statistics (%)

Industry	Geometric Mean	Arithmetic Mean	Standard Deviation
1-year	21.8	23.5	22.1
3-year	11.9	13.5	19.7
5-year	18.3	19.9	19.6

S&P 500 Index	Geometric Mean	Arithmetic Mean	Standard Deviation
1-year	17.2	17.4	7.2
3-year	10.4	10.9	11.5
5-year	13.3	13.9	11.5

Total Assets (in millions)

Three Largest Companies
Thermo Fisher Scientific Inc.	$45,907.5
KLA-Tencor Corp.	4,962.4
Waters Corp.	4,662.1

Three Smallest Companies
MOCON Inc.	$47.4
InTEST Corp.	42.8
Electro-Sensors Inc.	13.4

Return Ratios (%)

	Return on Assets Latest	5-Yr Avg	Return on Equity Latest	5-Yr Avg	Dividend Yield Latest	5-Yr Avg
Median (24)	6.2	6.1	9.3	8.3	0.0	0.2
SIC Composite (24)	6.0	6.1	2.9	3.6	0.5	1.0
Large Composite (3)	5.9	5.8	3.5	4.2	0.7	1.7
Small Composite (3)	2.8	4.5	2.8	5.1	0.0	0.4
High-Financial Risk (6)	1.7	1.6	1.1	1.4	0.0	0.0

Liquidity Ratio

	Current Ratio Latest	5-Yr Avg
Median (24)	4.0	4.1
SIC Composite (24)	2.6	2.8
Large Composite (3)	1.8	2.2
Small Composite (3)	–	–
High-Financial Risk (6)	1.8	1.8

Profitability Ratio (%)

	Operating Margin Latest	5-Yr Avg
Median (24)	13.0	11.1
SIC Composite (24)	17.3	16.2
Large Composite (3)	18.4	17.0
Small Composite (3)	5.8	7.9
High-Financial Risk (6)	7.2	6.5

Growth Rates (%)

	Long-term EPS Analyst Estimates
Median (24)	10.7
SIC Composite (24)	10.7
Large Composite (3)	11.0
Small Composite (3)	10.7
High-Financial Risk (6)	18.5

Betas (Levered)

	Raw (OLS)	Blume Adjusted	Peer Group	Vasicek Adjusted	Sum	Downside
Median	0.93	0.96	0.93	0.93	1.18	1.33
SIC Composite	1.12	1.08	0.93	1.11	1.37	1.35
Large Composite	1.20	1.13	0.94	1.15	1.48	1.24
Small Composite	0.57	0.73	0.93	0.66	0.79	0.85
High Financial Risk	1.28	1.18	0.91	1.21	0.77	1.53

Betas (Unlevered)

	Raw (OLS)	Blume Adjusted	Peer Group	Vasicek Adjusted	Sum	Downside
Median	0.87	0.90	0.90	0.87	1.07	1.25
SIC Composite	0.99	0.96	0.82	0.97	1.20	1.19
Large Composite	0.99	0.94	0.78	0.95	1.22	1.02
Small Composite	0.56	0.72	0.91	0.65	0.77	0.83
High Financial Risk	1.19	1.10	0.85	1.13	0.72	1.41

Equity Valuation Multiples

	Price/Sales Latest	5-Yr Avg	Price/Earnings Latest	5-Yr Avg	Market/Book Latest	5-Yr Avg
Median	2.8	2.2	33.8	25.7	3.0	2.0
SIC Composite	4.1	3.2	34.8	27.8	4.0	2.9
Large Composite	3.7	3.0	28.2	23.8	3.5	2.5
Small Composite	1.6	1.3	36.3	19.7	1.2	1.1
High Financial Risk	1.2	1.0	91.6	70.7	3.3	2.4

Enterprise Valuation (EV) Multiples

	EV/Sales Latest	5-Yr Avg	EV/EBITDA Latest	5-Yr Avg
Median	2.8	1.8	15.9	11.0
SIC Composite	4.4	3.4	18.1	14.7
Large Composite	4.4	3.4	16.6	14.0
Small Composite	1.2	0.9	19.5	7.7
High Financial Risk	1.3	1.1	12.2	10.3

Enterprise Valuation SIC Composite
- EV/Sales: Latest 4.4, 5-Yr Avg 3.4
- EV/EBITDA: Latest 18.1, 5-Yr Avg 14.7

Fama-French (F-F) 5-Factor Model

	F-F Beta	SMB Premium	HML Premium	RMW Premium	CMA Premium
Median	0.6	5.0	-1.0	-0.3	-0.3
SIC Composite	–	–	–	–	–
Large Composite	–	–	–	–	–
Small Composite	0.5	3.1	-0.8	-0.1	-0.2
High Financial Risk	–	–	–	–	–

Leverage Ratios (%)

	Debt/MV Equity Latest	5-Yr Avg	Debt/Total Capital Latest	5-Yr Avg
Median	5.3	6.7	5.1	6.3
SIC Composite	15.3	16.1	13.3	13.9
Large Composite	23.4	23.3	19.0	18.9
Small Composite	3.6	4.9	3.5	4.7
High Financial Risk	10.1	15.0	9.1	13.0

Cost of Debt

	Cost of Debt (%) Latest
Median	6.1
SIC Composite	5.0
Large Composite	4.8
Small Composite	7.1
High Financial Risk	6.2

Capital Structure

SIC Composite (%) Latest
- D/TC: 13.3
- E/TC: 86.7

Cost of Equity Capital (%)

	CRSP Deciles CAPM	CAPM +Size Prem	Build-Up	Risk Premium Report CAPM +Size Prem	Build-Up	Discounted Cash Flow 1-Stage	3-Stage	Fama-French 5-Factor Model
Median	8.6	11.2	9.8	13.7	13.9	11.0	8.9	10.5
SIC Composite	9.6	10.0	8.9	13.7	11.8	11.2	8.6	–
Large Composite	9.8	10.0	8.7	13.6	10.7	11.7	9.8	–
Small Composite	7.1	12.7	14.1	13.8	16.7	10.7	10.0	8.0
High Financial Risk	–	–	–	12.8	17.0	–	–	–

Cost of Equity Capital (%) SIC Composite
- Avg CRSP: 9.5
- Avg RPR: 12.7
- 1-Stage: 11.2
- 3-Stage: 8.6
- 5-Factor Model: n/a

Weighted Average Cost of Capital (WACC) (%)

	CRSP Deciles CAPM	CAPM +Size Prem	Build-Up	Risk Premium Report CAPM +Size Prem	Build-Up	Discounted Cash Flow 1-Stage	3-Stage	Fama-French 5-Factor Model
Median	8.4	11.1	9.7	13.6	13.6	10.7	8.7	10.4
SIC Composite	8.9	9.3	8.3	12.4	10.8	10.3	8.0	–
Large Composite	8.8	9.0	7.9	11.9	9.5	10.4	8.8	–
Small Composite	7.1	12.5	13.8	13.5	16.3	10.6	9.8	8.0
High Financial Risk	–	–	–	12.2	16.0	–	–	–

WACC (%) SIC Composite
- Low: 8.0
- High: 12.4
- Average: 9.8
- Median: 9.8

© 2017 Duff & Phelps. All Rights Reserved. Duff & Phelps has used the utmost care in compiling the data presented herein, but cannot guarantee the accuracy, completeness, or timeliness of the information.

Data Updated Through March 31, 2017

3823

Number of Companies: 5
Industrial Instruments for Measurement, Display, and Control of Process Variables; and Related Products

Industry Description
Establishments primarily engaged in manufacturing industrial instruments and related products for measuring, displaying (indicating and/or recording), transmitting, and controlling process variables in manufacturing, energy conversion, and public service utilities.

Sales (in millions)

Three Largest Companies
MKS Instruments Inc.	$1,295.3
Cognex Corp.	520.8
Rudolph Technologies Inc.	232.8

Three Smallest Companies
Rudolph Technologies Inc.	$232.8
Hurco Companies Inc.	227.3
Electro-Sensors Inc.	7.6

Total Assets (in millions)

Three Largest Companies
MKS Instruments Inc.	$2,212.2
Cognex Corp.	1,038.6
Rudolph Technologies Inc.	338.7

Three Smallest Companies
Rudolph Technologies Inc.	$338.7
Hurco Companies Inc.	251.9
Electro-Sensors Inc.	13.4

Annualized Monthly Performance Statistics (%)

Industry	Geometric Mean	Arithmetic Mean	Standard Deviation	S&P 500 Index	Geometric Mean	Arithmetic Mean	Standard Deviation
1-year	97.8	101.7	41.7	1-year	17.2	17.4	7.2
3-year	33.8	37.2	31.6	3-year	10.4	10.9	11.5
5-year	26.0	28.8	27.5	5-year	13.3	13.9	11.5

Return Ratios (%)

	Return on Assets		Return on Equity		Dividend Yield	
	Latest	5-Yr Avg	Latest	5-Yr Avg	Latest	5-Yr Avg
Median (5)	8.9	6.6	10.1	7.9	0.9	0.8
SIC Composite (5)	7.9	7.9	2.6	3.9	0.8	1.0
Large Composite (−)	−	−	−	−	−	−
Small Composite (−)	−	−	−	−	−	−
High-Financial Risk (−)	−	−	−	−	−	−

Liquidity Ratio

	Current Ratio	
	Latest	5-Yr Avg
Median (5)	−	−
SIC Composite (5)	−	−

Profitability Ratio (%)

	Operating Margin	
	Latest	5-Yr Avg
Median (5)	15.8	11.0
SIC Composite (5)	18.6	17.4

Growth Rates (%)

	Long-term EPS
	Analyst Estimates
Median (5)	10.7
SIC Composite (5)	11.1

Betas (Levered)

	Raw (OLS)	Blume Adjusted	Peer Group	Vasicek Adjusted	Sum	Downside
Median	1.05	1.04	0.91	1.02	0.97	1.11
SIC Composite	1.26	1.17	0.91	1.18	1.30	1.50
Large Composite	−	−	−	−	−	−
Small Composite	−	−	−	−	−	−
High Financial Risk	−	−	−	−	−	−

Betas (Unlevered)

	Raw (OLS)	Blume Adjusted	Peer Group	Vasicek Adjusted	Sum	Downside
Median	0.94	0.93	0.90	0.92	0.97	1.00
SIC Composite	1.22	1.13	0.88	1.14	1.25	1.44
Large Composite	−	−	−	−	−	−
Small Composite	−	−	−	−	−	−
High Financial Risk	−	−	−	−	−	−

Equity Valuation Multiples

	Price/Sales		Price/Earnings		Market/Book	
	Latest	5-Yr Avg	Latest	5-Yr Avg	Latest	5-Yr Avg
Median	2.8	2.0	18.9	20.8	2.4	1.5
SIC Composite	5.2	3.3	38.6	25.4	4.3	2.4
Large Composite	−	−	−	−	−	−
Small Composite	−	−	−	−	−	−
High Financial Risk	−	−	−	−	−	−

Enterprise Valuation (EV) Multiples

	EV/Sales		EV/EBITDA	
	Latest	5-Yr Avg	Latest	5-Yr Avg
Median	2.5	1.4	13.2	9.1
SIC Composite	5.0	2.8	21.8	13.8
Large Composite	−	−	−	−
Small Composite	−	−	−	−
High Financial Risk	−	−	−	−

Enterprise Valuation SIC Composite
- EV/Sales: Latest 5.0, 5-Yr Avg 2.8
- EV/EBITDA: Latest 21.8, 5-Yr Avg 13.8

Fama-French (F-F) 5-Factor Model

Fama-French (F-F) Components

	F-F Beta	SMB Premium	HML Premium	RMW Premium	CMA Premium
Median	0.9	2.8	2.8	0.3	-4.5
SIC Composite	1.2	2.9	1.5	-0.2	-4.6
Large Composite	−	−	−	−	−
Small Composite	−	−	−	−	−
High Financial Risk	−	−	−	−	−

Leverage Ratios (%)

	Debt/MV Equity		Debt/Total Capital	
	Latest	5-Yr Avg	Latest	5-Yr Avg
Median	0.7	1.7	0.7	1.7
SIC Composite	5.2	3.0	4.9	2.9

Cost of Debt

	Cost of Debt (%)
	Latest
Median	6.1
SIC Composite	6.1

Capital Structure

SIC Composite (%) Latest
- D/TC: 4.9
- E/TC: 95.1

Cost of Equity Capital (%)

	CRSP Deciles			Risk Premium Report		Discounted Cash Flow		Fama-French
	CAPM	CAPM +Size Prem	Build-Up	CAPM +Size Prem	Build-Up	1-Stage	3-Stage	5-Factor Model
Median	9.1	11.6	10.6	13.9	15.5	11.6	10.1	9.9
SIC Composite	10.0	11.1	9.6	14.5	13.6	11.7	7.9	9.5
Large Composite	−	−	−	−	−	−	−	−
Small Composite	−	−	−	−	−	−	−	−
High Financial Risk	−	−	−	−	−	−	−	−

Cost of Equity Capital (%) SIC Composite
- Avg CRSP: 10.3
- Avg RPR: 14.0
- 1-Stage: 11.7
- 3-Stage: 7.9
- 5-Factor Model: 9.5

Weighted Average Cost of Capital (WACC) (%)

	CRSP Deciles			Risk Premium Report		Discounted Cash Flow		Fama-French
	CAPM	CAPM +Size Prem	Build-Up	CAPM +Size Prem	Build-Up	1-Stage	3-Stage	5-Factor Model
Median	8.4	11.6	10.6	13.9	15.5	11.5	9.2	9.0
SIC Composite	9.7	10.7	9.3	14.0	13.1	11.3	7.7	9.2
Large Composite	−	−	−	−	−	−	−	−
Small Composite	−	−	−	−	−	−	−	−
High Financial Risk	−	−	−	−	−	−	−	−

WACC (%) SIC Composite
- Low: 7.7
- High: 14.0
- Average: 10.8
- Median: 10.7

© 2017 Duff & Phelps. All Rights Reserved. Duff & Phelps has used the utmost care in compiling the data presented herein, but cannot guarantee the accuracy, completeness, or timeliness of the information.

Data Updated Through March 31, 2017

3826

Number of Companies: 7
Laboratory Analytical Instruments

Industry Description
Establishments primarily engaged in manufacturing laboratory instruments and instrumentation systems for chemical or physical analysis of the composition or concentration of samples of solid, fluid, gaseous, or composite material.

Sales (in millions)

Three Largest Companies
Thermo Fisher Scientific Inc.	$18,274.1
Mettler-Toledo Int'l Inc.	2,508.3
Illumina Inc.	2,398.4

Three Smallest Companies
Bio-Rad Laboratories Inc.	$2,068.2
Bruker Corp.	1,611.3
Coherent Inc.	857.4

Annualized Monthly Performance Statistics (%)

Industry	Geometric Mean	Arithmetic Mean	Standard Deviation
1-year	14.3	16.7	25.0
3-year	10.6	12.6	21.6
5-year	20.3	22.2	21.8

Total Assets (in millions)

Three Largest Companies
Thermo Fisher Scientific Inc.	$45,907.5
Waters Corp.	4,662.1
Illumina Inc.	4,280.6

Three Smallest Companies
Mettler-Toledo Int'l Inc.	$2,166.8
Bruker Corp.	1,808.4
Coherent Inc.	1,161.1

S&P 500 Index	Geometric Mean	Arithmetic Mean	Standard Deviation
1-year	17.2	17.4	7.2
3-year	10.4	10.9	11.5
5-year	13.3	13.9	11.5

Return Ratios (%)

	Return on Assets Latest	5-Yr Avg	Return on Equity Latest	5-Yr Avg	Dividend Yield Latest	5-Yr Avg
Median (7)	8.7	7.3	21.5	12.4	0.0	0.0
SIC Composite (7)	5.7	5.7	2.9	3.4	0.2	0.3
Large Composite (–)	–	–	–	–	–	–
Small Composite (–)	–	–	–	–	–	–
High-Financial Risk (–)	–	–	–	–	–	–

Liquidity Ratio

	Current Ratio Latest	5-Yr Avg
Median (7)	3.3	3.6
SIC Composite (7)	2.3	2.4
Large Composite (–)	–	–
Small Composite (–)	–	–
High-Financial Risk (–)	–	–

Profitability Ratio (%)

	Operating Margin Latest	5-Yr Avg
Median (7)	16.1	14.3
SIC Composite (7)	17.0	16.0
Large Composite (–)	–	–
Small Composite (–)	–	–
High-Financial Risk (–)	–	–

Growth Rates (%)

	Long-term EPS Analyst Estimates
Median (7)	10.1
SIC Composite (7)	10.6
Large Composite (–)	–
Small Composite (–)	–
High-Financial Risk (–)	–

Betas (Levered)

	Raw (OLS)	Blume Adjusted	Peer Group	Vasicek Adjusted	Sum	Downside
Median	0.91	0.95	0.93	0.93	1.34	1.40
SIC Composite	1.01	1.01	0.93	0.96	1.41	1.34
Large Composite	–	–	–	–	–	–
Small Composite	–	–	–	–	–	–
High Financial Risk	–	–	–	–	–	–

Betas (Unlevered)

	Raw (OLS)	Blume Adjusted	Peer Group	Vasicek Adjusted	Sum	Downside
Median	0.86	0.89	0.88	0.87	1.23	1.29
SIC Composite	0.88	0.88	0.82	0.84	1.22	1.16
Large Composite	–	–	–	–	–	–
Small Composite	–	–	–	–	–	–
High Financial Risk	–	–	–	–	–	–

Equity Valuation Multiples

	Price/Sales Latest	5-Yr Avg	Price/Earnings Latest	5-Yr Avg	Market/Book Latest	5-Yr Avg
Median	5.0	2.8	32.4	26.0	5.4	4.3
SIC Composite	4.2	3.4	34.1	29.0	3.7	3.0
Large Composite	–	–	–	–	–	–
Small Composite	–	–	–	–	–	–
High Financial Risk	–	–	–	–	–	–

Enterprise Valuation (EV) Multiples

	EV/Sales Latest	5-Yr Avg	EV/EBITDA Latest	5-Yr Avg
Median	5.3	3.5	19.5	13.4
SIC Composite	4.7	3.7	18.6	15.8
Large Composite	–	–	–	–
Small Composite	–	–	–	–
High Financial Risk	–	–	–	–

Enterprise Valuation SIC Composite
Latest: EV/Sales 4.7, EV/EBITDA 18.6
5-Yr Avg: EV/Sales 3.7, EV/EBITDA 15.8

Fama-French (F-F) 5-Factor Model

	Fama-French (F-F) Components				
	F-F Beta	SMB Premium	HML Premium	RMW Premium	CMA Premium
Median	0.8	2.1	-1.9	-1.8	1.9
SIC Composite	–	–	–	–	–
Large Composite	–	–	–	–	–
Small Composite	–	–	–	–	–
High Financial Risk	–	–	–	–	–

Leverage Ratios (%)

	Debt/MV Equity Latest	5-Yr Avg	Debt/Total Capital Latest	5-Yr Avg
Median	7.4	10.5	6.9	9.5
SIC Composite	17.0	18.2	14.5	15.4
Large Composite	–	–	–	–
Small Composite	–	–	–	–
High Financial Risk	–	–	–	–

Cost of Debt

	Cost of Debt (%) Latest
Median	6.1
SIC Composite	5.0
Large Composite	–
Small Composite	–
High Financial Risk	–

Capital Structure

SIC Composite (%) Latest
D/TC: 14.5
E/TC: 85.5

Cost of Equity Capital (%)

	CRSP Deciles CAPM	CAPM +Size Prem	Build-Up	Risk Premium Report CAPM +Size Prem	Build-Up	Discounted Cash Flow 1-Stage	3-Stage	Fama-French 5-Factor Model
Median	8.6	9.5	9.1	13.6	12.5	10.1	7.1	8.3
SIC Composite	8.8	9.0	8.7	13.7	11.3	10.8	8.4	–
Large Composite	–	–	–	–	–	–	–	–
Small Composite	–	–	–	–	–	–	–	–
High Financial Risk	–	–	–	–	–	–	–	–

Cost of Equity Capital (%) SIC Composite
Avg CRSP: 8.9, Avg RPR: 12.5, 1-Stage: 10.8, 3-Stage: 8.4, 5-Factor Model: n/a

Weighted Average Cost of Capital (WACC) (%)

	CRSP Deciles CAPM	CAPM +Size Prem	Build-Up	Risk Premium Report CAPM +Size Prem	Build-Up	Discounted Cash Flow 1-Stage	3-Stage	Fama-French 5-Factor Model
Median	8.4	9.1	8.8	11.8	12.1	9.6	7.0	8.8
SIC Composite	8.1	8.3	8.1	12.3	10.3	9.8	7.8	–
Large Composite	–	–	–	–	–	–	–	–
Small Composite	–	–	–	–	–	–	–	–
High Financial Risk	–	–	–	–	–	–	–	–

WACC (%) SIC Composite
Low 7.8 — High 12.3
Average 9.4, Median 9.1

© 2017 Duff & Phelps. All Rights Reserved. Duff & Phelps has used the utmost care in compiling the data presented herein, but cannot guarantee the accuracy, completeness, or timeliness of the information.

Data Updated Through March 31, 2017

384

Number of Companies: 32
Surgical, Medical, and Dental Instruments and Supplies

Industry Description
Establishments primarily engaged in surgical and medical instruments and apparatus; orthopedic, prosthetic, and surgical appliances and supplies; dental equipment and supplies; x-ray apparatus and tubes and related irradiation apparatus; and electromedical and electrotherapeutic apparatus.

Sales (in millions)

Three Largest Companies
Stryker Corp.	$11,325.0
Zimmer Biomet Holdings, Inc.	7,683.9
DENTSPLY SIRONA Inc.	3,745.3

Three Smallest Companies
IRIDEX Corp.	$46.2
Utah Medical Products Inc.	39.3
Electromed, Inc.	23.0

Annualized Monthly Performance Statistics (%)

Industry	Geometric Mean	Arithmetic Mean	Standard Deviation
1-year	23.4	24.4	16.2
3-year	19.3	20.3	15.6
5-year	16.8	17.7	15.1

S&P 500 Index	Geometric Mean	Arithmetic Mean	Standard Deviation
1-year	17.2	17.4	7.2
3-year	10.4	10.9	11.5
5-year	13.3	13.9	11.5

Total Assets (in millions)

Three Largest Companies
Zimmer Biomet Holdings, Inc.	$26,684.4
Stryker Corp.	20,435.0
DENTSPLY SIRONA Inc.	11,656.1

Three Smallest Companies
IRIDEX Corp.	$48.1
Intricon Corp.	43.8
Electromed, Inc.	20.6

Return Ratios (%)

	Return on Assets Latest	Return on Assets 5-Yr Avg	Return on Equity Latest	Return on Equity 5-Yr Avg	Dividend Yield Latest	Dividend Yield 5-Yr Avg
Median (32)	7.1	6.1	10.3	8.4	0.0	0.0
SIC Composite (32)	5.9	6.8	2.7	3.4	0.6	0.7
Large Composite (3)	4.1	5.2	2.7	3.5	1.1	1.2
Small Composite (3)	1.8	8.6	0.7	3.9	0.9	1.2
High-Financial Risk (10)	1.8	-3.9	1.1	-3.9	0.0	0.0

Liquidity Ratio

	Current Ratio Latest	Current Ratio 5-Yr Avg
Median (32)	2.8	3.3
SIC Composite (32)	2.6	2.9
Large Composite (3)	2.3	2.7
Small Composite (3)	–	4.6
High-Financial Risk (10)	1.1	1.5

Profitability Ratio (%)

	Operating Margin Latest	Operating Margin 5-Yr Avg
Median (32)	16.6	13.1
SIC Composite (32)	20.7	20.1
Large Composite (3)	21.2	21.0
Small Composite (3)	15.5	16.7
High-Financial Risk (10)	15.2	12.8

Growth Rates (%)

	Long-term EPS Analyst Estimates
Median (32)	11.4
SIC Composite (32)	12.0
Large Composite (3)	9.5
Small Composite (3)	11.8
High-Financial Risk (10)	12.0

Betas (Levered)

	Raw (OLS)	Blume Adjusted	Peer Group	Vasicek Adjusted	Sum	Downside
Median	0.86	0.92	0.91	0.88	1.01	1.29
SIC Composite	0.83	0.90	0.91	0.84	0.85	0.84
Large Composite	1.00	1.01	0.91	0.98	0.97	0.98
Small Composite	0.81	0.89	0.91	0.84	0.47	0.93
High Financial Risk	1.07	1.05	0.91	1.05	1.15	1.26

Betas (Unlevered)

	Raw (OLS)	Blume Adjusted	Peer Group	Vasicek Adjusted	Sum	Downside
Median	0.80	0.83	0.86	0.81	0.90	1.15
SIC Composite	0.74	0.81	0.82	0.75	0.77	0.76
Large Composite	0.83	0.83	0.75	0.81	0.80	0.81
Small Composite	0.81	0.88	0.91	0.84	0.47	0.92
High Financial Risk	0.92	0.91	0.79	0.90	0.99	1.08

Equity Valuation Multiples

	Price/Sales Latest	Price/Sales 5-Yr Avg	Price/Earnings Latest	Price/Earnings 5-Yr Avg	Market/Book Latest	Market/Book 5-Yr Avg
Median	3.7	2.6	41.3	32.7	3.5	2.6
SIC Composite	4.5	3.5	37.2	29.0	4.0	3.4
Large Composite	3.9	3.2	37.0	28.5	2.8	2.7
Small Composite	3.6	3.0	–	25.8	3.0	2.6
High Financial Risk	3.6	2.4	93.7	–	4.3	2.3

Enterprise Valuation (EV) Multiples

	EV/Sales Latest	EV/Sales 5-Yr Avg	EV/EBITDA Latest	EV/EBITDA 5-Yr Avg
Median	4.3	2.7	17.2	14.0
SIC Composite	4.8	3.6	17.6	14.1
Large Composite	4.5	3.5	15.5	12.7
Small Composite	3.1	2.8	14.6	12.9
High Financial Risk	4.2	3.0	16.5	13.1

Enterprise Valuation SIC Composite
- Latest: EV/Sales 4.8, EV/EBITDA 17.6
- 5-Yr Avg: EV/Sales 3.6, EV/EBITDA 14.1

Fama-French (F-F) 5-Factor Model

	F-F Beta	SMB Premium	HML Premium	RMW Premium	CMA Premium
Median	1.2	1.4	-5.2	-1.8	5.4
SIC Composite	0.8	1.6	-3.6	-0.7	2.0
Large Composite	–	–	–	–	–
Small Composite	0.8	4.6	-1.5	1.7	5.6
High Financial Risk	–	–	–	–	–

Leverage Ratios (%)

	Debt/MV Equity Latest	Debt/MV Equity 5-Yr Avg	Debt/Total Capital Latest	Debt/Total Capital 5-Yr Avg
Median	8.4	6.0	7.8	5.6
SIC Composite	13.1	12.0	11.6	10.7
Large Composite	22.3	18.6	18.2	15.7
Small Composite	0.3	2.3	0.3	2.3
High Financial Risk	19.8	32.9	16.5	24.7

Cost of Debt

	Cost of Debt (%) Latest
Median	7.1
SIC Composite	5.1
Large Composite	4.5
Small Composite	7.1
High Financial Risk	5.4

Capital Structure

SIC Composite (%) Latest
- D/TC: 11.6
- E/TC: 88.4

Cost of Equity Capital (%)

	CRSP Deciles CAPM	CRSP Deciles CAPM +Size Prem	CRSP Deciles Build-Up	Risk Premium Report CAPM +Size Prem	Risk Premium Report Build-Up	Discounted Cash Flow 1-Stage	Discounted Cash Flow 3-Stage	Fama-French 5-Factor Model
Median	8.4	10.0	10.1	12.7	14.0	12.0	8.4	9.7
SIC Composite	8.1	8.6	9.0	11.0	12.0	12.6	8.7	7.1
Large Composite	8.9	9.0	8.6	11.0	11.0	10.6	8.1	–
Small Composite	8.1	13.7	14.1	11.9	16.6	12.9	8.7	18.2
High Financial Risk	–	–	–	15.9	18.0	–	–	–

Cost of Equity Capital (%) SIC Composite
- Avg CRSP: 8.8
- Avg RPR: 11.5
- 1-Stage: 12.6
- 3-Stage: 8.7
- 5-Factor Model: 7.1

Weighted Average Cost of Capital (WACC) (%)

	CRSP Deciles CAPM	CRSP Deciles CAPM +Size Prem	CRSP Deciles Build-Up	Risk Premium Report CAPM +Size Prem	Risk Premium Report Build-Up	Discounted Cash Flow 1-Stage	Discounted Cash Flow 3-Stage	Fama-French 5-Factor Model
Median	8.1	9.7	9.5	11.7	13.1	11.9	7.9	9.6
SIC Composite	7.7	8.1	8.5	10.3	11.2	11.7	8.2	6.8
Large Composite	8.0	8.1	7.8	9.7	9.7	9.4	7.4	–
Small Composite	8.1	13.7	14.1	11.9	16.6	12.9	8.7	18.1
High Financial Risk	–	–	–	13.9	15.7	–	–	–

WACC (%) SIC Composite
- Low: 6.8
- High: 11.7
- Average: 9.2
- Median: 8.5

© 2017 Duff & Phelps. All Rights Reserved. Duff & Phelps has used the utmost care in compiling the data presented herein, but cannot guarantee the accuracy, completeness, or timeliness of the information.

Data Updated Through March 31, 2017

3841

Number of Companies: 9
Surgical and Medical Instruments and Apparatus

Industry Description
Establishments primarily engaged in manufacturing medical, surgical, ophthalmic, and veterinary instruments and apparatus.

Sales (in millions)

Three Largest Companies
CR Bard Inc.	$3,714.0
Teleflex Inc.	1,868.0
NuVasive, Inc.	962.1

Three Smallest Companies
ABIOMED, Inc.	$329.5
ATRION Corp.	145.7
LeMaitre Vascular, Inc.	89.2

Total Assets (in millions)

Three Largest Companies
CR Bard Inc.	$5,306.1
Teleflex Inc.	3,891.2
NuVasive, Inc.	1,570.8

Three Smallest Companies
ABIOMED, Inc.	$423.9
ATRION Corp.	164.3
LeMaitre Vascular, Inc.	101.9

Annualized Monthly Performance Statistics (%)

Industry	Geometric Mean	Arithmetic Mean	Standard Deviation		S&P 500 Index	Geometric Mean	Arithmetic Mean	Standard Deviation
1-year	28.5	29.6	17.4		1-year	17.2	17.4	7.2
3-year	24.4	25.8	19.3		3-year	10.4	10.9	11.5
5-year	23.4	24.8	19.6		5-year	13.3	13.9	11.5

Return Ratios (%)

	Return on Assets Latest	5-Yr Avg	Return on Equity Latest	5-Yr Avg	Dividend Yield Latest	5-Yr Avg	Current Ratio Latest	5-Yr Avg	Operating Margin Latest	5-Yr Avg	Long-term EPS Analyst Estimates
Median (9)	9.5	7.3	10.2	8.3	0.5	0.6	2.8	3.6	20.1	12.9	12.1
SIC Composite (9)	6.3	5.5	2.1	2.8	0.5	0.6	2.7	2.9	19.9	18.9	13.6
Large Composite (−)	−	−	−	−	−	−	−	−	−	−	−
Small Composite (−)	−	−	−	−	−	−	−	−	−	−	−
High-Financial Risk (−)	−	−	−	−	−	−	−	−	−	−	−

Liquidity Ratio | Profitability Ratio (%) | Growth Rates (%)

Betas (Levered)

	Raw (OLS)	Blume Adjusted	Peer Group	Vasicek Adjusted	Sum	Downside
Median	0.85	0.91	0.91	0.88	1.07	1.24
SIC Composite	0.71	0.82	0.91	0.77	0.71	0.75
Large Composite	−	−	−	−	−	−
Small Composite	−	−	−	−	−	−
High Financial Risk	−	−	−	−	−	−

Betas (Unlevered)

	Raw (OLS)	Blume Adjusted	Peer Group	Vasicek Adjusted	Sum	Downside
Median	0.76	0.82	0.84	0.82	0.99	1.24
SIC Composite	0.67	0.77	0.85	0.73	0.67	0.70
Large Composite	−	−	−	−	−	−
Small Composite	−	−	−	−	−	−
High Financial Risk	−	−	−	−	−	−

Equity Valuation Multiples

	Price/Sales Latest	5-Yr Avg	Price/Earnings Latest	5-Yr Avg	Market/Book Latest	5-Yr Avg
Median	4.9	2.7	43.2	36.5	5.1	2.7
SIC Composite	4.8	3.3	47.3	35.2	5.9	3.6
Large Composite	−	−	−	−	−	−
Small Composite	−	−	−	−	−	−
High Financial Risk	−	−	−	−	−	−

Enterprise Valuation (EV) Multiples

	EV/Sales Latest	5-Yr Avg	EV/EBITDA Latest	5-Yr Avg
Median	4.9	3.0	18.1	13.5
SIC Composite	4.9	3.4	18.5	13.6
Large Composite	−	−	−	−
Small Composite	−	−	−	−
High Financial Risk	−	−	−	−

Enterprise Valuation SIC Composite
- Latest: EV/Sales 4.9, EV/EBITDA 18.5
- 5-Yr Avg: EV/Sales 3.4, EV/EBITDA 13.6

Fama-French (F-F) 5-Factor Model

	F-F Beta	SMB Premium	HML Premium	RMW Premium	CMA Premium
Median	0.5	5.1	-1.2	2.9	-2.8
SIC Composite	0.6	2.5	-2.9	0.9	0.8
Large Composite	−	−	−	−	−
Small Composite	−	−	−	−	−
High Financial Risk	−	−	−	−	−

Leverage Ratios (%)

	Debt/MV Equity Latest	5-Yr Avg	Debt/Total Capital Latest	5-Yr Avg
Median	9.1	12.2	8.3	10.9
SIC Composite	9.4	13.8	8.6	12.2
Large Composite	−	−	−	−
Small Composite	−	−	−	−
High Financial Risk	−	−	−	−

Cost of Debt

	Cost of Debt (%) Latest
Median	6.1
SIC Composite	5.6
Large Composite	−
Small Composite	−
High Financial Risk	−

Capital Structure

SIC Composite (%) Latest
- D/TC: 8.6
- E/TC: 91.4

Cost of Equity Capital (%)

	CRSP Deciles CAPM	CAPM +Size Prem	Build-Up	Risk Premium Report CAPM +Size Prem	Build-Up	Discounted Cash Flow 1-Stage	3-Stage	Fama-French 5-Factor Model
Median	8.3	9.8	10.0	12.7	14.1	13.0	6.8	10.2
SIC Composite	7.8	8.7	9.4	10.9	13.1	14.0	7.7	8.3
Large Composite	−	−	−	−	−	−	−	−
Small Composite	−	−	−	−	−	−	−	−
High Financial Risk	−	−	−	−	−	−	−	−

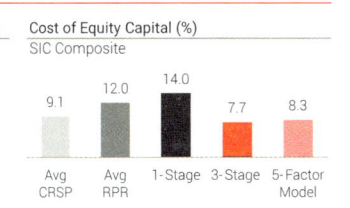

Cost of Equity Capital (%) SIC Composite:
- Avg CRSP: 9.1
- Avg RPR: 12.0
- 1-Stage: 14.0
- 3-Stage: 7.7
- 5-Factor Model: 8.3

Weighted Average Cost of Capital (WACC) (%)

	CRSP Deciles CAPM	CAPM +Size Prem	Build-Up	Risk Premium Report CAPM +Size Prem	Build-Up	Discounted Cash Flow 1-Stage	3-Stage	Fama-French 5-Factor Model
Median	8.1	9.2	9.5	11.9	12.9	13.0	6.7	11.2
SIC Composite	7.5	8.4	9.1	10.4	12.4	13.3	7.5	8.0
Large Composite	−	−	−	−	−	−	−	−
Small Composite	−	−	−	−	−	−	−	−
High Financial Risk	−	−	−	−	−	−	−	−

WACC (%) SIC Composite: Low 7.5, High 13.3. Average 9.9, Median 9.1

© 2017 Duff & Phelps. All Rights Reserved. Duff & Phelps has used the utmost care in compiling the data presented herein, but cannot guarantee the accuracy, completeness, or timeliness of the information.

Data Updated Through March 31, 2017

3842

Number of Companies: 6
Orthopedic, Prosthetic, and Surgical Appliances and Supplies

Industry Description
Establishments primarily engaged in manufacturing orthopedic, prosthetic, and surgical appliances and supplies, arch supports and other foot appliances; fracture appliances, elastic hosiery, abdominal supporters, braces, and trusses; bandages; surgical gauze and dressings; sutures; adhesive tapes and medicated plasters; and personal safety appliances and equipment.

Sales (in millions)

Three Largest Companies
Zimmer Biomet Holdings, Inc.	$7,683.9
Edwards Lifesciences Corp.	2,963.7
MSA Safety Inc.	1,149.5

Three Smallest Companies
Integra Lifesciences Holdings	$992.1
Exactech Inc.	257.6
Intricon Corp.	68.0

Annualized Monthly Performance Statistics (%)

Industry
	Geometric Mean	Arithmetic Mean	Standard Deviation
1-year	13.7	18.3	34.2
3-year	19.4	22.0	25.3
5-year	17.2	19.5	23.4

Total Assets (in millions)

Three Largest Companies
Zimmer Biomet Holdings, Inc.	$26,684.4
Edwards Lifesciences Corp.	4,510.0
Integra Lifesciences Holdings	1,808.0

Three Smallest Companies
MSA Safety Inc.	$1,353.9
Exactech Inc.	294.2
Intricon Corp.	43.8

S&P 500 Index
	Geometric Mean	Arithmetic Mean	Standard Deviation
1-year	17.2	17.4	7.2
3-year	10.4	10.9	11.5
5-year	13.3	13.9	11.5

Return Ratios (%)

	Return on Assets Latest	5-Yr Avg	Return on Equity Latest	5-Yr Avg	Dividend Yield Latest	5-Yr Avg
Median (6)	2.6	4.1	5.1	6.2	0.0	0.0
SIC Composite (6)	3.0	5.1	2.1	3.3	0.5	0.6
Large Composite (–)	–	–	–	–	–	–
Small Composite (–)	–	–	–	–	–	–
High-Financial Risk (–)	–	–	–	–	–	–

Liquidity Ratio

	Current Ratio Latest	5-Yr Avg
Median (6)	3.1	3.6
SIC Composite (6)	2.4	3.5

Profitability Ratio (%)

	Operating Margin Latest	5-Yr Avg
Median (6)	14.8	12.3
SIC Composite (6)	23.2	23.3

Growth Rates (%)

	Long-term EPS Analyst Estimates
Median (6)	11.1
SIC Composite (6)	12.5

Betas (Levered)

	Raw (OLS)	Blume Adjusted	Peer Group	Vasicek Adjusted	Sum	Downside
Median	0.81	0.89	0.91	0.83	1.38	1.14
SIC Composite	0.96	0.98	0.91	0.95	0.98	0.99
Large Composite	–	–	–	–	–	–
Small Composite	–	–	–	–	–	–
High Financial Risk	–	–	–	–	–	–

Betas (Unlevered)

	Raw (OLS)	Blume Adjusted	Peer Group	Vasicek Adjusted	Sum	Downside
Median	0.76	0.78	0.83	0.76	0.99	1.03
SIC Composite	0.79	0.80	0.74	0.78	0.80	0.81
Large Composite	–	–	–	–	–	–
Small Composite	–	–	–	–	–	–
High Financial Risk	–	–	–	–	–	–

Equity Valuation Multiples

	Price/Sales Latest	5-Yr Avg	Price/Earnings Latest	5-Yr Avg	Market/Book Latest	5-Yr Avg
Median	2.7	1.8	55.3	29.2	3.3	2.2
SIC Composite	3.9	3.5	48.7	29.9	3.0	2.8
Large Composite	–	–	–	–	–	–
Small Composite	–	–	–	–	–	–
High Financial Risk	–	–	–	–	–	–

Enterprise Valuation (EV) Multiples

	EV/Sales Latest	5-Yr Avg	EV/EBITDA Latest	5-Yr Avg
Median	3.2	2.2	15.5	12.8
SIC Composite	4.7	3.9	14.6	12.6
Large Composite	–	–	–	–
Small Composite	–	–	–	–
High Financial Risk	–	–	–	–

Enterprise Valuation SIC Composite
Latest: FV/Sales 4.7, EV/EBITDA 14.6
5-Yr Avg: FV/Sales 3.9, EV/EBITDA 12.6

Fama-French (F-F) 5-Factor Model

Fama-French (F-F) Components
	F-F Beta	SMB Premium	HML Premium	RMW Premium	CMA Premium
Median	0.6	4.4	-7.0	1.8	2.7
SIC Composite	0.9	2.8	-5.4	-0.3	3.9
Large Composite	–	–	–	–	–
Small Composite	–	–	–	–	–
High Financial Risk	–	–	–	–	–

Leverage Ratios (%)

	Debt/MV Equity Latest	5-Yr Avg	Debt/Total Capital Latest	5-Yr Avg
Median	16.8	22.4	14.3	18.2
SIC Composite	26.0	20.1	20.6	16.7

Cost of Debt

	Cost of Debt (%) Latest
Median	6.6
SIC Composite	5.0

Capital Structure

SIC Composite (%) Latest
D/TC: 20.6
E/TC: 79.4

Cost of Equity Capital (%)

	CRSP Deciles CAPM	CAPM +Size Prem	Build-Up	Risk Premium Report CAPM +Size Prem	Build-Up	Discounted Cash Flow 1-Stage	3-Stage	Fama-French 5-Factor Model
Median	8.1	10.4	10.0	13.3	13.8	11.3	9.5	8.4
SIC Composite	8.7	9.2	8.9	11.5	11.7	13.0	9.4	9.2
Large Composite	–	–	–	–	–	–	–	–
Small Composite	–	–	–	–	–	–	–	–
High Financial Risk	–	–	–	–	–	–	–	–

Cost of Equity Capital (%) SIC Composite
Avg CRSP 9.1, Avg RPR 11.6, 1-Stage 13.0, 3-Stage 9.4, 5-Factor Model 9.2

Weighted Average Cost of Capital (WACC) (%)

	CRSP Deciles CAPM	CAPM +Size Prem	Build-Up	Risk Premium Report CAPM +Size Prem	Build-Up	Discounted Cash Flow 1-Stage	3-Stage	Fama-French 5-Factor Model
Median	7.6	9.7	9.3	11.4	12.5	10.2	9.0	8.0
SIC Composite	7.8	8.1	7.9	10.0	10.1	11.1	8.3	8.1
Large Composite	–	–	–	–	–	–	–	–
Small Composite	–	–	–	–	–	–	–	–
High Financial Risk	–	–	–	–	–	–	–	–

WACC (%) SIC Composite
Low 7.9, Average 9.1, Median 8.3, High 11.1

© 2017 Duff & Phelps. All Rights Reserved. Duff & Phelps has used the utmost care in compiling the data presented herein, but cannot guarantee the accuracy, completeness, or timeliness of the information.

Data Updated Through March 31, 2017

3845

Number of Companies: 13
Electromedical and Electrotherapeutic Apparatus

Industry Description
Establishments primarily engaged in manufacturing electromedical and electrotherapeutic apparatus.

Sales (in millions)

Three Largest Companies
Varian Medical Systems Inc.	$3,217.8
Intuitive Surgical, Inc.	2,704.4
ResMed Inc.	1,838.7

Three Smallest Companies
IRIDEX Corp.	$46.2
Utah Medical Products Inc.	39.3
Electromed, Inc.	23.0

Total Assets (in millions)

Three Largest Companies
Intuitive Surgical, Inc.	$6,486.9
Varian Medical Systems Inc.	3,816.0
ResMed Inc.	3,258.9

Three Smallest Companies
Utah Medical Products Inc.	$76.6
IRIDEX Corp.	48.1
Electromed, Inc.	20.6

Annualized Monthly Performance Statistics (%)

Industry	Geometric Mean	Arithmetic Mean	Standard Deviation		S&P 500 Index	Geometric Mean	Arithmetic Mean	Standard Deviation
1-year	29.4	30.5	17.9		1-year	17.2	17.4	7.2
3-year	17.2	18.5	17.7		3-year	10.4	10.9	11.5
5-year	11.0	12.4	17.8		5-year	13.3	13.9	11.5

Return Ratios (%)

	Return on Assets Latest	5-Yr Avg	Return on Equity Latest	5-Yr Avg	Dividend Yield Latest	5-Yr Avg
Median (13)	10.8	6.3	13.6	8.3	0.0	0.0
SIC Composite (13)	9.2	10.2	3.1	3.7	0.4	0.4
Large Composite (3)	11.0	12.9	3.1	3.8	0.4	0.4
Small Composite (3)	1.8	8.6	0.7	3.9	0.9	1.2
High-Financial Risk (−)	−	−	−	−	−	−

Liquidity Ratio

	Current Ratio Latest	5-Yr Avg
Median (13)	5.0	3.6
SIC Composite (13)	2.7	2.9
Large Composite (3)	2.6	2.8
Small Composite (3)	−	4.6
High-Financial Risk (−)	−	−

Profitability Ratio (%)

	Operating Margin Latest	5-Yr Avg
Median (13)	15.3	13.0
SIC Composite (13)	20.9	21.1
Large Composite (3)	25.4	25.8
Small Composite (3)	15.5	16.7
High-Financial Risk (−)	−	−

Growth Rates (%)

	Long-term EPS Analyst Estimates
Median (13)	11.4
SIC Composite (13)	11.4
Large Composite (3)	11.0
Small Composite (3)	11.8
High-Financial Risk (−)	−

Betas (Levered)

	Raw (OLS)	Blume Adjusted	Peer Group	Vasicek Adjusted	Sum	Downside
Median	0.86	0.92	0.91	0.89	0.86	1.44
SIC Composite	0.68	0.80	0.91	0.73	0.84	0.88
Large Composite	0.61	0.76	0.91	0.78	0.74	0.81
Small Composite	0.81	0.89	0.91	0.84	0.47	0.93
High Financial Risk	−	−	−	−	−	−

Betas (Unlevered)

	Raw (OLS)	Blume Adjusted	Peer Group	Vasicek Adjusted	Sum	Downside
Median	0.83	0.90	0.90	0.86	0.80	1.23
SIC Composite	0.66	0.77	0.87	0.71	0.81	0.84
Large Composite	0.60	0.74	0.89	0.76	0.72	0.80
Small Composite	0.81	0.88	0.91	0.84	0.47	0.92
High Financial Risk	−	−	−	−	−	−

Equity Valuation Multiples

	Price/Sales Latest	5-Yr Avg	Price/Earnings Latest	5-Yr Avg	Market/Book Latest	5-Yr Avg
Median	3.4	2.6	35.2	32.6	3.1	2.7
SIC Composite	5.0	4.1	31.8	26.7	4.6	4.0
Large Composite	6.2	5.1	32.5	26.2	5.2	4.8
Small Composite	3.6	3.0	−	25.8	3.0	2.6
High Financial Risk	−	−	−	−	−	−

Enterprise Valuation (EV) Multiples

	EV/Sales Latest	5-Yr Avg	EV/EBITDA Latest	5-Yr Avg
Median	3.1	2.4	15.3	14.2
SIC Composite	4.9	3.9	19.2	15.4
Large Composite	5.9	4.8	20.1	15.9
Small Composite	3.1	2.8	14.6	12.9
High Financial Risk	−	−	−	−

Enterprise Valuation SIC Composite
EV/Sales Latest 4.9, 5-Yr Avg 3.9
EV/EBITDA Latest 19.2, 5-Yr Avg 15.4

Fama-French (F-F) 5-Factor Model

	F-F Beta	SMB Premium	HML Premium	RMW Premium	CMA Premium
Median	1.6	2.2	-8.5	-2.7	6.7
SIC Composite	0.6	1.6	-3.9	-1.5	1.1
Large Composite	−	−	−	−	−
Small Composite	0.8	4.6	-1.5	1.7	5.6
High Financial Risk	−	−	−	−	−

Leverage Ratios (%)

	Debt/MV Equity Latest	5-Yr Avg	Debt/Total Capital Latest	5-Yr Avg
Median	1.3	3.4	1.2	3.3
SIC Composite	6.9	4.9	6.5	4.7
Large Composite	3.8	2.6	3.7	2.5
Small Composite	0.3	2.3	0.3	2.3
High Financial Risk	−	−	−	−

Cost of Debt

	Cost of Debt (%) Latest
Median	7.1
SIC Composite	7.1
Large Composite	7.1
Small Composite	7.1
High Financial Risk	−

Capital Structure

SIC Composite (%) Latest
D/TC 6.5
E/TC 93.5

Cost of Equity Capital (%)

	CRSP Deciles CAPM	CAPM +Size Prem	Build-Up	Risk Premium Report CAPM +Size Prem	Build-Up	Discounted Cash Flow 1-Stage	3-Stage	Fama-French 5-Factor Model
Median	8.4	10.3	10.2	12.3	14.7	11.9	8.6	10.0
SIC Composite	7.5	8.1	9.1	11.2	12.4	11.8	8.9	4.3
Large Composite	7.8	8.1	8.8	10.3	11.9	11.4	8.9	−
Small Composite	8.1	13.7	14.1	11.9	16.6	12.9	8.7	18.2
High Financial Risk	−	−	−	−	−	−	−	−

Cost of Equity Capital (%) SIC Composite
Avg CRSP 8.6, Avg RPR 11.8, 1-Stage 11.8, 3-Stage 8.9, 5-Factor Model 4.3

Weighted Average Cost of Capital (WACC) (%)

	CRSP Deciles CAPM	CAPM +Size Prem	Build-Up	Risk Premium Report CAPM +Size Prem	Build-Up	Discounted Cash Flow 1-Stage	3-Stage	Fama-French 5-Factor Model
Median	8.3	9.9	9.7	11.7	13.8	11.9	8.4	10.3
SIC Composite	7.4	8.0	8.9	10.8	11.9	11.4	8.7	4.4
Large Composite	7.7	8.0	8.7	10.1	11.7	11.2	8.8	−
Small Composite	8.1	13.7	14.1	11.9	16.6	12.9	8.7	18.1
High Financial Risk	−	−	−	−	−	−	−	−

WACC (%) SIC Composite
Low 4.4, High 11.9
▲ Average 9.2 ◆ Median 8.9

© 2017 Duff & Phelps. All Rights Reserved. Duff & Phelps has used the utmost care in compiling the data presented herein, but cannot guarantee the accuracy, completeness, or timeliness of the information.

Data Updated Through March 31, 2017

39

Number of Companies: 9
Miscellaneous Manufacturing Industries

Industry Description
This major group includes establishments primarily engaged in manufacturing products not classified in any other manufacturing major group. Industries in this group fall into the following categories: jewelry, silverware, and plated ware; musical instruments; dolls, toys, games, and sporting and athletic goods; pens, pencils, and artists' materials; buttons, costume novelties, miscellaneous notions; brooms and brushes; caskets; and other miscellaneous manufacturing industries.

Sales (in millions)

Three Largest Companies

Mattel, Inc.	$5,456.6
Hasbro Inc.	5,019.8
Kingold Jewelry, Inc.	1,000.2

Three Smallest Companies

Nautilus Inc.	$406.0
Escalade Inc.	167.6
Gaming Partners Int'l Corp.	78.2

Annualized Monthly Performance Statistics (%)

Industry

	Geometric Mean	Arithmetic Mean	Standard Deviation
1-year	6.6	7.7	16.2
3-year	5.5	7.2	19.6
5-year	10.7	12.5	20.4

Total Assets (in millions)

Three Largest Companies

Mattel, Inc.	$6,493.8
Hasbro Inc.	5,091.4
Callaway Golf Company	801.3

Three Smallest Companies

Nautilus Inc.	$333.1
Escalade Inc.	150.8
Gaming Partners Int'l Corp.	77.2

S&P 500 Index

	Geometric Mean	Arithmetic Mean	Standard Deviation
1-year	17.2	17.4	7.2
3-year	10.4	10.9	11.5
5-year	13.3	13.9	11.5

Return Ratios (%)

	Return on Assets Latest	Return on Assets 5-Yr Avg	Return on Equity Latest	Return on Equity 5-Yr Avg	Dividend Yield Latest	Dividend Yield 5-Yr Avg	Current Ratio Latest	Current Ratio 5-Yr Avg	Operating Margin Latest	Operating Margin 5-Yr Avg	Long-term EPS Analyst Estimates
Median (9)	8.1	7.6	12.3	9.8	0.4	1.3	2.0	2.3	9.3	8.6	10.6
SIC Composite (9)	8.3	8.4	4.6	5.1	3.3	3.4	2.1	2.3	11.2	12.1	9.8
Large Composite (−)	−	−	−	−	−	−	−	−	−	−	−
Small Composite (−)	−	−	−	−	−	−	−	−	−	−	−
High-Financial Risk (−)	−	−	−	−	−	−	−	−	−	−	−

Betas (Levered)

	Raw (OLS)	Blume Adjusted	Peer Group	Vasicek Adjusted	Sum	Downside
Median	1.04	1.03	0.97	1.01	1.10	1.30
SIC Composite	0.89	0.94	0.97	0.90	0.73	1.12
Large Composite	−	−	−	−	−	−
Small Composite	−	−	−	−	−	−
High Financial Risk	−	−	−	−	−	−

Betas (Unlevered)

	Raw (OLS)	Blume Adjusted	Peer Group	Vasicek Adjusted	Sum	Downside
Median	0.99	0.98	0.91	0.95	1.09	1.04
SIC Composite	0.78	0.82	0.85	0.78	0.64	0.97
Large Composite	−	−	−	−	−	−
Small Composite	−	−	−	−	−	−
High Financial Risk	−	−	−	−	−	−

Equity Valuation Multiples

	Price/Sales Latest	Price/Sales 5-Yr Avg	Price/Earnings Latest	Price/Earnings 5-Yr Avg	Market/Book Latest	Market/Book 5-Yr Avg
Median	1.2	1.1	16.1	19.2	2.1	2.2
SIC Composite	1.8	1.6	21.5	19.6	4.1	3.6
Large Composite	−	−	−	−	−	−
Small Composite	−	−	−	−	−	−
High Financial Risk	−	−	−	−	−	−

Enterprise Valuation (EV) Multiples

	EV/Sales Latest	EV/Sales 5-Yr Avg	EV/EBITDA Latest	EV/EBITDA 5-Yr Avg
Median	1.2	1.2	13.1	10.2
SIC Composite	1.9	1.7	13.1	10.9
Large Composite	−	−	−	−
Small Composite	−	−	−	−
High Financial Risk	−	−	−	−

Enterprise Valuation SIC Composite: EV/Sales Latest 1.9, 5-Yr Avg 1.7; EV/EBITDA Latest 13.1, 5-Yr Avg 10.9.

Fama-French (F-F) 5-Factor Model

	F-F Beta	SMB Premium	HML Premium	RMW Premium	CMA Premium
Median	0.2	4.1	1.7	2.7	-0.8
SIC Composite	0.9	-0.5	0.8	2.5	1.5
Large Composite	−	−	−	−	−
Small Composite	−	−	−	−	−
High Financial Risk	−	−	−	−	−

Leverage Ratios (%)

	Debt/MV Equity Latest	Debt/MV Equity 5-Yr Avg	Debt/Total Capital Latest	Debt/Total Capital 5-Yr Avg
Median	11.8	11.5	10.5	10.3
SIC Composite	17.0	17.2	14.5	14.7
Large Composite	−	−	−	−
Small Composite	−	−	−	−
High Financial Risk	−	−	−	−

Cost of Debt

	Cost of Debt (%) Latest
Median	7.1
SIC Composite	4.9
Large Composite	−
Small Composite	−
High Financial Risk	−

Capital Structure

SIC Composite (%) Latest: D/TC 14.5, E/TC 85.5

Cost of Equity Capital (%)

	CAPM	CRSP Deciles CAPM +Size Prem	CRSP Deciles Build-Up	Risk Premium Report CAPM +Size Prem	Risk Premium Report Build-Up	Discounted Cash Flow 1-Stage	Discounted Cash Flow 3-Stage	Fama-French 5-Factor Model
Median	9.0	11.5	11.5	14.2	15.1	10.6	13.3	12.2
SIC Composite	8.5	9.4	9.8	10.7	12.5	13.2	10.5	13.0
Large Composite	−	−	−	−	−	−	−	−
Small Composite	−	−	−	−	−	−	−	−
High Financial Risk	−	−	−	−	−	−	−	−

Cost of Equity Capital (%) SIC Composite: Avg CRSP 9.6, Avg RPR 11.6, 1-Stage 13.2, 3-Stage 10.5, 5-Factor Model 13.0

Weighted Average Cost of Capital (WACC) (%)

	CAPM	CRSP Deciles CAPM +Size Prem	CRSP Deciles Build-Up	Risk Premium Report CAPM +Size Prem	Risk Premium Report Build-Up	Discounted Cash Flow 1-Stage	Discounted Cash Flow 3-Stage	Fama-French 5-Factor Model
Median	8.7	11.2	10.5	14.1	14.6	10.6	12.0	12.0
SIC Composite	7.8	8.6	9.0	9.7	11.3	11.8	9.5	11.7
Large Composite	−	−	−	−	−	−	−	−
Small Composite	−	−	−	−	−	−	−	−
High Financial Risk	−	−	−	−	−	−	−	−

WACC (%) SIC Composite: Low 8.6, High 11.8, Average 10.2, Median 9.7

© 2017 Duff & Phelps. All Rights Reserved. Duff & Phelps has used the utmost care in compiling the data presented herein, but cannot guarantee the accuracy, completeness, or timeliness of the information.

Data Updated Through March 31, 2017

394

Number of Companies: 5
Dolls, Toys, Games and Sporting and Athletic Goods

Industry Description
Establishments primarily engaged in manufacturing in dolls and stuffed toys; games, toys, and children's vehicles, except dolls and bicycles; and sporting and athletic goods, not elsewhere classified.

Sales (in millions)

Three Largest Companies
Mattel, Inc.	$5,456.6
Hasbro Inc.	5,019.8
Callaway Golf Company	871.2

Three Smallest Companies
Callaway Golf Company	$871.2
Nautilus Inc.	406.0
Escalade Inc.	167.6

Total Assets (in millions)

Three Largest Companies
Mattel, Inc.	$6,493.8
Hasbro Inc.	5,091.4
Callaway Golf Company	801.3

Three Smallest Companies
Callaway Golf Company	$801.3
Nautilus Inc.	333.1
Escalade Inc.	150.8

Annualized Monthly Performance Statistics (%)

Industry	Geometric Mean	Arithmetic Mean	Standard Deviation	S&P 500 Index	Geometric Mean	Arithmetic Mean	Standard Deviation
1-year	3.0	4.3	17.1	1-year	17.2	17.4	7.2
3-year	5.2	7.1	20.7	3-year	10.4	10.9	11.5
5-year	10.3	12.3	21.4	5-year	13.3	13.9	11.5

Return Ratios (%)

	Return on Assets Latest	Return on Assets 5-Yr Avg	Return on Equity Latest	Return on Equity 5-Yr Avg	Dividend Yield Latest	Dividend Yield 5-Yr Avg
Median (5)	10.8	8.9	21.7	19.3	2.4	2.9
SIC Composite (5)	8.6	8.5	4.8	5.1	3.5	3.6
Large Composite (–)	–	–	–	–	–	–
Small Composite (–)	–	–	–	–	–	–
High-Financial Risk (–)	–	–	–	–	–	–

Liquidity Ratio

	Current Ratio Latest	Current Ratio 5-Yr Avg
Median (5)	2.0	2.2
SIC Composite (5)	2.0	2.3
Large Composite	–	–
Small Composite	–	–
High-Financial Risk	–	–

Profitability Ratio (%)

	Operating Margin Latest	Operating Margin 5-Yr Avg
Median (5)	10.3	11.1
SIC Composite (5)	12.5	13.3
Large Composite	–	–
Small Composite	–	–
High-Financial Risk	–	–

Growth Rates (%)

	Long-term EPS Analyst Estimates
Median (5)	10.6
SIC Composite (5)	9.7
Large Composite	–
Small Composite	–
High-Financial Risk	–

Betas (Levered)

	Raw (OLS)	Blume Adjusted	Peer Group	Vasicek Adjusted	Sum	Downside
Median	0.86	0.91	0.97	0.88	0.80	1.30
SIC Composite	0.88	0.93	0.97	0.90	0.71	1.11
Large Composite	–	–	–	–	–	–
Small Composite	–	–	–	–	–	–
High Financial Risk	–	–	–	–	–	–

Betas (Unlevered)

	Raw (OLS)	Blume Adjusted	Peer Group	Vasicek Adjusted	Sum	Downside
Median	0.76	0.81	0.90	0.78	0.75	1.04
SIC Composite	0.76	0.80	0.84	0.77	0.61	0.96
Large Composite	–	–	–	–	–	–
Small Composite	–	–	–	–	–	–
High Financial Risk	–	–	–	–	–	–

Equity Valuation Multiples

	Price/Sales Latest	Price/Sales 5-Yr Avg	Price/Earnings Latest	Price/Earnings 5-Yr Avg	Market/Book Latest	Market/Book 5-Yr Avg
Median	1.4	1.3	16.1	19.2	3.2	3.4
SIC Composite	1.9	1.7	20.8	19.7	4.4	3.9
Large Composite	–	–	–	–	–	–
Small Composite	–	–	–	–	–	–
High Financial Risk	–	–	–	–	–	–

Enterprise Valuation (EV) Multiples

	EV/Sales Latest	EV/Sales 5-Yr Avg	EV/EBITDA Latest	EV/EBITDA 5-Yr Avg
Median	1.3	1.2	13.1	10.3
SIC Composite	2.1	1.9	13.0	11.1
Large Composite	–	–	–	–
Small Composite	–	–	–	–
High Financial Risk	–	–	–	–

Enterprise Valuation SIC Composite
EV/Sales: Latest 2.1, 5-Yr Avg 1.9
EV/EBITDA: Latest 13.0, 5-Yr Avg 11.1

Fama-French (F-F) 5-Factor Model

	F-F Beta	SMB Premium	HML Premium	RMW Premium	CMA Premium
Median	1.6	1.5	-2.7	-6.1	7.9
SIC Composite	1.0	-0.9	0.6	2.7	2.1
Large Composite	–	–	–	–	–
Small Composite	–	–	–	–	–
High Financial Risk	–	–	–	–	–

Leverage Ratios (%)

	Debt/MV Equity Latest	Debt/MV Equity 5-Yr Avg	Debt/Total Capital Latest	Debt/Total Capital 5-Yr Avg
Median	13.8	15.3	12.1	13.2
SIC Composite	18.1	18.3	15.3	15.4
Large Composite	–	–	–	–
Small Composite	–	–	–	–
High Financial Risk	–	–	–	–

Cost of Debt

	Cost of Debt (%) Latest
Median	7.1
SIC Composite	4.8
Large Composite	–
Small Composite	–
High Financial Risk	–

Capital Structure

SIC Composite (%) Latest
D/TC: 15.3
E/TC: 84.7

Cost of Equity Capital (%)

	CRSP Deciles CAPM	CRSP Deciles CAPM +Size Prem	CRSP Deciles Build-Up	Risk Premium Report CAPM +Size Prem	Risk Premium Report Build-Up	Discounted Cash Flow 1-Stage	Discounted Cash Flow 3-Stage	Fama-French 5-Factor Model
Median	8.4	11.7	10.6	13.9	14.8	11.0	13.2	13.1
SIC Composite	8.4	9.3	9.7	10.4	12.3	13.4	10.6	13.3
Large Composite	–	–	–	–	–	–	–	–
Small Composite	–	–	–	–	–	–	–	–
High Financial Risk	–	–	–	–	–	–	–	–

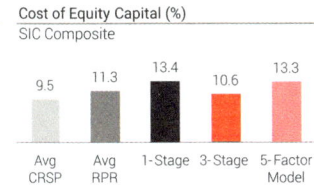

Cost of Equity Capital (%) SIC Composite
Avg CRSP: 9.5, Avg RPR: 11.3, 1-Stage: 13.4, 3-Stage: 10.6, 5-Factor Model: 13.3

Weighted Average Cost of Capital (WACC) (%)

	CRSP Deciles CAPM	CRSP Deciles CAPM +Size Prem	CRSP Deciles Build-Up	Risk Premium Report CAPM +Size Prem	Risk Premium Report Build-Up	Discounted Cash Flow 1-Stage	Discounted Cash Flow 3-Stage	Fama-French 5-Factor Model
Median	7.7	11.1	10.5	13.1	14.5	11.0	12.0	12.5
SIC Composite	7.7	8.5	8.8	9.4	11.0	12.0	9.5	11.8
Large Composite	–	–	–	–	–	–	–	–
Small Composite	–	–	–	–	–	–	–	–
High Financial Risk	–	–	–	–	–	–	–	–

WACC (%) SIC Composite
Low 8.5, High 12.0, Average 10.1, Median 9.5

© 2017 Duff & Phelps. All Rights Reserved. Duff & Phelps has used the utmost care in compiling the data presented herein, but cannot guarantee the accuracy, completeness, or timeliness of the information.

Division E:
Transportation, Communications, Electric, Gas, and Sanitary Services

This division includes establishments providing, to the general public or to other business enterprises, passenger and freight transportation, communications services, or electricity, gas, steam, water or sanitary services. Major groups between "40" and "49" are in this division.

Data Updated Through March 31, 2017

4

Number of Companies: 168
Transportation, Communications, Electric, Gas, and Sanitary Services

Industry Description
This division includes establishments providing, to the general public or to other business enterprises, passenger and freight transportation, communications services, or electricity, gas, steam, water or sanitary services.

Sales (in millions)

Three Largest Companies
AT&T Inc.	$163,763.0
Verizon Communications Inc.	125,980.0
Comcast Corp.	80,403.0

Three Smallest Companies
RGC Resources, Inc.	$59.1
York Water Co.	47.6
U.S. Geothermal Inc.	31.2

Total Assets (in millions)

Three Largest Companies
AT&T Inc.	$403,821.0
Verizon Communications Inc.	244,180.0
Comcast Corp.	180,500.0

Three Smallest Companies
Gas Natural Inc.	$197.4
RGC Resources, Inc.	165.6
Hudson Technologies Inc.	122.5

Annualized Monthly Performance Statistics (%)

Industry	Geometric Mean	Arithmetic Mean	Standard Deviation
1-year	14.5	14.9	9.6
3-year	9.1	9.6	10.9
5-year	13.2	13.7	10.8

S&P 500 Index	Geometric Mean	Arithmetic Mean	Standard Deviation
1-year	17.2	17.4	7.2
3-year	10.4	10.9	11.5
5-year	13.3	13.9	11.5

Return Ratios (%)

	Return on Assets Latest	Return on Assets 5-Yr Avg	Return on Equity Latest	Return on Equity 5-Yr Avg	Dividend Yield Latest	Dividend Yield 5-Yr Avg
Median (168)	3.3	3.4	7.2	7.7	2.2	2.5
SIC Composite (168)	3.3	3.5	4.8	5.4	3.1	3.2
Large Composite (16)	3.7	3.9	5.4	5.9	3.4	3.5
Small Composite (16)	2.8	4.6	2.7	6.0	2.1	2.8
High-Financial Risk (31)	-4.0	-2.8	-11.7	-9.2	4.7	4.6

Liquidity Ratio

	Current Ratio Latest	Current Ratio 5-Yr Avg
Median (168)	1.0	1.1
SIC Composite (168)	0.8	0.9
Large Composite (16)	0.8	0.9
Small Composite (16)	2.1	1.8
High-Financial Risk (31)	0.8	1.2

Profitability Ratio (%)

	Operating Margin Latest	Operating Margin 5-Yr Avg
Median (168)	17.6	16.4
SIC Composite (168)	17.5	16.4
Large Composite (16)	16.2	15.2
Small Composite (16)	17.2	18.7
High-Financial Risk (31)	7.0	6.0

Growth Rates (%)

	Long-term EPS Analyst Estimates
Median (168)	6.9
SIC Composite (168)	7.3
Large Composite (16)	7.3
Small Composite (16)	12.6
High-Financial Risk (31)	6.3

Betas (Levered)

	Raw (OLS)	Blume Adjusted	Peer Group	Vasicek Adjusted	Sum	Downside
Median	0.76	0.85	0.78	0.76	0.83	1.13
SIC Composite	0.69	0.81	0.78	0.69	0.60	0.69
Large Composite	0.67	0.80	0.89	0.68	0.55	0.66
Small Composite	0.57	0.73	0.78	0.60	0.48	0.74
High Financial Risk	1.14	1.09	0.67	1.11	1.45	1.30

Betas (Unlevered)

	Raw (OLS)	Blume Adjusted	Peer Group	Vasicek Adjusted	Sum	Downside
Median	0.56	0.64	0.58	0.58	0.60	0.83
SIC Composite	0.49	0.56	0.55	0.49	0.43	0.49
Large Composite	0.48	0.56	0.62	0.48	0.40	0.47
Small Composite	0.49	0.61	0.65	0.51	0.42	0.62
High Financial Risk	0.62	0.61	0.44	0.61	0.75	0.69

Equity Valuation Multiples

	Price/Sales Latest	Price/Sales 5-Yr Avg	Price/Earnings Latest	Price/Earnings 5-Yr Avg	Market/Book Latest	Market/Book 5-Yr Avg
Median	2.0	1.6	23.4	19.6	1.8	1.6
SIC Composite	1.8	1.5	20.8	18.6	1.8	1.7
Large Composite	1.6	1.3	18.6	17.1	1.9	1.8
Small Composite	3.2	2.3	36.9	16.8	2.1	1.7
High Financial Risk	0.8	0.7	–	–	1.2	1.0

Enterprise Valuation (EV) Multiples

	EV/Sales Latest	EV/Sales 5-Yr Avg	EV/EBITDA Latest	EV/EBITDA 5-Yr Avg
Median	2.9	2.5	10.3	9.2
SIC Composite	2.7	2.3	9.3	8.5
Large Composite	2.3	1.9	8.4	7.6
Small Composite	3.9	3.2	14.1	10.6
High Financial Risk	1.9	1.6	8.8	8.7

Enterprise Valuation SIC Composite
EV/Sales: Latest 2.7, 5-Yr Avg 2.3
EV/EBITDA: Latest 9.3, 5-Yr Avg 8.5

Fama-French (F-F) 5-Factor Model

	F-F Beta	SMB Premium	HML Premium	RMW Premium	CMA Premium
Median	0.5	2.1	-0.1	2.7	0.8
SIC Composite	0.7	0.1	-1.7	0.6	3.8
Large Composite	0.8	0.1	-1.8	1.1	1.5
Small Composite	0.6	1.5	-1.4	-1.0	5.9
High Financial Risk	–	–	–	–	–

Leverage Ratios (%)

	Debt/MV Equity Latest	Debt/MV Equity 5-Yr Avg	Debt/Total Capital Latest	Debt/Total Capital 5-Yr Avg
Median	51.6	54.6	34.0	35.3
SIC Composite	55.1	55.7	35.5	35.8
Large Composite	53.1	50.8	34.7	33.7
Small Composite	31.4	47.3	23.9	32.1
High Financial Risk	150.8	158.6	60.1	61.3

Cost of Debt

	Cost of Debt (%) Latest
Median	6.1
SIC Composite	5.0
Large Composite	4.9
Small Composite	5.9
High Financial Risk	6.6

Capital Structure

SIC Composite (%) Latest: D/TC 35.5, E/TC 64.5

Cost of Equity Capital (%)

	CAPM	CRSP Deciles CAPM +Size Prem	Build-Up	Risk Premium Report CAPM +Size Prem	Build-Up	Discounted Cash Flow 1-Stage	3-Stage	Fama-French 5-Factor Model
Median	7.7	9.0	8.8	11.6	12.7	9.6	7.5	11.5
SIC Composite	7.3	7.6	7.8	8.4	10.2	10.4	7.7	10.1
Large Composite	7.2	7.3	8.0	7.5	9.3	10.6	8.2	8.7
Small Composite	6.8	9.3	9.8	11.2	15.5	14.0	10.1	11.7
High Financial Risk	–	–	–	27.1	28.3	–	–	–

Cost of Equity Capital (%) SIC Composite
Avg CRSP 7.7, Avg RPR 9.3, 1-Stage 10.4, 3-Stage 7.7, 5-Factor Model 10.1

Weighted Average Cost of Capital (WACC) (%)

	CAPM	CRSP Deciles CAPM +Size Prem	Build-Up	Risk Premium Report CAPM +Size Prem	Build-Up	Discounted Cash Flow 1-Stage	3-Stage	Fama-French 5-Factor Model
Median	6.8	7.6	7.5	9.2	9.6	7.7	6.6	9.2
SIC Composite	6.2	6.3	6.4	6.9	8.0	8.1	6.4	8.0
Large Composite	6.2	6.2	6.7	6.3	7.5	8.4	6.8	7.1
Small Composite	6.4	8.3	8.7	9.7	13.0	11.9	8.9	10.1
High Financial Risk	–	–	–	14.3	14.7	–	–	–

WACC (%) SIC Composite
Low 6.3, High 8.1, Average 7.2, Median 6.9

© 2017 Duff & Phelps. All Rights Reserved. Duff & Phelps has used the utmost care in compiling the data presented herein, but cannot guarantee the accuracy, completeness, or timeliness of the information.

Data Updated Through March 31, 2017

40

Number of Companies: 5
Railroad Transportation

Industry Description
This major group includes establishments furnishing transportation by line-haul railroad, and switching and terminal establishments.

Sales (in millions)

Three Largest Companies
Union Pacific Corp.	$19,941.0
CSX Corp.	11,069.0
Norfolk Southern Corp.	9,888.0

Three Smallest Companies
Norfolk Southern Corp.	$9,888.0
Kansas City Southern	2,334.2
Genesee & Wyoming Inc.	2,001.5

Total Assets (in millions)

Three Largest Companies
Union Pacific Corp.	$55,718.0
CSX Corp.	35,414.0
Norfolk Southern Corp.	34,892.0

Three Smallest Companies
Norfolk Southern Corp.	$34,892.0
Kansas City Southern	8,817.5
Genesee & Wyoming Inc.	7,635.0

Annualized Monthly Performance Statistics (%)

Industry	Geometric Mean	Arithmetic Mean	Standard Deviation
1-year	42.5	45.2	30.0
3-year	8.1	10.2	22.2
5-year	15.8	17.5	20.4

S&P 500 Index	Geometric Mean	Arithmetic Mean	Standard Deviation
1-year	17.2	17.4	7.2
3-year	10.4	10.9	11.5
5-year	13.3	13.9	11.5

Return Ratios (%)

	Return on Assets Latest	5-Yr Avg	Return on Equity Latest	5-Yr Avg	Dividend Yield Latest	5-Yr Avg
Median (5)	4.9	5.7	8.1	9.6	2.1	2.1
SIC Composite (5)	5.8	6.6	4.7	6.0	2.2	2.1
Large Composite (–)	–	–	–	–	–	–
Small Composite (–)	–	–	–	–	–	–
High-Financial Risk (–)	–	–	–	–	–	–

Liquidity Ratio

	Current Ratio Latest	5-Yr Avg
Median (5)	1.0	1.1
SIC Composite (5)	1.0	1.2
Large Composite (–)	–	–
Small Composite (–)	–	–
High-Financial Risk (–)	–	–

Profitability Ratio (%)

	Operating Margin Latest	5-Yr Avg
Median (5)	31.1	29.6
SIC Composite (5)	33.0	32.0
Large Composite (–)	–	–
Small Composite (–)	–	–
High-Financial Risk (–)	–	–

Growth Rates (%)

	Long-term EPS Analyst Estimates
Median (5)	11.3
SIC Composite (5)	11.4
Large Composite (–)	–
Small Composite (–)	–
High-Financial Risk (–)	–

Betas (Levered)

	Raw (OLS)	Blume Adjusted	Peer Group	Vasicek Adjusted	Sum	Downside
Median	1.28	1.18	–	–	1.46	1.64
SIC Composite	1.02	1.02	–	–	1.09	1.33
Large Composite	–	–	–	–	–	–
Small Composite	–	–	–	–	–	–
High Financial Risk	–	–	–	–	–	–

Betas (Unlevered)

	Raw (OLS)	Blume Adjusted	Peer Group	Vasicek Adjusted	Sum	Downside
Median	1.04	0.95	–	–	1.16	1.25
SIC Composite	0.84	0.84	–	–	0.90	1.09
Large Composite	–	–	–	–	–	–
Small Composite	–	–	–	–	–	–
High Financial Risk	–	–	–	–	–	–

Equity Valuation Multiples

	Price/Sales Latest	5-Yr Avg	Price/Earnings Latest	5-Yr Avg	Market/Book Latest	5-Yr Avg
Median	3.9	2.6	20.4	17.2	1.7	1.4
SIC Composite	3.9	3.0	21.3	16.8	2.0	1.8
Large Composite	–	–	–	–	–	–
Small Composite	–	–	–	–	–	–
High Financial Risk	–	–	–	–	–	–

Enterprise Valuation (EV) Multiples

	EV/Sales Latest	5-Yr Avg	EV/EBITDA Latest	5-Yr Avg
Median	4.8	3.8	10.8	9.1
SIC Composite	4.7	3.7	10.7	8.9
Large Composite	–	–	–	–
Small Composite	–	–	–	–
High Financial Risk	–	–	–	–

Enterprise Valuation SIC Composite
Latest: EV/Sales 4.7, EV/EBITDA 10.7
5-Yr Avg: EV/Sales 3.7, EV/EBITDA 8.9

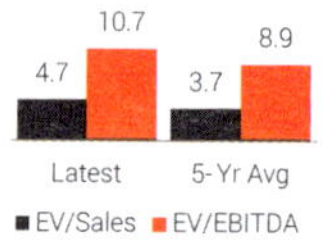

Fama-French (F-F) 5-Factor Model

	F-F Beta	SMB Premium	HML Premium	RMW Premium	CMA Premium
Median	1.2	2.1	0.5	0.2	0.9
SIC Composite	1.0	1.5	0.3	-0.2	2.8
Large Composite	–	–	–	–	–
Small Composite	–	–	–	–	–
High Financial Risk	–	–	–	–	–

Leverage Ratios (%)

	Debt/MV Equity Latest	5-Yr Avg	Debt/Total Capital Latest	5-Yr Avg
Median	27.2	36.0	21.4	26.5
SIC Composite	23.7	24.4	19.2	19.6
Large Composite	–	–	–	–
Small Composite	–	–	–	–
High Financial Risk	–	–	–	–

Cost of Debt

	Cost of Debt (%) Latest
Median	4.8
SIC Composite	4.6
Large Composite	–
Small Composite	–
High Financial Risk	–

Capital Structure

SIC Composite (%) Latest: D/TC 19.2, E/TC 80.8

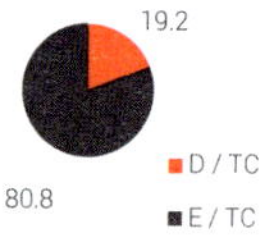

Cost of Equity Capital (%)

	CRSP Deciles CAPM	CAPM +Size Prem	Risk Premium Report Build-Up	CAPM +Size Prem	Build-Up	Discounted Cash Flow 1-Stage	3-Stage	Fama-French 5-Factor Model
Median	–	–	9.0	14.3	10.4	13.5	10.5	14.0
SIC Composite	–	–	9.1	11.2	10.3	13.6	10.3	13.2
Large Composite	–	–	–	–	–	–	–	–
Small Composite	–	–	–	–	–	–	–	–
High Financial Risk	–	–	–	–	–	–	–	–

Cost of Equity Capital (%) SIC Composite
Avg CRSP 9.1, Avg RPR 10.7, 1-Stage 13.6, 3-Stage 10.3, 5-Factor Model 13.2

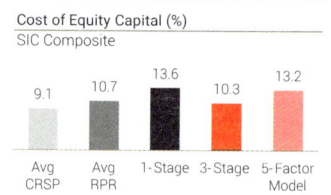

Weighted Average Cost of Capital (WACC) (%)

	CRSP Deciles CAPM	CAPM +Size Prem	Risk Premium Report Build-Up	CAPM +Size Prem	Build-Up	Discounted Cash Flow 1-Stage	3-Stage	Fama-French 5-Factor Model
Median	–	–	8.1	11.8	8.9	11.3	8.8	11.8
SIC Composite	–	–	7.9	9.6	8.9	11.6	8.9	11.3
Large Composite	–	–	–	–	–	–	–	–
Small Composite	–	–	–	–	–	–	–	–
High Financial Risk	–	–	–	–	–	–	–	–

WACC (%) SIC Composite: Low 7.9, High 11.6, Average 9.7, Median 9.3

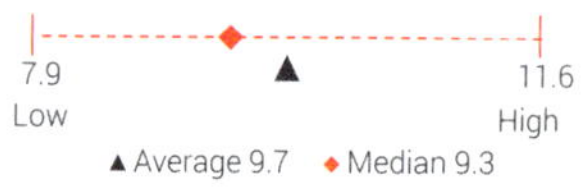

© 2017 Duff & Phelps. All Rights Reserved. Duff & Phelps has used the utmost care in compiling the data presented herein, but cannot guarantee the accuracy, completeness, or timeliness of the information.

Data Updated Through March 31, 2017

42

Number of Companies: 14
Motor Freight Transportation and Warehousing

Industry Description
This major group includes establishments furnishing local or long-distance trucking or transfer services, or those engaged in the storage of farm products, furniture and other household goods, or commercial goods of any nature.

Sales (in millions)

Three Largest Companies
United Parcel Service, Inc.	$60,906.0
JB Hunt Transport Services Inc.	6,555.5
Landstar System Inc.	3,169.1

Three Smallest Companies
Marten Transport LTD	$671.1
Heartland Express, Inc.	612.9
P.A.M. Transportation Services	417.0

Annualized Monthly Performance Statistics (%)

Industry	Geometric Mean	Arithmetic Mean	Standard Deviation
1-year	7.1	7.8	12.8
3-year	6.6	7.8	16.1
5-year	9.7	10.7	15.5

S&P 500 Index	Geometric Mean	Arithmetic Mean	Standard Deviation
1-year	17.2	17.4	7.2
3-year	10.4	10.9	11.5
5-year	13.3	13.9	11.5

Total Assets (in millions)

Three Largest Companies
United Parcel Service, Inc.	$40,377.0
JB Hunt Transport Services Inc.	3,829.0
Old Dominion Freight	2,696.2

Three Smallest Companies
Covenant Transportation Group	$647.4
Forward Air Corp.	641.3
P.A.M. Transportation Services	358.0

Return Ratios (%)

	Return on Assets Latest	5-Yr Avg	Return on Equity Latest	5-Yr Avg	Dividend Yield Latest	5-Yr Avg
Median (14)	6.6	8.0	9.8	11.2	0.6	1.0
SIC Composite (14)	8.3	8.7	3.8	4.0	2.4	2.4
Large Composite (3)	8.8	9.0	3.7	3.8	2.7	2.6
Small Composite (3)	6.4	6.9	4.4	4.5	0.4	1.3
High-Financial Risk (–)	–	–	–	–	–	–

Liquidity Ratio

	Current Ratio Latest	5-Yr Avg
	1.5	1.4
	1.3	1.5
	1.2	1.5
	1.8	1.8
	–	–

Profitability Ratio (%)

	Operating Margin Latest	5-Yr Avg
	8.1	7.1
	9.0	9.6
	9.1	9.9
	9.1	8.2
	–	–

Growth Rates (%)

	Long-term EPS Analyst Estimates
	10.3
	9.1
	8.9
	3.8
	–

Betas (Levered)

	Raw (OLS)	Blume Adjusted	Peer Group	Vasicek Adjusted	Sum	Downside
Median	0.84	0.91	0.87	0.85	0.98	1.17
SIC Composite	0.88	0.93	0.87	0.88	0.71	0.94
Large Composite	0.87	0.92	0.87	0.87	0.66	0.94
Small Composite	0.66	0.79	0.87	0.72	0.87	0.83
High Financial Risk	–	–	–	–	–	–

Betas (Unlevered)

	Raw (OLS)	Blume Adjusted	Peer Group	Vasicek Adjusted	Sum	Downside
Median	0.75	0.81	0.83	0.74	0.73	0.91
SIC Composite	0.77	0.81	0.76	0.77	0.62	0.83
Large Composite	0.75	0.80	0.75	0.75	0.57	0.81
Small Composite	0.64	0.77	0.83	0.69	0.84	0.81
High Financial Risk	–	–	–	–	–	–

Equity Valuation Multiples

	Price/Sales Latest	5-Yr Avg	Price/Earnings Latest	5-Yr Avg	Market/Book Latest	5-Yr Avg
Median	1.1	0.9	23.9	21.9	2.3	2.1
SIC Composite	1.5	1.4	26.3	25.1	–	8.9
Large Composite	1.5	1.5	26.7	26.0	–	–
Small Composite	1.5	1.4	22.8	22.2	1.9	2.0
High Financial Risk	–	–	–	–	–	–

Enterprise Valuation (EV) Multiples

	EV/Sales Latest	5-Yr Avg	EV/EBITDA Latest	5-Yr Avg
Median	1.1	1.0	7.8	7.1
SIC Composite	1.6	1.5	12.0	11.1
Large Composite	1.7	1.6	13.1	12.0
Small Composite	1.5	1.4	6.3	6.6
High Financial Risk	–	–	–	–

Enterprise Valuation SIC Composite

	Latest	5-Yr Avg
EV/Sales	1.6	1.5
EV/EBITDA	12.0	11.1

Fama-French (F-F) 5-Factor Model

Fama-French (F-F) Components

	F-F Beta	SMB Premium	HML Premium	RMW Premium	CMA Premium
Median	0.9	0.8	0.1	0.2	6.2
SIC Composite	0.9	1.2	0.6	1.3	2.5
Large Composite	0.9	1.0	0.5	1.3	1.8
Small Composite	0.6	3.1	1.4	0.9	2.6
High Financial Risk	–	–	–	–	–

Leverage Ratios (%)

	Debt/MV Equity Latest	5-Yr Avg	Debt/Total Capital Latest	5-Yr Avg
Median	8.0	7.2	7.4	6.7
SIC Composite	15.0	13.5	13.1	11.9
Large Composite	16.1	14.2	13.9	12.4
Small Composite	6.3	6.2	5.9	5.8
High Financial Risk	–	–	–	–

Cost of Debt

	Cost of Debt (%) Latest
Median	7.1
SIC Composite	4.4
Large Composite	4.1
Small Composite	7.1
High Financial Risk	–

Capital Structure

SIC Composite (%) Latest
- D/TC: 13.1
- E/TC: 86.9

Cost of Equity Capital (%)

	CRSP Deciles CAPM	CAPM +Size Prem	Build-Up	Risk Premium Report CAPM +Size Prem	Build-Up	Discounted Cash Flow 1-Stage	3-Stage	Fama-French 5-Factor Model
Median	8.2	9.6	9.9	12.4	14.2	11.6	8.4	15.5
SIC Composite	8.3	8.6	8.6	9.4	10.7	11.7	8.6	13.8
Large Composite	8.3	8.4	8.4	8.9	10.3	11.9	8.7	13.0
Small Composite	7.4	9.4	10.2	12.6	14.4	4.3	5.9	14.9
High Financial Risk	–	–	–	–	–	–	–	–

Cost of Equity Capital (%) SIC Composite
- Avg CRSP: 8.6
- Avg RPR: 10.1
- 1-Stage: 11.7
- 3-Stage: 8.6
- 5-Factor Model: 13.8

Weighted Average Cost of Capital (WACC) (%)

	CRSP Deciles CAPM	CAPM +Size Prem	Build-Up	Risk Premium Report CAPM +Size Prem	Build-Up	Discounted Cash Flow 1-Stage	3-Stage	Fama-French 5-Factor Model
Median	7.7	9.3	9.4	11.2	12.7	10.7	8.1	13.8
SIC Composite	7.8	8.0	8.0	8.7	9.9	10.7	8.0	12.5
Large Composite	7.6	7.7	7.7	8.2	9.4	10.7	8.0	11.8
Small Composite	7.3	9.1	9.9	12.2	13.8	4.3	5.9	14.3
High Financial Risk	–	–	–	–	–	–	–	–

WACC (%) SIC Composite
- Low: 8.0
- High: 12.5
- ▲ Average 9.4 ♦ Median 8.7

© 2017 Duff & Phelps. All Rights Reserved. Duff & Phelps has used the utmost care in compiling the data presented herein, but cannot guarantee the accuracy, completeness, or timeliness of the information.

Data Updated Through March 31, 2017

4213

Number of Companies: 12
Trucking, Except Local

Industry Description
Establishments primarily engaged in furnishing "over-the-road" trucking services or trucking services and storage services, including household goods either as common carriers or under special or individual contracts or agreements, for freight generally weighing more than 100 pounds. Such operations are principally outside a single municipality, outside one group of contiguous municipalities, or outside a single municipality and its suburban areas.

Sales (in millions)

Three Largest Companies

JB Hunt Transport Services Inc.	$6,555.5
Landstar System Inc.	3,169.1
Old Dominion Freight	2,991.5

Three Smallest Companies

Marten Transport LTD	$671.1
Heartland Express, Inc.	612.9
P.A.M. Transportation Services	417.0

Annualized Monthly Performance Statistics (%)

Industry

	Geometric Mean	Arithmetic Mean	Standard Deviation
1-year	15.5	17.8	25.3
3-year	8.1	10.1	21.7
5-year	12.7	14.4	20.0

Total Assets (in millions)

Three Largest Companies

JB Hunt Transport Services Inc.	$3,829.0
Old Dominion Freight	2,696.2
Werner Enterprises Inc.	1,793.0

Three Smallest Companies

Marten Transport LTD	$653.7
Covenant Transportation Group	647.4
P.A.M. Transportation Services	358.0

S&P 500 Index

	Geometric Mean	Arithmetic Mean	Standard Deviation
1-year	17.2	17.4	7.2
3-year	10.4	10.9	11.5
5-year	13.3	13.9	11.5

Return Ratios (%)

	Return on Assets Latest	5-Yr Avg	Return on Equity Latest	5-Yr Avg	Dividend Yield Latest	5-Yr Avg
Median (12)	6.6	7.0	9.8	10.2	0.5	0.9
SIC Composite (12)	8.0	8.5	4.3	4.7	0.6	0.9
Large Composite (3)	11.4	11.8	4.2	4.6	0.6	0.7
Small Composite (3)	6.4	6.9	4.4	4.5	0.4	1.3
High-Financial Risk (–)	–	–	–	–	–	–

Liquidity Ratio

	Current Ratio Latest	5-Yr Avg
Median (12)	1.5	1.4
SIC Composite (12)	1.6	1.5
Large Composite (3)	1.7	1.5
Small Composite (3)	1.8	1.8
High-Financial Risk (–)	–	–

Profitability Ratio (%)

	Operating Margin Latest	5-Yr Avg
Median (12)	7.2	6.9
SIC Composite (12)	8.8	8.6
Large Composite (3)	11.3	10.8
Small Composite (3)	9.1	8.2
High-Financial Risk (–)	–	–

Growth Rates (%)

	Long-term EPS Analyst Estimates
Median (12)	10.3
SIC Composite (12)	11.4
Large Composite (3)	12.3
Small Composite (3)	3.8
High-Financial Risk (–)	–

Betas (Levered)

	Raw (OLS)	Blume Adjusted	Peer Group	Vasicek Adjusted	Sum	Downside
Median	0.79	0.87	0.87	0.83	0.98	1.28
SIC Composite	0.85	0.91	0.87	0.85	0.73	0.94
Large Composite	0.86	0.91	0.87	0.86	0.61	0.97
Small Composite	0.66	0.79	0.87	0.72	0.87	0.83
High Financial Risk	–	–	–	–	–	–

Betas (Unlevered)

	Raw (OLS)	Blume Adjusted	Peer Group	Vasicek Adjusted	Sum	Downside
Median	0.73	0.81	0.83	0.73	0.73	0.91
SIC Composite	0.80	0.86	0.82	0.81	0.69	0.88
Large Composite	0.82	0.87	0.82	0.82	0.59	0.92
Small Composite	0.64	0.77	0.83	0.69	0.84	0.81
High Financial Risk	–	–	–	–	–	–

Equity Valuation Multiples

	Price/Sales Latest	5-Yr Avg	Price/Earnings Latest	5-Yr Avg	Market/Book Latest	5-Yr Avg
Median	1.0	0.9	23.7	21.2	1.7	1.7
SIC Composite	1.3	1.2	23.5	21.3	2.9	2.9
Large Composite	1.6	1.4	24.1	21.8	4.3	4.2
Small Composite	1.5	1.4	22.8	22.2	1.9	2.0
High Financial Risk	–	–	–	–	–	–

Enterprise Valuation (EV) Multiples

	EV/Sales Latest	5-Yr Avg	EV/EBITDA Latest	5-Yr Avg
Median	1.1	0.9	6.9	6.4
SIC Composite	1.4	1.2	8.9	8.4
Large Composite	1.7	1.5	10.9	10.1
Small Composite	1.5	1.4	6.3	6.6
High Financial Risk	–	–	–	–

Enterprise Valuation SIC Composite

	Latest	5-Yr Avg
EV/Sales	1.4	1.2
EV/EBITDA	8.9	8.4

Fama-French (F-F) 5-Factor Model

	F-F Beta	SMB Premium	HML Premium	RMW Premium	CMA Premium
Median	1.0	2.0	3.0	2.8	-0.9
SIC Composite	0.8	1.6	0.8	0.8	3.5
Large Composite	0.9	1.0	1.0	1.0	1.3
Small Composite	0.6	3.1	1.4	0.9	2.6
High Financial Risk	–	–	–	–	–

Leverage Ratios (%)

	Debt/MV Equity Latest	5-Yr Avg	Debt/Total Capital Latest	5-Yr Avg
Median	8.0	7.2	7.4	6.7
SIC Composite	8.8	9.4	8.1	8.6
Large Composite	6.1	7.1	5.7	6.7
Small Composite	6.3	6.2	5.9	5.8
High Financial Risk	–	–	–	–

Cost of Debt

	Cost of Debt (%) Latest
Median	7.1
SIC Composite	6.3
Large Composite	5.3
Small Composite	7.1
High Financial Risk	–

Capital Structure

SIC Composite (%) Latest
- D/TC: 8.1
- E/TC: 91.9

Cost of Equity Capital (%)

	CRSP Deciles CAPM	CAPM +Size Prem	Build-Up	Risk Premium Report CAPM +Size Prem	Build-Up	Discounted Cash Flow 1-Stage	3-Stage	Fama-French 5-Factor Model
Median	8.1	9.6	9.9	12.4	14.2	11.6	8.6	15.9
SIC Composite	8.2	9.4	9.5	10.9	13.0	12.0	8.9	14.7
Large Composite	8.2	9.1	9.2	10.0	12.5	13.0	9.5	12.7
Small Composite	7.4	9.4	10.2	12.6	14.4	4.3	5.9	14.9
High Financial Risk	–	–	–	–	–	–	–	–

Cost of Equity Capital (%) SIC Composite

Avg CRSP	Avg RPR	1-Stage	3-Stage	5-Factor Model
9.4	12.0	12.0	8.9	14.7

Weighted Average Cost of Capital (WACC) (%)

	CRSP Deciles CAPM	CAPM +Size Prem	Build-Up	Risk Premium Report CAPM +Size Prem	Build-Up	Discounted Cash Flow 1-Stage	3-Stage	Fama-French 5-Factor Model
Median	7.7	9.4	9.4	11.2	12.7	10.7	8.5	14.7
SIC Composite	7.9	9.0	9.1	10.4	12.3	11.4	8.6	13.9
Large Composite	8.0	8.8	8.9	9.7	12.0	12.5	9.2	12.2
Small Composite	7.3	9.1	9.9	12.2	13.8	4.3	5.9	14.3
High Financial Risk	–	–	–	–	–	–	–	–

WACC (%) SIC Composite
Low 8.6 — Average 10.7 — Median 10.4 — High 13.9

© 2017 Duff & Phelps. All Rights Reserved. Duff & Phelps has used the utmost care in compiling the data presented herein, but cannot guarantee the accuracy, completeness, or timeliness of the information.

Data Updated Through March 31, 2017

45

Number of Companies: 15
Transportation By Air

Industry Description
This major group includes establishments engaged in furnishing domestic and foreign transportation by air and also those operating airports and flying fields and furnishing terminal services.

Sales (in millions)

Three Largest Companies
American Airlines Group Inc.	$40,180.0
Delta Air Lines Inc.	39,639.0
United Continental Holdings Inc.	36,556.0

Three Smallest Companies
Air Methods Corp.	$1,170.5
Air Transport Services Group, Inc.	768.9
PHI Inc.	634.1

Total Assets (in millions)

Three Largest Companies
American Airlines Group Inc.	$51,274.0
Delta Air Lines Inc.	51,261.0
United Continental Holdings Inc.	40,140.0

Three Smallest Companies
Allegiant Travel Co.	$1,671.6
PHI Inc.	1,448.4
Air Transport Services Group, Inc.	1,259.3

Annualized Monthly Performance Statistics (%)

Industry
	Geometric Mean	Arithmetic Mean	Standard Deviation
1-year	8.2	12.1	31.7
3-year	15.4	18.7	29.3
5-year	34.9	38.7	33.5

S&P 500 Index
	Geometric Mean	Arithmetic Mean	Standard Deviation
1-year	17.2	17.4	7.2
3-year	10.4	10.9	11.5
5-year	13.3	13.9	11.5

Return Ratios (%)

	Return on Assets Latest	5-Yr Avg	Return on Equity Latest	5-Yr Avg	Dividend Yield Latest	5-Yr Avg
Median (15)	5.9	5.4	16.8	13.3	0.0	0.4
SIC Composite (15)	6.5	6.1	9.6	11.0	0.9	0.7
Large Composite (3)	6.5	6.3	12.1	13.8	1.1	0.7
Small Composite (3)	2.1	3.6	3.4	5.2	0.0	0.7
High-Financial Risk (–)	–	–	–	–	–	–

Liquidity Ratio

	Current Ratio Latest	5-Yr Avg
Median (15)	0.9	1.0
SIC Composite (15)	0.7	0.8
Large Composite (3)	0.6	0.7
Small Composite (3)	2.9	2.6
High-Financial Risk	–	–

Profitability Ratio (%)

	Operating Margin Latest	5-Yr Avg
Median (15)	16.5	12.6
SIC Composite (15)	16.2	11.7
Large Composite (3)	15.4	11.0
Small Composite (3)	9.9	13.2
High-Financial Risk	–	–

Growth Rates (%)

	Long-term EPS Analyst Estimates
Median (15)	5.5
SIC Composite (15)	3.1
Large Composite (3)	-1.4
Small Composite (3)	12.4
High-Financial Risk	–

Betas (Levered)

	Raw (OLS)	Blume Adjusted	Peer Group	Vasicek Adjusted	Sum	Downside
Median	1.27	1.18	1.32	1.28	1.46	1.40
SIC Composite	0.98	0.99	1.32	1.01	0.50	1.06
Large Composite	0.98	0.99	1.32	1.00	0.34	1.29
Small Composite	1.57	1.36	–	–	1.67	1.51
High Financial Risk	–	–	–	–	–	–

Betas (Unlevered)

	Raw (OLS)	Blume Adjusted	Peer Group	Vasicek Adjusted	Sum	Downside
Median	0.86	0.81	1.00	0.86	0.79	1.03
SIC Composite	0.77	0.78	1.01	0.80	0.44	0.83
Large Composite	0.73	0.74	0.95	0.74	0.32	0.93
Small Composite	1.05	0.93	–	–	1.11	1.01
High Financial Risk	–	–	–	–	–	–

Equity Valuation Multiples

	Price/Sales Latest	5-Yr Avg	Price/Earnings Latest	5-Yr Avg	Market/Book Latest	5-Yr Avg
Median	1.0	0.7	14.0	14.5	2.2	2.3
SIC Composite	0.9	0.7	10.5	9.1	2.6	2.5
Large Composite	0.7	0.5	8.3	7.3	3.1	4.1
Small Composite	1.1	1.1	29.3	19.2	1.4	1.5
High Financial Risk	–	–	–	–	–	–

Enterprise Valuation (EV) Multiples

	EV/Sales Latest	5-Yr Avg	EV/EBITDA Latest	5-Yr Avg
Median	1.2	1.0	6.7	5.8
SIC Composite	1.1	0.9	5.1	5.2
Large Composite	0.9	0.7	4.4	4.9
Small Composite	1.7	1.7	8.4	7.2
High Financial Risk	–	–	–	–

Enterprise Valuation SIC Composite
- EV/Sales: Latest 1.1, 5-Yr Avg 0.9
- EV/EBITDA: Latest 5.1, 5-Yr Avg 5.2

Fama-French (F-F) 5-Factor Model

	F-F Beta	SMB Premium	HML Premium	RMW Premium	CMA Premium
Median	1.4	3.3	-1.6	0.6	3.8
SIC Composite	0.9	2.8	-0.6	2.6	3.6
Large Composite	1.0	3.7	-1.4	2.4	3.2
Small Composite	1.5	4.2	0.1	2.3	3.5
High Financial Risk	–	–	–	–	–

Leverage Ratios (%)

	Debt/MV Equity Latest	5-Yr Avg	Debt/Total Capital Latest	5-Yr Avg
Median	48.1	52.3	32.5	34.3
SIC Composite	42.4	52.3	29.8	34.3
Large Composite	56.1	66.6	36.0	40.0
Small Composite	73.7	60.3	42.4	37.6
High Financial Risk	–	–	–	–

Cost of Debt

	Cost of Debt (%) Latest
Median	6.1
SIC Composite	6.1
Large Composite	6.1
Small Composite	7.1
High Financial Risk	–

Capital Structure

SIC Composite (%) Latest
- D/TC: 29.8
- E/TC: 70.2

Cost of Equity Capital (%)

	CRSP Deciles CAPM	CAPM +Size Prem	Build-Up	Risk Premium Report CAPM +Size Prem	Build-Up	Discounted Cash Flow 1-Stage	3-Stage	Fama-French 5-Factor Model
Median	10.5	12.3	12.3	15.5	13.1	9.5	8.1	17.4
SIC Composite	9.1	9.5	11.2	8.3	10.8	–	8.9	16.9
Large Composite	9.0	9.3	11.1	6.9	10.0	–	8.3	16.8
Small Composite	–	–	12.9	16.8	14.1	12.4	11.4	21.9
High Financial Risk	–	–	–	–	–	–	–	–

Cost of Equity Capital (%) SIC Composite
- Avg CRSP: 10.4
- Avg RPR: 9.5
- 1-Stage: n/a
- 3-Stage: 8.9
- 5-Factor Model: 16.9

Weighted Average Cost of Capital (WACC) (%)

	CRSP Deciles CAPM	CAPM +Size Prem	Build-Up	Risk Premium Report CAPM +Size Prem	Build-Up	Discounted Cash Flow 1-Stage	3-Stage	Fama-French 5-Factor Model
Median	8.4	8.9	9.9	10.1	10.1	8.5	7.5	13.9
SIC Composite	8.0	8.3	9.4	7.4	9.1	4.4	7.8	13.4
Large Composite	7.9	8.1	9.3	6.6	8.6	–	7.5	12.9
Small Composite	–	–	10.3	12.5	11.0	10.0	9.4	15.5
High Financial Risk	–	–	–	–	–	–	–	–

WACC (%) SIC Composite
- Low: 4.4
- High: 13.4
- Average: 8.5
- Median: 8.3

© 2017 Duff & Phelps. All Rights Reserved. Duff & Phelps has used the utmost care in compiling the data presented herein, but cannot guarantee the accuracy, completeness, or timeliness of the information.

Data Updated Through March 31, 2017

451

Number of Companies: 11
Air Transportation, Scheduled, and Air Courier

Industry Description
Establishments primarily engaged in air transportation, scheduled; and air courier services.

Sales (in millions)

Three Largest Companies
American Airlines Group Inc.	$40,180.0
Delta Air Lines Inc.	39,639.0
United Continental Holdings Inc.	36,556.0

Three Smallest Companies
Spirit Airlines, Inc.	$2,322.0
Allegiant Travel Co.	1,362.8
Air Transport Services Group, Inc.	768.9

Total Assets (in millions)

Three Largest Companies
American Airlines Group Inc.	$51,274.0
Delta Air Lines Inc.	51,261.0
United Continental Holdings Inc.	40,140.0

Three Smallest Companies
Hawaiian Holdings Inc.	$2,708.6
Allegiant Travel Co.	1,671.6
Air Transport Services Group, Inc.	1,259.3

Annualized Monthly Performance Statistics (%)

	Industry Geometric Mean	Arithmetic Mean	Standard Deviation	S&P 500 Index Geometric Mean	Arithmetic Mean	Standard Deviation
1-year	8.1	12.2	32.2	17.2	17.4	7.2
3-year	16.8	20.4	30.5	10.4	10.9	11.5
5-year	37.8	42.3	36.6	13.3	13.9	11.5

Return Ratios (%)

	Return on Assets Latest	5-Yr Avg	Return on Equity Latest	5-Yr Avg	Dividend Yield Latest	5-Yr Avg
Median (11)	8.4	5.5	25.1	21.6	0.8	0.8
SIC Composite (11)	6.9	6.3	9.8	11.3	1.0	0.7
Large Composite (3)	6.5	6.3	12.1	13.8	1.1	0.7
Small Composite (3)	8.3	9.2	6.9	6.2	0.7	0.7
High-Financial Risk (–)	–	–	–	–	–	–

Liquidity Ratio

	Current Ratio Latest	5-Yr Avg
Median (11)	0.8	0.9
SIC Composite (11)	0.7	0.7
Large Composite (3)	0.6	0.7
Small Composite (3)	1.4	1.6
High-Financial Risk (–)	–	–

Profitability Ratio (%)

	Operating Margin Latest	5-Yr Avg
Median (11)	18.6	12.9
SIC Composite (11)	16.5	11.7
Large Composite (3)	15.4	11.0
Small Composite (3)	20.7	18.7
High-Financial Risk (–)	–	–

Growth Rates (%)

	Long-term EPS Analyst Estimates
Median (11)	4.3
SIC Composite (11)	3.1
Large Composite (3)	-1.4
Small Composite (3)	5.5
High-Financial Risk (–)	–

Betas (Levered)

	Raw (OLS)	Blume Adjusted	Peer Group	Vasicek Adjusted	Sum	Downside
Median	0.98	0.99	1.32	1.02	0.79	1.25
SIC Composite	0.94	0.97	1.32	0.98	0.42	1.09
Large Composite	0.98	0.99	1.32	1.00	0.34	1.29
Small Composite	0.52	0.70	1.32	0.61	0.27	0.94
High Financial Risk	–	–	–	–	–	–

Betas (Unlevered)

	Raw (OLS)	Blume Adjusted	Peer Group	Vasicek Adjusted	Sum	Downside
Median	0.86	0.81	1.10	0.86	0.70	1.03
SIC Composite	0.75	0.77	1.02	0.78	0.38	0.86
Large Composite	0.73	0.74	0.95	0.74	0.32	0.93
Small Composite	0.47	0.61	1.08	0.54	0.28	0.79
High Financial Risk	–	–	–	–	–	–

Equity Valuation Multiples

	Price/Sales Latest	5-Yr Avg	Price/Earnings Latest	5-Yr Avg	Market/Book Latest	5-Yr Avg
Median	1.0	0.7	12.1	11.0	2.7	2.4
SIC Composite	0.9	0.7	10.2	8.8	2.7	2.7
Large Composite	0.7	0.5	8.3	7.3	3.1	4.1
Small Composite	1.6	1.7	14.4	16.1	2.7	3.1
High Financial Risk	–	–	–	–	–	–

Enterprise Valuation (EV) Multiples

	EV/Sales Latest	5-Yr Avg	EV/EBITDA Latest	5-Yr Avg
Median	1.2	1.0	6.5	5.2
SIC Composite	1.1	0.8	5.1	5.1
Large Composite	0.9	0.7	4.4	4.9
Small Composite	1.9	1.7	6.6	6.9
High Financial Risk	–	–	–	–

Enterprise Valuation SIC Composite
- Latest: EV/Sales 1.1, EV/EBITDA 5.1
- 5-Yr Avg: EV/Sales 0.8, EV/EBITDA 5.1

Fama-French (F-F) 5-Factor Model

	F-F Beta	SMB Premium	HML Premium	RMW Premium	CMA Premium
Median	0.7	2.1	-0.9	3.1	4.4
SIC Composite	0.9	2.8	-1.1	2.6	4.3
Large Composite	1.0	3.7	-1.4	2.4	3.2
Small Composite	0.6	2.9	-0.5	4.2	3.4
High Financial Risk	–	–	–	–	–

Leverage Ratios (%)

	Debt/MV Equity Latest	5-Yr Avg	Debt/Total Capital Latest	5-Yr Avg
Median	27.2	52.3	21.4	34.3
SIC Composite	40.3	51.0	28.7	33.8
Large Composite	56.1	66.6	36.0	40.0
Small Composite	31.1	20.0	23.7	16.7
High Financial Risk	–	–	–	–

Cost of Debt

	Cost of Debt (%) Latest
Median	6.1
SIC Composite	6.1
Large Composite	6.1
Small Composite	6.3
High Financial Risk	–

Capital Structure

SIC Composite (%) Latest: D/TC 28.7, E/TC 71.3

Cost of Equity Capital (%)

	CRSP Deciles CAPM	CAPM +Size Prem	Build-Up	Risk Premium Report CAPM +Size Prem	Build-Up	Discounted Cash Flow 1-Stage	3-Stage	Fama-French 5-Factor Model
Median	9.1	9.4	11.7	10.5	12.0	10.4	8.2	16.2
SIC Composite	8.9	9.3	11.2	7.8	10.7	4.0	9.0	16.9
Large Composite	9.0	9.3	11.1	6.9	10.0	–	8.3	16.8
Small Composite	6.9	8.2	12.1	8.6	13.2	6.1	7.9	16.6
High Financial Risk	–	–	–	–	–	–	–	–

Cost of Equity Capital (%) SIC Composite: Avg CRSP 10.2, Avg RPR 9.2, 1-Stage 4.0, 3-Stage 9.0, 5-Factor Model 16.9

Weighted Average Cost of Capital (WACC) (%)

	CRSP Deciles CAPM	CAPM +Size Prem	Build-Up	Risk Premium Report CAPM +Size Prem	Build-Up	Discounted Cash Flow 1-Stage	3-Stage	Fama-French 5-Factor Model
Median	8.5	8.6	10.1	9.5	10.1	9.2	7.6	14.1
SIC Composite	7.8	8.1	9.5	7.0	9.1	4.4	7.9	13.6
Large Composite	7.9	8.1	9.3	6.6	8.6	–	7.5	12.9
Small Composite	6.4	7.4	10.4	7.7	11.3	5.8	7.2	13.8
High Financial Risk	–	–	–	–	–	–	–	–

WACC (%) SIC Composite: Low 4.4, High 13.6, Average 8.5, Median 8.1

© 2017 Duff & Phelps. All Rights Reserved. Duff & Phelps has used the utmost care in compiling the data presented herein, but cannot guarantee the accuracy, completeness, or timeliness of the information.

Data Updated Through March 31, 2017

4512

Number of Companies: 10
Air Transportation, Scheduled

Industry Description
Establishments primarily engaged in furnishing air transportation over regular routes and on regular schedules.

Sales (in millions)

Three Largest Companies
American Airlines Group Inc.	$40,180.0
Delta Air Lines Inc.	39,639.0
United Continental Holdings Inc.	36,556.0

Three Smallest Companies
Hawaiian Holdings Inc.	$2,450.6
Spirit Airlines, Inc.	2,322.0
Allegiant Travel Co.	1,362.8

Total Assets (in millions)

Three Largest Companies
American Airlines Group Inc.	$51,274.0
Delta Air Lines Inc.	51,261.0
United Continental Holdings Inc.	40,140.0

Three Smallest Companies
Spirit Airlines, Inc.	$3,151.9
Hawaiian Holdings Inc.	2,708.6
Allegiant Travel Co.	1,671.6

Annualized Monthly Performance Statistics (%)

Industry	Geometric Mean	Arithmetic Mean	Standard Deviation
1-year	8.2	12.2	32.2
3-year	16.7	20.3	30.5
5-year	38.0	42.5	36.8

S&P 500 Index	Geometric Mean	Arithmetic Mean	Standard Deviation
1-year	17.2	17.4	7.2
3-year	10.4	10.9	11.5
5-year	13.3	13.9	11.5

Return Ratios (%)

	Return on Assets Latest	5-Yr Avg	Return on Equity Latest	5-Yr Avg	Dividend Yield Latest	5-Yr Avg
Median (10)	8.7	6.1	25.4	22.7	0.8	0.8
SIC Composite (10)	6.9	6.3	9.8	11.4	1.0	0.7
Large Composite (3)	6.5	6.3	12.1	13.8	1.1	0.7
Small Composite (3)	9.6	8.8	8.2	7.1	0.6	0.7
High-Financial Risk (−)	−	−	−	−	−	−

Liquidity Ratio

	Current Ratio Latest	5-Yr Avg
Median (10)	0.8	0.9
SIC Composite (10)	0.7	0.7
Large Composite (3)	0.6	0.7
Small Composite (3)	1.3	1.3
High-Financial Risk (−)	−	−

Profitability Ratio (%)

	Operating Margin Latest	5-Yr Avg
Median (10)	19.2	13.0
SIC Composite (10)	16.5	11.7
Large Composite (3)	15.4	11.0
Small Composite (3)	22.2	17.2
High-Financial Risk (−)	−	−

Growth Rates (%)

	Long-term EPS Analyst Estimates
Median (10)	3.3
SIC Composite (10)	3.1
Large Composite (3)	-1.4
Small Composite (3)	1.5
High-Financial Risk (−)	−

Betas (Levered)

	Raw (OLS)	Blume Adjusted	Peer Group	Vasicek Adjusted	Sum	Downside
Median	0.91	0.95	1.32	0.96	0.72	1.23
SIC Composite	0.94	0.97	1.32	0.97	0.41	1.09
Large Composite	0.98	0.99	1.32	1.00	0.34	1.29
Small Composite	0.56	0.73	1.32	0.78	0.28	0.86
High Financial Risk	−	−	−	−	−	−

Betas (Unlevered)

	Raw (OLS)	Blume Adjusted	Peer Group	Vasicek Adjusted	Sum	Downside
Median	0.78	0.81	1.11	0.82	0.66	1.02
SIC Composite	0.75	0.77	1.02	0.77	0.38	0.86
Large Composite	0.73	0.74	0.95	0.74	0.32	0.93
Small Composite	0.50	0.64	1.11	0.68	0.28	0.74
High Financial Risk	−	−	−	−	−	−

Equity Valuation Multiples

	Price/Sales Latest	5-Yr Avg	Price/Earnings Latest	5-Yr Avg	Market/Book Latest	5-Yr Avg
Median	1.0	0.7	11.3	10.4	2.8	2.6
SIC Composite	0.9	0.7	10.2	8.8	2.8	2.8
Large Composite	0.7	0.5	8.3	7.3	3.1	4.1
Small Composite	1.4	1.3	12.3	14.2	2.8	3.3
High Financial Risk	−	−	−	−	−	−

Enterprise Valuation (EV) Multiples

	EV/Sales Latest	5-Yr Avg	EV/EBITDA Latest	5-Yr Avg
Median	1.2	0.9	5.7	5.2
SIC Composite	1.1	0.8	5.0	5.1
Large Composite	0.9	0.7	4.4	4.9
Small Composite	1.5	1.3	5.6	6.2
High Financial Risk	−	−	−	−

Enterprise Valuation SIC Composite
- EV/Sales: Latest 1.1, 5-Yr Avg 0.8
- EV/EBITDA: Latest 5.0, 5-Yr Avg 5.1

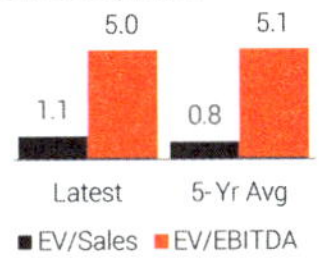

Fama-French (F-F) 5-Factor Model

	Fama-French (F-F) Components				
	F-F Beta	SMB Premium	HML Premium	RMW Premium	CMA Premium
Median	0.7	2.1	-0.9	3.1	4.4
SIC Composite	0.9	2.8	-1.1	2.6	4.3
Large Composite	1.0	3.7	-1.4	2.4	3.2
Small Composite	0.6	3.4	-0.2	4.6	3.3
High Financial Risk	−	−	−	−	−

Leverage Ratios (%)

	Debt/MV Equity Latest	5-Yr Avg	Debt/Total Capital Latest	5-Yr Avg
Median	26.6	44.5	21.0	30.6
SIC Composite	40.2	50.9	28.7	33.7
Large Composite	56.1	66.6	36.0	40.0
Small Composite	26.8	24.1	21.1	19.4
High Financial Risk	−	−	−	−

Cost of Debt

	Cost of Debt (%) Latest
Median	6.1
SIC Composite	6.0
Large Composite	6.1
Small Composite	6.1
High Financial Risk	−

Capital Structure

SIC Composite (%) Latest
- D/TC: 28.7
- E/TC: 71.3

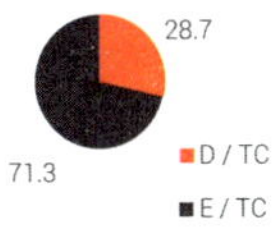

Cost of Equity Capital (%)

	CRSP Deciles			Risk Premium Report		Discounted Cash Flow		Fama-French
	CAPM	CAPM +Size Prem	Build-Up	CAPM +Size Prem	Build-Up	1-Stage	3-Stage	5-Factor Model
Median	8.8	9.4	11.5	9.5	11.8	11.3	8.3	16.2
SIC Composite	8.9	9.2	11.2	7.7	10.7	4.0	9.0	16.9
Large Composite	9.0	9.3	11.1	6.9	10.0	−	8.3	16.8
Small Composite	7.8	9.1	12.1	8.6	13.1	−	6.8	17.9
High Financial Risk	−	−	−	−	−	−	−	−

Cost of Equity Capital (%) SIC Composite
- Avg CRSP: 10.2
- Avg RPR: 9.2
- 1-Stage: 4.0
- 3-Stage: 9.0
- 5-Factor Model: 16.9

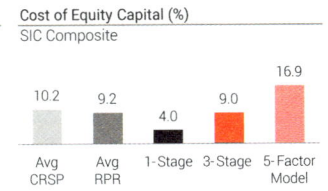

Weighted Average Cost of Capital (WACC) (%)

	CRSP Deciles			Risk Premium Report		Discounted Cash Flow		Fama-French
	CAPM	CAPM +Size Prem	Build-Up	CAPM +Size Prem	Build-Up	1-Stage	3-Stage	5-Factor Model
Median	8.1	8.3	10.0	8.9	10.1	9.8	7.7	13.9
SIC Composite	7.8	8.1	9.5	7.0	9.1	4.4	7.9	13.5
Large Composite	7.9	8.1	9.3	6.6	8.6	−	7.5	12.9
Small Composite	7.2	8.2	10.6	7.8	11.4	−	6.4	15.2
High Financial Risk	−	−	−	−	−	−	−	−

WACC (%) SIC Composite
- Low: 4.4
- High: 13.5
- Average: 8.5
- Median: 8.1

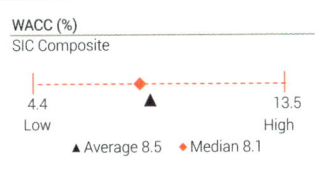

© 2017 Duff & Phelps. All Rights Reserved. Duff & Phelps has used the utmost care in compiling the data presented herein, but cannot guarantee the accuracy, completeness, or timeliness of the information.

Data Updated Through March 31, 2017

46

Number of Companies: 6
Pipelines, Except Natural Gas

Industry Description
This major group includes establishments primarily engaged in the pipeline transportation of petroleum and other commodities, except natural gas. Pipelines operated by petroleum producing or refining companies and separately reported are included. Establishments primarily engaged in natural gas transmission are classified in Industry 4922.

Sales (in millions)

Three Largest Companies
Sunoco Logistics Partners LP	$9,151.0
Buckeye Partners, LP	3,248.4
Magellan Midstream Partners LP	2,205.4

Three Smallest Companies
Tesoro Logistics LP	$1,220.0
Holly Energy Partners LP	402.0
Transmontaigne Partners LP	152.5

Total Assets (in millions)

Three Largest Companies
Sunoco Logistics Partners LP	$18,849.0
Buckeye Partners, LP	9,421.1
Magellan Midstream Partners LP	6,772.1

Three Smallest Companies
Tesoro Logistics LP	$5,860.0
Holly Energy Partners LP	1,884.2
Transmontaigne Partners LP	656.7

Annualized Monthly Performance Statistics (%)

Industry
	Geometric Mean	Arithmetic Mean	Standard Deviation
1-year	13.8	14.8	16.3
3-year	1.5	3.4	20.1
5-year	14.6	16.5	21.5

S&P 500 Index
	Geometric Mean	Arithmetic Mean	Standard Deviation
1-year	17.2	17.4	7.2
3-year	10.4	10.9	11.5
5-year	13.3	13.9	11.5

Return Ratios (%)

	Return on Assets Latest	Return on Assets 5-Yr Avg	Return on Equity Latest	Return on Equity 5-Yr Avg	Dividend Yield Latest	Dividend Yield 5-Yr Avg
Median (6)	6.2	5.9	16.3	14.9	6.9	5.3
SIC Composite (6)	5.9	5.6	5.8	5.1	6.1	5.0
Large Composite (–)	–	–	–	–	–	–
Small Composite (–)	–	–	–	–	–	–
High-Financial Risk (–)	–	–	–	–	–	–

Liquidity Ratio

	Current Ratio Latest	Current Ratio 5-Yr Avg
Median (6)	1.1	1.1
SIC Composite (6)	1.7	1.2
Large Composite	–	–
Small Composite	–	–
High-Financial Risk	–	–

Profitability Ratio (%)

	Operating Margin Latest	Operating Margin 5-Yr Avg
Median (6)	31.8	31.4
SIC Composite (6)	19.1	11.1
Large Composite	–	–
Small Composite	–	–
High-Financial Risk	–	–

Growth Rates (%)

	Long-term EPS Analyst Estimates
Median (6)	11.4
SIC Composite (6)	14.2
Large Composite	–
Small Composite	–
High-Financial Risk	–

Betas (Levered)

	Raw (OLS)	Blume Adjusted	Peer Group	Vasicek Adjusted	Sum	Downside
Median	0.98	0.99	1.10	1.04	1.29	1.26
SIC Composite	1.01	1.01	1.10	1.03	1.40	1.23
Large Composite	–	–	–	–	–	–
Small Composite	–	–	–	–	–	–
High Financial Risk	–	–	–	–	–	–

Betas (Unlevered)

	Raw (OLS)	Blume Adjusted	Peer Group	Vasicek Adjusted	Sum	Downside
Median	0.64	0.70	0.80	0.73	0.92	0.90
SIC Composite	0.72	0.73	0.78	0.74	0.99	0.87
Large Composite	–	–	–	–	–	–
Small Composite	–	–	–	–	–	–
High Financial Risk	–	–	–	–	–	–

Equity Valuation Multiples

	Price/Sales Latest	Price/Sales 5-Yr Avg	Price/Earnings Latest	Price/Earnings 5-Yr Avg	Market/Book Latest	Market/Book 5-Yr Avg
Median	4.7	4.5	17.5	19.1	2.7	2.8
SIC Composite	2.7	1.7	17.1	19.7	2.5	2.6
Large Composite	–	–	–	–	–	–
Small Composite	–	–	–	–	–	–
High Financial Risk	–	–	–	–	–	–

Enterprise Valuation (EV) Multiples

	EV/Sales Latest	EV/Sales 5-Yr Avg	EV/EBITDA Latest	EV/EBITDA 5-Yr Avg
Median	6.9	6.7	12.7	13.9
SIC Composite	3.9	2.4	13.8	14.9
Large Composite	–	–	–	–
Small Composite	–	–	–	–
High Financial Risk	–	–	–	–

Enterprise Valuation SIC Composite
EV/Sales: Latest 3.9, 5-Yr Avg 13.8
EV/EBITDA: Latest 2.4, 5-Yr Avg 14.9

Fama-French (F-F) 5-Factor Model

Fama-French (F-F) Components
	F-F Beta	SMB Premium	HML Premium	RMW Premium	CMA Premium
Median	1.3	-0.7	-2.5	-2.1	3.6
SIC Composite	1.0	-1.6	-1.7	-2.1	4.7
Large Composite	–	–	–	–	–
Small Composite	–	–	–	–	–
High Financial Risk	–	–	–	–	–

Leverage Ratios (%)

	Debt/MV Equity Latest	Debt/MV Equity 5-Yr Avg	Debt/Total Capital Latest	Debt/Total Capital 5-Yr Avg
Median	49.7	46.8	33.1	31.8
SIC Composite	49.3	39.6	33.0	28.4
Large Composite	–	–	–	–
Small Composite	–	–	–	–
High Financial Risk	–	–	–	–

Cost of Debt

	Cost of Debt (%) Latest
Median	5.5
SIC Composite	5.1
Large Composite	–
Small Composite	–
High Financial Risk	–

Capital Structure

SIC Composite (%) Latest
D/TC: 33.0
E/TC: 67.0

Cost of Equity Capital (%)

	CRSP Deciles CAPM	CRSP Deciles CAPM +Size Prem	CRSP Deciles Build-Up	Risk Premium Report CAPM +Size Prem	Risk Premium Report Build-Up	Discounted Cash Flow 1-Stage	Discounted Cash Flow 3-Stage	Fama-French 5-Factor Model
Median	9.2	10.5	10.5	14.1	12.4	12.2	11.5	8.9
SIC Composite	9.2	10.0	10.4	14.1	12.1	20.7	9.6	8.5
Large Composite	–	–	–	–	–	–	–	–
Small Composite	–	–	–	–	–	–	–	–
High Financial Risk	–	–	–	–	–	–	–	–

Cost of Equity Capital (%) SIC Composite
Avg CRSP: 10.2
Avg RPR: 13.1
1-Stage: 20.7
3-Stage: 9.6
5-Factor Model: 8.5

Weighted Average Cost of Capital (WACC) (%)

	CRSP Deciles CAPM	CRSP Deciles CAPM +Size Prem	CRSP Deciles Build-Up	Risk Premium Report CAPM +Size Prem	Risk Premium Report Build-Up	Discounted Cash Flow 1-Stage	Discounted Cash Flow 3-Stage	Fama-French 5-Factor Model
Median	7.2	8.0	8.4	10.2	9.7	10.1	8.8	7.7
SIC Composite	7.2	7.8	8.1	10.5	9.2	15.0	7.5	6.8
Large Composite	–	–	–	–	–	–	–	–
Small Composite	–	–	–	–	–	–	–	–
High Financial Risk	–	–	–	–	–	–	–	–

WACC (%) SIC Composite
Low 6.8 — High 15.0
Average 9.3 ◆ Median 8.1

© 2017 Duff & Phelps. All Rights Reserved. Duff & Phelps has used the utmost care in compiling the data presented herein, but cannot guarantee the accuracy, completeness, or timeliness of the information.

Data Updated Through March 31, 2017

47

Number of Companies: 7
Transportation Services

Industry Description
This major group includes establishments furnishing services incidental to transportation, such as forwarding and packing services, and the arrangement of passenger and freight transportation.

Sales (in millions)

Three Largest Companies

Expedia Inc.	$8,773.6
Expeditors Int'l of Washington Inc.	6,098.0
Hub Group Inc.	3,572.8

Three Smallest Companies

Echo Global Logistics, Inc.	$1,716.2
GATX Corp.	1,418.3
Radiant Logistics, Inc.	782.5

Annualized Monthly Performance Statistics (%)

Industry	Geometric Mean	Arithmetic Mean	Standard Deviation
1-year	16.6	17.4	14.1
3-year	13.2	14.6	18.2
5-year	14.1	15.3	17.4

Total Assets (in millions)

Three Largest Companies

Expedia Inc.	$15,777.5
GATX Corp.	7,105.4
Expeditors Int'l of Washington Inc.	2,790.9

Three Smallest Companies

Roadrunner Transportation Systems	$1,326.1
Echo Global Logistics, Inc.	766.8
Radiant Logistics, Inc.	263.5

S&P 500 Index	Geometric Mean	Arithmetic Mean	Standard Deviation
1-year	17.2	17.4	7.2
3-year	10.4	10.9	11.5
5-year	13.3	13.9	11.5

Return Ratios (%)

	Return on Assets Latest	Return on Assets 5-Yr Avg	Return on Equity Latest	Return on Equity 5-Yr Avg	Dividend Yield Latest	Dividend Yield 5-Yr Avg
Median (7)	3.7	3.9	7.0	8.8	0.4	0.5
SIC Composite (7)	3.7	4.7	3.2	4.3	1.2	1.2
Large Composite (−)	−	−	−	−	−	−
Small Composite (−)	−	−	−	−	−	−
High-Financial Risk (−)	−	−	−	−	−	−

Liquidity Ratio / Profitability Ratio (%) / Growth Rates (%)

	Current Ratio Latest	Current Ratio 5-Yr Avg	Operating Margin Latest	Operating Margin 5-Yr Avg	Long-term EPS Analyst Estimates
Median (7)	1.5	1.7	5.0	5.5	17.0
SIC Composite (7)	0.9	1.0	7.7	8.4	17.0
Large Composite	−	−	−	−	−
Small Composite	−	−	−	−	−
High-Financial Risk	−	−	−	−	−

Betas (Levered)

	Raw (OLS)	Blume Adjusted	Peer Group	Vasicek Adjusted	Sum	Downside
Median	0.98	0.99	0.91	0.92	0.68	1.42
SIC Composite	0.82	0.89	0.91	0.84	0.51	0.86
Large Composite	−	−	−	−	−	−
Small Composite	−	−	−	−	−	−
High Financial Risk	−	−	−	−	−	−

Betas (Unlevered)

	Raw (OLS)	Blume Adjusted	Peer Group	Vasicek Adjusted	Sum	Downside
Median	0.68	0.81	0.79	0.76	0.47	0.95
SIC Composite	0.69	0.74	0.75	0.70	0.43	0.71
Large Composite	−	−	−	−	−	−
Small Composite	−	−	−	−	−	−
High Financial Risk	−	−	−	−	−	−

Equity Valuation Multiples

	Price/Sales Latest	Price/Sales 5-Yr Avg	Price/Earnings Latest	Price/Earnings 5-Yr Avg	Market/Book Latest	Market/Book 5-Yr Avg
Median	0.4	0.5	23.6	22.1	1.9	2.1
SIC Composite	1.4	1.3	31.4	23.1	3.1	2.8
Large Composite	−	−	−	−	−	−
Small Composite	−	−	−	−	−	−
High Financial Risk	−	−	−	−	−	−

Enterprise Valuation (EV) Multiples

	EV/Sales Latest	EV/Sales 5-Yr Avg	EV/EBITDA Latest	EV/EBITDA 5-Yr Avg
Median	0.5	0.7	9.9	10.3
SIC Composite	1.6	1.4	12.1	10.9
Large Composite	−	−	−	−
Small Composite	−	−	−	−
High Financial Risk	−	−	−	−

Enterprise Valuation SIC Composite: EV/Sales Latest 1.6, 5-Yr Avg 1.4; EV/EBITDA Latest 12.1, 5-Yr Avg 10.9

Fama-French (F-F) 5-Factor Model

	F-F Beta	SMB Premium	HML Premium	RMW Premium	CMA Premium
Median	1.1	3.4	1.5	1.1	1.0
SIC Composite	0.8	0.4	-1.1	0.7	-0.7
Large Composite	−	−	−	−	−
Small Composite	−	−	−	−	−
High Financial Risk	−	−	−	−	−

Leverage Ratios (%)

	Debt/MV Equity Latest	Debt/MV Equity 5-Yr Avg	Debt/Total Capital Latest	Debt/Total Capital 5-Yr Avg
Median	16.7	18.7	14.3	15.7
SIC Composite	24.3	26.4	19.5	20.9
Large Composite	−	−	−	−
Small Composite	−	−	−	−
High Financial Risk	−	−	−	−

Cost of Debt

	Cost of Debt (%) Latest
Median	7.1
SIC Composite	5.0
Large Composite	−
Small Composite	−
High Financial Risk	−

Capital Structure

SIC Composite (%) Latest: D/TC 19.5, E/TC 80.5

Cost of Equity Capital (%)

	CAPM	CRSP Deciles CAPM +Size Prem	CRSP Deciles Build-Up	Risk Premium Report CAPM +Size Prem	Risk Premium Report Build-Up	Discounted Cash Flow 1-Stage	Discounted Cash Flow 3-Stage	Fama-French 5-Factor Model
Median	8.6	11.2	10.1	11.6	14.0	17.5	10.4	16.6
SIC Composite	8.1	9.0	9.3	9.2	12.2	18.2	11.4	7.3
Large Composite	−	−	−	−	−	−	−	−
Small Composite	−	−	−	−	−	−	−	−
High Financial Risk	−	−	−	−	−	−	−	−

Cost of Equity Capital (%) SIC Composite: Avg CRSP 9.2, Avg RPR 10.7, 1-Stage 18.2, 3-Stage 11.4, 5-Factor Model 7.3

Weighted Average Cost of Capital (WACC) (%)

	CAPM	CRSP Deciles CAPM +Size Prem	CRSP Deciles Build-Up	Risk Premium Report CAPM +Size Prem	Risk Premium Report Build-Up	Discounted Cash Flow 1-Stage	Discounted Cash Flow 3-Stage	Fama-French 5-Factor Model
Median	7.7	8.8	9.0	8.6	12.3	14.7	9.7	13.2
SIC Composite	7.4	8.1	8.4	8.2	10.6	15.5	10.0	6.7
Large Composite	−	−	−	−	−	−	−	−
Small Composite	−	−	−	−	−	−	−	−
High Financial Risk	−	−	−	−	−	−	−	−

WACC (%) SIC Composite: Low 6.7, High 15.5, Average 9.7, Median 8.4

© 2017 Duff & Phelps. All Rights Reserved. Duff & Phelps has used the utmost care in compiling the data presented herein, but cannot guarantee the accuracy, completeness, or timeliness of the information.

Data Updated Through March 31, 2017

473

Number of Companies: 5
Arrangement Of Transportation Of Freight and Cargo

Industry Description
Establishments primarily engaged in furnishing shipping information and acting as agents in arranging transportation for freight and cargo.

Sales (in millions)

Three Largest Companies
Expeditors Int'l of Washington Inc.	$6,098.0
Hub Group Inc.	3,572.8
Roadrunner Transportation Systems	1,995.0

Three Smallest Companies
Roadrunner Transportation Systems, Inc.	$1,995.0
Echo Global Logistics, Inc.	1,716.2
Radiant Logistics, Inc.	782.5

Annualized Monthly Performance Statistics (%)

Industry	Geometric Mean	Arithmetic Mean	Standard Deviation
1-year	12.2	12.9	13.4
3-year	9.3	10.7	17.9
5-year	4.3	5.7	18.0

Total Assets (in millions)

Three Largest Companies
Expeditors Int'l of Washington Inc.	$2,790.9
Hub Group Inc.	1,360.3
Roadrunner Transportation System	1,326.1

Three Smallest Companies
Roadrunner Transportation Systems	$1,326.1
Echo Global Logistics, Inc.	766.8
Radiant Logistics, Inc.	263.5

S&P 500 Index	Geometric Mean	Arithmetic Mean	Standard Deviation
1-year	17.2	17.4	7.2
3-year	10.4	10.9	11.5
5-year	13.3	13.9	11.5

Return Ratios (%)

	Return on Assets Latest	5-Yr Avg	Return on Equity Latest	5-Yr Avg	Dividend Yield Latest	5-Yr Avg
Median (5)	3.7	5.0	7.0	8.6	0.0	0.0
SIC Composite (5)	8.5	9.2	4.3	4.5	1.2	1.2
Large Composite (–)	–	–	–	–	–	–
Small Composite (–)	–	–	–	–	–	–
High-Financial Risk (–)	–	–	–	–	–	–

Liquidity Ratio | Profitability Ratio (%) | Growth Rates (%)

	Current Ratio Latest	5-Yr Avg	Operating Margin Latest	5-Yr Avg	Long-term EPS Analyst Estimates
Median (5)	1.6	1.8	3.5	3.4	17.0
SIC Composite (5)	2.0	2.1	6.6	6.6	8.8
Large Composite	–	–	–	–	–
Small Composite	–	–	–	–	–
High-Financial Risk	–	–	–	–	–

Betas (Levered)

	Raw (OLS)	Blume Adjusted	Peer Group	Vasicek Adjusted	Sum	Downside
Median	0.98	0.99	0.90	0.91	0.68	1.80
SIC Composite	0.82	0.89	0.90	0.84	0.51	0.78
Large Composite	–	–	–	–	–	–
Small Composite	–	–	–	–	–	–
High Financial Risk	–	–	–	–	–	–

Betas (Unlevered)

	Raw (OLS)	Blume Adjusted	Peer Group	Vasicek Adjusted	Sum	Downside
Median	0.91	0.92	0.83	0.85	0.56	1.31
SIC Composite	0.79	0.86	0.86	0.81	0.50	0.75
Large Composite	–	–	–	–	–	–
Small Composite	–	–	–	–	–	–
High Financial Risk	–	–	–	–	–	–

Equity Valuation Multiples

	Price/Sales Latest	5-Yr Avg	Price/Earnings Latest	5-Yr Avg	Market/Book Latest	5-Yr Avg
Median	0.3	0.5	23.6	22.1	1.9	2.1
SIC Composite	0.9	0.9	23.4	22.3	3.3	3.2
Large Composite	–	–	–	–	–	–
Small Composite	–	–	–	–	–	–
High Financial Risk	–	–	–	–	–	–

Enterprise Valuation (EV) Multiples

	EV/Sales Latest	5-Yr Avg	EV/EBITDA Latest	5-Yr Avg
Median	0.5	0.5	9.9	10.3
SIC Composite	0.9	0.8	11.2	10.9
Large Composite	–	–	–	–
Small Composite	–	–	–	–
High Financial Risk	–	–	–	–

Enterprise Valuation SIC Composite
- Latest: EV/Sales 0.9, EV/EBITDA 11.2
- 5-Yr Avg: EV/Sales 0.8, EV/EBITDA 10.9

Fama-French (F-F) 5-Factor Model

	F-F Beta	SMB Premium	HML Premium	RMW Premium	CMA Premium
Median	0.7	7.3	5.5	2.5	-3.2
SIC Composite	0.8	1.6	1.7	1.2	-1.2
Large Composite	–	–	–	–	–
Small Composite	–	–	–	–	–
High Financial Risk	–	–	–	–	–

Leverage Ratios (%)

	Debt/MV Equity Latest	5-Yr Avg	Debt/Total Capital Latest	5-Yr Avg
Median	12.8	14.2	11.4	12.5
SIC Composite	6.7	4.3	6.3	4.1
Large Composite	–	–	–	–
Small Composite	–	–	–	–
High Financial Risk	–	–	–	–

Cost of Debt | Capital Structure

	Cost of Debt (%) Latest	SIC Composite (%) Latest
Median	7.1	
SIC Composite	7.1	D/TC 6.3, E/TC 93.7

Cost of Equity Capital (%)

	CRSP Deciles CAPM	CAPM +Size Prem	Build-Up	Risk Premium Report CAPM +Size Prem	Build-Up	Discounted Cash Flow 1-Stage	3-Stage	Fama-French 5-Factor Model
Median	8.5	11.3	10.5	11.6	14.4	17.0	8.5	19.7
SIC Composite	8.1	9.4	9.7	9.6	12.8	10.0	9.3	11.1
Large Composite	–	–	–	–	–	–	–	–
Small Composite	–	–	–	–	–	–	–	–
High Financial Risk	–	–	–	–	–	–	–	–

Cost of Equity Capital (%) SIC Composite
- Avg CRSP: 9.5
- Avg RPR: 11.2
- 1-Stage: 10.0
- 3-Stage: 9.3
- 5-Factor Model: 11.1

Weighted Average Cost of Capital (WACC) (%)

	CRSP Deciles CAPM	CAPM +Size Prem	Build-Up	Risk Premium Report CAPM +Size Prem	Build-Up	Discounted Cash Flow 1-Stage	3-Stage	Fama-French 5-Factor Model
Median	8.0	9.6	9.3	10.4	12.4	14.7	8.5	15.0
SIC Composite	7.9	9.1	9.4	9.3	12.3	9.7	9.0	10.7
Large Composite	–	–	–	–	–	–	–	–
Small Composite	–	–	–	–	–	–	–	–
High Financial Risk	–	–	–	–	–	–	–	–

WACC (%) SIC Composite: Low 9.0, High 12.3, Average 9.9, Median 9.4

© 2017 Duff & Phelps. All Rights Reserved. Duff & Phelps has used the utmost care in compiling the data presented herein, but cannot guarantee the accuracy, completeness, or timeliness of the information.

Data Updated Through March 31, 2017

48

Number of Companies: 38
Communications

Industry Description
This major group includes establishments furnishing point-to-point communications services, whether intended to be received aurally or visually; and radio and television broadcasting.

Sales (in millions)

Three Largest Companies
AT&T Inc.	$163,763.0
Verizon Communications Inc.	125,980.0
Comcast Corp.	80,403.0

Three Smallest Companies
Spok Holdings, Inc.	$179.6
Saga Communications	132.9
Beasley Broadcast Group Inc.	105.9

Total Assets (in millions)

Three Largest Companies
AT&T Inc.	$403,821.0
Verizon Communications Inc.	244,180.0
Comcast Corp.	180,500.0

Three Smallest Companies
Beasley Broadcast Group Inc.	$311.4
RigNet, Inc.	258.1
Saga Communications	204.6

Annualized Monthly Performance Statistics (%)

Industry	Geometric Mean	Arithmetic Mean	Standard Deviation	S&P 500 Index	Geometric Mean	Arithmetic Mean	Standard Deviation
1-year	13.2	14.0	14.1	1-year	17.2	17.4	7.2
3-year	9.2	10.1	13.8	3-year	10.4	10.9	11.5
5-year	13.7	14.5	13.3	5-year	13.3	13.9	11.5

Return Ratios (%)

	Return on Assets Latest	5-Yr Avg	Return on Equity Latest	5-Yr Avg	Dividend Yield Latest	5-Yr Avg	Current Ratio Latest	5-Yr Avg	Operating Margin Latest	5-Yr Avg	Long-term EPS Analyst Estimates
Median (38)	3.6	4.1	7.2	9.1	1.2	1.2	1.8	1.7	16.2	18.4	7.1
SIC Composite (38)	4.0	4.1	5.3	5.6	3.1	3.2	0.9	1.0	18.1	18.4	5.9
Large Composite (3)	4.2	4.0	5.5	5.8	3.8	4.0	0.8	0.9	18.2	18.4	7.2
Small Composite (3)	3.7	6.9	3.5	8.1	3.4	3.7	3.0	2.6	15.8	19.8	5.7
High-Financial Risk (15)	-1.6	-3.3	-4.8	-11.5	4.9	6.2	0.7	1.2	6.6	5.0	5.8

Betas (Levered)

	Raw (OLS)	Blume Adjusted	Peer Group	Vasicek Adjusted	Sum	Downside
Median	1.06	1.04	0.78	1.01	1.11	1.48
SIC Composite	0.76	0.85	0.78	0.76	0.61	0.77
Large Composite	0.57	0.73	0.78	0.60	0.40	0.68
Small Composite	0.87	0.92	0.76	0.85	0.81	0.91
High Financial Risk	1.14	1.09	0.76	1.08	1.40	1.76

Betas (Unlevered)

	Raw (OLS)	Blume Adjusted	Peer Group	Vasicek Adjusted	Sum	Downside
Median	0.78	0.77	0.59	0.72	0.81	1.05
SIC Composite	0.55	0.61	0.57	0.55	0.45	0.56
Large Composite	0.41	0.52	0.56	0.43	0.29	0.48
Small Composite	0.80	0.85	0.71	0.79	0.75	0.85
High Financial Risk	0.65	0.63	0.50	0.62	0.75	0.89

Equity Valuation Multiples

	Price/Sales Latest	5-Yr Avg	Price/Earnings Latest	5-Yr Avg	Market/Book Latest	5-Yr Avg
Median	2.0	1.8	24.3	17.4	2.1	2.3
SIC Composite	1.8	1.6	19.1	18.0	1.9	1.9
Large Composite	1.7	1.5	18.2	17.1	1.9	1.7
Small Composite	2.3	1.7	28.4	12.4	1.4	1.2
High Financial Risk	0.8	0.6	–	–	1.0	0.9

Enterprise Valuation (EV) Multiples

	EV/Sales Latest	5-Yr Avg	EV/EBITDA Latest	5-Yr Avg
Median	2.8	2.7	9.1	8.8
SIC Composite	2.7	2.4	8.2	7.2
Large Composite	2.5	2.2	7.6	6.7
Small Composite	2.2	1.7	10.1	6.8
High Financial Risk	2.1	1.6	7.7	7.5

Enterprise Valuation SIC Composite

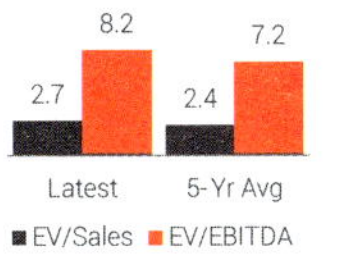

Latest: EV/Sales 2.7, EV/EBITDA 8.2
5-Yr Avg: EV/Sales 2.4, EV/EBITDA 7.2

Fama-French (F-F) 5-Factor Model

	F-F Beta	SMB Premium	HML Premium	RMW Premium	CMA Premium
Median	1.6	1.8	-1.4	-0.9	2.7
SIC Composite	0.8	-0.2	-2.0	0.8	4.8
Large Composite	0.7	-0.5	-2.4	1.3	1.8
Small Composite	0.8	3.9	-2.5	-0.5	6.4
High Financial Risk	–	–	–	–	–

Leverage Ratios (%)

	Debt/MV Equity Latest	5-Yr Avg	Debt/Total Capital Latest	5-Yr Avg
Median	55.1	50.7	35.5	33.6
SIC Composite	50.9	50.5	33.7	33.6
Large Composite	46.3	47.0	31.6	32.0
Small Composite	12.9	22.0	11.5	18.0
High Financial Risk	162.8	177.6	61.9	64.0

Cost of Debt

	Cost of Debt (%) Latest
Median	6.1
SIC Composite	5.1
Large Composite	4.6
Small Composite	6.8
High Financial Risk	7.3

Capital Structure

SIC Composite (%) Latest
D/TC: 33.7
E/TC: 66.3

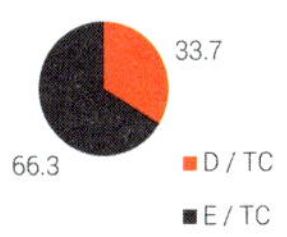

Cost of Equity Capital (%)

	CRSP Deciles CAPM	CAPM +Size Prem	Build-Up	Risk Premium Report CAPM +Size Prem	Build-Up	Discounted Cash Flow 1-Stage	3-Stage	Fama-French 5-Factor Model
Median	9.0	10.5	9.3	13.3	13.6	9.2	9.9	14.2
SIC Composite	7.7	7.8	7.8	7.9	9.3	9.0	9.0	11.1
Large Composite	6.8	6.8	7.7	6.2	8.7	11.2	10.8	7.5
Small Composite	8.2	10.9	10.4	13.2	15.8	8.0	10.8	15.2
High Financial Risk	–	–	–	27.3	28.7	–	–	–

Cost of Equity Capital (%) SIC Composite
Avg CRSP 7.8, Avg RPR 8.6, 1-Stage 9.0, 3-Stage 9.0, 5-Factor Model 11.1

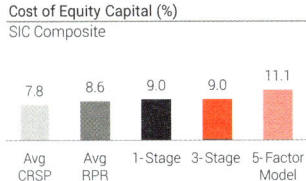

Weighted Average Cost of Capital (WACC) (%)

	CRSP Deciles CAPM	CAPM +Size Prem	Build-Up	Risk Premium Report CAPM +Size Prem	Build-Up	Discounted Cash Flow 1-Stage	3-Stage	Fama-French 5-Factor Model
Median	7.9	8.8	7.8	10.5	10.0	7.8	8.8	10.3
SIC Composite	6.6	6.7	6.7	6.7	7.7	7.5	7.5	8.8
Large Composite	5.9	5.9	6.5	5.5	7.2	8.9	8.7	6.4
Small Composite	8.0	10.3	9.9	12.4	14.7	7.8	10.3	14.1
High Financial Risk	–	–	–	14.7	15.2	–	–	–

WACC (%) SIC Composite
Low 6.7, Average 7.4, Median 7.5, High 8.8

© 2017 Duff & Phelps. All Rights Reserved. Duff & Phelps has used the utmost care in compiling the data presented herein, but cannot guarantee the accuracy, completeness, or timeliness of the information.

Data Updated Through March 31, 2017

481

Number of Companies: 12
Telephone Communications

Industry Description
Establishments primarily engaged in radiotelephone communications; telephone communications, except radiotelephone.

Sales (in millions)

Three Largest Companies
Verizon Communications Inc.	$125,980.0
Centurylink, Inc.	17,470.0
Level 3 Communications Inc.	8,172.0

Three Smallest Companies
Hawaiian Telcom Holdco, Inc.	$393.0
Alaska Communications Sys. Group	226.9
Spok Holdings, Inc.	179.6

Total Assets (in millions)

Three Largest Companies
Verizon Communications Inc.	$244,180.0
Centurylink, Inc.	47,017.0
Level 3 Communications Inc.	24,888.0

Three Smallest Companies
LDT Corp.	$469.7
Alaska Communications Sys. Group	442.4
Spok Holdings, Inc.	388.1

Annualized Monthly Performance Statistics (%)

Industry	Geometric Mean	Arithmetic Mean	Standard Deviation	S&P 500 Index	Geometric Mean	Arithmetic Mean	Standard Deviation
1-year	-5.5	-4.4	14.7	1-year	17.2	17.4	7.2
3-year	5.4	6.5	16.2	3-year	10.4	10.9	11.5
5-year	8.9	10.1	16.4	5-year	13.3	13.9	11.5

Return Ratios (%)

	Return on Assets Latest	5-Yr Avg	Return on Equity Latest	5-Yr Avg	Dividend Yield Latest	5-Yr Avg
Median (12)	1.2	3.4	2.5	10.7	3.0	2.7
SIC Composite (12)	4.4	3.7	6.0	5.7	4.3	4.4
Large Composite (3)	4.6	3.8	6.2	5.8	4.3	4.4
Small Composite (3)	1.1	5.6	2.3	14.2	2.1	2.0
High-Financial Risk (8)	-1.0	-3.1	-3.3	-11.4	7.3	7.9

Liquidity Ratio

	Current Ratio Latest	5-Yr Avg
	1.2	1.2
	1.0	1.1
	0.9	1.1
	1.5	1.5
	0.6	1.2

Profitability Ratio (%)

	Operating Margin Latest	5-Yr Avg
	13.3	14.5
	18.9	18.4
	19.8	19.3
	8.0	10.5
	6.7	4.8

Growth Rates (%)

	Long-term EPS Analyst Estimates
	3.6
	-1.2
	-1.7
	3.6
	5.4

Betas (Levered)

	Raw (OLS)	Blume Adjusted	Peer Group	Vasicek Adjusted	Sum	Downside
Median	0.90	0.94	0.76	0.80	0.60	1.29
SIC Composite	0.54	0.71	0.76	0.59	0.30	0.62
Large Composite	0.52	0.70	0.76	0.56	0.28	0.62
Small Composite	0.78	0.87	–	–	0.71	0.93
High Financial Risk	1.01	1.01	0.76	0.90	1.11	1.79

Betas (Unlevered)

	Raw (OLS)	Blume Adjusted	Peer Group	Vasicek Adjusted	Sum	Downside
Median	0.70	0.74	0.57	0.65	0.56	0.86
SIC Composite	0.39	0.50	0.53	0.42	0.24	0.44
Large Composite	0.37	0.49	0.53	0.40	0.22	0.44
Small Composite	0.60	0.66	–	–	0.56	0.69
High Financial Risk	0.59	0.59	0.50	0.55	0.63	0.89

Equity Valuation Multiples

	Price/Sales Latest	5-Yr Avg	Price/Earnings Latest	5-Yr Avg	Market/Book Latest	5-Yr Avg
Median	1.6	1.4	50.2	21.7	1.7	1.7
SIC Composite	1.5	1.4	16.6	17.5	2.3	2.3
Large Composite	1.5	1.4	16.1	17.3	2.4	2.4
Small Composite	0.9	0.8	42.9	7.0	1.0	1.0
High Financial Risk	0.8	0.6	–	–	0.9	0.9

Enterprise Valuation (EV) Multiples

	EV/Sales Latest	5-Yr Avg	EV/EBITDA Latest	5-Yr Avg
Median	2.0	1.9	7.0	5.5
SIC Composite	2.4	2.1	7.0	6.2
Large Composite	2.4	2.1	7.0	6.3
Small Composite	1.3	1.3	5.2	4.8
High Financial Risk	2.0	1.5	7.4	7.1

Enterprise Valuation SIC Composite
Latest: EV/Sales 2.4, EV/EBITDA 7.0
5-Yr Avg: EV/Sales 2.1, EV/EBITDA 6.2

Fama-French (F-F) 5-Factor Model

	F-F Beta	SMB Premium	HML Premium	RMW Premium	CMA Premium
Median	0.6	3.6	-0.6	1.1	4.5
SIC Composite	0.6	-1.6	-2.6	1.6	6.5
Large Composite	0.7	-1.8	-2.6	1.7	2.2
Small Composite	0.7	3.1	-0.1	0.3	3.2
High Financial Risk	–	–	–	–	–

Leverage Ratios (%)

	Debt/MV Equity Latest	5-Yr Avg	Debt/Total Capital Latest	5-Yr Avg
Median	57.4	63.6	36.4	38.7
SIC Composite	59.8	61.0	37.4	37.9
Large Composite	59.7	61.0	37.4	37.9
Small Composite	63.5	95.6	38.8	48.9
High Financial Risk	166.8	181.8	62.5	64.5

Cost of Debt

	Cost of Debt (%) Latest
Median	6.1
SIC Composite	5.1
Large Composite	5.1
Small Composite	6.8
High Financial Risk	7.1

Capital Structure

SIC Composite (%) Latest
D/TC: 37.4
E/TC: 62.6

Cost of Equity Capital (%)

	CRSP Deciles CAPM	CAPM +Size Prem	Build-Up	Risk Premium Report CAPM +Size Prem	Build-Up	Discounted Cash Flow 1-Stage	3-Stage	Fama-French 5-Factor Model
Median	7.9	9.9	9.4	10.9	14.4	8.2	7.6	15.5
SIC Composite	6.8	6.9	7.8	6.0	9.1	–	6.9	10.9
Large Composite	6.6	6.7	7.8	5.7	9.0	–	6.8	7.0
Small Composite	–	–	10.7	12.2	15.2	5.7	13.7	14.0
High Financial Risk	–	–	–	26.0	29.0	–	–	–

Cost of Equity Capital (%) SIC Composite
Avg CRSP: 7.4; Avg RPR: 7.6; 1-Stage: n/a; 3-Stage: 6.9; 5-Factor Model: 10.9

Weighted Average Cost of Capital (WACC) (%)

	CRSP Deciles CAPM	CAPM +Size Prem	Build-Up	Risk Premium Report CAPM +Size Prem	Build-Up	Discounted Cash Flow 1-Stage	3-Stage	Fama-French 5-Factor Model
Median	7.4	8.4	8.2	9.9	10.2	7.2	7.4	10.6
SIC Composite	5.5	5.6	6.2	5.1	7.0	–	5.6	8.1
Large Composite	5.4	5.4	6.1	4.9	6.9	–	5.5	5.6
Small Composite	–	–	9.1	10.0	11.9	6.1	10.9	11.1
High Financial Risk	–	–	–	14.1	15.2	–	–	–

WACC (%) SIC Composite
Low: 5.1; High: 8.1; Average: 6.3; Median: 5.9

© 2017 Duff & Phelps. All Rights Reserved. Duff & Phelps has used the utmost care in compiling the data presented herein, but cannot guarantee the accuracy, completeness, or timeliness of the information.

Data Updated Through March 31, 2017

4813

Number of Companies: 7
Telephone Communications, Except Radiotelephone

Industry Description
Establishments primarily engaged in furnishing telephone voice and data communications, except radiotelephone and telephone answering services.

Sales (in millions)

Three Largest Companies
Centurylink, Inc.	$17,470.0
Level 3 Communications Inc.	8,172.0
LDT Corp.	1,496.3

Three Smallest Companies
Cogent Communications Holdings	$446.9
Hawaiian Telcom Holdco, Inc.	393.0
Alaska Communications Sys. Group	226.9

Total Assets (in millions)

Three Largest Companies
Centurylink, Inc.	$47,017.0
Level 3 Communications Inc.	24,888.0
Consolidated Comm. Holdings Inc	2,092.8

Three Smallest Companies
Cogent Communications Holdings	$737.9
LDT Corp.	469.7
Alaska Communications Sys. Group	442.4

Annualized Monthly Performance Statistics (%)

Industry	Geometric Mean	Arithmetic Mean	Standard Deviation
1-year	-4.0	-2.9	15.3
3-year	4.9	6.5	19.2
5-year	5.5	7.2	19.4

S&P 500 Index	Geometric Mean	Arithmetic Mean	Standard Deviation
1-year	17.2	17.4	7.2
3-year	10.4	10.9	11.5
5-year	13.3	13.9	11.5

Return Ratios (%)

	Return on Assets Latest	5-Yr Avg	Return on Equity Latest	5-Yr Avg	Dividend Yield Latest	5-Yr Avg
Median (7)	1.3	3.4	3.3	14.8	4.0	3.4
SIC Composite (7)	1.8	2.0	3.6	4.2	3.6	4.2
Large Composite (−)	−	−	−	−	−	−
Small Composite (−)	−	−	−	−	−	−
High-Financial Risk (−)	−	−	−	−	−	−

Liquidity Ratio

	Current Ratio Latest	5-Yr Avg
Median (7)	1.0	1.1
SIC Composite (7)	1.2	1.0
Large Composite (−)	−	−
Small Composite (−)	−	−
High-Financial Risk (−)	−	−

Profitability Ratio (%)

	Operating Margin Latest	5-Yr Avg
Median (7)	12.0	11.9
SIC Composite (7)	14.5	14.1
Large Composite (−)	−	−
Small Composite (−)	−	−
High-Financial Risk (−)	−	−

Growth Rates (%)

	Long-term EPS Analyst Estimates
Median (7)	3.6
SIC Composite (7)	-17.8
Large Composite (−)	−
Small Composite (−)	−
High-Financial Risk (−)	−

Betas (Levered)

	Raw (OLS)	Blume Adjusted	Peer Group	Vasicek Adjusted	Sum	Downside
Median	1.06	1.04	0.76	0.86	0.81	1.37
SIC Composite	0.90	0.94	0.76	0.86	0.47	1.01
Large Composite	−	−	−	−	−	−
Small Composite	−	−	−	−	−	−
High Financial Risk	−	−	−	−	−	−

Betas (Unlevered)

	Raw (OLS)	Blume Adjusted	Peer Group	Vasicek Adjusted	Sum	Downside
Median	0.69	0.70	0.54	0.64	0.63	0.87
SIC Composite	0.62	0.64	0.54	0.60	0.39	0.67
Large Composite	−	−	−	−	−	−
Small Composite	−	−	−	−	−	−
High Financial Risk	−	−	−	−	−	−

Equity Valuation Multiples

	Price/Sales Latest	5-Yr Avg	Price/Earnings Latest	5-Yr Avg	Market/Book Latest	5-Yr Avg
Median	0.7	1.1	39.8	15.7	1.9	2.0
SIC Composite	1.3	1.2	27.4	23.6	1.3	1.3
Large Composite	−	−	−	−	−	−
Small Composite	−	−	−	−	−	−
High Financial Risk	−	−	−	−	−	−

Enterprise Valuation (EV) Multiples

	EV/Sales Latest	5-Yr Avg	EV/EBITDA Latest	5-Yr Avg
Median	1.9	2.2	4.9	5.6
SIC Composite	2.3	2.3	6.8	6.7
Large Composite	−	−	−	−
Small Composite	−	−	−	−
High Financial Risk	−	−	−	−

Enterprise Valuation SIC Composite
Latest: EV/Sales 2.3, EV/EBITDA 6.8
5-Yr Avg: EV/Sales 2.3, EV/EBITDA 6.7

Fama-French (F-F) 5-Factor Model

Fama-French (F-F) Components	F-F Beta	SMB Premium	HML Premium	RMW Premium	CMA Premium
Median	1.0	-1.6	-3.7	4.4	8.1
SIC Composite	1.0	-1.9	0.1	3.0	2.1
Large Composite	−	−	−	−	−
Small Composite	−	−	−	−	−
High Financial Risk	−	−	−	−	−

Leverage Ratios (%)

	Debt/MV Equity Latest	5-Yr Avg	Debt/Total Capital Latest	5-Yr Avg
Median	112.1	105.5	52.8	51.3
SIC Composite	88.9	95.2	47.1	48.8
Large Composite	−	−	−	−
Small Composite	−	−	−	−
High Financial Risk	−	−	−	−

Cost of Debt

	Cost of Debt (%) Latest
Median	6.1
SIC Composite	6.2
Large Composite	−
Small Composite	−
High Financial Risk	−

Capital Structure

SIC Composite (%) Latest
D/TC: 47.1
E/TC: 52.9

Cost of Equity Capital (%)

	CRSP Deciles CAPM	CAPM +Size Prem	Build-Up	Risk Premium Report CAPM	CAPM +Size Prem	Build-Up	Discounted Cash Flow 1-Stage	3-Stage	Fama-French 5-Factor Model
Median	8.2	10.7	9.4	10.6		14.6	9.2	7.2	16.4
SIC Composite	8.2	9.0	8.4	8.2		11.1	−	−	12.4
Large Composite	−	−	−	−		−	−	−	−
Small Composite	−	−	−	−		−	−	−	−
High Financial Risk	−	−	−	−		−	−	−	−

Cost of Equity Capital (%) SIC Composite
Avg CRSP: 8.7, Avg RPR: 9.7, 1-Stage: n/a, 3-Stage: n/a, 5-Factor Model: 12.4

Weighted Average Cost of Capital (WACC) (%)

	CRSP Deciles CAPM	CAPM +Size Prem	Build-Up	Risk Premium Report CAPM	CAPM +Size Prem	Build-Up	Discounted Cash Flow 1-Stage	3-Stage	Fama-French 5-Factor Model
Median	7.6	8.5	8.5	9.8		10.1	7.6	6.3	11.1
SIC Composite	6.6	7.0	6.7	6.6		8.1	−	−	8.8
Large Composite	−	−	−	−		−	−	−	−
Small Composite	−	−	−	−		−	−	−	−
High Financial Risk	−	−	−	−		−	−	−	−

WACC (%) SIC Composite
Low: 6.6, High: 8.8, Average 7.4, Median 7.0

© 2017 Duff & Phelps. All Rights Reserved. Duff & Phelps has used the utmost care in compiling the data presented herein, but cannot guarantee the accuracy, completeness, or timeliness of the information.

Data Updated Through March 31, 2017

483

Number of Companies: 12
Radio and Television Broadcasting Stations

Industry Description
Establishments primarily engaged in radio broadcasting stations; television broadcasting stations.

Sales (in millions)

Three Largest Companies
Viacom, Inc.	$12,488.0
Sirius XM Holdings Inc.	5,017.2
Scripps Networks Interactive	3,401.4

Three Smallest Companies
Entravision Communications	$258.5
Saga Communications	132.9
Beasley Broadcast Group Inc.	105.9

Total Assets (in millions)

Three Largest Companies
Viacom, Inc.	$22,508.0
Sirius XM Holdings Inc.	8,003.6
Scripps Networks Interactive	6,200.3

Three Smallest Companies
Entravision Communications	$517.9
Beasley Broadcast Group Inc.	311.4
Saga Communications	204.6

Annualized Monthly Performance Statistics (%)

Industry	Geometric Mean	Arithmetic Mean	Standard Deviation
1-year	22.8	24.5	21.8
3-year	0.1	2.0	20.2
5-year	11.3	13.2	20.7

S&P 500 Index	Geometric Mean	Arithmetic Mean	Standard Deviation
1-year	17.2	17.4	7.2
3-year	10.4	10.9	11.5
5-year	13.3	13.9	11.5

Return Ratios (%)

	Return on Assets Latest	5-Yr Avg	Return on Equity Latest	5-Yr Avg	Dividend Yield Latest	5-Yr Avg
Median (12)	4.1	6.6	10.5	17.5	1.8	1.2
SIC Composite (12)	6.5	8.7	5.4	6.8	1.3	1.3
Large Composite (3)	7.8	10.5	5.4	7.0	1.4	1.3
Small Composite (3)	3.9	6.8	3.6	7.8	2.0	2.6
High-Financial Risk (–)	–	–	–	–	–	–

Liquidity Ratio
	Current Ratio Latest	5-Yr Avg
Median	2.2	2.4
SIC Composite	1.2	1.3
Large Composite	1.0	1.2
Small Composite	3.6	3.0
High-Financial Risk	–	–

Profitability Ratio (%)
	Operating Margin Latest	5-Yr Avg
Median	22.0	24.5
SIC Composite	25.5	27.6
Large Composite	26.2	29.2
Small Composite	18.4	22.3
High-Financial Risk	–	–

Growth Rates (%)
	Long-term EPS Analyst Estimates
Median	7.1
SIC Composite	7.1
Large Composite	7.5
Small Composite	7.1
High-Financial Risk	–

Betas (Levered)

	Raw (OLS)	Blume Adjusted	Peer Group	Vasicek Adjusted	Sum	Downside
Median	1.52	1.34	0.85	1.31	1.59	1.87
SIC Composite	1.27	1.18	0.85	1.25	1.27	1.18
Large Composite	1.24	1.16	0.85	0.93	1.14	1.12
Small Composite	1.24	1.16	0.76	1.14	1.54	1.36
High Financial Risk	–	–	–	–	–	–

Betas (Unlevered)

	Raw (OLS)	Blume Adjusted	Peer Group	Vasicek Adjusted	Sum	Downside
Median	1.06	0.95	0.64	0.92	1.14	1.32
SIC Composite	0.91	0.85	0.63	0.90	0.92	0.85
Large Composite	0.93	0.87	0.65	0.71	0.86	0.84
Small Composite	0.99	0.93	0.64	0.91	1.21	1.07
High Financial Risk	–	–	–	–	–	–

Equity Valuation Multiples

	Price/Sales Latest	5-Yr Avg	Price/Earnings Latest	5-Yr Avg	Market/Book Latest	5-Yr Avg
Median	2.0	1.8	19.2	16.0	3.0	3.3
SIC Composite	2.2	2.4	18.4	14.8	6.6	6.0
Large Composite	2.5	2.7	18.6	14.4	9.2	6.6
Small Composite	2.3	1.9	28.0	12.9	2.1	2.0
High Financial Risk	–	–	–	–	–	–

Enterprise Valuation (EV) Multiples

	EV/Sales Latest	5-Yr Avg	EV/EBITDA Latest	5-Yr Avg
Median	2.9	3.1	9.9	9.5
SIC Composite	3.3	3.4	10.8	10.4
Large Composite	3.5	3.5	11.6	10.6
Small Composite	2.9	2.7	12.2	9.9
High Financial Risk	–	–	–	–

Enterprise Valuation SIC Composite
- EV/Sales: Latest 3.3, 5-Yr Avg 3.4
- EV/EBITDA: Latest 10.8, 5-Yr Avg 10.4

Fama-French (F-F) 5-Factor Model

	F-F Beta	SMB Premium	HML Premium	RMW Premium	CMA Premium
Median	1.8	2.6	1.4	-4.5	2.9
SIC Composite	1.2	0.1	-0.4	-1.2	0.6
Large Composite	1.2	-0.4	-0.3	-0.8	-1.0
Small Composite	1.1	5.7	-4.4	-0.5	7.5
High Financial Risk	–	–	–	–	–

Leverage Ratios (%)

	Debt/MV Equity Latest	5-Yr Avg	Debt/Total Capital Latest	5-Yr Avg
Median	58.3	62.4	36.7	38.3
SIC Composite	49.5	42.4	33.1	29.8
Large Composite	39.5	33.2	28.3	24.9
Small Composite	36.8	56.5	26.9	36.1
High Financial Risk	–	–	–	–

Cost of Debt

	Cost of Debt (%) Latest
Median	6.1
SIC Composite	5.6
Large Composite	5.2
Small Composite	6.3
High Financial Risk	–

Capital Structure

SIC Composite (%) Latest
- D/TC: 33.1
- E/TC: 66.9

Cost of Equity Capital (%)

	CAPM	CRSP Deciles CAPM +Size Prem	Build-Up	Risk Premium Report CAPM +Size Prem	Build-Up	Discounted Cash Flow 1-Stage	3-Stage	Fama-French 5-Factor Model
Median	10.7	13.1	9.3	16.6	13.8	8.0	13.4	15.8
SIC Composite	10.4	11.0	8.3	13.1	11.6	8.3	13.2	9.4
Large Composite	8.6	9.0	8.1	12.1	11.1	8.8	13.3	7.8
Small Composite	9.7	12.4	10.4	17.2	15.7	8.8	11.2	18.0
High Financial Risk	–	–	–	–	–	–	–	–

Cost of Equity Capital (%) SIC Composite
- Avg CRSP: 9.6
- Avg RPR: 12.3
- 1-Stage: 8.3
- 3-Stage: 13.2
- 5-Factor Model: 9.4

Weighted Average Cost of Capital (WACC) (%)

	CAPM	CRSP Deciles CAPM +Size Prem	Build-Up	Risk Premium Report CAPM +Size Prem	Build-Up	Discounted Cash Flow 1-Stage	3-Stage	Fama-French 5-Factor Model
Median	9.0	9.7	7.8	11.6	10.2	7.1	9.8	11.9
SIC Composite	8.7	9.1	7.3	10.5	9.5	7.3	10.6	8.1
Large Composite	7.6	7.9	7.2	10.1	9.4	7.8	11.0	7.0
Small Composite	8.7	10.6	9.1	14.1	13.0	7.9	9.7	14.7
High Financial Risk	–	–	–	–	–	–	–	–

WACC (%) SIC Composite
Low 7.3 — High 10.6
▲ Average 8.9 ◆ Median 9.1

© 2017 Duff & Phelps. All Rights Reserved. Duff & Phelps has used the utmost care in compiling the data presented herein, but cannot guarantee the accuracy, completeness, or timeliness of the information.

Data Updated Through March 31, 2017

4833

Number of Companies: 8
Television Broadcasting Stations

Industry Description
Establishments primarily engaged in broadcasting visual programs by television to the public, except cable and other pay television services.

Sales (in millions)

Three Largest Companies
Viacom, Inc.	$12,488.0
Scripps Networks Interactive	3,401.4
AMC Networks Inc.	2,755.7

Three Smallest Companies
The E. W. Scripps Company	$943.0
Gray Television Inc.	812.5
Entravision Communications	258.5

Total Assets (in millions)

Three Largest Companies
Viacom, Inc.	$22,508.0
Scripps Networks Interactive	6,200.3
Sinclair Broadcast Group, Inc.	5,963.2

Three Smallest Companies
Gray Television Inc.	$2,783.3
The E. W. Scripps Company	1,728.4
Entravision Communications	517.9

Annualized Monthly Performance Statistics (%)

	Industry Geometric Mean	Arithmetic Mean	Standard Deviation		S&P 500 Index Geometric Mean	Arithmetic Mean	Standard Deviation
1-year	17.8	19.6	22.4	1-year	17.2	17.4	7.2
3-year	-7.0	-4.2	23.4	3-year	10.4	10.9	11.5
5-year	8.1	10.8	24.6	5-year	13.3	13.9	11.5

Return Ratios (%)

	Return on Assets Latest	5-Yr Avg	Return on Equity Latest	5-Yr Avg	Dividend Yield Latest	5-Yr Avg
Median (8)	4.1	6.8	27.7	28.9	1.7	1.3
SIC Composite (8)	6.1	7.9	6.8	7.2	1.7	1.7
Large Composite (–)	–	–	–	–	–	–
Small Composite (–)	–	–	–	–	–	–
High-Financial Risk (–)	–	–	–	–	–	–

Liquidity Ratio

	Current Ratio Latest	5-Yr Avg
Median (8)	2.1	2.4
SIC Composite (8)	1.6	1.7
Large Composite	–	–
Small Composite	–	–
High-Financial Risk	–	–

Profitability Ratio (%)

	Operating Margin Latest	5-Yr Avg
Median (8)	24.8	26.6
SIC Composite (8)	24.8	27.7
Large Composite	–	–
Small Composite	–	–
High-Financial Risk	–	–

Growth Rates (%)

	Long-term EPS Analyst Estimates
Median (8)	6.8
SIC Composite (8)	7.1
Large Composite	–
Small Composite	–
High-Financial Risk	–

Betas (Levered)

	Raw (OLS)	Blume Adjusted	Peer Group	Vasicek Adjusted	Sum	Downside
Median	1.71	1.46	0.88	1.45	2.05	2.17
SIC Composite	1.32	1.21	0.88	1.28	1.41	1.39
Large Composite	–	–	–	–	–	–
Small Composite	–	–	–	–	–	–
High Financial Risk	–	–	–	–	–	–

Betas (Unlevered)

	Raw (OLS)	Blume Adjusted	Peer Group	Vasicek Adjusted	Sum	Downside
Median	1.10	0.96	0.60	0.93	1.45	1.42
SIC Composite	0.87	0.80	0.60	0.85	0.93	0.91
Large Composite	–	–	–	–	–	–
Small Composite	–	–	–	–	–	–
High Financial Risk	–	–	–	–	–	–

Equity Valuation Multiples

	Price/Sales Latest	5-Yr Avg	Price/Earnings Latest	5-Yr Avg	Market/Book Latest	5-Yr Avg
Median	1.7	1.9	15.9	15.6	3.5	4.2
SIC Composite	1.7	2.1	14.7	14.0	4.1	5.2
Large Composite	–	–	–	–	–	–
Small Composite	–	–	–	–	–	–
High Financial Risk	–	–	–	–	–	–

Enterprise Valuation (EV) Multiples

	EV/Sales Latest	5-Yr Avg	EV/EBITDA Latest	5-Yr Avg
Median	2.9	3.2	9.4	9.7
SIC Composite	2.7	3.0	9.3	9.3
Large Composite	–	–	–	–
Small Composite	–	–	–	–
High Financial Risk	–	–	–	–

Enterprise Valuation SIC Composite
- EV/Sales: Latest 2.7, 5-Yr Avg 3.0
- EV/EBITDA: Latest 9.3, 5-Yr Avg 9.3

Fama-French (F-F) 5-Factor Model

	F-F Beta	SMB Premium	HML Premium	RMW Premium	CMA Premium
Median	1.3	-0.7	-0.3	1.9	2.8
SIC Composite	1.3	0.1	-0.7	-0.8	1.5
Large Composite	–	–	–	–	–
Small Composite	–	–	–	–	–
High Financial Risk	–	–	–	–	–

Leverage Ratios (%)

	Debt/MV Equity Latest	5-Yr Avg	Debt/Total Capital Latest	5-Yr Avg
Median	67.7	62.4	40.4	38.3
SIC Composite	64.2	49.9	39.1	33.3
Large Composite	–	–	–	–
Small Composite	–	–	–	–
High Financial Risk	–	–	–	–

Cost of Debt

	Cost of Debt (%) Latest
Median	6.1
SIC Composite	5.4
Large Composite	–
Small Composite	–
High Financial Risk	–

Capital Structure

SIC Composite (%) Latest: D/TC 39.1, E/TC 60.9

Cost of Equity Capital (%)

	CAPM	CRSP Deciles CAPM +Size Prem	Build-Up	Risk Premium Report CAPM +Size Prem	Build-Up	Discounted Cash Flow 1-Stage	3-Stage	Fama-French 5-Factor Model
Median	11.5	13.3	9.0	19.1	13.1	8.5	14.5	14.2
SIC Composite	10.5	11.4	8.6	13.9	11.6	8.8	15.4	10.8
Large Composite	–	–	–	–	–	–	–	–
Small Composite	–	–	–	–	–	–	–	–
High Financial Risk	–	–	–	–	–	–	–	–

Cost of Equity Capital (%) SIC Composite
- Avg CRSP: 10.0
- Avg RPR: 12.7
- 1-Stage: 8.8
- 3-Stage: 15.4
- 5-Factor Model: 10.8

Weighted Average Cost of Capital (WACC) (%)

	CAPM	CRSP Deciles CAPM +Size Prem	Build-Up	Risk Premium Report CAPM +Size Prem	Build-Up	Discounted Cash Flow 1-Stage	3-Stage	Fama-French 5-Factor Model
Median	8.7	9.8	7.6	13.5	9.8	7.0	10.2	10.6
SIC Composite	8.4	9.0	7.3	10.5	9.1	7.4	11.4	8.6
Large Composite	–	–	–	–	–	–	–	–
Small Composite	–	–	–	–	–	–	–	–
High Financial Risk	–	–	–	–	–	–	–	–

WACC (%) SIC Composite
Low 7.3 — Average 9.0 ▲ — Median 9.0 ♦ — High 11.4

© 2017 Duff & Phelps. All Rights Reserved. Duff & Phelps has used the utmost care in compiling the data presented herein, but cannot guarantee the accuracy, completeness, or timeliness of the information.

Data Updated Through March 31, 2017

489

Number of Companies: 7
Communications Services, Not Elsewhere Classified

Industry Description
Establishments primarily engaged in furnishing communications services, not elsewhere classified.

Sales (in millions)

Three Largest Companies
NeuStar, Inc.	$1,209.8
Vonage Holdings Corp.	955.6
DigitalGlobe, Inc.	725.4

Three Smallest Companies
RigNet, Inc.	$271.3
8X8 Inc.	209.3
Lumos Networks Corp.	206.9

Annualized Monthly Performance Statistics (%)

Industry	Geometric Mean	Arithmetic Mean	Standard Deviation
1-year	48.4	50.3	24.4
3-year	3.1	5.0	20.2
5-year	8.7	10.6	21.0

S&P 500 Index	Geometric Mean	Arithmetic Mean	Standard Deviation
1-year	17.2	17.4	7.2
3-year	10.4	10.9	11.5
5-year	13.3	13.9	11.5

Total Assets (in millions)

Three Largest Companies
Iridium Communications Inc.	$3,499.6
DigitalGlobe, Inc.	3,009.9
NeuStar, Inc.	2,098.7

Three Smallest Companies
Lumos Networks Corp.	$753.4
8X8 Inc.	313.5
RigNet, Inc.	258.1

Return Ratios (%)

	Return on Assets Latest	5-Yr Avg	Return on Equity Latest	5-Yr Avg	Dividend Yield Latest	5-Yr Avg
Median (7)	0.9	3.3	1.7	7.3	0.0	0.0
SIC Composite (7)	2.8	3.3	3.6	4.3	0.0	0.1
Large Composite (−)	−	−	−	−	−	−
Small Composite (−)	−	−	−	−	−	−
High-Financial Risk (5)	-6.1	-11.2	-4.9	-10.4	0.0	0.0

Liquidity Ratio

	Current Ratio Latest	5-Yr Avg
Median (7)	2.1	2.0
SIC Composite (7)	1.7	2.0
Large Composite	−	−
Small Composite	−	−
High-Financial Risk	0.7	0.8

Profitability Ratio (%)

	Operating Margin Latest	5-Yr Avg
Median (7)	15.0	11.4
SIC Composite (7)	18.0	18.2
Large Composite	−	−
Small Composite	−	−
High-Financial Risk	-4.8	-9.9

Growth Rates (%)

	Long-term EPS Analyst Estimates
Median (7)	16.6
SIC Composite (7)	16.6
Large Composite	−
Small Composite	−
High-Financial Risk	10.6

Betas (Levered)

	Raw (OLS)	Blume Adjusted	Peer Group	Vasicek Adjusted	Sum	Downside
Median	0.52	0.70	0.77	0.64	1.68	1.59
SIC Composite	0.96	0.98	0.77	0.93	1.18	1.28
Large Composite	−	−	−	−	−	−
Small Composite	−	−	−	−	−	−
High Financial Risk	1.70	1.45	0.76	1.47	2.79	2.41

Betas (Unlevered)

	Raw (OLS)	Blume Adjusted	Peer Group	Vasicek Adjusted	Sum	Downside
Median	0.52	0.70	0.64	0.63	0.91	1.29
SIC Composite	0.73	0.75	0.61	0.72	0.88	0.94
Large Composite	−	−	−	−	−	−
Small Composite	−	−	−	−	−	−
High Financial Risk	1.31	1.13	0.64	1.15	2.09	1.82

Equity Valuation Multiples

	Price/Sales Latest	5-Yr Avg	Price/Earnings Latest	5-Yr Avg	Market/Book Latest	5-Yr Avg
Median	2.0	2.0	89.4	35.4	1.9	2.5
SIC Composite	2.1	2.0	29.5	24.4	1.7	1.6
Large Composite	−	−	−	−	−	−
Small Composite	−	−	−	−	−	−
High Financial Risk	3.6	3.8	−	−	5.6	3.9

Enterprise Valuation (EV) Multiples

	EV/Sales Latest	5-Yr Avg	EV/EBITDA Latest	5-Yr Avg
Median	3.9	3.2	9.3	7.9
SIC Composite	3.0	2.8	8.0	7.6
Large Composite	−	−	−	−
Small Composite	−	−	−	−
High Financial Risk	5.0	5.2	40.3	−

Enterprise Valuation SIC Composite

	Latest	5-Yr Avg
EV/Sales	3.0	2.8
EV/EBITDA	8.0	7.6

Fama-French (F-F) 5-Factor Model

	F-F Beta	SMB Premium	HML Premium	RMW Premium	CMA Premium
Median	1.5	1.1	2.2	-2.3	2.6
SIC Composite	0.8	3.0	-0.6	-1.6	5.0
Large Composite	−	−	−	−	−
Small Composite	−	−	−	−	−
High Financial Risk	−	−	−	−	−

Leverage Ratios (%)

	Debt/MV Equity Latest	5-Yr Avg	Debt/Total Capital Latest	5-Yr Avg
Median	44.4	39.1	30.8	28.1
SIC Composite	55.6	53.2	35.7	34.7
Large Composite	−	−	−	−
Small Composite	−	−	−	−
High Financial Risk	40.7	41.5	28.9	29.3

Cost of Debt

	Cost of Debt (%) Latest
Median	7.1
SIC Composite	6.9
Large Composite	−
Small Composite	−
High Financial Risk	7.4

Capital Structure

SIC Composite (%) Latest
- D / TC: 35.7
- E / TC: 64.3

Cost of Equity Capital (%)

	CAPM	CRSP Deciles CAPM +Size Prem	Build-Up	Risk Premium Report CAPM +Size Prem	Build-Up	Discounted Cash Flow 1-Stage	3-Stage	Fama-French 5-Factor Model
Median	7.0	9.5	9.4	16.4	14.4	10.0	8.8	15.7
SIC Composite	8.6	10.4	9.5	14.1	14.1	16.6	10.9	13.8
Large Composite	−	−	−	−	−	−	−	−
Small Composite	−	−	−	−	−	−	−	−
High Financial Risk	−	−	−	31.9	25.6	−	−	−

Cost of Equity Capital (%) SIC Composite
- Avg CRSP: 10.0
- Avg RPR: 14.1
- 1-Stage: 16.6
- 3-Stage: 10.9
- 5-Factor Model: 13.8

Weighted Average Cost of Capital (WACC) (%)

	CAPM	CRSP Deciles CAPM +Size Prem	Build-Up	Risk Premium Report CAPM +Size Prem	Build-Up	Discounted Cash Flow 1-Stage	3-Stage	Fama-French 5-Factor Model
Median	7.0	8.7	8.4	12.1	10.8	9.3	8.4	11.4
SIC Composite	7.6	8.8	8.2	11.2	11.2	12.8	9.1	11.0
Large Composite	−	−	−	−	−	−	−	−
Small Composite	−	−	−	−	−	−	−	−
High Financial Risk	−	−	−	24.5	20.0	−	−	−

WACC (%) SIC Composite
Low 8.2 — High 12.8
▲ Average 10.3   ◆ Median 11.0

© 2017 Duff & Phelps. All Rights Reserved. Duff & Phelps has used the utmost care in compiling the data presented herein, but cannot guarantee the accuracy, completeness, or timeliness of the information.

Data Updated Through March 31, 2017

49

Number of Companies: 74
Electric, Gas, and Sanitary Services

Industry Description
This major group includes establishments engaged in the generation, transmission, and/or distribution of electricity or gas or steam. Such establishments may be combinations of any of the above three services and also include other types of services, such as transportation, communications, and refrigeration. Water and irrigation systems, and sanitary systems engaged in the collection and disposal of garbage, sewage, and other wastes by means of destroying or processing materials, are also included.

Sales (in millions)

Three Largest Companies
Energy Transfer Equity, L.P.	$34,024.0
Exelon Corp.	31,360.0
Duke Energy Corp.	22,754.0

Three Smallest Companies
RGC Resources, Inc.	$59.1
York Water Co.	47.6
U.S. Geothermal Inc.	31.2

Total Assets (in millions)

Three Largest Companies
Duke Energy Corp.	$132,761.0
Exelon Corp.	114,904.0
Southern Co.	109,697.0

Three Smallest Companies
Gas Natural Inc.	$197.4
RGC Resources, Inc.	165.6
Hudson Technologies Inc.	122.5

Annualized Monthly Performance Statistics (%)

Industry
	Geometric Mean	Arithmetic Mean	Standard Deviation
1-year	13.6	14.1	12.1
3-year	8.6	9.4	13.0
5-year	10.7	11.4	12.7

S&P 500 Index
	Geometric Mean	Arithmetic Mean	Standard Deviation
1-year	17.2	17.4	7.2
3-year	10.4	10.9	11.5
5-year	13.3	13.9	11.5

Return Ratios (%)

	Return on Assets Latest	Return on Assets 5-Yr Avg	Return on Equity Latest	Return on Equity 5-Yr Avg	Dividend Yield Latest	Dividend Yield 5-Yr Avg
Median (74)	2.8	2.8	6.4	6.5	3.1	3.5
SIC Composite (74)	2.1	2.3	4.0	4.7	3.7	3.8
Large Composite (7)	1.5	2.0	3.9	4.9	4.7	4.6
Small Composite (7)	3.0	2.7	3.4	4.3	2.1	2.9
High-Financial Risk (8)	-7.9	-2.6	–	-8.5	5.5	4.5

Liquidity Ratio

	Current Ratio Latest	Current Ratio 5-Yr Avg
Median (74)	0.8	0.9
SIC Composite (74)	0.8	0.9
Large Composite (7)	0.8	0.9
Small Composite (7)	1.4	1.3
High-Financial Risk (8)	0.8	1.0

Profitability Ratio (%)

	Operating Margin Latest	Operating Margin 5-Yr Avg
Median (74)	20.1	18.6
SIC Composite (74)	19.5	17.7
Large Composite (7)	16.6	14.4
Small Composite (7)	23.9	21.7
High-Financial Risk (8)	9.9	8.1

Growth Rates (%)

	Long-term EPS Analyst Estimates
Median (74)	6.1
SIC Composite (74)	7.4
Large Composite (7)	7.3
Small Composite (7)	8.5
High-Financial Risk (8)	2.1

Betas (Levered)

	Raw (OLS)	Blume Adjusted	Peer Group	Vasicek Adjusted	Sum	Downside
Median	0.40	0.62	0.48	0.42	0.27	0.67
SIC Composite	0.46	0.67	0.48	0.47	0.43	0.55
Large Composite	0.46	0.66	0.47	0.46	0.53	0.57
Small Composite	0.28	0.55	0.47	0.33	-0.07	0.48
High Financial Risk	0.80	0.88	0.56	0.78	1.10	1.02

Betas (Unlevered)

	Raw (OLS)	Blume Adjusted	Peer Group	Vasicek Adjusted	Sum	Downside
Median	0.27	0.42	0.34	0.29	0.20	0.47
SIC Composite	0.30	0.42	0.31	0.30	0.28	0.35
Large Composite	0.27	0.37	0.27	0.27	0.30	0.33
Small Composite	0.24	0.44	0.38	0.28	-0.02	0.39
High Financial Risk	0.45	0.48	0.35	0.44	0.57	0.54

Equity Valuation Multiples

	Price/Sales Latest	Price/Sales 5-Yr Avg	Price/Earnings Latest	Price/Earnings 5-Yr Avg	Market/Book Latest	Market/Book 5-Yr Avg
Median	2.3	1.8	24.1	20.3	1.4	1.2
SIC Composite	2.1	1.6	25.3	21.3	1.4	1.3
Large Composite	1.5	1.2	26.1	20.4	1.1	1.0
Small Composite	3.8	2.7	29.7	23.5	1.9	1.4
High Financial Risk	1.0	0.8	–	–	1.8	1.1

Enterprise Valuation (EV) Multiples

	EV/Sales Latest	EV/Sales 5-Yr Avg	EV/EBITDA Latest	EV/EBITDA 5-Yr Avg
Median	3.6	3.0	11.0	10.1
SIC Composite	3.6	2.9	10.8	9.8
Large Composite	3.0	2.3	10.2	9.4
Small Composite	4.9	3.9	16.4	12.6
High Financial Risk	2.3	2.0	10.3	10.7

Enterprise Valuation SIC Composite

Latest: EV/Sales 3.6, EV/EBITDA 10.8
5-Yr Avg: EV/Sales 2.9, EV/EBITDA 9.8

Fama-French (F-F) 5-Factor Model

	F-F Beta	SMB Premium	HML Premium	RMW Premium	CMA Premium
Median	0.5	0.4	-4.1	-0.2	5.7
SIC Composite	0.5	-0.4	-2.3	0.2	3.8
Large Composite	–	–	–	–	–
Small Composite	0.3	0.8	0.3	-0.2	4.4
High Financial Risk	–	–	–	–	–

Leverage Ratios (%)

	Debt/MV Equity Latest	Debt/MV Equity 5-Yr Avg	Debt/Total Capital Latest	Debt/Total Capital 5-Yr Avg
Median	56.0	68.3	35.9	40.6
SIC Composite	76.0	77.9	43.2	43.8
Large Composite	103.1	91.1	50.8	47.7
Small Composite	32.4	47.7	24.5	32.3
High Financial Risk	136.9	149.7	57.8	60.0

Cost of Debt

	Cost of Debt (%) Latest
Median	4.8
SIC Composite	4.8
Large Composite	4.7
Small Composite	4.9
High Financial Risk	5.5

Capital Structure

SIC Composite (%) Latest: D/TC 43.2, E/TC 56.8

Cost of Equity Capital (%)

	CRSP Deciles CAPM	CRSP Deciles CAPM +Size Prem	CRSP Deciles Build-Up	Risk Premium Report CAPM +Size Prem	Risk Premium Report Build-Up	Discounted Cash Flow 1-Stage	Discounted Cash Flow 3-Stage	Fama-French 5-Factor Model
Median	5.8	7.1	7.0	8.1	11.9	9.1	6.7	7.8
SIC Composite	6.1	6.4	6.5	7.7	10.7	11.2	6.7	7.5
Large Composite	6.0	6.1	6.2	7.7	9.9	12.1	6.3	–
Small Composite	5.3	8.4	9.1	8.5	16.0	10.6	6.5	10.5
High Financial Risk	–	–	–	24.8	27.8	–	–	–

Cost of Equity Capital (%) SIC Composite

Avg CRSP 6.5, Avg RPR 9.2, 1-Stage 11.2, 3-Stage 6.7, 5-Factor Model 7.5

Weighted Average Cost of Capital (WACC) (%)

	CRSP Deciles CAPM	CRSP Deciles CAPM +Size Prem	CRSP Deciles Build-Up	Risk Premium Report CAPM +Size Prem	Risk Premium Report Build-Up	Discounted Cash Flow 1-Stage	Discounted Cash Flow 3-Stage	Fama-French 5-Factor Model
Median	5.1	5.7	5.7	6.8	8.8	7.1	5.6	6.2
SIC Composite	5.0	5.2	5.3	6.0	7.6	7.9	5.4	5.8
Large Composite	4.9	4.9	4.9	5.7	6.8	7.9	5.0	–
Small Composite	4.9	7.2	7.8	7.3	13.0	8.9	5.8	8.8
High Financial Risk	–	–	–	12.9	14.1	–	–	–

WACC (%) SIC Composite

Low 5.2, High 7.9, Average 6.2, Median 5.8

© 2017 Duff & Phelps. All Rights Reserved. Duff & Phelps has used the utmost care in compiling the data presented herein, but cannot guarantee the accuracy, completeness, or timeliness of the information.

Data Updated Through March 31, 2017

491

Number of Companies: 16
Electric Services

Industry Description
Establishments engaged in the generation, transmission, and/or distribution of electric energy for sale.

Sales (in millions)

Three Largest Companies
Exelon Corp.	$31,360.0
Southern Co.	19,896.0
American Electric Power Co.	16,380.1

Three Smallest Companies
IdaCorp Inc.	$1,262.0
El Paso Electric Co.	886.9
Ormat Technologies, Inc.	662.6

Total Assets (in millions)

Three Largest Companies
Exelon Corp.	$114,904.0
Southern Co.	109,697.0
NextEra Energy Inc.	89,993.0

Three Smallest Companies
IdaCorp Inc.	$6,289.9
El Paso Electric Co.	3,376.3
Ormat Technologies, Inc.	2,461.6

Annualized Monthly Performance Statistics (%)

Industry	Geometric Mean	Arithmetic Mean	Standard Deviation	S&P 500 Index	Geometric Mean	Arithmetic Mean	Standard Deviation
1-year	6.6	7.6	14.9	1-year	17.2	17.4	7.2
3-year	11.0	12.1	15.8	3-year	10.4	10.9	11.5
5-year	12.0	13.0	15.1	5-year	13.3	13.9	11.5

Return Ratios (%)

	Return on Assets Latest	Return on Assets 5-Yr Avg	Return on Equity Latest	Return on Equity 5-Yr Avg	Dividend Yield Latest	Dividend Yield 5-Yr Avg
Median (16)	2.7	2.6	6.3	6.3	3.4	3.7
SIC Composite (16)	2.1	2.4	4.2	5.3	3.6	3.8
Large Composite (3)	1.5	2.3	3.7	5.3	4.0	4.3
Small Composite (3)	3.2	2.7	4.3	4.9	2.1	2.4
High-Financial Risk (–)	–	–	–	–	–	–

Liquidity Ratio

	Current Ratio Latest	Current Ratio 5-Yr Avg
Median (16)	0.7	0.8
SIC Composite (16)	0.7	0.8
Large Composite (3)	0.8	0.9
Small Composite (3)	1.5	1.4
High-Financial Risk (–)	–	–

Profitability Ratio (%)

	Operating Margin Latest	Operating Margin 5-Yr Avg
Median (16)	21.8	21.2
SIC Composite (16)	22.1	21.2
Large Composite (3)	18.8	19.1
Small Composite (3)	24.5	21.7
High-Financial Risk (–)	–	–

Growth Rates (%)

	Long-term EPS Analyst Estimates
Median (16)	5.0
SIC Composite (16)	3.9
Large Composite (3)	2.6
Small Composite (3)	6.9
High-Financial Risk (–)	–

Betas (Levered)

	Raw (OLS)	Blume Adjusted	Peer Group	Vasicek Adjusted	Sum	Downside
Median	0.33	0.58	0.47	0.40	0.11	0.65
SIC Composite	0.28	0.55	0.47	0.35	0.11	0.48
Large Composite	0.21	0.50	0.47	0.40	0.13	0.47
Small Composite	0.66	0.79	0.47	0.62	0.31	0.70
High Financial Risk	–	–	–	–	–	–

Betas (Unlevered)

	Raw (OLS)	Blume Adjusted	Peer Group	Vasicek Adjusted	Sum	Downside
Median	0.23	0.38	0.31	0.27	0.08	0.39
SIC Composite	0.18	0.33	0.29	0.22	0.08	0.30
Large Composite	0.12	0.28	0.26	0.22	0.08	0.26
Small Composite	0.50	0.59	0.37	0.47	0.26	0.52
High Financial Risk	–	–	–	–	–	–

Equity Valuation Multiples

	Price/Sales Latest	Price/Sales 5-Yr Avg	Price/Earnings Latest	Price/Earnings 5-Yr Avg	Market/Book Latest	Market/Book 5-Yr Avg
Median	2.3	1.7	21.1	18.2	1.2	1.1
SIC Composite	2.3	1.9	24.0	19.2	1.3	1.2
Large Composite	1.7	1.6	27.5	19.1	1.0	1.0
Small Composite	3.2	2.3	23.3	20.4	1.5	1.1
High Financial Risk	–	–	–	–	–	–

Enterprise Valuation (EV) Multiples

	EV/Sales Latest	EV/Sales 5-Yr Avg	EV/EBITDA Latest	EV/EBITDA 5-Yr Avg
Median	3.9	3.1	10.0	8.7
SIC Composite	4.0	3.2	10.4	9.3
Large Composite	3.3	2.8	10.0	8.9
Small Composite	4.6	3.6	11.5	9.6
High Financial Risk	–	–	–	–

Enterprise Valuation SIC Composite
Latest: EV/Sales 4.0, EV/EBITDA 10.4
5-Yr Avg: EV/Sales 3.2, EV/EBITDA 9.3

Fama-French (F-F) 5-Factor Model

	F-F Beta	SMB Premium	HML Premium	RMW Premium	CMA Premium
Median	0.4	-0.5	-4.4	-0.1	5.8
SIC Composite	0.3	-1.2	-3.0	0.1	4.0
Large Composite	–	–	–	–	–
Small Composite	0.7	0.8	-2.0	-0.1	2.4
High Financial Risk	–	–	–	–	–

Leverage Ratios (%)

	Debt/MV Equity Latest	Debt/MV Equity 5-Yr Avg	Debt/Total Capital Latest	Debt/Total Capital 5-Yr Avg
Median	67.1	74.6	40.2	42.7
SIC Composite	75.0	77.1	42.9	43.5
Large Composite	93.1	78.6	48.2	44.0
Small Composite	44.9	63.5	31.0	38.8
High Financial Risk	–	–	–	–

Cost of Debt

	Cost of Debt (%) Latest
Median	4.8
SIC Composite	4.4
Large Composite	4.3
Small Composite	5.1
High Financial Risk	–

Capital Structure

SIC Composite (%) Latest
D/TC: 42.9
E/TC: 57.1

Cost of Equity Capital (%)

	CRSP Deciles CAPM	CRSP Deciles CAPM +Size Prem	CRSP Deciles Build-Up	Risk Premium Report CAPM +Size Prem	Risk Premium Report Build-Up	Discounted Cash Flow 1-Stage	Discounted Cash Flow 3-Stage	Fama-French 5-Factor Model
Median	5.7	6.6	6.8	6.7	11.2	8.4	6.2	6.7
SIC Composite	5.4	5.6	6.2	5.7	10.3	7.5	6.0	5.2
Large Composite	5.7	5.7	6.1	5.5	9.9	6.5	5.9	–
Small Composite	6.9	8.2	7.4	8.6	13.0	9.0	6.4	8.1
High Financial Risk	–	–	–	–	–	–	–	–

Cost of Equity Capital (%) SIC Composite
Avg CRSP: 5.9; Avg RPR: 8.0; 1-Stage: 7.5; 3-Stage: 6.0; 5-Factor Model: 5.2

Weighted Average Cost of Capital (WACC) (%)

	CRSP Deciles CAPM	CRSP Deciles CAPM +Size Prem	CRSP Deciles Build-Up	Risk Premium Report CAPM +Size Prem	Risk Premium Report Build-Up	Discounted Cash Flow 1-Stage	Discounted Cash Flow 3-Stage	Fama-French 5-Factor Model
Median	4.8	5.2	5.5	5.2	8.2	6.7	5.1	5.4
SIC Composite	4.5	4.6	5.0	4.7	7.3	5.7	4.8	4.4
Large Composite	4.5	4.5	4.7	4.4	6.6	4.9	4.6	–
Small Composite	5.8	6.7	6.2	7.0	10.1	7.3	5.5	6.7
High Financial Risk	–	–	–	–	–	–	–	–

WACC (%) SIC Composite
Low 4.4, High 7.3
Average 5.2, Median 4.8

© 2017 Duff & Phelps. All Rights Reserved. Duff & Phelps has used the utmost care in compiling the data presented herein, but cannot guarantee the accuracy, completeness, or timeliness of the information.

Data Updated Through March 31, 2017

492
Number of Companies: 15
Gas Production and Distribution

Industry Description
Establishments engaged in natural gas transmission; natural gas transmission and distribution; natural gas distribution; mixed, manufactured, or liquefied petroleum gas production and/or distribution.

Sales (in millions)

Three Largest Companies
Energy Transfer Equity, L.P.	$34,024.0
Energy Transfer Partners, L.P.	21,827.0
Kinder Morgan, Inc.	13,058.0

Three Smallest Companies
Chesapeake Utilities Corp.	$498.9
Gas Natural Inc.	99.4
RGC Resources, Inc.	59.1

Total Assets (in millions)

Three Largest Companies
Kinder Morgan, Inc.	$80,305.0
Energy Transfer Equity, L.P.	79,011.0
Energy Transfer Partners, L.P.	70,191.0

Three Smallest Companies
Chesapeake Utilities Corp.	$1,229.2
Gas Natural Inc.	197.4
RGC Resources, Inc.	165.6

Annualized Monthly Performance Statistics (%)

Industry	Geometric Mean	Arithmetic Mean	Standard Deviation
1-year	44.5	45.7	19.9
3-year	-2.3	0.4	23.4
5-year	4.3	6.3	20.7

S&P 500 Index	Geometric Mean	Arithmetic Mean	Standard Deviation
1-year	17.2	17.4	7.2
3-year	10.4	10.9	11.5
5-year	13.3	13.9	11.5

Return Ratios (%)

	Return on Assets Latest	5-Yr Avg	Return on Equity Latest	5-Yr Avg	Dividend Yield Latest	5-Yr Avg
Median (15)	2.5	2.5	7.2	6.8	3.3	4.5
SIC Composite (15)	1.4	1.9	3.0	3.7	5.2	5.0
Large Composite (3)	0.9	1.3	2.3	3.0	5.5	5.2
Small Composite (3)	3.2	3.4	3.6	5.0	2.2	2.8
High-Financial Risk (–)	–	–	–	–	–	–

Liquidity Ratio

	Current Ratio Latest	5-Yr Avg
Median (15)	0.5	0.7
SIC Composite (15)	0.7	0.8
Large Composite (3)	0.8	0.9
Small Composite (3)	0.5	0.6
High-Financial Risk	–	–

Profitability Ratio (%)

	Operating Margin Latest	5-Yr Avg
Median (15)	19.0	14.5
SIC Composite (15)	16.1	12.0
Large Composite (3)	13.9	10.5
Small Composite (3)	14.8	13.8
High-Financial Risk	–	–

Growth Rates (%)

	Long-term EPS Analyst Estimates
Median (15)	10.0
SIC Composite (15)	17.8
Large Composite (3)	23.5
Small Composite (3)	8.4
High-Financial Risk	–

Betas (Levered)

	Raw (OLS)	Blume Adjusted	Peer Group	Vasicek Adjusted	Sum	Downside
Median	0.64	0.78	0.52	0.61	0.92	1.05
SIC Composite	1.00	1.01	0.52	0.93	1.65	1.22
Large Composite	1.07	1.05	0.47	0.99	1.78	1.39
Small Composite	0.19	0.49	0.47	0.46	0.09	0.73
High Financial Risk	–	–	–	–	–	–

Betas (Unlevered)

	Raw (OLS)	Blume Adjusted	Peer Group	Vasicek Adjusted	Sum	Downside
Median	0.42	0.50	0.37	0.40	0.60	0.67
SIC Composite	0.58	0.59	0.34	0.55	0.91	0.69
Large Composite	0.55	0.54	0.29	0.52	0.86	0.69
Small Composite	0.16	0.39	0.37	0.37	0.09	0.57
High Financial Risk	–	–	–	–	–	–

Equity Valuation Multiples

	Price/Sales Latest	5-Yr Avg	Price/Earnings Latest	5-Yr Avg	Market/Book Latest	5-Yr Avg
Median	2.3	1.3	25.9	20.3	1.6	1.4
SIC Composite	1.6	1.3	34.5	27.1	1.7	1.8
Large Composite	1.3	1.0	48.2	33.9	1.5	1.7
Small Composite	2.2	1.4	27.8	20.1	1.7	1.3
High Financial Risk	–	–	–	–	–	–

Enterprise Valuation (EV) Multiples

	EV/Sales Latest	5-Yr Avg	EV/EBITDA Latest	5-Yr Avg
Median	3.4	2.0	12.0	11.4
SIC Composite	3.3	2.4	11.8	12.1
Large Composite	3.0	2.1	12.0	12.0
Small Composite	2.9	2.0	13.2	10.0
High Financial Risk	–	–	–	–

Enterprise Valuation SIC Composite: Latest EV/Sales 3.3, EV/EBITDA 11.8; 5-Yr Avg EV/Sales 2.4, EV/EBITDA 12.1

Fama-French (F-F) 5-Factor Model

	F-F Beta	SMB Premium	HML Premium	RMW Premium	CMA Premium
Median	0.3	2.0	-0.6	0.2	4.1
SIC Composite	0.9	1.8	0.5	0.0	1.4
Large Composite	1.0	2.4	0.9	0.6	0.8
Small Composite	0.2	0.7	0.2	0.0	2.9
High Financial Risk	–	–	–	–	–

Leverage Ratios (%)

	Debt/MV Equity Latest	5-Yr Avg	Debt/Total Capital Latest	5-Yr Avg
Median	53.6	69.6	34.9	41.0
SIC Composite	102.0	89.4	50.5	47.2
Large Composite	132.8	111.0	57.0	52.6
Small Composite	33.5	42.1	25.1	29.6
High Financial Risk	–	–	–	–

Cost of Debt

	Cost of Debt (%) Latest
Median	4.8
SIC Composite	5.3
Large Composite	5.3
Small Composite	4.8
High Financial Risk	–

Capital Structure

SIC Composite (%) Latest: D/TC 50.5, E/TC 49.5

Cost of Equity Capital (%)

	CRSP Deciles CAPM	CAPM +Size Prem	Build-Up	Risk Premium Report CAPM	CAPM +Size Prem	Build-Up	Discounted Cash Flow 1-Stage	3-Stage	Fama-French 5-Factor Model
Median	6.8	7.9	7.0	11.0		12.0	11.6	7.5	10.6
SIC Composite	8.6	9.1	6.6	14.6		10.8	23.5	7.8	12.4
Large Composite	8.9	9.2	6.4	14.8		10.1	29.8	7.3	13.8
Small Composite	6.0	8.5	8.6	8.7		15.0	10.5	6.2	8.4
High Financial Risk	–	–	–	–		–	–	–	–

Cost of Equity Capital (%) SIC Composite: Avg CRSP 7.9, Avg RPR 12.7, 1-Stage 23.5, 3-Stage 7.8, 5-Factor Model 12.4

Weighted Average Cost of Capital (WACC) (%)

	CRSP Deciles CAPM	CAPM +Size Prem	Build-Up	Risk Premium Report CAPM	CAPM +Size Prem	Build-Up	Discounted Cash Flow 1-Stage	3-Stage	Fama-French 5-Factor Model
Median	5.4	6.3	5.6	8.3		8.6	8.6	5.9	7.3
SIC Composite	6.3	6.5	5.3	9.2		7.3	13.6	5.9	8.1
Large Composite	6.3	6.4	5.2	8.8		6.8	15.2	5.5	8.3
Small Composite	5.4	7.3	7.3	7.4		12.1	8.7	5.5	7.2
High Financial Risk	–	–	–	–		–	–	–	–

WACC (%) SIC Composite: Low 5.3, High 13.6, Average 8.0, Median 7.3

© 2017 Duff & Phelps. All Rights Reserved. Duff & Phelps has used the utmost care in compiling the data presented herein, but cannot guarantee the accuracy, completeness, or timeliness of the information.

Data Updated Through March 31, 2017

4922

Number of Companies: 6
Natural Gas Transmission

Industry Description
Establishments engaged in the transmission and/or storage of natural gas for sale.

Sales (in millions)

Three Largest Companies
Energy Transfer Equity, L.P.	$34,024.0
Energy Transfer Partners, L.P.	21,827.0
ONEOK Partners LP	8,918.5

Three Smallest Companies
Williams Cos. Inc.	$7,499.0
Spectra Energy Partners, LP	2,533.0
Boardwalk Pipeline Partners LP	1,294.5

Total Assets (in millions)

Three Largest Companies
Energy Transfer Equity, L.P.	$79,011.0
Energy Transfer Partners, L.P.	70,191.0
Williams Cos. Inc.	46,835.0

Three Smallest Companies
Spectra Energy Partners, LP	$21,606.0
ONEOK Partners LP	15,469.3
Boardwalk Pipeline Partners LP	8,637.8

Annualized Monthly Performance Statistics (%)

Industry	Geometric Mean	Arithmetic Mean	Standard Deviation
1-year	61.2	64.0	32.5
3-year	0.1	4.0	29.2
5-year	8.3	11.2	25.7

S&P 500 Index	Geometric Mean	Arithmetic Mean	Standard Deviation
1-year	17.2	17.4	7.2
3-year	10.4	10.9	11.5
5-year	13.3	13.9	11.5

Return Ratios (%)

	Return on Assets Latest	5-Yr Avg	Return on Equity Latest	5-Yr Avg	Dividend Yield Latest	5-Yr Avg
Median (6)	2.4	2.7	8.6	9.1	6.4	5.0
SIC Composite (6)	1.4	2.2	3.6	4.5	7.1	5.7
Large Composite (–)	–	–	–	–	–	–
Small Composite (–)	–	–	–	–	–	–
High-Financial Risk (–)	–	–	–	–	–	–

Liquidity Ratio

	Current Ratio Latest	5-Yr Avg
Median (6)	0.5	0.7
SIC Composite (6)	0.8	0.9
Large Composite	–	–
Small Composite	–	–
High-Financial Risk	–	–

Profitability Ratio (%)

	Operating Margin Latest	5-Yr Avg
Median	19.2	15.8
SIC Composite	13.8	9.6
Large Composite	–	–
Small Composite	–	–
High-Financial Risk	–	–

Growth Rates (%)

	Long-term EPS Analyst Estimates
Median	12.4
SIC Composite	20.0
Large Composite	–
Small Composite	–
High-Financial Risk	–

Betas (Levered)

	Raw (OLS)	Blume Adjusted	Peer Group	Vasicek Adjusted	Sum	Downside
Median	1.02	1.02	0.54	0.86	1.66	1.43
SIC Composite	1.27	1.18	0.54	1.12	2.28	1.55
Large Composite	–	–	–	–	–	–
Small Composite	–	–	–	–	–	–
High Financial Risk	–	–	–	–	–	–

Betas (Unlevered)

	Raw (OLS)	Blume Adjusted	Peer Group	Vasicek Adjusted	Sum	Downside
Median	0.53	0.58	0.37	0.49	0.79	0.84
SIC Composite	0.68	0.64	0.35	0.61	1.13	0.81
Large Composite	–	–	–	–	–	–
Small Composite	–	–	–	–	–	–
High Financial Risk	–	–	–	–	–	–

Equity Valuation Multiples

	Price/Sales Latest	5-Yr Avg	Price/Earnings Latest	5-Yr Avg	Market/Book Latest	5-Yr Avg
Median	2.2	1.7	17.6	17.9	1.6	1.5
SIC Composite	1.3	1.0	28.2	22.0	1.7	1.8
Large Composite	–	–	–	–	–	–
Small Composite	–	–	–	–	–	–
High Financial Risk	–	–	–	–	–	–

Enterprise Valuation (EV) Multiples

	EV/Sales Latest	5-Yr Avg	EV/EBITDA Latest	5-Yr Avg
Median	4.3	3.9	10.6	11.5
SIC Composite	2.8	2.0	10.9	11.7
Large Composite	–	–	–	–
Small Composite	–	–	–	–
High Financial Risk	–	–	–	–

Enterprise Valuation SIC Composite
Latest: EV/Sales 2.8, EV/EBITDA 10.9
5-Yr Avg: EV/Sales 2.0, EV/EBITDA 11.7

Fama-French (F-F) 5-Factor Model

Fama-French (F-F) Components	F-F Beta	SMB Premium	HML Premium	RMW Premium	CMA Premium
Median	1.3	-0.5	0.4	-0.3	1.3
SIC Composite	1.2	1.5	1.3	-1.3	-0.7
Large Composite	–	–	–	–	–
Small Composite	–	–	–	–	–
High Financial Risk	–	–	–	–	–

Leverage Ratios (%)

	Debt/MV Equity Latest	5-Yr Avg	Debt/Total Capital Latest	5-Yr Avg
Median	91.8	71.3	47.6	41.6
SIC Composite	124.9	96.1	55.5	49.0
Large Composite	–	–	–	–
Small Composite	–	–	–	–
High Financial Risk	–	–	–	–

Cost of Debt

	Cost of Debt (%) Latest
Median	4.8
SIC Composite	5.5
Large Composite	–
Small Composite	–
High Financial Risk	–

Capital Structure

SIC Composite (%) Latest
D/TC: 44.5
E/TC: 55.5

Cost of Equity Capital (%)

	CRSP Deciles CAPM	CAPM +Size Prem	Build-Up	Risk Premium Report CAPM +Size Prem	Build-Up	Discounted Cash Flow 1-Stage	3-Stage	Fama-French 5-Factor Model
Median	8.2	8.8	6.7	14.8	10.8	13.3	10.9	11.2
SIC Composite	9.7	10.3	6.7	17.9	10.7	27.8	8.3	11.0
Large Composite	–	–	–	–	–	–	–	–
Small Composite	–	–	–	–	–	–	–	–
High Financial Risk	–	–	–	–	–	–	–	–

Cost of Equity Capital (%) SIC Composite
Avg CRSP: 8.5; Avg RPR: 14.3; 1-Stage: 27.8; 3-Stage: 8.3; 5-Factor Model: 11.0

Weighted Average Cost of Capital (WACC) (%)

	CRSP Deciles CAPM	CAPM +Size Prem	Build-Up	Risk Premium Report CAPM +Size Prem	Build-Up	Discounted Cash Flow 1-Stage	3-Stage	Fama-French 5-Factor Model
Median	6.2	6.6	5.4	9.0	7.7	9.0	7.6	7.6
SIC Composite	6.7	7.0	5.4	10.4	7.1	14.7	6.1	7.3
Large Composite	–	–	–	–	–	–	–	–
Small Composite	–	–	–	–	–	–	–	–
High Financial Risk	–	–	–	–	–	–	–	–

WACC (%) SIC Composite
Low 5.4 — High 14.7; Average 8.3; Median 7.1

© 2017 Duff & Phelps. All Rights Reserved. Duff & Phelps has used the utmost care in compiling the data presented herein, but cannot guarantee the accuracy, completeness, or timeliness of the information.

Data Updated Through March 31, 2017

4924

Number of Companies: 5
Natural Gas Distribution

Industry Description
Establishments engaged in the distribution of natural gas for sale.

Sales (in millions)

Three Largest Companies
New Jersey Resources Corp.	$1,880.9
Spire Inc.	1,537.3
Northwest Natural Gas Co.	693.1

Three Smallest Companies
Northwest Natural Gas Co.	$693.1
Gas Natural Inc.	99.4
RGC Resources, Inc.	59.1

Total Assets (in millions)

Three Largest Companies
Spire Inc.	$6,077.4
New Jersey Resources Corp.	3,727.1
Northwest Natural Gas Co.	3,079.8

Three Smallest Companies
Northwest Natural Gas Co.	$3,079.8
Gas Natural Inc.	197.4
RGC Resources, Inc.	165.6

Annualized Monthly Performance Statistics (%)

Industry	Geometric Mean	Arithmetic Mean	Standard Deviation
1-year	9.7	11.1	18.4
3-year	17.6	19.0	18.4
5-year	13.8	14.9	16.2

S&P 500 Index	Geometric Mean	Arithmetic Mean	Standard Deviation
1-year	17.2	17.4	7.2
3-year	10.4	10.9	11.5
5-year	13.3	13.9	11.5

Return Ratios (%)

	Return on Assets Latest	5-Yr Avg	Return on Equity Latest	5-Yr Avg	Dividend Yield Latest	5-Yr Avg
Median (5)	2.5	2.5	6.5	6.0	3.2	3.8
SIC Composite (5)	2.6	2.7	4.0	5.0	3.0	3.5
Large Composite (–)	–	–	–	–	–	–
Small Composite (–)	–	–	–	–	–	–
High-Financial Risk (–)	–	–	–	–	–	–

Liquidity Ratio

	Current Ratio Latest	5-Yr Avg
Median (5)	1.0	0.8
SIC Composite (5)	0.7	0.8
Large Composite	–	–
Small Composite	–	–
High-Financial Risk	–	–

Profitability Ratio (%)

	Operating Margin Latest	5-Yr Avg
Median	19.0	13.5
SIC Composite	14.3	10.4
Large Composite	–	–
Small Composite	–	–
High-Financial Risk	–	–

Growth Rates (%)

	Long-term EPS Analyst Estimates
Median	6.0
SIC Composite	5.4
Large Composite	–
Small Composite	–
High-Financial Risk	–

Betas (Levered)

	Raw (OLS)	Blume Adjusted	Peer Group	Vasicek Adjusted	Sum	Downside
Median	0.37	0.61	0.48	0.45	0.17	0.63
SIC Composite	0.40	0.63	0.48	0.46	0.12	0.64
Large Composite	–	–	–	–	–	–
Small Composite	–	–	–	–	–	–
High Financial Risk	–	–	–	–	–	–

Betas (Unlevered)

	Raw (OLS)	Blume Adjusted	Peer Group	Vasicek Adjusted	Sum	Downside
Median	0.23	0.41	0.34	0.33	0.13	0.50
SIC Composite	0.27	0.42	0.32	0.31	0.09	0.43
Large Composite	–	–	–	–	–	–
Small Composite	–	–	–	–	–	–
High Financial Risk	–	–	–	–	–	–

Equity Valuation Multiples

	Price/Sales Latest	5-Yr Avg	Price/Earnings Latest	5-Yr Avg	Market/Book Latest	5-Yr Avg
Median	2.0	1.3	27.3	20.4	1.3	1.1
SIC Composite	2.0	1.1	24.9	19.9	1.5	1.3
Large Composite	–	–	–	–	–	–
Small Composite	–	–	–	–	–	–
High Financial Risk	–	–	–	–	–	–

Enterprise Valuation (EV) Multiples

	EV/Sales Latest	5-Yr Avg	EV/EBITDA Latest	5-Yr Avg
Median	3.5	2.0	12.7	11.1
SIC Composite	3.1	1.8	13.7	11.9
Large Composite	–	–	–	–
Small Composite	–	–	–	–
High Financial Risk	–	–	–	–

Enterprise Valuation SIC Composite
- Latest: EV/Sales 3.1, EV/EBITDA 13.7
- 5-Yr Avg: EV/Sales 1.8, EV/EBITDA 11.9

Fama-French (F-F) 5-Factor Model

	F-F Beta	SMB Premium	HML Premium	RMW Premium	CMA Premium
Median	0.6	-1.3	-1.8	0.5	3.9
SIC Composite	0.4	-0.4	-2.2	0.7	3.7
Large Composite	–	–	–	–	–
Small Composite	–	–	–	–	–
High Financial Risk	–	–	–	–	–

Leverage Ratios (%)

	Debt/MV Equity Latest	5-Yr Avg	Debt/Total Capital Latest	5-Yr Avg
Median	45.7	65.9	31.3	39.7
SIC Composite	54.4	61.3	35.3	38.0
Large Composite	–	–	–	–
Small Composite	–	–	–	–
High Financial Risk	–	–	–	–

Cost of Debt

	Cost of Debt (%) Latest
Median	4.8
SIC Composite	4.3
Large Composite	–
Small Composite	–
High Financial Risk	–

Capital Structure

SIC Composite (%) Latest
- D / TC: 35.3
- E / TC: 64.7

Cost of Equity Capital (%)

	CRSP Deciles CAPM	CAPM +Size Prem	Build-Up	Risk Premium Report CAPM +Size Prem	Build-Up	Discounted Cash Flow 1-Stage	3-Stage	Fama-French 5-Factor Model
Median	6.0	7.7	7.7	8.1	13.7	8.7	6.2	8.2
SIC Composite	6.0	7.7	7.8	7.7	13.3	8.3	6.0	7.7
Large Composite	–	–	–	–	–	–	–	–
Small Composite	–	–	–	–	–	–	–	–
High Financial Risk	–	–	–	–	–	–	–	–

Cost of Equity Capital (%) SIC Composite
- Avg CRSP: 7.7
- Avg RPR: 10.5
- 1-Stage: 8.3
- 3-Stage: 6.0
- 5-Factor Model: 7.7

Weighted Average Cost of Capital (WACC) (%)

	CRSP Deciles CAPM	CAPM +Size Prem	Build-Up	Risk Premium Report CAPM +Size Prem	Build-Up	Discounted Cash Flow 1-Stage	3-Stage	Fama-French 5-Factor Model
Median	5.1	6.3	6.4	6.6	10.4	7.2	5.1	6.2
SIC Composite	5.0	6.1	6.1	6.1	9.7	6.5	5.0	6.1
Large Composite	–	–	–	–	–	–	–	–
Small Composite	–	–	–	–	–	–	–	–
High Financial Risk	–	–	–	–	–	–	–	–

WACC (%) SIC Composite
- Low: 5.0
- High: 9.7
- Average: 6.5
- Median: 6.1

© 2017 Duff & Phelps. All Rights Reserved. Duff & Phelps has used the utmost care in compiling the data presented herein, but cannot guarantee the accuracy, completeness, or timeliness of the information.

Data Updated Through March 31, 2017

493

Number of Companies: 14
Combination Electric and Gas, and Other Utility

Industry Description
Establishments primarily engaged in providing electric services in combination with other services; providing gas services in combination with other services; providing combinations of electric, gas, and other services, not elsewhere classified.

Sales (in millions)

Three Largest Companies
Duke Energy Corp.	$22,754.0
PG&E Corp.	17,666.0
Xcel Energy Inc.	11,106.9

Three Smallest Companies
Avista Corp.	$1,442.5
Northwestern Corp.	1,257.2
MGE Energy Inc.	544.7

Annualized Monthly Performance Statistics (%)

Industry	Geometric Mean	Arithmetic Mean	Standard Deviation
1-year	8.3	9.3	15.3
3-year	12.9	14.2	17.6
5-year	13.2	14.4	16.4

S&P 500 Index	Geometric Mean	Arithmetic Mean	Standard Deviation
1-year	17.2	17.4	7.2
3-year	10.4	10.9	11.5
5-year	13.3	13.9	11.5

Total Assets (in millions)

Three Largest Companies
Duke Energy Corp.	$132,761.0
PG&E Corp.	68,598.0
Xcel Energy Inc.	41,155.3

Three Smallest Companies
Northwestern Corp.	$5,499.3
Avista Corp.	5,309.8
MGE Energy Inc.	1,801.1

Return Ratios (%)

	Return on Assets Latest	5-Yr Avg	Return on Equity Latest	5-Yr Avg	Dividend Yield Latest	5-Yr Avg	Current Ratio Latest	5-Yr Avg	Operating Margin Latest	5-Yr Avg	Long-term EPS Analyst Estimates
Median (14)	2.9	2.9	6.0	6.5	3.3	3.6	0.8	0.9	22.3	20.7	5.2
SIC Composite (14)	2.4	2.4	4.6	5.2	3.5	3.8	0.8	0.9	21.4	20.3	4.2
Large Composite (3)	2.1	2.1	4.5	5.0	3.7	4.0	0.8	0.9	21.4	20.3	3.5
Small Composite (3)	3.0	2.8	5.0	5.6	3.1	3.4	0.8	0.9	20.5	17.6	4.7
High-Financial Risk (–)	–	–	–	–	–	–	–	–	–	–	–

Betas (Levered)

	Raw (OLS)	Blume Adjusted	Peer Group	Vasicek Adjusted	Sum	Downside
Median	0.35	0.60	0.47	0.43	0.08	0.61
SIC Composite	0.25	0.53	0.47	0.37	-0.08	0.50
Large Composite	0.19	0.49	0.47	0.45	-0.14	0.48
Small Composite	0.38	0.61	0.47	0.47	-0.01	0.64
High Financial Risk	–	–	–	–	–	–

Betas (Unlevered)

	Raw (OLS)	Blume Adjusted	Peer Group	Vasicek Adjusted	Sum	Downside
Median	0.26	0.39	0.32	0.29	0.11	0.41
SIC Composite	0.17	0.34	0.30	0.24	-0.04	0.32
Large Composite	0.12	0.29	0.28	0.27	-0.07	0.29
Small Composite	0.28	0.43	0.34	0.34	0.03	0.44
High Financial Risk	–	–	–	–	–	–

Equity Valuation Multiples

	Price/Sales Latest	5-Yr Avg	Price/Earnings Latest	5-Yr Avg	Market/Book Latest	5-Yr Avg
Median	2.4	2.0	20.9	18.2	1.2	1.1
SIC Composite	2.3	1.8	21.9	19.2	1.2	1.0
Large Composite	2.2	1.8	22.4	20.1	1.1	1.0
Small Composite	2.3	1.7	20.2	17.9	1.3	1.1
High Financial Risk	–	–	–	–	–	–

Enterprise Valuation (EV) Multiples

	EV/Sales Latest	5-Yr Avg	EV/EBITDA Latest	5-Yr Avg
Median	3.9	3.2	11.1	9.5
SIC Composite	3.7	3.1	10.5	9.2
Large Composite	3.8	3.2	10.3	9.3
Small Composite	3.7	2.8	11.2	10.0
High Financial Risk	–	–	–	–

Enterprise Valuation SIC Composite: EV/Sales 3.7 (Latest), 3.1 (5-Yr Avg); EV/EBITDA 10.5 (Latest), 9.2 (5-Yr Avg)

Fama-French (F-F) 5-Factor Model

	F-F Beta	SMB Premium	HML Premium	RMW Premium	CMA Premium
Median	0.3	-1.3	-2.4	-0.3	5.2
SIC Composite	0.3	-0.9	-3.5	0.2	4.9
Large Composite	–	–	–	–	–
Small Composite	0.4	1.2	-3.5	0.2	4.1
High Financial Risk	–	–	–	–	–

Leverage Ratios (%)

	Debt/MV Equity Latest	5-Yr Avg	Debt/Total Capital Latest	5-Yr Avg
Median	57.1	68.3	36.3	40.6
SIC Composite	64.5	70.7	39.2	41.4
Large Composite	73.9	80.4	42.5	44.6
Small Composite	57.4	67.3	36.5	40.2
High Financial Risk	–	–	–	–

Cost of Debt

	Cost of Debt (%) Latest
Median	4.8
SIC Composite	4.3
Large Composite	4.2
Small Composite	4.9
High Financial Risk	–

Capital Structure
SIC Composite (%) Latest: D/TC 39.2, E/TC 60.8

Cost of Equity Capital (%)

	CRSP Deciles CAPM	CAPM +Size Prem	Build-Up	Risk Premium Report CAPM +Size Prem	Build-Up	Discounted Cash Flow 1-Stage	3-Stage	Fama-French 5-Factor Model
Median	5.8	6.5	6.7	7.4	11.0	8.4	6.5	6.4
SIC Composite	5.5	6.0	6.5	4.8	10.5	7.8	6.3	5.8
Large Composite	6.0	6.1	6.2	4.1	10.0	7.2	5.9	–
Small Composite	6.1	7.6	7.6	6.9	13.2	7.9	6.7	7.7
High Financial Risk	–	–	–	–	–	–	–	–

Cost of Equity Capital (%) SIC Composite: Avg CRSP 6.2, Avg RPR 7.7, 1-Stage 7.8, 3-Stage 6.3, 5-Factor Model 5.8

Weighted Average Cost of Capital (WACC) (%)

	CRSP Deciles CAPM	CAPM +Size Prem	Build-Up	Risk Premium Report CAPM +Size Prem	Build-Up	Discounted Cash Flow 1-Stage	3-Stage	Fama-French 5-Factor Model
Median	5.0	5.4	5.7	6.2	8.4	6.4	5.4	5.2
SIC Composite	4.7	5.0	5.3	4.3	7.8	6.1	5.2	4.9
Large Composite	4.9	5.0	5.0	3.8	7.2	5.6	4.9	–
Small Composite	5.2	6.1	6.1	5.7	9.7	6.3	5.5	6.2
High Financial Risk	–	–	–	–	–	–	–	–

WACC (%) SIC Composite: Low 4.3, High 7.8, Average 5.5, Median 5.2

© 2017 Duff & Phelps. All Rights Reserved. Duff & Phelps has used the utmost care in compiling the data presented herein, but cannot guarantee the accuracy, completeness, or timeliness of the information.

Data Updated Through March 31, 2017

494

Number of Companies: 9
Water Supply

Industry Description
Establishments primarily engaged in distributing water for sale for domestic, commercial, and industrial use.

Sales (in millions)

Three Largest Companies
American Water Works Co. Inc.	$3,302.0
Aqua America Inc.	819.9
California Water Service Group	609.4

Three Smallest Companies
Connecticut Water Service Inc.	$99.4
Artesian Resources	79.1
York Water Co.	47.6

Total Assets (in millions)

Three Largest Companies
American Water Works Co. Inc.	$17,264.0
Aqua America Inc.	6,159.0
California Water Service Group	2,411.7

Three Smallest Companies
Middlesex Water Co.	$620.2
Artesian Resources	451.0
York Water Co.	320.5

Annualized Monthly Performance Statistics (%)

Industry
	Geometric Mean	Arithmetic Mean	Standard Deviation
1-year	14.5	16.3	21.9
3-year	18.5	20.0	19.2
5-year	19.1	20.2	16.5

S&P 500 Index
	Geometric Mean	Arithmetic Mean	Standard Deviation
1-year	17.2	17.4	7.2
3-year	10.4	10.9	11.5
5-year	13.3	13.9	11.5

Return Ratios (%)

	Return on Assets Latest	5-Yr Avg	Return on Equity Latest	5-Yr Avg	Dividend Yield Latest	5-Yr Avg
Median (9)	3.7	3.1	7.9	7.4	2.1	2.5
SIC Composite (9)	3.0	3.1	3.6	4.5	2.1	2.5
Large Composite (–)	–	–	–	–	–	–
Small Composite (–)	–	–	–	–	–	–
High-Financial Risk (–)	–	–	–	–	–	–

Liquidity Ratio

	Current Ratio Latest	5-Yr Avg
Median (9)	0.6	0.7
SIC Composite (9)	0.4	0.6
Large Composite (–)	–	–
Small Composite (–)	–	–
High-Financial Risk (–)	–	–

Profitability Ratio (%)

	Operating Margin Latest	5-Yr Avg
Median (9)	32.3	31.3
SIC Composite (9)	31.3	31.2
Large Composite (–)	–	–
Small Composite (–)	–	–
High-Financial Risk (–)	–	–

Growth Rates (%)

	Long-term EPS Analyst Estimates
Median (9)	6.8
SIC Composite (9)	6.8
Large Composite (–)	–
Small Composite (–)	–
High-Financial Risk (–)	–

Betas (Levered)

	Raw (OLS)	Blume Adjusted	Peer Group	Vasicek Adjusted	Sum	Downside
Median	0.43	0.64	0.47	0.46	0.04	0.67
SIC Composite	0.35	0.59	0.47	0.40	-0.07	0.54
Large Composite	–	–	–	–	–	–
Small Composite	–	–	–	–	–	–
High Financial Risk	–	–	–	–	–	–

Betas (Unlevered)

	Raw (OLS)	Blume Adjusted	Peer Group	Vasicek Adjusted	Sum	Downside
Median	0.34	0.51	0.40	0.36	0.03	0.55
SIC Composite	0.27	0.44	0.36	0.31	-0.02	0.40
Large Composite	–	–	–	–	–	–
Small Composite	–	–	–	–	–	–
High Financial Risk	–	–	–	–	–	–

Equity Valuation Multiples

	Price/Sales Latest	5-Yr Avg	Price/Earnings Latest	5-Yr Avg	Market/Book Latest	5-Yr Avg
Median	4.3	3.1	26.6	21.9	1.8	1.6
SIC Composite	4.5	3.3	28.0	22.0	1.8	1.5
Large Composite	–	–	–	–	–	–
Small Composite	–	–	–	–	–	–
High Financial Risk	–	–	–	–	–	–

Enterprise Valuation (EV) Multiples

	EV/Sales Latest	5-Yr Avg	EV/EBITDA Latest	5-Yr Avg
Median	5.7	4.6	13.6	10.8
SIC Composite	6.3	5.1	13.9	11.4
Large Composite	–	–	–	–
Small Composite	–	–	–	–
High Financial Risk	–	–	–	–

Enterprise Valuation SIC Composite
- Latest: EV/Sales 6.3, EV/EBITDA 13.9
- 5-Yr Avg: EV/Sales 5.1, EV/EBITDA 11.4

Fama-French (F-F) 5-Factor Model

Fama-French (F-F) Components
	F-F Beta	SMB Premium	HML Premium	RMW Premium	CMA Premium
Median	0.4	1.7	-2.3	-2.8	7.8
SIC Composite	0.4	-0.4	-3.9	-1.1	6.6
Large Composite	–	–	–	–	–
Small Composite	–	–	–	–	–
High Financial Risk	–	–	–	–	–

Leverage Ratios (%)

	Debt/MV Equity Latest	5-Yr Avg	Debt/Total Capital Latest	5-Yr Avg
Median	37.3	48.4	27.2	32.6
SIC Composite	42.8	53.2	30.0	34.7
Large Composite	–	–	–	–
Small Composite	–	–	–	–
High Financial Risk	–	–	–	–

Cost of Debt

	Cost of Debt (%) Latest
Median	4.1
SIC Composite	4.6
Large Composite	–
Small Composite	–
High Financial Risk	–

Capital Structure

SIC Composite (%) Latest
- D/TC: 30.0
- E/TC: 70.0

Cost of Equity Capital (%)

	CRSP Deciles CAPM	CAPM +Size Prem	Build-Up	Risk Premium Report CAPM +Size Prem	Build-Up	Discounted Cash Flow 1-Stage	3-Stage	Fama-French 5-Factor Model
Median	6.0	7.7	8.2	8.9	14.4	8.8	6.6	10.2
SIC Composite	5.7	6.7	7.1	6.1	12.4	9.0	6.6	6.6
Large Composite	–	–	–	–	–	–	–	–
Small Composite	–	–	–	–	–	–	–	–
High Financial Risk	–	–	–	–	–	–	–	–

Cost of Equity Capital (%) SIC Composite
- Avg CRSP: 6.9
- Avg RPR: 9.3
- Build-Up: 9.0
- 1-Stage: 6.6
- 3-Stage: 6.6
- 5-Factor Model: 6.6

Weighted Average Cost of Capital (WACC) (%)

	CRSP Deciles CAPM	CAPM +Size Prem	Build-Up	Risk Premium Report CAPM +Size Prem	Build-Up	Discounted Cash Flow 1-Stage	3-Stage	Fama-French 5-Factor Model
Median	5.6	6.9	7.0	7.8	11.7	7.6	6.1	8.7
SIC Composite	5.2	5.9	6.2	5.5	9.9	7.5	5.9	5.9
Large Composite	–	–	–	–	–	–	–	–
Small Composite	–	–	–	–	–	–	–	–
High Financial Risk	–	–	–	–	–	–	–	–

WACC (%) SIC Composite
- Low: 5.5
- High: 9.9
- Average: 6.7
- Median: 5.9

© 2017 Duff & Phelps. All Rights Reserved. Duff & Phelps has used the utmost care in compiling the data presented herein, but cannot guarantee the accuracy, completeness, or timeliness of the information.

Data Updated Through March 31, 2017

495

Number of Companies: 8
Sanitary Services

Industry Description
Establishments primarily engaged in sewerage systems; refuse systems; furnishing sanitary services, not elsewhere classified.

Sales (in millions)

Three Largest Companies
Waste Management, Inc.	$13,609.0
Republic Services, Inc.	9,387.7
Stericycle Inc.	3,562.3

Three Smallest Companies
US Ecology Inc.	$477.7
Heritage-Crystal Clean, Inc.	347.6
Hudson Technologies Inc.	105.5

Total Assets (in millions)

Three Largest Companies
Waste Management, Inc.	$20,859.0
Republic Services, Inc.	20,629.6
Stericycle Inc.	6,980.1

Three Smallest Companies
US Ecology Inc.	$776.4
Heritage-Crystal Clean, Inc.	314.3
Hudson Technologies Inc.	122.5

Annualized Monthly Performance Statistics (%)

Industry	Geometric Mean	Arithmetic Mean	Standard Deviation		S&P 500 Index	Geometric Mean	Arithmetic Mean	Standard Deviation
1-year	16.1	17.0	15.1		1-year	17.2	17.4	7.2
3-year	15.6	16.3	13.1		3-year	10.4	10.9	11.5
5-year	13.7	14.4	12.7		5-year	13.3	13.9	11.5

Return Ratios (%)

	Return on Assets Latest	5-Yr Avg	Return on Equity Latest	5-Yr Avg	Dividend Yield Latest	5-Yr Avg
Median (8)	3.0	3.4	6.2	8.8	0.8	0.9
SIC Composite (8)	3.5	3.3	3.0	3.5	2.1	2.3
Large Composite (–)	–	–	–	–	–	–
Small Composite (–)	–	–	–	–	–	–
High-Financial Risk (–)	–	–	–	–	–	–

Liquidity Ratio

	Current Ratio Latest	5-Yr Avg
Median (8)	1.6	1.7
SIC Composite (8)	1.0	1.0
Large Composite	–	–
Small Composite	–	–
High-Financial Risk	–	–

Profitability Ratio (%)

	Operating Margin Latest	5-Yr Avg
Median (8)	15.5	14.7
SIC Composite (8)	15.4	15.3
Large Composite	–	–
Small Composite	–	–
High-Financial Risk	–	–

Growth Rates (%)

	Long-term EPS Analyst Estimates
Median (8)	10.4
SIC Composite (8)	11.1
Large Composite	–
Small Composite	–
High-Financial Risk	–

Betas (Levered)

	Raw (OLS)	Blume Adjusted	Peer Group	Vasicek Adjusted	Sum	Downside
Median	0.77	0.86	0.52	0.66	0.76	0.91
SIC Composite	0.58	0.74	0.52	0.58	0.48	0.65
Large Composite	–	–	–	–	–	–
Small Composite	–	–	–	–	–	–
High Financial Risk	–	–	–	–	–	–

Betas (Unlevered)

	Raw (OLS)	Blume Adjusted	Peer Group	Vasicek Adjusted	Sum	Downside
Median	0.60	0.67	0.43	0.56	0.60	0.70
SIC Composite	0.45	0.57	0.41	0.45	0.37	0.50
Large Composite	–	–	–	–	–	–
Small Composite	–	–	–	–	–	–
High Financial Risk	–	–	–	–	–	–

Equity Valuation Multiples

	Price/Sales Latest	5-Yr Avg	Price/Earnings Latest	5-Yr Avg	Market/Book Latest	5-Yr Avg
Median	2.1	1.6	38.2	30.7	2.6	2.3
SIC Composite	2.1	1.7	34.2	28.5	3.2	2.5
Large Composite	–	–	–	–	–	–
Small Composite	–	–	–	–	–	–
High Financial Risk	–	–	–	–	–	–

Enterprise Valuation (EV) Multiples

	EV/Sales Latest	5-Yr Avg	EV/EBITDA Latest	5-Yr Avg
Median	2.7	2.4	11.1	10.7
SIC Composite	2.9	2.4	11.2	10.0
Large Composite	–	–	–	–
Small Composite	–	–	–	–
High Financial Risk	–	–	–	–

Enterprise Valuation SIC Composite

	Latest	5-Yr Avg
EV/Sales	2.9	2.4
EV/EBITDA	11.2	10.0

Fama-French (F-F) 5-Factor Model

	Fama-French (F-F) Components				
	F-F Beta	SMB Premium	HML Premium	RMW Premium	CMA Premium
Median	0.9	0.1	4.5	2.1	1.2
SIC Composite	0.6	-0.1	-0.4	0.8	1.4
Large Composite	–	–	–	–	–
Small Composite	–	–	–	–	–
High Financial Risk	–	–	–	–	–

Leverage Ratios (%)

	Debt/MV Equity Latest	5-Yr Avg	Debt/Total Capital Latest	5-Yr Avg
Median	32.5	34.4	24.5	25.3
SIC Composite	36.5	44.2	26.7	30.7
Large Composite	–	–	–	–
Small Composite	–	–	–	–
High Financial Risk	–	–	–	–

Cost of Debt

	Cost of Debt (%) Latest
Median	6.1
SIC Composite	4.7
Large Composite	–
Small Composite	–
High Financial Risk	–

Capital Structure

SIC Composite (%) Latest: D/TC 26.7, E/TC 73.3

Cost of Equity Capital (%)

	CRSP Deciles			Risk Premium Report		Discounted Cash Flow		Fama-French
	CAPM	CAPM +Size Prem	Build-Up	CAPM	Build-Up	1-Stage	3-Stage	5-Factor Model
				+Size Prem				
Median	7.2	8.7	7.7	12.3	13.2	11.9	9.2	16.1
SIC Composite	6.7	7.1	6.5	8.6	11.5	13.3	8.9	8.5
Large Composite	–	–	–	–	–	–	–	–
Small Composite	–	–	–	–	–	–	–	–
High Financial Risk	–	–	–	–	–	–	–	–

Cost of Equity Capital (%) SIC Composite: Avg CRSP 6.8, Avg RPR 10.0, 1-Stage 13.3, 3-Stage 8.9, 5-Factor Model 8.5

Weighted Average Cost of Capital (WACC) (%)

	CRSP Deciles			Risk Premium Report		Discounted Cash Flow		Fama-French
	CAPM	CAPM +Size Prem	Build-Up	CAPM +Size Prem	Build-Up	1-Stage	3-Stage	5-Factor Model
Median	6.7	7.4	6.8	9.4	10.0	10.5	7.6	12.7
SIC Composite	5.9	6.3	5.8	7.3	9.4	10.8	7.6	7.3
Large Composite	–	–	–	–	–	–	–	–
Small Composite	–	–	–	–	–	–	–	–
High Financial Risk	–	–	–	–	–	–	–	–

WACC (%) SIC Composite: Low 5.8, High 10.8, Average 7.8, Median 7.3

© 2017 Duff & Phelps. All Rights Reserved. Duff & Phelps has used the utmost care in compiling the data presented herein, but cannot guarantee the accuracy, completeness, or timeliness of the information.

Division F: Wholesale Trade

This division includes establishments or places of business primarily engaged in selling merchandise to retailers; to industrial, commercial, institutional, farm, construction contractors, or professional business users; or to other wholesalers; or acting as agents or brokers in buying merchandise for or selling merchandise to such persons or companies. Major groups between "50" and "51" are in this division.

Data Updated Through March 31, 2017

5

Number of Companies: 192
Wholesale Trade & Retail Trade

Industry Description
Wholesale Trade division includes establishments or places of business primarily engaged in selling merchandise to retailers; to industrial, commercial, institutional, farm, construction contractors, or professional business users; or to other wholesalers; or acting as agents or brokers in buying merchandise for or selling merchandise to such persons or companies. Retail Trade division includes establishments engaged in selling merchandise for personal or household consumption and rendering services incidental to the sale of the goods.

Sales (in millions)

Three Largest Companies
Wal-Mart Stores Inc.	$479,962.0
McKesson Corp.	190,884.0
CVS Health Corp.	177,526.0

Three Smallest Companies
Educational Development Corp.	$63.6
ADDvantage Technologies Group	38.7
Envirostar, Inc.	36.0

Annualized Monthly Performance Statistics (%)

Industry	Geometric Mean	Arithmetic Mean	Standard Deviation
1-year	7.5	7.8	8.5
3-year	10.7	11.2	11.4
5-year	13.8	14.4	11.8

Total Assets (in millions)

Three Largest Companies
Wal-Mart Stores Inc.	$199,581.0
CVS Health Corp.	94,462.0
Amazon.com Inc.	83,402.0

Three Smallest Companies
Appliance Recycling Centers	$46.8
Coffee Holding Co. Inc.	37.0
Envirostar, Inc.	10.2

S&P 500 Index	Geometric Mean	Arithmetic Mean	Standard Deviation
1-year	17.2	17.4	7.2
3-year	10.4	10.9	11.5
5-year	13.3	13.9	11.5

Return Ratios (%)

	Return on Assets Latest	Return on Assets 5-Yr Avg	Return on Equity Latest	Return on Equity 5-Yr Avg	Dividend Yield Latest	Dividend Yield 5-Yr Avg
Median (192)	5.3	5.8	11.9	12.7	1.4	1.4
SIC Composite (192)	6.6	6.8	4.3	4.6	1.7	1.8
Large Composite (19)	6.6	6.4	4.1	4.4	1.5	1.7
Small Composite (19)	7.7	7.6	5.6	6.3	2.1	2.2
High-Financial Risk (23)	1.7	-0.6	1.9	-0.7	1.5	1.5

Liquidity Ratio

	Current Ratio Latest	Current Ratio 5-Yr Avg
Median (192)	1.7	1.7
SIC Composite (192)	1.2	1.3
Large Composite (19)	1.1	1.1
Small Composite (19)	2.4	2.3
High-Financial Risk (23)	1.3	1.2

Profitability Ratio (%)

	Operating Margin Latest	Operating Margin 5-Yr Avg
Median	5.4	6.0
SIC Composite	5.4	5.5
Large Composite	4.5	4.5
Small Composite	7.8	7.2
High-Financial Risk	5.2	3.6

Growth Rates (%)

	Long-term EPS Analyst Estimates
Median	10.9
SIC Composite	15.8
Large Composite	16.7
Small Composite	15.9
High-Financial Risk	12.4

Betas (Levered)

	Raw (OLS)	Blume Adjusted	Peer Group	Vasicek Adjusted	Sum	Downside
Median	0.96	0.98	0.87	0.94	0.94	1.36
SIC Composite	0.87	0.92	0.87	0.87	0.83	0.85
Large Composite	0.86	0.92	0.87	0.86	0.86	0.84
Small Composite	0.96	0.98	1.03	0.96	0.81	1.06
High Financial Risk	0.82	0.89	0.89	0.82	0.81	0.94

Betas (Unlevered)

	Raw (OLS)	Blume Adjusted	Peer Group	Vasicek Adjusted	Sum	Downside
Median	0.79	0.80	0.75	0.75	0.71	1.02
SIC Composite	0.74	0.79	0.74	0.74	0.71	0.72
Large Composite	0.74	0.79	0.75	0.74	0.74	0.73
Small Composite	0.88	0.90	0.94	0.88	0.75	0.97
High Financial Risk	0.60	0.64	0.63	0.60	0.59	0.67

Equity Valuation Multiples

	Price/Sales Latest	Price/Sales 5-Yr Avg	Price/Earnings Latest	Price/Earnings 5-Yr Avg	Market/Book Latest	Market/Book 5-Yr Avg
Median	0.6	0.7	20.7	20.0	2.2	2.4
SIC Composite	0.7	0.7	23.5	21.8	4.7	3.9
Large Composite	0.7	0.6	24.4	22.6	5.0	4.1
Small Composite	0.9	0.7	17.9	15.9	2.6	2.2
High Financial Risk	0.7	0.6	54.5	–	–	8.8

Enterprise Valuation (EV) Multiples

	EV/Sales Latest	EV/Sales 5-Yr Avg	EV/EBITDA Latest	EV/EBITDA 5-Yr Avg
Median	0.7	0.8	9.3	9.5
SIC Composite	0.8	0.8	11.4	10.5
Large Composite	0.7	0.7	11.7	10.6
Small Composite	0.9	0.7	9.5	8.0
High Financial Risk	1.1	0.9	12.5	13.7

Enterprise Valuation SIC Composite: EV/Sales 0.8 (Latest), 0.8 (5-Yr Avg); EV/EBITDA 11.4 (Latest), 10.5 (5-Yr Avg)

Fama-French (F-F) 5-Factor Model

	F-F Beta	SMB Premium	HML Premium	RMW Premium	CMA Premium
Median	0.7	1.3	1.8	3.9	-0.6
SIC Composite	0.9	0.7	-2.2	0.4	1.7
Large Composite	0.9	0.1	-3.2	-0.1	-0.1
Small Composite	0.9	3.6	1.1	2.3	0.1
High Financial Risk	–	–	–	–	–

Leverage Ratios (%)

	Debt/MV Equity Latest	Debt/MV Equity 5-Yr Avg	Debt/Total Capital Latest	Debt/Total Capital 5-Yr Avg
Median	22.8	16.7	18.5	14.3
SIC Composite	20.3	19.0	16.9	16.0
Large Composite	17.1	17.7	14.6	15.1
Small Composite	14.2	12.5	12.5	11.1
High Financial Risk	72.4	63.1	42.0	38.7

Cost of Debt

	Cost of Debt (%) Latest
Median	6.1
SIC Composite	5.0
Large Composite	4.4
Small Composite	7.0
High Financial Risk	6.5

Capital Structure

SIC Composite (%) Latest: D/TC 16.9, E/TC 83.1

Cost of Equity Capital (%)

	CRSP Deciles CAPM	CRSP Deciles CAPM +Size Prem	CRSP Deciles Build-Up	Risk Premium Report CAPM +Size Prem	Risk Premium Report Build-Up	Discounted Cash Flow 1-Stage	Discounted Cash Flow 3-Stage	Fama-French 5-Factor Model
Median	8.7	10.6	10.6	12.2	13.6	13.0	11.8	13.6
SIC Composite	8.3	8.5	8.9	9.8	10.4	17.6	12.0	8.9
Large Composite	8.2	8.3	8.9	9.4	9.7	18.3	11.3	5.1
Small Composite	8.8	12.6	12.4	13.5	16.2	17.4	15.8	15.4
High Financial Risk	–	–	–	23.6	28.2	–	–	–

Cost of Equity Capital (%) SIC Composite: Avg CRSP 8.7, Avg RPR 10.1, 1-Stage 17.6, 3-Stage 12.0, 5-Factor Model 8.9

Weighted Average Cost of Capital (WACC) (%)

	CRSP Deciles CAPM	CRSP Deciles CAPM +Size Prem	CRSP Deciles Build-Up	Risk Premium Report CAPM +Size Prem	Risk Premium Report Build-Up	Discounted Cash Flow 1-Stage	Discounted Cash Flow 3-Stage	Fama-French 5-Factor Model
Median	7.7	9.1	9.1	10.2	11.5	11.4	10.1	11.5
SIC Composite	7.6	7.8	8.0	8.8	9.3	15.3	10.6	8.0
Large Composite	7.5	7.6	8.1	8.5	8.7	16.2	10.1	4.8
Small Composite	8.4	11.7	11.5	12.5	14.9	16.0	14.5	14.2
High Financial Risk	–	–	–	16.2	18.8	–	–	–

WACC (%) SIC Composite: Low 7.8, High 15.3, Average 9.7, Median 8.8

© 2017 Duff & Phelps. All Rights Reserved. Duff & Phelps has used the utmost care in compiling the data presented herein, but cannot guarantee the accuracy, completeness, or timeliness of the information.

Data Updated Through March 31, 2017

50

Number of Companies: 38
Wholesale Trade- durable Goods

Industry Description
This major group includes establishments primarily engaged in the wholesale distribution of durable goods.

Sales (in millions)

Three Largest Companies
Tech Data Corp.	$26,234.9
Avnet, Inc.	26,219.3
Arrow Electronics, Inc.	23,825.3

Three Smallest Companies
BSQUARE Corp.	$106.6
ADDvantage Technologies Group	38.7
Envirostar, Inc.	36.0

Total Assets (in millions)

Three Largest Companies
Arrow Electronics, Inc.	$14,206.4
Avnet, Inc.	11,239.8
Genuine Parts Co.	8,859.4

Three Smallest Companies
BSQUARE Corp.	$55.3
ADDvantage Technologies Group	50.3
Envirostar, Inc.	10.2

Annualized Monthly Performance Statistics (%)

Industry	Geometric Mean	Arithmetic Mean	Standard Deviation	S&P 500 Index	Geometric Mean	Arithmetic Mean	Standard Deviation
1-year	9.8	10.5	13.6	1-year	17.2	17.4	7.2
3-year	5.7	6.6	14.4	3-year	10.4	10.9	11.5
5-year	10.2	11.1	14.3	5-year	13.3	13.9	11.5

Return Ratios (%)

	Return on Assets Latest	5-Yr Avg	Return on Equity Latest	5-Yr Avg	Dividend Yield Latest	5-Yr Avg
Median (38)	4.1	4.8	11.1	11.9	1.1	1.3
SIC Composite (38)	5.1	5.8	4.7	5.5	1.2	1.4
Large Composite (3)	3.7	4.0	7.8	9.4	0.6	0.5
Small Composite (3)	7.0	3.0	2.8	3.0	0.8	4.1
High-Financial Risk (—)	—	—	—	—	—	—

Liquidity Ratio

	Current Ratio Latest	5-Yr Avg
Median (38)	2.1	2.2
SIC Composite (38)	1.8	1.9
Large Composite (3)	1.6	1.6
Small Composite (3)	3.3	3.2
High-Financial Risk (—)	—	—

Profitability Ratio (%)

	Operating Margin Latest	5-Yr Avg
Median (38)	5.1	5.8
SIC Composite (38)	5.0	5.2
Large Composite (3)	2.8	2.7
Small Composite (3)	5.4	3.6
High-Financial Risk (—)	—	—

Growth Rates (%)

	Long-term EPS Analyst Estimates
Median (38)	10.0
SIC Composite (38)	10.6
Large Composite (3)	4.3
Small Composite (3)	10.5
High-Financial Risk (—)	—

Betas (Levered)

	Raw (OLS)	Blume Adjusted	Peer Group	Vasicek Adjusted	Sum	Downside
Median	1.18	1.12	1.07	1.15	1.09	1.50
SIC Composite	1.02	1.02	1.07	1.02	0.94	1.05
Large Composite	1.16	1.11	1.07	1.11	0.83	1.21
Small Composite	1.88	1.57	1.07	1.64	1.34	1.58
High Financial Risk	—	—	—	—	—	—

Betas (Unlevered)

	Raw (OLS)	Blume Adjusted	Peer Group	Vasicek Adjusted	Sum	Downside
Median	0.92	0.93	0.92	0.93	0.87	1.06
SIC Composite	0.87	0.87	0.91	0.87	0.81	0.90
Large Composite	0.84	0.80	0.78	0.81	0.61	0.88
Small Composite	1.86	1.55	1.06	1.62	1.32	1.56
High Financial Risk	—	—	—	—	—	—

Equity Valuation Multiples

	Price/Sales Latest	5-Yr Avg	Price/Earnings Latest	5-Yr Avg	Market/Book Latest	5-Yr Avg
Median	0.6	0.5	22.0	19.3	2.0	2.0
SIC Composite	0.6	0.5	21.2	18.1	2.7	2.4
Large Composite	0.2	0.2	12.8	10.7	1.4	1.2
Small Composite	1.6	0.6	35.8	33.1	3.5	1.4
High Financial Risk	—	—	—	—	—	—

Enterprise Valuation (EV) Multiples

	EV/Sales Latest	5-Yr Avg	EV/EBITDA Latest	5-Yr Avg
Median	0.7	0.7	10.7	9.6
SIC Composite	0.7	0.6	11.3	9.8
Large Composite	0.2	0.2	8.9	6.9
Small Composite	1.4	0.5	21.1	9.8
High Financial Risk	—	—	—	—

Enterprise Valuation SIC Composite

EV/Sales: Latest 0.7, 5-Yr Avg 0.6
EV/EBITDA: Latest 11.3, 5-Yr Avg 9.8

Fama-French (F-F) 5-Factor Model

	F-F Beta	SMB Premium	HML Premium	RMW Premium	CMA Premium
Median	1.0	2.1	-3.4	0.2	6.2
SIC Composite	1.0	2.1	0.0	0.5	1.6
Large Composite	1.1	2.2	1.7	0.7	0.9
Small Composite	1.9	1.3	3.5	-0.5	5.7
High Financial Risk	—	—	—	—	—

Leverage Ratios (%)

	Debt/MV Equity Latest	5-Yr Avg	Debt/Total Capital Latest	5-Yr Avg
Median	25.3	22.6	20.2	18.5
SIC Composite	23.2	20.6	18.9	17.1
Large Composite	42.4	39.1	29.8	28.1
Small Composite	1.5	3.5	1.5	3.4
High Financial Risk	—	—	—	—

Cost of Debt

	Cost of Debt (%) Latest
Median	7.1
SIC Composite	5.8
Large Composite	4.8
Small Composite	7.1
High Financial Risk	—

Capital Structure

SIC Composite (%) Latest
D/TC: 18.9
E/TC: 81.1

Cost of Equity Capital (%)

	CRSP Deciles CAPM	CAPM +Size Prem	Build-Up	Risk Premium Report CAPM +Size Prem	Build-Up	Discounted Cash Flow 1-Stage	3-Stage	Fama-French 5-Factor Model
Median	9.8	11.7	11.1	13.8	13.6	11.2	11.7	13.8
SIC Composite	9.1	10.1	10.4	11.7	12.4	11.9	12.1	12.9
Large Composite	9.6	10.6	10.4	10.7	12.0	4.9	12.0	14.9
Small Composite	12.5	18.1	15.0	16.8	16.7	10.7	5.5	23.9
High Financial Risk	—	—	—	—	—	—	—	—

Cost of Equity Capital (%) SIC Composite

Avg CRSP: 10.3; Avg RPR: 12.1; 1-Stage: 11.9; 3-Stage: 12.1; 5-Factor Model: 12.9

Weighted Average Cost of Capital (WACC) (%)

	CRSP Deciles CAPM	CAPM +Size Prem	Build-Up	Risk Premium Report CAPM +Size Prem	Build-Up	Discounted Cash Flow 1-Stage	3-Stage	Fama-French 5-Factor Model
Median	8.5	9.6	9.5	11.2	11.4	9.5	10.3	12.0
SIC Composite	8.3	9.1	9.4	10.5	11.0	10.6	10.7	11.4
Large Composite	8.0	8.8	8.6	8.8	9.7	4.7	9.7	11.7
Small Composite	12.4	17.9	14.8	16.6	16.5	10.6	5.5	23.6
High Financial Risk	—	—	—	—	—	—	—	—

WACC (%) SIC Composite
Low 9.1; High 11.4; Average 10.4; Median 10.6

© 2017 Duff & Phelps. All Rights Reserved. Duff & Phelps has used the utmost care in compiling the data presented herein, but cannot guarantee the accuracy, completeness, or timeliness of the information.

Data Updated Through March 31, 2017

504

Number of Companies: 10
Professional and Commercial Equipment and Supplies

Industry Description
Establishments primarily engaged in the wholesale distribution of photographic equipment and supplies; office equipment; computers and computer peripheral equipment and software; commercial equipment, not elsewhere classified; medical, dental, and hospital equipment and supplies; opthalmic goods; professional equipment and supplies, not elsewhere classified.

Sales (in millions)

Three Largest Companies
Tech Data Corp.	$26,234.9
SYNNEX Corp.	14,061.8
Henry Schein, Inc.	11,571.7

Three Smallest Companies
ePlus Inc.	$1,204.2
Wayside Technology Group Inc.	418.1
BSQUARE Corp.	106.6

Annualized Monthly Performance Statistics (%)

Industry	Geometric Mean	Arithmetic Mean	Standard Deviation
1-year	3.6	4.8	16.6
3-year	10.7	11.9	16.4
5-year	13.7	14.9	16.6

Total Assets (in millions)

Three Largest Companies
Tech Data Corp.	$7,931.9
Henry Schein, Inc.	6,730.4
SYNNEX Corp.	5,223.3

Three Smallest Companies
ePlus Inc.	$616.7
Wayside Technology Group Inc.	113.7
BSQUARE Corp.	55.3

S&P 500 Index	Geometric Mean	Arithmetic Mean	Standard Deviation
1-year	17.2	17.4	7.2
3-year	10.4	10.9	11.5
5-year	13.3	13.9	11.5

Return Ratios (%)

	Return on Assets Latest	5-Yr Avg	Return on Equity Latest	5-Yr Avg	Dividend Yield Latest	5-Yr Avg
Median (10)	5.3	4.4	12.2	11.7	0.8	0.5
SIC Composite (10)	4.6	4.9	4.7	5.4	0.5	0.5
Large Composite (3)	4.7	4.9	4.4	5.4	0.2	0.1
Small Composite (3)	7.2	6.5	5.1	6.8	3.8	4.3
High-Financial Risk (–)	–	–	–	–	–	–

Liquidity Ratio

	Current Ratio Latest	5-Yr Avg
Median (10)	1.7	1.7
SIC Composite (10)	1.6	1.7
Large Composite (3)	1.6	1.5
Small Composite (3)	1.7	1.7
High-Financial Risk (–)	–	–

Profitability Ratio (%)

	Operating Margin Latest	5-Yr Avg
Median (10)	2.8	2.6
SIC Composite (10)	3.1	3.1
Large Composite (3)	2.9	2.7
Small Composite (3)	5.4	4.9
High-Financial Risk (–)	–	–

Growth Rates (%)

	Long-term EPS Analyst Estimates
Median (10)	7.9
SIC Composite (10)	8.4
Large Composite (3)	9.5
Small Composite (3)	5.5
High-Financial Risk (–)	–

Betas (Levered)

	Raw (OLS)	Blume Adjusted	Peer Group	Vasicek Adjusted	Sum	Downside
Median	1.10	1.07	1.07	1.09	0.94	1.38
SIC Composite	1.07	1.05	1.07	1.07	0.76	1.09
Large Composite	1.04	1.03	1.07	1.05	0.66	1.09
Small Composite	1.20	1.13	1.09	1.19	1.10	1.20
High Financial Risk	–	–	–	–	–	–

Betas (Unlevered)

	Raw (OLS)	Blume Adjusted	Peer Group	Vasicek Adjusted	Sum	Downside
Median	0.90	0.90	0.96	0.90	0.74	0.98
SIC Composite	0.93	0.92	0.94	0.94	0.67	0.95
Large Composite	0.92	0.92	0.95	0.94	0.60	0.97
Small Composite	1.17	1.10	1.06	1.16	1.07	1.17
High Financial Risk	–	–	–	–	–	–

Equity Valuation Multiples

	Price/Sales Latest	5-Yr Avg	Price/Earnings Latest	5-Yr Avg	Market/Book Latest	5-Yr Avg
Median	0.3	0.2	18.0	15.9	2.1	1.8
SIC Composite	0.4	0.3	21.5	18.6	2.6	2.2
Large Composite	0.4	0.3	22.7	18.6	3.0	2.3
Small Composite	0.6	0.4	19.5	14.8	2.8	1.9
High Financial Risk	–	–	–	–	–	–

Enterprise Valuation (EV) Multiples

	EV/Sales Latest	5-Yr Avg	EV/EBITDA Latest	5-Yr Avg
Median	0.3	0.3	10.3	7.8
SIC Composite	0.4	0.4	12.7	9.9
Large Composite	0.4	0.3	14.5	10.5
Small Composite	0.6	0.4	11.2	6.9
High Financial Risk	–	–	–	–

Enterprise Valuation SIC Composite
- EV/Sales: Latest 0.4, 5-Yr Avg 0.4
- EV/EBITDA: Latest 12.7, 5-Yr Avg 9.9

Fama-French (F-F) 5-Factor Model

	F-F Beta	SMB Premium	HML Premium	RMW Premium	CMA Premium
Median	1.1	1.6	1.6	-3.3	1.1
SIC Composite	1.0	1.8	-2.9	0.7	2.0
Large Composite	1.0	1.8	-3.7	0.9	1.2
Small Composite	1.1	1.1	1.6	-2.6	1.7
High Financial Risk	–	–	–	–	–

Leverage Ratios (%)

	Debt/MV Equity Latest	5-Yr Avg	Debt/Total Capital Latest	5-Yr Avg
Median	17.6	19.2	14.9	16.1
SIC Composite	19.5	16.5	16.3	14.2
Large Composite	16.7	12.9	14.3	11.5
Small Composite	4.3	7.6	4.1	7.0
High Financial Risk	–	–	–	–

Cost of Debt

	Cost of Debt (%) Latest
Median	7.1
SIC Composite	6.3
Large Composite	6.2
Small Composite	7.1
High Financial Risk	–

Capital Structure

SIC Composite (%) Latest
- D/TC: 16.3
- E/TC: 83.7

Cost of Equity Capital (%)

	CRSP Deciles CAPM	CAPM +Size Prem	Build-Up	Risk Premium Report CAPM +Size Prem	Build-Up	Discounted Cash Flow 1-Stage	3-Stage	Fama-French 5-Factor Model
Median	9.5	11.3	11.1	12.2	13.5	11.1	11.2	10.4
SIC Composite	9.4	10.4	10.4	10.8	12.6	8.9	10.7	10.8
Large Composite	9.3	10.1	10.2	10.0	12.2	9.7	10.5	9.4
Small Composite	10.0	12.6	11.9	14.3	15.0	5.8	8.5	11.5
High Financial Risk	–	–	–	–	–	–	–	–

Cost of Equity Capital (%) SIC Composite
- Avg CRSP: 10.4
- Avg RPR: 11.7
- 1-Stage: 8.9
- 3-Stage: 10.7
- 5-Factor Model: 10.8

Weighted Average Cost of Capital (WACC) (%)

	CRSP Deciles CAPM	CAPM +Size Prem	Build-Up	Risk Premium Report CAPM +Size Prem	Build-Up	Discounted Cash Flow 1-Stage	3-Stage	Fama-French 5-Factor Model
Median	8.5	9.8	9.8	10.2	11.6	9.4	9.7	10.8
SIC Composite	8.7	9.6	9.6	9.9	11.4	8.3	9.8	9.9
Large Composite	8.8	9.5	9.6	9.4	11.3	9.1	9.8	8.9
Small Composite	9.8	12.3	11.6	13.9	14.6	5.7	8.4	11.2
High Financial Risk	–	–	–	–	–	–	–	–

WACC (%) SIC Composite
Low 8.3 — Average 9.8 — Median 9.8 — High 11.4

© 2017 Duff & Phelps. All Rights Reserved. Duff & Phelps has used the utmost care in compiling the data presented herein, but cannot guarantee the accuracy, completeness, or timeliness of the information.

Data Updated Through March 31, 2017

5045

Number of Companies: 7

Computers and Computer Peripheral Equipment and Software

Industry Description

Establishments primarily engaged in the wholesale distribution of computers, computer peripheral equipment, and computer software.

Sales (in millions)

Three Largest Companies
Tech Data Corp.	$26,234.9
SYNNEX Corp.	14,061.8
Insight Enterprises Inc.	5,485.5

Three Smallest Companies
ePlus Inc.	$1,204.2
Wayside Technology Group Inc.	418.1
BSQUARE Corp.	106.6

Total Assets (in millions)

Three Largest Companies
Tech Data Corp.	$7,931.9
SYNNEX Corp.	5,223.3
Insight Enterprises Inc.	2,219.3

Three Smallest Companies
ePlus Inc.	$616.7
Wayside Technology Group Inc.	113.7
BSQUARE Corp.	55.3

Annualized Monthly Performance Statistics (%)

Industry	Geometric Mean	Arithmetic Mean	Standard Deviation
1-year	17.6	20.9	30.0
3-year	13.6	15.8	23.1
5-year	14.1	16.5	24.1

S&P 500 Index	Geometric Mean	Arithmetic Mean	Standard Deviation
1-year	17.2	17.4	7.2
3-year	10.4	10.9	11.5
5-year	13.3	13.9	11.5

Return Ratios (%)

	Return on Assets Latest	5-Yr Avg	Return on Equity Latest	5-Yr Avg	Dividend Yield Latest	5-Yr Avg
Median (7)	4.9	4.1	12.2	11.5	0.8	0.5
SIC Composite (7)	3.5	3.7	5.8	7.4	0.7	0.5
Large Composite (–)	–	–	–	–	–	–
Small Composite (–)	–	–	–	–	–	–
High-Financial Risk (–)	–	–	–	–	–	–

Liquidity Ratio

	Current Ratio Latest	5-Yr Avg
Median (7)	1.6	1.6
SIC Composite (7)	1.6	1.6
Large Composite	–	–
Small Composite	–	–
High-Financial Risk	–	–

Profitability Ratio (%)

	Operating Margin Latest	5-Yr Avg
Median (7)	2.8	2.6
SIC Composite (7)	2.0	2.0
Large Composite	–	–
Small Composite	–	–
High-Financial Risk	–	–

Growth Rates (%)

	Long-term EPS Analyst Estimates
Median (7)	8.4
SIC Composite (7)	8.3
Large Composite	–
Small Composite	–
High-Financial Risk	–

Betas (Levered)

	Raw (OLS)	Blume Adjusted	Peer Group	Vasicek Adjusted	Sum	Downside
Median	1.21	1.14	1.07	1.17	1.07	1.51
SIC Composite	1.20	1.13	1.07	1.18	0.71	1.44
Large Composite	–	–	–	–	–	–
Small Composite	–	–	–	–	–	–
High Financial Risk	–	–	–	–	–	–

Betas (Unlevered)

	Raw (OLS)	Blume Adjusted	Peer Group	Vasicek Adjusted	Sum	Downside
Median	1.00	0.96	0.98	0.99	1.06	1.35
SIC Composite	0.98	0.93	0.88	0.97	0.60	1.17
Large Composite	–	–	–	–	–	–
Small Composite	–	–	–	–	–	–
High Financial Risk	–	–	–	–	–	–

Equity Valuation Multiples

	Price/Sales Latest	5-Yr Avg	Price/Earnings Latest	5-Yr Avg	Market/Book Latest	5-Yr Avg
Median	0.3	0.2	17.0	14.0	2.0	1.6
SIC Composite	0.2	0.2	17.1	13.6	1.8	1.4
Large Composite	–	–	–	–	–	–
Small Composite	–	–	–	–	–	–
High Financial Risk	–	–	–	–	–	–

Enterprise Valuation (EV) Multiples

	EV/Sales Latest	5-Yr Avg	EV/EBITDA Latest	5-Yr Avg
Median	0.3	0.2	9.6	7.4
SIC Composite	0.2	0.2	11.6	7.3
Large Composite	–	–	–	–
Small Composite	–	–	–	–
High Financial Risk	–	–	–	–

Enterprise Valuation SIC Composite

- Latest: EV/Sales 0.2, EV/EBITDA 11.6
- 5-Yr Avg: EV/Sales 0.2, EV/EBITDA 7.3

Fama-French (F-F) 5-Factor Model

	F-F Beta	SMB Premium	HML Premium	RMW Premium	CMA Premium
Median	1.0	5.6	2.3	2.5	-3.8
SIC Composite	1.1	4.0	1.7	0.5	-0.9
Large Composite	–	–	–	–	–
Small Composite	–	–	–	–	–
High Financial Risk	–	–	–	–	–

Leverage Ratios (%)

	Debt/MV Equity Latest	5-Yr Avg	Debt/Total Capital Latest	5-Yr Avg
Median	13.4	19.5	11.8	16.3
SIC Composite	29.3	26.8	22.6	21.1

Cost of Debt

	Cost of Debt (%) Latest
Median	7.1
SIC Composite	5.9

Capital Structure

SIC Composite (%) Latest
- D/TC: 22.6
- E/TC: 77.4

Cost of Equity Capital (%)

	CAPM	CRSP Deciles CAPM +Size Prem	Build-Up	Risk Premium Report CAPM +Size Prem	Build-Up	Discounted Cash Flow 1-Stage	3-Stage	Fama-French 5-Factor Model
Median	10.0	12.0	11.5	14.2	13.7	12.4	11.2	15.4
SIC Composite	10.0	11.5	10.9	10.8	13.1	8.9	11.8	14.6
Large Composite	–	–	–	–	–	–	–	–
Small Composite	–	–	–	–	–	–	–	–
High Financial Risk	–	–	–	–	–	–	–	–

Cost of Equity Capital (%) SIC Composite
- Avg CRSP: 11.2
- Avg RPR: 12.0
- 1-Stage: 8.9
- 3-Stage: 11.8
- 5-Factor Model: 14.6

Weighted Average Cost of Capital (WACC) (%)

	CAPM	CRSP Deciles CAPM +Size Prem	Build-Up	Risk Premium Report CAPM +Size Prem	Build-Up	Discounted Cash Flow 1-Stage	3-Stage	Fama-French 5-Factor Model
Median	9.2	11.6	10.6	13.7	12.9	10.8	10.4	12.0
SIC Composite	8.9	10.0	9.6	9.5	11.3	8.0	10.2	12.4
Large Composite	–	–	–	–	–	–	–	–
Small Composite	–	–	–	–	–	–	–	–
High Financial Risk	–	–	–	–	–	–	–	–

WACC (%) SIC Composite
- Low: 8.0
- High: 12.4
- Average: 10.2
- Median: 10.0

© 2017 Duff & Phelps. All Rights Reserved. Duff & Phelps has used the utmost care in compiling the data presented herein, but cannot guarantee the accuracy, completeness, or timeliness of the information.

Data Updated Through March 31, 2017

506

Number of Companies: 5
Electrical Goods

Industry Description
This industry group includes establishments primarily engaged in the wholesale distribution of electrical generating, distributing, and wiring equipment. It also includes household appliances, whether electrically, manually, or mechanically powered.

Sales (in millions)

Three Largest Companies
Anixter Int'l Inc.	$7,622.8
WESCO Int'l Inc.	7,336.0
TESSCO Technologies Inc.	530.7

Three Smallest Companies
TESSCO Technologies Inc.	$530.7
Houston Wire & Cable Co.	261.6
ADDvantage Technologies Group	38.7

Total Assets (in millions)

Three Largest Companies
WESCO Int'l Inc.	$4,491.0
Anixter Int'l Inc.	4,093.6
Houston Wire & Cable Co.	175.8

Three Smallest Companies
Houston Wire & Cable Co.	$175.8
TESSCO Technologies Inc.	169.4
ADDvantage Technologies Group	50.3

Annualized Monthly Performance Statistics (%)

Industry	Geometric Mean	Arithmetic Mean	Standard Deviation
1-year	35.7	41.5	44.1
3-year	-7.6	-3.6	29.3
5-year	2.0	5.3	27.5

S&P 500 Index	Geometric Mean	Arithmetic Mean	Standard Deviation
1-year	17.2	17.4	7.2
3-year	10.4	10.9	11.5
5-year	13.3	13.9	11.5

Return Ratios (%)

	Return on Assets Latest	Return on Assets 5-Yr Avg	Return on Equity Latest	Return on Equity 5-Yr Avg	Dividend Yield Latest	Dividend Yield 5-Yr Avg
Median (5)	2.2	4.3	4.7	10.4	0.0	1.3
SIC Composite (5)	2.5	4.4	3.5	6.6	0.0	1.2
Large Composite (–)	–	–	–	–	–	–
Small Composite (–)	–	–	–	–	–	–
High-Financial Risk (–)	–	–	–	–	–	–

Liquidity Ratio

	Current Ratio Latest	Current Ratio 5-Yr Avg
Median (5)	2.6	2.4
SIC Composite (5)	2.3	2.4
Large Composite	–	–
Small Composite	–	–
High-Financial Risk	–	–

Profitability Ratio (%)

	Operating Margin Latest	Operating Margin 5-Yr Avg
Median (5)	2.0	5.2
SIC Composite (5)	4.1	5.2
Large Composite	–	–
Small Composite	–	–
High-Financial Risk	–	–

Growth Rates (%)

	Long-term EPS Analyst Estimates
Median (5)	8.5
SIC Composite (5)	9.1
Large Composite	–
Small Composite	–
High-Financial Risk	–

Betas (Levered)

	Raw (OLS)	Blume Adjusted	Peer Group	Vasicek Adjusted	Sum	Downside
Median	1.34	1.22	1.07	1.22	1.51	1.79
SIC Composite	1.75	1.48	1.07	1.58	2.19	1.81
Large Composite	–	–	–	–	–	–
Small Composite	–	–	–	–	–	–
High Financial Risk	–	–	–	–	–	–

Betas (Unlevered)

	Raw (OLS)	Blume Adjusted	Peer Group	Vasicek Adjusted	Sum	Downside
Median	1.28	1.11	0.84	1.14	1.30	1.29
SIC Composite	1.30	1.11	0.83	1.18	1.60	1.34
Large Composite	–	–	–	–	–	–
Small Composite	–	–	–	–	–	–
High Financial Risk	–	–	–	–	–	–

Equity Valuation Multiples

	Price/Sales Latest	Price/Sales 5-Yr Avg	Price/Earnings Latest	Price/Earnings 5-Yr Avg	Market/Book Latest	Market/Book 5-Yr Avg
Median	0.4	0.4	33.3	16.5	1.2	1.7
SIC Composite	0.4	0.4	28.3	15.3	1.7	1.7
Large Composite	–	–	–	–	–	–
Small Composite	–	–	–	–	–	–
High Financial Risk	–	–	–	–	–	–

Enterprise Valuation (EV) Multiples

	EV/Sales Latest	EV/Sales 5-Yr Avg	EV/EBITDA Latest	EV/EBITDA 5-Yr Avg
Median	0.5	0.6	8.9	9.5
SIC Composite	0.6	0.6	11.3	9.5
Large Composite	–	–	–	–
Small Composite	–	–	–	–
High Financial Risk	–	–	–	–

Enterprise Valuation SIC Composite
Latest: EV/Sales 0.6, EV/EBITDA 11.3
5-Yr Avg: EV/Sales 0.6, EV/EBITDA 9.5

Fama-French (F-F) 5-Factor Model

	F-F Beta	SMB Premium	HML Premium	RMW Premium	CMA Premium
Median	1.1	5.2	-0.6	0.3	1.5
SIC Composite	1.6	3.3	4.7	-0.3	-0.1
Large Composite	–	–	–	–	–
Small Composite	–	–	–	–	–
High Financial Risk	–	–	–	–	–

Leverage Ratios (%)

	Debt/MV Equity Latest	Debt/MV Equity 5-Yr Avg	Debt/Total Capital Latest	Debt/Total Capital 5-Yr Avg
Median	41.8	29.3	29.5	22.6
SIC Composite	45.4	48.2	31.2	32.5
Large Composite	–	–	–	–
Small Composite	–	–	–	–
High Financial Risk	–	–	–	–

Cost of Debt

	Cost of Debt (%) Latest
Median	7.1
SIC Composite	6.2
Large Composite	–
Small Composite	–
High Financial Risk	–

Capital Structure

SIC Composite (%) Latest
D/TC: 31.2
E/TC: 68.8

Cost of Equity Capital (%)

	CRSP Deciles CAPM	CRSP Deciles CAPM +Size Prem	CRSP Deciles Build-Up	Risk Premium Report CAPM +Size Prem	Risk Premium Report Build-Up	Discounted Cash Flow 1-Stage	Discounted Cash Flow 3-Stage	Fama-French 5-Factor Model
Median	10.2	14.0	15.0	17.8	16.3	8.0	13.7	16.2
SIC Composite	12.2	13.9	11.1	18.9	13.0	9.1	13.8	20.0
Large Composite	–	–	–	–	–	–	–	–
Small Composite	–	–	–	–	–	–	–	–
High Financial Risk	–	–	–	–	–	–	–	–

Cost of Equity Capital (%) SIC Composite
Avg CRSP: 12.5
Avg RPR: 16.0
1-Stage: 9.1
3-Stage: 13.8
5-Factor Model: 20.0

Weighted Average Cost of Capital (WACC) (%)

	CRSP Deciles CAPM	CRSP Deciles CAPM +Size Prem	CRSP Deciles Build-Up	Risk Premium Report CAPM +Size Prem	Risk Premium Report Build-Up	Discounted Cash Flow 1-Stage	Discounted Cash Flow 3-Stage	Fama-French 5-Factor Model
Median	9.4	12.0	11.4	14.2	12.6	6.9	11.2	16.0
SIC Composite	9.9	11.0	9.1	14.5	10.4	7.8	11.0	15.3
Large Composite	–	–	–	–	–	–	–	–
Small Composite	–	–	–	–	–	–	–	–
High Financial Risk	–	–	–	–	–	–	–	–

WACC (%) SIC Composite
Low: 7.8
High: 15.3
Average: 11.3
Median: 11.0

© 2017 Duff & Phelps. All Rights Reserved. Duff & Phelps has used the utmost care in compiling the data presented herein, but cannot guarantee the accuracy, completeness, or timeliness of the information.

Data Updated Through March 31, 2017

508

Number of Companies: 8
Machinery, Equipment, and Supplies

Industry Description

Establishments primarily engaged in the wholesale distribution of construction and mining machinery and equipment; farm and garden machinery and equipment; industrial machinery and equipment; industrial supplies; services establishment equipment and supplies; transportation equipment and supplies.

Sales (in millions)

Three Largest Companies
MSC Industrial Direct	$2,863.5
Applied Industrial Tech. Inc.	2,519.4
Kaman Corporation	1,808.4

Three Smallest Companies
DXP Enterprises Inc.	$1,247.0
H&E Equipment Services, Inc.	978.1
Envirostar, Inc.	36.0

Annualized Monthly Performance Statistics (%)

Industry	Geometric Mean	Arithmetic Mean	Standard Deviation
1-year	32.2	34.9	29.6
3-year	1.8	3.8	21.6
5-year	7.0	8.8	20.5

Total Assets (in millions)

Three Largest Companies
MSC Industrial Direct	$2,065.0
Wesco Aircraft Holdings, Inc.	1,956.2
AAR Corp.	1,442.1

Three Smallest Companies
H&E Equipment Services, Inc.	$1,241.6
DXP Enterprises Inc.	684.0
Envirostar, Inc.	10.2

S&P 500 Index	Geometric Mean	Arithmetic Mean	Standard Deviation
1-year	17.2	17.4	7.2
3-year	10.4	10.9	11.5
5-year	13.3	13.9	11.5

Return Ratios (%)

	Return on Assets Latest	Return on Assets 5-Yr Avg	Return on Equity Latest	Return on Equity 5-Yr Avg	Dividend Yield Latest	Dividend Yield 5-Yr Avg
Median (8)	3.5	4.3	10.5	12.5	1.9	2.4
SIC Composite (8)	4.5	5.3	3.4	4.6	2.0	2.6
Large Composite (–)	–	–	–	–	–	–
Small Composite (–)	–	–	–	–	–	–
High-Financial Risk (–)	–	–	–	–	–	–

Liquidity Ratio / Profitability Ratio (%) / Growth Rates (%)

	Current Ratio Latest	Current Ratio 5-Yr Avg	Operating Margin Latest	Operating Margin 5-Yr Avg	Long-term EPS Analyst Estimates
Median (8)	2.1	2.6	7.1	7.0	11.4
SIC Composite (8)	2.6	3.0	8.2	9.3	11.3
Large Composite	–	–	–	–	–
Small Composite	–	–	–	–	–
High-Financial Risk	–	–	–	–	–

Betas (Levered)

	Raw (OLS)	Blume Adjusted	Peer Group	Vasicek Adjusted	Sum	Downside
Median	1.10	1.07	1.07	1.04	1.28	1.66
SIC Composite	0.94	0.96	1.07	0.95	1.13	1.01
Large Composite						
Small Composite						
High Financial Risk						

Betas (Unlevered)

	Raw (OLS)	Blume Adjusted	Peer Group	Vasicek Adjusted	Sum	Downside
Median	1.07	1.02	0.94	0.98	1.16	1.37
SIC Composite	0.81	0.83	0.92	0.82	0.96	0.87
Large Composite	–	–	–	–	–	–
Small Composite	–	–	–	–	–	–
High Financial Risk	–	–	–	–	–	–

Equity Valuation Multiples

	Price/Sales Latest	Price/Sales 5-Yr Avg	Price/Earnings Latest	Price/Earnings 5-Yr Avg	Market/Book Latest	Market/Book 5-Yr Avg
Median	0.8	0.8	26.7	21.3	2.7	2.8
SIC Composite	1.1	1.0	29.8	22.0	2.8	2.3
Large Composite	–	–	–	–	–	–
Small Composite	–	–	–	–	–	–
High Financial Risk	–	–	–	–	–	–

Enterprise Valuation (EV) Multiples

	EV/Sales Latest	EV/Sales 5-Yr Avg	EV/EBITDA Latest	EV/EBITDA 5-Yr Avg
Median	1.2	0.8	11.3	9.8
SIC Composite	1.3	1.2	11.0	9.3
Large Composite	–	–	–	–
Small Composite	–	–	–	–
High Financial Risk	–	–	–	–

Enterprise Valuation SIC Composite
Latest: EV/Sales 1.3, EV/EBITDA 11.0
5-Yr Avg: EV/Sales 1.2, EV/EBITDA 9.3

Fama-French (F-F) 5-Factor Model

Fama-French (F-F) Components

	F-F Beta	SMB Premium	HML Premium	RMW Premium	CMA Premium
Median	1.3	6.4	0.6	-2.5	-2.2
SIC Composite	0.8	3.4	3.7	-0.6	1.3
Large Composite	–	–	–	–	–
Small Composite	–	–	–	–	–
High Financial Risk	–	–	–	–	–

Leverage Ratios (%)

	Debt/MV Equity Latest	Debt/MV Equity 5-Yr Avg	Debt/Total Capital Latest	Debt/Total Capital 5-Yr Avg
Median	23.1	33.5	18.3	25.1
SIC Composite	26.2	27.6	20.7	21.6
Large Composite	–	–	–	–
Small Composite	–	–	–	–
High Financial Risk	–	–	–	–

Cost of Debt

	Cost of Debt (%) Latest
Median	6.6
SIC Composite	6.7
Large Composite	–
Small Composite	–
High Financial Risk	–

Capital Structure

SIC Composite (%) Latest
D/TC: 20.7
E/TC: 79.3

Cost of Equity Capital (%)

	CAPM	CRSP Deciles CAPM +Size Prem	CRSP Deciles Build-Up	Risk Premium Report CAPM +Size Prem	Risk Premium Report Build-Up	Discounted Cash Flow 1-Stage	Discounted Cash Flow 3-Stage	Fama-French 5-Factor Model
Median	9.2	11.8	11.1	15.5	14.1	13.0	10.7	13.2
SIC Composite	8.7	10.1	10.8	13.5	13.5	13.0	10.6	15.7
Large Composite	–	–	–	–	–	–	–	–
Small Composite	–	–	–	–	–	–	–	–
High Financial Risk	–	–	–	–	–	–	–	–

Cost of Equity Capital (%) SIC Composite
Avg CRSP: 10.5
Avg RPR: 13.5
1-Stage: 13.0
3-Stage: 10.6
5-Factor Model: 15.7

Weighted Average Cost of Capital (WACC) (%)

	CAPM	CRSP Deciles CAPM +Size Prem	CRSP Deciles Build-Up	Risk Premium Report CAPM +Size Prem	Risk Premium Report Build-Up	Discounted Cash Flow 1-Stage	Discounted Cash Flow 3-Stage	Fama-French 5-Factor Model
Median	8.7	10.2	9.6	13.8	11.8	12.0	9.2	12.6
SIC Composite	7.9	9.0	9.6	11.7	11.7	11.3	9.4	13.4
Large Composite	–	–	–	–	–	–	–	–
Small Composite	–	–	–	–	–	–	–	–
High Financial Risk	–	–	–	–	–	–	–	–

WACC (%) SIC Composite
Low: 9.0, High: 13.4
Average 10.9, Median 11.3

© 2017 Duff & Phelps. All Rights Reserved. Duff & Phelps has used the utmost care in compiling the data presented herein, but cannot guarantee the accuracy, completeness, or timeliness of the information.

Data Updated Through March 31, 2017

51

Number of Companies: 29
Wholesale Trade- non- durable Goods

Industry Description
This major group includes establishments primarily engaged in the wholesale distribution of nondurable goods.

Sales (in millions)

Three Largest Companies
McKesson Corp.	$190,884.0
AmerisourceBergen Corp.	146,849.7
Cardinal Health, Inc.	121,546.0

Three Smallest Companies
Natural Health Trends Corp.	$287.7
Coffee Holding Co. Inc.	78.9
Educational Development Corp.	63.6

Total Assets (in millions)

Three Largest Companies
McKesson Corp.	$56,563.0
Cardinal Health, Inc.	34,122.0
AmerisourceBergen Corp.	33,656.2

Three Smallest Companies
AMCON Distributing Co.	$112.3
Educational Development Corp.	49.7
Coffee Holding Co. Inc.	37.0

Annualized Monthly Performance Statistics (%)

	Industry Geometric Mean	Arithmetic Mean	Standard Deviation		S&P 500 Index Geometric Mean	Arithmetic Mean	Standard Deviation
1-year	7.5	9.0	19.2	1-year	17.2	17.4	7.2
3-year	2.0	3.1	15.3	3-year	10.4	10.9	11.5
5-year	11.8	12.8	15.0	5-year	13.3	13.9	11.5

Return Ratios (%)

	Return on Assets Latest	5-Yr Avg	Return on Equity Latest	5-Yr Avg	Dividend Yield Latest	5-Yr Avg
Median (29)	3.6	3.8	8.2	9.6	1.7	1.3
SIC Composite (29)	3.7	3.8	4.9	4.5	3.0	2.9
Large Composite (3)	4.1	3.3	6.7	4.3	2.1	1.8
Small Composite (3)	25.3	21.6	15.6	11.7	3.2	1.4
High-Financial Risk (−)	—	—	—	—	—	—

Liquidity Ratio

	Current Ratio Latest	5-Yr Avg
Median	2.2	1.7
SIC Composite	1.2	1.2
Large Composite	1.0	1.1
Small Composite	2.3	2.2
High Financial Risk	—	—

Profitability Ratio (%)

	Operating Margin Latest	5-Yr Avg
Median	3.3	3.5
SIC Composite	2.1	2.1
Large Composite	1.7	1.7
Small Composite	16.6	10.4
High Financial Risk	—	—

Growth Rates (%)

	Long-term EPS Analyst Estimates
Median	12.0
SIC Composite	12.4
Large Composite	8.6
Small Composite	9.1
High Financial Risk	—

Betas (Levered)

	Raw (OLS)	Blume Adjusted	Peer Group	Vasicek Adjusted	Sum	Downside
Median	1.17	1.12	1.01	1.06	1.23	1.55
SIC Composite	0.93	0.96	1.01	0.94	1.15	1.01
Large Composite	0.94	0.97	1.01	0.98	1.37	1.18
Small Composite	2.02	1.65	1.01	1.20	1.77	2.91
High Financial Risk	—	—	—	—	—	—

Betas (Unlevered)

	Raw (OLS)	Blume Adjusted	Peer Group	Vasicek Adjusted	Sum	Downside
Median	0.84	0.80	0.82	0.77	1.03	1.20
SIC Composite	0.72	0.75	0.78	0.73	0.89	0.78
Large Composite	0.77	0.79	0.82	0.80	1.11	0.96
Small Composite	1.90	1.56	0.96	1.14	1.67	2.73
High Financial Risk	—	—	—	—	—	—

Equity Valuation Multiples

	Price/Sales Latest	5-Yr Avg	Price/Earnings Latest	5-Yr Avg	Market/Book Latest	5-Yr Avg
Median	0.3	0.4	26.6	23.6	1.6	1.8
SIC Composite	0.2	0.3	20.7	22.2	2.9	3.1
Large Composite	0.2	0.2	14.9	23.4	3.2	4.1
Small Composite	0.9	0.8	6.4	8.6	3.2	3.4
High Financial Risk	—	—	—	—	—	—

Enterprise Valuation (EV) Multiples

	EV/Sales Latest	5-Yr Avg	EV/EBITDA Latest	5-Yr Avg
Median	0.6	0.5	9.9	10.6
SIC Composite	0.3	0.3	10.9	11.3
Large Composite	0.2	0.2	8.9	11.3
Small Composite	0.6	0.6	3.8	5.6
High Financial Risk	—	—	—	—

Enterprise Valuation SIC Composite: EV/Sales Latest 0.3, 5-Yr Avg 0.3; EV/EBITDA Latest 10.9, 5-Yr Avg 11.3

Fama-French (F-F) 5-Factor Model

	F-F Beta	SMB Premium	HML Premium	RMW Premium	CMA Premium
Median	0.6	1.4	0.0	1.8	3.7
SIC Composite	0.9	1.6	-2.2	-0.4	3.1
Large Composite	0.9	1.8	-3.7	-1.0	-1.3
Small Composite	2.0	5.4	-0.1	8.8	-4.3
High Financial Risk	—	—	—	—	—

Leverage Ratios (%)

	Debt/MV Equity Latest	5-Yr Avg	Debt/Total Capital Latest	5-Yr Avg
Median	27.4	26.2	21.5	20.7
SIC Composite	34.9	28.5	25.9	22.2
Large Composite	23.8	19.1	19.2	16.0
Small Composite	7.6	3.4	7.0	3.3
High Financial Risk	—	—	—	—

Cost of Debt

	Cost of Debt (%) Latest
Median	7.1
SIC Composite	5.2
Large Composite	4.4
Small Composite	6.9
High Financial Risk	—

Capital Structure

SIC Composite (%) Latest: D/TC 25.9, E/TC 74.1

Cost of Equity Capital (%)

	CRSP Deciles CAPM	CAPM +Size Prem	Build-Up	Risk Premium Report CAPM +Size Prem	Build-Up	Discounted Cash Flow 1-Stage	3-Stage	Fama-French 5-Factor Model
Median	9.3	11.5	10.8	14.2	13.9	12.7	10.4	13.7
SIC Composite	8.7	9.1	9.5	11.8	11.0	14.8	11.5	10.4
Large Composite	8.9	9.1	9.2	12.4	10.1	9.9	11.8	4.1
Small Composite	10.1	13.2	12.2	18.7	16.2	12.3	19.9	24.3
High Financial Risk	—	—	—	—	—	—	—	—

Cost of Equity Capital (%) SIC Composite: Avg CRSP 9.3, Avg RPR 11.4, 1-Stage 14.8, 3-Stage 11.5, 5-Factor Model 10.4

Weighted Average Cost of Capital (WACC) (%)

	CRSP Deciles CAPM	CAPM +Size Prem	Build-Up	Risk Premium Report CAPM +Size Prem	Build-Up	Discounted Cash Flow 1-Stage	3-Stage	Fama-French 5-Factor Model
Median	8.3	9.7	9.5	11.7	11.4	10.8	9.1	11.8
SIC Composite	7.6	7.9	8.2	9.9	9.3	12.1	9.7	8.8
Large Composite	7.9	8.0	8.2	10.8	8.9	8.7	10.2	4.1
Small Composite	9.9	12.7	11.8	17.9	15.6	11.9	19.0	23.1
High Financial Risk	—	—	—	—	—	—	—	—

WACC (%) SIC Composite: Low 7.9, High 12.1, Average 9.4, Median 9.3

© 2017 Duff & Phelps. All Rights Reserved. Duff & Phelps has used the utmost care in compiling the data presented herein, but cannot guarantee the accuracy, completeness, or timeliness of the information.

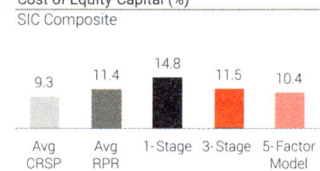

Data Updated Through March 31, 2017

512

Number of Companies: 6
Drugs, Drug Proprietaries, and Druggists' Sundries

Industry Description
Establishments primarily engaged in the wholesale distribution of prescription drugs, proprietary drugs, druggists' sundries, and toiletries.

Sales (in millions)

Three Largest Companies
McKesson Corp.	$190,884.0
AmerisourceBergen Corp.	146,849.7
Cardinal Health, Inc.	121,546.0

Three Smallest Companies
PharMerica Corp.	$2,091.1
Prestige Brands Holdings	806.2
Natural Health Trends Corp.	287.7

Annualized Monthly Performance Statistics (%)

Industry	Geometric Mean	Arithmetic Mean	Standard Deviation
1-year	-0.6	2.3	25.2
3-year	2.8	4.8	21.0
5-year	15.0	17.0	21.4

Total Assets (in millions)

Three Largest Companies
McKesson Corp.	$56,563.0
Cardinal Health, Inc.	34,122.0
AmerisourceBergen Corp.	33,656.2

Three Smallest Companies
Prestige Brands Holdings	$2,948.8
PharMerica Corp.	1,299.5
Natural Health Trends Corp.	148.1

S&P 500 Index	Geometric Mean	Arithmetic Mean	Standard Deviation
1-year	17.2	17.4	7.2
3-year	10.4	10.9	11.5
5-year	13.3	13.9	11.5

Return Ratios (%)

	Return on Assets Latest	5-Yr Avg	Return on Equity Latest	5-Yr Avg	Dividend Yield Latest	5-Yr Avg
Median (6)	4.3	3.7	20.8	17.5	2.0	1.5
SIC Composite (6)	4.1	3.3	6.6	4.3	2.0	1.8
Large Composite (–)	–	–	–	–	–	–
Small Composite (–)	–	–	–	–	–	–
High-Financial Risk (–)	–	–	–	–	–	–

Liquidity Ratio
	Current Ratio Latest	5-Yr Avg
	1.7	1.6
	1.0	1.1

Profitability Ratio (%)
	Operating Margin Latest	5-Yr Avg
	2.8	3.1
	1.8	1.8

Growth Rates (%)
	Long-term EPS Analyst Estimates
	8.9
	8.7

Betas (Levered)

	Raw (OLS)	Blume Adjusted	Peer Group	Vasicek Adjusted	Sum	Downside
Median	1.12	1.08	1.01	1.06	1.60	1.68
SIC Composite	0.96	0.98	1.01	0.97	1.38	1.19
Large Composite	–	–	–	–	–	–
Small Composite	–	–	–	–	–	–
High Financial Risk	–	–	–	–	–	–

Betas (Unlevered)

	Raw (OLS)	Blume Adjusted	Peer Group	Vasicek Adjusted	Sum	Downside
Median	0.85	0.83	0.82	0.82	1.22	1.27
SIC Composite	0.78	0.80	0.82	0.79	1.12	0.96
Large Composite	–	–	–	–	–	–
Small Composite	–	–	–	–	–	–
High Financial Risk	–	–	–	–	–	–

Equity Valuation Multiples

	Price/Sales Latest	5-Yr Avg	Price/Earnings Latest	5-Yr Avg	Market/Book Latest	5-Yr Avg
Median	0.3	0.3	15.6	24.5	2.9	3.6
SIC Composite	0.2	0.2	15.1	23.4	3.1	4.0
Large Composite	–	–	–	–	–	–
Small Composite	–	–	–	–	–	–
High Financial Risk	–	–	–	–	–	–

Enterprise Valuation (EV) Multiples

	EV/Sales Latest	5-Yr Avg	EV/EBITDA Latest	5-Yr Avg
Median	0.4	0.4	9.1	10.5
SIC Composite	0.2	0.2	9.1	11.3
Large Composite	–	–	–	–
Small Composite	–	–	–	–
High Financial Risk	–	–	–	–

Enterprise Valuation SIC Composite
- EV/Sales: Latest 0.2, 5-Yr Avg 0.2
- EV/EBITDA: Latest 9.1, 5-Yr Avg 11.3

Fama-French (F-F) 5-Factor Model

	F-F Beta	SMB Premium	HML Premium	RMW Premium	CMA Premium
Median	0.9	2.7	-4.4	0.9	4.2
SIC Composite	0.9	1.8	-3.6	-1.0	2.7
Large Composite	–	–	–	–	–
Small Composite	–	–	–	–	–
High Financial Risk	–	–	–	–	–

Leverage Ratios (%)

	Debt/MV Equity Latest	5-Yr Avg	Debt/Total Capital Latest	5-Yr Avg
Median	24.6	20.0	19.8	16.7
SIC Composite	25.2	20.5	20.1	17.0

Cost of Debt
	Cost of Debt (%) Latest
Median	4.8
SIC Composite	4.7

Capital Structure
SIC Composite (%) Latest
- D/TC: 20.1
- E/TC: 79.9

Cost of Equity Capital (%)

	CRSP Deciles CAPM	CAPM +Size Prem	Build-Up	Risk Premium Report CAPM +Size Prem	Build-Up	Discounted Cash Flow 1-Stage	3-Stage	Fama-French 5-Factor Model
Median	9.3	10.4	10.1	14.8	11.9	11.3	10.4	11.6
SIC Composite	8.8	9.1	9.3	12.6	10.3	9.9	11.7	8.2
Large Composite	–	–	–	–	–	–	–	–
Small Composite	–	–	–	–	–	–	–	–
High Financial Risk	–	–	–	–	–	–	–	–

Cost of Equity Capital (%) SIC Composite
- Avg CRSP: 9.2
- Avg RPR: 11.5
- 1-Stage: 9.9
- 3-Stage: 11.7
- 5-Factor Model: 8.2

Weighted Average Cost of Capital (WACC) (%)

	CRSP Deciles CAPM	CAPM +Size Prem	Build-Up	Risk Premium Report CAPM +Size Prem	Build-Up	Discounted Cash Flow 1-Stage	3-Stage	Fama-French 5-Factor Model
Median	8.3	9.0	8.9	12.2	10.1	9.8	9.1	10.2
SIC Composite	7.9	8.0	8.2	10.9	9.1	8.7	10.2	7.4
Large Composite	–	–	–	–	–	–	–	–
Small Composite	–	–	–	–	–	–	–	–
High Financial Risk	–	–	–	–	–	–	–	–

WACC (%) SIC Composite
Low 7.4 — High 10.9
▲ Average 8.9   ◆ Median 8.7

© 2017 Duff & Phelps. All Rights Reserved. Duff & Phelps has used the utmost care in compiling the data presented herein, but cannot guarantee the accuracy, completeness, or timeliness of the information.

Data Updated Through March 31, 2017

514

Number of Companies: 5
Groceries and Related Products

Industry Description
Establishment primarily engaged in the wholesale distribution of a general line of groceries; packaged frozen foods; dairy products, except dried or canned; poultry and poultry products; confectionery; fish and seafood's; meats and meat products; fresh fruits and vegetables; and groceries and related products, not elsewhere classified.

Sales (in millions)

Three Largest Companies
Sysco Corp.	$50,366.9
United Natural Foods, Inc.	8,470.3
SpartanNash Co.	7,734.6

Three Smallest Companies
SpartanNash Co.	$7,734.6
The Chefs' Warehouse, Inc.	1,192.9
Coffee Holding Co. Inc.	78.9

Annualized Monthly Performance Statistics (%)

Industry	Geometric Mean	Arithmetic Mean	Standard Deviation
1-year	12.2	13.7	19.7
3-year	12.3	13.5	17.3
5-year	13.1	14.2	15.8

S&P 500 Index	Geometric Mean	Arithmetic Mean	Standard Deviation
1-year	17.2	17.4	7.2
3-year	10.4	10.9	11.5
5-year	13.3	13.9	11.5

Total Assets (in millions)

Three Largest Companies
Sysco Corp.	$16,721.8
United Natural Foods, Inc.	2,852.2
SpartanNash Co.	1,930.3

Three Smallest Companies
SpartanNash Co.	$1,930.3
The Chefs' Warehouse, Inc.	633.5
Coffee Holding Co. Inc.	37.0

Return Ratios (%)

	Return on Assets Latest	5-Yr Avg	Return on Equity Latest	5-Yr Avg	Dividend Yield Latest	5-Yr Avg
Median (5)	4.7	3.7	8.2	9.6	0.0	0.5
SIC Composite (5)	5.1	5.9	3.6	4.2	1.7	2.6
Large Composite (–)	–	–	–	–	–	–
Small Composite (–)	–	–	–	–	–	–
High-Financial Risk (–)	–	–	–	–	–	–

Liquidity Ratio

	Current Ratio Latest	5-Yr Avg
Median (5)	2.5	2.4
SIC Composite (5)	2.3	1.7
Large Composite	–	–
Small Composite	–	–
High-Financial Risk	–	–

Profitability Ratio (%)

	Operating Margin Latest	5-Yr Avg
Median	3.2	3.0
SIC Composite	3.6	3.6
Large Composite	–	–
Small Composite	–	–
High-Financial Risk	–	–

Growth Rates (%)

	Long-term EPS Analyst Estimates
Median	11.2
SIC Composite	11.1
Large Composite	–
Small Composite	–
High-Financial Risk	–

Betas (Levered)

	Raw (OLS)	Blume Adjusted	Peer Group	Vasicek Adjusted	Sum	Downside
Median	1.19	1.13	1.01	1.06	0.74	1.50
SIC Composite	0.64	0.78	1.01	0.70	0.31	0.75
Large Composite	–	–	–	–	–	–
Small Composite	–	–	–	–	–	–
High Financial Risk	–	–	–	–	–	–

Betas (Unlevered)

	Raw (OLS)	Blume Adjusted	Peer Group	Vasicek Adjusted	Sum	Downside
Median	0.87	0.86	0.85	0.86	0.66	1.22
SIC Composite	0.53	0.64	0.82	0.58	0.27	0.62
Large Composite	–	–	–	–	–	–
Small Composite	–	–	–	–	–	–
High Financial Risk	–	–	–	–	–	–

Equity Valuation Multiples

	Price/Sales Latest	5-Yr Avg	Price/Earnings Latest	5-Yr Avg	Market/Book Latest	5-Yr Avg
Median	0.3	0.4	23.0	24.0	1.4	2.1
SIC Composite	0.5	0.4	28.1	23.9	5.1	3.7
Large Composite	–	–	–	–	–	–
Small Composite	–	–	–	–	–	–
High Financial Risk	–	–	–	–	–	–

Enterprise Valuation (EV) Multiples

	EV/Sales Latest	5-Yr Avg	EV/EBITDA Latest	5-Yr Avg
Median	0.4	0.5	9.1	11.2
SIC Composite	0.5	0.5	11.7	10.6
Large Composite	–	–	–	–
Small Composite	–	–	–	–
High Financial Risk	–	–	–	–

Enterprise Valuation SIC Composite
- EV/Sales: Latest 0.5, 5-Yr Avg 0.5
- EV/EBITDA: Latest 11.7, 5-Yr Avg 10.6

Fama-French (F-F) 5-Factor Model

	F-F Beta	SMB Premium	HML Premium	RMW Premium	CMA Premium
Median	1.2	6.3	0.6	6.9	1.2
SIC Composite	0.6	2.3	-0.1	2.6	3.5
Large Composite	–	–	–	–	–
Small Composite	–	–	–	–	–
High Financial Risk	–	–	–	–	–

Leverage Ratios (%)

	Debt/MV Equity Latest	5-Yr Avg	Debt/Total Capital Latest	5-Yr Avg
Median	27.4	20.9	21.5	17.3
SIC Composite	27.6	21.6	21.6	17.7
Large Composite	–	–	–	–
Small Composite	–	–	–	–
High Financial Risk	–	–	–	–

Cost of Debt

	Cost of Debt (%) Latest
Median	7.1
SIC Composite	5.2
Large Composite	–
Small Composite	–
High Financial Risk	–

Capital Structure

SIC Composite (%) Latest
- D/TC: 21.6
- E/TC: 78.4

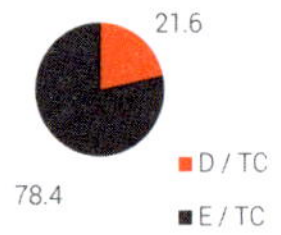

Cost of Equity Capital (%)

	CRSP Deciles CAPM	CAPM +Size Prem	Build-Up	Risk Premium Report CAPM	CAPM +Size Prem	Build-Up	Discounted Cash Flow 1-Stage	3-Stage	Fama-French 5-Factor Model
Median	9.3	11.2	10.8	11.3		13.9	11.2	9.8	24.8
SIC Composite	7.4	7.6	9.3	7.4		11.2	13.1	10.0	15.2
Large Composite	–	–	–	–		–	–	–	–
Small Composite	–	–	–	–		–	–	–	–
High Financial Risk	–	–	–	–		–	–	–	–

Cost of Equity Capital (%) SIC Composite
- Avg CRSP: 8.4
- Avg RPR: 9.3
- 1-Stage: 13.1
- 3-Stage: 10.0
- 5-Factor Model: 15.2

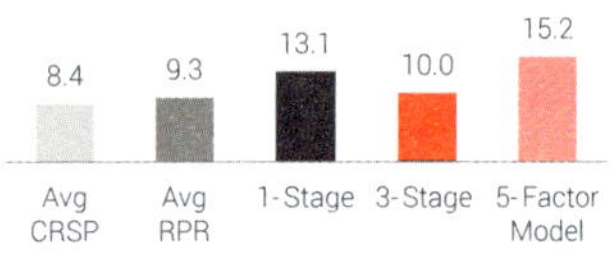

Weighted Average Cost of Capital (WACC) (%)

	CRSP Deciles CAPM	CAPM +Size Prem	Build-Up	Risk Premium Report CAPM	CAPM +Size Prem	Build-Up	Discounted Cash Flow 1-Stage	3-Stage	Fama-French 5-Factor Model
Median	8.2	9.6	9.4	9.8		11.5	9.5	8.6	20.0
SIC Composite	6.5	6.7	8.0	6.5		9.5	11.0	8.6	12.7
Large Composite	–	–	–	–		–	–	–	–
Small Composite	–	–	–	–		–	–	–	–
High Financial Risk	–	–	–	–		–	–	–	–

WACC (%) SIC Composite
- Low: 6.5
- High: 12.7
- Average: 9.0
- Median: 8.6

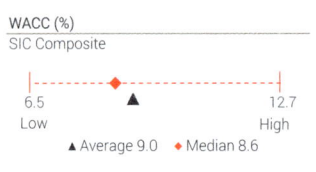

© 2017 Duff & Phelps. All Rights Reserved. Duff & Phelps has used the utmost care in compiling the data presented herein, but cannot guarantee the accuracy, completeness, or timeliness of the information.

Data Updated Through March 31, 2017

517

Number of Companies: 7
Petroleum and Petroleum Products

Industry Description
Establishments primarily engaged in the wholesale distribution of petroleum bulk stations and terminals; petroleum and petroleum products wholesalers.

Sales (in millions)

Three Largest Companies
World Fuel Services Corp.	$27,015.8
Plains All American Pipeline LP	20,182.0
Global Partners LP	8,239.6

Three Smallest Companies
Genesis Energy, L.P.	$1,712.5
SemGroup Corporation	1,332.2
Martin Midstream Partners LP	827.4

Total Assets (in millions)

Three Largest Companies
Plains All American Pipeline LP	$24,210.0
Genesis Energy, L.P.	5,702.6
World Fuel Services Corp.	5,412.6

Three Smallest Companies
Global Partners LP	$2,564.0
Martin Midstream Partners LP	1,246.4
Adams Resources & Energy Inc.	243.2

Annualized Monthly Performance Statistics (%)

Industry	Geometric Mean	Arithmetic Mean	Standard Deviation	S&P 500 Index	Geometric Mean	Arithmetic Mean	Standard Deviation
1-year	35.9	37.7	23.5	1-year	17.2	17.4	7.2
3-year	-10.1	-7.8	21.4	3-year	10.4	10.9	11.5
5-year	2.6	4.8	21.3	5-year	13.3	13.9	11.5

Return Ratios (%)

	Return on Assets Latest	5-Yr Avg	Return on Equity Latest	5-Yr Avg	Dividend Yield Latest	5-Yr Avg
Median (7)	2.0	4.1	5.4	10.4	7.8	5.6
SIC Composite (7)	1.9	4.1	2.5	5.5	7.1	5.1
Large Composite (–)	–	–	–	–	–	–
Small Composite (–)	–	–	–	–	–	–
High-Financial Risk (–)	–	–	–	–	–	–

Liquidity Ratio

	Current Ratio Latest	5-Yr Avg
Median (7)	1.4	1.4
SIC Composite (7)	1.2	1.2
Large Composite	–	–
Small Composite	–	–
High-Financial Risk	–	–

Profitability Ratio (%)

	Operating Margin Latest	5-Yr Avg
Median	4.7	3.1
SIC Composite	2.6	2.3
Large Composite	–	–
Small Composite	–	–
High-Financial Risk	–	–

Growth Rates (%)

	Long-term EPS Analyst Estimates
Median	12.0
SIC Composite	22.4
Large Composite	–
Small Composite	–
High-Financial Risk	–

Betas (Levered)

	Raw (OLS)	Blume Adjusted	Peer Group	Vasicek Adjusted	Sum	Downside
Median	1.17	1.12	1.01	1.12	1.77	1.64
SIC Composite	1.08	1.06	1.01	1.06	1.24	1.34
Large Composite	–	–	–	–	–	–
Small Composite	–	–	–	–	–	–
High Financial Risk	–	–	–	–	–	–

Betas (Unlevered)

	Raw (OLS)	Blume Adjusted	Peer Group	Vasicek Adjusted	Sum	Downside
Median	0.83	0.77	0.69	0.75	1.12	0.96
SIC Composite	0.72	0.70	0.67	0.71	0.81	0.87
Large Composite	–	–	–	–	–	–
Small Composite	–	–	–	–	–	–
High Financial Risk	–	–	–	–	–	–

Equity Valuation Multiples

	Price/Sales Latest	5-Yr Avg	Price/Earnings Latest	5-Yr Avg	Market/Book Latest	5-Yr Avg
Median	0.9	0.5	35.0	24.2	1.6	1.8
SIC Composite	0.5	0.3	46.4	18.5	2.2	2.1
Large Composite	–	–	–	–	–	–
Small Composite	–	–	–	–	–	–
High Financial Risk	–	–	–	–	–	–

Enterprise Valuation (EV) Multiples

	EV/Sales Latest	5-Yr Avg	EV/EBITDA Latest	5-Yr Avg
Median	1.7	0.8	10.6	11.4
SIC Composite	0.8	0.4	15.9	13.0
Large Composite	–	–	–	–
Small Composite	–	–	–	–
High Financial Risk	–	–	–	–

Enterprise Valuation SIC Composite
- Latest: EV/Sales 0.8, EV/EBITDA 15.9
- 5-Yr Avg: EV/Sales 0.4, EV/EBITDA 13.0

Fama-French (F-F) 5-Factor Model

	F-F Beta	SMB Premium	HML Premium	RMW Premium	CMA Premium
Median	1.0	-0.7	-2.4	-2.6	9.3
SIC Composite	1.1	0.0	-1.3	-1.8	5.6
Large Composite	–	–	–	–	–
Small Composite	–	–	–	–	–
High Financial Risk	–	–	–	–	–

Leverage Ratios (%)

	Debt/MV Equity Latest	5-Yr Avg	Debt/Total Capital Latest	5-Yr Avg
Median	63.1	49.0	38.7	32.9
SIC Composite	66.7	55.1	40.0	35.5
Large Composite	–	–	–	–
Small Composite	–	–	–	–
High Financial Risk	–	–	–	–

Cost of Debt

	Cost of Debt (%) Latest
Median	7.1
SIC Composite	5.5
Large Composite	–
Small Composite	–
High Financial Risk	–

Capital Structure

SIC Composite (%) Latest: D/TC 40.0, E/TC 60.0

Cost of Equity Capital (%)

	CRSP Deciles CAPM	CAPM +Size Prem	Build-Up	Risk Premium Report CAPM +Size Prem	Build-Up	Discounted Cash Flow 1-Stage	3-Stage	Fama-French 5-Factor Model
Median	9.6	11.2	10.7	16.4	13.3	14.6	10.3	12.5
SIC Composite	9.3	10.2	10.0	12.9	11.7	29.2	10.7	11.9
Large Composite	–	–	–	–	–	–	–	–
Small Composite	–	–	–	–	–	–	–	–
High Financial Risk	–	–	–	–	–	–	–	–

Cost of Equity Capital (%) SIC Composite: Avg CRSP 10.1, Avg RPR 12.3, 1-Stage 29.2, 3-Stage 10.7, 5-Factor Model 11.9

Weighted Average Cost of Capital (WACC) (%)

	CRSP Deciles CAPM	CAPM +Size Prem	Build-Up	Risk Premium Report CAPM +Size Prem	Build-Up	Discounted Cash Flow 1-Stage	3-Stage	Fama-French 5-Factor Model
Median	7.4	8.2	8.0	10.8	9.3	11.5	8.0	9.6
SIC Composite	7.8	8.3	8.1	9.9	9.2	19.7	8.6	9.3
Large Composite	–	–	–	–	–	–	–	–
Small Composite	–	–	–	–	–	–	–	–
High Financial Risk	–	–	–	–	–	–	–	–

WACC (%) SIC Composite: Low 8.1, High 19.7, Average 10.4, Median 9.2

© 2017 Duff & Phelps. All Rights Reserved. Duff & Phelps has used the utmost care in compiling the data presented herein, but cannot guarantee the accuracy, completeness, or timeliness of the information.

Division G: Retail Trade

This division includes establishments engaged in selling merchandise for personal or household consumption and rendering services incidental to the sale of the goods. Major groups between "52" and "59" are in this division.

Data Updated Through March 31, 2017

52

Number of Companies: 5
Building Materials, Hardware, Garden Supply, and Mobile Home Dealers

Industry Description
This major group includes retail establishments primarily engaged in selling lumber and other building materials, paint, glass, wallpaper, nursery stock, lawn and garden supplies, and mobile homes.

Sales (in millions)

Three Largest Companies
Home Depot, Inc.	$94,595.0
Lowe's Companies Inc.	65,017.0
Tractor Supply Co.	6,779.6

Three Smallest Companies
Tractor Supply Co.	$6,779.6
Fastenal Co.	3,962.0
Lumber Liquidators Holdings, Inc.	960.6

Total Assets (in millions)

Three Largest Companies
Home Depot, Inc.	$42,966.0
Lowe's Companies Inc.	34,408.0
Tractor Supply Co.	2,674.9

Three Smallest Companies
Tractor Supply Co.	$2,674.9
Fastenal Co.	2,668.9
Lumber Liquidators Holdings, Inc.	488.6

Annualized Monthly Performance Statistics (%)

Industry	Geometric Mean	Arithmetic Mean	Standard Deviation	S&P 500 Index	Geometric Mean	Arithmetic Mean	Standard Deviation
1-year	10.1	11.3	17.0	1-year	17.2	17.4	7.2
3-year	21.0	22.5	19.2	3-year	10.4	10.9	11.5
5-year	22.5	24.0	19.2	5-year	13.3	13.9	11.5

Return Ratios (%)

	Return on Assets Latest	5-Yr Avg	Return on Equity Latest	5-Yr Avg	Dividend Yield Latest	5-Yr Avg
Median (5)	17.3	15.2	30.7	26.3	1.8	1.6
SIC Composite (5)	14.3	12.2	4.4	4.6	2.1	1.9
Large Composite (–)	–	–	–	–	–	–
Small Composite (–)	–	–	–	–	–	–
High-Financial Risk (–)	–	–	–	–	–	–

Liquidity Ratio

	Current Ratio Latest	5-Yr Avg
Median (5)	1.9	2.1
SIC Composite (5)	1.2	1.3
Large Composite (–)	–	–
Small Composite (–)	–	–
High-Financial Risk (–)	–	–

Profitability Ratio (%)

	Operating Margin Latest	5-Yr Avg
Median (5)	10.2	10.1
SIC Composite (5)	12.4	11.1
Large Composite (–)	–	–
Small Composite (–)	–	–
High-Financial Risk (–)	–	–

Growth Rates (%)

	Long-term EPS Analyst Estimates
Median (5)	13.3
SIC Composite (5)	12.5
Large Composite (–)	–
Small Composite (–)	–
High-Financial Risk (–)	–

Betas (Levered)

	Raw (OLS)	Blume Adjusted	Peer Group	Vasicek Adjusted	Sum	Downside
Median	1.18	1.12	–	–	1.16	1.23
SIC Composite	1.11	1.08	–	–	1.09	1.10
Large Composite	–	–	–	–	–	–
Small Composite	–	–	–	–	–	–
High Financial Risk	–	–	–	–	–	–

Betas (Unlevered)

	Raw (OLS)	Blume Adjusted	Peer Group	Vasicek Adjusted	Sum	Downside
Median	1.00	0.95	–	–	1.00	1.20
SIC Composite	0.97	0.94	–	–	0.95	0.97
Large Composite	–	–	–	–	–	–
Small Composite	–	–	–	–	–	–
High Financial Risk	–	–	–	–	–	–

Equity Valuation Multiples

	Price/Sales Latest	5-Yr Avg	Price/Earnings Latest	5-Yr Avg	Market/Book Latest	5-Yr Avg
Median	1.3	1.5	23.0	26.5	7.4	7.2
SIC Composite	1.6	1.4	22.9	21.8	–	8.7
Large Composite	–	–	–	–	–	–
Small Composite	–	–	–	–	–	–
High Financial Risk	–	–	–	–	–	–

Enterprise Valuation (EV) Multiples

	EV/Sales Latest	5-Yr Avg	EV/EBITDA Latest	5-Yr Avg
Median	1.4	1.7	11.1	14.0
SIC Composite	1.8	1.6	12.5	11.7
Large Composite	–	–	–	–
Small Composite	–	–	–	–
High Financial Risk	–	–	–	–

Enterprise Valuation SIC Composite
Latest: EV/Sales 1.8, EV/EBITDA 12.5
5-Yr Avg: EV/Sales 1.6, EV/EBITDA 11.7

Fama-French (F-F) 5-Factor Model

	F-F Beta	SMB Premium	HML Premium	RMW Premium	CMA Premium
Median	0.9	2.1	3.2	0.7	2.1
SIC Composite	1.1	1.3	-0.8	-0.6	0.5
Large Composite	–	–	–	–	–
Small Composite	–	–	–	–	–
High Financial Risk	–	–	–	–	–

Leverage Ratios (%)

	Debt/MV Equity Latest	5-Yr Avg	Debt/Total Capital Latest	5-Yr Avg
Median	6.7	1.3	6.3	1.3
SIC Composite	14.7	14.2	12.8	12.4
Large Composite	–	–	–	–
Small Composite	–	–	–	–
High Financial Risk	–	–	–	–

Cost of Debt

	Cost of Debt (%) Latest
Median	6.1
SIC Composite	4.1
Large Composite	–
Small Composite	–
High Financial Risk	–

Capital Structure

SIC Composite (%) Latest
D/TC: 12.8
E/TC: 87.2

Cost of Equity Capital (%)

	CAPM	CRSP Deciles CAPM +Size Prem	Build-Up	Risk Premium Report CAPM +Size Prem	Build-Up	Discounted Cash Flow 1-Stage	3-Stage	Fama-French 5-Factor Model
Median	–	–	9.6	11.8	12.1	14.9	11.0	16.6
SIC Composite	–	–	9.1	10.9	10.0	14.7	11.3	9.7
Large Composite	–	–	–	–	–	–	–	–
Small Composite	–	–	–	–	–	–	–	–
High Financial Risk	–	–	–	–	–	–	–	–

Cost of Equity Capital (%) SIC Composite
Avg CRSP: 9.1, Avg RPR: 10.5, 1-Stage: 14.7, 3-Stage: 11.3, 5-Factor Model: 9.7

Weighted Average Cost of Capital (WACC) (%)

	CAPM	CRSP Deciles CAPM +Size Prem	Build-Up	Risk Premium Report CAPM +Size Prem	Build-Up	Discounted Cash Flow 1-Stage	3-Stage	Fama-French 5-Factor Model
Median	–	–	9.5	10.4	11.9	14.5	10.0	16.2
SIC Composite	–	–	8.3	9.9	9.1	13.2	10.2	8.8
Large Composite	–	–	–	–	–	–	–	–
Small Composite	–	–	–	–	–	–	–	–
High Financial Risk	–	–	–	–	–	–	–	–

WACC (%) SIC Composite
Low: 8.3, High: 13.2
Average 9.9, Median 9.5

© 2017 Duff & Phelps. All Rights Reserved. Duff & Phelps has used the utmost care in compiling the data presented herein, but cannot guarantee the accuracy, completeness, or timeliness of the information.

Data Updated Through March 31, 2017

53

Number of Companies: 11
General Merchandise Stores

Industry Description
This major group includes retail stores which sell a number of lines of merchandise, such as dry goods, apparel and accessories, furniture and home furnishings, small wares, hardware, and food.

Sales (in millions)

Three Largest Companies
Wal-Mart Stores Inc.	$479,962.0
Costco Wholesale Corp.	118,719.0
Target Corp.	69,495.0

Three Smallest Companies
Big Lots Inc.	$5,200.4
PriceSmart Inc.	2,904.8
Fred's Inc.	2,150.7

Total Assets (in millions)

Three Largest Companies
Wal-Mart Stores Inc.	$199,581.0
Target Corp.	37,431.0
Costco Wholesale Corp.	33,163.0

Three Smallest Companies
Big Lots Inc.	$1,607.7
PriceSmart Inc.	1,096.7
Fred's Inc.	730.5

Annualized Monthly Performance Statistics (%)

Industry	Geometric Mean	Arithmetic Mean	Standard Deviation	S&P 500 Index	Geometric Mean	Arithmetic Mean	Standard Deviation
1-year	-0.6	0.0	11.4	1-year	17.2	17.4	7.2
3-year	2.8	3.7	13.8	3-year	10.4	10.9	11.5
5-year	6.9	7.8	13.9	5-year	13.3	13.9	11.5

Return Ratios (%)

	Return on Assets Latest	5-Yr Avg	Return on Equity Latest	5-Yr Avg	Dividend Yield Latest	5-Yr Avg
Median (11)	6.9	7.1	14.7	17.5	1.5	2.0
SIC Composite (11)	6.9	7.4	6.1	6.1	2.4	2.5
Large Composite (3)	7.3	7.5	6.0	6.2	2.6	2.7
Small Composite (3)	6.8	7.4	4.3	4.5	1.2	0.9
High-Financial Risk (−)	−	−	−	−	−	−

Liquidity Ratio

	Current Ratio Latest	5-Yr Avg
Median	1.4	1.6
SIC Composite	1.0	1.0
Large Composite	0.9	1.0
Small Composite	1.5	1.7
High Financial Risk	−	−

Profitability Ratio (%)

	Operating Margin Latest	5-Yr Avg
Median	5.3	6.6
SIC Composite	4.9	5.4
Large Composite	4.6	5.0
Small Composite	4.0	4.1
High Financial Risk	−	−

Growth Rates (%)

	Long-term EPS Analyst Estimates
Median	8.6
SIC Composite	5.9
Large Composite	5.1
Small Composite	21.6
High Financial Risk	−

Betas (Levered)

	Raw (OLS)	Blume Adjusted	Peer Group	Vasicek Adjusted	Sum	Downside
Median	0.86	0.92	0.42	0.66	0.49	1.11
SIC Composite	0.42	0.64	0.42	0.42	0.29	0.64
Large Composite	0.32	0.58	0.42	0.34	0.22	0.62
Small Composite	1.18	1.12	0.42	1.01	1.26	1.27
High Financial Risk	−	−	−	−	−	−

Betas (Unlevered)

	Raw (OLS)	Blume Adjusted	Peer Group	Vasicek Adjusted	Sum	Downside
Median	0.72	0.69	0.37	0.54	0.38	0.80
SIC Composite	0.35	0.52	0.35	0.35	0.25	0.53
Large Composite	0.27	0.48	0.35	0.28	0.18	0.52
Small Composite	1.13	1.08	0.41	0.97	1.21	1.22
High Financial Risk	−	−	−	−	−	−

Equity Valuation Multiples

	Price/Sales Latest	5-Yr Avg	Price/Earnings Latest	5-Yr Avg	Market/Book Latest	5-Yr Avg
Median	0.4	0.6	15.1	15.9	2.6	2.8
SIC Composite	0.5	0.5	16.5	16.3	2.8	3.0
Large Composite	0.5	0.5	16.5	16.2	3.0	3.1
Small Composite	0.5	0.5	23.3	22.1	3.2	3.1
High Financial Risk	−	−	−	−	−	−

Enterprise Valuation (EV) Multiples

	EV/Sales Latest	5-Yr Avg	EV/EBITDA Latest	5-Yr Avg
Median	0.6	0.8	7.8	7.9
SIC Composite	0.6	0.6	8.1	8.2
Large Composite	0.6	0.6	8.2	8.3
Small Composite	0.5	0.5	8.9	9.2
High Financial Risk	−	−	−	−

Enterprise Valuation SIC Composite
- EV/Sales: Latest 0.6, 5-Yr Avg 0.6
- EV/EBITDA: Latest 8.1, 5-Yr Avg 8.2

Fama-French (F-F) 5-Factor Model

Fama-French (F-F) Components

	F-F Beta	SMB Premium	HML Premium	RMW Premium	CMA Premium
Median	1.2	0.7	2.8	0.9	2.5
SIC Composite	0.4	0.2	-3.5	1.5	5.6
Large Composite	0.4	-0.1	-3.7	1.4	1.9
Small Composite	1.2	1.7	1.0	3.3	0.3
High Financial Risk	−	−	−	−	−

Leverage Ratios (%)

	Debt/MV Equity Latest	5-Yr Avg	Debt/Total Capital Latest	5-Yr Avg
Median	22.5	21.5	18.4	17.7
SIC Composite	23.4	22.4	18.9	18.3
Large Composite	20.9	21.4	17.3	17.6
Small Composite	4.9	4.0	4.7	3.8
High Financial Risk	−	−	−	−

Cost of Debt

	Cost of Debt (%) Latest
Median	4.8
SIC Composite	4.2
Large Composite	3.9
Small Composite	5.8
High Financial Risk	−

Capital Structure

SIC Composite (%) Latest
- D/TC: 18.9
- E/TC: 81.1

Cost of Equity Capital (%)

	CRSP Deciles CAPM	CAPM +Size Prem	Build-Up	Risk Premium Report CAPM +Size Prem	Build-Up	Discounted Cash Flow 1-Stage	3-Stage	Fama-French 5-Factor Model
Median	7.1	8.2	6.7	8.4	11.3	12.1	11.4	16.8
SIC Composite	5.8	5.9	5.9	6.2	9.4	8.5	10.6	9.6
Large Composite	5.4	5.4	5.8	5.5	9.1	7.8	9.9	5.4
Small Composite	9.1	10.7	7.5	14.3	13.6	23.0	16.8	16.5
High Financial Risk	−	−	−	−	−	−	−	−

Cost of Equity Capital (%) SIC Composite
- Avg CRSP: 5.9
- Avg RPR: 7.8
- 1-Stage: 8.5
- 3-Stage: 10.6
- 5-Factor Model: 9.6

Weighted Average Cost of Capital (WACC) (%)

	CRSP Deciles CAPM	CAPM +Size Prem	Build-Up	Risk Premium Report CAPM +Size Prem	Build-Up	Discounted Cash Flow 1-Stage	3-Stage	Fama-French 5-Factor Model
Median	6.1	6.9	5.8	7.5	9.4	10.3	9.9	12.1
SIC Composite	5.2	5.3	5.3	5.5	8.2	7.4	9.2	8.3
Large Composite	4.9	4.9	5.2	5.0	7.9	6.9	8.6	4.9
Small Composite	8.9	10.5	7.4	13.9	13.2	22.2	16.3	16.0
High Financial Risk	−	−	−	−	−	−	−	−

WACC (%) SIC Composite
- Low: 5.3
- High: 9.2
- Average: 7.0
- Median: 7.4

© 2017 Duff & Phelps. All Rights Reserved. Duff & Phelps has used the utmost care in compiling the data presented herein, but cannot guarantee the accuracy, completeness, or timeliness of the information.

Data Updated Through March 31, 2017

533

Number of Companies: 7
Variety Stores

Industry Description
Establishments primarily engaged in the retail sale of a variety of merchandise in the low and popular price ranges.

Sales (in millions)

Three Largest Companies
Wal-Mart Stores Inc.	$479,962.0
Target Corp.	69,495.0
Dollar General Corp.	21,986.6

Three Smallest Companies
Big Lots Inc.	$5,200.4
PriceSmart Inc.	2,904.8
Fred's Inc.	2,150.7

Total Assets (in millions)

Three Largest Companies
Wal-Mart Stores Inc.	$199,581.0
Target Corp.	37,431.0
Dollar Tree Inc.	15,701.6

Three Smallest Companies
Big Lots Inc.	$1,607.7
PriceSmart Inc.	1,096.7
Fred's Inc.	730.5

Annualized Monthly Performance Statistics (%)

Industry	Geometric Mean	Arithmetic Mean	Standard Deviation		S&P 500 Index	Geometric Mean	Arithmetic Mean	Standard Deviation
1-year	-0.6	0.0	11.4		1-year	17.2	17.4	7.2
3-year	1.8	2.9	15.4		3-year	10.4	10.9	11.5
5-year	5.9	7.0	15.5		5-year	13.3	13.9	11.5

Return Ratios (%)

	Return on Assets Latest	5-Yr Avg	Return on Equity Latest	5-Yr Avg	Dividend Yield Latest	5-Yr Avg
Median (7)	7.3	8.7	17.3	18.4	1.4	0.9
SIC Composite (7)	7.4	7.7	6.7	6.5	2.6	2.4
Large Composite (–)	–	–	–	–	–	–
Small Composite (–)	–	–	–	–	–	–
High-Financial Risk (–)	–	–	–	–	–	–

Liquidity Ratio

	Current Ratio Latest	5-Yr Avg
Median (7)	1.4	1.6
SIC Composite (7)	1.0	1.0
Large Composite	–	–
Small Composite	–	–
High-Financial Risk	–	–

Profitability Ratio (%)

	Operating Margin Latest	5-Yr Avg
Median	5.3	5.3
SIC Composite	5.2	5.6
Large Composite	–	–
Small Composite	–	–
High-Financial Risk	–	–

Growth Rates (%)

	Long-term EPS Analyst Estimates
Median	10.9
SIC Composite	4.9
Large Composite	–
Small Composite	–
High-Financial Risk	–

Betas (Levered)

	Raw (OLS)	Blume Adjusted	Peer Group	Vasicek Adjusted	Sum	Downside
Median	0.83	0.90	0.42	0.70	0.27	0.92
SIC Composite	0.26	0.54	0.42	0.28	0.15	0.64
Large Composite	–	–	–	–	–	–
Small Composite	–	–	–	–	–	–
High Financial Risk	–	–	–	–	–	–

Betas (Unlevered)

	Raw (OLS)	Blume Adjusted	Peer Group	Vasicek Adjusted	Sum	Downside
Median	0.72	0.78	0.39	0.64	0.26	0.80
SIC Composite	0.22	0.44	0.34	0.23	0.13	0.52
Large Composite	–	–	–	–	–	–
Small Composite	–	–	–	–	–	–
High Financial Risk	–	–	–	–	–	–

Equity Valuation Multiples

	Price/Sales Latest	5-Yr Avg	Price/Earnings Latest	5-Yr Avg	Market/Book Latest	5-Yr Avg
Median	0.5	0.6	15.3	17.9	2.7	2.9
SIC Composite	0.5	0.5	15.0	15.5	2.7	2.9
Large Composite	–	–	–	–	–	–
Small Composite	–	–	–	–	–	–
High Financial Risk	–	–	–	–	–	–

Enterprise Valuation (EV) Multiples

	EV/Sales Latest	5-Yr Avg	EV/EBITDA Latest	5-Yr Avg
Median	0.6	0.8	9.1	10.1
SIC Composite	0.6	0.7	7.7	8.1
Large Composite	–	–	–	–
Small Composite	–	–	–	–
High Financial Risk	–	–	–	–

Enterprise Valuation SIC Composite

EV/Sales: Latest 0.6, 5-Yr Avg 0.7
EV/EBITDA: Latest 7.7, 5-Yr Avg 8.1

Fama-French (F-F) 5-Factor Model

Fama-French (F-F) Components

	F-F Beta	SMB Premium	HML Premium	RMW Premium	CMA Premium
Median	1.4	0.0	0.3	1.5	0.6
SIC Composite	0.3	0.2	-4.2	1.3	6.7
Large Composite	–	–	–	–	–
Small Composite	–	–	–	–	–
High Financial Risk	–	–	–	–	–

Leverage Ratios (%)

	Debt/MV Equity Latest	5-Yr Avg	Debt/Total Capital Latest	5-Yr Avg
Median	16.7	14.9	14.3	13.0
SIC Composite	24.5	23.0	19.7	18.7

Cost of Debt

	Cost of Debt (%) Latest
Median	4.8
SIC Composite	4.1

Capital Structure

SIC Composite (%) Latest
D/TC: 19.7
E/TC: 80.3

Cost of Equity Capital (%)

	CRSP Deciles CAPM	CAPM +Size Prem	Build-Up	Risk Premium Report CAPM +Size Prem	Build-Up	Discounted Cash Flow 1-Stage	3-Stage	Fama-French 5-Factor Model
Median	7.4	8.2	6.4	8.6	11.3	13.0	11.0	13.4
SIC Composite	5.0	5.1	5.9	5.3	9.2	7.6	10.6	9.0
Large Composite	–	–	–	–	–	–	–	–
Small Composite	–	–	–	–	–	–	–	–
High Financial Risk	–	–	–	–	–	–	–	–

Cost of Equity Capital (%) SIC Composite

Avg CRSP 5.5, Avg RPR 7.2, 1-Stage 7.6, 3-Stage 10.6, 5-Factor Model 9.0

Weighted Average Cost of Capital (WACC) (%)

	CRSP Deciles CAPM	CAPM +Size Prem	Build-Up	Risk Premium Report CAPM +Size Prem	Build-Up	Discounted Cash Flow 1-Stage	3-Stage	Fama-French 5-Factor Model
Median	6.9	7.4	5.9	7.4	9.9	11.3	9.3	12.7
SIC Composite	4.6	4.7	5.3	4.8	7.9	6.7	9.1	7.8
Large Composite	–	–	–	–	–	–	–	–
Small Composite	–	–	–	–	–	–	–	–
High Financial Risk	–	–	–	–	–	–	–	–

WACC (%) SIC Composite
Low 4.7, High 9.1
Average 6.6, Median 6.7

© 2017 Duff & Phelps. All Rights Reserved. Duff & Phelps has used the utmost care in compiling the data presented herein, but cannot guarantee the accuracy, completeness, or timeliness of the information.

Data Updated Through March 31, 2017

54

Number of Companies: 8
Food Stores

Industry Description
This major group includes retail stores primarily engaged in selling food for home preparation and consumption.

Sales (in millions)

Three Largest Companies
Kroger Co.	$115,337.0
Whole Foods Market, Inc.	15,724.0
Caseys General Stores, Inc.	7,121.3

Three Smallest Companies
GNC Holdings, Inc.	$2,540.0
Village Super Market	1,634.9
Vitamin Shoppe, Inc.	1,289.2

Total Assets (in millions)

Three Largest Companies
Kroger Co.	$36,505.0
Whole Foods Market, Inc.	6,341.0
Caseys General Stores, Inc.	2,726.1

Three Smallest Companies
Weis Markets Inc.	$1,431.3
Vitamin Shoppe, Inc.	734.2
Village Super Market	450.3

Annualized Monthly Performance Statistics (%)

Industry	Geometric Mean	Arithmetic Mean	Standard Deviation	S&P 500 Index	Geometric Mean	Arithmetic Mean	Standard Deviation
1-year	-17.1	-16.0	13.9	1-year	17.2	17.4	7.2
3-year	0.3	1.9	18.7	3-year	10.4	10.9	11.5
5-year	8.0	9.7	19.5	5-year	13.3	13.9	11.5

Return Ratios (%)

	Return on Assets Latest	5-Yr Avg	Return on Equity Latest	5-Yr Avg	Dividend Yield Latest	5-Yr Avg
Median (8)	5.6	6.0	10.0	12.6	1.8	1.6
SIC Composite (8)	5.0	6.1	5.8	5.4	1.6	1.5
Large Composite (–)	–	–	–	–	–	–
Small Composite (–)	–	–	–	–	–	–
High-Financial Risk (–)	–	–	–	–	–	–

Liquidity Ratio

	Current Ratio Latest	5-Yr Avg
	1.7	1.6
	0.9	0.9
	–	–
	–	–
	–	–

Profitability Ratio (%)

	Operating Margin Latest	5-Yr Avg
	4.4	3.8
	3.6	3.7
	–	–
	–	–
	–	–

Growth Rates (%)

	Long-term EPS Analyst Estimates
	4.2
	4.2
	–
	–
	–

Betas (Levered)

	Raw (OLS)	Blume Adjusted	Peer Group	Vasicek Adjusted	Sum	Downside
Median	0.67	0.80	0.82	0.80	0.58	1.07
SIC Composite	0.68	0.80	0.82	0.79	0.20	0.86
Large Composite	–	–	–	–	–	–
Small Composite	–	–	–	–	–	–
High Financial Risk	–	–	–	–	–	–

Betas (Unlevered)

	Raw (OLS)	Blume Adjusted	Peer Group	Vasicek Adjusted	Sum	Downside
Median	0.53	0.63	0.72	0.69	0.47	0.92
SIC Composite	0.52	0.60	0.61	0.59	0.18	0.64

Equity Valuation Multiples

	Price/Sales Latest	5-Yr Avg	Price/Earnings Latest	5-Yr Avg	Market/Book Latest	5-Yr Avg
Median	0.3	0.5	18.5	19.5	2.1	2.7
SIC Composite	0.3	0.4	17.2	18.5	2.8	3.4
Large Composite	–	–	–	–	–	–
Small Composite	–	–	–	–	–	–
High Financial Risk	–	–	–	–	–	–

Enterprise Valuation (EV) Multiples

	EV/Sales Latest	5-Yr Avg	EV/EBITDA Latest	5-Yr Avg
Median	0.5	0.5	7.0	8.1
SIC Composite	0.4	0.5	7.0	8.1

Enterprise Valuation SIC Composite
- EV/Sales: Latest 0.4, 5-Yr Avg 0.5
- EV/EBITDA: Latest 7.0, 5-Yr Avg 8.1

Fama-French (F-F) 5-Factor Model

	F-F Beta	SMB Premium	HML Premium	RMW Premium	CMA Premium
Median	0.6	2.8	0.4	1.4	-1.3
SIC Composite	0.7	1.0	-2.6	0.4	3.2

Leverage Ratios (%)

	Debt/MV Equity Latest	5-Yr Avg	Debt/Total Capital Latest	5-Yr Avg
Median	23.7	17.3	19.0	14.4
SIC Composite	41.4	29.4	29.3	22.7

Cost of Debt

	Cost of Debt (%) Latest
Median	6.1
SIC Composite	5.0

Capital Structure

SIC Composite (%) Latest
- D / TC: 29.3
- E / TC: 70.7

Cost of Equity Capital (%)

	CAPM	CRSP Deciles CAPM +Size Prem	Build-Up	Risk Premium Report CAPM +Size Prem	Build-Up	Discounted Cash Flow 1-Stage	3-Stage	Fama-French 5-Factor Model
Median	7.9	9.8	9.9	10.4	13.8	6.2	8.8	9.9
SIC Composite	7.8	8.3	8.5	6.6	11.1	5.8	9.0	9.2
Large Composite	–	–	–	–	–	–	–	–
Small Composite	–	–	–	–	–	–	–	–
High Financial Risk	–	–	–	–	–	–	–	–

Cost of Equity Capital (%) SIC Composite
- Avg CRSP: 8.4
- Avg RPR: 8.8
- 1-Stage: 5.8
- 3-Stage: 9.0
- 5-Factor Model: 9.2

Weighted Average Cost of Capital (WACC) (%)

	CAPM	CRSP Deciles CAPM +Size Prem	Build-Up	Risk Premium Report CAPM +Size Prem	Build-Up	Discounted Cash Flow 1-Stage	3-Stage	Fama-French 5-Factor Model
Median	7.5	8.3	8.5	9.2	11.3	6.2	7.4	8.4
SIC Composite	6.7	7.0	7.1	5.8	8.9	5.2	7.5	7.6
Large Composite	–	–	–	–	–	–	–	–
Small Composite	–	–	–	–	–	–	–	–
High Financial Risk	–	–	–	–	–	–	–	–

WACC (%) SIC Composite
- Low: 5.2
- High: 8.9
- Average: 7.0
- Median: 7.1

© 2017 Duff & Phelps. All Rights Reserved. Duff & Phelps has used the utmost care in compiling the data presented herein, but cannot guarantee the accuracy, completeness, or timeliness of the information.

Data Updated Through March 31, 2017

541

Number of Companies: 6
Grocery Stores

Industry Description
Stores, commonly known as supermarkets, food stores, and grocery stores, primarily engaged in the retail sale of all sorts of canned foods and dry goods, such as tea, coffee, spices, sugar, and flour; fresh fruits and vegetables; and fresh and prepared me

Sales (in millions)

Three Largest Companies
Kroger Co.	$115,337.0
Whole Foods Market, Inc.	15,724.0
Caseys General Stores, Inc.	7,121.3

Three Smallest Companies
Ingles Markets, Inc.	$3,795.0
Weis Markets Inc.	3,136.7
Village Super Market	1,634.9

Total Assets (in millions)

Three Largest Companies
Kroger Co.	$36,505.0
Whole Foods Market, Inc.	6,341.0
Caseys General Stores, Inc.	2,726.1

Three Smallest Companies
Ingles Markets, Inc.	$1,686.5
Weis Markets Inc.	1,431.3
Village Super Market	450.3

Annualized Monthly Performance Statistics (%)

Industry	Geometric Mean	Arithmetic Mean	Standard Deviation
1-year	-14.3	-13.3	14.5
3-year	3.0	4.7	19.4
5-year	10.2	12.0	20.4

S&P 500 Index	Geometric Mean	Arithmetic Mean	Standard Deviation
1-year	17.2	17.4	7.2
3-year	10.4	10.9	11.5
5-year	13.3	13.9	11.5

Return Ratios (%)

	Return on Assets Latest	5-Yr Avg	Return on Equity Latest	5-Yr Avg	Dividend Yield Latest	5-Yr Avg
Median (6)	6.1	6.0	12.4	12.1	1.8	2.6
SIC Composite (6)	5.8	6.1	6.5	5.5	1.5	1.5
Large Composite (–)	–	–	–	–	–	–
Small Composite (–)	–	–	–	–	–	–
High-Financial Risk (–)	–	–	–	–	–	–

Liquidity Ratio

	Current Ratio Latest	5-Yr Avg
Median (6)	1.5	1.5
SIC Composite (6)	0.9	0.9

Profitability Ratio (%)

	Operating Margin Latest	5-Yr Avg
Median (6)	3.3	3.5
SIC Composite (6)	3.5	3.4

Growth Rates (%)

	Long-term EPS Analyst Estimates
Median (6)	4.2
SIC Composite (6)	4.4

Betas (Levered)

	Raw (OLS)	Blume Adjusted	Peer Group	Vasicek Adjusted	Sum	Downside
Median	0.67	0.80	0.82	0.80	0.40	1.05
SIC Composite	0.69	0.81	0.82	0.79	0.13	0.89
Large Composite	–	–	–	–	–	–
Small Composite	–	–	–	–	–	–
High Financial Risk	–	–	–	–	–	–

Betas (Unlevered)

	Raw (OLS)	Blume Adjusted	Peer Group	Vasicek Adjusted	Sum	Downside
Median	0.57	0.66	0.74	0.70	0.38	0.94
SIC Composite	0.53	0.61	0.62	0.60	0.12	0.67
Large Composite	–	–	–	–	–	–
Small Composite	–	–	–	–	–	–
High Financial Risk	–	–	–	–	–	–

Equity Valuation Multiples

	Price/Sales Latest	5-Yr Avg	Price/Earnings Latest	5-Yr Avg	Market/Book Latest	5-Yr Avg
Median	0.3	0.3	17.2	17.7	2.1	2.2
SIC Composite	0.3	0.3	15.3	18.1	2.9	3.4
Large Composite	–	–	–	–	–	–
Small Composite	–	–	–	–	–	–
High Financial Risk	–	–	–	–	–	–

Enterprise Valuation (EV) Multiples

	EV/Sales Latest	5-Yr Avg	EV/EBITDA Latest	5-Yr Avg
Median	0.5	0.4	7.2	7.1
SIC Composite	0.4	0.4	7.1	8.0
Large Composite	–	–	–	–
Small Composite	–	–	–	–
High Financial Risk	–	–	–	–

Enterprise Valuation SIC Composite
- EV/Sales: Latest 0.4, 5-Yr Avg 0.4
- EV/EBITDA: Latest 7.1, 5-Yr Avg 8.0

Fama-French (F-F) 5-Factor Model

	F-F Beta	SMB Premium	HML Premium	RMW Premium	CMA Premium
Median	0.6	2.8	0.4	1.4	-1.3
SIC Composite	0.7	1.0	-2.4	0.5	3.0
Large Composite	–	–	–	–	–
Small Composite	–	–	–	–	–
High Financial Risk	–	–	–	–	–

Leverage Ratios (%)

	Debt/MV Equity Latest	5-Yr Avg	Debt/Total Capital Latest	5-Yr Avg
Median	15.4	17.3	13.3	14.4
SIC Composite	38.6	29.2	27.8	22.6

Cost of Debt

	Cost of Debt (%) Latest
Median	6.1
SIC Composite	4.9

Capital Structure

SIC Composite (%) Latest
- D/TC: 27.8
- E/TC: 72.2

Cost of Equity Capital (%)

	CRSP Deciles CAPM	CAPM +Size Prem	Build-Up	Risk Premium Report CAPM +Size Prem	Build-Up	Discounted Cash Flow 1-Stage	3-Stage	Fama-French 5-Factor Model
Median	7.9	9.1	9.3	9.7	13.4	6.7	7.6	9.9
SIC Composite	7.8	8.2	8.4	6.2	11.0	5.9	8.8	9.2
Large Composite	–	–	–	–	–	–	–	–
Small Composite	–	–	–	–	–	–	–	–
High Financial Risk	–	–	–	–	–	–	–	–

Cost of Equity Capital (%) SIC Composite
- Avg CRSP: 8.3
- Avg RPR: 8.6
- 1-Stage: 5.9
- 3-Stage: 8.8
- 5-Factor Model: 9.2

Weighted Average Cost of Capital (WACC) (%)

	CRSP Deciles CAPM	CAPM +Size Prem	Build-Up	Risk Premium Report CAPM +Size Prem	Build-Up	Discounted Cash Flow 1-Stage	3-Stage	Fama-French 5-Factor Model
Median	7.5	8.3	8.5	9.2	11.3	6.2	7.2	8.5
SIC Composite	6.7	7.0	7.1	5.5	9.0	5.3	7.4	7.7
Large Composite	–	–	–	–	–	–	–	–
Small Composite	–	–	–	–	–	–	–	–
High Financial Risk	–	–	–	–	–	–	–	–

WACC (%) SIC Composite
Low 5.3 — Average 7.0 — Median 7.1 — High 9.0

© 2017 Duff & Phelps. All Rights Reserved. Duff & Phelps has used the utmost care in compiling the data presented herein, but cannot guarantee the accuracy, completeness, or timeliness of the information.

Data Updated Through March 31, 2017

5411

Number of Companies: 5
Grocery Stores

Industry Description
Stores, commonly known as supermarkets, food stores, and grocery stores, primarily engaged in the retail sale of all sorts of canned foods and dry goods, such as tea, coffee, spices, sugar, and flour; fresh fruits and vegetables; and fresh and prepared meats, fish, and poultry.

Sales (in millions)

Three Largest Companies
Kroger Co.	$115,337.0
Whole Foods Market, Inc.	15,724.0
Ingles Markets, Inc.	3,795.0

Three Smallest Companies
Ingles Markets, Inc.	$3,795.0
Weis Markets Inc.	3,136.7
Village Super Market	1,634.9

Total Assets (in millions)

Three Largest Companies
Kroger Co.	$36,505.0
Whole Foods Market, Inc.	6,341.0
Ingles Markets, Inc.	1,686.5

Three Smallest Companies
Ingles Markets, Inc.	$1,686.5
Weis Markets Inc.	1,431.3
Village Super Market	450.3

Annualized Monthly Performance Statistics (%)

	Industry Geometric Mean	Arithmetic Mean	Standard Deviation		S&P 500 Index Geometric Mean	Arithmetic Mean	Standard Deviation
1-year	-15.6	-14.5	15.0	1-year	17.2	17.4	7.2
3-year	1.7	3.6	20.3	3-year	10.4	10.9	11.5
5-year	9.7	11.7	21.4	5-year	13.3	13.9	11.5

Return Ratios (%)

	Return on Assets Latest	5-Yr Avg	Return on Equity Latest	5-Yr Avg	Dividend Yield Latest	5-Yr Avg
Median (5)	5.7	5.9	10.4	9.8	1.8	2.6
SIC Composite (5)	5.7	6.0	6.7	5.6	1.5	1.5
Large Composite (–)	–	–	–	–	–	–
Small Composite (–)	–	–	–	–	–	–
High-Financial Risk (–)	–	–	–	–	–	–

Liquidity Ratio

	Current Ratio Latest	5-Yr Avg
Median (5)	1.6	1.6
SIC Composite (5)	0.9	0.9
Large Composite (–)	–	–
Small Composite (–)	–	–
High-Financial Risk (–)	–	–

Profitability Ratio (%)

	Operating Margin Latest	5-Yr Avg
Median (5)	3.1	3.4
SIC Composite (5)	3.3	3.4
Large Composite (–)	–	–
Small Composite (–)	–	–
High-Financial Risk (–)	–	–

Growth Rates (%)

	Long-term EPS Analyst Estimates
Median (5)	4.2
SIC Composite (5)	3.9
Large Composite (–)	–
Small Composite (–)	–
High-Financial Risk (–)	–

Betas (Levered)

	Raw (OLS)	Blume Adjusted	Peer Group	Vasicek Adjusted	Sum	Downside
Median	0.70	0.82	0.82	0.81	0.26	1.07
SIC Composite	0.70	0.82	0.82	0.81	0.09	0.94
Large Composite	–	–	–	–	–	–
Small Composite	–	–	–	–	–	–
High Financial Risk	–	–	–	–	–	–

Betas (Unlevered)

	Raw (OLS)	Blume Adjusted	Peer Group	Vasicek Adjusted	Sum	Downside
Median	0.60	0.72	0.74	0.74	0.26	0.94
SIC Composite	0.53	0.61	0.61	0.60	0.09	0.70
Large Composite	–	–	–	–	–	–
Small Composite	–	–	–	–	–	–
High Financial Risk	–	–	–	–	–	–

Equity Valuation Multiples

	Price/Sales Latest	5-Yr Avg	Price/Earnings Latest	5-Yr Avg	Market/Book Latest	5-Yr Avg
Median	0.2	0.3	16.1	17.6	1.6	1.7
SIC Composite	0.3	0.3	14.9	17.8	2.9	3.4
Large Composite	–	–	–	–	–	–
Small Composite	–	–	–	–	–	–
High Financial Risk	–	–	–	–	–	–

Enterprise Valuation (EV) Multiples

	EV/Sales Latest	5-Yr Avg	EV/EBITDA Latest	5-Yr Avg
Median	0.5	0.4	7.2	7.1
SIC Composite	0.4	0.4	6.9	7.9
Large Composite	–	–	–	–
Small Composite	–	–	–	–
High Financial Risk	–	–	–	–

Enterprise Valuation SIC Composite
Latest: EV/Sales 0.4, EV/EBITDA 6.9
5-Yr Avg: EV/Sales 0.4, EV/EBITDA 7.9

Fama-French (F-F) 5-Factor Model

	F-F Beta	SMB Premium	HML Premium	RMW Premium	CMA Premium
Median	0.4	6.7	2.6	-2.2	-2.3
SIC Composite	0.7	0.8	-2.4	0.5	3.2
Large Composite	–	–	–	–	–
Small Composite	–	–	–	–	–
High Financial Risk	–	–	–	–	–

Leverage Ratios (%)

	Debt/MV Equity Latest	5-Yr Avg	Debt/Total Capital Latest	5-Yr Avg
Median	11.8	10.6	10.6	9.6
SIC Composite	40.7	29.7	28.9	22.9
Large Composite	–	–	–	–
Small Composite	–	–	–	–
High Financial Risk	–	–	–	–

Cost of Debt

	Cost of Debt (%) Latest
Median	6.1
SIC Composite	4.9
Large Composite	–
Small Composite	–
High Financial Risk	–

Capital Structure

SIC Composite (%) Latest: D/TC 28.9, E/TC 71.1

Cost of Equity Capital (%)

	CRSP Deciles CAPM	CAPM +Size Prem	Build-Up	Risk Premium Report CAPM +Size Prem	Build-Up	Discounted Cash Flow 1-Stage	3-Stage	Fama-French 5-Factor Model
Median	8.0	9.6	9.6	9.7	14.0	6.7	7.8	10.5
SIC Composite	7.9	8.3	8.3	5.8	10.8	5.6	8.9	9.4
Large Composite	–	–	–	–	–	–	–	–
Small Composite	–	–	–	–	–	–	–	–
High Financial Risk	–	–	–	–	–	–	–	–

Cost of Equity Capital (%) SIC Composite
Avg CRSP 8.3, Avg RPR 8.3, 1-Stage 5.6, 3-Stage 8.9, 5-Factor Model 9.4

Weighted Average Cost of Capital (WACC) (%)

	CRSP Deciles CAPM	CAPM +Size Prem	Build-Up	Risk Premium Report CAPM +Size Prem	Build-Up	Discounted Cash Flow 1-Stage	3-Stage	Fama-French 5-Factor Model
Median	7.6	8.4	8.5	9.2	11.0	6.2	7.2	9.7
SIC Composite	6.7	6.9	7.0	5.1	8.7	5.0	7.4	7.7
Large Composite	–	–	–	–	–	–	–	–
Small Composite	–	–	–	–	–	–	–	–
High Financial Risk	–	–	–	–	–	–	–	–

WACC (%) SIC Composite
Low 5.0, High 8.7, Average 6.8, Median 7.0

© 2017 Duff & Phelps. All Rights Reserved. Duff & Phelps has used the utmost care in compiling the data presented herein, but cannot guarantee the accuracy, completeness, or timeliness of the information.

Data Updated Through March 31, 2017

55

Number of Companies: 13
Automotive Dealers and Gasoline Service Stations

Industry Description
This major group includes retail dealers selling new and used automobiles, boats, recreational vehicles, utility trailers, and motorcycles including mopeds; those selling new automobile parts and accessories; and gasoline service stations. Automobile repair shops maintained by establishments engaged in the sale of new automobiles are also included.

Sales (in millions)

Three Largest Companies
AutoNation Inc.	$21,609.0
Penske Automotive Group Inc.	20,118.5
Carmax Inc.	15,832.2

Three Smallest Companies
Rush Enterprises, Inc.	$4,214.6
Marinemax Inc.	942.0
West Marine Inc.	703.4

Annualized Monthly Performance Statistics (%)

Industry	Geometric Mean	Arithmetic Mean	Standard Deviation
1-year	2.8	4.4	19.4
3-year	9.7	11.7	21.3
5-year	15.1	16.9	21.1

S&P 500 Index	Geometric Mean	Arithmetic Mean	Standard Deviation
1-year	17.2	17.4	7.2
3-year	10.4	10.9	11.5
5-year	13.3	13.9	11.5

Total Assets (in millions)

Three Largest Companies
Carmax Inc.	$14,481.6
AutoNation Inc.	10,060.0
Penske Automotive Group Inc.	8,861.1

Three Smallest Companies
TravelCenters Of America LLC	$1,635.1
Marinemax Inc.	546.7
West Marine Inc.	406.1

Return Ratios (%)

	Return on Assets Latest	5-Yr Avg	Return on Equity Latest	5-Yr Avg	Dividend Yield Latest	5-Yr Avg
Median (13)	4.4	4.7	14.7	14.8	0.0	0.0
SIC Composite (13)	5.3	5.3	5.7	5.4	0.3	0.3
Large Composite (3)	4.2	4.4	7.2	6.0	1.1	0.8
Small Composite (3)	2.0	2.7	3.4	5.2	0.0	0.0
High-Financial Risk (–)	–	–	–	–	–	–

Liquidity Ratio

	Current Ratio Latest	5-Yr Avg
Median	1.2	1.2
SIC Composite	1.1	1.2
Large Composite	1.0	1.2
Small Composite	1.4	1.4
High Financial Risk	–	–

Profitability Ratio (%)

	Operating Margin Latest	5-Yr Avg
Median	3.8	3.4
SIC Composite	5.2	5.1
Large Composite	4.3	4.3
Small Composite	2.4	2.7
High Financial Risk	–	–

Growth Rates (%)

	Long-term EPS Analyst Estimates
Median	13.1
SIC Composite	13.7
Large Composite	11.7
Small Composite	17.4
High Financial Risk	–

Betas (Levered)

	Raw (OLS)	Blume Adjusted	Peer Group	Vasicek Adjusted	Sum	Downside
Median	1.30	1.20	0.91	1.14	1.50	1.83
SIC Composite	1.03	1.03	0.91	1.01	0.90	1.21
Large Composite	1.23	1.15	0.92	0.99	1.35	1.67
Small Composite	1.17	1.11	0.90	1.04	1.62	1.29
High Financial Risk	–	–	–	–	–	–

Betas (Unlevered)

	Raw (OLS)	Blume Adjusted	Peer Group	Vasicek Adjusted	Sum	Downside
Median	0.76	0.75	0.61	0.73	0.85	1.01
SIC Composite	0.75	0.75	0.67	0.74	0.67	0.87
Large Composite	0.71	0.67	0.56	0.60	0.76	0.91
Small Composite	0.82	0.79	0.66	0.75	1.08	0.89
High Financial Risk	–	–	–	–	–	–

Equity Valuation Multiples

	Price/Sales Latest	5-Yr Avg	Price/Earnings Latest	5-Yr Avg	Market/Book Latest	5-Yr Avg
Median	0.2	0.3	11.6	15.1	1.7	1.8
SIC Composite	0.5	0.5	17.7	18.6	3.5	3.4
Large Composite	0.3	0.4	13.8	16.8	2.5	2.8
Small Composite	0.4	0.3	29.6	19.3	1.2	1.1
High Financial Risk	–	–	–	–	–	–

Enterprise Valuation (EV) Multiples

	EV/Sales Latest	5-Yr Avg	EV/EBITDA Latest	5-Yr Avg
Median	0.5	0.5	11.1	12.3
SIC Composite	0.8	0.8	12.7	12.6
Large Composite	0.7	0.7	14.0	14.9
Small Composite	0.6	0.5	15.1	13.7
High Financial Risk	–	–	–	–

Enterprise Valuation SIC Composite
Latest: EV/Sales 0.8, EV/EBITDA 12.7
5-Yr Avg: EV/Sales 0.8, EV/EBITDA 12.6

Fama-French (F-F) 5-Factor Model

	F-F Beta	SMB Premium	HML Premium	RMW Premium	CMA Premium
Median	1.3	6.3	2.6	2.2	-5.1
SIC Composite	0.9	3.3	0.0	0.8	-0.2
Large Composite	1.0	5.3	1.4	0.2	0.3
Small Composite	1.0	3.6	4.3	0.5	-2.1
High Financial Risk	–	–	–	–	–

Leverage Ratios (%)

	Debt/MV Equity Latest	5-Yr Avg	Debt/Total Capital Latest	5-Yr Avg
Median	111.1	82.9	52.6	45.3
SIC Composite	57.5	51.8	36.5	34.1
Large Composite	115.9	86.4	53.7	46.4
Small Composite	72.8	86.0	42.1	46.2
High Financial Risk	–	–	–	–

Cost of Debt

	Cost of Debt (%) Latest
Median	6.1
SIC Composite	6.2
Large Composite	6.2
Small Composite	7.0
High Financial Risk	–

Capital Structure

SIC Composite (%) Latest
D/TC: 36.5
E/TC: 63.5

Cost of Equity Capital (%)

	CRSP Deciles CAPM	CAPM +Size Prem	Build-Up	Risk Premium Report CAPM +Size Prem	Build-Up	Discounted Cash Flow 1-Stage	3-Stage	Fama-French 5-Factor Model
Median	9.8	11.4	10.1	14.8	13.1	13.1	12.9	16.5
SIC Composite	9.1	9.7	9.1	11.2	11.9	14.0	13.0	12.5
Large Composite	8.9	9.7	9.2	13.5	11.7	12.3	14.3	16.3
Small Composite	9.2	11.6	10.9	16.7	14.3	17.4	8.9	15.4
High Financial Risk	–	–	–	–	–	–	–	–

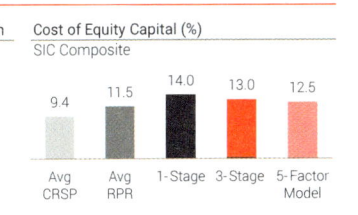

Cost of Equity Capital (%) SIC Composite
Avg CRSP 9.4, Avg RPR 11.5, 1-Stage 14.0, 3-Stage 13.0, 5-Factor Model 12.5

Weighted Average Cost of Capital (WACC) (%)

	CRSP Deciles CAPM	CAPM +Size Prem	Build-Up	Risk Premium Report CAPM +Size Prem	Build-Up	Discounted Cash Flow 1-Stage	3-Stage	Fama-French 5-Factor Model
Median	7.5	8.2	8.1	9.8	8.7	9.5	9.4	10.7
SIC Composite	7.5	7.9	7.5	8.8	9.2	10.6	10.0	9.6
Large Composite	6.6	6.9	6.7	8.6	7.8	8.1	9.1	10.0
Small Composite	7.9	9.3	8.9	12.2	10.9	12.6	7.7	11.5
High Financial Risk	–	–	–	–	–	–	–	–

WACC (%) SIC Composite
Low 7.5, High 10.6
Average 9.1, Median 9.2

© 2017 Duff & Phelps. All Rights Reserved. Duff & Phelps has used the utmost care in compiling the data presented herein, but cannot guarantee the accuracy, completeness, or timeliness of the information.

Data Updated Through March 31, 2017

56

Number of Companies: 24
Apparel and Accessory Stores

Industry Description
This major group includes retail stores primarily engaged in selling new clothing, shoes, hats, underwear, and related articles for personal wear and adornment. Furriers and custom tailors carrying stocks are included.

Sales (in millions)

Three Largest Companies
TJX Companies, Inc.	$33,183.7
Gap Inc.	15,516.0
Nordstrom Inc.	14,757.0

Three Smallest Companies
Citi Trends Inc.	$683.8
Destination Maternity Corp.	498.8
Francesca's Holdings Corporation	487.2

Total Assets (in millions)

Three Largest Companies
TJX Companies, Inc.	$12,883.8
Nordstrom Inc.	7,858.0
Gap Inc.	7,610.0

Three Smallest Companies
Citi Trends Inc.	$314.5
Destination Maternity Corp.	219.1
Francesca's Holdings Corporation	189.6

Annualized Monthly Performance Statistics (%)

Industry	Geometric Mean	Arithmetic Mean	Standard Deviation	S&P 500 Index	Geometric Mean	Arithmetic Mean	Standard Deviation
1-year	-3.1	-1.8	17.3	1-year	17.2	17.4	7.2
3-year	4.3	5.5	16.6	3-year	10.4	10.9	11.5
5-year	8.1	9.4	16.8	5-year	13.3	13.9	11.5

Return Ratios (%)

	Return on Assets Latest	5-Yr Avg	Return on Equity Latest	5-Yr Avg	Dividend Yield Latest	5-Yr Avg	Current Ratio Latest	5-Yr Avg	Operating Margin Latest	5-Yr Avg	Long-term EPS Analyst Estimates
Median (24)	7.1	8.7	13.9	14.2	1.7	1.8	2.4	2.3	5.7	8.0	9.7
SIC Composite (24)	10.4	12.1	5.1	5.5	1.7	1.8	1.8	1.9	9.0	10.1	9.6
Large Composite (3)	11.7	14.3	4.8	5.6	1.9	1.8	1.5	1.7	9.7	11.2	9.3
Small Composite (3)	7.3	8.5	6.0	4.4	0.4	0.1	2.0	2.3	5.2	6.1	9.9
High-Financial Risk (—)	—	—	—	—	—	—	—	—	—	—	—

Betas (Levered)

	Raw (OLS)	Blume Adjusted	Peer Group	Vasicek Adjusted	Sum	Downside
Median	0.85	0.91	0.76	0.80	0.63	1.24
SIC Composite	0.83	0.90	0.76	0.82	0.52	0.78
Large Composite	0.78	0.87	0.77	0.77	0.45	0.74
Small Composite	0.59	0.75	0.73	0.66	0.61	0.95
High Financial Risk	—	—	—	—	—	—

Betas (Unlevered)

	Raw (OLS)	Blume Adjusted	Peer Group	Vasicek Adjusted	Sum	Downside
Median	0.79	0.78	0.75	0.70	0.52	1.01
SIC Composite	0.78	0.85	0.72	0.77	0.50	0.74
Large Composite	0.72	0.80	0.71	0.72	0.42	0.69
Small Composite	0.58	0.73	0.71	0.64	0.60	0.92
High Financial Risk	—	—	—	—	—	—

Equity Valuation Multiples

	Price/Sales Latest	5-Yr Avg	Price/Earnings Latest	5-Yr Avg	Market/Book Latest	5-Yr Avg
Median	0.6	0.9	18.4	19.1	2.1	2.5
SIC Composite	1.0	1.1	19.7	18.3	4.8	4.7
Large Composite	1.1	1.2	20.6	17.8	8.0	7.6
Small Composite	0.5	0.8	16.8	22.7	2.1	3.2
High Financial Risk	—	—	—	—	—	—

Enterprise Valuation (EV) Multiples

	EV/Sales Latest	5-Yr Avg	EV/EBITDA Latest	5-Yr Avg
Median	0.5	0.7	6.1	6.8
SIC Composite	1.0	1.1	8.6	8.1
Large Composite	1.1	1.2	8.5	8.4
Small Composite	0.5	0.8	5.7	8.4
High Financial Risk	—	—	—	—

Enterprise Valuation SIC Composite: EV/Sales Latest 1.0, 5-Yr Avg 1.1; EV/EBITDA Latest 8.6, 5-Yr Avg 8.1

Fama-French (F-F) 5-Factor Model

	F-F Beta	SMB Premium	HML Premium	RMW Premium	CMA Premium
Median	1.4	5.8	-2.9	1.6	0.4
SIC Composite	0.8	2.2	-1.5	2.8	1.4
Large Composite	0.8	2.0	-1.9	3.0	4.1
Small Composite	0.6	1.3	-0.1	-0.1	3.0
High Financial Risk	—	—	—	—	—

Leverage Ratios (%)

	Debt/MV Equity Latest	5-Yr Avg	Debt/Total Capital Latest	5-Yr Avg
Median	1.4	1.6	1.4	1.5
SIC Composite	7.8	6.2	7.3	5.8
Large Composite	9.4	8.7	8.6	8.0
Small Composite	4.6	1.7	4.4	1.7
High Financial Risk	—	—	—	—

Cost of Debt

	Cost of Debt (%) Latest
Median	6.1
SIC Composite	5.2
Large Composite	4.8
Small Composite	7.1
High Financial Risk	—

Capital Structure

SIC Composite (%) Latest:
D/TC: 7.3
E/TC: 92.7

Cost of Equity Capital (%)

	CAPM	CRSP Deciles CAPM +Size Prem	Build-Up	Risk Premium Report CAPM +Size Prem	Build-Up	Discounted Cash Flow 1-Stage	3-Stage	Fama-French 5-Factor Model
Median	7.9	10.4	9.6	10.3	13.9	10.8	15.3	16.2
SIC Composite	8.0	8.5	8.0	8.8	11.4	11.5	11.8	12.8
Large Composite	7.8	8.0	7.7	7.9	10.7	11.3	11.9	15.1
Small Composite	7.1	10.4	10.8	12.1	15.7	10.4	13.5	10.8
High Financial Risk	—	—	—	—	—	—	—	—

Cost of Equity Capital (%) SIC Composite: Avg CRSP 8.2, Avg RPR 10.1, 1-Stage 11.5, 3-Stage 11.8, 5-Factor Model 12.8

Weighted Average Cost of Capital (WACC) (%)

	CAPM	CRSP Deciles CAPM +Size Prem	Build-Up	Risk Premium Report CAPM +Size Prem	Build-Up	Discounted Cash Flow 1-Stage	3-Stage	Fama-French 5-Factor Model
Median	7.4	8.9	9.0	9.8	13.1	10.7	13.1	13.4
SIC Composite	7.7	8.1	7.7	8.4	10.9	10.9	11.2	12.1
Large Composite	7.4	7.6	7.3	7.5	10.1	10.6	11.1	14.1
Small Composite	7.0	10.2	10.5	11.8	15.2	10.1	13.1	10.6
High Financial Risk	—	—	—	—	—	—	—	—

WACC (%) SIC Composite: Low 7.7, High 12.1, Average 9.9, Median 10.9

© 2017 Duff & Phelps. All Rights Reserved. Duff & Phelps has used the utmost care in compiling the data presented herein, but cannot guarantee the accuracy, completeness, or timeliness of the information.

Data Updated Through March 31, 2017

562

Number of Companies: 5
Women's Clothing Stores

Industry Description
Establishments primarily engaged in the retail sale of a general line of women's ready-to-wear clothing.

Sales (in millions)

Three Largest Companies
Ascena Retail Group Inc.	$6,998.6
Chico's Fas Inc.	2,476.4
Cato Corp.	956.6

Three Smallest Companies
Cato Corp.	$956.6
Destination Maternity Corp.	498.8
Francesca's Holdings Corporation	487.2

Total Assets (in millions)

Three Largest Companies
Ascena Retail Group Inc.	$5,506.3
Chico's Fas Inc.	1,109.0
Cato Corp.	606.3

Three Smallest Companies
Cato Corp.	$606.3
Destination Maternity Corp.	219.1
Francesca's Holdings Corporation	189.6

Annualized Monthly Performance Statistics (%)

Industry	Geometric Mean	Arithmetic Mean	Standard Deviation	S&P 500 Index	Geometric Mean	Arithmetic Mean	Standard Deviation
1-year	-30.6	-26.9	25.3	1-year	17.2	17.4	7.2
3-year	-16.4	-13.2	24.5	3-year	10.4	10.9	11.5
5-year	-12.2	-9.5	22.9	5-year	13.3	13.9	11.5

Return Ratios (%)

	Return on Assets Latest	5-Yr Avg	Return on Equity Latest	5-Yr Avg	Dividend Yield Latest	5-Yr Avg
Median (5)	7.6	6.9	11.9	13.7	1.3	0.9
SIC Composite (5)	2.2	4.1	4.2	3.6	1.8	1.3
Large Composite (–)	–	–	–	–	–	–
Small Composite (–)	–	–	–	–	–	–
High-Financial Risk (–)	–	–	–	–	–	–

Liquidity Ratio

	Current Ratio Latest	5-Yr Avg
Median (5)	1.6	1.8
SIC Composite (5)	1.5	1.7
Large Composite	–	–
Small Composite	–	–
High-Financial Risk	–	–

Profitability Ratio (%)

	Operating Margin Latest	5-Yr Avg
Median (5)	4.8	7.6
SIC Composite (5)	5.4	6.9
Large Composite	–	–
Small Composite	–	–
High-Financial Risk	–	–

Growth Rates (%)

	Long-term EPS Analyst Estimates
Median (5)	9.5
SIC Composite (5)	11.5
Large Composite	–
Small Composite	–
High-Financial Risk	–

Betas (Levered)

	Raw (OLS)	Blume Adjusted	Peer Group	Vasicek Adjusted	Sum	Downside
Median	0.82	0.89	0.73	0.80	0.74	1.36
SIC Composite	1.09	1.06	0.73	1.01	0.43	1.21
Large Composite	–	–	–	–	–	–
Small Composite	–	–	–	–	–	–
High Financial Risk	–	–	–	–	–	–

Betas (Unlevered)

	Raw (OLS)	Blume Adjusted	Peer Group	Vasicek Adjusted	Sum	Downside
Median	0.73	0.77	0.71	0.67	0.45	1.02
SIC Composite	0.84	0.82	0.59	0.79	0.39	0.93
Large Composite	–	–	–	–	–	–
Small Composite	–	–	–	–	–	–
High Financial Risk	–	–	–	–	–	–

Equity Valuation Multiples

	Price/Sales Latest	5-Yr Avg	Price/Earnings Latest	5-Yr Avg	Market/Book Latest	5-Yr Avg
Median	0.6	0.9	20.0	19.9	1.5	2.4
SIC Composite	0.3	0.7	23.6	27.9	1.1	2.0
Large Composite	–	–	–	–	–	–
Small Composite	–	–	–	–	–	–
High Financial Risk	–	–	–	–	–	–

Enterprise Valuation (EV) Multiples

	EV/Sales Latest	5-Yr Avg	EV/EBITDA Latest	5-Yr Avg
Median	0.3	0.7	6.1	6.2
SIC Composite	0.4	0.7	4.3	6.3
Large Composite	–	–	–	–
Small Composite	–	–	–	–
High Financial Risk	–	–	–	–

Enterprise Valuation SIC Composite: Latest EV/Sales 0.4, 5-Yr Avg 0.7; Latest EV/EBITDA 4.3, 5-Yr Avg 6.3

Fama-French (F-F) 5-Factor Model

	F-F Beta	SMB Premium	HML Premium	RMW Premium	CMA Premium
Median	1.0	0.7	0.4	1.3	0.9
SIC Composite	1.0	6.0	4.1	6.6	-2.5
Large Composite	–	–	–	–	–
Small Composite	–	–	–	–	–
High Financial Risk	–	–	–	–	–

Leverage Ratios (%)

	Debt/MV Equity Latest	5-Yr Avg	Debt/Total Capital Latest	5-Yr Avg
Median	4.6	1.5	4.4	1.5
SIC Composite	45.7	8.1	31.4	7.5
Large Composite	–	–	–	–
Small Composite	–	–	–	–
High Financial Risk	–	–	–	–

Cost of Debt

	Cost of Debt (%) Latest
Median	7.1
SIC Composite	6.2
Large Composite	–
Small Composite	–
High Financial Risk	–

Capital Structure

SIC Composite (%) Latest: D/TC 31.4, E/TC 68.6

Cost of Equity Capital (%)

	CRSP Deciles CAPM	CAPM +Size Prem	Build-Up	Risk Premium Report CAPM +Size Prem	Build-Up	Discounted Cash Flow 1-Stage	3-Stage	Fama-French 5-Factor Model
Median	7.9	9.9	9.6	10.9	14.6	13.1	15.2	12.2
SIC Composite	9.1	11.0	9.4	10.0	14.0	13.7	11.4	22.9
Large Composite	–	–	–	–	–	–	–	–
Small Composite	–	–	–	–	–	–	–	–
High Financial Risk	–	–	–	–	–	–	–	–

Cost of Equity Capital (%) SIC Composite: Avg CRSP 10.2, Avg RPR 12.0, 1-Stage 13.7, 3-Stage 11.4, 5-Factor Model 22.9

Weighted Average Cost of Capital (WACC) (%)

	CRSP Deciles CAPM	CAPM +Size Prem	Build-Up	Risk Premium Report CAPM +Size Prem	Build-Up	Discounted Cash Flow 1-Stage	3-Stage	Fama-French 5-Factor Model
Median	7.3	9.0	9.6	10.5	13.4	12.8	15.2	14.0
SIC Composite	7.6	9.0	7.9	8.2	11.0	10.8	9.2	17.1
Large Composite	–	–	–	–	–	–	–	–
Small Composite	–	–	–	–	–	–	–	–
High Financial Risk	–	–	–	–	–	–	–	–

WACC (%) SIC Composite: Low 7.9, High 17.1, Average 10.5, Median 9.2

© 2017 Duff & Phelps. All Rights Reserved. Duff & Phelps has used the utmost care in compiling the data presented herein, but cannot guarantee the accuracy, completeness, or timeliness of the information.

Data Updated Through March 31, 2017

565

Number of Companies: 11
Family Clothing Stores

Industry Description
Establishments primarily engaged in the retail sale of clothing, furnishings, and accessories for men, women, and children, without specializing in sales for an individual sex or age group.

Sales (in millions)

Three Largest Companies
TJX Companies, Inc.	$33,183.7
Gap Inc.	15,516.0
Nordstrom Inc.	14,757.0

Three Smallest Companies
Buckle, Inc.	$974.9
Zumiez, Inc.	836.3
Citi Trends Inc.	683.8

Total Assets (in millions)

Three Largest Companies
TJX Companies, Inc.	$12,883.8
Nordstrom Inc.	7,858.0
Gap Inc.	7,610.0

Three Smallest Companies
Stein Mart Inc.	$527.8
Zumiez, Inc.	426.7
Citi Trends Inc.	314.5

Annualized Monthly Performance Statistics (%)

Industry	Geometric Mean	Arithmetic Mean	Standard Deviation	S&P 500 Index	Geometric Mean	Arithmetic Mean	Standard Deviation
1-year	-1.9	-0.7	16.8	1-year	17.2	17.4	7.2
3-year	5.1	6.3	16.4	3-year	10.4	10.9	11.5
5-year	9.9	11.1	17.1	5-year	13.3	13.9	11.5

Return Ratios (%)

	Return on Assets Latest	5-Yr Avg	Return on Equity Latest	5-Yr Avg	Dividend Yield Latest	5-Yr Avg
Median (11)	6.2	8.6	17.8	17.8	3.1	2.3
SIC Composite (11)	11.8	13.8	4.8	5.4	1.7	1.8
Large Composite (3)	11.7	14.3	4.8	5.6	1.9	1.8
Small Composite (3)	10.6	14.5	8.6	6.2	4.7	4.8
High-Financial Risk (—)	—	—	—	—	—	—

Liquidity Ratio / Profitability Ratio (%) / Growth Rates (%)

	Current Ratio Latest	5-Yr Avg	Operating Margin Latest	5-Yr Avg	Long-term EPS Analyst Estimates
Median (11)	2.3	2.2	6.6	9.0	9.9
SIC Composite (11)	1.6	1.7	9.5	10.9	9.9
Large Composite (3)	1.5	1.7	9.7	11.2	9.3
Small Composite (3)	3.1	2.8	8.7	11.7	9.9
High-Financial Risk (—)	—	—	—	—	—

Betas (Levered)

	Raw (OLS)	Blume Adjusted	Peer Group	Vasicek Adjusted	Sum	Downside
Median	0.85	0.91	0.76	0.79	0.45	1.20
SIC Composite	0.83	0.90	0.76	0.81	0.51	0.77
Large Composite	0.78	0.87	0.77	0.77	0.45	0.74
Small Composite	0.94	0.97	0.73	0.90	0.37	1.04
High Financial Risk	—	—	—	—	—	—

Betas (Unlevered)

	Raw (OLS)	Blume Adjusted	Peer Group	Vasicek Adjusted	Sum	Downside
Median	0.75	0.76	0.73	0.71	0.45	0.84
SIC Composite	0.78	0.84	0.72	0.77	0.48	0.73
Large Composite	0.72	0.80	0.71	0.72	0.42	0.69
Small Composite	—	—	—	—	—	—
High Financial Risk	—	—	—	—	—	—

Equity Valuation Multiples

	Price/Sales Latest	5-Yr Avg	Price/Earnings Latest	5-Yr Avg	Market/Book Latest	5-Yr Avg
Median	0.5	0.9	22.2	19.7	2.1	3.4
SIC Composite	1.1	1.2	21.0	18.4	6.5	6.2
Large Composite	1.1	1.2	20.6	17.8	8.0	7.6
Small Composite	0.6	1.2	11.6	16.1	1.7	3.3
High Financial Risk	—	—	—	—	—	—

Enterprise Valuation (EV) Multiples

	EV/Sales Latest	5-Yr Avg	EV/EBITDA Latest	5-Yr Avg
Median	0.6	0.9	5.9	7.6
SIC Composite	1.1	1.2	9.3	8.6
Large Composite	1.1	1.2	8.5	8.4
Small Composite	0.5	1.0	10.8	7.7
High Financial Risk	—	—	—	—

Enterprise Valuation SIC Composite: EV/Sales Latest 1.1, 5-Yr Avg 1.2; EV/EBITDA Latest 9.3, 5-Yr Avg 8.6

Fama-French (F-F) 5-Factor Model

	F-F Beta	SMB Premium	HML Premium	RMW Premium	CMA Premium
Median	0.7	1.3	1.8	3.9	-0.6
SIC Composite	0.8	1.8	-2.1	2.6	2.0
Large Composite	0.8	2.0	-1.9	3.0	4.1
Small Composite	1.0	4.7	-2.1	4.4	5.5
High Financial Risk	—	—	—	—	—

Leverage Ratios (%)

	Debt/MV Equity Latest	5-Yr Avg	Debt/Total Capital Latest	5-Yr Avg
Median	4.7	3.7	4.5	3.6
SIC Composite	7.5	6.8	7.0	6.4
Large Composite	9.4	8.7	8.6	8.0
Small Composite	0.0	0.0	0.0	0.0
High Financial Risk	—	—	—	—

Cost of Debt

	Cost of Debt (%) Latest
Median	4.8
SIC Composite	4.9
Large Composite	4.8
Small Composite	—
High Financial Risk	—

Capital Structure
SIC Composite (%) Latest: D/TC 7.0, E/TC 93.0

Cost of Equity Capital (%)

	CRSP Deciles CAPM	CAPM +Size Prem	Build-Up	Risk Premium Report CAPM +Size Prem	Build-Up	Discounted Cash Flow 1-Stage	3-Stage	Fama-French 5-Factor Model
Median	7.9	10.4	9.6	9.4	13.4	11.8	16.6	13.6
SIC Composite	8.0	8.3	7.8	8.5	11.1	11.8	11.9	12.3
Large Composite	7.8	8.0	7.7	7.9	10.7	11.3	11.9	15.1
Small Composite	8.5	11.3	10.3	10.2	14.8	15.9	18.8	21.3
High Financial Risk	—	—	—	—	—	—	—	—

Cost of Equity Capital (%) SIC Composite: Avg CRSP 8.0, Avg RPR 9.8, 1-Stage 11.8, 3-Stage 11.9, 5-Factor Model 12.3

Weighted Average Cost of Capital (WACC) (%)

	CRSP Deciles CAPM	CAPM +Size Prem	Build-Up	Risk Premium Report CAPM +Size Prem	Build-Up	Discounted Cash Flow 1-Stage	3-Stage	Fama-French 5-Factor Model
Median	7.4	8.4	8.2	8.5	11.0	11.5	11.2	12.0
SIC Composite	7.7	7.9	7.5	8.1	10.5	11.2	11.3	11.6
Large Composite	7.4	7.6	7.3	7.5	10.1	10.6	11.1	14.1
Small Composite	8.5	11.3	10.3	10.2	14.8	15.9	18.8	21.3
High Financial Risk	—	—	—	—	—	—	—	—

WACC (%) SIC Composite: Low 7.5, High 11.6, Average 9.7, Median 10.5

© 2017 Duff & Phelps. All Rights Reserved. Duff & Phelps has used the utmost care in compiling the data presented herein, but cannot guarantee the accuracy, completeness, or timeliness of the information.

Data Updated Through March 31, 2017

566

Number of Companies: 5
Shoe Stores

Industry Description
Establishments primarily engaged in the retail sale of men's, women's, and children's footwear, including athletic footwear.

Sales (in millions)

Three Largest Companies
Foot Locker, Inc.	$7,766.0
Genesco Inc.	2,868.3
DSW Inc.	2,711.4

Three Smallest Companies
DSW Inc.	$2,711.4
Finish Line Inc.	1,888.9
Shoe Carnival Inc.	1,001.1

Total Assets (in millions)

Three Largest Companies
Foot Locker, Inc.	$3,840.0
Genesco Inc.	1,448.9
DSW Inc.	1,428.5

Three Smallest Companies
DSW Inc.	$1,428.5
Finish Line Inc.	817.5
Shoe Carnival Inc.	458.5

Annualized Monthly Performance Statistics (%)

Industry	Geometric Mean	Arithmetic Mean	Standard Deviation	S&P 500 Index	Geometric Mean	Arithmetic Mean	Standard Deviation
1-year	2.9	5.2	23.2	1-year	17.2	17.4	7.2
3-year	5.7	7.6	21.2	3-year	10.4	10.9	11.5
5-year	10.4	12.2	20.3	5-year	13.3	13.9	11.5

Return Ratios (%)

	Return on Assets Latest	5-Yr Avg	Return on Equity Latest	5-Yr Avg	Dividend Yield Latest	5-Yr Avg
Median (5)	6.5	8.8	13.5	12.3	1.7	1.8
SIC Composite (5)	11.7	11.0	6.8	6.5	1.8	1.7
Large Composite (–)	–	–	–	–	–	–
Small Composite (–)	–	–	–	–	–	–
High-Financial Risk (–)	–	–	–	–	–	–

Liquidity Ratio

	Current Ratio Latest	5-Yr Avg
	2.4	3.0
	3.2	3.2
	–	–
	–	–
	–	–

Profitability Ratio (%)

	Operating Margin Latest	5-Yr Avg
	4.7	6.8
	8.8	9.2
	–	–
	–	–
	–	–

Growth Rates (%)

	Long-term EPS Analyst Estimates
	9.5
	8.9
	–
	–
	–

Betas (Levered)

	Raw (OLS)	Blume Adjusted	Peer Group	Vasicek Adjusted	Sum	Downside
Median	0.79	0.88	0.78	0.79	0.69	1.39
SIC Composite	0.67	0.79	0.78	0.70	0.71	0.80
Large Composite	–	–	–	–	–	–
Small Composite	–	–	–	–	–	–
High Financial Risk	–	–	–	–	–	–

Betas (Unlevered)

	Raw (OLS)	Blume Adjusted	Peer Group	Vasicek Adjusted	Sum	Downside
Median	0.79	0.88	0.78	0.79	0.69	1.32
SIC Composite	0.66	0.79	0.77	0.70	0.70	0.79
Large Composite	–	–	–	–	–	–
Small Composite	–	–	–	–	–	–
High Financial Risk	–	–	–	–	–	–

Equity Valuation Multiples

	Price/Sales Latest	5-Yr Avg	Price/Earnings Latest	5-Yr Avg	Market/Book Latest	5-Yr Avg
Median	0.5	0.6	14.8	15.6	1.8	2.1
SIC Composite	0.8	0.9	14.6	15.4	3.0	2.6
Large Composite	–	–	–	–	–	–
Small Composite	–	–	–	–	–	–
High Financial Risk	–	–	–	–	–	–

Enterprise Valuation (EV) Multiples

	EV/Sales Latest	5-Yr Avg	EV/EBITDA Latest	5-Yr Avg
Median	0.4	0.5	6.9	6.7
SIC Composite	0.8	0.8	9.2	7.2
Large Composite	–	–	–	–
Small Composite	–	–	–	–
High Financial Risk	–	–	–	–

Enterprise Valuation SIC Composite

	Latest	5-Yr Avg
EV/Sales	0.8	0.8
EV/EBITDA	9.2	7.2

Fama-French (F-F) 5-Factor Model

Fama-French (F-F) Components

	F-F Beta	SMB Premium	HML Premium	RMW Premium	CMA Premium
Median	0.6	4.5	-2.1	5.1	3.2
SIC Composite	0.6	2.8	0.6	3.1	-0.8
Large Composite	–	–	–	–	–
Small Composite	–	–	–	–	–
High Financial Risk	–	–	–	–	–

Leverage Ratios (%)

	Debt/MV Equity Latest	5-Yr Avg	Debt/Total Capital Latest	5-Yr Avg
Median	0.0	0.0	0.0	0.0
SIC Composite	1.5	1.5	1.5	1.5
Large Composite	–	–	–	–
Small Composite	–	–	–	–
High Financial Risk	–	–	–	–

Cost of Debt

	Cost of Debt (%) Latest
Median	6.1
SIC Composite	6.1
Large Composite	–
Small Composite	–
High Financial Risk	–

Capital Structure

SIC Composite (%) Latest
- D/TC: 1.5
- E/TC: 98.5

Cost of Equity Capital (%)

	CRSP Deciles CAPM	CAPM +Size Prem	Build-Up	Risk Premium Report CAPM +Size Prem	Build-Up	Discounted Cash Flow 1-Stage	3-Stage	Fama-French 5-Factor Model
Median	7.8	10.5	9.2	12.1	13.9	10.5	15.4	17.6
SIC Composite	7.4	8.5	8.6	10.5	12.5	10.7	12.7	12.5
Large Composite	–	–	–	–	–	–	–	–
Small Composite	–	–	–	–	–	–	–	–
High Financial Risk	–	–	–	–	–	–	–	–

Cost of Equity Capital (%) SIC Composite

Avg CRSP	Avg RPR	1-Stage	3-Stage	5-Factor Model
8.6	11.5	10.7	12.7	12.5

Weighted Average Cost of Capital (WACC) (%)

	CRSP Deciles CAPM	CAPM +Size Prem	Build-Up	Risk Premium Report CAPM +Size Prem	Build-Up	Discounted Cash Flow 1-Stage	3-Stage	Fama-French 5-Factor Model
Median	7.8	10.3	9.1	12.1	13.6	10.5	14.8	17.6
SIC Composite	7.3	8.5	8.6	10.5	12.3	10.6	12.6	12.4
Large Composite	–	–	–	–	–	–	–	–
Small Composite	–	–	–	–	–	–	–	–
High Financial Risk	–	–	–	–	–	–	–	–

WACC (%) SIC Composite
Low 8.5 — High 12.6
Average 10.8   Median 10.6

© 2017 Duff & Phelps. All Rights Reserved. Duff & Phelps has used the utmost care in compiling the data presented herein, but cannot guarantee the accuracy, completeness, or timeliness of the information.

Data Updated Through March 31, 2017

57

Number of Companies: 7
Home Furniture, Furnishings, and Equipment Stores

Industry Description
This major group includes retail stores selling goods used for furnishing the home, such as furniture, floor coverings, draperies, glass and chinaware, domestic stoves, refrigerators, and other household electrical and gas appliances.

Sales (in millions)

Three Largest Companies
Best Buy Co. Inc.	$39,403.0
Bed Bath & Beyond Inc.	12,103.9
GameStop Corp.	8,607.9

Three Smallest Companies
Pier 1 Imports, Inc.	$1,892.2
Haverty Furniture	821.8
Trans World Entertainment Corporation	334.7

Total Assets (in millions)

Three Largest Companies
Best Buy Co. Inc.	$13,856.0
Bed Bath & Beyond Inc.	6,498.9
GameStop Corp.	4,975.9

Three Smallest Companies
Pier 1 Imports, Inc.	$819.2
Haverty Furniture	454.5
Trans World Entertainment Corporati	271.6

Annualized Monthly Performance Statistics (%)

Industry	Geometric Mean	Arithmetic Mean	Standard Deviation	S&P 500 Index	Geometric Mean	Arithmetic Mean	Standard Deviation
1-year	13.2	15.6	25.0	1-year	17.2	17.4	7.2
3-year	0.7	2.6	20.5	3-year	10.4	10.9	11.5
5-year	5.3	8.3	25.4	5-year	13.3	13.9	11.5

Return Ratios (%)

	Return on Assets Latest	5-Yr Avg	Return on Equity Latest	5-Yr Avg	Dividend Yield Latest	5-Yr Avg	Current Ratio Latest	5-Yr Avg	Operating Margin Latest	5-Yr Avg	Long-term EPS Analyst Estimates
Median (7)	7.6	5.7	16.1	16.9	3.0	3.7	2.0	2.2	5.3	6.7	8.9
SIC Composite (7)	9.5	8.0	9.5	7.0	3.4	3.2	1.6	1.5	6.3	6.1	8.9
Large Composite (–)	–	–	–	–	–	–	–	–	–	–	–
Small Composite (–)	–	–	–	–	–	–	–	–	–	–	–
High-Financial Risk (–)	–	–	–	–	–	–	–	–	–	–	–

Betas (Levered)

	Raw (OLS)	Blume Adjusted	Peer Group	Vasicek Adjusted	Sum	Downside
Median	1.09	1.06	1.30	1.20	1.25	1.41
SIC Composite	1.01	1.01	1.30	1.12	1.03	1.23
Large Composite	–	–	–	–	–	–
Small Composite	–	–	–	–	–	–
High Financial Risk	–	–	–	–	–	–

Betas (Unlevered)

	Raw (OLS)	Blume Adjusted	Peer Group	Vasicek Adjusted	Sum	Downside
Median	0.96	0.95	1.20	1.07	1.21	1.41
SIC Composite	0.90	0.91	1.16	1.00	0.92	1.10
Large Composite	–	–	–	–	–	–
Small Composite	–	–	–	–	–	–
High Financial Risk	–	–	–	–	–	–

Equity Valuation Multiples

	Price/Sales Latest	5-Yr Avg	Price/Earnings Latest	5-Yr Avg	Market/Book Latest	5-Yr Avg
Median	0.4	0.6	15.0	15.0	2.0	2.5
SIC Composite	0.4	0.5	10.6	14.3	2.5	2.8
Large Composite	–	–	–	–	–	–
Small Composite	–	–	–	–	–	–
High Financial Risk	–	–	–	–	–	–

Enterprise Valuation (EV) Multiples

	EV/Sales Latest	5-Yr Avg	EV/EBITDA Latest	5-Yr Avg
Median	0.4	0.6	5.2	6.5
SIC Composite	0.4	0.4	4.8	5.5
Large Composite	–	–	–	–
Small Composite	–	–	–	–
High Financial Risk	–	–	–	–

Enterprise Valuation SIC Composite
- Latest: EV/Sales 0.4, EV/EBITDA 4.8
- 5-Yr Avg: EV/Sales 0.4, EV/EBITDA 5.5

Fama-French (F-F) 5-Factor Model

	F-F Beta	SMB Premium	HML Premium	RMW Premium	CMA Premium
Median	0.8	6.8	2.4	3.6	0.6
SIC Composite	0.9	4.0	-0.2	5.3	2.0
Large Composite	–	–	–	–	–
Small Composite	–	–	–	–	–
High Financial Risk	–	–	–	–	–

Leverage Ratios (%)

	Debt/MV Equity Latest	5-Yr Avg	Debt/Total Capital Latest	5-Yr Avg
Median	10.8	6.3	9.7	5.9
SIC Composite	13.8	8.5	12.1	7.8
Large Composite	–	–	–	–
Small Composite	–	–	–	–
High Financial Risk	–	–	–	–

Cost of Debt

	Cost of Debt (%) Latest
Median	7.1
SIC Composite	5.2
Large Composite	–
Small Composite	–
High Financial Risk	–

Capital Structure
SIC Composite (%) Latest: D/TC 12.1, E/TC 87.9

Cost of Equity Capital (%)

	CRSP Deciles CAPM	CAPM +Size Prem	Build-Up	Risk Premium Report CAPM +Size Prem	Build-Up	Discounted Cash Flow 1-Stage	3-Stage	Fama-French 5-Factor Model
Median	10.1	12.0	12.3	13.7	12.7	13.7	14.7	21.2
SIC Composite	9.6	10.5	11.5	11.7	11.8	11.5	15.1	19.8
Large Composite	–	–	–	–	–	–	–	–
Small Composite	–	–	–	–	–	–	–	–
High Financial Risk	–	–	–	–	–	–	–	–

Cost of Equity Capital (%) SIC Composite
- Avg CRSP: 11.0
- Avg RPR: 11.8
- 1-Stage: 11.5
- 3-Stage: 15.1
- 5-Factor Model: 19.8

Weighted Average Cost of Capital (WACC) (%)

	CRSP Deciles CAPM	CAPM +Size Prem	Build-Up	Risk Premium Report CAPM +Size Prem	Build-Up	Discounted Cash Flow 1-Stage	3-Stage	Fama-French 5-Factor Model
Median	9.4	10.9	11.2	13.3	12.3	11.9	13.3	18.5
SIC Composite	9.0	9.8	10.7	10.9	11.0	10.6	13.9	18.0
Large Composite	–	–	–	–	–	–	–	–
Small Composite	–	–	–	–	–	–	–	–
High Financial Risk	–	–	–	–	–	–	–	–

WACC (%) SIC Composite: Low 9.8, High 18.0. ▲ Average 12.1, ♦ Median 10.9

© 2017 Duff & Phelps. All Rights Reserved. Duff & Phelps has used the utmost care in compiling the data presented herein, but cannot guarantee the accuracy, completeness, or timeliness of the information.

Data Updated Through March 31, 2017

58

Number of Companies: 26
Eating and Drinking Places

Industry Description
This major group includes retail establishments selling prepared foods and drinks for consumption on the premises; and also lunch counters and refreshment stands selling prepared foods and drinks for immediate consumption.

Sales (in millions)

Three Largest Companies
McDonald's Corp.	$24,621.9
Starbucks Corp.	21,315.9
Darden Restaurants, Inc.	6,933.5

Three Smallest Companies
Flanigans Enterprises Inc.	$103.6
Nathan's Famous Inc.	100.9
Famous Dave's of America Inc.	99.2

Annualized Monthly Performance Statistics (%)

Industry	Geometric Mean	Arithmetic Mean	Standard Deviation
1-year	6.0	6.5	11.1
3-year	12.3	12.9	11.6
5-year	11.3	11.9	11.9

Total Assets (in millions)

Three Largest Companies
McDonald's Corp.	$31,023.9
Starbucks Corp.	14,329.5
Yum Brands, Inc.	5,478.0

Three Smallest Companies
Ark Restaurants Corp.	$68.3
Flanigans Enterprises Inc.	56.6
Famous Dave's of America Inc.	50.9

S&P 500 Index	Geometric Mean	Arithmetic Mean	Standard Deviation
1-year	17.2	17.4	7.2
3-year	10.4	10.9	11.5
5-year	13.3	13.9	11.5

Return Ratios (%)

	Return on Assets Latest	5-Yr Avg	Return on Equity Latest	5-Yr Avg	Dividend Yield Latest	5-Yr Avg
Median (26)	8.4	8.3	12.5	16.3	1.5	1.0
SIC Composite (26)	13.4	12.1	3.8	4.0	2.2	2.1
Large Composite (3)	15.7	13.6	3.9	4.2	2.4	2.5
Small Composite (3)	3.5	7.0	1.9	3.5	0.5	0.1
High-Financial Risk (8)	3.2	4.4	0.8	1.8	0.9	0.9

Liquidity Ratio

	Current Ratio Latest	5-Yr Avg
	1.0	1.0
	1.1	1.2
	1.1	1.4
	2.7	2.2
	1.0	1.1

Profitability Ratio (%)

	Operating Margin Latest	5-Yr Avg
	9.4	10.0
	19.1	18.1
	23.3	22.3
	9.0	7.9
	8.0	7.7

Growth Rates (%)

	Long-term EPS Analyst Estimates
	15.6
	18.2
	11.7
	17.9
	18.0

Betas (Levered)

	Raw (OLS)	Blume Adjusted	Peer Group	Vasicek Adjusted	Sum	Downside
Median	0.52	0.70	0.66	0.58	0.58	1.01
SIC Composite	0.65	0.79	0.66	0.65	0.51	0.71
Large Composite	0.71	0.82	0.66	0.70	0.50	0.73
Small Composite	0.64	0.78	0.71	0.66	0.05	0.96
High Financial Risk	0.50	0.69	0.66	0.55	0.01	0.92

Betas (Unlevered)

	Raw (OLS)	Blume Adjusted	Peer Group	Vasicek Adjusted	Sum	Downside
Median	0.46	0.61	0.59	0.52	0.52	0.84
SIC Composite	0.58	0.69	0.58	0.58	0.46	0.63
Large Composite	0.63	0.73	0.58	0.62	0.44	0.65
Small Composite	0.54	0.64	0.59	0.56	0.14	0.76
High Financial Risk	0.47	0.61	0.59	0.51	0.09	0.80

Equity Valuation Multiples

	Price/Sales Latest	5-Yr Avg	Price/Earnings Latest	5-Yr Avg	Market/Book Latest	5-Yr Avg
Median	1.5	1.4	25.5	25.2	5.7	4.9
SIC Composite	3.1	2.8	26.2	24.9	–	8.6
Large Composite	3.8	3.3	25.6	23.7	–	8.8
Small Composite	1.1	1.1	53.9	28.3	–	7.4
High Financial Risk	1.8	1.3	–	56.8	–	–

Enterprise Valuation (EV) Multiples

	EV/Sales Latest	5-Yr Avg	EV/EBITDA Latest	5-Yr Avg
Median	1.6	1.5	11.2	10.8
SIC Composite	3.6	3.1	14.5	12.9
Large Composite	4.3	3.6	14.6	12.9
Small Composite	1.4	1.2	11.9	11.2
High Financial Risk	2.3	1.7	19.3	15.0

Enterprise Valuation SIC Composite

EV/Sales: 3.6 (Latest), 3.1 (5-Yr Avg)
EV/EBITDA: 14.5 (Latest), 12.9 (5-Yr Avg)

Fama-French (F-F) 5-Factor Model

	Fama-French (F-F) Components				
	F-F Beta	SMB Premium	HML Premium	RMW Premium	CMA Premium
Median	0.3	4.1	0.2	4.0	-2.2
SIC Composite	0.6	0.7	-0.7	1.2	0.1
Large Composite	0.8	-0.2	-0.5	1.0	1.4
Small Composite	0.6	2.0	-0.9	0.8	3.7
High Financial Risk	–	–	–	–	–

Leverage Ratios (%)

	Debt/MV Equity Latest	5-Yr Avg	Debt/Total Capital Latest	5-Yr Avg
Median	23.6	17.4	19.1	14.8
SIC Composite	18.0	13.9	15.2	12.2
Large Composite	14.9	13.3	13.0	11.7
Small Composite	45.8	22.9	31.4	18.6
High Financial Risk	28.3	38.6	22.1	27.8

Cost of Debt

	Cost of Debt (%) Latest
Median	6.1
SIC Composite	5.3
Large Composite	4.7
Small Composite	7.0
High Financial Risk	7.4

Capital Structure

SIC Composite (%) Latest

D/TC: 15.2
E/TC: 84.8

Cost of Equity Capital (%)

	CRSP Deciles			Risk Premium Report		Discounted Cash Flow		Fama-French
	CAPM	CAPM +Size Prem	Build-Up	CAPM +Size Prem	Build-Up	1-Stage	3-Stage	5-Factor Model
Median	6.7	8.5	8.7	10.5	13.7	16.3	12.0	11.4
SIC Composite	7.1	7.4	7.4	8.5	10.9	20.6	12.3	8.4
Large Composite	7.4	7.4	7.2	8.0	10.3	14.2	9.4	9.3
Small Composite	7.1	12.7	12.7	9.6	16.5	18.1	14.6	12.7
High Financial Risk	–	–	–	19.9	29.0	–	–	–

Cost of Equity Capital (%) SIC Composite

Avg CRSP: 7.4
Avg RPR: 9.7
1-Stage: 20.6
3-Stage: 12.3
5-Factor Model: 8.4

Weighted Average Cost of Capital (WACC) (%)

	CRSP Deciles			Risk Premium Report		Discounted Cash Flow		Fama-French
	CAPM	CAPM +Size Prem	Build-Up	CAPM +Size Prem	Build-Up	1-Stage	3-Stage	5-Factor Model
Median	6.4	7.6	7.8	9.6	12.4	13.5	10.6	9.3
SIC Composite	6.7	7.0	7.0	7.9	10.0	18.2	11.1	7.8
Large Composite	7.0	7.0	6.8	7.6	9.5	12.9	8.8	8.7
Small Composite	6.3	10.2	10.2	8.0	12.7	13.8	11.5	10.1
High Financial Risk	–	–	–	16.6	23.7	–	–	–

WACC (%) SIC Composite

Low: 7.0, High: 18.2
Average 9.9, Median 7.9

© 2017 Duff & Phelps. All Rights Reserved. Duff & Phelps has used the utmost care in compiling the data presented herein, but cannot guarantee the accuracy, completeness, or timeliness of the information.

Data Updated Through March 31, 2017

5812

Number of Companies: 25
Eating Places

Industry Description
Establishments primarily engaged in the retail sale of prepared food and drinks for on-premise or immediate consumption.

Sales (in millions)

Three Largest Companies
McDonald's Corp.	$24,621.9
Starbucks Corp.	21,315.9
Darden Restaurants, Inc.	6,933.5

Three Smallest Companies
Flanigans Enterprises Inc.	$103.6
Nathan's Famous Inc.	100.9
Famous Dave's of America Inc.	99.2

Total Assets (in millions)

Three Largest Companies
McDonald's Corp.	$31,023.9
Starbucks Corp.	14,329.5
Yum Brands, Inc.	5,478.0

Three Smallest Companies
Ark Restaurants Corp.	$68.3
Flanigans Enterprises Inc.	56.6
Famous Dave's of America Inc.	50.9

Annualized Monthly Performance Statistics (%)

Industry	Geometric Mean	Arithmetic Mean	Standard Deviation	S&P 500 Index	Geometric Mean	Arithmetic Mean	Standard Deviation
1-year	6.0	6.5	11.1	1-year	17.2	17.4	7.2
3-year	12.3	12.9	11.6	3-year	10.4	10.9	11.5
5-year	11.3	11.9	11.9	5-year	13.3	13.9	11.5

Return Ratios (%)

	Return on Assets Latest	5-Yr Avg	Return on Equity Latest	5-Yr Avg	Dividend Yield Latest	5-Yr Avg
Median (25)	8.9	8.8	13.1	17.1	1.6	1.0
SIC Composite (25)	13.4	12.1	3.8	4.0	2.2	2.1
Large Composite (3)	15.7	13.6	3.9	4.2	2.4	2.5
Small Composite (3)	3.5	7.0	1.9	3.5	0.5	0.1
High-Financial Risk (–)	–	–	–	–	–	–

Liquidity Ratio

	Current Ratio Latest	5-Yr Avg
Median (25)	1.0	1.0
SIC Composite (25)	1.1	1.2
Large Composite (3)	1.1	1.4
Small Composite (3)	2.7	2.2
High-Financial Risk (–)	–	–

Profitability Ratio (%)

	Operating Margin Latest	5-Yr Avg
Median (25)	9.2	9.6
SIC Composite (25)	19.1	18.1
Large Composite (3)	23.3	22.3
Small Composite (3)	9.0	7.9
High-Financial Risk (–)	–	–

Growth Rates (%)

	Long-term EPS Analyst Estimates
Median (25)	15.5
SIC Composite (25)	18.2
Large Composite (3)	11.7
Small Composite (3)	17.9
High-Financial Risk (–)	–

Betas (Levered)

	Raw (OLS)	Blume Adjusted	Peer Group	Vasicek Adjusted	Sum	Downside
Median	0.48	0.67	0.66	0.56	0.56	0.99
SIC Composite	0.65	0.79	0.66	0.65	0.51	0.71
Large Composite	0.71	0.82	0.66	0.70	0.50	0.73
Small Composite	0.64	0.78	0.71	0.66	0.05	0.96
High Financial Risk	–	–	–	–	–	–

Betas (Unlevered)

	Raw (OLS)	Blume Adjusted	Peer Group	Vasicek Adjusted	Sum	Downside
Median	0.45	0.63	0.59	0.52	0.52	0.84
SIC Composite	0.58	0.69	0.58	0.58	0.46	0.63
Large Composite	0.63	0.73	0.58	0.62	0.44	0.65
Small Composite	0.54	0.64	0.59	0.56	0.14	0.76
High Financial Risk	–	–	–	–	–	–

Equity Valuation Multiples

	Price/Sales Latest	5-Yr Avg	Price/Earnings Latest	5-Yr Avg	Market/Book Latest	5-Yr Avg
Median	1.6	1.4	25.6	25.7	6.6	5.0
SIC Composite	3.1	2.8	26.2	24.9	–	8.7
Large Composite	3.8	3.3	25.6	23.7	–	8.8
Small Composite	1.1	1.1	53.9	28.3	–	7.4
High Financial Risk	–	–	–	–	–	–

Enterprise Valuation (EV) Multiples

	EV/Sales Latest	5-Yr Avg	EV/EBITDA Latest	5-Yr Avg
Median	1.6	1.6	11.4	10.9
SIC Composite	3.6	3.1	14.5	13.0
Large Composite	4.3	3.6	14.6	12.9
Small Composite	1.4	1.2	11.9	11.2
High Financial Risk	–	–	–	–

Enterprise Valuation SIC Composite

	Latest	5-Yr Avg
EV/Sales	3.6	3.1
EV/EBITDA	14.5	13.0

Fama-French (F-F) 5-Factor Model

Fama-French (F-F) Components

	F-F Beta	SMB Premium	HML Premium	RMW Premium	CMA Premium
Median	0.3	4.1	0.2	4.0	-2.2
SIC Composite	0.6	0.7	-0.7	1.2	0.1
Large Composite	0.8	-0.2	-0.5	1.0	1.4
Small Composite	0.6	2.0	-0.9	0.8	3.7
High Financial Risk	–	–	–	–	–

Leverage Ratios (%)

	Debt/MV Equity Latest	5-Yr Avg	Debt/Total Capital Latest	5-Yr Avg
Median	22.7	15.6	18.5	13.5
SIC Composite	17.9	13.9	15.2	12.2
Large Composite	14.9	13.3	13.0	11.7
Small Composite	45.8	22.9	31.4	18.6
High Financial Risk	–	–	–	–

Cost of Debt

	Cost of Debt (%) Latest
Median	6.1
SIC Composite	5.3
Large Composite	4.7
Small Composite	7.0
High Financial Risk	–

Capital Structure

SIC Composite (%) Latest
- D/TC: 15.2
- E/TC: 84.8

Cost of Equity Capital (%)

	CRSP Deciles CAPM	CAPM +Size Prem	Build-Up	Risk Premium Report CAPM +Size Prem	Build-Up	Discounted Cash Flow 1-Stage	3-Stage	Fama-French 5-Factor Model
Median	6.6	8.2	8.6	10.4	13.7	16.2	11.9	11.4
SIC Composite	7.1	7.4	7.4	8.5	10.9	20.6	12.3	8.4
Large Composite	7.4	7.4	7.2	8.0	10.3	14.2	9.4	9.3
Small Composite	7.1	12.7	12.7	9.6	16.5	18.1	14.6	12.7
High Financial Risk	–	–	–	–	–	–	–	–

Cost of Equity Capital (%) SIC Composite

Avg CRSP	Avg RPR	1-Stage	3-Stage	5-Factor Model
7.4	9.7	20.6	12.3	8.4

Weighted Average Cost of Capital (WACC) (%)

	CRSP Deciles CAPM	CAPM +Size Prem	Build-Up	Risk Premium Report CAPM +Size Prem	Build-Up	Discounted Cash Flow 1-Stage	3-Stage	Fama-French 5-Factor Model
Median	6.4	7.5	7.8	9.3	12.4	13.4	10.6	9.3
SIC Composite	6.7	7.0	7.0	7.9	10.0	18.2	11.1	7.8
Large Composite	7.0	7.0	6.8	7.6	9.5	12.9	8.8	8.7
Small Composite	6.3	10.2	10.2	8.0	12.7	13.8	11.5	10.1
High Financial Risk	–	–	–	–	–	–	–	–

WACC (%) SIC Composite
- Low: 7.0
- High: 18.2
- Average: 9.9
- Median: 7.9

© 2017 Duff & Phelps. All Rights Reserved. Duff & Phelps has used the utmost care in compiling the data presented herein, but cannot guarantee the accuracy, completeness, or timeliness of the information.

Data Updated Through March 31, 2017

59
Number of Companies: 27
Miscellaneous Retail

Industry Description
This major group includes retail establishments, not elsewhere classified. These establishments fall into the following categories: drug stores, liquor stores, used merchandise stores, miscellaneous shopping goods stores, non-store retailers, fuel dealers, and miscellaneous retail stores, not elsewhere classified.

Sales (in millions)

Three Largest Companies
CVS Health Corp.	$177,526.0
Amazon.com Inc.	135,987.0
Walgreens Boots Alliance, Inc.	117,351.0

Three Smallest Companies
Nutrisystem, Inc.	$545.5
PetMed Express Inc.	234.7
Tandy Leather Factory, Inc.	82.9

Total Assets (in millions)

Three Largest Companies
CVS Health Corp.	$94,462.0
Amazon.com Inc.	83,402.0
Walgreens Boots Alliance, Inc.	72,688.0

Three Smallest Companies
Nutrisystem, Inc.	$154.2
PetMed Express Inc.	90.3
Tandy Leather Factory, Inc.	70.6

Annualized Monthly Performance Statistics (%)

Industry	Geometric Mean	Arithmetic Mean	Standard Deviation
1-year	19.4	19.9	11.5
3-year	19.3	20.8	19.4
5-year	22.5	24.0	19.5

S&P 500 Index	Geometric Mean	Arithmetic Mean	Standard Deviation
1-year	17.2	17.4	7.2
3-year	10.4	10.9	11.5
5-year	13.3	13.9	11.5

Return Ratios (%)

	Return on Assets Latest	Return on Assets 5-Yr Avg	Return on Equity Latest	Return on Equity 5-Yr Avg	Dividend Yield Latest	Dividend Yield 5-Yr Avg
Median (27)	5.9	6.2	13.9	11.5	1.2	0.7
SIC Composite (27)	5.0	4.5	2.6	2.8	0.7	0.8
Large Composite (3)	4.7	4.5	2.0	2.3	0.6	0.7
Small Composite (3)	19.8	15.9	2.9	4.4	2.0	3.2
High-Financial Risk (−)	−	−	−	−	−	−

Liquidity Ratio

	Current Ratio Latest	Current Ratio 5-Yr Avg
Median (27)	1.5	1.6
SIC Composite (27)	1.2	1.3
Large Composite (3)	1.2	1.2
Small Composite (3)	3.0	3.0
High-Financial Risk (−)	−	−

Profitability Ratio (%)

	Operating Margin Latest	Operating Margin 5-Yr Avg
Median (27)	5.9	7.2
SIC Composite (27)	5.1	4.9
Large Composite (3)	4.9	4.6
Small Composite (3)	11.4	9.4
High-Financial Risk (−)	−	−

Growth Rates (%)

	Long-term EPS Analyst Estimates
Median (27)	15.0
SIC Composite (27)	25.7
Large Composite (3)	27.9
Small Composite (3)	25.7
High-Financial Risk (−)	−

Betas (Levered)

	Raw (OLS)	Blume Adjusted	Peer Group	Vasicek Adjusted	Sum	Downside
Median	1.06	1.04	1.25	1.10	0.96	1.45
SIC Composite	1.21	1.14	1.25	1.21	1.28	1.30
Large Composite	1.26	1.17	1.25	1.25	1.26	1.41
Small Composite	1.18	1.12	1.26	1.25	1.24	1.57
High Financial Risk	−	−	−	−	−	−

Betas (Unlevered)

	Raw (OLS)	Blume Adjusted	Peer Group	Vasicek Adjusted	Sum	Downside
Median	0.91	0.84	1.09	0.91	0.81	1.28
SIC Composite	1.06	1.00	1.10	1.06	1.12	1.14
Large Composite	1.13	1.06	1.13	1.13	1.13	1.27
Small Composite	1.17	1.12	1.26	1.25	1.24	1.56
High Financial Risk	−	−	−	−	−	−

Equity Valuation Multiples

	Price/Sales Latest	Price/Sales 5-Yr Avg	Price/Earnings Latest	Price/Earnings 5-Yr Avg	Market/Book Latest	Market/Book 5-Yr Avg
Median	0.7	0.8	19.7	20.1	2.3	2.3
SIC Composite	1.1	0.9	38.1	35.5	5.2	3.8
Large Composite	1.4	1.1	50.2	43.7	6.4	4.5
Small Composite	2.5	1.3	34.2	23.0	9.2	5.0
High Financial Risk	−	−	−	−	−	−

Enterprise Valuation (EV) Multiples

	EV/Sales Latest	EV/Sales 5-Yr Avg	EV/EBITDA Latest	EV/EBITDA 5-Yr Avg
Median	0.7	0.9	8.7	9.1
SIC Composite	1.2	1.0	16.0	14.0
Large Composite	1.4	1.2	19.4	16.6
Small Composite	2.4	1.2	18.2	10.7
High Financial Risk	−	−	−	−

Enterprise Valuation SIC Composite
- Latest: EV/Sales 1.2, EV/EBITDA 16.0
- 5-Yr Avg: EV/Sales 1.0, EV/EBITDA 14.0

Fama-French (F-F) 5-Factor Model

	F-F Beta	SMB Premium	HML Premium	RMW Premium	CMA Premium
Median	1.3	0.2	-1.7	-0.7	4.6
SIC Composite	1.2	-0.6	-3.1	-1.2	-0.2
Large Composite	−	−	−	−	−
Small Composite	1.0	4.1	1.8	2.5	-6.3
High Financial Risk	−	−	−	−	−

Leverage Ratios (%)

	Debt/MV Equity Latest	Debt/MV Equity 5-Yr Avg	Debt/Total Capital Latest	Debt/Total Capital 5-Yr Avg
Median	18.0	14.7	15.2	12.8
SIC Composite	15.3	16.6	13.3	14.2
Large Composite	11.2	11.4	10.1	10.2
Small Composite	0.3	0.5	0.3	0.5
High Financial Risk	−	−	−	−

Cost of Debt

	Cost of Debt (%) Latest
Median	7.1
SIC Composite	5.1
Large Composite	4.5
Small Composite	7.1
High Financial Risk	−

Capital Structure

SIC Composite (%) Latest
- D/TC: 13.3
- E/TC: 86.7

Cost of Equity Capital (%)

	CRSP Deciles CAPM	CRSP Deciles CAPM +Size Prem	CRSP Deciles Build-Up	Risk Premium Report CAPM +Size Prem	Risk Premium Report Build-Up	Discounted Cash Flow 1-Stage	Discounted Cash Flow 3-Stage	Fama-French 5-Factor Model
Median	9.5	11.5	12.1	11.9	13.5	13.1	16.9	13.2
SIC Composite	10.1	10.2	10.5	11.9	9.9	26.5	13.6	5.1
Large Composite	10.4	10.4	10.4	11.5	9.6	28.7	12.8	−
Small Composite	10.4	12.4	12.4	15.4	15.4	26.9	13.0	11.1
High Financial Risk	−	−	−	−	−	−	−	−

Cost of Equity Capital (%) SIC Composite
- Avg CRSP: 10.4
- Avg RPR: 10.9
- 1-Stage: 26.5
- 3-Stage: 13.6
- 5-Factor Model: 5.1

Weighted Average Cost of Capital (WACC) (%)

	CRSP Deciles CAPM	CRSP Deciles CAPM +Size Prem	CRSP Deciles Build-Up	Risk Premium Report CAPM +Size Prem	Risk Premium Report Build-Up	Discounted Cash Flow 1-Stage	Discounted Cash Flow 3-Stage	Fama-French 5-Factor Model
Median	8.6	10.5	11.0	10.4	12.1	10.8	14.6	10.6
SIC Composite	9.4	9.5	9.7	10.9	9.2	23.5	12.4	5.0
Large Composite	9.7	9.7	9.8	10.8	9.1	26.2	11.9	−
Small Composite	10.4	12.4	12.4	15.3	15.4	26.8	12.9	11.1
High Financial Risk	−	−	−	−	−	−	−	−

WACC (%) SIC Composite
- Low: 5.0
- High: 23.5
- Average: 11.5
- Median: 9.7

© 2017 Duff & Phelps. All Rights Reserved. Duff & Phelps has used the utmost care in compiling the data presented herein, but cannot guarantee the accuracy, completeness, or timeliness of the information.

Data Updated Through March 31, 2017

591

Number of Companies: 5
Drug Stores and Proprietary Stores

Industry Description
Establishments engaged in the retail sale of prescription drugs, proprietary drugs, and nonprescription medicines, and which may carry a number of related lines, such as cosmetics, toiletries, tobacco, and novelty merchandise.

Sales (in millions)

Three Largest Companies
CVS Health Corp.	$177,526.0
Walgreens Boots Alliance, Inc.	117,351.0
Express Scripts Holding Co.	100,287.5

Three Smallest Companies
Express Scripts Holding Co.	$100,287.5
Rite Aid Corp.	30,736.7
PetMed Express Inc.	234.7

Total Assets (in millions)

Three Largest Companies
CVS Health Corp.	$94,462.0
Walgreens Boots Alliance, Inc.	72,688.0
Express Scripts Holding Co.	51,744.9

Three Smallest Companies
Express Scripts Holding Co.	$51,744.9
Rite Aid Corp.	11,277.0
PetMed Express Inc.	90.3

Annualized Monthly Performance Statistics (%)

	Industry Geometric Mean	Arithmetic Mean	Standard Deviation		S&P 500 Index Geometric Mean	Arithmetic Mean	Standard Deviation
1-year	-12.0	-11.7	7.4	1-year	17.2	17.4	7.2
3-year	3.5	4.6	15.8	3-year	10.4	10.9	11.5
5-year	13.6	14.9	17.1	5-year	13.3	13.9	11.5

Return Ratios (%)

	Return on Assets Latest	5-Yr Avg	Return on Equity Latest	5-Yr Avg	Dividend Yield Latest	5-Yr Avg	Current Ratio Latest	5-Yr Avg	Operating Margin Latest	5-Yr Avg	Long-term EPS Analyst Estimates
Median (5)	5.9	6.2	16.5	11.3	1.8	1.6	1.5	1.4	5.6	5.1	12.3
SIC Composite (5)	5.7	5.4	6.0	4.9	1.5	1.3	1.2	1.2	5.4	5.2	11.1
Large Composite (–)	–	–	–	–	–	–	–	–	–	–	–
Small Composite (–)	–	–	–	–	–	–	–	–	–	–	–
High-Financial Risk (–)	–	–	–	–	–	–	–	–	–	–	–

Betas (Levered)

	Raw (OLS)	Blume Adjusted	Peer Group	Vasicek Adjusted	Sum	Downside
Median	1.06	1.04	1.25	1.13	1.27	1.32
SIC Composite	0.98	0.99	1.25	1.01	1.05	1.05
Large Composite	–	–	–	–	–	–
Small Composite	–	–	–	–	–	–
High Financial Risk	–	–	–	–	–	–

Betas (Unlevered)

	Raw (OLS)	Blume Adjusted	Peer Group	Vasicek Adjusted	Sum	Downside
Median	0.96	0.83	0.96	0.78	0.92	1.06
SIC Composite	0.77	0.78	0.98	0.79	0.82	0.82
Large Composite	–	–	–	–	–	–
Small Composite	–	–	–	–	–	–
High Financial Risk	–	–	–	–	–	–

Equity Valuation Multiples

	Price/Sales Latest	5-Yr Avg	Price/Earnings Latest	5-Yr Avg	Market/Book Latest	5-Yr Avg
Median	0.5	0.6	20.1	18.7	2.8	2.6
SIC Composite	0.5	0.6	16.6	20.4	2.3	2.3
Large Composite	–	–	–	–	–	–
Small Composite	–	–	–	–	–	–
High Financial Risk	–	–	–	–	–	–

Enterprise Valuation (EV) Multiples

	EV/Sales Latest	5-Yr Avg	EV/EBITDA Latest	5-Yr Avg
Median	0.6	0.7	8.7	9.5
SIC Composite	0.6	0.7	9.1	10.0
Large Composite	–	–	–	–
Small Composite	–	–	–	–
High Financial Risk	–	–	–	–

Enterprise Valuation SIC Composite
- Latest: EV/Sales 0.6, EV/EBITDA 9.1
- 5-Yr Avg: EV/Sales 0.7, EV/EBITDA 10.0

Fama-French (F-F) 5-Factor Model

	F-F Beta	SMB Premium	HML Premium	RMW Premium	CMA Premium
Median	1.3	-0.9	-2.8	-1.2	2.2
SIC Composite	1.0	-0.5	-2.5	-1.3	2.5
Large Composite	–	–	–	–	–
Small Composite	–	–	–	–	–
High Financial Risk	–	–	–	–	–

Leverage Ratios (%)

	Debt/MV Equity Latest	5-Yr Avg	Debt/Total Capital Latest	5-Yr Avg
Median	33.1	20.6	24.8	17.1
SIC Composite	31.8	23.2	24.1	18.8
Large Composite	–	–	–	–
Small Composite	–	–	–	–
High Financial Risk	–	–	–	–

Cost of Debt

	Cost of Debt (%) Latest
Median	4.8
SIC Composite	5.0

Capital Structure
SIC Composite (%) Latest
- D/TC: 24.1
- E/TC: 75.9

Cost of Equity Capital (%)

	CRSP Deciles CAPM	CAPM +Size Prem	Build-Up	Risk Premium Report CAPM	CAPM +Size Prem	Build-Up	Discounted Cash Flow 1-Stage	3-Stage	Fama-French 5-Factor Model
Median	9.7	10.4	10.4	11.8		9.7	12.9	13.7	8.0
SIC Composite	9.0	9.1	10.5	10.4		9.7	12.9	13.6	7.1
Large Composite	–	–	–	–		–	–	–	–
Small Composite	–	–	–	–		–	–	–	–
High Financial Risk	–	–	–	–		–	–	–	–

Cost of Equity Capital (%) SIC Composite
- Avg CRSP: 9.8
- Avg RPR: 10.1
- 1-Stage: 12.9
- 3-Stage: 13.6
- 5-Factor Model: 7.1

Weighted Average Cost of Capital (WACC) (%)

	CRSP Deciles CAPM	CAPM +Size Prem	Build-Up	Risk Premium Report CAPM	CAPM +Size Prem	Build-Up	Discounted Cash Flow 1-Stage	3-Stage	Fama-French 5-Factor Model
Median	7.9	8.3	8.8	9.7		8.3	10.5	11.7	7.1
SIC Composite	7.7	7.8	8.8	8.8		8.2	10.7	11.2	6.3
Large Composite	–	–	–	–		–	–	–	–
Small Composite	–	–	–	–		–	–	–	–
High Financial Risk	–	–	–	–		–	–	–	–

WACC (%) SIC Composite
- Low: 6.3
- High: 11.2
- Average: 8.8
- Median: 8.8

© 2017 Duff & Phelps. All Rights Reserved. Duff & Phelps has used the utmost care in compiling the data presented herein, but cannot guarantee the accuracy, completeness, or timeliness of the information.

Data Updated Through March 31, 2017

594

Number of Companies: 6
Miscellaneous Shopping Goods Stores

Industry Description
Establishments primarily engaged in sporting goods stores and bicycle shops; book stores, stationary stores; jewelry stores; hobby, toy, and game shops; camera and photographic supply stores; gift, novelty, and souvenir shops; luggage and leather goods stores; sewing, needlework, and piece goods stores.

Sales (in millions)

Three Largest Companies
Office Depot, Inc.	$11,021.0
Dicks Sporting Goods Inc.	7,922.0
Cabela's Inc.	4,365.2

Three Smallest Companies
Tiffany & Co.	$4,001.8
Big 5 Sporting Goods Corp.	1,021.2
Hibbett Sports, Inc.	973.0

Annualized Monthly Performance Statistics (%)

Industry	Geometric Mean	Arithmetic Mean	Standard Deviation
1-year	9.9	13.1	28.0
3-year	0.1	2.5	22.8
5-year	5.4	7.8	23.3

Total Assets (in millions)

Three Largest Companies
Cabela's Inc.	$8,970.8
Office Depot, Inc.	5,540.0
Tiffany & Co.	5,097.6

Three Smallest Companies
Dicks Sporting Goods Inc.	$4,058.3
Hibbett Sports, Inc.	458.9
Big 5 Sporting Goods Corp.	433.6

S&P 500 Index	Geometric Mean	Arithmetic Mean	Standard Deviation
1-year	17.2	17.4	7.2
3-year	10.4	10.9	11.5
5-year	13.3	13.9	11.5

Return Ratios (%)

	Return on Assets Latest	Return on Assets 5-Yr Avg	Return on Equity Latest	Return on Equity 5-Yr Avg	Dividend Yield Latest	Dividend Yield 5-Yr Avg	Current Ratio Latest	Current Ratio 5-Yr Avg	Operating Margin Latest	Operating Margin 5-Yr Avg	Long-term EPS Analyst Estimates
Median (6)	8.1	6.2	15.2	12.9	1.5	1.1	2.2	2.5	6.7	8.1	11.3
SIC Composite (6)	6.7	4.6	6.8	4.4	1.6	1.4	2.3	2.3	7.3	7.0	9.9
Large Composite (–)	–	–	–	–	–	–	–	–	–	–	–
Small Composite (–)	–	–	–	–	–	–	–	–	–	–	–
High-Financial Risk (–)	–	–	–	–	–	–	–	–	–	–	–

Betas (Levered)

	Raw (OLS)	Blume Adjusted	Peer Group	Vasicek Adjusted	Sum	Downside
Median	0.63	0.77	1.26	0.67	0.82	1.72
SIC Composite	1.40	1.26	1.26	1.40	1.63	1.58
Large Composite	–	–	–	–	–	–
Small Composite	–	–	–	–	–	–
High Financial Risk	–	–	–	–	–	–

Betas (Unlevered)

	Raw (OLS)	Blume Adjusted	Peer Group	Vasicek Adjusted	Sum	Downside
Median	0.63	0.77	1.20	0.67	0.65	1.66
SIC Composite	1.16	1.05	1.05	1.15	1.33	1.29
Large Composite	–	–	–	–	–	–
Small Composite	–	–	–	–	–	–
High Financial Risk	–	–	–	–	–	–

Equity Valuation Multiples

	Price/Sales Latest	Price/Sales 5-Yr Avg	Price/Earnings Latest	Price/Earnings 5-Yr Avg	Market/Book Latest	Market/Book 5-Yr Avg
Median	0.7	0.9	19.2	19.2	1.9	2.6
SIC Composite	0.8	0.8	14.8	23.2	2.6	2.8
Large Composite	–	–	–	–	–	–
Small Composite	–	–	–	–	–	–
High Financial Risk	–	–	–	–	–	–

Enterprise Valuation (EV) Multiples

	EV/Sales Latest	EV/Sales 5-Yr Avg	EV/EBITDA Latest	EV/EBITDA 5-Yr Avg
Median	0.6	1.0	7.2	8.5
SIC Composite	1.0	0.9	9.8	9.8
Large Composite	–	–	–	–
Small Composite	–	–	–	–
High Financial Risk	–	–	–	–

Enterprise Valuation SIC Composite
- EV/Sales: Latest 1.0, 5-Yr Avg 0.9
- EV/EBITDA: Latest 9.8, 5-Yr Avg 9.8

Fama-French (F-F) 5-Factor Model

	F-F Beta	SMB Premium	HML Premium	RMW Premium	CMA Premium
Median	0.7	3.6	-3.4	2.3	6.2
SIC Composite	1.3	2.3	-0.6	1.2	2.9
Large Composite	–	–	–	–	–
Small Composite	–	–	–	–	–
High Financial Risk	–	–	–	–	–

Leverage Ratios (%)

	Debt/MV Equity Latest	Debt/MV Equity 5-Yr Avg	Debt/Total Capital Latest	Debt/Total Capital 5-Yr Avg
Median	6.7	13.4	6.2	11.8
SIC Composite	29.1	26.5	22.5	21.0
Large Composite	–	–	–	–
Small Composite	–	–	–	–
High Financial Risk	–	–	–	–

Cost of Debt

	Cost of Debt (%) Latest
Median	7.1
SIC Composite	6.8
Large Composite	–
Small Composite	–
High Financial Risk	–

Capital Structure

SIC Composite (%) Latest
- D/TC: 22.5
- E/TC: 77.5

Cost of Equity Capital (%)

	CRSP Deciles CAPM	CRSP Deciles CAPM +Size Prem	CRSP Deciles Build-Up	Risk Premium Report CAPM +Size Prem	Risk Premium Report Build-Up	Discounted Cash Flow 1-Stage	Discounted Cash Flow 3-Stage	Fama-French 5-Factor Model
Median	7.2	9.6	11.7	11.8	12.7	12.2	11.0	16.2
SIC Composite	11.2	12.1	11.4	15.5	12.4	11.5	9.6	16.6
Large Composite	–	–	–	–	–	–	–	–
Small Composite	–	–	–	–	–	–	–	–
High Financial Risk	–	–	–	–	–	–	–	–

Cost of Equity Capital (%) SIC Composite
- Avg CRSP: 11.7
- Avg RPR: 13.9
- 1-Stage: 11.5
- 3-Stage: 9.6
- 5-Factor Model: 16.6

Weighted Average Cost of Capital (WACC) (%)

	CRSP Deciles CAPM	CRSP Deciles CAPM +Size Prem	CRSP Deciles Build-Up	Risk Premium Report CAPM +Size Prem	Risk Premium Report Build-Up	Discounted Cash Flow 1-Stage	Discounted Cash Flow 3-Stage	Fama-French 5-Factor Model
Median	7.2	9.5	11.0	11.0	11.8	10.0	10.3	16.3
SIC Composite	10.0	10.7	10.2	13.4	11.0	10.3	8.8	14.2
Large Composite	–	–	–	–	–	–	–	–
Small Composite	–	–	–	–	–	–	–	–
High Financial Risk	–	–	–	–	–	–	–	–

WACC (%) SIC Composite
- Low: 8.8
- High: 14.2
- Average: 11.2
- Median: 10.7

© 2017 Duff & Phelps. All Rights Reserved. Duff & Phelps has used the utmost care in compiling the data presented herein, but cannot guarantee the accuracy, completeness, or timeliness of the information.

Data Updated Through March 31, 2017

596

Number of Companies: 7
Nonstore Retailers

Industry Description
Establishments primarily engaged in catalog and mail-order houses; automatic merchandising machine operators; direct selling establishments.

Sales (in millions)

Three Largest Companies
Amazon.com Inc.	$135,987.0
Liberty Interactive Corporation	10,219.0
HSN, Inc.	3,567.5

Three Smallest Companies
PCM, Inc.	$2,250.6
Overstock.com Inc.	1,800.0
Nutrisystem, Inc.	545.5

Total Assets (in millions)

Three Largest Companies
Amazon.com Inc.	$83,402.0
Liberty Interactive Corporation	14,357.0
HSN, Inc.	1,304.5

Three Smallest Companies
PCM, Inc.	$633.0
Overstock.com Inc.	485.1
Nutrisystem, Inc.	154.2

Annualized Monthly Performance Statistics (%)

Industry	Geometric Mean	Arithmetic Mean	Standard Deviation	S&P 500 Index	Geometric Mean	Arithmetic Mean	Standard Deviation
1-year	46.0	48.4	28.1	1-year	17.2	17.4	7.2
3-year	35.4	40.0	37.3	3-year	10.4	10.9	11.5
5-year	32.8	36.9	34.5	5-year	13.3	13.9	11.5

Return Ratios (%)

	Return on Assets Latest	5-Yr Avg	Return on Equity Latest	5-Yr Avg	Dividend Yield Latest	5-Yr Avg	Current Ratio Latest	5-Yr Avg	Operating Margin Latest	5-Yr Avg	Long-term EPS Analyst Estimates
Median (7)	3.2	7.6	13.9	11.5	0.0	0.0	1.5	1.5	3.1	2.9	25.7
SIC Composite (7)	3.0	1.9	0.7	0.6	0.0	0.1	1.1	1.1	3.5	2.8	34.3
Large Composite (−)	−	−	−	−	−	−	−	−	−	−	−
Small Composite (−)	−	−	−	−	−	−	−	−	−	−	−
High-Financial Risk (−)	−	−	−	−	−	−	−	−	−	−	−

Betas (Levered)

	Raw (OLS)	Blume Adjusted	Peer Group	Vasicek Adjusted	Sum	Downside
Median	1.22	1.14	1.24	1.24	1.20	1.76
SIC Composite	1.42	1.28	1.24	1.32	1.37	1.72
Large Composite	−	−	−	−	−	−
Small Composite	−	−	−	−	−	−
High Financial Risk	−	−	−	−	−	−

Betas (Unlevered)

	Raw (OLS)	Blume Adjusted	Peer Group	Vasicek Adjusted	Sum	Downside
Median	0.99	0.95	1.14	1.10	1.07	1.63
SIC Composite	1.35	1.20	1.18	1.25	1.29	1.62
Large Composite	−	−	−	−	−	−
Small Composite	−	−	−	−	−	−
High Financial Risk	−	−	−	−	−	−

Equity Valuation Multiples

	Price/Sales Latest	5-Yr Avg	Price/Earnings Latest	5-Yr Avg	Market/Book Latest	5-Yr Avg
Median	0.5	0.8	19.4	23.8	2.5	3.6
SIC Composite	2.8	2.0	−	−	−	−
Large Composite	−	−	−	−	−	−
Small Composite	−	−	−	−	−	−
High Financial Risk	−	−	−	−	−	−

Enterprise Valuation (EV) Multiples

	EV/Sales Latest	5-Yr Avg	EV/EBITDA Latest	5-Yr Avg
Median	0.7	0.9	8.6	9.1
SIC Composite	2.8	2.0	32.6	28.4
Large Composite	−	−	−	−
Small Composite	−	−	−	−
High Financial Risk	−	−	−	−

Enterprise Valuation SIC Composite: EV/Sales Latest 2.8, 5-Yr Avg 2.0; EV/EBITDA Latest 32.6, 5-Yr Avg 28.4

Fama-French (F-F) 5-Factor Model

	F-F Beta	SMB Premium	HML Premium	RMW Premium	CMA Premium
Median	1.3	0.2	−1.7	−0.7	4.6
SIC Composite	−	−	−	−	−
Large Composite	−	−	−	−	−
Small Composite	−	−	−	−	−
High Financial Risk	−	−	−	−	−

Leverage Ratios (%)

	Debt/MV Equity Latest	5-Yr Avg	Debt/Total Capital Latest	5-Yr Avg
Median	13.5	6.4	11.9	6.0
SIC Composite	6.3	8.6	5.9	8.0
Large Composite	−	−	−	−
Small Composite	−	−	−	−
High Financial Risk	−	−	−	−

Cost of Debt

	Cost of Debt (%) Latest
Median	7.1
SIC Composite	4.7

Capital Structure

SIC Composite (%) Latest: D/TC 5.9, E/TC 94.1

Cost of Equity Capital (%)

	CRSP Deciles CAPM	CAPM +Size Prem	Build-Up	Risk Premium Report CAPM +Size Prem	Build-Up	Discounted Cash Flow 1-Stage	3-Stage	Fama-French 5-Factor Model
Median	10.3	12.0	12.1	13.2	14.9	20.1	17.1	13.2
SIC Composite	10.8	10.8	10.5	12.2	9.7	34.3	7.0	−
Large Composite	−	−	−	−	−	−	−	−
Small Composite	−	−	−	−	−	−	−	−
High Financial Risk	−	−	−	−	−	−	−	−

Cost of Equity Capital (%) SIC Composite: Avg CRSP 10.6, Avg RPR 11.0, 1-Stage 34.3, 3-Stage 7.0, 5-Factor Model n/a

Weighted Average Cost of Capital (WACC) (%)

	CRSP Deciles CAPM	CAPM +Size Prem	Build-Up	Risk Premium Report CAPM +Size Prem	Build-Up	Discounted Cash Flow 1-Stage	3-Stage	Fama-French 5-Factor Model
Median	9.7	11.1	11.3	12.5	13.3	18.8	15.9	11.1
SIC Composite	10.4	10.4	10.1	11.8	9.4	32.5	6.9	−
Large Composite	−	−	−	−	−	−	−	−
Small Composite	−	−	−	−	−	−	−	−
High Financial Risk	−	−	−	−	−	−	−	−

WACC (%) SIC Composite: Low 6.9, High 32.5, ▲ Average 13.5, ◆ Median 10.3

© 2017 Duff & Phelps. All Rights Reserved. Duff & Phelps has used the utmost care in compiling the data presented herein, but cannot guarantee the accuracy, completeness, or timeliness of the information.

Division H: Finance, Insurance, and Real Estate

This division includes establishments operating primarily in the fields of finance, insurance, and real estate. Major groups between "60" and "67" are in this division.

Data Updated Through March 31, 2017

6
Number of Companies: 678
Finance, Insurance, and Real Estate

Industry Description
This division includes establishments operating primarily in the fields of finance, insurance, and real estate. Finance includes depository institutions, non-depository credit institutions, holding (but not predominantly operating) companies, other investment companies, brokers and dealers in securities and commodity contracts, and security and commodity exchanges. Insurance covers carriers of all types of insurance, and insurance agents and brokers. Real estate includes owners, lessors, lessees, buyers, sellers, agents, and developers of real estate.

Sales (in millions)

Three Largest Companies
UnitedHealth Group Inc.	$184,840.0
JPMorgan Chase & Co.	105,486.0
Bank of America Corp.	93,662.0

Three Smallest Companies
Mesa Royalty Trust	$2.1
Kayne Anderson Energy Development	1.8
CKX Lands Inc.	1.1

Annualized Monthly Performance Statistics (%)

Industry	Geometric Mean	Arithmetic Mean	Standard Deviation
1-year	26.9	27.7	15.1
3-year	11.7	12.6	14.8
5-year	15.4	16.3	14.6

Total Assets (in millions)

Three Largest Companies
JPMorgan Chase & Co.	$2,490,972.0
Bank of America Corp	2,187,702.0
Wells Fargo & Co.	1,930,115.0

Three Smallest Companies
Permian Basin Royalty Trust	$2.1
North European Oil Royalty Trust	1.2
BP Prudhoe Bay Royalty Trust	1.0

S&P 500 Index	Geometric Mean	Arithmetic Mean	Standard Deviation
1-year	17.2	17.4	7.2
3-year	10.4	10.9	11.5
5-year	13.3	13.9	11.5

Return Ratios (%)

	Return on Assets Latest	5-Yr Avg	Return on Equity Latest	5-Yr Avg	Dividend Yield Latest	5-Yr Avg
Median (678)	1.1	1.2	8.8	8.4	2.4	2.4
SIC Composite (678)	1.2	1.1	5.6	6.4	2.4	2.4
Large Composite (67)	1.1	1.0	6.1	7.2	2.0	1.8
Small Composite (67)	1.1	1.8	4.9	8.4	2.7	3.1
High-Financial Risk (73)	0.5	0.9	2.6	5.0	3.7	4.0

Liquidity Ratio

	Current Ratio Latest	5-Yr Avg
	1.6	1.5
	1.1	1.1
	1.1	1.1
	1.5	1.5
	1.0	1.2

Profitability Ratio (%)

	Operating Margin Latest	5-Yr Avg
	29.3	27.7
	21.4	22.0
	19.1	19.9
	26.6	37.2
	18.5	18.9

Growth Rates (%)

	Long-term EPS Analyst Estimates
	8.5
	11.2
	11.2
	9.7
	18.3

Betas (Levered)

	Raw (OLS)	Blume Adjusted	Peer Group	Vasicek Adjusted	Sum	Downside
Median	0.83	0.90	1.11	0.91	0.91	1.10
SIC Composite	1.08	1.06	1.11	1.09	1.24	1.17
Large Composite	1.20	1.13	1.13	1.20	1.45	1.34
Small Composite	0.51	0.69	1.08	0.61	0.62	0.63
High Financial Risk	1.09	1.06	1.08	1.09	1.12	1.14

Betas (Unlevered)

	Raw (OLS)	Blume Adjusted	Peer Group	Vasicek Adjusted	Sum	Downside
Median	0.56	0.63	0.80	0.63	0.60	0.75
SIC Composite	0.60	0.59	0.62	0.60	0.69	0.65
Large Composite	0.61	0.58	0.58	0.61	0.74	0.68
Small Composite	0.38	0.51	0.79	0.45	0.46	0.47
High Financial Risk	0.49	0.49	0.49	0.49	0.50	0.51

Enterprise Valuation (EV) Multiples

	EV/EBITDA Latest	5-Yr Avg
Median	15.3	13.1
SIC Composite	12.7	11.0
Large Composite	10.8	9.3
Small Composite	18.4	11.6
High Financial Risk	30.0	29.1

Equity Valuation Multiples

	Price/Sales Latest	5-Yr Avg	Price/Earnings Latest	5-Yr Avg	Price/TBV* Latest	5-Yr Avg	Price/EBT** Latest	5-Yr Avg
Median	3.9	3.0	20.0	16.7	1.9	1.5	13.7	11.2
SIC Composite	2.4	2.0	18.7	16.2	2.4	2.0	12.4	10.2
Large Composite	2.0	1.6	17.2	14.3	2.3	1.9	11.2	9.0
Small Composite	4.8	4.1	20.4	12.0	1.6	1.5	19.3	12.1
High Financial Risk	1.8	1.7	43.9	21.8	1.6	1.6	15.5	12.0

Equity Valuation
SIC Composite
- Price/TBV: Latest 2.4, 5-Yr Avg 2.0
- Price/EBT: Latest 12.4, 5-Yr Avg 10.2

Fama-French (F-F) 5-Factor Model

	F-F Beta	SMB Premium	HML Premium	RMW Premium	CMA Premium
Median	0.7	2.6	5.4	-0.9	-3.0
SIC Composite	1.0	0.7	2.8	-1.1	-1.9
Large Composite	1.1	0.4	4.2	-1.6	-2.2
Small Composite	0.5	-0.9	2.1	-1.2	-0.7
High Financial Risk	–	–	–	–	–

Leverage Ratios (%)

	Debt/MV Equity Latest	5-Yr Avg	Debt/Total Capital Latest	5-Yr Avg
Median	44.7	55.2	30.9	35.5
SIC Composite	90.4	116.3	47.5	53.8
Large Composite	105.6	138.0	51.4	58.0
Small Composite	42.6	47.7	29.9	32.3
High Financial Risk	–	–	72.8	74.9

Cost of Debt

	Cost of Debt (%) Latest
Median	4.8
SIC Composite	4.6
Large Composite	4.5
Small Composite	4.8
High Financial Risk	6.2

Capital Structure
SIC Composite (%) Latest
- D/TC: 47.5
- E/TC: 52.5

Cost of Equity Capital (%)

	CRSP Deciles CAPM	CAPM +Size Prem	Build-Up	Risk Premium Report CAPM +Size Prem	Build-Up	Discounted Cash Flow 1-Stage	3-Stage	Fama-French 5-Factor Model
Median	8.5	11.0	11.9	–	–	11.3	11.7	11.4
SIC Composite	9.5	9.9	10.0	–	–	13.7	12.6	9.8
Large Composite	10.1	10.2	10.2	–	–	13.2	13.7	10.4
Small Composite	6.8	11.9	13.9	–	–	11.3	12.5	5.5
High Financial Risk	–	–	–	–	–	–	–	–

Cost of Equity Capital (%) SIC Composite
- Avg CRSP: 9.9
- Avg RPR: n/a
- 1-Stage: 13.7
- 3-Stage: 12.6
- 5-Factor Model: 9.8

Weighted Average Cost of Capital (WACC) (%)

	CRSP Deciles CAPM	CAPM +Size Prem	Build-Up	Risk Premium Report CAPM +Size Prem	Build-Up	Discounted Cash Flow 1-Stage	3-Stage	Fama-French 5-Factor Model
Median	6.9	8.5	8.9	–	–	9.0	8.9	8.7
SIC Composite	6.6	6.9	6.9	–	–	8.9	8.3	6.8
Large Composite	6.7	6.8	6.8	–	–	8.2	8.5	6.9
Small Composite	5.8	9.4	10.7	–	–	9.0	9.8	4.9
High Financial Risk	–	–	–	–	–	–	–	–

WACC (%) SIC Composite
- Low 6.8, High 8.9
- Average 7.6, Median 6.9

*TBV = Tangible Book Value
**EBT = Earnings Before Taxes

© 2017 Duff & Phelps. All Rights Reserved. Duff & Phelps has used the utmost care in compiling the data presented herein, but cannot guarantee the accuracy, completeness, or timeliness of the information.

Data Updated Through March 31, 2017

60

Number of Companies: 347
Depository Institutions

Industry Description
This major group includes institutions that are engaged in deposit banking or closely related functions, including fiduciary activities.

Sales (in millions)

Three Largest Companies
JPMorgan Chase & Co.	$105,486.0
Bank of America Corp.	93,662.0
Wells Fargo & Co.	93,512.0

Three Smallest Companies
AMB Financial Corp.	$9.0
Great American Bancorp Inc.	8.3
WVS Financial Corp.	7.4

Annualized Monthly Performance Statistics (%)

Industry	Geometric Mean	Arithmetic Mean	Standard Deviation
1-year	37.6	39.5	24.3
3-year	12.8	14.3	19.1
5-year	17.5	18.8	18.1

Total Assets (in millions)

Three Largest Companies
JPMorgan Chase & Co.	$2,490,972.0
Bank of America Corp.	2,187,702.0
Wells Fargo & Co.	1,930,115.0

Three Smallest Companies
AMB Financial Corp.	$189.9
Great American Bancorp Inc.	182.1
Payment Data Systems, Inc.	68.4

S&P 500 Index	Geometric Mean	Arithmetic Mean	Standard Deviation
1-year	17.2	17.4	7.2
3-year	10.4	10.9	11.5
5-year	13.3	13.9	11.5

Return Ratios (%)

	Return on Assets Latest	5-Yr Avg	Return on Equity Latest	5-Yr Avg	Dividend Yield Latest	5-Yr Avg	Current Ratio Latest	5-Yr Avg	Operating Margin Latest	5-Yr Avg	Long-term EPS Analyst Estimates
Median (347)	0.9	0.9	8.6	8.3	2.0	2.1	1.6	1.5	29.1	26.6	8.1
SIC Composite (347)	1.1	1.0	6.1	7.3	2.0	2.0	1.8	1.7	32.8	30.7	9.4
Large Composite (34)	1.1	1.0	6.4	7.5	2.0	1.9	1.8	1.7	32.8	30.9	9.4
Small Composite (34)	0.7	0.6	4.2	5.1	2.0	2.2	1.1	1.1	22.6	18.7	9.2
High-Financial Risk (11)	-1.2	-0.3	-9.3	-1.4	0.3	0.1	–	–	-3.7	5.6	14.8

Betas (Levered)

	Raw (OLS)	Blume Adjusted	Peer Group	Vasicek Adjusted	Sum	Downside
Median	0.77	0.86	1.14	0.90	0.93	1.02
SIC Composite	1.13	1.09	1.14	1.13	1.43	1.30
Large Composite	1.15	1.10	1.14	1.15	1.46	1.34
Small Composite	0.19	0.49	1.14	0.25	0.33	0.25
High Financial Risk	1.32	1.21	1.14	1.25	2.08	2.20

Betas (Unlevered)

	Raw (OLS)	Blume Adjusted	Peer Group	Vasicek Adjusted	Sum	Downside
Median	0.51	0.57	0.80	0.59	0.65	0.68
SIC Composite	0.60	0.58	0.61	0.60	0.76	0.69
Large Composite	0.59	0.56	0.59	0.59	0.75	0.68
Small Composite	0.15	0.35	0.77	0.19	0.24	0.19
High Financial Risk	0.55	0.52	0.51	0.53	0.72	0.74

Enterprise Valuation (EV) Multiples

	EV/EBITDA Latest	5-Yr Avg
Median	15.4	12.9
SIC Composite	10.9	9.0
Large Composite	10.2	8.4
Small Composite	17.8	13.9
High Financial Risk	–	20.4

Equity Valuation Multiples

	Price/Sales Latest	5-Yr Avg	Price/Earnings Latest	5-Yr Avg	Price/TBV* Latest	5-Yr Avg	Price/EBT** Latest	5-Yr Avg
Median	3.9	2.8	19.8	15.5	1.9	1.4	13.3	10.3
SIC Composite	3.7	2.8	17.2	14.4	2.4	1.9	11.2	9.1
Large Composite	3.6	2.7	16.7	14.1	2.4	2.0	10.9	8.8
Small Composite	3.7	2.7	23.9	19.9	1.3	1.1	16.5	14.5
High Financial Risk	0.7	1.3	–	–	–	–	–	22.2

Equity Valuation SIC Composite
Latest: Price/TBV 2.4, Price/EBT 11.2
5-Yr Avg: Price/TBV 1.9, Price/EBT 9.1

Fama-French (F-F) 5-Factor Model

Fama-French (F-F) Components	F-F Beta	SMB Premium	HML Premium	RMW Premium	CMA Premium
Median	0.6	2.7	4.7	0.4	-3.1
SIC Composite	1.1	0.6	5.2	-1.8	-4.0
Large Composite	1.0	0.2	5.2	-2.1	-2.8
Small Composite	0.2	0.1	1.2	-0.6	-0.6
High Financial Risk	–	–	–	–	–

Leverage Ratios (%)

	Debt/MV Equity Latest	5-Yr Avg	Debt/Total Capital Latest	5-Yr Avg
Median	48.9	70.2	32.8	41.2
SIC Composite	94.8	126.1	48.7	55.8
Large Composite	102.0	134.1	50.5	57.3
Small Composite	54.4	66.6	35.2	40.0
High Financial Risk	–	176.8	77.6	63.9

Cost of Debt

	Cost of Debt (%) Latest
Median	4.8
SIC Composite	4.3
Large Composite	4.3
Small Composite	4.8
High Financial Risk	7.0

Capital Structure

SIC Composite (%) Latest: D/TC 48.7, E/TC 51.3

Cost of Equity Capital (%)

	CRSP Deciles CAPM	CAPM +Size Prem	Build-Up	Risk Premium Report CAPM +Size Prem	Build-Up	Discounted Cash Flow 1-Stage	3-Stage	Fama-French 5-Factor Model
Median	8.4	11.2	12.5	–	–	10.4	11.0	11.7
SIC Composite	9.7	10.0	10.1	–	–	11.3	12.3	9.4
Large Composite	9.8	9.9	9.9	–	–	11.3	12.6	9.6
Small Composite	4.9	10.5	15.4	–	–	10.8	9.6	4.4
High Financial Risk	–	–	–	–	–	–	–	–

Cost of Equity Capital (%) SIC Composite
Avg CRSP 10.1, Avg RPR n/a, 1-Stage 11.3, 3-Stage 12.3, 5-Factor Model 9.4

Weighted Average Cost of Capital (WACC) (%)

	CRSP Deciles CAPM	CAPM +Size Prem	Build-Up	Risk Premium Report CAPM +Size Prem	Build-Up	Discounted Cash Flow 1-Stage	3-Stage	Fama-French 5-Factor Model
Median	6.5	8.6	9.3	–	–	7.9	8.4	8.7
SIC Composite	6.3	6.5	6.6	–	–	7.2	7.7	6.2
Large Composite	6.5	6.5	6.5	–	–	7.2	7.8	6.3
Small Composite	4.3	8.0	11.1	–	–	8.2	7.4	4.0
High Financial Risk	–	–	–	–	–	–	–	–

WACC (%) SIC Composite
Low 6.2, High 7.7, Average 6.8, Median 6.6

*TBV = Tangible Book Value
**EBT = Earnings Before Taxes

© 2017 Duff & Phelps. All Rights Reserved. Duff & Phelps has used the utmost care in compiling the data presented herein, but cannot guarantee the accuracy, completeness, or timeliness of the information.

Data Updated Through March 31, 2017

602

Number of Companies: 259
Commercial Banks

Industry Description
Commercial banks and trust companies engaged in the business of accepting deposits from the public.

Sales (in millions)

Three Largest Companies
JPMorgan Chase & Co.	$105,486.0
Bank of America Corp.	93,662.0
Wells Fargo & Co.	93,512.0

Three Smallest Companies
Glen Burnie Bancorp	$14.9
FNBH Bancorp Inc.	12.6
AMB Financial Corp.	9.0

Total Assets (in millions)

Three Largest Companies
JPMorgan Chase & Co.	$2,490,972.0
Bank of America Corp.	2,187,702.0
Wells Fargo & Co.	1,930,115.0

Three Smallest Companies
FNBH Bancorp Inc.	$348.2
Carolina Trust BancShares, Inc.	334.0
AMB Financial Corp.	189.9

Annualized Monthly Performance Statistics (%)

	Industry			S&P 500 Index		
	Geometric Mean	Arithmetic Mean	Standard Deviation	Geometric Mean	Arithmetic Mean	Standard Deviation
1-year	43.7	46.8	32.1	17.2	17.4	7.2
3-year	11.8	13.8	21.8	10.4	10.9	11.5
5-year	16.4	18.1	20.4	13.3	13.9	11.5

Return Ratios (%)

	Return on Assets		Return on Equity		Dividend Yield		Current Ratio		Operating Margin		Long-term EPS
	Latest	5-Yr Avg	Latest	5-Yr Avg	Latest	5-Yr Avg	Latest	5-Yr Avg	Latest	5-Yr Avg	Analyst Estimates
Median (259)	0.9	0.9	8.8	8.7	2.0	2.1	–	–	29.9	27.7	8.1
SIC Composite (259)	1.0	0.9	6.9	8.2	2.3	2.2	–	–	31.5	29.7	8.1
Large Composite (25)	1.0	0.9	7.2	8.5	2.3	2.2	–	–	31.3	29.6	7.9
Small Composite (25)	0.7	0.7	5.5	7.4	2.3	2.4	–	–	24.4	21.5	8.1
High-Financial Risk (–)	–	–	–	–	–	–	–	–	–	–	–

Betas (Levered)

	Raw (OLS)	Blume Adjusted	Peer Group	Vasicek Adjusted	Sum	Downside
Median	0.86	0.92	1.14	0.96	1.04	1.11
SIC Composite	1.16	1.11	1.14	1.16	1.56	1.38
Large Composite	1.18	1.12	1.14	1.16	1.60	1.42
Small Composite	0.24	0.52	1.14	0.35	0.39	0.29
High Financial Risk	–	–	–	–	–	–

Betas (Unlevered)

	Raw (OLS)	Blume Adjusted	Peer Group	Vasicek Adjusted	Sum	Downside
Median	0.59	0.63	0.81	0.66	0.72	0.76
SIC Composite	0.57	0.54	0.56	0.57	0.75	0.67
Large Composite	0.54	0.52	0.53	0.54	0.73	0.65
Small Composite	0.18	0.38	0.79	0.26	0.29	0.22
High Financial Risk	–	–	–	–	–	–

Enterprise Valuation (EV) Multiples / Equity Valuation Multiples

	EV/EBITDA		Price/Sales		Price/Earnings		Price/TBV*		Price/EBT**	
	Latest	5-Yr Avg	Latest	5-Yr Avg	Latest	5-Yr Avg	Latest	5-Yr Avg	Latest	5-Yr Avg
Median	15.1	11.9	3.9	2.8	19.6	14.9	2.0	1.5	13.0	10.2
SIC Composite	9.8	8.0	3.2	2.4	15.5	12.9	2.0	1.6	10.2	8.1
Large Composite	9.0	7.5	3.0	2.3	14.8	12.6	1.9	1.6	9.7	7.8
Small Composite	11.5	7.8	3.1	2.1	18.5	14.0	1.4	1.1	12.7	9.9
High Financial Risk	–	–	–	–	–	–	–	–	–	–

Equity Valuation SIC Composite
Price/TBV: Latest 2.0, 5-Yr Avg 1.6
Price/EBT: Latest 10.2, 5-Yr Avg 8.1

Fama-French (F-F) 5-Factor Model

	F-F Beta	SMB Premium	HML Premium	RMW Premium	CMA Premium
Median	0.5	3.4	6.9	-0.6	-3.3
SIC Composite	1.1	0.9	6.9	-2.1	-4.6
Large Composite	1.0	0.5	7.1	-2.4	-3.3
Small Composite	0.2	0.3	1.5	-0.7	-0.4
High Financial Risk	–	–	–	–	–

Leverage Ratios (%)

	Debt/MV Equity		Debt/Total Capital	
	Latest	5-Yr Avg	Latest	5-Yr Avg
Median	47.9	66.4	32.4	39.9
SIC Composite	113.4	153.1	53.1	60.5
Large Composite	126.8	167.9	55.9	62.7
Small Composite	50.0	64.8	33.4	39.3
High Financial Risk	–	–	–	–

Cost of Debt

	Cost of Debt (%) Latest
Median	4.8
SIC Composite	4.3
Large Composite	4.3
Small Composite	4.8
High Financial Risk	–

Capital Structure

SIC Composite (%) Latest
D/TC 53.1
E/TC 46.9

Cost of Equity Capital (%)

	CRSP Deciles			Risk Premium Report		Discounted Cash Flow		Fama-French 5-Factor Model
	CAPM	CAPM +Size Prem	Build-Up	CAPM +Size Prem	Build-Up	1-Stage	3-Stage	
Median	8.8	11.3	11.9	–	–	10.1	10.7	12.5
SIC Composite	9.9	10.2	10.2	–	–	10.2	12.4	10.6
Large Composite	9.9	10.0	9.9	–	–	10.1	12.8	11.0
Small Composite	5.4	11.0	15.4	–	–	10.0	11.0	5.4
High Financial Risk	–	–	–	–	–	–	–	–

Cost of Equity Capital (%) SIC Composite
Avg CRSP 10.2, Avg RPR n/a, 1-Stage 10.2, 3-Stage 12.4, 5-Factor Model 10.6

Weighted Average Cost of Capital (WACC) (%)

	CRSP Deciles			Risk Premium Report		Discounted Cash Flow		Fama-French 5-Factor Model
	CAPM	CAPM +Size Prem	Build-Up	CAPM +Size Prem	Build-Up	1-Stage	3-Stage	
Median	6.9	8.8	9.3	–	–	7.8	8.2	9.7
SIC Composite	6.2	6.4	6.4	–	–	6.4	7.4	6.6
Large Composite	6.0	6.1	6.0	–	–	6.1	7.3	6.5
Small Composite	4.7	8.4	11.3	–	–	7.8	8.4	4.6
High Financial Risk	–	–	–	–	–	–	–	–

WACC (%) SIC Composite
Low 6.4, High 7.4, Average 6.6, Median 6.4

*TBV = Tangible Book Value
**EBT = Earnings Before Taxes

© 2017 Duff & Phelps. All Rights Reserved. Duff & Phelps has used the utmost care in compiling the data presented herein, but cannot guarantee the accuracy, completeness, or timeliness of the information.

Data Updated Through March 31, 2017

603

Number of Companies: 83
Savings Institutions

Industry Description
Chartered savings institutions (accepting deposits).

Sales (in millions)

Three Largest Companies
New York Community Bancorp Inc.	$1,820.4
People's United Financial Inc.	1,470.0
Flagstar Bancorp Inc.	904.0

Three Smallest Companies
Ottawa Bancorp, Inc.	$9.2
Great American Bancorp Inc.	8.3
WVS Financial Corp.	7.4

Total Assets (in millions)

Three Largest Companies
New York Community Bancorp Inc	$48,926.6
People's United Financial Inc.	40,609.8
Investors Bancorp Inc.	23,174.7

Three Smallest Companies
Ottawa Bancorp, Inc.	$213.6
Home Loan Financial Corp.	200.3
Great American Bancorp Inc.	182.1

Annualized Monthly Performance Statistics (%)

Industry	Geometric Mean	Arithmetic Mean	Standard Deviation	S&P 500 Index	Geometric Mean	Arithmetic Mean	Standard Deviation
1-year	19.2	20.6	19.6	1-year	17.2	17.4	7.2
3-year	12.3	13.2	14.3	3-year	10.4	10.9	11.5
5-year	15.0	15.8	13.2	5-year	13.3	13.9	11.5

Return Ratios (%)

	Return on Assets Latest	5-Yr Avg	Return on Equity Latest	5-Yr Avg	Dividend Yield Latest	5-Yr Avg
Median (83)	0.8	0.7	6.3	5.7	1.7	1.8
SIC Composite (83)	0.8	0.8	5.0	5.1	2.8	3.1
Large Composite (8)	0.9	0.8	6.0	5.8	3.2	4.0
Small Composite (8)	0.6	0.6	3.4	4.4	2.4	2.7
High-Financial Risk (6)	-1.5	-0.8	-14.7	-2.6	0.1	0.0

Liquidity Ratio

	Current Ratio Latest	5-Yr Avg
Median (83)	–	–
SIC Composite (83)	–	–
Large Composite (8)	–	–
Small Composite (8)	–	–
High-Financial Risk (6)	–	–

Profitability Ratio (%)

	Operating Margin Latest	5-Yr Avg
Median (83)	26.8	21.8
SIC Composite (83)	31.2	25.7
Large Composite (8)	31.6	25.0
Small Composite (8)	23.0	20.0
High-Financial Risk (6)	-10.8	3.4

Growth Rates (%)

	Long-term EPS Analyst Estimates
Median (83)	10.3
SIC Composite (83)	9.1
Large Composite (8)	8.1
Small Composite (8)	9.9
High-Financial Risk (6)	14.7

Betas (Levered)

	Raw (OLS)	Blume Adjusted	Peer Group	Vasicek Adjusted	Sum	Downside
Median	0.41	0.63	1.14	0.66	0.59	0.71
SIC Composite	0.63	0.77	1.14	0.70	0.68	0.79
Large Composite	0.71	0.82	1.14	0.79	0.78	0.92
Small Composite	0.21	0.51	1.14	0.61	0.48	0.27
High Financial Risk	1.14	1.09	1.14	1.14	2.05	2.42

Betas (Unlevered)

	Raw (OLS)	Blume Adjusted	Peer Group	Vasicek Adjusted	Sum	Downside
Median	0.26	0.41	0.71	0.43	0.36	0.47
SIC Composite	0.35	0.43	0.62	0.39	0.38	0.44
Large Composite	0.35	0.40	0.53	0.38	0.38	0.44
Small Composite	0.15	0.32	0.67	0.38	0.30	0.19
High Financial Risk	0.44	0.43	0.44	0.44	0.57	0.62

Enterprise Valuation (EV) Multiples

	EV/EBITDA Latest	5-Yr Avg
Median	18.8	19.3
SIC Composite	21.9	23.9
Large Composite	22.1	26.0
Small Composite	24.1	19.6
High Financial Risk	–	38.1

Equity Valuation Multiples

	Price/Sales Latest	5-Yr Avg	Price/Earnings Latest	5-Yr Avg	Price/TBV* Latest	5-Yr Avg	Price/EBT** Latest	5-Yr Avg
Median	3.9	2.9	21.6	18.1	1.5	1.1	14.0	12.2
SIC Composite	4.1	3.4	20.5	20.1	1.8	1.5	13.0	13.2
Large Composite	3.3	2.9	17.4	17.9	1.8	1.7	10.6	11.6
Small Composite	4.4	3.1	29.7	22.7	1.3	1.1	18.9	15.6
High Financial Risk	0.7	1.8	–	–	–	–	–	52.5

Equity Valuation SIC Composite
Latest: Price/TBV 1.8, Price/EBT 13.0
5-Yr Avg: Price/TBV 1.5, Price/EBT 13.2

Fama-French (F-F) 5-Factor Model

	F-F Beta	SMB Premium	HML Premium	RMW Premium	CMA Premium
Median	0.6	1.6	4.4	0.4	-4.4
SIC Composite	0.5	2.3	4.0	0.2	-3.5
Large Composite	0.6	1.8	4.5	0.2	0.2
Small Composite	0.2	-0.1	1.1	-0.4	0.0
High Financial Risk	–	–	–	–	–

Leverage Ratios (%)

	Debt/MV Equity Latest	5-Yr Avg	Debt/Total Capital Latest	5-Yr Avg
Median	69.1	89.6	40.9	47.3
SIC Composite	100.1	122.1	50.0	55.0
Large Composite	137.4	164.7	57.9	62.2
Small Composite	80.1	103.7	44.5	50.9
High Financial Risk	–	188.9	86.0	65.4

Cost of Debt

	Cost of Debt (%) Latest
Median	4.8
SIC Composite	4.8
Large Composite	4.8
Small Composite	4.8
High Financial Risk	7.0

Capital Structure

SIC Composite (%) Latest: D/TC 50.0, E/TC 50.0

Cost of Equity Capital (%)

	CRSP Deciles CAPM	CAPM +Size Prem	Build-Up	Risk Premium Report CAPM +Size Prem	Build-Up	Discounted Cash Flow 1-Stage	3-Stage	Fama-French 5-Factor Model
Median	7.1	11.5	15.4	–	–	11.6	10.6	8.7
SIC Composite	7.3	9.2	11.7	–	–	11.8	10.2	9.5
Large Composite	7.8	9.0	11.0	–	–	11.4	10.7	13.5
Small Composite	6.9	12.5	15.4	–	–	12.2	9.1	5.3
High Financial Risk	–	–	–	–	–	–	–	–

Cost of Equity Capital (%) SIC Composite
Avg CRSP: 10.4; Avg RPR: n/a; 1-Stage: 11.8; 3-Stage: 10.2; 5-Factor Model: 9.5

Weighted Average Cost of Capital (WACC) (%)

	CRSP Deciles CAPM	CAPM +Size Prem	Build-Up	Risk Premium Report CAPM +Size Prem	Build-Up	Discounted Cash Flow 1-Stage	3-Stage	Fama-French 5-Factor Model
Median	5.6	7.9	9.3	–	–	8.4	7.1	6.6
SIC Composite	5.3	6.2	7.4	–	–	7.5	6.7	6.3
Large Composite	5.2	5.7	6.5	–	–	6.7	6.4	7.6
Small Composite	5.2	8.4	10.5	–	–	8.2	6.5	4.4
High Financial Risk	–	–	–	–	–	–	–	–

WACC (%) SIC Composite
Low 6.2 — Average 6.8 — High 7.5; Median 6.7

*TBV = Tangible Book Value
**EBT = Earnings Before Taxes

© 2017 Duff & Phelps. All Rights Reserved. Duff & Phelps has used the utmost care in compiling the data presented herein, but cannot guarantee the accuracy, completeness, or timeliness of the information.

Data Updated Through March 31, 2017

6035

Number of Companies: 61
Savings Institutions, Federally Chartered

Industry Description
Federally chartered savings institutions (accepting deposits) operating under Federal charter.

Sales (in millions)

Three Largest Companies
Flagstar Bancorp Inc.	$904.0
Banc of California Inc.	656.9
Astoria Financial Corp.	505.8

Three Smallest Companies
Kentucky First Federal Bancorp	$12.0
Ottawa Bancorp, Inc.	9.2
Great American Bancorp Inc.	8.3

Total Assets (in millions)

Three Largest Companies
Astoria Financial Corp.	$14,558.7
Flagstar Bancorp Inc.	14,053.0
TFS Financial Corp.	12,914.1

Three Smallest Companies
Kentucky First Federal Bancorp	$291.9
Ottawa Bancorp, Inc.	213.6
Great American Bancorp Inc.	182.1

Annualized Monthly Performance Statistics (%)

Industry	Geometric Mean	Arithmetic Mean	Standard Deviation		S&P 500 Index	Geometric Mean	Arithmetic Mean	Standard Deviation
1-year	22.7	24.1	19.6		1-year	17.2	17.4	7.2
3-year	14.4	15.2	14.5		3-year	10.4	10.9	11.5
5-year	16.7	17.4	13.1		5-year	13.3	13.9	11.5

Return Ratios (%)

	Return on Assets Latest	5-Yr Avg	Return on Equity Latest	5-Yr Avg	Dividend Yield Latest	5-Yr Avg	Current Ratio Latest	5-Yr Avg	Operating Margin Latest	5-Yr Avg	Long-term EPS Analyst Estimates
Median (61)	0.8	0.7	6.1	5.5	1.8	2.0	–	–	26.8	21.4	10.3
SIC Composite (61)	0.8	0.7	4.6	4.8	2.3	2.4	–	–	29.8	23.5	10.3
Large Composite (6)	0.9	0.7	4.7	4.5	1.9	1.8	–	–	30.3	19.6	10.4
Small Composite (6)	0.5	0.5	2.7	3.6	2.0	2.4	–	–	19.4	16.3	10.3
High-Financial Risk (–)	–	–	–	–	–	–	–	–	–	–	–

Betas (Levered)

	Raw (OLS)	Blume Adjusted	Peer Group	Vasicek Adjusted	Sum	Downside
Median	0.38	0.61	1.14	0.62	0.57	0.69
SIC Composite	0.58	0.74	1.14	0.66	0.62	0.72
Large Composite	0.58	0.74	1.14	0.73	0.68	0.87
Small Composite	0.20	0.50	1.14	0.81	0.42	0.27
High Financial Risk	–	–	–	–	–	–

Betas (Unlevered)

	Raw (OLS)	Blume Adjusted	Peer Group	Vasicek Adjusted	Sum	Downside
Median	0.25	0.41	0.74	0.41	0.36	0.47
SIC Composite	0.36	0.44	0.67	0.40	0.38	0.43
Large Composite	0.34	0.42	0.63	0.42	0.39	0.49
Small Composite	0.17	0.38	0.85	0.61	0.32	0.21
High Financial Risk	–	–	–	–	–	–

Enterprise Valuation (EV) Multiples

	EV/EBITDA Latest	5-Yr Avg
Median	18.5	18.9
SIC Composite	20.7	23.1
Large Composite	20.8	28.3
Small Composite	19.6	14.9
High Financial Risk	–	–

Equity Valuation Multiples

	Price/Sales Latest	5-Yr Avg	Price/Earnings Latest	5-Yr Avg	Price/TBV* Latest	5-Yr Avg	Price/EBT** Latest	5-Yr Avg
Median	3.9	2.9	21.7	17.9	1.5	1.1	14.1	12.2
SIC Composite	4.2	3.4	22.7	21.7	1.8	1.4	14.1	14.4
Large Composite	3.9	3.2	22.8	24.4	2.1	1.7	12.8	16.3
Small Composite	4.5	3.2	37.7	28.2	1.3	1.1	23.2	19.4
High Financial Risk	–	–	–	–	–	–	–	–

Equity Valuation SIC Composite
Latest: Price/TBV 1.8, Price/EBT 14.1
5-Yr Avg: Price/TBV 1.4, Price/EBT 14.4

Fama-French (F-F) 5-Factor Model

	F-F Beta	SMB Premium	HML Premium	RMW Premium	CMA Premium
Median	0.4	2.4	4.0	0.6	-3.9
SIC Composite	0.5	2.8	3.6	0.2	-3.0
Large Composite	0.4	3.0	4.0	0.0	0.1
Small Composite	0.2	0.2	0.9	-0.3	0.0
High Financial Risk	–	–	–	–	–

Leverage Ratios (%)

	Debt/MV Equity Latest	5-Yr Avg	Debt/Total Capital Latest	5-Yr Avg
Median	61.8	82.4	38.2	45.2
SIC Composite	82.2	106.2	45.1	51.5
Large Composite	94.1	115.4	48.5	53.6
Small Composite	39.1	58.1	28.1	36.8
High Financial Risk	–	–	–	–

Cost of Debt

	Cost of Debt (%) Latest
Median	4.8
SIC Composite	4.8
Large Composite	4.8
Small Composite	4.8
High Financial Risk	–

Capital Structure SIC Composite (%) Latest
D/TC 45.1, E/TC 54.9

Cost of Equity Capital (%)

	CRSP Deciles CAPM	CAPM +Size Prem	Build-Up	Risk Premium Report CAPM +Size Prem	Build-Up	Discounted Cash Flow 1-Stage	3-Stage	Fama-French 5-Factor Model
Median	6.9	11.6	15.4	–	–	11.8	11.0	8.7
SIC Composite	7.1	9.3	12.0	–	–	12.6	10.1	9.7
Large Composite	7.5	9.0	11.2	–	–	12.5	9.8	12.8
Small Composite	8.0	13.6	15.4	–	–	12.2	8.1	5.2
High Financial Risk	–	–	–	–	–	–	–	–

Cost of Equity Capital (%) SIC Composite
Avg CRSP 10.6, Avg RPR n/a, 1-Stage 12.6, 3-Stage 10.1, 5-Factor Model 9.7

Weighted Average Cost of Capital (WACC) (%)

	CRSP Deciles CAPM	CAPM +Size Prem	Build-Up	Risk Premium Report CAPM +Size Prem	Build-Up	Discounted Cash Flow 1-Stage	3-Stage	Fama-French 5-Factor Model
Median	5.5	8.0	9.4	–	–	8.7	8.0	6.7
SIC Composite	5.3	6.5	8.0	–	–	8.3	7.0	6.7
Large Composite	5.5	6.2	7.4	–	–	8.1	6.7	8.2
Small Composite	6.6	10.7	12.0	–	–	9.7	6.7	4.6
High Financial Risk	–	–	–	–	–	–	–	–

WACC (%) SIC Composite
Low 6.5, High 8.3, Average 7.3, Median 7.0

*TBV = Tangible Book Value
**EBT = Earnings Before Taxes

© 2017 Duff & Phelps. All Rights Reserved. Duff & Phelps has used the utmost care in compiling the data presented herein, but cannot guarantee the accuracy, completeness, or timeliness of the information.

Data Updated Through March 31, 2017

6036

Number of Companies: 22
Savings Institutions, Not Federally Chartered

Industry Description
State-chartered savings institutions (accepting deposits) which do not operate under Federal charter.

Sales (in millions)

Three Largest Companies
New York Community Bancorp Inc.	$1,820.4
People's United Financial Inc.	1,470.0
Investors Bancorp Inc.	830.7

Three Smallest Companies
Jacksonville Bancorp Inc.	$15.7
Home Loan Financial Corp.	10.4
WVS Financial Corp.	7.4

Total Assets (in millions)

Three Largest Companies
New York Community Bancorp Inc.	$48,926.6
People's United Financial Inc.	40,609.8
Investors Bancorp Inc.	23,174.7

Three Smallest Companies
WVS Financial Corp.	$335.7
Jacksonville Bancorp Inc.	319.3
Home Loan Financial Corp.	200.3

Annualized Monthly Performance Statistics (%)

Industry	Geometric Mean	Arithmetic Mean	Standard Deviation
1-year	14.9	16.5	21.0
3-year	9.8	10.8	15.1
5-year	13.0	13.8	14.4

S&P 500 Index	Geometric Mean	Arithmetic Mean	Standard Deviation
1-year	17.2	17.4	7.2
3-year	10.4	10.9	11.5
5-year	13.3	13.9	11.5

Return Ratios (%)

	Return on Assets Latest	Return on Assets 5-Yr Avg	Return on Equity Latest	Return on Equity 5-Yr Avg	Dividend Yield Latest	Dividend Yield 5-Yr Avg
Median (22)	0.9	0.8	6.9	6.0	1.7	1.6
SIC Composite (22)	0.8	0.8	5.5	5.4	3.4	4.0
Large Composite (3)	0.9	0.8	5.7	5.2	3.8	4.5
Small Composite (3)	0.9	0.9	6.1	8.0	2.7	3.4
High-Financial Risk (−)	−	−	−	−	−	−

Liquidity Ratio

	Current Ratio Latest	Current Ratio 5-Yr Avg
Median (22)	−	−
SIC Composite (22)	−	−
Large Composite (3)	−	−
Small Composite (3)	−	−
High-Financial Risk (−)	−	−

Profitability Ratio (%)

	Operating Margin Latest	Operating Margin 5-Yr Avg
Median (22)	28.5	23.5
SIC Composite (22)	32.9	28.4
Large Composite (3)	36.5	30.6
Small Composite (3)	32.3	31.1
High-Financial Risk (−)	−	−

Growth Rates (%)

	Long-term EPS Analyst Estimates
Median (22)	7.9
SIC Composite (22)	7.4
Large Composite (3)	7.0
Small Composite (3)	7.9
High-Financial Risk (−)	−

Betas (Levered)

	Raw (OLS)	Blume Adjusted	Peer Group	Vasicek Adjusted	Sum	Downside
Median	0.51	0.70	1.14	0.83	0.66	0.72
SIC Composite	0.67	0.80	1.14	0.78	0.73	0.89
Large Composite	0.71	0.82	1.14	1.00	0.76	0.95
Small Composite	0.09	0.43	1.14	0.44	0.44	0.36
High Financial Risk	−	−	−	−	−	−

Betas (Unlevered)

	Raw (OLS)	Blume Adjusted	Peer Group	Vasicek Adjusted	Sum	Downside
Median	0.30	0.43	0.63	0.48	0.42	0.49
SIC Composite	0.35	0.40	0.56	0.39	0.37	0.44
Large Composite	0.34	0.39	0.53	0.47	0.37	0.45
Small Composite	0.08	0.22	0.50	0.22	0.22	0.19
High Financial Risk	−	−	−	−	−	−

Enterprise Valuation (EV) Multiples

	EV/EBITDA Latest	EV/EBITDA 5-Yr Avg
Median	22.3	19.7
SIC Composite	23.4	24.7
Large Composite	24.2	26.5
Small Composite	24.6	20.9
High Financial Risk	−	−

Equity Valuation Multiples

	Price/Sales Latest	Price/Sales 5-Yr Avg	Price/Earnings Latest	Price/Earnings 5-Yr Avg	Price/TBV* Latest	Price/TBV* 5-Yr Avg	Price/EBT** Latest	Price/EBT** 5-Yr Avg
Median	3.9	2.9	19.8	18.1	1.5	1.1	13.9	12.2
SIC Composite	3.9	3.4	18.1	18.4	1.8	1.7	11.8	12.1
Large Composite	4.1	3.7	17.5	19.1	1.8	1.8	11.2	12.2
Small Composite	3.7	2.8	16.3	12.6	1.2	1.0	11.5	8.9
High Financial Risk	−	−	−	−	−	−	−	−

Equity Valuation SIC Composite
Latest: Price/TBV 1.8, Price/EBT 11.8
5-Yr Avg: Price/TBV 1.7, Price/EBT 12.1

Fama-French (F-F) 5-Factor Model

	F-F Beta	SMB Premium	HML Premium	RMW Premium	CMA Premium
Median	0.1	1.9	1.7	0.5	0.2
SIC Composite	0.6	1.7	4.6	0.3	-4.2
Large Composite	0.6	1.6	4.6	0.3	0.4
Small Composite	0.1	-0.6	0.8	-0.5	0.9
High Financial Risk	−	−	−	−	−

Leverage Ratios (%)

	Debt/MV Equity Latest	Debt/MV Equity 5-Yr Avg	Debt/Total Capital Latest	Debt/Total Capital 5-Yr Avg
Median	94.6	101.3	48.6	50.3
SIC Composite	124.5	141.2	55.5	58.5
Large Composite	139.5	152.0	58.3	60.3
Small Composite	154.3	181.7	60.7	64.5
High Financial Risk	−	−	−	−

Cost of Debt

	Cost of Debt (%) Latest
Median	4.8
SIC Composite	4.8
Large Composite	4.8
Small Composite	4.8
High Financial Risk	−

Capital Structure

SIC Composite (%) Latest: D/TC 55.5, E/TC 44.5

Cost of Equity Capital (%)

	CRSP Deciles CAPM	CRSP Deciles CAPM +Size Prem	CRSP Deciles Build-Up	Risk Premium Report CAPM +Size Prem	Risk Premium Report Build-Up	Discounted Cash Flow 1-Stage	Discounted Cash Flow 3-Stage	Fama-French 5-Factor Model
Median	8.0	11.0	12.5	−	−	9.5	10.0	8.6
SIC Composite	7.8	9.2	11.2	−	−	10.7	10.2	9.3
Large Composite	9.0	9.9	10.7	−	−	11.0	10.0	13.6
Small Composite	5.9	11.5	15.4	−	−	10.6	12.1	4.6
High Financial Risk	−	−	−	−	−	−	−	−

Cost of Equity Capital (%) SIC Composite
Avg CRSP 10.2, Avg RPR n/a, 1-Stage 10.7, 3-Stage 10.2, 5-Factor Model 9.3

Weighted Average Cost of Capital (WACC) (%)

	CRSP Deciles CAPM	CRSP Deciles CAPM +Size Prem	CRSP Deciles Build-Up	Risk Premium Report CAPM +Size Prem	Risk Premium Report Build-Up	Discounted Cash Flow 1-Stage	Discounted Cash Flow 3-Stage	Fama-French 5-Factor Model
Median	5.8	7.5	8.2	−	−	6.7	6.3	5.9
SIC Composite	5.2	5.9	6.8	−	−	6.6	6.3	5.9
Large Composite	5.6	6.0	6.3	−	−	6.5	6.1	7.5
Small Composite	4.2	6.4	8.0	−	−	6.1	6.7	3.7
High Financial Risk	−	−	−	−	−	−	−	−

WACC (%) SIC Composite
Low 5.9, High 6.8, Average 6.3, Median 6.3

*TBV = Tangible Book Value
**EBT = Earnings Before Taxes

© 2017 Duff & Phelps. All Rights Reserved. Duff & Phelps has used the utmost care in compiling the data presented herein, but cannot guarantee the accuracy, completeness, or timeliness of the information.

Data Updated Through March 31, 2017

609
Number of Companies: 5
Functions Related To Depository Banking

Industry Description
Trust companies engaged in fiduciary business, but not regularly engaged in deposit banking; establishments primarily engaged in performing functions related to depository banking, not elsewhere classified.

Sales (in millions)

Three Largest Companies
Visa Inc.	$15,082.0
MasterCard Inc.	10,776.0
Western Union Co.	5,422.9

Three Smallest Companies
Western Union Co.	$5,422.9
Euronet Worldwide Inc.	1,958.6
Payment Data Systems, Inc.	14.4

Total Assets (in millions)

Three Largest Companies
Visa Inc.	$64,035.0
MasterCard Inc.	18,675.0
Western Union Co.	9,419.6

Three Smallest Companies
Western Union Co.	$9,419.6
Euronet Worldwide Inc.	2,712.9
Payment Data Systems, Inc.	68.4

Annualized Monthly Performance Statistics (%)

Industry	Geometric Mean	Arithmetic Mean	Standard Deviation	S&P 500 Index	Geometric Mean	Arithmetic Mean	Standard Deviation
1-year	17.8	18.8	15.8	1-year	17.2	17.4	7.2
3-year	17.5	19.0	19.4	3-year	10.4	10.9	11.5
5-year	23.5	25.0	19.8	5-year	13.3	13.9	11.5

Return Ratios (%)

	Return on Assets Latest	5-Yr Avg	Return on Equity Latest	5-Yr Avg	Dividend Yield Latest	5-Yr Avg	Current Ratio Latest	5-Yr Avg	Operating Margin Latest	5-Yr Avg	Long-term EPS Analyst Estimates
Median (5)	7.1	7.8	19.0	38.2	0.8	0.7	1.6	1.5	17.8	18.6	14.7
SIC Composite (5)	11.0	13.1	3.1	3.7	0.8	0.8	1.8	1.7	51.9	49.2	15.4
Large Composite (–)	–	–	–	–	–	–	–	–	–	–	–
Small Composite (–)	–	–	–	–	–	–	–	–	–	–	–
High-Financial Risk (–)	–	–	–	–	–	–	–	–	–	–	–

Betas (Levered)

	Raw (OLS)	Blume Adjusted	Peer Group	Vasicek Adjusted	Sum	Downside
Median	1.19	1.13	1.14	1.17	1.05	1.54
SIC Composite	1.06	1.04	1.14	1.09	0.98	1.16
Large Composite	–	–	–	–	–	–
Small Composite	–	–	–	–	–	–
High Financial Risk	–	–	–	–	–	–

Betas (Unlevered)

	Raw (OLS)	Blume Adjusted	Peer Group	Vasicek Adjusted	Sum	Downside
Median	0.96	0.97	1.04	1.06	1.05	1.26
SIC Composite	0.98	0.96	1.05	1.01	0.90	1.06
Large Composite	–	–	–	–	–	–
Small Composite	–	–	–	–	–	–
High Financial Risk	–	–	–	–	–	–

Enterprise Valuation (EV) Multiples / Equity Valuation Multiples

	EV/EBITDA Latest	5-Yr Avg	Price/Sales Latest	5-Yr Avg	Price/Earnings Latest	5-Yr Avg	Price/TBV* Latest	5-Yr Avg	Price/EBT** Latest	5-Yr Avg
Median	14.5	12.6	2.3	2.5	30.0	25.9	–	–	20.8	18.3
SIC Composite	19.0	15.7	10.3	8.6	32.7	26.7	–	–	20.3	17.5
Large Composite	–	–	–	–	–	–	–	–	–	–
Small Composite	–	–	–	–	–	–	–	–	–	–
High Financial Risk	–	–	–	–	–	–	–	–	–	–

Equity Valuation SIC Composite: Price/TBV Latest 20.3, 5-Yr Avg 17.5; Price/EBT Latest 0.0, 5-Yr Avg 0.0

Fama-French (F-F) 5-Factor Model

	F-F Beta	SMB Premium	HML Premium	RMW Premium	CMA Premium
Median	1.2	-0.4	-0.8	0.0	-1.1
SIC Composite	1.1	-0.7	-1.9	-0.9	-1.1
Large Composite	–	–	–	–	–
Small Composite	–	–	–	–	–
High Financial Risk	–	–	–	–	–

Leverage Ratios (%)

	Debt/MV Equity Latest	5-Yr Avg	Debt/Total Capital Latest	5-Yr Avg
Median	10.5	2.9	9.5	2.9
SIC Composite	8.8	4.2	8.1	4.0

Cost of Debt

	Cost of Debt (%) Latest
Median	4.8
SIC Composite	4.2

Capital Structure SIC Composite (%)
D/TC 8.1, E/TC 91.9

Cost of Equity Capital (%)

	CAPM	CRSP Deciles CAPM +Size Prem	Build-Up	Risk Premium Report CAPM +Size Prem	Build-Up	Discounted Cash Flow 1-Stage	3-Stage	Fama-French 5-Factor Model
Median	9.9	10.8	10.7	–	–	15.2	11.4	7.6
SIC Composite	9.5	9.5	9.8	–	–	16.3	11.0	4.8
Large Composite	–	–	–	–	–	–	–	–
Small Composite	–	–	–	–	–	–	–	–
High Financial Risk	–	–	–	–	–	–	–	–

Cost of Equity Capital (%) SIC Composite: Avg CRSP 9.7, Avg RPR n/a, 1-Stage 16.3, 3-Stage 11.0, 5-Factor Model 4.8

Weighted Average Cost of Capital (WACC) (%)

	CAPM	CRSP Deciles CAPM +Size Prem	Build-Up	Risk Premium Report CAPM +Size Prem	Build-Up	Discounted Cash Flow 1-Stage	3-Stage	Fama-French 5-Factor Model
Median	9.4	9.6	9.5	–	–	14.3	11.1	7.4
SIC Composite	9.0	9.0	9.3	–	–	15.2	10.3	4.6
Large Composite	–	–	–	–	–	–	–	–
Small Composite	–	–	–	–	–	–	–	–
High Financial Risk	–	–	–	–	–	–	–	–

WACC (%) SIC Composite: Low 4.6, High 15.2, Average 9.7, Median 9.3

*TBV = Tangible Book Value
**EBT = Earnings Before Taxes

© 2017 Duff & Phelps. All Rights Reserved. Duff & Phelps has used the utmost care in compiling the data presented herein, but cannot guarantee the accuracy, completeness, or timeliness of the information.

Data Updated Through March 31, 2017

61

Number of Companies: 21
Non-depository Credit Institutions

Industry Description
This major group includes establishments engaged in extending credit in the form of loans, but not engaged in deposit banking.

Sales (in millions)

Three Largest Companies
American Express Co.	$33,823.0
Discover Financial Services Inc.	10,497.0
CIT Group Inc.	3,327.2

Three Smallest Companies
Marlin Business Services Inc.	$100.0
Asta Funding Inc.	58.7
California First National Bancorp	32.6

Total Assets (in millions)

Three Largest Companies
American Express Co.	$158,893.0
Discover Financial Services Inc.	92,308.0
CIT Group Inc.	64,190.7

Three Smallest Companies
Regional Management Corp.	$712.2
LendingTree, Inc.	323.4
Asta Funding Inc.	256.0

Annualized Monthly Performance Statistics (%)

Industry	Geometric Mean	Arithmetic Mean	Standard Deviation	S&P 500 Index	Geometric Mean	Arithmetic Mean	Standard Deviation
1-year	32.0	33.8	23.0	1-year	17.2	17.4	7.2
3-year	-0.4	1.7	20.6	3-year	10.4	10.9	11.5
5-year	9.9	11.8	20.1	5-year	13.3	13.9	11.5

Return Ratios (%)

	Return on Assets Latest	5-Yr Avg	Return on Equity Latest	5-Yr Avg	Dividend Yield Latest	5-Yr Avg	Current Ratio Latest	5-Yr Avg	Operating Margin Latest	5-Yr Avg	Long-term EPS Analyst Estimates
Median (21)	2.1	2.5	13.2	14.2	0.1	0.2	1.8	2.1	21.6	24.6	7.5
SIC Composite (21)	2.2	2.5	7.3	7.6	1.6	1.3	1.6	1.6	24.6	27.6	7.4
Large Composite (3)	2.4	2.7	7.1	7.4	1.8	1.4	–	–	25.9	28.6	7.2
Small Composite (3)	1.7	1.8	5.8	5.8	2.3	4.7	–	–	30.6	28.3	10.0
High-Financial Risk (–)	–	–	–	–	–	–	–	–	–	–	–

Betas (Levered)

	Raw (OLS)	Blume Adjusted	Peer Group	Vasicek Adjusted	Sum	Downside
Median	1.27	1.18	1.61	1.46	1.13	1.82
SIC Composite	1.22	1.15	1.61	1.27	1.50	1.43
Large Composite	1.24	1.16	1.62	1.44	1.59	1.47
Small Composite	0.84	0.90	1.49	1.00	0.74	0.87
High Financial Risk	–	–	–	–	–	–

Betas (Unlevered)

	Raw (OLS)	Blume Adjusted	Peer Group	Vasicek Adjusted	Sum	Downside
Median	0.59	0.60	0.85	0.68	0.54	0.77
SIC Composite	0.61	0.58	0.78	0.63	0.73	0.70
Large Composite	0.72	0.67	0.92	0.82	0.90	0.84
Small Composite	0.74	0.79	1.29	0.87	0.66	0.76
High Financial Risk	–	–	–	–	–	–

Enterprise Valuation (EV) Multiples

	EV/EBITDA Latest	5-Yr Avg
Median	15.4	12.6
SIC Composite	14.7	13.7
Large Composite	11.3	10.9
Small Composite	8.6	8.8
High Financial Risk	–	–

Equity Valuation Multiples

	Price/Sales Latest	5-Yr Avg	Price/Earnings Latest	5-Yr Avg	Price/TBV* Latest	5-Yr Avg	Price/EBT** Latest	5-Yr Avg
Median	1.9	2.2	12.3	14.5	2.6	2.0	9.3	9.2
SIC Composite	2.1	2.2	14.0	13.3	4.1	3.4	9.0	8.6
Large Composite	2.2	2.3	14.3	13.6	4.2	3.4	9.2	8.7
Small Composite	3.1	3.2	17.4	17.3	1.6	1.0	10.0	11.5
High Financial Risk	–	–	–	–	–	–	–	–

Equity Valuation SIC Composite
Price/TBV: Latest 4.1, 5-Yr Avg 3.4
Price/EBT: Latest 9.0, 5-Yr Avg 8.6

Fama-French (F-F) 5-Factor Model

	F-F Beta	SMB Premium	HML Premium	RMW Premium	CMA Premium
Median	1.2	2.2	2.3	-2.4	1.9
SIC Composite	1.1	2.3	4.2	0.3	-3.2
Large Composite	1.1	2.0	4.3	0.4	0.6
Small Composite	0.8	1.1	1.9	-1.8	1.8
High Financial Risk	–	–	–	–	–

Leverage Ratios (%)

	Debt/MV Equity Latest	5-Yr Avg	Debt/Total Capital Latest	5-Yr Avg
Median	116.1	96.7	53.7	49.2
SIC Composite	135.9	134.1	57.6	57.3
Large Composite	87.6	92.8	46.7	48.1
Small Composite	19.0	14.6	16.0	12.7
High Financial Risk	–	–	–	–

Cost of Debt

	Cost of Debt (%) Latest
Median	6.1
SIC Composite	5.3
Large Composite	5.0
Small Composite	5.6
High Financial Risk	–

Capital Structure

SIC Composite (%) Latest
D/TC: 42.4
E/TC: 57.6

Cost of Equity Capital (%)

	CRSP Deciles CAPM	CAPM +Size Prem	Build-Up	Risk Premium Report CAPM +Size Prem	Build-Up	Discounted Cash Flow 1-Stage	3-Stage	Fama-French 5-Factor Model
Median	11.5	13.3	14.6	–	–	9.0	13.3	13.8
SIC Composite	10.5	10.8	13.2	–	–	8.9	13.0	13.4
Large Composite	11.4	11.5	12.9	–	–	8.9	12.4	17.0
Small Composite	9.0	13.0	16.8	–	–	12.2	12.1	10.7
High Financial Risk	–	–	–	–	–	–	–	–

Cost of Equity Capital (%) SIC Composite
Avg CRSP: 12.0; Avg RPR: n/a; 1-Stage: 8.9; 3-Stage: 13.0; 5-Factor Model: 13.4

Weighted Average Cost of Capital (WACC) (%)

	CRSP Deciles CAPM	CAPM +Size Prem	Build-Up	Risk Premium Report CAPM +Size Prem	Build-Up	Discounted Cash Flow 1-Stage	3-Stage	Fama-French 5-Factor Model
Median	7.2	7.9	8.9	–	–	6.9	8.6	7.8
SIC Composite	6.8	6.9	7.9	–	–	6.1	7.8	8.0
Large Composite	7.9	7.9	8.7	–	–	6.5	8.4	10.8
Small Composite	8.2	11.6	14.8	–	–	10.9	10.8	9.7
High Financial Risk	–	–	–	–	–	–	–	–

WACC (%) SIC Composite
Low 6.1, High 8.0
Average 7.4, Median 7.8

*TBV = Tangible Book Value
**EBT = Earnings Before Taxes

© 2017 Duff & Phelps. All Rights Reserved. Duff & Phelps has used the utmost care in compiling the data presented herein, but cannot guarantee the accuracy, completeness, or timeliness of the information.

Data Updated Through March 31, 2017

614

Number of Companies: 5
Personal Credit Institutions

Industry Description
Establishments primarily engaged in providing loans to individuals.

Sales (in millions)

Three Largest Companies
Discover Financial Services Inc.	$10,497.0
Nelnet Inc.	1,181.2
Credit Acceptance Corp.	969.2

Three Smallest Companies
Credit Acceptance Corp.	$969.2
World Acceptance Corp.	557.5
Regional Management Corp.	240.5

Total Assets (in millions)

Three Largest Companies
Discover Financial Services Inc.	$92,308.0
Nelnet Inc.	27,180.1
Credit Acceptance Corp.	4,218.0

Three Smallest Companies
Credit Acceptance Corp.	$4,218.0
World Acceptance Corp.	806.2
Regional Management Corp.	712.2

Annualized Monthly Performance Statistics (%)

	Industry				S&P 500 Index		
	Geometric Mean	Arithmetic Mean	Standard Deviation		Geometric Mean	Arithmetic Mean	Standard Deviation
1-year	31.3	34.8	33.2	1-year	17.2	17.4	7.2
3-year	7.1	9.7	24.8	3-year	10.4	10.9	11.5
5-year	15.1	17.4	23.9	5-year	13.3	13.9	11.5

Return Ratios (%)

	Return on Assets		Return on Equity		Dividend Yield	
	Latest	5-Yr Avg	Latest	5-Yr Avg	Latest	5-Yr Avg
Median (5)	3.6	4.4	21.9	23.2	0.6	0.8
SIC Composite (5)	2.5	2.6	9.4	10.1	1.6	1.5
Large Composite (–)	–	–	–	–	–	–
Small Composite (–)	–	–	–	–	–	–
High-Financial Risk (–)	–	–	–	–	–	–

Liquidity Ratio

	Current Ratio	
	Latest	5-Yr Avg
Median (5)	–	–
SIC Composite (5)	–	–
Large Composite (–)	–	–
Small Composite (–)	–	–
High-Financial Risk (–)	–	–

Profitability Ratio (%)

	Operating Margin	
	Latest	5-Yr Avg
Median (5)	32.8	34.8
SIC Composite (5)	41.0	43.6
Large Composite (–)	–	–
Small Composite (–)	–	–
High-Financial Risk (–)	–	–

Growth Rates (%)

	Long-term EPS Analyst Estimates
Median (5)	7.4
SIC Composite (5)	7.6
Large Composite (–)	–
Small Composite (–)	–
High-Financial Risk (–)	–

Betas (Levered)

	Raw (OLS)	Blume Adjusted	Peer Group	Vasicek Adjusted	Sum	Downside
Median	1.36	1.24	1.69	1.42	1.20	1.74
SIC Composite	1.25	1.16	1.69	1.31	1.36	1.38
Large Composite	–	–	–	–	–	–
Small Composite	–	–	–	–	–	–
High Financial Risk	–	–	–	–	–	–

Betas (Unlevered)

	Raw (OLS)	Blume Adjusted	Peer Group	Vasicek Adjusted	Sum	Downside
Median	0.66	0.61	0.89	0.76	0.58	0.77
SIC Composite	0.53	0.50	0.70	0.56	0.58	0.58
Large Composite	–	–	–	–	–	–
Small Composite	–	–	–	–	–	–
High Financial Risk	–	–	–	–	–	–

Enterprise Valuation (EV) Multiples

	EV/EBITDA	
	Latest	5-Yr Avg
Median	11.8	11.1
SIC Composite	13.0	12.8
Large Composite	–	–
Small Composite	–	–
High Financial Risk	–	–

Equity Valuation Multiples

	Price/Sales		Price/Earnings		Price/TBV*		Price/EBT**	
	Latest	5-Yr Avg	Latest	5-Yr Avg	Latest	5-Yr Avg	Latest	5-Yr Avg
Median	1.6	1.5	9.3	10.3	1.2	2.0	5.5	6.2
SIC Composite	2.5	2.4	10.8	10.0	2.3	2.3	6.9	6.2
Large Composite	–	–	–	–	–	–	–	–
Small Composite	–	–	–	–	–	–	–	–
High Financial Risk	–	–	–	–	–	–	–	–

Equity Valuation SIC Composite
- Price/TBV: Latest 2.3, 5-Yr Avg 2.3
- Price/EBT: Latest 6.9, 5-Yr Avg 6.2

Fama-French (F-F) 5-Factor Model

	F-F Beta	SMB Premium	HML Premium	RMW Premium	CMA Premium
Median	1.3	1.5	5.3	-0.3	-1.4
SIC Composite	1.2	2.0	4.3	-0.1	-1.2
Large Composite	–	–	–	–	–
Small Composite	–	–	–	–	–
High Financial Risk	–	–	–	–	–

Leverage Ratios (%)

	Debt/MV Equity		Debt/Total Capital	
	Latest	5-Yr Avg	Latest	5-Yr Avg
Median	97.8	96.7	49.4	49.2
SIC Composite	163.7	174.0	62.1	63.5
Large Composite	–	–	–	–
Small Composite	–	–	–	–
High Financial Risk	–	–	–	–

Cost of Debt

	Cost of Debt (%) Latest
Median	6.1
SIC Composite	4.9
Large Composite	–
Small Composite	–
High Financial Risk	–

Capital Structure

SIC Composite (%) Latest
- D/TC: 37.9
- E/TC: 62.1

Cost of Equity Capital (%)

	CRSP Deciles			Risk Premium Report		Discounted Cash Flow		Fama-French
	CAPM	CAPM +Size Prem	Build-Up	CAPM +Size Prem	Build-Up	1-Stage	3-Stage	5-Factor Model
Median	11.3	12.0	14.5	–	–	7.4	17.5	15.6
SIC Composite	10.7	11.0	13.1	–	–	9.2	16.7	15.0
Large Composite	–	–	–	–	–	–	–	–
Small Composite	–	–	–	–	–	–	–	–
High Financial Risk	–	–	–	–	–	–	–	–

Cost of Equity Capital (%) SIC Composite
- Avg CRSP: 12.1
- Avg RPR: n/a
- 1-Stage: 9.2
- 3-Stage: 16.7
- 5-Factor Model: 15.0

Weighted Average Cost of Capital (WACC) (%)

	CRSP Deciles			Risk Premium Report		Discounted Cash Flow		Fama-French
	CAPM	CAPM +Size Prem	Build-Up	CAPM +Size Prem	Build-Up	1-Stage	3-Stage	5-Factor Model
Median	8.0	8.1	9.9	–	–	6.5	10.7	6.7
SIC Composite	6.9	7.0	7.8	–	–	6.3	9.1	8.5
Large Composite	–	–	–	–	–	–	–	–
Small Composite	–	–	–	–	–	–	–	–
High Financial Risk	–	–	–	–	–	–	–	–

WACC (%) SIC Composite
Low 6.3 — High 9.1; Average 7.8, Median 7.8

*TBV = Tangible Book Value
**EBT = Earnings Before Taxes

© 2017 Duff & Phelps. All Rights Reserved. Duff & Phelps has used the utmost care in compiling the data presented herein, but cannot guarantee the accuracy, completeness, or timeliness of the information.

Data Updated Through March 31, 2017

615

Number of Companies: 5
Business Credit Institutions

Industry Description
Establishments primarily engaged in extending credit to business enterprises for relatively short periods; furnishing intermediate or long-term general and industrial credit, including the finance leasing of automobiles, trucks, and machinery and equipment.

Sales (in millions)

Three Largest Companies
Encore Capital Group, Inc.	$1,029.3
PRA Group, Inc.	830.6
Consumer Portfolio Services Inc.	363.6

Three Smallest Companies
Consumer Portfolio Services Inc.	$363.6
NewStar Financial, Inc.	273.6
California First National Bancorp	32.6

Annualized Monthly Performance Statistics (%)

Industry	Geometric Mean	Arithmetic Mean	Standard Deviation
1-year	16.1	21.7	39.1
3-year	-13.7	-8.9	31.0
5-year	5.5	10.5	34.7

Total Assets (in millions)

Three Largest Companies
NewStar Financial, Inc.	$4,040.6
Encore Capital Group, Inc.	3,670.5
PRA Group, Inc.	3,164.0

Three Smallest Companies
PRA Group, Inc.	$3,164.0
Consumer Portfolio Services Inc.	2,142.9
California First National Bancorp	888.2

S&P 500 Index	Geometric Mean	Arithmetic Mean	Standard Deviation
1-year	17.2	17.4	7.2
3-year	10.4	10.9	11.5
5-year	13.3	13.9	11.5

Return Ratios (%)

	Return on Assets Latest	Return on Assets 5-Yr Avg	Return on Equity Latest	Return on Equity 5-Yr Avg	Dividend Yield Latest	Dividend Yield 5-Yr Avg
Median (5)	1.7	2.1	7.8	14.2	0.0	0.0
SIC Composite (5)	1.7	2.6	7.7	7.1	0.2	0.2
Large Composite (–)	–	–	–	–	–	–
Small Composite (–)	–	–	–	–	–	–
High-Financial Risk (–)	–	–	–	–	–	–

Liquidity Ratio

	Current Ratio Latest	Current Ratio 5-Yr Avg
Median (5)	–	–
SIC Composite (5)	–	–
Large Composite (–)	–	–
Small Composite (–)	–	–
High-Financial Risk (–)	–	–

Profitability Ratio (%)

	Operating Margin Latest	Operating Margin 5-Yr Avg
Median (5)	16.4	17.1
SIC Composite (5)	11.9	21.2
Large Composite (–)	–	–
Small Composite (–)	–	–
High-Financial Risk (–)	–	–

Growth Rates (%)

	Long-term EPS Analyst Estimates
Median (5)	7.5
SIC Composite (5)	13.2
Large Composite (–)	–
Small Composite (–)	–
High-Financial Risk (–)	–

Betas (Levered)

	Raw (OLS)	Blume Adjusted	Peer Group	Vasicek Adjusted	Sum	Downside
Median	1.51	1.33	1.66	1.57	1.17	1.88
SIC Composite	1.51	1.33	1.66	1.55	1.23	1.70
Large Composite	–	–	–	–	–	–
Small Composite	–	–	–	–	–	–
High Financial Risk	–	–	–	–	–	–

Betas (Unlevered)

	Raw (OLS)	Blume Adjusted	Peer Group	Vasicek Adjusted	Sum	Downside
Median	0.49	0.54	0.59	0.58	0.48	0.53
SIC Composite	0.58	0.54	0.61	0.59	0.51	0.62
Large Composite	–	–	–	–	–	–
Small Composite	–	–	–	–	–	–
High Financial Risk	–	–	–	–	–	–

Enterprise Valuation (EV) Multiples

	EV/EBITDA Latest	EV/EBITDA 5-Yr Avg
Median	31.3	18.5
SIC Composite	33.3	20.8
Large Composite	–	–
Small Composite	–	–
High Financial Risk	–	–

Equity Valuation Multiples

	Price/Sales Latest	Price/Sales 5-Yr Avg	Price/Earnings Latest	Price/Earnings 5-Yr Avg	Price/TBV* Latest	Price/TBV* 5-Yr Avg	Price/EBT** Latest	Price/EBT** 5-Yr Avg
Median	1.7	2.7	16.0	14.9	1.3	1.6	11.5	8.8
SIC Composite	1.2	1.8	13.0	14.0	4.3	2.8	10.2	8.5
Large Composite	–	–	–	–	–	–	–	–
Small Composite	–	–	–	–	–	–	–	–
High Financial Risk	–	–	–	–	–	–	–	–

Equity Valuation SIC Composite: Latest Price/TBV 4.3, Price/EBT 10.2; 5-Yr Avg Price/TBV 2.8, Price/EBT 8.5

Fama-French (F-F) 5-Factor Model

	F-F Beta	SMB Premium	HML Premium	RMW Premium	CMA Premium
Median	1.7	6.9	2.5	1.2	-6.6
SIC Composite	1.3	5.0	6.5	0.2	-5.5
Large Composite	–	–	–	–	–
Small Composite	–	–	–	–	–
High Financial Risk	–	–	–	–	–

Leverage Ratios (%)

	Debt/MV Equity Latest	Debt/MV Equity 5-Yr Avg	Debt/Total Capital Latest	Debt/Total Capital 5-Yr Avg
Median	–	–	78.1	72.0
SIC Composite	–	184.8	76.4	64.9
Large Composite	–	–	–	–
Small Composite	–	–	–	–
High Financial Risk	–	–	–	–

Cost of Debt

	Cost of Debt (%) Latest
Median	6.1
SIC Composite	6.1
Large Composite	–
Small Composite	–
High Financial Risk	–

Capital Structure
SIC Composite (%) Latest: D/TC 76.4, E/TC 23.6

Cost of Equity Capital (%)

	CAPM	CRSP Deciles CAPM +Size Prem	Build-Up	Risk Premium Report CAPM +Size Prem	Risk Premium Report Build-Up	Discounted Cash Flow 1-Stage	Discounted Cash Flow 3-Stage	Fama-French 5-Factor Model
Median	12.1	14.7	15.5	–	–	10.5	17.8	16.6
SIC Composite	12.1	14.4	15.2	–	–	13.4	21.6	17.1
Large Composite	–	–	–	–	–	–	–	–
Small Composite	–	–	–	–	–	–	–	–
High Financial Risk	–	–	–	–	–	–	–	–

Cost of Equity Capital (%) SIC Composite: Avg CRSP 14.8, Avg RPR n/a, 1-Stage 13.4, 3-Stage 21.6, 5-Factor Model 17.1

Weighted Average Cost of Capital (WACC) (%)

	CAPM	CRSP Deciles CAPM +Size Prem	Build-Up	Risk Premium Report CAPM +Size Prem	Risk Premium Report Build-Up	Discounted Cash Flow 1-Stage	Discounted Cash Flow 3-Stage	Fama-French 5-Factor Model
Median	6.5	8.0	8.0	–	–	8.0	9.2	8.8
SIC Composite	7.2	7.7	7.9	–	–	7.5	9.4	8.4
Large Composite	–	–	–	–	–	–	–	–
Small Composite	–	–	–	–	–	–	–	–
High Financial Risk	–	–	–	–	–	–	–	–

WACC (%) SIC Composite: Low 7.5, High 9.4, Average 8.2, Median 7.9

*TBV = Tangible Book Value
**EBT = Earnings Before Taxes

© 2017 Duff & Phelps. All Rights Reserved. Duff & Phelps has used the utmost care in compiling the data presented herein, but cannot guarantee the accuracy, completeness, or timeliness of the information.

Data Updated Through March 31, 2017

616

Number of Companies: 5
Mortgage Bankers and Brokers

Industry Description
Establishments primarily engaged in originating mortgage loans, selling mortgage loans to permanent investors, and servicing these loans; arranging loans for others.

Sales (in millions)

Three Largest Companies
Nationstar Mortgage Holdings Inc.	$2,340.0
Walker & Dunlop, Inc.	611.9
HFF, Inc.	517.4

Three Smallest Companies
HFF, Inc.	$517.4
Impac Mortgage Holdings, Inc.	443.8
LendingTree, Inc.	384.4

Annualized Monthly Performance Statistics (%)

Industry	Geometric Mean	Arithmetic Mean	Standard Deviation
1-year	35.6	38.5	30.1
3-year	1.1	4.0	24.9
5-year	17.9	22.8	35.6

Total Assets (in millions)

Three Largest Companies
Nationstar Mortgage Holdings Inc	$19,593.0
Impac Mortgage Holdings, Inc.	5,211.3
Walker & Dunlop, Inc.	3,052.4

Three Smallest Companies
Walker & Dunlop, Inc.	$3,052.4
HFF, Inc.	716.7
LendingTree, Inc.	323.4

S&P 500 Index	Geometric Mean	Arithmetic Mean	Standard Deviation
1-year	17.2	17.4	7.2
3-year	10.4	10.9	11.5
5-year	13.3	13.9	11.5

Return Ratios (%)

	Return on Assets Latest	5-Yr Avg	Return on Equity Latest	5-Yr Avg	Dividend Yield Latest	5-Yr Avg
Median (5)	3.5	3.2	17.0	13.1	0.0	0.2
SIC Composite (5)	1.1	1.3	5.9	6.3	1.3	1.4
Large Composite (–)	–	–	–	–	–	–
Small Composite (–)	–	–	–	–	–	–
High-Financial Risk (–)	–	–	–	–	–	–

Liquidity Ratio

	Current Ratio Latest	5-Yr Avg
Median (5)	1.8	2.1
SIC Composite (5)	1.6	1.6
Large Composite	–	–
Small Composite	–	–
High-Financial Risk	–	–

Profitability Ratio (%)

	Operating Margin Latest	5-Yr Avg
Median (5)	13.7	10.3
SIC Composite (5)	10.4	12.3
Large Composite	–	–
Small Composite	–	–
High-Financial Risk	–	–

Growth Rates (%)

	Long-term EPS Analyst Estimates
Median (5)	14.4
SIC Composite (5)	12.6
Large Composite	–
Small Composite	–
High-Financial Risk	–

Betas (Levered)

	Raw (OLS)	Blume Adjusted	Peer Group	Vasicek Adjusted	Sum	Downside
Median	1.37	1.24	1.70	1.61	0.91	2.26
SIC Composite	1.27	1.18	1.70	1.49	0.89	1.67
Large Composite	–	–	–	–	–	–
Small Composite	–	–	–	–	–	–
High Financial Risk	–	–	–	–	–	–

Betas (Unlevered)

	Raw (OLS)	Blume Adjusted	Peer Group	Vasicek Adjusted	Sum	Downside
Median	0.71	0.66	0.81	0.78	0.55	0.89
SIC Composite	0.48	0.46	0.57	0.52	0.41	0.56
Large Composite	–	–	–	–	–	–
Small Composite	–	–	–	–	–	–
High Financial Risk	–	–	–	–	–	–

Enterprise Valuation (EV) Multiples

	EV/EBITDA Latest	5-Yr Avg
Median	23.5	25.1
SIC Composite	41.8	37.1
Large Composite	–	–
Small Composite	–	–
High Financial Risk	–	–

Equity Valuation Multiples

	Price/Sales Latest	5-Yr Avg	Price/Earnings Latest	5-Yr Avg	Price/TBV* Latest	5-Yr Avg	Price/EBT** Latest	5-Yr Avg
Median	2.0	1.5	13.7	16.3	14.3	8.3	9.3	11.7
SIC Composite	1.3	1.4	17.1	16.0	–	–	12.2	10.9
Large Composite	–	–	–	–	–	–	–	–
Small Composite	–	–	–	–	–	–	–	–
High Financial Risk	–	–	–	–	–	–	–	–

Equity Valuation SIC Composite
Price/TBV Latest: 12.2, 5-Yr Avg: 10.9
Price/EBT: n.a, n/a

Fama-French (F-F) 5-Factor Model

	F-F Beta	SMB Premium	HML Premium	RMW Premium	CMA Premium
Median	0.8	1.1	7.2	-3.0	-0.5
SIC Composite	1.2	2.4	3.4	-1.4	-0.2
Large Composite	–	–	–	–	–
Small Composite	–	–	–	–	–
High Financial Risk	–	–	–	–	–

Leverage Ratios (%)

	Debt/MV Equity Latest	5-Yr Avg	Debt/Total Capital Latest	5-Yr Avg
Median	174.9	–	63.6	72.4
SIC Composite	–	–	80.5	78.7
Large Composite	–	–	–	–
Small Composite	–	–	–	–
High Financial Risk	–	–	–	–

Cost of Debt

	Cost of Debt (%) Latest
Median	6.1
SIC Composite	6.1
Large Composite	–
Small Composite	–
High Financial Risk	–

Capital Structure

SIC Composite (%) Latest
D/TC: 19.5
E/TC: 80.5

Cost of Equity Capital (%)

	CRSP Deciles CAPM	CAPM +Size Prem	Build-Up	Risk Premium Report CAPM +Size Prem	Build-Up	Discounted Cash Flow 1-Stage	3-Stage	Fama-French 5-Factor Model
Median	12.4	14.1	14.6	–	–	15.2	16.7	12.6
SIC Composite	11.7	13.5	14.7	–	–	13.8	18.5	14.1
Large Composite	–	–	–	–	–	–	–	–
Small Composite	–	–	–	–	–	–	–	–
High Financial Risk	–	–	–	–	–	–	–	–

Cost of Equity Capital (%) SIC Composite
Avg CRSP: 14.1, Avg RPR: n/a, 1-Stage: 13.8, 3-Stage: 18.5, 5-Factor Model: 14.1

Weighted Average Cost of Capital (WACC) (%)

	CRSP Deciles CAPM	CAPM +Size Prem	Build-Up	Risk Premium Report CAPM +Size Prem	Build-Up	Discounted Cash Flow 1-Stage	3-Stage	Fama-French 5-Factor Model
Median	7.0	7.6	7.8	–	–	10.6	9.8	7.0
SIC Composite	6.4	6.8	7.0	–	–	6.8	7.7	6.9
Large Composite	–	–	–	–	–	–	–	–
Small Composite	–	–	–	–	–	–	–	–
High Financial Risk	–	–	–	–	–	–	–	–

WACC (%) SIC Composite
Low: 6.8, High: 7.7, Average 7.0, Median 6.9

*TBV = Tangible Book Value
**EBT = Earnings Before Taxes

© 2017 Duff & Phelps. All Rights Reserved. Duff & Phelps has used the utmost care in compiling the data presented herein, but cannot guarantee the accuracy, completeness, or timeliness of the information.

Data Updated Through March 31, 2017

62

Number of Companies: 49

Security and Commodity Brokers, Dealers, Exchanges, and Services

Industry Description
This major group includes establishments engaged in the underwriting, purchase, sale, or brokerage of securities and other financial contracts on their own account or for the account of others; and exchanges, exchange clearinghouses, and other services allied with the exchange of securities and commodities.

Sales (in millions)

Three Largest Companies
Morgan Stanley	$37,949.0
Goldman Sachs Group, Inc.	37,712.0
Ameriprise Financial, Inc.	11,739.0

Three Smallest Companies
Pzena Investment Management	$108.3
Ellington Financial LLC	80.2
Hennessy Advisors, Inc.	51.4

Annualized Monthly Performance Statistics (%)

Industry	Geometric Mean	Arithmetic Mean	Standard Deviation
1-year	33.3	35.7	27.2
3-year	9.4	11.3	20.9
5-year	15.9	17.9	22.2

Total Assets (in millions)

Three Largest Companies
Goldman Sachs Group, Inc.	$860,165.0
Morgan Stanley	814,949.0
Charles Schwab Corp.	223,383.0

Three Smallest Companies
Pzena Investment Management	$179.1
GAMCO Investors Inc.	149.2
Hennessy Advisors, Inc.	85.4

S&P 500 Index	Geometric Mean	Arithmetic Mean	Standard Deviation
1-year	17.2	17.4	7.2
3-year	10.4	10.9	11.5
5-year	13.3	13.9	11.5

Return Ratios (%)

	Return on Assets Latest	5-Yr Avg	Return on Equity Latest	5-Yr Avg	Dividend Yield Latest	5-Yr Avg
Median (49)	4.2	3.5	13.4	14.3	2.5	2.3
SIC Composite (49)	1.2	1.1	5.6	6.2	2.3	2.3
Large Composite (4)	0.9	0.8	6.9	7.7	2.0	1.8
Small Composite (4)	-1.4	1.9	-5.6	7.8	8.0	8.6
High-Financial Risk (7)	-3.2	-1.1	–	-3.7	0.6	5.0

Liquidity Ratio

	Current Ratio Latest	5-Yr Avg
Median (49)	2.8	2.6
SIC Composite (49)	1.1	1.1
Large Composite (4)	–	–
Small Composite (4)	0.9	1.2
High-Financial Risk (7)	1.4	1.2

Profitability Ratio (%)

	Operating Margin Latest	5-Yr Avg
Median (49)	29.5	32.9
SIC Composite (49)	31.4	34.8
Large Composite (4)	30.1	31.1
Small Composite (4)	-5.7	28.0
High-Financial Risk (7)	3.0	18.9

Growth Rates (%)

	Long-term EPS Analyst Estimates
Median (49)	13.5
SIC Composite (49)	13.9
Large Composite (4)	12.8
Small Composite (4)	14.4
High-Financial Risk (7)	12.8

Betas (Levered)

	Raw (OLS)	Blume Adjusted	Peer Group	Vasicek Adjusted	Sum	Downside
Median	1.51	1.33	1.55	1.52	1.83	1.76
SIC Composite	1.52	1.34	1.55	1.52	1.84	1.66
Large Composite	1.69	1.44	1.54	1.60	2.10	1.92
Small Composite	0.70	0.81	1.56	0.73	0.92	0.75
High Financial Risk	1.61	1.40	1.55	1.60	2.62	2.04

Betas (Unlevered)

	Raw (OLS)	Blume Adjusted	Peer Group	Vasicek Adjusted	Sum	Downside
Median	1.26	1.10	1.31	1.24	1.52	1.39
SIC Composite	0.66	0.58	0.67	0.66	0.79	0.71
Large Composite	0.47	0.41	0.44	0.45	0.57	0.53
Small Composite	0.30	0.34	0.61	0.31	0.38	0.32
High Financial Risk	0.57	0.52	0.55	0.57	0.77	0.65

Enterprise Valuation (EV) Multiples

	EV/EBITDA Latest	5-Yr Avg
Median	9.0	9.9
SIC Composite	14.6	12.6
Large Composite	19.0	18.1
Small Composite	–	23.0
High Financial Risk	42.6	9.8

Equity Valuation Multiples

	Price/Sales Latest	5-Yr Avg	Price/Earnings Latest	5-Yr Avg	Price/TBV* Latest	5-Yr Avg	Price/EBT** Latest	5-Yr Avg
Median	2.5	3.0	19.7	18.5	5.4	5.8	10.9	10.3
SIC Composite	3.2	2.6	18.5	16.5	3.1	2.6	11.2	8.4
Large Composite	2.6	2.1	15.1	13.5	1.8	1.5	10.1	8.5
Small Composite	2.6	2.4	–	12.8	–	1.3	–	8.5
High Financial Risk	0.6	0.9	–	–	–	–	19.5	5.0

Equity Valuation SIC Composite
Price/TBV: Latest 3.1, 5-Yr Avg 2.6
Price/EBT: Latest 11.2, 5-Yr Avg 8.4

Fama-French (F-F) 5-Factor Model

	F-F Beta	SMB Premium	HML Premium	RMW Premium	CMA Premium
Median	1.1	4.4	5.8	-1.4	-5.4
SIC Composite	1.4	1.3	4.7	-1.7	-2.9
Large Composite	1.5	0.6	7.3	-2.7	-3.6
Small Composite	0.7	0.4	0.8	-1.0	0.0
High Financial Risk	–	–	–	–	–

Leverage Ratios (%)

	Debt/MV Equity Latest	5-Yr Avg	Debt/Total Capital Latest	5-Yr Avg
Median	17.9	20.6	15.2	17.0
SIC Composite	148.9	–	59.8	67.1
Large Composite	–	–	75.6	81.1
Small Composite	181.0	–	64.4	68.7
High Financial Risk	–	153.8	79.6	60.6

Cost of Debt

	Cost of Debt (%) Latest
Median	4.8
SIC Composite	4.7
Large Composite	4.8
Small Composite	4.8
High Financial Risk	6.3

Capital Structure

SIC Composite (%) Latest
D/TC: 40.2
E/TC: 59.8

Cost of Equity Capital (%)

	CRSP Deciles CAPM	CAPM +Size Prem	Build-Up	Risk Premium Report CAPM	Build-Up	Discounted Cash Flow 1-Stage	3-Stage	Fama-French 5-Factor Model
Median	11.9	13.3	13.6	–	–	15.6	13.6	12.8
SIC Composite	11.9	12.2	12.4	–	–	16.2	13.8	12.9
Large Composite	12.3	12.4	12.1	–	–	14.8	14.6	13.6
Small Composite	7.5	11.5	16.0	–	–	23.7	18.7	7.3
High Financial Risk	–	–	–	–	–	–	–	–

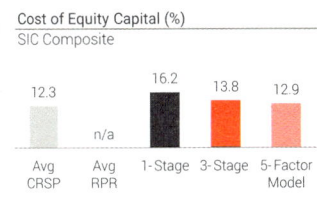

Cost of Equity Capital (%) SIC Composite
Avg CRSP: 12.3
Avg RPR: n/a
1-Stage: 16.2
3-Stage: 13.8
5-Factor Model: 12.9

Weighted Average Cost of Capital (WACC) (%)

	CRSP Deciles CAPM	CAPM +Size Prem	Build-Up	Risk Premium Report CAPM	Build-Up	Discounted Cash Flow 1-Stage	3-Stage	Fama-French 5-Factor Model
Median	10.2	11.3	11.6	–	–	12.7	11.2	11.3
SIC Composite	7.1	7.3	7.3	–	–	8.9	7.9	7.5
Large Composite	6.1	6.1	6.0	–	–	6.7	6.7	6.4
Small Composite	4.9	6.3	7.9	–	–	10.7	8.9	4.8
High Financial Risk	–	–	–	–	–	–	–	–

WACC (%) SIC Composite
Low 7.3 ... High 8.9
▲ Average 7.8 ◆ Median 7.5

*TBV = Tangible Book Value
**EBT = Earnings Before Taxes

© 2017 Duff & Phelps. All Rights Reserved. Duff & Phelps has used the utmost care in compiling the data presented herein, but cannot guarantee the accuracy, completeness, or timeliness of the information.

Data Updated Through March 31, 2017

621

Number of Companies: 11
Security Brokers, Dealers, and Flotation

Industry Description
Establishments primarily engaged in the purchase, sale, and brokerage of securities; and those, generally known as investment bankers, primarily engaged in originating, underwriting, and distributing issues of securities.

Sales (in millions)

Three Largest Companies
Goldman Sachs Group, Inc.	$37,712.0
Ameriprise Financial, Inc.	11,739.0
Raymond James Financial Corp.	5,520.3

Three Smallest Companies
Interactive Brokers Group	$1,475.0
Piper Jaffray Cos. Inc.	769.9
FBR & Co.	119.7

Total Assets (in millions)

Three Largest Companies
Goldman Sachs Group, Inc.	$860,165.0
Ameriprise Financial, Inc.	139,821.0
Interactive Brokers Group	54,673.0

Three Smallest Companies
BGC Partners Inc.	$3,508.4
Piper Jaffray Cos. Inc.	2,125.5
FBR & Co.	1,037.9

Annualized Monthly Performance Statistics (%)

Industry	Geometric Mean	Arithmetic Mean	Standard Deviation
1-year	43.7	48.3	40.4
3-year	11.1	13.9	26.4
5-year	16.0	18.8	26.4

S&P 500 Index	Geometric Mean	Arithmetic Mean	Standard Deviation
1-year	17.2	17.4	7.2
3-year	10.4	10.9	11.5
5-year	13.3	13.9	11.5

Return Ratios (%)

	Return on Assets Latest	5-Yr Avg	Return on Equity Latest	5-Yr Avg	Dividend Yield Latest	5-Yr Avg
Median (11)	0.9	1.3	9.5	9.9	1.4	1.4
SIC Composite (11)	0.9	0.9	6.5	8.0	1.6	1.7
Large Composite (3)	0.9	0.9	7.3	9.2	1.6	1.6
Small Composite (3)	0.0	0.2	-0.1	4.0	1.1	1.5
High-Financial Risk (5)	-9.1	-1.2	–	-6.2	3.6	2.8

Liquidity Ratio

	Current Ratio Latest	5-Yr Avg
Median (11)	–	–
SIC Composite (11)	–	–
Large Composite (3)	–	–
Small Composite (3)	–	–
High-Financial Risk (5)	1.5	1.2

Profitability Ratio (%)

	Operating Margin Latest	5-Yr Avg
Median (11)	14.0	14.4
SIC Composite (11)	28.9	29.1
Large Composite (3)	31.1	31.7
Small Composite (3)	33.7	32.9
High-Financial Risk (5)	-5.4	2.2

Growth Rates (%)

	Long-term EPS Analyst Estimates
Median (11)	13.2
SIC Composite (11)	13.0
Large Composite (3)	12.9
Small Composite (3)	15.9
High-Financial Risk (5)	14.9

Betas (Levered)

	Raw (OLS)	Blume Adjusted	Peer Group	Vasicek Adjusted	Sum	Downside
Median	1.53	1.34	1.53	1.53	1.91	1.88
SIC Composite	1.56	1.36	1.53	1.55	1.96	1.76
Large Composite	1.59	1.38	1.53	1.56	2.02	1.84
Small Composite	1.16	1.11	–	–	1.20	1.43
High Financial Risk	1.50	1.32	1.54	1.51	2.40	2.05

Betas (Unlevered)

	Raw (OLS)	Blume Adjusted	Peer Group	Vasicek Adjusted	Sum	Downside
Median	1.05	0.96	1.19	1.14	1.50	1.36
SIC Composite	0.47	0.42	0.47	0.47	0.58	0.53
Large Composite	0.41	0.36	0.39	0.40	0.50	0.46
Small Composite	0.64	0.61	–	–	0.66	0.78
High Financial Risk	0.62	0.58	0.64	0.63	0.86	0.77

Enterprise Valuation (EV) Multiples

	EV/EBITDA Latest	5-Yr Avg
Median	10.1	10.7
SIC Composite	15.3	15.3
Large Composite	18.1	17.4
Small Composite	–	–
High Financial Risk	–	20.0

Equity Valuation Multiples

	Price/Sales Latest	5-Yr Avg	Price/Earnings Latest	5-Yr Avg	Price/TBV* Latest	5-Yr Avg	Price/EBT** Latest	5-Yr Avg
Median	1.6	1.3	24.4	21.6	2.7	2.0	12.2	10.3
SIC Composite	2.4	1.9	15.9	12.9	1.9	1.6	10.3	7.9
Large Composite	2.3	1.8	14.1	11.3	1.6	1.3	9.8	7.2
Small Composite	1.4	1.2	–	25.1	2.2	1.6	4.1	3.6
High Financial Risk	0.3	0.5	–	–	2.9	3.4	–	21.9

Equity Valuation SIC Composite: Price/TBV Latest 1.9, 5-Yr Avg 1.6; Price/EBT Latest 10.3, 5-Yr Avg 7.9

Fama-French (F-F) 5-Factor Model

	F-F Beta	SMB Premium	HML Premium	RMW Premium	CMA Premium
Median	1.2	3.9	4.4	-1.8	-4.4
SIC Composite	1.5	1.3	7.6	-2.5	-4.6
Large Composite	1.4	0.5	8.6	-2.4	-3.2
Small Composite	1.0	4.0	3.8	2.0	-5.7
High Financial Risk	–	–	–	–	–

Leverage Ratios (%)

	Debt/MV Equity Latest	5-Yr Avg	Debt/Total Capital Latest	5-Yr Avg
Median	30.4	47.8	23.3	32.3
SIC Composite	–	–	73.5	79.4
Large Composite	–	–	78.4	83.2
Small Composite	95.4	171.3	48.8	63.1
High Financial Risk	179.6	73.8	64.2	

Cost of Debt

	Cost of Debt (%) Latest
Median	4.8
SIC Composite	4.8
Large Composite	4.8
Small Composite	4.8
High Financial Risk	6.6

Capital Structure

SIC Composite (%) Latest: D/TC 26.5, E/TC 73.5

Cost of Equity Capital (%)

	CRSP Deciles CAPM	CAPM +Size Prem	Build-Up	Risk Premium Report CAPM +Size Prem	Build-Up	Discounted Cash Flow 1-Stage	3-Stage	Fama-French 5-Factor Model
Median	11.9	13.0	13.0	–	–	16.1	12.0	12.3
SIC Composite	12.0	12.4	12.4	–	–	14.6	15.0	13.4
Large Composite	12.1	12.2	12.2	–	–	14.5	16.2	14.9
Small Composite	–	–	14.0	–	–	17.1	12.1	13.1
High Financial Risk	–	–	–	–	–	–	–	–

Cost of Equity Capital (%) SIC Composite: Avg CRSP 12.4, Avg RPR n/a, 1-Stage 14.6, 3-Stage 15.0, 5-Factor Model 13.4

Weighted Average Cost of Capital (WACC) (%)

	CRSP Deciles CAPM	CAPM +Size Prem	Build-Up	Risk Premium Report CAPM +Size Prem	Build-Up	Discounted Cash Flow 1-Stage	3-Stage	Fama-French 5-Factor Model
Median	9.9	10.7	10.6	–	–	11.0	8.5	8.4
SIC Composite	6.3	6.4	6.4	–	–	7.0	7.1	6.7
Large Composite	5.9	6.0	6.0	–	–	6.5	6.8	6.5
Small Composite	–	–	8.7	–	–	10.3	7.7	8.2
High Financial Risk	–	–	–	–	–	–	–	–

WACC (%) SIC Composite: Low 6.4, High 7.1, Average 6.7, Median 6.7

*TBV = Tangible Book Value
**EBT = Earnings Before Taxes

© 2017 Duff & Phelps. All Rights Reserved. Duff & Phelps has used the utmost care in compiling the data presented herein, but cannot guarantee the accuracy, completeness, or timeliness of the information.

Data Updated Through March 31, 2017

628

Number of Companies: 30
Services Allied With The Exchange Of Securities

Industry Description
Establishments primarily engaged in investment advice; services allied with the exchange of securities or commodities not elsewhere classified.

Sales (in millions)

Three Largest Companies
Blackrock, Inc.	$11,155.0
Charles Schwab Corp.	7,628.0
Franklin Resources Inc.	6,618.0

Three Smallest Companies
Pzena Investment Management	$108.3
Ellington Financial LLC	80.2
Hennessy Advisors, Inc.	51.4

Total Assets (in millions)

Three Largest Companies
Charles Schwab Corp.	$223,383.0
Blackrock, Inc.	220,177.0
KKR & Co. L.P.	39,002.9

Three Smallest Companies
Pzena Investment Management	$179.1
GAMCO Investors Inc.	149.2
Hennessy Advisors, Inc.	85.4

Annualized Monthly Performance Statistics (%)

Industry	Geometric Mean	Arithmetic Mean	Standard Deviation
1-year	18.6	20.5	22.5
3-year	4.3	6.2	20.4
5-year	13.4	15.4	21.5

S&P 500 Index	Geometric Mean	Arithmetic Mean	Standard Deviation
1-year	17.2	17.4	7.2
3-year	10.4	10.9	11.5
5-year	13.3	13.9	11.5

Return Ratios (%)

	Return on Assets Latest	5-Yr Avg	Return on Equity Latest	5-Yr Avg	Dividend Yield Latest	5-Yr Avg
Median (30)	8.1	7.9	16.3	18.1	3.1	3.3
SIC Composite (30)	2.1	2.0	5.0	5.6	2.6	2.8
Large Composite (3)	1.5	1.6	4.8	5.7	1.9	1.9
Small Composite (3)	0.5	2.2	1.8	8.9	8.4	10.5
High-Financial Risk (−)	−	−	−	−	−	−

Liquidity Ratio

	Current Ratio Latest	5-Yr Avg
Median (30)	3.2	2.7
SIC Composite (30)	3.0	2.7
Large Composite (3)	−	−
Small Composite (3)	0.9	1.2
High-Financial Risk	−	−

Profitability Ratio (%)

	Operating Margin Latest	5-Yr Avg
Median (30)	32.3	36.7
SIC Composite (30)	37.6	46.2
Large Composite (3)	40.0	38.2
Small Composite (3)	2.5	47.2
High-Financial Risk	−	−

Growth Rates (%)

	Long-term EPS Analyst Estimates
Median (30)	14.5
SIC Composite (30)	15.5
Large Composite (3)	12.1
Small Composite (3)	14.6
High-Financial Risk	−

Betas (Levered)

	Raw (OLS)	Blume Adjusted	Peer Group	Vasicek Adjusted	Sum	Downside
Median	1.53	1.34	1.56	1.54	1.84	1.77
SIC Composite	1.60	1.39	1.56	1.60	1.89	1.68
Large Composite	1.71	1.46	1.56	1.58	2.05	1.82
Small Composite	0.62	0.76	1.56	0.64	0.79	0.68
High Financial Risk	−	−	−	−	−	−

Betas (Unlevered)

	Raw (OLS)	Blume Adjusted	Peer Group	Vasicek Adjusted	Sum	Downside
Median	1.34	1.18	1.41	1.34	1.63	1.55
SIC Composite	1.30	1.13	1.27	1.30	1.54	1.37
Large Composite	1.57	1.34	1.43	1.45	1.88	1.67
Small Composite	0.26	0.30	0.56	0.26	0.31	0.28
High Financial Risk	−	−	−	−	−	−

Enterprise Valuation (EV) Multiples

	EV/EBITDA Latest	5-Yr Avg
Median	8.3	9.7
SIC Composite	10.4	7.3
Large Composite	9.9	8.0
Small Composite	−	24.0
High Financial Risk	−	−

Equity Valuation Multiples

	Price/Sales Latest	5-Yr Avg	Price/Earnings Latest	5-Yr Avg	Price/TBV* Latest	5-Yr Avg	Price/EBT** Latest	5-Yr Avg
Median	3.0	3.8	18.3	17.0	6.2	6.1	9.4	10.3
SIC Composite	4.2	3.5	20.3	18.0	5.5	5.5	11.3	7.6
Large Composite	5.5	4.6	21.2	17.9	5.5	5.6	14.0	12.3
Small Composite	3.3	3.5	55.1	11.2	−	1.5	−	7.3
High Financial Risk	−	−	−	−	−	−	−	−

Equity Valuation SIC Composite

	Latest	5-Yr Avg
Price/TBV	5.5	5.5
Price/EBT	11.3	7.6

Fama-French (F-F) 5-Factor Model

	F-F Beta	SMB Premium	HML Premium	RMW Premium	CMA Premium
Median	1.2	0.9	3.6	-1.0	1.6
SIC Composite	1.5	1.6	2.7	-0.7	-1.6
Large Composite	1.6	1.5	3.7	-0.8	-1.1
Small Composite	0.6	0.8	0.0	-0.7	1.1
High Financial Risk	−	−	−	−	−

Leverage Ratios (%)

	Debt/MV Equity Latest	5-Yr Avg	Debt/Total Capital Latest	5-Yr Avg
Median	10.8	12.0	9.8	10.7
SIC Composite	23.7	27.2	19.2	21.4
Large Composite	9.0	11.2	8.2	10.1
Small Composite	−	−	67.6	72.9
High Financial Risk	−	−	−	−

Cost of Debt

	Cost of Debt (%) Latest
Median	4.8
SIC Composite	4.2
Large Composite	4.0
Small Composite	4.8
High Financial Risk	−

Capital Structure

SIC Composite (%) Latest: D/TC 19.2, E/TC 80.8

Cost of Equity Capital (%)

	CRSP Deciles CAPM	CAPM +Size Prem	Build-Up	Risk Premium Report CAPM +Size Prem	Build-Up	Discounted Cash Flow 1-Stage	3-Stage	Fama-French 5-Factor Model
Median	12.0	13.5	13.6	−	−	17.0	15.2	15.4
SIC Composite	12.3	12.8	12.5	−	−	18.2	14.7	13.9
Large Composite	12.2	12.3	12.2	−	−	14.0	12.0	15.6
Small Composite	7.0	10.8	15.8	−	−	24.6	20.6	7.8
High Financial Risk	−	−	−	−	−	−	−	−

Cost of Equity Capital (%) SIC Composite
Avg CRSP 12.7, Avg RPR n/a, 1-Stage 18.2, 3-Stage 14.7, 5-Factor Model 13.9

Weighted Average Cost of Capital (WACC) (%)

	CRSP Deciles CAPM	CAPM +Size Prem	Build-Up	Risk Premium Report CAPM +Size Prem	Build-Up	Discounted Cash Flow 1-Stage	3-Stage	Fama-French 5-Factor Model
Median	10.8	12.3	12.0	−	−	14.0	13.1	13.2
SIC Composite	10.6	11.0	10.8	−	−	15.4	12.5	11.9
Large Composite	11.5	11.6	11.5	−	−	13.2	11.3	14.7
Small Composite	4.5	5.7	7.3	−	−	10.2	8.9	4.7
High Financial Risk	−	−	−	−	−	−	−	−

WACC (%) SIC Composite
Low 10.8, High 15.4, Average 12.3, Median 11.9

*TBV = Tangible Book Value
**EBT = Earnings Before Taxes

© 2017 Duff & Phelps. All Rights Reserved. Duff & Phelps has used the utmost care in compiling the data presented herein, but cannot guarantee the accuracy, completeness, or timeliness of the information.

Data Updated Through March 31, 2017

63

Number of Companies: 64
Insurance Carriers

Industry Description
This major group includes carriers of insurance of all types, including reinsurance. Agents and brokers dealing in insurance and organizations rendering services to insurance carriers or to policyholders are classified in Major Group 64.

Sales (in millions)

Three Largest Companies
UnitedHealth Group Inc.	$184,840.0
Aetna Inc.	63,155.0
Metlife, Inc.	63,110.0

Three Smallest Companies
National Sec Group Inc.	$64.1
Kingstone Cos. Inc.	63.8
Unico American Corp.	33.3

Annualized Monthly Performance Statistics (%)

Industry	Geometric Mean	Arithmetic Mean	Standard Deviation
1-year	20.9	21.5	13.0
3-year	16.3	17.2	14.8
5-year	19.1	20.1	15.5

Total Assets (in millions)

Three Largest Companies
Metlife, Inc.	$898,764.0
American International Group	498,264.0
Lincoln National Corporation	261,627.0

Three Smallest Companies
Kingstone Cos. Inc.	$149.1
National Sec Group Inc.	148.1
Unico American Corp.	140.2

S&P 500 Index	Geometric Mean	Arithmetic Mean	Standard Deviation
1-year	17.2	17.4	7.2
3-year	10.4	10.9	11.5
5-year	13.3	13.9	11.5

Return Ratios (%)

	Return on Assets Latest	Return on Assets 5-Yr Avg	Return on Equity Latest	Return on Equity 5-Yr Avg	Dividend Yield Latest	Dividend Yield 5-Yr Avg
Median (64)	2.0	1.9	8.4	8.4	2.1	2.0
SIC Composite (64)	1.0	1.3	4.5	7.3	1.9	1.8
Large Composite (6)	0.6	1.1	2.9	6.6	1.8	1.6
Small Composite (6)	1.2	1.2	3.2	3.4	0.6	0.6
High-Financial Risk (7)	0.9	1.5	6.5	11.4	1.9	2.0

Liquidity Ratio

	Current Ratio Latest	Current Ratio 5-Yr Avg
Median (64)	1.4	1.2
SIC Composite (64)	1.1	1.0
Large Composite (6)	1.0	1.0
Small Composite (6)	–	–
High-Financial Risk (7)	–	–

Profitability Ratio (%)

	Operating Margin Latest	Operating Margin 5-Yr Avg
Median (64)	10.9	10.1
SIC Composite (64)	7.5	9.5
Large Composite (6)	5.5	8.3
Small Composite (6)	7.1	6.9
High-Financial Risk (7)	17.2	14.3

Growth Rates (%)

	Long-term EPS Analyst Estimates
Median (64)	12.9
SIC Composite (64)	15.2
Large Composite (6)	19.8
Small Composite (6)	13.8
High-Financial Risk (7)	8.3

Betas (Levered)

	Raw (OLS)	Blume Adjusted	Peer Group	Vasicek Adjusted	Sum	Downside
Median	0.92	0.95	0.98	0.93	0.84	1.22
SIC Composite	1.00	1.00	0.98	1.00	1.00	1.06
Large Composite	1.01	1.01	0.99	1.01	1.00	1.08
Small Composite	0.93	0.96	0.97	0.94	0.71	1.36
High Financial Risk	1.39	1.25	0.98	1.36	1.41	1.57

Betas (Unlevered)

	Raw (OLS)	Blume Adjusted	Peer Group	Vasicek Adjusted	Sum	Downside
Median	0.78	0.82	0.85	0.82	0.70	0.97
SIC Composite	0.80	0.80	0.79	0.80	0.80	0.85
Large Composite	0.78	0.78	0.76	0.78	0.77	0.84
Small Composite	0.89	0.92	0.93	0.90	0.68	1.30
High Financial Risk	0.80	0.72	0.56	0.78	0.81	0.90

Enterprise Valuation (EV) Multiples

	EV/EBITDA Latest	EV/EBITDA 5-Yr Avg
Median	9.0	6.6
SIC Composite	9.5	6.2
Large Composite	10.9	6.5
Small Composite	14.1	11.9
High Financial Risk	8.3	9.7

Equity Valuation Multiples

	Price/Sales Latest	Price/Sales 5-Yr Avg	Price/Earnings Latest	Price/Earnings 5-Yr Avg	Price/TBV* Latest	Price/TBV* 5-Yr Avg	Price/EBT** Latest	Price/EBT** 5-Yr Avg
Median	1.0	0.9	17.4	13.3	1.5	1.2	11.3	9.3
SIC Composite	0.9	0.8	22.2	13.8	2.1	1.5	13.6	9.1
Large Composite	0.8	0.7	35.0	15.2	2.8	1.8	17.3	9.6
Small Composite	1.4	1.2	31.9	30.0	1.6	1.3	20.6	19.7
High Financial Risk	1.1	1.0	15.5	8.8	0.8	0.9	7.7	6.1

Equity Valuation SIC Composite: 13.6, 9.1, 2.1, 1.5 (Latest, 5-Yr Avg, Price/TBV, Price/EBT)

Fama-French (F-F) 5-Factor Model

Fama-French (F-F) Components	F-F Beta	SMB Premium	HML Premium	RMW Premium	CMA Premium
Median	1.1	0.3	0.8	0.7	0.8
SIC Composite	0.9	1.6	1.4	-0.4	-0.4
Large Composite	0.9	1.6	2.4	-1.0	-1.4
Small Composite	0.7	5.2	6.3	2.2	-6.5
High Financial Risk	–	–	–	–	–

Leverage Ratios (%)

	Debt/MV Equity Latest	Debt/MV Equity 5-Yr Avg	Debt/Total Capital Latest	Debt/Total Capital 5-Yr Avg
Median	16.9	22.8	14.4	18.5
SIC Composite	27.4	32.1	21.5	24.3
Large Composite	32.2	37.6	24.4	27.3
Small Composite	5.4	7.5	5.1	7.0
High Financial Risk	75.5	96.2	43.0	49.0

Cost of Debt

	Cost of Debt (%) Latest
Median	4.8
SIC Composite	4.6
Large Composite	4.6
Small Composite	4.8
High Financial Risk	4.1

Capital Structure

SIC Composite (%) Latest: D/TC 21.5, E/TC 78.5

Cost of Equity Capital (%)

	CRSP Deciles CAPM	CRSP Deciles CAPM +Size Prem	CRSP Deciles Build-Up	Risk Premium Report CAPM +Size Prem	Risk Premium Report Build-Up	Discounted Cash Flow 1-Stage	Discounted Cash Flow 3-Stage	Fama-French 5-Factor Model
Median	8.6	10.2	10.4	–	–	14.5	15.6	12.4
SIC Composite	9.0	9.3	9.2	–	–	17.2	17.5	10.8
Large Composite	9.0	9.1	8.9	–	–	21.8	20.2	10.1
Small Composite	8.7	12.3	12.4	–	–	14.0	8.9	14.6
High Financial Risk	–	–	–	–	–	–	–	–

Cost of Equity Capital (%) SIC Composite: Avg CRSP 9.3, Avg RPR n/a, 1-Stage 17.2, 3-Stage 17.5, 5-Factor Model 10.8

Weighted Average Cost of Capital (WACC) (%)

	CRSP Deciles CAPM	CRSP Deciles CAPM +Size Prem	CRSP Deciles Build-Up	Risk Premium Report CAPM +Size Prem	Risk Premium Report Build-Up	Discounted Cash Flow 1-Stage	Discounted Cash Flow 3-Stage	Fama-French 5-Factor Model
Median	8.0	9.0	9.0	–	–	12.0	13.8	10.8
SIC Composite	7.8	8.1	8.0	–	–	14.3	14.5	9.3
Large Composite	7.7	7.8	7.6	–	–	17.4	16.2	8.5
Small Composite	8.4	11.8	12.0	–	–	13.5	8.6	14.0
High Financial Risk	–	–	–	–	–	–	–	–

WACC (%) SIC Composite: Low 8.0, High 14.5, Average 10.8, Median 9.3

*TBV = Tangible Book Value
**EBT = Earnings Before Taxes

© 2017 Duff & Phelps. All Rights Reserved. Duff & Phelps has used the utmost care in compiling the data presented herein, but cannot guarantee the accuracy, completeness, or timeliness of the information.

Data Updated Through March 31, 2017

632

Number of Companies: 10
Accident and Health Insurance and Medical

Industry Description
Establishments primarily engaged in accident and health insurance; and hospital and medical service plans.

Sales (in millions)

Three Largest Companies
UnitedHealth Group Inc.	$184,840.0
Aetna Inc.	63,155.0
Humana Inc.	54,962.0

Three Smallest Companies
Unum Group	$11,047.4
CNO Financial Group, Inc.	3,992.4
Independence Holding Co.	521.3

Total Assets (in millions)

Three Largest Companies
UnitedHealth Group Inc.	$122,810.0
Aetna Inc.	69,146.0
Unum Group	61,941.5

Three Smallest Companies
Molina Healthcare, Inc.	$7,449.0
WellCare Health Plans Inc.	6,152.8
Independence Holding Co.	1,198.0

Annualized Monthly Performance Statistics (%)

Industry	Geometric Mean	Arithmetic Mean	Standard Deviation
1-year	21.7	23.0	19.1
3-year	24.0	25.6	21.0
5-year	22.6	24.3	20.8

S&P 500 Index	Geometric Mean	Arithmetic Mean	Standard Deviation
1-year	17.2	17.4	7.2
3-year	10.4	10.9	11.5
5-year	13.3	13.9	11.5

Return Ratios (%)

	Return on Assets Latest	5-Yr Avg	Return on Equity Latest	5-Yr Avg	Dividend Yield Latest	5-Yr Avg
Median (10)	2.9	3.6	11.5	10.7	0.7	0.9
SIC Composite (10)	3.4	3.7	4.6	6.4	1.1	1.2
Large Composite (3)	4.6	5.2	4.3	6.3	1.4	1.4
Small Composite (3)	1.4	1.1	9.0	9.5	1.9	1.8
High-Financial Risk (–)	–	–	–	–	–	–

Liquidity Ratio

	Current Ratio Latest	5-Yr Avg
Median (10)	1.4	1.2
SIC Composite (10)	1.1	1.0
Large Composite (3)	1.0	1.0
Small Composite (3)	–	–
High-Financial Risk (–)	–	–

Profitability Ratio (%)

	Operating Margin Latest	5-Yr Avg
Median (10)	7.2	6.8
SIC Composite (10)	6.6	7.0
Large Composite (3)	6.8	7.0
Small Composite (3)	13.0	11.8
High-Financial Risk (–)	–	–

Growth Rates (%)

	Long-term EPS Analyst Estimates
Median (10)	13.6
SIC Composite (10)	14.3
Large Composite (3)	14.9
Small Composite (3)	7.9
High-Financial Risk (–)	–

Betas (Levered)

	Raw (OLS)	Blume Adjusted	Peer Group	Vasicek Adjusted	Sum	Downside
Median	0.79	0.87	0.99	0.91	0.64	1.33
SIC Composite	0.71	0.82	0.99	0.78	0.55	0.83
Large Composite	0.68	0.80	1.00	0.86	0.35	0.76
Small Composite	1.47	1.31	0.97	1.41	1.87	1.65
High Financial Risk	–	–	–	–	–	–

Betas (Unlevered)

	Raw (OLS)	Blume Adjusted	Peer Group	Vasicek Adjusted	Sum	Downside
Median	0.55	0.64	0.80	0.65	0.52	0.94
SIC Composite	0.58	0.67	0.81	0.64	0.45	0.68
Large Composite	0.56	0.66	0.82	0.70	0.30	0.62
Small Composite	0.98	0.87	0.65	0.94	1.24	1.09
High Financial Risk	–	–	–	–	–	–

Enterprise Valuation (EV) Multiples

	EV/EBITDA Latest	5-Yr Avg
Median	7.7	6.7
SIC Composite	9.6	7.4
Large Composite	10.4	7.8
Small Composite	7.7	6.7
High Financial Risk	–	–

Equity Valuation Multiples

	Price/Sales Latest	5-Yr Avg	Price/Earnings Latest	5-Yr Avg	Price/TBV* Latest	5-Yr Avg	Price/EBT** Latest	5-Yr Avg
Median	0.7	0.5	21.0	15.2	4.1	3.4	10.6	8.9
SIC Composite	0.7	0.6	21.9	15.6	15.1	8.7	11.7	9.0
Large Composite	0.8	0.6	23.4	15.9	–	–	12.2	9.1
Small Composite	0.9	0.7	11.1	10.5	1.1	0.9	8.4	7.4
High Financial Risk	–	–	–	–	–	–	–	–

Equity Valuation — SIC Composite
Latest: Price/TBV 15.1, Price/EBT 11.7
5-Yr Avg: Price/TBV 8.7, Price/EBT 9.0

Fama-French (F-F) 5-Factor Model

	F-F Beta	SMB Premium	HML Premium	RMW Premium	CMA Premium
Median	0.8	3.6	1.7	-1.6	0.5
SIC Composite	0.6	3.3	-0.7	-0.5	1.9
Large Composite	0.6	3.1	-0.5	-0.4	-0.5
Small Composite	1.3	1.9	5.9	-1.8	-3.7
High Financial Risk	–	–	–	–	–

Leverage Ratios (%)

	Debt/MV Equity Latest	5-Yr Avg	Debt/Total Capital Latest	5-Yr Avg
Median	26.1	25.9	20.6	20.5
SIC Composite	25.5	27.0	20.3	21.3
Large Composite	24.9	25.6	19.9	20.4
Small Composite	52.0	60.6	34.2	37.7
High Financial Risk	–	–	–	–

Cost of Debt

	Cost of Debt (%) Latest
Median	4.8
SIC Composite	4.7
Large Composite	4.8
Small Composite	4.1
High Financial Risk	–

Capital Structure

SIC Composite (%) Latest
D/TC: 20.3
E/TC: 79.7

Cost of Equity Capital (%)

	CRSP Deciles CAPM	CAPM +Size Prem	Build-Up	Risk Premium Report CAPM +Size Prem	Build-Up	Discounted Cash Flow 1-Stage	3-Stage	Fama-French 5-Factor Model
Median	8.5	9.3	9.6	–	–	14.2	14.7	12.0
SIC Composite	7.8	7.9	9.0	–	–	15.5	14.3	10.7
Large Composite	8.2	8.2	8.9	–	–	16.4	14.3	8.5
Small Composite	11.3	12.2	9.8	–	–	9.6	15.9	12.9
High Financial Risk	–	–	–	–	–	–	–	–

Cost of Equity Capital (%) — SIC Composite
Avg CRSP: 8.4; Avg RPR: n/a; 1-Stage: 15.5; 3-Stage: 14.3; 5-Factor Model: 10.7

Weighted Average Cost of Capital (WACC) (%)

	CRSP Deciles CAPM	CAPM +Size Prem	Build-Up	Risk Premium Report CAPM +Size Prem	Build-Up	Discounted Cash Flow 1-Stage	3-Stage	Fama-French 5-Factor Model
Median	7.2	7.9	8.2	–	–	11.7	11.8	9.5
SIC Composite	6.9	7.0	7.8	–	–	13.0	12.1	9.2
Large Composite	7.2	7.2	7.8	–	–	13.8	12.1	7.5
Small Composite	8.4	9.1	7.5	–	–	7.4	11.5	9.5
High Financial Risk	–	–	–	–	–	–	–	–

WACC (%) — SIC Composite
Low 7.0, High 13.0; Average 9.8, Median 9.2

*TBV = Tangible Book Value
**EBT = Earnings Before Taxes

© 2017 Duff & Phelps. All Rights Reserved. Duff & Phelps has used the utmost care in compiling the data presented herein, but cannot guarantee the accuracy, completeness, or timeliness of the information.

Data Updated Through March 31, 2017

6324

Number of Companies: 7
Hospital and Medical Service Plans

Industry Description
Establishments primarily engaged in providing hospital, medical, and other health services to subscribers or members in accordance with prearranged agreements or service plans.

Sales (in millions)

Three Largest Companies
UnitedHealth Group Inc.	$184,840.0
Aetna Inc.	63,155.0
Humana Inc.	54,962.0

Three Smallest Companies
Cigna Corp.	$39,668.0
Molina Healthcare, Inc.	17,782.0
WellCare Health Plans Inc.	14,237.1

Annualized Monthly Performance Statistics (%)

	Industry			S&P 500 Index		
	Geometric Mean	Arithmetic Mean	Standard Deviation	Geometric Mean	Arithmetic Mean	Standard Deviation
1-year	20.8	22.1	19.3	17.2	17.4	7.2
3-year	25.0	26.8	21.9	10.4	10.9	11.5
5-year	22.9	24.7	21.5	13.3	13.9	11.5

Total Assets (in millions)

Three Largest Companies
UnitedHealth Group Inc.	$122,810.0
Aetna Inc.	69,146.0
Cigna Corp.	59,360.0

Three Smallest Companies
Centene Corp.	$20,197.0
Molina Healthcare, Inc.	7,449.0
WellCare Health Plans Inc.	6,152.8

Return Ratios (%)

	Return on Assets		Return on Equity		Dividend Yield		Current Ratio		Operating Margin		Long-term EPS
	Latest	5-Yr Avg	Latest	5-Yr Avg	Latest	5-Yr Avg	Latest	5-Yr Avg	Latest	5-Yr Avg	Analyst Estimates
Median (7)	3.7	4.1	13.3	14.2	0.0	0.0	1.4	1.2	4.4	4.7	13.7
SIC Composite (7)	4.1	4.6	4.3	6.2	1.1	1.1	1.1	1.0	6.4	6.8	14.6
Large Composite (–)	–	–	–	–	–	–	–	–	–	–	–
Small Composite (–)	–	–	–	–	–	–	–	–	–	–	–
High-Financial Risk (–)	–	–	–	–	–	–	–	–	–	–	–

Liquidity Ratio
Profitability Ratio (%)
Growth Rates (%)

Betas (Levered)

	Raw (OLS)	Blume Adjusted	Peer Group	Vasicek Adjusted	Sum	Downside
Median	0.73	0.83	0.99	0.96	0.57	1.10
SIC Composite	0.66	0.79	0.99	0.87	0.46	0.80
Large Composite	–	–	–	–	–	–
Small Composite	–	–	–	–	–	–
High Financial Risk	–	–	–	–	–	–

Betas (Unlevered)

	Raw (OLS)	Blume Adjusted	Peer Group	Vasicek Adjusted	Sum	Downside
Median	0.55	0.63	0.84	0.72	0.46	0.89
SIC Composite	0.55	0.65	0.82	0.72	0.39	0.66
Large Composite	–	–	–	–	–	–
Small Composite	–	–	–	–	–	–
High Financial Risk	–	–	–	–	–	–

Enterprise Valuation (EV) Multiples

	EV/EBITDA	
	Latest	5-Yr Avg
Median	8.0	6.8
SIC Composite	9.7	7.5
Large Composite	–	–
Small Composite	–	–
High Financial Risk	–	–

Equity Valuation Multiples

	Price/Sales		Price/Earnings		Price/TBV*		Price/EBT**	
	Latest	5-Yr Avg	Latest	5-Yr Avg	Latest	5-Yr Avg	Latest	5-Yr Avg
Median	0.6	0.4	22.3	18.6	5.3	5.9	11.4	9.6
SIC Composite	0.7	0.6	23.0	16.1	–	19.3	11.9	9.1
Large Composite	–	–	–	–	–	–	–	–
Small Composite	–	–	–	–	–	–	–	–
High Financial Risk	–	–	–	–	–	–	–	–

Equity Valuation SIC Composite
- Price/TBV: Latest 11.9, 5-Yr Avg 19.3
- Price/EBT: Latest n/a, 5-Yr Avg 9.1

Fama-French (F-F) 5-Factor Model

	Fama-French (F-F) Components				
	F-F Beta	SMB Premium	HML Premium	RMW Premium	CMA Premium
Median	0.6	3.0	-1.4	-0.1	2.2
SIC Composite	0.5	3.4	-1.1	-0.4	2.1
Large Composite	–	–	–	–	–
Small Composite	–	–	–	–	–
High Financial Risk	–	–	–	–	–

Leverage Ratios (%)

	Debt/MV Equity		Debt/Total Capital	
	Latest	5-Yr Avg	Latest	5-Yr Avg
Median	21.1	24.6	17.4	19.8
SIC Composite	24.1	24.9	19.4	20.0
Large Composite	–	–	–	–
Small Composite	–	–	–	–
High Financial Risk	–	–	–	–

Cost of Debt

	Cost of Debt (%) Latest
Median	4.8
SIC Composite	4.8
Large Composite	–
Small Composite	–
High Financial Risk	–

Capital Structure

SIC Composite (%) Latest
- D/TC: 19.4
- E/TC: 80.6

Cost of Equity Capital (%)

	CRSP Deciles			Risk Premium Report		Discounted Cash Flow		Fama-French
	CAPM	CAPM +Size Prem	Build-Up	CAPM +Size Prem	Build-Up	1-Stage	3-Stage	5-Factor Model
Median	8.8	8.9	8.9	–	–	14.6	12.9	10.5
SIC Composite	8.3	8.3	8.9	–	–	15.8	14.2	10.5
Large Composite	–	–	–	–	–	–	–	–
Small Composite	–	–	–	–	–	–	–	–
High Financial Risk	–	–	–	–	–	–	–	–

Cost of Equity Capital (%) SIC Composite
- Avg CRSP: 8.6
- Avg RPR: n/a
- 1-Stage: 15.8
- 3-Stage: 14.2
- 5-Factor Model: 10.5

Weighted Average Cost of Capital (WACC) (%)

	CRSP Deciles			Risk Premium Report		Discounted Cash Flow		Fama-French
	CAPM	CAPM +Size Prem	Build-Up	CAPM +Size Prem	Build-Up	1-Stage	3-Stage	5-Factor Model
Median	7.7	8.1	8.2	–	–	12.6	11.1	9.3
SIC Composite	7.3	7.4	7.8	–	–	13.4	12.1	9.1
Large Composite	–	–	–	–	–	–	–	–
Small Composite	–	–	–	–	–	–	–	–
High Financial Risk	–	–	–	–	–	–	–	–

WACC (%) SIC Composite
- Low: 7.4
- High: 13.4
- Average: 10.0
- Median: 9.1

*TBV = Tangible Book Value
**EBT = Earnings Before Taxes

© 2017 Duff & Phelps. All Rights Reserved. Duff & Phelps has used the utmost care in compiling the data presented herein, but cannot guarantee the accuracy, completeness, or timeliness of the information.

Data Updated Through March 31, 2017

633

Number of Companies: 34
Fire, Marine, and Casualty Insurance

Industry Description
Establishments primarily engaged in underwriting fire, marine, and casualty insurance.

Sales (in millions)

Three Largest Companies
Allstate Corp.	$36,128.0
Travelers Cos. Inc.	27,499.0
Progressive Corp	23,417.4

Three Smallest Companies
National Sec Group Inc.	$64.1
Kingstone Cos. Inc.	63.8
Unico American Corp.	33.3

Total Assets (in millions)

Three Largest Companies
Hartford Financial Services	$223,432.0
Allstate Corp.	108,610.0
Travelers Cos. Inc.	100,245.0

Three Smallest Companies
Kingstone Cos. Inc.	$149.1
National Sec Group Inc.	148.1
Unico American Corp.	140.2

Annualized Monthly Performance Statistics (%)

Industry	Geometric Mean	Arithmetic Mean	Standard Deviation	S&P 500 Index	Geometric Mean	Arithmetic Mean	Standard Deviation
1-year	16.5	17.1	13.3	1-year	17.2	17.4	7.2
3-year	15.9	16.8	15.1	3-year	10.4	10.9	11.5
5-year	18.3	19.3	15.2	5-year	13.3	13.9	11.5

Return Ratios (%)

	Return on Assets Latest	Return on Assets 5-Yr Avg	Return on Equity Latest	Return on Equity 5-Yr Avg	Dividend Yield Latest	Dividend Yield 5-Yr Avg	Current Ratio Latest	Current Ratio 5-Yr Avg	Operating Margin Latest	Operating Margin 5-Yr Avg	Long-term EPS Analyst Estimates
Median (34)	2.1	2.0	8.2	8.3	2.5	2.7	–	–	11.6	11.4	13.8
SIC Composite (34)	1.6	1.6	6.1	8.0	2.5	2.7	–	–	10.7	12.1	9.1
Large Composite (3)	2.4	2.7	6.9	9.3	2.1	2.5	–	–	10.3	12.9	8.6
Small Composite (3)	2.4	1.5	4.8	4.2	–	–	–	–	10.7	8.9	17.8
High-Financial Risk (–)	–	–	–	–	–	–	–	–	–	–	–

Betas (Levered)

	Raw (OLS)	Blume Adjusted	Peer Group	Vasicek Adjusted	Sum	Downside
Median	0.88	0.93	0.98	0.89	0.77	0.99
SIC Composite	0.95	0.97	0.98	0.95	0.82	0.96
Large Composite	0.98	0.99	0.97	0.97	0.79	0.99
Small Composite	0.08	0.42	0.97	0.73	0.60	0.55
High Financial Risk	–	–	–	–	–	–

Betas (Unlevered)

	Raw (OLS)	Blume Adjusted	Peer Group	Vasicek Adjusted	Sum	Downside
Median	0.78	0.82	0.86	0.79	0.67	0.89
SIC Composite	0.81	0.83	0.83	0.81	0.70	0.82
Large Composite	0.83	0.85	0.83	0.83	0.67	0.84
Small Composite	0.08	0.39	0.90	0.68	0.56	0.51
High Financial Risk	–	–	–	–	–	–

Enterprise Valuation (EV) Multiples

	EV/EBITDA Latest	EV/EBITDA 5-Yr Avg
Median	10.1	6.8
SIC Composite	8.7	5.9
Large Composite	7.2	5.4
Small Composite	9.6	4.4
High Financial Risk	–	–

Equity Valuation Multiples

	Price/Sales Latest	Price/Sales 5-Yr Avg	Price/Earnings Latest	Price/Earnings 5-Yr Avg	Price/TBV* Latest	Price/TBV* 5-Yr Avg	Price/EBT** Latest	Price/EBT** 5-Yr Avg
Median	1.2	1.0	17.7	13.4	1.5	1.2	12.5	9.7
SIC Composite	1.2	1.0	16.6	12.7	1.6	1.3	12.1	8.8
Large Composite	1.0	0.9	14.9	10.9	1.9	1.6	10.5	7.5
Small Composite	1.3	1.0	20.7	23.8	1.4	1.0	13.7	13.3
High Financial Risk	–	–	–	–	–	–	–	–

Equity Valuation SIC Composite
Price/TBV: Latest 1.6, 5-Yr Avg 1.3
Price/EBT: Latest 12.1, 5-Yr Avg 8.8

Fama-French (F-F) 5-Factor Model

	F-F Beta	SMB Premium	HML Premium	RMW Premium	CMA Premium
Median	1.2	0.3	-0.9	1.3	2.2
SIC Composite	0.9	0.8	-0.2	0.8	1.2
Large Composite	1.0	0.2	-1.1	1.1	1.4
Small Composite	0.1	-0.5	2.8	-0.3	-0.6
High Financial Risk	–	–	–	–	–

Leverage Ratios (%)

	Debt/MV Equity Latest	Debt/MV Equity 5-Yr Avg	Debt/Total Capital Latest	Debt/Total Capital 5-Yr Avg
Median	15.6	19.1	13.5	16.0
SIC Composite	19.1	22.8	16.1	18.6
Large Composite	18.5	20.2	15.6	16.8
Small Composite	8.4	14.4	7.7	12.6
High Financial Risk	–	–	–	–

Cost of Debt

	Cost of Debt (%) Latest
Median	4.8
SIC Composite	4.7
Large Composite	4.5
Small Composite	4.8
High Financial Risk	–

Capital Structure

SIC Composite (%) Latest
D/TC: 16.1
E/TC: 83.9

Cost of Equity Capital (%)

	CRSP Deciles CAPM	CRSP Deciles CAPM +Size Prem	CRSP Deciles Build-Up	Risk Premium Report CAPM +Size Prem	Risk Premium Report Build-Up	Discounted Cash Flow 1-Stage	Discounted Cash Flow 3-Stage	Fama-French 5-Factor Model
Median	8.4	10.1	10.5	–	–	15.6	12.7	12.7
SIC Composite	8.7	9.3	9.5	–	–	11.7	14.1	11.2
Large Composite	8.9	9.0	9.0	–	–	10.7	16.2	10.7
Small Composite	7.5	13.1	14.4	–	–	17.8	12.2	5.2
High Financial Risk	–	–	–	–	–	–	–	–

Cost of Equity Capital (%) SIC Composite
Avg CRSP: 9.4
Avg RPR: n/a
1-Stage: 11.7
3-Stage: 14.1
5-Factor Model: 11.2

Weighted Average Cost of Capital (WACC) (%)

	CRSP Deciles CAPM	CRSP Deciles CAPM +Size Prem	CRSP Deciles Build-Up	Risk Premium Report CAPM +Size Prem	Risk Premium Report Build-Up	Discounted Cash Flow 1-Stage	Discounted Cash Flow 3-Stage	Fama-French 5-Factor Model
Median	8.0	9.1	9.6	–	–	14.3	11.7	11.0
SIC Composite	7.9	8.4	8.5	–	–	10.4	12.4	10.0
Large Composite	8.0	8.2	8.1	–	–	9.5	14.2	9.6
Small Composite	7.2	12.4	13.6	–	–	16.7	11.5	5.1
High Financial Risk	–	–	–	–	–	–	–	–

WACC (%) SIC Composite
Low 8.4, High 12.4
Average 9.9, Median 10.0

*TBV = Tangible Book Value
**EBT = Earnings Before Taxes

© 2017 Duff & Phelps. All Rights Reserved. Duff & Phelps has used the utmost care in compiling the data presented herein, but cannot guarantee the accuracy, completeness, or timeliness of the information.

Data Updated Through March 31, 2017

64

Number of Companies: 8
Insurance Agents, Brokers, and Service

Industry Description
This major group includes agents and brokers dealing in insurance, and also organizations offering services to insurance companies and to policyholders.

Sales (in millions)

Three Largest Companies
Marsh & Mclennan Cos.	$13,200.0
Arthur J Gallagher & Co.	5,594.8
Verisk Analytics, Inc.	1,995.2

Three Smallest Companies
Crawford & Co.	$1,177.6
CorVel Corp.	503.6
HMS Holdings Corp.	496.0

Total Assets (in millions)

Three Largest Companies
Marsh & Mclennan Cos.	$18,190.0
Arthur J Gallagher & Co.	11,489.6
Brown & Brown Inc.	5,287.3

Three Smallest Companies
HMS Holdings Corp.	$882.8
Crawford & Co.	735.9
CorVel Corp.	220.3

Annualized Monthly Performance Statistics (%)

Industry	Geometric Mean	Arithmetic Mean	Standard Deviation	S&P 500 Index	Geometric Mean	Arithmetic Mean	Standard Deviation
1-year	20.9	21.4	11.8	1-year	17.2	17.4	7.2
3-year	14.0	14.7	13.2	3-year	10.4	10.9	11.5
5-year	15.2	15.9	12.2	5-year	13.3	13.9	11.5

Return Ratios (%)

	Return on Assets Latest	5-Yr Avg	Return on Equity Latest	5-Yr Avg	Dividend Yield Latest	5-Yr Avg
Median (8)	6.9	4.6	23.2	16.5	1.9	2.2
SIC Composite (8)	7.5	5.7	4.2	4.6	1.7	1.8
Large Composite (–)	–	–	–	–	–	–
Small Composite (–)	–	–	–	–	–	–
High-Financial Risk (–)	–	–	–	–	–	–

Liquidity Ratio

	Current Ratio Latest	5-Yr Avg
	1.3	1.4
	1.1	1.2
	–	–
	–	–
	–	–

Profitability Ratio (%)

	Operating Margin Latest	5-Yr Avg
	16.0	16.0
	19.4	18.4
	–	–
	–	–
	–	–

Growth Rates (%)

	Long-term EPS Analyst Estimates
	10.1
	10.1
	–
	–
	–

Betas (Levered)

	Raw (OLS)	Blume Adjusted	Peer Group	Vasicek Adjusted	Sum	Downside
Median	0.84	0.91	0.88	0.85	1.00	1.18
SIC Composite	0.86	0.91	0.88	0.86	0.80	0.95
Large Composite	–	–	–	–	–	–
Small Composite	–	–	–	–	–	–
High Financial Risk	–	–	–	–	–	–

Betas (Unlevered)

	Raw (OLS)	Blume Adjusted	Peer Group	Vasicek Adjusted	Sum	Downside
Median	0.77	0.84	0.77	0.80	0.94	1.00
SIC Composite	0.75	0.80	0.77	0.75	0.71	0.83
Large Composite	–	–	–	–	–	–
Small Composite	–	–	–	–	–	–
High Financial Risk	–	–	–	–	–	–

Enterprise Valuation (EV) Multiples

	EV/EBITDA Latest	5-Yr Avg
Median	12.8	10.5
SIC Composite	13.5	10.2
Large Composite	–	–
Small Composite	–	–
High Financial Risk	–	–

Equity Valuation Multiples

	Price/Sales Latest	5-Yr Avg	Price/Earnings Latest	5-Yr Avg	Price/TBV* Latest	5-Yr Avg	Price/EBT** Latest	5-Yr Avg
Median	3.1	1.8	26.6	23.6	–	–	18.6	13.8
SIC Composite	2.9	2.2	24.0	21.6	–	–	16.6	12.8
Large Composite	–	–	–	–	–	–	–	–
Small Composite	–	–	–	–	–	–	–	–
High Financial Risk	–	–	–	–	–	–	–	–

Equity Valuation SIC Composite: Price/TBV n/a Latest, n/a 5-Yr Avg; Price/EBT 16.6 Latest, 12.8 5-Yr Avg

Fama-French (F-F) 5-Factor Model

Fama-French (F-F) Components

	F-F Beta	SMB Premium	HML Premium	RMW Premium	CMA Premium
Median	0.8	5.7	-4.2	-1.3	3.3
SIC Composite	0.8	0.9	-1.2	-0.3	2.0
Large Composite	–	–	–	–	–
Small Composite	–	–	–	–	–
High Financial Risk	–	–	–	–	–

Leverage Ratios (%)

	Debt/MV Equity Latest	5-Yr Avg	Debt/Total Capital Latest	5-Yr Avg
Median	15.1	15.5	13.1	13.4
SIC Composite	15.0	15.6	13.0	13.5
Large Composite	–	–	–	–
Small Composite	–	–	–	–
High Financial Risk	–	–	–	–

Cost of Debt

	Cost of Debt (%) Latest
Median	4.8
SIC Composite	4.5
Large Composite	–
Small Composite	–
High Financial Risk	–

Capital Structure

SIC Composite (%) Latest: D/TC 13.0; E/TC 87.0

Cost of Equity Capital (%)

	CRSP Deciles CAPM	CAPM +Size Prem	Build-Up	Risk Premium Report CAPM +Size Prem	Build-Up	Discounted Cash Flow 1-Stage	3-Stage	Fama-French 5-Factor Model
Median	8.2	9.2	9.2	–	–	12.2	10.0	11.5
SIC Composite	8.2	8.7	8.8	–	–	11.8	9.8	9.4
Large Composite	–	–	–	–	–	–	–	–
Small Composite	–	–	–	–	–	–	–	–
High Financial Risk	–	–	–	–	–	–	–	–

Cost of Equity Capital (%) SIC Composite: Avg CRSP 8.7; Avg RPR n/a; 1-Stage 11.8; 3-Stage 9.8; 5-Factor Model 9.4

Weighted Average Cost of Capital (WACC) (%)

	CRSP Deciles CAPM	CAPM +Size Prem	Build-Up	Risk Premium Report CAPM +Size Prem	Build-Up	Discounted Cash Flow 1-Stage	3-Stage	Fama-French 5-Factor Model
Median	7.8	8.5	8.8	–	–	11.1	9.2	9.7
SIC Composite	7.6	8.0	8.1	–	–	10.7	8.9	8.6
Large Composite	–	–	–	–	–	–	–	–
Small Composite	–	–	–	–	–	–	–	–
High Financial Risk	–	–	–	–	–	–	–	–

WACC (%) SIC Composite: Low 8.0; High 10.7; Average 8.9; Median 8.6

*TBV = Tangible Book Value
**EBT = Earnings Before Taxes

© 2017 Duff & Phelps. All Rights Reserved. Duff & Phelps has used the utmost care in compiling the data presented herein, but cannot guarantee the accuracy, completeness, or timeliness of the information.

Data Updated Through March 31, 2017

65

Number of Companies: 15
Real Estate

Industry Description
This major group includes real estate operators, and owners and lessors of real property, as well as buyers, sellers, developers, agents, and brokers.

Sales (in millions)

Three Largest Companies
CBRE Group, Inc.	$13,071.6
Jones Lang Lasalle Inc.	6,803.8
Wyndham Worldwide Corp.	5,599.0

Three Smallest Companies
Griffin Industrial Realty, Inc.	$30.9
JW Mays Inc.	18.6
Income Opportunity Realty Investors	4.4

Total Assets (in millions)

Three Largest Companies
CBRE Group, Inc.	$10,779.6
Wyndham Worldwide Corp.	9,819.0
Kennedy-Wilson Holdings, Inc.	7,659.1

Three Smallest Companies
Income Opportunity Realty Investors	$84.3
JW Mays Inc.	63.5
Maui Land & Pineapple Company, Inc	38.9

Annualized Monthly Performance Statistics (%)

Industry	Geometric Mean	Arithmetic Mean	Standard Deviation	S&P 500 Index	Geometric Mean	Arithmetic Mean	Standard Deviation
1-year	12.4	14.0	20.2	1-year	17.2	17.4	7.2
3-year	2.8	5.1	22.4	3-year	10.4	10.9	11.5
5-year	11.1	13.0	20.9	5-year	13.3	13.9	11.5

Return Ratios (%)

	Return on Assets Latest	5-Yr Avg	Return on Equity Latest	5-Yr Avg	Dividend Yield Latest	5-Yr Avg	Current Ratio Latest	5-Yr Avg	Operating Margin Latest	5-Yr Avg	Long-term EPS Analyst Estimates
Median (15)	3.3	3.7	5.9	4.2	0.2	0.1	1.1	1.2	22.6	20.3	11.3
SIC Composite (15)	4.2	4.1	5.3	4.6	1.1	0.8	1.1	1.1	13.6	13.9	12.1
Large Composite (3)	5.3	5.3	5.8	5.6	1.1	0.9	1.1	1.1	11.7	12.7	10.9
Small Composite (3)	1.0	1.0	1.3	1.4	0.6	0.5	1.6	2.2	21.9	20.0	11.3
High-Financial Risk (5)	-0.8	-1.1	-3.6	-2.8	0.0	0.0	2.8	2.4	17.9	13.4	14.7

Betas (Levered)

	Raw (OLS)	Blume Adjusted	Peer Group	Vasicek Adjusted	Sum	Downside
Median	1.26	1.17	1.50	1.31	1.07	1.46
SIC Composite	1.50	1.32	1.50	1.50	1.75	1.51
Large Composite	1.58	1.37	1.49	1.56	1.90	1.59
Small Composite	0.77	0.86	1.51	0.82	0.95	0.87
High Financial Risk	0.98	0.99	1.45	1.32	0.77	0.98

Betas (Unlevered)

	Raw (OLS)	Blume Adjusted	Peer Group	Vasicek Adjusted	Sum	Downside
Median	0.83	0.84	1.12	0.96	0.69	1.12
SIC Composite	1.05	0.94	1.05	1.05	1.21	1.06
Large Composite	1.15	1.00	1.09	1.14	1.37	1.16
Small Composite	0.63	0.69	1.15	0.66	0.76	0.70
High Financial Risk	0.52	0.52	0.65	0.62	0.45	0.52

Enterprise Valuation (EV) Multiples

	EV/EBITDA Latest	5-Yr Avg
Median	14.0	11.8
SIC Composite	10.9	11.8
Large Composite	9.4	10.0
Small Composite	17.9	18.6
High Financial Risk	18.8	30.7

Equity Valuation Multiples

	Price/Sales Latest	5-Yr Avg	Price/Earnings Latest	5-Yr Avg	Price/TBV* Latest	5-Yr Avg	Price/EBT** Latest	5-Yr Avg
Median	4.3	3.9	23.1	20.9	1.9	1.9	15.8	14.7
SIC Composite	1.3	1.5	18.8	21.6	10.2	9.8	11.9	13.3
Large Composite	1.0	1.2	17.1	18.0	–	–	9.9	10.7
Small Composite	5.1	5.0	75.9	69.5	1.2	1.1	44.8	55.5
High Financial Risk	1.5	2.8	–	–	2.5	4.6	–	–

Equity Valuation SIC Composite: Price/TBV Latest 10.2, 5-Yr Avg 11.9; Price/EBT Latest 9.8, 5-Yr Avg 13.3

Fama-French (F-F) 5-Factor Model

	F-F Beta	SMB Premium	HML Premium	RMW Premium	CMA Premium
Median	1.0	3.2	0.2	-2.0	1.5
SIC Composite	1.4	1.9	0.6	-0.1	-2.3
Large Composite	1.5	1.5	0.8	-0.2	-0.2
Small Composite	0.7	0.3	0.0	-2.7	-0.6
High Financial Risk	–	–	–	–	–

Leverage Ratios (%)

	Debt/MV Equity Latest	5-Yr Avg	Debt/Total Capital Latest	5-Yr Avg
Median	38.7	37.4	27.9	27.2
SIC Composite	54.2	44.7	35.1	30.9
Large Composite	43.6	40.1	30.4	28.6
Small Composite	42.7	39.3	29.9	28.2
High Financial Risk	–	134.0	70.7	57.3

Cost of Debt

	Cost of Debt (%) Latest
Median	6.1
SIC Composite	5.8
Large Composite	5.2
Small Composite	6.1
High Financial Risk	6.8

Capital Structure

SIC Composite (%) Latest: D/TC 35.1, E/TC 64.9

Cost of Equity Capital (%)

	CRSP Deciles CAPM	CAPM +Size Prem	Build-Up	Risk Premium Report CAPM +Size Prem	Build-Up	Discounted Cash Flow 1-Stage	3-Stage	Fama-French 5-Factor Model
Median	10.7	13.1	14.5	–	–	11.4	13.7	11.9
SIC Composite	11.7	12.8	12.9	–	–	13.2	9.3	11.4
Large Composite	12.1	12.9	12.6	–	–	12.0	14.2	13.6
Small Composite	8.0	13.6	17.4	–	–	11.9	4.7	4.2
High Financial Risk	–	–	–	–	–	–	–	–

Cost of Equity Capital (%) SIC Composite: Avg CRSP 12.9, Avg RPR n/a, 1-Stage 13.2, 3-Stage 9.3, 5-Factor Model 11.4

Weighted Average Cost of Capital (WACC) (%)

	CRSP Deciles CAPM	CAPM +Size Prem	Build-Up	Risk Premium Report CAPM +Size Prem	Build-Up	Discounted Cash Flow 1-Stage	3-Stage	Fama-French 5-Factor Model
Median	8.9	10.9	11.2	–	–	9.8	11.8	9.6
SIC Composite	9.4	10.1	10.2	–	–	10.4	7.9	9.2
Large Composite	9.8	10.4	10.2	–	–	9.7	11.3	10.8
Small Composite	7.3	11.3	14.0	–	–	10.1	5.0	4.7
High Financial Risk	–	–	–	–	–	–	–	–

WACC (%) SIC Composite: Low 7.9, High 10.4, Average 9.6, Median 10.1

*TBV = Tangible Book Value
**EBT = Earnings Before Taxes

© 2017 Duff & Phelps. All Rights Reserved. Duff & Phelps has used the utmost care in compiling the data presented herein, but cannot guarantee the accuracy, completeness, or timeliness of the information.

Data Updated Through March 31, 2017

651

Number of Companies: 5
Real Estate Operators (except Developers) and Lessors

Industry Description
Establishments primarily engaged in the operation of nonresidential buildings; apartment buildings; dwellings other than apartment buildings, mobile home sites; lessors of railroad property; lessors of real property, not elsewhere classified.

Sales (in millions)

Three Largest Companies
Kennedy-Wilson Holdings, Inc.	$703.4
Consolidated Tomoka Land Co.	71.1
FRP Holdings, Inc.	37.5

Three Smallest Companies
FRP Holdings, Inc.	$37.5
Griffin Industrial Realty, Inc.	30.9
JW Mays Inc.	18.6

Total Assets (in millions)

Three Largest Companies
Kennedy-Wilson Holdings, Inc.	$7,659.1
Consolidated Tomoka Land Co.	408.6
FRP Holdings, Inc.	265.7

Three Smallest Companies
FRP Holdings, Inc.	$265.7
Griffin Industrial Realty, Inc.	223.6
JW Mays Inc.	63.5

Annualized Monthly Performance Statistics (%)

Industry	Geometric Mean	Arithmetic Mean	Standard Deviation	S&P 500 Index	Geometric Mean	Arithmetic Mean	Standard Deviation
1-year	6.0	7.3	17.4	1-year	17.2	17.4	7.2
3-year	2.8	5.3	23.9	3-year	10.4	10.9	11.5
5-year	12.2	14.4	22.7	5-year	13.3	13.9	11.5

Return Ratios (%)

	Return on Assets Latest	5-Yr Avg	Return on Equity Latest	5-Yr Avg	Dividend Yield Latest	5-Yr Avg
Median (5)	2.3	2.1	2.9	2.6	0.3	0.2
SIC Composite (5)	0.4	0.7	1.0	1.4	2.1	1.5
Large Composite (–)	–	–	–	–	–	–
Small Composite (–)	–	–	–	–	–	–
High-Financial Risk (–)	–	–	–	–	–	–

Liquidity Ratio

	Current Ratio Latest	5-Yr Avg
Median (5)	1.6	1.9
SIC Composite (5)	1.6	1.5
Large Composite (–)	–	–
Small Composite (–)	–	–
High-Financial Risk (–)	–	–

Profitability Ratio (%)

	Operating Margin Latest	5-Yr Avg
Median (5)	39.2	20.8
SIC Composite (5)	39.8	27.3
Large Composite (–)	–	–
Small Composite (–)	–	–
High-Financial Risk (–)	–	–

Growth Rates (%)

	Long-term EPS Analyst Estimates
Median (5)	11.3
SIC Composite (5)	11.3
Large Composite (–)	–
Small Composite (–)	–
High-Financial Risk (–)	–

Betas (Levered)

	Raw (OLS)	Blume Adjusted	Peer Group	Vasicek Adjusted	Sum	Downside
Median	1.24	1.16	1.44	1.37	1.53	1.44
SIC Composite	1.28	1.18	1.44	1.34	1.57	1.27
Large Composite	–	–	–	–	–	–
Small Composite	–	–	–	–	–	–
High Financial Risk	–	–	–	–	–	–

Betas (Unlevered)

	Raw (OLS)	Blume Adjusted	Peer Group	Vasicek Adjusted	Sum	Downside
Median	0.83	0.84	1.04	0.96	0.79	0.97
SIC Composite	0.69	0.65	0.75	0.71	0.80	0.69
Large Composite	–	–	–	–	–	–
Small Composite	–	–	–	–	–	–
High Financial Risk	–	–	–	–	–	–

Enterprise Valuation (EV) Multiples

	EV/EBITDA Latest	5-Yr Avg
Median	15.5	20.0
SIC Composite	13.9	18.9
Large Composite	–	–
Small Composite	–	–
High Financial Risk	–	–

Equity Valuation Multiples

	Price/Sales Latest	5-Yr Avg	Price/Earnings Latest	5-Yr Avg	Price/TBV* Latest	5-Yr Avg	Price/EBT** Latest	5-Yr Avg
Median	4.3	5.2	52.7	64.6	1.9	1.7	30.7	39.0
SIC Composite	4.1	4.9	–	85.6	2.4	2.1	26.1	78.3
Large Composite	–	–	–	–	–	–	–	–
Small Composite	–	–	–	–	–	–	–	–
High Financial Risk	–	–	–	–	–	–	–	–

Equity Valuation SIC Composite: Price/TBV Latest 2.4, 5-Yr Avg 2.1; Price/EBT Latest 26.1, 5-Yr Avg 78.3

Fama-French (F-F) 5-Factor Model

	F-F Beta	SMB Premium	HML Premium	RMW Premium	CMA Premium
Median	1.2	1.7	-0.7	-2.3	-1.1
SIC Composite	1.1	3.4	-0.4	-1.1	-3.4
Large Composite	–	–	–	–	–
Small Composite	–	–	–	–	–
High Financial Risk	–	–	–	–	–

Leverage Ratios (%)

	Debt/MV Equity Latest	5-Yr Avg	Debt/Total Capital Latest	5-Yr Avg
Median	54.4	40.4	35.2	28.8
SIC Composite	148.8	108.6	59.8	52.1
Large Composite	–	–	–	–
Small Composite	–	–	–	–
High Financial Risk	–	–	–	–

Cost of Debt

	Cost of Debt (%) Latest
Median	6.1
SIC Composite	6.1
Large Composite	–
Small Composite	–
High Financial Risk	–

Capital Structure

SIC Composite (%) Latest: D/TC 40.2, E/TC 59.8

Cost of Equity Capital (%)

	CAPM	CRSP Deciles CAPM +Size Prem	Build-Up	Risk Premium Report CAPM +Size Prem	Build-Up	Discounted Cash Flow 1-Stage	3-Stage	Fama-French 5-Factor Model
Median	11.0	13.4	14.5	–	–	11.6	4.7	8.0
SIC Composite	10.9	12.9	13.8	–	–	13.5	–	8.2
Large Composite	–	–	–	–	–	–	–	–
Small Composite	–	–	–	–	–	–	–	–
High Financial Risk	–	–	–	–	–	–	–	–

Cost of Equity Capital (%) SIC Composite: Avg CRSP 13.4, Avg RPR 13.5, 1-Stage n/a, 3-Stage n/a, 5-Factor Model 8.2

Weighted Average Cost of Capital (WACC) (%)

	CAPM	CRSP Deciles CAPM +Size Prem	Build-Up	Risk Premium Report CAPM +Size Prem	Build-Up	Discounted Cash Flow 1-Stage	3-Stage	Fama-French 5-Factor Model
Median	9.0	11.5	12.7	–	–	9.8	4.8	8.4
SIC Composite	7.8	8.6	9.0	–	–	8.9	–	6.7
Large Composite	–	–	–	–	–	–	–	–
Small Composite	–	–	–	–	–	–	–	–
High Financial Risk	–	–	–	–	–	–	–	–

WACC (%) SIC Composite: Low 6.7, High 9.0, Average 8.3, Median 8.7

*TBV = Tangible Book Value
**EBT = Earnings Before Taxes

© 2017 Duff & Phelps. All Rights Reserved. Duff & Phelps has used the utmost care in compiling the data presented herein, but cannot guarantee the accuracy, completeness, or timeliness of the information.

Data Updated Through March 31, 2017

655

Number of Companies: 6
Land Subdividers and Developers

Industry Description
Establishments primarily engaged in subdividing real property into lots, and in developing for resale on their own account.

Sales (in millions)

Three Largest Companies
The Howard Hughes Corporation	$1,035.0
The St. Joe Company	95.7
Stratus Properties Inc.	80.3

Three Smallest Companies
Maui Land & Pineapple Company, Inc.	$47.4
China HGS Real Estate Inc.	38.5
Income Opportunity Realty Investors	4.4

Total Assets (in millions)

Three Largest Companies
The Howard Hughes Corporation	$6,367.4
The St. Joe Company	1,027.9
Stratus Properties Inc.	452.2

Three Smallest Companies
China HGS Real Estate Inc.	$356.4
Income Opportunity Realty Investors	84.3
Maui Land & Pineapple Company, Inc	38.9

Annualized Monthly Performance Statistics (%)

	Industry			S&P 500 Index		
	Geometric Mean	Arithmetic Mean	Standard Deviation	Geometric Mean	Arithmetic Mean	Standard Deviation
1-year	10.0	11.2	16.7	17.2	17.4	7.2
3-year	-5.0	-2.9	20.7	10.4	10.9	11.5
5-year	8.8	11.0	22.4	13.3	13.9	11.5

Return Ratios (%)

	Return on Assets		Return on Equity		Dividend Yield		Current Ratio		Operating Margin		Long-term EPS
	Latest	5-Yr Avg	Latest	5-Yr Avg	Latest	5-Yr Avg	Latest	5-Yr Avg	Latest	5-Yr Avg	Analyst Estimates
Median (6)	1.6	5.3	2.7	2.4	0.0	0.0	1.4	0.6	29.9	35.6	11.3
SIC Composite (6)	2.9	2.0	3.7	2.1	0.1	0.0	1.6	0.9	32.2	24.9	17.6
Large Composite (−)	−	−	−	−	−	−	−	−	−	−	−
Small Composite (−)	−	−	−	−	−	−	−	−	−	−	−
High-Financial Risk (−)	−	−	−	−	−	−	−	−	−	−	−

Betas (Levered)

	Raw (OLS)	Blume Adjusted	Peer Group	Vasicek Adjusted	Sum	Downside
Median	0.92	0.95	1.51	1.11	0.46	1.37
SIC Composite	1.31	1.20	1.51	1.33	1.43	1.46
Large Composite	−	−	−	−	−	−
Small Composite	−	−	−	−	−	−
High Financial Risk	−	−	−	−	−	−

Betas (Unlevered)

	Raw (OLS)	Blume Adjusted	Peer Group	Vasicek Adjusted	Sum	Downside
Median	0.64	0.62	1.21	0.84	0.36	1.15
SIC Composite	0.98	0.91	1.11	0.99	1.06	1.08
Large Composite	−	−	−	−	−	−
Small Composite	−	−	−	−	−	−
High Financial Risk	−	−	−	−	−	−

Enterprise Valuation (EV) Multiples / Equity Valuation Multiples

	EV/EBITDA		Price/Sales		Price/Earnings		Price/TBV*		Price/EBT**	
	Latest	5-Yr Avg	Latest	5-Yr Avg	Latest	5-Yr Avg	Latest	5-Yr Avg	Latest	5-Yr Avg
Median	16.3	12.2	4.6	4.3	23.7	15.9	1.7	1.5	15.9	14.4
SIC Composite	16.6	22.9	5.0	6.0	27.0	47.4	1.7	1.9	19.9	30.6
Large Composite	−	−	−	−	−	−	−	−	−	−
Small Composite	−	−	−	−	−	−	−	−	−	−
High Financial Risk	−	−	−	−	−	−	−	−	−	−

Equity Valuation SIC Composite: Price/TBV Latest 1.7, 5-Yr Avg 1.9; Price/EBT Latest 19.9, 5-Yr Avg 30.6

Fama-French (F-F) 5-Factor Model

	F-F Beta	SMB Premium	HML Premium	RMW Premium	CMA Premium
Median	0.9	-1.4	-0.3	-4.9	10.5
SIC Composite	1.2	1.9	1.4	-0.1	-2.1
Large Composite	−	−	−	−	−
Small Composite	−	−	−	−	−
High Financial Risk	−	−	−	−	−

Leverage Ratios (%)

	Debt/MV Equity		Debt/Total Capital	
	Latest	5-Yr Avg	Latest	5-Yr Avg
Median	38.0	39.5	26.0	28.3
SIC Composite	51.3	35.5	33.9	26.2

Cost of Debt

	Cost of Debt (%) Latest
Median	6.1
SIC Composite	6.9

Capital Structure

SIC Composite (%) Latest: D/TC 33.9, E/TC 66.1

Cost of Equity Capital (%)

	CRSP Deciles			Risk Premium Report		Discounted Cash Flow		Fama-French
	CAPM	CAPM +Size Prem	Build-Up	CAPM +Size Prem	Build-Up	1-Stage	3-Stage	5-Factor Model
Median	9.6	13.4	17.4	−	−	11.3	16.4	12.4
SIC Composite	10.8	12.3	13.3	−	−	17.7	5.1	11.4
Large Composite	−	−	−	−	−	−	−	−
Small Composite	−	−	−	−	−	−	−	−
High Financial Risk	−	−	−	−	−	−	−	−

Cost of Equity Capital (%) SIC Composite: Avg CRSP 12.8, Avg RPR n/a, 1-Stage 17.7, 3-Stage 5.1, 5-Factor Model 11.4

Weighted Average Cost of Capital (WACC) (%)

	CRSP Deciles			Risk Premium Report		Discounted Cash Flow		Fama-French
	CAPM	CAPM +Size Prem	Build-Up	CAPM +Size Prem	Build-Up	1-Stage	3-Stage	5-Factor Model
Median	8.4	10.6	11.5	−	−	10.5	15.6	9.7
SIC Composite	9.4	10.4	11.1	−	−	14.0	5.6	9.8
Large Composite	−	−	−	−	−	−	−	−
Small Composite	−	−	−	−	−	−	−	−
High Financial Risk	−	−	−	−	−	−	−	−

WACC (%) SIC Composite: Low 5.6, High 14.0, Average 10.2, Median 10.4

*TBV = Tangible Book Value
**EBT = Earnings Before Taxes

© 2017 Duff & Phelps. All Rights Reserved. Duff & Phelps has used the utmost care in compiling the data presented herein, but cannot guarantee the accuracy, completeness, or timeliness of the information.

Data Updated Through March 31, 2017

67

Number of Companies: 168
Holding and Other Investment Offices

Industry Description
This major group includes investment trusts, investment companies, holding companies, and miscellaneous investment offices.

Sales (in millions)

Three Largest Companies
Simon Property Group, Inc.	$5,788.6
American Tower Corp.	5,785.7
Host Hotels & Resorts, Inc.	5,454.0

Three Smallest Companies
Rand Capital Corporation	$2.8
Mesa Royalty Trust	2.1
Kayne Anderson Energy Development	1.8

Total Assets (in millions)

Three Largest Companies
Annaly Capital Management, Inc.	$87,905.0
Starwood Property Trust, Inc.	77,256.3
Simon Property Group, Inc.	31,103.6

Three Smallest Companies
Permian Basin Royalty Trust	$2.1
North European Oil Royalty Trust	1.2
BP Prudhoe Bay Royalty Trust	1.0

Annualized Monthly Performance Statistics (%)

Industry	Geometric Mean	Arithmetic Mean	Standard Deviation	S&P 500 Index	Geometric Mean	Arithmetic Mean	Standard Deviation
1-year	6.1	6.8	13.3	1-year	17.2	17.4	7.2
3-year	11.1	12.1	15.1	3-year	10.4	10.9	11.5
5-year	10.8	11.7	14.3	5-year	13.3	13.9	11.5

Return Ratios (%)

	Return on Assets Latest	5-Yr Avg	Return on Equity Latest	5-Yr Avg	Dividend Yield Latest	5-Yr Avg	Current Ratio Latest	5-Yr Avg	Operating Margin Latest	5-Yr Avg	Long-term EPS Analyst Estimates
Median (168)	3.7	3.3	8.7	7.3	4.5	4.5	1.5	1.4	46.7	44.3	12.2
SIC Composite (168)	3.5	2.7	4.0	3.5	4.2	4.3	1.4	1.6	44.2	40.1	12.2
Large Composite (16)	4.4	2.8	4.2	3.0	3.9	3.8	1.2	1.2	45.8	39.2	12.5
Small Composite (16)	6.9	11.7	5.2	9.7	8.0	7.4	3.0	2.5	51.6	86.4	10.7
High-Financial Risk (39)	0.7	0.6	1.9	1.9	4.8	5.7	0.7	1.0	30.9	30.9	24.8

Betas (Levered)

	Raw (OLS)	Blume Adjusted	Peer Group	Vasicek Adjusted	Sum	Downside
Median	0.70	0.82	0.66	0.69	0.61	1.01
SIC Composite	0.62	0.76	0.66	0.62	0.39	0.76
Large Composite	0.59	0.74	0.66	0.60	0.32	0.73
Small Composite	0.71	0.82	0.66	0.69	0.96	1.00
High Financial Risk	0.80	0.88	0.66	0.79	0.74	0.85

Betas (Unlevered)

	Raw (OLS)	Blume Adjusted	Peer Group	Vasicek Adjusted	Sum	Downside
Median	0.47	0.55	0.47	0.47	0.39	0.66
SIC Composite	0.42	0.51	0.45	0.42	0.28	0.51
Large Composite	0.40	0.50	0.45	0.41	0.23	0.49
Small Composite	0.59	0.68	0.55	0.58	0.79	0.83
High Financial Risk	0.45	0.48	0.40	0.45	0.43	0.47

Enterprise Valuation (EV) Multiples

	EV/EBITDA Latest	5-Yr Avg
Median	21.7	21.9
SIC Composite	22.3	24.2
Large Composite	20.9	24.8
Small Composite	24.6	11.5
High Financial Risk	34.3	36.7

Equity Valuation Multiples

	Price/Sales Latest	5-Yr Avg	Price/Earnings Latest	5-Yr Avg	Price/TBV* Latest	5-Yr Avg	Price/EBT** Latest	5-Yr Avg
Median	7.0	6.2	24.5	27.8	2.1	2.0	22.5	23.5
SIC Composite	6.9	6.5	25.9	30.8	3.0	2.7	23.0	26.5
Large Composite	7.2	6.9	24.6	35.3	4.9	4.2	22.0	29.3
Small Composite	12.5	9.2	19.2	10.3	2.4	2.3	32.0	12.5
High Financial Risk	4.2	4.2	74.6	76.2	2.4	2.0	32.5	43.9

Equity Valuation SIC Composite: Price/TBV 23.0 Latest, 26.5 5-Yr Avg; Price/EBT 3.0 Latest, 2.7 5-Yr Avg

Fama-French (F-F) 5-Factor Model

Fama-French (F-F) Components
	F-F Beta	SMB Premium	HML Premium	RMW Premium	CMA Premium
Median	0.4	3.9	4.3	0.0	-3.9
SIC Composite	0.6	-0.1	-3.0	0.4	2.2
Large Composite	0.7	-0.8	-3.3	0.6	0.8
Small Composite	0.7	-1.2	2.9	-1.5	1.5
High Financial Risk	–	–	–	–	–

Leverage Ratios (%)

	Debt/MV Equity Latest	5-Yr Avg	Debt/Total Capital Latest	5-Yr Avg
Median	50.3	56.2	33.5	36.0
SIC Composite	58.8	67.7	37.0	40.4
Large Composite	57.3	66.6	36.4	40.0
Small Composite	22.9	25.0	18.6	20.0
High Financial Risk	198.9	–	66.5	70.1

Cost of Debt

	Cost of Debt (%) Latest
Median	4.8
SIC Composite	4.8
Large Composite	4.7
Small Composite	4.8
High Financial Risk	6.1

Capital Structure

SIC Composite (%) Latest: D/TC 37.0, E/TC 63.0

Cost of Equity Capital (%)

	CRSP Deciles CAPM	CAPM +Size Prem	Build-Up	Risk Premium Report CAPM +Size Prem	Build-Up	Discounted Cash Flow 1-Stage	3-Stage	Fama-French 5-Factor Model
Median	7.3	9.0	8.8	–	–	15.4	10.2	10.0
SIC Composite	6.9	7.6	7.8	–	–	16.8	9.2	6.4
Large Composite	6.8	7.0	7.3	–	–	16.8	8.6	4.4
Small Composite	7.3	11.2	11.1	–	–	11.8	15.5	9.2
High Financial Risk	–	–	–	–	–	–	–	–

Cost of Equity Capital (%) SIC Composite: Avg CRSP 7.7, Avg RPR n/a, 1-Stage 16.8, 3-Stage 9.2, 5-Factor Model 6.4

Weighted Average Cost of Capital (WACC) (%)

	CRSP Deciles CAPM	CAPM +Size Prem	Build-Up	Risk Premium Report CAPM +Size Prem	Build-Up	Discounted Cash Flow 1-Stage	3-Stage	Fama-French 5-Factor Model
Median	6.3	7.3	7.2	–	–	11.8	8.1	7.7
SIC Composite	6.1	6.6	6.7	–	–	12.4	7.6	5.8
Large Composite	6.1	6.2	6.4	–	–	12.5	7.2	4.5
Small Composite	6.6	9.8	9.7	–	–	10.3	13.3	8.2
High Financial Risk	–	–	–	–	–	–	–	–

WACC (%) SIC Composite: Low 5.8, High 12.4, Average 7.8, Median 6.7

*TBV = Tangible Book Value
**EBT = Earnings Before Taxes

© 2017 Duff & Phelps. All Rights Reserved. Duff & Phelps has used the utmost care in compiling the data presented herein, but cannot guarantee the accuracy, completeness, or timeliness of the information.

Data Updated Through March 31, 2017

6794

Number of Companies: 10
Patent Owners and Lessors

Industry Description
Establishments primarily engaged in owning or leasing franchises, patents, and copyrights which they in turn license others to use.

Sales (in millions)

Three Largest Companies
Dolby Laboratories, Inc.	$1,025.7
InterDigital Inc.	665.9
DineEquity Inc.	634.0

Three Smallest Companies
Cherokee Inc.	$34.7
Xcel Brands, Inc.	32.8
Network-1 Technologies, Inc.	11.9

Total Assets (in millions)

Three Largest Companies
Dolby Laboratories, Inc.	$2,310.1
DineEquity Inc.	2,278.6
InterDigital Inc.	1,727.9

Three Smallest Companies
Cherokee Inc.	$70.5
Winmark Corp.	48.6
Network-1 Technologies, Inc.	30.4

Annualized Monthly Performance Statistics (%)

	Industry Geometric Mean	Arithmetic Mean	Standard Deviation		S&P 500 Index Geometric Mean	Arithmetic Mean	Standard Deviation
1-year	14.6	15.7	16.6	1-year	17.2	17.4	7.2
3-year	10.1	11.3	17.0	3-year	10.4	10.9	11.5
5-year	11.1	12.3	17.0	5-year	13.3	13.9	11.5

Return Ratios (%)

	Return on Assets Latest	5-Yr Avg	Return on Equity Latest	5-Yr Avg	Dividend Yield Latest	5-Yr Avg	Current Ratio Latest	5-Yr Avg	Operating Margin Latest	5-Yr Avg	Long-term EPS Analyst Estimates
Median (10)	7.1	8.2	8.2	12.5	0.4	0.5	3.0	2.9	22.9	25.3	12.2
SIC Composite (10)	8.0	7.4	5.2	5.4	1.3	2.0	2.6	3.0	33.0	31.8	12.8
Large Composite (3)	9.4	8.1	6.4	6.2	1.8	2.7	2.5	3.0	38.7	35.5	11.8
Small Composite (3)	6.0	7.1	6.4	5.4	0.7	0.2	2.5	2.6	20.8	25.0	12.2
High-Financial Risk (–)	–	–	–	–	–	–	–	–	–	–	–

Betas (Levered)

	Raw (OLS)	Blume Adjusted	Peer Group	Vasicek Adjusted	Sum	Downside
Median	0.96	0.98	0.66	0.75	0.90	1.45
SIC Composite	0.74	0.84	0.66	0.73	0.55	0.89
Large Composite	0.62	0.76	0.66	0.62	0.33	0.85
Small Composite	0.82	0.89	0.66	0.77	0.91	1.35
High Financial Risk	–	–	–	–	–	–

Betas (Unlevered)

	Raw (OLS)	Blume Adjusted	Peer Group	Vasicek Adjusted	Sum	Downside
Median	0.93	0.93	0.63	0.72	0.76	1.33
SIC Composite	0.68	0.77	0.61	0.67	0.52	0.81
Large Composite	0.57	0.69	0.60	0.57	0.32	0.77
Small Composite	0.73	0.79	0.60	0.69	0.80	1.16
High Financial Risk	–	–	–	–	–	–

Enterprise Valuation (EV) Multiples / Equity Valuation Multiples

	EV/EBITDA Latest	5-Yr Avg	Price/Sales Latest	5-Yr Avg	Price/Earnings Latest	5-Yr Avg	Price/TBV* Latest	5-Yr Avg	Price/EBT** Latest	5-Yr Avg
Median	13.8	10.1	4.4	4.1	24.0	19.8	6.8	6.2	19.8	13.4
SIC Composite	8.6	8.2	4.0	3.6	19.1	18.7	9.4	8.1	13.4	13.3
Large Composite	8.6	8.4	4.0	3.5	15.6	16.0	10.3	9.7	11.3	11.4
Small Composite	12.0	14.2	3.0	4.1	15.6	18.4	15.3	–	17.1	19.3
High Financial Risk	–	–	–	–	–	–	–	–	–	–

Equity Valuation SIC Composite: Price/TBV Latest 9.4, 5-Yr Avg 13.4; Price/EBT Latest 8.1, 5-Yr Avg 13.3

Fama-French (F-F) 5-Factor Model

	F-F Beta	SMB Premium	HML Premium	RMW Premium	CMA Premium
Median	0.6	3.5	0.8	1.1	0.7
SIC Composite	0.6	3.4	-0.9	-0.1	2.0
Large Composite	0.6	3.1	-2.4	-0.1	-0.1
Small Composite	0.6	2.5	-0.3	-2.5	-2.0
High Financial Risk	–	–	–	–	–

Leverage Ratios (%)

	Debt/MV Equity Latest	5-Yr Avg	Debt/Total Capital Latest	5-Yr Avg
Median	10.4	11.2	9.4	9.9
SIC Composite	16.0	19.2	13.8	16.1
Large Composite	18.1	22.9	15.3	18.6
Small Composite	23.3	21.2	18.9	17.5
High Financial Risk	–	–	–	–

Cost of Debt

	Cost of Debt (%) Latest
Median	7.1
SIC Composite	6.4
Large Composite	6.3
Small Composite	7.1
High Financial Risk	–

Capital Structure
SIC Composite (%) Latest: D/TC 13.8, E/TC 86.2

Cost of Equity Capital (%)

	CRSP Deciles CAPM	CAPM +Size Prem	Build-Up	Risk Premium Report CAPM +Size Prem	Build-Up	Discounted Cash Flow 1-Stage	3-Stage	Fama-French 5-Factor Model
Median	7.6	10.2	9.2	–	–	12.4	12.8	13.0
SIC Composite	7.5	9.0	8.6	–	–	14.2	13.8	11.4
Large Composite	6.9	8.2	8.4	–	–	13.7	13.6	7.1
Small Composite	7.7	13.3	12.7	–	–	12.8	16.2	4.7
High Financial Risk	–	–	–	–	–	–	–	–

Cost of Equity Capital (%) SIC Composite: Avg CRSP 8.8, Avg RPR n/a, 1-Stage 14.2, 3-Stage 13.8, 5-Factor Model 11.4

Weighted Average Cost of Capital (WACC) (%)

	CRSP Deciles CAPM	CAPM +Size Prem	Build-Up	Risk Premium Report CAPM +Size Prem	Build-Up	Discounted Cash Flow 1-Stage	3-Stage	Fama-French 5-Factor Model
Median	7.4	9.8	8.9	–	–	11.8	10.8	11.7
SIC Composite	7.2	8.6	8.2	–	–	13.0	12.7	10.6
Large Composite	6.7	7.8	7.9	–	–	12.4	12.3	6.9
Small Composite	7.4	11.9	11.4	–	–	11.5	14.2	4.9
High Financial Risk	–	–	–	–	–	–	–	–

WACC (%) SIC Composite: Low 8.2, High 13.0, Average 10.6, Median 10.6

*TBV = Tangible Book Value
**EBT = Earnings Before Taxes

© 2017 Duff & Phelps. All Rights Reserved. Duff & Phelps has used the utmost care in compiling the data presented herein, but cannot guarantee the accuracy, completeness, or timeliness of the information.

Data Updated Through March 31, 2017

6798

Number of Companies: 115
Real Estate Investment Trusts

Industry Description
Establishments primarily engaged in closed-end investments in real estate or related mortgage assets operating so that they could meet the requirements of the Real Estate Investment Trust Act of 1960 as amended.

Sales (in millions)

Three Largest Companies
Simon Property Group, Inc.	$5,788.6
American Tower Corp.	5,785.7
Host Hotels & Resorts, Inc.	5,454.0

Three Smallest Companies
One Liberty Properties, Inc.	$72.0
Universal Health Realty Income Trust	71.5
Manhattan Bridge Capital, Inc.	4.0

Total Assets (in millions)

Three Largest Companies
Annaly Capital Management, Inc.	$87,905.0
Starwood Property Trust, Inc.	77,256.3
Simon Property Group, Inc.	31,103.6

Three Smallest Companies
CorEnergy Infrastructure Trust	$650.7
Universal Health Realty Income Trust	524.8
Manhattan Bridge Capital, Inc.	31.7

Annualized Monthly Performance Statistics (%)

Industry	Geometric Mean	Arithmetic Mean	Standard Deviation	S&P 500 Index	Geometric Mean	Arithmetic Mean	Standard Deviation
1-year	4.9	5.7	13.7	1-year	17.2	17.4	7.2
3-year	11.6	12.7	15.9	3-year	10.4	10.9	11.5
5-year	11.2	12.1	15.0	5-year	13.3	13.9	11.5

Return Ratios (%)

	Return on Assets Latest	5-Yr Avg	Return on Equity Latest	5-Yr Avg	Dividend Yield Latest	5-Yr Avg
Median (115)	3.4	2.7	8.2	6.0	4.2	4.4
SIC Composite (115)	3.5	2.5	4.0	3.3	4.1	4.2
Large Composite (11)	3.8	2.6	3.0	2.3	3.5	3.3
Small Composite (11)	2.0	1.8	3.4	4.4	5.1	6.1
High-Financial Risk (32)	0.8	0.6	2.3	1.9	4.8	5.7

Liquidity Ratio

	Current Ratio Latest	5-Yr Avg
	1.4	1.4
	1.2	1.2
	1.2	1.2
	1.5	1.8
	0.4	0.5

Profitability Ratio (%)

	Operating Margin Latest	5-Yr Avg
	42.7	36.8
	44.1	39.1
	35.2	33.1
	48.6	50.5
	30.0	29.9

Growth Rates (%)

	Long-term EPS Analyst Estimates
	12.3
	12.3
	13.8
	10.7
	25.1

Betas (Levered)

	Raw (OLS)	Blume Adjusted	Peer Group	Vasicek Adjusted	Sum	Downside
Median	0.69	0.81	0.66	0.68	0.55	0.97
SIC Composite	0.60	0.75	0.66	0.61	0.36	0.78
Large Composite	0.63	0.77	0.66	0.63	0.41	0.75
Small Composite	0.65	0.78	0.66	0.65	0.27	0.74
High Financial Risk	0.78	0.87	0.66	0.78	0.73	0.84

Betas (Unlevered)

	Raw (OLS)	Blume Adjusted	Peer Group	Vasicek Adjusted	Sum	Downside
Median	0.44	0.54	0.47	0.45	0.33	0.63
SIC Composite	0.41	0.50	0.44	0.42	0.26	0.52
Large Composite	0.47	0.57	0.49	0.47	0.32	0.56
Small Composite	0.35	0.41	0.35	0.35	0.17	0.39
High Financial Risk	0.45	0.48	0.40	0.44	0.43	0.47

Enterprise Valuation (EV) Multiples

	EV/EBITDA Latest	5-Yr Avg
Median	23.8	26.1
SIC Composite	22.9	25.5
Large Composite	22.2	24.0
Small Composite	31.9	34.1
High Financial Risk	35.8	38.4

Equity Valuation Multiples

	Price/Sales Latest	5-Yr Avg	Price/Earnings Latest	5-Yr Avg	Price/TBV* Latest	5-Yr Avg	Price/EBT** Latest	5-Yr Avg
Median	7.2	6.1	27.6	34.1	2.2	2.1	23.8	27.7
SIC Composite	7.0	6.5	26.4	33.1	3.2	2.8	23.5	28.2
Large Composite	7.0	6.7	34.4	44.7	6.2	5.2	30.4	35.4
Small Composite	7.9	6.5	34.3	26.6	2.2	1.6	28.7	22.3
High Financial Risk	4.3	4.2	58.8	77.9	2.3	1.9	34.5	49.7

Equity Valuation SIC Composite: Price/TBV Latest 3.2, 5-Yr Avg 2.8; Price/EBT Latest 23.5, 5-Yr Avg 28.2

Fama-French (F-F) 5-Factor Model

	F-F Beta	SMB Premium	HML Premium	RMW Premium	CMA Premium
Median	1.0	-0.4	-0.6	-1.0	2.6
SIC Composite	0.6	-0.2	-3.2	0.4	2.2
Large Composite	0.7	-0.9	-3.4	0.7	0.9
Small Composite	0.7	1.5	-2.4	0.5	3.4
High Financial Risk	–	–	–	–	–

Leverage Ratios (%)

	Debt/MV Equity Latest	5-Yr Avg	Debt/Total Capital Latest	5-Yr Avg
Median	50.3	58.7	33.5	37.0
SIC Composite	59.7	69.5	37.4	41.0
Large Composite	42.4	49.1	29.8	32.9
Small Composite	109.6	173.2	52.3	63.4
High Financial Risk	195.0	–	66.1	70.3

Cost of Debt

	Cost of Debt (%) Latest
Median	4.8
SIC Composite	4.8
Large Composite	4.8
Small Composite	4.8
High Financial Risk	6.0

Capital Structure

SIC Composite (%) Latest: D/TC 37.4, E/TC 62.6

Cost of Equity Capital (%)

	CRSP Deciles CAPM	CAPM +Size Prem	Build-Up	Risk Premium Report CAPM +Size Prem	Build-Up	Discounted Cash Flow 1-Stage	3-Stage	Fama-French 5-Factor Model
Median	7.2	8.6	8.1	–	–	15.6	8.7	9.7
SIC Composite	6.9	7.5	7.7	–	–	16.9	8.9	6.1
Large Composite	7.0	7.1	7.3	–	–	17.7	8.1	4.7
Small Composite	7.1	9.2	9.2	–	–	16.0	8.8	10.0
High Financial Risk	–	–	–	–	–	–	–	–

Cost of Equity Capital (%) SIC Composite: Avg CRSP 7.6, Avg RPR n/a, 1-Stage 16.9, 3-Stage 8.9, 5-Factor Model 6.1

Weighted Average Cost of Capital (WACC) (%)

	CRSP Deciles CAPM	CAPM +Size Prem	Build-Up	Risk Premium Report CAPM +Size Prem	Build-Up	Discounted Cash Flow 1-Stage	3-Stage	Fama-French 5-Factor Model
Median	6.3	7.1	7.1	–	–	12.2	7.2	7.5
SIC Composite	6.1	6.5	6.7	–	–	12.4	7.4	5.7
Large Composite	6.3	6.5	6.5	–	–	13.9	7.1	4.8
Small Composite	5.9	7.0	7.0	–	–	10.2	6.8	7.3
High Financial Risk	–	–	–	–	–	–	–	–

WACC (%) SIC Composite: Low 5.7, High 12.4, Average 7.7, Median 6.7

*TBV = Tangible Book Value
**EBT = Earnings Before Taxes

© 2017 Duff & Phelps. All Rights Reserved. Duff & Phelps has used the utmost care in compiling the data presented herein, but cannot guarantee the accuracy, completeness, or timeliness of the information.

Data Updated Through March 31, 2017

6799

Number of Companies: 5
Investors, Not Elsewhere Classified

Industry Description
Establishments primarily engaged in investing, not elsewhere classified.

Sales (in millions)

Three Largest Companies
TC Pipelines, LP	$357.0
AllianceBernstein Holding L.P.	239.4
America First Multifamily LP	64.6

Three Smallest Companies
America First Multifamily LP	$64.6
MMA Capital Management, LLC	29.3
Kayne Anderson Energy Development	1.8

Total Assets (in millions)

Three Largest Companies
TC Pipelines, LP	$3,158.0
AllianceBernstein Holding L.P.	1,540.5
America First Multifamily LP	872.5

Three Smallest Companies
America First Multifamily LP	$872.5
MMA Capital Management, LLC	599.1
Kayne Anderson Energy Developmen	346.0

Annualized Monthly Performance Statistics (%)

Industry	Geometric Mean	Arithmetic Mean	Standard Deviation		S&P 500 Index	Geometric Mean	Arithmetic Mean	Standard Deviation
1-year	21.6	22.9	19.0		1-year	17.2	17.4	7.2
3-year	10.0	12.1	22.3		3-year	10.4	10.9	11.5
5-year	14.2	16.1	21.3		5-year	13.3	13.9	11.5

Return Ratios (%)

	Return on Assets Latest	5-Yr Avg	Return on Equity Latest	5-Yr Avg	Dividend Yield Latest	5-Yr Avg
Median (5)	7.2	2.9	13.8	10.2	8.3	7.5
SIC Composite (5)	8.0	5.3	7.5	5.7	7.3	6.9
Large Composite (–)	–	–	–	–	–	–
Small Composite (–)	–	–	–	–	–	–
High-Financial Risk (–)	–	–	–	–	–	–

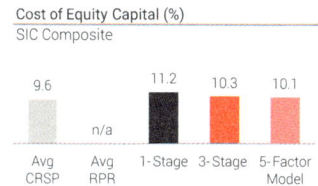

Liquidity Ratio

	Current Ratio Latest	5-Yr Avg
Median (5)	1.5	0.7
SIC Composite (5)	1.5	0.7
Large Composite	–	–
Small Composite	–	–
High-Financial Risk	–	–

Profitability Ratio (%)

	Operating Margin Latest	5-Yr Avg
Median (5)	86.6	85.5
SIC Composite (5)	83.3	78.5
Large Composite	–	–
Small Composite	–	–
High-Financial Risk	–	–

Growth Rates (%)

	Long-term EPS Analyst Estimates
Median (5)	12.2
SIC Composite (5)	4.5
Large Composite	–
Small Composite	–
High-Financial Risk	–

Betas (Levered)

	Raw (OLS)	Blume Adjusted	Peer Group	Vasicek Adjusted	Sum	Downside
Median	1.05	1.04	0.66	0.85	1.51	1.47
SIC Composite	1.14	1.10	0.66	1.03	1.46	1.33
Large Composite	–	–	–	–	–	–
Small Composite	–	–	–	–	–	–
High Financial Risk	–	–	–	–	–	–

Betas (Unlevered)

	Raw (OLS)	Blume Adjusted	Peer Group	Vasicek Adjusted	Sum	Downside
Median	0.68	0.70	0.47	0.61	0.83	0.97
SIC Composite	0.84	0.81	0.49	0.76	1.07	0.97
Large Composite	–	–	–	–	–	–
Small Composite	–	–	–	–	–	–
High Financial Risk	–	–	–	–	–	–

Enterprise Valuation (EV) Multiples

	EV/EBITDA Latest	5-Yr Avg
Median	12.6	23.2
SIC Composite	14.4	15.7
Large Composite	–	–
Small Composite	–	–
High Financial Risk	–	–

Equity Valuation Multiples

	Price/Sales Latest	5-Yr Avg	Price/Earnings Latest	5-Yr Avg	Price/TBV* Latest	5-Yr Avg	Price/EBT** Latest	5-Yr Avg
Median	9.2	11.4	10.2	22.7	1.2	1.4	14.7	25.5
SIC Composite	10.2	10.5	13.4	17.5	2.2	1.9	14.5	16.9
Large Composite	–	–	–	–	–	–	–	–
Small Composite	–	–	–	–	–	–	–	–
High Financial Risk	–	–	–	–	–	–	–	–

Equity Valuation SIC Composite
Latest: Price/TBV 2.2, Price/EBT 14.5
5-Yr Avg: Price/TBV 1.9, Price/EBT 16.9

Fama-French (F-F) 5-Factor Model

	F-F Beta	SMB Premium	HML Premium	RMW Premium	CMA Premium
Median	1.1	-3.0	-3.0	-1.6	7.0
SIC Composite	1.2	-1.5	-0.8	-1.7	4.1
Large Composite	–	–	–	–	–
Small Composite	–	–	–	–	–
High Financial Risk	–	–	–	–	–

Leverage Ratios (%)

	Debt/MV Equity Latest	5-Yr Avg	Debt/Total Capital Latest	5-Yr Avg
Median	49.4	47.7	33.1	32.3
SIC Composite	40.2	42.0	28.7	29.6
Large Composite	–	–	–	–
Small Composite	–	–	–	–
High Financial Risk	–	–	–	–

Cost of Debt

	Cost of Debt (%) Latest
Median	4.8
SIC Composite	4.8
Large Composite	–
Small Composite	–
High Financial Risk	–

Capital Structure

SIC Composite (%) Latest
D/TC: 28.7
E/TC: 71.3

Cost of Equity Capital (%)

	CRSP Deciles CAPM	CAPM +Size Prem	Build-Up	Risk Premium Report CAPM +Size Prem	Build-Up	Discounted Cash Flow 1-Stage	3-Stage	Fama-French 5-Factor Model
Median	8.2	11.3	9.8	–	–	11.3	8.7	9.2
SIC Composite	9.2	10.7	8.6	–	–	11.2	10.3	10.1
Large Composite	–	–	–	–	–	–	–	–
Small Composite	–	–	–	–	–	–	–	–
High Financial Risk	–	–	–	–	–	–	–	–

Cost of Equity Capital (%) SIC Composite
Avg CRSP: 9.6; Avg RPR: n/a; 1-Stage: 11.2; 3-Stage: 10.3; 5-Factor Model: 10.1

Weighted Average Cost of Capital (WACC) (%)

	CRSP Deciles CAPM	CAPM +Size Prem	Build-Up	Risk Premium Report CAPM +Size Prem	Build-Up	Discounted Cash Flow 1-Stage	3-Stage	Fama-French 5-Factor Model
Median	6.5	7.8	7.6	–	–	11.3	6.8	7.9
SIC Composite	7.4	8.5	7.0	–	–	8.9	8.2	8.1
Large Composite	–	–	–	–	–	–	–	–
Small Composite	–	–	–	–	–	–	–	–
High Financial Risk	–	–	–	–	–	–	–	–

WACC (%) SIC Composite
Low 7.0 — High 8.9
Average 8.2, Median 8.2

*TBV = Tangible Book Value
**EBT = Earnings Before Taxes

© 2017 Duff & Phelps. All Rights Reserved. Duff & Phelps has used the utmost care in compiling the data presented herein, but cannot guarantee the accuracy, completeness, or timeliness of the information.

Division I: Services

This division includes establishments primarily engaged in providing a wide variety of services for individuals, business and government establishments, and other organizations. Major groups between "70" and "89" are in this division.

Data Updated Through March 31, 2017

7

Number of Companies: 186
Services

Industry Description
This division includes establishments primarily engaged in providing a wide variety of services for individuals, business and government establishments, and other organizations. Hotels and other lodging places; establishments providing personal, business, repair, and amusement services; health, legal, engineering, and other professional services; educational institutions; membership organizations, and other miscellaneous services, are included.

Sales (in millions)

Three Largest Companies
Alphabet Inc.	$90,272.0
Microsoft Corp.	85,320.0
Int'l Business Machines Corp.	79,920.0

Three Smallest Companies
Bowl America Inc.	$24.1
Aware, Inc.	22.4
Issuer Direct Corp.	11.7

Annualized Monthly Performance Statistics (%)

Industry
	Geometric Mean	Arithmetic Mean	Standard Deviation
1-year	19.9	20.5	13.2
3-year	12.9	13.9	15.4
5-year	15.3	16.2	15.0

Total Assets (in millions)

Three Largest Companies
Microsoft Corp.	$193,694.0
Alphabet Inc.	167,497.0
Int'l Business Machines Corp.	117,470.0

Three Smallest Companies
Auxilio, Inc.	$26.5
MAM Software Group, Inc.	22.4
Issuer Direct Corp.	12.9

S&P 500 Index
	Geometric Mean	Arithmetic Mean	Standard Deviation
1-year	17.2	17.4	7.2
3-year	10.4	10.9	11.5
5-year	13.3	13.9	11.5

Return Ratios (%)

	Return on Assets Latest	Return on Assets 5-Yr Avg	Return on Equity Latest	Return on Equity 5-Yr Avg	Dividend Yield Latest	Dividend Yield 5-Yr Avg
Median (186)	5.5	5.6	11.0	11.2	0.0	0.6
SIC Composite (186)	7.7	8.6	3.6	4.6	1.3	1.3
Large Composite (18)	8.9	10.0	4.0	5.0	1.5	1.5
Small Composite (18)	12.6	9.1	5.9	4.7	1.6	3.2
High-Financial Risk (58)	-4.2	-2.0	-4.8	-2.9	0.4	0.5

Liquidity Ratio

	Current Ratio Latest	Current Ratio 5-Yr Avg
	1.5	1.7
	1.9	1.9
	2.1	2.0
	1.8	1.8
	1.0	1.1

Profitability Ratio (%)

	Operating Margin Latest	Operating Margin 5-Yr Avg
	13.5	13.1
	19.3	20.7
	21.0	22.9
	14.8	12.0
	6.3	7.3

Growth Rates (%)

	Long-term EPS Analyst Estimates
	12.4
	14.2
	14.7
	13.6
	20.8

Betas (Levered)

	Raw (OLS)	Blume Adjusted	Peer Group	Vasicek Adjusted	Sum	Downside
Median	1.10	1.07	1.08	1.09	1.03	1.39
SIC Composite	1.10	1.07	1.08	1.10	1.00	1.06
Large Composite	1.07	1.05	1.08	1.07	0.97	1.02
Small Composite	0.87	0.92	1.17	0.91	0.78	1.05
High Financial Risk	1.36	1.23	1.22	1.35	1.21	1.35

Betas (Unlevered)

	Raw (OLS)	Blume Adjusted	Peer Group	Vasicek Adjusted	Sum	Downside
Median	0.99	0.97	1.00	0.99	0.91	1.22
SIC Composite	0.99	0.96	0.98	0.99	0.90	0.95
Large Composite	0.97	0.95	0.97	0.97	0.87	0.92
Small Composite	0.86	0.91	1.16	0.90	0.77	1.03
High Financial Risk	0.98	0.90	0.89	0.97	0.88	0.97

Equity Valuation Multiples

	Price/Sales Latest	Price/Sales 5-Yr Avg	Price/Earnings Latest	Price/Earnings 5-Yr Avg	Market/Book Latest	Market/Book 5-Yr Avg
Median	2.6	2.4	30.7	26.1	3.7	3.2
SIC Composite	4.0	3.2	27.8	21.8	4.9	4.1
Large Composite	4.3	3.4	25.0	20.1	5.2	4.5
Small Composite	2.6	2.4	17.0	21.1	3.0	2.7
High Financial Risk	1.6	1.2	–	–	4.9	3.3

Enterprise Valuation (EV) Multiples

	EV/Sales Latest	EV/Sales 5-Yr Avg	EV/EBITDA Latest	EV/EBITDA 5-Yr Avg
Median	2.9	2.6	12.8	11.9
SIC Composite	3.9	3.1	14.6	11.3
Large Composite	4.1	3.2	14.3	10.9
Small Composite	2.4	2.2	12.7	13.0
High Financial Risk	2.3	2.0	12.3	10.7

Enterprise Valuation SIC Composite

Latest: EV/Sales 3.9, EV/EBITDA 14.6
5-Yr Avg: EV/Sales 3.1, EV/EBITDA 11.3

Fama-French (F-F) 5-Factor Model

Fama-French (F-F) Components
	F-F Beta	SMB Premium	HML Premium	RMW Premium	CMA Premium
Median	0.8	4.4	-0.2	1.8	-2.6
SIC Composite	1.1	-0.8	0.4	-0.3	-3.2
Large Composite	1.1	-1.5	1.3	0.0	0.0
Small Composite	0.8	1.7	-0.9	-1.8	1.7
High Financial Risk	–	–	–	–	–

Leverage Ratios (%)

	Debt/MV Equity Latest	Debt/MV Equity 5-Yr Avg	Debt/Total Capital Latest	Debt/Total Capital 5-Yr Avg
Median	12.0	10.8	10.7	9.8
SIC Composite	12.4	12.0	11.0	10.7
Large Composite	11.0	10.3	9.9	9.3
Small Composite	2.2	2.4	2.1	2.3
High Financial Risk	58.8	77.4	37.0	43.6

Cost of Debt

	Cost of Debt (%) Latest
Median	6.1
SIC Composite	4.8
Large Composite	4.2
Small Composite	6.8
High Financial Risk	6.9

Capital Structure

SIC Composite (%) Latest

D/TC: 11.0
E/TC: 89.0

Cost of Equity Capital (%)

	CRSP Deciles CAPM	CRSP Deciles CAPM +Size Prem	CRSP Deciles Build-Up	Risk Premium Report CAPM +Size Prem	Risk Premium Report Build-Up	Discounted Cash Flow 1-Stage	Discounted Cash Flow 3-Stage	Fama-French 5-Factor Model
Median	9.5	11.2	11.0	13.0	14.0	13.5	10.6	11.1
SIC Composite	9.6	9.8	9.7	10.5	10.2	15.4	11.3	5.8
Large Composite	9.4	9.4	9.5	9.7	9.2	16.1	11.9	9.1
Small Composite	8.5	13.1	14.2	13.6	16.5	15.1	12.7	8.5
High Financial Risk	–	–	–	25.2	27.6	–	–	–

Cost of Equity Capital (%) SIC Composite

Avg CRSP: 9.7
Avg RPR: 10.4
1-Stage: 15.4
3-Stage: 11.3
5-Factor Model: 5.8

Weighted Average Cost of Capital (WACC) (%)

	CRSP Deciles CAPM	CRSP Deciles CAPM +Size Prem	CRSP Deciles Build-Up	Risk Premium Report CAPM +Size Prem	Risk Premium Report Build-Up	Discounted Cash Flow 1-Stage	Discounted Cash Flow 3-Stage	Fama-French 5-Factor Model
Median	9.0	10.3	10.2	11.7	12.6	12.5	9.9	9.7
SIC Composite	9.0	9.2	9.1	9.9	9.5	14.2	10.5	5.6
Large Composite	8.8	8.9	8.9	9.1	8.7	14.9	11.1	8.6
Small Composite	8.4	13.0	14.0	13.4	16.3	14.9	12.6	8.4
High Financial Risk	–	–	–	18.2	19.7	–	–	–

WACC (%) SIC Composite

Low: 5.6, High: 14.2
Average 9.7, Median 9.5

© 2017 Duff & Phelps. All Rights Reserved. Duff & Phelps has used the utmost care in compiling the data presented herein, but cannot guarantee the accuracy, completeness, or timeliness of the information.

Data Updated Through March 31, 2017

73

Number of Companies: 155
Business Services

Industry Description
This major group includes establishments primarily engaged in rendering services, not elsewhere classified, to business establishments on a contract or fee basis, such as advertising, credit reporting, collection of claims, mailing, reproduction, stenographic, news syndicates, computer programming, photocopying, duplicating, data processing, services to buildings, and help supply services.

Sales (in millions)

Three Largest Companies
Alphabet Inc.	$90,272.0
Microsoft Corp.	85,320.0
Int'l Business Machines Corp.	79,920.0

Three Smallest Companies
Evolving Systems Inc.	$25.6
Aware, Inc.	22.4
Issuer Direct Corp.	11.7

Annualized Monthly Performance Statistics (%)

Industry	Geometric Mean	Arithmetic Mean	Standard Deviation
1-year	19.3	19.9	13.1
3-year	13.2	14.2	15.4
5-year	15.1	16.0	14.8

Total Assets (in millions)

Three Largest Companies
Microsoft Corp.	$193,694.0
Alphabet Inc.	167,497.0
Int'l Business Machines Corp.	117,470.0

Three Smallest Companies
Auxilio, Inc.	$26.5
MAM Software Group, Inc.	22.4
Issuer Direct Corp.	12.9

S&P 500 Index	Geometric Mean	Arithmetic Mean	Standard Deviation
1-year	17.2	17.4	7.2
3-year	10.4	10.9	11.5
5-year	13.3	13.9	11.5

Return Ratios (%)

	Return on Assets Latest	Return on Assets 5-Yr Avg	Return on Equity Latest	Return on Equity 5-Yr Avg	Dividend Yield Latest	Dividend Yield 5-Yr Avg
Median (155)	5.6	5.9	11.2	11.8	0.0	0.0
SIC Composite (155)	8.0	8.9	3.7	4.7	1.2	1.2
Large Composite (15)	9.3	10.1	4.2	5.1	1.4	1.4
Small Composite (15)	12.2	8.7	5.6	4.4	1.3	2.7
High-Financial Risk (43)	-1.7	-2.4	-1.0	-1.8	0.4	0.5

Liquidity Ratio / Profitability Ratio (%) / Growth Rates (%)

	Current Ratio Latest	Current Ratio 5-Yr Avg	Operating Margin Latest	Operating Margin 5-Yr Avg	Long-term EPS Analyst Estimates
Median (155)	1.7	1.8	13.8	13.9	12.6
SIC Composite (155)	2.0	2.0	20.1	21.4	12.9
Large Composite (15)	2.2	2.1	21.7	23.6	12.7
Small Composite (15)	1.8	2.0	15.6	12.4	15.0
High-Financial Risk (43)	1.1	1.3	2.3	4.4	23.4

Betas (Levered)

	Raw (OLS)	Blume Adjusted	Peer Group	Vasicek Adjusted	Sum	Downside
Median	1.12	1.08	1.06	1.10	1.07	1.45
SIC Composite	1.09	1.06	1.06	1.09	1.00	1.04
Large Composite	1.05	1.03	1.07	1.05	0.96	0.99
Small Composite	1.04	1.03	1.07	1.04	0.94	1.20
High Financial Risk	1.30	1.19	1.06	1.27	1.08	1.39

Betas (Unlevered)

	Raw (OLS)	Blume Adjusted	Peer Group	Vasicek Adjusted	Sum	Downside
Median	1.05	0.99	0.99	1.00	0.96	1.26
SIC Composite	0.98	0.96	0.96	0.98	0.90	0.94
Large Composite	0.94	0.94	0.96	0.95	0.86	0.90
Small Composite	1.02	1.01	1.04	1.02	0.92	1.17
High Financial Risk	1.12	1.03	0.92	1.09	0.94	1.19

Equity Valuation Multiples

	Price/Sales Latest	Price/Sales 5-Yr Avg	Price/Earnings Latest	Price/Earnings 5-Yr Avg	Market/Book Latest	Market/Book 5-Yr Avg
Median	3.0	2.8	31.2	26.4	3.9	3.4
SIC Composite	4.1	3.3	27.1	21.5	4.8	4.0
Large Composite	4.3	3.5	23.9	19.6	5.1	4.3
Small Composite	2.9	2.7	18.0	22.7	3.1	2.7
High Financial Risk	2.7	1.9	–	–	6.9	4.6

Enterprise Valuation (EV) Multiples

	EV/Sales Latest	EV/Sales 5-Yr Avg	EV/EBITDA Latest	EV/EBITDA 5-Yr Avg
Median	3.1	2.8	13.4	12.3
SIC Composite	4.0	3.2	14.7	11.4
Large Composite	4.0	3.2	14.3	10.9
Small Composite	2.7	2.4	13.8	14.0
High Financial Risk	3.0	2.1	25.3	15.6

Enterprise Valuation SIC Composite
- Latest: EV/Sales 4.0, EV/EBITDA 14.7
- 5-Yr Avg: EV/Sales 3.2, EV/EBITDA 11.4

Fama-French (F-F) 5-Factor Model

	F-F Beta	SMB Premium	HML Premium	RMW Premium	CMA Premium
Median	1.0	-0.1	2.1	1.1	-1.5
SIC Composite	1.1	-0.9	0.5	-0.3	-3.3
Large Composite	1.0	-1.6	1.3	0.0	0.0
Small Composite	0.9	2.3	-0.6	-1.6	0.8
High Financial Risk	–	–	–	–	–

Leverage Ratios (%)

	Debt/MV Equity Latest	Debt/MV Equity 5-Yr Avg	Debt/Total Capital Latest	Debt/Total Capital 5-Yr Avg
Median	10.5	7.1	9.5	6.6
SIC Composite	11.6	11.0	10.4	9.9
Large Composite	10.7	9.8	9.7	8.9
Small Composite	3.4	2.1	3.3	2.1
High Financial Risk	21.5	25.5	17.7	20.3

Cost of Debt

	Cost of Debt (%) Latest
Median	6.1
SIC Composite	4.7
Large Composite	4.1
Small Composite	6.9
High Financial Risk	6.4

Capital Structure
SIC Composite (%) Latest
- D/TC: 10.4
- E/TC: 89.6

Cost of Equity Capital (%)

	CRSP Deciles CAPM	CRSP Deciles CAPM +Size Prem	CRSP Deciles Build-Up	Risk Premium Report CAPM +Size Prem	Risk Premium Report Build-Up	Discounted Cash Flow 1-Stage	Discounted Cash Flow 3-Stage	Fama-French 5-Factor Model
Median	9.5	11.2	10.8	13.3	14.0	13.6	10.2	10.4
SIC Composite	9.5	9.7	9.5	10.4	10.0	14.0	10.9	5.7
Large Composite	9.3	9.3	9.3	9.6	9.1	14.0	11.3	9.1
Small Composite	9.2	13.9	13.9	14.4	16.5	16.2	13.1	9.4
High Financial Risk	–	–	–	25.4	28.5	–	–	–

Cost of Equity Capital (%) SIC Composite
- Avg CRSP: 9.6
- Avg RPR: 10.2
- 1-Stage: 14.0
- 3-Stage: 10.9
- 5-Factor Model: 5.7

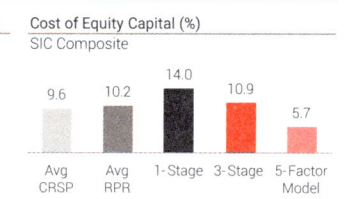

Weighted Average Cost of Capital (WACC) (%)

	CRSP Deciles CAPM	CRSP Deciles CAPM +Size Prem	CRSP Deciles Build-Up	Risk Premium Report CAPM +Size Prem	Risk Premium Report Build-Up	Discounted Cash Flow 1-Stage	Discounted Cash Flow 3-Stage	Fama-French 5-Factor Model
Median	9.1	10.4	10.1	12.2	12.7	12.6	9.7	9.4
SIC Composite	8.9	9.1	9.0	9.8	9.4	13.0	10.2	5.5
Large Composite	8.7	8.8	8.8	9.0	8.6	13.0	10.6	8.6
Small Composite	9.1	13.6	13.7	14.2	16.2	15.8	12.8	9.3
High Financial Risk	–	–	–	22.0	24.5	–	–	–

WACC (%) SIC Composite
- Low: 5.5
- High: 13.0
- Average: 9.4
- Median: 9.4

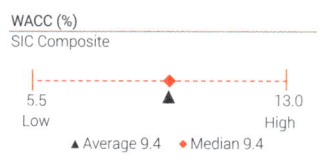

© 2017 Duff & Phelps. All Rights Reserved. Duff & Phelps has used the utmost care in compiling the data presented herein, but cannot guarantee the accuracy, completeness, or timeliness of the information.

Data Updated Through March 31, 2017

735

Number of Companies: 6
Miscellaneous Equipment Rental and Leasing

Industry Description
Establishments primarily engaged in renting or leasing in medical equipment rental and leasing; heavy construction equipment rental and leasing; equipment rental and leasing, not elsewhere classified.

Sales (in millions)

Three Largest Companies
United Rentals, Inc.	$5,762.0
Aaron's, Inc.	3,207.7
Air Lease Corporation	1,339.0

Three Smallest Companies
Mobile Mini, Inc.	$508.4
McGrath Rentcorp	424.1
General Finance Corp.	285.9

Annualized Monthly Performance Statistics (%)

Industry	Geometric Mean	Arithmetic Mean	Standard Deviation
1-year	52.9	58.4	46.6
3-year	4.2	9.1	34.1
5-year	15.4	19.7	33.0

Total Assets (in millions)

Three Largest Companies
Air Lease Corporation	$13,975.6
United Rentals, Inc.	11,988.0
Aaron's, Inc.	2,615.7

Three Smallest Companies
Mobile Mini, Inc.	$2,004.9
McGrath Rentcorp	1,128.3
General Finance Corp.	675.8

S&P 500 Index	Geometric Mean	Arithmetic Mean	Standard Deviation
1-year	17.2	17.4	7.2
3-year	10.4	10.9	11.5
5-year	13.3	13.9	11.5

Return Ratios (%)

	Return on Assets Latest	5-Yr Avg	Return on Equity Latest	5-Yr Avg	Dividend Yield Latest	5-Yr Avg
Median (6)	3.1	3.2	6.9	7.4	0.6	0.4
SIC Composite (6)	3.6	3.1	6.1	6.0	0.6	0.5
Large Composite (−)	−	−	−	−	−	−
Small Composite (−)	−	−	−	−	−	−
High-Financial Risk (−)	−	−	−	−	−	−

Liquidity Ratio
	Current Ratio Latest	5-Yr Avg
	1.1	1.1
	1.1	1.1
	−	−
	−	−
	−	−

Profitability Ratio (%)
	Operating Margin Latest	5-Yr Avg
	21.1	22.4
	23.7	22.9
	−	−
	−	−
	−	−

Growth Rates (%)
	Long-term EPS Analyst Estimates
	13.6
	13.8
	−
	−
	−

Betas (Levered)

	Raw (OLS)	Blume Adjusted	Peer Group	Vasicek Adjusted	Sum	Downside
Median	1.40	1.26	1.06	1.37	1.59	1.71
SIC Composite	1.82	1.53	1.06	1.76	2.05	2.05
Large Composite	−	−	−	−	−	−
Small Composite	−	−	−	−	−	−
High Financial Risk	−	−	−	−	−	−

Betas (Unlevered)

	Raw (OLS)	Blume Adjusted	Peer Group	Vasicek Adjusted	Sum	Downside
Median	0.74	0.69	0.74	0.73	0.78	0.93
SIC Composite	1.02	0.87	0.63	0.99	1.13	1.13
Large Composite	−	−	−	−	−	−
Small Composite	−	−	−	−	−	−
High Financial Risk	−	−	−	−	−	−

Equity Valuation Multiples

	Price/Sales Latest	5-Yr Avg	Price/Earnings Latest	5-Yr Avg	Market/Book Latest	5-Yr Avg
Median	1.9	1.6	19.7	17.3	1.2	1.3
SIC Composite	1.6	1.4	16.4	16.6	1.7	1.5
Large Composite	−	−	−	−	−	−
Small Composite	−	−	−	−	−	−
High Financial Risk	−	−	−	−	−	−

Enterprise Valuation (EV) Multiples

	EV/Sales Latest	5-Yr Avg	EV/EBITDA Latest	5-Yr Avg
Median	2.9	2.8	8.1	7.1
SIC Composite	3.2	3.0	6.0	6.0
Large Composite	−	−	−	−
Small Composite	−	−	−	−
High Financial Risk	−	−	−	−

Enterprise Valuation SIC Composite: EV/Sales Latest 3.2, 5-Yr Avg 3.0; EV/EBITDA Latest 6.0, 5-Yr Avg 6.0

Fama-French (F-F) 5-Factor Model

| | Fama-French (F-F) Components |
	F-F Beta	SMB Premium	HML Premium	RMW Premium	CMA Premium
Median	1.1	0.9	4.3	1.2	0.7
SIC Composite	1.7	4.2	5.0	0.8	−1.7
Large Composite	−	−	−	−	−
Small Composite	−	−	−	−	−
High Financial Risk	−	−	−	−	−

Leverage Ratios (%)

	Debt/MV Equity Latest	5-Yr Avg	Debt/Total Capital Latest	5-Yr Avg
Median	71.7	82.5	41.7	43.7
SIC Composite	98.6	111.2	49.6	52.7
Large Composite	−	−	−	−
Small Composite	−	−	−	−
High Financial Risk	−	−	−	−

Cost of Debt
	Cost of Debt (%) Latest
Median	6.6
SIC Composite	5.6
Large Composite	−
Small Composite	−
High Financial Risk	−

Capital Structure
SIC Composite (%) Latest: D/TC 50.4, E/TC 49.6

Cost of Equity Capital (%)

	CRSP Deciles CAPM	CAPM +Size Prem	Build-Up	Risk Premium Report CAPM	CAPM +Size Prem	Build-Up	Discounted Cash Flow 1-Stage	3-Stage	Fama-French 5-Factor Model
Median	11.0	14.2	11.0	16.4	13.6	13.8	10.0	16.4	
SIC Composite	13.2	14.3	10.4	17.7	12.2	14.4	9.9	21.1	
Large Composite	−	−	−	−	−	−	−	−	
Small Composite	−	−	−	−	−	−	−	−	
High Financial Risk	−	−	−	−	−	−	−	−	

Cost of Equity Capital (%) SIC Composite: Avg CRSP 12.4, Avg RPR 14.9, 1-Stage 14.4, 3-Stage 9.9, 5-Factor Model 21.1

Weighted Average Cost of Capital (WACC) (%)

	CRSP Deciles CAPM	CAPM +Size Prem	Build-Up	Risk Premium Report CAPM	Build-Up	Discounted Cash Flow 1-Stage	3-Stage	Fama-French 5-Factor Model
Median	7.9	9.3	9.0	10.5	9.9	10.3	8.1	12.8
SIC Composite	8.8	9.4	7.4	11.1	8.3	9.4	7.2	12.8
Large Composite	−	−	−	−	−	−	−	−
Small Composite	−	−	−	−	−	−	−	−
High Financial Risk	−	−	−	−	−	−	−	−

WACC (%) SIC Composite: Low 7.2, High 12.8, Average 9.4, Median 9.4

© 2017 Duff & Phelps. All Rights Reserved. Duff & Phelps has used the utmost care in compiling the data presented herein, but cannot guarantee the accuracy, completeness, or timeliness of the information.

Data Updated Through March 31, 2017

7359

Number of Companies: 5
Equipment Rental and Leasing, Not Elsewhere Classified

Industry Description
Establishments primarily engaged in renting or leasing (except finance leasing) equipment, not elsewhere classified.

Sales (in millions)

Three Largest Companies
Aaron's, Inc.	$3,207.7
Air Lease Corporation	1,339.0
Mobile Mini, Inc.	508.4

Three Smallest Companies
Mobile Mini, Inc.	$508.4
McGrath Rentcorp	424.1
General Finance Corp.	285.9

Annualized Monthly Performance Statistics (%)

Industry	Geometric Mean	Arithmetic Mean	Standard Deviation
1-year	16.8	19.1	25.4
3-year	-1.1	1.6	24.3
5-year	7.4	9.9	23.8

S&P 500 Index	Geometric Mean	Arithmetic Mean	Standard Deviation
1-year	17.2	17.4	7.2
3-year	10.4	10.9	11.5
5-year	13.3	13.9	11.5

Total Assets (in millions)

Three Largest Companies
Air Lease Corporation	$13,975.6
Aaron's, Inc.	2,615.7
Mobile Mini, Inc.	2,004.9

Three Smallest Companies
Mobile Mini, Inc.	$2,004.9
McGrath Rentcorp	1,128.3
General Finance Corp.	675.8

Return Ratios (%)

	Return on Assets Latest	Return on Assets 5-Yr Avg	Return on Equity Latest	Return on Equity 5-Yr Avg	Dividend Yield Latest	Dividend Yield 5-Yr Avg
Median (5)	2.8	2.4	5.7	6.6	0.8	0.5
SIC Composite (5)	2.9	2.7	7.1	5.8	1.3	0.9
Large Composite (–)	–	–	–	–	–	–
Small Composite (–)	–	–	–	–	–	–
High-Financial Risk (–)	–	–	–	–	–	–

Liquidity Ratio

	Current Ratio Latest	Current Ratio 5-Yr Avg
Median (5)	–	–
SIC Composite (5)	–	–
Large Composite	–	–
Small Composite	–	–
High-Financial Risk	–	–

Profitability Ratio (%)

	Operating Margin Latest	Operating Margin 5-Yr Avg
Median (5)	18.7	20.4
SIC Composite (5)	21.9	21.2
Large Composite	–	–
Small Composite	–	–
High-Financial Risk	–	–

Growth Rates (%)

	Long-term EPS Analyst Estimates
Median (5)	13.8
SIC Composite (5)	14.5
Large Composite	–
Small Composite	–
High-Financial Risk	–

Betas (Levered)

	Raw (OLS)	Blume Adjusted	Peer Group	Vasicek Adjusted	Sum	Downside
Median	1.12	1.08	1.06	1.11	1.24	1.52
SIC Composite	1.32	1.21	1.06	1.30	1.08	1.57
Large Composite	–	–	–	–	–	–
Small Composite	–	–	–	–	–	–
High Financial Risk	–	–	–	–	–	–

Betas (Unlevered)

	Raw (OLS)	Blume Adjusted	Peer Group	Vasicek Adjusted	Sum	Downside
Median	0.59	0.52	0.74	0.57	0.75	0.81
SIC Composite	0.65	0.60	0.53	0.64	0.54	0.76
Large Composite	–	–	–	–	–	–
Small Composite	–	–	–	–	–	–
High Financial Risk	–	–	–	–	–	–

Equity Valuation Multiples

	Price/Sales Latest	Price/Sales 5-Yr Avg	Price/Earnings Latest	Price/Earnings 5-Yr Avg	Market/Book Latest	Market/Book 5-Yr Avg
Median	1.9	2.0	21.0	18.6	1.2	1.2
SIC Composite	1.5	1.6	14.2	17.2	1.1	1.2
Large Composite	–	–	–	–	–	–
Small Composite	–	–	–	–	–	–
High Financial Risk	–	–	–	–	–	–

Enterprise Valuation (EV) Multiples

	EV/Sales Latest	EV/Sales 5-Yr Avg	EV/EBITDA Latest	EV/EBITDA 5-Yr Avg
Median	2.7	2.8	9.2	7.3
SIC Composite	3.2	3.3	5.5	6.0
Large Composite	–	–	–	–
Small Composite	–	–	–	–
High Financial Risk	–	–	–	–

Enterprise Valuation SIC Composite
EV/Sales: Latest 3.2, 5-Yr Avg 3.3
EV/EBITDA: Latest 5.5, 5-Yr Avg 6.0

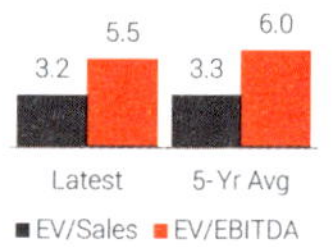

Fama-French (F-F) 5-Factor Model

	F-F Beta	SMB Premium	HML Premium	RMW Premium	CMA Premium
Median	1.1	0.9	4.3	1.2	0.7
SIC Composite	1.2	4.4	2.2	1.5	-1.6
Large Composite	–	–	–	–	–
Small Composite	–	–	–	–	–
High Financial Risk	–	–	–	–	–

Leverage Ratios (%)

	Debt/MV Equity Latest	Debt/MV Equity 5-Yr Avg	Debt/Total Capital Latest	Debt/Total Capital 5-Yr Avg
Median	69.4	53.1	41.0	34.7
SIC Composite	129.4	110.6	56.4	52.5
Large Composite	–	–	–	–
Small Composite	–	–	–	–
High Financial Risk	–	–	–	–

Cost of Debt

	Cost of Debt (%) Latest
Median	7.1
SIC Composite	5.2
Large Composite	–
Small Composite	–
High Financial Risk	–

Capital Structure

SIC Composite (%) Latest
D/TC: 43.6
E/TC: 56.4

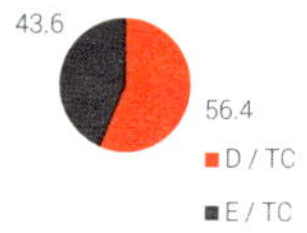

Cost of Equity Capital (%)

	CRSP Deciles CAPM	CRSP Deciles CAPM +Size Prem	CRSP Deciles Build-Up	Risk Premium Report CAPM +Size Prem	Risk Premium Report Build-Up	Discounted Cash Flow 1-Stage	Discounted Cash Flow 3-Stage	Fama-French 5-Factor Model
Median	9.6	13.4	11.0	13.5	14.0	14.2	8.9	16.4
SIC Composite	10.7	12.1	10.8	12.9	13.0	15.7	9.5	16.4
Large Composite	–	–	–	–	–	–	–	–
Small Composite	–	–	–	–	–	–	–	–
High Financial Risk	–	–	–	–	–	–	–	–

Cost of Equity Capital (%) SIC Composite
Avg CRSP 11.4, Avg RPR 13.0, 1-Stage 15.7, 3-Stage 9.5, 5-Factor Model 16.4

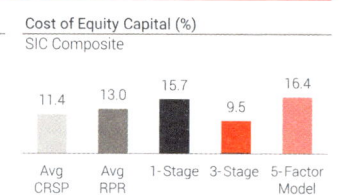

Weighted Average Cost of Capital (WACC) (%)

	CRSP Deciles CAPM	CRSP Deciles CAPM +Size Prem	CRSP Deciles Build-Up	Risk Premium Report CAPM +Size Prem	Risk Premium Report Build-Up	Discounted Cash Flow 1-Stage	Discounted Cash Flow 3-Stage	Fama-French 5-Factor Model
Median	7.6	9.0	9.0	10.1	10.7	10.8	7.7	10.1
SIC Composite	7.0	7.6	7.0	8.0	8.0	9.2	6.5	9.5
Large Composite	–	–	–	–	–	–	–	–
Small Composite	–	–	–	–	–	–	–	–
High Financial Risk	–	–	–	–	–	–	–	–

WACC (%) SIC Composite
Low 6.5, High 9.5, Average 8.0, Median 8.0

© 2017 Duff & Phelps. All Rights Reserved. Duff & Phelps has used the utmost care in compiling the data presented herein, but cannot guarantee the accuracy, completeness, or timeliness of the information.

Data Updated Through March 31, 2017

736

Number of Companies: 13
Personnel Supply Services

Industry Description
Establishments primarily engaged in providing employment services; and supplying temporary or continuing help on a contract or fee basis.

Sales (in millions)

Three Largest Companies
ManpowerGroup	$19,654.1
Kelly Services, Inc.	5,276.8
Robert Half Int'l Inc.	5,250.4

Three Smallest Companies
DHI Group, Inc.	$227.0
RCM Technologies Inc.	185.7
Mastech Digital, Inc.	132.0

Total Assets (in millions)

Three Largest Companies
ManpowerGroup	$7,574.2
Kelly Services, Inc.	2,028.1
Robert Half Int'l Inc.	1,778.0

Three Smallest Companies
DHI Group, Inc.	$310.1
RCM Technologies Inc.	81.3
Mastech Digital, Inc.	39.5

Annualized Monthly Performance Statistics (%)

	Industry Geometric Mean	Arithmetic Mean	Standard Deviation		S&P 500 Index Geometric Mean	Arithmetic Mean	Standard Deviation
1-year	20.8	23.4	26.8	1-year	17.2	17.4	7.2
3-year	10.6	12.5	21.4	3-year	10.4	10.9	11.5
5-year	16.2	18.5	24.0	5-year	13.3	13.9	11.5

Return Ratios (%)

	Return on Assets Latest	5-Yr Avg	Return on Equity Latest	5-Yr Avg	Dividend Yield Latest	5-Yr Avg
Median (13)	6.1	4.9	16.0	10.2	1.4	1.7
SIC Composite (13)	6.7	5.9	5.3	5.3	1.5	1.5
Large Composite (3)	8.0	6.6	6.5	6.0	2.1	1.7
Small Composite (3)	0.7	4.2	1.1	3.6	0.0	2.1
High-Financial Risk (–)	–	–	–	–	–	–

Liquidity Ratio

	Current Ratio Latest	5-Yr Avg
Median (13)	1.6	1.6
SIC Composite (13)	1.5	1.5
Large Composite (3)	1.5	1.5
Small Composite (3)	1.1	1.2
High-Financial Risk (–)	–	–

Profitability Ratio (%)

	Operating Margin Latest	5-Yr Avg
Median (13)	4.2	4.6
SIC Composite (13)	5.0	4.3
Large Composite (3)	4.6	3.9
Small Composite (3)	8.0	11.1
High-Financial Risk (–)	–	–

Growth Rates (%)

	Long-term EPS Analyst Estimates
Median (13)	11.2
SIC Composite (13)	11.2
Large Composite (3)	7.9
Small Composite (3)	11.2
High-Financial Risk (–)	–

Betas (Levered)

	Raw (OLS)	Blume Adjusted	Peer Group	Vasicek Adjusted	Sum	Downside
Median	1.22	1.14	1.05	1.15	1.02	1.56
SIC Composite	1.37	1.24	1.05	1.34	1.16	1.31
Large Composite	1.32	1.21	1.05	1.16	1.08	1.29
Small Composite	0.76	0.85	1.06	0.83	0.87	0.99
High Financial Risk	–	–	–	–	–	–

Betas (Unlevered)

	Raw (OLS)	Blume Adjusted	Peer Group	Vasicek Adjusted	Sum	Downside
Median	1.19	1.13	0.95	1.15	1.02	1.49
SIC Composite	1.27	1.15	0.98	1.24	1.08	1.22
Large Composite	1.25	1.15	1.00	1.10	1.02	1.23
Small Composite	0.64	0.70	0.85	0.69	0.72	0.81
High Financial Risk	–	–	–	–	–	–

Equity Valuation Multiples

	Price/Sales Latest	5-Yr Avg	Price/Earnings Latest	5-Yr Avg	Market/Book Latest	5-Yr Avg
Median	0.5	0.5	19.6	23.7	2.7	2.7
SIC Composite	0.5	0.5	18.9	18.9	3.2	2.6
Large Composite	0.5	0.4	15.4	16.7	3.0	2.6
Small Composite	0.5	1.1	91.4	27.7	1.8	2.4
High Financial Risk	–	–	–	–	–	–

Enterprise Valuation (EV) Multiples

	EV/Sales Latest	5-Yr Avg	EV/EBITDA Latest	5-Yr Avg
Median	0.5	0.4	8.5	8.6
SIC Composite	0.6	0.5	9.5	8.9
Large Composite	0.5	0.4	8.9	8.5
Small Composite	0.7	1.2	6.7	8.1
High Financial Risk	–	–	–	–

Enterprise Valuation SIC Composite
Latest: EV/Sales 0.6, EV/EBITDA 9.5
5-Yr Avg: EV/Sales 0.5, EV/EBITDA 8.9

Fama-French (F-F) 5-Factor Model

Fama-French (F-F) Components

	F-F Beta	SMB Premium	HML Premium	RMW Premium	CMA Premium
Median	1.0	3.2	4.5	1.4	-4.5
SIC Composite	1.3	3.5	3.2	1.1	-4.0
Large Composite	1.2	3.1	4.7	1.2	1.5
Small Composite	0.6	3.6	-1.1	-0.7	2.5
High Financial Risk	–	–	–	–	–

Leverage Ratios (%)

	Debt/MV Equity Latest	5-Yr Avg	Debt/Total Capital Latest	5-Yr Avg
Median	12.0	12.5	10.7	11.1
SIC Composite	9.9	10.0	9.0	9.1
Large Composite	5.9	6.2	5.6	5.9
Small Composite	40.4	18.7	28.8	15.7
High Financial Risk	–	–	–	–

Cost of Debt

	Cost of Debt (%) Latest
Median	7.1
SIC Composite	5.8
Large Composite	4.8
Small Composite	6.9
High Financial Risk	–

Capital Structure

SIC Composite (%) Latest
D/TC: 9.0
E/TC: 91.0

Cost of Equity Capital (%)

	CRSP Deciles CAPM	CAPM +Size Prem	Build-Up	Risk Premium Report CAPM	Build-Up	CAPM +Size Prem	Discounted Cash Flow 1-Stage	3-Stage	Fama-French 5-Factor Model
Median	9.8	12.5	11.4	14.2	14.4		11.3	12.2	13.7
SIC Composite	10.9	12.2	10.6	13.4	13.2		12.6	11.8	14.2
Large Composite	9.9	10.9	10.3	12.4	12.4		9.9	11.0	20.4
Small Composite	8.1	13.7	14.9	13.7	16.1		11.2	18.1	11.3
High Financial Risk	–	–	–	–	–		–	–	–

Cost of Equity Capital (%) SIC Composite
Avg CRSP: 11.4, Avg RPR: 13.3, 1-Stage: 12.6, 3-Stage: 11.8, 5-Factor Model: 14.2

Weighted Average Cost of Capital (WACC) (%)

	CRSP Deciles CAPM	CAPM +Size Prem	Build-Up	Risk Premium Report CAPM	Build-Up	Discounted Cash Flow 1-Stage	3-Stage	Fama-French 5-Factor Model
Median	9.8	12.0	10.8	13.6	13.6	10.6	11.5	14.7
SIC Composite	10.4	11.6	10.2	12.7	12.5	12.0	11.3	13.4
Large Composite	9.6	10.5	10.0	12.0	12.0	9.6	10.6	19.5
Small Composite	7.1	11.1	12.0	11.2	12.9	9.4	14.3	9.5
High Financial Risk	–	–	–	–	–	–	–	–

WACC (%) SIC Composite
Low 10.2, High 13.4, Average 12.0, Median 12.0

© 2017 Duff & Phelps. All Rights Reserved. Duff & Phelps has used the utmost care in compiling the data presented herein, but cannot guarantee the accuracy, completeness, or timeliness of the information.

Data Updated Through March 31, 2017

7363

Number of Companies: 9
Help Supply Services

Industry Description
Establishments primarily engaged in supplying temporary or continuing help on a contract or fee basis.

Sales (in millions)

Three Largest Companies
ManpowerGroup	$19,654.1
Kelly Services, Inc.	5,276.8
Robert Half Int'l Inc.	5,250.4

Three Smallest Companies
Kforce Inc.	$1,319.7
Barrett Business Services Inc.	840.6
RCM Technologies Inc.	185.7

Total Assets (in millions)

Three Largest Companies
ManpowerGroup	$7,574.2
Kelly Services, Inc.	2,028.1
Robert Half Int'l Inc.	1,778.0

Three Smallest Companies
Barrett Business Services Inc.	$597.8
Kforce Inc.	365.4
RCM Technologies Inc.	81.3

Annualized Monthly Performance Statistics (%)

Industry	Geometric Mean	Arithmetic Mean	Standard Deviation
1-year	22.8	25.9	29.5
3-year	9.5	11.7	22.3
5-year	16.1	18.7	25.2

S&P 500 Index	Geometric Mean	Arithmetic Mean	Standard Deviation
1-year	17.2	17.4	7.2
3-year	10.4	10.9	11.5
5-year	13.3	13.9	11.5

Return Ratios (%)

	Return on Assets Latest	5-Yr Avg	Return on Equity Latest	5-Yr Avg	Dividend Yield Latest	5-Yr Avg
Median (9)	6.1	4.9	16.8	10.2	1.5	1.7
SIC Composite (9)	6.9	6.0	5.4	5.4	1.7	1.6
Large Composite (–)	–	–	–	–	–	–
Small Composite (–)	–	–	–	–	–	–
High-Financial Risk (–)	–	–	–	–	–	–

Liquidity Ratio

Current Ratio	Latest	5-Yr Avg
	1.7	2.1
	1.5	1.6
	–	–
	–	–
	–	–

Profitability Ratio (%)

Operating Margin	Latest	5-Yr Avg
	4.2	3.8
	4.7	4.1
	–	–
	–	–
	–	–

Growth Rates (%)

Long-term EPS	Analyst Estimates
	11.2
	11.1
	–
	–
	–

Betas (Levered)

	Raw (OLS)	Blume Adjusted	Peer Group	Vasicek Adjusted	Sum	Downside
Median	1.27	1.18	1.05	1.17	1.22	1.66
SIC Composite	1.43	1.28	1.05	1.40	1.16	1.38
Large Composite	–	–	–	–	–	–
Small Composite	–	–	–	–	–	–
High Financial Risk	–	–	–	–	–	–

Betas (Unlevered)

	Raw (OLS)	Blume Adjusted	Peer Group	Vasicek Adjusted	Sum	Downside
Median	1.26	1.17	0.98	1.17	1.09	1.50
SIC Composite	1.33	1.19	0.98	1.30	1.08	1.28
Large Composite	–	–	–	–	–	–
Small Composite	–	–	–	–	–	–
High Financial Risk	–	–	–	–	–	–

Equity Valuation Multiples

	Price/Sales Latest	5-Yr Avg	Price/Earnings Latest	5-Yr Avg	Market/Book Latest	5-Yr Avg
Median	0.5	0.4	19.6	23.7	2.7	2.3
SIC Composite	0.5	0.4	18.5	18.6	3.2	2.6
Large Composite	–	–	–	–	–	–
Small Composite	–	–	–	–	–	–
High Financial Risk	–	–	–	–	–	–

Enterprise Valuation (EV) Multiples

	EV/Sales Latest	5-Yr Avg	EV/EBITDA Latest	5-Yr Avg
Median	0.5	0.4	8.9	8.6
SIC Composite	0.5	0.4	9.6	8.9
Large Composite	–	–	–	–
Small Composite	–	–	–	–
High Financial Risk	–	–	–	–

Enterprise Valuation SIC Composite
- Latest: EV/Sales 0.5, EV/EBITDA 9.6
- 5-Yr Avg: EV/Sales 0.4, EV/EBITDA 8.9

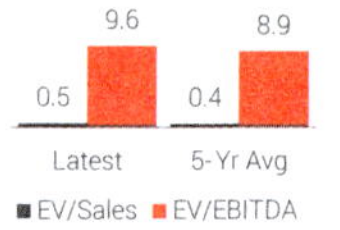

Fama-French (F-F) 5-Factor Model

	F-F Beta	SMB Premium	HML Premium	RMW Premium	CMA Premium
Median	1.0	3.2	4.5	1.4	-4.5
SIC Composite	1.3	3.4	3.4	1.2	-4.3
Large Composite	–	–	–	–	–
Small Composite	–	–	–	–	–
High Financial Risk	–	–	–	–	–

Leverage Ratios (%)

	Debt/MV Equity Latest	5-Yr Avg	Debt/Total Capital Latest	5-Yr Avg
Median	11.9	11.1	10.7	10.0
SIC Composite	9.0	9.1	8.2	8.4
Large Composite	–	–	–	–
Small Composite	–	–	–	–
High Financial Risk	–	–	–	–

Cost of Debt

Cost of Debt (%)	Latest
Median	7.1
SIC Composite	5.7
Large Composite	–
Small Composite	–
High Financial Risk	–

Capital Structure

SIC Composite (%) Latest
- D / TC: 8.2
- E / TC: 91.8

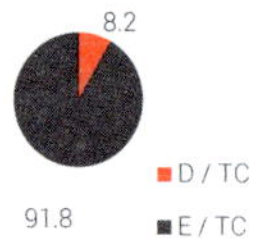

Cost of Equity Capital (%)

	CRSP Deciles CAPM	CAPM +Size Prem	Build-Up	Risk Premium Report CAPM +Size Prem	Build-Up	Discounted Cash Flow 1-Stage	3-Stage	Fama-French 5-Factor Model
Median	9.9	12.3	11.0	14.0	14.2	11.3	12.1	13.7
SIC Composite	11.2	12.4	10.5	13.3	13.0	12.7	11.9	14.4
Large Composite	–	–	–	–	–	–	–	–
Small Composite	–	–	–	–	–	–	–	–
High Financial Risk	–	–	–	–	–	–	–	–

Cost of Equity Capital (%) SIC Composite:
- Avg CRSP: 11.5
- Avg RPR: 13.1
- 1-Stage: 12.7
- 3-Stage: 11.9
- 5-Factor Model: 14.4

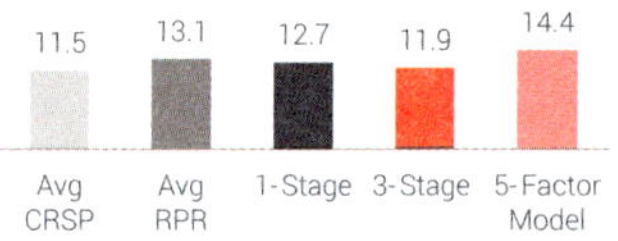

Weighted Average Cost of Capital (WACC) (%)

	CRSP Deciles CAPM	CAPM +Size Prem	Build-Up	Risk Premium Report CAPM +Size Prem	Build-Up	Discounted Cash Flow 1-Stage	3-Stage	Fama-French 5-Factor Model
Median	9.9	12.0	10.7	13.6	13.6	10.6	11.4	14.7
SIC Composite	10.7	11.8	10.1	12.6	12.4	12.1	11.3	13.7
Large Composite	–	–	–	–	–	–	–	–
Small Composite	–	–	–	–	–	–	–	–
High Financial Risk	–	–	–	–	–	–	–	–

WACC (%) SIC Composite
Low 10.1 — High 13.7
▲ Average 12.0 ◆ Median 12.1

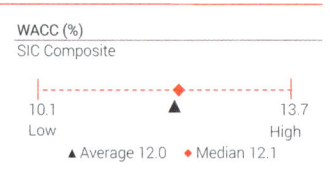

© 2017 Duff & Phelps. All Rights Reserved. Duff & Phelps has used the utmost care in compiling the data presented herein, but cannot guarantee the accuracy, completeness, or timeliness of the information.

Data Updated Through March 31, 2017

737

Number of Companies: 115
Computer Programming, Data Processing, and Other Computer Related Services

Industry Description
Establishments primarily engaged in computer programming services; prepackaged software; computer integrated systems design; computer processing and data preparation and processing services; information retrieval services; computer facilities management services; computer rental and leasing; computer maintenance and repair; computer related services, not elsewhere classified.

Sales (in millions)

Three Largest Companies
Alphabet Inc.	$90,272.0
Microsoft Corp.	85,320.0
Int'l Business Machines Corp.	79,920.0

Three Smallest Companies
Evolving Systems Inc.	$25.6
Aware, Inc.	22.4
Issuer Direct Corp.	11.7

Total Assets (in millions)

Three Largest Companies
Microsoft Corp.	$193,694.0
Alphabet Inc.	167,497.0
Int'l Business Machines Corp.	117,470.0

Three Smallest Companies
Auxilio, Inc.	$26.5
MAM Software Group, Inc.	22.4
Issuer Direct Corp.	12.9

Annualized Monthly Performance Statistics (%)

Industry	Geometric Mean	Arithmetic Mean	Standard Deviation
1-year	18.9	19.6	13.4
3-year	13.1	14.1	15.6
5-year	14.8	15.7	14.8

S&P 500 Index	Geometric Mean	Arithmetic Mean	Standard Deviation
1-year	17.2	17.4	7.2
3-year	10.4	10.9	11.5
5-year	13.3	13.9	11.5

Return Ratios (%)

	Return on Assets Latest	5-Yr Avg	Return on Equity Latest	5-Yr Avg	Dividend Yield Latest	5-Yr Avg
Median (115)	6.1	6.9	10.8	11.8	0.0	0.0
SIC Composite (115)	8.2	9.3	3.6	4.7	1.2	1.1
Large Composite (11)	9.6	10.6	4.1	5.1	1.3	1.3
Small Composite (11)	14.3	9.5	7.3	5.1	0.2	2.6
High-Financial Risk (31)	-2.1	-2.8	-1.0	-1.7	0.0	0.0

Liquidity Ratio / Profitability Ratio (%) / Growth Rates (%)

	Current Ratio Latest	5-Yr Avg	Operating Margin Latest	5-Yr Avg	Long-term EPS Analyst Estimates
Median (115)	1.8	1.9	16.2	15.0	13.1
SIC Composite (115)	2.1	2.1	21.7	23.5	13.0
Large Composite (11)	2.3	2.2	23.6	25.9	12.8
Small Composite (11)	1.8	1.9	17.4	11.8	15.4
High-Financial Risk (31)	1.1	1.3	0.5	2.9	24.0

Betas (Levered)

	Raw (OLS)	Blume Adjusted	Peer Group	Vasicek Adjusted	Sum	Downside
Median	1.10	1.07	1.06	1.08	1.07	1.41
SIC Composite	1.07	1.05	1.06	1.07	0.97	1.02
Large Composite	1.04	1.03	1.07	1.04	0.95	0.99
Small Composite	0.70	0.82	1.06	0.77	0.97	1.03
High Financial Risk	1.32	1.21	1.06	1.28	1.05	1.42

Betas (Unlevered)

	Raw (OLS)	Blume Adjusted	Peer Group	Vasicek Adjusted	Sum	Downside
Median	1.02	0.99	1.01	1.01	0.99	1.27
SIC Composite	0.98	0.96	0.97	0.98	0.88	0.93
Large Composite	0.94	0.93	0.97	0.94	0.86	0.89
Small Composite	0.69	0.80	1.04	0.76	0.95	1.01
High Financial Risk	1.20	1.10	0.97	1.17	0.96	1.29

Equity Valuation Multiples

	Price/Sales Latest	5-Yr Avg	Price/Earnings Latest	5-Yr Avg	Market/Book Latest	5-Yr Avg
Median	3.8	3.3	33.2	28.9	4.0	3.7
SIC Composite	4.7	3.8	27.5	21.5	4.7	4.0
Large Composite	4.8	3.9	24.1	19.7	5.1	4.3
Small Composite	3.1	2.9	13.8	19.5	2.7	2.5
High Financial Risk	3.3	2.2	–	–	7.1	4.9

Enterprise Valuation (EV) Multiples

	EV/Sales Latest	5-Yr Avg	EV/EBITDA Latest	5-Yr Avg
Median	3.6	3.1	15.2	13.6
SIC Composite	4.5	3.5	15.4	11.7
Large Composite	4.5	3.6	14.5	11.0
Small Composite	2.8	2.6	12.6	14.6
High Financial Risk	3.4	2.2	41.7	22.1

Enterprise Valuation SIC Composite
- EV/Sales: Latest 4.5, 5-Yr Avg 3.5
- EV/EBITDA: Latest 15.4, 5-Yr Avg 11.7

Fama-French (F-F) 5-Factor Model

	F-F Beta	SMB Premium	HML Premium	RMW Premium	CMA Premium
Median	1.3	2.0	-7.3	-3.5	7.2
SIC Composite	1.1	-1.1	0.6	-0.3	-3.5
Large Composite	1.0	-1.7	1.4	0.0	0.1
Small Composite	0.6	2.9	-1.9	-2.6	1.7
High Financial Risk	–	–	–	–	–

Leverage Ratios (%)

	Debt/MV Equity Latest	5-Yr Avg	Debt/Total Capital Latest	5-Yr Avg
Median	7.9	4.5	7.3	4.4
SIC Composite	10.5	9.7	9.5	8.8
Large Composite	10.4	9.4	9.4	8.6
Small Composite	2.7	2.0	2.7	2.0
High Financial Risk	12.2	14.1	10.8	12.4

Cost of Debt

	Cost of Debt (%) Latest
Median	6.1
SIC Composite	4.5
Large Composite	4.0
Small Composite	6.6
High Financial Risk	6.0

Capital Structure

SIC Composite (%) Latest
- D/TC: 9.5
- E/TC: 90.5

Cost of Equity Capital (%)

	CRSP Deciles CAPM	CAPM +Size Prem	Build-Up	Risk Premium Report CAPM +Size Prem	Build-Up	Discounted Cash Flow 1-Stage	3-Stage	Fama-French 5-Factor Model
Median	9.5	10.9	10.8	13.0	13.9	14.3	9.9	9.2
SIC Composite	9.4	9.6	9.5	10.2	9.9	14.1	10.9	5.3
Large Composite	9.2	9.2	9.3	9.5	9.0	14.0	11.3	9.0
Small Composite	7.7	12.6	14.2	14.7	16.6	15.5	14.6	6.7
High Financial Risk	–	–	–	25.2	28.5	–	–	–

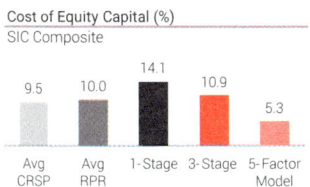

Cost of Equity Capital (%) SIC Composite
- Avg CRSP: 9.5
- Avg RPR: 10.0
- 1-Stage: 14.1
- 3-Stage: 10.9
- 5-Factor Model: 5.3

Weighted Average Cost of Capital (WACC) (%)

	CRSP Deciles CAPM	CAPM +Size Prem	Build-Up	Risk Premium Report CAPM +Size Prem	Build-Up	Discounted Cash Flow 1-Stage	3-Stage	Fama-French 5-Factor Model
Median	9.1	10.3	10.1	12.2	12.9	13.4	9.5	9.0
SIC Composite	8.9	9.1	9.0	9.6	9.3	13.1	10.3	5.2
Large Composite	8.7	8.7	8.8	9.0	8.5	13.1	10.6	8.5
Small Composite	7.7	12.5	14.0	14.5	16.4	15.3	14.3	6.7
High Financial Risk	–	–	–	23.1	26.0	–	–	–

WACC (%) SIC Composite
Low 5.2 — Average 9.4 ◆ Median 9.3 — High 13.1

© 2017 Duff & Phelps. All Rights Reserved. Duff & Phelps has used the utmost care in compiling the data presented herein, but cannot guarantee the accuracy, completeness, or timeliness of the information.

Data Updated Through March 31, 2017

7372

Number of Companies: 31
Prepackaged Software

Industry Description
Establishments primarily engaged in the design, development, and production of prepackaged computer software.

Sales (in millions)

Three Largest Companies
Microsoft Corp.	$85,320.0
Activision Blizzard, Inc.	6,608.0
Adobe Systems Inc.	5,854.4

Three Smallest Companies
American Software	$113.9
GlobalSCAPE Inc.	33.3
Aware, Inc.	22.4

Total Assets (in millions)

Three Largest Companies
Microsoft Corp.	$193,694.0
Activision Blizzard, Inc.	17,452.0
Adobe Systems Inc.	12,707.1

Three Smallest Companies
American Software	$136.7
Aware, Inc.	62.0
GlobalSCAPE Inc.	50.2

Annualized Monthly Performance Statistics (%)

Industry
	Geometric Mean	Arithmetic Mean	Standard Deviation
1-year	25.2	26.2	16.6
3-year	20.8	22.7	22.0
5-year	18.6	20.1	19.4

S&P 500 Index
	Geometric Mean	Arithmetic Mean	Standard Deviation
1-year	17.2	17.4	7.2
3-year	10.4	10.9	11.5
5-year	13.3	13.9	11.5

Return Ratios (%)

	Return on Assets Latest	Return on Assets 5-Yr Avg	Return on Equity Latest	Return on Equity 5-Yr Avg	Dividend Yield Latest	Dividend Yield 5-Yr Avg
Median (31)	6.5	6.9	8.4	11.4	0.0	0.0
SIC Composite (31)	7.7	9.4	2.8	4.4	1.9	2.0
Large Composite (3)	8.5	10.5	3.1	4.8	2.2	2.4
Small Composite (3)	7.4	12.9	3.7	7.1	0.7	13.1
High-Financial Risk (–)	–	–	–	–	–	–

Liquidity Ratio

	Current Ratio Latest	Current Ratio 5-Yr Avg
Median	1.8	1.8
SIC Composite	2.1	2.1
Large Composite	2.3	2.5
Small Composite	2.8	3.2
High Financial Risk	–	–

Profitability Ratio (%)

	Operating Margin Latest	Operating Margin 5-Yr Avg
Median	16.4	15.2
SIC Composite	23.2	27.4
Large Composite	24.8	30.9
Small Composite	14.9	14.9
High Financial Risk	–	–

Growth Rates (%)

	Long-term EPS Analyst Estimates
Median	11.9
SIC Composite	11.3
Large Composite	10.4
Small Composite	10.8
High Financial Risk	–

Betas (Levered)

	Raw (OLS)	Blume Adjusted	Peer Group	Vasicek Adjusted	Sum	Downside
Median	1.06	1.04	1.06	1.06	0.92	1.33
SIC Composite	1.06	1.04	1.06	1.06	1.02	1.07
Large Composite	1.04	1.03	1.06	1.06	1.09	1.10
Small Composite	0.41	0.63	1.06	0.54	0.26	0.72
High Financial Risk	–	–	–	–	–	–

Betas (Unlevered)

	Raw (OLS)	Blume Adjusted	Peer Group	Vasicek Adjusted	Sum	Downside
Median	1.03	1.01	1.03	1.02	0.91	1.26
SIC Composite	0.97	0.96	0.97	0.97	0.94	0.98
Large Composite	0.94	0.93	0.96	0.96	0.99	1.00
Small Composite	–	–	–	–	–	–
High Financial Risk	–	–	–	–	–	–

Equity Valuation Multiples

	Price/Sales Latest	Price/Sales 5-Yr Avg	Price/Earnings Latest	Price/Earnings 5-Yr Avg	Market/Book Latest	Market/Book 5-Yr Avg
Median	4.9	4.0	43.0	33.8	4.9	4.4
SIC Composite	6.0	4.2	35.1	22.8	6.5	4.2
Large Composite	6.2	4.4	32.3	20.7	6.8	4.3
Small Composite	2.9	2.8	26.9	14.0	2.7	2.4
High Financial Risk	–	–	–	–	–	–

Enterprise Valuation (EV) Multiples

	EV/Sales Latest	EV/Sales 5-Yr Avg	EV/EBITDA Latest	EV/EBITDA 5-Yr Avg
Median	4.9	3.8	20.1	17.0
SIC Composite	5.4	3.7	17.5	10.9
Large Composite	5.6	3.7	17.0	9.9
Small Composite	2.1	1.9	10.2	9.6
High Financial Risk	–	–	–	–

Enterprise Valuation — SIC Composite
- EV/Sales: Latest 5.4, 5-Yr Avg 3.7
- EV/EBITDA: Latest 17.5, 5-Yr Avg 10.9

Fama-French (F-F) 5-Factor Model

Fama-French (F-F) Components
	F-F Beta	SMB Premium	HML Premium	RMW Premium	CMA Premium
Median	1.3	4.9	1.1	-0.2	-7.8
SIC Composite	1.1	-2.1	2.4	-0.1	-5.7
Large Composite	1.1	-3.1	3.9	0.3	0.4
Small Composite	0.3	4.3	-2.4	-0.6	2.8
High Financial Risk	–	–	–	–	–

Leverage Ratios (%)

	Debt/MV Equity Latest	Debt/MV Equity 5-Yr Avg	Debt/Total Capital Latest	Debt/Total Capital 5-Yr Avg
Median	3.1	2.5	3.0	2.5
SIC Composite	9.1	7.7	8.4	7.2
Large Composite	9.9	8.2	9.0	7.5
Small Composite	0.0	0.5	0.0	0.5
High Financial Risk	–	–	–	–

Cost of Debt

	Cost of Debt (%) Latest
Median	6.1
SIC Composite	4.2
Large Composite	3.8
Small Composite	–
High Financial Risk	–

Capital Structure

SIC Composite (%) Latest
- D/TC: 8.4
- E/TC: 91.6

Cost of Equity Capital (%)

	CRSP Deciles CAPM	CRSP Deciles CAPM +Size Prem	CRSP Deciles Build-Up	Risk Premium Report CAPM +Size Prem	Risk Premium Report Build-Up	Discounted Cash Flow 1-Stage	Discounted Cash Flow 3-Stage	Fama-French 5-Factor Model
Median	9.3	10.3	10.3	12.4	13.9	13.3	8.4	8.7
SIC Composite	9.3	9.5	9.5	10.5	10.0	13.0	9.1	4.2
Large Composite	9.3	9.3	9.3	10.3	9.1	12.6	9.1	10.9
Small Composite	6.5	10.3	13.1	10.7	16.5	11.1	15.5	9.1
High Financial Risk	–	–	–	–	–	–	–	–

Cost of Equity Capital (%) — SIC Composite
- Avg CRSP: 9.5
- Avg RPR: 10.3
- 1-Stage: 13.0
- 3-Stage: 9.1
- 5-Factor Model: 4.2

Weighted Average Cost of Capital (WACC) (%)

	CRSP Deciles CAPM	CRSP Deciles CAPM +Size Prem	CRSP Deciles Build-Up	Risk Premium Report CAPM +Size Prem	Risk Premium Report Build-Up	Discounted Cash Flow 1-Stage	Discounted Cash Flow 3-Stage	Fama-French 5-Factor Model
Median	9.2	10.3	10.2	11.9	13.3	12.8	8.3	8.2
SIC Composite	8.9	9.0	9.0	10.0	9.5	12.3	8.7	4.2
Large Composite	8.8	8.8	8.8	9.7	8.6	11.8	8.6	10.3
Small Composite	6.5	10.3	13.1	10.7	16.5	11.1	15.5	9.1
High Financial Risk	–	–	–	–	–	–	–	–

WACC (%) — SIC Composite
Low 4.2 — High 12.3
▲ Average 9.0   ◆ Median 9.0

© 2017 Duff & Phelps. All Rights Reserved. Duff & Phelps has used the utmost care in compiling the data presented herein, but cannot guarantee the accuracy, completeness, or timeliness of the information.

Data Updated Through March 31, 2017

7373

Number of Companies: 19
Computer Integrated Systems Design

Industry Description
Establishments primarily engaged in developing or modifying computer software and packaging or bundling the software with purchased computer hardware to create and market an integrated system for specific application.

Sales (in millions)

Three Largest Companies
VMware, Inc.	$7,093.0
Leidos Holdings, Inc.	7,043.0
Cerner Corp.	4,796.5

Three Smallest Companies
Medidata Solutions	$463.4
Computer Programs & Systems	267.3
CSP Inc.	103.4

Annualized Monthly Performance Statistics (%)

Industry	Geometric Mean	Arithmetic Mean	Standard Deviation
1-year	34.6	35.4	14.8
3-year	4.7	5.9	16.0
5-year	5.7	7.2	18.1

Total Assets (in millions)

Three Largest Companies
VMware, Inc.	$16,643.0
Leidos Holdings, Inc.	9,132.0
Cerner Corp.	5,630.0

Three Smallest Companies
Computer Programs & Systems	$339.1
Manhattan Associates Inc.	297.1
CSP Inc.	48.7

S&P 500 Index	Geometric Mean	Arithmetic Mean	Standard Deviation
1-year	17.2	17.4	7.2
3-year	10.4	10.9	11.5
5-year	13.3	13.9	11.5

Return Ratios (%)

	Return on Assets Latest	Return on Assets 5-Yr Avg	Return on Equity Latest	Return on Equity 5-Yr Avg	Dividend Yield Latest	Dividend Yield 5-Yr Avg
Median (19)	5.4	7.3	11.4	11.7	0.0	0.0
SIC Composite (19)	6.4	7.0	3.0	3.1	1.4	0.7
Large Composite (3)	6.6	6.7	3.2	2.8	2.0	0.7
Small Composite (3)	2.9	5.5	0.9	1.4	0.6	0.9
High-Financial Risk (–)	–	–	–	–	–	–

Liquidity Ratio

	Current Ratio Latest	Current Ratio 5-Yr Avg
Median (19)	1.6	1.8
SIC Composite (19)	1.8	1.9
Large Composite (3)	1.9	2.1
Small Composite (3)	3.3	3.2
High-Financial Risk (–)	–	–

Profitability Ratio (%)

	Operating Margin Latest	Operating Margin 5-Yr Avg
Median (19)	10.8	16.1
SIC Composite (19)	14.9	14.9
Large Composite (3)	15.8	15.1
Small Composite (3)	9.1	11.4
High-Financial Risk (–)	–	–

Growth Rates (%)

	Long-term EPS Analyst Estimates
Median (19)	11.7
SIC Composite (19)	11.7
Large Composite (3)	10.9
Small Composite (3)	20.2
High-Financial Risk (–)	–

Betas (Levered)

	Raw (OLS)	Blume Adjusted	Peer Group	Vasicek Adjusted	Sum	Downside
Median	1.12	1.08	1.06	1.09	1.14	1.57
SIC Composite	1.05	1.04	1.06	1.05	1.07	1.24
Large Composite	0.94	0.97	1.06	0.96	1.07	1.32
Small Composite	1.38	1.25	1.10	1.33	2.06	1.56
High Financial Risk	–	–	–	–	–	–

Betas (Unlevered)

	Raw (OLS)	Blume Adjusted	Peer Group	Vasicek Adjusted	Sum	Downside
Median	1.00	1.00	1.00	1.02	1.07	1.29
SIC Composite	0.99	0.97	0.99	0.99	1.00	1.16
Large Composite	0.89	0.91	0.99	0.90	1.00	1.23
Small Composite	1.28	1.16	1.03	1.23	1.88	1.44
High Financial Risk	–	–	–	–	–	–

Equity Valuation Multiples

	Price/Sales Latest	Price/Sales 5-Yr Avg	Price/Earnings Latest	Price/Earnings 5-Yr Avg	Market/Book Latest	Market/Book 5-Yr Avg
Median	3.2	2.8	31.4	26.3	3.5	4.5
SIC Composite	3.2	3.0	33.6	32.1	4.0	4.1
Large Composite	3.4	3.5	31.3	35.5	4.1	4.5
Small Composite	4.5	4.6	–	69.3	6.5	7.8
High Financial Risk	–	–	–	–	–	–

Enterprise Valuation (EV) Multiples

	EV/Sales Latest	EV/Sales 5-Yr Avg	EV/EBITDA Latest	EV/EBITDA 5-Yr Avg
Median	3.1	2.8	15.2	13.6
SIC Composite	3.2	2.8	15.9	14.8
Large Composite	3.2	3.2	15.2	16.0
Small Composite	4.5	4.5	34.3	31.6
High Financial Risk	–	–	–	–

Enterprise Valuation SIC Composite

	Latest	5-Yr Avg
EV/Sales	3.2	2.8
EV/EBITDA	15.9	14.8

Fama-French (F-F) 5-Factor Model

Fama-French (F-F) Components

	F-F Beta	SMB Premium	HML Premium	RMW Premium	CMA Premium
Median	1.1	0.2	0.4	2.2	-3.4
SIC Composite	1.0	1.2	-0.1	-0.3	-4.0
Large Composite	0.8	1.0	0.0	0.3	0.4
Small Composite	1.2	2.6	-5.9	-8.6	7.2
High Financial Risk	–	–	–	–	–

Leverage Ratios (%)

	Debt/MV Equity Latest	Debt/MV Equity 5-Yr Avg	Debt/Total Capital Latest	Debt/Total Capital 5-Yr Avg
Median	7.9	5.2	7.3	5.0
SIC Composite	8.5	6.8	7.9	6.4
Large Composite	8.3	5.3	7.6	5.0
Small Composite	11.1	7.8	10.0	7.2
High Financial Risk	–	–	–	–

Cost of Debt

	Cost of Debt (%) Latest
Median	7.1
SIC Composite	6.0
Large Composite	5.7
Small Composite	7.1
High Financial Risk	–

Capital Structure

SIC Composite (%) Latest
- D / TC: 7.9
- E / TC: 92.1

Cost of Equity Capital (%)

	CAPM	CRSP Deciles CAPM +Size Prem	Build-Up	Risk Premium Report CAPM +Size Prem	Build-Up	Discounted Cash Flow 1-Stage	3-Stage	Fama-French 5-Factor Model
Median	9.5	10.9	10.3	13.8	13.6	14.3	9.4	9.0
SIC Composite	9.3	10.0	10.0	12.4	12.3	13.0	9.2	5.8
Large Composite	8.8	9.1	9.6	11.8	11.4	12.9	8.9	10.0
Small Composite	10.8	12.5	11.0	19.3	14.7	20.9	8.5	5.2
High Financial Risk	–	–	–	–	–	–	–	–

Cost of Equity Capital (%) SIC Composite
- Avg CRSP: 10.0
- Avg RPR: 12.4
- Build-Up: 13.0
- 3-Stage: 9.2
- 5-Factor Model: 5.8

Weighted Average Cost of Capital (WACC) (%)

	CAPM	CRSP Deciles CAPM +Size Prem	Build-Up	Risk Premium Report CAPM +Size Prem	Build-Up	Discounted Cash Flow 1-Stage	3-Stage	Fama-French 5-Factor Model
Median	9.1	10.4	10.1	12.6	12.6	13.7	9.4	8.8
SIC Composite	9.0	9.6	9.7	11.8	11.8	12.4	8.9	5.8
Large Composite	8.6	8.8	9.3	11.4	11.0	12.3	8.7	9.6
Small Composite	10.4	11.9	10.6	18.0	13.9	19.5	8.3	5.4
High Financial Risk	–	–	–	–	–	–	–	–

WACC (%) SIC Composite
- Low: 5.8
- High: 12.4
- ▲ Average 10.0
- ◆ Median 9.7

© 2017 Duff & Phelps. All Rights Reserved. Duff & Phelps has used the utmost care in compiling the data presented herein, but cannot guarantee the accuracy, completeness, or timeliness of the information.

Data Updated Through March 31, 2017

7374

Number of Companies: 17
Computer Processing and Data Preparation and Processing Services

Industry Description
Establishments primarily engaged in providing computer processing and data preparation services.

Sales (in millions)

Three Largest Companies
Automatic Data Processing, Inc.	$11,667.8
Fidelity National Info. Services	9,241.0
Fiserv, Inc.	5,505.0

Three Smallest Companies
Information Services Group, Inc.	$216.5
Auxilio, Inc.	60.2
Planet Payment, Inc.	54.3

Total Assets (in millions)

Three Largest Companies
Automatic Data Processing, Inc.	$43,670.0
Fidelity National Info. Services	26,031.0
Global Payments Inc.	10,664.3

Three Smallest Companies
Information Services Group, Inc.	$235.1
Planet Payment, Inc.	58.6
Auxilio, Inc.	26.5

Annualized Monthly Performance Statistics (%)

Industry	Geometric Mean	Arithmetic Mean	Standard Deviation
1-year	16.0	16.2	7.6
3-year	17.4	18.1	13.0
5-year	21.5	22.2	13.6

S&P 500 Index	Geometric Mean	Arithmetic Mean	Standard Deviation
1-year	17.2	17.4	7.2
3-year	10.4	10.9	11.5
5-year	13.3	13.9	11.5

Return Ratios (%)

	Return on Assets Latest	5-Yr Avg	Return on Equity Latest	5-Yr Avg	Dividend Yield Latest	5-Yr Avg
Median (17)	5.2	5.2	12.4	14.0	0.0	0.0
SIC Composite (17)	3.6	4.4	2.9	3.9	1.1	1.3
Large Composite (3)	3.8	4.4	3.1	3.9	1.5	1.7
Small Composite (3)	7.4	4.8	6.4	3.3	0.0	0.3
High-Financial Risk (–)	–	–	–	–	–	–

Liquidity Ratio

	Current Ratio Latest	5-Yr Avg
Median (17)	1.4	1.3
SIC Composite (17)	1.1	1.1
Large Composite (3)	1.1	1.1
Small Composite (3)	2.0	2.0
High-Financial Risk (–)	–	–

Profitability Ratio (%)

	Operating Margin Latest	5-Yr Avg
Median (17)	16.9	13.9
SIC Composite (17)	19.1	18.6
Large Composite (3)	20.0	20.0
Small Composite (3)	5.1	4.6
High-Financial Risk (–)	–	–

Growth Rates (%)

	Long-term EPS Analyst Estimates
Median (17)	13.1
SIC Composite (17)	13.1
Large Composite (3)	12.2
Small Composite (3)	18.1
High-Financial Risk (–)	–

Betas (Levered)

	Raw (OLS)	Blume Adjusted	Peer Group	Vasicek Adjusted	Sum	Downside
Median	0.82	0.89	1.05	0.95	1.00	1.24
SIC Composite	0.95	0.97	1.05	0.95	0.79	0.83
Large Composite	0.84	0.91	1.04	1.02	0.57	0.73
Small Composite	0.51	0.70	1.06	0.98	0.74	1.31
High Financial Risk	–	–	–	–	–	–

Betas (Unlevered)

	Raw (OLS)	Blume Adjusted	Peer Group	Vasicek Adjusted	Sum	Downside
Median	0.70	0.76	0.90	0.84	0.68	0.91
SIC Composite	0.81	0.83	0.89	0.81	0.68	0.71
Large Composite	0.73	0.78	0.90	0.88	0.50	0.63
Small Composite	0.45	0.59	0.85	0.80	0.62	1.04
High Financial Risk	–	–	–	–	–	–

Equity Valuation Multiples

	Price/Sales Latest	5-Yr Avg	Price/Earnings Latest	5-Yr Avg	Market/Book Latest	5-Yr Avg
Median	2.6	2.1	30.7	25.1	3.1	2.8
SIC Composite	3.5	2.8	34.3	25.4	4.3	3.5
Large Composite	3.7	3.1	32.4	25.8	4.8	3.7
Small Composite	1.1	1.0	15.6	30.5	3.4	3.9
High Financial Risk	–	–	–	–	–	–

Enterprise Valuation (EV) Multiples

	EV/Sales Latest	5-Yr Avg	EV/EBITDA Latest	5-Yr Avg
Median	2.7	2.6	13.4	11.9
SIC Composite	4.1	3.2	15.2	12.4
Large Composite	4.2	3.4	15.1	12.9
Small Composite	1.3	1.1	15.6	13.4
High Financial Risk	–	–	–	–

Enterprise Valuation SIC Composite
- EV/Sales Latest: 4.1; 5-Yr Avg: 3.2
- EV/EBITDA Latest: 15.2; 5-Yr Avg: 12.4

Fama-French (F-F) 5-Factor Model

	F-F Beta	SMB Premium	HML Premium	RMW Premium	CMA Premium
Median	0.9	0.5	-1.9	1.9	1.4
SIC Composite	0.9	0.6	-0.7	0.8	0.2
Large Composite	0.9	0.4	-0.6	1.1	1.5
Small Composite	0.3	3.8	-1.8	-1.7	-0.1
High Financial Risk	–	–	–	–	–

Leverage Ratios (%)

	Debt/MV Equity Latest	5-Yr Avg	Debt/Total Capital Latest	5-Yr Avg
Median	24.8	23.4	19.9	19.0
SIC Composite	22.6	22.2	18.5	18.1
Large Composite	17.6	17.0	15.0	14.5
Small Composite	36.4	23.8	26.7	19.2
High Financial Risk	–	–	–	–

Cost of Debt

	Cost of Debt (%) Latest
Median	6.1
SIC Composite	5.4
Large Composite	4.7
Small Composite	6.1
High Financial Risk	–

Capital Structure

SIC Composite (%) Latest
- D/TC: 18.5
- E/TC: 81.5

Cost of Equity Capital (%)

	CRSP Deciles CAPM	CAPM +Size Prem	Build-Up	Risk Premium Report CAPM +Size Prem	Build-Up	Discounted Cash Flow 1-Stage	3-Stage	Fama-French 5-Factor Model
Median	8.7	10.7	10.8	12.9	13.1	13.1	11.7	10.2
SIC Composite	8.7	9.1	9.7	10.3	11.5	14.2	10.7	9.5
Large Composite	9.1	9.1	9.3	8.7	10.8	13.8	10.2	10.8
Small Composite	8.9	14.5	14.9	13.5	16.7	18.1	12.6	5.4
High Financial Risk	–	–	–	–	–	–	–	–

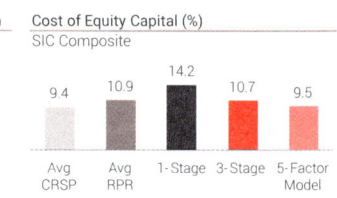

Cost of Equity Capital (%) SIC Composite
- Avg CRSP: 9.4
- Avg RPR: 10.9
- 1-Stage: 14.2
- 3-Stage: 10.7
- 5-Factor Model: 9.5

Weighted Average Cost of Capital (WACC) (%)

	CRSP Deciles CAPM	CAPM +Size Prem	Build-Up	Risk Premium Report CAPM +Size Prem	Build-Up	Discounted Cash Flow 1-Stage	3-Stage	Fama-French 5-Factor Model
Median	8.1	9.1	9.5	10.8	10.9	11.4	9.9	10.3
SIC Composite	8.0	8.3	8.8	9.3	10.2	12.5	9.6	8.7
Large Composite	8.4	8.4	8.5	8.0	9.8	12.3	9.3	9.8
Small Composite	7.9	12.0	12.3	11.3	13.7	14.7	10.7	5.4
High Financial Risk	–	–	–	–	–	–	–	–

WACC (%) SIC Composite
Low 8.3 — High 12.5; Average 9.6; Median 9.3

© 2017 Duff & Phelps. All Rights Reserved. Duff & Phelps has used the utmost care in compiling the data presented herein, but cannot guarantee the accuracy, completeness, or timeliness of the information.

Data Updated Through March 31, 2017

738

Number of Companies: 14
Miscellaneous Business Services

Industry Description
Establishments primarily engaged in detective, guard, and armored car services; security systems services; news syndicates; photofinishing laboratories; business services not elsewhere classified.

Sales (in millions)

Three Largest Companies
Total System Services, Inc.	$4,170.1
KAR Auction Services, Inc.	3,150.1
Brink's Co.	3,020.6

Three Smallest Companies
Spar Group Inc.	$119.3
National Research Corp.	102.3
Collectors Universe Inc.	61.0

Total Assets (in millions)

Three Largest Companies
KAR Auction Services, Inc.	$6,557.6
Total System Services, Inc.	6,366.2
Sotheby's	2,504.4

Three Smallest Companies
Spar Group Inc.	$43.4
Command Security Corp.	36.1
Collectors Universe Inc.	28.2

Annualized Monthly Performance Statistics (%)

	Industry				S&P 500 Index		
	Geometric Mean	Arithmetic Mean	Standard Deviation		Geometric Mean	Arithmetic Mean	Standard Deviation
1-year	20.1	20.3	7.9	1-year	17.2	17.4	7.2
3-year	14.3	15.6	17.9	3-year	10.4	10.9	11.5
5-year	15.9	17.4	18.9	5-year	13.3	13.9	11.5

Return Ratios (%)

	Return on Assets		Return on Equity		Dividend Yield		Current Ratio		Operating Margin		Long-term EPS
	Latest	5-Yr Avg	Latest	5-Yr Avg	Latest	5-Yr Avg	Latest	5-Yr Avg	Latest	5-Yr Avg	Analyst Estimates
Median (14)	3.1	3.7	10.8	9.5	1.2	1.5	1.6	1.7	8.1	9.1	12.4
SIC Composite (14)	3.6	3.9	3.2	4.0	1.3	1.9	1.4	1.5	11.0	10.7	12.4
Large Composite (3)	3.9	4.0	3.1	3.8	1.5	1.8	1.3	1.4	12.6	11.3	12.0
Small Composite (3)	13.0	13.8	3.6	4.4	3.7	3.8	1.5	1.6	15.1	15.4	12.8
High-Financial Risk (–)	–	–	–	–	–	–	–	–	–	–	–

Liquidity Ratio header spans Current Ratio. *Profitability Ratio (%)* spans Operating Margin. *Growth Rates (%)* spans Long-term EPS.

Betas (Levered)

	Raw (OLS)	Blume Adjusted	Peer Group	Vasicek Adjusted	Sum	Downside
Median	1.22	1.15	1.06	1.14	1.09	1.53
SIC Composite	1.24	1.16	1.06	1.23	1.06	1.29
Large Composite	1.19	1.13	1.06	1.16	1.16	1.26
Small Composite	1.33	1.22	1.06	1.22	0.59	1.53
High Financial Risk	–	–	–	–	–	–

Betas (Unlevered)

	Raw (OLS)	Blume Adjusted	Peer Group	Vasicek Adjusted	Sum	Downside
Median	1.09	1.06	0.91	0.94	0.81	1.12
SIC Composite	0.97	0.92	0.84	0.97	0.85	1.01
Large Composite	0.90	0.85	0.81	0.88	0.88	0.95
Small Composite	1.32	1.20	1.04	1.20	0.58	1.51
High Financial Risk	–	–	–	–	–	–

Equity Valuation Multiples

	Price/Sales		Price/Earnings		Market/Book	
	Latest	5-Yr Avg	Latest	5-Yr Avg	Latest	5-Yr Avg
Median	1.4	1.1	30.7	23.8	3.5	2.6
SIC Composite	1.6	1.3	31.6	25.2	3.3	2.5
Large Composite	1.8	1.5	31.9	26.6	4.1	3.0
Small Composite	2.6	2.3	28.2	22.8	6.4	5.1
High Financial Risk	–	–	–	–	–	–

Enterprise Valuation (EV) Multiples

	EV/Sales		EV/EBITDA	
	Latest	5-Yr Avg	Latest	5-Yr Avg
Median	1.3	1.0	9.7	8.5
SIC Composite	1.9	1.6	11.2	9.3
Large Composite	2.4	1.9	12.3	10.5
Small Composite	2.4	2.2	13.7	11.8
High Financial Risk	–	–	–	–

Enterprise Valuation SIC Composite

	Latest	5-Yr Avg
EV/Sales	1.9	1.6
EV/EBITDA	11.2	9.3

Fama-French (F-F) 5-Factor Model

	F-F Beta	SMB Premium	HML Premium	RMW Premium	CMA Premium
Median	0.8	2.8	2.1	1.4	-1.9
SIC Composite	1.2	2.0	0.6	0.3	-2.5
Large Composite	1.1	0.9	-0.5	0.0	0.0
Small Composite	1.3	1.1	0.3	0.6	0.9
High Financial Risk	–	–	–	–	–

Leverage Ratios (%)

	Debt/MV Equity		Debt/Total Capital	
	Latest	5-Yr Avg	Latest	5-Yr Avg
Median	22.6	18.6	18.3	15.7
SIC Composite	34.5	31.1	25.7	23.7
Large Composite	41.0	39.2	29.1	28.2
Small Composite	1.8	2.8	1.8	2.7
High Financial Risk	–	–	–	–

Cost of Debt

	Cost of Debt (%) Latest
Median	6.1
SIC Composite	5.6
Large Composite	5.5
Small Composite	7.1
High Financial Risk	–

Capital Structure

SIC Composite (%) Latest: D/TC 25.7, E/TC 74.3

Cost of Equity Capital (%)

	CRSP Deciles			Risk Premium Report		Discounted Cash Flow		Fama-French
	CAPM	CAPM +Size Prem	Build-Up	CAPM +Size Prem	Build-Up	1-Stage	3-Stage	5-Factor Model
Median	9.7	12.1	11.2	12.8	14.5	14.2	10.9	12.2
SIC Composite	10.2	11.6	10.6	12.9	13.1	13.8	11.9	10.3
Large Composite	9.9	10.9	10.3	13.0	12.5	13.6	11.8	10.1
Small Composite	10.2	13.9	13.0	12.3	16.2	16.1	11.1	13.7
High Financial Risk	–	–	–	–	–	–	–	–

Cost of Equity Capital (%) SIC Composite

Avg CRSP	Avg RPR	1-Stage	3-Stage	5-Factor Model
11.1	13.0	13.8	11.9	10.3

Weighted Average Cost of Capital (WACC) (%)

	CRSP Deciles			Risk Premium Report		Discounted Cash Flow		Fama-French
	CAPM	CAPM +Size Prem	Build-Up	CAPM +Size Prem	Build-Up	1-Stage	3-Stage	5-Factor Model
Median	9.1	11.1	10.5	11.1	13.0	12.0	9.8	11.3
SIC Composite	8.8	9.8	9.1	10.8	10.9	11.5	10.0	8.8
Large Composite	8.3	9.0	8.6	10.5	10.2	10.9	9.6	8.5
Small Composite	10.1	13.7	12.9	12.2	16.0	15.9	11.0	13.5
High Financial Risk	–	–	–	–	–	–	–	–

WACC (%) SIC Composite: Low 8.8, High 11.5, Average 10.1, Median 10.0

© 2017 Duff & Phelps. All Rights Reserved. Duff & Phelps has used the utmost care in compiling the data presented herein, but cannot guarantee the accuracy, completeness, or timeliness of the information.

Data Updated Through March 31, 2017

7389

Number of Companies: 12
Business Services, Not Elsewhere Classified

Industry Description
Establishments primarily engaged in furnishing business services, not elsewhere classified, such as bondspersons, drafting services, lecture bureaus, notaries public, sign painting, speakers' bureaus, water softening services, and auctioneering services, on a commission or fee basis.

Sales (in millions)

Three Largest Companies
Total System Services, Inc.	$4,170.1
KAR Auction Services, Inc.	3,150.1
Convergys Corp.	2,913.6

Three Smallest Companies
Spar Group Inc.	$119.3
National Research Corp.	102.3
Collectors Universe Inc.	61.0

Annualized Monthly Performance Statistics (%)

Industry	Geometric Mean	Arithmetic Mean	Standard Deviation
1-year	17.0	17.3	7.7
3-year	13.4	14.7	17.8
5-year	15.6	17.1	19.1

Total Assets (in millions)

Three Largest Companies
KAR Auction Services, Inc.	$6,557.6
Total System Services, Inc.	6,366.2
Sotheby's	2,504.4

Three Smallest Companies
National Research Corp.	$129.1
Spar Group Inc.	43.4
Collectors Universe Inc.	28.2

S&P 500 Index	Geometric Mean	Arithmetic Mean	Standard Deviation
1-year	17.2	17.4	7.2
3-year	10.4	10.9	11.5
5-year	13.3	13.9	11.5

Return Ratios (%)

	Return on Assets Latest	Return on Assets 5-Yr Avg	Return on Equity Latest	Return on Equity 5-Yr Avg	Dividend Yield Latest	Dividend Yield 5-Yr Avg
Median (12)	3.8	4.3	11.3	11.4	1.4	1.6
SIC Composite (12)	3.7	4.2	3.4	4.1	1.4	1.9
Large Composite (3)	4.4	4.6	3.8	4.1	1.6	1.7
Small Composite (3)	13.0	13.8	3.6	4.4	3.7	3.8
High-Financial Risk (–)	–	–	–	–	–	–

Liquidity Ratio

	Current Ratio Latest	Current Ratio 5-Yr Avg
Median (12)	1.7	1.7
SIC Composite (12)	1.4	1.6
Large Composite (3)	1.5	1.6
Small Composite (3)	1.5	1.6
High-Financial Risk (–)	–	–

Profitability Ratio (%)

	Operating Margin Latest	Operating Margin 5-Yr Avg
Median (12)	11.9	12.5
SIC Composite (12)	12.3	12.7
Large Composite (3)	13.2	13.3
Small Composite (3)	15.1	15.4
High-Financial Risk (–)	–	–

Growth Rates (%)

	Long-term EPS Analyst Estimates
Median (12)	12.4
SIC Composite (12)	12.4
Large Composite (3)	12.0
Small Composite (3)	12.8
High-Financial Risk (–)	–

Betas (Levered)

	Raw (OLS)	Blume Adjusted	Peer Group	Vasicek Adjusted	Sum	Downside
Median	1.22	1.15	1.06	1.13	1.09	1.54
SIC Composite	1.21	1.14	1.06	1.20	1.02	1.29
Large Composite	1.10	1.07	1.06	1.08	1.00	1.15
Small Composite	1.33	1.22	1.06	1.22	0.59	1.53
High Financial Risk	–	–	–	–	–	–

Betas (Unlevered)

	Raw (OLS)	Blume Adjusted	Peer Group	Vasicek Adjusted	Sum	Downside
Median	1.09	1.06	0.92	0.92	0.81	1.12
SIC Composite	0.95	0.90	0.84	0.94	0.81	1.01
Large Composite	0.83	0.81	0.80	0.82	0.76	0.87
Small Composite	1.32	1.20	1.04	1.20	0.58	1.51
High Financial Risk	–	–	–	–	–	–

Equity Valuation Multiples

	Price/Sales Latest	Price/Sales 5-Yr Avg	Price/Earnings Latest	Price/Earnings 5-Yr Avg	Market/Book Latest	Market/Book 5-Yr Avg
Median	2.1	1.5	30.5	23.3	3.5	2.6
SIC Composite	1.7	1.6	29.7	24.3	3.2	2.5
Large Composite	1.7	1.7	26.3	24.4	3.1	2.5
Small Composite	2.6	2.3	28.2	22.8	6.4	5.1
High Financial Risk	–	–	–	–	–	–

Enterprise Valuation (EV) Multiples

	EV/Sales Latest	EV/Sales 5-Yr Avg	EV/EBITDA Latest	EV/EBITDA 5-Yr Avg
Median	2.2	1.7	11.1	8.5
SIC Composite	2.2	1.9	11.5	9.8
Large Composite	2.4	2.2	11.7	10.6
Small Composite	2.4	2.2	13.7	11.8
High Financial Risk	–	–	–	–

Enterprise Valuation SIC Composite

	Latest	5-Yr Avg
EV/Sales	2.2	1.9
EV/EBITDA	11.5	9.8

Fama-French (F-F) 5-Factor Model

	F-F Beta	SMB Premium	HML Premium	RMW Premium	CMA Premium
Median	0.8	2.8	2.1	1.4	-1.9
SIC Composite	1.1	2.0	0.6	0.3	-2.6
Large Composite	1.0	0.9	-0.5	0.0	0.0
Small Composite	1.3	1.1	0.3	0.6	0.9
High Financial Risk	–	–	–	–	–

Leverage Ratios (%)

	Debt/MV Equity Latest	Debt/MV Equity 5-Yr Avg	Debt/Total Capital Latest	Debt/Total Capital 5-Yr Avg
Median	22.6	15.3	18.3	13.2
SIC Composite	36.4	31.2	26.7	23.8
Large Composite	42.0	35.9	29.6	26.4
Small Composite	1.8	2.8	1.8	2.7
High Financial Risk	–	–	–	–

Cost of Debt

	Cost of Debt (%) Latest
Median	6.1
SIC Composite	5.7
Large Composite	5.5
Small Composite	7.1
High Financial Risk	–

Capital Structure

SIC Composite (%) Latest
- D/TC: 26.7
- E/TC: 73.3

Cost of Equity Capital (%)

	CRSP Deciles CAPM	CRSP Deciles CAPM +Size Prem	CRSP Deciles Build-Up	Risk Premium Report CAPM +Size Prem	Risk Premium Report Build-Up	Discounted Cash Flow 1-Stage	Discounted Cash Flow 3-Stage	Fama-French 5-Factor Model
Median	9.7	11.4	11.2	12.7	14.5	14.4	11.1	12.2
SIC Composite	10.1	11.4	10.6	12.6	13.1	13.9	12.6	10.1
Large Composite	9.5	10.4	10.3	12.1	12.5	13.7	13.3	9.6
Small Composite	10.2	13.9	13.0	12.3	16.2	16.1	11.1	13.7
High Financial Risk	–	–	–	–	–	–	–	–

Cost of Equity Capital (%) SIC Composite
- Avg CRSP: 11.0
- Avg RPR: 12.9
- 1-Stage: 13.9
- 3-Stage: 12.6
- 5-Factor Model: 10.1

Weighted Average Cost of Capital (WACC) (%)

	CRSP Deciles CAPM	CRSP Deciles CAPM +Size Prem	CRSP Deciles Build-Up	Risk Premium Report CAPM +Size Prem	Risk Premium Report Build-Up	Discounted Cash Flow 1-Stage	Discounted Cash Flow 3-Stage	Fama-French 5-Factor Model
Median	9.1	11.0	10.5	11.1	13.0	12.1	9.9	11.3
SIC Composite	8.6	9.6	9.0	10.5	10.8	11.4	10.5	8.6
Large Composite	7.9	8.6	8.5	9.8	10.1	10.9	10.6	8.1
Small Composite	10.1	13.7	12.9	12.2	16.0	15.9	11.0	13.5
High Financial Risk	–	–	–	–	–	–	–	–

WACC (%) SIC Composite
- Low: 8.6
- High: 11.4
- Average: 10.1
- Median: 10.5

© 2017 Duff & Phelps. All Rights Reserved. Duff & Phelps has used the utmost care in compiling the data presented herein, but cannot guarantee the accuracy, completeness, or timeliness of the information.

Data Updated Through March 31, 2017

79
Number of Companies: 16
Amusement and Recreation Services

Industry Description
This major group includes establishments engaged in providing amusement or entertainment services, not elsewhere classified.

Sales (in millions)

Three Largest Companies
Las Vegas Sands Corp.	$11,410.0
Wynn Resorts LTD	4,466.3
Vail Resorts Inc.	1,604.8

Three Smallest Companies
Canterbury Park Holding Corp.	$52.3
Dover Motorsports Inc.	45.9
Bowl America Inc.	24.1

Annualized Monthly Performance Statistics (%)

Industry	Geometric Mean	Arithmetic Mean	Standard Deviation
1-year	19.7	22.9	29.6
3-year	-4.1	-0.7	27.0
5-year	8.0	11.9	30.7

S&P 500 Index	Geometric Mean	Arithmetic Mean	Standard Deviation
1-year	17.2	17.4	7.2
3-year	10.4	10.9	11.5
5-year	13.3	13.9	11.5

Total Assets (in millions)

Three Largest Companies
Las Vegas Sands Corp.	$20,469.0
Wynn Resorts LTD	11,953.6
Six Flags Entertainment Corp.	2,487.7

Three Smallest Companies
Canterbury Park Holding Corp.	$45.3
Wilhelmina International, Inc.	43.8
Bowl America Inc.	31.9

Return Ratios (%)

	Return on Assets Latest	5-Yr Avg	Return on Equity Latest	5-Yr Avg	Dividend Yield Latest	5-Yr Avg
Median (16)	4.7	4.2	7.8	5.5	3.1	3.2
SIC Composite (16)	5.7	7.0	3.3	4.2	4.5	4.4
Large Composite (3)	5.9	7.8	3.2	4.2	4.6	4.4
Small Composite (3)	5.5	4.3	4.3	3.5	3.5	3.4
High-Financial Risk (8)	-9.2	-3.5	—	-11.0	0.2	0.1

Liquidity Ratio / Profitability Ratio (%) / Growth Rates (%)

	Current Ratio Latest	5-Yr Avg	Operating Margin Latest	5-Yr Avg	Long-term EPS Analyst Estimates
Median (16)	1.3	1.6	13.1	13.6	5.5
SIC Composite (16)	1.3	1.6	19.5	21.8	5.2
Large Composite (3)	1.4	1.7	19.8	22.5	4.9
Small Composite (3)	2.7	2.2	10.5	10.2	5.4
High-Financial Risk (8)	0.8	0.8	10.4	9.4	14.7

Betas (Levered)

	Raw (OLS)	Blume Adjusted	Peer Group	Vasicek Adjusted	Sum	Downside
Median	0.91	0.95	1.55	1.09	0.93	1.15
SIC Composite	1.60	1.39	1.55	1.59	1.17	1.51
Large Composite	1.73	1.47	1.54	1.70	1.24	1.66
Small Composite	0.33	0.58	1.46	0.66	0.56	0.49
High Financial Risk	1.29	1.19	1.56	1.32	1.31	1.29

Betas (Unlevered)

	Raw (OLS)	Blume Adjusted	Peer Group	Vasicek Adjusted	Sum	Downside
Median	0.82	0.85	1.32	0.94	0.74	0.87
SIC Composite	1.27	1.10	1.23	1.26	0.94	1.20
Large Composite	1.36	1.16	1.22	1.34	0.99	1.31
Small Composite	0.33	0.57	1.42	0.65	0.55	0.49
High Financial Risk	0.78	0.73	0.90	0.79	0.78	0.78

Equity Valuation Multiples

	Price/Sales Latest	5-Yr Avg	Price/Earnings Latest	5-Yr Avg	Market/Book Latest	5-Yr Avg
Median	2.0	1.7	23.5	25.0	1.4	1.3
SIC Composite	3.4	3.1	30.6	23.9	6.7	5.8
Large Composite	3.7	3.3	31.4	23.7	8.5	7.7
Small Composite	1.6	1.7	23.2	28.7	1.5	1.5
High Financial Risk	1.0	0.7	—	—	3.3	2.0

Enterprise Valuation (EV) Multiples

	EV/Sales Latest	5-Yr Avg	EV/EBITDA Latest	5-Yr Avg
Median	2.1	2.1	9.8	9.0
SIC Composite	4.3	3.8	14.3	12.5
Large Composite	4.6	4.0	15.1	12.9
Small Composite	1.6	1.7	9.9	10.6
High Financial Risk	1.9	1.8	9.5	12.0

Enterprise Valuation SIC Composite: EV/Sales Latest 4.3, 5-Yr Avg 3.8; EV/EBITDA Latest 14.3, 5-Yr Avg 12.5

Fama-French (F-F) 5-Factor Model

	F-F Beta	SMB Premium	HML Premium	RMW Premium	CMA Premium
Median	1.9	-0.1	-10.4	-1.8	9.1
SIC Composite	1.6	1.2	-4.2	-0.2	3.7
Large Composite	1.7	1.3	-4.8	0.1	0.1
Small Composite	0.3	-0.4	1.0	-0.6	0.7
High Financial Risk	—	—	—	—	—

Leverage Ratios (%)

	Debt/MV Equity Latest	5-Yr Avg	Debt/Total Capital Latest	5-Yr Avg
Median	20.5	20.6	17.0	17.1
SIC Composite	31.5	30.9	24.0	23.6
Large Composite	31.5	29.5	24.0	22.8
Small Composite	3.5	6.0	3.4	5.6
High Financial Risk	119.4	199.0	54.4	66.6

Cost of Debt

	Cost of Debt (%) Latest
Median	7.1
SIC Composite	5.6
Large Composite	5.5
Small Composite	7.1
High Financial Risk	7.3

Capital Structure

SIC Composite (%) Latest: D/TC 24.0, E/TC 76.0

Cost of Equity Capital (%)

	CRSP Deciles CAPM	CAPM +Size Prem	Build-Up	Risk Premium Report CAPM	CAPM +Size Prem	Build-Up	Discounted Cash Flow 1-Stage	3-Stage	Fama-French 5-Factor Model
Median	9.5	12.6	14.7	11.9	15.8	9.9	7.1	10.9	
SIC Composite	12.2	12.6	12.5	12.4	11.5	9.5	7.2	12.6	
Large Composite	12.8	13.1	12.3	12.6	11.1	9.2	7.0	9.8	
Small Composite	7.1	12.7	17.7	12.5	16.7	9.1	7.7	6.1	
High Financial Risk	—	—	—	22.1	23.8	—	—	—	

Cost of Equity Capital (%) SIC Composite: Avg CRSP 12.6, Avg RPR 12.0, 1-Stage 9.5, 3-Stage 7.2, 5-Factor Model 12.6

Weighted Average Cost of Capital (WACC) (%)

	CRSP Deciles CAPM	CAPM +Size Prem	Build-Up	Risk Premium Report CAPM	CAPM +Size Prem	Build-Up	Discounted Cash Flow 1-Stage	3-Stage	Fama-French 5-Factor Model
Median	8.6	10.4	12.3	10.7	12.4	8.9	6.8	9.1	
SIC Composite	10.6	10.9	10.8	10.7	10.0	8.5	6.7	10.8	
Large Composite	11.0	11.2	10.6	10.8	9.7	8.3	6.6	8.7	
Small Composite	7.1	12.5	17.3	12.3	16.3	9.0	7.6	6.1	
High Financial Risk	—	—	—	13.8	14.6	—	—	—	

WACC (%) SIC Composite: Low 6.7, High 10.9; Average 9.8, Median 10.7

© 2017 Duff & Phelps. All Rights Reserved. Duff & Phelps has used the utmost care in compiling the data presented herein, but cannot guarantee the accuracy, completeness, or timeliness of the information.

Data Updated Through March 31, 2017

799

Number of Companies: 10
Miscellaneous Amusement and Recreation

Industry Description
Establishments primarily engaged in physical fitness facilities; public golf courses; coin-operated amusement devices; amusement parks; membership sports and recreation clubs; amusement and recreation services, not elsewhere classified.

Sales (in millions)

Three Largest Companies
Las Vegas Sands Corp.	$11,410.0
Wynn Resorts LTD	4,466.3
Vail Resorts Inc.	1,604.8

Three Smallest Companies
Dover Downs Gaming & Ent.	$182.3
Century Casinos Inc.	131.1
Full House Resorts Inc.	124.6

Annualized Monthly Performance Statistics (%)

Industry
	Geometric Mean	Arithmetic Mean	Standard Deviation
1-year	20.5	23.9	30.8
3-year	-4.3	-0.7	28.0
5-year	8.1	12.3	31.8

Total Assets (in millions)

Three Largest Companies
Las Vegas Sands Corp.	$20,469.0
Wynn Resorts LTD	11,953.6
Six Flags Entertainment Corp.	2,487.7

Three Smallest Companies
Century Casinos Inc.	$187.1
Dover Downs Gaming & Ent.	170.3
Full House Resorts Inc.	142.8

S&P 500 Index
	Geometric Mean	Arithmetic Mean	Standard Deviation
1-year	17.2	17.4	7.2
3-year	10.4	10.9	11.5
5-year	13.3	13.9	11.5

Return Ratios (%)

	Return on Assets Latest	Return on Assets 5-Yr Avg	Return on Equity Latest	Return on Equity 5-Yr Avg	Dividend Yield Latest	Dividend Yield 5-Yr Avg
Median (10)	5.4	4.5	13.0	8.6	3.2	4.5
SIC Composite (10)	5.9	7.5	3.2	4.2	4.6	4.5
Large Composite (3)	5.9	7.8	3.2	4.2	4.6	4.4
Small Composite (3)	2.3	1.5	4.3	3.4	0.0	1.1
High-Financial Risk (7)	-10.2	-3.7	–	-13.2	0.3	0.2

Liquidity Ratio

	Current Ratio Latest	Current Ratio 5-Yr Avg
Median (10)	1.1	1.5
SIC Composite (10)	1.3	1.6
Large Composite (3)	1.4	1.7
Small Composite (3)	1.0	1.0
High-Financial Risk (7)	0.7	0.7

Profitability Ratio (%)

	Operating Margin Latest	Operating Margin 5-Yr Avg
Median (10)	14.9	13.6
SIC Composite (10)	19.8	22.2
Large Composite (3)	19.8	22.5
Small Composite (3)	4.3	4.4
High-Financial Risk (7)	13.5	11.5

Growth Rates (%)

	Long-term EPS Analyst Estimates
Median (10)	5.4
SIC Composite (10)	5.2
Large Composite (3)	4.9
Small Composite (3)	5.3
High-Financial Risk (7)	13.2

Betas (Levered)

	Raw (OLS)	Blume Adjusted	Peer Group	Vasicek Adjusted	Sum	Downside
Median	1.01	1.01	1.55	1.20	0.93	1.15
SIC Composite	1.63	1.40	1.55	1.61	1.19	1.54
Large Composite	1.73	1.47	1.54	1.70	1.24	1.66
Small Composite	-0.15	0.27	1.56	–	0.00	0.67
High Financial Risk	1.37	1.24	1.56	1.39	1.40	1.44

Betas (Unlevered)

	Raw (OLS)	Blume Adjusted	Peer Group	Vasicek Adjusted	Sum	Downside
Median	0.98	0.93	1.22	1.02	0.74	0.86
SIC Composite	1.28	1.11	1.22	1.27	0.95	1.22
Large Composite	1.36	1.16	1.22	1.34	0.99	1.31
Small Composite	0.01	0.30	1.15	–	0.11	0.56
High Financial Risk	0.77	0.72	0.85	0.78	0.79	0.80

Equity Valuation Multiples

	Price/Sales Latest	Price/Sales 5-Yr Avg	Price/Earnings Latest	Price/Earnings 5-Yr Avg	Market/Book Latest	Market/Book 5-Yr Avg
Median	2.5	1.8	33.6	24.8	3.4	2.2
SIC Composite	3.5	3.2	31.1	23.8	8.8	7.4
Large Composite	3.7	3.3	31.4	23.7	8.5	7.7
Small Composite	0.6	0.5	23.4	29.1	0.9	0.7
High Financial Risk	1.1	0.7	–	–	3.1	1.9

Enterprise Valuation (EV) Multiples

	EV/Sales Latest	EV/Sales 5-Yr Avg	EV/EBITDA Latest	EV/EBITDA 5-Yr Avg
Median	3.2	2.4	10.6	11.4
SIC Composite	4.5	3.9	14.8	12.7
Large Composite	4.6	4.0	15.1	12.9
Small Composite	0.8	0.7	7.7	6.6
High Financial Risk	2.3	2.1	9.1	12.1

Enterprise Valuation SIC Composite
Latest: EV/Sales 4.5, EV/EBITDA 14.8
5-Yr Avg: EV/Sales 3.9, EV/EBITDA 12.7

Fama-French (F-F) 5-Factor Model

Fama-French (F-F) Components
	F-F Beta	SMB Premium	HML Premium	RMW Premium	CMA Premium
Median	1.9	-0.1	-10.4	-1.8	9.1
SIC Composite	1.6	1.2	-4.5	-0.2	3.8
Large Composite	1.7	1.3	-4.8	0.1	0.1
Small Composite	–	–	–	–	–
High Financial Risk	–	–	–	–	–

Leverage Ratios (%)

	Debt/MV Equity Latest	Debt/MV Equity 5-Yr Avg	Debt/Total Capital Latest	Debt/Total Capital 5-Yr Avg
Median	35.5	41.8	26.1	29.4
SIC Composite	31.9	31.0	24.2	23.7
Large Composite	31.5	29.5	24.0	22.8
Small Composite	51.2	57.7	33.8	36.6
High Financial Risk	140.9	–	58.5	70.1

Cost of Debt

	Cost of Debt (%) Latest
Median	7.1
SIC Composite	5.6
Large Composite	5.5
Small Composite	7.1
High Financial Risk	7.4

Capital Structure

SIC Composite (%) Latest
D/TC: 24.2
E/TC: 75.8

Cost of Equity Capital (%)

	CRSP Deciles CAPM	CRSP Deciles CAPM +Size Prem	CRSP Deciles Build-Up	Risk Premium Report CAPM +Size Prem	Risk Premium Report Build-Up	Discounted Cash Flow 1-Stage	Discounted Cash Flow 3-Stage	Fama-French 5-Factor Model
Median	10.1	12.8	13.9	11.9	14.6	11.6	7.3	10.9
SIC Composite	12.4	12.7	12.4	12.5	11.4	9.6	7.2	12.6
Large Composite	12.8	13.1	12.3	12.6	11.1	9.2	7.0	9.8
Small Composite	–	–	17.7	9.4	16.7	5.3	7.8	–
High Financial Risk	–	–	–	21.3	22.5	–	–	–

Cost of Equity Capital (%) SIC Composite
Avg CRSP: 12.6, Avg RPR: 11.9, 1-Stage: 9.6, 3-Stage: 7.2, 5-Factor Model: 12.6

Weighted Average Cost of Capital (WACC) (%)

	CRSP Deciles CAPM	CRSP Deciles CAPM +Size Prem	CRSP Deciles Build-Up	Risk Premium Report CAPM +Size Prem	Risk Premium Report Build-Up	Discounted Cash Flow 1-Stage	Discounted Cash Flow 3-Stage	Fama-French 5-Factor Model
Median	8.9	9.6	11.4	10.7	11.4	9.9	6.9	9.1
SIC Composite	10.7	10.9	10.7	10.7	9.9	8.5	6.7	10.8
Large Composite	11.0	11.2	10.6	10.8	9.7	8.3	6.6	8.7
Small Composite	–	–	14.0	8.5	13.3	5.8	7.4	–
High Financial Risk	–	–	–	12.8	13.3	–	–	–

WACC (%) SIC Composite
Low: 6.7, Average: 9.8, Median: 10.7, High: 10.9

© 2017 Duff & Phelps. All Rights Reserved. Duff & Phelps has used the utmost care in compiling the data presented herein, but cannot guarantee the accuracy, completeness, or timeliness of the information.

Data Updated Through March 31, 2017

8

Number of Companies: 58
Services

Industry Description
This division includes establishments primarily engaged in providing a wide variety of services for individuals, business and government establishments, and other organizations. Hotels and other lodging places; establishments providing personal, business, repair, and amusement services; health, legal, engineering, and other professional services; educational institutions; membership organizations, and other miscellaneous services, are included.

Sales (in millions)

Three Largest Companies
Universal Health Services Inc.	$9,765.2
Laboratory Corp. of America Holding	9,641.8
Quest Diagnostics Inc.	7,515.0

Three Smallest Companies
DLH Holdings Corp.	$85.6
Fonar Corp.	73.4
Psychemedics Corp.	39.0

Annualized Monthly Performance Statistics (%)

Industry	Geometric Mean	Arithmetic Mean	Standard Deviation
1-year	16.5	17.1	12.4
3-year	11.0	11.8	13.6
5-year	14.3	15.2	14.4

Total Assets (in millions)

Three Largest Companies
Envision Healthcare Corporation	$16,708.9
Laboratory Corp. of America Holdi	14,247.0
Universal Health Services Inc.	10,317.8

Three Smallest Companies
DLH Holdings Corp.	$65.1
Ecology And Environment, Inc.	59.5
Psychemedics Corp.	25.0

S&P 500 Index	Geometric Mean	Arithmetic Mean	Standard Deviation
1-year	17.2	17.4	7.2
3-year	10.4	10.9	11.5
5-year	13.3	13.9	11.5

Return Ratios (%)

	Return on Assets Latest	5-Yr Avg	Return on Equity Latest	5-Yr Avg	Dividend Yield Latest	5-Yr Avg
Median (58)	5.6	5.8	11.4	10.1	0.0	0.0
SIC Composite (58)	4.5	5.5	3.8	4.8	0.6	0.7
Large Composite (5)	5.2	5.7	5.1	6.1	0.6	0.7
Small Composite (5)	7.0	7.3	5.5	6.8	1.5	2.3
High-Financial Risk (18)	-0.3	1.3	-0.6	2.8	0.1	1.1

Liquidity Ratio

	Current Ratio Latest	5-Yr Avg
Median (58)	1.6	1.8
SIC Composite (58)	1.4	1.4
Large Composite (5)	1.4	1.5
Small Composite (5)	2.1	2.0
High-Financial Risk (18)	1.4	1.4

Profitability Ratio (%)

	Operating Margin Latest	5-Yr Avg
Median (58)	9.9	9.3
SIC Composite (58)	12.4	13.0
Large Composite (5)	11.7	12.7
Small Composite (5)	6.5	6.6
High-Financial Risk (18)	9.7	9.9

Growth Rates (%)

	Long-term EPS Analyst Estimates
Median (58)	11.5
SIC Composite (58)	10.5
Large Composite (5)	8.2
Small Composite (5)	10.4
High-Financial Risk (18)	11.3

Betas (Levered)

	Raw (OLS)	Blume Adjusted	Peer Group	Vasicek Adjusted	Sum	Downside
Median	0.97	0.99	0.92	0.94	1.05	1.39
SIC Composite	0.94	0.97	0.92	0.94	0.96	1.01
Large Composite	0.89	0.94	0.92	0.90	0.96	1.08
Small Composite	1.24	1.16	0.90	1.19	0.90	1.31
High Financial Risk	0.92	0.96	0.92	0.92	1.24	1.37

Betas (Unlevered)

	Raw (OLS)	Blume Adjusted	Peer Group	Vasicek Adjusted	Sum	Downside
Median	0.88	0.88	0.85	0.84	0.90	1.20
SIC Composite	0.79	0.81	0.77	0.79	0.80	0.84
Large Composite	0.69	0.72	0.71	0.70	0.74	0.82
Small Composite	1.15	1.08	0.85	1.11	0.84	1.22
High Financial Risk	0.55	0.56	0.55	0.55	0.66	0.71

Equity Valuation Multiples

	Price/Sales Latest	5-Yr Avg	Price/Earnings Latest	5-Yr Avg	Market/Book Latest	5-Yr Avg
Median	1.2	1.2	24.0	20.8	2.4	2.3
SIC Composite	1.5	1.4	26.0	21.0	2.7	2.6
Large Composite	1.2	1.1	19.5	16.5	2.4	2.2
Small Composite	1.0	0.8	18.2	14.7	2.1	2.0
High Financial Risk	0.4	0.5	—	35.7	—	—

Enterprise Valuation (EV) Multiples

	EV/Sales Latest	5-Yr Avg	EV/EBITDA Latest	5-Yr Avg
Median	1.4	1.2	10.8	9.3
SIC Composite	1.9	1.7	11.3	9.7
Large Composite	1.6	1.5	9.8	8.6
Small Composite	0.9	0.7	14.2	7.7
High Financial Risk	1.2	1.2	8.2	8.1

Enterprise Valuation SIC Composite: EV/Sales Latest 1.9, 5-Yr Avg 1.7; EV/EBITDA Latest 11.3, 5-Yr Avg 9.7

Fama-French (F-F) 5-Factor Model

Fama-French (F-F) Components	F-F Beta	SMB Premium	HML Premium	RMW Premium	CMA Premium
Median	0.4	2.7	3.4	0.9	-0.6
SIC Composite	0.8	2.5	-1.1	-0.5	0.2
Large Composite	0.8	1.8	-1.4	-0.5	-0.6
Small Composite	1.2	3.2	-1.5	1.7	0.5
High Financial Risk	—	—	—	—	—

Leverage Ratios (%)

	Debt/MV Equity Latest	5-Yr Avg	Debt/Total Capital Latest	5-Yr Avg
Median	14.3	12.1	12.5	10.8
SIC Composite	28.3	25.9	22.1	20.6
Large Composite	38.8	41.4	28.0	29.3
Small Composite	11.0	10.9	9.9	9.8
High Financial Risk	180.3	163.5	64.3	62.1

Cost of Debt

	Cost of Debt (%) Latest
Median	7.1
SIC Composite	6.1
Large Composite	5.3
Small Composite	7.1
High Financial Risk	7.2

Capital Structure

SIC Composite (%) Latest: D/TC 22.1, E/TC 77.9

Cost of Equity Capital (%)

	CRSP Deciles CAPM	CAPM +Size Prem	Build-Up	Risk Premium Report CAPM +Size Prem	Build-Up	Discounted Cash Flow 1-Stage	3-Stage	Fama-French 5-Factor Model
Median	8.7	10.6	10.5	13.6	14.7	12.9	10.8	12.2
SIC Composite	8.6	9.8	9.7	12.0	12.7	11.0	10.8	9.3
Large Composite	8.5	9.2	9.3	11.4	11.7	8.8	11.5	7.3
Small Composite	10.0	15.6	14.1	14.3	16.7	11.9	12.1	14.0
High Financial Risk	—	—	—	26.2	28.5	—	—	—

Cost of Equity Capital (%) SIC Composite: Avg CRSP 9.7, Avg RPR 12.4, 1-Stage 11.0, 3-Stage 10.8, 5-Factor Model 9.3

Weighted Average Cost of Capital (WACC) (%)

	CRSP Deciles CAPM	CAPM +Size Prem	Build-Up	Risk Premium Report CAPM +Size Prem	Build-Up	Discounted Cash Flow 1-Stage	3-Stage	Fama-French 5-Factor Model
Median	8.2	10.0	9.9	12.0	13.4	11.7	9.9	11.4
SIC Composite	7.8	8.7	8.6	10.5	11.0	9.6	9.5	8.3
Large Composite	7.3	7.8	7.9	9.4	9.6	7.5	9.5	6.5
Small Composite	9.7	14.7	13.3	13.5	15.7	11.3	11.6	13.2
High Financial Risk	—	—	—	13.9	14.7	—	—	—

WACC (%) SIC Composite: Low 8.3, High 11.0, Average 9.5, Median 9.5

© 2017 Duff & Phelps. All Rights Reserved. Duff & Phelps has used the utmost care in compiling the data presented herein, but cannot guarantee the accuracy, completeness, or timeliness of the information.

Data Updated Through March 31, 2017

80

Number of Companies: 23
Health Services

Industry Description
This major group includes establishments primarily engaged in furnishing medical, surgical, and other health services to persons. Establishments of associations or groups, such as Health Maintenance Organizations (HMOs), primarily engaged in providing medical or other health services to members are included, but those which limit their services to the provision of insurance against hospitalization or medical costs are classified in Insurance, Major Group 63.

Sales (in millions)

Three Largest Companies
Universal Health Services Inc.	$9,765.2
Quest Diagnostics Inc.	7,515.0
LifePoint Health, Inc.	6,364.0

Three Smallest Companies
DLH Holdings Corp.	$85.6
Fonar Corp.	73.4
Psychemedics Corp.	39.0

Annualized Monthly Performance Statistics (%)

Industry
	Geometric Mean	Arithmetic Mean	Standard Deviation
1-year	9.9	11.0	16.5
3-year	12.5	13.7	17.3
5-year	16.3	17.6	17.4

Total Assets (in millions)

Three Largest Companies
Envision Healthcare Corporation	$16,708.9
Universal Health Services Inc.	10,317.8
Quest Diagnostics Inc.	10,100.0

Three Smallest Companies
Fonar Corp.	$84.9
DLH Holdings Corp.	65.1
Psychemedics Corp.	25.0

S&P 500 Index
	Geometric Mean	Arithmetic Mean	Standard Deviation
1-year	17.2	17.4	7.2
3-year	10.4	10.9	11.5
5-year	13.3	13.9	11.5

Return Ratios (%)

	Return on Assets Latest	5-Yr Avg	Return on Equity Latest	5-Yr Avg	Dividend Yield Latest	5-Yr Avg
Median (23)	6.2	6.0	12.4	12.0	0.0	0.0
SIC Composite (23)	3.6	4.9	4.2	5.6	0.7	0.9
Large Composite (3)	5.5	5.7	5.2	6.4	1.0	1.0
Small Composite (3)	14.7	14.0	9.0	9.6	1.2	1.8
High-Financial Risk (12)	0.3	1.8	0.7	4.2	0.1	1.3

Liquidity Ratio

	Current Ratio Latest	5-Yr Avg
	1.6	1.8
	1.5	1.5
	1.5	1.4
	1.7	1.6
	1.5	1.5

Profitability Ratio (%)

	Operating Margin Latest	5-Yr Avg
	10.0	8.2
	12.5	13.4
	12.2	13.2
	14.4	11.4
	10.2	10.5

Growth Rates (%)

	Long-term EPS Analyst Estimates
	10.1
	10.4
	8.3
	10.1
	11.4

Betas (Levered)

	Raw (OLS)	Blume Adjusted	Peer Group	Vasicek Adjusted	Sum	Downside
Median	0.91	0.95	0.92	0.92	1.19	1.46
SIC Composite	0.86	0.92	0.92	0.87	1.03	1.11
Large Composite	0.86	0.92	0.92	0.88	1.00	1.12
Small Composite	1.56	1.36	0.92	1.42	1.04	1.53
High Financial Risk	0.82	0.89	0.92	0.85	1.09	1.30

Betas (Unlevered)

	Raw (OLS)	Blume Adjusted	Peer Group	Vasicek Adjusted	Sum	Downside
Median	0.65	0.71	0.77	0.77	0.97	1.11
SIC Composite	0.67	0.71	0.72	0.68	0.79	0.84
Large Composite	0.69	0.73	0.73	0.70	0.78	0.87
Small Composite	1.44	1.26	0.87	1.32	0.98	1.42
High Financial Risk	0.51	0.54	0.55	0.53	0.61	0.69

Equity Valuation Multiples

	Price/Sales Latest	5-Yr Avg	Price/Earnings Latest	5-Yr Avg	Market/Book Latest	5-Yr Avg
Median	1.2	1.1	20.9	18.9	2.2	2.2
SIC Composite	1.2	1.1	23.8	18.1	2.0	2.0
Large Composite	1.2	1.1	19.1	15.7	2.4	2.0
Small Composite	1.4	1.2	11.1	10.4	2.8	3.1
High Financial Risk	0.4	0.4	–	24.0	–	–

Enterprise Valuation (EV) Multiples

	EV/Sales Latest	5-Yr Avg	EV/EBITDA Latest	5-Yr Avg
Median	1.6	1.3	12.1	9.3
SIC Composite	1.8	1.6	10.7	9.1
Large Composite	1.6	1.5	9.7	8.5
Small Composite	1.5	1.2	13.1	9.2
High Financial Risk	1.1	1.2	7.9	7.7

Enterprise Valuation SIC Composite

Latest: EV/Sales 1.8, EV/EBITDA 10.7
5-Yr Avg: EV/Sales 1.6, EV/EBITDA 9.1

Fama-French (F-F) 5-Factor Model

	F-F Beta	SMB Premium	HML Premium	RMW Premium	CMA Premium
Median	0.6	2.7	-1.0	1.4	-0.7
SIC Composite	0.8	2.1	-2.0	-1.5	1.3
Large Composite	0.8	1.4	-1.4	-0.9	-1.2
Small Composite	1.6	4.8	-5.2	4.6	5.9
High Financial Risk	–	–	–	–	–

Leverage Ratios (%)

	Debt/MV Equity Latest	5-Yr Avg	Debt/Total Capital Latest	5-Yr Avg
Median	27.8	21.3	21.7	17.6
SIC Composite	47.8	45.4	32.4	31.2
Large Composite	38.4	43.7	27.7	30.4
Small Composite	10.6	9.3	9.6	8.5
High Financial Risk	176.9	171.2	63.9	63.1

Cost of Debt

	Cost of Debt (%) Latest
Median	7.1
SIC Composite	6.4
Large Composite	5.7
Small Composite	7.1
High Financial Risk	7.2

Capital Structure

SIC Composite (%) Latest
D/TC: 32.4
E/TC: 67.6

Cost of Equity Capital (%)

	CAPM	CRSP Deciles CAPM +Size Prem	Build-Up	Risk Premium Report CAPM +Size Prem	Build-Up	Discounted Cash Flow 1-Stage	3-Stage	Fama-French 5-Factor Model
Median	8.5	10.5	10.7	13.8	14.8	11.8	11.4	9.3
SIC Composite	8.3	9.3	9.6	12.2	12.4	11.1	11.3	7.5
Large Composite	8.4	9.1	9.3	11.6	11.7	9.3	11.4	5.7
Small Composite	11.3	16.9	14.2	15.1	16.7	11.4	14.1	22.3
High Financial Risk	–	–	–	25.4	28.5	–	–	–

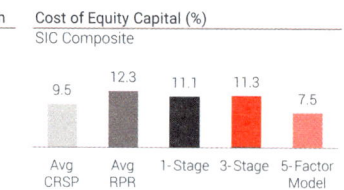

Cost of Equity Capital (%) SIC Composite

Avg CRSP: 9.5
Avg RPR: 12.3
1-Stage: 11.1
3-Stage: 11.3
5-Factor Model: 7.5

Weighted Average Cost of Capital (WACC) (%)

	CAPM	CRSP Deciles CAPM +Size Prem	Build-Up	Risk Premium Report CAPM +Size Prem	Build-Up	Discounted Cash Flow 1-Stage	3-Stage	Fama-French 5-Factor Model
Median	7.9	9.3	9.8	11.9	12.7	10.3	9.9	8.5
SIC Composite	7.2	7.9	8.1	9.9	10.0	9.1	9.2	6.7
Large Composite	7.1	7.6	7.8	9.5	9.5	7.8	9.3	5.2
Small Composite	10.9	16.0	13.5	14.3	15.7	10.9	13.4	20.8
High Financial Risk	–	–	–	13.6	14.8	–	–	–

WACC (%) SIC Composite

Low: 6.7, High: 10.0
Average 8.7, Median 9.1

© 2017 Duff & Phelps. All Rights Reserved. Duff & Phelps has used the utmost care in compiling the data presented herein, but cannot guarantee the accuracy, completeness, or timeliness of the information.

Data Updated Through March 31, 2017

806

Number of Companies: 6
Hospitals

Industry Description
Establishments primarily engaged in general medical and surgical hospitals, psychiatric hospitals and specialty hospitals.

Sales (in millions)

Three Largest Companies
Universal Health Services Inc.	$9,765.2
LifePoint Health, Inc.	6,364.0
Select Medical Holdings Corp.	4,286.0

Three Smallest Companies
HEALTHSOUTH Corp.	$3,646.0
Acadia Healthcare Company, Inc.	2,810.9
AAC Holdings, Inc.	279.8

Total Assets (in millions)

Three Largest Companies
Universal Health Services Inc.	$10,317.8
LifePoint Health, Inc.	6,319.0
Acadia Healthcare Company, Inc.	6,024.7

Three Smallest Companies
Select Medical Holdings Corp.	$4,944.4
HEALTHSOUTH Corp.	4,681.9
AAC Holdings, Inc.	383.9

Annualized Monthly Performance Statistics (%)

Industry	Geometric Mean	Arithmetic Mean	Standard Deviation	S&P 500 Index	Geometric Mean	Arithmetic Mean	Standard Deviation
1-year	-2.8	-1.0	20.4	1-year	17.2	17.4	7.2
3-year	9.1	11.3	22.7	3-year	10.4	10.9	11.5
5-year	19.7	22.1	24.7	5-year	13.3	13.9	11.5

Return Ratios (%)

	Return on Assets Latest	5-Yr Avg	Return on Equity Latest	5-Yr Avg	Dividend Yield Latest	5-Yr Avg
Median (6)	2.2	3.2	8.1	9.9	0.0	0.4
SIC Composite (6)	3.7	4.5	4.9	5.7	0.5	0.8
Large Composite	(–)	–	–	–	–	–
Small Composite	(–)	–	–	–	–	–
High-Financial Risk	(–)	–	–	–	–	–

Liquidity Ratio

	Current Ratio Latest	5-Yr Avg
Median (6)	1.4	1.5
SIC Composite (6)	1.4	1.5

Profitability Ratio (%)

	Operating Margin Latest	5-Yr Avg
Median (6)	10.1	11.2
SIC Composite (6)	11.4	12.4

Growth Rates (%)

	Long-term EPS Analyst Estimates
Median (6)	10.1
SIC Composite (6)	9.6

Betas (Levered)

	Raw (OLS)	Blume Adjusted	Peer Group	Vasicek Adjusted	Sum	Downside
Median	0.94	0.97	0.92	0.93	1.24	1.52
SIC Composite	1.09	1.06	0.92	0.98	1.33	1.39
Large Composite	–	–	–	–	–	–
Small Composite	–	–	–	–	–	–
High Financial Risk	–	–	–	–	–	–

Betas (Unlevered)

	Raw (OLS)	Blume Adjusted	Peer Group	Vasicek Adjusted	Sum	Downside
Median	0.62	0.65	0.64	0.64	1.00	0.96
SIC Composite	0.78	0.76	0.68	0.71	0.93	0.96
Large Composite	–	–	–	–	–	–
Small Composite	–	–	–	–	–	–
High Financial Risk	–	–	–	–	–	–

Equity Valuation Multiples

	Price/Sales Latest	5-Yr Avg	Price/Earnings Latest	5-Yr Avg	Market/Book Latest	5-Yr Avg
Median	0.9	1.1	19.0	17.3	1.7	2.5
SIC Composite	0.9	1.0	20.3	18.0	2.2	2.2
Large Composite	–	–	–	–	–	–
Small Composite	–	–	–	–	–	–
High Financial Risk	–	–	–	–	–	–

Enterprise Valuation (EV) Multiples

	EV/Sales Latest	5-Yr Avg	EV/EBITDA Latest	5-Yr Avg
Median	1.5	1.8	9.3	8.7
SIC Composite	1.5	1.5	9.2	9.0
Large Composite	–	–	–	–
Small Composite	–	–	–	–
High Financial Risk	–	–	–	–

Enterprise Valuation SIC Composite: EV/Sales Latest 1.5, 5-Yr Avg 1.5; EV/EBITDA Latest 9.2, 5-Yr Avg 9.0

Fama-French (F-F) 5-Factor Model

	F-F Beta	SMB Premium	HML Premium	RMW Premium	CMA Premium
Median	1.1	0.5	-3.0	-3.7	3.6
SIC Composite	1.0	1.5	-3.4	-2.6	2.9
Large Composite	–	–	–	–	–
Small Composite	–	–	–	–	–
High Financial Risk	–	–	–	–	–

Leverage Ratios (%)

	Debt/MV Equity Latest	5-Yr Avg	Debt/Total Capital Latest	5-Yr Avg
Median	90.3	62.9	47.4	38.3
SIC Composite	67.3	59.5	40.2	37.3

Cost of Debt

	Cost of Debt (%) Latest
Median	6.6
SIC Composite	6.5

Capital Structure

SIC Composite (%) Latest: D/TC 40.2, E/TC 59.8

Cost of Equity Capital (%)

	CRSP Deciles CAPM	CAPM +Size Prem	Build-Up	Risk Premium Report CAPM +Size Prem	Build-Up	Discounted Cash Flow 1-Stage	3-Stage	Fama-French 5-Factor Model
Median	8.6	9.5	9.8	13.3	12.6	10.1	12.8	6.9
SIC Composite	8.9	9.8	9.5	13.7	12.1	10.2	11.8	7.5
Large Composite	–	–	–	–	–	–	–	–
Small Composite	–	–	–	–	–	–	–	–
High Financial Risk	–	–	–	–	–	–	–	–

Cost of Equity Capital (%) SIC Composite: Avg CRSP 9.7, Avg RPR 12.9, 1-Stage 10.2, 3-Stage 11.8, 5-Factor Model 7.5

Weighted Average Cost of Capital (WACC) (%)

	CRSP Deciles CAPM	CAPM +Size Prem	Build-Up	Risk Premium Report CAPM +Size Prem	Build-Up	Discounted Cash Flow 1-Stage	3-Stage	Fama-French 5-Factor Model
Median	7.7	8.1	8.1	10.6	9.7	8.7	9.8	6.2
SIC Composite	7.5	8.0	7.8	10.3	9.4	8.2	9.2	6.6
Large Composite	–	–	–	–	–	–	–	–
Small Composite	–	–	–	–	–	–	–	–
High Financial Risk	–	–	–	–	–	–	–	–

WACC (%) SIC Composite: Low 6.6, High 10.3, Average 8.5, Median 8.2

© 2017 Duff & Phelps. All Rights Reserved. Duff & Phelps has used the utmost care in compiling the data presented herein, but cannot guarantee the accuracy, completeness, or timeliness of the information.

Data Updated Through March 31, 2017

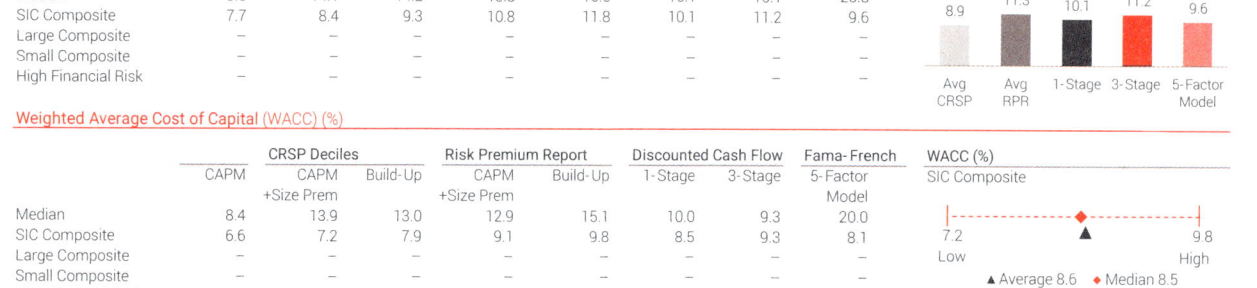

807

Number of Companies: 5
Medical and Dental Laboratories

Industry Description
Establishments primarily engaged in medical laboratories; dental laboratories.

Sales (in millions)

Three Largest Companies
Quest Diagnostics Inc.	$7,515.0
RadNet Inc.	809.6
Digirad Corporation	125.5

Three Smallest Companies
Digirad Corporation	$125.5
Fonar Corp.	73.4
Psychemedics Corp.	39.0

Total Assets (in millions)

Three Largest Companies
Quest Diagnostics Inc.	$10,100.0
RadNet Inc.	838.4
Digirad Corporation	106.3

Three Smallest Companies
Digirad Corporation	$106.3
Fonar Corp.	84.9
Psychemedics Corp.	25.0

Annualized Monthly Performance Statistics (%)

Industry	Geometric Mean	Arithmetic Mean	Standard Deviation	S&P 500 Index	Geometric Mean	Arithmetic Mean	Standard Deviation
1-year	39.3	40.4	18.3	1-year	17.2	17.4	7.2
3-year	21.4	23.2	21.4	3-year	10.4	10.9	11.5
5-year	12.2	13.9	19.8	5-year	13.3	13.9	11.5

Return Ratios (%)

	Return on Assets Latest	5-Yr Avg	Return on Equity Latest	5-Yr Avg	Dividend Yield Latest	5-Yr Avg
Median (5)	16.8	12.5	34.3	16.0	1.9	1.9
SIC Composite (5)	6.2	6.7	4.9	6.9	1.9	1.9
Large Composite (−)	−	−	−	−	−	−
Small Composite (−)	−	−	−	−	−	−
High-Financial Risk (−)	−	−	−	−	−	−

Liquidity Ratio / Profitability Ratio (%) / Growth Rates (%)

	Current Ratio Latest	5-Yr Avg	Operating Margin Latest	5-Yr Avg	Long-term EPS Analyst Estimates
Median (5)	1.6	1.9	15.8	16.1	10.1
SIC Composite (5)	1.6	1.3	14.7	15.2	8.3
Large Composite	−	−	−	−	−
Small Composite	−	−	−	−	−
High-Financial Risk	−	−	−	−	−

Betas (Levered)

	Raw (OLS)	Blume Adjusted	Peer Group	Vasicek Adjusted	Sum	Downside
Median	1.30	1.20	0.92	1.09	1.03	1.46
SIC Composite	0.74	0.84	0.92	0.75	0.85	1.02
Large Composite	−	−	−	−	−	−
Small Composite	−	−	−	−	−	−
High Financial Risk	−	−	−	−	−	−

Betas (Unlevered)

	Raw (OLS)	Blume Adjusted	Peer Group	Vasicek Adjusted	Sum	Downside
Median	0.88	0.92	0.82	0.89	0.68	1.04
SIC Composite	0.59	0.67	0.73	0.61	0.68	0.81
Large Composite	−	−	−	−	−	−
Small Composite	−	−	−	−	−	−
High Financial Risk	−	−	−	−	−	−

Equity Valuation Multiples

	Price/Sales Latest	5-Yr Avg	Price/Earnings Latest	5-Yr Avg	Market/Book Latest	5-Yr Avg
Median	1.6	1.3	16.4	12.9	2.8	2.9
SIC Composite	1.6	1.2	20.4	14.5	2.8	2.2
Large Composite	−	−	−	−	−	−
Small Composite	−	−	−	−	−	−
High Financial Risk	−	−	−	−	−	−

Enterprise Valuation (EV) Multiples

	EV/Sales Latest	5-Yr Avg	EV/EBITDA Latest	5-Yr Avg
Median	1.6	1.3	7.6	8.7
SIC Composite	2.1	1.7	10.9	8.6
Large Composite	−	−	−	−
Small Composite	−	−	−	−
High Financial Risk	−	−	−	−

Enterprise Valuation SIC Composite
Latest: EV/Sales 2.1, EV/EBITDA 10.9
5-Yr Avg: EV/Sales 1.7, EV/EBITDA 8.6

Fama-French (F-F) 5-Factor Model

	F-F Beta	SMB Premium	HML Premium	RMW Premium	CMA Premium
Median	0.8	6.7	1.0	5.9	−0.7
SIC Composite	0.7	2.7	−1.0	1.5	−0.7
Large Composite	−	−	−	−	−
Small Composite	−	−	−	−	−
High Financial Risk	−	−	−	−	−

Leverage Ratios (%)

	Debt/MV Equity Latest	5-Yr Avg	Debt/Total Capital Latest	5-Yr Avg
Median	20.3	10.8	16.9	9.7
SIC Composite	31.3	40.6	23.9	28.9
Large Composite	−	−	−	−
Small Composite	−	−	−	−
High Financial Risk	−	−	−	−

Cost of Debt

	Cost of Debt (%) Latest
Median	7.1
SIC Composite	5.1
Large Composite	−
Small Composite	−
High Financial Risk	−

Capital Structure SIC Composite (%) Latest

D/TC: 23.9
E/TC: 76.1

Cost of Equity Capital (%)

	CRSP Deciles CAPM	CAPM +Size Prem	Build-Up	Risk Premium Report CAPM +Size Prem	Build-Up	Discounted Cash Flow 1-Stage	3-Stage	Fama-French 5-Factor Model
Median	9.5	14.1	14.2	13.8	16.6	10.1	15.1	20.8
SIC Composite	7.7	8.4	9.3	10.8	11.8	10.1	11.2	9.6
Large Composite	−	−	−	−	−	−	−	−
Small Composite	−	−	−	−	−	−	−	−
High Financial Risk	−	−	−	−	−	−	−	−

Cost of Equity Capital (%) SIC Composite
Avg CRSP: 8.9; Avg RPR: 11.3; 1-Stage: 10.1; 3-Stage: 11.2; 5-Factor Model: 9.6

Weighted Average Cost of Capital (WACC) (%)

	CRSP Deciles CAPM	CAPM +Size Prem	Build-Up	Risk Premium Report CAPM +Size Prem	Build-Up	Discounted Cash Flow 1-Stage	3-Stage	Fama-French 5-Factor Model
Median	8.4	13.9	13.0	12.9	15.1	10.0	9.3	20.0
SIC Composite	6.6	7.2	7.9	9.1	9.8	8.5	9.3	8.1
Large Composite	−	−	−	−	−	−	−	−
Small Composite	−	−	−	−	−	−	−	−
High Financial Risk	−	−	−	−	−	−	−	−

WACC (%) SIC Composite
Low: 7.2; High: 9.8; Average 8.6; Median 8.5

© 2017 Duff & Phelps. All Rights Reserved. Duff & Phelps has used the utmost care in compiling the data presented herein, but cannot guarantee the accuracy, completeness, or timeliness of the information.

Data Updated Through March 31, 2017

82

Number of Companies: 11
Educational Services

Industry Description
This major group includes establishments providing academic or technical instruction. Also included are establishments providing educational services such as libraries, student exchange programs, and curriculum development.

Sales (in millions)

Three Largest Companies
Graham Holdings Company	$2,481.9
DeVry Education Group Inc.	1,843.5
Grand Canyon Education Inc.	873.3

Three Smallest Companies
American Public Education	$313.1
Franklin Covey Co.	200.1
National American University Holdings	96.1

Annualized Monthly Performance Statistics (%)

Industry	Geometric Mean	Arithmetic Mean	Standard Deviation
1-year	50.3	53.3	33.1
3-year	8.5	10.3	20.5
5-year	12.2	15.0	25.7

S&P 500 Index	Geometric Mean	Arithmetic Mean	Standard Deviation
1-year	17.2	17.4	7.2
3-year	10.4	10.9	11.5
5-year	13.3	13.9	11.5

Total Assets (in millions)

Three Largest Companies
Graham Holdings Company	$4,432.7
DeVry Education Group Inc.	2,097.0
Grand Canyon Education Inc.	1,092.5

Three Smallest Companies
Capella Education Co.	$277.3
Franklin Covey Co.	190.9
National American University Holding	70.7

Return Ratios (%)

	Return on Assets Latest	5-Yr Avg	Return on Equity Latest	5-Yr Avg	Dividend Yield Latest	5-Yr Avg
Median (11)	3.8	8.1	6.0	13.2	0.0	0.0
SIC Composite (11)	3.6	6.5	2.8	6.0	0.7	0.9
Large Composite (3)	4.1	5.8	3.5	6.0	0.7	1.0
Small Composite (3)	4.4	9.1	3.7	5.9	0.0	0.0
High-Financial Risk (−)	—	—	—	—	—	—

Liquidity Ratio / Profitability Ratio (%) / Growth Rates (%)

	Current Ratio Latest	5-Yr Avg	Operating Margin Latest	5-Yr Avg	Long-term EPS Analyst Estimates
Median (11)	2.4	2.0	11.0	12.0	11.9
SIC Composite (11)	2.1	2.0	11.8	12.1	11.9
Large Composite (3)	1.9	1.7	14.4	12.4	12.5
Small Composite (3)	2.7	2.5	9.6	13.6	12.4
High-Financial Risk	—	—	—	—	—

Betas (Levered)

	Raw (OLS)	Blume Adjusted	Peer Group	Vasicek Adjusted	Sum	Downside
Median	1.03	1.02	0.83	0.93	0.98	1.39
SIC Composite	1.02	1.02	0.83	0.99	0.78	1.19
Large Composite	1.08	1.06	0.83	0.95	0.85	1.27
Small Composite	1.13	1.09	0.85	0.99	1.19	1.35
High Financial Risk	—	—	—	—	—	—

Betas (Unlevered)

	Raw (OLS)	Blume Adjusted	Peer Group	Vasicek Adjusted	Sum	Downside
Median	0.95	0.94	0.82	0.89	0.94	1.37
SIC Composite	0.99	0.98	0.80	0.95	0.76	1.14
Large Composite	1.04	1.01	0.80	0.91	0.81	1.21
Small Composite	1.08	1.04	0.81	0.94	1.13	1.28
High Financial Risk	—	—	—	—	—	—

Equity Valuation Multiples

	Price/Sales Latest	5-Yr Avg	Price/Earnings Latest	5-Yr Avg	Market/Book Latest	5-Yr Avg
Median	1.2	1.2	25.7	17.0	1.6	2.2
SIC Composite	1.5	1.2	35.3	16.8	1.9	1.6
Large Composite	1.7	1.3	28.6	16.6	1.7	1.4
Small Composite	1.2	1.4	27.3	17.1	1.7	2.2
High Financial Risk	—	—	—	—	—	—

Enterprise Valuation (EV) Multiples

	EV/Sales Latest	5-Yr Avg	EV/EBITDA Latest	5-Yr Avg
Median	1.0	1.0	8.2	5.9
SIC Composite	1.3	1.0	8.6	6.0
Large Composite	1.5	1.1	8.7	6.4
Small Composite	0.9	1.2	6.4	6.6
High Financial Risk	—	—	—	—

Enterprise Valuation SIC Composite
Latest: EV/Sales 1.3, EV/EBITDA 8.6
5-Yr Avg: EV/Sales 1.0, EV/EBITDA 6.0

Fama-French (F-F) 5-Factor Model

	F-F Beta	SMB Premium	HML Premium	RMW Premium	CMA Premium
Median	1.2	3.4	7.1	-0.3	-6.8
SIC Composite	0.9	4.7	1.7	0.4	-2.1
Large Composite	0.9	4.8	-0.2	1.1	1.5
Small Composite	1.0	2.4	4.0	-0.7	-1.9
High Financial Risk	—	—	—	—	—

Leverage Ratios (%)

	Debt/MV Equity Latest	5-Yr Avg	Debt/Total Capital Latest	5-Yr Avg
Median	2.9	5.0	2.8	4.8
SIC Composite	5.4	6.8	5.2	6.4
Large Composite	6.6	7.9	6.2	7.3
Small Composite	7.2	4.8	6.7	4.6
High Financial Risk	—	—	—	—

Cost of Debt

	Cost of Debt (%) Latest
Median	7.1
SIC Composite	6.4
Large Composite	6.3
Small Composite	6.4
High Financial Risk	—

Capital Structure
SIC Composite (%) Latest
D/TC: 5.2
E/TC: 94.8

Cost of Equity Capital (%)

	CRSP Deciles CAPM	CAPM +Size Prem	Build-Up	Risk Premium Report CAPM +Size Prem	Build-Up	Discounted Cash Flow 1-Stage	3-Stage	Fama-French 5-Factor Model
Median	8.6	10.8	10.1	13.5	14.8	13.2	13.1	13.4
SIC Composite	8.9	10.7	9.9	11.8	13.8	12.5	11.5	13.0
Large Composite	8.7	10.3	9.6	11.8	13.3	13.2	11.0	15.9
Small Composite	8.9	11.8	11.0	15.4	15.8	12.4	15.8	12.7
High Financial Risk	—	—	—	—	—	—	—	—

Cost of Equity Capital (%) SIC Composite
Avg CRSP: 10.3
Avg RPR: 12.8
1-Stage: 12.5
3-Stage: 11.5
5-Factor Model: 13.0

Weighted Average Cost of Capital (WACC) (%)

	CRSP Deciles CAPM	CAPM +Size Prem	Build-Up	Risk Premium Report CAPM +Size Prem	Build-Up	Discounted Cash Flow 1-Stage	3-Stage	Fama-French 5-Factor Model
Median	8.3	10.7	10.0	13.2	14.8	12.6	12.4	13.9
SIC Composite	8.7	10.4	9.6	11.4	13.4	12.1	11.1	12.6
Large Composite	8.5	9.9	9.3	11.3	12.7	12.6	10.6	15.2
Small Composite	8.6	11.3	10.5	14.6	15.0	11.9	15.0	12.2
High Financial Risk	—	—	—	—	—	—	—	—

WACC (%) SIC Composite
Low: 9.6
High: 13.4
Average 11.5 ♦ Median 11.4

© 2017 Duff & Phelps. All Rights Reserved. Duff & Phelps has used the utmost care in compiling the data presented herein, but cannot guarantee the accuracy, completeness, or timeliness of the information.

Data Updated Through March 31, 2017

87

Number of Companies: 22
Engineering, Accounting, Research, Management, and Related Services

Industry Description
This major group includes establishments primarily engaged in providing engineering, architectural, and surveying services; accounting, auditing, and bookkeeping services; research, development, and testing services; and management and public relations services.

Sales (in millions)

Three Largest Companies
Magellan Health, Inc.	$4,836.9
Paychex Inc.	2,951.9
Tetra Tech Inc.	2,583.5

Three Smallest Companies
Willdan Group, Inc.	$208.9
PRGX Global Inc.	140.8
Ecology And Environment, Inc.	105.8

Annualized Monthly Performance Statistics (%)

Industry	Geometric Mean	Arithmetic Mean	Standard Deviation
1-year	15.8	16.7	15.3
3-year	10.3	11.2	14.4
5-year	14.8	15.7	14.3

S&P 500 Index	Geometric Mean	Arithmetic Mean	Standard Deviation
1-year	17.2	17.4	7.2
3-year	10.4	10.9	11.5
5-year	13.3	13.9	11.5

Total Assets (in millions)

Three Largest Companies
Paychex Inc.	$6,440.8
Magellan Health, Inc.	2,443.7
Gartner Inc.	2,367.3

Three Smallest Companies
Willdan Group, Inc.	$108.3
PRGX Global Inc.	93.5
Ecology And Environment, Inc.	59.5

Return Ratios (%)

	Return on Assets Latest	Return on Assets 5-Yr Avg	Return on Equity Latest	Return on Equity 5-Yr Avg	Dividend Yield Latest	Dividend Yield 5-Yr Avg
Median (22)	5.3	4.7	9.0	8.2	0.0	0.0
SIC Composite (22)	6.6	6.2	3.4	3.6	0.4	0.4
Large Composite (3)	8.6	7.9	3.7	4.0	0.6	0.4
Small Composite (3)	4.4	0.8	2.5	0.8	0.5	0.7
High-Financial Risk (−)	−	−	−	−	−	−

Liquidity Ratio

	Current Ratio Latest	Current Ratio 5-Yr Avg
Median (22)	1.5	1.7
SIC Composite (22)	1.3	1.3
Large Composite (3)	1.2	1.2
Small Composite (3)	1.6	1.9
High-Financial Risk (−)	−	−

Profitability Ratio (%)

	Operating Margin Latest	Operating Margin 5-Yr Avg
Median (22)	9.6	8.5
SIC Composite (22)	11.6	11.8
Large Composite (3)	14.1	14.0
Small Composite (3)	4.2	3.0
High-Financial Risk (−)	−	−

Growth Rates (%)

	Long-term EPS Analyst Estimates
Median (22)	11.8
SIC Composite (22)	10.7
Large Composite (3)	8.3
Small Composite (3)	10.7
High-Financial Risk (−)	−

Betas (Levered)

	Raw (OLS)	Blume Adjusted	Peer Group	Vasicek Adjusted	Sum	Downside
Median	1.02	1.02	0.94	0.98	1.05	1.30
SIC Composite	0.96	0.98	0.94	0.96	0.92	0.97
Large Composite	0.90	0.94	0.94	0.91	0.71	1.00
Small Composite	1.02	1.02	0.94	1.00	1.07	1.16
High Financial Risk	−	−	−	−	−	−

Betas (Unlevered)

	Raw (OLS)	Blume Adjusted	Peer Group	Vasicek Adjusted	Sum	Downside
Median	0.92	0.95	0.88	0.91	0.89	1.15
SIC Composite	0.91	0.92	0.89	0.90	0.86	0.91
Large Composite	0.87	0.91	0.91	0.89	0.69	0.97
Small Composite	1.01	1.00	0.92	0.98	1.05	1.14
High Financial Risk	−	−	−	−	−	−

Equity Valuation Multiples

	Price/Sales Latest	Price/Sales 5-Yr Avg	Price/Earnings Latest	Price/Earnings 5-Yr Avg	Market/Book Latest	Market/Book 5-Yr Avg
Median	1.2	1.1	26.8	26.1	2.9	2.4
SIC Composite	2.0	1.8	29.5	28.1	4.9	4.2
Large Composite	2.4	2.2	27.3	24.7	6.3	5.0
Small Composite	1.0	0.6	39.6	−	3.2	1.9
High Financial Risk	−	−	−	−	−	−

Enterprise Valuation (EV) Multiples

	EV/Sales Latest	EV/Sales 5-Yr Avg	EV/EBITDA Latest	EV/EBITDA 5-Yr Avg
Median	1.3	1.1	11.9	10.5
SIC Composite	2.0	1.9	13.6	12.4
Large Composite	2.4	2.1	14.3	12.4
Small Composite	0.9	0.5	13.5	8.7
High Financial Risk	−	−	−	−

Enterprise Valuation SIC Composite: EV/Sales Latest 2.0, 5-Yr Avg 1.9; EV/EBITDA Latest 13.6, 5-Yr Avg 12.4

Fama-French (F-F) 5-Factor Model

Fama-French (F-F) Components	F-F Beta	SMB Premium	HML Premium	RMW Premium	CMA Premium
Median	0.2	6.5	5.8	2.3	-5.4
SIC Composite	0.9	2.4	-0.5	0.3	0.0
Large Composite	0.9	1.6	-0.7	1.4	1.8
Small Composite	1.0	2.0	4.6	1.1	-0.6
High Financial Risk	−	−	−	−	−

Leverage Ratios (%)

	Debt/MV Equity Latest	Debt/MV Equity 5-Yr Avg	Debt/Total Capital Latest	Debt/Total Capital 5-Yr Avg
Median	10.2	11.2	9.2	10.1
SIC Composite	9.4	8.2	8.6	7.6
Large Composite	3.8	2.2	3.7	2.2
Small Composite	2.4	4.3	2.4	4.1
High Financial Risk	−	−	−	−

Cost of Debt

	Cost of Debt (%) Latest
Median	6.1
SIC Composite	6.1
Large Composite	5.6
Small Composite	6.2
High Financial Risk	−

Capital Structure

SIC Composite (%) Latest: D/TC 8.6, E/TC 91.4

Cost of Equity Capital (%)

	CRSP Deciles CAPM	CRSP Deciles CAPM +Size Prem	CRSP Deciles Build-Up	Risk Premium Report CAPM +Size Prem	Risk Premium Report Build-Up	Discounted Cash Flow 1-Stage	Discounted Cash Flow 3-Stage	Fama-French 5-Factor Model
Median	8.9	10.6	10.6	13.2	14.5	12.9	10.0	13.6
SIC Composite	8.8	10.0	9.8	12.0	13.0	11.0	9.4	10.6
Large Composite	8.5	9.3	9.4	10.3	12.0	8.4	8.8	12.5
Small Composite	9.0	12.8	12.5	15.3	16.7	11.1	4.5	16.0
High Financial Risk	−	−	−	−	−	−	−	−

Cost of Equity Capital (%) SIC Composite: Avg CRSP 9.9, Avg RPR 12.5, 1-Stage 11.0, 3-Stage 9.4, 5-Factor Model 10.6

Weighted Average Cost of Capital (WACC) (%)

	CRSP Deciles CAPM	CRSP Deciles CAPM +Size Prem	CRSP Deciles Build-Up	Risk Premium Report CAPM +Size Prem	Risk Premium Report Build-Up	Discounted Cash Flow 1-Stage	Discounted Cash Flow 3-Stage	Fama-French 5-Factor Model
Median	8.6	9.9	9.7	12.3	12.9	11.7	9.4	11.8
SIC Composite	8.5	9.5	9.4	11.4	12.3	10.4	9.1	10.1
Large Composite	8.4	9.1	9.2	10.0	11.7	8.2	8.6	12.2
Small Composite	8.9	12.7	12.4	15.1	16.4	11.0	4.5	15.7
High Financial Risk	−	−	−	−	−	−	−	−

WACC (%) SIC Composite: Low 9.1, High 12.3, Average 10.3, Median 10.1

© 2017 Duff & Phelps. All Rights Reserved. Duff & Phelps has used the utmost care in compiling the data presented herein, but cannot guarantee the accuracy, completeness, or timeliness of the information.

Data Updated Through March 31, 2017

871

Number of Companies: 5
Engineering, Architectural, and Surveying

Industry Description
Establishments primarily engaged in engineering services; architectural services; surveying services.

Sales (in millions)

Three Largest Companies
Tetra Tech Inc.	$2,583.5
Mistras Group, Inc.	719.2
Argan, Inc.	411.7

Three Smallest Companies
Argan, Inc.	$411.7
Willdan Group, Inc.	208.9
Ecology And Environment, Inc.	105.8

Total Assets (in millions)

Three Largest Companies
Tetra Tech Inc.	$1,800.8
Mistras Group, Inc.	482.7
Argan, Inc.	410.9

Three Smallest Companies
Argan, Inc.	$410.9
Willdan Group, Inc.	108.3
Ecology And Environment, Inc.	59.5

Annualized Monthly Performance Statistics (%)

Industry	Geometric Mean	Arithmetic Mean	Standard Deviation
1-year	40.0	41.5	21.6
3-year	14.9	17.2	23.7
5-year	11.6	13.9	23.2

S&P 500 Index	Geometric Mean	Arithmetic Mean	Standard Deviation
1-year	17.2	17.4	7.2
3-year	10.4	10.9	11.5
5-year	13.3	13.9	11.5

Return Ratios (%)

	Return on Assets Latest	Return on Assets 5-Yr Avg	Return on Equity Latest	Return on Equity 5-Yr Avg	Dividend Yield Latest	Dividend Yield 5-Yr Avg
Median (5)	5.2	3.9	9.2	6.8	1.0	0.7
SIC Composite (5)	5.4	4.4	3.6	3.9	1.0	0.7
Large Composite (−)	−	−	−	−	−	−
Small Composite (−)	−	−	−	−	−	−
High-Financial Risk (−)	−	−	−	−	−	−

Liquidity Ratio / Profitability Ratio / Growth Rates (%)

	Current Ratio Latest	Current Ratio 5-Yr Avg	Operating Margin Latest	Operating Margin 5-Yr Avg	Long-term EPS Analyst Estimates
Median (5)	1.9	1.8	6.1	4.9	10.7
SIC Composite (5)	1.9	1.8	7.3	5.9	11.8
Large Composite	−	−	−	−	−
Small Composite	−	−	−	−	−
High-Financial Risk	−	−	−	−	−

Betas (Levered)

	Raw (OLS)	Blume Adjusted	Peer Group	Vasicek Adjusted	Sum	Downside
Median	1.11	1.07	0.94	1.01	1.39	1.51
SIC Composite	1.02	1.02	0.94	0.99	0.89	1.08
Large Composite	−	−	−	−	−	−
Small Composite	−	−	−	−	−	−
High Financial Risk	−	−	−	−	−	−

Betas (Unlevered)

	Raw (OLS)	Blume Adjusted	Peer Group	Vasicek Adjusted	Sum	Downside
Median	1.04	1.01	0.92	0.95	1.32	1.34
SIC Composite	0.95	0.95	0.88	0.93	0.84	1.01
Large Composite	−	−	−	−	−	−
Small Composite	−	−	−	−	−	−
High Financial Risk	−	−	−	−	−	−

Equity Valuation Multiples

	Price/Sales Latest	Price/Sales 5-Yr Avg	Price/Earnings Latest	Price/Earnings 5-Yr Avg	Market/Book Latest	Market/Book 5-Yr Avg
Median	0.9	0.7	27.9	31.3	2.5	2.3
SIC Composite	1.1	0.8	27.8	25.7	2.8	2.0
Large Composite	−	−	−	−	−	−
Small Composite	−	−	−	−	−	−
High Financial Risk	−	−	−	−	−	−

Enterprise Valuation (EV) Multiples

	EV/Sales Latest	EV/Sales 5-Yr Avg	EV/EBITDA Latest	EV/EBITDA 5-Yr Avg
Median	1.0	0.7	10.0	9.4
SIC Composite	1.1	0.8	11.2	9.3
Large Composite	−	−	−	−
Small Composite	−	−	−	−
High Financial Risk	−	−	−	−

Enterprise Valuation SIC Composite
- EV/Sales: Latest 1.1, 5-Yr Avg 0.8
- EV/EBITDA: Latest 11.2, 5-Yr Avg 9.3

Fama-French (F-F) 5-Factor Model

	F-F Beta	SMB Premium	HML Premium	RMW Premium	CMA Premium
Median	0.9	2.0	3.3	-0.1	-1.6
SIC Composite	0.9	3.6	2.5	0.7	-1.8
Large Composite	−	−	−	−	−
Small Composite	−	−	−	−	−
High Financial Risk	−	−	−	−	−

Leverage Ratios (%)

	Debt/MV Equity Latest	Debt/MV Equity 5-Yr Avg	Debt/Total Capital Latest	Debt/Total Capital 5-Yr Avg
Median	2.4	10.7	2.4	9.6
SIC Composite	10.7	10.5	9.7	9.5
Large Composite	−	−	−	−
Small Composite	−	−	−	−
High Financial Risk	−	−	−	−

Cost of Debt

	Cost of Debt (%) Latest
Median	7.1
SIC Composite	6.9
Large Composite	−
Small Composite	−
High Financial Risk	−

Capital Structure

SIC Composite (%) Latest
- D/TC: 9.7
- E/TC: 90.3

Cost of Equity Capital (%)

	CRSP Deciles CAPM	CRSP Deciles CAPM +Size Prem	CRSP Deciles Build-Up	Risk Premium Report CAPM +Size Prem	Risk Premium Report Build-Up	Discounted Cash Flow 1-Stage	Discounted Cash Flow 3-Stage	Fama-French 5-Factor Model
Median	9.1	11.1	10.8	16.0	15.1	14.5	10.1	12.2
SIC Composite	9.0	10.9	10.6	12.7	14.4	12.4	10.0	13.4
Large Composite	−	−	−	−	−	−	−	−
Small Composite	−	−	−	−	−	−	−	−
High Financial Risk	−	−	−	−	−	−	−	−

Cost of Equity Capital (%) SIC Composite
- Avg CRSP: 10.7
- Avg RPR: 13.5
- 1-Stage: 12.4
- 3-Stage: 10.0
- 5-Factor Model: 13.4

Weighted Average Cost of Capital (WACC) (%)

	CRSP Deciles CAPM	CRSP Deciles CAPM +Size Prem	CRSP Deciles Build-Up	Risk Premium Report CAPM +Size Prem	Risk Premium Report Build-Up	Discounted Cash Flow 1-Stage	Discounted Cash Flow 3-Stage	Fama-French 5-Factor Model
Median	8.8	10.7	10.8	15.2	15.1	13.5	9.7	13.5
SIC Composite	8.7	10.5	10.2	12.1	13.6	11.9	9.7	12.7
Large Composite	−	−	−	−	−	−	−	−
Small Composite	−	−	−	−	−	−	−	−
High Financial Risk	−	−	−	−	−	−	−	−

WACC (%) SIC Composite
- Low: 9.7
- High: 13.6
- Average: 11.5
- Median: 11.9

© 2017 Duff & Phelps. All Rights Reserved. Duff & Phelps has used the utmost care in compiling the data presented herein, but cannot guarantee the accuracy, completeness, or timeliness of the information.

Data Updated Through March 31, 2017

874

Number of Companies: 9
Management and Public Relations Services

Industry Description
Establishments primarily engaged in management services; management consulting services; public relations services; facilities supporting management services; business consulting services, not elsewhere classified.

Sales (in millions)

Three Largest Companies
Magellan Health, Inc.	$4,836.9
MAXIMUS, Inc.	2,403.4
ICF International Inc.	1,185.1

Three Smallest Companies
Huron Consulting Group Inc.	$798.0
Exponent Inc.	315.1
Hackett Group, Inc.	288.6

Total Assets (in millions)

Three Largest Companies
Magellan Health, Inc.	$2,443.7
Advisory Board Co.	2,036.6
CEB Inc.	1,412.6

Three Smallest Companies
Navigant Consulting Inc.	$1,054.8
Exponent Inc.	403.7
Hackett Group, Inc.	158.9

Annualized Monthly Performance Statistics (%)

Industry	Geometric Mean	Arithmetic Mean	Standard Deviation		S&P 500 Index	Geometric Mean	Arithmetic Mean	Standard Deviation
1-year	17.2	18.0	13.7		1-year	17.2	17.4	7.2
3-year	4.3	5.9	19.0		3-year	10.4	10.9	11.5
5-year	12.9	14.4	19.5		5-year	13.3	13.9	11.5

Return Ratios (%)

	Return on Assets Latest	5-Yr Avg	Return on Equity Latest	5-Yr Avg	Dividend Yield Latest	5-Yr Avg
Median (9)	4.6	5.0	16.1	9.9	0.0	0.0
SIC Composite (9)	4.8	5.0	3.5	3.6	0.7	0.5
Large Composite (−)	−	−	−	−	−	−
Small Composite (−)	−	−	−	−	−	−
High-Financial Risk (−)	−	−	−	−	−	−

Liquidity Ratio

	Current Ratio Latest	5-Yr Avg
	1.3	1.6
	1.3	1.4
	−	−
	−	−
	−	−

Profitability Ratio (%)

	Operating Margin Latest	5-Yr Avg
	10.3	10.0
	7.9	8.6
	−	−
	−	−
	−	−

Growth Rates (%)

	Long-term EPS Analyst Estimates
	12.5
	12.1
	−
	−
	−

Betas (Levered)

	Raw (OLS)	Blume Adjusted	Peer Group	Vasicek Adjusted	Sum	Downside
Median	0.92	0.95	0.94	0.93	0.86	1.39
SIC Composite	1.07	1.05	0.94	1.06	1.01	1.16
Large Composite	−	−	−	−	−	−
Small Composite	−	−	−	−	−	−
High Financial Risk	−	−	−	−	−	−

Betas (Unlevered)

	Raw (OLS)	Blume Adjusted	Peer Group	Vasicek Adjusted	Sum	Downside
Median	0.89	0.87	0.79	0.83	0.74	1.22
SIC Composite	0.94	0.92	0.83	0.92	0.88	1.01
Large Composite	−	−	−	−	−	−
Small Composite	−	−	−	−	−	−
High Financial Risk	−	−	−	−	−	−

Equity Valuation Multiples

	Price/Sales Latest	5-Yr Avg	Price/Earnings Latest	5-Yr Avg	Market/Book Latest	5-Yr Avg
Median	1.7	1.6	22.6	22.0	3.1	2.9
SIC Composite	1.2	1.2	28.3	27.8	3.2	2.9
Large Composite	−	−	−	−	−	−
Small Composite	−	−	−	−	−	−
High Financial Risk	−	−	−	−	−	−

Enterprise Valuation (EV) Multiples

	EV/Sales Latest	5-Yr Avg	EV/EBITDA Latest	5-Yr Avg
Median	1.7	1.8	11.5	11.3
SIC Composite	1.3	1.3	11.2	10.6
Large Composite	−	−	−	−
Small Composite	−	−	−	−
High Financial Risk	−	−	−	−

Enterprise Valuation SIC Composite
- Latest: EV/Sales 1.3, EV/EBITDA 11.2
- 5-Yr Avg: EV/Sales 1.3, EV/EBITDA 10.6

Fama-French (F-F) 5-Factor Model

	F-F Beta	SMB Premium	HML Premium	RMW Premium	CMA Premium
Median	0.8	4.0	-0.8	-2.8	4.8
SIC Composite	0.9	4.1	-1.2	0.1	-0.5
Large Composite	−	−	−	−	−
Small Composite	−	−	−	−	−
High Financial Risk	−	−	−	−	−

Leverage Ratios (%)

	Debt/MV Equity Latest	5-Yr Avg	Debt/Total Capital Latest	5-Yr Avg
Median	31.2	15.1	23.8	13.1
SIC Composite	19.7	13.8	16.5	12.1

Cost of Debt

	Cost of Debt (%) Latest
Median	6.1
SIC Composite	5.9

Capital Structure
SIC Composite (%) Latest
- D/TC: 16.5
- E/TC: 83.5

Cost of Equity Capital (%)

	CRSP Deciles CAPM	CAPM +Size Prem	Build-Up	Risk Premium Report CAPM +Size Prem	Build-Up	Discounted Cash Flow 1-Stage	3-Stage	Fama-French 5-Factor Model
Median	8.6	10.7	10.4	12.7	14.4	13.5	12.4	12.9
SIC Composite	9.3	10.9	10.2	13.1	14.0	12.8	11.0	11.2
Large Composite	−	−	−	−	−	−	−	−
Small Composite	−	−	−	−	−	−	−	−
High Financial Risk	−	−	−	−	−	−	−	−

Cost of Equity Capital (%) SIC Composite: Avg CRSP 10.5, Avg RPR 13.6, 1-Stage 12.8, 3-Stage 11.0, 5-Factor Model 11.2

Weighted Average Cost of Capital (WACC) (%)

	CRSP Deciles CAPM	CAPM +Size Prem	Build-Up	Risk Premium Report CAPM +Size Prem	Build-Up	Discounted Cash Flow 1-Stage	3-Stage	Fama-French 5-Factor Model
Median	8.2	9.5	9.5	11.3	12.4	12.0	10.8	11.6
SIC Composite	8.6	9.9	9.4	11.8	12.6	11.5	10.0	10.2
Large Composite	−	−	−	−	−	−	−	−
Small Composite	−	−	−	−	−	−	−	−
High Financial Risk	−	−	−	−	−	−	−	−

WACC (%) SIC Composite: Low 9.4, High 12.6, Average 10.8, Median 10.2

© 2017 Duff & Phelps. All Rights Reserved. Duff & Phelps has used the utmost care in compiling the data presented herein, but cannot guarantee the accuracy, completeness, or timeliness of the information.

Data Updated Through March 31, 2017

8742

Number of Companies: 7
Management Consulting Services

Industry Description
Establishments primarily engaged in furnishing operating counsel and assistance to managements of private, nonprofit, and public organizations.

Sales (in millions)

Three Largest Companies
ICF International Inc.	$1,185.1
Navigant Consulting Inc.	1,034.5
CEB Inc.	949.8

Three Smallest Companies
Huron Consulting Group Inc.	$798.0
Exponent Inc.	315.1
Hackett Group, Inc.	288.6

Total Assets (in millions)

Three Largest Companies
Advisory Board Co.	$2,036.6
CEB Inc.	1,412.6
Huron Consulting Group Inc.	1,153.2

Three Smallest Companies
Navigant Consulting Inc.	$1,054.8
Exponent Inc.	403.7
Hackett Group, Inc.	158.9

Annualized Monthly Performance Statistics (%)

Industry	Geometric Mean	Arithmetic Mean	Standard Deviation	S&P 500 Index	Geometric Mean	Arithmetic Mean	Standard Deviation
1-year	20.3	20.8	12.2	1-year	17.2	17.4	7.2
3-year	1.6	3.7	21.6	3-year	10.4	10.9	11.5
5-year	10.3	12.3	21.9	5-year	13.3	13.9	11.5

Return Ratios (%)

	Return on Assets Latest	5-Yr Avg	Return on Equity Latest	5-Yr Avg	Dividend Yield Latest	5-Yr Avg	Current Ratio Latest	5-Yr Avg	Operating Margin Latest	5-Yr Avg	Long-term EPS Analyst Estimates
Median (7)	4.6	4.5	16.1	9.9	0.0	0.0	1.3	1.5	10.3	10.0	12.5
SIC Composite (7)	3.7	3.7	2.9	2.9	0.9	0.7	1.2	1.2	10.2	11.1	12.1
Large Composite (–)	–	–	–	–	–	–	–	–	–	–	–
Small Composite (–)	–	–	–	–	–	–	–	–	–	–	–
High-Financial Risk (–)	–	–	–	–	–	–	–	–	–	–	–

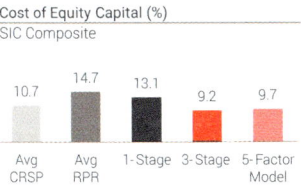

Liquidity Ratio · **Profitability Ratio (%)** · **Growth Rates (%)**

Betas (Levered)

	Raw (OLS)	Blume Adjusted	Peer Group	Vasicek Adjusted	Sum	Downside
Median	0.92	0.95	0.94	0.93	1.07	1.41
SIC Composite	1.06	1.04	0.94	1.04	1.30	1.27
Large Composite	–	–	–	–	–	–
Small Composite	–	–	–	–	–	–
High Financial Risk	–	–	–	–	–	–

Betas (Unlevered)

	Raw (OLS)	Blume Adjusted	Peer Group	Vasicek Adjusted	Sum	Downside
Median	0.89	0.87	0.79	0.84	0.89	1.24
SIC Composite	0.92	0.90	0.82	0.90	1.11	1.08
Large Composite	–	–	–	–	–	–
Small Composite	–	–	–	–	–	–
High Financial Risk	–	–	–	–	–	–

Equity Valuation Multiples

	Price/Sales Latest	5-Yr Avg	Price/Earnings Latest	5-Yr Avg	Market/Book Latest	5-Yr Avg
Median	1.9	1.6	23.2	22.0	3.1	2.9
SIC Composite	1.7	1.7	34.2	35.0	3.3	3.0
Large Composite	–	–	–	–	–	–
Small Composite	–	–	–	–	–	–
High Financial Risk	–	–	–	–	–	–

Enterprise Valuation (EV) Multiples

	EV/Sales Latest	5-Yr Avg	EV/EBITDA Latest	5-Yr Avg
Median	1.9	1.8	14.2	11.3
SIC Composite	2.0	1.9	12.7	12.1
Large Composite	–	–	–	–
Small Composite	–	–	–	–
High Financial Risk	–	–	–	–

Enterprise Valuation SIC Composite: EV/Sales Latest 2.0, 5-Yr Avg 1.9; EV/EBITDA Latest 12.7, 5-Yr Avg 12.1

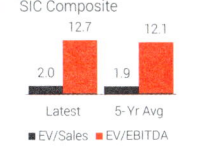

Fama-French (F-F) 5-Factor Model

	F-F Beta	SMB Premium	HML Premium	RMW Premium	CMA Premium
Median	0.8	4.0	-0.8	-2.8	4.8
SIC Composite	0.9	4.2	0.4	-0.8	-2.5
Large Composite	–	–	–	–	–
Small Composite	–	–	–	–	–
High Financial Risk	–	–	–	–	–

Leverage Ratios (%)

	Debt/MV Equity Latest	5-Yr Avg	Debt/Total Capital Latest	5-Yr Avg
Median	31.2	15.7	23.8	13.6
SIC Composite	23.2	18.0	18.9	15.2
Large Composite	–	–	–	–
Small Composite	–	–	–	–
High Financial Risk	–	–	–	–

Cost of Debt

	Cost of Debt (%) Latest
Median	6.1
SIC Composite	6.1
Large Composite	–
Small Composite	–
High Financial Risk	–

Capital Structure

SIC Composite (%) Latest: D/TC 18.9, E/TC 81.1

Cost of Equity Capital (%)

	CAPM	CRSP Deciles CAPM +Size Prem	Build-Up	Risk Premium Report CAPM +Size Prem	Build-Up	Discounted Cash Flow 1-Stage	3-Stage	Fama-French 5-Factor Model
Median	8.6	10.7	10.4	13.8	14.5	13.4	11.1	12.9
SIC Composite	9.2	11.0	10.4	15.0	14.4	13.1	9.2	9.7
Large Composite	–	–	–	–	–	–	–	–
Small Composite	–	–	–	–	–	–	–	–
High Financial Risk	–	–	–	–	–	–	–	–

Cost of Equity Capital (%) SIC Composite: Avg CRSP 10.7, Avg RPR 14.7, 1-Stage 13.1, 3-Stage 9.2, 5-Factor Model 9.7

Weighted Average Cost of Capital (WACC) (%)

	CAPM	CRSP Deciles CAPM +Size Prem	Build-Up	Risk Premium Report CAPM +Size Prem	Build-Up	Discounted Cash Flow 1-Stage	3-Stage	Fama-French 5-Factor Model
Median	8.2	9.5	9.6	11.9	12.4	11.7	10.7	10.7
SIC Composite	8.5	9.9	9.4	13.1	12.6	11.6	8.5	8.8
Large Composite	–	–	–	–	–	–	–	–
Small Composite	–	–	–	–	–	–	–	–
High Financial Risk	–	–	–	–	–	–	–	–

WACC (%) SIC Composite: Low 8.5, High 13.1, Average 10.6, Median 9.9

© 2017 Duff & Phelps. All Rights Reserved. Duff & Phelps has used the utmost care in compiling the data presented herein, but cannot guarantee the accuracy, completeness, or timeliness of the information.

Size Groupings:
Large-, Mid-, Low-, and Micro- Capitalization Companies

Size groupings based on the Center for Research in Security Prices at the University of Chicago School of Business (CRSP®), as reported in the *2017 Valuation Handbook – U.S. Guide to Cost of Capital*.

Data Updated Through March 31, 2017

Large-Cap

Number of Companies: 330
Large-Cap Companies

Industry Description
Based on the Center for Research in Security Prices at the University of Chicago Booth School of Business (CRSP®) deciles 1-2. Includes all companies with market capitalization greater than $10,711.194 million.

Sales (in millions)

Three Largest Companies
Wal-Mart Stores Inc.	$479,962.0
Apple Inc.	215,091.0
Exxon Mobil Corp.	197,518.0

Three Smallest Companies
Mid-America Apartment Communities,	$1,126.3
Realty Income Corporation	1,103.2
Liberty Bancorp Inc.	21.7

Total Assets (in millions)

Three Largest Companies
JPMorgan Chase & Co.	$2,490,972.0
Bank of America Corp.	2,187,702.0
Wells Fargo & Co.	1,930,115.0

Three Smallest Companies
Chipotle Mexican Grill, Inc.	$2,026.1
IDEXX Labs. Inc.	1,530.7
Liberty Bancorp Inc.	435.9

Annualized Monthly Performance Statistics (%)

Industry	Geometric Mean	Arithmetic Mean	Standard Deviation
1-year	18.6	18.9	7.7
3-year	11.4	12.0	11.5
5-year	14.1	14.7	11.4

S&P 500 Index	Geometric Mean	Arithmetic Mean	Standard Deviation
1-year	17.2	17.4	7.2
3-year	10.4	10.9	11.5
5-year	13.3	13.9	11.5

Return Ratios (%)

	Return on Assets Latest	5-Yr Avg	Return on Equity Latest	5-Yr Avg	Dividend Yield Latest	5-Yr Avg
Median (330)	5.4	5.7	14.0	14.8	2.1	2.1
SIC Composite (330)	2.7	2.8	4.6	5.6	2.3	2.3
Large Composite (33)	2.5	2.7	5.0	6.3	2.3	2.3
Small Composite (33)	4.5	3.5	4.0	3.6	2.7	2.8
High-Financial Risk (28)	-2.2	-1.1	-2.6	-1.6	0.9	1.1

Liquidity Ratio

	Current Ratio Latest	5-Yr Avg
	1.3	1.4
	1.3	1.4
	1.2	1.2
	2.0	1.9
	1.1	1.2

Profitability Ratio (%)

	Operating Margin Latest	5-Yr Avg
	18.4	18.1
	14.8	15.0
	11.5	12.4
	32.4	34.1
	5.9	7.1

Growth Rates (%)

	Long-term EPS Analyst Estimates
	9.7
	12.8
	14.3
	11.8
	17.0

Betas (Levered)

	Raw (OLS)	Blume Adjusted	Peer Group	Vasicek Adjusted	Sum	Downside
Median	0.96	0.98	0.99	0.97	0.99	1.16
SIC Composite	0.98	0.99	0.99	0.98	0.98	0.98
Large Composite	0.98	0.99	0.97	0.98	1.02	0.97
Small Composite	0.76	0.85	0.87	0.77	0.64	0.85
High Financial Risk	1.04	1.03	0.92	1.04	1.17	1.02

Betas (Unlevered)

	Raw (OLS)	Blume Adjusted	Peer Group	Vasicek Adjusted	Sum	Downside
Median	0.76	0.79	0.81	0.77	0.80	0.91
SIC Composite	0.71	0.72	0.72	0.71	0.72	0.71
Large Composite	0.68	0.69	0.67	0.68	0.71	0.68
Small Composite	0.56	0.63	0.64	0.57	0.48	0.63
High Financial Risk	0.81	0.80	0.72	0.80	0.90	0.79

Equity Valuation Multiples

	Price/Sales Latest	5-Yr Avg	Price/Earnings Latest	5-Yr Avg	Market/Book Latest	5-Yr Avg
Median	2.8	2.3	23.3	20.9	3.2	2.9
SIC Composite	2.0	1.6	22.2	18.2	2.8	2.4
Large Composite	1.4	1.2	20.4	16.1	2.5	2.1
Small Composite	7.8	6.7	25.6	28.8	3.3	2.8
High Financial Risk	2.3	1.7	–	–	2.8	2.0

Enterprise Valuation (EV) Multiples

	EV/Sales Latest	5-Yr Avg	EV/EBITDA Latest	5-Yr Avg
Median	3.4	2.7	12.8	10.8
SIC Composite	2.3	1.9	11.7	9.8
Large Composite	1.6	1.4	10.3	8.4
Small Composite	10.6	9.7	31.6	35.8
High Financial Risk	3.1	2.4	14.3	11.2

Enterprise Valuation SIC Composite: EV/Sales Latest 2.3, 5-Yr Avg 1.9; EV/EBITDA Latest 11.7, 5-Yr Avg 9.8

Fama-French (F-F) 5-Factor Model

	F-F Beta	SMB Premium	HML Premium	RMW Premium	CMA Premium
Median	1.2	1.4	-5.2	-1.8	5.4
SIC Composite	1.0	0.0	0.0	0.0	-0.2
Large Composite	1.0	-0.4	0.9	0.5	0.7
Small Composite	0.7	0.7	-2.2	-0.4	0.2
High Financial Risk	–	–	–	–	–

Leverage Ratios (%)

	Debt/MV Equity Latest	5-Yr Avg	Debt/Total Capital Latest	5-Yr Avg
Median	24.8	23.8	19.9	19.2
SIC Composite	40.7	45.7	28.9	31.4
Large Composite	47.1	54.0	32.0	35.1
Small Composite	41.1	50.3	29.1	33.5
High Financial Risk	40.9	47.7	29.0	32.3

Cost of Debt

	Cost of Debt (%) Latest
Median	4.8
SIC Composite	4.6
Large Composite	4.4
Small Composite	4.7
High Financial Risk	5.9

Capital Structure

SIC Composite (%) Latest — D/TC 28.9, E/TC 71.1

Cost of Equity Capital (%)

	CRSP Deciles CAPM	CAPM +Size Prem	Build-Up	Risk Premium Report CAPM +Size Prem	Build-Up	Discounted Cash Flow 1-Stage	3-Stage	Fama-French 5-Factor Model
Median	8.8	9.1	9.3	11.0	10.8	11.7	10.5	9.7
SIC Composite	8.9	9.0	9.2	10.2	9.8	15.0	–	8.7
Large Composite	8.9	8.9	9.3	9.8	8.9	16.7	13.5	10.7
Small Composite	7.7	8.2	8.6	9.6	11.6	14.5	8.8	5.7
High Financial Risk	–	–	–	24.0	26.4	–	–	–

Cost of Equity Capital (%) SIC Composite: Avg CRSP 9.1, Avg RPR 10.0, 1-Stage 15.0, 3-Stage n/a, 5-Factor Model 8.7

Weighted Average Cost of Capital (WACC) (%)

	CRSP Deciles CAPM	CAPM +Size Prem	Build-Up	Risk Premium Report CAPM +Size Prem	Build-Up	Discounted Cash Flow 1-Stage	3-Stage	Fama-French 5-Factor Model
Median	7.7	8.0	8.2	9.4	9.3	10.1	9.3	8.3
SIC Composite	7.4	7.5	7.7	8.4	8.1	11.8	–	7.3
Large Composite	7.2	7.2	7.5	7.8	7.2	12.5	10.3	8.4
Small Composite	6.7	7.1	7.4	8.1	9.5	11.6	7.5	5.3
High Financial Risk	–	–	–	18.6	20.3	–	–	–

WACC (%) SIC Composite: Low 7.3, High 11.8, Average 8.4, Median 7.9

© 2017 Duff & Phelps. All Rights Reserved. Duff & Phelps has used the utmost care in compiling the data presented herein, but cannot guarantee the accuracy, completeness, or timeliness of the information.

Data Updated Through March 31, 2017

Mid-Cap

Number of Companies: 527
Mid-Cap Companies

Industry Description
Based on the Center for Research in Security Prices at the University of Chicago Booth School of Business (CRSP®) deciles 3-5. Includes all companies with market capitalization between $2,392.689 and $10,711.194 million.

Sales (in millions)

Three Largest Companies
Rite Aid Corp.	$30,736.7
World Fuel Services Corp.	27,015.8
Tech Data Corp.	26,234.9

Three Smallest Companies
EastGroup Properties, Inc.	$254.1
National Health Investors Inc.	247.3
Universal Display Corp.	198.9

Total Assets (in millions)

Three Largest Companies
Starwood Property Trust, Inc.	$77,256.3
CIT Group Inc.	64,190.7
Zions Bancorporation	63,239.2

Three Smallest Companies
Aspen Technology, Inc.	$419.7
National Beverage Corp.	305.5
Manhattan Associates Inc.	297.1

Annualized Monthly Performance Statistics (%)

Industry	Geometric Mean	Arithmetic Mean	Standard Deviation	S&P 500 Index	Geometric Mean	Arithmetic Mean	Standard Deviation
1-year	17.2	17.5	9.4	1-year	17.2	17.4	7.2
3-year	7.8	8.5	12.7	3-year	10.4	10.9	11.5
5-year	13.0	13.7	12.9	5-year	13.3	13.9	11.5

Return Ratios (%)

	Return on Assets Latest	5-Yr Avg	Return on Equity Latest	5-Yr Avg	Dividend Yield Latest	5-Yr Avg
Median (527)	4.6	4.7	11.4	11.4	1.5	1.5
SIC Composite (527)	2.9	3.1	4.2	4.9	2.1	2.0
Large Composite (52)	3.9	4.5	6.1	6.6	2.1	1.9
Small Composite (52)	2.4	2.2	3.1	3.4	2.6	2.8
High-Financial Risk (42)	-1.3	-0.7	-3.6	-2.3	2.7	2.9

Liquidity Ratio

	Current Ratio Latest	5-Yr Avg
	1.8	1.8
	1.6	1.7
	1.5	1.5
	3.9	4.2
	1.3	1.5

Profitability Ratio (%)

	Operating Margin Latest	5-Yr Avg
	15.4	14.8
	12.3	12.0
	6.1	6.3
	37.5	35.8
	6.3	7.9

Growth Rates (%)

	Long-term EPS Analyst Estimates
	10.9
	11.6
	11.5
	13.8
	17.4

Betas (Levered)

	Raw (OLS)	Blume Adjusted	Peer Group	Vasicek Adjusted	Sum	Downside
Median	1.06	1.05	1.00	1.05	1.09	1.31
SIC Composite	1.04	1.03	1.00	1.04	1.04	1.04
Large Composite	1.10	1.07	0.96	1.10	1.07	1.13
Small Composite	0.87	0.92	0.94	0.87	0.77	0.88
High Financial Risk	1.26	1.17	1.00	1.25	1.36	1.31

Betas (Unlevered)

	Raw (OLS)	Blume Adjusted	Peer Group	Vasicek Adjusted	Sum	Downside
Median	0.86	0.85	0.83	0.84	0.87	1.04
SIC Composite	0.81	0.80	0.78	0.81	0.81	0.81
Large Composite	0.83	0.81	0.73	0.83	0.80	0.84
Small Composite	0.68	0.72	0.73	0.68	0.60	0.68
High Financial Risk	0.65	0.61	0.55	0.64	0.69	0.67

Equity Valuation Multiples

	Price/Sales Latest	5-Yr Avg	Price/Earnings Latest	5-Yr Avg	Market/Book Latest	5-Yr Avg
Median	2.4	2.0	24.0	21.5	2.8	2.5
SIC Composite	1.6	1.3	24.2	20.5	2.5	2.2
Large Composite	0.5	0.5	16.5	15.2	2.0	2.1
Small Composite	8.4	6.6	34.0	31.4	2.7	2.2
High Financial Risk	1.3	1.1	—	—	1.7	1.5

Enterprise Valuation (EV) Multiples

	EV/Sales Latest	5-Yr Avg	EV/EBITDA Latest	5-Yr Avg
Median	3.0	2.4	12.5	11.1
SIC Composite	2.0	1.7	12.4	10.6
Large Composite	0.6	0.6	7.6	7.3
Small Composite	10.6	8.9	38.4	36.4
High Financial Risk	3.3	3.3	22.2	20.7

Enterprise Valuation SIC Composite
- Latest: EV/Sales 2.0, EV/EBITDA 12.4
- 5-Yr Avg: EV/Sales 1.7, EV/EBITDA 10.6

Fama-French (F-F) 5-Factor Model

	F-F Beta	SMB Premium	HML Premium	RMW Premium	CMA Premium
Median	0.2	3.2	-0.1	4.6	-0.5
SIC Composite	1.0	1.7	0.1	0.0	0.1
Large Composite	1.1	2.0	0.4	1.1	1.4
Small Composite	0.8	1.8	-1.8	-0.2	0.7
High Financial Risk	—	—	—	—	—

Leverage Ratios (%)

	Debt/MV Equity Latest	5-Yr Avg	Debt/Total Capital Latest	5-Yr Avg
Median	27.2	27.8	21.4	21.8
SIC Composite	35.3	37.4	26.1	27.2
Large Composite	43.9	38.7	30.5	27.9
Small Composite	33.5	42.7	25.1	29.9
High Financial Risk	171.3	—	63.1	67.9

Cost of Debt

	Cost of Debt (%) Latest
Median	6.1
SIC Composite	5.4
Large Composite	5.6
Small Composite	5.0
High Financial Risk	6.2

Capital Structure

SIC Composite (%) Latest: D/TC 26.1, E/TC 73.9

Cost of Equity Capital (%)

	CRSP Deciles CAPM	CAPM +Size Prem	Build-Up	Risk Premium Report CAPM +Size Prem	Build-Up	Discounted Cash Flow 1-Stage	3-Stage	Fama-French 5-Factor Model
Median	9.3	10.3	10.3	12.8	12.8	12.5	10.1	11.9
SIC Composite	9.2	10.2	10.1	12.4	12.6	13.6	—	10.7
Large Composite	9.5	10.5	9.9	12.0	11.9	13.7	13.9	14.3
Small Composite	8.3	9.5	9.8	11.4	13.4	16.4	9.0	8.3
High Financial Risk	—	—	—	25.6	27.0	—	—	—

Cost of Equity Capital (%) SIC Composite:
- Avg CRSP 10.1, Avg RPR 12.5, 1-Stage 13.6, 3-Stage n/a, 5-Factor Model 10.7

Weighted Average Cost of Capital (WACC) (%)

	CRSP Deciles CAPM	CAPM +Size Prem	Build-Up	Risk Premium Report CAPM +Size Prem	Build-Up	Discounted Cash Flow 1-Stage	3-Stage	Fama-French 5-Factor Model
Median	8.2	9.1	9.1	10.8	11.0	10.6	8.9	10.3
SIC Composite	8.0	8.7	8.6	10.3	10.5	11.3	—	9.1
Large Composite	8.2	8.8	8.4	9.9	9.8	11.0	11.2	11.4
Small Composite	7.3	8.2	8.4	9.7	11.2	13.4	7.9	7.4
High Financial Risk	—	—	—	13.1	13.6	—	—	—

WACC (%) SIC Composite: Low 8.6, High 11.3, Average 9.8, Median 9.7

© 2017 Duff & Phelps. All Rights Reserved. Duff & Phelps has used the utmost care in compiling the data presented herein, but cannot guarantee the accuracy, completeness, or timeliness of the information.

Data Updated Through March 31, 2017

Low-Cap

Number of Companies: 550
Low-Cap Companies

Industry Description
Based on the Center for Research in Security Prices at the University of Chicago Booth School of Business (CRSP®) deciles 6-8. Includes all companies with market capitalization between $569.279 million and $2,390.899 million.

Sales (in millions)

Three Largest Companies
Core Mark Holding Co. Inc.	$11,507.4
Group 1 Automotive Inc.	10,887.6
Sonic Automotive Inc.	9,731.8

Three Smallest Companies
CEVA Inc.	$72.7
Universal Health Realty Income Trust	71.5
Texas Pacific Land Trust	59.9

Annualized Monthly Performance Statistics (%)

Industry
	Geometric Mean	Arithmetic Mean	Standard Deviation
1-year	18.3	19.2	16.0
3-year	4.1	5.1	15.3
5-year	9.4	10.5	15.1

Total Assets (in millions)

Three Largest Companies
American Equity Invst. Life Holding	$56,053.5
Interactive Brokers Group	54,673.0
Nelnet Inc.	27,180.1

Three Smallest Companies
GAMCO Investors Inc.	$149.2
Heska Corp.	109.7
Texas Pacific Land Trust	62.5

S&P 500 Index
	Geometric Mean	Arithmetic Mean	Standard Deviation
1-year	17.2	17.4	7.2
3-year	10.4	10.9	11.5
5-year	13.3	13.9	11.5

Return Ratios (%)

	Return on Assets Latest	5-Yr Avg	Return on Equity Latest	5-Yr Avg	Dividend Yield Latest	5-Yr Avg
Median (550)	3.5	3.8	9.0	9.1	1.4	1.4
SIC Composite (550)	2.0	2.4	4.2	5.0	2.3	2.3
Large Composite (55)	3.2	4.4	5.5	6.1	1.7	1.9
Small Composite (55)	1.6	1.9	3.9	5.3	2.9	3.3
High-Financial Risk (87)	-4.1	-1.4	-17.6	-5.3	1.7	1.5

Liquidity Ratio / Profitability Ratio (%) / Growth Rates (%)

	Current Ratio Latest	5-Yr Avg	Operating Margin Latest	5-Yr Avg	Long-term EPS Analyst Estimates
Median (550)	2.2	2.3	12.9	12.8	10.0
SIC Composite (550)	2.0	2.0	10.2	10.1	10.9
Large Composite (55)	1.6	1.6	4.0	4.4	10.4
Small Composite (55)	2.3	2.8	47.0	45.3	11.2
High-Financial Risk (87)	1.4	1.4	5.0	6.0	13.5

Betas (Levered)

	Raw (OLS)	Blume Adjusted	Peer Group	Vasicek Adjusted	Sum	Downside
Median	1.02	1.02	1.04	1.03	1.10	1.40
SIC Composite	1.09	1.06	1.04	1.09	1.12	1.14
Large Composite	1.23	1.15	0.94	1.22	1.11	1.31
Small Composite	0.80	0.88	1.01	0.82	0.81	0.86
High Financial Risk	1.57	1.37	1.05	1.54	1.89	1.69

Betas (Unlevered)

	Raw (OLS)	Blume Adjusted	Peer Group	Vasicek Adjusted	Sum	Downside
Median	0.81	0.82	0.89	0.83	0.86	1.14
SIC Composite	0.79	0.78	0.76	0.79	0.81	0.83
Large Composite	0.90	0.85	0.71	0.89	0.82	0.95
Small Composite	0.61	0.67	0.77	0.63	0.62	0.66
High Financial Risk	0.72	0.65	0.55	0.71	0.83	0.76

Equity Valuation Multiples

	Price/Sales Latest	5-Yr Avg	Price/Earnings Latest	5-Yr Avg	Market/Book Latest	5-Yr Avg
Median	1.8	1.7	22.8	19.9	2.0	1.8
SIC Composite	1.1	1.0	24.0	20.1	1.9	1.8
Large Composite	0.3	0.4	18.3	16.3	1.5	1.7
Small Composite	6.9	5.3	26.1	19.1	2.0	1.6
High Financial Risk	0.5	0.5	—	—	2.0	1.7

Enterprise Valuation (EV) Multiples

	EV/Sales Latest	5-Yr Avg	EV/EBITDA Latest	5-Yr Avg
Median	2.2	1.8	11.7	10.5
SIC Composite	1.5	1.4	11.8	10.7
Large Composite	0.5	0.5	7.3	6.9
Small Composite	8.5	6.7	22.2	17.6
High Financial Risk	1.3	1.3	11.9	11.4

Enterprise Valuation SIC Composite: Latest EV/Sales 1.5, EV/EBITDA 11.8; 5-Yr Avg EV/Sales 1.4, EV/EBITDA 10.7

Fama-French (F-F) 5-Factor Model

Fama-French (F-F) Components
	F-F Beta	SMB Premium	HML Premium	RMW Premium	CMA Premium
Median	0.9	3.6	3.7	0.3	-1.8
SIC Composite	1.0	3.5	1.7	0.4	-0.6
Large Composite	1.1	3.5	1.8	1.9	2.5
Small Composite	0.7	2.9	1.4	0.1	-0.5
High Financial Risk	—	—	—	—	—

Leverage Ratios (%)

	Debt/MV Equity Latest	5-Yr Avg	Debt/Total Capital Latest	5-Yr Avg
Median	25.3	22.7	20.2	18.5
SIC Composite	50.2	50.1	33.4	33.4
Large Composite	55.9	41.7	35.9	29.4
Small Composite	35.8	43.0	26.4	30.1
High Financial Risk	165.4	66.7	62.3	—

Cost of Debt / Capital Structure

	Cost of Debt (%) Latest
Median	6.1
SIC Composite	5.6
Large Composite	6.4
Small Composite	4.9
High Financial Risk	6.7

SIC Composite (%) Latest: D/TC 33.4, E/TC 66.6

Cost of Equity Capital (%)

	CRSP Deciles CAPM	CAPM +Size Prem	Build-Up	Risk Premium Report Build-Up +Size Prem	Build-Up	Discounted Cash Flow 1-Stage	3-Stage	Fama-French 5-Factor Model
Median	9.1	10.9	11.3	13.9	14.3	11.8	10.7	14.0
SIC Composite	9.5	11.3	11.0	13.8	14.1	13.1	—	13.8
Large Composite	10.2	11.9	10.5	13.3	13.4	12.3	14.4	19.5
Small Composite	8.0	9.9	10.6	12.6	14.8	13.9	10.6	11.2
High Financial Risk	—	—	—	26.9	25.4	—	—	—

Cost of Equity Capital (%) SIC Composite: Avg CRSP 11.2, Avg RPR 13.9, 1-Stage 13.1, 3-Stage n/a, 5-Factor Model 13.8

Weighted Average Cost of Capital (WACC) (%)

	CRSP Deciles CAPM	CAPM +Size Prem	Build-Up	Risk Premium Report CAPM +Size Prem	Build-Up	Discounted Cash Flow 1-Stage	3-Stage	Fama-French 5-Factor Model
Median	8.1	9.5	9.6	11.6	12.4	10.2	9.0	11.5
SIC Composite	7.9	9.0	8.9	10.7	10.9	10.3	—	10.7
Large Composite	8.5	9.6	8.7	10.5	10.6	9.9	11.2	14.5
Small Composite	6.9	8.3	8.8	10.3	11.9	11.2	8.8	9.3
High Financial Risk	—	—	—	13.1	12.5	—	—	—

WACC (%) SIC Composite: Low 8.9, High 10.9, Average 10.1, Median 10.5

© 2017 Duff & Phelps. All Rights Reserved. Duff & Phelps has used the utmost care in compiling the data presented herein, but cannot guarantee the accuracy, completeness, or timeliness of the information.

Data Updated Through March 31, 2017

Micro-Cap

Number of Companies: 579
Micro-Cap Companies

Industry Description
Based on the Center for Research in Security Prices at the University of Chicago Booth School of Business (CRSP®) deciles 9-10. Includes all companies with market capitalization between $2.516 million and $567.843 million.

Sales (in millions)

Three Largest Companies
TravelCenters Of America LLC	$5,850.6
Essendant Inc.	5,369.0
GNC Holdings, Inc.	2,540.0

Three Smallest Companies
Mesa Royalty Trust	$2.1
Kayne Anderson Energy Development	1.8
CKX Lands Inc.	1.1

Total Assets (in millions)

Three Largest Companies
OFG Bancorp	$6,501.8
Anworth Mortgage Asset Corp.	5,395.8
Impac Mortgage Holdings, Inc.	5,211.3

Three Smallest Companies
Permian Basin Royalty Trust	$2.1
North European Oil Royalty Trust	1.2
BP Prudhoe Bay Royalty Trust	1.0

Annualized Monthly Performance Statistics (%)

	Industry Geometric Mean	Arithmetic Mean	Standard Deviation		S&P 500 Index Geometric Mean	Arithmetic Mean	Standard Deviation
1-year	17.7	18.8	16.8	1-year	17.2	17.4	7.2
3-year	-0.7	0.2	14.0	3-year	10.4	10.9	11.5
5-year	4.9	5.8	14.0	5-year	13.3	13.9	11.5

Return Ratios (%)

	Return on Assets Latest	5-Yr Avg	Return on Equity Latest	5-Yr Avg	Dividend Yield Latest	5-Yr Avg
Median (579)	1.3	2.5	7.8	8.1	1.4	1.4
SIC Composite (579)	1.5	2.2	4.4	6.1	2.1	2.5
Large Composite (57)	1.6	3.5	3.9	5.7	1.5	1.4
Small Composite (57)	1.5	3.1	4.4	8.2	3.0	3.5
High-Financial Risk (212)	-5.8	-2.6	–	-8.1	1.6	2.9

Liquidity Ratio

	Current Ratio Latest	5-Yr Avg
	2.4	2.3
	2.1	2.1
	1.8	1.9
	2.3	2.4
	1.3	1.5

Profitability Ratio (%)

	Operating Margin Latest	5-Yr Avg
	14.8	15.0
	9.3	10.1
	3.4	4.3
	37.4	45.3
	-3.3	3.3

Growth Rates (%)

	Long-term EPS Analyst Estimates
	10.3
	11.7
	14.2
	10.8
	14.6

Betas (Levered)

	Raw (OLS)	Blume Adjusted	Peer Group	Vasicek Adjusted	Sum	Downside
Median	0.78	0.87	1.02	0.87	0.91	1.22
SIC Composite	1.00	1.00	1.02	1.00	1.06	1.03
Large Composite	1.22	1.15	0.96	1.21	1.33	1.34
Small Composite	0.55	0.72	1.08	0.64	0.64	0.75
High Financial Risk	1.41	1.27	1.12	1.40	1.74	1.58

Betas (Unlevered)

	Raw (OLS)	Blume Adjusted	Peer Group	Vasicek Adjusted	Sum	Downside
Median	0.60	0.69	0.85	0.68	0.70	0.95
SIC Composite	0.71	0.71	0.72	0.71	0.74	0.73
Large Composite	0.83	0.79	0.68	0.82	0.89	0.90
Small Composite	0.44	0.58	0.86	0.52	0.52	0.60
High Financial Risk	0.62	0.58	0.55	0.61	0.70	0.66

Equity Valuation Multiples

	Price/Sales Latest	5-Yr Avg	Price/Earnings Latest	5-Yr Avg	Market/Book Latest	5-Yr Avg
Median	1.8	1.6	20.9	17.6	1.5	1.3
SIC Composite	0.9	0.9	22.8	16.5	1.4	1.5
Large Composite	0.3	0.4	25.9	17.7	1.0	1.5
Small Composite	5.5	5.2	22.6	12.3	1.7	1.7
High Financial Risk	0.4	0.6	–	–	1.1	1.3

Enterprise Valuation (EV) Multiples

	EV/Sales Latest	5-Yr Avg	EV/EBITDA Latest	5-Yr Avg
Median	1.9	1.6	10.6	–
SIC Composite	1.2	1.2	11.8	10.3
Large Composite	0.4	0.5	6.7	7.4
Small Composite	6.0	5.4	17.7	10.9
High Financial Risk	1.4	1.4	21.3	10.5

Enterprise Valuation SIC Composite
- EV/Sales: Latest 1.2, 5-Yr Avg 1.2
- EV/EBITDA: Latest 11.8, 5-Yr Avg 10.3

Fama-French (F-F) 5-Factor Model

	F-F Beta	SMB Premium	HML Premium	RMW Premium	CMA Premium
Median	0.6	1.5	4.5	-1.6	1.0
SIC Composite	0.9	3.3	1.4	0.2	0.9
Large Composite	1.1	4.9	0.5	1.0	1.4
Small Composite	0.5	-1.0	2.0	-1.2	-0.3
High Financial Risk	–	–	–	–	–

Leverage Ratios (%)

	Debt/MV Equity Latest	5-Yr Avg	Debt/Total Capital Latest	5-Yr Avg
Median	26.7	29.2	21.0	22.6
SIC Composite	58.8	58.3	37.0	36.8
Large Composite	76.3	47.4	43.3	32.2
Small Composite	28.8	22.9	22.4	18.6
High Financial Risk	–	161.3	75.8	61.7

Cost of Debt

	Cost of Debt (%) Latest
Median	6.1
SIC Composite	5.8
Large Composite	6.7
Small Composite	4.8
High Financial Risk	7.9

Capital Structure

SIC Composite (%) Latest
- D/TC: 37.0
- E/TC: 63.0

Cost of Equity Capital (%)

	CRSP Deciles CAPM	CAPM +Size Prem	Build-Up	Risk Premium Report CAPM +Size Prem	Build-Up	Discounted Cash Flow 1-Stage	3-Stage	Fama-French 5-Factor Model
Median	8.3	12.5	14.4	14.1	16.5	11.2	12.1	12.4
SIC Composite	9.0	12.6	12.9	14.6	15.8	13.5	–	14.1
Large Composite	10.1	13.3	12.2	15.5	14.9	15.7	14.3	17.4
Small Composite	7.0	11.9	13.5	12.8	16.5	12.4	13.0	5.9
High Financial Risk	–	–	–	26.4	25.7	–	–	–

Cost of Equity Capital (%) SIC Composite
- Avg CRSP: 12.8
- Avg RPR: 15.2
- 1-Stage: 13.5
- 3-Stage: n/a
- 5-Factor Model: 14.1

Weighted Average Cost of Capital (WACC) (%)

	CRSP Deciles CAPM	CAPM +Size Prem	Build-Up	Risk Premium Report CAPM +Size Prem	Build-Up	Discounted Cash Flow 1-Stage	3-Stage	Fama-French 5-Factor Model
Median	7.4	10.5	11.3	11.3	13.8	9.4	10.0	10.1
SIC Composite	7.3	9.6	9.8	10.9	11.6	10.1	–	10.6
Large Composite	8.2	10.0	9.4	11.2	10.9	11.4	10.6	12.3
Small Composite	6.3	10.0	11.3	10.7	13.6	10.4	10.8	5.4
High Financial Risk	–	–	–	12.0	11.8	–	–	–

WACC (%) SIC Composite: Low 9.6, High 11.6. Average 10.4, Median 10.4.

© 2017 Duff & Phelps. All Rights Reserved. Duff & Phelps has used the utmost care in compiling the data presented herein, but cannot guarantee the accuracy, completeness, or timeliness of the information.